THE TIMES
FOOTBALL
YEARBOOK 2004-05

Times Books
an imprint of
Collins
HarperCollins Publishers
77-85 Fulham Palace Road
London
W6 8JB

First published 2004
10 9 8 7 6 5 4 3 2 1
2005 2004

Printed and bound in the UK by
Butler & Tanner, Frome, Somerset
ISBN 0 00 719328 9

THE TIMES
FOOTBALL
YEARBOOK 2004-05

EDITED BY RICHARD WHITEHEAD AND KEITH PIKE

Collins

CONTENTS

MEET THE EDITORS   10
Richard Whitehead
and Keith Pike

INTRODUCTION   11
Keith Blackmore,
Head of Sport, *The Times*

**FIVE FOOTBALLERS
OF THE YEAR**
Steven Gerrard   **14-15**
Thierry Henry   **16-17**
Frank Lampard   **18-19**
Michael McIndoe   **20-21**
Wayne Rooney   **22-23**

OTHER AWARDS   24

THE BIG READS
Simon Barnes   **25-28**
Tony Cascarino   **29-32**
Martin Samuel   **33-36**
Daniel Finkelstein   **37-40**

**THE 2004 EUROPEAN
CHAMPIONSHIP REVIEW**
Matt Dickinson,
Chief Football
Correspondent   **41-54**

**THE PREMIERSHIP REVIEW
2003-04**
Matt Dickinson,
Chief Football
Correspondent   **55-58**

THE PREMIERSHIP CLUBS

Arsenal   59-70
Catherine Riley

Aston Villa   71-80
Richard Guy

Birmingham City   81-90
Tim Austin

Blackburn Rovers   91-100
John Dawkins

Bolton Wanderers 101-110
Alan Kay

Charlton Athletic   111-120
Nigel Williamson

Chelsea   121-132
Geoff Harwood

Everton   133-142
Chris Gill

Fulham   143-152
Tim Miller

Leeds United   153-162
Rick Broadbent

Leicester City   163-172
Jim Wheildon

Liverpool   173-184
Alyson Rudd

Manchester City   185-194
Paul Connolly

Manchester United   195-206
Mick Hume

Middlesbrough   207-216
Shaun Keogh

Newcastle United   217-228
Angus Batey

Portsmouth   229-238
Richard Holledge

Southampton   239-248
Steve Keenan

**Tottenham
Hotspur**   249-258
Phil Myers

**Wolverhampton
Wanderers**   259-268
Peter Lansley

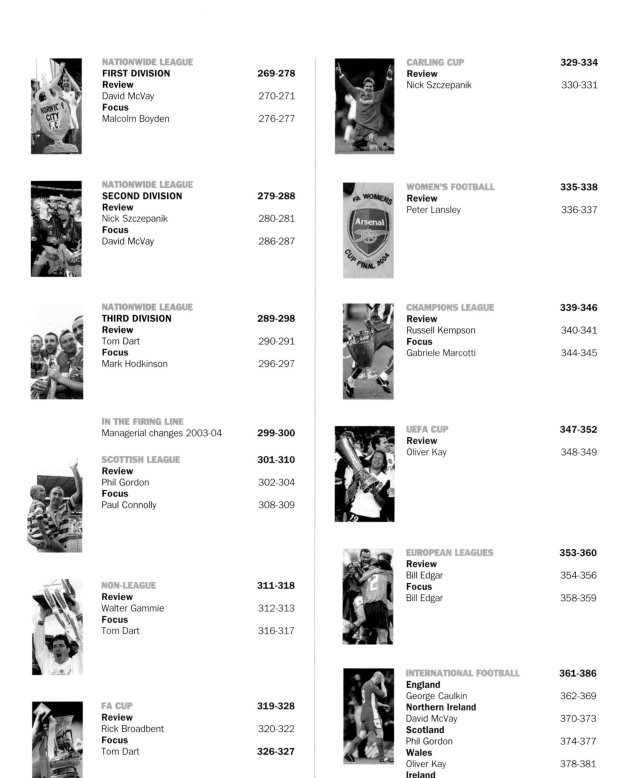

NATIONWIDE LEAGUE
FIRST DIVISION **269-278**
Review
David McVay 270-271
Focus
Malcolm Boyden 276-277

NATIONWIDE LEAGUE
SECOND DIVISION **279-288**
Review
Nick Szczepanik 280-281
Focus
David McVay 286-287

NATIONWIDE LEAGUE
THIRD DIVISION **289-298**
Review
Tom Dart 290-291
Focus
Mark Hodkinson 296-297

IN THE FIRING LINE
Managerial changes 2003-04 **299-300**

SCOTTISH LEAGUE **301-310**
Review
Phil Gordon 302-304
Focus
Paul Connolly 308-309

NON-LEAGUE **311-318**
Review
Walter Gammie 312-313
Focus
Tom Dart 316-317

FA CUP **319-328**
Review
Rick Broadbent 320-322
Focus
Tom Dart **326-327**

CARLING CUP **329-334**
Review
Nick Szczepanik 330-331

WOMEN'S FOOTBALL **335-338**
Review
Peter Lansley 336-337

CHAMPIONS LEAGUE **339-346**
Review
Russell Kempson 340-341
Focus
Gabriele Marcotti 344-345

UEFA CUP **347-352**
Review
Oliver Kay 348-349

EUROPEAN LEAGUES **353-360**
Review
Bill Edgar 354-356
Focus
Bill Edgar 358-359

INTERNATIONAL FOOTBALL **361-386**
England
George Caulkin 362-369
Northern Ireland
David McVay 370-373
Scotland
Phil Gordon 374-377
Wales
Oliver Kay 378-381
Ireland
Russell Kempson 380-383
International dates for 2004-05 384

OBITUARIES **387-393**
Daniel Crewe

KEY DATES IN 2004-05 **394-395**

THE TIMES FOOTBALL

EDITORS
Richard Whitehead and Keith Pike

DESIGN
Kit Gregory

COVER DESIGN
Mike Krage

PICTURE RESEARCH
Richard Horton

RESULTS AND TABLES
Tim Greenwell

PROOF-READING
Robert Hands

PHOTOGRAPHIC IMAGING
Gary Hedgman

THANKS
Myles Archibald, Keith Blackmore, Alastair Brett, Marion Brinton, George Brock, Jim Brown, Anthony Cappaert, Clive Cardy, Magnus Cohen, Bill Edgar, Tony Evans, Matt Gibbs, Steve Gibbs, Mark Giles, Gary Jacob, Jan Pike, Wendy Showell, Sue and Steve Turner, Tom Wyett

SIMON BARNES
Voted Sports Writer of the Year in the *What The Papers Say* awards, the Chief Sports Writer of *The Times* reflects on the remarkable impact made by Roman Abramovich in his first year at Chelsea.

MATT DICKINSON
Chief Football Correspondent of *The Times* and the most authoritative writer in the game, he gives his verdict on the 2004 European Championship and an historic 2003-04 Premiership season.

MARTIN SAMUEL
Football's most provocative columnist appears in *The Times* every Wednesday, producing seven days' worth of talking points. His strident view of Euro 2004 is as outspoken as ever.

TONY CASCARINO
Some ex-pros make a career out of sitting on the fence — not the former Ireland striker. His insider's view of the game's "season of shame" is as direct and forthright as a Jack Charlton team talk.

DANIEL FINKELSTEIN
Who ever said football statistics were dry and uninteresting? Taking a radical new approach to the subject, his weekly Fink Tank column in the Saturday *Times* has become essential reading.

MARC ASPLAND
The Barclaycard Football Photographer of the Year is making his debut in *The Times Football Yearbook* and his dramatic and brilliant pictures add immeasurably to the style and impact of the book.

YEARBOOK TEAM

CONTRIBUTORS

TIM AUSTIN — Birmingham City review

ANGUS BATEY — Newcastle United review

RICK BROADBENT — Thierry Henry, FA Cup review, Leeds United review

GEORGE CAULKIN — Steven Gerrard and England review

PAUL CONNOLLY — Manchester City review, Scottish focus

DANIEL CREWE — Obituaries

TOM DART — Michael McIndoe, third division review, Non-League focus, FA Cup focus

JOHN DAWKINS — Blackburn Rovers review

BILL EDGAR — European leagues review, European focus

WALTER GAMMIE — Non-League review

CHRIS GILL — Everton review

PHIL GORDON — Scottish League review, Scotland review

RICHARD GUY — Aston Villa review

GEOFF HARWOOD — Chelsea review

MARK HODKINSON — Third division focus

RICHARD HOLLEDGE — Portsmouth review

MICK HUME — Manchester United review

ALAN KAY — Bolton Wanderers review

OLIVER KAY — Wayne Rooney, Uefa Cup review, Wales review

STEVE KEENAN — Southampton review

RUSSELL KEMPSON — Champions League review, Ireland review

SHAUN KEOGH — Middlesbrough review

PETER LANSLEY — Wolverhampton Wanderers review, women's review

GABRIELE MARCOTTI — Champions League focus

DAVID McVAY — First division review, second division focus, Northern Ireland review

TIM MILLER — Fulham review

PHIL MYERS — Tottenham Hotspur review

CATHERINE RILEY — Arsenal review

ALYSON RUDD — Frank Lampard, Liverpool review

NICK SZCZEPANIK — Carling Cup review, second division review

JIM WHEILDON — Leicester City review

NIGEL WILLIAMSON — Charlton Athletic review

THE EDITORS

RICHARD WHITEHEAD

After joining the sports desk of *The Times* in late 1995, Richard Whitehead, 43, is now in charge of the paper's sports supplements — including the innovative Handbook series. He has been in journalism for 25 years and is a keen student of football history, contributing regular nostalgia features for the newspaper. As well as co-editing *The Times Football Yearbook*, he is the author of *Children of the Revolution: Aston Villa in the 1970s* and his greatest sporting ambition is to see his beloved club win the FA Cup — but not before he has completed his mammoth history of the club in the competition.

KEITH PIKE

A regular member of *The Times*'s football reporting team and a key part of the sports production department, Keith Pike, 49, joined the paper in 1990 after working on various newspapers in his native North London. His writing and statistical talents have been put to good use in compiling the summaries of every Premiership match that are one of the main attractions of this book. However, the glamour of the Premiership does not stop him asking "Has anyone heard the Barnet score?" whenever he catches sight of a press-room television at ten to five on a Saturday afternoon.

INTRODUCTION
Keith Blackmore, Head of Sport, The Times

WHEN THE FIRST *TIMES FOOTBALL YEARBOOK* went to press last summer, the world was a different place. Manchester United and Arsenal had divided up the main honours in their familiar way and David Beckham, although bound for Real Madrid, was still indisputably the biggest star in the British game. Twenty-fours after the last page had been sent to the printers, Roman Abramovich bought Chelsea and nothing has been the same since. Not everything is Mr Abramovich's doing, of course (Wayne Rooney replaced Beckham in the nation's affections without his help), but as Simon Barnes, the Sports Writer of the Year, argues in these pages, much of it had something to do with him. An unprecedented spending spree helped to insert Chelsea between the former Big Two and carried them farther than any other British team in the Champions League. And, it seems, this was only the beginning.

So this edition of the *Yearbook* chronicles the first season of a new era, and to make sense of a season of sometimes overwhelming change, the editors have once again been able to draw on the kind of talent that is otherwise only available to Chelsea managers. Readers of *The Times* and particularly our weekly football supplement, *TheGame*, will be familiar with the award-winning team of reporters led by Matt Dickinson, Barnes and Tony Cascarino. This year, the editors have been able to rotate a couple of extra *galacticos* into the line-up. Danny Finkelstein explains how his scientific theories of football have made him a better bet than the bookies for predictions and Martin Samuel, our regular Wednesday columnist, runs his critical eye over the aftermath of the European Championship.

This summer, the *Yearbook* deadline was extended to allow full coverage of Euro 2004. Greece's triumph in Portugal brought an amazing end to an amazing year. Relive it all again in these pages.

FIVE FOOTBALLERS OF THE YEAR

STEVEN GERRARD
by George Caulkin   **14-15**

THIERRY HENRY
by Rick Broadbent   **16-17**

FRANK LAMPARD
by Alyson Rudd   **18-19**

MICHAEL McINDOE
by Tom Dart   **20-21**

WAYNE ROONEY
by Oliver Kay   **22-23**

STEVEN GERRARD

George Caulkin

IT WAS A BITTER-SWEET compliment and it made Liverpool supporters wince. "If you were looking for the player you would replace Keane with, it's Gerrard, without question," Sir Alex Ferguson said, in the verbal equivalent of a two-footed tackle on Manchester United's great rivals. "He has become the most influential player in England, bar none. More than Vieira. Absolutely more than Vieira."

In spite of signing a contract extension in November, nominally binding him to his only club until 2007, the prospect of Gerrard leaving Anfield did not dissipate. In fact, after another season of scrabbling under-achievement, which was to cost Gerard Houllier his job, it seemed certain that he would be joining Chelsea after the European Championship. However, at the eleventh hour — and after a tournament in which he did not do himself justice — he elected to stay at Anfield.

For all that, the reasons why he might have considered heading south were obvious, even to the most one-eyed of Merseysiders.

"Named captain, he propelled Liverpool towards a Champions League place"

Gerrard was brilliant, of course, in the Liverpool midfield, but there was more to it than that. Twenty-four at the end of May, he finally emerged as the driving, dominant presence that his brittle body appeared destined to prevent. In all, he made 44 starts, a total only bettered by Harry Kewell and Sami Hyypia.

Named captain midway through the campaign, Gerrard responded vigorously (he also took the skipper's armband for England's friendly in Sweden, which — irony of ironies — was to be his first defeat as an international footballer). Becoming a father for the first time gave added weight to the sense of responsibility and maturity. The Football Association declared him their "Lion of the Season".

And how he roared, wading through Liverpool's general stagnation, propelling them — almost alone — towards fourth place in the Premiership and the final qualifying position for the Champions League. "To me, Gerrard is where Keane was when Roy came to us in 1993," Ferguson said. "When the ball is in their penalty area, he is right there. When it's in his own team's area, he is back there. Anyone would take Gerrard."

No wonder United and Chelsea were taking sneaky glances in the direction of Gerrard, who spoke of his "hurt" at finishing 30 points behind Arsenal. "I think it is well-documented that I'm not happy with the way it has gone at Liverpool over the past two seasons," he said. "Everyone knows how desperate I am to win the league."

Regulars at Anfield share the sentiment. Cue more wincing.

THIERRY HENRY

Rick Broadbent

BEFORE DISAPPEARING INTO a nether world of beach football, beer bellies and suspect French art movies, Eric Cantona proved his philosophical musings did not stop at trying to pin it on the seagulls. "There is no salvation without the artist," he said. Thierry Henry is the lip-smacking, hip-shaking, living proof.

No longer does Arsenal-esque mean boring and lucky and dirty and petulant and rich and mean, as Nick Hornby once claimed. Henry is that rare sort of player who has transcended the parochialism that defines club football to become an Everyhero. It is why Portsmouth fans chanted his name after he had demolished their side in the FA Cup.

To be as consistent as he has been over two seasons, when the bedrock of his game is the unexpected, puts him on another plane to most great players. The likes of Patrick Vieira and Frank Lampard had their backers in the end-of-season votes, but they are athletes where Henry is an aesthete. That so many of his goals are forged beyond the normal parameters is remarkable and

"He can drop deep as a creator or use his pace to breach static defences"

if he could add the two-yard tap-in off his shin to his repertoire, he might just be the best we have ever seen.

Certainly, he must now stand alongside knights of the round ball fable — Tom Finney, Stanley Matthews and Bobby Charlton — as well as lustrous mavericks such as George Best, Kenny Dalglish and Cantona. He has created a new, all-encompassing role. Like Dalglish, he can drop deep and work as a "schemer", or he can use his raw, gazelle-like pace to breach static defences, as Michael Owen does. He conjures memories of Best with his luminosity and thwacks a ball like Charlton in his pomp.

It has been a remarkable blossoming for a man who was killing time as a wing back at Juventus and resembled a slightly tipsy Darren Huckerby as he charged down blind alleys on his introduction to Britain. Who could have imagined that one day the Italian press would carry banner headlines commanding us to "Kneel

Down Before The King" after a mesmerising 5-1 Arsenal victory over Inter Milan in the San Siro?

The European Championship may have been an anti-climax to his triumphant season — but then so it was to all his jaded France team-mates.

Some people still claim Henry is not a natural finisher. It sounds fatuous, given his strike record, but they merely mean he is not a poacher in the manner of Gary Lineker and Ruud van Nistelrooy. Henry is so much more than that. He is, as Cantona could have told them, an artist.

FRANK LAMPARD

Alyson Rudd

HE KISSES THE BADGE on his shirt when he scores, and why not? West Ham United may have nurtured his talents, but it was at Chelsea that Frank Lampard blossomed. He was always popular with Claudio Ranieri, but last season you could be forgiven for thinking Ranieri was obsessed with him. Ranieri, now forever known as the Tinkerman, played Lampard from the start in every Premiership match. Lampard missed only the game against Notts County in the Carling Cup and played for a half in those against Aston Villa, again in the Carling Cup, and Sparta Prague.

For all the glamour, the ambition, the access to vast sums of cash that Chelsea represents, Lampard stands for the one thing in football that money cannot buy: commitment. And what makes Lampard such a marvellous talent is that while his commitment sets him apart from some of Chelsea's other players, he is not the archetypal English midfield player who everyone loves because he gets stuck in but leaves the flair to the foreigners.

"His goals in Euro 2004 were a testament to his stamina and athleticism"

Lampard is better than the flashy overseas stars in terms of work-rate and skill. He must owe the rest a debt of gratitude, though. Those neat, extremely deft first touches can only have been honed in training alongside the likes of Adrian Mutu, Hernan Crespo and Eidur Gudjohnsen. But while many of Chelsea's players seemed prepared to drift through games or to pout when a move broke down, Lampard never forgot that, cultured player though he is, there is no substitute for hard work.

He was a sight to behold last season. With his chest puffed out he would power though midfield. When he could not leave an opponent with his energy or his pace, he would unleash a neat swerve or full-circle twirl.

While many of his contemporaries find the oxygen vanishes from their brains after a surging run, Lampard's athleticism ensures that the end product of one of his bursts is either an astute pass or a shot on target — as his two goals for England in Euro 2004 testified.

Oh, and he is chatty, down to earth and modest, too. He wants to win trophies, who doesn't? — but he can talk about his ambitions without seeming grasping or naive.

Did Chelsea underperform last season? No, given that only one outfield player was consistently playing better than ever, forever improving and always trying, they probably finished a few places higher than they deserved.

MICHAEL McINDOE

Tom Dart

DISMISSIVE COMMENTS ABOUT the low calibre of most Scottish players may be common, but the discerning third-division supporter would not be so snide. Not after last season.

David Graham, of Torquay United, and Steven MacLean, who spent the season on loan at Scunthorpe United from Rangers, were among the division's highest scorers. Michael McIndoe, of Doncaster Rovers, was less prolific but no less impressive.

An artist in a division of artisans, the left winger with the white boots possesses pace, the ability to snap over a penetrating cross, quick feet and a sharp footballing brain. Ambitious, confident, and durable, he started all but one league match in 2003-04.

Still, there is room for improvement. More goals from open play would be nice: six of his ten strikes were penalties. McIndoe's mid-season form did not match the blistering fashion in which he started and finished the campaign. But the feeling is that the player, like his club,

"The winger in the white boots has pace, a sharp brain and crossing ability"

are on the up and neither has yet fully realised their potential. It is one thing to look good in the basement division; McIndoe looks as if he is capable of playing at a much higher level.

Born in Edinburgh, he left the city aged 16 for Luton Town, spending two years in Bedfordshire before dropping out of the League to join Hereford United in 2000. It was only a brief stay — Yeovil Town snapped him up for £25,000. Not that they are so enamoured with the 24-year-old at Huish Park any more.

Accusations of avarice were levelled at McIndoe and his agent as a £50,000 move to Doncaster was engineered last August. Why, Somerset wondered, would McIndoe want to leave the 2002-03 Nationwide Conference champions for a club that finished 18 points below them? But he was proved right as the tables were turned: last season it was Doncaster who finished 18

points clear of Yeovil as they cantered to the third-division championship. Now it might cost potential suitors a seven-figure sum to prise him away from Belle Vue. And several clubs have considered trying.

Last December, McIndoe was called up to the Scotland Future squad for a game against Turkey and played a half. The achievement underlined the extent of his recovery from alcohol and gambling problems that blighted his teenage years. Stays in The Priory are not just for superstars. McIndoe spent a month there in rehabilitation after he amassed gambling debts of £48,000 by the age of 19. Now teetotal, his renaissance continues.

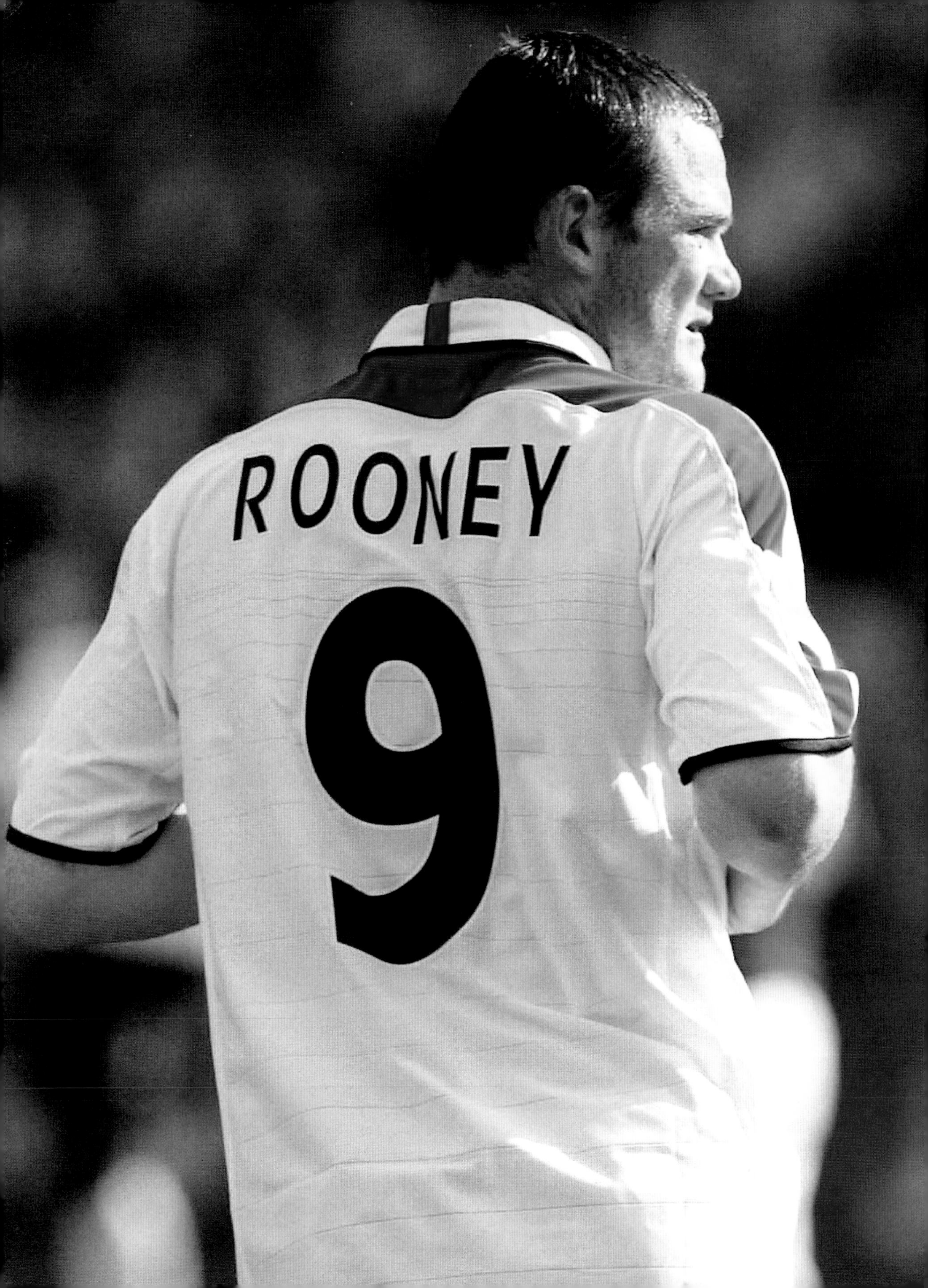
ROONEY
9

WAYNE ROONEY

Oliver Kay

SVEN-GORAN ERIKSSON compared him to Pele; a team of scientists said that the genius of Mozart was more appropriate; sales of England shirts with his No 9 on the back far outstripped those bearing the names of David Beckham and Michael Owen, while the Half Moon pub, in Paignton, Devon, renamed itself The Half Roon. It was the summer of 2004 and the whole country, it seemed, was going mad about the boy.

The boy was Wayne Rooney, two years out of school and suddenly a star on an enormous scale. He was not quite an overnight success, with a number of smaller outbreaks of "Roo-mania" witnessed over the previous 18 months, but now the whole world, or at least the whole of Europe, was talking about him. *AS*, the Spanish sports daily, called him the "Messiah", while the Italian *Corriere dello Sport* christened him "the Baby Bomber".

For once, the hype was justified. Rooney had taken the European Championship finals by storm, showing a maturity that belied his 18 years in England's opening match, against France, before exploding into life with two goals in each of the group games against Switzerland and

> "Two years out of school,
> suddenly he was a
> star on an enormous scale"

Croatia. Who knows what would have happened had he not limped off with a broken foot just 22 minutes into the quarter-final, when England were leading Portugal 1-0?

Nonetheless, Rooney's heroics in Portugal — which Eriksson, not usually given to hyperbole, described as the biggest impact made by a teenager in a leading tournament since Pele in the 1958 World Cup — had catapulted him on to football's A-list. Eighteen months earlier, he had been on a £90-a-week youth contract at Everton. Now Manchester United and Chelsea led a queue of clubs prepared to pay whatever it took to spirit him away from Goodison Park.

Quite what David Moyes, his club manager at Everton, made of it is not clear. He said he was delighted at the performances of his prodigy, but that pride may have been tempered by frustration at the young forward's

inconsistency at club level. His second full season had been a disappointment, with a poor return of nine goals in 40 appearances — as many as he managed in 12 outings for England — and no fewer than 12 yellow cards.

Perhaps that says more about Everton than about Rooney. Perhaps he has already outgrown them, the so-called street footballer having found that the Goodison stage is no longer big enough for his talents. Either way, with or without Everton, Rooney is on his way to superstardom. A frightening thought for the rest of Europe, but "Roo-mania" has only just begun.

AWARDS

THIERRY HENRY insists that the team comes first, but while there is no doubt that claiming the championship trophy will have given him most pleasure at the end of an historic season, it must have been a special source of pride for the Arsenal striker to create another record when he became the first man to capture back-to-back PFA Player of the Year and Football Writers' Association Footballer of the Year awards.

"It's difficult to find new words for Henry every time," Arsene Wenger said of a player who scored 30 league goals in a season's haul of 39. "I don't think there's a better striker in the world." Henry beat off the challenge of Alan Shearer, Jay-Jay Okocha, Steven Gerrard, Frank Lampard and Patrick Vieira to top the PFA poll.

Scott Parker's selection as PFA Young Player of the Year reflected his contribution first to Charlton Athletic and then to Chelsea, while at the other end of the age range, Dario Gradi received a PFA merit award after completing more than 1,000 games in charge of Crewe Alexandra.

PFA AWARDS
Player of the Year: Thierry Henry (Arsenal)
Young Player of the Year: Scott Parker (Chelsea)
Merit Award: Dario Gradi (Crewe Alexandra)
Premiership team of the year: Tim Howard (Manchester United) – **Lauren** (Arsenal), **Sol Campbell** (Arsenal), **John Terry** (Chelsea), **Ashley Cole** (Arsenal) – **Steven Gerrard** (Liverpool), **Frank Lampard** (Chelsea), **Patrick Vieira** (Arsenal), **Robert Pires** (Arsenal) – **Thierry Henry** (Arsenal), **Ruud van Nistelrooy** (Manchester United)

BARCLAYCARD PREMIERSHIP AWARD
Manager of the Year: Arsene Wenger (Arsenal)

BARCLAYCARD MERIT AWARD
Paul Durkin

LEAGUE MANAGERS ASSOCIATION AWARDS
Manager of the Year: Arsene Wenger (Arsenal)
First division: Nigel Worthington (Norwich City)
Second division: Paul Sturrock (Plymouth Argyle)
Third division: Dave Penney (Doncaster Rovers)
Merit Award: Don Howe

ROMAN: FROM POWER TO GLORY

Simon Barnes

IT WAS WIMBLEDON. The Wimbledon that happens in Wimbledon, not the other one. Two things occupied the mind: a new star, a new book. Was Roger Federer the magical being he seemed? And how was Harry Potter going to get out of this one? And then all at once we were faced with a story far less credible than either Harry or Roger's tale. It was the story of Roman Abramovich and the Wallet of Fire.

At the tennis, it seemed that we had all been doing a decent job of keeping football off the back pages. There was the David Beckham transfer story, true, and some stuff about Ronaldinho and Harry Kewell. But that apart, football seemed to be behaving with an altogether admirable sense of restraint. Tennis. Test matches. The Open golf coming up.

And then, just after first edition one evening in SW19, the most improbable football story in years exploded in our faces. A Russian multibillionaire had bought Chelsea Football Club — apparently on a whim, apparently with the handful of cash he had found lying on his dressing-table. He was going to spend millions more on footballers. A new word entered the football language: Chelski.

The first questions we asked were: who is this man? And why is he doing this thing? They are the questions we are all still asking.

The most obvious and immediate truth was that The Abramovich Purchase broke all the established rules. These state that football clubs spend money generated by football clubs. A big club has more to spend than a small club, but both are bound by the same basic rule: football can only spend football's money. Abramovich brought to football the financial rules of racing.

Very few owners buy racehorses with money generated by racing. Racing is not self-sufficient, it is subsidised by those who wish to buy into dreamland. Racehorses have always been the glorious folly of the wealthy. As the song has it, you race them just for a laugh, ha ha ha.

Now Abramovich, it seemed, had bought a football

HOW CHELSEA SPENT ABRAMOVICH MILLIONS			
July 15, 2003	Glen Johnson	West Ham United	£6m
July 16	Geremi	Real Madrid	£7m
July 21	Damien Duff	Blackburn Rovers	£17m
July 21	Wayne Bridge	Southampton	£7m
August 6	Joe Cole	West Ham United	£6.6m
August 7	Juan Sebastian Veron	Manchester United	£15m
August 11	Adrian Mutu	Parma	£15.8m
August 25	Alexei Smertin	Bordeaux	£3.45m
August 26	Hernan Crespo	Inter Milan	£16.8m
Sept 1	Claude Makelele	Real Madrid	£16.6m
Jan 19, 2004	Scott Parker	Charlton Athletic	£10m
February 10	Petr Cech	Rennes	£7m
March 2	Arjen Robben	PSV Eindhoven	£12m
July 2	Mateja Kezman	PSV Eindhoven	£7m

club for the same reason. He then spent in jigtime £111 million on players, ha ha ha. Experts gave their opinions on what it would do to a transfer market that had, until that moment, looked moribund. Mention Chelsea and the asking price doubled.

A new season dawned. I abandoned the World Athletics Championships in Paris before they had finished in order to get my first look at Chelsea. Intriguingly, they were held to a 2-2 draw by Blackburn Rovers at Stamford Bridge. A most instructive comparison here. Because everybody had been asking: "Can a man really buy the Premiership title?"

It was a question hoping for the answer "no", because this massive transfusion of cash looked so unnatural and unfair. But, of course, you can buy a title: Blackburn themselves did it in 1995. Jack Walker liked the title so much that he bought it.

But there were significant differences. Walker was a local boy made good, a salt-of-the-earth millionaire who never betrayed his roots. He simply lived out the dream of all small-town boys: made his pile, bought the club he had supported as a lad and made it great again. He did so without buying any black players, though we are supposed to believe that this was mere coincidence. Whatever the truth behind all that, it emphasises an earthy, homespun, east-west-home's-best philosophy: none of your fancy foreign ways here. As if to prove the point, the attack was led by Alan Shearer, an embodiment of solid, unvarnished, English virtues.

The Abramovich takeover was nothing like this.

Abramovich liked the club so much he bought it from Ken Bates. The former Chelsea chairman was soon heading for the exit

Abramovich was no lifelong Chelsea supporter. He wasn't even a football supporter. But for reasons not easily apparent, he was prepared to buy a lorryload of expensive footballers and to chuck them together and see if they could become a football team.

It was a wonderful, elegant experiment in the very nature of teams. How long does it take for a group of individuals to become a team? How much shared experience is necessary before the right kind of trust builds up? How long does it take to establish a culture of excellence?

Outsiders looked on, longing to witness a pratfall. Is there anything in life quite as amusing as seeing those who fancy themselves taken down a peg? Football offers this to a greater extent than any other sport in the calendar. That alone is enough to explain football's disproportionate appeal.

But what was the appeal of football for Abramovich? Nobody knew. Nobody knew anything about him. He looked absurdly young. That was because he *is* absurdly young. He was born in October 1966; so that was the second extraordinary thing to happen to English football in that year.

A lad of 37, smiling enigmatically from the directors' box. How could anybody get so much money so young? What did he do? What is he good at? Where is the steel, where is the diamond-hardness required to achieve so much in so little time? Abramovich gave nothing away, smiling, clapping, refusing most interviews, well aware that there is more power in mystery than in self-revelation.

And so, for want of a better theory, Chelsea were looked on as a rich man's toy: a string of human racehorses. A man who had worked with, presumably, dedication and fanaticism in order to gather all that money was now able to loosen up and have a bit of fun. Chelsea gave him the chance to reflect on the fact that he had led a stimulating, if somewhat one-track sort of life, and could now afford to indulge himself. It was time to revel in the fruits of his achievement.

The serious flaw in this view is that Abramovich has never for one instant looked like a man who has outgrown ambition. One look at him seems to indicate that the power remains switched on, the ambitions unfulfilled, the thirst unquenched. So what is the Chelsea deal really all about? Most business deals — most agreements of any kind — make sense as soon as you know what's in it for the other bloke. But no one knew what was in it for Abramovich.

Claude Makelele joins the Roman revolution at Stamford Bridge after a £16.6 million move from Real Madrid

His first season was a tremendously successful loosener. Or perhaps it was an exercise in running a football club by means of chaos theory. Second in the Premiership, semi-finals of the European Cup — it looked pretty good. But the absurdity of the public dealings with Claudio Ranieri, the head coach, made the club and Abramovich look not only cruel and hard-hearted but also daft and indecisive.

Some observers see Abramovich as an owner of the kind more often found on the mainland of Europe than on Pudding Island, an owner who insists on having his say in player acquisition and team selection. Then Jose Mourinho, appointed in the close season as Ranieri's successor, made public statements long before he was offered the job, saying that he would never work under such constraints. Which leaves the situation more enigmatic than ever — and we are still no wiser about the question of who Abramovich is and why he has bought a football club.

It was *The Sunday Times* Rich List that gave us a clue. It placed Abramovich as supreme champion: the richest individual living in Britain. He overtook the perennial winner, the Duke of Westminster, to do so, his £7.5 billion beating Westminster's cheeseparing £5.5 billion. In third and fourth were Hans Rausing and Philip Green.

If you are not an expert in business, you will ask: who are those last two? But you do not need to ask about the No 1. Everyone knows who Abramovich is. He is the man who bought Chelsea Football Club.

He has, through this one act, acquired a name. It is a name that has a resonance everywhere football is played — that is to say, the entire world outside the United States. Abramovich has, at a stroke, acquired clout, presence, reputation: even, if you like, charisma. All that adds up to power.

That's what it comes down to. Abramovich is clearly a man unsated. He has achieved greatness, he has revealed nothing less than genius, in so far as these things can be measured in fiscal terms. But Abramovich wants more. That seems clear from the cut of his jib. Exactly what sort of more is unclear, but his acquisition of Chelsea has opened up a great new world of opportunities. It is a slightly humbling thing for football's *amour-propre*.

Football is a small world that likes to think of itself as the most important thing in life. But for Abramovich, football is just another piece on the chessboard.

Abramovich may be part of football now, but football is also part of Abramovich's schemes. And he will demand more, something better than second place and semi-finalists. He wants to be associated with excellence: he wants, above all, to be associated with victory.

Abramovich made the new Chelsea: now Chelsea are required to do him credit. If Chelsea fail to make Abramovich took great, then Chelsea have failed and people must suffer. Chelsea have a long-term place in Abramovich's plans: it is his flagship, his mascot, his totem. Chelsea!

Look on my works, ye mighty, and despair.

The introduction of a transfer window did nothing to stop Abramovich launching a £100 million-plus raid on clubs across Europe after the Russian took control of Chelsea

MEN BEHAVING BADLY

Tony Cascarino

IT HAD BEEN A TYPICAL tour: a few days of relaxation in Hong Kong, some friendly matches, evenings spent (foolishly) being amused at nightclubs. Drink, women, the odd player disappearing — the usual stuff. Then we were invited to watch an execution.

It was a couple of days before we were scheduled to fly back. The army officer who was acting as our guide and guard asked us if we fancied going into Kuala Lumpur to watch someone being put to death. "It's a local boy," he said, as if that would help us to make up our minds. Cue laughter from some of my Aston Villa team-mates.

Naturally, none of us went. But even then, in 1991, before the popularity of the game exploded and players were thrust into the public spotlight as never before, it was evidence of the kind of privileges — if being invited to watch an execution could be called a privilege — that

Lineker thought standards of behaviour had hit rock bottom

were on offer. Now there can be few lifestyles that can offer the same in terms of money, attention, pampering … and, yes, women.

Players have always been at their happiest when they have been together and out on the town. There is this sense of invincibility that comes from being rich and famous. It is hard to refuse when gorgeous women offer all kinds of flattery and sexual temptations. It matters little whether the players are nice to them or if they behave like complete idiots. They are trinkets that the women can exhibit to their friends. Some players can resist. More often than not, I was one who succumbed.

Many people have suggested that the last season in England was when the game finally veered out of control as far as the behaviour of the players was concerned. Among those to raise his concerns was Gary Lineker, who suggested at the football writers' dinner just before the FA Cup Final that standards had slipped alarmingly over the past few years and had now hit rock bottom.

Of course, there were several high-profile incidents, with allegations of rape made against players from Newcastle United, Leeds United and Leicester City. Sections of the media were quick to convict such well-known players, all of whom were exonerated. But in previous recent seasons, too, there have been unconnected trials of Leeds and Chelsea players accused of assault. Was 2003-04 really the season when the game reached its lowest ebb?

Perhaps the only difference last season was that the events were more concentrated than before. For a while it seemed that hardly a day would go by without some high-profile footballer being accused of something. Even the saintly figure of David Beckham — who has built much of his image around the idea that he is a "perfect" family man — was the cause of a blizzard of newspaper headlines in April when allegations of an extra-marital affair, which he strongly denied, first appeared.

In the past, players have been too quick to forget the warnings on offer when their colleagues got into trouble. Maybe now a few of them will be more wary about where they go, what they do, who they are seen with. But I suspect the majority will not.

I've little doubt that the behaviour of some players has

Court Entrance

NOT
DVLA

The game's most
high-profile players,
such as George Best,
have always lived
their private lives in
the media glare

been worse in the past. The biggest difference is that the incidents never came to light. During my career, players would frequent nightclubs where they knew the staff. It was easier to cover things up, like Paul McGrath's drinking, other players' sexual adventures. Now there are people seeking to profit financially from players' misdemeanours, individuals ready to tip off tabloids and women no longer embarrassed about their exploits and showing their faces. They are only too aware that they can sell their story to a newspaper, or visit their lawyer.

The really top players, such as George Best, have always been celebrities whose lives have interested the public and media. Best and Mary Stavin have been superseded by David and Victoria Beckham. Back in Best's day, though, the majority of players were never considered stars. Yet as media coverage of all aspects of football has intensified, some outlets now choose to treat any professional as a celebrity if it suits their agenda.

Players and, increasingly, their partners and parents are instantly recognisable and, as a consequence, it is easier to uncover their transgressions. Perhaps society demands a higher level of responsibility from players than they feel they owe to anyone other than their families. Players are human: they fail, they are susceptible to an affair — just, indeed, like individuals in the media, whom players feel can be frustratingly hypocritical at times. We all have faults and I found myself empathising with Beckham. I erred, but I was not nearly so famous that my infidelity was splashed over the newspapers.

As players have earned more, their mentality has changed. When I began my career, players would play well and take their money. Now, some want their money first and then they may play well. It's often greed, a competition to have the latest artefact all the time. One player I heard about received dismissive looks from his team-mates for owning a Ferrari that was two years old. Another couldn't decide which watch to buy, so he bought three. Surrounded by yes-men and spoilt from a young age, they rarely receive anything but praise and largely believe their own publicity.

In a player's cossetted life, money buys a feeling of power they sometimes abuse. Some display a nonchalant attitude, typified so patently by Rio Ferdinand failing to take a drugs test in September. Until I was 27, I was little different. Surrounded by footballing mates, I believed I was special. A player I knew at Liverpool had a chauffeur, others have drivers-cum-bodyguards that follow them around to deal with any problems. It is understandable, though, because there are people, often ignited by

Paul McGrath, left, the defender notorious for his drinking habits, played at a time when it was far easier for footballers' excesses to be kept out of the public spotlight

jealousy, who seek to provoke them — at bars, in nightclubs — into being aggressive.

The crazy notion of fame hit home for me at a nightclub in Ireland, when a girl I had not long met pretended that she did not recognise me as an international player. "My friend had to tell me who you were and I am not talking to you as you're a footballer, it's because I like you," she said. Her words massaged my ego, something I was susceptible to, and after a few more drinks she said: "You are not going to take me home and sleep with me." I wasn't intending to, I replied. "I will have sex with you now, though," she added.

The Ireland players, treated like heroes, would have to fend off girls who wanted to have sex with them. Mobbed in nightclubs, people would scramble to meet and kiss us. It's why club managers prefer their players not to be single, so they know there is someone to answer to.

On another occasion I met a girl in a nightclub in Dublin. She wanted me to go back to her house to introduce me to her father, who thought I was a great player. Sat on her settee at 5am, she offered to make me a coffee. She went to the kitchen and returned wearing only a red bra, knickers and suspenders. Wait a moment, she said, and I heard her pounding upstairs to return with her father. Wait a moment, she said again, and she came back with his football album and trophies, which he guided me through as his daughter paraded around in the skimpiest of garments. I sat there so embarrassed. And then he went to work.

Yes, I upset people, did things wrong. But the temptation and opportunities were there and I took them. When I had six or seven pints, laughing, joking, something would go wrong in my head and I found people attractive. Some people can walk away, others can't. Some never put themselves into a situation where they can do anything wrong. Now, I consider how I would feel if my second wife strayed — the feeling of being let down, devastated. I wouldn't want her to feel like that. It was easy for me to get caught up in that glamorous world, which has only magnified since I hung up my boots.

So, was Gary Lineker right? I don't think so. It is only the public awareness of the players' misdemeanours that has changed. The problem is, we are never going to go back to the days when players' lives were a well-kept secret. Football is now such a huge, glamorous, rich business that players — from the top of their profession to the bottom — are targets. It might be unfair, but what none of them can say in their defence in future is that they have not been warned.

GREECE LEAVE GIANTS IN RUINS

Martin Samuel

MUST TRY HARDER. THE abiding feeling on leaving Portugal in the summer was that the biggest nations, the best players, the self-proclaimed stars of European football, had only themselves to blame for an outcome that was as deserved as it was unexpected.

Instead of cursing Otto Rehhagel and Greek efficiency — and when did you hear those two words in the same sentence in the build-up to the Athens Olympic Games? — it might be better if the vanquished looked closer to home in the wake of events at Euro 2004 and raised their game and their standards in time to avoid a repeat in Germany. When many of the top nations underachieved at the World Cup in 2002, the proximity of the competition to the climax of the club football season in

Europe was a convenient, and believable, explanation. For it to happen a second time smacks of complacency.

That a team of well-organised, honest battlers should win, fair and square, a European Championship that was held up as the most complete and consistent test in international football says as much about the also-rans as it does about the winners. Before lifting the trophy, Greece overcame the hosts (twice), the holders and the form team of the tournament, and at the group stage they helped to remove the nation with the best domestic league in Europe. This was no fluke — but does anyone seriously consider Greece to possess the best football team in Europe if the rival nations perform to their potential?

The consensus is that this was a triumph of the Greek will and the tactical skill of a coach whose previous term of employment had ended with his club team, 1FC Kaiserslautern, 15th of 18 in the Bundesliga. Ugly ducklings together, Rehhagel was out of work when handed the Greece job and his adopted country had previously qualified for one European Championship finals, in 1980, returning with a single point from three games. Even topping Spain's qualifying group did little to encourage confidence on a bigger stage and Greece were given a starting price between 80-1 and 100-1 (only Switzerland and Latvia were more poorly regarded).

Having beaten Portugal, France and the Czech Republic, and helped to dispose of Spain, it is now impossible to question the worthiness of Greece's win on any logical level, so critics have instead focused on an area that is impossible to quantify, decrying their football as a retrograde presence, built solidly on defence and putting the emphasis on the opposition to break down a man-for-man marking system, complete with sweeper.

The question remains, though: is that a bad thing? Greece may represent a throwback to the days when flair was stifled by (mostly German) tactics at the big tournaments, but look what came out of that. Sick of leaving empty-handed, the best worked harder and grew fitter and more technically adept, while coaches became more daring. Football entered an era in which Real

Luiz Felipe Scolari, the Portugal coach, had one of the stars of Euro 2004 in Ronaldo, but Greek efficiency won through

Eriksson, left, was guilty of tactical errors while Robben, above, and Holland paid for Advocaat's substitution blunder

negative tactics meant that they were no more lamented than the cumbersome Germans.

If Euro 2004 was an endorsement of the worth of the coach, the validation did not apply to all. Rehhagel went safety-first but also changed formations and tactics to win matches, made aggressive substitutions and responded swiftly to movements in the balance of power during the game. That is not the same as taking off your best player at 1-0 up, retreating to a foxhole on the edge of your own 18-yard box and handing the initiative to the opposition.

Dick Advocaat's removal of Arjen Robben, the best player on the field against the Czech Republic, snatched defeat from the jaws of victory. The same is true of Eriksson's decision to put Emile Heskey on for Rooney against France. Even if Heskey had not given away the senseless free kick that turned the game in France's favour in injury time, the Alamo-like assault on England's goal that followed Rooney's withdrawal was evidence that a grave misjudgment had been made.

Hanging on for grim death is not a game-plan. It is ironic that Euro 2004 should go down as a triumph for the men with the chalkboards, because at the halfway stage a campaign to keep coaches out of football would have found many willing supporters. The Dutch said it best. A banner held up at their quarter-final with Sweden read: "*Dick, begrupt je vrouw je weer?*" Translation: "Dick, does your wife understand you?"

The biggest losers of all came from football's aristocracy. A cutting from *The Times* dated Saturday, June 12 — the opening day of the tournament — gives the measure of the revolution that took place in Europe.

Beneath a giant headline with the legend "Go for it!" was a full-page advertisement from the G-14 group, the self-appointed "voice of the clubs" (a preposterous boast, considering G-14 represents just 18 of football's most privileged throughout Europe, including some, like Borussia Dortmund, that have been dismally run and remain financially fragile). The announcement was an overblown exercise in swaggering arrogance. "G-14 members are providing a third of all players at Euro 2004," it bragged, "including the vast majority of the tournament's stars. We are confident that G-14's players will help to make this year's championship the best yet. Go for it!" Printed below was a list of the 139 footballers appearing in Euro 2004 that were contracted to G-14 clubs (including, rather shamelessly, those that had been sold to non-G-14 members before the competition, such as Paulo Ferreira, who had agreed to go from FC Porto to

Madrid, on their day, played some of the most devastatingly beautiful football ever seen, the English championship was won by an Arsenal team many consider to be the greatest, or at least the most enthralling, to play on these shores and, at international level, a high-water mark was reached by the standard set at Euro 2000. Greece's win was not a reaction to that, but a warning regarding what happens if contentment sets in.

There were too many self-satisfied superstars in Portugal, too many coaches without the imagination to seek the creative best from their players. Sven-Goran Eriksson is far guiltier of betraying football's brave new world than Rehhagel, considering the players at his disposal; Giovanni Trapattoni, of Italy, too. Given Paul Scholes, Frank Lampard, David Beckham, Steven Gerrard, Wayne Rooney and Michael Owen, it is possible that Rehhagel would not have been so centred on rugged defence.

Eriksson had a truly talented group yet turned his two most important games into a version of Ali's rope-a-dope, minus the flurry of killer punches at the end. England got what they deserved; so did Greece. Italy went home unbeaten with five points from three games (one more than Greece had in the group stage), yet their

Chelsea). Only Latvia did not have a representative on the page. So how many of this glittering 139 did the victors have to call upon in the final against Portugal? Answer: none. Georgios Karagounis was the only G-14 representative in the Greece squad and he was suspended for their finest hour. Far from providing the vast majority of the tournament's stars, the playground bullies of European football donated many of its greatest flops.

A team of G-14 disappointments would include Fabien Barthez in goal, a defence of Ferreira (well, they wanted him), dropped after one game when put against the Bolton Wanderers outside left, Jens Nowotny and the Real Madrid duo, Ivan Helguera and Raul Bravo; a midfield of Beckham, Bernd Schneider and Robert Pires; and more strikers than you could shake a stick at. Take your pick from Pauleta, Thierry Henry, David Trezeguet, Christian Vieri and Raul.

Does this mean the tide is turning in the European game? No, but it would suggest that the margins at international level are so small these days that it is not possible for any player to coast or for any coach to fail to make the best use of his team without falling short of the target.

There is hope, of course, not least because the majority of success stories at the tournament — the unfortunate and brilliant Pavel Nedved aside — were teenagers (Cristiano Ronaldo and Rooney) or men in their early twenties (Robben and Philipp Lahm). On a purely selfish note, it is also pleasing that three of that quartet will play in the Premiership this season. Yet the emergence of a handful of future stars hardly means that the World Cup in Germany will be easier for the favoured nations. Take France. In 2006, Zinedine Zidane and Lilian Thuram will be 34, Claude Makelele and Pires 33, Bixente Lizarazu 36, Patrick Vieira 30. At least these players have something to show for their efforts.

By the time a ball is kicked in Germany, Beckham, Scholes, Sol Campbell and Gary Neville will be 31 — and the nagging fear remains that the tournament just passed saw a generation of English footballers at their peak and an opportunity wasted. Like Portugal's famed golden boys, the expectations have always exceeded the reality. So, too, for the Italians: Vieri, Alessandro Del Piero, Fabio Cannavaro and Alessandro Nesta will all be men in their thirties by the time of the next tournament.

Will they be any match for another invasion of well-drilled, ambitious nobodies, culled from the reserve teams of Europe? Not without a fight.

Rehhagel's flexibility was a key element in Greece's triumph

SCHOOL OF SCIENCE

Daniel Finkelstein

IT HAPPENED, AS most things in my life do, because of a political meeting and a free-market think-tank. Before it did, I was an enthusiastic football fan, but hardly someone whose view on the game you would pay much attention to. Now I feel increasingly excited. I think I'm playing a part, a tiny part but still a part, in a revolution that is going to change soccer profoundly.

Just before the last World Cup, I was heading back in the car from a political meeting, an interminable dinner where someone had been droning on about policy on something or other of importance, I forget what. That's when I tuned in to one of those late-night radio talk shows and heard "Henry from Warwick" say what he thought would happen when the tournament kicked off.

Now, normally I would have turned over straight away, but Henry was making sense, so I kept listening. This is what he had to say: "When two sides meet we all think

we know which is the better one and which is more likely to win, and we've all got views about the favourites to lift the cup. We justify our guesses with all sorts of theories, but in the end they remain just that, guesses. And pretty often they're not very good ones, either.

"There are so many different possibilities in a football tournament, millions in fact, that the human brain can't integrate them and reach a sensible estimation of their chances."

Thank you, Henry from Warwick, and now the weather… except that he didn't stop there. Henry Stott, an academic at Warwick University, had created a computer model, input every international result for the past two years, simulated millions of different outcomes and was able to provide probabilities for different games and the overall competition.

Any temptation I had to dismiss Stott as an eccentric disappeared two days later when France met Senegal in the opening game. The bookies thought that Senegal had a one in eight chance. Wrong, Stott's computer model said. These are the two most inconsistent sides in the 2002 World Cup finals. Senegal have a 25 per cent chance. Senegal duly won. Henry from Warwick certainly had my attention now.

Throughout the rest of the competition, "amazing" upsets happened that the model did not regard as "amazing" at all. When South Korea beat Italy in the second round, for instance, the modellers, having taken home advantage properly into account, were comparatively unsurprised.

Soon after Brazil won the trophy, *The Times* and Warwick University began collaborating on Premiership data. Stott and I were joined by Dr Alex Morton and a new model, the Fink Tank Predictor, was created, using data for goals scored and conceded (their role was to do all the work, mine was to ring every couple of days and ask how they were getting on). Adding in home advantage and weighting so that more recent results counted for more allowed the Warwick statisticians to provide probabilities of different match outcomes, rank attacks and defences and suggest the likelihood of title challenges or relegation. All this was very interesting, of

Stott proved that playing the percentage game can work

Senegal's defeat of France in the 2002 World Cup finals may have been considered a shock, but a computer model had predicted it

course, and it enabled *Times* readers to do pretty well at the bookmakers. But it does not justify my earlier claim to be playing a small part in a revolution. That's where the free-market think-tank came in.

Hearing of my interest in football stats, a friend recommended that I read an article in the journal of one of Margaret Thatcher's favourite organisations, the Institute of Economic Affairs. Two economists were trying to work out how important managers were to companies. Since football clubs provide years of consistent data, it struck them that they could use football to help them to work out the contribution made by managers.

Their conclusion? Sacking the gaffer is a much over-rated pastime. True, clubs often seem to do better in the short run, but that is because the old manager was only sacked when results were uncommonly bad anyway. A bit of a rebound was almost bound to happen with or without a new manager.

The moment I read this article, I realised that if economists could use soccer stats to analyse the benefits of sacking a manager, then the same rigour could be used to examine a wide range of ideas about the sport. All that commentating guff ("the form-book flies out of the window in derbies", "just before half-time is the worst time to concede", and so on) could be shown to be true or false.

I told Stott all this excitedly. He smiled indulgently. It had already occurred to him and Morton. It had occurred to a few people in the United States, too. The Oakland Athletics baseball team is much poorer than many of its big, successful rivals. So Billy Beane, their general manager, and a number of other visionaries began to think how they might use their resources more efficiently.

Using information gathered from the internet (and reading the ideas of people such as Bill James, the data-mad baseball writer), they worked out, for instance, that most clubs were using their annual pick of new players, called the draft, very poorly. They were selecting high-school players who looked good rather than college graduates with a record. Of course, when you picked from the former group, you stood a greater chance of recruiting a star before anyone else. But on average, given how many didn't work out, you would do worse.

The Oakland A's went on to pursue an entirely different strategy to their rivals in terms of the skills they valued and the data they regarded as truly important. The views of backroom boys with computers has become more valuable to the A's than that of their traditional scouting operation. And the computer work is

A book about the work of Beane, above, did not go down well in baseball circles, but his methods were vindicated

The likes of Aston Villa and Birmingham City now have proof that form does indeed go out of the window in derbies

influencing their tactics, too. The new ideas have been an almost complete success and others are now copying them. But success has not come without controversy.

When Michael Lewis recorded Beane's work in his book *Moneyball* many in the baseball establishment did not react well. They said it was nonsense (which it clearly isn't) or that it took the romance out of the game (which it clearly doesn't). They just wanted the geeks and their computers to go away. They won't. And let me explain why.

Using football data for journalism has produced interesting results. Among them: the form-book, it turns out, does fly out of the window in derby games; conceding just before half-time has no additional impact on conceding at any other time; the league table sometimes does lie, because a league season is not long enough to guarantee in most cases that the leaders are really the best side; and most surprisingly of all, there is no evidence whatsoever that short-term bursts of form change the probability of results in the next game.

Yet if all it did was to produce ripostes to commentators, this work would be little more than entertainment and certainly not a revolution. However, it does far more than that. Pioneers such as the late Charles

Reep or Charles Hughes, of the FA, have for years been using carefully recorded data to estimate the correct number of passes before trying to score, or the best way to take a corner. It's from this that "direct football" was derived.

Now the use of computers and models such as the Fink Tank Predictor can make this work more accurate and deeper. Claudio Ranieri, for instance, believed that he was on to something at Chelsea with his tinkering, but simple computer work showed he wasn't, that tinkering damages teams. John Terry's performance may be highly rated by the pundits, but carefully tracking his play might show he does not complete enough successful passes. The optimal strategy for substitution or even for professional fouls could be calculated.

But this isn't where the big money is. That is in player selection. In the close season, huge transfer fees and wages are on offer for the best players. But are they really worth it? Derivatives traders in the US have been helping baseball clubs to value stars properly. No more watching a video a couple of times and guessing. If we could do that in football, it would deserve the title "a revolution". The computer geeks aren't going away. We're here to stay.

EUROPEAN CHAMPIONSHIP

Uplifting moment: Angelos Charisteas, the man whose goal won Euro 2004 for Greece, gets his hands on the trophy

THE GAMES

Matt Dickinson, Chief Football Correspondent

Saturday June 12
Group A   *Dragao Stadium*
PORTUGAL (0) **1**   **GREECE** (2) **2**
Ronaldo 90   Karagounis 7
48,761   Basinas 52 (pen)

PORTUGAL Ricardo — Paulo Ferreira, F Couto, Jorge
Andrade, Rui Jorge — Costinha (sub: Nuno Gomes,
66min), Maniche — L Figo, Rui Costa (sub: Deco, ht), S
Simao (sub: C Ronaldo, ht) — Pauleta *Substitutes not
used* Quim, Moreira, Miguel, Beto, Nuno Valente, Ricardo
Carvalho, Petit, Tiago, H Postiga
Booked **Costinha, Pauleta**

GREECE A Nikopolidis — G Seitaridis, T Dellas, M Kapsis,
P Fyssas — S Giannakopoulos (sub: T Nikolaidis, 68), T
Zagorakis, A Basinas, G Karagounis (sub: K Katsouranis,
ht) — Z Vryzas, A Charisteas (sub: V Lakis, 74)
Substitutes not used K Chalkias, T Katergiannakis, I
Goumas, N Dabizas, S Venetidis, P Kafes, V Tsiartas, G
Georgiadis, D Papadopoulos
Booked **Karagounis, Seitaridis**
Referee **P Collina** (Italy)

                                                     Algarve Stadium
SPAIN (0) **1**   **RUSSIA** (0) **0**
Valeron 60   30,000

SPAIN I Casillas — C Puyol, I Helguera, C Marchena, Raul
Bravo — D Albelda — J Etxeberria, R Baraja (sub: Xabi
Alonso, 59min), Vicente — Raul (sub: Fernando Torres,
78), F Morientes (sub: J C Valeron, 59) *Substitutes not
used* S Canizares, D Aranzubia, J Capdevila, A Luque,
Gabri, Cesar, Joaquin, Xavi, Juanito
Booked **Baraja, Marchena, Albelda**

RUSSIA S Ovchinnikov — V Evseev, A Smertin, R
Sharonov, D Sennikov — D Alenichev, E Aldonin (sub: D
Sytchev, 68), A Mostovoi — R Gusev (sub: V Radimov, ht),
M Izmailov (sub: A Kariaka, 74) — D Bulykin *Substitutes
not used* V Malafeev, I Akinfeev, I Semshov, A Kerzhakov,
A Aniukov, D Kirichenko, V Bystrov, D Loskov, A Bugaev
Booked **Gusev, Sharonov, Smertin, Aldonin, Radimov**
Sent off **Sharonov** (88)
Referee **U Meier** (Switzerland)

Sunday June 13
Group B
SWITZERLAND (0) 0   *Dr Magalhaes Pessoa Stadium*
SWITZERLAND (0) **0**   **CROATIA** (0) **0**
24,090

SWITZERLAND J Stiel — B Haas, M Yakin, P Muller, C
Spycher — B Huggel, J Vogel, R Wicky (sub: S Henchoz,
83min) — H Yakin (sub: D Gygax, 87) — A Frei, S
Chapuisat (sub: F Celestini, 54) *Substitutes not used* B
Berner, M Zwyssig, L Magnin, T Barnetta, M Rama, J
Vonlanthen, P Zuberbuhler
Booked **Vogel, Huggel, Stiel**
Sent off **Vogel** (50)

CROATIA T Butina — D Simic (sub: D Srna, 61), R Kovac,
J Simunic, B Zivkovic — N Kovac, N Bjelica (sub: G Rosso,
74) — I Mornar, D Prso, I Olic (sub: M Rapaic, ht) — T
Sokota *Substitutes not used* M Tokic, S Tomas, M
Neretljak, J Leko, M Babic, I Klasnic, V Vasilj, J A Didulica
Booked **Prso, Bjelica, Rapaic, Zivkovic, Mornar**
Referee **L Batista** (Portugal)

WAS A GREAT DAY FOR GREECE a bad one for football? From the reaction of some people, including the hugely influential Michel Platini, you would have guessed that Uefa had no sooner presented the European Championship trophy to the most unlikely winners in the tournament's history than they were working out how to make sure that it never happened again.

Greece deserved better because, however defensive in style, they had won Euro 2004 on merit. The first team to beat the holders (France) and the hosts (Portugal, twice), they also knocked out Spain and the Czech Republic. At least Luiz Felipe Scolari, the coach of Portugal, was gracious after defeat in the final. "It is up to us, the more offensive sides, to work out how to beat them," he said.

Scolari's words will have come too late to stop crisis meetings at the European governing body. The failure of any of the favourites to reach the semi-finals will have caused alarm, if only because maximising broadcasting and sponsorship revenues depends on the likes of England, Italy and Spain enjoying success.

No one should discourage Uefa from discussing the big issues — Are the top stars playing too much? Should there be quotas of home-grown players in the top leagues? — but the haste with which those investigations began undermined Greece's achievement. There was a sense that Otto Rehhagel's team had lowered the tone of the party, which was rich coming from the English, in particular, given that Sven-Goran Eriksson's men had hardly set standards of footballing excellence.

No one could doubt that the tournament did not hit the heights of Euro 2000, but that was not Greece's fault. On the back of a disappointing 2002 World Cup finals, their unlikely triumph has been interpreted as further proof that the international game is in crisis, but the quality of Euro 2000, when four top-class sides collided memorably in the last three matches, was the exception rather than the rule. Germany hardly raised the pulse on their way to winning Euro 96 and the France team of 1998, which may have had Zinedine Zidane but had no centre forward, had an easier route to the final than Greece did in Portugal.

Some of the leading stars were jaded but, while Thierry Henry disappointed, his Arsenal team-mates, Ashley Cole and Sol Campbell, were in brilliant form. Zidane, Raul and David Beckham may have been paying the price for Real Madrid's policy of squeezing every appearance out of their *galacticos*, but it was a decent tournament for Luis Figo, despite the finale.

According to Arsene Wenger, one of football's wisest heads, sweeping conclusions should be avoided, with each country's failings

Barthez saves Beckham's penalty to keep France alive against England

examined individually. Those inquests will have become even more pointed on the basis that, if Theodoros Zagorakis could lift the trophy, why not Zidane, Raul, Alessandro Del Piero or Beckham?

In England's case, the disappointment was intense because there had been a genuine belief, not least among the players, that this was a team that could win the first big trophy since the World Cup in 1966. For a long time in their opening match against France, it did not seem an entirely fanciful notion as, thanks to Frank Lampard's first-half header, England looked capable of beating the holders, even if their goal had come against the run of play.

When Mikael Silvestre scythed down Wayne Rooney, Beckham should have finished off the match, but his spot kick — not his worst of the tournament, as it turned out — was a nice height for Fabien Barthez. England were punished to the maximum when, in three extraordinary minutes, Zidane turned the game on its head with a free kick from the edge of the area and, after a sloppy back-pass by Steven Gerrard, an impeccable penalty.

The tone of England's tournament was set that evening. In the plus column there was the prodigiousness of Rooney and the excellence of Campbell and Cole. Among the minuses were the inability to retain possession, the habit of dropping far too deep and the inability of Beckham to score from 12 yards.

After victories over Switzerland and Croatia carried England to the quarter-final against Portugal, all of those weaknesses came to

---

Stadium of Light

FRANCE (0) **2**   **ENGLAND** (1) **1**
Zidane 90, 90 (pen)   Lampard 38
64,000

FRANCE F Barthez — W Gallas, L Thuram, M Silvestre (sub: W Sagnol, 69min), B Lizarazu — R Pires (sub: S Wiltord, 75), P Vieira, C Makelele, Z Zidane — T Henry, D Trezeguet *Substitutes not used* M Landreau, G Coupet, J-A Boumsong, M Desailly, L Saha, J Rothen, O Dacourt, B Pedretti, S Marlet, S Gouvou
Booked Pires, Silvestre

ENGLAND D James — G Neville, S Campbell, L King, A Cole — D Beckham, F Lampard, S Gerrard, P Scholes (sub: O Hargreaves, 76) — M Owen (sub: D Vassell, 69), W Rooney (sub: E Heskey, 76) *Substitutes not used* P Robinson, I Walker, J Terry, W Bridge, P Neville, J Carragher, N Butt, J Cole, K Dyer
Booked Scholes, Lampard
Referee **M Merk** (Germany)

Monday June 14
Group C   *D Afonso Henriques Stadium*
DENMARK (0) **0**   **ITALY** (0) **0**
29,595

DENMARK T Sorensen — T Helveg, M Laursen, R Henriksen, N Jensen — C Poulsen (sub: B Priske, 76min), J D Tomasson, D Jensen — M Jorgensen (sub: K Perez, 72), E Sand (sub: C Jensen, 69), D Rommedahl *Substitutes not used* P Skov-Jensen, S Andersen, K Bogelund, T Kahlenberg, P Kroldrup, P Madsen, P Lovenkrands
Booked Tomasson, Helveg

ITALY G Buffon — C Panucci, A Nesta, F Cannavaro, G Zambrotta — C Zanetti (sub: G Gattuso, 57), S Perrotta — M Camoranesi (sub: S Fiore, 68), F Totti, A Del Piero (sub: A Cassano, 64) — C Vieri *Substitutes not used* F Toldo, A Peruzzi, M Oddo, M Ferrari, B Corradi, G Favalli, M Di Vaio, A Pirlo, M Materazzi
Booked Cannavaro, Cassano, Gattuso, Totti
Referee **M E Mejuto Gonzalez** (Spain)

Jose Alvalade Stadium

SWEDEN (1) **5**   **BULGARIA** (0) **0**
Ljungberg 32   52,000
Larsson 57, 58
Ibrahimovic 78 (pen)
Allback 90

SWEDEN A Isaksson — T Lucic (sub: C Wilhelmsson, 41min), A Jakobsson, O Mellberg, E Edman — M Nilsson, T Linderoth, A Svensson (sub: K Kallstrom, 77), F Ljungberg — Z Ibrahimovic (sub: M Allback, 82), H Larsson *Substitutes not used* M Hedman, M Kihlstedt, J Mjallby, P Hansson, A Ostlund, A Andersson, M Jonson, P Farnerud, E Wahlstedt
Booked Linderoth, Ibrahimovic

BULGARIA Z Zdravkov — V Ivanov, R Kirilov, P Pajin, I Petkov — G Peev, S Petrov, M Hristov, M Petrov (sub: Z Lazarov, 84) — Z Jankovich (sub: V Dimitrov, 62) — D Berbatov (sub: V Manchev, 77) *Substitutes not used* S Kolev, D Ivankov, Z Zagorcic, K Kotev, D Borimirov, M Petkov, G Chilikov, V Bozhinov, I Stoianov
Booked I Petkov, Kirilov, Jankovich, Ivanov
Referee **M Riley** (England)

The despair felt by Beckham, left, contrasts with Henry's Lisbon delight

the fore on what was a memorable but ultimately distressing night in Lisbon's magnificent Stadium of Light. After seizing the lead through Michael Owen's first goal of the tournament, England's defence came under almost unbearable pressure. The loss of Rooney compounded the problem because the Everton teenager had not only become his team's leading goalscorer but also its most effective player.

After his two goals against Croatia had followed his brace against Switzerland, Eriksson, normally a man of restraint, had been moved to compare the striker to Pele, although with not quite the unqualified abandon that it may have appeared in the following day's papers. "I don't remember anyone of his age having this sort of impact on a major tournament since Pele in 1958," Eriksson said. "That was the World Cup in Sweden. I don't remember how many goals Pele scored in the tournament, but he scored twice in the final and he was 17. So to compare a football player of today with Pele is not bad, not bad at all. I'm a little frightened about saying it because of the pressure it will put on him but, when you have someone who has scored four goals in a tournament like this, you can't stop that. I hope Wayne will go on to be one of the greats of football. He seems to be a complete football player."

England were so dependent on Rooney's astute link play that, when he was forced to hobble off after 27 minutes against Portugal with a broken bone in his foot, Eriksson's men could not escape their

Tuesday June 15
Group D   Municipal Stadium, Aveiro
CZECH REPUBLIC (0) **2**   **LATVIA** (1) **1**
Baros 73, Heinz 85   Verpakovskis 45
20,000

CZECH REPUBLIC P Cech — Z Grygera (sub: M Heinz, 56min), T Ujfalusi, R Bolf, M Jankulovski — T Galasek (sub: V Smicer, 65) — K Poborsky, T Rosicky, P Nedved — J Koller, M Baros (sub: M Jiranek, 87) *Substitutes not used* J Blazek, A Kinsky, P Mares, V Lokvenc, S Vachousek, T Hubschman, R Tyce, J Plasil, D Rozehnal

LATVIA A Kolinko — A Isakovs, M Zemlinskis, I Stepanovs, O Blagonadezdins — V Lobanovs (sub: V Rimkus, 90) — I Bleidelis, V Astafjevs, A Rubins — M Verpakovskis (sub: M Pahars, 82), A Prohorenkovs (sub: J Laizans, 71) *Substitutes not used* A Piedels, A Pavlovs, J Pucinsks, M Smirnovs, D Zirnis, I Korablovs, A Stolcers, M Miholaps, A Zakresevskis
Referee **G Veissiere** (France)

                                          Dragao Stadium
GERMANY (1) **1**   **HOLLAND** (0) **1**
Frings 30   Van Nistelrooy 81
46,000

GERMANY O Kahn — A Friedrich, C Worns, J Nowotny, P Lahm — B Schneider (sub: B Schweinsteiger, 68min), D Hamann, F Baumann, T Frings (sub: F Ernst, 79) — M Ballack — K Kuranyi (sub: F Bobic, 85) *Substitutes not used* A Hinkel, T Brdaric, C Ziege, S Kehl, J Jeremies, L Podolski, M Klose, J Lehmann, T Hildebrand
Booked **Kuranyi, Ballack**

HOLLAND E van der Sar — J Heitinga (sub: P van Hooijdonk, 73), J Stam, W Bouma, G van Bronckhorst — A van der Meyde, P Cocu, E Davids (sub: W Sneijder, ht), B Zenden (sub: M Overmars, ht) — R van der Vaart — R van Nistelrooy *Substitutes not used* M Reiziger, F de Boer, P Bosvelt, A Robben, P Kluivert, R Makaay, S Westerveld, R Waterreus
Booked **Cocu, Stam**
Referee **A Frisk** (Sweden)

Wednesday June 16
Group A   *Bessa Stadium*
GREECE (0) **1**   **SPAIN** (1) **1**
Charisteas 66   Morientes 28
25,444

GREECE A Nikopolidis — M Kapsis, T Dellas, K Katsouranis — G Seitaridis, T Zagorakis, G Karagounis (sub: V Tsiartas, 35min), P Fyssas (sub: S Venetidis, 86) — S Giannakopoulos (sub: T Nikolaidis, 49) — A Charisteas, Z Vryzas *Substitutes not used* A Basinas, P Kafes, G Georgiadis, V Lakis, D Papadopoulos, K Chalkias, T Katergiannakis
Booked **Katsouranis, Giannakopoulos, Karagounis, Zagorakis, Vryzas**

SPAIN I Casillas — C Puyol, I Helguera, C Marchena, Raul Bravo — J Etxeberria (sub: Joaquin, ht), D Albelda, R Baraja, Vicente — F Morientes (sub: J C Valeron, 65), Raul (sub: F Torres, 80) *Substitutes not used* J Capdevila, Gabri, Cesar, Juanito, Xabi Alonso, Xavi, A Luque, S Canizares, D Aranzubia
Booked **Marchena, Helguera**
Referee **L Michel** (Slovakia)

RUSSIA (0) **0**   *Stadium of Light*
58,000   **PORTUGAL** (1) **2**
                                         Maniche 7, Rui Costa 89

RUSSIA S Ovchinnikov — V Evseev, A Smertin, A Bugayev, D Sennikov — E Aldonin (sub: V Malafeev, 45min) — D Alenichev, D Loskov, A Kariaka (sub: D Bulykin, 79) — A Kerzhakov, M Izmailov (sub: V Bystrov, 72) *Substitutes not used* I Akinfeev, V Radimov, D Sychev, I Semshov, R Gusev, A Anyukov, D Kirichenko
Booked **Smertin, Evseev, Alenichev**
Sent off **Ovchinnikov** (45)

PORTUGAL Ricardo — Miguel, Jorge Andrade, Ricardo Carvalho, Nuno Valente — Costinha — L Figo (sub: C Ronaldo, 78), Maniche, Deco, S Simao (sub: Rui Costa, 63) — Pauleta (sub: Nuno Gomes, 57) *Substitutes not used* Quim, Moreira, Paulo Ferreira, Rui Jorge, F Couto, Petit, Beto, Tiago, H Postiga
Booked **Ricardo Carvalho, Deco**
Referee **T Hauge** (Norway)

Thursday June 17
Group B
ENGLAND (1) **3**   *Coimbra Stadium*
Rooney 23, 76   **SWITZERLAND** (0) **0**
Gerrard 82   30,616

ENGLAND D James — G Neville, J Terry, S Campbell, A Cole — D Beckham, F Lampard, S Gerrard, P Scholes (sub: O Hargreaves, 70min) — M Owen (sub: D Vassell, 72), W Rooney (sub: K Dyer, 83) *Substitutes not used* P Robinson, I Walker, W Bridge, P Neville, L King, J Carragher, N Butt, J Cole, E Heskey
Booked **Rooney**

SWITZERLAND J Stiel — B Haas, P Muller, M Yakin, C Spycher — R Wicky, F Celestini (sub: R Cabanas, 53), B Huggel — H Yakin (sub: J Vonlanthen, 83) — S Chapuisat (sub: D Gygax, ht), A Frei *Substitutes not used* P Zuberbuhler, S Roth, B Berner, S Henchoz, M Zwyssig, L Magnin, T Barnetta, M Rama
Booked **Celestini, Haas**
Sent off **Haas** (60)
Referee **V Ivanov** (Russia)

                                         Dr Magalhaes Pessoa Stadium
CROATIA (0) **2**   **FRANCE** (1) **2**
Rapaic 48 (pen)   Tudor 23 (og)
Prso 52   Trezeguet 64
30,000

CROATIA T Butina — D Simic, I Tudor, R Kovac, J Simunic — G Rosso, N Bjelica (sub: J Leko, 68min), N Kovac, M Rapaic (sub: I Mornar, 87) — D Prso — T Sokota (sub: I Olic, 73) *Substitutes not used* M Tokic, S Tomas, B Zivkovic, D Srna, M Neretljak, M Babic, I Klasnic, V Vasilj, J A Didulica
Booked **Tudor, Rosso, R Kovac, Leko**

FRANCE F Barthez — W Gallas (sub: W Sagnol, 81), L Thuram, M Desailly, M Silvestre — S Wiltord (sub: R Pires, 70), P Vieira, O Dacourt (sub: B Pedretti, 79), Z Zidane — T Henry, D Trezeguet *Substitutes not used* J-A Boumsong, B Lizarazu, C Makelele, J Rothen, L Saha, S Marlet, S Gouvou, M Landreau, G Coupet
Booked **Vieira, Dacourt**
Referee **K M Nielsen** (Denmark)

Vassell is in tears after defeat to Portugal follows his shoot-out failure

own half. Darius Vassell was so poor as Rooney's replacement that, by the time penalties came around, it was no surprise that his kick lacked any conviction.

Such was Portugal's territorial domination that England were lucky to have taken the game to spot kicks in any case. Only after Rui Costa had given Portugal the lead in extra time did England attack with any forcefulness and, from a corner, Lampard equalised for his third goal of the competition; evidence that he had been the best of a disappointing quartet in midfield.

England's history of failure in penalty shoot-outs was to come back to haunt them and the final insult came when Ricardo, the Portugal goalkeeper, drove the last kick past David James and into the bottom corner. It was England's third defeat in competitive matches under Eriksson and, because of the expectations, the most dispiriting.

The tournament was not a total calamity for the FA, with the supporters, who travelled in greater numbers than those of any other country, awarded nine out of ten by Uefa. Rooney's enjoyment of the big stage was something for the fans to savour but, otherwise, the FA's contention that England will peak at the 2006 World Cup finals did not look justified. Gerrard is still on the upslope of his career, but Beckham and Paul Scholes appeared to be coming down the other side, with no young replacements obvious.

The total absence of penetration down the flanks was highlighted

Rooney limps off against Portugal — and Beckham sees England's quarter-final hopes going with him

Friday June 18
Group C
Municipal Stadium, Braga
BULGARIA (0) **0**
DENMARK (1) **2**
24,131
Tomasson 44, Gronkjaer 90

BULGARIA Z Zdravkov — V Ivanov (sub: Z Lazarov, 52min), R Kirilov, I Stoianov, I Petkov (sub: Z Zagorcic, 40) — G Peev, S Petrov, M Hristov, M Petrov — Z Jankovich (sub: M Petkov, 81) — D Berbatov *Substitutes not used* S Kolev, D Ivankov, K Kotev, D Borimirov, V Dimitrov, G Chilikov, V Manchev, P Pazin, V Bozhinov
Booked **Kirilov, Stoianov, S Petrov, Zagorcic, Hristov, M Petrov**
Sent off **S Petrov** (83)

DENMARK T Sorensen — T Helveg, M Laursen, R Henriksen, N Jensen — T Gravesen, J D Tomasson, D Jensen — M Jorgensen (sub: C Jensen, 72), E Sand, D Rommedahl (sub: J Gronkjaer, 24) *Substitutes not used* P Skov-Jensen, S Andersen, K Bogelund, T Kahlenberg, P Kroldrup, C Poulsen, B Priske, K Perez, P Madsen, P Lovenkrands
Booked **N Jensen, Sand**
Referee **L Batista** (Portugal)

Dragao Stadium
ITALY (1) **1**
SWEDEN (0) **1**
Cassano 37
Ibrahimovic 85
44,926

ITALY G Buffon — C Panucci, A Nesta, F Cannavaro, G Zambrotta — G Gattuso (sub: G Favalli, 76min), A Pirlo, S Perrotta — A Cassano (sub: S Fiore, 70) — C Vieri, A Del Piero (sub: M Camoranesi, 82) *Substitutes not used* M Oddo, M Ferrari, M Materazzi, C Zanetti, B Corradi, M Di Vaio, F Toldo, A Peruzzi
Booked **Gattuso, Cannavaro, Zambrotta**

SWEDEN A Isaksson — M Nilsson, O Mellberg, A Jakobsson, E Edman (sub: M Allback, 82) — T Linderoth — C Wilhelmsson (sub: M Jonson, 67), A Svensson (sub: K Kallstrom, 55), F Ljungberg — Z Ibrahimovic, H Larsson *Substitutes not used* T Lucic, J Mjallby, P Hansson, A Ostlund, E Wahlstedt, A Andersson, P Farnerud, M Hedman, M Kihlstedt
Booked **Edman, Linderoth**
Referee **U Meier** (Switzerland)

Saturday June 19
Group D
Bessa Stadium
LATVIA (0) **0**
GERMANY (0) **0**
30,000

LATVIA A Kolinko — A Isakovs, M Zemlinskis, I Stepanovs, O Blagonadezdins — I Bleidelis, V Lobanovs (sub: J Laizans, 70min), V Astafjevs, A Rubins — M Verpakovskis (sub: D Zirnis, 90), A Prohorenkovs (sub: M Pahars, 67) *Substitutes not used* A Piedels, J Pucinskis, M Smirnovs, I Korablovs, A Stolcers, A Pavlovs, M Miholaps, A Zakreskevskis, V Rimkus
Booked **Isakovs, Astafjevs**

GERMANY O Kahn — A Friedrich, C Worns, F Baumann, P Lahm — B Schneider (sub: B Schweinsteiger, ht), D Hamann, M Ballack, T Frings — F Bobic (sub: M Klose, 67), K Kuranyi (sub: T Brdaric, 78) *Substitutes not used* A Hinkel, J Nowotny, J Lehmann, S Kehl, J Jeremies, C Ziege, F Ernst, L Podolski, T Hildebrand
Booked **Friedrich, Hamann, Frings**
Referee **M Riley** (England)

Campbell's goal against Portugal is disallowed — and England are out

by sparkling displays elsewhere in Portugal. To Manchester United's delight, Cristiano Ronaldo emerged as a player of real distinction at the highest level, while Arjen Robben, Chelsea's new signing, also impressed until he was booked for diving in Holland's defeat to Portugal in the semi-final.

It was not a tournament blessed with great games — the Czech Republic's victory over Holland was the best — but there was enough drama that more than 15 million English viewers were still tuning in by the time the final came around. Their outstanding memory not involving England? Who can forget Antonio Cassano running to the Italy bench after his superb winner against Bulgaria, his joy turning to despair as he was told that, thanks to Sweden's 2-2 draw with Denmark, his goal did not matter? And, if the joy of sport is not knowing how it will end, then what better example of glorious unpredictability than Greece knocking out Raul, Henry, Zidane and Nedved before beating Figo for a second time in the final? Rehhagel and his durable, defensive team may not set the pulses racing, but England would have happily bored their way to the trophy.

"I don't remember anyone getting a championship trophy just for being part of an attractive side," Nikos Dabizas, the Leicester City and Greece centre half, said. "In 40 years' time, no one will remember this side as boring." With that, he left for the biggest party that Athens has seen since the days of Dionysus.

STATS AND FACTS

● The record for the youngest goalscorer at a European Championship finals, previously held by Dragan Stojkovic, of Yugoslavia, was broken three times: Cristiano Ronaldo (19 years 128 days, for Portugal v Greece), Wayne Rooney (18 years 236 days, for England v Switzerland) and Johann Vonlanthen (18 years 141 days, for Switzerland v France).

● England scored more goals in the group stage than on any of their previous 16 appearances at a leading tournament finals.

● Just as at the World Cup finals two years earlier, when England were knocked out by Brazil, they lost the first quarter-final of the tournament against a team coached by Luiz Felipe Scolari after Michael Owen had given them an early lead.

● Last season, Wayne Rooney scored nine goals in 12 games for England and nine in 40 appearances for Everton.

● France were the only team in group B not to field a pair of brothers. Gary and Phil Neville played for England, Niko and Robert Kovac appeared for Croatia and Hakan and Murat Yakin did so for Switzerland.

● England, under Sven-Goran Eriksson, were one of three teams at Euro 2004 with a foreign coach. The other two contested the final: Greece, guided by Otto Rehhagel, a German, and Portugal, led by Scolari, a Brazilian.

● Greece won 1-0 through a headed goal in the quarter-final, semi-final and final (against France, the Czech Republic and Portugal respectively).

Bill Edgar

Baros was top marksman

LEADING GOALSCORERS

Milan Baros	Czech Republic	5
Wayne Rooney	England	4
Ruud van Nistelrooy	Holland	4
Frank Lampard	England	3
Henrik Larsson	Sweden	3
Jon Dahl Tomasson	Denmark	3
Zinedine Zidane	France	3

Municipal Stadium, Aveiro

HOLLAND (2) **2**	CZECH REPUBLIC (1) **3**
Bouma 4	Koller 23
Van Nistelrooy 19	Baros 71
30,000	Smicer 88

HOLLAND E van der Sar — J Stam, P Cocu, W Bouma — J Heitinga, C Seedorf (sub: R van der Vaart, 86min), E Davids, G van Bronckhorst — A van der Meyde (sub: M Reiziger, 79), R van Nistelrooy, A Robben (sub: P Bosvelt, 59) *Substitutes not used* F de Boer, W Sneijder, M Overmars, B Zenden, P Kluivert, R Makaay, P van Hooijdonk, S Westerveld, R Waterreus
Booked **Seedorf, Heitinga**
Sent off **Heitinga** (75)

CZECH REPUBLIC P Cech — Z Grygera (sub: V Smicer, 25), M Jiranek, T Ujfalusi, M Jankulovski — T Galasek (sub: M Heinz, 62) — K Poborsky, T Rosicky, P Nedved — J Koller (sub: D Rozehnal, 75), M Baros *Substitutes not used* P Mares, R Bolf, T Hubschmann, S Vachousek, R Tyce, J Plasil, V Lokvenc, J Blazek, A Kinsky
Booked **Galasek**
Referee **M M Gonzalez** (Spain)

Sunday June 20
Group A   *Jose Alvalade Stadium*

SPAIN (0) **0**	PORTUGAL (0) **1**
47,491	Nuno Gomes 57

SPAIN I Casillas — C Puyol, Juanito (sub: F Morientes, 80min), I Helguera, Raul Bravo — Xabi Alonso, D Albelda (sub: R Baraja, 66) — Joaquin (sub: A Luque, 72), Raul, Vicente — F Torres *Substitutes not used* S Canizares, D Aranzubia, J Capdevila, Gabri, J Etxeberria, Cesar, Xavi, J C Valeron
Booked **Albelda, Juanito, Puyol**

PORTUGAL Ricardo — Miguel, Jorge Andrade, Ricardo Carvalho, Nuno Valente — Costinha — L Figo (sub: Petit, 78), Maniche, Deco, C Ronaldo (sub: F Couto, 84) — Pauleta (sub: Nuno Gomes, ht) *Substitutes not used* Quim, Moreira, Paulo Ferreira, Rui Jorge, Rui Costa, S Simao, Beto, Tiago, H Postiga
Booked **Pauleta, Nuno Gomes**
Referee **A Frisk** (Sweden)

Algarve Stadium

RUSSIA (2) **2**	GREECE (1) **1**
Kirichenko 2	Vryzas 43
Bulykin 17	*25,000*

RUSSIA V Malafeev — A Aniukov, R Sharonov (sub: D Sennikov, 56min), A Bugaev, V Evseev — R Gusev, V Radimov, A Kariaka — D Alenichev — D Bulykin (sub: D Sytchev, ht), D Kirichenko *Substitutes not used* I Akinfeev, I Semshov, M Izmailov, A Kerzhakov, B Bystrov, D Loskov, E Aldonin
Booked **Sharonov, Aniukov, Kariaka, Alenichev, Radimov, Malafeev**

GREECE A Nikopolidis — G Seitaridis, M Kapsis, T Dellas, S Venetidis (sub: P Fyssas, 89) — T Zagorakis, A Basinas (sub: T Siartas, 43) — A Charisteas, K Katsouranis, D Papadopoulos (sub: T Nikolaidis, 70) — Z Vryzas *Substitutes not used* K Chalkias, T Katergiannakis, N Dabizas, S Giannakopoulos, P Kafes, G Georgiadis, I Goumas, V Lakis
Booked **Vryzas, Dellas**
Referee **G Veissiere** (France)

GROUP A
FINAL TABLE

	P	W	D	L	F	A	Pts
Portugal	3	2	0	1	4	2	6
Greece	3	1	1	1	4	4	4
Spain	3	1	1	1	2	2	4
Russia	3	1	0	2	2	4	3

Monday June 21   *Coimbra Stadium*

Group B

SWITZERLAND (1) **1**   **FRANCE** (1) **3**

Vonlanthen 26   Zidane 20

30,000   Henry 76, 84

SWITZERLAND J Stiel — S Henchoz (sub: L Magnin, 86min), M Yakin, P Muller, C Spycher — J Vogel, R Cabanas — D Gygax (sub: M Rama, 86), H Yakin (sub: B Huggel, 60), R Wicky — J Vonlanthen *Substitutes not used* B Berner, M Zwyssig, F Celestini, T Barnetta, S Chapuisat, P Zuberbuhler, S Roth

Booked **H Yakin, Wicky, Huggel**

FRANCE F Barthez — W Sagnol (sub: W Gallas, ht; sub: J-A Boumsong, 90), L Thuram, M Silvestre, B Lizarazu — C Makelele, Z Zidane, P Vieira, R Pires — D Trezeguet (sub: L Saha, 75), T Henry *Substitutes not used* M Desailly, O Dacourt, B Pedretti, J Rothen, S Wiltord, S Marlet, S Govou, M Landreau, G Coupet

Booked **Henry**

Referee **L Michel** (Slovakia)

                                         Stadium of Light

CROATIA (1) **2**   **ENGLAND** (2) **4**

N Kovac 6   Scholes 40

Tudor 74   Rooney 45, 68

57,047   Lampard 79

CROATIA T Butina — D Simic (sub: D Srna, 67min), B Zivkovic, R Kovac (sub: I Mornar, ht), J Simunic — G Rosso, I Tudor, N Kovac, M Rapaic (sub: I Olic, 55) — D Prso, T Sokota *Substitutes not used* V Vasilj, M Tokic, S Tomas, M Neretljak, J Leko, M Babic, I Klasnic, N Bjelica, J Didulica

Booked **Simic**

ENGLAND D James — G Neville, J Terry, S Campbell, A Cole — D Beckham, F Lampard (sub: P Neville, 84), P Scholes (sub: L King, 70), S Gerrard — W Rooney (sub: D Vassell, 72), M Owen *Substitutes not used* W Bridge, P Robinson, J Carragher, O Hargreaves, J Cole, K Dyer, E Heskey, I Walker

Referee **P Collina** (Italy)

GROUP B

FINAL TABLE

	P	W	D	L	F	A	Pts
France	3	2	1	0	7	4	7
England	3	2	0	1	8	4	6
Croatia	3	0	2	1	4	6	2
Switzerland	3	0	1	2	1	6	1

Tuesday June 22

Group C   *D Afonso Henriques Stadium*

ITALY (0) **2**   **BULGARIA** (1) **1**

Perrotta 48   M Petrov 45 (pen)

Cassano 90   16,003

ITALY G Buffon — C Panucci, M Materazzi (sub: M Di Vaio, 83min), A Nesta — S Perrotta (sub: M Oddo, 68), A Pirlo, S Fiore, G Zambrotta — A Cassano, B Corradi (sub: C Vieri, 53), A Del Piero *Substitutes not used* F Toldo, A Peruzzi, C Zanetti, M Ferrari, G Favalli, M Camoranesi

Booked **Materazzi**

BULGARIA Z Zdravkov — D Borimirov, Z Zagorcic, P Pazin (sub: K Kotev, 64), I Stoianov — Z Lazarov, M Petrov, Z Jankovich (sub: V Bojinov, ht), M Hristov (sub: V Dimitrov, 79), M Petkov — D Berbatov *Substitutes not used* S Kolev, D Ivankov, V Ivanov, I Petkov, G Peev, G Chilikov, V Manchev

Booked **M Petrov, Bojinov, Stoianov, Lazarov**

Referee **V Ivanov** (Russia)

MATCH OF THE TOURNAMENT

Holland 2 Czech Republic 3

Municipal Stadium, Aveiro, Saturday June 19 2004

Oliver Kay

IF LOOKS COULD KILL, THE so-called group of death would have claimed its first victim at about 9.30 on Saturday night. It was then, with four minutes of a pulsating game remaining, that Dick Advocaat, the Holland coach, sent on Rafael van der Vaart to play in a free role, the third and last of a series of truly baffling substitutions. "Don't shoot the messenger," Van der Vaart seemed to tell his team-mates, but Edgar Davids had no intention, having already set his sights on Advocaat, the recipient of a menacing glare that penetrated the midfield player's famous goggles.

Within two minutes, Holland, who had led by 2-0, had conceded the winning goal to Vladimir Smicer and the Czech Republic were in the quarter-finals. Again, Davids glared at Advocaat, this time with greater contempt, but, when the final whistle blew, he chose a different policy, marching past the bench and down the tunnel without looking his coach in the eye. An hour later, on his way to the team bus, he was asked what had gone wrong. "You will have to ask the coach," he said. "I can't speak for the coach."

Nor, it seemed, would anyone else. Ruud van Nistelrooy, whose nineteenth-minute effort had put Holland two goals ahead, tried to be diplomatic, but Patrick Kluivert, already furious at having to watch the game from the bench, was in no mood to suggest collective responsibility. "Why did it happen?" the Barcelona forward asked. "Why? Maybe because some of the substitutions weren't good. [Arjen] Robben played a very good match and, if I was the trainer, that's not a change I would have made. It's always easy to say these things after the match, but I personally think it had to do with the changes."

Kluivert, of course, has an agenda against Advocaat for what he called the "bizarre" decision to keep him on the bench throughout the team's first two matches, but even less outspoken individuals such as Edwin van der Sar questioned the decision to replace the excellent Robben, who had set up both goals, with Paul Bosvelt, a second-rate scrapper from Manchester City. It was that substitution that caused the greatest outrage, but it seemed that Advocaat, often accused of being too clever for his own good, conceded further ground with every reshuffle he made.

Part of the problem, perhaps, was that each of Advocaat's changes was a belated, and usually flawed, reaction to events on the pitch, whereas Karel Bruckner, the Czech Republic coach, was far more proactive and, it must be said, far more bold.

The Czech Republic were 2-0 down to a header from Wilfred Bouma and a tap-in by Van Nistelrooy — both from crosses by the left boot of Robben, who will join Chelsea from PSV Eindhoven on

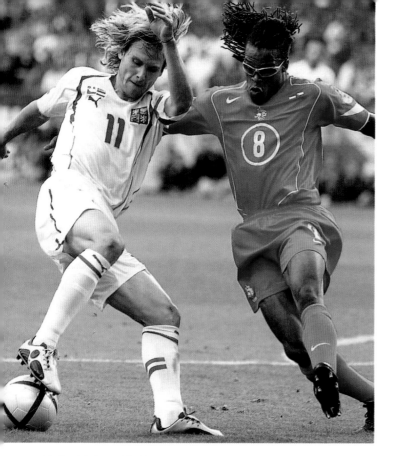

Nedved, left, and Davids are involved in a titanic midfield struggle

July 1 — when Bruckner decided to replace Zdenek Grygera, a full back, with Smicer, the Liverpool forward. It helped that Jan Koller, profiting from good work by Milan Baros after a careless pass by Phillip Cocu, reduced the arrears while Smicer was waiting to come on, but Bruckner stuck with his instinct. What ensued, with each team having just three defenders on the pitch, was a spectacle that is unlikely to be bettered in this tournament. Before the interval, Johnny Heitinga, Clarence Seedorf and Davids all went close from long range, Davids hitting the post, but the Czech Republic were increasingly playing the better football.

The first half was compelling, but the second was even better, with Pavel Nedved the dominant figure. It was in an attempt to deny the Czech Republic captain space that Advocaat sent on Bosvelt, but, if anything, it had the opposite effect. With Bruckner sending on yet another attacking player, Marek Heinz, in place of Ivan Galasek, the Czech Republic were now almost totally committed to attack.

Baros, Smicer's Liverpool team-mate, struck a deserved equaliser with 19 minutes remaining and, four minutes later, Heitinga was sent off for a second caution. The Czech Republic pushed forward in ever greater numbers, Nedved striking the crossbar from 30 yards, and, with Advocaat's final substitution compounding the sense of

---

Bessa Stadium

DENMARK (1) 2 **SWEDEN (0) 2**
Tomasson 28, 66 Larsson 47 (pen)
29,000 Jonson 89

DENMARK T Sorensen — T Helveg, M Laursen, R Henriksen, N Jensen (sub: K Bogelund, ht) — D Jensen (sub: C Poulsen, 65), T Gravesen — J Gronkjaer, J D Tomasson, M Jorgensen (sub: D Rommedahl, 57) — E Sand *Substitutes not used* P Kroldrup, B Priske, T Kahlenburg, C Jensen, K Perez, P Madsen, P Lovenkrands, P Skov-Jensen, S Andersen

SWEDEN A Isaksson — M Nilsson, O Mellberg, A Jakobsson, E Edman — A Andersson (sub: M Allback, 81) — M Jonson, K Kallstrom (sub: C Wilhelmsson, 72), F Ljungberg — Z Ibrahimovic, H Larsson *Substitutes not used* T Lucic, J Mjallby, P Hansson, A Ostlund, E Wahlstedt, A Svensson, P Farnerud, M Hedman, M Kihlstedt
Booked **Edman, Kallstrom**
Referee M Merk (Germany)

GROUP C
FINAL TABLE

	P	W	D	L	F	A	Pts
Sweden	3	1	2	0	8	3	5
Denmark	3	1	2	0	4	2	5
Italy	3	1	2	0	3	2	5
Bulgaria	3	0	0	3	1	9	0

Wednesday June 23
Group D Municipal Stadium, Braga
HOLLAND (2) 3 **LATVIA (0) 0**
Van Nistelrooy 27 (pen), 35 30,000
Makaay 84

HOLLAND E van der Sar — M Reiziger, J Stam, F de Boer, G van Bronckhorst — P Cocu — C Seedorf, E Davids (sub: W Sneijder, 77min) — A van der Meyde (sub: M Overmars, 63), R van Nistelrooy (sub: R Makaay, 70), A Robben *Substitutes not used* W Bouma, P Bosvelt, B Zenden, R van der Vaart, P Kluivert, P van Hooijdonk, S Westerveld, R Waterreus

LATVIA A Kolinko — A Isakovs, M Zemlinskis, I Stepanovs, O Blagonadezdins — I Bleidelis (sub: A Stolcers, 83), V Lobanovs, V Astafjevs, A Rubins — A Prohorenkovs (sub: J Laizans, 74), M Verpakovskis (sub: M Pahars, 62) *Substitutes not used* M Smirnovs, D Zirnis, I Korablovs, A Zakresevskis, J Pucinsks, M Miholaps, V Rimkus, A Piedels, A Pavlovs
Booked **Lobanovs**

Jose Alvalade Stadium

GERMANY (1) 1 **CZECH REPUBLIC (1) 2**
Ballack 21 Heinz 30
46,849 Baros 77

GERMANY O Kahn — A Friedrich, J Nowotny, C Worns — T Frings (sub: L Podolski, ht), D Hamann (sub: M Klose, 79), P Lahm — B Schneider, M Ballack, B Schweinsteiger (sub: J Jeremies, 86) — K Kuranyi *Substitutes not used* J Lehmann, T Hildebrand, A Hinkel, F Baumann, F Bobic, T Brdaric, S Kehl, C Ziege, F Ernst
Booked **Nowotny, Lahm, Worns**

CZECH REPUBLIC J Blazek — M Jiranek, R Bolf, D Rozehnal, P Mares — T Galasek (sub: T Hubschman, ht) — J Plasil (sub: K Poborsky, 70), R Tyce, S Vachousek — M Heinz, V Lokvenc (sub: M Baros, 59) *Substitutes not used* P Cech, A Kinsky, Z Grygera, M Jankulovski, V Smicer, J Koller, T Rosicky, P Nedved, T Ujfalusi
Booked **Tyce**
Referee T Hauge (Norway)

GROUP D
FINAL TABLE

	P	W	D	L	F	A	Pts
Czech Republic	3	3	0	0	7	4	9
Holland	3	1	1	1	6	4	4
Germany	3	0	2	1	2	3	2
Latvia	3	0	1	2	1	5	1

QUARTER-FINALS

Thursday June 24   *Stadium of Light*
PORTUGAL (0) **2**   **ENGLAND** (1) **2**
Postiga 83   Owen 3
Rui Costa 110   Lampard 115
65,000

(aet; 1-1 at 90min; Portugal win 6-5 on pens)

PORTUGAL Ricardo — Miguel (sub: Rui Costa, 79min),
Jorge Andrade, Carvalho, Nuno Valente — Costinha (sub:
S Simao, 63) — C Ronaldo, Maniche, Deco, L Figo (sub: H
Postiga, 75) — Nuno Gomes *Substitutes not used* Quim,
Moreira, Paulo Ferreira, Rui Jorge, F Couto, Petit, Beto,
Tiago
Booked **Costinha, Deco, Ricardo Carvalho**

ENGLAND D James — G Neville, J Terry, S Campbell, A
Cole — D Beckham, F Lampard, S Gerrard (sub: O
Hargreaves, 82), P Scholes (sub: P Neville, 57) — M Owen,
W Rooney (sub: D Vassell, 27) *Substitutes not used* W
Bridge, P Robinson, J Carragher, N Butt, J Cole, K Dyer, E
Heskey, I Walker
Booked **Gerrard, G Neville, P Neville**
Referee **U Meier** (Switzerland)

Friday June 25   *Jose Alvalade Stadium*
FRANCE (0) **0**   **GREECE** (0) **1**
50,000   Charisteas 65

FRANCE F Barthez — W Gallas, L Thuram, M Silvestre, B
Lizarazu — Z Zidane, O Dacourt (sub: S Wiltord, 72min), C
Makelele, R Pires (sub: J Rothen, 79) — T Henry, D
Trezeguet (sub: L Saha, 72) *Substitutes not used* M
Landreau, G Coupet, J-A Boumsong, P Vieira, M Desailly, B
Pedretti, W Sagnol, S Marlet, S Govou

GREECE A Nikopolidis — G Seitaridis, M Kapsis, T Dellas,
P Fyssas — T Zagorakis, A Basinas (sub: V Tsiartas, 85) —
G Karagounis, K Katsouranis, T Nikolaidis (sub: V Lakis,
61) — A Charisteas *Substitutes not used* K Chalkias, T
Katergiannakis, S Venetidis, N Dabizas, S
Giannakopoulos, P Kafes, G Georgiadis, I Goumas, D
Papadopoulos
Booked **Karagounis, Zagorakis**
Referee **A Frisk** (Sweden)

Saturday June 26   *Algarve Stadium*
SWEDEN (0) **0**   **HOLLAND** (0) **0**
30,000

(aet; Holland won 5-4 on pens)

SWEDEN A Isaksson — A Ostlund, O Mellberg, A
Jakobsson, M Nilsson — T Linderoth — M Jonson (sub: C
Wilhelmsson, 65min), F Ljungberg — A Svensson (sub: K
Kallstrom, 81) — Z Ibrahimovic, H Larsson *Substitutes not
used* M Hedman, M Kihlstedt, T Lucic, J Mjallby, P
Hansson, A Andersson, P Farnerud, M Allback, E
Wahlstedt
Booked **Ibrahimovic, Ostlund**

HOLLAND E van der Sar — M Reiziger, J Stam, F de Boer
(sub: W Bouma, 36), G van Bronckhorst — E Davids (sub: J
Heitinga, 62), C Seedorf, P Cocu — A van der Meyde (sub:
R Makaay, 87), R van Nistelrooy, A Robben *Substitutes not
used* S Westerveld, R Waterreus, P Kluivert, R van der
Vaart, W Sneijder, M Overmars, P van Hooijdonk, P
Bosvelt, B Zenden
Booked **De Boer, Van der Meyde, Makaay**
Referee **L Michel** (Slovakia)

The Czechs are ecstatic after victory over Holland put them through

chaos in the opposition ranks, the inevitable winning goal arrived,
Smicer tapping in from close range after Karel Poborsky followed up
another shot by Nedved. The Czech Republic celebrated wildly,
having become the first team through to the last eight, while Davids
and company stormed off in bitter disbelief. Even victory over Latvia
on Wednesday might not be enough for Holland, with Bruckner
likely to rest several players for his team's match against Germany.
"We can't worry about that. We have to look after ourselves,"
Advocaat said. After this, though, his biggest problem will be
quelling the prospect of revolt in the ranks.

HOLLAND (3-4-3): **E van der Sar** (Fulham) — **J Stam** (Lazio), **P Cocu** (Barcelona), **W Bouma** (PSV
Eindhoven) — **J Heitinga** (Ajax), **C Seedorf** (AC Milan; sub: **R van der Vaart**, Ajax, 86min), **E Davids**
(Barcelona), **G van Bronckhorst** (Barcelona) — **A van der Meyde** (Inter Milan; sub: **M Reiziger**,
Barcelona, 79), **R van Nistelrooy** (Manchester United), **A Robben** (PSV Eindhoven; sub: **P Bosvelt**,
Manchester City, 59). **Substitutes not used:** F de Boer (Rangers), W Sneijder (Ajax), M Overmars
(Barcelona), B Zenden (Middlesbrough), P Kluivert (Barcelona), R Makaay (Bayern Munich), P van
Hooijdonk (Fenerbahce), S Westerveld (Real Sociedad), R Waterreus (PSV Eindhoven). **Booked:**
Seedorf, Heitinga. **Sent off:** Heitinga (75).
CZECH REPUBLIC (4-1-3-2): **P Cech** (Rennes) — **Z Grygera** (Ajax; sub: **V Smicer**, Liverpool, 25),
M Jiranek (Reggina), **T Ujfalusi** (SV Hamburg), **M Jankulovski** (Udinese) — **T Galasek** (Ajax; sub:
M Heinz, Banik Ostrava, 62) — **K Poborsky** (Sparta Prague), **T Rosicky** (Borussia Dortmund),
P Nedved (Juventus) — **J Koller** (Borussia Dortmund; sub: **D Rozehnal**, FC Bruges, 75), **M Baros**
(Liverpool). **Substitutes not used:** P Mares (Zenit St Petersburg), R Bolf (Banik Ostrava), T Hub-
schmann (Sparta Prague), S Vachousek (Marseilles), R Tyce (TSV 1860 Munich), J Plasil (AS
Monaco), V Lokvenc (1FC Kaiserslautern), J Blazek (Sparta Prague), A Kinsky (FC Saturn
Moskovskaya Oblast). **Booked:** Galasek.
Referee: M E Mejuto Gonzalez (Spain).

PLAYER OF THE TOURNAMENT
Theodoros Zagorakis

With four goals leaving him just one behind Milan Baros, the Golden Boot winner, Wayne Rooney deserves to be high on the shortlist, but, just as Uefa's panel picked Theo Zagorakis, so this vote goes to the man who lifted the trophy as captain of Greece. The midfield labourer could not claim to be his country's best player — that honour must go to Giourkas Seitaridis, the right back — but he was an inspirational leader as he flew into tackles, cajoled his team-mates and occasionally raged at their sloppy mistakes. In and out of the Leicester City side under Martin O'Neill, Zagorakis was one of the least likely heroes of Euro 2004, which is why he deserves the recognition. David Beckham and Zinedine Zidane must have imagined lifting the cup; Zagorakis actually did it.

Matt Dickinson

Sunday June 27

Dragao Stadium

CZECH REPUBLIC (0) **3**   **DENMARK** (0) **0**
Koller 49   45,000
Baros 63, 65

CZECH REPUBLIC P Cech — M Jiranek (sub: Z Grygera, 39min), T Ujfalusi, R Bolf (sub: D Rozenhal, 64), M Jankulovski — T Galasek — K Poborsky, T Rosicky, P Nedved — J Koller, M Baros (sub: M Heinz, 71) *Substitutes not used* J Blazek, A Kinsky, P Mares, V Smicer, V Lokvenc, S Vachousek, T Hubschman, R Tyce, J Plasil
Booked **Jankulovski, Ujfalusi, Nedved**

DENMARK T Sorensen — T Helveg, M Laursen, R Henriksen, K Bogelund — C Poulsen, C Jensen (sub: P Madsen, 71), T Gravesen — J Gronkjaer (sub: D Rommedahl, 77), J D Tomasson, M Jorgensen (sub: P Lovenkrands, 85) *Substitutes not used* P Skov-Jensen, S Andersen, N Jensen, E Sand, T Kahlenberg, P Kroldrup, D Jensen, B Priske, K Perez
Booked **Paulsen, Bogelund, Gravesen**
Referee **V Ivanov** (Russia)

SEMI-FINALS

Wednesday June 30

PORTUGAL (1) **2**   **HOLLAND** (0) **1**
Ronaldo 26   Jorge Andrade 63 (og)
Maniche 58   46,679

PORTUGAL Ricardo — Miguel, Ricardo Carvalho, Jorge Andrade, Nuno Valente — Maniche (sub: F Couto, 87min), Costinha — C Ronaldo (sub: Petit, 67), Deco, L Figo — Pauleta (sub: Nuno Gomes, 75) *Substitutes not used* Quim, Moreira, Paulo Ferreira, Rui Jorge, Rui Costa, S Simao, Beto, Tiago, H Postiga
Booked **Ronaldo, Nuno Valente, Figo**

HOLLAND E van der Sar — M Reiziger, J Stam, W Bouma (sub: R van der Vaart, 55), G van Bronckhorst — P Cocu — M Overmars (sub: R Makaay, ht), C Seedorf, E Davids, A Robben (sub: P van Hooijdonk, 81) — R van Nistelrooy *Substitutes not used* S Westerveld, R Waterreus, A van der Meyde, P Kluivert, W Sneijder, J Heitinga, P Bosvelt, B Zenden
Booked **Overmars, Robben**
Referee **A Frisk** (Sweden)

Thursday July 1   *Dragao Stadium*
GREECE (0) **1**   **CZECH REPUBLIC** (0) **0**
Dellas 105   48,000
(aet; Greece win on silver goal)

GREECE A Nikopolidis — G Seitaridis, M Kapsis, T Dellas, P Fyssas — T Zagorakis, K Katsouranis, A Basinas (sub: S Giannakopoulos, 72min) — A Charisteas, Z Vryzas (sub: V Tsiartas, 90), G Karagounis *Substitutes not used* K Chalkias, T Katergiannakis, S Venetidis, N Dabizas, T Nikolaidis, P Kafes, G Georgiadis, I Goumas, D Papadopoulos, V Lakis
Booked **Seitaridis, Charisteas, Karagounis**

CZECH REPUBLIC P Cech — Z Grygera, T Ujfalusi, R Bolf, M Jankulovski, T Galasek — K Poborsky, T Rosicky, P Nedved (sub: V Smicer, 40) — M Baros, J Koller *Substitutes not used* J Blazek, A Kinsky, P Mares, V Lokvenc, M Jiranek, S Vachousek, T Hubschmann, M Heinz, R Tyce, J Plasil, D Rozehnal
Booked **Galasek, Smicer, Baros**
Referee **P Collina** (Italy)

THE FINAL

Sunday July 4, Stadium of Light

PORTUGAL (0) **0**
62,865

GREECE (0) **1**
Charisteas 57

They will be called the most unexpected and least attractive European champions in history, but no one can say that Greece were not deserving of their triumph. Portugal had been anticipating the coronation of their "golden generation", but the party had to be cancelled. Instead, the Stadium of Light was forced to salute a former Sheffield United defender and a one-time Leicester City midfield player who were two of the cogs in Otto Rehhagel's durable Greece machine. Once the hosts had failed to score an early goal, there was an inevitability about the winner. Predictably, it came from a set-piece, Greece's only corner of the game, as Angelos Charisteas overpowered Costinha to head home.

PORTUGAL (4-2-3-1): Ricardo — Miguel (sub: Paulo Ferreira, 43min), Jorge Andrade, Ricardo Carvalho, Nuno Valente — Maniche, Costinha (sub: Rui Costa, 61) — C Ronaldo, Deco, L Figo — Pauleta (sub: Nuno Gomes, 74). **Substitutes not used:** Quim, J Moreira, Rui Jorge, F Couto, Petit, S Simao, Beto, Tiago, H Postiga. **Booked:** Costinha, Nuno Valente.

GREECE (4-1-2-2-1): A Nikopolidis — G Seitaridis, M Kapsis, T Dellas, P Fyssas — K Katsouranis — T Zagorakis, A Basinas — S Giannakopoulos (sub: S Venetidis, 76), A Charisteas — Z Vryzas (sub: D Papadopoulos, 81). **Substitutes not used:** K Chalkias, T Katergiannakis, N Dabizas, V Tsiartas, P Kafes, G Georgiadis, I Goumas, V Lakis. **Booked:** Basinas, Seitaridis, Fyssas, Papadopoulos.

Referee: M Merk (Germany).

Charisteas heads the only goal of the final, sparking delight in Greek ranks but only dismay among the host nation

IMMORTAL AND INVINCIBLE

Matt Dickinson, Chief Football Correspondent

AS THEY CROSSED THE finishing line unbeaten, Arsene Wenger believed that his players had not grasped the epic scale of their achievement. Perhaps none of us have. For all the praise showered on Arsenal after they survived 38 league games without a single defeat, it may be impossible to put it in proper context for another 10 or 20 years.

With each season that passes without their unbeaten campaign being replicated, the legend of Wenger's Invincibles will grow in stature.

Those of us who saw them play, often thrillingly, will be able to bore our grandchildren that we saw the team which, in their manager's words, "refused to lose". The Frenchman believes that it will not be done again in his lifetime and he may be right; it had been 115 years since Preston North End, the previous Invincibles of the English league.

The special quality of Arsenal's championship provided a memorably uplifting climax to a Premiership season that did not have too much else to recommend it. On the back of the Russian revolution at Stamford Bridge, Chelsea secured their highest place in almost 50 years but still sacked Claudio Ranieri. Liverpool parted with Gerard Houllier while Manchester United and Newcastle United had good cause to consider their manager's positions.

It was the season of rape investigations, roasting and Rio Ferdinand's failure to provide a urine sample; of Rock Of Gibraltar and Sir Alex Ferguson's battle with two of United's biggest shareholders. It was the season when the footballing *Titanic* that is Leeds United finally sank from the top division, probably for many years.

Thank goodness, then, for Thierry Henry, Patrick

FINAL PREMIERSHIP TABLE

| | Played | HOME | | | | | AWAY | | | | | Points | Goal Diff |
		Won	Drawn	Lost	For	Against	Won	Drawn	Lost	For	Against		
Arsenal	38	15	4	0	40	14	11	8	0	33	12	90	47
Chelsea	38	12	4	3	34	13	12	3	4	33	17	79	37
Manchester United	38	12	4	3	37	15	11	2	6	27	20	75	29
Liverpool	38	10	4	5	29	15	6	8	5	26	22	60	18
Newcastle United	38	11	5	3	33	14	2	12	5	19	26	56	12
Aston Villa	38	9	6	4	24	19	6	5	8	24	25	56	4
Charlton Athletic	38	7	6	6	29	29	7	5	7	22	22	53	0
Bolton Wanderers	38	6	8	5	24	21	8	3	8	24	35	53	-8
Fulham	38	9	4	6	29	21	5	6	8	23	25	52	6
Birmingham City	38	8	5	6	26	24	4	9	6	17	24	50	-5
Middlesbrough	38	8	4	7	25	23	5	5	9	19	29	48	-8
Southampton	38	8	6	5	24	17	4	5	10	20	28	47	-1
Portsmouth	38	10	4	5	35	19	2	5	12	12	35	45	-7
Tottenham Hotspur	38	9	4	6	33	27	4	2	13	14	30	45	-10
Blackburn Rovers	38	5	4	10	25	31	7	4	8	26	28	44	-8
Manchester City	38	5	9	5	31	24	4	5	10	24	30	41	1
Everton	38	8	5	6	27	20	1	7	11	18	37	39	-12
Leicester City	38	3	10	6	19	28	3	5	11	29	37	33	-17
Leeds United	38	5	7	7	25	31	3	2	14	15	48	33	-39
Wolverhampton Wanderers	38	7	5	7	23	35	0	7	12	15	42	33	-39

LEADING GOALSCORERS		Total
Thierry Henry	Arsenal	30
Alan Shearer	Newcastle United	22
Louis Saha	Manchester United	20
Ruud van Nistelrooy	Manchester United	20
Mikael Forssell	Birmingham City	17
Nicolas Anelka	Manchester City	17
Juan Pablo Angel	Aston Villa	16
Michael Owen	Liverpool	16
Yakubu Ayegbeni	Portsmouth	16
James Beattie	Southampton	14
Robbie Keane	Tottenham Hotspur	14
Robert Pires	Arsenal	14
Les Ferdinand	Leicester City	12
Jimmy Floyd Hasselbaink	Chelsea	12
Kevin Phillips	Southampton	12
Andrew Cole	Blackburn Rovers	11
Paul Dickov	Leicester City	11
Mark Viduka	Leeds United	11

Saha's total includes 13 Premiership goals for Fulham

Wenger and Ferguson agree to differ at Highbury in March

Vieira, Robert Pires and the rest of Arsenal's unbeatables although even they had their dark side. The season was only six matches old when they travelled to Old Trafford for perhaps the most significant game of the entire campaign.

If Arsenal should have lost any of their 38 matches it was to their arch rivals, but Ruud van Nistelrooy whacked his late penalty against the crossbar with the game goalless. "That was in September and you could not have imagined then that we would still be unbeaten in May," Wenger said. Particularly not when, after the final whistle at Old Trafford, Martin Keown led a mugging of Van Nistelrooy. Arsenal were hit with suspensions and record fines by the Football Association, but they learnt their lesson. For the next eight months, they played with a rare grace and behaved impeccably.

Their title was Wenger's third in seven full seasons at Highbury and all the more admirable given that few experts had given them much chance back in August. To the team which had blown the previous championship and allowed United to pass them on the finishing straight, Wenger had added only Jens Lehmann, an able but highly strung German goalkeeper.

Without a new centre half, it was hard to see how Arsenal could mount a more robust challenge but Kolo Toure stepped into the breach and was a revelation alongside Sol Campbell. A renascent Dennis Bergkamp and an imperious Vieira were among the many stars of a team in which, of the regular XI, only Fredrik Ljungberg disappointed. They were led by the phenomenon that is Thierry Henry, who set a record by becoming, for the second year running, both the PFA Players' Player and the Footballer of the Year.

Arsenal's unbeaten run persuaded Wenger to describe his team as immortal, a boast which drew snorts from Old Trafford where they regard their treble of 1999 as a more lasting achievement. Certainly Wenger did not convince when he said that he would not swap his team's achievement for success in the Champions League.

Their defeat to Chelsea in the quarter-finals of the European Cup was was a huge let-down, at least around Highbury, because they had looked irresistible. Winning the Continent's premier trophy, and retaining the title, were goals for Arsenal to take into the new season.

They could look forward with confidence which is more than could be said for many of the teams below them. Chelsea proved that, with Roman Abramovich's unprecedented financial backing, they are the coming force but their progress was overshadowed by the painfully protracted sacking of Claudio Ranieri.

Alan Smith came to symbolise the plight of Leeds United — but despite the tears he swiftly jumped ship for Old Trafford

So badly handled was removal of the Italian that he became a martyr despite failing to win a trophy in his four seasons at Stamford Bridge. His notorious compulsion to tinker cost his team a place in the European Cup final, but he departed Chelsea with his dignity intact. He had won the PR battle with Peter Kenyon, the club's chief executive, who was photographed through net curtains having clandestine and fruitless negotiations with Sven-Goran Eriksson, the England head coach.

Having spent £110 million on new players, the stars of Chelsea's campaign turned out to be Frank Lampard and John Terry rather than Hernan Crespo, Adrian Mutu and Juan Sebastian Veron. It was an expensive way to find out that, for all his billions, Abramovich did not yet have a strategy.

United, too, were undone by their own poor purchases, with David Bellion, Eric Djemba-Djemba and Kleberson sub-standard recruits at a club that had coveted Ronaldinho. Combined with his humiliation at the hands of the "Coolmore Mafia", Ferguson's position looked vulnerable for the first time in more than a decade. The development of Cristiano Ronaldo was one of the few

positives in a season of nine league defeats. United were poor and yet still finished 15 points above Liverpool who, in points terms, were closer to Leeds than Arsenal. While there was sympathy for Houllier after his dismissal, there were few people who did not feel that change was necessary at Anfield if the club was to rejoin the race for the title. The board was particularly worried that home-grown superstars such as Michael Owen and Steven Gerrard were developing itchy feet.

Liverpool finished the best of the rest in the Premiership but, while fourth place was nothing to celebrate, mid-table was a fine achievement for several clubs. Chris Coleman's Fulham had been widely tipped for relegation but finished in the top half of the table while Aston Villa, Charlton Athletic and Birmingham City all made progress and Steve McClaren led Middlesbrough to their first leading trophy by beating Bolton Wanderers to win the Carling Cup.

At the wrong end of the table, the Leeds soap opera continued to enthrall and appal in equal measure. Peter Reid was sacked in November but only after Professor John McKenzie, then the chairman, had consulted supporters over the dismissal. A consortium of local

The Premiership trophy returned to the marble halls

AVERAGE ATTENDANCES	
Manchester United	67,641
Newcastle United	51,966
Manchester City	46,834
Liverpool	42,706
Chelsea	41,234
Everton	38,837
Arsenal	38,078
Leeds United	36,666
Aston Villa	36,621
Tottenham Hotspur	34,876
Southampton	31,699
Leicester City	30,983
Middlesbrough	30,397
Birmingham City	29,077
Wolverhampton Wanderers	28,873
Bolton Wanderers	26,794
Charlton Athletic	26,293
Blackburn Rovers	24,376
Portsmouth	20,180
Fulham	16,342

businessmen bought the club in March but their money was borrowed and, in Gerald Krasner, they had a leader who made some fans long for the return of McKenzie or Peter Ridsdale. Three years after playing in a European Cup semi-final, relegation was confirmed away to Bolton Wanderers with a shambolic 4-1 defeat.

Eddie Gray, the caretaker manager, lost his job to join Houllier, Reid and Ranieri on the pile of discards. Also sacked was Glenn Hoddle, who was ousted at Tottenham Hotspur as early as September. David Pleat, the director of football who took charge of team affairs, was then kicked out at the end of the season.

Perhaps the most unexpected mid-season departure was at Southampton where Gordon Strachan announced that he wanted to take a sabbatical. Rather than wait until the summer, Rupert Lowe, the chairman, replaced him with Paul Sturrock, but only after flirting with the possibility of bringing back Hoddle, a move that did not endear him to the fans.

The single biggest story of the season was, in newspaper terms, the failure of Ferdinand to turn up for his drugs test in September. His England team-mates threatened to go on strike for the European Championship qualifier in Istanbul when he was dropped

from the international squad and, according to Ferguson, his absence through suspension from January transformed the Premiership season.

"There is absolutely no doubt in my mind that Ferdinand's ban made the difference," Ferguson said. "We were top of the league." He could, indeed, point out that United were four points clear in January with the Premiership's best defensive record, but the Scotsman is deluding himself if he cannot accept that Arsenal were the best team in the country.

They not only hit mesmerising peaks of form but showed a steely resolve when under pressure. Three days after they had been knocked out of the European Cup by Chelsea, they trailed Liverpool at home on Good Friday. They not only came from behind but did so breath-takingly, Henry capping a hat-trick with one of the goals of the season.

When Wenger had suggested 12 months earlier that his team was capable of surviving an entire campaign unbeaten, he had been mocked for his arrogance. In fact the Frenchman was just ahead of his time and, after securing the title at White Hart Lane, of all places, they kept going until the final victory over Leicester City. Invincibles, immortals; they had saved a poor Premiership campaign from being remembered for some unsavoury reasons.

PREMIERSHIP

	P	W	D	L	F	A	GD	Pts
Arsenal	38	26	12	0	73	26	47	**90**
Chelsea	38	24	7	7	67	30	37	**79**
Man Utd	38	23	6	9	64	35	29	**75**
Liverpool	38	16	12	10	55	37	18	**60**
Newcastle	38	13	17	8	52	40	12	**56**
Aston Villa	38	15	11	12	48	44	4	**56**
Charlton	38	14	11	13	51	51	0	**53**
Bolton	38	14	11	13	48	56	-8	**53**
Fulham	38	14	10	14	52	46	6	**52**
Birmingham	38	12	14	12	43	48	-5	**50**
Middlesbro	38	13	9	16	44	52	-8	**48**
Southampton	38	12	11	15	44	45	-1	**47**
Portsmouth	38	12	9	17	47	54	-7	**45**
Tottenham	38	13	6	19	47	57	-10	**45**
Blackburn	38	12	8	18	51	59	-8	**44**
Man City	38	9	14	15	55	54	1	**41**
Everton	38	9	12	17	45	57	-12	**39**
Leicester	38	6	15	17	48	65	-17	**33**
Leeds	38	8	9	21	40	79	-39	**33**
Wolves	38	7	12	19	38	77	-39	**33**

FA CUP
Semi-finals

CARLING CUP
Semi-finals

CHAMPIONS LEAGUE
Quarter-finals

Reflected glory: Patrick Vieira, who had another fine season at the heart of the Arsenal team, prepares to receive the Premiership trophy

Catherine Riley

Sunday August 10 2003
MANCHESTER UNITED
Community Shield (Cardiff)
Drew 1-1 (lost 4-3 on pens) HT **1-1** Att **59,293**
Lehmann — Lauren, Toure, Campbell, Cole — Parlour
(Pires ht), Vieira, Gilberto (Edu 60), Ljungberg
(Van Bronckhorst 65) — Henry (Wiltord ht), Bergkamp
(Jeffers 60) *Subs not used* Taylor, Cygan *Booked* Cole,
Vieira *Sent off* Jeffers 74
Scorer **Henry 20**
Report page 196

Saturday August 16
EVERTON (h)
Won 2-1 HT **1-0** Att **38,104** Position **4th**
Two matches into the season and Arsenal have already
had two players sent off, Campbell walking for a trip on
Gravesen. Henry's penalty, awarded for handball by
Stubbs, and a goal by Pires make Radzinski's late reply
irrelevant and Everton are also reduced to ten men
when Li Tie twice fouls Parlour.
Lehmann — Lauren, Toure, Campbell, Cole — Ljungberg,
Vieira, Gilberto, Pires (Parlour 70) — Henry, Wiltord
(Keown 30) *Subs not used* Jeffers, Bergkamp, Taylor
Booked Vieira *Sent off* Campbell 25
Scorers **Henry 35 (pen), Pires 58**
Referee **M Halsey**

Sunday August 24
MIDDLESBROUGH (a)
Won 4-0 HT **3-0** Att **29,450** Position **1st**
Lehmann — Lauren, Toure, Campbell, Cole —
Ljungberg (Parlour 74), Vieira, Gilberto, Pires (Edu 74) —
Henry, Wiltord (Bergkamp 74) *Subs not used* Taylor,
Keown
Scorers **Henry 5, Gilberto 13, Wiltord 22, 60**
Report page 208

Wednesday August 27
ASTON VILLA (h)
Won 2-0 HT **0-0** Att **38,010** Position **1st**
Capitalising on an error by Samuel, Campbell signs
off before a one-match ban with the header that
gives Arsenal the lead and Henry strikes with almost
the last kick of the match, but there are reports of a
tunnel skirmish at half-time in a game of seven
bookings. Despite defeat, David O'Leary is pleased with
Villa's performance.
Lehmann — Lauren, Toure, Campbell, Cole — Ljungberg
(Parlour 78), Vieira, Gilberto, Pires — Henry, Wiltord
(Bergkamp 66) *Subs not used* Keown, Taylor, Edu
Booked Toure, Vieira, Bergkamp
Scorers **Campbell 57, Henry 90**
Referee **M Dean**

Sunday August 31
MANCHESTER CITY (a)
Won 2-1 HT **0-1** Att **46,436** Position **1st**
Lehmann — Lauren, Toure, Keown, Cole — Ljungberg
(Parlour 77), Vieira, Gilberto, Pires (Edu 84) — Henry,
Wiltord (Bergkamp 77) *Subs not used* Taylor, Cygan
Booked Lauren, Cole
Scorers **Wiltord 48, Ljungberg 72**
Report page 187

A SEASON IN WHICH ARSENAL earned a place among the
greats, or an average season punctuated by moments of brilliance? A
team graced by the best player in the world, or a team built around
one man? However their fans look back at the 2003-04 season, it
certainly kept them guessing to the very end.

During the summer there had not been a great deal for them to
get excited about. With David Seaman gone to Manchester City, the
pressure was on to find a goalkeeper, and despite being linked with
name after name, to the surprise of many Arsene Wenger opted for
Jens Lehmann, of Borussia Dortmund. And that was it as far as
newcomers were concerned. With Patrick Vieira's future still
uncertain and Chelsea and Manchester United spending merrily in
the transfer market, it seemed that Arsenal would, at best, be
battling with Newcastle United and Liverpool for third place. And
when the traditional curtain-raiser, the Community Shield, ended in
defeat and took place in front of rows of empty seats at the Arsenal
end — those who stayed away missed the unedifying sight of
Francis Jeffers receiving a deserved red card for kicking out at Phil
Neville — the portents were not good. But then came Europe.

These days, the benchmark for a club's success is measured not by
domestic achievements but by those against the cream of the Continent. At the end of the season, Manchester United fans claimed that,
despite Arsenal's accomplishments, they should not be called a truly
great club because they had never won the European Cup. And
although Arsenal supporters gleefully dismissed this as sour grapes,
deep down each one will silently admit that they had a point.

The draw for the first group stage of the Champions League was
not a pretty one — Inter Milan, plus two trips east (one, of course,
being mandatory for Arsenal's European campaigns), to play
Dynamo Kiev and Lokomotiv Moscow. So it was with a sense of
some excitement that the first match was pencilled in fans' diaries
for September — Inter at Highbury. Cue one of Arsenal's most
humiliating European defeats. A 3-0 win for the Italian side left the
Gunners shell-shocked and things went from bad to worse with a
0-0 draw in Moscow and then a 2-1 defeat in Kiev, leaving Arsenal
at the bottom of their group and staring ignominy in the face.

And yet this was when they showed their true, new colours. In
previous seasons the team might have been strong individually, but
as a unit they were fragile. Although they were not the
overwhelming collection of egos found across London at Stamford
Bridge, Arsenal had still been capable at times of looking like a
group of workers sent forcibly on a bonding weekend in Cumbria.
Last season, however, things were different. The team started to

HONOURS BOARD

work, to fight for one another. Before a ball was kicked in a match, the players would go into a huddle and embrace. They had a mantra that they chanted at the start of each fixture. That word was "together".

Ultimately, it was not enough to take them to the European summit. But there is no doubt that it helped to sustain them during their remarkable, record-breaking march to the title.

Three successive Champions League victories followed, the highlight a glorious night at the San Siro when the sublime Thierry Henry danced through the Inter defence to score two and make two of Arsenal's goals in the 5-1 defeat of the Italian side. Arsenal progressed to the knockout stages as group winners, dispatching Celta Vigo 5-2 on aggregate. There was even time for a bit of crowing, with United being knocked out at this stage by FC Porto.

Come the quarter-final draw, however, come the inevitable: Arsenal v Chelsea. Given past form between the pair, the match was all but declared a bye for the Gunners, but after a 1-1 draw at Stamford Bridge, a resurgent Chelsea won 2-1 at Highbury. Arsenal's European ambitions had died again.

They were not the only dreams that lay shattered. The previous weekend had seen Manchester United end Arsenal's unbeaten run in the FA Cup, which stretched back to May 2001, when they lost in the final to Liverpool. The semi-final at Villa Park was a scrappy affair, the teams separated by a goal from Paul Scholes, but thankfully it was a far less charged affair than the league meeting between them at Old Trafford, when Vieira received a red card and six Arsenal players — plus the club itself — were charged by the FA.

So, at the start of a week when it looked as though Arsenal were heading for the treble, they were down simply to chasing the Premiership title — and even that looked shaky when Liverpool

Saturday September 13
PORTSMOUTH (h)
Drew 1-1 HT **1-1** Att **38,052** Position **1st**
Pires is roundly condemned for appearing to invent a trip by Stefanovic to earn the twice-taken penalty by which Arsenal salvage a draw from a match that even Arsene Wenger concedes they should have lost. Portsmouth, leading through Sheringham's header, are furious, but they pass their first big test with flying colours.

Lehmann — Lauren, Toure, Campbell, Cole — Parlour, Vieira, Edu (Ljungberg 70), Pires — Henry, Bergkamp (Wiltord 75) *Subs not used* Keown, Aliadiere, Stack
Booked Toure, Campbell
Scorer **Henry 40 (pen)**
Referee **A Wiley**

Wednesday September 17
INTER MILAN (h)
Champions League
Lost 0-3 HT **0-3** Att **34,393**
The day after Manchester United and Chelsea open their Champions League campaigns with victories, Arsenal suffer their heaviest home European defeat for 20 years and their first by an Italian side at Highbury. Cruz, Van der Meyde and Martins do the first-half damage, Toldo saving Henry's penalty at 0-2.

Lehmann — Lauren, Toure, Campbell, Cole — Ljungberg, Vieira, Gilberto (Kanu 65), Pires (Bergkamp 65) — Henry, Wiltord (Parlour 79) *Subs not used* Stack, Keown, Edu, Cygan
Referee **M E Mejuto Gonzalez (Spain)**

Sunday September 21
MANCHESTER UNITED (a)
Drew 0-0 HT **0-0** Att **67,639** Position **1st**
Lehmann — Lauren, Toure, Keown, Cole — Parlour, Vieira, Gilberto, Ljungberg — Henry, Bergkamp (Edu 82) *Subs not used* Cygan, Pires, Wiltord, Stack *Booked* Toure, Vieira, Keown *Sent off* Vieira 81
Report page 197

Friday September 26
NEWCASTLE UNITED (h)
Won 3-2 HT **1-1** Att **38,112** Position **1st**
Five days after the "Battle of Old Trafford", Arsene Wenger is still defiant and his team on their best behaviour. Twice Arsenal take the lead, twice Newcastle hit back, but there is no third reprieve after Jenas concedes the decisive penalty with a needless handball.

Lehmann — Lauren, Keown, Toure, Cole (Cygan 52) — Parlour (Pires 62), Vieira (Edu 25), Gilberto, Ljungberg — Henry, Wiltord *Subs not used* Stack
Scorers **Henry 18, 80 (pen), Gilberto 67**
Referee **M Riley**

Tuesday September 30
LOKOMOTIV MOSCOW (a)
Champions League
Drew 0-0 HT **0-0** Att **27,000**
After humiliation at Inter's hands this is a solid response by a weakened team in a city where Arsenal have never won, but they stay bottom of group B as their winless European run extends to seven games. Pires wastes the best chance, shooting too close to the goalkeeper.

Lehmann — Lauren, Keown, Toure, Cole — Parlour, Gilberto, Edu, Pires — Henry, Wiltord *Subs not used* Stack, Cygan, Kanu, Tavlaridis, Aliadiere, Bentley, Hoyte
Referee **J Wegereef (the Netherlands)**

Saturday October 4
LIVERPOOL (a)
Won 2-1 HT **1-1** Att **44,374** Position **1st**
Lehmann — Lauren, Toure, Campbell, Cole — Parlour, Gilberto, Edu, Pires — Henry, Aliadiere (Wiltord 73) *Subs not used* Keown, Cygan, Kanu, Stack *Booked* Cole, Parlour
Scorers **Hyypia 31 (og), Pires 68**
Report page 175

Togetherness was one of the principal ingredients of Arsenal's success

Saturday October 18
CHELSEA (h)
Won 2-1 HT **1-1** Att **38,172** Position **1st**
The second of the heavyweight clashes sees two unbeaten records collide at Highbury and it is Arsenal who retain theirs — and replace Chelsea at the top of the Premiership — after Cudicini's error presents Henry with the winner. Crespo earlier cancels out Edu's deflected free kick, curling in a beauty after running back on to the pitch — unseen by defenders — from tying up his bootlaces on the byline.

Lehmann — Lauren, Toure, Campbell, Cole — Parlour (Bergkamp 66), Gilberto, Edu, Pires (Cygan 90) — Henry, Wiltord (Kanu 66) *Subs not used* Aliadiere, Stack
Scorers **Edu 5, Henry 75**
Referee **P Durkin**

Tuesday October 21
DYNAMO KIEV (a)
Champions League
Lost 1-2 HT **0-1** Att **80,000**
It is now eight Champions League matches without a victory as Arsenal remain rooted to the bottom of group B. Pires hits the bar at 0-0 and Toure does the same at the death, but, in between, Shatskikh and Belkevich win the game for Dynamo, the latter after Lehmann's howler.

Lehmann — Lauren, Toure, Campbell, Cole — Parlour (Ljungberg 72), Gilberto (Kanu 72), Edu (Vieira 60) — Pires, Wiltord — Henry *Subs not used* Stack, Cygan, Clichy, Hoyte
Scorer **Henry 80**
Referee **K Plautz (Austria)**

Sunday October 26
CHARLTON ATHLETIC (a)
Drew 1-1 HT **1-1** Att **26,660** Position **1st**
Lehmann — Lauren, Toure, Campbell, Cole — Ljungberg (Kanu 71), Parlour, Gilberto, Pires — Henry, Bergkamp (Wiltord 71) *Subs not used* Stack, Edu, Cygan
Booked Lauren
Scorer **Henry 39**
Report page 114

Tuesday October 28
ROTHERHAM UNITED (h)
Carling Cup, 3rd rnd
Drew 1-1 (aet; won 9-8 on pens) HT 1-0 Att **27,451**
An extraordinary Arsenal line-up, an extraordinary climax to the tie: Wiltord, having missed their first kick, wins a protracted penalty shoot-out by converting the 22nd, getting a second turn from the spot because Rotherham have been reduced to ten men by the dismissal of Pollit, their goalkeeper. Fabregas becomes the youngest first-team player in Arsenal's history at 16 years 177 days.

Stack — Hoyte (Spicer 117), Tavlaridis, Cygan, Clichy — Wiltord, Fabregas (Owusu-Abeyie 85), Edu, Thomas (Smith 74) — Kanu, Aliadiere *Subs not used* Holloway, Skulason *Booked* Aliadiere
Scorer **Aliadiere 11**
Referee **B Knight**

Saturday November 1
LEEDS UNITED (a)
Won 4-1 HT **3-0** Att **36,491** Position **1st**
Lehmann — Lauren, Toure, Campbell, Cole — Ljungberg (Edu 70), Parlour, Gilberto, Pires — Henry, Bergkamp (Aliadiere 77) *Subs not used* Stack, Wiltord, Cygan
Scorers **Henry 8, 33, Pires 17, Gilberto 50**
Report page 156

came to Highbury the following weekend. "Together" had never been more important. Twice Arsenal came from behind and, on the final whistle, with a 4-2 victory secured, there was no doubting the club was on course for the championship, which was duly secured with four games in hand — and what better place to win it than at White Hart Lane? With Newcastle's defeat of Chelsea earlier in the day, Arsenal needed only a point, and even though they gave away a two-goal lead, never has a draw tasted sweeter.

The unbeaten record was maintained, too, and so the celebrations began with all talk of trebles forgotten — though it could even have been a quadruple: Arsenal's youngsters made it to the semi-finals of the Carling Cup, where they were beaten by the eventual winners, Middlesbrough.

That competition had been a wonderful showcase for some of the rising stars at Highbury, such as David Bentley and Gael Clichy, who then broke through into the first team. The second leg of the semi-final also marked the full debut of Wenger's winter transfer-window signing, Jose Antonio Reyes, from Seville. An own goal might not have been the ideal way to start his career, but Reyes has since shown pace, a deft touch and a willingness to battle for the ball. He is a tremendous addition to the squad.

And what for the new season? Retaining the Premiership in the face of what should be a reinvigorated challenge from United and Chelsea is imperative, but Europe is still the elusive prize and surely Arsenal are now better equipped to lift the trophy than at any other time. But they will have to do it together.

THE MANAGER — Arsene Wenger

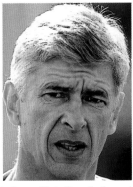

After Arsenal secured the title, David Dein, the vice-chairman, called Arsene Wenger "the miracle worker". "We have never seen such pretty football," Dein said. But 2003-04 will not just be remembered for Arsenal's own take on the beautiful game, but as the season that Wenger instilled real team spirit in the dressing-room. He has fostered a sense of self-belief as a team, rather than as individuals. His greatest achievement, however, may have been in holding the team together when the treble turned into the single and driving them on to finish the Premiership season unbeaten — a testament as much to the man as the team.

Catherine Riley

APPEARANCES

	Prem	FAC	CC	Euro	Total
J Aliadiere	3 (7)	1	3	0 (1)	7 (8)
D Bentley	1	0 (2)	5	0 (1)	6 (3)
D Bergkamp	21 (7)	3	-	4 (2)	29* (9)
S Campbell	35	5	-	9	50*
G Clichy	7 (5)	1 (3)	5	1	14 (8)
A Cole	32	4	1	9	47*
P Cygan	10 (8)	-	3	2 (1)	15 (9)
Edu	13 (17)	4 (1)	4	7 (1)	28 (20†)
F Fabregas	-	-	2 (1)	-	2 (1)
T Henry	37	2 (1)	-	10	50* (1)
J Hoyte	0 (1)	-	2	-	2 (1)
F Jeffers	-	-	-	-	0 (1†)
Kanu	3 (7)	1 (2)	4	1 (6)	9 (15)
M Keown	3 (7)	1	3	1	8 (7)
Lauren	30 (2)	5	1	8	45* (2)
J Lehmann	38	5	-	10	54*
F Ljungberg	27 (3)	4	-	8 (1)	40* (4)
Q Owuso-Abeyie	-	-	1 (2)	-	1 (2)
M Papadopulos	-	-	0 (1)	-	0 (1)
R Parlour	16 (9)	2 (1)	3	4 (1)	26* (11)
R Pires	33 (3)	3 (1)	-	10	46 (5†)
J A Reyes	7 (6)	2 (1)	1	2 (2)	12 (9)
Gilberto Silva	29 (3)	3	1	5 (3)	39* (6)
F Simek	-	-	1	-	1
O-I Skulason	-	-	0 (1)	-	0 (1)
R Smith	-	-	0 (3)	-	0 (3)
J Spicer	-	-	0 (1)	-	0 (1)
G Stack	-	-	5	-	5
E Tavlaridis	-	-	3	-	3
J Thomas	-	-	0 (2)	-	0 (2)
K Toure	36 (1)	4 (1)	2	10	53* (2)
G van Bronckhorst	-	-	-	-	0 (1†)
P Vieira	29	5	2	6 (1)	43* (1)
S Wiltord	8 (4)	-	3	3 (1)	14 (6†)

(* denotes appearance and † denotes substitute appearance in Community Shield)

Wednesday November 5
DYNAMO KIEV (h)
Champions League
Won 1-0 HT 0-0 Att **34,419**
While AS Monaco are putting eight goals past Deportivo in the highest-scoring Champions League match in history, Arsenal get just one — and they have to wait 88 minutes for that. But Cole's diving header is worth its weight in gold, Arsenal's first European win in a year preventing elimination.

Lehmann — Lauren, Toure, Campbell, Cole — Ljungberg (Wiltord 69), Parlour (Kanu 76), Gilberto, Pires — Henry, Bergkamp (Edu 90) *Subs not used* Stack, Cygan, Clichy, Aliadiere *Booked* Toure, Gilberto
Scorer **Cole 88**
Referee **L Cortez Batista (Portugal)**

Saturday November 8
TOTTENHAM HOTSPUR (h)
Won 2-1 HT 0-1 Att **38,101** Position **1st**
Arsenal need a large slice of luck against their most bitter rivals to keep their unbeaten run going. They trail to Anderton's first goal since February 2002 and hold their breath as Postiga misses two great chances, then win the game through Pires and Ljungberg, whose shot takes a wild deflection off Carr.

Lehmann — Lauren (Cygan 60), Toure, Campbell, Cole — Ljungberg, Parlour, Gilberto (Bergkamp 60), Pires — Henry, Kanu (Edu 82) *Subs not used* Stack, Hoyte *Booked* Parlour
Scorers **Pires 69, Ljungberg 79**
Referee **M Halsey**

Saturday November 22
BIRMINGHAM CITY (a)
Won 3-0 HT 1-0 Att **29,558** Position **1st**
Lehmann — Toure, Campbell, Cygan, Cole — Ljungberg, Edu, Pires (Hoyte 90), Clichy (Kanu 59) — Henry, Bergkamp (Aliadiere 90) *Subs not used* Stack, Tavlaridis *Booked* Toure, Edu
Scorers **Ljungberg 4, Bergkamp 80, Pires 88**
Report page 84

Tuesday November 25
INTER MILAN (a)
Champions League
Won 5-1 HT 1-1 Att **50,000**
The San Siro is stunned into silence as Arsenal, needing to win to stay alive, do that and much, much more, registering the biggest victory by an English side over Italian opposition and, at the same time, inflicting Inter's heaviest home defeat in Europe. Henry, who almost pulled out with injury, leads the way with a double and an assist.

Lehmann — Toure, Campbell, Cygan, Cole — Ljungberg, Edu, Parlour, Pires — Henry (Aliadiere 88), Kanu (Gilberto 73) *Subs not used* Stack, Keown, Clichy, Papadopulos, Hoyte *Booked* Cygan, Edu
Scorers **Henry 25, 85, Ljungberg 49, Edu 87, Pires 89**
Referee **W Stark (Germany)**

Sunday November 30
FULHAM (h)
Drew 0-0 HT 0-0 Att **38,063** Position **2nd**
Five days after putting five past Inter, Arsenal cannot once find a way past an inspired Van der Sar despite 26 goal attempts — the first time they have failed to score at Highbury for 46 matches. It costs them the lead in the Premiership, Chelsea taking over, while Fulham climb back to fourth place.

Lehmann — Toure, Campbell, Cygan, Cole — Ljungberg (Aliadiere 79), Gilberto (Kanu 66), Edu, Pires — Henry, Bergkamp *Subs not used* Clichy, Stack, Hoyte *Booked* Edu
Referee **G Barber**

Tuesday December 2
WOLVERHAMPTON WANDERERS (h)
Carling Cup, 4th rnd
Won 5-1 HT 1-0 Att **28,161**
Francesc Fabregas Soler ("Cesc" to his friends) becomes the youngest scorer in the club's history, at 16 years 212 days, as Arsenal's youngsters — plus the returning Vieira — humble a full-strength Wolves side. Aliadiere's second goal is the pick of the bunch, Kanu getting his first for more than a year.

Stack — Hoyte (Skulason 55), Simek, Tavlaridis, Clichy — Aliadiere (Papadopulos 83), Fabregas, Vieira, Bentley (Smith 78) — Kanu, Wiltord *Subs not used* Shaaban, Owusu-Abeyie *Booked* Simek, Tavlaridis
Scorers **Aliadiere 24, 71, Kanu 68, Wiltord 79, Fabregas 88**
Referee **D Gallagher**

Saturday December 6
LEICESTER CITY (a)
Drew 1-1 HT 0-0 Att **32,108** Position **2nd**
Lehmann — Toure, Campbell, Cygan, Cole — Ljungberg (Keown 87), Gilberto, Edu, Pires — Aliadiere (Wiltord 67), Bergkamp (Clichy 74) *Subs not used* Stack, Kanu *Booked* Lehmann *Sent off* Cole 73
Scorer **Gilberto 60**
Report page 167

Wednesday December 10
LOKOMOTIV MOSCOW (h)
Champions League
Won 2-0 HT 1-0 Att **35,343**
After taking one point from their first three games, Arsenal ensure they match Manchester United and Chelsea by finishing top of their group and earn seeding for the draw two days later. Lokomotiv, who have Lekgetho sent off on the stroke of half-time, also go through despite falling to two Henry-inspired goals.

Lehmann — Toure, Campbell, Cygan, Cole — Ljungberg, Gilberto, Vieira, Pires — Henry, Bergkamp (Kanu 75) *Subs not used* Stack, Keown, Wiltord, Parlour, Edu, Aliadiere *Booked* Vieira
Scorers **Pires 12, Ljungberg 67**
Referee **L Michel (Slovakia)**

Sunday December 14
BLACKBURN ROVERS (h)
Won 1-0 HT 1-0 Att **37,677** Position **1st**
Having confirmed before the game that they have received a formal approach from Chelsea for Henry, Arsenal beat Blackburn through Bergkamp's early goal to regain pole position from Manchester United. Rovers are a shade unlucky to have Babbel's headed equaliser disallowed for a foul on Toure.

Lehmann — Toure, Campbell, Cygan, Cole — Ljungberg (Edu 83), Gilberto, Vieira, Pires — Henry, Bergkamp (Parlour 73) *Subs not used* Keown, Kanu, Stack *Booked* Gilberto, Cygan
Scorer **Bergkamp 11**
Referee **A D'Urso**

Tuesday December 16
WEST BROMWICH ALBION (a)
Carling Cup, quarter-final
Won 2-0 HT 1-0 Att **20,369**
A mere 11 changes for Arsenal, who need a bit of luck at both ends to defeat the first-division leaders. Albion are denied two penalties, have a goal wrongly disallowed and hit the bar through Dobie, but Kanu and Aliadiere — the latter after a blunder by Hoult — see Arsenal through.

Stack — Lauren, Keown, Tavlaridis, Clichy — Wiltord, Parlour, Edu, Bentley (Thomas 82) — Kanu, Aliadiere (Fabregas 73) *Subs not used* Shaaban, Papadopulos, Simek *Booked* Tavlaridis
Scorers **Kanu 25, Aliadiere 57**
Referee **M Messias**

MATCH OF THE SEASON

Tottenham Hotspur 2 Arsenal 2
White Hart Lane, Sunday April 25 2004
Matt Dickinson

WINNING THE CHAMPIONSHIP AT White Hart Lane yesterday was not without its complications for Arsenal, who wanted to stay alive long enough to celebrate their Barclaycard Premiership title. A team jig in front of their fans was brought to an abrupt halt when a scuffle broke out on a nearby terrace. Patrick Vieira led a swift retreat to the dressing-room to ensure that they remained unbeaten in all respects.

Inside, the Arsenal players will have found Sol Campbell, who had made the quickest departure of all to avoid antagonising the Tottenham Hotspur supporters. Jens Lehmann, too, after he gave away the ridiculous late penalty which, Arsene Wenger admitted, had spoilt the finale. As the final whistle signalled that the championship trophy would be returning to Highbury, the Arsenal manager slapped his side in frustration.

"That tarnished it at first," Wenger admitted, but it was not long before the annoyance was swept away by a tidal wave of delight and deep fulfilment. "I don't want to diminish the other two [championships]," he said, but it was clear that, of the three titles he has won in seven full seasons in North London, this was the most special.

Special because his team have pushed back the boundaries of the game, setting records almost every week. Special, too, because they have not only come unscathed through 34 matches unbeaten but done so playing some of the most breathtaking football this country has ever seen thanks to masters of the game such as Vieira and Thierry Henry. A special championship will become an historic one if they can just find the energy to match Birmingham City, Portsmouth, Fulham and Leicester City in the last four games. "No champagne, just water," Wenger said as he entered the press conference clutching a drink. "We are serious."

Even if they slip before the end, the title is all the more impressive because, after surrendering the championship to Manchester United last May, Wenger went out and spent less than £2 million. Most of that was on Lehmann, who will surely be replaced this summer on grounds of suspect temperament. The Frenchman will know that the challenge of Chelsea will be augmented by another £50 million-plus in new signings this summer, but there are no reasons to doubt Arsenal's pre-eminence in England this morning. He has even made sense of the defeat to Chelsea in the European Cup quarter-final, which is the single significant regret. "You never forget a defeat like that in a big game, but what I would say is that the European Cup has become a complete cup," Wenger said. "One game not at your best and you are out. You can't base a season on that." Yesterday

Gilberto Silva steps up to get the better of Tottenham's Michael Brown

was not the day for wondering why this team of many talents has yet to fulfil its potential in Europe.

News of Chelsea's defeat away to Newcastle United found its way into the Arsenal dressing-room ten minutes before kick-off. A draw and the title would be theirs. Their resolve was evident when, with less than three minutes gone, Henry gathered the ball on the edge of his own penalty area and carried it over the halfway line. Henry found Dennis Bergkamp, who crossed for Vieira to score. From the Arsenal box to Tottenham's net, the move had taken 11.5 seconds.

More flowing passing brought the second goal before half-time when Bergkamp saw Vieira's break forward. The France midfield player, who was immense throughout despite Michael Brown's valiant attempts to bring the maestro down to size, cut the ball back for Robert Pires to sidefoot an easy finish. The Arsenal fans were jubilant, taunting their rivals that it had been 43 years since their last title. Victory seemed assured for Arsenal even after Jamie Redknapp beat Lehmann in the 62nd minute with a cracking first-time shot from outside the area.

Although guilty of defending far too deep, Arsenal seemed to have survived Tottenham's second-half rally until Lehmann, overreacting as usual, pushed Robbie Keane after the pair had jostled for a corner.

Saturday December 20
BOLTON WANDERERS (a)
Drew 1-1   HT **0-0**   Att **28,003**   Position **1st** (equal)
Lehmann — Toure, Campbell, Cygan, Clichy — Ljungberg, Gilberto, Vieira, Pires — Henry, Bergkamp (Parlour 69)
Subs not used Keown, Edu, Kanu, Stack Booked Vieira, Henry
Scorer **Pires 57**
Report page 105

Friday December 26
WOLVERHAMPTON WANDERERS (h)
Won 3-0   HT **2-0**   Att **38,003**   Position **2nd**
In a week in which he is named the second-best footballer in both Europe (behind Nedved) and the world (behind Zidane), Henry devours Wolves. The last thing Arsenal need is a helping hand, but they get one from the hapless Craddock, who puts through his own net and blunders for the first of Henry's double.
Lehmann — Toure, Campbell, Cygan, Clichy — Ljungberg (Edu 71), Parlour, Vieira, Pires (Aliadiere 71) — Henry, Bergkamp Subs not used Stack, Keown, Kanu Booked Vieira, Aliadiere
Scorers **Craddock 13 (og), Henry 20, 89**
Referee **P Dowd**

Monday December 29
SOUTHAMPTON (a)
Won 1-0   HT **1-0**   Att **32,151**   Position **2nd**
Lehmann — Toure, Campbell, Cygan, Clichy — Ljungberg (Edu 74), Parlour, Vieira, Pires (Lauren 88) — Henry, Bergkamp (Kanu 74) Subs not used Stack, Keown
Scorer **Pires 35**
Report page 244

Sunday January 4 2004
LEEDS UNITED (a)
FA Cup, 3rd rnd
Won 4-1   HT **2-1**   Att **31,207**
Lehmann — Lauren, Keown, Campbell, Cole — Ljungberg (Parlour 81), Gilberto, Vieira, Edu (Toure 81) — Kanu (Pires 81), Henry Subs not used Bentley, Shaaban Booked Gilberto
Scorers **Henry 26, Edu 33, Pires 87, Toure 90**
Report page 158

Wednesday January 7
EVERTON (a)
Drew 1-1   HT **1-0**   Att **38,726**   Position **2nd**
Lehmann — Toure (Lauren 20), Campbell, Cygan, Cole — Ljungberg (Gilberto 89), Parlour, Vieira, Pires — Kanu (Edu 81), Henry Subs not used Shaaban, Aliadiere Booked Lauren, Parlour, Ljungberg
Scorer **Kanu 29**
Report page 138

Saturday January 10
MIDDLESBROUGH (h)
Won 4-1   HT **2-0**   Att **38,117**   Position **1st** (equal)
Level three weeks ago with Chelsea, Arsenal now share first place in the Premiership with Manchester United, equal on points and goal difference after demolishing Middlesbrough in the first of four meetings between the clubs in three competitions spread over 19 days. They would have been top on their own but for Maccarone's late penalty.
Lehmann — Lauren, Campbell, Cygan, Cole — Ljungberg (Parlour 73), Vieira, Gilberto, Pires (Edu 67) — Aliadiere (Kanu ht), Henry Subs not used Stack, Keown Booked Gilberto
Scorers **Henry 38 (pen), Queudrue 45 (og), Pires 58, Ljungberg 68**
Referee **A D'Urso**

Sunday January 18
ASTON VILLA (a)
Won 2-0 **HT 1-0** Att **39,380** Position **1st**
Lehmann – Lauren, Campbell, Cygan, Cole – Ljungberg
(Parlour 76), Gilberto, Vieira, Pires (Edu 76) – Kanu
(Toure 76), Henry Subs not used Keown, Stack Booked
Vieira
Scorer **Henry 28, 53 (pen)**
Report page 77

Tuesday January 20
MIDDLESBROUGH (h)
Carling Cup, semi-final, 1st leg
Lost 0-1 **HT 0-0** Att **31,070**
Report and details page 332

Saturday January 24
MIDDLESBROUGH (h)
FA Cup, 4th rnd
Won 4-1 **HT 2-1** Att **37,256**
Henry is rested, but the returning Bergkamp sends
Arsenal on their way to a place in the last 16. However,
Job's equaliser, Ljungberg's double and Boateng's
sending-off for two bookable offences are all
overshadowed by the peach of a goal chipped in by
Bentley, the 19-year-old Arsenal substitute, at the death.

Lehmann – Lauren, Toure, Campbell, Cole – Parlour,
Vieira (Clichy 75), Edu, Pires – Bergkamp (Bentley 84),
Ljungberg Subs not used Keown, Stack, Owusu-Abeyie
Scorers **Bergkamp 19, Ljungberg 28, 68, Bentley 90**
Referee **M Dean**

Sunday February 1
MANCHESTER CITY (h)
Won 2-1 **HT 1-0** Att **38,103** Position **1st**
Highbury is treated to 20 minutes of Reyes, Arsenal's
new Spanish import, who shows several nice touches.
But his debut takes second billing to another superb goal
from Henry, rifled into the far corner, and by the melee
that follows Anelka's late reply and the Manchester City
striker's dismissal.

Lehmann – Lauren, Toure, Campbell, Cole – Ljungberg
(Edu 59), Parlour, Gilberto, Pires (Cygan 84) – Bergkamp
(Reyes 70), Henry Subs not used Stack, Bentley Booked
Cole, Parlour, Edu
Scorers **Tarnat 39 (og), Henry 83**
Referee **A Wiley**

Tuesday February 3
MIDDLESBROUGH (a)
Carling Cup, semi-final, 2nd leg
Lost 1-2 (lost 1-3 on agg) **HT 0-0** Att **28,781**
Report and details page 333

Saturday February 7
WOLVERHAMPTON WANDERERS (a)
Won 3-1 **HT 1-1** Att **29,392** Position **1st**
Lehmann – Lauren, Toure, Campbell, Cole – Gilberto,
Vieira, Edu, Pires – Bergkamp (Reyes 55), Henry Subs
not used Parlour, Cygan, Clichy, Stack Booked Bergkamp
Scorers **Bergkamp 9, Henry 58, Toure 63**
Report page 266

Tuesday February 10
SOUTHAMPTON (h)
Won 2-0 **HT 1-0** Att **38,007** Position **1st**
Earlier in the day, Real Madrid admit that Henry is on
their summer shopping list; in the evening, he shows
why, scoring both of the goals – the first prompting
Southampton complaints about offside – that take
Arsenal five points clear. The first is Henry's 100th in
the Premiership, on his 160th appearance.

Lehmann – Lauren, Toure, Campbell, Cole – Parlour,
Gilberto, Vieira, Pires – Reyes (Clichy 75), Henry Subs
not used Stack, Edu, Cygan, Bentley Booked Parlour,
Vieira
Scorer **Henry 31, 90**
Referee **N Barry**

Needing just a point to secure the title, Arsenal swept into an early lead at White Hart Lane through Patrick Vieira, second left

After booking both of them, Mark Halsey pointed to the penalty spot. Keane scored and, from White Hart Lane's celebrations, you would have thought that Spurs had just secured the title themselves. The final whistle went and Lehmann stalked to the dressing-room.

"It has become a game to wind him up," Wenger said, but the Germany goalkeeper has brought most of the trouble on himself. His team-mates must be tiring of his antics because they have been impeccably behaved since the shameful scenes at Old Trafford in September, when they mugged Ruud van Nistelrooy after he missed a late penalty. "That was 28 games ago and we are still unbeaten," Wenger said. "That shows you how precarious it all is. This championship was closer than people think." Retaining the crown for the first time is now the task for Wenger and more records could fall if his players can match the 42-game unbeaten run by Brian Clough's Nottingham Forest spread over two seasons. Worryingly for Chelsea and United, Wenger believes that the best is yet to come from this youthful, admirable and special team.

TOTTENHAM HOTSPUR (4-4-2): K Keller – S Kelly (sub: G Poyet, 79min), A Gardner, L King, M Taricco (sub: G Bunjevcevic, 90) – S Davies, J Redknapp, M Brown, J Jackson (sub: J Defoe, 46) – R Keane, F Kanoute. **Substitutes not used:** L Hirschfeld, R Ricketts. **Booked:** Redknapp, Keane.
ARSENAL (4-4-2): J Lehmann – Lauren, K Toure, S Campbell, A Cole – R Parlour (sub: Edu, 67), P Vieira, Gilberto Silva – R Pires – D Bergkamp (sub: J A Reyes, 81), T Henry. **Substitutes not used:** G Stack, M Keown, G Clichy. **Booked:** Lehmann.

STATS AND FACTS

- Arsenal scored in 46 successive home league games until drawing 0-0 against Fulham in October.

- Thierry Henry has faced Charlton Athletic seven times and scored nine goals.

- What was strange about the following Arsenal scorelines: Leeds United 1, Arsenal 4; Arsenal 4, Middlesbrough 1; Arsenal 2, Chelsea 1? Answer: they all occurred in both the Premiership and the FA Cup last season.

- Arsenal have lost four of their past 57 away games in the Premiership.

- Arsenal's FA Cup semi-final loss to Manchester United was only their fourth in 43 games in the competition (including one in a penalty shoot-out).

- Robert Pires, who supplied 14 league goals from midfield, scored more than three times as many as Arsenal's second most prolific striker, Dennis Bergkamp, who managed four.

- Only two teams have completed a league double over Arsenal in the past six years: Blackburn in 2002-03 and Liverpool in 1999-2000.

- Arsenal became the third team to remain unbeaten throughout a league campaign in England. The other two were Preston North End in the old first division in 1888-89 and Liverpool in the old second division in 1893-94.

- Arsenal are unbeaten in 14 away London derbies in the Premiership.

- In the past 14 league meetings between Manchester United and Arsenal at Old Trafford there has been a winner on nine occasions and each time that team has finished above the other one in the table.

Bill Edgar

GOALSCORERS

	Prem	FAC	CC	Euro	Total
J Aliadiere	-	-	4	-	4
D Bentley	-	1	-	-	1
D Bergkamp	4	1	-	-	5
S Campbell	1	-	-	-	1
A Cole	-	-	-	1	1
Edu	2	1	1	3	7
F Fabregas	-	-	1	-	1
T Henry	30 (7p)	3	-	5	39† (7p)
Kanu	1	-	2	-	3
F Ljungberg	4	4	-	2	10
R Pires	14	1	-	4	19
J A Reyes	2	2	-	1	5
Gilberto Silva	4	-	-	-	4
K Toure	1	2	-	-	3
P Vieira	3	-	-	-	3
S Wiltord	3	-	1	-	4
Own goals	4	-	-	-	4

(† Total includes goal in Community Shield)

Sunday February 15
CHELSEA (h)
FA Cup, 5th rnd
Won 2-1   HT 0-1   Att 38,136
Chelsea, who have a header by Gronkjaer wrongly disallowed before Mutu gives them the lead, are beaten in the FA Cup by Arsenal for the fourth season in succession, Reyes proving an able deputy for the injured Henry with his first goals — in the right end, at least — of his career in England, the opener a superb 25-yard shot into the top corner.

Lehmann — Lauren, Toure, Campbell, Cole — Parlour (Edu 51), Gilberto, Vieira, Pires — Reyes (Clichy 82), Bergkamp *Subs not used* Cygan, Stack, Bentley *Booked* Campbell, Vieira, Gilberto
Scorer **Reyes 56, 61**
Referee **P Durkin**

Saturday February 21
CHELSEA (a)
Won 2-1   HT 2-1   Att 41,847   Position 1st
Lehmann — Lauren, Toure, Campbell, Clichy — Gilberto, Vieira, Edu, Pires — Bergkamp (Ljungberg 78), Henry *Subs not used* Stack, Reyes, Cygan, Kanu *Booked* Lauren, Henry
Scorers **Vieira 15, Edu 21**
Report page 129

Tuesday February 24
CELTA VIGO (a)
European Cup, 1st knockout rnd, 1st leg
Won 3-2   HT 1-1   Att 21,000
Arsenal's first win in seven attempts on Spanish soil puts them within reach of the quarter-finals. The unlikely hero is Edu, who twice puts them ahead, the second time with a fabulous individual goal (his namesake, Luis Edu, and Jose Ignacio reply for Celta). Pires hits the winner after a great exchange with Henry.

Lehmann — Lauren, Toure, Campbell, Clichy (Cygan 90) — Ljungberg (Bentley 90), Vieira, Edu, Pires — Henry, Reyes (Kanu 78) *Subs not used* Stack, Keown, Hoyte, Fabregas *Booked* Edu, Henry
Scorers **Edu 18, 58, Pires 80**
Referee **A Frisk (Sweden)**

Saturday February 28
CHARLTON ATHLETIC (h)
Won 2-1   HT 2-0   Att 38,137   Position 1st
Two goals up before you can blink after a devastating opening, Arsenal are forced to hang on uncomfortably by the end. Jensen replies with a free kick and both Stuart, with a header, and Johansson, with an overhead kick that hits the inside of a post, go desperately close for Charlton. Arsenal, though, are now nine points clear of the field.

Lehmann — Lauren, Toure, Campbell, Cole — Ljungberg (Gilberto 75), Vieira, Edu, Pires (Cygan 89) — Henry, Bergkamp (Reyes 75) *Subs not used* Taylor, Kanu
Scorers **Pires 2, Henry 4**
Referee **G Barber**

Saturday March 6
PORTSMOUTH (a)
FA Cup, 6th rnd
Won 5-1   HT 3-0   Att 20,137
Lehmann — Lauren, Toure, Campbell, Cole — Gilberto, Vieira (Clichy 73), Edu, Ljungberg (Bentley 73) — Reyes, Henry (Kanu 73) *Subs not used* Taylor, Cygan
Scorers **Henry 25, 50, Ljungberg 43, 57, Toure 45**
Report page 236

Wednesday March 10
CELTA VIGO (h)
European Cup, 1st knockout rnd, 2nd leg
Won 2-0 (won 5-2 on agg) HT 2-0 Att **35,402**
"Are you watching Manchester?" The chant reflects the glee at Highbury as, 24 hours after United's elimination, Arsenal stroll through to the last eight with another superb performance capped by Henry's goals, the first after more sublime work by Bergkamp. Celta, happy to indulge in damage-limitation, have Contreras sent off 20 minutes from time.

Lehmann — Lauren, Toure, Campbell, Cole — Ljungberg, Vieira, Edu (Gilberto 70), Pires (Reyes 70) — Bergkamp (Kanu 77), Henry Subs not used Stack, Keown, Cygan, Clichy
Scorer **Henry 14, 34**
Referee **P Collina (Italy)**

Saturday March 13
BLACKBURN ROVERS (a)
Won 2-0 HT 0-0 Att **28,627** Position **1st**
Lehmann — Lauren, Toure, Campbell, Cole — Gilberto, Vieira, Edu, Pires (Cygan 89) — Reyes (Clichy 77), Henry Subs not used Stack, Bentley, Kanu Booked Edu
Scorers **Henry 57, Pires 87**
Report page 98

Saturday March 20
BOLTON WANDERERS (h)
Won 2-1 HT 2-1 Att **38,053** Position **1st**
The first landmarks are reached in what is threatening to turn into a record-breaking season for Arsenal, who equal the feat of Liverpool and Leeds in going 29 matches unbeaten from the start of a season and eclipse their own mark of 30 Premiership games undefeated. However, 2-0 ahead and imperious early on, they suffer an anxious second half after Campo replies twice for Bolton.

Lehmann — Lauren, Toure, Campbell, Cole — Gilberto (Ljungberg 69), Vieira, Edu, Pires (Cygan 88) — Bergkamp, Henry Subs not used Stack, Reyes, Kanu Booked Cole
Scorers **Pires 16, Bergkamp 24**
Referee **G Barber**

Wednesday March 24
CHELSEA (a)
European Cup, quarter-final, 1st leg
Drew 1-1 HT 0-0 Att **40,778**
Lehmann — Lauren, Toure, Campbell, Cole — Ljungberg (Reyes 78), Vieira, Edu, Pires — Bergkamp (Gilberto 72), Henry Subs not used Stack, Keown, Cygan, Clichy, Kanu
Scorer **Pires 59**
Report page 130

Sunday March 28
MANCHESTER UNITED (h)
Drew 1-1 HT 0-0 Att **38,184** Position **1st**
A pulsating match lives up to its billing as Arsenal duly claim the record of 30 matches unbeaten from the start of a season and United prove their equal on the day. Henry's stunning, swerving, 30-yard shot gives Arsenal the lead, but United — angered by the refusal of a penalty for Campbell's apparent foul on Giggs — level through Saha from 25 yards closer.

Lehmann — Lauren, Toure, Campbell, Clichy — Ljungberg (Cygan 82), Vieira, Edu, Pires (Bergkamp 86) — Reyes (Gilberto 78), Henry Subs not used Stack, Kanu Booked Clichy
Scorer **Henry 50**
Referee **G Poll**

THE PLAYERS

JEREMIE ALIADIERE (forward) **Born** March 30, 1983, Rambouillet, France **Ht** 6ft 0in **Wt** 11st 0lb **Signed from** trainee, March 2000

DAVID BENTLEY (forward) **Born** August 27, 1984, Peterborough **Ht** 5ft 11in **Wt** 11st 0lb **Signed from** trainee, summer 2000

DENNIS BERGKAMP (forward) **Born** May 18, 1969, Amsterdam **Ht** 6ft 0in **Wt** 12st 5lb **Signed from** Inter Milan, July 1995, £7.5m

SOL CAMPBELL (defender) **Born** September 18, 1974, Newham **Ht** 6ft 2in **Wt** 14st 1lb **Signed from** Tottenham Hotspur, July 2001, free

ASHLEY COLE (defender) **Born** December 20, 1980, Stepney **Ht** 5ft 8in **Wt** 10st 10lb **Signed from** trainee, November 1998

FRANCESC FABREGAS (midfield) **Born** May 4, 1987, Arenyes de Mar, Spain **Ht** 5ft 10in **Wt** 10st 12lb **Signed from** Barcelona, July 2003, free

GAEL CLICHY (defender) **Born** July 26, 1985, Clichy, France **Ht** 5ft 11in **Wt** 11st 5lb **Signed from** Cannes, August 2003, nominal

PASCAL CYGAN (defender) **Born** April 29, 1974, Lens **Ht** 6ft 3in **Wt** 13st 10lb **Signed from** Lille, July 2002, £2.1m

EDU (midfield) **Born** May 15, 1978, Sao Paulo **Ht** 6ft 1in **Wt** 11st 4lb **Signed from** Corinthians, Brazil, January 2001, £6m

GILBERTO SILVA (midfield) **Born** October 7, 1976, Lagoa da Prata, Brazil **Ht** 6ft 3in **Wt** 12st 7lb **Signed from** Atletico Mineiro, July 2002, £4.5m

THIERRY HENRY (forward) **Born** August 17, 1977, Paris **Ht** 6ft 2in **Wt** 12st 6lb **Signed from** Juventus, August 1999, £10.5m

JUSTIN HOYTE (defender) **Born** November 20, 1984, Waltham Forest **Ht** 5ft 11in **Wt** 10st 7lb **Signed from** trainee, June 2001

FRANCIS JEFFERS (forward) **Born** January 25, 1981, Liverpool **Ht** 5ft 9in **Wt** 10st 8lb **Signed from** Everton, June 2001, £8m

KANU (forward) **Born** August 1, 1976, Owerri, Nigeria **Ht** 6ft 6in **Wt** 12st 8lb **Signed from** Inter Milan, February 1999, £4.5m

MARTIN KEOWN (defender) **Born** July 24, 1966, Oxford **Ht** 6ft 1in **Wt** 12st 4lb **Signed from** Everton, February 1993, £2m

LAUREN (defender) **Born** January 19, 1977, Lodhji Krib, Cameroon **Ht** 5ft 11in **Wt** 11st 3lb **Signed from** Real Mallorca, June 2000, £7.2m

JENS LEHMANN (goalkeeper) **Born** November 10, 1969, Essen, Germany **Ht** 6ft 3in **Wt** 13st 5lb **Signed from** Borussia Dortmund, July 2003, undisclosed

FREDRIK LJUNGBERG (midfield) **Born** April 16, 1977, Vittsjo, Sweden **Ht** 5ft 9in **Wt** 11st 11lb **Signed from** BK Halmstad, September 1998, £3m

QUINCY OWUSU-ABEYIE (forward) **Born** April 15, 1986, Amsterdam **Ht** 5ft 10in **Wt** 12st 0lb **Signed from** September 2002, Ajax

MICHAL PAPADOPULOS (forward) **Born** April 14, 1985, Czech Republic **Ht** 6ft 0in **Wt** 12st 4lb **Signed from** Banik Ostrava (loan), July 2003

RAY PARLOUR (midfield) **Born** March 7, 1973, Romford **Ht** 5ft 10in **Wt** 11st 13lb **Signed from** trainee, July 1989

ROBERT PIRES (midfield) **Born** October 29, 1973, Reims **Ht** 6ft 1in **Wt** 11st 9lb **Signed from** Marseilles, July 2000, £6m

JOSE ANTONIO REYES (forward) **Born** September 1, 1983, Utrera, Spain **Ht** 5ft 10in **Wt** 11st 10lb **Signed from** Seville, January 2004, £10.78m (rising to £17.61m)

FRANKIE SIMEK (defender) **Born** October 13, 1984, Missouri **Ht** 5ft 10in **Wt** 11st 9lb **Signed from** trainee, August 2001

OLAFUR-INGI SKULASON (defender) **Born** April 1, 1983, Reykjavik **Ht** 6ft 0in **Wt** 11st 10lb **Signed from** Fylkir AC, Iceland, July 2001

RYAN SMITH (midfield) **Born** November 10, 1986, Islington **Ht** 5ft 10in **Wt** 10st 10lb **Signed from** trainee, July 2003

JOHN SPICER (midfield) **Born** September 13, 1983, Romford **Ht** 5ft 11in **Wt** 11st 7lb **Signed from** trainee, August 2001

GRAHAM STACK (goalkeeper) **Born** September 26, 1981, Hampstead **Ht** 6ft 2in **Wt** 12st 6lb **Signed from** trainee, July 2000

EFSTATHIOS TAVLARIDIS (defender) **Born** January 25, 1980, Greece **Ht** 6ft 0in **Wt** 12st 11lb **Signed from** Iraklis, Greece, September 2001, £600,000

JEROME THOMAS (midfield) **Born** March 23, 1983, Brent **Ht** 5ft 10in **Wt** 11st 10in **Signed from** trainee, August 2001

KOLO TOURE (defender) **Born** March 19, 1981, Abidjan, Ivory Coast **Ht** 6ft 0in **Wt** 12st 0lb **Signed from** Asec Mimosas, February 2002, free

GIOVANNI VAN BRONCKHORST (midfield) **Born** February 5, 1975, Rotterdam **Ht** 5ft 10in **Wt** 11st 9lb **Signed from** Rangers, June 2001, £8.5m

PATRICK VIEIRA (midfield) **Born** June 23, 1976, Dakar, Senegal **Ht** 6ft 4in **Wt** 13st 0lb **Signed from** AC Milan, August 1996, £3.5m

SYLVAIN WILTORD (forward) **Born** May 10, 1974, Paris **Ht** 5ft 9in **Wt** 12st 4lb **Signed from** Bordeaux, August 2000, £13m

Saturday April 3
MANCHESTER UNITED
FA Cup, semi-final (Villa Park)
Lost 0-1 HT **0-1** Att **39,939**
Report and details, page 328

Tuesday April 6
CHELSEA (h)
European Cup, quarter-final, 2nd leg
Lost 1-2 (lost 2-3 on agg) HT **1-0** Att **35,486**
Within four painful days, Arsenal's targets have been reduced to one. Their 17-match unbeaten run against Chelsea counts for nothing as, coming from behind after Reyes strikes on the stroke of half-time, Lampard — when Lehmann fails to hold Makelele's shot — and Bridge, after a one-two with Gudjohnsen three minutes from time, put a tearful Claudio Ranieri's side through to the last four, not to face Real Madrid but AS Monaco.

Lehmann — Lauren, Toure, Campbell, Cole — Ljungberg, Vieira, Edu, Pires — Reyes, Henry (Bergkamp 81) *Subs not used* Stack, Keown, Wiltord, Gilberto, Clichy, Kanu *Booked* Lauren
Scorer **Reyes 45**
Referee **M Merk (Germany)**

Friday April 9
LIVERPOOL (h)
Won 4-2 HT **1-2** Att **38,119** Position **1st**
Write off Arsenal — and Henry — at your peril. After their two numbing cup exits, Arsene Wenger's side recover their form to overcome a determined Liverpool and establish a seven-point lead at the top. Gerard Houllier's side lead twice but they cannot contain Henry, whose middle goal in a hat-trick follows a superb slaloming run.

Lehmann — Lauren, Toure, Campbell, Cole — Ljungberg (Keown 90), Gilberto, Vieira, Pires (Edu 71) — Bergkamp — Henry *Subs not used* Reyes, Clichy, Shaaban *Booked* Lauren, Vieira, Cole
Scorers **Henry 31, 50, 78, Pires 49**
Referee **A Wiley**

Sunday April 11
NEWCASTLE UNITED (a)
Drew 0-0 HT **0-0** Att **52,141** Position **1st**
Lehmann — Lauren, Toure, Campbell, Cole (Clichy 90) — Wiltord (Pires 79), Gilberto, Vieira, Edu — Reyes (Bergkamp 79), Henry *Subs not used* Shaaban, Keown *Booked* Vieira
Report page 227

Friday April 16
LEEDS UNITED (h)
Won 5-0 HT **3-0** Att **38,094** Position **1st**
A masterclass in finishing by the peerless Henry takes Arsenal ten points clear and within touching distance of the Premiership title — and pushes Leeds nearer the drop. The Frenchman's four-timer, including an audacious chipped penalty, takes his tally to 150 goals in 250 games for his club.

Lehmann — Lauren, Toure, Campbell, Clichy — Wiltord, Gilberto (Edu 69), Vieira, Pires (Parlour 72) — Bergkamp (Reyes 72), Henry *Subs not used* Keown, Stack
Scorers **Pires 6, Henry 27, 33 (pen), 50, 67**
Referee **D Gallagher**

PLAYER OF THE SEASON
Kolo Toure

Logic dictates that you should be reading about Thierry Henry here. The striker certainly did have a sensational season — 30 league goals out of a personal haul of 39 bringing him the Golden Boot — and there is no doubt that Arsenal would be half the team without him. And yet Henry is really only doing what we expect, what we hope, of him. A better choice is Kolo Toure, who, like Henry, is another man transformed by Arsene Wenger. The Ivory Coast player started life at Arsenal in midfield, where he seemed ill at ease — charging forward, charging back — but since Wenger introduced him alongside Sol Campbell at the heart of the defence he has blossomed, showing maturity beyond his 23 years. His reading of the game is excellent and if Wenger pulled a masterstroke in the conversion of Henry from winger to striker, time may prove his re-casting of Toure a stroke of genius.

Catherine Riley

Sunday April 25
TOTTENHAM HOTSPUR (a)
Drew 2-2   HT 2-0   Att 36,097   Position 1st
Lehmann — Lauren, Toure, Campbell, Cole — Parlour (Edu 67), Gilberto, Vieira, Pires — Bergkamp (Reyes 81), Henry Subs not used Stack, Keown, Clichy Booked Lehmann
Scorers **Vieira 3, Pires 35**
Report page 258

Saturday May 1
BIRMINGHAM CITY (h)
Drew 0-0   HT 0-0   Att 38,061   Position 1st
The champions are given an ecstatic welcome home, but while they extend their season-long unbeaten league record there is very little else to get excited about as Birmingham stand firm in a match in which there is not a single clear-cut chance.

Lehmann — Lauren, Toure, Campbell, Cole — Bergkamp (Keown 90), Vieira, Gilberto, Ljungberg (Pires 69) — Henry, Reyes (Aliadiere 79) Subs not used Parlour, Shaaban
Referee **G Poll**

Tuesday May 4
PORTSMOUTH (a)
Drew 1-1   HT 0-1   Att 20,140   Position 1st
Lehmann — Lauren, Toure, Campbell, Cole — Bentley (Kanu 61), Parlour, Vieira, Ljungberg (Aliadiere 90) — Reyes (Keown 90), Henry Subs not used Shaaban, Clichy Booked Campbell, Parlour
Scorer **Reyes 50**
Report page 238

Sunday May 9
FULHAM (a)
Won 1-0   HT 1-0   Att 18,102   Position 1st
Lehmann — Lauren, Toure, Campbell, Cole — Ljungberg (Keown 87), Parlour, Vieira, Pires (Clichy 78) — Reyes (Aliadiere 71), Henry Subs not used Stack, Bergkamp Booked Vieira, Henry, Parlour
Scorer **Reyes 9**
Report page 152

Saturday May 15
LEICESTER CITY (h)
Won 2-1   HT 0-1   Att 38,419   Position 1st
Can Arsenal join the immortals? Needing to avoid defeat against already relegated opposition, they go behind to Dickov, their former player, but complete the first unbeaten top-flight campaign for 115 years with second-half goals from Henry, his 30th in the league coming from the penalty spot, and Vieira. Then the party begins.

Lehmann — Lauren, Toure, Campbell, Cole — Ljungberg (Keown 86), Gilberto, Vieira, Pires (Edu 69) — Bergkamp (Reyes 82) — Henry Subs not used Parlour, Stack
Scorers **Henry 47 (pen), Vieira 66**
Referee **P Durkin**

ASTON VILLA

PREMIERSHIP

	P	W	D	L	F	A	GD	Pts
Arsenal	38	26	12	0	73	26	47	**90**
Chelsea	38	24	7	7	67	30	37	**79**
Man Utd	38	23	6	9	64	35	29	**75**
Liverpool	38	16	12	10	55	37	18	**60**
Newcastle	38	13	17	8	52	40	12	**56**
Aston Villa	38	15	11	12	48	44	4	**56**
Charlton	38	14	11	13	51	51	0	**53**
Bolton	38	14	11	13	48	56	-8	**53**
Fulham	38	14	10	14	52	46	6	**52**
Birmingham	38	12	14	12	43	48	-5	**50**
Middlesbro	38	13	9	16	44	52	-8	**48**
Southampton	38	12	11	15	44	45	-1	**47**
Portsmouth	38	12	9	17	47	54	-7	**45**
Tottenham	38	13	6	19	47	57	-10	**45**
Blackburn	38	12	8	18	51	59	-8	**44**
Man City	38	9	14	15	55	54	1	**41**
Everton	38	9	12	17	45	57	-12	**39**
Leicester	38	6	15	17	48	65	-17	**33**
Leeds	38	8	9	21	40	79	-39	**33**
Wolves	38	7	12	19	38	77	-39	**33**

FA CUP
Third round

CARLING CUP
Semi-finals

Quick reviver: In his first season
back in management, David
O'Leary swiftly lifted Villa back up
the Premiership table

Saturday August 16 2003
PORTSMOUTH (a)
Lost 1-2   HT 0-1   Att 20,101   Position 16th
Sorensen — Delaney, Johnsen, Alpay, Samuel — Hendrie, McCann, Barry, Whittingham (Hitzlsperger 60) — Allback, Angel (Crouch 76) *Subs not used* Postma, Mellberg, De La Cruz *Booked* Hendrie, McCann *Sent off* Barry 87
Scorer **Barry 84 (pen)**
Report page 230

Sunday August 24
LIVERPOOL (h)
Drew 0-0   HT 0-0   Att 42,573   Position 16th
Having started his Villa managerial career with a defeat, David O'Leary must make do with a point from a dull first match in charge at Villa Park. Kewell misses a sitter for Liverpool and Sorensen saves well from Murphy, while Angel hits a post at the other end. But a live TV audience snoozes on a Sunday afternoon.
Sorensen — Delaney, Mellberg, Johnsen, Samuel — Hendrie (De La Cruz 87), McCann, Barry, Whittingham — Vassell, Angel (Dublin 90) *Subs not used* Alpay, Hitzlsperger, Postma
Referee **P Durkin**

Wednesday August 27
ARSENAL (a)
Lost 0-2   HT 0-0   Att 38,010   Position 17th
Sorensen — Delaney, Mellberg, Johnsen, Samuel — De La Cruz, Hendrie, Kinsella (Vassell 60), Barry, Whittingham — Angel *Subs not used* Alpay, Hitzlsperger, Postma, Kachloul *Booked* Delaney, Hendrie, Whittingham, Angel
Report page 60

Saturday August 30
LEICESTER CITY (h)
Won 3-1   HT 3-0   Att 32,274   Position 12th
Angel, who says later that he would have left in the summer had Graham Taylor stayed as manager, describes it as a "perfect day" after his double helps Villa to settle the match within 16 minutes. Leicester, who lose Curtis and Howey to early injuries and Ferdinand to two quickfire yellow cards, are not so amused.
Sorensen — Delaney, Mellberg, Johnsen (Alpay 78), Samuel — Hendrie (De La Cruz 83), McCann, Hitzlsperger, Whittingham — Angel, Vassell (Dublin 83) *Subs not used* Postma, Kinsella *Booked* Johnsen
Scorers **Thatcher 8 (og), Angel 10, 16**
Referee **S Bennett**

Sunday September 14
MANCHESTER CITY (a)
Lost 1-4   HT 1-0   Att 46,687   Position 15th
Sorensen — Delaney, Mellberg (Alpay 37), Johnsen (Hadji 66), Samuel — Hendrie, McCann, Hitzlsperger, Whittingham — Angel (Dublin 76), Allback *Subs not used* Postma, Kinsella *Booked* Johnsen
Scorer **Angel 31**
Report page 187

A CHEQUEBOOK MANAGER WHO talks to the media too much? Or a great coach whose achievements with Leeds United were overshadowed by financial mismanagement beyond his control? Whatever the answer — and Villa fans were certainly divided last summer — the 2003-04 season was going to be as much about David O'Leary as Aston Villa.

O'Leary went into the job with his eyes open. Even though he had spent a year out of the game, he was aware of the parsimonious reputation of Doug Ellis, the chairman, and the fact that Villa, on the field at least, were in a mess. But he was unfazed and immediately rectified two glaring weaknesses in the side by spending his £4 million transfer budget on Thomas Sorensen, the goalkeeper, and Gavin McCann, a holding midfield player — hardly names guaranteed to sell season tickets, but the right thing to do at the start of a serious reconstruction programme.

Any optimism quickly disappeared as Villa lost to Portsmouth. An away fixture against a team playing their first Premiership game is the last thing you want on the opening day, but the manner of the defeat was the biggest cause for concern as there seemed to be no change in style, technique or attitude from the dismal second Graham Taylor era. Most alarming was O'Leary's decision to play Alpay ahead of an apparently uninjured Olof Mellberg, the player of the year in 2002-03. (Let's deal with Alpay now. Villa fans were glad to see the back of him, not because of his baiting of David Beckham in Istanbul, but because he had been a liability for the club since his return from the World Cup in 2002. As it turned out, Villa managed a rare PR coup by terminating his contract in the face of hyperbolic national anti-Alpay feeling. He wasn't missed.)

It was unrealistic to expect a quick fix from O'Leary, but in the early months there were signs of improvement. Before the end of September, Villa were unlucky to return from London with nothing after difficult trips to Highbury and Stamford Bridge. In both games, O'Leary replaced his normal 4-4-2 system with 4-5-1 in an attempt to stifle markedly better sides. It did not lead to the most exciting football to watch, but it was effective and it forced Claudio Ranieri into a bit of early-season tinkering with his formation to combat a resolute Villa. They even got a point at St Andrew's, which, after the previous season, went a long way to increasing O'Leary's standing in the eyes of the Villa fans, as did three goals in the first 15 minutes at home to Leicester City, their former bogey side.

Yet despite the positives, Villa were still a long way short. There was amazement as O'Leary trotted out his 4-5-1 at home to Everton. It was one thing playing like that away to Arsenal and Chelsea, quite

HONOURS BOARD

FOOTBALL LEAGUE
Champions 1894, 1896, 1897, 1899, 1900, 1910, 1981
Runners-up 1889, 1903, 1908, 1911, 1913, 1914, 1931, 1933, 1990
PREMIERSHIP
Runners-up 1993
FA CUP
Winners 1887, 1895, 1897, 1905, 1913, 1920, 1957
Runners-up 1892, 1924, 2000

LEAGUE CUP
Winners 1961, 1975, 1977, 1994, 1996
Runners-up 1963, 1971
EUROPEAN CUP
Winners 1982

Record attendance 76,588 (v Derby County, FA Cup 6th rnd, March 2, 1946)
Current capacity 42,602
Record victory 13-0 (v Wednesbury Old Athletic, FA Cup 1st rnd, October 30, 1886)
Record defeat 1-8 (v Blackburn Rovers, FA Cup 3rd rnd, February 16, 1889)

another in a game that they were expected to win, and the dour 0-0 draw was not a surprise. A terrible home performance against Middlesbrough, twice shipping four goals in Manchester and losing a game they really should have won away to Spurs, meant that Villa found themselves in the bottom three in December.

Wolves visited Villa Park on December 14 for a crucial derby — there were only three points between the sides at kick-off — that Villa won, albeit somewhat shakily. Then, the following Wednesday, Chelsea arrived for a Carling Cup quarter-final and, to the surprise of supporters, were beaten by a goal from McCann after Juan Pablo Angel's screaming opener. Not only had Villa beaten Chelsea (and Chelsea were trying, too), they had come back after conceding an equaliser. This was a Villa side with fight, outplaying one of the top teams in the land.

All that was missing was an away win in the league (previous two: Middlesbrough, January 28, 2003; Chelsea, May 11, 2002) and that duly happened against Blackburn Rovers at Ewood Park three days later to cap the week that changed Villa's season.

From then on, Villa's league form was bettered only by Arsenal and Chelsea. There were five more away wins, including a rout of Leicester (out of the 48 Premiership goals Villa scored, eight came in the space of 26 minutes in the two games against the Foxes). There was still the occasional hiccup as Villa lost at home to Blackburn, dropped points from winning situations against Bolton Wanderers and Manchester City and, most galling of all, shipped a

Saturday September 20
CHARLTON ATHLETIC (h)
Won 2-1   HT 1-0   Att 31,410   Position 11th
Alpay's first goal for the club he wants to leave is booed by some home fans and Samuel also gets his first for Villa, but they are very lucky to take all three points. Fortune hits the bar and has a goal wrongly disallowed, while Bartlett is denied a clear penalty before Lisbie's late reply for Charlton.

Sorensen — De La Cruz, Delaney, Alpay, Samuel — Hendrie, McCann, Barry, Whittingham — Angel, Allback (Vassell 64) *Subs not used* Dublin, Hitzlsperger, Postma, S Moore *Booked* McCann, Whittingham, Angel
Scorers **Alpay 37, Samuel 55**
Referee **C Foy**

Tuesday September 23
WYCOMBE WANDERERS (a)
Carling Cup, 2nd rnd
Won 5-0   HT 2-0   Att 6,072
Having managed just three goals throughout last season, Angel scores as many inside 24 minutes during the rout of the struggling second-division side, who concede five goals for the second match running. Whittingham starts the spree, Vassell ends it with Villa's second penalty of the night.

Sorensen — De La Cruz, Delaney, Dublin, Samuel — Hendrie (Ridgewell 76), McCann, Barry, Whittingham — Angel (Vassell 62), Allback (S Moore 76) *Subs not used* Postma, Hitzlsperger
Scorers **Whittingham 14, Angel 31, 50 (pen), 55, Vassell 86 (pen)**
Referee **A Butler**

Saturday September 27
CHELSEA (a)
Lost 0-1   HT 0-1   Att 41,182   Position 11th
Sorensen — Delaney, Alpay, Samuel — De La Cruz, Hendrie, McCann, Barry, Whittingham (Vassell 54) — Angel *Subs not used* Postma, Hitzlsperger, Allback, Ridgewell *Booked* Delaney, Samuel
Report page 123

Sunday October 5
BOLTON WANDERERS (h)
Drew 1-1   HT 0-0   Att 30,229   Position 13th
Villa come from behind to earn a point, but after getting the equaliser and then winning a highly controversial late penalty with his fall under Campo's challenge, Angel has his spot kick saved by Jaaskelainen. Nolan gives Bolton the lead, beating Postma, the substitute goalkeeper, a minute after his arrival.

Sorensen (Postma ht) — Delaney, Mellberg, Alpay, Samuel — Hendrie, McCann, Barry, Whittingham (Allback 57) — Angel, Vassell *Subs not used* Dublin, De La Cruz, Kinsella *Booked* Hendrie
Scorer **Angel 58**
Referee **R Styles**

Sunday October 19
BIRMINGHAM CITY (a)
Drew 0-0   HT 0-0   Att 29,546   Position 14th
Sorensen — Delaney, Mellberg, Johnsen, Samuel —
Hendrie (Whittingham 41), McCann, Barry — De La Cruz,
Angel, Vassell *Subs not used* Dublin, Postma, Allback,
Kinsella *Booked* Hendrie
Report page 84

Saturday October 25
EVERTON (h)
Drew 0-0   HT 0-0   Att 36,146   Position 14th
A Villa defence now without Alpay, released in the wake
of the Beckham tunnel bust-up in Istanbul, copes easily
enough in a bore draw, although Campbell has a header
turned on to the bar by Sorensen. The day after his 18th
birthday, Rooney makes no impact, but, at the other
end, Whittingham hits a post.

Sorensen — Delaney, Mellberg, Dublin, Samuel — Kinsella
(Hitzlsperger ht), McCann, Barry (De La Cruz 81),
Whittingham, Vassell — Angel *Subs not used* Postma,
Allback, Ridgewell
Referee **A D'Urso**

Wednesday October 29
LEICESTER CITY (h)
Carling Cup, 3rd rnd
Won 1-0   HT 0-0   Att 26,729
Micky Adams makes no fewer than ten changes to the
Leicester side that turned a 3-0 lead into a 4-3 defeat
against Wolves, but although Coyne, the goalkeeper, is
especially impressive, another defeat follows as
Hitzlsperger, a substitute, rewards Villa's dominance with
the only goal.

Sorensen — Delaney, Mellberg (Dublin 85), Johnsen,
Samuel — De La Cruz (Allback 57), McCann, Barry,
Whittingham — Angel, Vassell (Hitzlsperger 65) *Subs not
used* Postma, Ridgewell *Booked* Johnsen
Scorer **Hitzlsperger 75**
Referee **M Halsey**

Saturday November 1
NEWCASTLE UNITED (a)
Drew 1-1   HT 1-1   Att 51,975   Position 13th
Sorensen — Delaney, Dublin, Johnsen, Samuel —
De La Cruz (S Moore 51), Hitzlsperger, McCann, Barry,
Whittingham — Angel (Allback 63) *Subs not used* Postma,
Ridgewell, Kinsella *Booked* Johnsen, McCann,
Hitzlsperger *Sent off* McCann 70
Scorer **Dublin 11**
Report page 221

Saturday November 8
MIDDLESBROUGH (h)
Lost 0-2   HT 0-1   Att 29,898   Position 15th
After four successive Premiership draws, Villa are well
beaten by a Middlesbrough side putting together an
impressive run. Zenden's diving header from Queudrue's
cross and Ricketts's penalty, after Hendrie's foul on
Zenden, settle an uninspiring game. "We were poor,"
David O'Leary admits.

Sorensen — Delaney, Mellberg, Johnsen, Samuel —
Hendrie (Vassell 51), McCann, Barry (Hitzlsperger 51),
Whittingham — Angel, Allback (Dublin 71) *Subs not used*
Postma, S Moore *Booked* Mellberg
Referee **D Gallagher**

McCann's winner against Chelsea was the turning point in Villa's season

stoppage-time equaliser to Birmingham City after having led 2-0
and murdered them for an hour.

For consolation, Villa fans can look at the final table and take
heart from some of the performances the team put in. Once he
settled, Sorensen was excellent; Jlloyd Samuel, although frustrating
at times, deserved his England call-up; and Mellberg was once again
outstanding. The midfield had the right balance between hard work
and creativity as they fed Angel and Darius Vassell — on their day a
front two to strike fear into any defence. But it was as much the
team as individuals that made Villa, on occasions, a joy to watch.

O'Leary cannot be faulted for the way he used his meagre funds
and, by finishing ten places higher than last year, Villa earned some
£5 million more in prize-money. How much of that Ellis earmarks
for team building remains to be seen, if indeed it is Ellis in control.
During the season he stepped down from the role of chief executive
and appointed Bruce Langham, who worked under Mohamed Al
Fayed at Fulham, so will be used to autocrats. Whether or not this is
a cosmetic appointment to appease his detractors or whether Ellis,
an octogenarian, is indeed relinquishing some of his hold on the
club, time will tell.

This was a season of overachievement for Aston Villa, a
remarkable turnaround with a threadbare squad. The club has found
itself one or two players away from having a consistently good side
on a number of occasions in the past ten years, yet has failed each
time to make the final push. The reserves won their league, the
youth team were runners-up in the FA Youth Cup. Will the board
rely on promising youngsters or spend money to capitalise on the
best season for years?

THE MANAGER

David O'Leary

According to David O'Leary, his brief at Villa was "to lose 12 players from the squad, reduce the wage bill and not be relegated". Mission accomplished. On top of that, he almost got them into Europe by playing some of the best football seen from Villa for a long time. Transfer dealings excellent, spouting off in the media much reduced from his Leeds United days. His challenge is to improve next season — Doug Ellis's "minimum requirement" is fourth place, which is a little optimistic with the present squad. But if the chairman backs him, and O'Leary does not get a better offer from elsewhere, who knows?

Richard Guy

APPEARANCES

	Prem	FAC	CC	Total
M Allback	7 (8)	-	1 (3)	8 (11)
Alpay Ozalan	4 (2)	-	-	4 (2)
J P Angel	33	1	5	39
G Barry	36	1	6	43
P Crouch	6 (10)	-	1 (1)	7 (11)
U De La Cruz	20 (8)	1	3	24 (8)
M Delaney	23 (2)	-	5	28 (2)
D Dublin	12 (11)	-	4 (1)	16 (12)
M Hadji	0 (1)	-	-	0 (1)
L Hendrie	32	1	4	37
T Hitzlsperger	22 (10)	0 (1)	2 (3)	24 (14)
R Johnsen	21 (2)	1	2 (1)	24 (3)
M Kinsella	2	-	-	2
G McCann	28	1	6	35
O Mellberg	33	1	5	39
L Moore	0 (7)	-	-	0 (7)
S Moore	2 (6)	0 (1)	1 (2)	3 (9)
S Postma	0 (2)	-	-	0 (2)
L Ridgewell	5 (6)	-	0 (2)	5 (8)
J Samuel	38	1	6	45
N Solano	10	-	-	10
T Sorensen	38	1	6	45
D Vassell	26 (6)	1	5 (1)	32 (7)
P Whittingham	20 (12)	1	4 (2)	25 (14)

Sunday November 23
TOTTENHAM HOTSPUR (a)
Lost 1-2   HT 0-0   Att 33,140   Position 18th
Sorensen — Delaney (Dublin 80), Mellberg, Johnsen, Samuel — Hendrie (S Moore 87), McCann, Barry, Whittingham — Allback, Vassell *Subs not used* Postma, Ridgewell, Kinsella *Booked* Hendrie
Scorer **Allback 66**
Report page 253

Saturday November 29
SOUTHAMPTON (h)
Won 1-0   HT 1-0   Att 31,285   Position 17th
Around 2,000 Villa fans stage a pre-match "Ellis Out" demonstration, but their mood is eased by Dublin's bicycle kick winner on the stroke of half-time after Beattie fails to clear a corner. Niemi prevents a heavier defeat for a Southampton side who have now failed to score in seven out of eight league games.

Sorensen — De La Cruz, Mellberg, Dublin, Samuel — Hendrie (S Moore 65), McCann, Whittingham (Hitzlsperger 85), Barry — Angel (Allback 77), Vassell *Subs not used* Postma, Johnsen
Scorer **Dublin 45**
Referee **M Messias**

Wednesday December 3
CRYSTAL PALACE (h)
Carling Cup, 4th rnd
Won 3-0   HT 1-0   Att 24,258
Given the kick-start of an own goal by Symons, the Palace caretaker manager, Villa score more than one for the first time in ten matches as McCann — with his first for the club — and Angel, ending a six-game barren run, ease them through to the quarter-finals.

Sorensen — De La Cruz, Mellberg, Dublin (Ridgewell 80), Samuel — S Moore, McCann, Hitzlsperger, Barry (Whittingham 73) — Angel, Vassell (Allback 73) *Subs not used* Hendrie, Postma *Booked* Hitzlsperger
Scorers **Symons 22 (og), McCann 70, Angel 79**
Referee **M Dean**

Saturday December 6
MANCHESTER UNITED (a)
Lost 0-4   HT 0-2   Att 67,621   Position 17th
Sorensen — Delaney, Mellberg, Dublin, Samuel — Vassell, Hendrie, McCann, Whittingham (Hitzlsperger 72), Barry — Angel (Allback 65) *Subs not used* Postma, De La Cruz, Ridgewell *Booked* Hendrie
Report page 200

Sunday December 14
WOLVERHAMPTON WANDERERS (h)
Won 3-2   HT 2-1   Att 36,964   Position 16th
So, that's one relegation place settled: Wolves are condemned to being bottom of the Premiership at Christmas and, as they are endlessly reminded, no side has escaped from such a position. Angel hits a rapid double but misses a sitter near the end after Wolves had twice halved the two-goal deficit.

Sorensen (Postma 51) — Delaney, Mellberg, Dublin, Samuel — McCann, Hitzlsperger, Barry — Vassell, Angel, Allback (De La Cruz 58) *Subs not used* Crouch, Whittingham, Johnsen *Booked* Delaney, Samuel, McCann
Scorers **Angel 21, 23, Barry 48**
Referee **G Poll**

Wednesday December 17
CHELSEA (h)
Carling Cup, quarter-final
Won 2-1   HT 1-0   Att 30,414
With Chelsea uncomfortable in an initial 3-4-3 formation, Villa take control through Angel's sensational opener, a swerving 25-yard shot after beating two challenges. Though Cole levels from Crespo's pass, McCann's goal — and Sorensen's brilliant save from Terry — secures a deserved semi-final place.

Sorensen — Delaney, Mellberg, Johnsen, Samuel — Hendrie (Hitzlsperger 69), McCann, Whittingham, Barry — Angel (Crouch 83), Vassell (S Moore 52) *Subs not used* Postma, Ridgewell *Booked* Sorensen, Delaney
Scorers **Angel 16, McCann 78**
Referee **N Barry**

Saturday December 20
BLACKBURN ROVERS (a)
Won 2-0   HT 0-0   Att 20,722   Position 13th
Sorensen — Delaney, Mellberg, Dublin, Samuel — Hendrie (De La Cruz 89), McCann, Whittingham, Barry (Hitzlsperger 78) — Angel, S Moore (Vassell 68) *Subs not used* Postma, Johnsen
Scorers **S Moore 62, Angel 75**
Report page 96

Friday December 26
LEEDS UNITED (a)
Drew 0-0   HT 0-0   Att 38,513   Position 12th
Sorensen — Delaney, Mellberg, Dublin, Samuel — Hendrie (Vassell 66), McCann, Whittingham, Barry — Angel, S Moore (Hitzlsperger 66) *Subs not used* Postma, De La Cruz, Johnsen *Booked* Whittingham, Dublin
Report page 158

Sunday December 28
FULHAM (h)
Won 3-0   HT 1-0   Att 35,617   Position 10th
With only four days to go until the anniversary, Vassell gets his first goals at Villa Park since January 1 — both at the Holte End — to see off Fulham, who "fold" in the second half, according to Chris Coleman. The Fulham manager also reiterates that Saha will not be sold when the transfer window opens.

Sorensen — Delaney (Ridgewell 61), Mellberg, Johnsen, Samuel — Hendrie (Hitzlsperger 74), McCann, Whittingham, Barry — Angel (S Moore 83), Vassell *Subs not used* Postma, Crouch
Scorers **Angel 33, Vassell 69, 82**
Referee **B Knight**

MATCH OF THE SEASON

Aston Villa 1   Tottenham Hotspur 0
Villa Park, Sunday May 2 2004
Russell Kempson

WHEN ASTON VILLA LEFT WHITE Hart Lane after a 2-1 defeat against Tottenham Hotspur in November, they were in eighteenth place in the Barclaycard Premiership. Unkind words were being said about David O'Leary, in his first year as Villa manager, and the threat of relegation appeared real. Today, Villa sit in fifth place and a place in the Champions League is still not beyond them. The turnaround is remarkable and in stark contrast to Tottenham, who have slid in the opposite direction.

Since that day in North London, the statistical fortunes of the clubs make fascinating reading. Villa fans should sit in wonderment; Tottenham supporters should look away now. Villa: P23, W13, D5, L5, 44pts; Tottenham: P23, W7, D3, L13, 24pts. If Villa fail to earn a place among the elite next season, a Uefa Cup berth can be considered a worthwhile consolation. O'Leary, on his 46th birthday yesterday, accepted that his side has overachieved but is grateful nonetheless. "Sure, we've comfortably exceeded our own expectations," he said. "But I'll take that. When we lost at Tottenham we were 1-0 up and we got mugged. I just hoped that that wouldn't happen today, but we're a better team now and we're still learning. We try to play good football, we've been climbing the league and we'll see where we end up."

Villa made the perfect start. Five minutes in, Thomas Hitzlsperger curled over a free kick to the far post, Gareth Barry nodded it back and Juan Pablo Angel rose to head past Kasey Keller. It was his 22nd goal of the season, further backing his claims for a new four-year contract. However, Villa failed to build on their lead.

Jamie Redknapp got the better of his midfield duel with Gavin McCann, despite McCann's persistent ankle-tapping, and Tottenham could have equalised. Dean Richards nodded over at the far post from Redknapp's free kick — it summed up his afternoon — and Jermain Defoe wasted a similar chance from a centre by Simon Davies. Tottenham play as individuals, not as a team; Villa offer the reverse. At times it is a spectacular sight, a free-flowing rhythm that matches Arsenal at their best. Too often, though, they become absorbed with their own game, allowing their opponents space that should not be there. Villa's concentration wavers dangerously.

Not that Tottenham could take advantage of it and they were fortunate not to lose further ground early in the second half. First, Hitzlsperger crashed a trademark 20-yard left-foot shot against the crossbar; then Barry, also with his left boot, skimmed a post from distance. McCann also sent in a long-range effort that fizzed past the same upright. Tottenham recoiled in discomfort. Though Robbie Keane, Redknapp and Defoe continued to probe, Tottenham's

Time to celebrate after Juan Pablo Angel's headed goal against Spurs

collective effort was, again, almost non-existent. The fear of failure haunted them.

That they held on and could have equalised had Keane and Defoe been more accurate when presented with half-chances said more about Villa's nervousness in the closing stages than any show of ability from Tottenham. Only when David Pleat, the director of football, is replaced by a permanent manager this summer will they be able to rediscover their direction.

"I never really thought we were in danger of relegation," Pleat said, "but there has been a certain amount of tension as we've gone into a spiral." Indeed, two points out of a possible 24 is one big spiral. "We deserve to be in the Premiership because we've had good runs as well as bad, but this certainly is a bad one."

While Pleat said a private prayer for the fall of Leeds, O'Leary felt nothing but sorrow. "It is very sad," he said. "I know that they have lost a lot of players and were never going to finish in the top six, but I still thought that they'd finish in the top ten. I always thought that they had too much quality to go down and I just can't understand it. A lot of the players really won't fancy playing in the first division."

O'Leary set off to celebrate the victory and his birthday with his family last night. "I'm not quite sure what they've got me," he said. What better than a belated present on May 15, the final day of the season, when Villa could secure a place in the Champions League.

ASTON VILLA (4-4-2): T Sorensen — U De La Cruz, O Mellberg, L Ridgewell, J Samuel — N Solano (sub: M Delaney, 90min), G McCann, T Hitzlsperger, G Barry — J P Angel (sub: M Allback, 69), P Crouch (sub: D Dublin, 86). **Substitutes not used:** S Postma, P Whittingham. **Booked:** Solano, Sorensen.
TOTTENHAM HOTSPUR (4-3-1-2): K Keller — S Kelly (sub: R Ricketts, 71), D Richards, A Gardner, M Taricco — S Davies, J Redknapp, M Brown — R Keane — F Kanoute (sub: G Doherty, 79), J Defoe. **Substitutes not used:** G Bunjevcevic, M Mabizela, L Hirschfeld. **Booked:** Defoe.

Sunday January 4 2004
MANCHESTER UNITED (h)
FA Cup, 3rd rnd
Lost 1-2 HT **1-0** Att **40,371**
Sir Alex Ferguson hails Scholes as "a genius" after his double turns the Cup tide against Villa, who lead through Barry's bobbling, deflected, long-range shot. Giggs is involved in both second-half goals, but it is the arrival of Keane as a substitute that proves every bit as influential for United.

Sorensen — De La Cruz, Mellberg, Johnsen, Samuel — Hendrie (Hitzlsperger ht), McCann, Whittingham, Barry — Vassell (S Moore 74), Angel, Crouch, Ridgewell *Subs not used* Postma, Crouch, Ridgewell
Scorer **Barry 19**
Referee **M Riley**

Tuesday January 6
PORTSMOUTH (h)
Won 2-1 HT **1-0** Att **28,625** Position **6th**
In the relegation zone less than six weeks earlier, Villa are up to the giddy heights of sixth place, if only for 24 hours, after a freak late winner by Vassell, whose midriff sends a clearance back over the line. Angel and Yakubu had earlier exchanged headers. Injury-ravaged Portsmouth include Knight, 44, the retired goalkeeping veteran, on the bench.

Sorensen — Delaney, Mellberg, Dublin, Samuel — Hendrie, McCann, Whittingham (Hitzlsperger 66), Barry — Vassell (S Moore 85), Angel (Crouch 87) *Subs not used* Postma, Ridgewell
Scorers **Angel 22, Vassell 85**
Referee **J Winter**

Saturday January 10
LIVERPOOL (a)
Lost 0-1 HT **0-1** Att **43,771** Position **10th**
Sorensen — Delaney, Mellberg, Dublin, Samuel — Hendrie (Johnsen 69), McCann (Hitzlsperger 40), Whittingham, Barry — Vassell (S Moore ht), Angel *Subs not used* Postma, De La Cruz *Booked* McCann
Report page 179

Sunday January 18
ARSENAL (h)
Lost 0-2 HT **0-1** Att **39,380** Position **12th**
Arsenal capitalise on Manchester United's defeat at Molineux the day before with Henry's double, but his quickly taken free kick for the opener infuriates Villa, who are none too pleased, either, with the penalty awarded when Kanu appears to run into Mellberg. Mark Halsey, the referee, later explains and stands by his decisions.

Sorensen — Delaney, Mellberg, Johnsen, Samuel — Hendrie (De La Cruz 86), Hitzlsperger, Whittingham, Barry (Ridgewell 86) — Allback (Crouch 86), Angel *Subs not used* Dublin, Postma *Booked* Delaney, Barry, Whittingham, Mellberg
Referee **M Halsey**

Wednesday January 21
BOLTON WANDERERS (a)
Carling Cup, semi-final, 1st leg
Lost 2-5 HT **1-3** Att **16,302**
Report and details page 332

Tuesday January 27
BOLTON WANDERERS (h)
Carling Cup, semi-final, 2nd leg
Won 2-0 (lost 4-5 on agg)   HT 1-0   Att 36,883
Report and details page 333

Saturday January 31
LEICESTER CITY (a)
Won 5-0   HT 0-0   Att 31,056   Position 11th
Sorensen — Delaney (De La Cruz 82), Mellberg, Dublin, Samuel — Solano, McCann, Hitzlsperger (Whittingham 71), Barry — Crouch, Vassell (Allback 71) *Subs not used* Postma, Ridgewell *Booked* Mellberg
Scorers **Vassell 50, 60, Crouch 57, 68, Dublin 64**
Report page 169

Saturday February 7
LEEDS UNITED (h)
Won 2-0   HT 1-0   Att 39,171   Position 8th
The crossbar is hit no fewer than four times in total, on three separate occasions by Villa, but when the home side do lower their sights, Angel — with a debatable penalty awarded for Domi's alleged foul on Vassell — and Johnsen, with a glancing header, inflict yet another defeat on Leeds.

Sorensen — De La Cruz, Mellberg, Dublin (Johnsen 49), Samuel — Solano, Hendrie (Ridgewell 86), Hitzlsperger, Barry — Angel, Vassell (Crouch 86) *Subs not used* Postma, Allback *Booked* Mellberg, De La Cruz
Scorers **Angel 45 (pen), Johnsen 59**
Referee **U Rennie**

Wednesday February 11
FULHAM (a)
Won 2-1   HT 2-1   Att 16,153   Position 7th
Sorensen — Delaney (De La Cruz 77), Mellberg, Johnsen, Samuel — Solano, Hendrie (Ridgewell 87), Hitzlsperger, Barry (Whittingham 80) — Angel, Vassell *Subs not used* Postma, Crouch *Booked* Barry
Scorers **Angel 13, Vassell 32**
Report page 149

Sunday February 22
BIRMINGHAM CITY (h)
Drew 2-2   HT 1-0   Att 40,061   Position 7th
Villa are 2-0 up and heading for sixth place when, according to David O'Leary, "too many of our players stopped playing". Vassell's three misses and Angel's failure in front of goal come back to haunt them when Birmingham, back in the hunt through Forssell, play their get-out-of-jail card via John in the fourth and final minute of stoppage time. Cue Blue delirium.

Sorensen — De La Cruz, Mellberg, Johnsen (Dublin 52), Samuel — Solano, Hendrie (L Moore 81), Hitzlsperger, Barry (Whittingham 56) — Angel, Vassell *Subs not used* Postma, Crouch
Scorers **Vassell 21, Hitzlsperger 47**
Referee **J Winter**

Saturday February 28
EVERTON (a)
Lost 0-2   HT 0-0   Att 39,353   Position 7th
Sorensen — De La Cruz, Mellberg, Johnsen, Samuel — Solano, Hendrie, Hitzlsperger, Barry — Vassell (Crouch 77), Angel *Subs not used* Dublin, Postma, Whittingham, Ridgewell *Booked* Samuel, Hendrie
Report page 140

THE PLAYERS

MARCUS ALLBACK (forward) **Born** July 5, 1973, Stockholm **Ht** 6ft 0in **Wt** 12st 0lb **Signed from** Heerenveen, May 2002, £2m

ALPAY OZALAN (defender) **Born** May 29, 1973, Izmir, Turkey **Ht** 6ft 2in **Wt** 13st 7lb **Signed from** Fenerbahce, July 2000, £5.6m

JUAN PABLO ANGEL (forward) **Born** October 21, 1975, Medellin, Colombia **Ht** 5ft 11in **Wt** 11st 3lb **Signed from** River Plate, January 2001, £9.5m

GARETH BARRY (midfield) **Born** February 23, 1981, Hastings **Ht** 6ft 0in **Wt** 12st 6lb **Signed from** trainee, February 1998

PETER CROUCH (forward) **Born** January 30, 1981, Macclesfield **Ht** 6ft 7in **Wt** 11st 12lb **Signed from** Portsmouth, March 2002, £5m

ULISES DE LA CRUZ (defender) **Born** February 8, 1974, Chota, Ecuador **Ht** 5ft 11in **Wt** 11st 6lb **Signed from** Hibernian, July 2002, £1.5m

MARK DELANEY (defender) **Born** May 13, 1976, Haverfordwest **Ht** 6ft 1in **Wt** 11st 7lb **Signed from** Cardiff City, March 1999, £250,000

DION DUBLIN (forward) **Born** April 22, 1969, Leicester **Ht** 6ft 2in **Wt** 12st 4lb **Signed from** Coventry City, November 1998, £5.75m

MOUSTAPHA HADJI (midfield) **Born** November 16, 1971, Ifrane, Morocco **Ht** 6ft 0in **Wt** 12st 2lb **Signed from** Coventry City, July 2001, £4.5m

LEE HENDRIE (midfield) **Born** May 18, 1977, Birmingham **Ht** 5ft 10in **Wt** 11st 0lb **Signed from** trainee, May 1994

THOMAS HITZLSPERGER (midfield) **Born** April 5, 1982, Munich **Ht** 6ft 0in **Wt** 11st 12lb **Signed from** Bayern Munich, August 2000, free

RONNY JOHNSEN (defender) **Born** June 10, 1969, Sandefjord, Norway **Ht** 6ft 3in **Wt** 13st 1lb **Signed from** Manchester United, August 2002, free

MARK KINSELLA (midfield) **Born** August 12, 1972, Dublin **Ht** 5ft 9in **Wt** 10st 10lb **Signed from** Charlton Athletic, August 2002, free

GAVIN McCANN (midfield) **Born** January 10, 1978, Blackpool **Ht** 6ft 1in **Wt** 12st 8lb **Signed from** Sunderland, July 2003, £2.25m

OLOF MELLBERG (defender) **Born** September 3, 1977, Gullspang, Sweden **Ht** 6ft 1in **Wt** 12st 10lb **Signed from** Racing Santander, July 2001, £5m

LUKE MOORE (forward) **Born** February 13, 1986, Birmingham **Ht** 5ft 11in **Wt** 11st 13lb **Signed from** trainee, July 2003

STEFAN MOORE (forward) **Born** September 28, 1983, Birmingham **Ht** 5ft 11in **Wt** 10st 12lb **Signed from** trainee, July 2000

STEFAN POSTMA (goalkeeper) **Born** June 10, 1976, Utrecht **Ht** 6ft 7in **Wt** 14st 6lb **Signed from** De Graafschap, May 2002, £1.5m

LIAM RIDGEWELL (defender) **Born** July 21, 1984, London **Ht** 5ft 10in **Wt** 10st 5lb **Signed from** trainee, August 2001

JLLOYD SAMUEL (defender) **Born** March 29, 1981, San Fernando, Trinidad **Ht** 5ft 11in **Wt** 11st 4lb **Signed from** trainee, February 1999

NOLBERTO SOLANO (midfield) **Born** December 12, 1974, Callao, Peru **Ht** 5ft 9in **Wt** 11st 2lb **Signed from** Newcastle United, January 2004, £1.5m

THOMAS SORENSEN (goalkeeper) **Born** June 12, 1976, Odense, Denmark **Ht** 6ft 4in **Wt** 13st 8lb **Signed from** Sunderland, July 2003, £2.25m

DARIUS VASSELL (forward) **Born** June 30, 1980, Birmingham **Ht** 5ft 7in **Wt** 12st 0lb **Signed from** trainee, April 1998

PETER WHITTINGHAM (midfield) **Born** September 8, 1984, Nuneaton **Ht** 5ft 10in **Wt** 9st 13lb **Signed from** trainee, April 2003

● Three Villa players scored their first goal for the club in the space of six days in September — Alpay, Jlloyd Samuel and Peter Whittingham.

● Only once in the past six years have Villa conceded five goals: when they lost 5-2 to Bolton Wanderers in the first leg of their Carling Cup semi-final.

● Villa beat Leicester City three times out of three last season having won just one of their previous 17 meetings.

● The club has finished in the top eight for the eighth time in nine seasons.

● Villa rose from sixteenth in 2002-03 to sixth, but they improved even more in 1996, jumping from 18th in 1995 (when the Premiership had 22 teams) to fourth the following year.

● Villa have won three of their past 37 league matches against Manchester United.

Bill Edgar

GOALSCORERS

	Prem	FAC	CC	Total
M Allback	1	-	-	1
Alpay Ozalan	1	-	-	1
J P Angel	16 (2p)	-	7 (1p)	23 (3p)
G Barry	3 (1p)	1	-	4 (1p)
P Crouch	4	-	-	4
D Dublin	3	-	-	3
L Hendrie	2	-	-	2
T Hitzlsperger	3	-	2	5
R Johnsen	1	-	-	1
G McCann	-	-	2	2
O Mellberg	1	-	-	1
S Moore	1	-	-	1
J Samuel	2	-	1	3
D Vassell	9 (1p)	-	1 (p)	10 (2p)
P Whittingham	-	-	1	1
Own goals	1	-	1	2

Sunday March 14
WOLVERHAMPTON WANDERERS (a)
Won 4-0   HT 3-0   Att **28,386**   Position **7th**
Sorensen — De La Cruz, Mellberg, Johnsen, Samuel — Solano, Hendrie (Whittingham 83), Hitzlsperger, Barry — Angel (Crouch 78), Vassell (L Moore 60) *Subs not used* Postma, Dublin *Booked* Samuel, Hitzlsperger
Scorers **Hitzlsperger 7, Mellberg 18, Angel 24, 59**
Report page 266

Saturday March 20
BLACKBURN ROVERS (h)
Lost 0-2   HT 0-2   Att **37,532**   Position **8th**
After a dreadful week in which Graeme Souness comes to blows with Yorke (literally) and Cole (metaphorically), his Blackburn side beat one of the Premiership's form teams, Stead claiming his third goal in four games as talk of Villa making the Champions League is made to look extremely optimistic.

Sorensen — De La Cruz, Mellberg, Ridgewell, Samuel — Solano (L Moore ht), Hendrie, Hitzlsperger, Barry (Whittingham 29) — Vassell (Crouch 81), Angel *Subs not used* Postma, Dublin
Referee **A D'Urso**

Saturday March 27
CHARLTON ATHLETIC (a)
Won 2-1   HT 1-1   Att **26,250**   Position **7th**
Sorensen — De La Cruz, Mellberg, Johnsen, Samuel — Hendrie, McCann, Hitzlsperger, Barry (Ridgewell 85) — Angel (L Moore 89) *Subs not used* Postma, Dublin, Crouch *Booked* Hendrie
Scorers **Vassell 24, Samuel 54**
Report page 119

Sunday April 4
MANCHESTER CITY (h)
Drew 1-1   HT 1-0   Att **37,602**   Position **7th**
Arthur Cox, the City assistant manager, liaises with Kevin Keegan — still absent after back surgery — before dropping Anelka and Fowler to the bench. Villa take the lead when Angel heads in at the far post from a right-wing corner, only for Distin to reply in identical fashion eight minutes from time.

Sorensen — De La Cruz, Mellberg, Johnsen, Samuel — Hendrie, McCann, Hitzlsperger, Barry — Angel (Crouch ht), Vassell (L Moore 67) *Subs not used* Postma, Whittingham, Ridgewell *Booked* Samuel
Scorer **Angel 26**
Referee **U Rennie**

Saturday April 10
BOLTON WANDERERS (a)
Drew 2-2   HT 1-0   Att **26,374**   Position **7th**
Sorensen — De La Cruz, Mellberg, Ridgewell, Samuel — Hendrie (Whittingham 80), McCann, Hitzlsperger, Barry — Crouch (Dublin 69), Vassell (L Moore 65) *Subs not used* Postma, Johnsen *Booked* Hendrie, Crouch, L Moore
Scorers **Crouch 18, Hendrie 53**
Report page 109

Monday April 12
CHELSEA (h)
Won 3-2   HT 1-1   Att **41,112**   Position **6th**
Claudio Ranieri's halo slips a bit with this defeat, two days before a scheduled meeting with the Stamford Bridge hierarchy to discuss his future. Having made eight changes to his team, he sees Crespo score twice, but in between Villa are at their fluent best and thoroughly deserve victory.

Sorensen — De La Cruz, Mellberg, Johnsen, Samuel — Hendrie (Whittingham 55), McCann, Hitzlsperger, Barry — Crouch (L Moore 82), Vassell (Dublin 89) *Subs not used* Postma, Ridgewell
Scorers **Vassell 39 (pen), Hitzlsperger 49, Hendrie 52**
Referee **J Winter**

PLAYER OF THE SEASON
Juan Pablo Angel

The first Villa player to score 20 goals in a season for seven years, Juan Pablo Angel delivered consistently what he had only shown in flashes since arriving in early 2001. He was always the best player at the club, but now he has a manager who appreciates him, no off-field problems (when he first came his child was seriously ill and his family unceremoniously kicked out of the hotel where they were staying after a booking error), and he has realised the limitations of his team-mates. Appears to enjoy playing for Villa after nearly leaving last summer; and crucial to the future.
Richard Guy

Sunday April 18
NEWCASTLE UNITED (h)
Drew 0-0   HT 0-0   Att 40,786   Position 6th
The prize for the winners is fourth place, but neither side can take it. Newcastle's disappointment is compounded by injuries to Bellamy and Jenas, four days before the Uefa Cup semi-final, but they battle well, playing for 80 minutes with ten men after the dismissal of O'Brien for a professional foul on Vassell.

Sorensen — De La Cruz, Mellberg, Johnsen (Ridgewell 89), Samuel — Solano (Whittingham 69), Hendrie, Hitzlsperger, Barry — Vassell, Crouch (Allback 62) *Subs not used* Delaney, Postma *Booked* De La Cruz
Referee **B Knight**

Saturday April 24
MIDDLESBROUGH (a)
Won 2-1   HT 1-1   Att 31,322   Position 5th
Sorensen — De La Cruz, Mellberg, Johnsen, Samuel — Solano, McCann, Hitzlsperger, Barry (Whittingham 53) — Angel (Crouch 74), Vassell (Delaney 58) *Subs not used* Ridgewell, Postma *Booked* Barry *Sent off* Solano 57
Scorers **Barry 45, Crouch 89**
Report page 216

Sunday May 2
TOTTENHAM HOTSPUR (h)
Won 1-0   HT 1-0   Att 42,573   Position 5th
Angel's 22nd goal of the season, an early close-range header, keeps Villa on an unlikely course for the Champions League. David O'Leary later talks of his sadness at Leeds United's relegation, but it his former club's defeat against Bolton which brings joy to the Spurs camp — they are now safe.

Sorensen — De La Cruz, Mellberg, Ridgewell, Samuel — Solano (Delaney 90), McCann, Hitzlsperger, Barry — Angel (Allback 69), Crouch (Dublin 86) *Subs not used* Postma, Whittingham *Booked* Sorensen, Solano
Scorer **Angel 5**
Referee **N Barry**

Saturday May 8
SOUTHAMPTON (a)
Drew 1-1   HT 1-1   Att 32,054   Position 5th
Sorensen — De La Cruz, Johnsen, Ridgewell, Samuel — Hendrie (Whittingham 90), McCann, Hitzlsperger, Barry — Angel (Dublin 86), Vassell (Crouch 68) *Subs not used* Postma, Delaney
Scorer **Angel 39 (pen)**
Report page 248

Saturday May 15
MANCHESTER UNITED (h)
Lost 0-2   HT 0-2   Att 42,573   Position 6th
Villa's bid to cap a fine season by reaching the Uefa Cup is over within ten minutes, the time it takes United to open a 2-0 lead. The real talking points are the two red cards incurred by the Cup Finalists, Fletcher and Ronaldo seeing the fifteenth and sixteenth brandished by Rob Styles this season, both for two bookable offences.

Sorensen — De La Cruz, Mellberg, Ridgewell, Samuel — Hendrie (Whittingham 76), McCann, Hitzlsperger, Barry (Dublin 82) — Angel, Crouch (Allback 58) *Subs not used* Delaney, Postma *Booked* Samuel, Hitzlsperger, Angel, Hendrie
Referee **R Styles**

BIRMINGHAM CITY

PREMIERSHIP

	P	W	D	L	F	A	GD	Pts
Arsenal	38	26	12	0	73	26	47	90
Chelsea	38	24	7	7	67	30	37	79
Man Utd	38	23	6	9	64	35	29	75
Liverpool	38	16	12	10	55	37	18	60
Newcastle	38	13	17	8	52	40	12	56
Aston Villa	38	15	11	12	48	44	4	56
Charlton	38	14	11	13	51	51	0	53
Bolton	38	14	11	13	48	56	-8	53
Fulham	38	14	10	14	52	46	6	52
Birmingham	38	12	14	12	43	48	-5	50
Middlesbro	38	13	9	16	44	52	-8	48
Southampton	38	12	11	15	44	45	-1	47
Portsmouth	38	12	9	17	47	54	-7	45
Tottenham	38	13	6	19	47	57	-10	45
Blackburn	38	12	8	18	51	59	-8	44
Man City	38	9	14	15	55	54	1	41
Everton	38	9	12	17	45	57	-12	39
Leicester	38	6	15	17	48	65	-17	33
Leeds	38	8	9	21	40	79	-39	33
Wolves	38	7	12	19	38	77	-39	33

FA CUP
Fifth round

CARLING CUP
Quarter-finals

CHAMPIONS LEAGUE
Semi-finals

Point well made: Olivier Tebily offers thanks to the heavens after Stern John's injury-time goal secured a draw at Villa Park

Saturday August 16 2003
TOTTENHAM HOTSPUR (h)
Won 1-0   HT 1-0   Att 29,358   Position 6th
Steve Bruce celebrates signing a new five-year contract with a lucky victory, secured when Savage wins a contentious penalty after his initial foul on Gardner. After Keane hits a post and Zamora heads over the bar, Glenn Hoddle invites trouble with his post-match criticism of Rob Styles, the referee — and the FA does not disappoint him.

Maik Taylor — Kenna, Purse, Cunningham, Clapham — Johnson, Savage (Tebily 90), Clemence, Dunn — Horsfield (John 69), Dugarry (Devlin 72) *Subs not used* Lazaridis, Bennett *Booked* Savage, Clemence, Dunn
Scorer **Dunn 36 (pen)**
Referee **R Styles**

Saturday August 23
SOUTHAMPTON (a)
Drew 0-0   HT 0-0   Att 31,656   Position 6th
Maik Taylor — Kenna, Cunningham, Upson, Clapham — Johnson, Savage (Tebily 89), Clemence — Dunn — Horsfield (Lazaridis 60), John (Morrison 80) *Subs not used* Bennett, Tebily *Booked* Savage
Report page 240

Saturday August 30
NEWCASTLE UNITED (a)
Won 1-0   HT 0-0   Att 52,006   Position 6th
Maik Taylor — Kenna, Cunningham, Upson, Clapham — Johnson, Savage, Clemence, Lazaridis (Cisse 79) — Dunn (Tebily 88) — John (Horsfield 71) *Subs not used* Bennett, Morrison *Booked* Kenna
Scorer **Dunn 61**
Report page 219

Sunday September 14
FULHAM (h)
Drew 2-2   HT 1-1   Att 27,250   Position 8th
The bad blood between these sides resurfaces with the dismissals of Legwinski (two bookings) and Purse, who wrestles Boa Morte to the ground in what Steve Bruce describes as an act of "absolute lunacy". Fulham lead twice after Saha, inside 40 seconds, and Boa Morte breach the Birmingham defence for the first time this season.

Maik Taylor — Kenna (Tebily ht), Purse, Upson, Clapham — Johnson, Savage, Clemence (Lazaridis 64), Dunn — Forssell, John (Morrison 70) *Subs not used* Bennett, Cisse *Booked* Johnson, Dunn *Sent off* Purse 82
Scorer **Forssell 45, 82**
Referee **S Dunn**

IT IS A MEASURE OF HOW far Birmingham City have progressed in Steve Bruce's 2½ years in charge that many Blues fans regarded finishing tenth in the Premiership as a serious disappointment. In certain respects, of course, it was: for the whole season the team, amazingly, never fell below tenth, occupying fourth position in October and early November and, as late as mid-April, apparently challenging for a Uefa Cup spot at least. But a wretched dip in form once Premiership safety had been secured with a 4-1 win over Leeds United on March 27 — only one win in the final 11 games was relegation form — meant a season that had started so well ended in mediocrity and anticlimax.

On the positive side, however, the club has indeed progressed. The tally of 50 points was two better than the previous season's and tenth position was an obvious improvement on thirteenth in their first Premiership finish in May 2003.

So this was a season of consolidation, just as Bruce and his excellent board had always intended. The dreams of Europe were, frankly, never realistic at this stage. The ubiquitous and sneering terrace chant of "Champions League? You're having a laugh!" could have been invented specially for the Blues.

All this, however, should not mask the many plus-points about Birmingham and the underlying optimism that this is still a club on the rise. Bruce has instilled a ferocious work ethic into his small squad, epitomised by the manic efforts of the blond bombshell, Robbie Savage, and even in that awful last quarter the team could never be accused of not giving 100 per cent.

Moreover, for most of the season the defence looked among the best in the Premiership. The central pairing of Matthew Upson and Kenny Cunningham, ahead of the excellent Maik Taylor, finally secured from Fulham after a season-long loan, provided a solid foundation and made Birmingham a difficult team to beat. Early results, such as the 1-0 wins away to Newcastle United and Bolton Wanderers, set the pattern, though when Upson was injured the cracks started to appear, especially with Cunningham beginning to show his age towards the end of the campaign. But brave rearguard actions to achieve two 0-0 draws with Chelsea and another stalemate against Arsenal at Highbury showed the mettle, as well as the organisation, of Bruce's defensive warriors.

Perhaps it was a reflection on the overall mediocrity of the Premiership, apart from the top three, that Birmingham's season looked so promising for so long. Maybe this was an overachieving side, but they were given little credit (especially by the London media) for their workrate and never-say-die spirit. Nevertheless, the

HONOURS BOARD

England's No 1: Blues' greatest keeper, Harry Hibbs

FA CUP
Runners-up 1931, 1956
LEAGUE CUP
Winners 1963
Runners-up 2001
FAIRS CUP/UEFA CUP
Runners-up 1960, 1961

Record attendance 66,844 (v Everton, FA Cup 5th rnd, February 11, 1939)
Current capacity 30,009
Record victory 12-0 (v Walsall Town Swifts, second division, December 17, 1892)
Record defeat 1-9 (v Blackburn Rovers, first division, January 5, 1895 and v Sheffield Wednesday, first division, December 13, 1930)

turning point of the season came with the 2-0 home defeat by Sunderland, of the Nationwide League first division, in an FA Cup fifth-round replay on February 25, when the door to the quarter-final (and beyond) stood temptingly ajar. Indeed, Blues' failure to win games against apparently weaker opponents (0-1 at home to Leicester City, 2-2 at home to Wolverhampton Wanderers) was the season's biggest downside.

The other serious problem, of course, was the lack of goals. In fact, without the exceptional talents of Mikael Forssell, the on-loan Chelsea striker, who ended with 19 for the season, there is strong evidence that Blues would have been struggling against relegation. Forssell deservedly won all the awards and plaudits at Birmingham's end-of-season dinner and was coveted by a dozen top clubs, so for Bruce to have secured his services for the following season, again on loan, is a tremendous coup.

Consider, though, that Blues' next highest scorer was Forssell's striking partner, Clinton Morrison (cruelly labelled "the goal machine" by some supporters), with a meagre four Premiership goals, and the extent of the problem is obvious. Morrison, to his credit, did work hard and made runs that left space for Forssell, but doubts remain over his and Stern John's credentials as Premiership strikers. And this deficiency was hugely exacerbated with the sad departure of Christophe Dugarry, who returned to France in February after a half-season blighted by injury, loss of form and confidence, and family problems. His flair and creativity, which had done so much to inspire the team in the final third of the previous campaign, were horribly missed. Of the two other players capable

Saturday September 20
LEEDS UNITED (a)
Won 2-0 **HT 0-0** Att **34,305** Position **7th**
Maik Taylor — Johnson, Cunningham, Upson, Clapham — Dunn (Morrison 90), Savage, Clemence, Lazaridis — Forssell (Tebily 88), Dugarry (Cisse 85) *Subs not used* Bennett, John *Booked* Savage, Dugarry
Scorers **Savage 79 (pen), Forssell 84**
Report page 155

Tuesday September 23
BLACKPOOL (a)
Carling Cup, 2nd rnd
Lost 0-1 **HT 0-1** Att **7,370**
Much the biggest shock of the night. A full-strength Blues, unbeaten after five Premiership games, go down to Taylor's sixth-minute goal at Bloomfield Road, Clemence squandering the chance to keep them in it by putting a second-half penalty over the bar — Birmingham's third failure to convert from the spot so far.

Maik Taylor — Johnson, Cunningham (Kirovski 85), Upson, Clapham — Dunn, Cisse (Figueroa 65), Clemence, Lazaridis — Morrison, John (Forssell 56) *Subs not used* Bennett, Tebily
Referee **G Laws**

Saturday September 27
PORTSMOUTH (h)
Won 2-0 **HT 1-0** Att **29,057** Position **4th**
Played six, won four, drawn two: this is now Birmingham's best start to a top-division season. Clemence meets a free kick from Lazaridis for the opener and the roles are reversed for the second goal. In between, Yakubu's equaliser is disallowed for a marginal offside and Sheringham hits a post with Portsmouth 2-0 down.

Maik Taylor — Johnson, Cunningham, Upson, Clapham — Dunn, Savage, Clemence, Lazaridis (Tebily 84) — Forssell (Figueroa 88), Dugarry (Cisse 82) *Subs not used* Bennett, Morrison *Booked* Cisse
Scorers **Clemence 21, Lazaridis 50**
Referee **S Bennett**

Saturday October 4
MANCHESTER UNITED (a)
Lost 0-3 **HT 0-1** Att **67,633** Position **5th**
Maik Taylor — Johnson, Cunningham, Upson, Clapham — Dunn, Cisse, Clemence (Tebily 79), Lazaridis (Bennett 35) — Dugarry (Carter 66), Forssell *Subs not used* John, Morrison *Booked* Cisse *Sent off* Taylor 34
Report page 198

Tuesday October 14
CHELSEA (h)
Drew 0-0 **HT 0-0** Att **29,460** Position **4th**
Chelsea are denied the win that their second-half pressure merits, but a point is enough to take them above Arsenal on goal difference, four days before their Highbury summit meeting. Birmingham match them in the first half but have to hold on desperately in the second and strike lucky when Taylor saves unwittingly from Hasselbaink.

Maik Taylor — Tebily, Cunningham, Upson, Clapham — Johnson, Cisse, Clemence (Hughes 76), Lazaridis — Dunn — Dugarry (John 83) *Subs not used* Bennett, Kenna, Morrison *Booked* Dugarry, Cisse
Referee **N Barry**

Sunday October 19
ASTON VILLA (h)
Drew 0-0 HT 0-0 Att 29,546 Position 4th
Rarely can the authorities have been more grateful for a dull, goalless stalemate. After the renewal of hostilities sparked so much trouble last season (71 arrests, pitch invasions, etc), the fierce second-city rivals create just three chances between them while the supporters are largely on their best behaviour.

Bennett — Johnson (Tebily 82), Cunningham, Upson, Clapham — Dunn, Savage, Clemence, Lazaridis (Cisse 80) — Dugarry (Morrison 80), Forssell *Subs not used* Vaesen, Hughes *Booked* Savage, Clemence
Referee **M Riley**

Saturday October 25
BOLTON WANDERERS (a)
Won 1-0 HT 1-0 Att 25,023 Position 4th
Maik Taylor — Tebily (Kenna 57), Cunningham, Upson, Clapham — Dunn, Clemence, Cisse, Lazaridis (Hughes 77) — Forssell, Dugarry (Morrison 87) *Subs not used* Bennett, Figueroa *Booked* Dunn, Tebily
Scorer **Forssell 31**
Report page 103

Monday November 3
CHARLTON ATHLETIC (h)
Lost 1-2 HT 0-1 Att 27,225 Position 4th
An excellent match and a tale of two keepers. Taylor and Kiely are in magnificent form, the Charlton stopper producing sensational saves from headers by Dugarry and Forssell as Holland's first goals for the club (the second a fluke ricochet) keep their run going and inflict a first home defeat of the season on Birmingham.

Maik Taylor — Tebily (Morrison 77), Cunningham, Upson, Clapham — Dunn, Clemence, Cisse (Hughes 55), Lazaridis (John 89) — Forssell, Dugarry *Subs not used* Bennett, Kenna *Booked* Dugarry
Scorer **Dugarry 64**
Referee **P Dowd**

Saturday November 8
WOLVERHAMPTON WANDERERS (a)
Drew 1-1 HT 0-0 Att 28,831 Position 5th
Maik Taylor — Johnson, Cunningham, Upson, Clapham — Hughes (John 87), Savage, Dunn, Clemence — Forssell, Dugarry (Lazaridis 79) *Subs not used* Bennett, Cisse, Tebily *Booked* Dugarry
Scorer **Forssell 49**
Report page 262

Saturday November 22
ARSENAL (h)
Lost 0-3 HT 0-1 Att 29,588 Position 5th
Four of the miscreants from the "Battle of Old Trafford" begin their bans, but Arsenal are stronger than ever, tearing Birmingham apart with the speed of their counter-attacks for their thirteenth match unbeaten from the start of the season — a Premiership record. Henry is not on the scoresheet but is involved in all three goals.

Maik Taylor — Johnson, Cunningham, Upson, Clapham — Clemence, Savage, Cisse (John 64), Lazaridis (Hughes 85) — Dunn — Forssell (Morrison 87) *Subs not used* Bennett, Tebily *Booked* Cisse
Referee **P Durkin**

Despite his injuries, Lazaridis was one of Birmingham's star performers

of providing the flair and surprise so essential at this level, David Dunn — the club's record £5.5 million signing from Blackburn Rovers — missed half the season through injury (though displaying real sparkle, especially when roaming just behind the strikers), while Stan Lazaridis also missed too many games through injury. Going forward, only Lazaridis and Forssell were ever likely to provide the unexpected, to excite the loyal St Andrew's hordes.

So with injuries to key players, plus a ruthless pruning of fringe members of the playing staff — 18 were let go during the season, including (perhaps unwisely) Geoff Horsfield — Bruce was left with probably the smallest squad in the Premiership. He has opened the financial doors for an influx of four or five big signings, promising fans that they will be "exciting" names, and with Forssell booked in for at least another season, the prospects for Birmingham are encouraging again.

What the team needs most now, though, are players with that extra bit of class and flair; there are already more than enough journeymen in the Stephen Clemence mould.

Oh, and while Blues can still justifiably claim to be the "Pride of the Midlands", it did hurt that they finished four places below David O'Leary's lot from Aston. All the same, for most Bluenoses, John's injury-time equaliser in the 2-2 draw at Villa Park in February was probably the highlight of the campaign. Having a laugh? The blue half of Birmingham certainly did that day.

THE MANAGER

Steve Bruce

Steve Bruce continues to enhance his reputation as the best young English manager in the game. Honest, calm, straightforward, with a vast knowledge of football and hugely astute in the transfer market, he is the key to Birmingham City's patient progress to becoming a force in the land. If there is one criticism, perhaps (like any manager) he appears to have his favourites; Blues fans were never told what went wrong with Luciano Figueroa and Aliou Cisse. But there remains only one message from Bluenoses to Bruce: Keep Right On!

Tim Austin

APPEARANCES

	Prem	FAC	CC	Total
A Barrowman	0 (1)	-	-	0 (1)
I Bennett	4 (2)	-	-	4 (2)
D Carter	1 (4)	0 (3)	-	1 (7)
A Cisse	5 (10)	0 (1)	1	6 (11)
J Clapham	22 (3)	0 (1)	1	23 (4)
S Clemence	32 (3)	1 (1)	1	34 (4)
K Cunningham	36	4	1	41
P Devlin	0 (2)	-	-	0 (2)
C Dugarry	12 (2)	0 (1)	-	12 (3)
D Dunn	20 (1)	3	1	24 (1)
L Figueroa	0 (1)	-	0 (1)	0 (2)
M Forssell	32	3 (1)	0 (1)	35 (2)
M Grainger	3 (1)	-	-	3 (1)
G Horsfield	2 (1)	-	-	2 (1)
B Hughes	17 (9)	3 (1)	-	20 (10)
S John	7 (22)	1 (1)	1	9 (23)
D Johnson	35	4	1	40
J Kenna	14 (3)	4	-	18 (3)
J Kirovski	0 (6)	0 (1)	0 (1)	0 (8)
S Lazaridis	25 (5)	2	1	28 (5)
C Morrison	19 (13)	4	1	24 (13)
D Purse	9	3	-	12
R Savage	31	4	-	35
Maik Taylor	34	4	1	39
Martin Taylor	11 (1)	-	-	11 (1)
O Tebily	17 (10)	2	-	19 (10)
M Upson	30	2	1	33

Sunday November 30
LIVERPOOL (a)
Lost 1-3   HT 1-1   Att 42,683   Position 8th
Bennett — Johnson, Cunningham, Upson (Tebily 76), Clapham — Dunn, Savage, Clemence (Morrison 79), Lazaridis — Forssell, Dugarry (Kirovski 79) *Subs not used* Vaesen, Cisse *Booked* Johnson
Scorer **Forssell 33**
Report page 178

Saturday December 6
BLACKBURN ROVERS (h)
Lost 0-4   HT 0-0   Att 29,354   Position 8th
Rovers end a run of five successive away defeats as Birmingham implode. Trailing 2-0 after exquisite passes from Cole set up Ferguson and Neill, the home side have Dugarry sent off for his second bookable offence — he had previously escaped punishment for breaking Short's nose with his elbow — and then concede two more, including a thunderbolt from Tugay.

Maik Taylor — Kenna (Cisse 78), Tebily, Cunningham, Clapham — Johnson, Dunn, Savage (Clemence 82), Lazaridis (Morrison 72) — Forssell, Dugarry *Subs not used* Bennett, John *Booked* Dugarry *Sent off* Dugarry 72 Referee **G Barber**

Saturday December 13
LEICESTER CITY (a)
Won 2-0   HT 1-0   Att 30,639   Position 8th
Maik Taylor — Kenna, Cunningham, Upson, Clapham — Johnson, Savage (Cisse 72), Clemence (Lazaridis 66), Dunn — Morrison, Forssell (John 83) *Subs not used* Purse, Bennett *Booked* Johnson, Clemence
Scorers **Morrison 42, Forssell 66**
Report page 167

Friday December 26
MANCHESTER CITY (h)
Won 2-1   HT 0-1   Att 29,520   Position 8th
Without a win at St Andrew's for three months, Birmingham strike it lucky as Kevin Keegan's troubles pile up. Manchester City lead through Fowler's diving header, but a fortunate rebound allows Kenna to equalise and with three minutes left a ricochet off Forssell's backside earns victory for the home side.

Maik Taylor — Kenna, Cunningham, Upson, Lazaridis — Johnson, Savage, Clemence (Cisse 89), Dunn (Kirovski 62) — Morrison (John 62), Forssell *Subs not used* Bennett, Purse *Booked* Savage, Upson
Scorers **Kenna 81, Forssell 87**
Referee **U Rennie**

Sunday December 28
EVERTON (a)
Lost 0-1   HT 0-0   Att 39,631   Position 9th
Maik Taylor — Kenna (Kirovski 78), Cunningham, Upson, Lazaridis — Johnson, Savage, Clemence, Hughes (Cisse 66) — Forssell, John (Morrison 53) *Subs not used* Bennett, Purse
Report page 138

Saturday January 3 2004
BLACKBURN ROVERS (h)
FA Cup, 3rd rnd
Won 4-0 HT 2-0 Att 18,688
There is a 35-minute delay to kick-off because of
electrical problems, but Birmingham are super-charged
as they reverse the scoreline from their humiliating
league defeat a month earlier. Blackburn have no answer
to two goals in each half, but victory comes at a cost to
Birmingham, with Upson suffering damaged ankle
ligaments.

Maik Taylor — Kenna, Cunningham, Upson (Hughes 12),
Lazaridis (Carter 45) — Johnson, Savage, Clemence, Dunn
(Kirovski 76) — Forssell, Morrison *Subs not used* Bennett,
John
Scorers **Morrison 3, Clemence 36, Forssell 78,
Hughes 84**
Referee **P Durkin**

Wednesday January 7
TOTTENHAM HOTSPUR (a)
Lost 1-4 HT 0-3 Att 30,016 Position 10th
Maik Taylor — Kenna, Purse, Cunningham, Carter
(Tebily ht) — Johnson, Savage, Clemence (Hughes 80),
Dunn — Morrison, Forssell (Kirovski 83) *Subs not used*
Bennett, John
Scorer **Savage 68 (pen)**
Report page 255

Saturday January 10
SOUTHAMPTON (h)
Won 2-1 HT 1-1 Att 29,071 Position 8th
Not the best of times for Southampton. Two days after
fans wake to the shock news that Gordon Strachan is to
leave at the end of the season, the departing manager
sees his team surrender the early lead given them by
Ormerod and have Prutton sent off for an elbows-first
challenge on Kenna, the Birmingham match-winner.

Maik Taylor — Tebily, Cunningham, Purse, Kenna —
Johnson, Hughes, Clemence, Dunn (Carter 90) —
Morrison (Kirovski 90), Forssell *Subs not used* Bennett,
John, Cisse
Scorers **Clemence 16, Kenna 67**
Referee **S Bennnett**

Sunday January 18
CHELSEA (a)
Drew 0-0 HT 0-0 Att 41,073 Position 9th
Maik Taylor — Tebily, Purse, Cunningham, Kenna —
Johnson, Savage, Clemence, Hughes (Kirovski 82) — John
(Carter 90), Morrison (Lazaridis 66) *Subs not used*
Bennett, Barrowman *Booked* Savage, Tebily
Report page 128

Saturday January 24
WIMBLEDON (h)
FA Cup, 4th rnd
Won 1-0 HT 1-0 Att 22,159
Ahead after just four minutes against the side bottom of
the first division, who have been forced to sell their two
best players in the week, Birmingham unexpectedly
struggle to make their superior status tell. Taylor sees
Mackie hit his post and then saves from Lewington as
Wimbledon go down fighting.

Maik Taylor — Tebily, Cunningham, Purse, Kenna —
Johnson, Savage, Hughes, Dunn (Forssell 65) — John
(Clapham 69), Morrison *Subs not used* Bennett, Kirovski,
Carter *Booked* Purse
Scorer **Hughes 4**
Referee **U Rennie**

MATCH OF THE SEASON

Aston Villa 2 Birmingham City 2
Villa Park, Sunday February 22 2004
Rick Broadbent

POOR OLD DAVID O'LEARY. FOR AN hour of this second-city
slugfest he was probably dusting down one of his celebratory
addresses about young lads and big adventures, but by the end he
was not so much a latter-day Enid Blyton as the new Captain Bligh.
The Aston Villa ship that had been sailing along very nicely was
sunk when his players mutinied, threw all their good work
overboard and were last seen paddling for the shore in blind panic.

Had Villa won they would have leapfrogged Liverpool into sixth
place. That is partly a sign of their progress under O'Leary and
partly an indictment of the Barclaycard Premiership. Any side that
can be a dominant powerhouse and a mass of nervous tics within the
course of the same game is clearly far from the finished product.

So Birmingham are still able to laugh at their neighbours after
coming from two goals down to complete a rescue mission in the
fourth minute of injury time of a hugely entertaining derby. The
Holte End, all swaggering optimism for the first half, was suddenly
more angst-ridden than your average youth club disco. And then up
popped Robbie Savage to rub salt into the gaping wounds. "I'm
unbeaten in 16 matches against Villa," he said. "They'll be kicking
themselves, but the gaffer gave us a bollocking at half-time and told
us that if we were going to go down, we should go down fighting."

The turnaround in fortunes was dramatic. The first half was so
one-sided it suggested that O'Leary is, indeed, bringing about a
minor revolution in the Midlands. Unlike last season, they
approached this fixture with an air of confidence rather than in
mortal fear of their own shadows, let alone Savage. Nobody relishes
anti-hero status quite like the Welshman, but Villa threw a spanner
in the works of football's threshing machine and he toiled in vain.

Villa looked like a team who were beginning to believe again.
After 21 minutes they gained a deserved lead. Damien Johnson,
whose first-half display was the most pungent of several stinkers,
allowed Gareth Barry to turn the ball across the face of the goal and
Darius Vassell did the rest from six yards. The goal aside, he missed
three tremendous chances, side-footing one tamely at Maik Taylor,
forcing a good reaction save with a header and then lobbing a volley
over the bar. Had he been more clinical, or had Juan Pablo Angel
not wasted the best chance of the lot — not to mention the header
by Darren Purse that hit his own post — Villa would have been
home and dry. Even so, Thomas Hitzlsperger thundered a 20-yard
drive into the roof of the net 90 seconds after the restart and that
seemed like the game. But then the ship sprung a leak.

To blame it all on Villa's mental fragility would be to underplay
the gung-ho grit that accompanied Birmingham's recovery and the

Robbie Savage and David Dunn celebrate the great Villa Park escape

impact made from the bench by David Dunn and Clinton Morrison. Both exposed the pathetic commitment of Dugarry, who was big on incredulous looks but short on everything else.

From the moment Mikael Forssell stroked home his twelfth goal of the season after Morrison had shielded the ball from Dion Dublin just inside the area, Villa were in a nervous quandary. Birmingham dominated the second period, but it seemed they had run out of time until Thomas Sorensen palmed Morrison's shot out to Stern John, who could not miss from four yards. Cue pandemonium.

"It was incredible," Steve Bruce, the Birmingham manager, said. "We have got away with it. In the first half they could have been out of sight. We had three players. But I'm so pleased for Stern John because he, more than anyone, got us into the Premiership. For that I will always be grateful. But what's good for the city of Birmingham is that we are competing at the right end of the table this season."

He had a point. Birmingham had become a footballing backwater until O'Leary and Bruce got their hands on its clubs and the future now seems brighter than it had done for a long time. But sometimes football deals only in the here and the now, and the parochial takes precedence. This was one such occasion.

ASTON VILLA (4-4-2): T Sorensen — U De La Cruz, O Mellberg, R Johnsen (sub: D Dublin, 52min), J Samuel — N Solano, L Hendrie (sub: L Moore, 81), T Hitzlsperger, G Barry (sub: P Whittingham, 56) — J P Angel, D Vassell. **Substitutes not used:** S Postma, P Crouch.
BIRMINGHAM CITY (4-4-2): Maik Taylor — O Tebily, K Cunningham, D Purse, J Kenna (sub: S John, 83) — D Johnson, R Savage, S Clemence (sub: D Dunn, 56), B Hughes — M Forssell, C Dugarry (sub: C Morrison, 56). **Substitutes not used:** I Bennett, Martin Taylor. **Booked:** Johnson.

Saturday January 31
NEWCASTLE UNITED (h)
Drew 1-1   HT 0-1   Att 29,513   Position 9th
Ahead through Speed's splendid 30-yard shot, Newcastle leave St Andrew's in high dudgeon after conceding a last-gasp equaliser, a contentious free kick allowing John to rescue a point for Birmingham. Afterwards, Steve Bruce admits that his £5.5 million bid for Butt, the Manchester United midfield player, is doomed to failure.

Maik Taylor — Tebily, Purse, Cunningham, Kenna — Johnson (John 76), Savage, Hughes, Lazaridis — Morrison, Forssell *Subs not used* Bennett, Carter, Kirovski, Clapham *Booked* Savage
Scorer **John 90**
Referee **R Styles**

Sunday February 8
MANCHESTER CITY (a)
Drew 0-0   HT 0-0   Att 46,967   Position 10th
Maik Taylor — Tebily, Cunningham, Purse, Kenna (Clapham 70) — Johnson, Savage, Hughes, Lazaridis — John (Dugarry ht), Forssell (Morrison 77) *Subs not used* Upson, Bennett *Booked* Tebily
Report page 192

Wednesday February 11
EVERTON (h)
Won 3-0   HT 2-0   Att 29,004   Position 9th
Everton find themselves 3-0 down for the second successive match after Saturday's thriller against the champions, but this time there is no comeback. Birmingham show no signs of relaxing their grip after Lazaridis scores the pick of their three goals in the first 49 minutes.

Maik Taylor — Tebily, Cunningham, Purse, Upson — Johnson, Savage (Dugarry 63), Hughes, Lazaridis (John 75) — Forssell, Morrison (Martin Taylor 80) *Subs not used* Bennett, Kenna *Booked* Tebily
Scorers **Johnson 8, Lazaridis 39, Forssell 49**
Referee **M Halsey**

Saturday February 14
SUNDERLAND (a)
FA Cup, 5th rnd
Drew 1-1   HT 1-1   Att 24,966
Birmingham are the team grateful to be in the quarter-final draw after this teatime tie, Forssell giving them the lead in fine style but Sunderland dominating before and after Kyle heads the equaliser. Cisse, a late City substitute, is sent off within nine minutes for two bookable offences.

Maik Taylor — Kenna, Cunningham, Purse, Upson — Johnson, Savage (Cisse 81), Hughes (Carter 89), Lazaridis — Morrison (Dugarry 63), Forssell *Subs not used* Bennett, Cunningham, Johnson, Dugarry, Cisse *Sent off* Cisse 90
Scorer **Forssell 28**
Referee **G Barber**

Sunday February 22
ASTON VILLA (a)
Drew 2-2   HT 0-1   Att 40,061   Position 8th
Maik Taylor — Tebily, Cunningham, Purse, Kenna (John 83) — Johnson, Savage, Clemence (Dunn 56), Hughes — Forssell, Dugarry (Morrison 56) *Subs not used* Bennett, Martin Taylor *Booked* Johnson
Scorers **Forssell 60, John 90**
Report page 78

Wednesday February 25
SUNDERLAND (h)
FA Cup, 5th rnd replay
Lost 0-2 (aet)   HT 0-0   Att 25,645
Sometimes managers make excuses, sometimes not; Steve Bruce's summary of this defeat, inflicted by Smith's extra-time goals, says it all. "We started poorly and got worse . . . the worst display I've been associated with as a manager . . . dire . . . Sunderland were better than us in the first game and better than us tonight." Enough said.

Maik Taylor – Tebily (John 72), Cunningham, Purse, Kenna – Johnson, Savage, Hughes, Dunn (Clemence 10; Carter 96) – Forssell, Morrison *Subs not used* Bennett, Cisse
Referee **M Dean**

Wednesday March 3
MIDDLESBROUGH (h)
Won 3-1   HT 1-0   Att 29,369   Position 7th
Middlesbrough are plunged into a Carling Cup hangover three days after their historic Cardiff victory. Martin Taylor – on his full debut – and Savage, with a fine free kick, are among the Birmingham scorers, Savage having earlier almost come to blows with Mills, while Zenden sees red for his second bookable offence.

Maik Taylor – Tebily, Cunningham, Martin Taylor, Upson – Johnson, Savage (Kenna 90), Clemence, Hughes – Morrison (Carter 88), Forssell (John 83) *Subs not used* Bennett, Purse *Booked* Savage, Morrison, Forssell
Scorers **Martin Taylor 23, Savage 57, Forssell 79**
Referee **R Styles**

Saturday March 6
BOLTON WANDERERS (h)
Won 2-0   HT 1-0   Att 28,003   Position 5th
Three days after beating the Carling Cup winners, Birmingham account for the runners-up in Steve Bruce's 100th game in charge. Okocha makes plain his unhappiness at being substituted in between the goals from Forssell – not Jaaskelainen's finest hour – and Hughes that keep Blues on course for Europe.

Maik Taylor – Tebily, Cunningham, Martin Taylor, Upson – Johnson (Kenna 89), Savage, Clemence (Cisse 77), Hughes – Forssell (John 86), Morrison *Subs not used* Bennett, Purse *Booked* Savage
Scorers **Forssell 24, Hughes 69**
Referee **A D'Urso**

Saturday March 13
LEICESTER CITY (h)
Lost 0-1   HT 0-0   Att 29,491   Position 6th
After ten days from hell in the wake of the La Manga affair, with three of their players just returned from Spain on bail charged with serious sexual assault (all the allegations are subsequently dropped), Leicester produce the shock results of the season when Ferdinand's goal, stabbed home from unmissable range to settle a dire encounter, ends a run of 15 games without a win and inflicts a first defeat in nine Premiership outings on Birmingham.

Maik Taylor – Tebily, Cunningham (Barrowman 87), Martin Taylor, Upson – Hughes, Savage, Clemence (John 68), Lazaridis – Forssell, Morrison *Subs not used* Bennett, Carter, Cisse *Booked* Cunningham
Referee **M Messias**

THE PLAYERS

ANDREW BARROWMAN (forward) **Born** November 27, 1984, Glasgow **Ht** 6ft 0in **Wt** 12st 8lb **Signed from** trainee, August 2003

IAN BENNETT (goalkeeper) **Born** October 10, 1971, Worksop **Ht** 6ft 0in **Wt** 13st 1lb **Signed from** Peterborough United, December 1993, £325,000

DARREN CARTER (defender) **Born** December 18, 1983, Solihull **Ht** 6ft 2in **Wt** 12st 3lb **Signed from** trainee, August 2001

ALIOU CISSE (midfield) **Born** March 24, 1976, Zinguinchor, Senegal **Ht** 6ft 0in **Wt** 11st 5lb **Signed from** Montpellier, July 2002, £1.5m

JAMIE CLAPHAM (defender) **Born** December 7, 1975, Lincoln **Ht** 5ft 10in **Wt** 10st 8lb **Signed from** Ipswich Town, January 2003, £1.3m

STEPHEN CLEMENCE (midfield) **Born** March 31, 1978, Liverpool **Ht** 5ft 11in **Wt** 11st 7lb **Signed from** Tottenham Hotspur, January 2003, £250,000

KENNY CUNNINGHAM (defender) **Born** June 28, 1971, Dublin **Ht** 5ft 11in **Wt** 11st 4lb **Signed from** Wimbledon, July 2003, free

PAUL DEVLIN (midfield) **Born** April 14, 1972, Birmingham **Ht** 5ft 8in **Wt** 11st 1lb **Signed from** Sheffield United, February 2002, £200,000

CHRISTOPHE DUGARRY (forward) **Born** March 24, 1972, Bordeaux **Ht** 6ft 2in **Wt** 12st 4lb **Signed from** Bordeaux, January 2003, free

DAVID DUNN (midfield) **Born** December 27, 1979, Blackburn **Ht** 5ft 10in **Wt** 12st 3lb **Signed from** Blackburn Rovers, July 2003, £5.5m

LUCIANO FIGUEROA (forward) **Born** May 19, 1981, Santa Fe, Argentina **Ht** 6ft 0in **Wt** 11st 9lb **Signed from** Rosario Central, August 2003, £2.5m

MIKAEL FORSSELL (forward) **Born** March 15, 1981, Steinfurt, Finland **Ht** 5ft 10in **Wt** 10st 10lb **Signed from** Chelsea (loan), August 2003

MARTIN GRAINGER (defender) **Born** August 23, 1972, Enfield **Ht** 5ft 10in **Wt** 12st 10lb **Signed from** Brentford, March 1996, £400,000

GEOFF HORSFIELD (forward) **Born** November 1, 1973, Barnsley **Ht** 6ft 1in **Wt** 11st 7lb **Signed from** Fulham, July 2000, £2.25m

BRYAN HUGHES (midfield) **Born** June 19, 1976, Liverpool **Ht** 5ft 10in **Wt** 11st 2lb **Signed from** Wrexham, March 1997, £750,000

STERN JOHN (forward) **Born** October 30, 1976, Tunapuna, Trinidad **Ht** 5ft 11in **Wt** 13st 2lb **Signed from** Nottingham Forest, February 2002, free

DAMIEN JOHNSON (midfield) **Born** November 18, 1978, Lisburn **Ht** 5ft 9in **Wt** 11st 7lb **Signed from** Blackburn Rovers, March 2002, £100,000

JEFF KENNA (defender) **Born** August 27, 1907, Dublin **Ht** 5ft 11in **Wt** 12st 2lb **Signed from** Blackburn Rovers, December 2001, free

JOVAN KIROVSKI (forward) **Born** March 18, 1976, Escondido, California **Ht** 6ft 1in **Wt** 12st 4lb **Signed from** Crystal Palace, August 2002, free

STAN LAZARIDIS (midfield) **Born** August 16, 1972, Perth, Australia **Ht** 5ft 9in **Wt** 11st 12lb **Signed from** West Ham United, July 1999, £1.6m

CLINTON MORRISON (forward) **Born** May 14, 1979, Tooting **Ht** 6ft 1in **Wt** 11st 2lb **Signed from** Crystal Palace, July 2002, £4.25m

DARREN PURSE (defender) **Born** February 14, 1977, London **Ht** 6ft 2in **Wt** 13st 1lb **Signed from** Oxford United, February 1998, £700,000

ROBBIE SAVAGE (midfield) **Born** October 18, 1974, Wrexham **Ht** 5ft 11in **Wt** 10st 8lb **Signed from** Leicester City, May 2002, £1.25m

MAIK TAYLOR (goalkeeper) **Born** September 4, 1971, Hildeshein, Germany **Ht** 6ft 4in **Wt** 14st 2lb **Signed from** Fulham, August 2003 (initial loan), £1.5m

MARTIN TAYLOR (defender) **Born** November 9, 1979, Ashington **Ht** 6ft 4in **Wt** 15st 0lb **Signed from** Blackburn Rovers, February 2004, £1.25m

OLIVIER TEBILY (defender) **Born** December 19, 1975, Abidjan, Ivory Coast **Ht** 6ft 0in **Wt** 13st 3lb **Signed from** Celtic, March 2002, £700,000

MATTHEW UPSON (defender) **Born** April 18, 1979, Stowmarket **Ht** 6ft 1in **Wt** 11st 5lb **Signed from** Arsenal, January 2003, £1m

STATS AND FACTS

● Apart from Arsenal, Birmingham were the only side in the Premiership to avoid defeat by Chelsea last season.

● Birmingham recorded their first win away to Bolton Wanderers in 16 attempts

● Arsenal, the champions, hold the whip hand over City. Birmingham have won just two of the past 20 meetings with the Gunners.

● Blues' record against Liverpool is also miserable. They have won just one of their past 28 games at Anfield, and only one of their past 11 home matches against them.

● Mikael Forssell, on loan from Chelsea, scored more league goals than any of the four expensively acquired strikers at Stamford Bridge managed.

● Birmingham have not won in 14 meetings with Manchester United since beating them 5-1 at St Andrew's in 1978 — when the scorers were Buckley (2), Dillon, Givens and Calderwood.

Bill Edgar

GOALSCORERS

	Prem	FAC	CC	Total
S Clemence	2	1	-	3
C Dugarry	1	-	-	1
D Dunn	2 (1p)	-	-	2 (1p)
M Forssell	17 (1p)	2	-	19 (1p)
M Grainger	1	-	-	1
B Hughes	3	2	-	5
S John	4	-	-	4
D Johnson	1	-	-	1
J Kenna	2	-	-	2
S Lazaridis	2	-	-	2
C Morrison	4	1	-	5
R Savage	3 (2p)	-	-	3 (2p)
Martin Taylor	1	-	-	1

Saturday March 20
MIDDLESBROUGH (a)
Lost 3-5   HT 2-4   Att 30,244   Position 7th
Maik Taylor — Martin Taylor, Cunningham, Upson, Grainger — Johnson (John ht), Hughes, Clemence, Lazaridis — Morrison, Forssell *Subs not used* Bennett, Cisse, Carter, Barrowman
Scorers **Forssell 23, 59, Morrison 45**
Report page 215

Saturday March 27
LEEDS UNITED (h)
Won 4-1   HT 1-1   Att 29,069   Position 6th
Ahead within three minutes, Leeds are eventually overrun by a fluent Birmingham side who put two successive defeats behind them. Viduka misses a sitter after putting Leeds in front and Hughes is denied the chance of a hat-trick when Forssell grabs his second goal from the spot.

Maik Taylor — Martin Taylor, Cunningham, Upson, Grainger — Johnson, Hughes, Clemence, Lazaridis — Morrison (Tebily 83), Forssell (John 83) *Subs not used* Bennett, Cisse, Carter
Scorers **Hughes 12, 67, Forssell 69, 82 (pen)**
Referee **M Halsey**

Saturday April 3
FULHAM (a)
Drew 0-0   HT 0-0   Att 14,667   Position 6th
Maik Taylor — Martin Taylor, Cunningham, Upson, Grainger — Johnson (Clemence 38), Hughes (Clapham 90), Lazaridis — Forssell, Morrison (John 69) *Subs not used* Bennett, Tebily *Booked* Savage, Upson
Report page 151

Saturday April 10
MANCHESTER UNITED (h)
Lost 1-2   HT 1-0   Att 29,548   Position 6th
Birmingham threaten to continue their charge for Europe when Grainger's long-range free kick gives them the lead, but headers from Ronaldo and Saha, two players not noted for their aerial prowess, earn victory for United. Birmingham also lose Grainger to injury for the rest of the season.

Maik Taylor — Martin Taylor, Cunningham, Upson, Lazaridis (Grainger 14; Clapham ht) — Johnson, Savage, Clemence (John 79), Hughes — Forssell, Morrison *Subs not used* Bennett, Tebily
Scorer **Grainger 39**
Referee **D Gallagher**

Monday April 12
PORTSMOUTH (a)
Lost 1-3   HT 0-1   Att 20,104   Position 8th
Maik Taylor — Tebily (Bennett 45), Cunningham, Martin Taylor, Upson — Johnson, Savage (Clemence 58), Hughes, Clapham — Forssell (Morrison 79), John *Subs not used* Motteram, Cisse *Booked* Cunningham, Clemence *Sent off* Maik Taylor 45
Scorer **John 67**
Report page 237

PLAYER OF THE SEASON
Mikael Forssell

Maybe it's a bit odd to choose a Chelsea striker as Birmingham City's player of the season, but Mikael Forssell, on loan from Stamford Bridge, has been so far ahead of any of his team-mates — even Stan Lazaridis, Matthew Upson, Kenny Cunningham, Robbie Savage or Maik Taylor — that there was virtually no contest. His ability to score goals regularly, despite frankly poor service from midfield, has been inspirational to the whole team; his tight control and dribbling skills in the box are something that Blues have lacked for years. His common sense, hard work and modesty are also appealing. Huge credit to Steve Bruce and the board for securing Forssell's talents for at least another year: Chelsea's loss is definitely Birmingham's gain.
Tim Austin

Saturday April 17
CHARLTON ATHLETIC (a)
Drew 1-1   **HT 0-0**   Att **25,206**   Position **8th**
Maik Taylor — Martin Taylor, Cunningham, Upson, Clapham — Johnson, Savage, Clemence, Hughes — Forssell (John 89), Morrison *Subs not used* Bennett, Tebily, Barrowman, Motteram
Scorer **Morrison 84**
Report page 119

Sunday April 25
WOLVERHAMPTON WANDERERS (h)
Drew 2-2   **HT 2-1**   Att **29,494**   Position **9th**
Wolves are not down yet — "while there's hope we've got to believe", Dave Jones says — but they are nearer the drop after this draw. Cameron and Cort get the goals that keep Wolves hoping, Forssell, who scores a clever first and sets up the second for Morrison, providing Birmingham's inspiration.

Maik Taylor — Martin Taylor (John 81), Cunningham, Upson, Clapham — Johnson, Savage, Clemence, Lazaridis (Hughes 59) — Forssell, Morrison *Subs not used* Bennett, Tebily, Cisse *Booked* Savage
Scorers **Forssell 34, Morrison 41**
Referee **M Dean**

Saturday May 1
ARSENAL (a)
Drew 0-0   **HT 0-0**   Att **38,061**   Position **9th**
Bennett — Tebily, Cunningham, Upson, Clapham — Johnson, Savage, Clemence, Lazaridis — Dunn (Hughes 75) — Morrison (John 72) *Subs not used* Cisse, Doyle, Martin Taylor *Booked* Johnson, Savage
Report page 70

Saturday May 8
LIVERPOOL (h)
Lost 0-3   **HT 0-1**   Att **29,533**   Position **10th**
The race for fourth place takes a potentially decisive twist when Liverpool open a three-point gap over their nearest rivals with an emphatic win in which Heskey and Gerrard, both goalscorers, are on top form. Cunningham is sent off for an outclassed Birmingham side after a professional foul on Gerrard.

Bennett — Tebily, Cunningham, Upson, Clapham (John 60) — Johnson, Savage (Cisse 60), Clemence (Hughes 60), Lazaridis — Forssell, Morrison *Subs not used* Doyle, Martin Taylor *Booked* Johnson, Cisse *Sent off* Cunningham 64
Referee **S Dunn**

Saturday May 15
BLACKBURN ROVERS (a)
Drew 1-1   **HT 0-1**   Att **26,070**   Position **10th**
Maik Taylor — Tebily (John 60), Martin Taylor, Upson, Clapham — Johnson, Savage, Clemence (Hughes 57), Lazaridis — Forssell, Morrison *Subs not used* Bennett, Cunningham, Cisse
Scorer **John 83**
Report page 100

BLACKBURN ROVERS

PREMIERSHIP

	P	W	D	L	F	A	GD	Pts
Arsenal	38	26	12	0	73	26	47	**90**
Chelsea	38	24	7	7	67	30	37	**79**
Man Utd	38	23	6	9	64	35	29	**75**
Liverpool	38	16	12	10	55	37	18	**60**
Newcastle	38	13	17	8	52	40	12	**56**
Aston Villa	38	15	11	12	48	44	4	**56**
Charlton	38	14	11	13	51	51	0	**53**
Bolton	38	14	11	13	48	56	-8	**53**
Fulham	38	14	10	14	52	46	6	**52**
Birmingham	38	12	14	12	43	48	-5	**50**
Middlesbro	38	13	9	16	44	52	-8	**48**
Southampton	38	12	11	15	44	45	-1	**47**
Portsmouth	38	12	9	17	47	54	-7	**45**
Tottenham	38	13	6	19	47	57	-10	**45**
Blackburn	38	12	8	18	51	59	-8	**44**
Man City	38	9	14	15	55	54	1	**41**
Everton	38	9	12	17	45	57	-12	**39**
Leicester	38	6	15	17	48	65	-17	**33**
Leeds	38	8	9	21	40	79	-39	**33**
Wolves	38	7	12	19	38	77	-39	**33**

FA CUP
Third round

CARLING CUP
Third round

UEFA CUP
First round

All the rage: Graeme Souness cut an increasingly frustrated figure on the touchline as Blackburn's season failed to live up to expectations

THE REVIEW — John Dawkins

Saturday August 16 2003
WOLVERHAMPTON WANDERERS (h)
Won 5-1 HT 2-0 Att **26,270** Position **1st**
After a 19-year exile, Wolves return to the promised land
— and are promptly demolished by a rampant Rovers
side for whom Amoruso and the outstanding Emerton
score debut goals. Cole strikes twice from the bench as
Blackburn top the first table of the season. Bolton keep
Wolves off the bottom . . . for now.

Friedel — Neill, Taylor, Amoruso, Gresko — Thompson
(Grabbi 79), Tugay, Flitcroft, Emerton — Jansen (Cole 74),
Yorke Subs not used Johansson, Todd, Kelly Booked
Thompson
Scorers **Amoruso 17, Thompson 29, Emerton 53,
Cole 79, 87**
Referee **J Winter**

Saturday August 23
BOLTON WANDERERS (a)
Drew 2-2 HT 0-2 Att **27,423** Position **3rd**
Friedel — Neill, Taylor, Amoruso, Gresko (Grabbi 76) —
Thompson, Tugay, Flitcroft (Reid 76), Emerton —
Jansen (Cole 61), Yorke Subs not used Kelly, Johansson
Booked Neill, Thompson, Flitcroft, Emerton Sent off
Reid 88
Scorers **Jansen 50, Yorke 90**
Report page 102

Monday August 25
MANCHESTER CITY (h)
Lost 2-3 HT 1-1 Att **23,361** Position **5th**
Friedel, so consistent last season, takes the blame for
Tarnat's 40-yard opening goal and Anelka's
87th-minute winner, which is squeezed through the
goalkeeper's legs from a seemingly impossible angle.
Blackburn twice come from behind to level, but it is City
who are now top of the top division for the first time
since 1991.

Friedel — Neill, Taylor, Amoruso, Gresko — Emerton,
Tugay, Flitcroft (Grabbi 89), Reid (Thompson 64) — Cole,
Yorke (Jansen 57) Subs not used Johansson, Kelly
Booked Neill, Tugay
Scorers **Sinclair 44 (og), Amoruso 61**
Referee **A Wiley**

Saturday August 30
CHELSEA (a)
Drew 2-2 HT 1-1 Att **41,056** Position **8th**
Friedel — Neill, Babbel, Amoruso, Gresko — Reid
(Johansson 73), Tugay (Taylor 84), Flitcroft, Thompson —
Cole (Gallagher 73), Jansen Subs not used Grabbi, Kelly
Booked Amoruso, Thompson, Flitcroft, Reid
Scorer **Cole 1, 58**
Report page 123

HOW CAN A TEAM PLAY ABYSMALLY for most of the season, drive its supporters to distraction by flirting with relegation and then embark on a four-match winning run to ensure survival, defeating Manchester United in the process? Blackburn Rovers make a habit of putting their fans through an emotional wringer and last season was no exception.

Hopes were high that the previous year's sixth place could be followed by a genuine challenge for the Champions League and, having thrashed Wolverhampton Wanderers 5-1 on the opening day, the stage seemed set for an assault on the Premiership summit. After past disappointments, that Rovers spent most of the season scuffling in the foothills and, at one stage, looked ready to slip into the Football League, should perhaps not have been a surprise.

So where did it all go wrong? The departure of the talismanic Damien Duff on the eve of the pre-season tour to the United States was undoubtedly a blow. The £17 million release clause in his contract had frightened off Manchester United and Liverpool before Roman Abramovich arrived at Stamford Bridge, and the £5.5 million sale of David Dunn to Birmingham City after a fallout with Graeme Souness was seen by many as the sad waste of a local hero and potential England player. But Souness was pushing his luck by continually blaming "Lady Luck" — Rovers were not awarded one penalty all season — for the team's poor fortunes.

In his defence, Souness was entitled to point to the loss of Barry Ferguson, his £7 million signing from Rangers, and David Thompson with serious injuries for most of the season — and Lorenzo Amoruso, Steven Reid and Craig Short at different stages with a variety of ailments — while the failure of the highly regarded Brett Emerton to adapt to English football must have been a big disappointment for the manager. But that does not account for his failure to fill adequately the hole on the left side vacated by Duff, the decision to replace the dependable Henning Berg with the ponderous Amoruso, or his baffling selections and changes of tactics that made Claudio Ranieri look like a model of consistency. Nor did his well-publicised disputes with, among others, Andrew Cole, Andy Todd, Dwight Yorke and Short, or his weekly rant at match officials, do him any favours.

Souness, whose future at the club was questioned at one stage, admitted at the end of a difficult season that he had made a lot of mistakes, but those problems looked a long way off back in sunny August, when Wolves were sent packing and Rovers looked down on the rest from the top of the Premiership. Unfortunately, that first day proved to be the high point as their form soon started to

HONOURS BOARD

deteriorate. Defeat in the next home match, by Manchester City, revealed the defensive frailties that became more apparent as the season progressed and the decline accelerated to such an extent that yet another loss, away to Leicester City on November 2, put Rovers in the relegation zone. Away wins against Birmingham, Middlesbrough, Newcastle United and Aston Villa kept Rovers' heads just above water over the next few months, but their wretched home form, which saw the team fail to win at Ewood for five months, continued to frustrate the dwindling faithful.

Neither did the cups, in which Rovers fell at the first hurdle in all three competitions, offer much solace. The hard-won Uefa Cup place was thrown away against Genclerbirligi; in the League Cup, won so thrillingly at Cardiff two years before, Rovers lost at home to Liverpool; while in the FA Cup, a seemingly uninterested team succumbed tamely 4-0 to Birmingham at St Andrew's.

As spring arrived with the team apparently stumbling towards the first division, the lowest point in terms of morale was reached on April 10, when, after an abject defeat in the previous home game by Portsmouth, their relegation rivals, Rovers managed to lose at Ewood to Leeds United in a display so poor that even Souness ran out of excuses. The downcast players who headed shamefaced down the tunnel to a chorus of boos looked resigned to relegation.

What happened next, as Rovers proceeded to win their next four matches, defied logic. Three days after the Leeds debacle, with another change of formation by Souness — one that worked this time, with a stifling midfield and Amoruso restored to the centre of defence after months on the sidelines — Rovers travelled to Loftus Road and, playing with a spirit that had been sorely lacking for most of the season, secured a nailbiting but deserved 4-3 victory over Fulham. The winning goal was scored by the find of the season, Jonathan Stead, but Edwin van der Sar, the Fulham goalkeeper, contributed equally to the victory with horrendous mistakes that handed Rovers two priceless goals.

Having stumbled upon a winning method at the eleventh hour,

Saturday September 13
LIVERPOOL (h)
Lost 1-3   HT 1-1   Att 30,074   Position 10th
Baros has already suffered a broken ankle after an innocuous tackle by Babbel, the team-mate on loan to Blackburn, and Owen's penalty has cancelled out Jansen's superb opener, when Neill is sent off for a challenge that breaks Carragher's leg — and still only 13 minutes have gone. Owen and Kewell find the bottom corner in the second half to complete Liverpool's high-cost victory.
Friedel — Neill, Babbel, Amoruso, Gresko — Emerton, Flitcroft (Tugay 71), Ferguson, Thompson (Baggio 65) — Cole, Jansen (Yorke 65) *Subs not used* Johansson, Kelly *Booked* Amoruso, Baggio *Sent off* Neill 13
Scorer **Jansen 8**
Referee **N Barry**

Saturday September 20
PORTSMOUTH (a)
Won 2-1   HT 2-0   Att 20,024   Position 9th
Friedel — Neill (Johnson 90), Babbel, Amoruso, Gresko — Emerton, Tugay (Baggio 64), Ferguson, Thompson — Cole, Jansen (Yorke 64) *Subs not used* Kelly, Grabbi *Booked* Gresko, Cole
Scorers **Neill 35, Cole 43**
Report page 231

Wednesday September 24
GENCLERBIRLIGI (a)
Uefa Cup, 1st rnd, 1st leg
Lost 1-3   HT 0-2   Att 18,000
With Turkey and England preparing to lock European Championship horns in Istanbul, fears of trouble at club level prove groundless, but Rovers have problems enough on the pitch after Skoko's lob and Youla's double are met with only Emerton's goal — brilliantly created by Cole — in reply.
Friedel — Neill, Babbel, Amoruso, Gresko — Emerton, Tugay, Baggio (Reid 68), Thompson — Yorke (Grabbi 68), Jansen (Cole ht) *Subs not used* Kelly, Taylor, Johansson, Gallagher
Scorer **Emerton 57**
Referee **P Bertini (Italy)**

Sunday September 28
FULHAM (h)
Lost 0-2   HT 0-1   Att 21,985   Position 11th
Blackburn slip to their third successive home defeat as Fulham continue their solid start to the season. Malbranque does all the hard work for Boa Morte's early goal with a long run down the right and Saha easily outpaces Amoruso for the second. Cole lobs against the bar, but that is as good as it gets for Rovers.
Friedel — Babbel (Johansson 28), Taylor, Amoruso, Gresko (Grabbi 58) — Emerton, Flitcroft, Ferguson (Tugay 58), Thompson — Cole, Jansen *Subs not used* Yorke, Kelly *Booked* Tugay, Flitcroft
Referee **M Messias**

Saturday October 4
LEEDS UNITED (a)
Lost 1-2   HT 0-2   Att 35,039   Position 11th
Friedel — Reid (Baggio 65), Johansson, Taylor, Gresko — Emerton, Tugay (Grabbi 74), Flitcroft (Ferguson ht), Thompson — Cole, Yorke *Subs not used* Kelly, Jansen *Booked* Gresko
Scorer **Baggio 86**
Report page 155

Wednesday October 15
GENCLERBIRLIGI (h)
Uefa Cup, 1st rnd, 2nd leg
Drew 1-1 (lost 2-4 on agg)   HT 0-0   Att **14,573**
With Grabbi wasting three openings, Jansen another and Thompson striking the woodwork, Graeme Souness's side have more than enough chances to overturn a 3-1 deficit, but once Jansen does score, Ozkan equalises almost immediately and Blackburn are out, without a Uefa Cup victory in ten attempts.

Friedel — Reid, Todd (Taylor 77), Amoruso, Gresko (Yorke 62) — Emerton, Tugay, Flitcroft, Thompson — Jansen, Grabbi (Baggio 60) *Subs not used* Johansson, Gallagher, McEveley, Kelly *Booked* Thompson, Emerton, Todd
Scorer **Jansen 64**
Referee **E Braamhaar (the Netherlands)**

Monday October 20
CHARLTON ATHLETIC (h)
Lost 0-1   HT 0-1   Att **19,939**   Position **15th**
A new formation for Blackburn but the same result, a fourth straight home league defeat inflicted when Hreidarsson, on his return from injury, dives to head in Di Canio's corner — his first goal for Charlton. At the other end, Kiely saves well from Reid and Thompson to add to Rovers' frustration.

Friedel — Reid, Todd, Taylor, Gresko (Baggio 78) — Tugay, Ferguson, Flitcroft (Jansen ht) — Emerton (Gallagher 81), Thompson — Cole *Subs not used* Yelldell, Johansson *Booked* Thompson, Emerton, Cole
Referee **G Barber**

Saturday October 25
SOUTHAMPTON (a)
Lost 0-2   HT 0-0   Att **31,620**   Position **16th**
Friedel — Reid, Todd, Taylor, Gresko (Jansen 69) — Emerton (Gallagher 69), Flitcroft, Tugay, Ferguson, Thompson (Neill 72) — Cole *Subs not used* Yelldell, Johansson *Booked* Todd *Sent off* Cole 65
Report page 242

Wednesday October 29
LIVERPOOL (h)
Carling Cup, 3rd rnd
Lost 3-4   HT 1-1   Att **16,918**
Neill, whose sending-off in the league match between the clubs caused so much acrimony, sees red again, this time for a trip on Sinama-Pongolle, and the penalty that follows from Murphy helps the holders through. Heskey, who also has a penalty saved, scores with two headers, but from 4-1 up Liverpool are given a scare when Blackburn stage a late rally.

Friedel — Neill, Taylor, Babbel, Gresko (Johansson 85) — Thompson (Emerton 60), Ferguson, Tugay, Reid (Gallagher 82) — Cole, Yorke *Subs not used* Yelldell, Jansen *Sent off* Neill 40
Scorers **Yorke 35, 90, Ferguson 81**
Referee **M Riley**

Defeat at home by Leeds United in April deepened the Ewood gloom

Souness stuck with the line-up for the 1-0 victory over sinking Leicester — Rovers' first win at Ewood since Tottenham were defeated back in November — and similar 1-0 wins were ground out away to Everton and, always a pleasure, at home to Manchester United, the goals in the last two games being scored by the irrepressible Stead. In the blink of an eye, and after months of worry, Rovers had turned the season around and could breathe easily again after reaching 43 points and safety.

It was an uncomfortable season for the club, Souness in particular, but after the heroics of the previous campaign, perhaps expectations were unrealistic. Ten years after winning the championship, supporters who remember the grim days in the old third division are grateful that Jack Walker's legacy means they are able to watch top-flight football on a regular basis. The club cannot compete financially with the likes of Chelsea and Manchester United, but it is worth reminding those who still claim that unfashionable Blackburn "bought" their title that, in a period of four years, Walker spent a total of about £80 million on a new stadium, a new squad and bringing in a manager to take the club from the depths of the old second division all the way to the title. Chelsea have so far spent more than £150 million to move up two league places. Eat your Russian heart out, Roman.

THE MANAGER   Graeme Souness

After three successful seasons in which he hardly put a foot wrong, Graeme Souness sorely tested the supporters' faith, presiding over one of the worst home records in the Premiership and some of most dire performances seen at Ewood Park in many a year. Injuries to key players were one reason, but Souness was responsible for the bewildering changes of formations that confused players and supporters alike. Coupled with rows with senior players and skirmishes with the game's authorities, Souness was glad to see the back of a season he will want to forget. Rovers' brush with relegation gave him a fright; hopefully he will have learnt some hard lessons.

John Dawkins

APPEARANCES

	Prem	FAC	CC	Euro	Total
L Amoruso	11 (1)	-	-	2	13 (1)
M Andresen	11	-	-	-	11
M Babbel	23 (2)	1	1	1	26 (2)
D Baggio	0 (9)	0 (1)	-	1 (1)	1 (11)
A Cole	27 (7)	1	1	0 (1)	29 (8)
N Danns	0 (1)	-	-	-	0 (1)
J Douglas	14	-	-	-	14
B Emerton	31 (6)	-	0 (1)	2	33 (7)
P Enckelman	2	-	-	-	2
B Ferguson	14 (1)	-	1	-	15 (1)
G Flitcroft	29 (2)	1	-	1	31 (2)
B Friedel	36	1	1	2	40
P Gallagher	12 (14)	1	0 (1)	-	13 (15)
C Grabbi	0 (5)	-	-	1 (1)	1 (6)
M Gray	14	-	-	-	14
V Gresko	22 (2)	1	1	2	26 (2)
M Jansen	9 (10)	-	-	2	11 (10)
N-E Johansson	7 (7)	-	0 (1)	-	7 (8)
A Mahon	1 (2)	1	-	-	2 (2)
L Neill	30 (2)	1	1	1	33 (2)
S Reid	9 (7)	-	1	1 (1)	11 (8)
C Short	19	1	-	-	20
J Stead	13	-	-	-	13
M Taylor	10 (1)	0 (1)	1	0 (1)	11 (3)
D Thompson	10 (1)	-	1	2	13 (1)
A Todd	19	1	-	1	21
Tugay Kerimoglu	30 (6)	1	1	2	34 (6)
D Yorke	15 (8)	0 (1)	1	1 (1)	17 (10)

Sunday November 2
LEICESTER CITY (a)
Lost 0-2   **HT 0-0**   Att **30,975**   Position **19th**
Friedel — Neill, Todd, Babbel, Gresko (Reid 82) — Thompson, Flitcroft (Tugay 79), Ferguson, Emerton — Cole, Yorke *Subs not used* Yelldell, Jansen, Taylor
Booked Emerton
Report page 166

Monday November 10
EVERTON (h)
Won 2-1   **HT 2-0**   Att **22,179**   Position **16th**
After eight defeats in nine league and cup games, Blackburn find some relief at last to climb out of the Premiership's bottom three and send Everton into the danger zone in their place. Two headers exploit the shambolic nature of the visiting team's early defending, Radzinski replying in similar fashion after the break.
Friedel — Neill, Todd, Babbel, Gresko — Reid, Flitcroft, Ferguson, Emerton — Yorke (Gallagher ht), Jansen (Baggio 79) *Subs not used* Taylor, Tugay, Enckelman
Booked Gresko, Flitcroft, Ferguson
Scorers **Babbel 6, Yorke 13**
Referee **P Dowd**

Saturday November 22
MANCHESTER UNITED (a)
Lost 1-2   **HT 0-2**   Att **67,748**   Position **17th**
Friedel — Babbel, Todd, Short, Gresko — Reid (Johansson ht), Flitcroft (Baggio 78), Ferguson, Emerton — Yorke, Jansen (Gallagher ht) *Subs not used* Taylor, Enckelman *Booked* Ferguson
Scorer **Emerton 62**
Report page 199

Saturday November 29
TOTTENHAM HOTSPUR (h)
Won 1-0   **HT 0-0**   Att **22,802**   Position **16th**
Some overdue luck for Blackburn, who win when Gresko's shot takes a huge deflection off Carr, but even victory fails completely to satisfy Graeme Souness, who is sent to the stands once again after an exchange of views with the referee. Keane misses the only chance created by Spurs in a dreary contest.
Friedel — Babbel, Todd, Short, Gresko — Emerton, Ferguson, Tugay, Johansson (Reid ht) — Gallagher (Jansen 83), Yorke *Subs not used* Taylor, Baggio, Enckelman
Scorer **Gresko 78**
Referee **G Poll**

Saturday December 6
BIRMINGHAM CITY (a)
Won 4-0   **HT 0-0**   Att **29,354**   Position **14th**
Friedel — Babbel, Todd, Short, Gresko — Emerton, Tugay, Ferguson, Neill — Yorke (Cole 58), Gallagher *Subs not used* Enckelman, Reid, Jansen, Baggio
Booked Emerton
Scorers **Ferguson 66, Neill 68, Tugay 82, Gallagher 88**
Report page 85

Sunday December 14
ARSENAL (a)

Lost 0-1   **HT 0-1**   Att **37,677**   Position **14th**
Friedel — Babbel (Baggio 81), Todd, Short, Gresko
(Reid ht) — Emerton, Tugay, Ferguson, Neill — Yorke,
Gallagher (Cole 56) *Subs not used* Flitcroft, Enckelman
Booked Gresko, Todd, Babbel, Ferguson
Report page 64

Saturday December 20
ASTON VILLA (h)

Lost 0-2   **HT 0-0**   Att **20,722**   Position **16th**
Fresh from their conquest of Chelsea to reach the Carling
Cup semi-finals, Villa win on the road for the first time in
the league since January thanks to a brace of second-half
goals, including Angel's twelfth of the season. "I feel lower
than a snake's belly," Graeme Souness says after
Blackburn's defeat.

Friedel — Babbel, Todd, Short, Neill (Jansen 69) —
Emerton, Ferguson, Tugay (Flitcroft 60), Gallagher
(Gresko ht) — Yorke, Cole *Subs not used* Enckelman,
Taylor *Booked* Short
Referee **D Gallagher**

Friday December 26
MIDDLESBROUGH (h)

Drew 2-2   **HT 1-1**   Att **25,452**   Position **16th**
Unbreached for more than 11½ hours in the league,
Middlesbrough's defence cracks within three minutes and
again at the death, Babbel connecting with
corners each time. But, in between, Juninho also
scores twice, the first from a superb pass by Ricketts,
as Steve McClaren's team extend their unbeaten run to
11 games.

Friedel — Babbel, Todd, Taylor, Johansson (Mahon ht) —
Emerton, Ferguson, Flitcroft (Tugay 55), Neill — Gallagher,
Yorke (Cole ht) *Subs not used* Jansen, Enckelman *Booked*
Flitcroft, Gallagher
Scorer **Babbel 3, 90**
Referee **A Wiley**

Sunday December 28
NEWCASTLE UNITED (a)

Won 1-0   **HT 0-0**   Att **51,648**   Position **14th**
Friedel — Neill, Todd, Babbel, Gresko — Emerton,
Ferguson (Flitcroft 29), Tugay, Mahon — Cole (Yorke 87),
Gallagher (Jansen 90) *Subs not used* Enckelman, Taylor
Booked Todd
Scorer **Gallagher 71**
Report page 223

Saturday January 3 2004
BIRMINGHAM CITY (a)
FA Cup, 3rd rnd

Lost 0-4   **HT 0-2**   Att **16,688**
Friedel — Babbel, Todd, Short (Taylor 53), Gresko —
Neill, Tugay, Flitcroft, Mahon (Baggio ht) — Gallagher
(Yorke 59), Cole *Subs not used* Yelldell, Jansen
Booked Tugay
Report page 86

MATCH OF THE SEASON

Fulham 3   Blackburn Rovers 4
Loftus Road, Monday April 12 2004
Matt Dickinson

BLACKBURN ROVERS HAD TO TAKE the lead three times
before finally securing a vital win against Fulham last night, but all
the stress and strain was worth it. They remain a long way from
safety but, with Leicester City to come at home on Saturday,
Graeme Souness, the Blackburn manager, will hope that Jon Stead's
fine 75th-minute winner marks a turning point in their dire
campaign. In ending a run of three consecutive league defeats,
Rovers drew level on points with Manchester City, who will feel the
heat when they look at the table this morning. A lasting revival for
Blackburn will depend on better defending but, in Stead, they had a
striker who combined skill and perseverance. Plucked from
Huddersfield Town for £1.2 million in January, the 20-year-old
deserved his winner, a crisp volley from 20 yards.

His goal was the last decisive blow of a game that should have
made a hero of Collins John. The teenage striker had scored two
goals as a substitute on Saturday and, last night, he took his total to
four over the Easter weekend. Not a bad way to start his career in
England.

John spurned a good chance to make it 4-4 in the last few
minutes, but Fulham could not claim that defeat was an injustice.
They were lucky not to have been reduced to ten men before the
first of seven goals when Zat Knight head-butted Stead off the ball.
"I clipped his heel accidentally and he's turned around and nutted
me," Stead said, and Souness added: "The only four people in the
ground who didn't see it were the officials." The FA may take action
when it sees the video replays this morning.

Rovers struck back by taking the lead in the 23rd minute. Players
such as Tugay Kerimoglu, who was gracing a World Cup semi-final
for Turkey not so long ago, will always be capable of flashes of
brilliance even when their team is struggling and he set up Andrew
Cole with a wonderful pass off the outside of his right boot. Cole has
been demanding £75,000 a week from clubs interested in taking him
from Ewood Park and, with a chest-down and flash of his right boot,
he looked the striker of old.

Cole's finish was emphatic but it served only to rouse Fulham,
who were level within three minutes and ahead by half-time. Craig
Short and Lorenzo Amoruso looked vulnerable throughout and
neither was on hand when John bundled the ball in from close range
after Martin Djetou had struck the underside of the crossbar.
Moments before the interval, John struck again to prod home a free
kick from Sean Davis.

With the defence so flimsy and their position so desperate,
Souness had no choice other than to urge his team forward after the

Amoruso and Neill combine to thwart Boa Morte at Loftus Road

interval, but he could not have expected two goals within six minutes of the restart. From 2-1 down, Rovers were soon 3-2 up as Jonathan Douglas struck a powerful volley after Stead's flick-on.

In the 51st minute, a short free kick to Amoruso allowed the centre half to shoot around the Fulham defensive wall from 25 yards. Struck with power and wicked swerve, it was too much for a ponderous Edwin van der Sar. Having kept their lead for only three minutes in the first half, Blackburn held their advantage for the nine minutes that it took Luis Boa Morte to make a dramatic intervention. After a one-two with John, the Portugal winger raced half the length of the field before shooting past Brad Friedel. His goal celebration requires explanation; he mimicked a dog urinating against the corner flag. It was no stranger, perhaps, than anything else in a match that swung back Blackburn's way when Stead took advantage of more slow reactions from Van der Sar.

"That was a big win for us," Souness said. "We've a great chance against Leicester but we've failed against Leeds and Portsmouth at home in recent weeks. We pride ourselves on our football, but it's about scrapping now." For Chris Coleman, the Fulham manager, not even John's contribution could ease his frustration. "How do you score three goals at home against a team fighting relegation and still lose?" he said.

FULHAM (4-1-4-1): E van der Sar — M Volz, Z Knight, A Goma, C Bocanegra — M Djetou — S Malbranque (sub: B McBride, 84min), S Davis (sub: B Petta, 77), S Legwinski, L Boa Morte — C John (sub: B Hayles, 87). **Substitutes not used:** M Crossley, I Pearce.
BLACKBURN ROVERS (4-4-2): B Friedel — L Neill, L Amoruso, C Short, V Gresko — G Flitcroft, M Andresen, Tugay Kerimoglu, J Douglas — J Stead (sub: P Gallagher, 90), A Cole (sub: B Emerton, 89). **Substitutes not used:** P Enckelman, S Reid, N E Johansson.

Wednesday January 7
WOLVERHAMPTON WANDERERS (a)
Drew 2-2   HT 1-0   Att 27,393   Position 15th
Friedel — Babbel, Taylor, Short (Johansson 43), Neill — Emerton, Flitcroft, Tugay, Gresko (Baggio 75) — Cole, Gallagher (Yorke 62) *Subs not used* Yelldell, Jansen *Booked* Gresko
Scorers **Cole 14, Yorke 78**
Report page 264

Saturday January 10
BOLTON WANDERERS (h)
Lost 3-4   HT 3-2   Att 23,538   Position 16th
With a goal after 13 seconds, one of the fastest in the history of the Premiership, and another 12 minutes from time, Nolan starts and ends a seven-goal thriller full of defensive blunders and exceptional finishing. Bolton, who go from 1-0 up to 3-1 down, eventually take the points and the bragging rights.

Friedel — Neill (Jansen 83), Babbel, Taylor, Gresko — Emerton, Tugay, Douglas (Danns 74) — Yorke — Cole, Gallagher (Baggio 64) *Subs not used* Enckelman, Johansson *Booked* Gresko, Cole
Scorers **Gresko 3, Yorke 24, Cole 34**
Referee **S Dunn**

Saturday January 17
MANCHESTER CITY (a)
Drew 1-1   HT 0-0   Att 47,090   Position 16th
Friedel — Neill, Babbel, Johansson, Gresko — Emerton, Flitcroft, Tugay, Douglas — Cole, Yorke *Subs not used* Taylor, Danns, Mahon, Jansen, Enckelman *Booked* Flitcroft
Scorer **Flitcroft 55**
Report page 191

Sunday February 1
CHELSEA (h)
Lost 2-3   HT 1-2   Att 24,867   Position 16th
Chelsea, with Parker settling in nicely on his debut after a £10m move from Charlton Athletic, come from behind with a double from the ever-improving Lampard, but seem to slip farther out of the title picture when Gallagher grabs an equaliser for Blackburn three minutes from time. Johnson has other ideas, however, the defender hitting a terrific late winner into the top corner.

Friedel — Neill, Todd, Babbel, Gray — Emerton, Flitcroft, Tugay, Douglas (Mahon 56) — Yorke (Gallagher 56), Cole *Subs not used* Enckelman, Jansen, Johansson *Booked* Neill, Tugay
Scorers **Flitcroft 3, Gallagher 87**
Referee **D Gallagher**

Saturday February 7
MIDDLESBROUGH (a)
Won 1-0   HT 1-0   Att 28,307   Position 14th
Friedel — Neill, Babbel, Short, Todd, Flitcroft, Douglas — Gallagher (Jansen 65), Stead (Tugay 84) *Subs not used* Enckelman, Cole, Johansson *Booked* Douglas
Scorer **Stead 39**
Report page 213

Wednesday February 11
NEWCASTLE UNITED (h)
Drew 1-1   HT 0-0   Att 23,459   Position 14th
Bellamy, hurt by a challenge from Neill that has Sir Bobby
Robson spitting blood, recovers to score his first goal
after four months out with a serious knee injury, but
Stead, the new Ewood Park hero, makes it two goals in
two games with Blackburn's equaliser. It is Newcastle's
sixth successive away league draw.

Friedel — Neill, Todd, Babbel, Gray — Emerton, Flitcroft,
Tugay, Douglas (Gallagher 68) — Cole (Johansson 90),
Stead *Subs not used* Yorke, Andresen, Enckelman
Scorer Stead 85
Referee **M Messias**

Saturday February 21
CHARLTON ATHLETIC (a)
Lost 2-3   HT 0-2   Att 26,332   Position 15th
Friedel — Neill, Babbel, Short, Gray — Emerton, Flitcroft
(Tugay 30), Todd (Yorke 60), Douglas — Gallagher, Stead
(Cole ht) *Subs not used* Enckelman, Andresen
Scorers Cole 74, Friedel 90
Report page 118

Saturday February 28
SOUTHAMPTON (h)
Drew 1-1   HT 0-1   Att 21,970   Position 15th
Another home match without victory, another conspiracy
theory for Graeme Souness, who complains bitterly —
and with some justification — that Rovers should have
had a penalty for Le Saux's challenge on Emerton (they
have not had a spot kick all season, the manager points
out). Phillips's early goal, cancelled out by Cole, earns
Steve Wigley his second draw in two games in temporary
charge of Southampton.

Friedel — Neill, Babbel, Short, Gray — Emerton, Tugay,
Andresen, Douglas (Jansen ht) — Cole, Gallagher
(Yorke ht) *Subs not used* Gresko, Todd, Enckelman
Booked Babbel
Scorer Cole 52
Referee **M Dean**

Saturday March 13
ARSENAL (h)
Lost 0-2   HT 0-0   Att 28,627   Position 15th
Arsenal safely negotiate one of the trickier hurdles on
the title run-in, beating the side that defeated them
twice last season with Henry's trademark free kick —
controversially awarded for a foul on him by Short —
and a late second by Pires. It is Henry's 30th goal of
the season and extends Arsenal's unbeaten league run
to 30 games.

Friedel — Neill, Todd (Babbel 84), Short, Gray — Emerton,
Andresen, Tugay, Douglas (Gresko 77) — Cole, Jansen
(Yorke 73) *Subs not used* Enckelman, Johansson *Booked*
Andresen
Referee **A Wiley**

THE PLAYERS

LORENZO AMORUSO (defender)
Born June 28, 1971, Palese, Italy
Ht 6ft 2in **Wt** 13st 10lb **Signed from**
Rangers, July 2003, £1.4m

MARTIN ANDRESEN (midfield) **Born**
February 20, 1977, Norway
Ht 5ft 11in **Wt** 11st 5lb **Signed from**
Stabaek IF (loan), February 2004

MARKUS BABBEL (defender) **Born**
September 8, 1972, Munich
Ht 6ft 3in **Wt** 12st 10lb **Signed from**
Liverpool (loan), July 2003

DINO BAGGIO (forward) **Born** July 24,
1971, Camposampiero, Italy
Ht 6ft 1in **Wt** 11st 4lb **Signed from**
Lazio (loan), August 2003

ANDREW COLE (forward) **Born**
October 15, 1971, Nottingham
Ht 5ft 11in **Wt** 11st 12lb
Signed from Manchester United,
December 2001, £7.5m

NEIL DANNS (midfield) **Born**
November 23, 1982, Liverpool
Ht 5ft 11in **Wt** 11st 1lb **Signed from**
trainee, August 2002

JONATHAN DOUGLAS (midfield) **Born**
November 22, 1981, Monaghan
Ht 5ft 10in **Wt** 12st 12lb **Signed
from** trainee, February 2000

BRETT EMERTON (midfield) **Born**
February 22, 1979, Bankstown,
Australia **Ht** 6ft 2in **Wt** 13st 5lb
Signed from Feyenoord, July 2003,
£2.2m

PETER ENCKELMAN (goalkeeper)
Born March 10, 1977, Turku,
Finland **Ht** 6ft 2in **Wt** 12st 5lb
Signed from Aston Villa, January
2004, £150,000

BARRY FERGUSON (midfield) **Born**
February 2, 1978, Glasgow
Ht 5ft 10in **Wt** 11st 9lb **Signed from**
Rangers, August 2003, £7.5m

GARRY FLITCROFT (midfield) **Born**
November 6, 1972, Bolton **Ht** 6ft 0in
Wt 12st 2lb **Signed from** Manchester
City, March 1996, £3.2m

BRAD FRIEDEL (goalkeeper) **Born**
May 18, 1971, Lakewood, Ohio
Ht 6ft 3in **Wt** 14st 7lb **Signed from**
Liverpool, November 2000, free

PAUL GALLAGHER (forward) **Born**
August 9, 1984, Blackburn **Ht** 6ft 1in
Wt 11st 0lb **Signed from** trainee,
August 2002

CORRADO GRABBI (forward) **Born**
July 29, 1975, Turin **Ht** 5ft 11in
Wt 12st 12lb **Signed from** Ternana,
Italy, July 2001, £6.75m

MICHAEL GRAY (defender) **Born**
August 3, 1974, Sunderland
Ht 5ft 7in **Wt** 10st 10lb **Signed from**
Sunderland, January 2004, free

VRATISLAV GRESKO (defender)
Born July 24, 1977, Bratislava
Ht 6ft 0in **Wt** 11st 3lb **Signed from**
Parma (loan), January 2003

MATT JANSEN (forward) **Born**
October 20, 1977, Carlisle
Ht 5ft 11in **Wt** 10st 13lb **Signed
from** Crystal Palace, January 1999,
£4.1m

NILS-ERIC JOHANSSON (defender)
Born January 13, 1980, Stockholm
Ht 6ft 1in **Wt** 12st 7lb
Signed from Nuremberg, October
2001, £2.7m

ALAN MAHON (midfield) **Born**
April 4, 1978, Dublin **Ht** 5ft 10in
Wt 11st 5lb **Signed from** Tranmere
Rovers, December 2000, £1.5m

LUCAS NEILL (defender) **Born** March
9, 1978, Sydney **Ht** 6ft 1in
Wt 12st 0lb **Signed from** Millwall,
July 2001, £1m

STEVEN REID (midfield) **Born** March
10, 1981, Kingston **Ht** 5ft 11in
Wt 11st 10lb **Signed from** Millwall,
July 2003, £2.5m

CRAIG SHORT (defender) **Born** June
25, 1968, Bridlington **Ht** 6ft 1in
Wt 13st 8lb **Signed from** Everton,
August 1999, £1.7m

JONATHAN STEAD (forward) **Born**
April 7, 1983, Huddersfield **Ht** 6ft 3in
Wt 12st 2lb **Signed from**
Huddersfield Town, February 2004,
£1.25m

MARTIN TAYLOR
(see Birmingham City)

DAVID THOMPSON (midfield) **Born**
September 12, 1977, Birkenhead
Ht 5ft 7in **Wt** 10st 0lb **Signed from**
Coventry City, August 2002, £1.5m

ANDY TODD (defender) **Born**
September 21, 1974, Derby
Ht 5ft 10in **Wt** 11st 10lb **Signed
from** Charlton Athletic, May 2002,
£750,000

TUGAY KERIMOGLU (midfield) **Born**
August 24, 1970, Istanbul **Ht** 5ft 9in
Wt 11st 6lb **Signed from** Rangers,
July 2001, £1.3m

DWIGHT YORKE (forward) **Born**
November 3, 1971, Canaan, Tobago
Ht 5ft 10in **Wt** 12st 4lb
Signed from Manchester United, July
2002, £2m

STATS AND FACTS

● Between March 2000 and January 2004, Dwight Yorke and Andy Cole were at the same club for the equivalent of more than three seasons (at Manchester United, then Blackburn Rovers), but only once did they score in the same Premiership game in that period. Then they did so twice in four days, away to Wolverhampton Wanderers and at home to Bolton Wanderers.

● Brad Friedel, the Rovers goalkeeper, scored one league goal (against Charlton Athletic), only three fewer than Dwight Yorke.

● Rovers enjoy their visits to Stamford Bridge. They have not lost any of their past 11 matches away to Chelsea.

● Blackburn, however, have not beaten Liverpool in their past 11 league meetings.

● No wonder Graeme Souness gets upset — Blackburn were the only team not to be awarded a penalty in the Premiership last season.

● Blackburn's win over Manchester United in May was only their third in 31 meetings.

● In December, Blackburn suffered only the second defeat in their past 17 home games against Aston Villa.

Bill Edgar

GOALSCORERS

	Prem	FAC	CC	Euro	Total
L Amoruso	3	-	-	-	3
M Babbel	3	-	-	-	3
D Baggio	1	-	-	-	1
A Cole	11	-	-	-	11
J Douglas	1	-	-	-	1
B Emerton	2	-	-	1	3
B Ferguson	1	-	1	-	2
G Flitcroft	3	-	-	-	3
B Friedel	1	-	-	-	1
P Gallagher	3	-	-	-	3
V Gresko	2	-	-	-	2
M Jansen	2	-	-	1	3
L Neill	2	-	-	-	2
C Short	1	-	-	-	1
J Stead	6	-	-	-	6
D Thompson	1	-	-	-	1
Tugay Kerimoglu	1	-	-	-	1
D Yorke	4	-	2	-	6
Own goals	3	-	-	-	3

Saturday March 20
ASTON VILLA (a)
Won 2-0   HT 2-0   Att **37,532**   Position **15th**
Friedel — Neill (Babbel 60), Todd, Short, Gray — Emerton, Tugay, Flitcroft, Andresen — Stead (Amoruso 89), Cole
Subs not used Enckelman, Jansen, Yorke *Booked* Neill, Todd
Scorers **Flitcroft 26, Stead 36**
Report page 79

Saturday March 27
PORTSMOUTH (h)
Lost 1-2   HT 1-1   Att **22,855**   Position **16th**
Portsmouth's long-overdue first away league victory comes at the expense of the side who just cannot win at home. The first two goals need deflections, but Yakubu follows up his decisive strike against Southampton by securing back-to-back wins for Harry Redknapp's team for the first time this season. Cole squanders a great late chance to equalise.
Friedel — Neill, Todd, Short, Gray (Gallagher 83) — Emerton, Tugay, Flitcroft, Andresen (Yorke 70) — Stead (Reid 77), Cole *Subs not used* Amoruso, Enckelman
Scorer **Taylor 37 (og)**
Referee **P Durkin**

Sunday April 4
LIVERPOOL (a)
Lost 0-4   HT 0-3   Att **41,559**   Position **16th**
Friedel — Babbel, Todd, Short (Johansson ht), Gray — Emerton, Tugay, Flitcroft (Reid ht), Andresen — Gallagher (Cole 62), Stead *Subs not used* Enckelman, Yorke
Booked Flitcroft
Report page 183

Saturday April 10
LEEDS UNITED (h)
Lost 1-2   HT 0-1   Att **26,611**   Position **16th**
Blackburn have no home wins since November 29, Leeds none away since the same date, and it's Rovers, who are behind within two minutes and concede again just before Short's reply in stoppage time. For Leeds there is hope anew; for Graeme Souness a deepening foreboding.
Friedel — Neill, Amoruso, Short, Gray — Emerton, Tugay, Flitcroft, Reid (Gallagher ht) — Cole, Stead (Jansen 68) *Subs not used* Todd, Andresen, Enckelman *Booked* Flitcroft, Gray
Scorer **Short 90**
Referee **S Dunn**

Monday April 12
FULHAM (a)
Won 4-3   HT 1-2   Att **13,981**   Position **16th**
Friedel — Neill, Amoruso, Short, Gresko — Flitcroft, Tugay, Andresen, Douglas — Stead (Gallagher 90), Cole (Emerton 89) *Subs not used* Enckelman, Reid, Johansson
Scorers **Cole 23, Douglas 49, Amoruso 51, Stead 75**
Report page 151

PLAYER OF THE SEASON
Jonathan Stead

It is a tribute to a forward who has been at the club for only four months, or perhaps an indictment of the other players, that Jonathan Stead was Rovers' outstanding performer. Signed from Huddersfield in January, this gangly 21-year-old must be the best £1.2 million Rovers have spent. Quite simply, without his goals they would have been relegated. His impact on the season was remarkable: six goals, four of which were match-winners, in 13 games is impressive in itself, but of the six games in which Stead scored, Rovers were unbeaten, having accumulated 16 points from a possible 18. The club was going down when he arrived, but this confident Yorkshire lad stepped up three divisions and took the Premiership in his long stride. England have noticed, too: he has already been capped at under-21 level and if his form continues into 2004-05, a senior call-up may not be far away.

John Dawkins

Saturday April 17
LEICESTER CITY (h)
Won 1-0   HT 1-0   Att 22,749   Position 15th
Blackburn's most important game for years is predictably tense and is settled when Dabizas turns Cole's low cross into his own goal, with Walker, who saves well from Gresko and Stead, this time helpless. Graeme Souness has safety in sight, but while Micky Adams refuses to give up, Leicester's plight now looks hopeless.

Friedel — Neill, Amoruso, Short, Gresko — Flitcroft, Tugay, Andresen (Emerton 86), Douglas — Cole, Stead *Subs not used* Reid, Johansson, Gallagher, Enckelman *Booked* Amoruso, Douglas
Scorer **Dabizas 42 (og)**
Referee **R Styles**

Saturday April 24
EVERTON (a)
Won 1-0   HT 0-0   Att 38,884   Position 13th
Friedel — Neill, Amoruso, Short, Gray — Flitcroft, Tugay, Andresen (Emerton 74), Douglas — Stead, Cole (Gallagher 85) *Subs not used* Reid, Johansson, Enckelman *Booked* Neill, Tugay, Andresen, Douglas
Scorer **Stead 81**
Report page 142

Saturday May 1
MANCHESTER UNITED (h)
Won 1-0   HT 0-0   Att 29,616   Position 13th
After their united front in a press conference the day before, when Van Nistelrooy and Keane pledge their future to Old Trafford despite persistent transfer speculation, neither are fit to play as Blackburn, with yet another goal from the prolific Stead, guarantee their survival with a fourth successive win.

Friedel — Neill, Babbel, Johansson, Gray — Flitcroft, Tugay (Emerton 90), Andresen, Douglas — Cole (Gallagher 83), Stead *Subs not used* Reid, Yorke, Enckelman *Booked* Flitcroft, Gallagher
Scorer **Stead 85**
Referee **M Dean**

Saturday May 8
TOTTENHAM HOTSPUR (a)
Lost 0-1   HT 0-1   Att 35,698   Position 13th
Enckelman — Neill (Reid 61), Short, Johansson, Gray — Flitcroft (Gallagher 76), Tugay, Andresen (Emerton 64), Douglas — Cole, Stead *Subs not used* Yelldell, Babbel *Booked* Neill, Andresen
Report page 258

Saturday May 15
BIRMINGHAM CITY (h)
Drew 1-1   HT 1-0   Att 26,070   Position 15th
As Birmingham end the season on a run of eight games without a win, but in their highest position for 31 years, Rovers fans are left to ponder whether Cole's opening goal may prove to be his last for the club. Graeme Souness, fittingly, ends the campaign in an angry mood, complaining that John had pushed Neill before heading the equaliser.

Enckelman — Reid (Neill ht), Short, Johansson, Gray (Gallagher 87) — Flitcroft, Tugay, Andresen (Emerton ht), Douglas — Cole, Stead *Subs not used* Yelldell, Jansen
Scorer **Cole 24**
Referee **D Gallagher**

BOLTON WANDERERS

PREMIERSHIP

	P	W	D	L	F	A	GD	Pts
Arsenal	38	26	12	0	73	26	47	**90**
Chelsea	38	24	7	7	67	30	37	**79**
Man Utd	38	23	6	9	64	35	29	**75**
Liverpool	38	16	12	10	55	37	18	**60**
Newcastle	38	13	17	8	52	40	12	**56**
Aston Villa	38	15	11	12	48	44	4	**56**
Charlton	38	14	11	13	51	51	0	**53**
Bolton	38	14	11	13	48	56	-8	**53**
Fulham	38	14	10	14	52	46	6	**52**
Birmingham	38	12	14	12	43	48	-5	**50**
Middlesbro	38	13	9	16	44	52	-8	**48**
Southampton	38	12	11	15	44	45	-1	**47**
Portsmouth	38	12	9	17	47	54	-7	**45**
Tottenham	38	13	6	19	47	57	-10	**45**
Blackburn	38	12	8	18	51	59	-8	**44**
Man City	38	9	14	15	55	54	1	**41**
Everton	38	9	12	17	45	57	-12	**39**
Leicester	38	6	15	17	48	65	-17	**33**
Leeds	38	8	9	21	40	79	-39	**33**
Wolves	38	7	12	19	38	77	-39	**33**

FA CUP
Third round

CARLING CUP
Finalists

Sam-tastic: Allardyce salutes the fans after the victory away to Southampton that was a highlight of the late surge up the table

THE GAMES

Saturday August 16 2003
MANCHESTER UNITED (a)
Lost 0-4   HT 0-1   Att 67,647   Position 20th
Jaaskelainen — Hunt, N'Gotty, Laville, Gardner — Campo
— Giannakopoulos (Facey 76), Nolan (Frandsen 42),
Okocha, Pedersen (Djorkaeff 59) — Davies *Subs not
used* Barness, Poole *Booked* Jaaskelainen, N'Gotty,
Gardner, Giannakopoulos, Nolan
Report page 196

Saturday August 23
BLACKBURN ROVERS (h)
Drew 2-2   HT 2-0   Att 27,423   Position 16th
Just like last season, Bolton are unable to protect a lead,
this time from 2-0 up. Blackburn, who have Reid sent off
on his debut for a reckless challenge on
Giannakopoulos, hit back through Jansen and Yorke, the
latter with a stoppage-time header, as the fixture ends
all square for the fifth successive time.

Jaaskelainen — Hunt, N'Gotty, Laville, Gardner — Campo
— Nolan (Frandsen 66), Djorkaeff, Okocha
(Giannakopoulos 84) — Pedersen (Barness 77), Davies
Subs not used Poole, Jardel *Booked* Nolan, Davies
Scorers **Djorkaeff 3 (pen), Davies 25**
Referee **A D'Urso**

Tuesday August 26
PORTSMOUTH (a)
Lost 0-4   HT 0-0   Att 20,113   Position 19th
Jaaskelainen — Barness (Charlton 41), N'Gotty, Laville,
Gardner — Frandsen (Giannakopoulos 62), Campo,
Okocha — Djorkaeff — Pedersen, Davies (Jardel 62) *Subs
not used* Poole, Nolan *Booked* Laville, Giannakopoulos,
Davies, Charlton
Report page 230

Saturday August 30
CHARLTON ATHLETIC (h)
Drew 0-0   HT 0-0   Att 23,098   Position 17th
Bolton are left with most to regret after a dull goalless
draw: Okocha's thunderous free kick hits the bar,
Hreidarsson clears off the line from Djorkaeff and
Fortune gets away with a clear push on Davies in the
Charlton area. Parker and Holland miss the best
openings for Alan Curbishley's team.

Jaaskelainen — Hunt, N'Gotty, Thome, Gardner — Campo
— Djorkaeff, Nolan, Okocha — Pedersen
(Giannakopoulos ht), Davies *Subs not used* Poole,
Charlton, Frandsen, Facey *Booked* Jaaskelainen, Campo,
Okocha, Davies
Referee **A Wiley**

Saturday September 13
MIDDLESBROUGH (h)
Won 2-0   HT 1-0   Att 26,419   Position 14th
"The basics weren't there ... the will to win." Steve
McClaren, the Middlesbrough manager, issues a damning
verdict on the team that is booed off by travelling
supporters after headers from Davies — a thumping
effort — and N'Gotty earn Bolton a deserved victory.

Jaaskelainen — Hunt (Frandsen 69), Laville (N'Gotty 28),
Thome, Gardner — Campo — Giannakopoulos, Nolan,
Okocha — Davies, Djorkaeff (Pedersen 75) *Subs not
used* Poole, Jardel *Booked* Gardner, Djorkaeff, Thome
Scorers **Davies 23, N'Gotty 81**
Referee **P Dowd**

AT LEAST A FEW BOLTON FANS must have felt a little queasy when they picked up their papers on the morning of May Bank Holiday Monday. There, large as life on the sports pages, was the image of a young footballer, face contorted by pain, weeping inconsolably, his Wanderers shirt drenched in tears. His team had just been relegated. It took a moment for reality to kick in: ah, this is not a Bolton player, it's Alan Smith, after swapping shirts with Jay-Jay Okocha. It's Leeds United who are going down; Bolton Wanderers are not in danger. Not even nearly.

For anyone whose emotional balance has been upset by years of relegation stress, finding yourself seventh in the Premiership come May takes a bit of getting used to. Instead of having their bags packed, ready to slink back to the Football League, the Wanderers seemed to be little more than a long ball from Europe. Midweek mini-breaks in France or Spain were a tantalising possibility.

How had such a marvellous transformation been wrought, from relegation certainties to serious contenders for a Uefa Cup slot in three seasons? Even Sam Allardyce is not sure. "Sometimes I wonder," the manager said, "how we have managed to get this far, how we have managed to pull together cast-offs from all over the world and mould them into a unit that wants to play for this club."

If Allardyce is a little baffled by his own success, he is not alone. Never mind his famous cast-offs, he surprised his critics last season by regularly fielding a side with four or five British passport-holders and not a single loan player. He even managed to send one of his players — Mario Jardel — to help out a club in Italy's Serie A. Who could have imagined that a few years ago? Picture the scene in that Italian boardroom: "Giuseppe, things are looking up! We've got a top striker on loan from Bolton Wanderers ..."

As the once-prolific Jardel struggled to revive his ailing career, the striker that he had failed to dislodge at the Reebok Stadium was showing him how it should be done. Kevin Davies, a spent force at the tender age of 26, was the latest to benefit from Allardyce's healing powers. Dr Allardyce can hardly claim a perfect success rate for his therapeutic regime, but Davies was a model patient who rapidly recovered his confidence. Even when he didn't score, he made a big difference. Defenders don't like him. In his post-match interviews he seems such a nice lad, but in the penalty area he likes to put himself about, punching above his weight. David O'Leary, the Aston Villa manager, paid tribute to Davies's qualities after the first leg of the Carling Cup semi-final. "He bullied us from the very start," O'Leary said. "He knocked my mob around all night."

The revitalised Davies has much more to offer than his physical

FA CUP
Winners 1923, 1926, 1929, 1958
Runners-up 1894, 1904, 1953
LEAGUE CUP
Runners-up 1995, 2004

Record attendance 69,912 (v Manchester City, FA Cup 5th rnd, February 18, 1933)
Current capacity 27,879
Record victory 13-0 (v Sheffield United, FA Cup 2nd rnd, February 1, 1890)
Record defeat 1-9 (v Preston North End, FA Cup 2nd rnd, December 10, 1887)

presence and proved this at St Mary's Stadium in April, when he gave Southampton, who had released him the previous summer, a reminder of why they liked him so much they signed him twice. He created one goal then scored another to turn around the match in two second-half minutes.

Davies's sterling contribution to Bolton's best season since 1959-60 was matched by his fellow Englishmen, Nicky Hunt, and Kevin Nolan, both young graduates of the club's academy. They played with skill and passion to ensure their almost constant presence in the side. Nolan was top scorer with 13 goals from midfield. They are excellent players in their own right, but it cannot have hurt their progress to have been rubbing shoulders with the senior statesmen in Allardyce's global community: Okocha, Ivan Campo and Youri Djorkaeff.

Okocha's mid-season trip to the African Nations Cup, and the fatigue that blighted his return, annoyed his manager no end. But his talent is so prodigious that he is worth having even at half-strength. Forget that he failed to score a single Premiership goal; he hit the bar and post so many times that his zero tally was clearly an aberration, a freak of nature. Think back, instead, to his free kick in the Carling Cup semi-final, a goal to tell your grandchildren about. He hit it with power, swerve and military precision. Only a ballistics expert could have explained it.

Even so, the man is so much more than the sum of his goals. Coming from Africa and having played across Europe, he has four languages — five if you count the one that he speaks with his feet. And when Okocha is on the ball he is an orator: he grips us with his

Saturday September 20
NEWCASTLE UNITED (a)
Drew 0-0   HT 0-0   Att 52,014   Position 12th
Jaaskelainen — N'Gotty, Thome, Charlton, Gardner — Campo — Giannakopoulos (Pedersen 68), Nolan, Okocha, Djorkaeff (Frandsen 87) — Davies *Subs not used* Poole, Jardel, Hunt *Booked* Giannakopoulos
Report page 219

Wednesday September 24
WALSALL (h)
Carling Cup, 2nd rnd
Won 3-1   HT 1-0   Att 5,229
Mocked previously, a slimmer Jardel makes his full Bolton debut and, having had a thin time of it so far, scores twice — the first a header, the second on the rebound after Walker saves his penalty — as Walsall are routinely removed from the Carling Cup.
Poole — Hunt, N'Gotty (Comyn-Platt 81), Barness, Charlton — Ba (Giannakopoulos ht), Frandsen, Nolan, Okocha (Gardner ht) — Pedersen, Jardel *Subs not used* Bon, Davies *Booked* Barness, Hunt
Scorers Jardel 15, 80, Nolan 69
Referee **R Pearson**

Saturday September 27
WOLVERHAMPTON WANDERERS (h)
Drew 1-1   HT 0-1   Att 27,043   Position 13th
Naylor, the Wolves defender, has to be "peeled off the dressing-room wall" after allowing Thome to take the quick throw-in that leads to Davies's late equaliser for Bolton. Rae gives Wolves the lead with a sensational 30-yard volley into the top corner, their first league goal since the opening day.
Jaaskelainen — N'Gotty (Little 79), Thome, Charlton, Gardner — Nolan, Campo (Frandsen 61), Okocha, Djorkaeff — Davies, Pedersen (Jardel 61) *Subs not used* Poole, Hunt *Booked* Nolan, Thome
Scorer Davies 85
Referee **M Dean**

Sunday October 5
ASTON VILLA (a)
Drew 1-1   HT 0-0   Att 30,229   Position 15th
Jaaskelainen — N'Gotty, Thome, Charlton, Gardner — Campo — Nolan (Jardel 80), Frandsen, Okocha, Giannakopoulos (Little 90) — Davies *Subs not used* Poole, Pedersen, Hunt *Booked* Gardner, Campo, Okocha, Frandsen, Thome
Scorer Nolan 46
Report page 73

Saturday October 18
MANCHESTER CITY (a)
Lost 2-6   HT 1-1   Att 47,101   Position 16th
Jaaskelainen — N'Gotty, Thome (Little 79), Charlton, Gardner — Campo — Okocha, Frandsen (Jardel 53) — Nolan, Giannakopoulos — Davies *Subs not used* Poole, Barness, Pedersen *Booked* Davies
Scorers Nolan 25, Campo 60
Report page 188

Saturday October 25
BIRMINGHAM CITY (h)
Lost 0-1   HT 0-1   Att 25,023   Position 17th
A match in which five penalty appeals (three by Bolton, two by Birmingham) are rejected by Chris Foy — the referee might have given all of them, according to television replays — is settled by a combination of Forssell, who rounds off a City counter-attack with the only goal, and Taylor, who saves magnificently from Davies.
Jaaskelainen — N'Gotty, Thome, Charlton, Gardner — Campo (Jardel 64) — Nolan (Little 84), Okocha, Frandsen — Davies, Giannakopoulos (Pedersen 80) *Subs not used* Poole, Barness *Booked* Giannakopoulos
Referee **C Foy**

Tuesday October 28
GILLINGHAM (h)
Carling Cup, 3rd rnd
Won 2-0   HT 1-0   Att 5,258
A desperately thin crowd, a decidedly routine victory.
Giannakopoulos punishes a mistake by Brown, the
Gillingham goalkeeper, for Bolton's opener, his first goal
in English football, and Pedersen makes the game safe.
"We didn't need to get out of second gear," Sam
Allardyce says.

Poole — Hunt, Thome, Charlton, Barness — Nolan,
Campo, Ba (Okocha 66), Giannakopoulos (Gardner 50)
— Jardel, Pedersen *Subs not used* Jaaskelainen,
Comyn-Platt, Vaz Te
Scorers **Giannakopoulos 25, Pedersen 66**
Referee **P Dowd**

Saturday November 1
TOTTENHAM HOTSPUR (a)
Won 1-0   HT 0-0   Att 35,191   Position 15th
Jaaskelainen — Hunt, N'Gotty, Charlton, Gardner —
Campo — Nolan, Frandsen, Okocha — Davies,
Giannakopoulos (Pedersen 86) *Subs not used* Poole,
Barness, Jardel, Ba
Scorer **Nolan 73**
Report page 252

Saturday November 8
SOUTHAMPTON (h)
Drew 0-0   HT 0-0   Att 25,619   Position 14th
Okocha twice forces brilliant saves out of Niemi, but a
disappointing match is most notable for the late
sending-off of Michael Svensson, the Southampton
defender paying for Jardel's theatrics with a second
yellow card. The match is "mingin'" and Jardel is a "big
Jessie", according to Gordon Strachan.

Jaaskelainen — Hunt, N'Gotty, Charlton, Gardner —
Campo — Frandsen, Okocha — Nolan, Davies (Jardel 67),
Giannakopoulos (Pedersen 74) *Subs not used* Poole,
Barness, Ba *Booked* Campo, Jardel
Referee **H Webb**

Saturday November 22
LEEDS UNITED (a)
Won 2-0   HT 2-0   Att 36,558   Position 13th
Jaaskelainen — Campo, N'Gotty, Charlton — Hunt, Nolan
(Pedersen 73), Frandsen, Okocha, Gardner —
Giannakopoulos — Davies *Subs not used* Poole, Barness,
Djorkaeff, Jardel
Scorers **Davies 16, Giannakopoulos 17**
Report page 157

Saturday November 29
EVERTON (h)
Won 2-0   HT 1-0   Att 27,350   Position 10th
Inspired by Okocha, though he does not get on the
scoresheet, Bolton climb into the top half of the table as
Everton slip back into the bottom three. Their dismal
away form is reflected in the frustration shown by
Rooney, who stomps off in a huff after being replaced by
Jeffers. Bolton's second goal, initially credited to
Djorkaeff, is later awarded to Nolan.

Jaaskelainen — Hunt, N'Gotty, Charlton, Gardner — Nolan,
Frandsen, Campo, Okocha, Giannakopoulos
(Djorkaeff 30) — Davies *Subs not used* Poole, Pedersen,
Jardel, Thome
Scorers **Frandsen 26, Nolan 46**
Referee **P Durkin**

Kevin Davies celebrates the goal that climaxed a fine win at St Mary's

rhetoric and beguiles us with his wit. Defenders are entranced. How
does he *do* that? Then he grins and the entire stadium grins with
him. Is there a club in England whose fans would not be chuffed to
have him in their team?

If Okocha helped to ensure a memorable season, there are
elements that are best forgotten. Perhaps the disappointment of the
Carling Cup final, certainly the ticket fiasco that preceded it, and
possibly the unfortunately titled commemorative video that
followed it — *Sam's Heroes: A Journey to Remember.* The journey to
the Millennium Stadium was one that hundreds of season-ticket
holders were unable to make, let alone reminisce about.

But the team did the town proud, a feat reflected in the biggest
crowds for 44 years. Allardyce has said that the club should now
raise its sights and no longer be content to avoid relegation. He also
fears that having finished within three points (and a few goals) of a
Uefa Cup place will have left the fans with unrealistic expectations.
As the one who must try to fulfil them, he has good reason to be
worried. He knows that, in striving to reach Europe, his team could
end up playing in the exotic resorts of Brighton and Plymouth.

THE MANAGER Sam Allardyce

What a splendid season for Sam Allardyce. Not only did he lead Bolton Wanderers on magnificent league and cup campaigns, twice coming within a whisker of qualifying for Europe, but he also gave supporters the excitement of the great Rivaldo drama. This end-of-season soap opera, co-starring Martin O'Neill, featured a love triangle in which two earnest suitors vied for the hand of a comely maiden only to find out that she was really a brazen hussy on the brink of joining the harem of an Arab squillionaire. Gripping stuff. All things considered, it seems to have had a happy ending, too.

Alan Kay

APPEARANCES

	Prem	FAC	CC	Total
I Ba	0 (9)	1	5 (1)	6 (10)
A Barness	11 (4)	2	4 (2)	17 (6)
I Campo	37 (1)	-	6	43 (1)
S Charlton	28 (3)	-	5 (2)	33 (5)
C Comyn-Platt	0	2	0 (1)	2 (1)
K Davies	38	-	4 (1)	42 (1)
Y Djorkaeff	24 (3)	-	4 (1)	28 (4)
D Facey	0 (1)	2	-	2 (1)
P Frandsen	22 (11)	1 (1)	3	26 (12)
R Gardner	20 (2)	-	2 (2)	22 (4)
S Giannakopoulos	17 (14)	2	4 (2)	23 (16)
S Howey	2 (1)	-	-	2 (1)
N Hunt	28 (3)	1	6	35 (3)
J Jaaskelainen	38	-	3	41
M Jardel	0 (7)	1	3 (1)	4 (8)
F Laville	4	-	-	4
G Little	0 (4)	-	-	0 (4)
D Livesey	-	2	-	2
J Moreno	1 (7)	-	0 (2)	1 (9)
B N'Gotty	33 (1)	-	6	39 (1)
K Nolan	37	0 (2)	4 (1)	41 (3)
A Okocha	33 (2)	-	5 (1)	38 (3)
J Otsemobor	1	-	-	1
H Pedersen	19 (14)	2	4 (3)	25 (17)
K Poole	-	2	4	6
R Shakes	-	0 (1)	-	0 (1)
J Smith	-	2	-	2
C Taylor	0	0 (1)	-	0 (1)
E Thome	25 (1)	1	5	31 (1)
R Vaz Te	0 (1)	1 (1)	-	1 (2)

Wednesday December 3
LIVERPOOL (a)
Carling Cup, 4th rnd
Won 3-2   HT 1-0   Att 33,185
Poole — Barness, Thome, N'Gotty (Charlton 83), Gardner — Campo — Ba, Okocha, Pedersen — Jardel (Davies 63), Djorkaeff (Nolan 90) *Subs not used* Jaaskelainen, Frandsen
Scorers **Jardel 4, Okocha 79, Djorkaeff 90 (pen)**
Report page 178

Saturday December 6
FULHAM (a)
Lost 1-2   HT 0-0   Att 14,393   Position 12th
Jaaskelainen — Hunt, N'Gotty, Charlton, Gardner — Campo (Ba 89) — Nolan (Jardel 85), Frandsen (Giannakopoulos 82), Okocha, Djorkaeff — Davies *Subs not used* Poole, Thome *Booked* Frandsen, Gardner
Scorer **Davies 53**
Report page 147

Saturday December 13
CHELSEA (a)
Won 2-1   HT 1-1   Att 40,491   Position 10th
Jaaskelainen — Hunt, N'Gotty, Charlton, Gardner — Campo — Nolan (Giannakopoulos 61), Frandsen, Okocha, Djorkaeff (Pedersen 87) — Davies *Subs not used* Poole, Barness, Ba *Booked* Gardner, Frandsen
Scorers **N'Gotty 39, Terry 90 (og)**
Report page 126

Tuesday December 16
SOUTHAMPTON (h)
Carling Cup, quarter-final
Won 1-0 (aet)   HT 0-0   Att 13,957
Bolton leave it late to claim a semi-final place. Pedersen, having missed two good chances, finally finds a way past Niemi with a penalty shoot-out looming after Djorkaeff and Barness, the substitutes, combine at a corner. Southampton create little until the death, when Poole pushes Telfer's shot on to a post.

Poole — Hunt (Barness 110), N'Gotty, Charlton, Gardner — Ba, Campo, Okocha — Giannakopoulos (Djorkaeff 91), Davies (Jardel 77), Pedersen *Subs not used* Jaaskelainen, Nolan *Booked* Gardner, Campo, Giannakopoulos, Davies
Scorer **Pedersen 115**
Referee **P Dowd**

Saturday December 20
ARSENAL (h)
Drew 1-1   HT 0-0   Att 28,003   Position 10th
In front of a record Reebok crowd and on the ground where their title hopes were sunk last season, Arsenal have to be satisfied with a point despite taking the lead through Pires. Okocha hits a post with a free kick before Bolton gain a deserved draw through a fabulous left-foot volley by Pedersen, the substitute.

Jaaskelainen — Hunt, Thome, Charlton, Gardner — Campo (Ba 78) — Nolan (Pedersen 75), Frandsen, Okocha, Djorkaeff — Davies *Subs not used* Poole, Barness, Giannakopoulos *Booked* Campo, Nolan
Scorer **Pedersen 83**
Referee **G Poll**

Friday December 26
LIVERPOOL (a)
Lost 1-3   HT 0-1   Att 42,987   Position 10th
Jaaskelainen — N'Gotty, Thome, Charlton, Gardner — Campo (Ba 51) — Nolan, Frandsen, Okocha (Pedersen 51), Djorkaeff (Giannakopoulos 51) — Davies *Subs not used* Poole, Barness *Booked* Hunt, Frandsen
Scorer **Pedersen 85**
Report page 179

Sunday December 28
LEICESTER CITY (h)
Drew 2-2   HT 1-1   Att 28,353   Position 12th
Relegated to the Leicester substitutes' bench, Ferdinand refuses to sulk, arriving instead to earn a point with a trademark header from Izzet's corner two minutes into stoppage time. Bent gives Micky Adams's team the lead with a fine curling shot from distance, only for Bolton to take control and the lead.

Jaaskelainen — Hunt, N'Gotty, Charlton, Gardner — Campo — Giannakopoulos (Pedersen 76), Nolan, Okocha, Djorkaeff — Davies *Subs not used* Poole, Jardel, Ba, Thome *Booked* Campo
Scorers **N'Gotty 35, Campo 55**
Referee **N Barry**

Saturday January 3 2004
TRANMERE ROVERS (a)
FA Cup, 3rd rnd
Drew 1-1   HT 0-0   Att 10,587
With three regulars suspended and six more rested for what Sam Allardyce says are more important battles ahead, Bolton get the result their manager wants least of all when Nolan cancels out Haworth's goal for the second-division side.

Poole — Hunt (Frandsen ht), Livesey, Thome, Comyn-Platt, Smith (Vaz Te 54) — Ba (Nolan 71), Barness, Giannakopoulos — Facey, Pedersen *Subs not used* Ricketts, Talbot
Scorer **Nolan 78**
Referee **S Bennett**

Wednesday January 7
MANCHESTER UNITED (h)
Lost 1-2   HT 0-2   Att 27,668   Position 13th
Having surrendered four points to Bolton last season, United follow up their 4-0 opening-day win with victory at the Reebok. Scholes and Van Nistelrooy put them on top by half-time and they are worth the points despite Gary Neville heading through his own net for the second time in three weeks.

Jaaskelainen — Hunt, N'Gotty, Charlton, Gardner (Thome 18) — Campo (Ba 81) — Nolan (Moreno 63), Frandsen, Okocha — Davies, Djorkaeff *Subs not used* Giannakopoulos, Poole *Booked* Hunt, Frandsen
Scorer **G Neville 89 (og)**
Referee **D Gallagher**

Saturday January 10
BLACKBURN ROVERS (a)
Won 4-3   HT 2-3   Att 23,538   Position 11th
Jaaskelainen — Hunt, Thome, N'Gotty, Charlton (Moreno 69) — Campo — Nolan, Frandsen (Giannakopoulos 31), Okocha, Djorkaeff — Davies (Pedersen 86) *Subs not used* Barness, Poole *Booked* Hunt, Nolan, Davies
Scorers **Nolan 1, 78, Djorkaeff 43,**
Giannakopoulos 73
Report page 97

Tuesday January 13
TRANMERE ROVERS (h)
FA Cup, 3rd rnd replay
Lost 1-2 (aet; 1-1 after 90min)   HT 0-0   Att 8,759
"The bottom line is, I'm glad we're out." So says Sam Allardyce after his reserves are eliminated by second-division opposition in one of the greatest non-shocks in third-round history. Shakes almost upsets the plan by forcing extra time with a last-minute equaliser, but Hume's glorious winner soon puts Bolton out of their misery.

Poole — Barness, Livesey, Comyn-Platt, Smith — Frandsen — Facey (Taylor 80), Giannakopoulos (Shakes 86), Vaz Te, Pedersen — Jardel (Nolan ht) *Subs not used* Talbot, Ricketts *Booked* Nolan, Taylor
Scorer **Shakes 90**
Referee **H Webb**

MATCH OF THE SEASON

Bolton Wanderers 5   Aston Villa 2
Reebok Stadium, Wednesday January 21 2004
Oliver Kay

JAY-JAY OKOCHA IS A PLAYER whose mesmerising talents demand the biggest stage and so, when he returns next month from playing for Nigeria in the African Nations Cup, he will hope that there is a place at the Millennium Stadium waiting for him.

Whether that would be enough to keep him at Bolton Wanderers in the long term remains uncertain, with his contract due to expire in the summer, but last night he again demonstrated his strength of feeling for the club with a performance, capped with two goals, that put them firmly on course for a place in the Carling Cup final.

It left Sam Allardyce, the Bolton manager, acclaiming Okocha as the greatest player in the club's history — "even better than Nat Lofthouse and the like if we're talking about pure talent" — and describing his second goal, a thunderbolt of a free kick that provided a fitting conclusion to a breathless evening, as the goal of the season. It may have sounded like hyperbole at the end of a night that had sent most of those at the Reebok Stadium into a state of euphoria, but Okocha's display in the first leg of this semi-final was enough to justify that grand billing.

"I've been associated with this club for something like 17 years now and I've never seen anyone better," Allardyce said. "I think the two goals tonight proved what a player he is and what a man he is, having resisted the pressure to go away with Nigeria before now."

Having been asked for a farewell present from his manager, Okocha responded within two minutes, curling a magnificent free kick past Thomas Sorensen, but it was his second goal, another set-piece ten minutes from time, that summed up his night as, from the left-hand edge of the penalty area, he struck the ball with astonishing venom to beat Sorensen at his near post.

In between times there was much else to savour. Bolton built impressively on their early lead, with Kevin Nolan shooting into the bottom corner after running unopposed through the heart of the Villa defence and Stelios Giannakopoulos claiming a spectacular third, beating Sorensen with an overhead kick after Kevin Davies flicked on Bruno N'Gotty's free kick. Davies's more prosaic skills make him the antithesis of Okocha, but he was singled out by David O'Leary for the way in which he unsettled the Villa back four.

Then came the Villa fightback, led by Juan Pablo Angel. As badly as they defended, Villa could feasibly have scored three times themselves in that frenzied start to the game, but they finally got a foothold in the twentieth minute. There seemed little danger as the Colombia forward retrieved the ball from the right-hand touchline, but he slipped the ball through the legs of Davies before lofting it into the far corner from what looked an impossible angle. Villa

Nolan skates away from Delaney in Bolton's crushing first-leg victory

reduced the arrears still further ten minutes into the second half, again through Angel, but this time in controversial circumstances. After Jussi Jaaskelainen, the Bolton goalkeeper, had kept out shots from Lee Hendrie and Darius Vassell in a goalmouth scramble, Vassell's follow-up finally went in via Angel, who, television replays suggested, had been in an offside position no fewer than three times in the build-up.

By this stage the momentum appeared to be with Villa, but Bolton and Okocha roused themselves again. N'Gotty made it 4-2 in the 74th minute with a towering header from Youri Djorkaeff's corner and it was this goal, above all, that upset O'Leary. "It was a horror show defensively for us," the Villa manager said. "It was absolutely disgraceful. We've left ourselves with an Everest to climb in the second leg."

O'Leary claimed that even the fifth goal, Okocha's fabulous strike, was avoidable, but Allardyce begged to differ. "It was awesome, absolutely awesome," the Bolton manager said. "It's vital that we keep Jay-Jay — as long as he doesn't ask for silly money to stay, of course." On last night's evidence, as he put Bolton one step closer to their first piece of significant silverware for 46 years, he is worth his weight in gold.

BOLTON WANDERERS (4-1-2-3): J Jaaskelainen — N Hunt, E Thome, B N'Gotty, A Barness (sub: S Charlton, 63min) — I Campo — K Nolan, A Okocha — S Giannakopoulos (sub: H Pedersen, 69min), K Davies, Y Djorkaeff (sub: I Ba, 84). **Substitutes not used:** K Poole, J Moreno.
ASTON VILLA (4-4-2): T Sorensen — M Delaney, O Mellberg, O Dublin, J Samuel — L Hendrie, G McCann, P Whittingham, G Barry (sub: T Hitzlsperger, 56) — D Vassell (sub: M Allback, 78), J P Angel. **Substitutes not used:** S Postma, U De La Cruz. **Booked:** McCann, Vassell, Hendrie, Dublin.

Saturday January 17
PORTSMOUTH (h)
Won 1-0   HT 0-0   Att 26,558   Position 10th
After a poor first half, a flattering victory for Bolton is secured when Davies turns in Hunt's cross, after which Yakubu hits Jaaskelainen's post. Another poor away-day for Portsmouth is completed when Stefanovic curses his way to an early bath in the final minute after being refused a free kick.

Jaaskelainen — Hunt, Thome, N'Gotty, Barness — Nolan, Campo, Okocha (Giannakopoulos 90) — Moreno (Ba 61), Davies, Djorkaeff (Pedersen 85) *Subs not used* Poole, Charlton *Booked* Okocha
Scorer **Davies 53**
Referee **P Dowd**

Wednesday January 21
ASTON VILLA (h)
Carling Cup, semi-final, 1st leg
Won 5-2   HT 3-1   Att 16,302
Report and details page 332

Tuesday January 27
ASTON VILLA (a)
Carling Cup, semi-final, 2nd leg
Lost 0-2 (won 5-4 on agg)   HT 0-1   Att 36,883
Report and details page 333

Saturday January 31
CHARLTON ATHLETIC (a)
Won 2-1   HT 1-1   Att 26,249   Position 8th
Jaaskelainen — Hunt, Thome, N'Gotty, Barness — Campo — Giannakopoulos (Ba 15), Frandsen, Nolan — Davies (Moreno 69), Pedersen (Charlton 88) *Subs not used* Poole, Vaz Te
Scorers **Pedersen 1, Nolan 78**
Report page 117

Saturday February 7
LIVERPOOL (h)
Drew 2-2   HT 1-0   Att 27,552   Position 9th
Bolton show no signs of losing form as they twice take the lead. Hunt, the full back, follows his first senior goal by blocking a certain reply at the other end, but it is Liverpool who come closest to winning the match, Owen wasting a great chance as his mini-drought continues.

Jaaskelainen — Hunt, Thome, N'Gotty, Barness — Campo — Djorkaeff, Frandsen (Ba 24; Charlton 82), Nolan — Davies, Pedersen *Subs not used* Poole, Otsemobor, Moreno *Booked* Campo, Davies, Thome
Scorers **Nolan 11, Djorkaeff 58**
Referee **A Wiley**

Tuesday February 10
LEICESTER CITY (a)
Drew 1-1   HT 1-1   Att 26,674   Position 8th
Jaaskelainen — Barness, Thome, N'Gotty, Charlton — Campo — Pedersen, Frandsen, Nolan — Davies, Djorkaeff (Moreno 81) *Subs not used* Poole, Ba, Otsemobor, Vaz Te
Booked Nolan, Davies
Scorer **Walker 33 (og)**
Report page 170

Saturday February 21
MANCHESTER CITY (h)
Lost 1-3 HT 1-2 Att 27,301 Position 10th
Fourteen matches and nearly four months without a Premiership win, Manchester City end their torment against the side they put six past in October. Bolton, with half an eye on next week's Carling Cup final, take the lead and waste several other chances, paying when Fowler's double precedes an own goal by Charlton.

Jaaskelainen — Otsemobor (Hunt 69), Howey, Charlton, Barness — Campo — Djorkaeff (Okocha 58), Nolan, Frandsen (Moreno 58), Pedersen — Davies *Subs not used* Poole, N'Gotty
Scorer **Nolan 22**
Referee **S Dunn**

Sunday February 29
MIDDLESBROUGH (Cardiff)
Carling Cup, final
Lost 1-2 HT 1-2 Att 72,634
Report and details page 334

Saturday March 6
BIRMINGHAM CITY (a)
Lost 0-2 HT 0-1 Att 28,003 Position 11th
Jaaskelainen — Hunt, Thome, N'Gotty, Barness — Campo — Nolan, Frandsen (Giannakopoulos 79), Okocha (Ba 64), Djorkaeff (Pedersen 48) — Davies *Subs not used* Poole, Howey *Booked* Hunt
Report page 88

Saturday March 13
CHELSEA (h)
Lost 0-2 HT 0-0 Att 26,717 Position 12th
Chelsea are completely outplayed in the first half, when Ambrosio, their fourth-choice goalkeeper — and Graham Poll, who rejects two Bolton penalty apeals — keep them in the game. Then they show their skill on the counter-attack to register their fifth successive away league win and match Arsenal, with whom they were paired in the European Cup quarter-finals the day before.

Jaaskelainen — Hunt, Thome, N'Gotty, Charlton — Campo — Nolan, Okocha — Giannakopoulos (Ba 77), Davies, Pedersen *Subs not used* Poole, Frandsen, Moreno, Howey *Booked* Thome
Referee **G Poll**

Saturday March 20
ARSENAL (a)
Lost 1-2 HT 1-2 Att 38,053 Position 13th
Jaaskelainen — Hunt, Thome, N'Gotty, Charlton — Campo — Giannakopoulos, Nolan (Frandsen 76), Okocha, Pedersen — Davies *Subs not used* Poole, Barness, Vaz Te, Pezzarossi *Booked* Nolan, Pedersen
Scorer **Campo 41**
Report page 68

THE PLAYERS

IBRAHIM BA (midfield) **Born** January 12, 1973, Dato, Senegal **Ht** 5ft 10in **Wt** 11st 10lb **Signed from** AC Milan, September 2003, free

ANTHONY BARNESS (defender) **Born** February 25, 1973, Lewisham **Ht** 5ft 10in **Wt** 12st 1lb **Signed from** Charlton Athletic, July 2000, free

IVAN CAMPO (defender) **Born** February 21, 1974, San Sebastian, Spain **Ht** 6ft 1in **Wt** 12st 11lb **Signed from** Real Madrid (initial loan), July 2003, free

SIMON CHARLTON (defender) **Born** October 25, 1971, Huddersfield **Ht** 5ft 8in **Wt** 11st 4lb **Signed from** Birmingham City, July 2000, free

CHARLIE COMYN-PLATT (defender) **Born** October 2, 1985, Manchester **Ht** 6ft 2in **Wt** 12st 0lb **Signed from** trainee, July 2003

KEVIN DAVIES (forward) **Born** March 26, 1977, Sheffield **Ht** 6ft 0in **Wt** 12st 10lb **Signed from** Southampton, July 2003, free

YOURI DJORKAEFF (forward) **Born** March 9, 1968, Lyons **Ht** 5ft 10in **Wt** 11st 7lb **Signed from** 1FC Kaiserslautern, February 2002, free

DELROY FACEY (forward) **Born** April 22, 1980, Huddersfield **Ht** 6ft 0in **Wt** 13st 0lb **Signed from** Huddersfield Town, July 2002, free

PER FRANDSEN (midfield) **Born** February 6, 1970, Copenhagen **Ht** 6ft 1in **Wt** 12st 6lb **Signed from** Blackburn Rovers, July 2000, £16m

RICARDO GARDNER (midfield) **Born** September 25, 1978, St Andrews, Jamaica **Ht** 5ft 9in **Wt** 11st 0lb **Signed from** Harbour View, Jamaica, August 1998, £1m

STELIOS GIANNAKOPOULOS (forward) **Born** July 12, 1974, Greece **Ht** 5ft 8in **Wt** 11st 0lb **Signed from** Olympiakos, May 2003, free

STEVE HOWEY (defender) **Born** October 26, 1971, Sunderland **Ht** 6ft 2in **Wt** 13st 5lb **Signed from** Leicester City, January 2004, free

NICKY HUNT (defender) **Born** September 3, 1983, Bolton **Ht** 6ft 0in **Wt** 10st 6lb **Signed from** trainee, August 2000

MARIO JARDEL (forward) **Born** September 18, 1973, Fortaleza, Brazil **Ht** 6ft 2in **Wt** 12st 0lb **Signed from** Sporting Lisbon, August 2003, £15m

JUSSI JAASKELAINEN (goalkeeper) **Born** April 17, 1975, Vaasa, Finland **Ht** 6ft 4in **Wt** 12st 10lb **Signed from** VPS Vaasa, November 1997, £100,000

FLORENT LAVILLE (defender) **Born** August 7, 1973, Valence, France **Ht** 6ft 1in **Wt** 13st 1lb **Signed from** Lyons (initial loan), July 2003, £500,000

DANIEL LIVESEY (defender) **Born** December 31, 1984, Salford **Ht** 6ft 3in **Wt** 13st 1lb **Signed from** trainee, August 2002

GLEN LITTLE (midfield) **Born** October 15, 1975, Wimbledon **Ht** 6ft 3in **Wt** 13st 5lb **Signed from** Burnley (loan), September 2003

JAVI MORENO (forward) **Born** September 10, 1974, Silla, Spain **Ht** 5ft 11in **Wt** 12st 8lb **Signed from** Atletico Madrid (loan), January 2004

BRUNO N'GOTTY (defender) **Born** June 10, 1971, Lyons **Ht** 6ft 1in **Wt** 13st 8lb **Signed from** Marseilles, September 2001, £500,000

KEVIN NOLAN (midfield) **Born** June 24, 1982, Liverpool **Ht** 6ft 1in **Wt** 13st 5lb **Signed from** trainee, January 2000

AGUSTIN OKOCHA (midfield) **Born** August 14, 1973, Enugu, Nigeria **Ht** 5ft 10in **Wt** 11st 0lb **Signed from** Paris Saint-Germain, July 2002, free

JON OTSEMOBOR (defender) **Born** March 23, 1983, Liverpool **Ht** 5ft 10in **Wt** 12st 0lb **Signed from** Liverpool (loan), February 2004

HENRIK PEDERSEN (forward) **Born** June 10, 1975, Denmark **Ht** 6ft 1in **Wt** 13st 5lb **Signed from** Silkeborg, July 2001, £650,000

KEVIN POOLE (goalkeeper) **Born** July 21, 1963, Bromsgrove **Ht** 5ft 10in **Wt** 12st 11lb **Signed from** Birmingham City, October 2001, free

RICKY SHAKES (forward) **Born** January 25, 1985, Brixton **Ht** 5ft 10in **Wt** 12st 0lb **Signed from** trainee, January 2004

JEFF SMITH (midfield) **Born** June 28, 1980, Middlesbrough **Ht** 5ft 10in **Wt** 11st 8lb **Signed from** Bishop Auckland, March 2001, free

CLEVELAND TAYLOR (midfield) **Born** September 9, 1983, Leicester **Ht** 5ft 8in **Wt** 10st 8lb **Signed from** trainee, August 2000

EMERSON THOME (defender) **Born** March 30, 1972, Porto Alegre, Brazil **Ht** 6ft 1in **Wt** 13st 4lb **Signed from** Sunderland, August 2003, free

RICARDO VAZ TE (forward) **Born** October 1, 1986, Lisbon **Ht** 6ft 0in **Wt** 11st 8lb **Signed from** Farense, August 2003, free

STATS AND FACTS

- Bolton achieved their highest league placing since 1959-60, when they finished sixth in the old first division.

- Jay-Jay Okocha had 110 shots at goal in the Premiership without scoring.

- Bolton's win away to Chelsea in December ended a run of nine successive defeats at Stamford Bridge.

- Wanderers conceded six goals in a league game for the first time in eight years when they lost 6-2 away to Manchester City in October.

- Bolton have won none of their past 12 matches away to Newcastle United.

- Marks for good behaviour — Bolton were the only team to avoid a red card in the Premiership last season.

Bill Edgar

GOALSCORERS

	Prem	FAC	CC	Total
I Campo	4	-	-	4
K Davies	9	-	1	10
Y Djorkaeff	7 (1p)	-	1 (p)	8 (2p)
P Frandsen	1	-	-	1
S Giannakopoulos	2	-	2	4
N Hunt	1	-	-	1
M Jardel	-	-	3	3
B N'Gotty	3	-	1	4
K Nolan	10	1	2	13
A Okocha	-	-	3	3
H Pedersen	7	-	2	9
R Shakes	-	1	-	1
Own goals	4	-	-	4

Sunday March 28
NEWCASTLE UNITED (h)
Won 1-0 HT 1-0 Att 27,360 Position 13th
After five successive defeats, Bolton halt their slide towards the relegation zone courtesy of a freak early goal from Pedersen, who lobs the ball in from wide on the left. Bellamy and Bramble are guilty of bad misses for Newcastle as chances come at both ends, with Given the busier goalkeeper.

Jaaskelainen — Hunt (Frandsen 70), Thome, N'Gotty (Howey ht), Charlton — Campo — Giannakopoulos, Nolan, Okocha, Pedersen — Davies *Subs not used* Poole, Vaz Te, Pezzarossi *Booked* N'Gotty
Scorer **Pedersen 4**
Referee **M Dean**

Saturday April 3
MIDDLESBROUGH (a)
Lost 0-2 HT 0-1 Att 30,107 Position 13th
Jaaskelainen — Hunt, Howey, Thome, Barness — Nolan (Frandsen 56), Campo (Vaz Te 66), Okocha, Giannakopoulos — Davies (Moreno 56), Pedersen *Subs not used* Poole, Charlton *Booked* Hunt, Okocha
Report page 215

Saturday April 10
ASTON VILLA (h)
Drew 2-2 HT 0-1 Att 26,374 Position 12th
Bolton's sixth defeat in seven games looms when Crouch heads in at the far post and again when Hendrie lobs Jaaskelainen, but Pedersen and — four minutes from time — Davies earn a point. David O'Leary criticises Whittingham for shooting wide instead of passing to unmarked colleagues with Villa 2-1 up.

Jaaskelainen — Barness, N'Gotty, Thome, Charlton (Hunt ht) — Djorkaeff (Giannakopoulos 82), Nolan (Campo 80), Frandsen, Okocha — Pedersen, Davies *Subs not used* Poole, Moreno *Booked* Campo
Scorers **Pedersen 48, Davies 86**
Referee **M Messias**

Monday April 12
WOLVERHAMPTON WANDERERS (a)
Won 2-1 HT 1-1 Att 28,695 Position 12th
Jaaskelainen — Hunt, Thome, N'Gotty, Barness — Campo — Giannakopoulos (Djorkaeff 76), Frandsen (Okocha 61), Nolan, Pedersen — Davies *Subs not used* Poole, Charlton, Moreno *Booked* N'Gotty
Scorers **Pedersen 43, Davies 90**
Report page 267

Saturday April 17
TOTTENHAM HOTSPUR (h)
Won 2-0 HT 1-0 Att 26,440 Position 12th
The nightmare scenario — Arsenal winning the title at White Hart Lane next Sunday — looms larger for Spurs after this conclusive loss. They create virtually nothing as they suffer their fifth successive away defeat. Campo, from 25 yards, and Pedersen, after Gardner's slip, ensure that David Pleat's team are not safe yet.

Jaaskelainen — Hunt (Barness 77), Thome, N'Gotty, Charlton — Campo — Okocha (Frandsen 85), Nolan — Djorkaeff (Giannakopoulos 86), Pedersen, Davies *Subs not used* Poole, Moreno *Booked* Campo
Scorers **Campo 7, Pedersen 66**
Referee **J Winter**

PLAYER OF THE SEASON
Ivan Campo

It has been a delight to watch Ivan Campo complete his transformation from Real Madrid reject to Bolton hero. After his shaky start as a central defender in 2002, some pundits suggested that his act was more suited to a circus ring than a football stadium. Well, he is a bit of a tightrope walker: when he gets the ball on the edge of the Bolton box, you have the feeling that anything could happen, even with the safety net of the back four. But the hint of impending disaster is all part of the entertainment. He is a thrilling performer with excellent close control and a fabulous passing ability. It is players such as him who make football the greatest show on earth.
Alan Kay

Saturday April 24
SOUTHAMPTON (a)
Won 2-1   HT 0-1   Att 31,712   Position 10th
Jaaskelainen — Barness (Hunt ht), Thome, N'Gotty, Charlton — Nolan, Campo, Okocha, Djorkaeff (Giannakopoulos 77) — Davies, Pedersen (Frandsen 50) *Subs not used* Ricketts, Moreno *Booked* Thome, Campo, Nolan
Scorers **Nolan 77, Davies 78**
Report page 247

Sunday May 2
LEEDS UNITED (h)
Won 4-1   HT 0-1   Att 27,420   Position 7th
A fittingly shambolic end for Leeds: thrown a lifeline with Viduka's penalty, awarded for Thome's foul on Smith, they toss it away when the Australia striker's senseless dismissal for two crazy bookings is followed by a second-half collapse and their effective relegation. Smith ends the match in tears; Bolton in seventh heaven.

Jaaskelainen — Hunt, Thome (Barness 38), N'Gotty, Charlton — Campo — Djorkaeff, Nolan, Okocha, Pedersen (Moreno 69) — Davies (Giannakopoulos 84) *Subs not used* Poole, Frandsen *Booked* Hunt, Thome, Davies
Scorers **Djorkaeff 47, 53, Harte 55 (og), Nolan 78**
Referee **S Bennett**

Saturday May 8
EVERTON (a)
Won 2-1   HT 1-0   Att 40,190   Position 7th
Jaaskelainen — Hunt (Barness 83), Thome, N'Gotty, Charlton — Nolan (Gardner 85), Campo, Okocha, Pedersen (Frandsen 63) — Djorkaeff, Davies *Subs not used* Poole, Giannakopoulos
Scorer **Djorkaeff 14, 87**
Report page 142

Saturday May 15
FULHAM (h)
Lost 0-2   HT 0-1   Att 27,383   Position 8th
The victory that gives Fulham the best league placing in their history is achieved with two goals from McBride at the end of rare forays into Bolton territory. Home disappointment — especially for Davies, who wastes three clear chances — is eased as Bolton finish an equally fine campaign in their highest Premiership place.

Jaaskelainen — Hunt, Thome, N'Gotty, Charlton (Gardner ht) — Frandsen (Giannakopoulos 72), Campo, Okocha, Nolan — Djorkaeff (Pedersen 58) — Davies *Subs not used* Ricketts, Barness *Booked* Davies
Referee **G Barber**

CHARLTON ATHLETIC

PREMIERSHIP

	P	W	D	L	F	A	GD	Pts
Arsenal	38	26	12	0	73	26	47	**90**
Chelsea	38	24	7	7	67	30	37	**79**
Man Utd	38	23	6	9	64	35	29	**75**
Liverpool	38	16	12	10	55	37	18	**60**
Newcastle	38	13	17	8	52	40	12	**56**
Aston Villa	38	15	11	12	48	44	4	**56**
Charlton	38	14	11	13	51	51	0	**53**
Bolton	38	14	11	13	48	56	-8	**53**
Fulham	38	14	10	14	52	46	6	**52**
Birmingham	38	12	14	12	43	48	-5	**50**
Middlesbro	38	13	9	16	44	52	-8	**48**
Southampton	38	12	11	15	44	45	-1	**47**
Portsmouth	38	12	9	17	47	54	-7	**45**
Tottenham	38	13	6	19	47	57	-10	**45**
Blackburn	38	12	8	18	51	59	-8	**44**
Man City	38	9	14	15	55	54	1	**41**
Everton	38	9	12	17	45	57	-12	**39**
Leicester	38	6	15	17	48	65	-17	**33**
Leeds	38	8	9	21	40	79	-39	**33**
Wolves	38	7	12	19	38	77	-39	**33**

FA CUP
Third round

CARLING CUP
Third round

Yellow peril : Matt Holland is
ecstatic after scoring one of his two
goals in Charlton's victory over
Birmingham City at St Andrew's

THE GAMES

Sunday August 17 2003
MANCHESTER CITY (h)
Lost 0-3   HT 0-2   Att 25,780   Position 18th
Introduced to the Charlton crowd beforehand,
Di Canio sees his new side destroyed by Anelka, who
converts an early penalty — awarded for Parker's foul
on Wright-Phillips — and sets up Sibierski and Sun in
City's romp. Charlton are 2-0 down and almost out
before Fish is sent off for pulling Fowler back by the
shirt.

Royce — Rowett, Fish, Hreidarsson — Kishishev
(Young ht), Holland, Parker, Konchesky — Euell —
Lisbie (Johansson 78), Bartlett (Jensen ht) *Subs not
used* Leite, Fortune *Booked* Konchesky, Euell *Sent off*
Fish 71
Referee **M Dean**

Saturday August 23
WOLVERHAMPTON WANDERERS (a)
Won 4-0   HT 4-0   Att 27,327   Position 7th
Kiely — Young, Fortune, Fish, Hreidarsson — Kishishev
(Stuart 88), Holland, Parker, Jensen (Di Canio 79) —
Bartlett (Cole 77), Euell *Subs not used* Royce, Powell
Booked Parker *Sent off* Parker 71
Scorers **Euell 5, Jensen 15, Bartlett 25, 33**
Report page 260

Tuesday August 26
EVERTON (h)
Drew 2-2   HT 1-1   Att 26,336   Position 7th
David Moyes alleges a "vendetta" by officials after
Rooney's booking for a foul on Parker. Steve Dunn, the
referee, further riles Everton by awarding Charlton two
penalties, both converted by Euell. Rooney has the last
word, though, with a well-taken equaliser, Watson's goal
having kept Everton in the game.

Kiely — Young, Fish, Fortune, Hreidarsson — Kishishev
(Stuart 75), Holland, Parker, Jensen — Bartlett (Cole 74),
Euell *Subs not used* Royce, Powell, Johansson *Booked*
Jensen
Scorer **Euell 25 (pen), 49 (pen)**
Referee **S Dunn**

Saturday August 30
BOLTON WANDERERS (a)
Drew 0-0   HT 0-0   Att 23,098   Position 10th
Kiely — Young, Fortune, Fish, Hreidarsson — Kishishev,
Holland, Parker, Jensen (Lisbie 78) — Bartlett
(Johansson 66), Euell *Subs not used* Royce, Powell,
Stuart *Booked* Hreidarsson, Fortune
Report page 102

THAT FANS WERE LEFT DISAPPOINTED by the club's highest Premiership finish is an indication of just how far Charlton have come. Of course, there was pleasure and pride in what was undeniably a fine season. But there was also a frustration. The question on many lips when the final whistle blew on the last Saturday was: "What if Scott Parker had not been sold?"

The campaign turned on his departure and, for once, the stats tell a story. When Parker left for Chelsea at the end of January, Charlton had won ten and lost five out of 22 league games. With victories over Liverpool and Chelsea and a draw against Arsenal under their belts, it looked as if they genuinely might be the fourth-best side in the country. Once Parker had gone, they went on to lose eight and win only four of their last 16 matches. True, there were some memorable days without him, including a first win at Anfield in half a century. But far from that result heralding a revival, they failed to win again until the last day of the season. In the end, it was the inability of Charlton's main rivals to put a consistent run together that was to thank for a final position of seventh.

Asked to explain why — not for the first time — Charlton's season fell away in the latter stages, Alan Curbishley admitted that Parker's loss had been "a big hit". But he went on to suggest that a lack of fit bodies and insufficient depth in the squad were equally significant factors. Such protestations only made it all the more frustrating that the mishandled timing of Parker's sale meant there had been no opportunity to reinvest Chelsea's millions before the transfer window closed again. The money was left sitting in the bank for the last four months of the season.

Yet a poor finish should not be allowed to take the gloss off what, overall, was a magnificent season. Whereas mere survival in the top flight would, only two or three years ago, have been a cause for great rejoicing, last season there was an expectation of success around The Valley — although oddly, that became the place where it most stubbornly refused to come. Charlton had a better away record than Liverpool. Their home form was worse than that of Wolverhampton Wanderers. A couple of less nervy performances in front of the home fans and the club would surely have finished in the fourth spot it so proudly occupied for a lengthy spell in mid-season.

When you look at the squad and its lack of "name" players, Curbishley's achievement appears even more remarkable. Dean Kiely had another fine season in goal and it was no surprise that he won the fans' vote as player of the season. The defence was invariably well organised, although it often had a makeshift look. Chris Perry initially came in as a stop-gap loan signing, but with

HONOURS BOARD

Richard Rufus and Gary Rowett out all season and Mark Fish also sidelined in the latter stages, for a while he unexpectedly found himself the pivotal figure in the centre of the defence until he, too, was injured. Hermann Hreidarsson was a powerful force and Jon Fortune was a wholehearted performer, but Luke Young struggled with form and fitness, Chris Powell was clearly past his best and the inconsistent Radostin Kishishev and the gifted but unsettled Paul Konchesky were unsatisfyingly shuttled around the pitch.

The engine of Charlton's success was their midfield. The quartet of Parker, the cultured Claus Jensen, the tireless Jason Euell and the admirable Matt Holland, with a rejuvenated Graham Stuart as a further option, often played some flowing and creative football, even if the fans at times would have favoured a little more width of the kind that John Robinson used to lend.

Up front was more problematic. Paolo Di Canio at first appeared an inspirational figure, but by two-thirds of the way through the campaign he was showing his years. All of his four Premiership goals came from penalties (one of them on the rebound) and in the latter stages some of his most telling contributions were restricted to cameos from the bench. Carlton Cole, on an extended two-year loan from Chelsea, was strong and robust, but the manager clearly regarded him as a rookie and he was given a limited number of starts.

Both Jonatan Johansson and Shaun Bartlett had their moments, but it was Euell who comfortably ended as top scorer, even though he was seldom played as a striker. The biggest disappointment was the injury to Kevin Lisbie. The Jamaica striker has always possessed

Saturday September 13
MANCHESTER UNITED (h)
Lost 0-2   HT 0-0   Att 26,078   Position 12th
Not for the first time, Van Nistelrooy is the difference for United, his two scruffy second-half goals, both scored from close range, seeing off Charlton. The home team do not help their own cause when Euell, booked in the first minute for a trip on Howard, catches Gary Neville late and sees red.

Kiely — Kishishev, Fortune, Perry, Powell — Stuart, Holland (Bartlett 77), Parker (Lisbie 88), Jensen — Di Canio (Johansson 84) — Euell *Subs not used* Royce, Sankofa *Booked* Kishishev, Euell *Sent off* Euell 65
Referee **M Riley**

Saturday September 20
ASTON VILLA (a)
Lost 1-2   HT 0-1   Att 31,410   Position 15th
Kiely — Young, Fortune, Fish, Powell — Kishishev (Stuart 59), Holland, Parker, Jensen — Bartlett, Di Canio (Lisbie 82) *Subs not used* Johansson, Royce, Perry *Booked* Young, Fortune
Scorer **Lisbie 86**
Report page 73

Tuesday September 23
LUTON TOWN (h)
Carling Cup, 2nd rnd
Drew 4-4 (aet; 3-3 after 90min; won 8-7 on pens)
HT 1-2   Att 10,905
The goalkeepers have been beaten 23 times and it is approaching 11pm when Kiely finally settles this tie with the first save of the penalty shoot-out, from Coyne. Trailing 2-0 and 3-1, a full-strength Charlton side need Di Canio's first goal for the club, in the last minute, to force Luton into extra time.

Kiely — Young, Fortune, Fish, Powell (Euell 83) — Stuart (Johansson 68), Holland, Parker, Jensen — Lisbie (Campbell-Ryce 88), Di Canio *Subs not used* Leite, Rufus
Scorers **Parker 41, Lisbie 58, Di Canio 90, Jensen 95**
Referee **P Armstrong**

Sunday September 28
LIVERPOOL (h)
Won 3-2   HT 2-1   Att 26,508   Position 12th
Previously booed by his own fans, Lisbie wins them over in brilliant style and leaves Gerard Houllier distraught at Liverpool's "undeserved loss". At 2-2 and with seven minutes left, Lisbie sets off on a run from deep in his own half, but only has to beat one challenge, from Finnan, before completing the first hat-trick of his senior career.

Kiely — Young, Perry, Fish (Fortune 75), Powell — Stuart (Kishishev 72), Holland, Parker, Jensen — Lisbie (Johansson 90), Bartlett *Subs not used* Royce, Di Canio *Booked* Kishishev, Young
Scorer **Lisbie 31, 43, 83**
Referee **R Styles**

Saturday October 4
PORTSMOUTH (a)
Won 2-1   HT 0-1   Att **20,106**   Position **9th**
Kiely — Young, Perry, Fish (Fortune 65), Powell — Stuart,
Parker, Holland, Jensen (Di Canio 65) — Lisbie, Bartlett
Subs not used Royce, Kishishev, Johansson *Booked*
Bartlett, Perry
Scorers **Fortune 77, Bartlett 90**
Report page 231

Monday October 20
BLACKBURN ROVERS (a)
Won 1-0   HT 1-0   Att **19,939**   Position **7th**
Kiely — Young (Kishishev 19), Fish, Perry,
Hreidarsson — Holland, Parker, Jensen, Stuart —
Johansson (Euell 69), Di Canio (Fortune 87) *Subs not
used* Royce, Powell
Scorer **Hreidarsson 33**
Report page 94

Sunday October 26
ARSENAL (h)
Drew 1-1   HT 1-1   Att **26,660**   Position **9th**
The biter bit: after Pires's shenanigans against
Portsmouth the previous month, Arsenal are on the
receiving end when Holland makes the most of minimal
contact from Lauren to win a penalty, impudently
converted by Di Canio. Henry, though, shoots Arsenal
back to the top with a trademark free kick, his eighth
goal in six games against Charlton.

Kiely — Kishishev, Perry, Fish, Hreidarsson — Stuart,
Holland, Parker, Jensen — Johansson
(Campbell-Ryce 76), Di Canio (Euell 45) *Subs not used*
Powell, Royce, Fortune *Booked* Parker
Scorer **Di Canio 27 (pen)**
Referee **S Dunn**

Wednesday October 29
EVERTON (a)
Carling Cup, 3rd rnd
Lost 0-1   HT 0-1   Att **24,863**
Kiely — Kishishev, Fish (Fortune ht), Perry, Hreidarsson —
Holland (Campbell-Ryce 81), Parker, Jensen, Stuart
(Svensson 72) — Johansson, Euell *Subs not used* Royce,
Powell *Booked* Parker
Report page 136

Monday November 3
BIRMINGHAM CITY (a)
Won 2-1   HT 1-0   Att **27,225**   Position **7th**
Kiely — Kishishev, Perry, Fish, Hreidarsson — Holland,
Parker, Jensen, Stuart (Fortune 84) — Euell (Lisbie 68),
Johansson (Svensson 74) *Subs not used* Powell, Royce
Booked Parker
Scorer **Holland 11, 59**
Report page 84

With a precise, cool finish, Kevin Lisbie completes his hat-trick and secures a thrilling victory over Liverpool at The Valley in September

a blistering turn of pace that several Premiership defenders rate behind only Owen and Henry, but his development for several seasons was hindered by a lack of composure in front of goal. A wonderful hat-trick against Liverpool in late September, as part of a spree of five goals in nine days, suggested a significant corner had been turned. Soon after, he injured his back and, after just five Premiership starts, he was not seen again.

Even when not forced to do so, Curbishley chopped and changed his attacking options in a way that indicated he did not have confidence in any of his forwards as reliable goalscorers. Ultimately, half a dozen in-and-out strikers who might score four or five apiece are no substitute for an automatic first-choice marksman who can guarantee 15 to 20 goals a season. But then Charlton are far from the only Premiership club to rue the lack of such a superhero.

The one encouraging aspect of the Parker debacle was that it showed how close Charlton are to being not just a good side but a very fine one. After decades of mediocrity, Curbishley has instilled an organisation and attitude that are the envy of many so-called bigger clubs and he is particularly skilled at getting his players to punch above their weight. The message is surely that, with the addition of just one or two genuine big hitters, Charlton next term really could be challenging for a place in Europe.

THE MANAGER   Alan Curbishley

He has now been there so long that Charlton without Alan Curbishley is almost unthinkable. Yet during the season, questions were asked of the club's most successful manager in more than 50 years. For the fifth consecutive season, Charlton ended the campaign not with a surge but a limp. The cup record is so abysmal that it seems lower-division opponents are virtually guaranteed a giant-killing path to the next round. And there were those who felt that the Scott Parker affair was bungled. That said, Curbishley has worked footballing miracles and the job is his for life, if he wants it.

Nigel Williamson

APPEARANCES

	Prem	FAC	CC	Total
S Bartlett	13 (6)	-	-	13 (6)
J Campbell-Ryce	0 (2)	-	0 (2)	0 (4)
C Cole	8 (13)	1	-	9 (13)
P Di Canio	23 (8)	1	1	25 (8)
J Euell	24 (7)	0 (1)	1 (1)	25 (9)
M Fish	23	-	2	25
J Fortune	21 (7)	1	1 (1)	23 (8)
M Holland	38	1	2	41
H Hreidarsson	33	1	1	35
C Jensen	27 (4)	1	2	30 (4)
J Johansson	16 (10)	1	1 (1)	18 (11)
D Kiely	37	1	2	40
R Kishishev	30 (3)	1	1	32 (3)
P Konchesky	17 (4)	1	-	18 (4)
K Lisbie	5 (4)	-	1	6 (4)
S Parker	20	-	2	22
C Perry	25 (4)	1	1	27 (4)
C Powell	11 (5)	-	1	12 (5)
G Rowett	1	-	-	1
S Royce	1	-	-	1
G Stuart	23 (5)	1	2	26 (5)
M Svensson	1 (2)	-	0 (1)	1 (3)
J Thomas	0 (1)	-	-	0 (1)
L Young	21 (3)	-	1	22 (3)

Saturday November 8
FULHAM (h)
Won 3-1   **HT 1-0**   Att **26,344**   Position **4th**
Charlton's best start to a season for 40 years puts them in a Champions League place. Stuart gets his first goal for nearly two years and Johansson ends a 15-match scoreless streak before Davis, off the transfer list at Fulham, replies. Parker is again influential in Charlton's midfield, two days before Sven-Goran Eriksson names his England squad for the match against Denmark.

Kiely — Kishishev, Perry, Fish, Hreidarsson — Holland, Parker (Powell 80), Jensen (Euell 39), Stuart — Lisbie (Di Canio 85) — Johansson *Subs not used* Royce, Sankofa *Booked* Perry
Scorers **Stuart 10, Johansson 69, 76**
Referee **A D'Urso**

Saturday November 22
LEICESTER CITY (a)
Drew 1-1   **HT 0-1**   Att **30,242**   Position **4th**
Kiely — Fish (Svensson 17), Perry, Fortune, Hreidarsson — Kishishev, Euell, Holland, Stuart — Lisbie (Cole 64), Di Canio (Powell 88) *Subs not used* Royce, Hughes *Booked* Hreidarsson
Scorer **Di Canio 84 (pen)**
Report page 167

Saturday November 29
LEEDS UNITED (h)
Lost 0-1   **HT 0-1**   Att **26,445**   Position **4th**
Alan Curbishley's 400th match in charge of Charlton ends in a shock defeat against the bottom club as Eddie Gray is rewarded for dropping a number of Leeds's loan signings with a rare victory. Viduka finds Milner in space for the early winner and also has two shots cleared off the line. Holland hits the post with a header for Charlton.

Kiely — Kishishev (Fortune 88), Fish, Perry, Hreidarsson — Holland, Parker, Jensen (Campbell-Ryce 71), Stuart — Svensson (Cole ht), Euell *Subs not used* Leite, Powell *Booked* Kishishev, Parker
Referee **M Halsey**

Sunday December 7
SOUTHAMPTON (a)
Lost 2-3   **HT 0-2**   Att **30,513**   Position **6th**
Kiely — Kishishev, Fortune, Perry, Hreidarsson — Holland, Parker, Jensen, Stuart — Euell, Di Canio (Cole 76) *Subs not used* Royce, Sankofa, Powell, Svensson
Scorer **Parker 46, 65**
Report page 243

Saturday December 13
MIDDLESBROUGH (a)
Drew 0-0   **HT 0-0**   Att **26,721**   Position **7th**
Kiely — Kishishev, Fortune, Perry, Hreidarsson — Holland, Parker, Jensen, Stuart — Euell, Di Canio *Subs not used* Royce, Powell, Johansson, Turner, Cole *Booked* Hreidarsson
Report page 211

NEWCASTLE UNITED (h)
Drew 0-0   **HT 0-0**   **Att 26,508**   Position **6th**
Goalless draws are rarely as entertaining as this one.
Given, with a series of superb stops, pips Kiely to the
man-of-the-match award, the Charlton keeper saving
brilliantly from Robert as the battle for fourth place
resumes. Euell goes closest to a winner when he hits a
post in the first half.

Kiely — Kishishev, Fortune, Perry, Hreidarsson — Holland,
Parker, Jensen, Stuart — Euell, Di Canio (Cole 78) *Subs
not used* Royce, Powell, Johansson, Turner
Referee **S Bennett**

Friday December 26
CHELSEA (h)
Won 4-2   **HT 2-1**   **Att 26,768**   Position **5th**
The biggest crowd at The Valley since Charlton's return
11 years ago — plus a richly entertained lunchtime
television audience — see a Chelsea team recruited
for £108 million outplayed by one that cost a mere
£14 million. Behind after 42 seconds to
Hreidarsson's header, Chelsea slip to their third defeat
in four games.

Kiely — Kishishev, Fortune, Perry, Hreidarsson — Holland,
Parker, Euell, Stuart (Konchesky 77) — Johansson,
Di Canio (Powell 87) *Subs not used* Royce, Fish,
Campbell-Ryce *Booked* Parker
Scorers **Hreidarsson 1, Holland 35, Johansson 48,
Euell 53**
Referee **G Poll**

Sunday December 28
TOTTENHAM HOTSPUR (a)
Won 1-0   **HT 0-0**   **Att 34,534**   Position **4th**
Kiely — Kishishev, Fish, Perry, Hreidarsson — Holland,
Euell, Parker, Konchesky — Di Canio, Johansson (Cole ht)
Subs not used Powell, Stuart, Fortune, Royce
Scorer **Cole 69**
Report page 254

Saturday January 3 2004
GILLINGHAM (a)
FA Cup, 3rd rnd
Lost 2-3   **HT 1-3**   **Att 10,894**
Fourth in the Premiership, against a team forced to field
their fourth-choice goalkeeper, and then handed an own
goal after 35 seconds, Charlton are the biggest
fall-guys on third-round day as they are outbattled by
Gillingham. Bossu, the first-division side's French
stopper, bursts into tears in the dressing-room
afterwards.

Kiely — Kishishev (Euell 64), Fortune, Perry (Di Canio 57),
Hreidarsson — Stuart, Holland, Jensen, Konchesky — Cole,
Johansson *Subs not used* Fish, Royce, Hughes
Scorers **Cox 1 (og), Cole 90**
Referee **J Winter**

THE ✦ TIMES

MATCH OF THE SEASON

Charlton Athletic 4   Chelsea 2
The Valley, Friday December 26 2003
Tom Dart

AT LAST THERE WAS SOMETHING worth watching on
television this Christmas as Charlton Athletic put four goals past
Chelsea in a thrilling live lunchtime game. The scoreline was
stunning, yet no less noteworthy was that a two-goal margin of
victory was the least that Charlton deserved.

The assumption in August was that Chelsea's kinks would be
ironed out as time wore on, that their constellation of stars would
shine as understanding and familiarity developed. Displays such as
this appear to belie that notion. Frank Lampard and Joe Cole orbited
the centre circle to no real effect. Until Eidur Gudjohnsen's arrival
after half-time only Adrian Mutu, intermittently, dazzled. Communi-
cation between team-mates seemed to mean berating each other.

One theory about the origins of Boxing Day claims that it was an
occasion for the wealthy to give presents to those less well-off.
Charlton's fine performance was certainly aided by the generosity of
their opponents' defence. Chelsea's back four were uniformly awful.
Reliable rocks such as John Terry were reduced to jelly by the wit of
Paolo Di Canio and the will of his eager team-mates. Marcel
Desailly looked dizzy. In midfield, Lampard was utterly outshone by
Parker, a fellow contender for a place in England's European
Championship squad and a summer Chelsea transfer target.

Call it hunger, motivation, passion, desire, whatever — Charlton
had it, Chelsea did not. Physically assertive from the off, they bullied
and harried their opponents and Chelsea submitted. Claudio Ranieri
could have assembled a team culled from the lower reaches of the
Nationwide League for £111,000 rather than one hatched after a
£111 million trolley dash around Europe's elite and it might have
performed with more credit in the second half.

Roman Abramovich, the owner, sitting in the stands, wore a wan
grin-cum-grimace; around him swirled joy and perhaps a little
disbelief as Charlton carved Chelsea apart. Charlton's home record
before yesterday was no better than that of Wolverhampton
Wanderers, with only two wins, and Alan Curbishley, the manager,
emphasised the importance of three points in front of their own
fans. "We needed to win a game here, it was getting a bit of a
problem. Can we push on now?" he wondered. Charlton are fifth, 12
points behind Chelsea in third. No one could accuse Curbishley of
unrealistic ambitions. "I think Liverpool and Newcastle will be
fourth and fifth," he said. "We think we can get in the top half." They
were excellent yesterday and can surely do more than that.

There was barely time to digest any turkey leftovers before
Charlton took the lead. Only 42 seconds had gone when Di Canio's
corner was headed in by Hermann Hreidarsson, who rose above

Hreidarsson's fine header after just 42 seconds puts Charlton ahead

Terry in the six-yard box. Six days earlier, against Newcastle United, Di Canio was subdued, surly. Yesterday he was energised, not enervated, inspirational, not confrontational.

Inside ten minutes, Terry compensated for his defensive failure with a moment of attacking prowess. He directed Mutu's free kick into the net with a glancing header for the equaliser. Charlton reclaimed the lead ten minutes before the break. Di Canio's dummy set Jonatan Johansson clear on the left, though there was more than a hint of offside. Johansson crossed and Matt Holland rose above Desailly to thud in a header.

Early in the second half, Parker sprayed the ball out to Di Canio on the left and he twisted and turned Terry. Just as it seemed that the Italian would lose control, he crossed to the far post, where Johansson evaded scandalously static defending to tap in Charlton's third. Five minutes later, Wayne Bridge's hapless clearance dropped kindly for Jason Euell, who thundered in a low drive for the fourth. Chelsea were embarrassed into action. Gudjohnsen scored in the 73rd minute — Dean Kiely saved from Mutu, but Charlton failed to clear and the forward thumped the ball in. Charlton, though, closed the occasion out in front of 26,768, the biggest crowd since the return to The Valley 11 years ago.

CHARLTON ATHLETIC (4-4-2): D Kiely — R Kishishev, J Fortune, C Perry, H Hreidarsson — M Holland, S Parker, J Euell, G Stuart (sub: P Konchesky, 77min) — P Di Canio (sub: C Powell, 87), J Johansson. **Substitutes not used:** S Royce, M Fish, J Campbell-Ryce. **Booked:** Parker.
CHELSEA (4-4-2): C Cudicini — G Johnson, M Desailly, J Terry, W Bridge — J Cole (sub: W Gallas, 82), F Lampard (sub: Geremi, 65), C Makelele, J Gronkjaer (sub: E Gudjohnsen, 46) — A Mutu, J F Hasselbaink. **Substitutes not used:** N Sullivan, M Melchiot. **Booked:** Gronkjaer.

Wednesday January 7
MANCHESTER CITY (a)
Drew 1-1 HT **0-1** Att **44,307** Position **4th**
Kiely — Kishishev, Fish, Perry, Hreidarsson — Holland, Euell (Stuart 80), Parker, Konchesky (Cole 61) — Johansson (Jensen 74), Di Canio *Subs not used* Royce, Fortune
Scorer **Di Canio 84**
Report page 191

Saturday January 10
WOLVERHAMPTON WANDERERS (h)
Won 2-0 HT **1-0** Att **26,148** Position **4th**
Dave Jones is back in charge of Wolves after a bout of flu, but his luckless side are now eight points adrift of safety. Kiely is much the busier goalkeeper. Euell is contentiously adjudged onside for Charlton's opener and gets the credit for the second goal after Irwin's intended clearance flies in off him.

Kiely — Kishishev, Fish, Perry, Hreidarsson — Holland, Parker, Euell, Stuart (Konchesky 82) — Johansson, Di Canio (Cole 82) *Subs not used* Royce, Jensen, Fortune
Booked Euell
Scorer **Euell 38, 79**
Referee **R Styles**

Saturday January 17
EVERTON (a)
Won 1-0 HT **1-0** Att **36,322** Position **4th**
Kiely — Kishishev, Fish, Perry, Hreidarsson — Stuart (Young 90), Holland, Euell, Konchesky — Cole (Johansson 74), Di Canio (Fortune 86) *Subs not used* Jensen, Royce *Booked* Kishishev, Perry
Scorer **Stuart 41**
Report page 139

Saturday January 31
BOLTON WANDERERS (h)
Lost 1-2 HT **1-1** Att **26,249** Position **4th**
Through to the Carling Cup final and now up to eighth in the Premiership, life could hardly be better for Bolton, who take the lead inside 25 seconds and win through Nolan's sweet swivelled volley. Life without Parker for Charlton, though, begins ominously after his £10 million move to Chelsea two days earlier.

Kiely — Kishishev, Fish, Perry, Hreidarsson — Stuart, Holland, Euell (Cole 32), Jensen (Konchesky 74) — Johansson, Di Canio *Subs not used* Royce, Young, Fortune
Scorer **Johansson 12**
Referee **A D'Urso**

Sunday February 8
CHELSEA (a)
Lost 0-1 HT **0-1** Att **41,255** Position **5th**
Kiely — Kishishev, Fish, Perry, Hreidarsson — Stuart (Young 42), Holland, Jensen, Konchesky (Bartlett 76) — Di Canio, Johansson *Subs not used* Leite, Fortune, Hughes
Report page 128

Wednesday February 11
TOTTENHAM HOTSPUR (h)
Lost 2-4 HT 0-2 Att 26,660 Position 6th
After 3-4 and 4-3 scorelines in their previous two matches, Spurs settle for the comparatively mundane, just a 4-2 win at The Valley. Defoe's second goal in as many games helps them to open a 3-0 lead, but they need Jackson's first for the club to settle their nerves — and confirm Charlton's third successive defeat — after the home side fight back.

Kiely — Young, Fish, Perry, Hreidarsson — Holland, Kishishev (Stuart 33), Jensen, Konchesky — Cole (Euell 70), Bartlett (Di Canio 55) *Subs not used* Royce, Fortune *Booked* Fish, Young, Perry
Scorers **Stuart 51, Perry 81**
Referee **G Barber**

Saturday February 21
BLACKBURN ROVERS (h)
Won 3-2 HT 2-0 Att 26,332 Position 5th
The most dramatic finish of this and many other seasons. Unluckily trailing 2-0, Stead having hit the woodwork twice, Blackburn equalise in the last minute through none other than their goalkeeper, who goes up for a corner and scores, left-footed, from eight yards. But, seconds later, Friedel, the would-be hero, can only get his fingertips to a volley from Jensen, who ends Charlton's run of three successive defeats.

Kiely — Young, Fish (Fortune 16), Perry, Hreidarsson — Kishishev, Holland, Euell, Stuart — Di Canio (Konchesky 89), Cole (Jensen 78) *Subs not used* Royce, Johansson
Scorers **Cole 10, Euell 36, Jensen 90**
Referee **U Rennie**

Saturday February 28
ARSENAL (a)
Lost 1-2 HT 0-2 Att 38,137 Position 5th
Kiely — Young, Fish, Fortune, Hreidarsson — Kishishev (Johansson 79), Jensen, Holland, Stuart — Di Canio, Cole *Subs not used* Royce, Turner, Konchesky, Bartlett
Scorer **Jensen 59**
Report page 67

Saturday March 13
MIDDLESBROUGH (h)
Won 1-0 HT 1-0 Att 26,270 Position 4th
Zenden hits the post early on, Kiely is much the busier goalkeeper and Middlesbrough dominate possession in the second half, but all that counts for nothing as Holland curls in a beauty from the edge of the area to take Charlton back into the fourth Champions League place. "We can't believe we didn't win," Steve McClaren says.

Kiely — Young, Fish, Perry, Hreidarsson — Kishishev, Holland, Jensen, Konchesky — Cole (Bartlett 60), Di Canio (Johansson 73) *Subs not used* Royce, Fortune, Hughes
Scorer **Holland 25**
Referee **M Dean**

THE PLAYERS

SHAUN BARTLETT (forward) **Born** October 31, 1972, Cape Town **Ht** 6ft 1in **Wt** 12st 4lb **Signed from** FC Zurich, November 2000, £2m

JAMAL CAMPBELL-RYCE (midfield) **Born** April 6, 1983, Lambeth **Ht** 5ft 7in **Wt** 11st 10lb **Signed from** trainee, August 2001

CARLTON COLE (forward) **Born** November 12, 1983, Surrey **Ht** 6ft 3in **Wt** 12st 13lb **Signed from** Chelsea (loan), August 2003

PAOLO DI CANIO (forward) **Born** July 9, 1968, Rome **Ht** 5ft 9in **Wt** 11st 10lb **Signed from** West Ham United, August 2003, free

JASON EUELL (forward) **Born** February 6, 1977, Lambeth **Ht** 6ft 0in **Wt** 12st 7lb **Signed from** Wimbledon, July 2001, £4.75m

MARK FISH (defender) **Born** March 14, 1974, Cape Town **Ht** 6ft 3in **Wt** 13st 2lb **Signed from** Bolton Wanderers, November 2000, £700,000

JON FORTUNE (defender) **Born** August 23, 1980, Islington **Ht** 6ft 2in **Wt** 11st 4lb **Signed from** trainee, July 1988

MATT HOLLAND (midfield) **Born** April 11, 1974, Bury **Ht** 5ft 9in **Wt** 11st 0lb **Signed from** Ipswich Town, June 2003, £750,000

HERMANN HREIDARSSON (defender) **Born** July 7, 1974, Reykjavik **Ht** 6ft 3in **Wt** 12st 12lb **Signed from** Ipswich Town, March 2003, £900,000

CLAUS JENSEN (midfield) **Born** April 29, 1977, Nykobing, Denmark **Ht** 5ft 11in **Wt** 12st 6lb **Signed from** Bolton Wanderers, July 2000, £4m

JONATAN JOHANSSON (forward) **Born** August 16, 1975, Stockholm **Ht** 6ft 1in **Wt** 12st 8lb **Signed from** Rangers, August 2000, £3.25m

DEAN KIELY (goalkeeper) **Born** October 10, 1970, Salford **Ht** 6ft 1in **Wt** 13st 5lb **Signed from** Bury, May 1999, £1m

RADOSTIN KISHISHEV (midfield) **Born** July 30, 1974, Bourgas, Bulgaria **Ht** 5ft 10in **Wt** 12st 4lb **Signed from** Litex Lovech, Bulgaria, August 2000, £300,000

PAUL KONCHESKY (midfield) **Born** May 15, 1981, Barking **Ht** 5ft 10in **Wt** 10st 12lb **Signed from** trainee, May 1998

KEVIN LISBIE (forward) **Born** October 17, 1978, Hackney **Ht** 5ft 8in **Wt** 10st 12lb **Signed from** trainee, May 1996

SCOTT PARKER (midfield) **Born** October 13, 1980, Lambeth **Ht** 5ft 7in **Wt** 10st 7lb **Signed from** trainee, October 1997

CHRIS PERRY (defender) **Born** April 26, 1973, Carshalton **Ht** 5ft 8in **Wt** 10st 12lb **Signed from** Tottenham Hotspur (initial loan), November 2003, £100,000

CHRIS POWELL (defender) **Born** September 8, 1969, Lambeth **Ht** 5ft 10in **Wt** 11st 7lb **Signed from** Derby County, July 1998, £825,000

GARY ROWETT (defender) **Born** March 6, 1974, Bromsgrove **Ht** 6ft 0in **Wt** 12st 10lb **Signed from** Leicester City, May 2002, £2.5m

SIMON ROYCE (goalkeeper) **Born** September 9, 1971, Forest Gate **Ht** 6ft 2in **Wt** 12st 10lb **Signed from** Leicester City, June 2003, free

GRAHAM STUART (midfield) **Born** October 24, 1970, Tooting **Ht** 5ft 9in **Wt** 11st 10lb **Signed from** Sheffield United, March 1999, £1.1m

MATHIAS SVENSSON (forward) **Born** September 24, 1974, Boras, Sweden **Ht** 6ft 0in **Wt** 12st 4lb **Signed from** Crystal Palace, January 2000, £600,000

JEROME THOMAS (midfield) **Born** March 23, 1983, Brent **Ht** 5ft 10in **Wt** 11st 10lb **Signed from** Arsenal, February 2004, £100,000

LUKE YOUNG (defender) **Born** July 19, 1979, Harlow **Ht** 6ft 0in **Wt** 12st 4lb **Signed from** Tottenham Hotspur, July 2001, £3m

STATS AND FACTS

● Charlton's Carling Cup victory over Luton Town was the second time in five years that they had won a match on penalties after a 4-4 draw, having done so against Sunderland in the 1998 first division play-off final.

● Kevin Lisbie scored five times in three games in September, having scored five in his previous 55 appearances.

● Aside from one occasion when he played for Ireland instead of Ipswich Town, Matt Holland has started all of his clubs' past 329 league games (for Charlton, Ipswich and Bournemouth). He has lasted the whole 90 minutes in 326 of those matches.

● In the past three seasons Charlton have lost four domestic cup games to lower-division opposition: Oxford United and Watford have beaten them in the League Cup, Walsall and Gillingham have done so in the FA Cup.

● Half of Matt Holland's six league goals for the season came against Birmingham City — two at St Andrew's and one at The Valley.

● Charlton have won none of their past 12 Premiership meetings with Manchester United.

Bill Edgar

GOALSCORERS

	Prem	FAC	CC	Total
S Bartlett	5	-	-	5
C Cole	4	1	-	5
P Di Canio	4 (3p)	-	1	5 (3p)
J Euell	10 (3p)	-	-	10 (3p)
J Fortune	2	-	-	2
M Holland	6	-	-	6
H Hreidarsson	2	-	-	2
C Jensen	4	-	1	5
J Johansson	4	-	-	4
K Lisbie	4	-	1	5
S Parker	2	-	1	3
C Perry	1	-	-	1
G Stuart	3	-	-	3
Own goals	-	1	-	1

Saturday March 20
NEWCASTLE UNITED (a)
Lost 1-3   HT 0-2   Att 51,847   Position 6th
Kiely — Young, Fortune, Perry, Hreidarsson (Powell 89) — Kishishev (Johansson 67), Holland, Jensen, Konchesky — Di Canio, Cole (Bartlett 84) *Subs not used* Royce, Hughes *Booked* Young, Perry
Scorer **Jensen 54**
Report page 226

Saturday March 27
ASTON VILLA (h)
Lost 1-2   HT 1-1   Att 26,250   Position 8th
Villa leapfrog Charlton and take seventh place by completing a league double, leaving the home side to count the cost of Jensen's last-minute penalty miss. Both sides hit the woodwork between Cole's header and Samuel's winner, the Villa defender being rewarded with an England call-up for the match against Sweden.

Kiely — Young, Fortune, Perry, Konchesky — Kishishev (Johansson 69), Euell (Powell 79), Holland, Jensen — Cole, Di Canio (Bartlett 69) *Subs not used* Royce, Turner *Booked* Konchesky
Scorer **Cole 8**
Referee **B Knight**

Saturday April 10
PORTSMOUTH (h)
Drew 1-1   HT 1-0   Att 26,385   Position 9th
Alan Curbishley hints that his future may lie away from The Valley after Charlton are booed off, Yakubu's third goal in three games cancelling out Bartlett's stooping header to earn Portsmouth a vital point. "Perhaps it [the club] has to be freshened up," the Charlton manager says.

Kiely — Young, Fortune, Hreidarsson, Powell — Holland, Euell, Jensen, Konchesky — Johansson (Di Canio 79), Bartlett (Cole 72) *Subs not used* Royce, Thomas, Turner *Booked* Euell
Scorer **Bartlett 8**
Referee **A D'Urso**

Monday April 12
LIVERPOOL (a)
Won 1-0   HT 0-0   Att 40,003   Position 7th
Kiely — Young, Fortune, Hreidarsson, Powell — Kishishev, Holland, Jensen, Konchesky — Johansson (Euell 86), Bartlett *Subs not used* Perry, Thomas, Cole, Royce
Scorer **Bartlett 63**
Report page 183

Saturday April 17
BIRMINGHAM CITY (h)
Drew 1-1   HT 0-0   Att 25,206   Position 7th
Two teams striving for Europe produce the drabbest of draws, which only sparks into life when Morrison and Holland trade late headers and when Hughes embarrassingly miskicks in front of an open Charlton goal from eight yards. How expensive will that error prove for Birmingham?

Kiely — Young, Fortune, Hreidarsson, Powell — Kishishev (Cole 61), Holland, Jensen, Konchesky — Johansson (Euell 74), Bartlett (Di Canio ht) *Subs not used* Royce, Perry *Booked* Young
Scorer **Holland 86**
Referee **C Foy**

PLAYER OF THE SEASON
Scott Parker

This will be controversial in some quarters, but if you judge the player of the season as the individual who was instrumental in securing the greatest number of points, then Scott Parker achieved more in his 20 Premiership games than anyone who played in more. With him in the side, it often seemed that Charlton had 12 men. He was fierce in the tackle and a potent force driving forward. Matt Holland impressed in his first Charlton campaign and Dean Kiely was as dependable as ever, but it was Parker who put Charlton in sight of glory and they will long dream at The Valley of what might have been had he stayed.

Nigel Williamson

Saturday April 20
MANCHESTER UNITED (a)
Lost 0-2   HT 0-1   Att 67,477   Position 7th
Kiely — Young, Fortune, Hreidarsson, Powell (Perry 83) — Stuart (Di Canio 74), Holland, Jensen, Konchesky — Johansson (Euell 68), Bartlett *Subs not used* Royce, Cole
Booked Konchesky
Report page 205

Saturday April 24
FULHAM (a)
Lost 0-2   HT 0-1   Att 16,585   Position 8th
Kiely — Young, Fortune, Hreidarsson, Powell (Perry 72) — Stuart (Di Canio 72), Holland, Jensen, Konchesky — Cole (Johansson 72), Euell *Subs not used* Royce, Kishishev
Booked Powell
Report page 152

Saturday May 1
LEICESTER CITY (h)
Drew 2-2   HT 0-1   Att 26,034   Position 8th
Leicester's long fight against the seeming inevitability of relegation ends, although typically they do not go down without a fight. The referee's decision, three days later, to rescind Dabizas's red card for a foul on Johansson that concedes a penalty is of absolutely no consolation to the first team to exit the Premiership this season.

Kiely — Young, Fortune, Hreidarsson, Powell — Stuart, Holland, Euell, Konchesky (Thomas ht) — Di Canio (Perry 88), Johansson *Subs not used* Royce, Kishishev, Hughes *Booked* Di Canio
Scorers **Fortune 53, Di Canio 76 (pen)**
Referee **R Styles**

Saturday May 8
LEEDS UNITED (a)
Drew 3-3   HT 1-2   Att 38,986   Position 8th
Kiely — Young, Fortune, Hreidarsson, Powell (Perry 60) — Stuart (Kishishev 60), Holland, Euell, Konchesky — Johansson, Di Canio (Bartlett 60) *Subs not used* Leite, Fish
Scorers **Holland 11, Euell 76 (pen), 79**
Report page 162

Saturday May 15
SOUTHAMPTON (h)
Won 2-1   HT 1-0   Att 26,614   Position 7th
Charlton get the win that enables them to finish in their highest position for 51 years, Di Canio setting up Euell — their top scorer — for the first and Cole making it 2-0 before Prutton replies for an injury-hit Southampton side limping to the end of the season. Kiely makes a brave late save from the same player.

Kiely — Young, Fortune, Perry, Hreidarsson — Kishishev, Holland, Euell, Konchesky — Di Canio (Cole ht; Jensen 86), Bartlett *Subs not used* Royce, Powell, Fish
Scorers **Euell 36, Cole 53**
Referee **J Winter**

CHELSEA

PREMIERSHIP

	P	W	D	L	F	A	GD	Pts
Arsenal	38	26	12	0	73	26	47	**90**
Chelsea	38	24	7	7	67	30	37	**79**
Man Utd	38	23	6	9	64	35	29	**75**
Liverpool	38	16	12	10	55	37	18	**60**
Newcastle	38	13	17	8	52	40	12	**56**
Aston Villa	38	15	11	12	48	44	4	**56**
Charlton	38	14	11	13	51	51	0	**53**
Bolton	38	14	11	13	48	56	-8	**53**
Fulham	38	14	10	14	52	46	6	**52**
Birmingham	38	12	14	12	43	48	-5	**50**
Middlesbro	38	13	9	16	44	52	-8	**48**
Southampton	38	12	11	15	44	45	-1	**47**
Portsmouth	38	12	9	17	47	54	-7	**45**
Tottenham	38	13	6	19	47	57	-10	**45**
Blackburn	38	12	8	18	51	59	-8	**44**
Man City	38	9	14	15	55	54	1	**41**
Everton	38	9	12	17	45	57	-12	**39**
Leicester	38	6	15	17	48	65	-17	**33**
Leeds	38	8	9	21	40	79	-39	**33**
Wolves	38	7	12	19	38	77	-39	**33**

FA CUP
Fifth round

CARLING CUP
Quarter-finals

CHAMPIONS LEAGUE
Semi-finals

Bridge too far: After four seasons in charge and a year of speculation over his future, Claudio Ranieri bids a fond farewell to the Chelsea fans

Wednesday August 13 2003
MSK ZILINA (a)
Champions League, 3rd qualifying rnd, 1st leg
Won 2-0   **HT 1-0**   Att **6,160**
All eyes are on Chelsea after the summer's Roman
revolution at Stamford Bridge and they make a quietly
impressive start. Abramovich is watching on TV from a
boat off Alaska as Duff, the £17 million man, sets up
Gudjohnsen before an own goal puts them on the brink
of Champions League riches (as if they need them).

Cudicini — Johnson, Desailly, Terry, Bridge — Veron,
Lampard, Geremi, Duff (J Cole 70) — Forssell
(Gronkjaer 56), Gudjohnsen *Subs not used* Ambrosio,
Hasselbaink, Melchiot, Huth, C Cole
Scorers **Gudjohnsen 42, Drahno 75 (og)**
Referee **R Temmink (the Netherlands)**

Sunday August 17
LIVERPOOL (a)
Won 2-1   **HT 1-0**   Att **44,082**   Position **7th**
Cudicini — Johnson (Gallas 73), Desailly, Terry, Bridge —
Duff (J Cole 75), Lampard, Geremi, Gronkjaer — Veron —
Gudjohnsen (Hasselbaink ht) *Subs not used* Forssell,
Ambrosio *Booked* Lampard
Scorers **Veron 25, Hasselbaink 87**
Report page 174

Saturday August 23
LEICESTER CITY (h)
Won 2-1   **HT 2-1**   Att **41,073**   Position **2nd**
Three goals in the first half are followed by three red
cards in the second as Rob Styles sticks to the letter of
the law, dismissing Geremi (two-footed tackle on
Scimeca), Rogers (kicking out at Gronkjaer) and Scimeca
(two bookings) in turn. Mutu gets the winner on his
debut, a right-foot free kick hitting the wall but his left
foot finding the bottom corner from the rebound.

Cudicini — Melchiot, Desailly, Terry, Bridge — Duff
(J Cole 82), Lampard, Geremi, Veron — Hasselbaink
(Gudjohnsen 87), Mutu (Gronkjaer 69) *Subs not used*
Ambrosio, Gallas *Sent off* Geremi 67
Scorers **Nalis 3 (og), Mutu 45**
Referee **R Styles**

Tuesday August 26
MSK ZILINA (h)
Champions League, 3rd qualifying rnd, 2nd leg
Won 3-0 (won 5-0 on agg)   **HT 1-0**   Att **23,408**
Chelsea make routine progress. The excitement comes
with the introductory walk on to the pitch at half-time of
Crespo, dressed in black like a gunslinger, after
completing his £16.8 million move from Inter Milan.

Cudicini — Johnson, Desailly (Huth 64), Terry, Babayaro —
Gronkjaer (Stanic 69), Lampard (Petit ht), Geremi, J Cole
— Hasselbaink, Gudjohnsen *Subs not used* Ambrosio,
Duff, Melchiot, Forssell
Scorers **Johnson 32, Huth 67, Hasselbaink 78**
Referee **K Vassaras (Greece)**

LIKE A SCENE FROM A GLOSSY American soap, Roman
Abramovich rushed through a secret deal, swept into Stamford
Bridge — and Chelsea didn't know what had hit them. Private jets
flew in football luminaries, limousines ferried businessmen to and
fro and the yacht — mini-submarine and all — sat moored outside
Monte Carlo, too big to get into the marina. One day bankruptcy
beckoned, the next a place atop the game's rich list. Overnight,
Claudio Ranieri was pitched into a game of Russian roulette with
the gun loaded against him.

From his perch high in the West Stand, Abramovich, oil
billionaire and Britain's wealthiest man, ruthlessly went about
plotting the rise of his latest plaything, emotions pinned to his chest,
glamorous wife at his side. Remarkably, under the spotlight's glare,
the most expensive team assembled on English soil kept their feet
firmly on the ground.

Their task was to make it the greatest season in the club's history.
At the end of the first Abramovich year, only an unparalleled
unbeaten run by the Premiership champions and the tinkerfest that
blew the head coach's European Cup hopes out of the
Mediterranean had denied them. "Everybody knows I am crazy
man," Ranieri said, explaining the brainstorm against AS Monaco
that had cost a place in the European Cup final. At that moment, the
Italian, whose popularity had gone off the scale as the country
rallied behind him, could find no dissenters.

Yet fewer than 50 days after the takeover was sealed, the club that
could afford just one loan signing the previous summer had hit the
ground running with a dazzling array of new talent worth
approaching £100 million. It was high-fives all round for the new
Russian owner when Jimmy Floyd Hasselbaink's late winner earned
only Chelsea's third win at Anfield in 70 years. Juan Sebastian Veron
had put Chelsea ahead, but it was to be a desperately disappointing
season for the injury-plagued Argentinian — the first player to leave
in the end-of-season cull — and many of Ranieri's "champions" as
the fans lost patience with the expensive foreign imports.

"They'll take time to gel," the pundits had said gravely as more
and more big names arrived before the end of the summer transfer
window, Hernan Crespo and Claude Makelele among them, but the
players were out to prove them wrong. The banana skin of MSK
Zilina safely sidestepped in the Champions League qualifying round,
Chelsea were to go two months before tasting Premiership defeat.

Adrian Mutu marked his signing with a debut goal against
Leicester City to ease the fans' sense of loss over Gianfranco Zola
and the Romanian was soon being compared to Thierry Henry and

HONOURS BOARD

Ruud van Nistelrooy; by the season's end, injury and attitude had consigned him to training with the youth team.

If the flamboyance that might have been expected from such an exotic mix was missing, all the while solid progress was being made by the young Englishmen behind Ranieri's revolution. For once, Blackburn Rovers failed to return north with three points, although Chelsea twice had to show their grit in a hard-earned draw, and Wolverhampton Wanderers were crushed 5-0 away, Crespo's two goals producing a tiny return on the exorbitant outlay for a player who was once the world's most expensive signing. Chelsea's buzzword now was consistency and John Terry, marshalling a defence that could boast 21 clean sheets in the Premiership, had replaced Marcel Desailly as the rock on which it was built.

All the while, all-conquering Arsenal were looming on the horizon, though, and the customary league defeat at Highbury came courtesy of an uncharacteristic howler by Carlo Cudicini that left Henry merely to mutter *"merci"*. The goalkeeper's humiliation was forgotten in the next match as Lazio were outplayed at Stamford Bridge, a victory repeated in Rome a fortnight later by a 4-0 margin to send Ranieri into ecstasy in his home city and on the way to the Champions League knockout stage. November then brought a sequence of six unblemished defensive displays. Ten-man Newcastle United were humbled 5-0, but then came the biggest scalp of all, Manchester United dispatched by a penalty from Frank Lampard to illustrate his growing authority. The victory took his team past

---

Saturday August 30
BLACKBURN ROVERS (h)
Drew 2-2   HT 1-1   Att 41,066   Position 5th
At £16.7 million, Makelele is to take Chelsea's spending through the £100 million barrier 24 hours later, but for all their cash they twice trail to an impressive Blackburn as Andrew Cole punishes errors by Desailly — after 19 seconds — and Cudicini. Hasselbaink levels from the spot after Neill is somewhat harshly adjudged to have handled.

Cudicini — Johnson, Desailly, Terry, Bridge (J Cole 84) — Duff (Petit ht), Lampard, Geremi, Veron — Hasselbaink, Mutu (Crespo 75) *Subs not used* Ambrosio, Gallas
Scorers **Mutu 45, Hasselbaink 63 (pen)**
Referee **M Dean**

Saturday September 13
TOTTENHAM HOTSPUR (h)
Won 4-2   HT 2-1   Att 41,165   Position 3rd
Peter Kenyon, the chief executive recruited from Old Trafford, has started his gardening leave and now Chelsea prune their neighbours down to size — it is 26 league matches since Spurs won this fixture — despite falling behind. Mutu's double makes it four goals in three games as the pressure mounts on Glenn Hoddle.

Cudicini — Melchiot, Desailly, Terry, Babayaro — Gronkjaer (Gallas 71), Lampard, Petit (Makelele 65), Duff (J Cole 74) — Hasselbaink, Mutu *Subs not used* Ambrosio, Gudjohnsen *Booked* Hasselbaink, Petit
Scorers **Lampard 35, Mutu 37, 75, Hasselbaink 90**
Referee **G Poll**

Tuesday September 16
SPARTA PRAGUE (a)
Champions League
Won 1-0   HT 0-0   Att 18,597
Claudio Ranieri makes seven changes and gets a disjointed first-half performance, but the arrival of Lampard and Duff improves matters and another substitute, Hasselbaink, helps to get Chelsea off to a winning start in group G by flicking the ball on for Gallas to claim a late winner.

Cudicini — Johnson, Desailly, Gallas, Bridge — Geremi, Makelele, Petit (Lampard ht), Veron — Crespo (Hasselbaink 72), Mutu (Duff 47) *Subs not used* Ambrosio, J Cole, Gudjohnsen, Terry
Scorer **Gallas 85**
Referee **H Fleischer (Germany)**

Saturday September 20
WOLVERHAMPTON WANDERERS (a)
Won 5-0   HT 2-0   Position 1st
Cudicini — Johnson (Huth 74), Gallas, Terry, Babayaro — Gronkjaer (J Cole 57), Makelele, Lampard, Duff — Hasselbaink (Crespo 65), Gudjohnsen *Subs not used* Ambrosio, Petit *Booked* Terry, Gronkjaer, Huth
Scorers **Lampard 17, Hasselbaink 36, Duff 52, Crespo 67, 90**
Report page 261

Saturday September 27
ASTON VILLA (h)
Won 1-0   HT 1-0   Att 41,182   Position 2nd
They have just won 5-0 away from home, but Chelsea still make five changes for a match settled when Hasselbaink pounces after Sorensen fails to hold Lampard's low drive. Angel has three chances to get the draw Villa deserve but shoots wide of one post, then the other, followed by a complete miscue from six yards.

Cudicini — Johnson, Desailly, Gallas, Bridge — Veron (J Cole 80), Lampard, Petit (Makelele 74), Duff — Hasselbaink, Mutu (Gronkjaer 64) *Subs not used* Ambrosio, Crespo
Scorer **Hasselbaink 43**
Referee **J Winter**

Wednesday October 1
BESIKTAS (h)
Champions League
Lost 0-2 **HT 0-2** **Att 32,957**
Claudio Ranieri tinkers with both personnel and formation, but the result this time is a shock defeat as Sergen punishes a series of errors with two goals in four minutes. Despite increasingly desperate pressure, Chelsea cannot reply against a side down to ten men for 40 minutes after Ilhan's second yellow card.

Cudicini — Terry, Desailly, Gallas — Geremi, Lampard, Makelele, Babayaro (Bridge 23) — Veron, Crespo (Hasselbaink ht), Mutu (Duff ht) *Subs not used* Ambrosio, Johnson, J Cole, Gudjohnsen *Booked* Mutu
Referee **L Cardoso Cortez Batista (Portugal)**

Sunday October 5
MIDDLESBROUGH (a)
Won 2-1 **HT 1-0** **Att 29,170** Position **3rd**
Cudicini — Johnson, Terry, Huth, Bridge — Gronkjaer (J Cole 79), Makelele, Lampard, Duff — Hasselbaink (Crespo ht), Gudjohnsen (Mutu 79) *Subs not used* Ambrosio, Geremi *Booked* Hasselbaink, Huth
Scorers **Gudjohnsen 17, Crespo 88**
Report page 209

Tuesday October 14
BIRMINGHAM CITY (a)
Drew 0-0 **HT 0-0** **Att 29,460** Position **1st**
Cudicini — Johnson, Terry, Huth, Bridge — Makelele — Lampard, J Cole (Duff 65), Geremi — Hasselbaink (Gudjohnsen 76), Crespo *Subs not used* Ambrosio, Stanic, Melchiot *Booked* Johnson, Terry, Geremi, Huth
Report page 83

Saturday October 18
ARSENAL (a)
Lost 1-2 **HT 1-1** **Att 38,172** Position **3rd**
Cudicini — Johnson, Melchiot, Huth, Bridge — Geremi (Hasselbaink 78), Makelele, Lampard, Duff (J Cole 71) — Mutu (Gronkjaer 67), Crespo *Subs not used* Stanic, Ambrosio *Booked* Hasselbaink, Makelele
Scorer **Crespo 8**
Report page 62

Wednesday October 22
LAZIO (h)
Champions League
Won 2-1 **HT 0-1** **Att 40,405**
Behind to Inzaghi's header, Chelsea storm back for the victory that takes them top of group G with Lampard, having already hit the bar, swerving in a fine equaliser and Mutu pouncing on a rebound for the winner. Cudicini then defies the Italians with two great late saves.

Cudicini — Johnson, Gallas, Terry, Bridge — Makelele — Lampard, Veron (Gronkjaer 64), Duff (Geremi 79) — Mutu (J Cole 87), Gudjohnsen *Subs not used* Ambrosio, Hasselbaink, Melchiot, Huth *Booked* Terry, Veron
Scorers **Lampard 57, Mutu 65**
Referee **T Hauge (Norway)**

Saturday October 25
MANCHESTER CITY (h)
Won 1-0 **HT 1-0** **Att 41,040** Position **1st**
The meeting of the Premiership's two most free-scoring sides is a let-down, settled when Mutu's low cross deceives Seaman and is turned in almost involuntarily by Hasselbaink. Fowler's header is tipped on to the bar by Cudicini as Chelsea take advantage of Fulham's win at Old Trafford to reclaim top spot.

Cudicini — Melchiot, Gallas, Terry, Bridge — Gronkjaer (Geremi 67), Lampard, Makelele, J Cole (Duff 73) — Hasselbaink (Huth 83), Mutu *Subs not used* Ambrosio, Gudjohnsen
Scorer **Hasselbaink 34**
Referee **P Dowd**

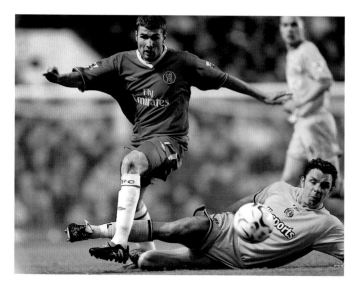
Adrian Mutu was one of the costly new arrivals who failed to impress

Arsenal to the top of the tree. It does not come sweeter. Chelsea's traditional Christmas holiday allowed Bolton Wanderers to steal away from London with the spoils and Charlton Athletic to accept a gift-wrapped 4-2 win on Boxing Day. Aston Villa ended interest in the Carling Cup and, in February, Arsenal — who else? — in the FA Cup, before Henry and Co galloped into the Premiership sunset six days later with a decisive second league victory.

When VfB Stuttgart were quietly overcome in the European Cup first knockout round, the draw could have been abandoned, so obvious did it seem that the bogeymen of Arsenal lay in wait. A 1-1 draw in the first leg enabled Wayne Bridge to earn his place in Chelsea folklore with a dramatic winner at Highbury to end 17 matches without victory against the red nemesis.

Two matches from the European Cup final, Ranieri had his chance to silence the boardroom backbiting, but, fatally, the Tinkerman blew it. A flurry of wild substitutions, with AS Monaco down to ten men and reeling, backfired and two late goals meant that there was no way back for Chelsea despite a first half at Stamford Bridge to stir the heart.

With a Champions League place secured by Easter, all that was left was for Chelsea's ten men to clinch second place in the Premiership with a draw at Old Trafford and for The Shed to shed a shedload of tears for an emotional Ranieri after the final-day defeat of Leeds United. Would he be back? Like all good storylines, the audience were kept waiting on the edge of their seats before Abramovich's dynasty moved on apace. Enter Jose Mourinho as the new manager in a blaze of European Cup glory. For Ranieri, staring down the barrel during the longest of long goodbyes, one thing had become inescapable — the bullet.

THE MANAGER

Claudio Ranieri

A Variety Club award for Man of the Year and his P45 were all that the dignified Italian had to show for a season of mind-blowing stress that started when Sven called on Roman for tea, but second place in the Premiership and a European Cup semi-final would have looked good on any other manager's CV. The Tinkerman worked wonders with the likes of Lampard, Terry and Bridge, but the cosmopolitan crew apparently chosen by others did the Tinkerman few favours. Manager of the Year? No way, Jose. But Man of the Year? No contest.

Geoff Harwood

APPEARANCES

	Prem	FAC	CC	Euro	Total
M Ambrosio	8	-	1	3	12
C Babayaro	5 (1)	2	3	3	13 (1)
W Bridge	33	2	-	11 (2)	46 (2)
J Cole	18 (17)	2 (1)	2 (1)	3 (6)	25 (25)
H Crespo	13 (6)	-	1 (1)	7 (3)	21 (10)
C Cudicini	26	3	-	11	40
M Desailly	15	1	1	7 (1)	24 (1)
D Duff	17 (6)	0 (1)	2	7 (4)	26 (11)
M Forssell	-	-	-	1	1
W Gallas	23 (6)	4	1	11	39 (6)
Geremi	19 (6)	1	3	7 (3)	30 (9)
J Gronkjaer	19 (12)	4	2 (1)	6 (4)	31 (17)
E Gudjohnsen	17 (9)	2 (2)	1	8 (2)	28 (13)
J F Hasselbaink	22 (8)	3	3	4 (4)	32 (12)
R Huth	8 (8)	0 (1)	1	0 (2)	9 (11)
G Johnson	17 (2)	1	3	8 (1)	29 (3)
F Lampard	38	4	1 (1)	13 (1)	56 (2)
C Makelele	26 (4)	3	1 (1)	11	41 (5)
M Melchiot	20 (3)	3	2	4 (1)	29 (4)
A Mutu	21 (4)	3	0 (1)	6 (1)	30 (6)
A Nicolas	1 (1)	1			2 (1)
F Oliveira	0 (1)	0 (1)	-	-	0 (2)
S Parker	7 (4)	1	-	4 (1)	12 (5)
E Petit	3 (1)	0 (1)	-	1 (1)	4 (3)
M Stanic	0 (2)	-	0 (2)	0 (1)	0 (5)
N Sullivan	4	1 (1)	2	-	7 (1)
J Terry	33	3	2	13	51
J S Veron	5 (2)	-	1	5 (1)	11 (3)

Wednesday October 29
NOTTS COUNTY (h)
Carling Cup, 3rd rnd
Won 4-2   HT 2-1   Att 35,997
Impoverished County run the millionaires too close for comfort, Joe Cole's first goal settling Chelsea's nerves.

Ambrosio — Johnson, Melchiot, Huth, Babayaro — Gronkjaer (J Cole 69), Geremi, Veron, Duff — Hasselbaink (Stanic ht), Gudjohnsen Subs not used Sullivan, Lampard, Bridge Booked Veron
Scorers **Hasselbaink 14, Gudjohnsen 36, 65 (pen), J Cole 87**
Referee **R Styles**

Saturday November 1
EVERTON (a)
Won 1-0   HT 0-0   Att 40,189   Position 1st
Cudicini — Melchiot, Gallas, Terry, Bridge — Makelele — Geremi, Lampard, J Cole (Gudjohnsen 87) — Hasselbaink, Mutu (Duff 78) Subs not used Johnson, Huth, Ambrosio
Scorer **Mutu 49**
Report page 136

Tuesday November 4
LAZIO (a)
Champions League
Won 4-0   HT 1-0   Att 50,000
Helped by the sending-off of Mihajlovic, who spits at Mutu, plus an almost comical display of goalkeeping by Sereni, Chelsea romp to their first win on Italian soil in the city where their head coach grew up. Only the last-minute dismissal of Johnson spoils their night.

Cudicini — Johnson, Gallas, Terry, Bridge — Lampard, Makelele, Veron (J Cole 74) — Duff — Crespo (Gudjohnsen 66), Mutu (Gronkjaer 57) Subs not used Ambrosio, Hasselbaink, Geremi, Huth Booked Cudicini, Johnson, Mutu Sent off Johnson 90
Scorers **Crespo 15, Gudjohnsen 70, Duff 75, Lampard 80**
Referee **V Ivanov (Russia)**

Sunday November 9
NEWCASTLE UNITED (h)
Won 5-0   HT 3-0   Att 41,332   Position 2nd
Chelsea are already 2-0 up when Mutu, slightly impeded by O'Brien outside the box, throws himself into it to earn a penalty and contribute towards the Newcastle defender's dismissal. Three more goals later, it all adds up to a "nightmare afternoon" for Sir Bobby Robson.

Cudicini — Johnson (Huth 89), Gallas, Terry, Bridge — Lampard, Makelele, Veron — Duff — Crespo (Gudjohnsen 69), Mutu (J Cole 64) Subs not used Ambrosio, Gronkjaer
Scorers **Johnson 25, Crespo 40, Lampard 42 (pen), Duff 78, Gudjohnsen 84**
Referee **P Durkin**

Saturday November 22
SOUTHAMPTON (a)
Won 1-0   HT 0-0   Att 32,149   Position 2nd
Cudicini — Melchiot, Gallas, Terry, Bridge — Lampard, Makelele, J Cole (Gronkjaer 59) — Duff (Stanic 74) — Hasselbaink (Mutu 80), Gudjohnsen Subs not used Ambrosio, Johnson Booked Terry
Scorer **Melchiot 47**
Report page 243

Wednesday November 26
SPARTA PRAGUE (h)
Champions League
Drew 0-0   HT 0-0   Att 40,152
Needing one point from their final two group games to go through, Chelsea get it despite a poor performance.

Cudicini — Melchiot, Gallas, Terry, Bridge — Makelele — Lampard, J Cole (Geremi 72) — Duff — Crespo (Gudjohnsen 72), Mutu Subs not used Ambrosio, Babayaro, Desailly, Hasselbaink, Gronkjaer
Referee **C B Larsen (Denmark)**

Sunday November 30
MANCHESTER UNITED (h)
Won 1-0   HT 1-0   Att 41,932   Position 1st
Clive Woodward is among the crowd for a heavyweight collision, settled by Lampard's penalty when Keane fells Joe Cole. Sir Alex Ferguson criticises the decision, but TV replays suggest Alan Wiley got it right and Chelsea deserve their victory, outplaying the champions to go top. They are now the bookmakers' title favourites.

Cudicini — Melchiot, Gallas, Terry, Bridge — Lampard, Makelele, Geremi — J Cole (Duff 58) — Crespo (Gronkjaer 61), Mutu (Hasselbaink 79) *Subs not used* Ambrosio, Desailly *Booked* Lampard, J Cole, Melchiot, Mutu
Scorer **Lampard 30 (pen)**
Referee **A Wiley**

Wednesday December 3
READING (a)
Carling Cup, 4th rnd
Won 1-0   HT 0-0   Att 24,107
Hahnemann's heroics in the Reading goal only delay the inevitable as Chelsea tear them apart, Hasselbaink finishing off a devastating move, though Lampard has to clear off the line from Ingimarsson to preserve a seventh successive clean sheet.

Sullivan — Johnson, Desailly, Terry, Babayaro — Geremi, Lampard, J Cole (Makelele ht) — Gronkjaer (Mutu 78) — Hasselbaink (Stanic 73), Crespo *Subs not used* Ambrosio, Gallas *Booked* Hasselbaink, Makelele
Scorer **Hasselbaink 57**
Referee **S Bennett**

Saturday December 6
LEEDS UNITED (a)
Drew 1-1   HT 0-1   Att 36,305   Position 1st
Cudicini — Melchiot, Gallas, Terry, Bridge — Lampard, Makelele, J Cole (Crespo ht) — Duff — Hasselbaink (Gronkjaer 75), Mutu *Subs not used* Sullivan, Geremi, Desailly *Booked* Hasselbaink, Mutu
Scorer **Duff 70**
Report page 157

Tuesday December 9
BESIKTAS (a*)
Champions League
Won 2-0   HT 0-0   Att 55,350   (*in Gelsenkirchen)
Chelsea join Manchester United as top seeds in Friday's draw with a courageous display in Gelsenkirchen, the neutral venue chosen after terrorist bombings in Istanbul. Play is delayed at the start of the second half when objects — mostly toilet rolls — are thrown on the pitch. Bridge scores his first goal for the club.

Cudicini — Gallas, Desailly, Terry — Johnson, Lampard, Makelele, Babayaro (Bridge 83) — Geremi — Hasselbaink, Gronkjaer (Duff 72) *Subs not used* Ambrosio, Mutu, J Cole, Stanic, Melchiot *Booked* Gronkjaer
Scorers **Hasselbaink 77, Bridge 85**
Referee **A Frisk (Sweden)**

Saturday December 13
BOLTON WANDERERS (h)
Lost 1-2   HT 1-1   Att 40,491   Position 2nd
Chelsea's first home defeat for ten months costs them the Premiership lead, but while Bolton's victory is only secured by a last-minute own goal from Terry, it is deserved. Terry earlier sets up Crespo's opener, N'Gotty levelling against the run of play with a thumping header.

Cudicini — Johnson, Desailly, Terry, Bridge — Lampard (Geremi 78), Makelele — Gronkjaer (Hasselbaink 70), Crespo (J Cole 78), Mutu, Duff *Subs not used* Ambrosio, Gallas *Booked* Gronkjaer, Mutu
Scorer **Crespo 22**
Referee **M Messias**

MATCH OF THE SEASON

Chelsea 1   Manchester United 0
Stamford Bridge, Sunday November 30 2003
Matt Dickinson

IT WAS ALMOST ENOUGH TO MAKE you feel sorry for Manchester United, the poor little underdogs battered and bullied by the loadsamoney brutes from Stamford Bridge. Outspent and now outplayed, Sir Alex Ferguson's men looked a sorry, bedraggled bunch as they trooped off in the drizzle yesterday to find that Chelsea had not only gone top but been installed by the bookmakers as favourites for the championship.

Of course, some of us said United were finished about this time last season and they went on one of the great title-winning runs of the past two decades, so let us not make the same mistake this time around. When Paul Scholes and Ole Gunnar Solskjaer return, Ferguson will be able to drop Quinton Fortune and Diego Forlan, who looked out of their depth against Chelsea. He should not have to deploy Ryan Giggs on the right wing.

Ferguson also plans to spend money on a forward in January but, whatever he has to play with, Chelsea have plenty more and that is what United fans left fearing yesterday. Their team and squad both looked inferior to Chelsea's and Roman Abramovich has barely started flexing his financial muscle. United might go shopping for Jermain Defoe or Louis Saha in January. The Russian billionaire is probably wondering how much it would take to lure Ronaldo or Thierry Henry.

It is a measure of Chelsea's growing stature at the top of the Barclaycard Premiership that Ferguson even honoured them with a post-defeat shot across the bows. "It was a great result for them but it's too early to say what it means, only 14 games into the season," he said. "It's when you are top in April that you start to feel the pressure."

Who can tell now how Chelsea will react in "squeaky bum time", as Ferguson likes to call the race for the finish line, but they showed few signs of cracking under the pressure yesterday. They fell too deep for their head coach's liking in the last 15 minutes, when United were searching for an equaliser to Frank Lampard's first-half penalty, but the hosts had resolute and composed leaders in Lampard, John Terry and Claude Makelele. "He's a great, great player," Claudio Ranieri said of the midfield stopper who cannot even be sure of getting into the France side that will face England in next summer's European Championship. "He gives us calm. He has good geometry."

After surviving a few self-inflicted scares in the opening quarter of an hour, Chelsea established a midfield platform that Roy Keane strived almost single-handedly to dismantle, but the old warrior found himself chasing around after the ball instead of winning it. He

Claude Makele employs his tackling skills on Cristiano Ronaldo

was haring around in the 29th minute when Hernan Crespo slipped the ball through to Joe Cole just inside the penalty area. Keane was on the wrong side of Cole when he attempted the tackle and clumsily stuck out a foot, over which the England midfield player happily tripped.

"Understandably, my players were disappointed," Ferguson said. "It was a major decision and disappointing for us because he was going away from the goal." Not even the most one-eyed Mancunian would agree after seeing a replay. "Jimmy Floyd Hasselbaink and Adrian Mutu are my top penalty-takers but Lampard keeps taking the ball," Ranieri said. The England player is in the form of his life and he firmly stroked his spot kick into the bottom corner to give Chelsea a fully merited lead.

They rarely looked like surrendering it because, although Cristiano Ronaldo whacked in a couple of late crosses after replacing Fortune, Chelsea's defence was excellently marshalled by Terry. It is now 11 hours and 31 minutes since Carlo Cudicini last conceded a goal, to Lazio in the Champions League.

Any complaints that Marcel Desailly and Glen Johnson may have had about not playing were answered by the doggedness of their team-mates in defence and even the questionable decision to rest Damien Duff, who was suffering from fatigue, according to Ranieri, could be said to have been vindicated. Of those in blue, only Geremi

Wednesday December 17
ASTON VILLA (a)
Carling Cup, quarter-final
Lost 1-2   HT 0-1   Att 30,414
Sullivan — Melchiot, Terry, Gallas — Johnson (Crespo 55), Geremi, Makelele (Lampard ht), Babayaro — Duff (Gronkjaer 55), Hasselbaink, J Cole *Subs not used* Desailly, Ambrosio *Booked* Terry, Gallas
Scorer **J Cole 69**
Report page 76

Saturday December 20
FULHAM (a)
Won 1-0   HT 0-0   Att 18,244   Position 1st (equal)
Cudicini — Johnson, Desailly, Terry, Bridge — Gronkjaer, Lampard, Makelele, Duff (J Cole 8; Geremi 84) — Crespo (Gallas 90), Mutu *Subs not used* Sullivan, Melchiot *Booked* Johnson, J Cole, Gronkjaer
Scorer **Crespo 62**
Report page 147

Friday December 26
CHARLTON ATHLETIC (a)
Lost 2-4   HT 1-2   Att 26,768   Position 3rd
Cudicini — Johnson, Desailly, Terry, Bridge — J Cole (Gallas 82), Lampard (Geremi 65), Makelele, Gronkjaer (Gudjohnsen ht) — Hasselbaink, Mutu *Subs not used* Sullivan, Melchiot *Booked* Gronkjaer
Scorers **Terry 10, Gudjohnsen 73**
Report page 116

Sunday December 28
PORTSMOUTH (h)
Won 3-0   HT 0-0   Att 41,552   Position 3rd
The turning point is Stone's departure through injury. He had forced Sullivan into a terrific save, but suddenly Portsmouth are swamped by fine strikes from Bridge, Lampard, brilliantly teed up by Mutu, and Geremi, whose first Chelsea goal is an unstoppable dipping volley.
Sullivan — Melchiot, Gallas, Terry, Bridge — Gronkjaer, Lampard, Makelele, Geremi — Gudjohnsen, Mutu *Subs not used* Ambrosio, Johnson, Desailly, Hasselbaink, J Cole
Scorers **Bridge 65, Lampard 73, Geremi 82**
Referee **G Barber**

Saturday January 3 2004
WATFORD (a)
FA Cup, 3rd rnd
Drew 2-2   HT 2-2   Att 21,121
On a muddy pitch and with their own on-loan goalkeeper, Pidgeley, between the opposition posts, the Cup favourites are happy to survive. Chelsea twice have to come back from behind, though replays show that Helguson's opener for Watford did not cross the line.
Sullivan — Johnson, Gallas, Desailly, Babayaro — Gronkjaer, Makelele, Lampard, Geremi — Mutu, Gudjohnsen *Subs not used* Hasselbaink, J Cole, Melchiot, Huth, Ambrosio
Scorers **Gudjohnsen 33 (pen), Lampard 41**
Referee **A Wiley**

Wednesday January 7
LIVERPOOL (h)
Lost 0-1   HT 0-1   Att 41,420   Position 3rd
Chelsea meet Liverpool at their most resilient and defeat leaves them seven points behind Manchester United, prompting a long debrief between Claudio Ranieri and Roman Abramovich. Heskey creates the winner for Cheyrou, his first Premiership goal. Two days later, Steve Dunn rescinds the second of Diouf's yellow cards (for tangling with Mutu), which had led to his sending-off.
Cudicini — Johnson, Gallas, Terry, Bridge — Lampard, Makelele, Geremi, J Cole (Gronkjaer 62) — Mutu, Crespo (Gudjohnsen 12) *Subs not used* Sullivan, Babayaro, Desailly
Referee **S Dunn**

Sunday January 11
LEICESTER CITY (a)
Won 4-0   HT 2-0   Att 31,547   Position 3rd
Cudicini — Melchiot, Desailly, Terry, Babayaro —
Gronkjaer (Geremi 65), Makelele, Lampard, J Cole
(Gallas 78) — Gudjohnsen (Mutu 74), Hasselbaink *Subs
not used* Sullivan, Huth *Booked* Hasselbaink
Scorers **Hasselbaink 12, 44, Mutu 88, Babayaro 90**
Report page 169

Wednesday January 14
WATFORD (h)
FA Cup, 3rd round replay
Won 4-0   HT 2-0   Att 38,763
Mutu, correctly adjudged onside, poaches the opening
goal and Chelsea are rarely troubled thereafter. Even
before the final whistle blows, the hype starts over their
fourth-round trip to the seaside and Scarborough.

Cudicini — Melchiot, Gallas (Huth 84), Terry, Babayaro —
Gronkjaer, Lampard, Makelele, J Cole — Hasselbaink
(Gudjohnsen 69), Mutu (Duff 79) *Subs not used* Sullivan,
Johnson
Scorers **Mutu 7, 76, Hasselbaink 34, Gudjohnsen 84**
Referee **A Wiley**

Sunday January 18
BIRMINGHAM CITY (h)
Drew 0-0   HT 0-0   Att 41,073   Position 3rd
Without five first-team regulars, Birmingham defend
superbly and have Taylor in inspired form, though they
need some good fortune when Joe Cole hits a post.

Cudicini — Johnson (Melchiot ht), Gallas, Desailly, Bridge
— Gronkjaer (Duff ht), Lampard, Makelele, J Cole
(Mutu 60) — Hasselbaink, Gudjohnsen *Subs not used*
Sullivan, Huth *Booked* Johnson, J Cole
Referee **J Winter**

Saturday January 24
SCARBOROUGH (a)
FA Cup, 4th rnd
Won 1-0   HT 1-0   Att 5,379
Scarborough bank half a million pounds from the clash
of princes and paupers, but were they robbed of a
replay? After Terry's early header from point-blank range
is followed by a string of Chelsea misses, the
Conference side are denied a penalty when Gallas's
handball goes unpunished.

Cudicini — Melchiot, Gallas, Terry, Bridge — J Cole,
Nicolas (Oliveira 67), Lampard, Gronkjaer (Petit ht) —
Hasselbaink, Gudjohnsen *Subs not used* Sullivan,
Johnson, Huth *Booked* Terry, Melchiot
Scorer **Terry 10**
Referee **B Knight**

Sunday February 1
BLACKBURN ROVERS (a)
Won 3-2   HT 2-1   Att 24,867   Position 3rd
Cudicini — Johnson, Gallas, Terry, Bridge — Petit
(Melchiot 81) — Parker (Gronkjaer 69), Makelele —
Lampard — Hasselbaink, Mutu (Gudjohnsen 90) *Subs not
used* Sullivan, Nicolas
Scorers **Lampard 25, 35, Johnson 88**
Report page 97

Sunday February 8
CHARLTON ATHLETIC (h)
Won 1-0   HT 1-0   Att 41,255   Position 3rd
With eight midfield players unavailable — including
Parker, prohibited from playing against the club he has
just left — Chelsea avenge their Boxing Day defeat
thanks to the penalty won and converted by Hasselbaink.

Sullivan — Melchiot, Gallas, Huth, Bridge — Johnson,
Lampard, Nicolas, Gronkjaer — Mutu, Hasselbaink
(Gudjohnsen 74) *Subs not used* Ambrosio, Desailly,
Oliveira, Rocastle *Booked* Gronkjaer, Mutu
Scorer **Hasselbaink 28 (pen)**
Referee **S Bennett**

No quarter given in this collision between Roy Keane and John Terry

was a disappointment and not just because he was so slow changing
boots that he arrived two minutes into the second half.

For United, there were plenty who fell short of the standards
demanded by their manager, who, if he was not so stubborn, might
reflect on how much David Beckham brought to his side. Failing to
lure Ronaldinho or Harry Kewell this summer could prove costly for
United.

A shortage of options is not troubling Chelsea, who are now top of
the league, vaulting over Arsenal after the North London club's
draw yesterday, four points clear of United and through to the last
16 of the European Cup. Ranieri continues to keep pace with the
expectations of Chelsea supporters and the club's owner, although
you will never get him to admit it. "I would like to be favourites
when we go to Manchester United [on May 8]," he said. It could be
some game, if they have not won the league already.

CHELSEA (4-3-1-2): C Cudicini — M Melchiot, W Gallas, J Terry, W Bridge — F Lampard, C Makelele,
Geremi — J Cole (sub: D Duff, 58min) — A Mutu (sub: J F Hasselbaink, 79), H Crespo (sub:
J Gronkjaer, 61). **Substitutes not used:** M Ambrosio, M Desailly. **Booked:** Cole, Melchiot, Lampard,
Mutu.
MANCHESTER UNITED (4-4-2): T Howard — G Neville, R Ferdinand, M Silvestre, J O'Shea — R Giggs,
P Neville (sub: Kleberson, 77), R Keane, Q Fortune (sub: C Ronaldo, 72) — D Forlan, R van Nistelrooy.
Substitutes not used: R Carroll, N Butt, D Bellion. **Booked:** Keane.

STATS AND FACTS

- The only teams to have beaten Chelsea in the FA Cup over the past nine seasons are Arsenal (four times) and Manchester United (three times). Chelsea won the competition in 1997 and 2000.

- Chelsea won 12 away league games — their previous best top-flight haul was 11.

- There were five goalless draws at Stamford Bridge between late November and mid-April.

- Roman Abramovich made his Stamford Bridge debut when Chelsea played at home to Leicester City; Chelsea's first game after the appointment of Claudio Ranieri three years before was also at home to Leicester.

- Both league matches between Chelsea and Liverpool were won by the away side, yet none of their previous 24 meetings had produced an away victory.

- Chelsea have lost just two of their past 20 meetings with Everton.

- For the first 25 minutes of the second half of the Carling Cup tie against Notts County in October, the Chelsea side included 11 different nationalities. They were Ambrosio (Italian), Johnson (English), Melchiot (Dutch), Huth (German), Babayaro (Nigerian), Gronkjaer (Danish), Geremi (Cameroonian), Veron (Argentine), Duff (Irish), Gudjohnsen (Icelandic) and Stanic (Croat).

- Chelsea have lost none of their past 15 home games against Newcastle United.

- They also have a good record against Manchester United, losing just three of their past 28 away league games.

Bill Edgar

GOALSCORERS

	Prem	FAC	CC	Euro	Total
C Babayaro	1	-	-	-	1
W Bridge	1	-	-	2	3
J Cole	1	-	2	-	3
H Crespo	10	-	-	2	12
D Duff	5	-	-	1	6
W Gallas	-	-	-	1	1
Geremi	1	-	-	-	1
J Gronkjaer	2	-	-	1	3
E Gudjohnsen	6	2 (1p)	2 (1p)	3	13 (2p)
J F Hasselbaink	13 (2p)	1	2	2	18 (2p)
R Huth	-	-	-	1	1
G Johnson	3	-	-	1	4
F Lampard	10 (2p)	1	-	4	15 (2p)
M Melchiot	2	-	-	-	2
A Mutu	6	3	-	1	10
S Parker	1	-	-	-	1
J Terry	2	1	-	-	3
J S Veron	1	-	-	-	1
Own goals	2	-	-	2	4

Wednesday February 11
PORTSMOUTH (a)
Won 2-0   HT 1-0   Att 20,140   Position 3rd
Sullivan — Melchiot, Gallas, Terry, Bridge — Parker (J Cole 73), Makelele, Lampard, Gronkjaer — Mutu (Crespo 62), Gudjohnsen (Hasselbaink 70) *Subs not used* Ambrosio, Huth *Booked* Crespo, Parker
Scorers **Parker 17, Crespo 79**
Report page 235

Sunday February 15
ARSENAL (a)
FA Cup, 5th rnd
Lost 1-2   HT 1-0   Att 38,136
Cudicini (Sullivan 61) — Melchiot, Gallas, Terry, Bridge — Gronkjaer (J Cole 69), Makelele, Lampard, Parker — Mutu (Gudjohnsen 64), Hasselbaink *Subs not used* Crespo, Huth *Booked* Hasselbaink, Melchiot, Mutu, Makelele
Scorer **Mutu 40**
Report page 67

Saturday February 21
ARSENAL (h)
Lost 1-2   HT 1-2   Att 41,487   Position 3rd
Is this the day the title was won? With Leeds getting a draw at Old Trafford in the other 12.30pm kick-off, Arsenal go seven points clear of Manchester United and nine ahead of Chelsea, prompting Claudio Ranieri to concede that his team are out of the race. Ahead through Gudjohnsen — sent off on the hour for two bookings — after just 28 seconds, Chelsea are beaten by the neighbours for the second time in seven days when Sullivan's flap allows Edu to poach the winner.

Sullivan — Melchiot, Gallas, Terry, Bridge — Parker (Gronkjaer 63), Makelele, Lampard, Geremi (J Cole 73) — Mutu (Hasselbaink 73), Gudjohnsen *Subs not used* Ambrosio, Desailly *Booked* Terry, Lampard, Gudjohnsen, Mutu *Sent off* Gudjohnsen 60
Scorer **Gudjohnsen 1**
Referee **M Riley**

Wednesday February 25
VFB STUTTGART (a)
European Cup, 1st knockout rnd, 1st leg
Won 1-0   HT 1-0   Att 50,000
Functional rather than inspired and with Claudio Ranieri still apparently on borrowed time, Chelsea are within reach of the quarter-finals after Meira, stretching to stop Johnson's cross reaching Crespo, puts through his own goal. One fine save from the returning Cudicini later in a low-key tie, victory is theirs.

Cudicini — Johnson, Gallas, Terry, Bridge — Geremi, Makelele, Lampard, Gronkjaer (Duff 66) — Gudjohnsen (Hasselbaink 73), Crespo (J Cole 89) *Subs not used* Sullivan, Desailly, Melchiot, Parker *Booked* Cudicini, Johnson
Scorer **Meira 12 (og)**
Referee **K Vassaras (Greece)**

Saturday February 28
MANCHESTER CITY (a)
Won 1-0   HT 0-0   Att 47,304   Position 2nd
Cudicini — Johnson, Gallas, Terry, Bridge — Geremi (Huth 71), Parker, Lampard, J Cole (Makelele ht) — Hasselbaink (Gudjohnsen 65), Crespo *Subs not used* Sullivan, Duff *Booked* Gallas
Scorer **Gudjohnsen 82**
Report page 192

Tuesday March 9
VFB STUTTGART (h)
European Cup, 1st knockout rnd, 2nd leg
Drew 0-0 (won 1-0 on agg)   HT 0-0   Att **36,657**
Chelsea are through to the last eight while Manchester United are out, but Claudio Ranieri still comes in for criticism for his decision to play with only one striker and protect his first-leg lead. Mutu almost scores three times near the end, but VfB rarely threaten as Chelsea record a fifth successive European clean sheet.

Cudicini — Johnson (Desailly 30), Gallas, Terry, Bridge — Makelele — Gronkjaer, Lampard, Parker (Geremi 61), Duff (Mutu 82) — Crespo *Subs not used* Ambrosio, J Cole, Gudjohnsen, Huth
Referee **K Milton Nielsen (Denmark)**

Saturday March 13
BOLTON WANDERERS (a)
Won 2-0   HT 0-0   Att **26,717**   Position **2nd**
Ambrosio — Gallas, Desailly, Terry, Bridge — Gronkjaer (Huth 89), Lampard, Geremi, Duff (Parker 90) — Crespo (J Cole 65), Duff *Subs not used* Makabu-Makalambay, Melchiot
Scorers **Terry 71, Duff 74**
Report page 108

Saturday March 20
FULHAM (h)
Won 2-1   HT 2-1   Att **41,169**   Position **2nd**
Chelsea match Arsenal's margin of victory for the second Saturday running, four days before they meet in the European Cup. Goals from Gudjohnsen — a superb 25-yard shot into the top corner — and Duff sandwich Pembridge's deflected free kick, but rumours of Claudio Ranieri's impending departure grow ever stronger.

Ambrosio — Gallas, Desailly, Terry, Bridge — Gronkjaer (Parker ht), Lampard, Geremi, Duff (J Cole 71) — Crespo, Gudjohnsen *Subs not used* Sullivan, Mutu, Huth *Booked* Parker
Scorers **Gudjohnsen 7, Duff 30**
Referee **N Barry**

Wednesday March 24
ARSENAL (h)
European Cup, quarter-final, 1st leg
Drew 1-1   HT 0-0   Att **40,778**
An absorbing game befitting its stature, but Arsenal hold the whip hand after their seventeenth fixture against Chelsea without defeat. The home side dream of ending that run for six minutes after Gudjohnsen charges down Lehmann's clearance to score from an angle before Pires heads in Ashley Cole's cross. Desailly sees red for two bookable offences.

Ambrosio — Gallas, Desailly, Terry, Bridge — Parker (J Cole 72), Makelele, Lampard, Duff — Gudjohnsen (Melchiot 86), Mutu (Crespo 72) *Subs not used* Sullivan, Geremi, Huth, Gronkjaer *Booked* Makelele, Desailly *Sent off* Desailly 84
Scorer **Gudjohnsen 53**
Referee **M E Mejuto Gonzalez (Spain)**

Saturday March 27
WOLVERHAMPTON WANDERERS (h)
Won 5-2   HT 1-1   Att **41,215**   Position **2nd**
Hasselbaink, with a superb 13-minute hat-trick after his arrival as a substitute — including his 100th Premiership goal — ends Wolves' hopes of a shock win after Craddock gives them a 2-1 lead. "There's only one Ranieri" is still the most popular chant as Sven-Goran Eriksson's employment plans dominate the sports pages.

Ambrosio — Melchiot, Gallas, Terry, Babayaro — Geremi (Hasselbaink 60), Makelele, Lampard, J Cole (Parker 81) — Crespo, Gudjohnsen (Duff ht) *Subs not used* Sullivan, Huth
Scorers **Melchiot 4, Lampard 70, Hasselbainck 77, 87, 90**
Referee **G Barber**

THE PLAYERS

MARCO AMBROSIO (goalkeeper) **Born** May 30, 1973, Brescia **Ht** 6ft 1in **Wt** 13st 4lb **Signed from** Chievo, June 2003, free

CELESTINE BABAYARO (defender) **Born** August 29, 1978, Kaduna, Nigeria **Ht** 5ft 8in **Wt** 11st 0lb **Signed from** Anderlecht, June 1997, £2.25m

WAYNE BRIDGE (defender) **Born** August 5, 1980, Southampton **Ht** 5ft 10in **Wt** 12st 8lb **Signed from** Southampton, July 2003, £7m

JOE COLE (midfield) **Born** November 8, 1981, Islington **Ht** 5ft 8in **Wt** 11st 13lb **Signed from** West Ham United, August 2003, £6.6m

HERNAN CRESPO (foward) **Born** July 5, 1975, Florida, Argentina **Ht** 6ft 1in **Wt** 12st 4lb **Signed from** Inter Milan, August 2003, £16.8m

CARLO CUDICINI (goalkeeper) **Born** September 6, 1973, Milan **Ht** 6ft 1in **Wt** 12st 3lb **Signed from** Castel Di Sangro, Italy, August 1999, £160,000

MARCEL DESAILLY (defender) **Born** September 7, 1968, Accra, Ghana **Ht** 6ft 1in **Wt** 13st 5lb **Signed from** AC Milan, July 1998, £4.6m

DAMIEN DUFF (midfield) **Born** March 2, 1979, Dublin **Ht** 5ft 10in **Wt** 12st 2lb **Signed from** Blackburn Rovers, July 2003, £17m

MIKAEL FORSSELL (foward) **Born** March 15, 1981, Steinfurt, Finland **Ht** 5ft 10in **Wt** 10st 10lb **Signed from** HJK Helsinki, July 1998, free

WILLIAM GALLAS (defender) **Born** August 17, 1977, Paris **Ht** 6ft 1in **Wt** 12st 7lb **Signed from** Marseilles, July 2001, £6.2m

GEREMI (midfield) **Born** December 20, 1978, Baffoussam, Cameroon **Ht** 5ft 9in **Wt** 13st 3lb **Signed from** Real Madrid, July 2003. £6.9m

JESPER GRONKJAER (midfield) **Born** August 12, 1977, Nuuk, Denmark **Ht** 6ft 1in **Wt** 12st 8lb **Signed from** Ajax, December 2000, £7.8m

EIDUR GUDJOHNSEN (foward) **Born** September 15, 1978, Reykjavik **Ht** 6ft 1in **Wt** 13st 0lb **Signed from** Bolton Wanderers, July 2000, £4m

JIMMY FLOYD HASSELBAINK (foward) **Born** March 27, 1972, Paramaribo, Surinam **Ht** 6ft 2in **Wt** 13st 4lb **Signed from** Atletico Madrid, July 2000, £15m

ROBERT HUTH (defender) **Born** August 18, 1984, Berlin **Ht** 6ft 2in **Wt** 12st 12lb **Signed from** trainee, August 2001

GLEN JOHNSON (defender) **Born** August 23, 1984, London **Ht** 5ft 11in **Wt** 12st 11lb **Signed from** West Ham United, July 2003, £6m

FRANK LAMPARD (midfield) **Born** June 20, 1978, Romford **Ht** 6ft 0in **Wt** 12st 6lb **Signed from** West Ham United, July 2001, £11m

CLAUDE MAKELELE (midfield) **Born** February 18, 1973, Kinshasa **Ht** 5ft 7in **Wt** 10st 8lb **Signed from** Real Madrid, August 2003, £16.7m

MARIO MELCHIOT (defender) **Born** November 4, 1976, Amsterdam **Ht** 6ft 1in **Wt** 11st 8lb **Signed from** Ajax, July 1999, free

ADRIAN MUTU (foward) **Born** January 8, 1979, Calinesti, Romania **Ht** 5ft 11in **Wt** 11st 11lb **Signed from** Parma, August 2003, £15.8m

ALEXIS NICOLAS (midfield) **Born** February 13, 1983, Westminster **Ht** 5ft 8in **Wt** 9st 13lb **Signed from** Aston Villa, December 2001, free

FILIPE OLIVEIRA (midfield) **Born** May 27, 1984, Braga, Portugal **Ht** 5ft 10in **Wt** 10st 12lb **Signed from** FC Porto, August 2001, £500,000

SCOTT PARKER (midfield) **Born** October 13, 1980, Lambeth **Ht** 5ft 7in **Wt** 10st 7lb **Signed from** Charlton Athletic, January 2004, £10m

EMMANUEL PETIT (midfield) **Born** September 22, 1970 **Ht** 6ft 1in **Wt** 12st 8lb **Signed from** Barcelona, July 2001, £7.5m

MARIO STANIC (defender) **Born** April 10, 1972, Sarajevo **Ht** 6ft 2in **Wt** 12st 12lb **Signed from** Parma, July 2000, £5.6m

NEIL SULLIVAN (goalkeeper) **Born** February 24, 1970, Sutton **Ht** 6ft 3in **Wt** 15st 4lb **Signed from** Tottenham Hotspur, September 2003, free

JOHN TERRY (defender) **Born** December 7, 1980, Barking **Ht** 6ft 0in **Wt** 12st 4lb **Signed from** trainee, March 1998

JUAN SEBASTIAN VERON (midfield) **Born** March 9, 1975, Buenos Aires **Ht** 6ft 1in **Wt** 12st 4lb **Signed from** Manchester United, August 2003, £15m

Saturday April 3
TOTTENHAM HOTSPUR (a)
Won 1-0   HT 1-0   Att 36,101   Position 2nd
Ambrosio — Melchiot, Gallas, Terry, Bridge — Parker (J Cole 73), Lampard, Makelele, Duff — Hasselbaink (Crespo 86), Gudjohnsen (Gronkjaer 78) Subs not used Sullivan, Huth
Scorer **Hasselbaink 38**
Report page 257

Tuesday April 6
ARSENAL (a)
European Cup, quarter-final, 2nd leg
Won 2-1 (won 3-2 on agg)   HT 0-1   Att 35,486
Ambrosio — Melchiot, Gallas, Terry, Bridge — Parker (Gronkjaer ht), Lampard, Makelele, Duff (J Cole 83) — Hasselbaink (Crespo 83), Gudjohnsen Subs not used Sullivan, Mutu, Geremi, Huth Booked Gallas, Hasselbaink, J Cole
Scorers **Lampard 51, Bridge 87**
Report page 69

Saturday April 10
MIDDLESBROUGH (h)
Drew 0-0   HT 0-0   Att 40,873   Position 2nd
Chelsea are afforded a heroes' return after their European Cup exploits, but after the Lord Mayor's Show comes an uneventful draw. Gudjohnsen hits a post, Lampard fluffs the rebound and Hasselbaink misses a late header, but Middlesbrough deserve a point.
Ambrosio — Gallas, Desailly, Terry, Babayaro (Huth 73) — Gronkjaer (Geremi ht), Makelele (Veron 57), Lampard, J Cole — Hasselbaink, Gudjohnsen Subs not used Sullivan, Crespo Booked Huth
Referee **M Halsey**

Monday April 12
ASTON VILLA (a)
Lost 2-3   HT 1-1   Att 41,112   Position 2nd
Ambrosio — Melchiot (Gallas 61), Huth, Terry, Bridge — Geremi, Parker, Lampard, Duff (Gronkjaer 71) — Crespo, Mutu (J Cole 71) Subs not used Gudjohnsen, Sullivan Booked Huth
Scorer **Crespo 11, 90**
Report page 79

Saturday April 17
EVERTON (h)
Drew 0-0   HT 0-0   Att 41,169   Position 2nd
Three days before the European Cup semi-finals, Chelsea are held to a second successive goalless draw at the Bridge, though Lampard does hit the woodwork twice. Rooney — not for sale by Everton for all of Roman Abramovich's money, according to David Moyes in the morning papers — forces a fine save from Ambrosio.
Ambrosio — Gallas (Melchiot 25), Huth, Desailly, Bridge — Geremi, Parker (Oliveira 80), Lampard, J Cole (Gronkjaer 80) — Mutu, Hasselbaink Subs not used Sullivan, Terry
Referee **G Poll**

Tuesday April 20
AS MONACO (a)
European Cup, semi-final, 1st leg
Lost 1-3   HT 1-1   Att 15,000
Claudio Ranieri, having allegedly criticised Roman Abramovich for "knowing nothing about football", is now the architect of his own side's destruction with his bizarre substitutions. In control at 1-1 against ten men, after Makelele's theatrics lead to the dismissal of Zikos, Chelsea concede twice in the last 12 minutes.
Ambrosio — Melchiot (Hasselbaink 62), Terry, Desailly, Bridge — Parker (Huth 69), Makelele, Lampard, Gronkjaer (Veron ht) — Gudjohnsen, Crespo Subs not used Sullivan, Mutu, J Cole, Geremi Booked Terry, Makelele, Melchiot
Scorer **Crespo 22**
Referee **U Meier (Switzerland)**

PLAYER OF THE SEASON
Frank Lampard

When Frank Lampard strolled into Stamford Bridge, many people saw a fee of £11 million as over the odds for a fine player as yet unproven. But the man around whom Claudio Ranieri built his team started every Premiership match in 2003-04 and, under the careful eye of the head coach, his learning curve has gone only one way — up. Fifteen goals from midfield compensated for the strikers' failure to fire fully and enabled him to see off the challenge from big-name arrivals such as Juan Sebastian Veron, while his tireless running thrust him to the forefront of Sven-Goran Eriksson's thinking for Euro 2004. Three years on and the doubts have been dispelled — Lampard is the real deal.

Geoff Harwood

Sunday April 25
NEWCASTLE UNITED (a)
Lost 1-2   HT 1-1   Att 52,016   Position 2nd
Ambrosio — Melchiot, Terry, Desailly (Huth 72), Bridge — Geremi, Makelele, Lampard, J Cole — Crespo (Hasselbaink 72), Gudjohnsen *Subs not used* Sullivan, Nicholas, Oliveira *Booked* Hasselbaink, Huth
Scorer **J Cole 5**
Report page 227

Saturday May 1
SOUTHAMPTON (h)
Won 4-0   HT 0-0   Att 41,321   Position 2nd
Chelsea warm up for AS Monaco, when they will need at least two goals, by plundering four in the second half against an injury-ravaged Southampton, who give them a head start when Cranie, the 17-year-old making his debut, puts through his own goal.
Cudicini — Melchiot, Huth, Terry, Bridge — Gronkjaer (Johnson 78), Geremi, Lampard (Makelele 86), J Cole (Veron 80) — Gudjohnsen, Hasselbaink *Subs not used* Ambrosio, Crespo
Scorers **Cranie 59 (og), Lampard 75, 83, Johnson 85**
Referee **P Durkin**

Wednesday May 5
AS MONACO (h)
European Cup, semi-final, 2nd leg
Drew 2-2 (lost 3-5 on agg)   HT 2-1   Att 37,132
A bridge too far for Chelsea. After a brilliant start, when Gronkjaer and Lampard wipe out Monaco's first-leg lead, they are pegged back by Ibarra on the stroke of half-time and killed off by Morientes as Monaco go through to a showdown with FC Porto, whose coach, Jose Mourinho — the firm favourite to replace Claudio Ranieri — watches from the stands.
Cudicini — Melchiot (Johnson 64), Gallas, Terry, Bridge — Geremi (Parker 69) — Gronkjaer, Lampard, J Cole — Hasselbaink (Crespo 69), Gudjohnsen *Subs not used* Ambrosio, Babayaro, Stanic, Huth *Booked* Johnson, Gronkjaer, J Cole
Scorers **Gronkjaer 22, Lampard 44**
Referee **A Frisk (Sweden)**

Saturday May 8
MANCHESTER UNITED (a)
Drew 1-1   HT 1-0   Att 67,609   Position 2nd
Cudicini — Melchiot (Johnson 75), Huth, Terry, Bridge — Gronkjaer (Babayaro 84), Lampard, Makelele, Geremi, J Cole (Parker 78) — Gudjohnsen *Subs not used* Stanic, Ambrosio *Booked* Terry, Huth *Sent off* Huth 73
Scorer **Gronkjaer 19**
Report page 206

Saturday May 15
LEEDS UNITED (h)
Won 1-0   HT 1-0   Att 41,276   Position 2nd
Claudio Ranieri's farewell? Still nobody knows for sure, especially not the Chelsea head coach, who goes on an emotional lap of honour after Gronkjaer's header earns a final-day victory. Leeds's fate, at least, is certain: with Kevin Blackwell in charge after the midweek removal of Eddie Gray as caretaker manager, they are heading out of the Premiership in disarray.
Cudicini — Melchiot, Gallas, Terry (Huth 86), Bridge — Makelele — Johnson (Stanic 83), Lampard (Nicolas 90), J Cole, Gronkjaer — Gudjohnsen *Subs not used* Ambrosio, Crespo
Scorer **Gronkjaer 20**
Referee **M Dean**

EVERTON

PREMIERSHIP

	P	W	D	L	F	A	GD	Pts
Arsenal	38	26	12	0	73	26	47	**90**
Chelsea	38	24	7	7	67	30	37	**79**
Man Utd	38	23	6	9	64	35	29	**75**
Liverpool	38	16	12	10	55	37	18	**60**
Newcastle	38	13	17	8	52	40	12	**56**
Aston Villa	38	15	11	12	48	44	4	**56**
Charlton	38	14	11	13	51	51	0	**53**
Bolton	38	14	11	13	48	56	-8	**53**
Fulham	38	14	10	14	52	46	6	**52**
Birmingham	38	12	14	12	43	48	-5	**50**
Middlesbro	38	13	9	16	44	52	-8	**48**
Southampton	38	12	11	15	44	45	-1	**47**
Portsmouth	38	12	9	17	47	54	-7	**45**
Tottenham	38	13	6	19	47	57	-10	**45**
Blackburn	38	12	8	18	51	59	-8	**44**
Man City	38	9	14	15	55	54	1	**41**
Everton	38	9	12	17	45	57	-12	**39**
Leicester	38	6	15	17	48	65	-17	**33**
Leeds	38	8	9	21	40	79	-39	**33**
Wolves	38	7	12	19	38	77	-39	**33**

FA CUP
Fourth round

CARLING CUP
Fourth round

Gripping stuff: until Euro 2004 Wayne Rooney's second season in the spotlight failed to live up to expectations as Everton struggled

Saturday August 16 2003
ARSENAL (a)
Lost 1-2   HT 0-1   Att 38,014   Position 17th
Wright — Pistone, Yobo, Stubbs, Unsworth (Li Tie 68) —
Watson, Linderoth (Rooney 58), Gravesen, Pembridge
(Naysmith 68) — Radzinski, Chadwick *Subs not used*
Weir, Simonsen *Booked* Gravesen, Li Tie, Rooney *Sent
off* Li Tie 87
Scorer **Radzinski 84**
Report page 60

Saturday August 23
FULHAM (h)
Won 3-1   HT 3-0   Att 37,604   Position 8th
With Marlet, a scorer in their opening-day victory,
omitted after handing in a transfer request on the eve of
the match, Fulham are beaten within 35 minutes.
Everton put defeat at Highbury behind them by racing
into a 3-0 lead that is never seriously threatened despite
a reply from Hayles.
Wright — Pistone, Yobo, Stubbs, Unsworth — Watson,
Linderoth, Pembridge, Naysmith — Radzinski, Rooney
(Chadwick 74) *Subs not used* Weir, Li Tie, Simonsen,
Osman *Booked* Pistone, Stubbs, Watson
Scorers **Naysmith 7, Unsworth 20, Watson 35**
Referee **N Barry**

Tuesday August 26
CHARLTON ATHLETIC (a)
Drew 2-2   HT 1-1   Att 26,336   Position 8th
Wright — Pistone, Yobo, Stubbs, Unsworth — Watson,
Linderoth, Pembridge, Naysmith — Radzinski, Rooney
Subs not used Simonsen, Weir, Li Tie, Hibbert, Chadwick
Booked Unsworth, Rooney
Scorers **Watson 26, Rooney 72**
Report page 112

Saturday August 30
LIVERPOOL (h)
Lost 0-3   HT 0-1   Att 40,200   Position 13th
The 169th Merseyside derby goes emphatically
Liverpool's way to ease the pressure on Gerard Houllier,
their manager, after two draws and a defeat in their first
three league games. Owen's double is followed by
Kewell's first for the Reds, while Rooney fluffs Everton's
three best chances and Ferguson hits the bar at 2-0
down.
Simonsen — Pistone, Yobo, Stubbs, Unsworth
(Gravesen ht) — Watson, Linderoth (Ferguson 71),
Pembridge, Naysmith — Radzinski, Rooney *Subs
not used* Weir, Chadwick, Turner *Booked* Watson,
Rooney, Naysmith
Referee **M Riley**

EVEN BY EVERTON'S PITIFUL standards it was a grim season.
Ten years on from Wimbledon and that narrow escape from relegation, it was a blessed relief that others were able to shape the survival
of a hopeless cause. Barely three hours of the campaign remained
when the ineptitude of a bankrupt and ailing Leeds United and the
swagger of Bolton Wanderers ensured that Everton's 125th season
was not to be their last in the top flight for the foreseeable future.

Everton's abysmal form, including a derisory haul of just two
points from their last six games of the season, led to yet another
stomach-churning, nail-biting finale. It was not what supporters,
who had thought their team's days of dancing on the Nationwide
League trapdoor had gone for ever, had expected.

The popular David Moyes had won the League Managers Association manager-of-the-season award after steering the Blues to
seventh place in the previous campaign, but, in retrospect, even that
effort, built largely on Moyes's motivational skills, was badly flawed.
Everton faded miserably well before the end of the campaign and
managed to concede not only a Champions League place but
squandered a Uefa Cup slot, too. The truth was that three points
from the last five games was a warning few had heeded as they
watched through their blue-tinted glasses. But the awful run-in to a
sunshine season had failed to dampen the ardour of Evertonians.
Moyes's magic had left the fans entranced and, of course, the arrival
of the Wonder Boy, Wayne Rooney, had lifted hopes sky-high.

So to August. Record season-ticket sales of 28,000 had led to a
waiting list and Moyes would be looking to produce a side worthy of
such faith. The tide of optimism had crashed over the breakwaters.
A new era of glory was about to begin at Goodison Park . . . or so fans
thought. Moyes had little or no money to spend. His main target,
Sean Davis, the Fulham midfield player, slipped away after a lengthy
cat-and-mouse chase. Moyes tried to prise Robbie Savage from
Birmingham City, but the starting day line-up was familiar — too
familiar, in fact. Moyes's pitiful budget stretched to deadline-day
deals for Nigel Martyn, the 37-year-old goalkeeper, who cost
virtually nothing, James McFadden, for whom he paid £1.25 million,
Kevin Kilbane, at £1 million and Francis Jeffers, who returned on
loan from Highbury.

The opening-day defeat away to Arsenal was to be put into
perspective as the Gunners sparkled throughout an unbeaten league
season. But the Everton rollercoaster was off and running.

At first it was hard to notice that the ride was bumpy. The patience
of saints has been instilled into these supporters and they were not
about to start doubting Moyes the messiah. However, ten points

HONOURS BOARD

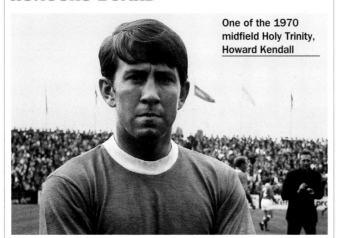

One of the 1970 midfield Holy Trinity, Howard Kendall

FOOTBALL LEAGUE
Champions 1891, 1915, 1928, 1932, 1939, 1963, 1970, 1985, 1987
Runners-up 1890, 1895, 1902, 1905, 1909, 1912, 1986
FA CUP
Winners 1906, 1933, 1966, 1984, 1995
Runners-up 1893, 1897, 1907, 1968, 1985, 1986, 1989
LEAGUE CUP
Runners-up 1977, 1984

CUP WINNERS' CUP
Winners 1985

Record attendance 78,299 (v Liverpool, first division, September 18, 1948)
Current capacity 40,228
Record victory 11-2 (v Derby County, FA Cup 1st rnd, January 18, 1890)
Record defeat 4-10 (v Tottenham Hotspur, first division, October 11, 1958)

from the first 12 games, including a Goodison mauling by Liverpool, still very much the Kings of Merseyside, saw shoulders slump. Coupled with the dismal return from the end of the previous season, the statistics were frightening: 13 points from 17 games. The finest of relegation form.

Everton's 3-0 defeat away to Spurs in October had brought the first murmurings of discontent, but November confirmed that all was not well. There was the first hint that Moyes had possibly begun to "lose" the dressing-room. A spat with Duncan Ferguson saw the forward hung out to dry for a fortnight. Moyes was later to have another row, this time with Jeffers, who did a U-turn after vowing never to play for the manager again.

The same month, ironically during a rare purple patch, Everton visited the Reebok Stadium, traditionally a happy hunting ground. Bolton won at a canter and Everton were jeered off the pitch by furious travelling fans. The expectations were great, the delivery non-existent. The honeymoon was well and truly over.

Rooney had become a fixture with England, but often seemed lost amid the mediocrity at Goodison. In December he scored one of the goals in his travel-sick side's only away win of the campaign, 2-1 over Portsmouth, but bizarrely, after an altercation with Steve Stone, the teenager sent himself off. Having left the pitch, he had to be ushered back on to it to receive a yellow card from Uriah Rennie, the referee, rather than the red he was expecting. It was an incident that

Saturday September 13
NEWCASTLE UNITED (h)
Drew 2-2 HT **0-0** Att **40,228** Position **13th**
Rooney, England's midweek hero against Liechtenstein, is injured early on, but even his explosive talent is hardly missed in a match of 11 yellow cards, two reds and three penalties. Two of those spot kicks are converted by Shearer (the second his 150th Newcastle goal), but Ferguson replies in identical fashion with a late equaliser, his first goal for 17 months.

Wright (Martyn 26) — Hibbert, Yobo, Stubbs, Naysmith — Watson (Ferguson 63), Linderoth, Gravesen, Kilbane — Radzinski, Rooney (Jeffers 30) *Subs not used* Weir, Unsworth *Booked* Stubbs, Watson, Linderoth, Ferguson, Jeffers *Sent off* Naysmith 58
Scorers **Radzinski 67, Ferguson 88 (pen)**
Referee **R Styles**

Sunday September 21
MIDDLESBROUGH (a)
Lost 0-1 HT **0-1** Att **28,113** Position **15th**
Martyn — Hibbert, Yobo, Stubbs, Naysmith — Watson (Carsley ht), Linderoth (Ferguson 70), Gravesen, Kilbane (McFadden 79) — Radzinski, Rooney *Subs not used* Turner, Pistone *Booked* Watson, Rooney, Kilbane
Report page 209

Wednesday September 24
STOCKPORT COUNTY (h)
Carling Cup, 2nd rnd
Won 3-0 HT **2-0** Att **19,807**
Managerless Stockport, of the second division, are brushed aside as Ferguson, starting a match for the first time in almost a year and a half, scores twice, first from the spot after a trip on Hibbert, then after being set up brilliantly by McFadden, who is making his full debut. Chadwick nets in between.

Martyn — Hibbert (Unsworth 61), Yobo (Clarke 61), Weir, Pistone — Watson, Carsley, Gravesen (Rooney 61), McFadden — Ferguson, Chadwick *Subs not used* Radzinski, Turner
Scorers **Ferguson 26 (pen), 56, Chadwick 44**
Referee **C Webster**

Sunday September 28
LEEDS UNITED (h)
Won 4-0 HT **3-0** Att **39,151** Position **10th**
This match is settled by the third Premiership hat-trick of the weekend — and the most unlikely, Watson following the example set by Van Nistelrooy and Lisbie. His first comes after a bad mistake by Roque Junior, Leeds's World Cup-winner, but his second is a superb finish from 40 yards with Robinson stranded. A cute chip from a narrow angle completes his treble. "We were outfought," Peter Reid admits.

Martyn — Hibbert, Yobo, Stubbs, Unsworth — Watson (Kilbane 75), Gravesen, Carsley, McFadden (Linderoth 87) — Ferguson, Radzinski (Rooney 75) *Subs not used* Weir, Turner
Scorers **Watson 27, 37, 52, Ferguson 39**
Referee **P Durkin**

Saturday October 4
TOTTENHAM HOTSPUR (a)
Lost 0-3 HT **0-1** Att **36,137** Position **12th**
Martyn — Hibbert, Yobo, Stubbs (Weir 33), Unsworth — Watson, Carsley, Gravesen, McFadden (Rooney 55) — Ferguson, Radzinski (Kilbane 55) *Subs not used* Turner, Campbell *Booked* Rooney, Hibbert
Report page 251

Sunday October 19
SOUTHAMPTON (h)
Drew 0-0   HT 0-0   Att 35,775   Position 13th
With Rooney and Phillips suspended — the Everton teenager is reportedly the subject of a £35 million transfer bid from Chelsea — this bore draw never gets off the ground. Southampton are slightly the more threatening side, Prutton wasting a late chance of a winner by shooting over with his first Premiership goal beckoning.

Martyn — Hibbert, Yobo, Weir, Naysmith — Watson, Carsley (Linderoth 64), Gravesen, McFadden (Kilbane 66) — Jeffers, Campbell *Subs not used* Unsworth, Li Tie, Wright *Booked* Carsley
Referee **M Messias**

Saturday October 25
ASTON VILLA (a)
Drew 0-0   HT 0-0   Att 36,146   Position 13th
Martyn — Hibbert, Yobo, Weir, Naysmith — Gravesen, Linderoth, Li Tie (Stubbs 80), Kilbane — Campbell (Ferguson 70), Rooney *Subs not used* Wright, Jeffers, McFadden *Booked* Ferguson
Report page 74

Wednesday October 29
CHARLTON ATHLETIC (h)
Carling Cup, 3rd rnd
Won 1-0   HT 1-0   Att 24,863
This is a tie notable for Nyarko's first Everton appearance for two years and Linderoth's overdue first goal, headed in after Rooney's deflected volley comes back off the bar. Euell misses two great chances either side of the goal, but Kiely is the busier goalkeeper and Charlton can have no complaints about defeat.

Martyn — Hibbert, Yobo, Weir, Naysmith — Gravesen (Li Tie 90), Linderoth, Nyarko (Stubbs 88), McFadden (Radzinski 75) — Ferguson, Rooney *Subs not used* Simonsen, Jeffers *Booked* Naysmith
Scorer **Linderoth 42**
Referee **A Wiley**

Saturday November 1
CHELSEA (h)
Lost 0-1   HT 0-0   Att 40,189   Position 16th
The tone for a fine contest is set when Mutu tries to score from the kick-off and Radzinski misses a great chance — all before a minute is up. Everton have the best and most of them, Nyarko rattling the bar and Jeffers missing a sitter with his head, but the match is settled by Mutu's 49th-minute header. Television replays suggest that the Romanian may also have used his hand.

Martyn — Hibbert, Yobo, Weir (Stubbs 33), Naysmith — Gravesen, Linderoth (McFadden 65), Nyarko, Kilbane — Radzinski (Jeffers 65), Rooney *Subs not used* Li Tie, Simonsen
Referee **J Winter**

Monday November 10
BLACKBURN ROVERS (a)
Lost 1-2   HT 0-2   Att 22,179   Position 18th
Martyn — Hibbert, Yobo, Clarke, Naysmith (Jeffers 82) — Gravesen, Linderoth, Nyarko (Unsworth ht), Kilbane (McFadden ht) — Campbell, Radzinski *Subs not used* Chadwick, Simonsen *Booked* Linderoth, Campbell
Scorer **Radzinski 49**
Report page 95

Yobo tangles with Savage at Goodison in the last game of 2003

summed up Everton's season. Rooney actually went on to collect more cards than he did goals.

A fortnight later it was off to Old Trafford and the start of an extraordinary pair of Premiership encounters with Manchester United. Everton, in total, put five goals past the mighty Reds — but got nothing for their trouble. That was to start something of a trend as they embarked on a spell of giving away late goals and points seven times in 14 matches. They led 3-1 away to Southampton with eight minutes to go, were ten seconds from a third successive league win away to Leicester City, and the disease permeated through the rest of the season. By May, only the inadequacies of the three relegated clubs ensured another season in the Premiership, secured with a record top-flight low of 39 points. Safe almost by default.

By the time that Everton lost at home for the sixth time in the season, a deserved double for Bolton, Moyes admitted that he was "ashamed" and "embarrassed" by his team's performances. Finally, there was the ignominy of that last-day 5-1 pounding away to Manchester City: a shoot-out for sixteenth and seventeenth places, a joust to decide the worst team not to go down.

Moyes, who had fed on scraps, was furious at such capitulation. He angrily announced that some players had worn the blue shirt for the last time. He should not have fretted too much — it's what they are used to down Goodison way. It was just a case of normal service being resumed.

THE MANAGER

David Moyes

After they finished seventh the previous season, David Moyes was expected to build on the Everton renaissance, but it all went wrong amid a lack of money for quality players, one away league victory and ripples of discontent from the Goodison Park dressing-room. Moyes, as candid as ever, admitted that if his quest to bring success to the club meant upsetting people, so be it. Disputes involving two of his forwards, Duncan Ferguson and Francis Jeffers, showed that he meant it, too. Moyes said that he was grateful to his under-fire board, which offered him a new deal, for their support, particularly as he had not done very well. Shockingly, he was serious.

Chris Gill

APPEARANCES

	Prem	FAC	CC	Total
K Campbell	8 (9)	0 (1)	-	8 (10)
L Carsley	15 (6)	2	2	19 (6)
N Chadwick	1 (2)	-	1	2 (2)
P Clarke	1	-	0 (1)	1 (1)
D Ferguson	13 (7)	2	2	17 (7)
T Gravesen	29 (1)	3	3	35 (1)
A Hibbert	24 (1)	3	3	30 (1)
F Jeffers	5 (13)	0 (3)	1	6 (16)
K Kilbane	26 (4)	3	-	29 (4)
Li Tie	4 (1)	-	1 (1)	5 (2)
T Linderoth	23 (4)	-	1 (1)	24 (5)
N Martyn	33 (1)	3	3	39 (1)
J McFadden	11 (12)	1	3	15 (12)
G Naysmith	27 (2)	2 (1)	2	31 (3)
A Nyarko	7 (4)	2	1	10 (4)
L Osman	3 (1)	-	0 (1)	3 (2)
M Pembridge	4	-	-	4
A Pistone	20 (1)	2	1	23 (1)
T Radzinski	28 (6)	2	0 (2)	30 (8)
W Rooney	26 (8)	3	2 (1)	31 (9)
S Simonsen	1	-	-	1
A Stubbs	26 (2)	2	1 (1)	29 (3)
D Unsworth	22 (4)	3	1 (1)	26 (5)
S Watson	22 (2)	0 (1)	1	23 (3)
D Weir	9 (1)	-	2	11 (1)
R Wright	4	-	-	4
J Yobo	26 (1)	0 (1)	2	28 (2)

Saturday November 22
WOLVERHAMPTON WANDERERS (h)
Won 2-0   HT 2-0   Att 40,190   Position 14th
Having been sucked into the relegation fight, Everton battle their way out of the bottom three with two early goals against their fellow strugglers. "It was murder out there," Alex Rae concedes after what amounts to a 2-0 stuffing for Wolves, Everton's first league win in six attempts.
Martyn – Hibbert, Yobo, Stubbs, Unsworth – McFadden (Osman 82), Linderoth, Gravesen, Kilbane – Radzinski, Rooney (Jeffers 82) *Subs not used* Simonsen, Nyarko, Clarke *Booked* Linderoth, McFadden
Scorers **Radzinski 16, Kilbane 19**
Referee **M Riley**

Saturday November 29
BOLTON WANDERERS (a)
Lost 0-2   HT 0-1   Att 27,350   Position 18th
Martyn – Hibbert, Yobo, Stubbs, Unsworth – Carsley, Gravesen (Nyarko 71), Linderoth (McFadden ht), Kilbane – Radzinski, Rooney (Jeffers 56) *Subs not used* Simonsen, Naysmith *Booked* Carsley, McFadden
Report page 104

Wednesday December 3
MIDDLESBROUGH (a)
Carling Cup, 4th rnd
Drew 0-0 (aet; lost 4-5 on pens)   HT 0-0   Att 18,568
Martyn – Hibbert, Stubbs, Unsworth, Naysmith – Carsley, Gravesen, Li Tie (Linderoth 117), McFadden – Jeffers (Osman 108), Rooney (Radzinski 98) *Subs not used* Simonsen, Clarke *Booked* Unsworth, Gravesen, Li Tie
Report page 211

Sunday December 7
MANCHESTER CITY (h)
Drew 0-0   HT 0-0   Att 37,871   Position 17th
Around 100 million Chinese tune in to see Sun Jihai and Li Tie go head to head, but 99.99 million probably tune out again before the end of a drab contest between sides short of confidence. Rooney is replaced again as his poor form continues, this time in the dressing-room as David Moyes abandons his new formation at half-time.
Martyn – Hibbert (Kilbane ht), Stubbs, Unsworth, Naysmith – Li Tie, Gravesen, Carsley – Rooney (McFadden ht) – Jeffers (Campbell 64), Radzinski *Subs not used* Linderoth, Simonsen *Booked* Naysmith
Referee **J Winter**

Saturday December 13
PORTSMOUTH (a)
Won 2-1   HT 2-1   Att 20,101   Position 15th
Martyn – Pistone, Stubbs, Unsworth, Naysmith – Watson (Rooney 24), Carsley, Gravesen, Kilbane – Radzinski (McFadden 84), Campbell *Subs not used* Simonsen, Jeffers, Li Tie *Booked* Rooney
Scorers **Carsley 27, Rooney 42**
Report page 233

Saturday December 20
LEICESTER CITY (h)
Won 3-2   HT 1-1   Att 37,007   Position 11th
David Moyes's Midas touch earns Everton their first back-to-back wins since April. Leicester, having turned a 1-0 deficit into a 2-1 lead, are undone first by one substitute, Rooney getting his second goal in two games from the bench, then by another, Ferguson heading down for Radzinski to get the winner.

Martyn — Pistone (Hibbert 27), Stubbs, Unsworth, Naysmith — McFadden (Rooney 60), Carsley, Gravesen, Kilbane — Radzinski, Campbell (Ferguson 77) *Subs not used* Li Tie, Simonsen *Booked* Stubbs, Ferguson
Scorers **Carsley 33, Rooney 71, Radzinski 79**
Referee **P Dowd**

Friday December 26
MANCHESTER UNITED (a)
Lost 2-3   HT 1-2   Att 67,642   Position 14th
Martyn — Hibbert, Stubbs, Unsworth, Naysmith — Li Tie, Linderoth (Jeffers 63), Gravesen, Kilbane — Campbell (Ferguson 83), Rooney (McFadden 70) *Subs not used* Simonsen, Yobo *Booked* Jeffers, Rooney
Scorers **G Neville 13 (og), Ferguson 90**
Report page 201

Sunday December 28
BIRMINGHAM CITY (h)
Won 1-0   HT 0-0   Att 39,631   Position 11th
Putting Rooney on the bench is proving to be a deadly weapon for Everton, who win for the third time in four matches with the help of a goal from their supersub. Rooney pounces when Taylor fails to hold Naysmith's corner under pressure, but City are convinced that their goalkeeper was fouled. "We feel aggrieved," Steve Bruce says.

Martyn — Hibbert, Stubbs, Unsworth, Naysmith — Carsley (Rooney ht), Nyarko (Yobo 84), Gravesen, Kilbane — Ferguson, Radzinski (Jeffers 78) *Subs not used* Simonsen, McFadden
Scorer **Rooney 69**
Referee **R Styles**

Saturday January 3 2004
NORWICH CITY (h)
FA Cup, 3rd rnd
Won 3-1   HT 2-1   Att 29,955
This tie is high on many lists of possible upsets, but Ferguson proves deadly from 12 yards to see off the first division leaders. Both penalties (dispatched into opposite corners) are awarded for fouls by Roberts on Stubbs, after Brennan's first goal for Norwich had cancelled out Kilbane's early header.

Martyn — Hibbert, Stubbs, Unsworth, Naysmith — McFadden (Jeffers 63), Gravesen (Yobo ht), Carsley, Kilbane — Rooney, Ferguson (Campbell 82) *Subs not used* Simonsen, Radzinski *Booked* Yobo, Naysmith, Hibbert
Scorers **Kilbane 15, Ferguson 38 (pen), 70 (pen)**
Referee **M Messias**

Wednesday January 7
ARSENAL (h)
Drew 1-1   HT 0-1   Att 38,726   Position 11th
Everton, who ended Arsenal's long unbeaten domestic run in this fixture last season, have to be content with a draw this time, but a deserved one. Kanu scores for the first time in a year to give Arsenal the lead, but — after Rooney spurns a header in front of an open goal — Radzinski levels after Lehmann can only parry a shot from Jeffers, the on-loan Gunner.

Martyn — Hibbert, Stubbs, Unsworth, Naysmith — Carsley, Li Tie (Linderoth ht), Kilbane (Jeffers 70), Rooney — Ferguson, Radzinski (Campbell 87) *Subs not used* Simonsen, Yobo
Scorer **Radzinski 75**
Referee **A Wiley**

MATCH OF THE SEASON

Everton 3   Tottenham Hotspur 1
Goodison Park, Friday April 9 2004
Nick Szczepanik

AFTER ARSENAL'S VICTORY OVER Liverpool at lunchtime, part two of yesterday's North West versus North London double-header went decisively the way of Merseyside. Everton, who have found Tottenham Hotspur unusually difficult opponents recently, defied history to earn only their second victory over the Londoners in 25 league matches. As a result, they put nine points between themselves and the bottom three which, together with Liverpool's defeat, gave their supporters a perfect start to the Easter weekend. "We didn't let them settle and played good, exciting football," David Moyes, the Everton manager, said. "It was an important win for us and the aim is to win the last six games."

Tottenham's followers, in contrast, had very little to cheer after an abject first half from their team, coupled with Arsenal's earlier win. They had seen Tottenham, for whom this was a fourth successive defeat, overrun by what looked like a weakened Everton side but which produced a series of fluent moves. A second-half improvement, which brought a goal by Stephen Carr, would have perked them up, but the Ireland defender then undid his good work when he was sent off for a second bookable offence.

Moyes had called for his defenders to cut out the individual errors that had cost the side dearly in the 4-2 defeat by Newcastle United at St James' Park last weekend, but, in the first 45 minutes, they had clearly decided that scoring goals was preferable to conceding them. In the absence of Wayne Rooney and Duncan Ferguson, who were suspended, and Kevin Campbell, who was unwell, defenders scored all three of Everton's goals. Moyes also praised James McFadden, the Scotland forward, who was behind the first two goals with running that unsettled the Tottenham defence.

After 16 minutes, McFadden's persistence in chasing a long forward pass by Gary Naysmith forced a corner and, when Thomas Gravesen bent the ball into the penalty area, Steve Watson nodded it on and David Unsworth turned it past Kasey Keller with his thigh. Unsworth had looked offside, but Tottenham's protests were in vain and, after 25 minutes, they were two behind. Again McFadden charged forward and his run at goal was ended illegally by Gary Doherty 20 yards out. From the free kick, Naysmith curled the ball around the wall with his left foot and past the right hand of Keller. "In Wayne Rooney, at 18, and James McFadden, at 20, we have two of the brightest young players in this country," Moyes said.

Tottenham did not manage a shot worthy of the name until Jermain Defoe's effort in the 28th minute and Everton resumed their rampage, scoring a third goal after 40 minutes. Doherty seemed to have made up for his own error when he headed clear

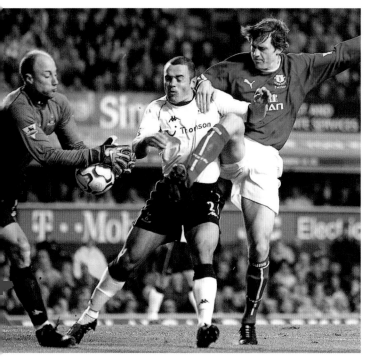

Kilbane is thwarted by Keller and Carr in his efforts to reach a cross

from an empty net with Keller out of his ground, but as Gravesen drove forward on to the loose ball, Doherty brought him down in more or less the same place that he had felled McFadden earlier. This time Gravesen took the free kick, which was hard, low and straight through the wall. Keller could only parry the ball into the path of Joseph Yobo, who scored with ease from a yard out. It was the second goal of his Everton career, only six days after his first.

With Frederic Kanoute on in the second half, Tottenham produced a more positive showing and it was rewarded with a goal after 74 minutes. Rohan Ricketts played a perfect pass inside Kevin Kilbane and Carr ran on to it, cut the ball back on to his left foot and beat Martyn with a low shot into the far corner. His moment of glory was brief: within seconds, he had tugged back McFadden and, having been booked in the first half for a foul on Gravesen, was shown the red card.

"The excellence of the two free kicks was decisive, but we were very poor," David Pleat, the acting Tottenham manager, said. "Everton's passion and aggression early on sent the whole game in their favour. I saw Real Madrid in the week and it can happen to the best players in the world. And we're not the best players in the world."

EVERTON (4-4-2): N Martyn — A Pistone, J Yobo, D Unsworth, G Naysmith — S Watson, T Gravesen (sub: L Carsley, 88min), T Linderoth, K Kilbane — T Radzinski, J McFadden (sub: F Jeffers, 78). **Substitutes not used:** R Wright, A Nyarko, A Hibbert. **Booked:** Linderoth.
TOTTENHAM HOTSPUR (4-4-2): K Keller — S Carr, G Doherty, A Gardner, S Kelly — S Davies (sub: R Ricketts, 73), M Brown, J Redknapp (sub: G Bunjevcevic, 73), C Ziege (sub: F Kanoute, 46min) — R Keane, J Defoe. **Substitutes not used:** J Jackson, L Hirschfeld. **Booked:** Redknapp, Doherty, Carr. **Sent off:** Carr.

Saturday January 10
FULHAM (a)
Lost 1-2   HT 0-1   Att 17,103   Position 12th
Martyn — Hibbert, Weir, Unsworth, Naysmith — Carsley (Rooney 57), Linderoth, Kilbane — Radzinski (McFadden 57), Campbell (Ferguson 57), Jeffers *Subs not used* Simonsen, Pistone
Scorer **Kilbane 81**
Report page 148

Saturday January 17
CHARLTON ATHLETIC (h)
Lost 0-1   HT 0-1   Att 36,322   Position 14th
Alan Curbishley's decision to omit Parker, because the midfield player has been unsettled by a bid from Chelsea, is vindicated as Charlton earn a slightly fortuitous win that leaves them five points clear in fourth place, with dreams of the Champions League growing. Fish clears off the line from Ferguson after Stuart, a former Evertonian, scores the decisive goal.
Martyn — Pistone, Stubbs, Unsworth, Naysmith — Rooney, Carsley (Campbell 82), Gravesen, Kilbane — Jeffers (Radzinski 57), Ferguson *Subs not used* Weir, Simonsen, Linderoth *Booked* Unsworth, Radzinski, Ferguson, Carsley
Referee **M Riley**

Sunday January 25
FULHAM (h)
FA Cup, 4th rnd
Drew 1-1   HT 0-0   Att 27,862
It has been a long time coming, but Jeffers finally gets off the mark after his return on loan to Goodison with a last-gasp equaliser to earn a replay when Van der Sar parries Ferguson's shot. Davis, a transfer target for the Merseysiders last season, gives Fulham the lead early in the first half.
Martyn — Hibbert, Stubbs, Unsworth (Naysmith 59), Pistone (Jeffers 84) — Gravesen, Nyarko, Kilbane — Rooney, Ferguson, Radzinski *Subs not used* Simonsen, Carsley, Campbell *Booked* Rooney
Scorer **Jeffers 90**
Referee **D Gallagher**

Saturday January 31
LIVERPOOL (a)
Drew 0-0   HT 0-0   Att 44,056   Position 14th
Martyn — Hibbert, Stubbs, Pistone, Naysmith — Gravesen, Nyarko (Carsley 58), Kilbane — Rooney (Watson 77), Ferguson, Radzinski (Jeffers 73) *Subs not used* Simonsen, Clarke *Booked* Gravesen
Report page 180

Wednesday February 4
FULHAM (a)
FA Cup, 4th rnd replay
Lost 1-2 (aet; 1-1 after 90min)   HT 0-0   Att 11,551
Martyn — Hibbert, Pistone, Unsworth, Naysmith — Carsley, Gravesen, Nyarko (Watson 62), Kilbane — Rooney, Radzinski (Jeffers 62) *Subs not used* Simonsen, Linderoth, Clarke *Booked* Carsley
Scorer **Jeffers 90**
Report page 149

Saturday February 7
MANCHESTER UNITED (h)
Lost 3-4   **HT 0-3**   Att **40,190**   Position **15th**
Probably the match of the season so far. United romp into a three-goal lead that could have been six or seven — after three half-time substitutions — fight back to 3-3 with three headers from three set-pieces (one an own goal), only for United to win anyway with Van Nistelrooy's late header, the Dutchman having earlier scored his 100th goal for the club. Football? Bloody hell . . .

Martyn — Hibbert, Stubbs, Unsworth, Pistone (Naysmith ht) — Watson (Rooney ht), Gravesen, Carsley, Kilbane — Jeffers (Radzinski ht), Ferguson *Subs not used* Linderoth, Simonsen *Booked* Gravesen
Scorers **Unsworth 49, O'Shea 65 (og), Kilbane 75**
Referee **N Barry**

Wednesday February 11
BIRMINGHAM CITY (a)
Lost 0-3   **HT 0-2**   Att **29,004**   Position **15th**
Martyn — Hibbert, Stubbs, Unsworth (Pistone ht), Naysmith — Radzinski (McFadden 59), Gravesen, Carsley, Kilbane — Ferguson (Campbell ht), Rooney *Subs not used* Simonsen, Linderoth
Report page 87

Saturday February 21
SOUTHAMPTON (a)
Drew 3-3   **HT 2-0**   Att **31,875**   Position **16th**
Martyn — Hibbert, Stubbs, Unsworth, Pistone — Watson, Gravesen, Linderoth, Kilbane — Ferguson, Rooney *Subs not used* Simonsen, McFadden, Naysmith, Radzinski, Campbell
Scorers **Rooney 7, 78, Ferguson 32**
Report page 246

Saturday February 28
ASTON VILLA (h)
Won 2-0   **HT 0-0**   Att **39,353**   Position **14th**
After four wins and a draw in five games, Aston Villa's revival ends when Radzinski, with a header from Rooney's clever cross, and Gravesen, a fine finish for his opening goal of the season, earn Everton their first win in ten league and cup games. "We're not good enough to strut and stroll around," David O'Leary complains.

Martyn — Hibbert, Yobo, Stubbs, Pistone (Unsworth 22) — Watson (Radzinski 67), Linderoth, Gravesen, Kilbane — Rooney, Ferguson (Campbell 88) *Subs not used* Simonsen, McFadden *Booked* Unsworth, Linderoth, Gravesen, Rooney
Scorers **Radzinski 78, Gravesen 83**
Referee **M Messias**

Saturday March 13
PORTSMOUTH (h)
Won 1-0   **HT 0-0**   Att **40,105**   Position **14th**
Another dismal away-day for Portsmouth is compounded when windows on their coach are shattered by bricks thrown as it departs Goodison. Rooney, with a quick change of feet and an unerring low shot, wins the match for Everton to mark David Moyes's second anniversary as manager.

Martyn — Hibbert, Yobo, Stubbs, Naysmith — Watson, Nyarko, Linderoth, Kilbane — Ferguson (Radzinski 32), Rooney *Subs not used* Wright, Unsworth, McFadden, Carsley
Scorer **Rooney 78**
Referee **N Barry**

THE PLAYERS

KEVIN CAMPBELL (forward) **Born** February 4, 1970, Lambeth **Ht** 6ft 1in **Wt** 14st 0lb **Signed from** Nottingham Forest, March 1999, £3m

LEE CARSLEY (midfield) **Born** February 28, 1974, Birmingham **Ht** 5ft 10in **Wt** 12st 0lb **Signed from** Coventry City, February 2002, £1.95m

NICK CHADWICK (forward) **Born** October 26, 1982, Market Drayton **Ht** 5ft 11in **Wt** 12st 12lb **Signed from** trainee, October 1999

PETER CLARKE (defender) **Born** January 3, 1982, Southport **Ht** 6ft 0in **Wt** 12st 1lb **Signed from** trainee, January 1999

DUNCAN FERGUSON (forward) **Born** December 27, 1971, Stirling **Ht** 6ft 4in **Wt** 13st 12lb **Signed from** Newcastle United, August 2000, £3.75m

THOMAS GRAVESEN (midfield) **Born** March 11, 1976, Vejle, Denmark **Ht** 6ft 0in **Wt** 13st 0lb **Signed from** SV Hamburg, August 2000, £2.5m

ANTHONY HIBBERT (defender) **Born** February 20, 1981, Liverpool **Ht** 5ft 9in **Wt** 11st 9lb **Signed from** trainee, July 1998

FRANCIS JEFFERS (forward) **Born** January 25, 1981, Liverpool **Ht** 5ft 9in **Wt** 10st 8lb **Signed from** Arsenal (loan), September 2003

KEVIN KILBANE (midfield) **Born** February 1, 1977, Preston **Ht** 6ft 0in **Wt** 13st 0lb **Signed from** Sunderland, September 2003, £1m

NIGEL MARTYN (goalkeeper) **Born** August 11, 1986, St Austell **Ht** 6ft 2in **Wt** 14st 7lb **Signed from** Leeds United, September 2003, nominal

JAMES McFADDEN (midfield) **Born** April 14, 1983, Glasgow **Ht** 5ft 10in **Wt** 11st 1lb **Signed from** Motherwell, September 2003, £1.25m

TOBIAS LINDEROTH (midfield) **Born** April 21, 1979, Marseilles **Ht** 5ft 9in **Wt** 11st 9lb **Signed from** Stabaek, Norway, February 2002, £2.5m

GARY NAYSMITH (defender) **Born** November 16, 1979, Edinburgh **Ht** 5ft 10in **Wt** 12st 1lb **Signed from** Heart of Midlothian, October 2000, £1.75m

ALEX NYARKO (midfield) **Born** October 15, 1973, Accra **Ht** 6ft 3in **Wt** 12st 0lb **Signed from** Lens, July 2001, £4.5m

LEON OSMAN (midfield) **Born** May 17, 1981, Billinge, Merseyside **Ht** 5ft 8in **Wt** 10st 7lb **Signed from** trainee, August 2000

MARK PEMBRIDGE (midfield) **Born** November 29, 1970, Merthyr Tydfil **Ht** 5ft 9in **Wt** 12st 0lb **Signed from** Sheffield Wednesday, August 1999, £800,000

ALESSANDRO PISTONE (defender) **Born** July 27, 1975, Milan **Ht** 6ft 1in **Wt** 13st 6lb **Signed from** Newcastle United, July 2000, £3m

TOMASZ RADZINSKI (forward) **Born** December 14, 1973, Poznan, Poland **Ht** 5ft 8in **Wt** 11st 10lb **Signed from** Anderlecht, August 2001, £4.5m

WAYNE ROONEY (forward) **Born** October 24, 1985, Croxteth, Liverpool **Ht** 5ft 10in **Wt** 12st 4lb **Signed from** trainee, April 2002

STEVE SIMONSEN (goalkeeper) **Born** April 3, 1979, South Shields **Ht** 6ft 3in **Wt** 13st 2lb **Signed from** Tranmere Rovers, September 1998, £3.3m

ALAN STUBBS (defender) **Born** October 6, 1971, Kirkby, Liverpool **Ht** 6ft 2in **Wt** 14st 4lb **Signed from** Celtic, July 2001, free

LI TIE (midfield) **Born** September 18, 1977, Liaoning, China **Ht** 6ft 0in **Wt** 12st 1lb **Signed from** Liaoning Bodao (initial loan), July 2002, undisclosed

DAVID UNSWORTH (defender) **Born** October 16, 1973, Chorley **Ht** 6ft 1in **Wt** 15st 0lb **Signed from** Aston Villa, August 1998, £3m

STEVE WATSON (midfield) **Born** April 1, 1974, North Shields **Ht** 6ft 1in **Wt** 13st 10lb **Signed from** Aston Villa, July 2000, £2.5m

DAVID WEIR (defender) **Born** May 10, 1970, Falkirk **Ht** 6ft 2in **Wt** 13st 12lb **Signed from** Heart of Midlothian, February 1999, £250,000

RICHARD WRIGHT (goalkeeper) **Born** November 5, 1977, Ipswich **Ht** 6ft 2in **Wt** 14st 1lb **Signed from** Arsenal, July 2002, £3.5m

JOSEPH YOBO (defender) **Born** September 5, 1980, Kano, Nigeria **Ht** 6ft 1in **Wt** 13st 2lb **Signed from** Marseilles, July 2002 (initial loan), £4.5m

STATS AND FACTS

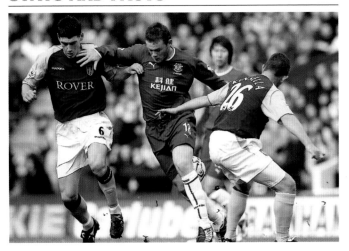

● A season after becoming the first club to compete in the top division for 100 seasons, Everton completed their fiftieth successive season in the top flight.

● Five penalties were scored against Everton in their first five Premiership games.

● Wayne Rooney has recorded more yellow cards (20) than goals (17) in his club career.

● Everton beat Tottenham Hotspur on Good Friday having won just once in their previous 24 league meetings.

● The club's past eight away games against Arsenal have ended in defeat.

● Everton have won none of their past 17 games away to Aston Villa.

● Everton suffered only their second home defeat to Charlton Athletic in 15 matches in January.

Bill Edgar

GOALSCORERS

	Prem	FAC	CC	Total
K Campbell	1	-	-	1
L Carsley	2	1	-	3
N Chadwick	-	-	1	1
D Ferguson	5 (1p)	2 (2p)	2 (1p)	9 (4p)
T Gravesen	2	-	-	2
F Jeffers	-	1	-	1
K Kilbane	3	1	-	4
T Linderoth	-	-	1	1
G Naysmith	2	-	-	2
L Osman	1	-	-	1
T Radzinski	8	-	-	8
W Rooney	9	-	-	9
D Unsworth	2	-	-	2
S Watson	6	-	-	6
J Yobo	2	-	-	2
Own goals	2	-	-	2

Saturday March 20
LEICESTER CITY (a)
Drew 1-1   HT 0-0   Att 31,650   Position 14th
Martyn – Pistone, Yobo, Stubbs, Naysmith – Watson, Linderoth, Gravesen, McFadden (Radzinski ht) – Rooney (Campbell 88), Ferguson Subs not used Wright, Unsworth, Nyarko Booked Gravesen, Radzinski, Rooney, Ferguson, McFadden Sent off Ferguson 41
Scorer **Rooney 75**
Report page 171

Saturday March 27
MIDDLESBROUGH (h)
Drew 1-1   HT 0-0   Att 38,210   Position 13th
Everton stretch their unbeaten run to five games but are disappointed to drop two points after taking the lead with only 12 minutes of a poor contest remaining. Rooney suffers ankle and back injuries four days before England's Euro 2004 warm-up match against Sweden.

Martyn – Pistone, Yobo, Stubbs (Unsworth ht), Naysmith – Watson (Jeffers 85), Linderoth, Gravesen, Kilbane – Radzinski, Rooney Subs not used Wright, Nyarko, McFadden
Scorer **Radzinski 78**
Referee **S Bennett**

Saturday April 3
NEWCASTLE UNITED (a)
Lost 2-4   HT 1-2   Att 42,155   Position 14th
Martyn – Pistone, Yobo, Unsworth, Naysmith – Watson, Linderoth (Nyarko 68), Gravesen, Kilbane (McFadden 68) – Campbell, Radzinski Subs not used Wright, Carsley, Hibbert
Scorers **Gravesen 12, Yobo 81**
Report page 226

Friday April 9
TOTTENHAM HOTSPUR (h)
Won 3-1   HT 3-0   Att 38,086   Position 12th
Suddenly Everton are nine points clear of the relegation zone. A first-half demolition of a ragged Spurs side, all three goals coming from defenders, eases the nerves at Goodison. Carr scores a fine reply, but the Spurs defender immediately blots his copybook by incurring his second booking.

Martyn – Pistone, Yobo, Unsworth, Naysmith – Watson, Gravesen (Carsley 88), Linderoth, Kilbane – Radzinski, McFadden (Jeffers 78) Subs not used Wright, Nyarko, Hibbert
Scorers **Unsworth 17, Naysmith 24, Yobo 40**
Referee **R Styles**

Tuesday April 13
LEEDS UNITED (a)
Drew 1-1   HT 1-0   Att 39,835   Position 13th
Martyn – Pistone, Yobo, Unsworth, Naysmith – Watson (McFadden 55), Gravesen (Carsley 77), Linderoth (Nyarko 55), Kilbane – Rooney, Radzinski Subs not used Wright, Hibbert Booked Nyarko
Scorer **Rooney 13**
Report page 161

PLAYER OF THE SEASON
Nigel Martyn

Some of the best things in life are free — and Nigel Martyn, 37, is testimony to that. The goalkeeper arrived at Goodison years late, but just in the nick of time as far as Everton were concerned.

He was coveted by the Toffees in 1996 but joined Leeds United after a bungled transfer bid. Joined in September 2003 and later stepped in for the injured Richard Wright. David Moyes said that Martyn was "one of the best signings I have ever made". Everyone else just felt that Martyn's magnificent form saved the club from relegation. The fact he was touted for a Euro 2004 squad place with England said it all.

Chris Gill

Saturday April 17
CHELSEA (a)
Drew 0-0   HT 0-0   Att 41,169   Position 13th
Martyn — Pistone, Yobo, Weir, Naysmith — McFadden (Carsley 57), Gravesen (Watson 85), Linderoth, Kilbane — Radzinski (Jeffers 78), Rooney *Subs not used* Wright, Nyarko
Report page 131

Saturday April 24
BLACKBURN ROVERS (h)
Lost 0-1   HT 0-0   Att 38,884   Position 14th
The magic 40-point mark is the prize for the winners of a poor match between the season's biggest underachievers — and Blackburn grab it thanks to Stead, who scores his fifth goal in ten games with a classical near-post header.

Martyn — Pistone, Yobo, Weir, Naysmith (Unsworth 63) — Watson, Gravesen (Nyarko 22), Linderoth, Kilbane — Rooney, Radzinski (McFadden 79) *Subs not used* Wright, Jeffers
Referee **P Dowd**

Saturday May 1
WOLVERHAMPTON WANDERERS (a)
Lost 1-2   HT 1-0   Att 29,395   Position 15th
Martyn — Hibbert, Yobo, Weir, Pistone — McFadden (Jeffers 82), Nyarko (Campbell 88), Carsley, Osman — Radzinski, Rooney *Subs not used* Wright, Stubbs, Linderoth *Booked* Rooney
Scorer **Osman 3**
Report page 268

Saturday May 8
BOLTON WANDERERS (h)
Lost 1-2   HT 0-1   Att 40,190   Position 16th
A season that David Moyes has called "an embarrassment" gets no better for the Everton manager as Djorkaeff's second successive double earns Bolton their fifth straight win. Ferguson sandwiches a reply between the Frenchman's first, scored after some clever footwork, and his late conversion of Charlton's low left-wing cross.

Martyn — Hibbert, Yobo, Weir (Campbell 90), Pistone (Radzinski ht) — Watson, Nyarko (Carsley ht), Osman, McFadden — Rooney, Ferguson *Subs not used* Wright, Linderoth *Booked* Weir
Scorer **Ferguson 68**
Referee **P Durkin**

Saturday May 15
MANCHESTER CITY (a)
Lost 1-5   HT 0-3   Att 47,284   Position 17th
Martyn — Yobo, Weir, Stubbs, Hibbert — Watson (Chadwick 72), Osman, Carsley, McFadden (Campbell ht) — Rooney, Radzinski (Linderoth 86) *Subs not used* Clarke, Wright *Booked* Rooney
Scorer **Campbell 60**
Report page 194

FULHAM

PREMIERSHIP

	P	W	D	L	F	A	GD	Pts
Arsenal	38	26	12	0	73	26	47	**90**
Chelsea	38	24	7	7	67	30	37	**79**
Man Utd	38	23	6	9	64	35	29	**75**
Liverpool	38	16	12	10	55	37	18	**60**
Newcastle	38	13	17	8	52	40	12	**56**
Aston Villa	38	15	11	12	48	44	4	**56**
Charlton	38	14	11	13	51	51	0	**53**
Bolton	38	14	11	13	48	56	-8	**53**
Fulham	38	14	10	14	52	46	6	**52**
Birmingham	38	12	14	12	43	48	-5	**50**
Middlesbro	38	13	9	16	44	52	-8	**48**
Southampton	38	12	11	15	44	45	-1	**47**
Portsmouth	38	12	9	17	47	54	-7	**45**
Tottenham	38	13	6	19	47	57	-10	**45**
Blackburn	38	12	8	18	51	59	-8	**44**
Man City	38	9	14	15	55	54	1	**41**
Everton	38	9	12	17	45	57	-12	**39**
Leicester	38	6	15	17	48	65	-17	**33**
Leeds	38	8	9	21	40	79	-39	**33**
Wolves	38	7	12	19	38	77	-39	**33**

FA CUP
Sixth round

CARLING CUP
Second round

Keeper of dreams: during 2003-04, Edwin van der Sar frequently showed why Jean Tigana paid Juventus £5 million for his services

Saturday August 16 2003
MIDDLESBROUGH (h)
Won 3-2 HT 1-1 Att 14,546 Position 3rd
Widely tipped for relegation, still in exile and with a
rookie manager at the helm, Fulham make the best
possible start by edging out Middlesbrough in an
excellent contest. Van der Sar's penalty save from
Christie with Fulham 2-1 up proves crucial, Nemeth
lobbing Middlesbrough's second goal nine minutes
from time

Van der Sar — Volz, Goma, Djetou, Bonnissel —
Legwinski — Marlet (Boa Morte 90), Clark, Inamoto,
Malbranque — Saha (Hayles 70) Subs not used Crossley,
Knight, Buari Booked Legwinski
Scorers **Marlet** 18, **Inamoto** 56, **Saha** 70
Referee **G Poll**

Saturday August 23
EVERTON (a)
Lost 1-3 HT 0-3 Att 37,604 Position 11th
Van der Sar — Volz, Goma, Djetou (Knight 57), Bonnissel
— Legwinski (Hayles ht) — Boa Morte, Clark, Inamoto
(Buari 62), Malbranque — Saha Subs not used Sava,
Crossley Booked Volz, Goma, Malbranque, Hayles
Scorer **Hayles** 69
Report page 134

Saturday August 30
TOTTENHAM HOTSPUR (a)
Won 3-0 HT 1-0 Att 33,421 Position 7th
Van der Sar — Volz, Goma, Knight, Bonnissel — Inamoto,
Legwinski — Malbranque, Clark, Boa Morte — Hayles
(Saha 83) Subs not used Crossley, Sava, Leacock, Buari
Booked Volz, Inamoto
Scorers **Hayles** 23, 60, **Boa Morte** 71
Report page 250

Sunday September 14
BIRMINGHAM CITY (a)
Drew 2-2 HT 1-1 Att 27,250 Position 9th
Van der Sar — Volz, Goma, Knight, Bonnissel — Inamoto
(Djetou 90), Legwinski — Malbranque (Pembridge 64),
Clark, Boa Morte — Saha (Sava 80) Subs not used
Crossley, Melville Booked Goma, Legwinski, Inamoto,
Boa Morte Sent off Legwinski 60
Scorers **Saha** 1, **Boa Morte** 78
Report page 82

Saturday September 20
MANCHESTER CITY (h)
Drew 2-2 HT 0-0 Att 16,124 Position 10th
Wanchope has waited 21 months for a goal and when
it comes — a header three minutes into stoppage time
— it earns City a point. Anelka gets their first with the aid
of a deflection off Knight, only for Fulham to take
control, Saha leaving Seaman (who turned 40 the day
before) stranded outside his penalty area to score the
second.

Van der Sar — Volz, Goma, Knight, Bonnissel — Inamoto,
Legwinski — Malbranque, Clark, Boa Morte
(Pembridge 84) — Saha Subs not used Crossley, Melville,
Sava, Djetou Booked Clark, Inamoto
Scorers **Malbranque** 73, **Saha** 79
Referee **P Dowd**

THE BAD NEWS? MANCHESTER UNITED ruined the season.
The good news? Fulham ruined theirs. The five points snatched
from the former champions by Fulham dealt a devastating blow to
Sir Alex Ferguson. And the stunning win at Old Trafford left many
Fulham fans wondering if this was their greatest victory of all time.

But despite this triumph, the season was dominated by the Reds'
revenge — the Louis Saha saga. Fulham may have recorded their
highest top-flight finish, but the loss of their rejuvenated striker left
the team emasculated and fans pondering the very point of life in
the Premiership.

Safe from any realistic prospect of relegation, but denied any
genuine hope of the coveted fourth place, Fulham were thrust into
mid-table mundanity. While many clubs long "to do a Charlton", the
Cottagers discovered what this dreary existence actually entails.
Every match becomes a friendly — passionless and pointless.

And not even the promise of fifth place will compensate. Having
already tasted Uefa Cup "glory", Fulham know what this really
means. It is a downgraded competition, with downgraded teams in
front of downgraded attendances. Matches — often against
unheard-of sides — are played at ridiculous times to satisfy German
television audiences. At least, that was Fulham's experience.

But apart from calling into question the point of life in the Premiership, it has — on paper — been an exceptionally good season.

The triumph at Old Trafford in October was spectacular and must
be a contender for Fulham's greatest win. Previous historic victories
may have more significance for fans — the FA Cup semi-final in
1975, the win away to Carlisle United in 1997 that thrust Micky
Adams into Fulham folklore, the FA Cup win away to Villa under
Kevin Keegan. But to beat the champions — the dominant force in
English football for more than a decade — was, arguably, more
impressive. Not only was it on their own turf, but it was in the
pre-eminent competition.

Credit must go to Chris Coleman, who took over a squad riven
with division and built a team. With Steve Finnan and Steve Marlet
gone and Sean Davis determined to join them, Coleman had an
unenviable task in stemming the haemorrhage. But his man-
management was superb. His tactics — unpopular at first — were
also incredibly effective. They brought out the very best in Saha,
who was played as a lone striker. And Coleman also scored points in
the transfer market. Moritz Volz was magnificent at right back and,
on the opposite flank, Jerome Bonnissel oozed class and confidence.
Collins John looks like an exciting prospect.

But it would be wrong to give Coleman all the credit. Jean Tigana

HONOURS BOARD

FA CUP
Runners-up 1975

Record attendance
49,335 (v Millwall, second division, October 8, 1938)
Current capacity
22,150
Record victory
10-1
(v Ipswich Town, first division, December 26, 1963)
Record defeat
0-10
(v Liverpool, League Cup 2nd rnd, 1st leg, September 23, 1986)

was the man who brought Saha to Fulham and it was Saha who had virtually secured Premiership safety by Christmas. In Davis, Steed Malbranque, Luis Boa Morte and Sylvain Legwinski, the Frenchman had assembled a midfield of diverse and prodigious talent — boasting, respectively, vision, skill, pace and grit. Tigana also secured the talents of Edwin van der Sar, who, despite his catastrophic blunder against Arsenal in May, had a stunning season. But it was Coleman who teased the best out of the talent available and got the individuals operating as a robust unit that could grind out a result anywhere.

And, by Coleman's own admission, results were everything. His determination to secure points led to some turgid tactics. With their five-man midfield and solitary striker, it is no accident that Fulham played out seven scoreless draws. When Saha was in the line-up, Fulham had the pace, skill and finishing prowess to catch opponents on the break, but once he had been lured away, the team was impotent.

While the loss of Saha did not lead to the expected collapse, it was confirmation that the goalposts have moved at Fulham. The chairman once boasted that he would make the club the "Manchester United of the South". Instead, he has made Fulham United's feeder club. However, fans can take solace not only in the win at Old Trafford, but also in the fact that United's cash will be paying for the return to Craven Cottage.

The club had previously announced that the cost of redeveloping the ground had spiralled out of control and claimed to be looking for a fresh site on which to build. But many fans feared that the temporary ground-share with Queens Park Rangers would become a longer-term arrangement. Fortunately, it was not possible to extend the two-year lease. Nor did Chelsea want to entertain the possibility of a ground-share at Stamford Bridge. And no other suitable site had emerged.

So by accident rather than design, the fans got their way. Fulham

Tuesday September 23
WIGAN ATHLETIC (a)
Carling Cup, 2nd rnd
Lost 0-1 HT 0-0 Att 4,874
For the second successive season, Fulham have to travel to Wigan in the League Cup and for the second successive season they are beaten, a largely second-string side falling to Ellington's soaring header. Crossley, the Fulham goalkeeper, comes closest to an equaliser, going up for a corner and forcing a great save out of Filan at the death.

Crossley — Leacock, Djetou, Melville, Green — Buari (Boa Morte 66), Legwinski, Inamoto (Rehman 57), Pembridge — Sava, Stolcers (Pratley 83) *Subs not used* Beasant, T Davis
Referee **A Kaye**

Sunday September 28
BLACKBURN ROVERS (a)
Won 2-0 HT 1-0 Att 21,985 Position 7th
Van der Sar — Volz (Leacock ht), Goma, Knight, Bonnissel — Malbranque, Inamoto, Clark, Pembridge, Boa Morte (Buari 84) — Saha *Subs not used* Melville, Djetou, Crossley *Booked* Inamoto, Boa Morte, Knight, Leacock
Scorers **Boa Morte 5, Saha 65**
Report page 93

Saturday October 4
LEICESTER CITY (h)
Won 2-0 HT 1-0 Att 14,562 Position 4th
Two teams going in opposite directions: Fulham are up to fourth after Boa Morte's double — the Portuguese is lucky to be on the pitch after his studs connect with Sinclair's stomach — while Leicester are back in the bottom three. Defeat would have been heavier but for Walker, who saves Malbranque's penalty and brilliantly denies Inamoto.

Van der Sar — Leacock (Djetou 80), Goma, Knight, Bonnissel — Pembridge, Inamoto (Legwinski 64) — Malbranque, Clark, Boa Morte — Saha (Hayles 84) *Subs not used* Crossley, Melville *Booked* Goma, Knight
Scorer **Boa Morte 36, 73**
Referee **C Foy**

Saturday October 18
WOLVERHAMPTON WANDERERS (h)
Drew 0-0 HT 0-0 Att 17,031 Position 5th
Wolves are off the bottom — above Leicester City — after another stubborn display, and though they get some luck when Malbranque hits the bar at the death, they deserve their point. Twice they are foiled by Van der Sar, who saves well from Camara and superbly from Blake with four minutes to go.

Van der Sar — Leacock, Goma, Knight, Bonnissel — Pembridge, Legwinski — Inamoto (Hayles 65), Clark, Malbranque — Saha *Subs not used* Crossley, Volz, Melville, Djetou *Booked* Inamoto, Leacock
Referee **H Webb**

Tuesday October 21
NEWCASTLE UNITED (h)
Lost 2-3 HT 2-1 Att 16,506 Position 6th
After kick-off is delayed for 30 minutes by a suspect vehicle outside Loftus Road, Fulham are straight into top gear, Clark and Saha scoring against their former club inside eight minutes. Then it is the Shearer Show: the Newcastle talisman sets up Robert, levels from the spot himself and then grabs the winner, though Fulham twice go desperately close to an equaliser in the closing stages.

Van der Sar — Leacock, Goma, Knight, Bonnissel — Buari (Hayles ht), Pembridge (Inamoto 77), Legwinski, Clark, Malbranque — Saha *Subs not used* Crossley, Melville, Djetou *Booked* Legwinski, Pembridge
Scorers **Clark 6, Saha 8**
Referee **B Knight**

Saturday October 25
MANCHESTER UNITED (a)
Won 3-1   HT 1-1   Att 67,727   Position 5th
Van der Sar — Volz, Goma, Knight, Bonnissel (Djetou 75)
— Malbranque, Pembridge (Inamoto 32), Legwinski, Clark,
Boa Morte (Hayles 86) — Saha *Subs not used* Crossley,
Melville *Booked* Inamoto, Knight
Scorers **Clark 3, Malbranque 66, Inamoto 79**
Report page 198

Sunday November 2
LIVERPOOL (h)
Lost 1-2   HT 1-1   Att 17,682   Position 6th
Gerard Houllier says that Owen is not for sale even at
£50 million after reports linking him with a move to Real
Madrid, but it is Heskey and Murphy, the latter with an
89th-minute penalty, who prove the match-winners here.
Boa Morte is sent off for a dreadful challenge on
Sinama-Pongolle.

Crossley — Volz, Melville, Knight, Bonnissel — Legwinski —
Malbranque, Pembridge (Djetou 20), Clark, Boa Morte —
Saha (Hayles 87) *Subs not used* Beasant, S Davis, Buari
Booked Boa Morte *Sent off* Boa Morte 90
Scorer **Saha 40**
Referee **R Styles**

Saturday November 8
CHARLTON ATHLETIC (a)
Lost 1-3   HT 0-1   Att 26,344   Position 7th
Van der Sar — Volz, Melville, Knight, Bonnissel —
Legwinski — Inamoto (S Davis 70), Clark, Malbranque,
Boa Morte (Hayles 63; Pratley 74) — Saha *Subs not used*
Crossley, Djetou *Booked* Legwinski, Inamoto
Scorer **S Davis 89**
Report page 115

Monday November 24
PORTSMOUTH (h)
Won 2-0   HT 2-0   Att 15,624   Position 5th
"We simply couldn't get a kick," the manager said. Harry
Redknapp reflecting on defeat? No, Chris Coleman, after
Fulham had been outplayed for half an hour.
Portsmouth's frustration is reflected in Berger's dismissal
for swearing after a rejected penalty appeal, Saha, with
two goals much against the run of play, having already
won the match.

Van der Sar — Volz, Melville, Knight, Bonnissel —
Legwinski — Malbranque, Clark, S Davis, Hayles
(Inamoto 68) — Saha (Sava 70) *Subs not used* Crossley,
Djetou, Pratley
Scorer **Saha 30, 33**
Referee **A Wiley**

Sunday November 30
ARSENAL (a)
Drew 0-0   HT 0-0   Att 38,063   Position 4th
Van der Sar — Volz, Melville, Knight, Bonnissel —
Legwinski — Inamoto, Clark, S Davis, Malbranque — Saha
(Hayles 75) *Subs not used* Sava, Crossley, Djetou, Goma
Booked Legwinski
Report page 63

Saha's goalscoring return to Loftus Road in a Manchester United shirt
rubbed salt into the wounds of Fulham fans aggrieved by his departure

were to head home. The terraces have gone, but the unique
ambience and the magical memories have not. It is supposed to be a
temporary stay while the search for a super-stadium goes on, but
many fans hope that commercial constraints will keep Fulham in
Fulham.

Converting the old Cottage into a Premiership stadium has not
been cheap. The renovation bill of around £5 million has been
funded by the sale of Saha. Many fans will find it hard to forgive a
striker who betrayed his club in such a public fashion. But he may
have provided Fulham with something even more priceless than his
goals — the capital to keep the club in the capital.

THE MANAGER
Chris Coleman

The mark of a good manager is one who is prepared to admit that things need changing — that basically, he got it wrong. Flexibility must be allowed to triumph over arrogance and pride. This is just one area in which Chris Coleman scores maximum points — chopping and changing his tactics in mid-match to get the required results. He does his homework, is shrewd in the transfer market and is enormously popular among fans and players. But, above all, the results speak for themselves. An extraordinary first full season in charge.

Tim Miller

APPEARANCES

	Prem	FAC	CC	Total
L Boa Morte	32 (1)	5	0 (1)	37 (2)
C Bocanegra	15	4	-	19
J Bonnissel	16	-	-	16
M Buari	1 (2)	-	1	2 (2)
L Clark	25	2	-	27
M Crossley	1	-	1	2
S Davis	22 (2)	6	-	28 (2)
M Djetou	19 (7)	4	1	24 (7)
A Goma	23	6	-	29
A Green	4	2	1	7
J Harley	3 (1)	-	-	3 (1)
B Hayles	10 (16)	3 (3)	-	13 (19)
J Inamoto	15 (7)	2	1	18 (7)
C John	3 (5)	-	-	3 (5)
Z Knight	30 (1)	5 (1)	-	35 (2)
D Leacock	3 (1)	-	1	4 (1)
S Legwinski	30 (2)	4	1	35 (2)
S Malbranque	38	6	-	44
S Marlet	1	-	-	1
B McBride	5 (11)	3	-	8 (11)
A Melville	9	0 (1)	1	10 (1)
I Pearce	12 (1)	-	-	12 (1)
M Pembridge	9 (3)	0 (1)	1	10 (4)
B Petta	3 (6)	2 (3)	-	5 (9)
D Pratley	0 (1)	-	0 (1)	0 (2)
Z Rehman	0 (1)	-	0 (1)	0 (2)
L Saha	20 (1)	1	-	21 (1)
F Sava	0 (6)	0 (2)	1	1 (8)
A Stolcers	-	-	1	1
E van der Sar	37	6	-	43
M Volz	32 (1)	5	-	37 (1)

Saturday December 6
BOLTON WANDERERS (h)
Won 2-1 HT 0-0 Att **14,393** Position **4th**
Bolton's players have "let themselves and the club down", Sam Allardyce says, which seems a harsh verdict on a narrow defeat. Ahead through Davies but conceding two goals in a minute, both created for Fulham by Hayles, Bolton almost snatch a draw in stoppage time when Jardel's header rebounds into Van der Sar's arms off a post.

Van der Sar — Volz, Melville, Knight, Bonnissel — Legwinski — Inamoto (Sava 58), S Davis (Djetou 81), Clark, Malbranque — Saha (Hayles 51) *Subs not used* Crossley, Goma
Scorers **S Davis 75, Sava 76**
Referee **A D'Urso**

Sunday December 14
LEEDS UNITED (a)
Lost 2-3 HT 0-1 Att **30,544** Position **4th**
Van der Sar — Volz (Hayles 63), Melville, Knight, Harley — Legwinski — Malbranque, Clark, S Davis, Boa Morte (Sava 77) — Saha *Subs not used* Crossley, Djetou, Goma
Booked Boa Morte
Scorer **Saha 47, 86**
Report page 157

Saturday December 20
CHELSEA (h)
Lost 0-1 HT 0-0 Att **18,244** Position **4th**
Fulham are still in a celebratory mood, three days after getting confirmation of their return to Craven Cottage next season, but Chelsea delight in spoiling the party, Crespo's header via a post ensuring that the gap between the neighbours widens. An injury to Duff, who suffers a dislocated shoulder, tempers their joy.

Van der Sar — Volz, Melville, Knight, Harley (Hayles 69) — Legwinski — Malbranque, Clark, S Davis (Djetou 37), Boa Morte — Saha *Subs not used* Crossley, Sava, Goma
Booked Clark, Saha
Referee **M Riley**

Friday December 26
SOUTHAMPTON (h)
Won 2-0 HT 1-0 Att **16,767** Position **4th**
Manchester United have inquired about Saha's availability in midweek and his price increases with the double — including a penalty when Marsden brings down Boa Morte — that beats Southampton and takes his tally for the season to 12. "He's in the form of his life — but he's not for sale," Chris Coleman says.

Van der Sar — Volz, Goma, Knight, Bonnissel (Harley 23) — Malbranque, Djetou — Inamoto, Clark, Boa Morte — Saha *Subs not used* Crossley, Melville, Sava, Hayles
Scorer **Saha 19, 63 (pen)**
Referee **D Gallagher**

Sunday December 28
ASTON VILLA (a)
Lost 0-3 HT 0-1 Att **35,617** Position **5th**
Van der Sar — Volz, Goma, Knight, Harley — Malbranque (Sava 82), Inamoto (Hayles 68), Djetou, Boa Morte — Clark — Saha *Subs not used* Melville, Crossley, Green
Report page 76

CHELTENHAM TOWN (h)
FA Cup, 3rd rnd
Won 2-1   HT 1-1   Att 10,303
Embarrassment looms when Fulham trail the third-division strugglers after five minutes, but Saha spares them with a clever lob and a last-minute header from a corner by Petta, who is making his debut. There is still time, though, for a thin, predominantly thankful crowd to see Van der Sar make the save of the game from Taylor.

Van der Sar – Djetou, Goma (Melville ht), Knight, Green – Legwinski – Malbranque, S Davis, Inamoto (Hayles 58), Petta – Saha *Subs not used* Crossley, Sava, Pratley
Scorer **Saha 13, 90**
Referee **P Walton**

Wednesday January 7
MIDDLESBROUGH (a)
Lost 1-2   HT 0-1   Att 27,869   Position 7th
Van der Sar – Djetou, Melville, Knight, Green – Malbranque, Clark, Legwinski (Hayles 70), S Davis, Boa Morte – Saha *Subs not used* Crossley, Inamoto, Hudson, Petta *Booked* Djetou, Davis
Scorer **Hayles 90**
Report page 212

Saturday January 10
EVERTON (h)
Won 2-1   HT 1-0   Att 17,103   Position 6th
Saha, in the Fulham side despite his fierce criticism of his club for blocking a move to Manchester United, scores the penalty that earns the lead. Malbranque is tripped by Naysmith to win the spot kick and nets himself immediately after half-time, Kilbane replying for an Everton side who squander three great chances with the score at 0-0.

Van der Sar – Djetou, Melville, Knight, Green – Legwinski – Malbranque, S Davis, Clark, Boa Morte (Petta 83) – Saha *Subs not used* Crossley, Inamoto, Sava, Hayles
Scorers **Saha 45 (pen), Malbranque 46**
Referee **G Poll**

Monday January 19
NEWCASTLE UNITED (a)
Lost 1-3   HT 0-2   Att 50,104   Position 7th
Van der Sar – Djetou, Goma, Knight, Bocanegra – Malbranque, Legwinski (Volz 18), Clark, S Davis, Boa Morte – Hayles (Sava 66) *Subs not used* Crossley, Petta, Green *Booked* Djetou
Scorer **S Davis 74**
Report page 223

Sunday January 25
EVERTON (a)
FA Cup, 4th rnd
Drew 1-1   HT 0-0   Att 27,862
Van der Sar – Volz, Goma, Knight, Bocanegra – Djetou – Malbranque, Clark, S Davis, Boa Morte – Hayles (Sava 81) *Subs not used* Crossley, Inamoto, Petta, Green *Booked* Goma, Djetou, Malbranque, Hayles
Scorer **S Davis 49**
Report page 139

THE ⚜ TIMES

MATCH OF THE SEASON

Manchester United 1 Fulham 3
Old Trafford, Saturday October 25 2003
Oliver Kay

THERE WAS THE UNMISTAKABLE feeling at Old Trafford on Saturday that something was missing. It was not Sir Alex Ferguson, who, while not on his usual perch in the dugout, could be found shuffling awkwardly in his seat on the back row of the directors' box. Nor was it Roy Keane, who, withdrawn from midfield duty to preserve his ageing limbs, was agitating on the row in the front of his manager. Finally, the answer became clear. It was David Beckham, whose departure to Real Madrid has left Manchester United lacking a certain *je ne sais quoi*.

For those who despair of the hype surrounding him, the decision to sell Beckham was perfectly understandable, but less so is Ferguson's apparent belief that one of his most influential players did not need to be replaced. Six players have been tried this season in Beckham's position on the right-hand side of midfield and, with the most convincing of them, Ole Gunnar Solskjaer, sidelined until December, Ferguson has yet to find a solution. With Beckham having made an impressive start to life in Madrid, the United manager does, for once, have the unmistakable look of a man who has dropped a clanger.

Beckham might not have made a huge difference had he been wearing a United shirt on Saturday, when Fulham produced what was, in both tactical and technical terms, the best performance by a visiting team at Old Trafford in recent memory. But, while it may seem churlish to damn a United team who are already six points better off than they were at the same stage last season, Ferguson's side, bereft of creativity and energy in midfield, appear to be missing the England captain a good deal more than he is missing them, homesickness notwithstanding.

To dwell too long on United's shortcomings post-Beckham, though, would be to do a gross injustice to Fulham, who performed so well that criticism of Ferguson's team selection, which saw Keane and Phil Neville rested and Paul Scholes on the bench, should be seen as largely irrelevant.

They took the game to their hosts from the third minute, when Lee Clark converted a cross from the excellent Steed Malbranque, and, while diligent in defence, continued to attack with such purpose that Tim Howard, the United goalkeeper, could be said to have enhanced his reputation further despite conceding three goals.

United claimed an equaliser on the stroke of half-time, Diego Forlan finding the bottom corner after Fulham's defence was carved open for the only time all afternoon by Ryan Giggs, but it did not have the anticipated effect. If anything, United were even worse after the interval, their chaotic display summed up by the incident that

Inamoto celebrates after his brilliant goal wrapped up a famous victory

saw Quinton Fortune booked four minutes into the second half because his half-time substitution had not been carried out in front of the referee.

Ferguson, consigned to the directors' box after a two-match touch-lineban, went a darker shade of red and glared at his coaching staff, presumably making a mental note to step up his search for an assistant manager.

Ferguson blamed "lethargy" and the rustiness of Nicky Butt and Eric Djemba-Djemba after seeing Malbranque and Junichi Inamoto, the substitute, secure Fulham's first victory at Old Trafford in 40 years, but Chris Coleman, the manager, was entitled to paint a rather different picture.

"It was a magnificent performance by us," Coleman said. "People can say that Roy Keane and Paul Scholes were missing for them, but the players that were playing were still world-class. I think you've got to give us some credit for the way we played. You don't win here without being at the top of your game. I thought every one of my lads was magnificent."

MANCHESTER UNITED (4-4-2): T Howard — G Neville, R Ferdinand, M Silvestre (sub: Q Fortune, 46min), J O'Shea — R Giggs, E Djemba-Djemba (sub: D Bellion, 79), N Butt, C Ronaldo (sub: P Scholes, 70) — D Forlan, R van Nistelrooy. **Substitutes not used:** D Fletcher, R Carroll. **Booked:** Forlan, Djemba-Djemba, Fortune, Giggs.
FULHAM (4-1-4-1): E van der Sar — M Volz, Z Knight, A Goma, J Bonnissel (sub: M Djetou, 74) — S Legwinski — S Malbranque, L Clark, M Pembridge (sub: J Inamoto, 33), L Boa Morte (sub: B Hayles, 87) — L Saha. **Substitutes not used:** A Melville, M Crossley. **Booked:** Inamoto, Knight.

Saturday January 31
TOTTENHAM HOTSPUR (h)
Won 2-1   HT 1-1   Att 17,024   Position 7th
Life without the £12.825 million Saha, who scores for his new club in the day's early kick-off, begins for Fulham with victory thanks to the £600,000 McBride, who marks his debut with the winner 11 minutes after coming on as a substitute. Keane (after Pearce's handball on his debut) and Malbranque trade first-half penalties.

Van der Sar — Volz, Knight, Pearce, Bocanegra — Djetou — Malbranque, S Davis, Clark, Boa Morte (Petta 88) — Hayles (McBride 56) *Subs not used* Crossley, Inamoto, Sava *Booked* Hayles
Scorers **Malbranque 45 (pen), McBride 67**
Referee **M Messias**

Wednesday February 4
EVERTON (h)
FA Cup, 4th rnd replay
Won 2-1 (aet; 1-1 after 90min)   HT 0-0   Att 11,551
Jeffers, whose last-gasp equaliser had earned a second chance, strikes in the final minute again for Everton, but then, astonishingly, squanders two golden chances to settle the replay in injury time. Malbranque makes no such mistake in extra time, Hayles helping to create both Fulham goals.

Van der Sar — Volz, Knight, Goma, Bocanegra — Malbranque, Inamoto (Petta 97), Djetou, S Davis — Hayles (Sava 81), Boa Morte *Subs not used* Crossley, Rehman, Green
Scorers **Inamoto 57, Malbranque 102**
Referee **P Durkin**

Saturday February 7
SOUTHAMPTON (a)
Drew 0-0   HT 0-0   Att 31,820   Position 7th
Van der Sar — Volz, Knight, Pearce, Bocanegra — Djetou — Malbranque (Petta 58), S Davis (Inamoto 89), Clark (Legwinski 65), Boa Morte — McBride *Subs not used* Crossley, Hayles *Booked* Volz, Malbranque
Report page 246

Wednesday February 11
ASTON VILLA (h)
Lost 1-2   HT 1-2   Att 16,153   Position 8th
If defeat after taking the lead inside a minute is not bad enough, Fulham also face trouble for events off the pitch (a bottle is thrown in the direction of a linesman, causing a brief hold-up) as well as on it, where Bocanegra's two-footed lunge at Delaney, to earn a red card, is a candidate for worst tackle of the season.

Van der Sar — Volz, Knight, Pearce, Bocanegra — Djetou (Hayles 70) — Malbranque, S Davis, Clark (Petta ht), Boa Morte — McBride *Subs not used* Crossley, Legwinski, Inamoto *Booked* Knight, S Davis *Sent off* Bocanegra 75
Scorer **Boa Morte 1**
Referee **B Knight**

Saturday February 14
WEST HAM UNITED (h)
FA Cup, 5th rnd
Drew 0-0   HT 0-0   Att 14,705
With West Ham in such fine form away from home in the first division, this hardly constitutes a shock. Indeed, Harewood almost scores inside 20 seconds and Van der Sar is the busier goalkeeper throughout, though Bocanegra hits the post with a curling shot. "No excuses," Chris Coleman says, "we were inept."

Van der Sar — Volz, Knight, Goma, Bocanegra — S Davis — Legwinski, Malbranque, Boa Morte (Petta 67) — McBride, Hayles *Subs not used* Crossley, Inamoto, Djetou, Green *Booked* Bocanegra, Hayles
Referee **G Poll**

Saturday February 21
WOLVERHAMPTON WANDERERS (a)
Lost 1-2   HT 0-1   Att **28,424**   Position **8th**
Van der Sar — Volz, Knight (Djetou 73), Pearce,
Bocanegra — Malbranque, S Davis, Legwinski, Boa Morte
— Hayles (Petta 67), McBride *Subs not used* Crossley,
Inamoto, Green
Scorer **Malbranque 84**
Report page 266

Tuesday February 24
WEST HAM UNITED (a)
FA Cup, 5th rnd replay
Won 3-0   HT 0-0   Att **27,934**
Struck down by a virus, Chris Coleman is not at the
game, but news of the result should help the manager's
recovery. Fulham's first win in five matches — McBride
sparking a late flurry with a fine 18-yard volley for the
pick of the goals — earns them a quarter-final tie away to
Manchester United.

Van der Sar — Volz, Goma, Djetou (Knight 48),
Bocanegra — Malbranque, S Davis, Legwinski, Petta
(Hayles 73) — Boa Morte, McBride *Subs not used*
Crossley, Inamoto, Pembridge
Scorers **McBride 76, Hayles 79, Boa Morte 90**
Referee **M Riley**

Saturday February 28
MANCHESTER UNITED (h)
Drew 1-1   HT 0-1   Att **18,306**   Position **8th**
Saha returns to Loftus Road and though Chris Coleman,
now in hospital with a viral infection, is not there to greet
him, Fulham fans make their feelings known. The striker
almost scores after 10 seconds and does after 14
minutes, but Boa Morte's equaliser — and the referee's
decision not to penalise Van der Sar's challenge on Saha
— perhaps leave Sir Alex Ferguson regretting the
decision to rest Van Nistelrooy, Howard and Giggs.

Van der Sar — Volz, Goma, Pearce, Green — Malbranque
(Inamoto 79), S Davis, Legwinski, Petta (Pembridge 65) —
McBride, Boa Morte *Subs not used* Crossley, Knight,
Rehman *Booked* S Davis
Scorer **Boa Morte 64**
Referee **A Wiley**

Saturday March 6
MANCHESTER UNITED (a)
FA Cup, 6th rnd
Lost 1-2   HT 1-1   Att **67,614**
Van der Sar — Volz, Knight, Goma, Green — Legwinski
(Pembridge 63), S Davis — Malbranque, Clark (Petta 81),
Boa Morte — McBride (Hayles 62) *Subs not used*
Crossley, Djetou *Booked* Volz, Goma, Boa Morte, Hayles
Scorer **Malbranque 23 (pen)**
Report page 204

Saturday March 13
LEEDS UNITED (h)
Won 2-0   HT 0-0   Att **17,104**   Position **8th**
Back in the Fulham dugout after three worrying weeks in
hospital, Chris Coleman enjoys a reasonably relaxed
afternoon as Leeds are easily dispatched, a glut of
pressure and near-misses preceding two goals in the last
19 minutes. "We're running out of games," Eddie Gray
says as Leeds remain rooted to the bottom.

Van der Sar — Volz, Knight, Pearce, Green — S Davis,
Legwinski, Pembridge — Malbranque, Hayles
(McBride 86), Boa Morte *Subs not used* Crossley,
Inamoto, Djetou, Petta *Booked* Volz, Legwinski,
Boa Morte, Green
Scorers **S Davis 71, Boa Morte 83**
Referee **S Dunn**

THE PLAYERS

LUIS BOA MORTE (midfield) **Born**
August 4, 1977, Lisbon **Ht** 5ft 10in
Wt 11st 5lb **Signed from** Southampton,
July 2000, £1.7m

CARLOS BOCANEGRA (defender) **Born**
May 25, 1979, Alta Loma, California
Ht 6ft 0in **Wt** 12st 4lb **Signed from**
Chicago Fire, January 2004, free

JEROME BONNISSEL (defender) **Born**
April 16, 1973, Montpellier **Ht** 5ft 9in
Wt 11st 11lb **Signed from** Rangers,
August 2003, free

MALIK BUARI (midfield) **Born** January
24, 1984, Accra **Ht** 6ft 0in **Wt** 11st 11lb
Signed from trainee, July 2003

LEE CLARK (midfield) **Born** October 27,
1972, Wallsend **Ht** 5ft 8in **Wt** 11st 7lb
Signed from Sunderland, July 1999,
£3m

MARK CROSSLEY (goalkeeper) **Born**
June 16, 1969, Barnsley **Ht** 6ft 0in
Wt 15st 9lb **Signed from** Middlesbrough,
August 2003, £500,000

SEAN DAVIS (midfield) **Born** September
20, 1979, Clapham **Ht** 5ft 9in
Wt 12st 0lb **Signed from** trainee, July
1998

MARTIN DJETOU (defender) **Born**
December 15, 1972, Abidjan, Ivory Coast
Ht 6ft 2in **Wt** 12st 6lb **Signed from**
Parma (loan), July 2002

ADAM GREEN (defender) **Born** January
12, 1984, Hillingdon **Ht** 5ft 10in
Wt 10st 11lb **Signed from** trainee, July
2003

ALAIN GOMA (defender) **Born** October
5, 1972, Sault, France **Ht** 6ft 0in
Wt 13st 0lb **Signed from** Newcastle
United, March 2001, £4m

JON HARLEY (defender) **Born**
September 26, 1979, Maidstone
Ht 5ft 9in **Wt** 10st 3lb **Signed from**
Chelsea, August 2001, £3.5m

BARRY HAYLES (forward) **Born** May 17,
1972, Lambeth **Ht** 5ft 9in **Wt** 11st 5lb
Signed from Bristol Rovers, November
1998, £2.1m

JUNICHI INAMOTO (midfield) **Born**
September 18, 1979, Kagashima, Japan
Ht 5ft 11in **Wt** 11st 11lb **Signed from**
Gamba Osaka (loan), July 2002

COLLINS JOHN (forward) **Born** October
7, 1985, Zwandru, Liberia **Ht** 5ft 11in
Wt 12st 4lb **Signed from** FC Twente,
January 2004, undisclosed

ZAT KNIGHT (defender) **Born** May 2,
1980, Solihull **Ht** 6ft 6in **Wt** 14st 0lb
Signed from Rushall Olympic, February
1999, free

DEAN LEACOCK (defender) **Born** June
10, 1984, Croydon **Ht** 6ft 2in

Wt 12st 4lb **Signed from** trainee,
August 2001

SYLVAIN LEGWINSKI (midfield) **Born**
October 6, 1973, Clermont-Ferrand,
France **Ht** 6ft 1in **Wt** 11st 7lb
Signed from Bordeaux, August 2001,
£3.5m

STEED MALBRANQUE (midfield) **Born**
January 6, 1980, Mouscron, Belgium
Ht 5ft 8in **Wt** 11st 5lb **Signed from**
Lyons, August 2001, £5m

STEVE MARLET (forward) **Born** January
10, 1974, Pithiviers, France **Ht** 5ft 11in
Wt 11st 5lb **Signed from** Lyons,
September 2001, £13.5m

BRIAN McBRIDE (forward) **Born** June
19, 1972, Arlington Hts, Illinois **Ht** 6ft 1in
Wt 12st 0lb **Signed from** Columbus
Crew, January 2004, undisclosed

ANDY MELVILLE (defender) **Born**
November 29, 1968, Swansea
Ht 6ft 0in **Wt** 13st 3lb **Signed from**
Sunderland, July 1999, free

IAN PEARCE (defender) **Born** May 7,
1974, Bury St Edmunds **Ht** 6ft 3in
Wt 14st 4lb **Signed from** West Ham
United, January 2004, undisclosed

MARK PEMBRIDGE (midfield) **Born**
November 29, 1970, Merthyr Tydfil
Ht 5ft 9in **Wt** 12st 0lb **Signed from**
Everton, September 2003, £500,000

BOBBY PETTA (midfield) **Born** August 6,
1974, Rotterdam **Ht** 5ft 7in **Wt** 11st 3lb
Signed from Celtic (loan), December
2003

DARREN PRATLEY (midfield) **Born** April
22, 1985, Barking **Ht** 6ft 1in
Wt 10st 13lb **Signed from** trainee, July
2003

ZESH REHMAN (midfield) **Born** October
14, 1983, Birmingham **Ht** 6ft 2in
Wt 12st 9lb **Signed from** trainee, July
2003

LOUIS SAHA
(see Manchester United)

FACUNDO SAVA (forward) **Born** July 3,
1974, Ituzaingo, Argentina **Ht** 6ft 1in
Wt 13st 1lb **Signed from** Gimnasia
y Esgrima La Plata, Argentina, £2m

ANDREJS STOLCERS (midfield) **Born**
July 8, 1974, Latvia **Ht** 5ft 11in
Wt 11st 0lb **Signed from** Shakhtar
Donetsk, December 2000, £2m

EDWIN VAN DER SAR (goalkeeper)
Born October 29, 1970, Leiden, Holland
Ht 6ft 5in **Wt** 13st 1lb **Signed from**
Juventus, August 2001, £5m

MORITZ VOLZ Born January 21, 1983,
Siegen, Germany **Ht** 6ft 0in **Wt** 11st 7lb
Signed from Schalke 04, June 1999,
free

STATS AND FACTS

● Fulham recorded their highest top-flight finish, ninth. Their previous best was tenth in 1959-60.

● Fulham's average league attendance, 16,342, was more than 500 lower than that of Hull City in the third division.

● Fulham won the fewest corners last season.

● Fulham have not won any of their past ten league matches at home to Birmingham City.

● Fulham achieved their first win in 18 attempts against Manchester United . . .

● . . . but after 23 visits they are still waiting for their first win at Anfield.

Bill Edgar

GOALSCORERS

	Prem	FAC	CC	Total
L Boa Morte	9	1	-	10
L Clark	2	-	-	2
S Davis	5	1	-	6
B Hayles	4	1	-	5
J Inamoto	2	1	-	3
C John	4	-	-	4
S Malbranque	6 (2p)	2 (1p)	-	8 (3p)
S Marlet	1	-	-	1
B McBride	4	1	-	5
M Pembridge	1	-	-	1
L Saha	13 (2p)	2	-	15 (2p)
F Sava	1	-	-	1

Saturday March 20
CHELSEA (a)
Lost 1-2   **HT 1-2**   Att **41,169**   Position **9th**
Van der Sar — Volz, Pearce, Knight, Bocanegra — S Davis, Legwinski, Pembridge (John 63) — Malbranque, Hayles (McBride 78), Boa Morte *Subs not used* Beasant, Djetou, Goma *Booked* Legwinski, Boa Morte
Scorer **Pembridge 19**
Report page 130

Saturday March 27
MANCHESTER CITY (a)
Drew 0-0   **HT 0-0**   Att **46,522**   Position **9th**
Van der Sar — Volz, Knight, Goma, Bocanegra — Djetou — Malbranque, S Davis, Pembridge, Boa Morte — Hayles (McBride 70) *Subs not used* Beasant, Inamoto, Sava, Rehman
Report page 193

Saturday April 3
BIRMINGHAM CITY (h)
Drew 0-0   **HT 0-0**   Att **14,667**   Position **10th**
A candidate for the least entertaining match of the season between sides who routinely bring out the worst in each other, though there are no red cards to go with the six yellows. Savage comes closest to winning it, hitting the bar from 25 yards, while Maik Taylor excels in the Birmingham goal.

Van der Sar — Volz, Knight, Goma, Bocanegra — Djetou (McBride 67) — Malbranque, S Davis, Legwinski — Hayles (Pearce 75), Boa Morte *Subs not used* Crossley, Inamoto, Petta *Booked* Djetou, Malbranque, Boa Morte, S Davis
Referee **M Riley**

Saturday April 10
LEICESTER CITY (a)
Won 2-0   **HT 0-0**   Att **28,392**   Position **8th**
Van der Sar — Volz, Knight, Goma, Bocanegra — Djetou — Malbranque (McBride 71), S Davis, Legwinski — Hayles (John 62), Boa Morte *Subs not used* Crossley, Petta, Pearce *Booked* Boa Morte
Scorer **John 66, 89**
Report page 171

Monday April 12
BLACKBURN ROVERS (h)
Lost 3-4   **HT 2-1**   Att **13,981**   Position **10th**
The Bank Holiday programme saves the best until last as Blackburn edge a seven-goal thriller for a crucial win. John makes it four goals in three days after his double against Leicester City, but Blackburn strike first through Cole and last through Stead to end their losing run just in time.

Van der Sar — Volz, Knight, Goma, Bocanegra — Djetou — Malbranque (McBride 84), S Davis (Petta 77), Legwinski, Boa Morte — John (Hayles 87) *Subs not used* Crossley, Pearce
Scorers **John 26, 45, Boa Morte 60**
Referee **M Dean**

PLAYER OF THE SEASON
Sylvain Legwinski

He is not a great goalscorer, not blessed with an abundance of pace or skill and has no particular gift when it comes to passing. But there is just something about Sylvain Legwinski that shouts "pick me". His role in the side is not glamorous, but vital. Gritty, tough in the tackle, energetic, he covers an enormous amount of ground, closing down and making decisive tackles. His quick thinking turns defence into attack in an instant. He is not a headline-grabber and those who cherry-pick from highlights will never appreciate his all-round contribution. But the fans do and it is mutual. His tireless efforts are complemented by his unstinting appreciation of those who support.
Tim Miller

Saturday April 17
LIVERPOOL (a)
Drew 0-0   HT 0-0   Att 42,042   Position 10th
Van der Sar — Volz, Pearce, Goma, Bocanegra (Inamoto 76) — Djetou — Malbranque, Legwinski, Petta (Rehman 88) — John (McBride 73), Boa Morte *Subs not used* Crossley, Hayles *Booked* Goma, Bocanegra, John
Report page 184

Saturday April 24
CHARLTON ATHLETIC (h)
Won 2-0   HT 1-0   Att 16,585   Position 7th
Sean Davis, recalled to the Fulham bench after being dropped for disciplinary reasons at Anfield, scores the goal that seals victory, a splendid dipping volley. Malbranque gets the lead from the spot, but Charlton are angry that they are not allowed to reply in kind when Djetou escapes after a clear handball.

Van der Sar — Volz, Pearce, Goma, Bocanegra — Djetou — Malbranque, Legwinski, Petta (S Davis ht) — Boa Morte (Inamoto 76), John (McBride 70) *Subs not used* Crossley, Knight *Booked* Volz
Scorers Malbranque 18 (pen), S Davis 64
Referee **M Messias**

Saturday May 1
PORTSMOUTH (a)
Drew 1-1   HT 0-0   Att 20,065   Position 7th
Van der Sar — Volz, Pearce, Goma, Bocanegra — S Davis, Djetou (McBride 77), Legwinski, Malbranque — Inamoto, Boa Morte (John 85) *Subs not used* Crossley, Petta, Hudson *Booked* Goma, Bocanegra, Legwinski, Inamoto
Scorer McBride 85
Report page 238

Sunday May 9
ARSENAL (h)
Lost 0-1   HT 0-1   Att 18,102   Position 9th
Now it's 37 down, one to go in Arsenal's quest for an unbeaten league season and, in Arsene Wenger's words after this victory, "football immortality". Reyes punishes Van der Sar's miscontrol of Djetou's routine backpass for the early winner, Fulham departing Loftus Road for Craven Cottage with a defeat.

Van der Sar — Volz, Pearce, Goma, Bocanegra — Djetou (John 59) — S Davis, Legwinski, Inamoto (McBride 59), Malbranque — Boa Morte *Subs not used* Crossley, Hudson, Petta *Booked* S Davis
Referee **M Dean**

Saturday May 15
BOLTON WANDERERS (a)
Won 2-0   HT 1-0   Att 27,383   Position 9th
Van der Sar — Volz, Pearce, Goma, Bocanegra — Legwinski, Djetou, S Davis, Malbranque — Boa Morte, McBride (John 90) *Subs not used* Crossley, Inamoto, Hudson, Petta *Booked* Boa Morte
Scorer McBride 45, 78
Report page 110

PREMIERSHIP

	P	W	D	L	F	A	GD	Pts
Arsenal	38	26	12	0	73	26	47	**90**
Chelsea	38	24	7	7	67	30	37	**79**
Man Utd	38	23	6	9	64	35	29	**75**
Liverpool	38	16	12	10	55	37	18	**60**
Newcastle	38	13	17	8	52	40	12	**56**
Aston Villa	38	15	11	12	48	44	4	**56**
Charlton	38	14	11	13	51	51	0	**53**
Bolton	38	14	11	13	48	56	-8	**53**
Fulham	38	14	10	14	52	46	6	**52**
Birmingham	38	12	14	12	43	48	-5	**50**
Middlesbro	38	13	9	16	44	52	-8	**48**
Southampton	38	12	11	15	44	45	-1	**47**
Portsmouth	38	12	9	17	47	54	-7	**45**
Tottenham	38	13	6	19	47	57	-10	**45**
Blackburn	38	12	8	18	51	59	-8	**44**
Man City	38	9	14	15	55	54	1	**41**
Everton	38	9	12	17	45	57	-12	**39**
Leicester	38	6	15	17	48	65	-17	**33**
Leeds	38	8	9	21	40	79	-39	**33**
Wolves	38	7	12	19	38	77	-39	**33**

FA CUP
Third round

CARLING CUP
Third round

Crying game: Paul Robinson hugs Alan Smith after Leeds's relegation was confirmed at Bolton — both swiftly signed for new clubs

THE GAMES

Sunday August 17 2003
NEWCASTLE UNITED (h)
Drew 2-2   HT 1-1   Att 36,766   Position **9th**
The Leeds old boys, Bowyer and Woodgate, get a hostile welcome back to Elland Road, but it is a Newcastle stalwart who makes the biggest impact, Shearer marking his 600th club game with the opener plus a late penalty equaliser after Radebe's trip on Dyer. Viduka and Smith, the latter after Bernard's error, are on target in between.

Robinson — Kelly, Camara, Radebe, Matteo — Wilcox (Batty 74), Morris, Seth Johnson, Sakho (Domi 60) — Viduka, Smith *Subs not used* Martyn, Lennon, Milner
Booked Wilcox, Morris, Seth Johnson, Domi
Scorers **Viduka 24, Smith 67**
Referee **A Wiley**

Saturday August 23
TOTTENHAM HOTSPUR (a)
Lost 1-2   HT 1-1   Att 34,354   Position **13th**
Robinson — Kelly, Camara, Radebe, Matteo — Wilcox (Pennant 55), Morris, Seth Johnson, Sakho (Domi 64) — Viduka (Lennon 79), Smith *Subs not used* Martyn, Batty
Booked Kelly, Matteo
Scorer **Smith 5**
Report page 250

Tuesday August 26
SOUTHAMPTON (h)
Drew 0-0   HT 0-0   Att 34,721   Position **13th**
Both sides are left looking for their first win of the campaign after Southampton's third successive draw, the second in three games for Leeds, although both managers express themselves happy with their team's performances in a dull affair. Smith goes closest for Leeds, Ormerod wastes Southampton's late and only chance.

Robinson — Kelly, Camara, Matteo, Harte (Richardson 82) — Pennant (Wilcox 90), Morris (Batty 67), Seth Johnson, Sakho — Viduka, Smith *Subs not used* Martyn, Lennon *Booked* Matteo, Sakho
Referee **P Durkin**

Saturday August 30
MIDDLESBROUGH (a)
Won 3-2   HT 1-0   Att 30,414   Position **11th**
Robinson — Kelly, Camara, Matteo, Harte (Lennon 71) — Pennant, Morris, Seth Johnson, Sakho (Radebe 84) — Viduka, Smith *Subs not used* Martyn, Wilcox, Batty
Booked Camara, Morris, Smith, Pennant
Scorers **Sakho 16, Camara 77, Viduka 89**
Report page 208

IT WAS THE PASSING OF A DECENT, honest giant that laid bare the folly of smaller men with bigger egos. That John Charles died in a season when tainted dreams were fired in the kiln of unbridled vanity and Fortress Elland Road was exposed as a house of cards was somehow apposite. The baton had been dropped and the soul had been sold. For Leeds United, it was a death by a 1,000 self-inflicted cuts. Three managers, two chairman, one almighty mess.

There was the threat of administration, the stain of suspicion caused by unfounded rape allegations against a player and the pomposity of a new regime that favoured a man who had taken Bradford City, their near neighbours, to the cusp of ruin. Then, when relegation and abject failure had turned the club into a morality tale, Alan Smith, the Leeds boy who had become a leading man, hotfooted it to Manchester United.

The eagerness of Smith to leave after such a desperate season was a wake-up call to supporters who remembered those gilt-edged days when Don Revie would merrily give his players a tot of whisky before matches. Three decades on and the full bottle was required to kill the pain. The vicarious pleasure that fans had taken in Smith's misplaced tackles and badge-kissing melodrama was unveiled as unrequited love. The very fabric of the club was fraying as Leeds were dragged kicking and screaming into cold, stark reality.

The omens had been there in August. Seth Johnson was found guilty of driving his Porsche at 135mph and Peter Reid admitted that an abject pre-season would have prompted him to hara-kiri were it not for the belief that his team would improve. They did not. A 4-0 defeat away to Leicester City was a stark reminder of how far and how quickly they had fallen. They lost by the same margin away to Everton and suffered the ignominy of a 6-1 humiliation against Portsmouth. Leeds, as the fans still viewed the club, was no more.

The farce was matched by the ineptitude off the pitch. Professor John McKenzie, the chairman, publicly wrestled with himself over Reid's position. He asked supporter groups for their opinion and then met Reid in a Halifax hotel, where he told him he would "sleep on it" before deciding whether to sack him. In the morning he rang him and asked: "Why aren't you at work?" Even Reid, a prosaic foghorn who had facilitated Leeds's decline with limited tactical nous and a job-lot of imported loans, did not merit such insensitive treatment.

Of those loans, Leeds will never forget Jose Roque Junior. Here was a veteran of World and European cup finals performing as if he had Toblerone-shaped boots and a lumberjack's finesse. In his first

HONOURS BOARD

FOOTBALL LEAGUE
Champions 1969, 1974, 1992
Runners-up 1965, 1966, 1970, 1971, 1972
FA CUP
Winners 1972
Runners-up 1965, 1970, 1973
LEAGUE CUP
Winners 1968
Runners-up 1996
EUROPEAN CUP
Runners-up 1975
CUP WINNERS' CUP

Runners-up 1973
FAIRS CUP/UEFA CUP
Winners 1968, 1971
Runners-up 1967

Record attendance 57,892 (v Sunderland,
FA Cup 5th rnd replay, March 15, 1967)
Current capacity 40,296
Record victory 10-0 (v Lyn, European Cup,
1st rnd, 1st leg, September 17, 1969)
Record defeat 1-8 (v Stoke City, first
division, August 27, 1934)

two games he conceded a penalty, got sent off and helped to ship six goals. Norman Hunter he was not.

The popularity of Eddie Gray as Reid's replacement was a result of nostalgia rather than his managerial ability and Leeds only tentatively suggested that they could avoid the drop. Gray went down with dignity, but his avuncular nature was lost on some of his players and a public rift with David Batty signalled the end of Batty's illustrious career for his home-town club.

By that point it was matters in the boardroom that were taking centre stage. As debts spiralled above the £100 million mark, McKenzie stepped down in December, the ludicrous contracts, scattered like confetti during the Ridsdale era, anathema to every dewy-eyed realist. Thereafter, Trevor Birch, the chief executive, skilfully negotiated a series of standstill agreements as he sought to placate anxious creditors.

A takeover was secured in March, but Leeds fans were now inured to mealy-mouthed platitudes and self-aggrandising saviours. When Gerald Krasner, the new chairman, finally admitted Geoffrey Richmond, a man with an outstanding tax bill and a tarnished reputation, had been acting as an adviser, the incredulity was palpable.

Details of the £23 million deal were protected by confidentiality agreements, which was a convenient way of hiding the fact they had borrowed most of their war chest. Indeed, Leeds ended the season seeking a second takeover and someone to pay off the loans taken

Monday September 15
LEICESTER CITY (a)
Lost 0-4   HT 0-2   Att 30,460   Position 14th
Robinson — Kelly, Camara, Roque Junior (Radebe 81), Domi (Olembe 54) — Pennant, Morris, Seth Johnson, Sakho (Lennon 69) — Viduka, Smith *Subs not used* Carson, Batty *Booked* Domi, Roque Junior
Report page 165

Saturday September 20
BIRMINGHAM CITY (h)
Lost 0-2   HT 0-0   Att 34,305   Position 16th
The opening goal sparks a controversy that keeps panellists on *The Premiership* busy as Robinson, the Leeds goalkeeper, brilliantly keeps out Dunn's penalty (Roque Junior is sent off for bringing down Forssell), only for a retake to be ordered because he has strayed inches from his line. Leeds are furious, the officials are heavily criticised, but Savage takes over from Dunn to put Birmingham on their way to victory.

Robinson — Kelly, Camara, Roque Junior, Harte — Pennant, Morris, Olembe, Sakho (Lennon 81) — Viduka, Smith *Subs not used* Carson, Radebe, Chapuis, Batty *Booked* Camara, Sakho, Roque Junior, Olembe *Sent off* Roque Junior 77
Referee **D Gallagher**

Wednesday September 24
SWINDON TOWN (h)
Carling Cup, 2nd rnd
Drew 2-2 (aet; 2-2 after 90min; won 4-3 on pens)
HT 0-1   Att 29,211
Lightning strikes twice as, imitating Poom's dramatic intervention for Derby County, Robinson becomes the second goalkeeper in four days to get himself on the scoresheet, heading the last-minute goal that forces extra time. Having trailed 2-0, Leeds then clinch a penalty shoot-out when Robinson saves from Gurney, Swindon having had their own goalkeeper, Griemink, sent off.

Robinson — Kelly (Radebe 37), Camara, Roque Junior, Harte — Lennon, Batty, Olembe, Wilcox (Domi ht) — Chapuis (Bridges 60), Smith *Subs not used* Carson, Seth Johnson *Booked* Camara, Radebe, Smith, Batty, Olembe
Scorers Harte 77, Robinson 90
Referee **M Clattenburg**

Sunday September 28
EVERTON (a)
Lost 0-4   HT 0-3   Att 39,151   Position 18th
Robinson — Kelly, Roque Junior, Camara, Matteo — Pennant (Lennon ht), Morris, Seth Johnson (Olembe ht), Sakho (Bridges ht) — Viduka, Smith *Subs not used* Harte, Carson *Booked* Camara, Bridges
Report page 135

Saturday October 4
BLACKBURN ROVERS (h)
Won 2-1   HT 2-0   Att 35,039   Position 14th
A triumphant end to a bizarre and humiliating week for Peter Reid, whose job is spared after a very public deliberation by his chairman, who consults fans before reaching his decision. Seth Johnson gets both goals, Baggio replying four minutes from time with his first goal in England, a close-range header.

Robinson — Kelly, Camara, Matteo, Olembe — Pennant (Sakho 85), Batty, Morris, Seth Johnson — Viduka (Bridges 67), Smith *Subs not used* Carson, Radebe, Milner *Booked* Robinson, Matteo, Johnson
Scorer Seth Johnson 11, 27
Referee **U Rennie**

Saturday October 18
MANCHESTER UNITED (h)
Lost 0-1 **HT 0-0** Att **40,153** Position **17th**
A deserved victory for the champions, secured by a rare header from Keane, is overshadowed by the FA's continuing investigation in the Rio Ferdinand affair, the defender having allegedly failed to take a drugs test and, as a result, been dropped for England's Euro 2004 qualifier against Turkey in Istanbul a week earlier.

Robinson — Kelly, Camara, Matteo, Olembe — Pennant (Lennon 86), Batty, Seth Johnson, Milner (Sakho 64) — Viduka (Bridges 69), Smith *Subs not used* Roque Junior, Carson *Booked* Seth Johnson, Smith, Batty, Pennant
Referee **G Poll**

Saturday October 25
LIVERPOOL (a)
Lost 1-3 **HT 1-1** Att **43,599** Position **18th**
Robinson — Kelly, Camara, Matteo, Olembe — Pennant (Lennon 82), Batty, Seth Johnson (Barmby 80), Milner (Sakho 74) — Viduka, Smith *Subs not used* Carson, Roque Junior *Booked* Matteo, Batty
Scorer **Smith 42**
Report page 176

Tuesday October 28
MANCHESTER UNITED (h)
Carling Cup, 3rd rnd
Lost 2-3 (aet; 1-1 after 90min) **HT 0-0** Att **37,546**
On the day that they announce record annual losses for an English club of £49.5m, and total debts of £78m, Leeds also go out of the Carling Cup to Djemba-Djemba's extra-time winner. Nothing else can go wrong, surely . . . except it can: Smith is also in trouble after throwing a plastic bottle back into the crowd, striking a female fan.

Robinson — Kelly, Roque Junior, Camara, Harte — Milner, Seth Johnson, Olembe (Lennon 59), Sakho (Chapuis 82) — Smith, Bridges (Domi 71) *Subs not used* Carson, Duberry *Booked* Smith, Roque Junior
Scorer **Roque Junior 49, 114**
Referee **P Durkin**

Saturday November 1
ARSENAL (h)
Lost 1-4 **HT 0-3** Att **36,491** Position **19th**
Viduka is dropped for disciplinary reasons and they are sent to the bottom the next day, but Leeds are not the only club with problems — Arsenal have just incurred fines totalling £275,000 and nine matches' worth of bans after September's "Battle of Old Trafford". The Londoners, though, appear completely unfazed, their speed on the counter-attack allowing them to race into a 4-0 lead inside 50 minutes.

Robinson — Kelly, Camara, Roque Junior, Olembe — Pennant, Batty, Seth Johnson, Sakho (Lennon 61) — Smith, Bridges (Milner ht) *Subs not used* Carson, Harte, Duberry *Booked* Batty, Olembe
Scorer **Smith 64**
Referee **M Dean**

Duberry tries to plug the gaps in the 6-1 humiliation at Fratton Park

out by the Krasner group. It was an unedifying denouement and entirely in keeping with the decline of a great club.

The list of key players to have been sold, spurned and sacrificed since the heady days of Europe now included Ferdinand, Woodgate, Bowyer, Dacourt, Kewell, Batty and Robinson. Leeds fans chaired Smith around Elland Road at the final home game as a conquering hero. They knew he was going and showed their affection. They even overlooked the arrogance that enabled Smith to renege on a previous vow to stay in the event of relegation. They would be less forgiving when talk of Manchester United surfaced. In a year in which their club had been torn asunder, age-old enmity and bitter tradition were all they had left.

It was a sign of how muddled the thinking had become that Mark Viduka wound down the season as a scapegoat. His crime was being sent off twice during the finale, yet Viduka had been the most talented striker Leeds had seen since the Revie era and had a record to prove it. It had also been a torrid time for Viduka, who missed part of the season to keep a bedside vigil as his father lay ill in a Melbourne hospital. That he will be remembered for two indiscretions is evidence of a revisionism more normally practised in the boardroom.

A packed memorial service for Charles at Elland Road was a poignant and timely reminder of the value of grace, honour and talent. Leeds now seem destined for the ranks of sleeping giants themselves.

THE MANAGER

Peter Reid

Having come perilously close to being in charge of two relegated sides during the same season, time finally caught up with Peter Reid. Barrack-room banter and a breath of foul-mouthed air will only get you so far and this time there was no Harry Kewell to produce a moment of magic to save him. At the end of a torrid year, Eddie Gray and Kevin Blackwell had also sat in the manager's chair while Reid had found another chairman prepared to believe that old school is not old hat. The damage was done before Reid arrived and the board had already ravaged the club by using a myopic version of paper, scissors, stone as their blueprint for implosion. An initial injection of motivation aside, Reid had more chance of staying with Diego Maradona in 1986 than he did of solving this conundrum.

Rick Broadbent

APPEARANCES

	Prem	FAC	CC	Total
E Bakke	8 (2)	1	-	9 (2)
N Barmby	1 (5)	-	-	1 (5)
D Batty	10 (2)	1	1	12 (2)
M Bridges	1 (9)	-	1 (1)	2 (10)
S Caldwell	13	-	-	13
Z Camara	13	-	2	15
S Carson	2 (1)	-	-	2 (1)
C Chapuis	0 (1)	-	1 (1)	1 (2)
D Domi	9 (3)	-	0 (2)	9 (5)
M Duberry	19	1	-	20
I Harte	21 (2)	1	2	24 (2)
Seth Johnson	24 (1)	-	1	25 (1)
Simon Johnson	1 (4)	-	-	1 (4)
G Kelly	37	-	2	39
M Kilgallon	7 (1)	1	-	8 (1)
A Lennon	0 (11)	0 (1)	1 (1)	1 (13)
D Matteo	33	1	-	34
S McPhail	8 (4)	-	-	8 (4)
J Milner	27 (3)	1	1	29 (3)
J Morris	11 (1)	-	-	11 (1)
S Olembe	8 (4)	-	2	10 (4)
J Pennant	34 (2)	-	-	34 (2)
P Robinson	36	1	2	39
L Radebe	11 (3)	-	0 (1)	11 (4)
F Richardson	2 (2)	1	-	3 (2)
Roque Junior	5	-	2	7
L Sakho	9 (8)	0 (1)	1	10 (9)
A Smith	35	1	2	38
M Viduka	30	1	-	31
J Wilcox	3 (3)	-	1	4 (3)

Saturday November 8
PORTSMOUTH (a)
Lost 1-6   HT 1-2   Att 20,112   Position 20th
Robinson — Kelly, Duberry, Matteo, Olembe — Pennant (Sakho 56), Morris, Roque Junior (Bridges 71), Seth Johnson — Smith, Milner *Subs not used* Carson, Harte, Camara *Booked* Matteo, Seth Johnson, Smith, Olembe
Scorer **Smith 19**
Report page 232

Saturday November 22
BOLTON WANDERERS (h)
Lost 0-2   HT 0-2   Att 36,558   Position 20th
With Peter Reid dismissed two days after the Fratton Park debacle, Eddie Gray is in charge against Bolton, but two goals in a minute condemn Leeds to a sixth straight defeat and some bookmakers have stopped taking bets on Gordon Strachan taking over. "You can't feel sympathy for a fellow manager — it's as brutal as that," Sam Allardyce says.
Robinson — Camara, Duberry, Radebe, Harte — Milner, Batty (Chapuis ht), Morris (Olembe 76), Seth Johnson (Barmby 76) — Viduka, Sakho *Subs not used* Carson, Domi *Booked* Sakho
Referee **G Poll**

Saturday November 29
CHARLTON ATHLETIC (a)
Won 1-0   HT 1-0   Att 26,445   Position 20th
Robinson — Kelly, Radebe, Duberry, Harte — Pennant, Smith, Batty, Matteo, Milner — Viduka *Subs not used* Carson, Morris, Bridges, McPhail, Domi *Booked* Smith
Scorer **Milner 9**
Report page 115

Saturday December 6
CHELSEA (h)
Drew 1-1   HT 1-0   Att 36,305   Position 19th
Bottom versus top, poorest v richest ... whatever way the game is labelled it ends all square. Pennant, on loan from Highbury, does Arsenal a favour by giving Leeds the lead after a fine slaloming run — his first goal for the club and the first Chelsea have conceded for more than 11 hours. Duff rewards the title contenders' pressure with the equaliser.
Robinson — Kelly, Radebe, Duberry, Harte — Pennant, Smith, Matteo, McPhail (Domi 64), Milner (Seth Johnson 63) — Viduka *Subs not used* Morris, Bridges, Carson *Booked* Radebe, Matteo, Smith
Scorer **Pennant 18**
Referee **M Dean**

Sunday December 14
FULHAM (h)
Won 3-2   HT 1-0   Att 30,544   Position 19th
The Leeds revival gather pace as Matteo's late header makes it seven points out of nine with victory over Fulham, who play their part in a thrilling second half. It looks all over when Viduka's superb curling shot makes it 2-0 just after half-time, only for the visiting team to hit back through Saha's double.
Robinson — Kelly, Radebe, Duberry, Harte — Pennant, Smith, Matteo, Batty, Milner — Viduka *Subs not used* Carson, Morris, Bridges, McPhail, Richardson *Booked* Smith, Batty
Scorers **Duberry 41, Viduka 46, Matteo 88**
Referee **N Barry**

Monday December 22
MANCHESTER CITY (a)
Drew 1-1   HT **1-0**   Att **47,126**   Position **19th**
Robinson — Kelly, Duberry, Radebe (McPhail 74), Harte —
Pennant (Bridges 81), Smith, Batty (Kilgallon 90), Matteo,
Milner — Viduka *Subs not used* Carson, Morris *Booked*
Batty, Bridges, Duberry
Scorer **Viduka** 24
Report page 190

Friday December 26
ASTON VILLA (h)
Drew 0-0   HT **0-0**   Att **38,513**   Position **19th**
David O'Leary returns to Elland Road for the first time
since his dismissal 18 months earlier and says that he
is happy with the reception he gets from the Leeds
supporters, He is also reasonably happy with a point
as two improving sides cancel each other out, though
Villa might have had a penalty for Kilgallon's push on
Moore.

Robinson — Kelly, Duberry, Kilgallon, Harte — Pennant
(Lennon 72), Batty, Smith, Matteo (Bakke 64), Milner —
Viduka *Subs not used* Carson, Sakho, McPhail
Referee **S Bennett**

Sunday December 28
WOLVERHAMPTON WANDERERS (a)
Lost 1-3   HT **1-1**   Att **29,139**   Position **19th**
Robinson — Kelly, Duberry, Kilgallon, Harte — Matteo —
Pennant (Sakho 82), Bakke, McPhail (Milner 62) —
Viduka, Smith *Subs not used* Carson, Seth Johnson,
Richardson *Booked* Matteo, Duberry, McPhail, Bakke
Sent off Matteo 76
Scorer **Duberry** 3
Report page 264

Sunday January 4 2004
ARSENAL (h)
FA Cup, 3rd rnd
Lost 1-4   HT **1-2**   Att **31,207**
Ahead when Lehmann's dreadful clearance goes
straight to Viduka, Leeds are swept aside again by
Arsenal, who repeat their winning league margin of
November as they go in pursuit of a fourth successive
Cup Final appearance. Henry, only playing because
Aliadiere drops out ill, leads the way with the equaliser
in an outstanding individual display.

Robinson — Richardson, Duberry, Kilgallon, Harte —
Bakke (Sakho 70), Batty, Matteo — Smith, Milner
(Lennon 84) — Viduka *Subs not used* Olembe, Seth
Johnson, Carson *Booked* Smith, Bakke
Scorer **Viduka** 8
Referee **R Styles**

Wednesday January 7
NEWCASTLE UNITED (a)
Lost 0-1   HT **0-1**   Att **52,130**   Position **19th**
Robinson — Kelly, Duberry, Kilgallon, Harte — Pennant,
Matteo, Batty (Olembe 30), Seth Johnson (Bridges 68),
Milner (Sakho 88) — Viduka *Subs not used* Carson,
Richardson *Booked* Kelly
Report page 223

MATCH OF THE SEASON

Leeds United 3 Fulham 2
Elland Road, Sunday December 14 2003
Rick Broadbent

IF EDDIE GRAY is not careful, he may be getting a poisoned
chalice for Christmas. It may be too early to talk of a phoenix rising
from the ashes of tainted dreams, but seven points from their past
three games amount to manna from heaven for a side that had been
dodo-esque during the last days of Peter Reid's reign. Having twice
lost his job at Elland Road in the past, the caretaker manager is now
staking a claim to be handed the role on a permanent basis.

It is no coincidence that Leeds's improvement has arrived with
Gray's policy of leaving out the job-lot of loan signings that Reid
recruited from abroad. "There are lots of players with ability, but you
have to use it," he said. "You need courage." The implication was
that home-grown players such as James Milner and worldly war-
horses such as Lucas Radebe are a better bet for a relegation scrap. A
rip-snorting finale left the game hanging in the balance until the
very last kick, but Leeds were worth their win.

Fulham must hope that their bubble has not burst after Dominic
Matteo, the Leeds captain, headed in Ian Harte's free kick in the
88th minute to claim the spoils with his first goal since he scored
against AC Milan in sepia days of success.

Having seen his side equalise only three minutes earlier, when
Paul Robinson fluffed Louis Saha's daisy-cutter, Chris Coleman felt
hard-done-by. He said that he felt his side deserved to win but was
happy to act as a seconder for Gray's claim on the manager's seat.
"No way are they one of the worst teams in the league," Coleman
said. "I think he's got them focused and has the players behind him."

Both sides had numerous chances and only a combination of
profligate finishing, good goalkeeping and the woodwork prevented
a goalfest. Jermaine Pennant twice hit the bar, once with a rasping
volley and then with a deflected cross, while Steed Malbranque drew
a fine save from Robinson in injury time. It was thrilling stuff and at
the centre of most of the frenzied action was Alan Smith.

Few fans will be devastated by Professor John McKenzie's
decision to step down, but they might be concerned that the chairman has always maintained that Smith would not be sold while he
was in charge. The local hero's manner of playing as if affronted by
the mere presence of opponents has cemented his place in Leeds
folklore and, if his billing as a regular goalscorer is something of a
myth, his passion and aggression are priceless. Every crisis club
should have a player such as him.

With Smith, Matteo and David Batty flooding the midfield, the
emphasis was on stifling rather than creating. It made for a first half
that was a good advertisement for Christmas shopping and it was
fitting that the breakthrough was a slapstick goal that owed much to

Jermaine Pennant gets the better of Sean Davis in Leeds's thrilling win

fortune, Michael Duberry scoring with his knee after Edwin van der Sar had parried Harte's disputed free kick.

Maybe it was the half-time singalong led by Allan Clarke, Mick Jones and Paul Reaney, three reminders that it used to be different, which galvanised the game. Seconds after the restart, Mark Viduka picked up Milner's throw and shuffled across the box with that familiar mincing gait that suggests his shorts are chafing. Yet Viduka's languid style masks the fact that he is the best finisher Leeds have had since Jimmy Floyd Hasselbaink and he proved it by caressing a wonderful 20-yard strike into the top corner. If he does depart in the January sales, it will leave Leeds bereft of a genuine goal threat. "He's very important to the system we're playing," Gray said.

This being Leeds, it was a fleeting stop in the comfort zone. Almost immediately, Sean Davis pushed a pass to Saha and the Frenchman threaded the ball between Radebe's legs and beyond the flailing hand of Robinson. Chances continued to come and go. Robinson stopped a volley from Saha, Malbranque flashed a drive just wide and then Matteo blazed over from eight yards. The last redeemed himself when it mattered, though, and Leeds can at least be assured of avoiding the hoodoo that dictates that the bottom side at Christmas ends up being relegated.

LEEDS UNITED (4-5-1): P Robinson — G Kelly, M Duberry, L Radebe, I Harte — J Pennant, A Smith, D Matteo, D Batty, J Milner — M Viduka. **Substitutes not used:** S Carson, J Morris, M Bridges, S McPhail, F Richardson. **Booked:** Batty, Smith.
FULHAM (4-1-4-1): E van der Sar — M Volz (sub: B Hayles, 63min), A Melville, Z Knight, J Harley — S Legwinski — S Malbranque, L Clark, S Davis, L Boa Morte (sub: F Sava, 77) — L Saha. **Substitutes not used:** M Crossley, M Djetou, A Goma. **Booked:** Boa Morte.

Saturday January 10
TOTTENHAM HOTSPUR (h)
Lost 0-1   HT 0-0   Att 35,365   Position 19th
They ride their luck initially, but another damaging defeat is inevitably inflicted on Leeds by their old boy, Keane. He reacts first to Taricco's quick free kick to make it three wins in eight days for Spurs, for whom Giovanni Trappatoni is the latest name to be linked with their managerial vacancy.

Robinson — Kelly, Duberry, Kilgallon, Harte — Pennant, Bakke, Matteo, Olembe (Sakho 66) — Viduka (Bridges ht), Barmby (Milner 66) *Subs not used* Carson, Richardson
Referee **M Halsey**

Saturday January 17
SOUTHAMPTON (a)
Lost 1-2   HT 0-2   Att 31,976   Position 20th
Robinson — Kelly, Camara, Kilgallon, Harte — Pennant, Bakke, Seth Johnson, Morris (Bridges 66), Milner — Smith *Subs not used* Carson, Roque Junior, Barmby, Richardson
Booked Camara
Scorer **Kilgallon 75**
Report page 245

Saturday January 31
MIDDLESBROUGH (h)
Lost 0-3   HT 0-0   Att 35,970   Position 20th
Leeds have negotiated two more extensions to their "standstill agreement" and the players have finally agreed to have part of their wages deferred, but progress off the pitch is not reflected on it. Middlesbrough romp away with three second-half goals, the last of which comes after Robinson trips Ricketts to incur a penalty and a sending-off.

Robinson — Kelly, Duberry, Kilgallon, Harte — Pennant, Bakke (Morris 78), Matteo, Seth Johnson (Bridges 67) — Smith, Milner (Carson 89) *Subs not used* Barmby, Richardson *Booked* Matteo *Sent off* Robinson 88
Referee **G Poll**

Saturday February 7
ASTON VILLA (a)
Lost 0-2   HT 0-1   Att 39,171   Position 20th
Robinson — Kelly, Caldwell, Matteo, Domi — Pennant (Lennon 63), Bakke (Richardson 86), Seth Johnson, Milner — Viduka, Smith *Subs not used* Harte, McPhail, Carson *Booked* Viduka, Domi
Report page 78

Tuesday February 10
WOLVERHAMPTON WANDERERS (h)
Won 4-1   HT 2-1   Att 36,867   Position 19th
Leeds end a run of six successive league defeats with an emphatic triumph over their fellow strugglers, a fine last-minute goal by the returning Viduka being enough to take them above Dave Jones's side on goal difference. There is no Batty in the Leeds team — the Elland Road stalwart has been told by Eddie Gray that he has already played his last game for the club.

Robinson — Kelly, Matteo, Caldwell, Domi (Harte ht) — Pennant, Bakke, Seth Johnson, Milner — Smith, Viduka *Subs not used* Carson, McPhail, Lennon, Richardson *Booked* Bakke
Scorers **Smith 14, Matteo 41, Milner 62, Viduka 90**
Referee **M Dean**

Saturday February 21
MANCHESTER UNITED (a)
Drew 1-1   HT 0-0   Att 67,744   Position 20th
Carson — Kelly, Caldwell, Matteo, Domi — Pennant,
Bakke, Seth Johnson, McPhail — Smith, Milner
(Sakho 73) *Subs not used* Radebe, Harte, Olembe,
Allaway *Booked* Pennant, McPhail
Scorer **Smith 67**
Report page 203

Sunday February 29
LIVERPOOL (h)
Drew 2-2   HT 2-2   Att 39,932   Position 20th
The creditors have just refused to extend their
"standstill agreement" again, pushing Leeds nearer to
administration, and they are still bottom despite a
good performance against Liverpool, when Kewell's
predictable goal against his former club and another
fine finish from Baros sandwich Bakke's first goal for
more than a year and a more predictable effort by
Viduka.

Robinson — Kelly, Caldwell, Matteo, Domi — Pennant,
Bakke (McPhail ht), Seth Johnson, Milner — Viduka,
Smith (Simon Johnson 82) *Subs not used* Carson,
Harte, Radebe
Scorers **Bakke 29, Viduka 34**
Referee **P Durkin**

Saturday March 13
FULHAM (a)
Lost 0-2   HT 0-0   Att 17,104   Position 20th
Robinson — Kelly, Caldwell, Matteo, Domi — Pennant,
McPhail, Seth Johnson, Milner (Simon Johnson 75) —
Smith, Viduka *Subs not used* Carson, Harte, Olembe,
Richardson *Booked* Caldwell, Domi, Pennant
Report page 150

Monday March 22
MANCHESTER CITY (h)
Won 2-1   HT 1-1   Att 36,998   Position 19th
Three days after a Yorkshire-based consortium agrees a
takeover that prevents the club from going into
administration and wipes out £60m of their £100m-plus
debts, Leeds begin life under new ownership by climbing
off the foot of the table thanks to a contentious penalty,
awarded for Van Buyten's foul on Smith, which, if any
contact is made, happens outside the area and results in
the defender's dismissal.

Robinson — Kelly, Caldwell, Matteo, Domi — Pennant,
Seth Johnson, McPhail, Milner — Smith, Viduka
Subs not used Carson, Harte, Radebe, Lennon,
Simon Johnson
Scorers **McPhail 23, Viduka 76 (pen)**
Referee **A Wiley**

THE PLAYERS

EIRIK BAKKE (midfield) **Born**
September 13, 1977, Sogndal, Norway
Ht 6ft 2in **Wt** 12st 9lb **Signed from**
Sogndal, July 1999, £1m

NICK BARMBY (midfield) **Born**
February 11, 1974, Hull **Ht** 5ft 7in
Wt 10st 8lb **Signed from** Liverpool,
August 2002, £2.75m

DAVID BATTY (midfield) **Born**
December 2, 1968, Leeds **Ht** 5ft 8in
Wt 12st 12lb **Signed from**
Newcastle United, December 1998,
£4.4m

MICHAEL BRIDGES (forward) **Born**
August 5, 1978, North Shields
Ht 6ft 1in **Wt** 12st 6lb **Signed from**
Sunderland, July 1999, £5m

STEVE CALDWELL (defender) **Born**
September 12, 1980, Stirling **Ht** 6ft 3in
Wt 11st 5lb **Signed from** Newcastle
United (loan), February 2004

SCOTT CARSON (goalkeeper) **Born**
September 3, 1985, Whitehaven
Ht 6ft 3in **Wt** 13st 3lb **Signed from**
trainee, July 2003

ZOUMANA CAMARA (defender) **Born**
March 4, 1979, Colombes, France
Ht 6ft 0in **Wt** 12st 4lb **Signed from**
Lens (loan), July 2003

CYRIL CHAPUIS (forward) **Born** March
21, 1979, Lyons **Ht** 6ft 0in
Wt 11st 11lb **Signed from** Marseilles
(loan), September 2003

DIDIER DOMI (defender) **Born** May 2,
1978, Sarcelles, France **Ht** 5ft 10in
Wt 11st 2lb **Signed from** Paris
Saint-Germain (loan), August 2003

MICHAEL DUBERRY (defender) **Born**
October 14, 1975, Enfield **Ht** 6ft 1in
Wt 14st 7lb **Signed from** Chelsea, July
1999, £4m

IAN HARTE (defender) **Born** August 31,
1977, Drogheda **Ht** 5ft 11in
Wt 12st 9lb **Signed from** trainee,
December 1995

SETH JOHNSON (midfield) **Born**
March 12, 1979, Birmingham
Ht 5ft 10in **Wt** 12st 5lb **Signed from**
Derby County, October 2001, £7m

SIMON JOHNSON (forward) **Born**
March 9, 1983, West Bromwich
Ht 5ft 9in **Wt** 11st 12lb **Signed from**
trainee, August 2002

GARY KELLY (defender) **Born** July 9,
1974, Drogheda **Ht** 5ft 10in
Wt 11st 5lb **Signed from** Home Farm,
September 1991, free

MATTHEW KILGALLON (defender)
Born January 8, 1984, York **Ht** 6ft 1in
Wt 12st 13lb **Signed from** trainee,
August 2002

AARON LENNON (midfield) **Born** April
16, 1987, Leeds **Ht** 5ft 6in **Wt** 10st
13lb **Signed from** trainee, August 2003

DOMINIC MATTEO (defender) **Born**
April 24, 1974, Dumfries **Ht** 6ft 1in
Wt 13st 4lb **Signed from** Liverpool,
August 2000, £4.75m

STEPHEN McPHAIL (midfield) **Born**
December 9, 1979, Westminster
Ht 5ft 10in **Wt** 12st 6lb **Signed from**
trainee, December 1996

JAMES MILNER (midfield) **Born** January
4, 1986, Leeds **Ht** 5ft 8in **Wt** 12st 7lb
Signed from trainee, August 2001

JODY MORRIS (midfield) **Born**
December 22, 1978, Hammersmith
Ht 5ft 5in **Wt** 10st 12lb **Signed from**
Chelsea, July 2003, free

SALOMON OLEMBE (midfield) **Born**
December 8, 1980, Yaounde,
Cameroon **Ht** 5ft 7in **Wt** 10st 5lb
Signed from Marseilles (loan), August
2003

JERMAINE PENNANT (midfield) **Born**
January 15, 1983, Nottingham
Ht 5ft 8in **Wt** 10st 1lb **Signed from**
Arsenal (loan), August 2003

LUCAS RADEBE (defender) **Born** April
12, 1969, Johannesburg **Ht** 6ft 1in
Wt 12st 4lb **Signed from** Kaizer Chiefs,
South Africa, September 1994,
£250,000

FRAZER RICHARDSON (defender)
Born October 29, 1982, Rotherham
Ht 5ft 11in **Wt** 11st 12lb **Signed from**
trainee, August 2001

PAUL ROBINSON (goalkeeper) **Born**
October 15, 1979, Beverley **Ht** 6ft 4in
Wt 14st 7lb **Signed from** trainee,
August 1997

ROQUE JUNIOR (defender) **Born**
August 31, 1976, Santa Rica do
Sapucai, Brazil **Ht** 6ft 1in **Wt** 11st 8lb
Signed from AC Milan (loan),
September 2003

LAMINE SAKHO (forward) **Born**
September 28, 1977, Senegal
Ht 5ft 10in **Wt** 11st 2lb **Signed from**
Marseilles (loan), August 2003

ALAN SMITH (forward) **Born** October
28, 1980, Rothwell **Ht** 5ft 9in
Wt 11st 10lb **Signed from** trainee,
March 1998

MARK VIDUKA (forward) **Born** October
9, 1975, Melbourne **Ht** 6ft 2in
Wt 14st 4lb **Signed from** Celtic, July
2000, £6m

JASON WILCOX (midfield) **Born** July 15,
1971, Bolton **Ht** 5ft 11in **Wt** 11st 10lb
Signed from Blackburn Rovers,
December 1999, £3m

STATS AND FACTS

● Between October 2002 and November 2003, Leeds did not draw a single away game in the league.

● On New Year's Day 2002, Leeds led Manchester United at the top of the Premiership, but since then Manchester United have picked up 94 points more than Leeds.

● Only one of the past 69 meetings between Leeds and Newcastle United has ended in a goalless draw.

● Leeds have won none of their past 13 games away to Everton.

● The rivalry may be intense, but Leeds have won just four of their past 36 meetings with Manchester United.

● Arsenal love travelling to Elland Road — the past three visits by Arsene Wenger's side have ended in 4-1 away wins.

● Leeds finished seven points ahead of Chelsea in 2001, two points ahead in 2002, 20

points behind in 2003 and 46 points behind in 2004.

Bill Edgar

GOALSCORERS

	Prem	FAC	CC	Total
E Bakke	1	-	-	1
S Caldwell	1	-	-	1
Z Camara	1	-	-	1
M Duberry	3	-	-	3
I Harte	1 (p)	-	1	2 (1p)
Seth Johnson	2	-	-	2
M Kilgallon	2	-	-	2
D Matteo	2	-	-	2
S McPhail	1	-	-	1
J Milner	3	-	-	3
J Pennant	2	-	-	2
P Robinson	-	-	1	1
Roque Junior	-	-	2	2
L Sakho	1	-	-	1
A Smith	9 (1p)	-	-	9 (1p)
M Viduka	11 (2p)	1	-	12 (2p)

Saturday March 27
BIRMINGHAM CITY (a)
Lost 1-4   HT 1-1   Att 29,069   Position 19th
Robinson — Kelly, Caldwell, Matteo, Domi — Pennant, Seth Johnson, McPhail, Milner (Simon Johnson 78) — Smith, Viduka *Subs not used* Carson, Harte, Radebe, Keegan *Booked* Domi
Scorer **Viduka 3**
Report page 89

Monday April 5
LEICESTER CITY (h)
Won 3-2   HT 2-0   Att 34,036   Position 19th
A huge win for Leeds against the team immediately above them in the relegation zone, courtesy of a late winner from Smith, who earlier in the week had criticised his team-mates for folding too easily in some matches. Viduka is sent off for two cautions as Leicester, having hit back from 2-0 down to 2-2, lose their six-match unbeaten run.

Robinson — Kelly, Caldwell, Duberry, Domi — Pennant, Matteo, Seth Johnson, Milner (Harte 88) — Viduka, Smith *Subs not used* Carson, Radebe, Lennon, Simon Johnson *Booked* Viduka, Milner *Sent off* Viduka 90
Scorers **Duberry 11, Viduka 13, Smith 86**
Referee **M Dean**

Saturday April 10
BLACKBURN ROVERS (a)
Won 2-1   HT 1-0   Att 26,611   Position 18th
Robinson — Kelly, Duberry, Caldwell, Harte — Pennant, Matteo, Seth Johnson (Bakke 56), Milner — Viduka, Smith (McPhail 90) *Subs not used* Radebe, Simon Johnson, Carson *Booked* Matteo, Milner
Scorers **Caldwell 2, Viduka 89**
Report page 99

Tuesday April 13
EVERTON (h)
Drew 1-1   HT 0-1   Att 39,835   Position 18th
Rooney, back from suspension, gives Everton an early lead, but Leeds reply via their own youthful prodigy, Milner, and are denied all three points by a magnificent display of goalkeeping from Martyn, their former No 1, who can rarely have played better in his 273 games for the Elland Road club.

Robinson — Kelly, Duberry, Caldwell, Harte — Pennant, Radebe, Matteo, Milner — Viduka, Smith *Subs not used* Carson, Barmby, Olembe, Lennon, Simon Johnson *Booked* Radebe, Caldwell
Scorer **Milner 50**
Referee **P Durkin**

Friday April 16
ARSENAL (a)
Lost 0-5   HT 0-3   Att 38,094   Position 18th
Robinson — Kelly, Duberry, Caldwell, Harte — Pennant, Radebe (Barmby 72), Matteo, Milner — Viduka (Simon Johnson 84), Smith *Subs not used* Lennon, Kilgallon, Carson
Report page 69

PLAYER OF THE SEASON
James Milner

Alan Smith deceived a lot of people by clutching his badge, donning the emperor's new clothes and maintaining his tradition of rarely scoring, but enhanced the myth of the committed local hero with a few tackles that were past their sell-by date. Mark Viduka was a far greater threat but more erratic than in past years and Jermaine Pennant dazzled fleetingly. That left two candidates. The first was Dominic Matteo, who employed the subtlety of a herd of rabid wildebeest but was a rock in a porous side, and James Milner. The teenager was sent out on loan by a befuddled Peter Reid, but returned to show the intelligence that prompted Claudio Ranieri to remark: "He has the brain of a 30-year-old." The academy system created by Howard Wilkinson yielded more fruit last season, Scott Carson, Matthew Kilgallon and Frazer Richardson all making their breakthroughs, but Milner was the pick of the lot.

Rick Broadbent

Sunday April 25
PORTSMOUTH (h)
Lost 1-2   HT 0-1   Att **39,273**   Position **18th**
One escape route is closed on Leeds as Portsmouth, the country's form side, score a deserved victory to reach 40 points, Yakubu and LuaLua making Harte's late penalty redundant. "It was a huge game for this club and we weren't up for it," Eddie Gray laments.
Robinson — Kelly, Duberry, Caldwell, Harte — Pennant, Radebe (Lennon 71), Matteo (McPhail ht), Milner — Simon Johnson (Barmby 59), Smith *Subs not used* Carson, Kilgallon *Booked* Kelly, Caldwell
Scorer **Harte 83 (pen)**
Referee **U Rennie**

Sunday May 2
BOLTON WANDERERS (a)
Lost 1-4   HT 1-0   Att **27,420**   Position **19th**
Robinson — Kelly, Duberry, Caldwell, Harte — Pennant, McPhail, Matteo, Milner (Wilcox 60) — Smith, Viduka *Subs not used* Carson, Barmby, Lennon, Kilgallon *Booked* Viduka, Pennant *Sent off* Viduka 33
Scorer **Viduka 27 (pen)**
Report page 110

Saturday May 8
CHARLTON ATHLETIC (h)
Drew 3-3   HT 2-1   Att **38,986**   Position **19th**
Extraordinary scenes greet the mathematical confirmation of Leeds's relegation as Smith is mobbed during a friendly pitch invasion, having signed off — or so it seems — from Elland Road with a goal from the spot. Ahead 1-0, then 3-1 behind, Charlton hit back with Euell's double, including another penalty, for a worthy draw.
Robinson — Richardson (Radebe 82), Duberry, Kilgallon, Harte — Kelly (Wilcox 73), Matteo, McPhail, Pennant — Smith, Milner *Subs not used* Carson, Barmby, Winter
Scorers **Kilgallon 29, Pennant 41, Smith 69 (pen)**
Referee **M Halsey**

Saturday May 15
CHELSEA (a)
Lost 0-1   HT 0-1   Att **41,276**   Position **19th**
Carson — Richardson, Duberry, Radebe, Harte — Milner, Matteo, Olembe (Barmby 80), Kelly, Wilcox (Pennant 62) — Smith *Subs not used* Allaway, McPhail, Kilgallon
Report page 132

LEICESTER CITY

PREMIERSHIP

	P	W	D	L	F	A	GD	Pts
Arsenal	38	26	12	0	73	26	47	**90**
Chelsea	38	24	7	7	67	30	37	**79**
Man Utd	38	23	6	9	64	35	29	**75**
Liverpool	38	16	12	10	55	37	18	**60**
Newcastle	38	13	17	8	52	40	12	**56**
Aston Villa	38	15	11	12	48	44	4	**56**
Charlton	38	14	11	13	51	51	0	**53**
Bolton	38	14	11	13	48	56	-8	**53**
Fulham	38	14	10	14	52	46	6	**52**
Birmingham	38	12	14	12	43	48	-5	**50**
Middlesbro	38	13	9	16	44	52	-8	**48**
Southampton	38	12	11	15	44	45	-1	**47**
Portsmouth	38	12	9	17	47	54	-7	**45**
Tottenham	38	13	6	19	47	57	-10	**45**
Blackburn	38	12	8	18	51	59	-8	**44**
Man City	38	9	14	15	55	54	1	**41**
Everton	38	9	12	17	45	57	-12	**39**
Leicester	38	6	15	17	48	65	-17	**33**
Leeds	38	8	9	21	40	79	-39	**33**
Wolves	38	7	12	19	38	77	-39	**33**

FA CUP
Third round

CARLING CUP
Third round

Walkers crunch: Micky Adams looks on as his side fail to secure a victory over Manchester City and edge closer to the precipice

THE GAMES

Saturday August 16 2003
SOUTHAMPTON (h)
Drew 2-2   HT 2-0   Att 31,621   Position 7th
Leading 2-0 within ten minutes, albeit that the decision to award a penalty for Michael Svensson's challenge on Ferdinand appears extremely harsh, Leicester's hopes of marking their return to the top flight with victory are undone by Phillips, a £3.25m signing two days earlier, who scores a brilliant 25-yard debut goal for Southampton, then hits a post for Beattie to tap in the rebound.

Walker – Curtis, Elliott, Thatcher, Rogers – Gillespie (Stewart 83), Scimeca, Izzet, Scowcroft – Ferdinand (Deane ht), Dickov (Nalis 71) *Subs not used* Coyne, Hignett *Booked* Scimeca, Izzet, Dickov
Scorers **Dickov 5 (pen), Ferdinand 10**
Referee **M Riley**

Saturday August 23
CHELSEA (a)
Lost 1-2   HT 1-2   Att 41,073   Position 14th
Walker – Curtis, Howey, Thatcher, Rogers – Impey (Gillespie 52), Scimeca, Izzet, Nalis (Hignett 73) – Scowcroft, Dickov (Deane 73) *Subs not used* Coyne, Taggart *Booked* Thatcher, Scimeca, Hignett, Howey *Sent off* Rogers 84, Scimeca 88
Scorer **Scowcroft 40**
Report page 122

Tuesday August 26
MIDDLESBROUGH (h)
Drew 0-0   HT 0-0   Att 30,823   Position 14th
A match that rarely looks likely to end in anything other than a goalless draw. Leicester are the better side in the first half, Schwarzer saving brilliantly from Izzet, but Middlesbrough improve in the second period and Mendieta, beginning his loan spell from Lazio, twice goes close from distance.

Walker – Curtis, Howey, Thatcher, Rogers – Gillespie, Scimeca, Izzet, Nalis (Deane 72) – Scowcroft, Dickov (Hignett 80) *Subs not used* Coyne, Taggart, Impey *Booked* Gillespie, Scimeca, Nalis
Referee **G Barber**

Saturday August 30
ASTON VILLA (a)
Lost 1-3   HT 0-3   Att 32,274   Position 16th
Walker – Curtis (Impey 4), Howey (Nalis 32), Thatcher, Rogers – Gillespie, Scimeca, Izzet, Scowcroft – Ferdinand, Dickov (Stewart 79) *Subs not used* Hignett, Deane *Booked* Ferdinand, Izzet *Sent off* Ferdinand 40
Scorer **Izzet 53**
Report page 72

THE REVIEW Jim Wheildon

THE TWO GAMES AGAINST Birmingham City encapsulated Leicester's season in a nutshell — a shambolic, even suicidal, defeat at home in mid-December (this was the game where the captain and the goalkeeper got themselves sent off and the manager was banned from the touchline) and a magnificent victory, hard on the heels of the infamous La Manga episode, at St Andrew's in March.

That win, against a then high-flying Birmingham, pulled City out of the bottom three and put paid to any excuses that the incidents in Spain — where, after a night of heavy drinking, eight players were interviewed by police and three found themselves incarcerated for a week while allegations of sexual assault were investigated — lay at the heart of the team's relegation.

La Manga is a stain that City will not find easy to remove. The three players at the centre of the storm, Paul Dickov, Keith Gillespie and Frank Sinclair, had all charges against them dropped after a three-month wait for the wheels of Spanish justice to turn, but the players' irresponsible behaviour on a club mid-season break will not easily be forgotten by fans.

Whatever the fallout from the incident, relegation was simply a case of not being good enough at home. After turning the Walkers Stadium into a fortress during the 2002-03 promotion season, Leicester managed just three home wins in the Premiership and one of those came once the pressure was off, with relegation confirmed. Away, City had more victories — albeit still only three — than Newcastle United, who won a place in Europe.

Yet at the start of the season there were good grounds for optimism. Muzzy Izzet, Leicester's best player, was — against all expectations — still at the club and Micky Adams, the manager, had bolstered the squad with numerous forays in the transfer market. These included half a dozen experienced Premiership players, adding weight to a team that had won promotion at the first attempt by some distance.

But then there is an adage about getting what you pay for and Leicester paid peanuts. Ben Thatcher, the defender signed from Tottenham Hotspur, and that old warhorse, Les Ferdinand, chosen as the players' and the fans' player of the year, more than paid back the faith shown in them by Adams. But John Curtis and Steve Howey were shown the door after only a handful of appearances and Gillespie and Craig Hignett never established themselves.

More Premiership experience in the shape of Steffen Freund, Nikos Dabizas and an old Filbert Street favourite, Steve Guppy, was imported as the season progressed. All three helped the cause, but it was not enough. Adams was always hamstrung by a lack of funds in

HONOURS BOARD

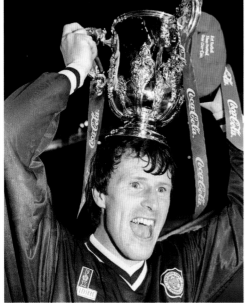

his Herculean efforts to keep City out of danger. The manager may have paid the price for winning promotion in his first full season in charge. When he took over, City were a busted flush, relegated from the Premiership and soon to go into administration. Although not all of his bargain-basement signings worked out, he made other shrewd investments, in particular Riccardo Scimeca, from Nottingham Forest, and Marcus Bent, on loan from Ipswich Town. Danny Coyne and Lilian Nalis also strengthened the squad, but too many of the senior players were on the wrong side of 30 and the Foxes were no longer able to rely on Matt Elliott to hold the side together. He started just three games, while another stalwart, Ian Walker, had a poor first half of the season in goal.

The arrival of younger players in the side, such as Peter Canero, 23, and Lee Morris, 24, as well as the form of 22-year-old Matt Heath, helped to dispel some of the gloom. James Scowcroft had another solid season and Paul Dickov, the diminutive striker, never threw in the towel, although his form understandably dipped after his Spanish trauma.

Aside from the dreadful home record, Leicester paid a heavy price for their inability to hold on to a lead, conceding goals again and again in the final minutes of games. The Premiership's highest tally of sendings-off (seven, albeit that one red card was rescinded), did not exactly help the cause, either. The multiple transfers, both in and out, the numerous suspensions and injuries, the inevitable struggle to adjust to the Premiership after the Nationwide League and, of course, La Manga, all added up to make the season a long, tough

Monday September 15
LEEDS UNITED (h)
Won 4-0 HT 2-0 Att 30,460 Position 11th
"We were second-best all over the pitch," Peter Reid, the Leeds manager, admits, although he also confesses that he "might have picked the wrong team". Leicester are sent on the way to their first win of the season by a stunning 25-yard dipping volley from Nalis, Dickov's double and a last-minute header by Scowcroft completing the rout.

Walker — Curtis, Sinclair, Taggart, Thatcher — Hignett (Stewart 77), Nalis, Izzet, Scowcroft — Bent (Deane 75), Dickov (Impey 86) Subs not used Coyne, Howey
Scorers **Nalis 20, Dickov 23, 83, Scowcroft 90**
Referee **J Winter**

Saturday September 20
LIVERPOOL (a)
Lost 1-2 HT 0-1 Att 44,094 Position 13th
Walker — Curtis, Sinclair, Taggart, Thatcher — Hignett (Stewart 7; Deane 71), Nalis (Scimeca 75), Izzet, Scowcroft — Bent, Dickov Subs not used Impey, Coyne
Scorer **Bent 90**
Report page 175

Tuesday September 23
CREWE ALEXANDRA (h)
Carling Cup, 2nd rnd
Won 1-0 HT 0-0 Att 27,675
Micky Adams indulges in some minor squad rotation — his opposite number, Dario Gradi, is recovering from heart surgery in hospital — and has to wait until eight minutes from time for the winner, when Wright concedes a penalty by holding back Stewart. Howey had earlier cleared off the line from Edwards.

Walker — Curtis, Sinclair, Howey, Impey — Brooker (Priet 89), Scimeca, Nalis, Scowcroft (Izzet ht) — Deane (Stewart 38), Dickov Subs not used Coyne, McKinlay
Booked Nalis, Sinclair
Scorer **Dickov 82 (pen)**
Referee **A Hall**

Saturday September 27
MANCHESTER UNITED (h)
Lost 1-4 HT 0-3 Att 32,044 Position 15th
Leicester's first home defeat for nine months — and their ninth successive reverse against the champions — is never in doubt once the returning Scholes picks out Keane for his first goal in 18 months. After that, Van Nistelrooy runs the show with his fifth United hat-trick. No wonder Walker is forced off with a back injury before Sinclair's consolation goal.

Walker (Coyne 64) — Curtis, Sinclair, Taggart (Stewart 56), Thatcher (Rogers 40) — Nalis, Scimeca, Izzet, Scowcroft — Bent, Dickov Subs not used Howey, Impey
Scorer **Sinclair 73**
Referee **G Poll**

Saturday October 4
FULHAM (a)
Lost 0-2 HT 0-1 Att 14,562 Position 19th
Walker — Sinclair, Howey (Dickov 61), Taggart — Impey, Nalis (Ferdinand 61), Izzet, Scimeca, Rogers — Bent (Gillespie 77), Scowcroft Subs not used Coyne, Stewart Booked Impey
Report page 145

Sunday October 19
TOTTENHAM HOTSPUR (h)
Lost 1-2   HT 1-0   Att 31,521   Position 20th
Ahead through Dickov's fluke, a shot that somehow
goes through Keller's arms and legs in turn, Leicester's
luck turns horribly when Mabizela makes an instant
impact on his Tottenham debut as a substitute with a
stunning 25-yard equaliser and Kanoute hits a
last-minute winner. Kanoute leaves the ground in pain
and on crutches, though, the victim of a poor challenge
by Izzet.

Walker — Curtis, Sinclair, Taggart, Rogers — Gillespie
(Stewart 76), Izzet, Scimeca, Scowcroft — Dickov
(Hignett 88), Ferdinand (Bent 64) *Subs not used* Coyne,
Elliott *Booked* Gillespie, Izzet, Sinclair
Scorer **Dickov 38**
Referee **A D'Urso**

Saturday October 25
WOLVERHAMPTON WANDERERS (a)
Lost 3-4   HT 3-0   Att 28,578   Position 20th
Walker — Curtis, Elliott, Taggart, Rogers — Gillespie
(Nalis 68), Izzet, Scimeca, Scowcroft — Dickov
(Hignett 68), Ferdinand (Bent 68) *Subs not used* Coyne,
Stewart *Booked* Scowcroft, Hignett
Scorers **Ferdinand 12, 15, Scimeca 35**
Report page 262

Wednesday October 29
ASTON VILLA (a)
Carling Cup, 3rd rnd
Lost 0-1   HT 0-0   Att 26,729
Coyne — Impey, Howey, Sinclair, Stewart — Brooker
(Scowcroft 82), Nalis, McKinlay (Izzet 82), Hignett
(Gillespie 65) — Dickov, Deane *Subs not used*
Murphy, Priet
Report page 74

Sunday November 2
BLACKBURN ROVERS (h)
Won 2-0   HT 0-0   Att 30,975   Position 18th
Leicester are off the bottom, leapfrogging Blackburn
in the process, after robbing them with two late goals,
having been on the back foot almost throughout.
Graeme Souness cannot bring himself to discuss
his side's defeat, their fifth in a row in the Premiership,
after replays show that they could have had two
penalties.

Walker — Impey, Howey, Sinclair (Elliott 73), Stewart —
Gillespie (Thatcher 61), McKinlay, Izzet, Scowcroft —
Ferdinand (Dickov 68), Bent *Subs not used* Coyne,
Hignett *Booked* Dickov, Howey
Scorers **Bent 75, Howey 82**
Referee **D Gallagher**

Marcus Bent scored the first of Leicester's two late goals to defeat
Blackburn on Remembrance Sunday, marked by one-off "poppy" kits

slog. The struggle to stay up was a valiant effort and fans suffered
three heavy home thrashings — Manchester United (4-1), Chelsea
(4-0) and Villa (5-0) — and an appalling April with four defeats,
including losses to Leeds United and Blackburn Rovers, their fellow
strugglers. However, Nalis provided the best goal in the best match
of the season, a 4-0 drubbing of Leeds in September, and November
was an unsurpassed month for City with three wins and a draw,
including back-to-back victories against Blackburn at home and 3-0
away to Manchester's light-blues.

There were two particularly memorable away draws, 3-3 at
Middlesbrough and 4-4 against Spurs. In both these, City conceded
late goals, two of them in the last two minutes at the Riverside, just
as they did in the third-round FA Cup replay defeat against
Manchester City. And no Leicester fan will need reminding of the
trauma of being 3-0 up at half-time at Molineux in October only to
walk off 4-3 losers. Arsenal were contained to a 1-1 draw at the Walkers Stadium in December, with City for once on the right side of a
last-minute goal. For 20 minutes on the last day of the season the
Foxes even threatened to end the Gunners' unbeaten league record.

Adams will have to continue to run the club on a shoestring in the
new season, one which sees City's 120th anniversary being
celebrated on November 1 — 120 years without the championship or
the FA Cup, but all of them spent in the top two divisions.

THE MANAGER
Micky Adams

One good thing did emerge emerge from the La Manga episode. Micky Adams was tested to the limit in explaining his decision to allow his highly paid and poorly performing players to take a mid-season break and he did so supremely well. Despite relegation, he has been an excellent manager in his two-year tenure. Fans hold two postwar managers in awe, Matt Gillies and Martin O'Neill. Both kept Leicester in the top division, took the team into Europe and brought home some modest silverware. If Adams stays and maintains the fighting spirit that has always marked the best Leicester teams, he may even surpass their achievements.

Jim Wheildon

APPEARANCES

	Prem	FAC	CC	Total
T Benjamin	2 (2)	-	-	2 (2)
M Bent	28 (5)	2	-	30 (5)
P Brooker	0 (3)	0 (1)	2	2 (4)
P Canero	2 (5)	-	-	2 (5)
D Coyne	1 (3)	-	1	2 (3)
J Curtis	14 (1)	1	1	16 (1)
N Dabizas	18	-	-	18
C Davidson	8 (5)	2	-	10 (5)
B Deane	0 (5)	-	2	2 (5)
P Dickov	28 (7)	2	2	32 (7)
M Elliott	3 (4)	0 (1)	-	3 (5)
L Ferdinand	20 (9)	1 (1)	-	21 (10)
S Freund	13 (1)	-	-	13 (1)
K Gillespie	7 (5)	-	0 (1)	7 (6)
S Guppy	9 (6)	-	-	9 (6)
M Heath	13	2	-	15
C Hignett	3 (10)	1	1	5 (10)
S Howey	13	-	2	15
A Impey	11 (2)	1	2	14 (2)
M Izzet	30	1	0 (2)	31 (2)
W McKinlay	15 (1)	2	1	18 (1)
L Nalis	11 (9)	-	2	13 (9)
N Priet	-	-	0 (1)	0 (1)
A Rogers	7 (1)	-	-	7 (1)
R Scimeca	28 (1)	1	1	30 (1)
J Scowcroft	33 (2)	2	1 (1)	36 (3)
F Sinclair	11 (3)	1	2	14 (3)
J Stewart	16 (9)	1 (1)	1 (1)	18 (11)
G Taggart	9	-	-	9
B Thatcher	28 (1)	-	-	28 (1)
I Walker	37	2	1	40

Sunday November 9
MANCHESTER CITY (a)
Won 3-0   HT 1-0   Att 46,966   Position 15th
Walker – Impey, Howey, Scimeca, Thatcher – Scowcroft, Izzet, McKinlay, Stewart – Dickov (Hignett 85), Bent (Ferdinand 78) *Subs not used* Coyne, Elliott, Gillespie
Booked Izzet, McKinlay
Scorers **Stewart 12, Dickov 53 (pen), Bent 58**
Report page 189

Saturday November 22
CHARLTON ATHLETIC (h)
Drew 1-1   HT 1-0   Att 30,242   Position 15th
Ahead when Ferdinand meets Thatcher's cross, Leicester then hit the post through Bent and go close via Izzet. Their frustration almost boils over when Di Canio goes to ground under the softest of challenges from Howey to win the late penalty that the Italian then converts to earn Charlton a draw.

Walker – Impey, Howey, Scimeca, Thatcher – Scowcroft, Izzet, McKinlay, Stewart – Ferdinand (Dickov 67), Bent *Subs not used* Coyne, Elliott, Gillespie, Hignett *Booked* Izzet, McKinlay
Scorer **Ferdinand 39**
Referee **G Barber**

Saturday November 29
PORTSMOUTH (a)
Won 2-0   HT 1-0   Att 20,061   Position 12th
Walker – Curtis, Howey, Scimeca, Thatcher – Scowcroft, Izzet, McKinlay, Stewart – Ferdinand (Davidson 79), Bent (Hignett 90) *Subs not used* Coyne, Elliott, Gillespie
Booked McKinlay
Scorers **Ferdinand 31, Bent 59**
Report page 233

Saturday December 6
ARSENAL (h)
Drew 1-1   HT 0-0   Att 32,108   Position 15th
Cole, sent off for an awful two-footed challenge on Thatcher, has the good grace to apologise – and it is not Arsenal's only regret on the day. Ahead when Gilberto finishes off a typically fluent break with a header, they concede an equaliser to Hignett with almost the last kick, which prevents them regaining the lead in the Premiership.

Walker – Impey, Howey, Scimeca, Thatcher – Scowcroft, McKinlay (Hignett 59), Davidson, Stewart – Ferdinand (Gillespie 76), Bent (Dickov 67) *Subs not used* Coyne, Elliott *Booked* Ferdinand
Scorer **Hignett 90**
Referee **R Styles**

Saturday December 13
BIRMINGHAM CITY (h)
Lost 0-2   HT 0-1   Att 30,639   Position 16th
Savage returns to Leicester and, perhaps predictably, there's trouble, though not of his making. Leicester have Elliott sent off for an arm-first aerial challenge on Dunn and Walker for handling yards outside his box, plus Micky Adams sent to the stands for his half-time protests to the referee. Morrison and Forssell get the goals that end Birmingham's poor run.

Walker – Impey, Elliott, Scimeca, Thatcher (Bent 72) – Scowcroft, Izzet, Davidson, Stewart – Ferdinand (Curtis ht), Dickov (Coyne 61) *Subs not used* Hignett, Gillespie *Booked* Scowcroft, Dickov *Sent off* Elliott 38, Walker 61
Referee **M Riley**

Saturday December 20
EVERTON (a)
Lost 2-3 **HT 1-1** Att **37,007** Position **17th**
Walker — Impey, Scimeca, Howey (Elliott 52), Thatcher —
Scowcroft, McKinlay (Dickov 84), Izzet, Stewart
(Davidson 76) — Ferdinand, Bent *Subs not used* Hignett,
Coyne *Booked* Thatcher, Scimeca, Bent
Scorers **Ferdinand 45, Scowcroft 58**
Report page 138

Friday December 26
NEWCASTLE UNITED (h)
Drew 1-1 **HT 0-0** Att **32,148** Position **18th**
Leicester's 4,000th league game is watched by a record
Walkers Stadium crowd, but they have little to entertain
them until Dickov pounces when O'Brien fails to clear.
Newcastle grab a point, though, when Ambrose, a late
substitute, nods in his first Premiership goal after Walker
parries Jenas's shot.
Walker — Curtis, Howey (Elliott 16), Scimeca, Thatcher —
Scowcroft, Izzet, McKinlay, Stewart (Davidson 69) —
Ferdinand, Dickov *Subs not used* Coyne, Bent, Hignett
Scorer **Dickov 67**
Referee **C Foy**

Sunday December 28
BOLTON WANDERERS (a)
Drew 2-2 **HT 1-1** Att **28,353** Position **17th**
Coyne — Curtis, Heath, Scimeca, Thatcher — Scowcroft,
Izzet, Davidson, Hignett (Brooker 72) — Dickov
(Ferdinand 71), Bent (Stewart 85) *Subs not used*
McKinlay, Impey *Booked* Thatcher, Izzet, Davidson
Scorers **Bent 18, Ferdinand 90**
Report page 106

Saturday January 3 2004
MANCHESTER CITY (a)
FA Cup, 3rd rnd
Drew 2-2 **HT 1-1** Att **30,617**
Walker — Impey, Heath, Scimeca (Stewart 55), Davidson
— Scowcroft, McKinlay, Izzet, Hignett — Bent (Brooker 85),
Dickov (Ferdinand 62) *Subs not used* Nalis, Coyne
Booked Dickov
Scorers **Dickov 4, Bent 66**
Report page 190

Wednesday January 7
SOUTHAMPTON (a)
Drew 0-0 **HT 0-0** Att **31,053** Position **17th**
Walker — Impey, Howey, Dabizas, Thatcher — Scowcroft,
Izzet, Davidson, Stewart — Bent, Ferdinand (Dickov 64)
Subs not used Coyne, Heath, Hignett, McKinlay *Booked*
Izzet
Report page 245

MATCH OF THE SEASON

Leicester City 4 Leeds United 0
Walkers Stadium, Monday September 15 2003
Peter Lansley

HE WOULD, ONE ASSUMES, PREFER not to suffer the scars in the first place, but there is nothing that Micky Adams prefers to work with than a wounded animal. The Leicester City manager admits that he has been like a snarling creature roaming his cage during an elongated international break, after a tummy-tickling from Aston Villa 17 days ago. Last night, his players proved that they have the stomach for the fight ahead.

Leicester's first win of the season was thoroughly deserved, Paul Dickov scoring twice after Lilian Nalis, signed on a free transfer from Chievo during the summer, had conjured up a wonderful goal to set the tone. The French midfield player, already favoured by the Leicester crowd for wearing the No 8 shirt and his hair long in the fashion of Robbie Savage, wrapped his left foot around Jody Morris's clearance, 30 yards out, 20 minutes in, and the ball flew into the top corner. "I've just been trying to explain to him what 'fluke' means," Adams joked.

James Scowcroft completed the scoring in the final minute as Leeds fell apart in a manner that alarmed Peter Reid. "In our four previous games, the attitude and work ethic has been tremendous, but tonight there are no excuses," the Leeds manager said. "We were second in too many departments to win a football match — or even to compete in it.

"We can learn from Leicester. Some goals were great, but we just weren't at the races. We told our players what to expect but, for some reason, they just weren't up for it."

The inconsistency being displayed by Leeds suggests that Leicester, adapting to the Barclaycard Premiership, may have taken three points from a rival. Last night, the home side overtook their opponents in the table, climbing out of the bottom three to the dizzy heights of eleventh place.

Adams clearly has been working on his team's start to matches since they went 3-0 down in the opening quarter of an hour at Villa Park. "I would have taken any margin of victory tonight," he said. "I wouldn't comment on Peter Reid's team, but I know I was bitterly disappointed by the defeat at Aston Villa. You've got to start fast and furious and we did that."

Marcus Bent, on loan from Ipswich Town, helped to establish the tempo with a superb debut, offering a ball-to-feet option in between the flurry of accurate crosses to the far post in which Leicester specialise. Paul Robinson, the England goalkeeper, was in splendid form, saving adroitly from Scowcroft and Gerry Taggart before Nalis's contender for goal of the season.

Three minutes later, Leicester confirmed their dominance.

Nalis is engulfed by team-mates after his stunning long-range strike

Scowcroft flicked on Ian Walker's long goal kick to Bent, who helped the ball on in similar fashion. Dickov chested the ball down, swivelled and volleyed beyond Robinson's clutches. The spectator who was advised over the public-address system at the interval that his wife had gone into labour must have been trusting that she would at least have the decency to wait until full-time before delivering. No Leicester supporter wanted to leave early last night.

Certainly Dickov remained right on his game as he scored his second of the night seven minutes from time, turning on to Muzzy Izzet's pass to leave Lucas Radebe on his backside and shoot beyond Robinson. The goalkeeper could do nothing to prevent Scowcroft heading in a fourth, from Izzet's free kick, in the final minute.

"We won't be getting complacent," Adams said. "We go to Anfield on Saturday and we have Manchester United after that. But I've been delighted with our level of performance apart from that first 20 minutes at Villa."

Leicester continue to play to their strengths, harassing the opposition and producing top-class deliveries into the penalty area. "We are what we are, I'm afraid," Adams said by way of an unnecessary apology. "We have to work at what we do every day."

LEICESTER CITY (4-4-2): I Walker — J Curtis, F Sinclair, G Taggart, B Thatcher — C Hignett (sub: J Stewart, 77min), L Nalis, M Izzet, J Scowcroft — B Bent (sub: B Deane, 75), P Dickov (sub: A Impey, 86). **Substitutes not used:** D Coyne, S Howey.
LEEDS UNITED (4-4-2): P Robinson — G Kelly, Z Camara, Roque Junior (sub: L Radebe, 81), D Domi (sub: S Olembe, 54) — J Pennant, J Morris, Seth Johnson, L Sakho (sub: A Lennon, 70) — A Smith, M Viduka. **Substitutes not used:** S Carson, D Batty. **Booked:** Domi, Roque Junior.

Sunday January 11
CHELSEA (h)
Lost 0-4   **HT 0-2**   Att **31,547**   Position **17th**
Claudio Ranieri recalls several members of the pre-Abramovich Chelsea "old guard" and is rewarded with an emphatic win, sparked by Hasselbaink's clever backheel and topped off with two goals in the last two minutes. "I didn't see much battling, to be honest," Micky Adams says as Leicester drop back into the relegation zone.

Walker — Impey, Dabizas, Howey, Davidson — Scowcroft, McKinlay (Hignett 82), Nalis (Brooker 69), Stewart — Dickov, Bent (Ferdinand 69) Subs not used Coyne, Heath
Referee **U Rennie**

Wednesday January 14
MANCHESTER CITY (h)
FA Cup, 3rd rnd replay
Lost 1-3   **HT 0-1**   Att **18,916**
The day after Seaman announces his retirement, Manchester City register their first victory in 15 matches when two goals in the last minute — Anelka punishing dreadful hesitancy by Sinclair and Macken plundering the next — ease the pressure on Kevin Keegan. "I'd forgotten what it was like to win," the relieved visiting manager says.

Walker — Curtis, Heath, Sinclair, Stewart — Scowcroft, McKinlay, Davidson, Dickov — Ferdinand (Elliott 83), Bent Subs not used Coyne, Hignett, Gillespie, Brooker Booked Scowcroft, Sinclair
Scorer **Ferdinand 73**
Referee **G Poll**

Saturday January 17
MIDDLESBROUGH (a)
Drew 3-3   **HT 0-1**   Att **27,125**   Position **18th**
Walker — Curtis, Dabizas, Scimeca, Davidson — Scowcroft, McKinlay (Gillespie 89), Stewart, Guppy — Dickov (Hignett 83), Bent (Ferdinand 83) Subs not used Coyne, Heath Booked Dickov, Stewart, McKinlay, Davidson, Dabizas
Scorers **Dickov 49, 65, Bent 76**
Report page 213

Saturday January 31
ASTON VILLA (h)
Lost 0-5   **HT 0-0**   Att **31,056**   Position **18th**
If conceding five goals in 18 minutes is not bad enough, Leicester have to endure the embarrassment of seeing one of their own disgruntled fans confronting Walker on the pitch and being pushed to the ground by the angry goalkeeper. The stewards are as slow to react as the Leicester defence as Villa — who include their £1.5 million new boy, Solano — win the fixture for the first time in 17 years.

Walker — Curtis (Sinclair 78), Dabizas, Scimeca, Thatcher — Gillespie (Hignett 61), McKinlay (Elliott 62), Davidson, Guppy — Scowcroft, Bent Subs not used Coyne, Stewart
Referee **J Winter**

Saturday February 7
NEWCASTLE UNITED (a)
Lost 1-3   HT 0-2   Att 52,125   Position 18th
Walker — Impey (Sinclair 62), Scimeca, Taggart, Thatcher — Scowcroft (Ferdinand 64), Davidson, Freund, Guppy (Stewart 73) — Dickov, Bent *Subs not used* Coyne, Hignett *Booked* Thatcher, Dickov
Scorer **Ferdinand 80**
Report page 224

Tuesday February 10
BOLTON WANDERERS (h)
Drew 1-1   HT 1-1   Att 26,674   Position 18th
A dreadful blunder by Walker, who cannot keep out of the spotlight, hands Bolton a point as he fumbles a weak shot by Davies over the line. Even Sam Allardyce is embarrassed by Bolton's exploitation of the new interpretation of the offside law as his side deliberately station two men in previously illegal positions at the free kick that precedes the equaliser.
Walker — Scimeca, Taggart, Dabizas, Thatcher — Bent (Scowcroft 36), Freund, Nalis (Davidson 76), Guppy (Stewart 83) — Dickov, Ferdinand *Subs not used* Coyne, Sinclair *Booked* Thatcher
Scorer **Ferdinand 16**
Referee **U Rennie**

Sunday February 22
TOTTENHAM HOTSPUR (a)
Drew 4-4   HT 1-3   Att 35,218   Position 19th
Walker — Scimeca, Dabizas, Taggart — Thatcher — Scowcroft, Freund, Nalis, Guppy — Dickov (Sinclair 88), Ferdinand (Bent 73) *Subs not used* Coyne, Stewart *Booked* Dickov, Taggart, Dabizas *Sent off* Scowcroft 70
Scorers **Doherty 9 (og), Ferdinand 51, Thatcher 72, Bent 77**
Report page 256

Saturday February 28
WOLVERHAMPTON WANDERERS (h)
Drew 0-0   HT 0-0   Att 31,768   Position 19th
They shared (unequally) seven goals at Molineux in October, but this time two struggling sides are unbreached thanks to the exploits of their goalkeepers. Jones saves brilliantly from Ferdinand and Walker matches him to deny Miller. Dickov and Rae escape punishment after going head to head in a predictably tense game.
Walker — Scimeca, Dabizas, Heath, Stewart — Scowcroft (Ferdinand 68), Freund, Izzet, Guppy — Dickov, Bent *Subs not used* Coyne, Canero, Nalis, Sinclair
Referee **J Winter**

Saturday March 13
BIRMINGHAM CITY (a)
Won 1-0   HT 0-0   Att 29,491   Position 17th
Walker — Scimeca, Dabizas, Heath, Thatcher — Freund (Nalis 90), Izzet, McKinlay, Benjamin (Canero 80) — Bent, Ferdinand *Subs not used* Elliott, Coyne, Priet *Booked* Izzet, Dabizas
Scorer **Ferdinand 53**
Report page 88

THE PLAYERS

TREVOR BENJAMIN (forward) **Born** February 8, 1979, Kettering **Ht** 6ft 2in **Wt** 14st 7lb **Signed from** Cambridge United, July 2000, £1.5m

MARCUS BENT (forward) **Born** May 19, 1978, Hammersmith **Ht** 6ft 2in **Wt** 12st 4lb **Signed from** Ipswich Town (loan), September 2003

PAUL BROOKER (midfield) **Born** November 25, 1976, Hammersmith **Ht** 5ft 8in **Wt** 10st 0lb **Signed from** Brighton & Hove Albion, June 2003, free

PETER CANERO (defender) **Born** January 18, 1981, Glasgow **Ht** 5ft 9in **Wt** 11st 4lb **Signed from** Kilmarnock, January 2004, £250,000

DANNY COYNE (goalkeeper) **Born** August 27, 1973, Prestatyn **Ht** 5ft 11in **Wt** 13st 0lb **Signed from** Grimsby Town, July 2003, free

JOHN CURTIS
(see Portsmouth)

NIKOS DABIZAS (defender) **Born** August 3, 1973, Ptolemaida, Greece **Ht** 6ft 2in **Wt** 12st 7lb **Signed from** Newcastle United, January 2004, free

CALLUM DAVIDSON (defender) **Born** June 25, 1976, Stirling **Ht** 5ft 10in **Wt** 12st 6lb **Signed from** Blackburn Rovers, July 2000, £1.75m

BRIAN DEANE (forward) **Born** February 7, 1968, Leeds **Ht** 6ft 3in **Wt** 14st 4lb **Signed from** Middlesbrough, November 2001, £150,000

PAUL DICKOV (forward) **Born** November 1, 1972, Livingston **Ht** 5ft 6in **Wt** 11st 9lb **Signed from** Manchester City, February 2002, nominal

MATT ELLIOTT (defender) **Born** November 1, 1968, Wandsworth **Ht** 6ft 3in **Wt** 14st 10lb **Signed from** Oxford United, January 1997, £1.6m

LES FERDINAND (forward) **Born** December 18, 1966, Acton **Ht** 5ft 11in **Wt** 13st 9lb **Signed from** West Ham United, July 2003, free

STEFFEN FREUND (midfield) **Born** January 19, 1970, Brandenburg, Germany **Ht** 5ft 11in **Wt** 12st 6lb **Signed from** 1FC Kaiserslautern, February 2004, free

KEITH GILLESPIE (midfield) **Born** February 18, 1975, Bangor **Ht** 5ft 10in **Wt** 11st 3lb **Signed from** Blackburn Rovers, July 2003, free

STEVE GUPPY (midfield) **Born** March 29, 1969, Winchester **Ht** 5ft 11in **Wt** 12st 0lb **Signed from** Celtic, January 2004, free

MATTHEW HEATH (defender) **Born** November 1, 1981, Leicester **Ht** 6ft 4in **Wt** 13st 13lb **Signed from** trainee, August 2001

CRAIG HIGNETT (midfield) **Born** January 12, 1970, Prescot **Ht** 5ft 9in **Wt** 11st 10lb **Signed from** Blackburn Rovers, July 2003, free

STEVE HOWEY
(see Bolton Wanderers)

ANDY IMPEY (defender) **Born** September 30, 1971, Hammersmith **Ht** 5ft 8in **Wt** 10st 8lb **Signed from** West Ham United, November 1998, £1.6m

MUZZY IZZET (midfield) **Born** October 31, 1974, Mile End **Ht** 5ft 10in **Wt** 11st 0lb **Signed from** Chelsea (initial loan), July 1996, £650,000

BILLY McKINLAY (midfield) **Born** April 22, 1969, Glasgow **Ht** 5ft 8in **Wt** 11st 7lb **Signed from** Clydebank, August 2002, free

LILIAN NALIS (midfield) **Born** September 29, 1971, Nogent-sur-Marne, France **Ht** 6ft 1in **Wt** 11st 0lb **Signed from** Chievo, July 2003, free

NICOLAS PRIET (defender) **Born** January 31, 1983, Villeurbanne, France **Ht** 6ft 4in **Signed from** Lyons, July 2003, free

ALAN ROGERS (defender) **Born** January 13, 1977, Liverpool **Ht** 5ft 10in **Wt** 11st 8lb **Signed from** Nottingham Forest, November 2001, £300,000

RICCARDO SCIMECA (defender) **Born** June 13, 1975, Leamington **Ht** 6ft 1in **Wt** 12st 9lb **Signed from** Nottingham Forest, June 2003, free

JAMES SCOWCROFT (forward) **Born** November 15, 1975, Bury St Edmunds **Ht** 6ft 2in **Wt** 14st 7lb **Signed from** Ipswich Town, August 2001, £3m

FRANK SINCLAIR (defender) **Born** December 3, 1971, Lambeth **Ht** 5ft 9in **Wt** 12st 2lb **Signed from** Chelsea, August 1998, £2m

JORDAN STEWART (defender) **Born** March 3, 1982, Birmingham **Ht** 6ft 0in **Wt** 12st 4lb **Signed from** trainee, August 1999

GERRY TAGGART (defender) **Born** October 18, 1970, Belfast **Ht** 6ft 1in **Wt** 14st 7lb **Signed from** Bolton Wanderers, July 1998, free

BEN THATCHER (defender) **Born** November 30, 1975, Swindon **Ht** 5ft 10in **Wt** 12st 7lb **Signed from** Tottenham Hotspur, July 2003, free

IAN WALKER (goalkeeper) **Born** October 31, 1971, Watford **Ht** 6ft 1in **Wt** 13st 0lb **Signed from** Tottenham Hotspur, July 2001, £2.5m

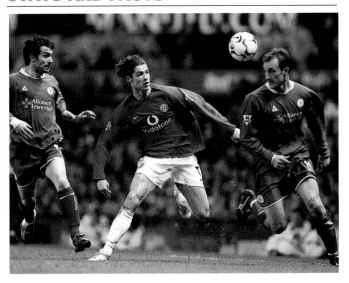

● Leicester have been either promoted or relegated 11 times in the past 26 years.

● Muzzy Izzet provided 14 goal assists, the most for any Premiership player.

● Leicester lost a lead in ten of 21 matches between October and February.

● The Foxes have joined Crystal Palace and Nottingham Forest as the only clubs relegated three times from the Premiership.

● Despite their relegation, Micky Adams's team scored ten more away goals in the league than Newcastle United, who qualified for the Uefa Cup.

● Leicester have won one of their past 23 league games against Arsenal.

● They are not much better against Manchester United, having lost their past ten games against Sir Alex Ferguson's team.

Bill Edgar

GOALSCORERS

	Prem	FAC	CC	Total
M Bent	9	1	-	10
P Dickov	11 (2p)	1	1 (p)	13 (3p)
L Ferdinand	12	1	-	13
C Hignett	1	-	-	1
S Howey	1	-	-	1
M Izzet	2	-	-	2
L Nalis	1	-	-	1
R Scimeca	1	-	-	1
J Scowcroft	5	-	-	5
F Sinclair	1	-	-	1
J Stewart	1	-	-	1
B Thatcher	1	-	-	1
Own goals	2	-	-	2

Saturday March 20
EVERTON (h)
Drew 1-1   HT 0-0   Att 31,650   Position 17th
The match has finished before players and crowd are made aware that a 40-year-old Everton fan has died while walking to the ground, struck by debris blown loose by gale-force winds. For the record, Bent equalises in the last minute, replying to Rooney's goal for an Everton side reduced to ten men by Ferguson's first-half dismissal.

Walker — Scimeca, Dabizas, Heath, Thatcher — Bent, Izzet, Freund (Nalis 84), Benjamin (Guppy ht) — Ferdinand (Canero 58), Dickov *Subs not used* Coyne, Davidson *Booked* Scimeca
Scorer **Bent 90**
Referee **B Knight**

Sunday March 28
LIVERPOOL (h)
Drew 0-0   HT 0-0   Att 32,013   Position 18th
A valuable point apiece, helping Liverpool to consolidate fourth place after their midweek Uefa Cup exit and Leicester to close the gap on Portsmouth. Cheyrou clips the post and Liverpool have the better chances, while Izzet misses from close range at the death.

Walker — Scimeca, Dabizas, Heath, Thatcher — Freund, Izzet, Nalis (Guppy ht) — Bent — Ferdinand, Dickov *Subs not used* Coyne, Benjamin, Canero, Gillespie *Booked* Dickov, Bent, Heath, Dabizas
Referee **P Dowd**

Monday April 5
LEEDS UNITED (a)
Lost 2-3   HT 0-2   Att 34,036   Position 18th
Walker — Scimeca, Dabizas, Heath, Thatcher — Scowcroft, Freund (Nalis 75), Izzet, Guppy (Dickov 37) — Ferdinand (Canero 75), Bent *Subs not used* Coyne, McKinlay *Booked* Thatcher
Scorers **Dickov 77, Izzet 79**
Report page 161

Saturday April 10
FULHAM (h)
Lost 0-2   HT 0-0   Att 28,392   Position 19th
Leicester rue their luck again as Izzet is denied a clear penalty and Dickov hits the bar, as well as having a goal rightly ruled out for his challenge on Van der Sar. Fulham unleash their match-winner from the bench, John, a Liberian teenager, scoring twice to round off a commendably determined team display.

Walker — Scimeca, Dabizas (Canero 79), Heath, Thatcher — Scowcroft, Freund (Nalis 73), Izzet, Guppy — Bent, Dickov *Subs not used* Stewart, Benjamin, McKinlay *Booked* Dickov, Freund
Referee **P Walton**

Tuesday April 13
MANCHESTER UNITED (a)
Lost 0-1   HT 0-0   Att 67,749   Position 19th
Walker — Scimeca, Dabizas, Heath, Thatcher — Freund (Gillespie 66), McKinlay, Izzet, Stewart (Scowcroft 66) — Dickov (Guppy 78), Bent *Subs not used* Nalis, Canero *Booked* Thatcher, Scimeca, Dabizas
Report page 205

PLAYER OF THE SEASON
Muzzy Izzet

Even in the season of his departure, Muzzy Izzet's claims were enough for him to finish ahead of Paul Dickov and Les Ferdinand, the next in line. He set up numerous goals in what was a respectable league tally of 48 for Leicester, including laying on the winner in the wonderful victory over Birmingham City. Izzet, a City player for eight years and one of the few survivors from the Martin O'Neill era, has been a class apart. Star performers in midfield are few and far between at this club, perhaps just five in the past five decades — David Gibson, Keith Weller, Gary McAllister, Neil Lennon and Izzet. Adams once said of him: "When he's in the team, we change from average to excellent."
Jim Wheildon

Saturday April 17
BLACKBURN ROVERS (a)
Lost 0-1   HT 0-1   Att 22,749   Position 19th
Walker — Sinclair, Dabizas, Heath (Canero 77), Thatcher — Bent, Izzet, McKinlay (Freund ht), Scowcroft — Dickov, Ferdinand (Guppy 62) *Subs not used* Gillespie, Nalis
Booked McKinlay
Report page 100

Saturday April 24
MANCHESTER CITY (h)
Drew 1-1   HT 0-1   Att 31,457   Position 19th
The FA demands to see the video of an ill-tempered six-minute hold-up in the second half, prompted by the award of a penalty to Leicester, which James eventually saves from Dickov as Manchester City keep Leicester at arm's length in a tense relegation battle. Tarnat's free kick and Scowcroft's header cancel each other out.

Walker — Sinclair (Guppy 63), Dabizas, Heath, Thatcher — Canero, Izzet, Freund (Nalis 71), Scowcroft — Dickov, Ferdinand (Bent ht) *Subs not used* McKinlay, Gillespie
Booked Bent
Scorer **Scowcroft 66**
Referee A D'Urso

Saturday May 1
CHARLTON ATHLETIC (a)
Drew 2-2   HT 1-0   Att 26,034   Position 20th
Walker — Sinclair, Dabizas, Heath, Stewart — Canero (Ferdinand 73), Izzet, Freund (McKinlay 59), Scowcroft — Bent, Dickov (Guppy 79) *Subs not used* Nalis, Gillespie
Sent off Dabizas 74
Scorers **Bent 5, Ferdinand 88**
Report page 120

Saturday May 8
PORTSMOUTH (h)
Won 3-1   HT 2-0   Att 31,536   Position 18th
Leicester's first home win since November 2 comes too late as the Walkers Stadium says farewell to the Premiership, plus Izzet and more likely than not a handful of his team-mates, with the team's fate already sealed. Harry Redknapp denies reports that he will be Tottenham's next manager after Portsmouth's eight-match unbeaten run is ended.

Walker — Sinclair, Dabizas, Heath, Stewart — Scowcroft, Izzet (Nalis 48), McKinlay, Guppy (Ferdinand 74) — Dickov, Bent (Benjamin 88) *Subs not used* Freund, Gillespie
Scorers **Taylor 6 (og), Dickov 27, Scowcroft 71**
Referee G Poll

Saturday May 15
ARSENAL (a)
Lost 1-2   HT 1-0   Att 38,419   Position 18th
Walker (Coyne 77) — Sinclair, Dabizas, Heath, Stewart — Bent, McKinlay, Freund (Brooker 75), Nalis, Scowcroft — Dickov (Benjamin 85) *Subs not used* Gillespie, Guppy
Booked Sinclair
Scorer **Dickov 26**
Report page 70

LIVERPOOL

PREMIERSHIP

	P	W	D	L	F	A	GD	Pts
Arsenal	38	26	12	0	73	26	47	**90**
Chelsea	38	24	7	7	67	30	37	**79**
Man Utd	38	23	6	9	64	35	29	**75**
Liverpool	38	16	12	10	55	37	18	**60**
Newcastle	38	13	17	8	52	40	12	**56**
Aston Villa	38	15	11	12	48	44	4	**56**
Charlton	38	14	11	13	51	51	0	**53**
Bolton	38	14	11	13	48	56	-8	**53**
Fulham	38	14	10	14	52	46	6	**52**
Birmingham	38	12	14	12	43	48	-5	**50**
Middlesbro	38	13	9	16	44	52	-8	**48**
Southampton	38	12	11	15	44	45	-1	**47**
Portsmouth	38	12	9	17	47	54	-7	**45**
Tottenham	38	13	6	19	47	57	-10	**45**
Blackburn	38	12	8	18	51	59	-8	**44**
Man City	38	9	14	15	55	54	1	**41**
Everton	38	9	12	17	45	57	-12	**39**
Leicester	38	6	15	17	48	65	-17	**33**
Leeds	38	8	9	21	40	79	-39	**33**
Wolves	38	7	12	19	38	77	-39	**33**

FA CUP
Fifth round

CARLING CUP
Fourth round

UEFA CUP
Fourth round

This is Anfield: Rafael Benitez meets the press after his arrival as the man to succeed Gerard Houllier and build a new Liverpool dynasty

Sunday August 17 2003
CHELSEA (h)
Lost 1-2 **HT 0-1** Att **44,082** Position **16th**
With Mutu awaiting international clearance as they continue their remarkable spending spree, Chelsea register only their third Anfield league victory since 1935 thanks to Hasselbaink's late goal. Liverpool, missing the suspended Gerrard, are second-best for long periods, despite Owen's twice-taken penalty.
Dudek — Carragher, Henchoz (Finnan 71), Hyypia, Riise — Murphy, Biscan (Baros 71), Cheyrou (Diouf 56) — Kewell — Owen, Heskey *Subs not used* Kirkland, Le Tallec *Booked* Henchoz, Biscan, Diouf
Scorer **Owen 79 (pen)**
Referee **S Bennett**

Sunday August 24
ASTON VILLA (a)
Drew 0-0 **HT 0-0** Att **42,573** Position **17th**
Dudek — Carragher, Henchoz, Hyypia, Riise — Kewell, Gerrard, Murphy (Biscan 87) — Diouf — Owen, Heskey (Baros 58) *Subs not used* Finnan, Smicer, Kirkland *Booked* Diouf
Report page 72

Wednesday August 27
TOTTENHAM HOTSPUR (h)
Drew 0-0 **HT 0-0** Att **43,778** Position **15th**
Gerrard Houllier drops Murphy and Riise and includes five forwards in a bold formation, but Liverpool still have only one goal and two points to show from three games after they are held by a well-organised Spurs side. Gerrard goes closest to a winner, forcing a fine 74th-minute save from Keller.
Dudek — Finnan, Biscan, Hyypia, Carragher — Gerrard — Diouf, Kewell, Smicer (Murphy 73) — Owen, Baros *Subs not used* Riise, Diao, Le Tallec, Kirkland *Booked* Diouf, Finnan
Referee **U Rennie**

Saturday August 30
EVERTON (a)
Won 3-0 **HT 1-0** Att **40,200** Position **9th**
Dudek — Finnan, Biscan, Hyypia, Carragher — Gerrard — Diouf (Riise 89), Smicer (Murphy 73), Kewell — Owen, Baros (Heskey 73) *Subs not used* Diao, Kirkland *Booked* Kewell, Finnan, Baros
Scorers **Owen 39, 52, Kewell 80**
Report page 134

Saturday September 13
BLACKBURN ROVERS (a)
Won 3-1 **HT 1-1** Att **30,074** Position **6th**
Dudek — Finnan, Biscan, Hyypia, Carragher (Riise 16) — Gerrard (Le Tallec 85) — Diouf, Smicer, Kewell — Owen, Baros (Heskey 4) *Subs not used* Traore, Luzi *Booked* Finnan, Smicer
Scorers **Owen 12 (pen), 68, Kewell 90**
Report page 93

NO ONE, I AM CERTAIN — NOT EVEN the Liverpool board — realised that the 2003-04 season would become known as the pre-Rafaelite era. Whether the pre-Rafaelite period is regarded as dour or relatively imaginative remains to be seen, but one thing is certain: something is wrong when your team is deemed worthy of a mention on Radio 4's *The News Quiz* and Andy Hamilton makes jokes about Danny Murphy being a Ladyboy. Oh yes, the proposed investment from Thailand was the butt of many, many gibes.

However, just as a mother determines how good a husband her son will become, Gerard Houllier reluctantly handed over a slightly spoilt but still highly desirable club. How much more difficult might it have been to prise Rafael Benitez away from Valencia had Liverpool not achieved qualification for the Champions League? Suddenly, all things seem possible and perhaps, in time, Houllier's role in what could be the start of a magnificent new era will be acknowledged.

The season started so badly, with a home defeat to Chelsea to be precise. It was a fall to the ground with an embarrassing bump. Liverpool had ended the previous season with a limp performance against the West London club and it looked as if nothing had changed. The 3-0 defeat of Everton three weeks later calmed the nerves, but that game was referred to too often. Houllier had a fit squad that day. On subsequent occasions, after a defeat, he would point out what he and the team could do when not ravaged by injuries.

By mid-October a title challenge already looked ludicrously fanciful. The pundits were kind after the home defeat by Arsenal, but they had been laughing a week earlier when the team had travelled to The Valley and lost against Charlton Athletic in the sort of thrilling match they had been used to winning. The inconsistency was glaring and painful.

Perhaps the first sign that something significant had to happen came with reports that Michael Owen was none too keen to sign a new contract. Owen overtook Ian Rush as Liverpool's all-time top scorer in European competition, but he was not fully fit for long spells. And it was not as if the club barely missed him when he was not there. The Kop started to sing his name, too proud actually to beg him to stay but hoping that his obvious loyalty could be massaged. We can only conjecture how much the spectre of Owen leaving had a bearing on the departure of Houllier.

Just as jokes on Radio 4 are not good, neither is it pleasant to hear players who form the spine of the team hinting that long-term

HONOURS BOARD

contracts are too risky. It would appear that 2003-04 was the season in which Liverpool finally became known officially as a club that was "languishing".

Even the highs were second-rate. The most impressive performance witnessed first hand by this reporter was in Bucharest in the second round of the Uefa Cup. The pitch was ridiculous. Heavy and constant rain had rendered it clearly unplayable, but the game went ahead in conditions that would obviously favour the home side. Houllier had complained about a fairly innocuous pitch in the previous round, when Liverpool had been held by Olimpija Ljubljana, so what hope was there of a spirited team performance when the pitch really was a factor?

In the event, Liverpool rolled up their sleeves and got stuck in. The ball floated in the puddles and become lodged in the mud, but the team kept on trying. Emile Heskey was a real hero that night, not caring that the water spread out in a wake from under his bottom as he slid here, there and everywhere. It is a shame he has gone.

With the title somewhere over the rainbow, Houllier needed a cup or two. But in Europe, Liverpool bowed out rather comically to Marseilles. There was nothing funny about the defeat to Portsmouth

---

Saturday September 20
LEICESTER CITY (h)
Won 2-1 **HT 1-0** Att **44,094** Position **6th**
Heskey, having donated £100,000 to help his old club to survive administration, has a less welcome gift this time, heading in Diouf's cross for Liverpool's second goal after Owen's third penalty of the season gives them the lead. Bent's first goal for Leicester comes too late to affect the result.

Dudek — Finnan, Biscan, Hyypia, Riise — Gerrard — Diouf (Le Tallec 89), Smicer (Murphy 76), Kewell — Owen, Heskey *Subs not used* Traore, Diao, Luzi
Scorers **Owen 20 (pen), Heskey 75**
Referee **M Halsey**

Wednesday September 24
OLIMPIJA LJUBLJANA (a)
Uefa Cup, 1st rnd, 1st leg
Drew 1-1 **HT 0-0** Att **10,000**
Trailing after 66 minutes, Zlogar pouncing when Dudek can only parry a shot by Jusufbegovic, Liverpool are saved from defeat against the Slovenian minnows by Owen's header from Riise's cross. It is his 21st European goal in 44 matches, beating the club record of 20 in 37 held by Ian Rush.

Dudek — Diao (Finnan 69), Biscan, Hyypia, Riise — Murphy (Gerrard 14) — Smicer, Le Tallec (Welsh 86), Kewell — Owen, Heskey *Subs not used* Luzi, Henchoz, Traore, Sinama-Pongolle *Booked* Kewell
Scorer **Owen 78**
Referee **J R Santiago (Spain)**

Sunday September 28
CHARLTON ATHLETIC (a)
Lost 2-3 **HT 1-2** Att **26,508** Position **8th**
Dudek — Finnan, Biscan, Hyypia, Riise — Diouf (Le Tallec 84), Gerrard, Smicer (Murphy 67), Kewell — Owen, Heskey *Subs not used* Luzi, Diao, Traore *Booked* Diouf
Scorers **Smicer 15, Owen 52 (pen)**
Report page 113

Saturday October 4
ARSENAL (h)
Lost 1-2 **HT 1-1** Att **44,374** Position **8th**
Dominant in the first half, when Kewell's volley gives them the lead, Liverpool slip nine points behind the leaders as Arsenal hit back through Edu's header, which goes in off Hyypia, and a fabulous winner curled in by Pires. Owen then collapses with a nasty shin injury only seven days before England's crucial European Championship appointment in Istanbul.

Dudek — Finnan, Biscan, Hyypia, Riise — Diouf, Gerrard, Diao (Welsh 83), Smicer (Le Tallec 42) — Owen (Heskey 72), Kewell *Subs not used* Henchoz, Kirkland *Booked* Biscan, Welsh
Scorer **Kewell 14**
Referee **G Barber**

Wednesday October 15
OLIMPIJA LJUBLJANA (h)
Uefa Cup, 2nd rnd, 2nd leg
Won 3-0 (won 4-1 on agg) HT **2-0** Att **42,880**
Liverpool's progress is never in doubt once Le Tallec
grabs his first goal for the club. Heskey follows with his
50th and crosses for Kewell to make it 3-0, with Diouf
able to afford a missed penalty.

Dudek — Finnan, Biscan, Hyypia, Riise — Gerrard
(Diao 76) — Diouf, Le Tallec (Sinama-Pongolle 61),
Smicer (Henchoz 67) — Heskey, Kewell Subs not used
Kirkland, Traore, Welsh, Potter
Scorers **Le Tallec 30, Heskey 37, Kewell 47**
Referee **S Messner (Austria)**

Saturday October 18
PORTSMOUTH (a)
Lost 0-1 HT **0-1** Att **20,123** Position **9th**
Dudek — Finnan, Henchoz, Hyypia, Riise — Gerrard,
Biscan, Diouf (Sinama-Pongolle 63) — Smicer
(Le Tallec 59) — Heskey, Kewell Subs not used Kirkland,
Traore, Welsh Booked Biscan, Diouf
Report page 231

Saturday October 25
LEEDS UNITED (h)
Won 3-1 HT **1-1** Att **43,599** Position **9th**
Liverpool end a run of three league defeats and consign
Leeds to their worst start for 15 years. Owen is back
with a goal, Smith replies with his 50th in the
Premiership, but the decisive moment comes when
Jeff Winter overrules a linesman flagging three players
offside as Murphy's free kick skids under Robinson to
put Liverpool 2-1 up.

Dudek — Finnan, Hyypia, Biscan, Riise — Diouf, Gerrard,
Smicer (Murphy 48), Kewell (Le Tallec 85) — Owen
(Sinama-Pongolle 59), Heskey Subs not used Kirkland,
Henchoz
Scorers **Owen 35, Murphy 57, Sinama-Pongolle 84**
Referee **J Winter**

Wednesday October 29
BLACKBURN ROVERS (a)
Carling Cup, 3rd rnd
Won 4-3 HT **1-1** Att **16,918**
Kirkland — Biscan, Henchoz, Hyypia (Riise ht), Traore —
Murphy, Gerrard (Hamann 80), Le Tallec, Diouf — Heskey,
Sinama-Pongolle (Kewell ht) Subs not used Dudek,
Finnan
Scorers **Murphy 41 (pen), Heskey 49, 61, Kewell 79**
Report page 94

Sunday November 2
FULHAM (a)
Won 2-1 HT **1-1** Att **17,682** Position **7th**
Dudek — Finnan, Biscan (Henchoz 66), Hyypia, Traore —
Gerrard — Murphy, Kewell — Smicer — Owen
(Sinama-Pongolle 77), Heskey (Le Tallec 82) Subs not
used Kirkland, Hamann Booked Murphy
Scorers **Heskey 17, Murphy 89 (pen)**
Report page 146

Harry Kewell failed to make the expected impact after his £5m signing

in the FA Cup, either. In some respects, then, the fact that the team
summoned an end-of-season run to secure Champions League entry
was quite a feat.

One of the very best goals of the season came in the final league
match, against Newcastle United, when a wonderful long pass from
Steven Gerrard was met with precision by Owen in a single fluid
movement. It was as if Gerrard and Owen were a form of Borg from
Star Trek and really the same person. Unfortunately, Liverpool had
increasingly looked like a one-man team. While it was lovely to see
Gerrard flourish in his role as captain, it was less lovely to see him at
left back one minute, right midfield the next. Were his team-mates
filing their nails, having a gossip, or what?

"I came here not to learn English, I came here to win," Benitez
said when he arrived at Anfield in the middle of the European
Championship finals. He will probably learn quite a bit of English,
though, if he stays the course that will be necessary for Liverpool to
become a team that can win the Premiership.

These are strange times for Liverpool fans. The club does not even
pretend its foreign appointments are honorary Scousers any more.
In many respects, Benitez is very brave. He may think he is in a
no-lose situation, but he is not. The tide of resentment grows ever
stronger as the fans yearn for a return to the good old days. The days
of dominating Radio 5 Live and not Radio 4 are gone. The former
did not even carry live commentary on Manchester United v
Liverpool in April; a worrying sign of the times that, even though
Liverpool beat United, it was not considered overly significant.

THE MANAGER — Gerard Houllier

The fans whined for most of the season, but they never actually believed that Gerard Houllier would be fired. And perhaps the man himself only realised it might happen very close to the end, when he became bitter and almost hysterically blasted those who keep harking back to the successes of the 1960s and 70s. Thankfully, that was not his parting shot. Instead he left with grace, saying he remained a supporter of the club he loves. Houllier had to go because he could provide no evidence that the next season would be better. The proof was there, though, that he desperately wanted it to be otherwise.

Alyson Rudd

APPEARANCES

	Prem	FAC	CC	Euro	Total
M Baros	6 (7)	0 (1)	-	2 (2)	8 (10)
I Biscan	27 (2)	1	2	5 (2)	35 (4)
J Carragher	22	3	-	4	29
B Cheyrou	9 (3)	3 (1)	-	1 (2)	13 (6)
S Diao	2 (1)	-	1	2 (1)	5 (2)
E-H Diouf	20 (6)	1	2	3 (1)	26 (7)
J Dudek	30	3	1	4	38
S Finnan	19 (3)	3	-	5 (1)	27 (4)
S Gerrard	33	3	1 (1)	7 (1)	44 (2)
D Hamann	25	4	0 (1)	5	34 (1)
S Henchoz	15 (3)	4	1	3 (1)	23 (4)
E Heskey	24 (10)	3 (1)	2	4 (2)	33 (13)
S Hyypia	38	4	1	8	51
P Jones	2	-	-	-	2
H Kewell	36	3	0 (2)	8	47 (2)
C Kirkland	6	1	1	4	12
A Le Tallec	3 (10)	1 (3)	2	2 (2)	8 (15)
P Luzi	0 (1)	-	-	-	0 (1)
D Murphy	19 (12)	1 (1)	2	6 (1)	28 (14)
J Otsemobor	4	-	1	-	5
M Owen	29	3	-	6	38
J A Riise	22 (6)	1	1 (1)	4	28 (7)
F Sinama-Pongolle	3 (12)	1 (2)	1 (1)	1 (2)	6 (17)
V Smicer	15 (5)	1	1	2 (1)	19 (6)
D Traore	7	-	2	2	11
J Welsh	0 (1)	-	-	0 (1)	0 (2)

Thursday November 6
STEAUA BUCHAREST (a)
Uefa Cup, 2nd rnd, 1st leg
Drew 1-1 HT 1-0 Att 25,000
Liverpool dig in on a barely playable bog of a pitch and stun Southampton's conquerors when Traore finds the bottom corner for his first Liverpool goal. Raducanu equalises in the 69th minute and only a magnificent save by Dudek, who pushes Mutica's volley on to the bar, preserves parity.

Dudek — Finnan, Biscan, Hyypia, Traore — Diouf (Le Tallec 56), Gerrard, Murphy, Riise — Heskey, Kewell *Subs not used* Kirkland, Henchoz, Smicer, Diao, Hamann, Sinama-Pongolle *Booked* Murphy, Diouf
Scorer **Traore 23**
Referee **S Farina (Italy)**

Sunday November 9
MANCHESTER UNITED (h)
Lost 1-2 HT 0-0 Att 44,159 Position 8th
A flattering victory for United in a strangely uneventful game. Giggs's double does the trick, his first an intended cross that eludes forwards and defenders alike, but after Kewell halves the deficit, Liverpool are denied a penalty when Ferdinand brings down Sinama-Pongolle, then Heskey fluffs a great chance in stoppage time.

Dudek — Finnan, Biscan, Hyypia, Traore — Diouf (Le Tallec 69), Gerrard, Murphy, Kewell — Smicer (Sinama-Pongolle 63) — Heskey *Subs not used* Riise, Diao, Kirkland *Booked* Diouf
Scorer **Kewell 76**
Referee **G Poll**

Saturday November 22
MIDDLESBROUGH (a)
Drew 0-0 HT 0-0 Att 34,268 Position 9th
Kirkland — Finnan (Diao 47), Biscan, Hyypia, Traore — Diouf (Smicer 74), Gerrard, Murphy, Kewell — Heskey, Owen (Sinama-Pongolle 68) *Subs not used* Dudek, Le Tallec *Booked* Hyypia, Kewell
Report page 210

Thursday November 27
STEAUA BUCHAREST (h)
Uefa Cup, 2nd rnd, 2nd leg
Won 1-0 (won 2-1 on agg) HT 0-0 Att 42,837
Fortunate not to concede a penalty for Biscan's trip on Raducanu, Liverpool settle the tie almost immediately when Kewell rises highest to meet Gerrard's cross, but Owen limps off with a worrying new muscle strain before the end.

Kirkland — Diao, Biscan, Hyypia, Traore — Diouf (Smicer 70), Gerrard, Hamann, Kewell — Owen (Murphy 89), Sinama-Pongolle (Heskey 70) *Subs not used* Dudek, Riise, Le Tallec, Otsemobor
Scorer **Kewell 49**
Referee **F Meyer (Germany)**

Sunday November 30
BIRMINGHAM CITY (h)
Won 3-1   HT 1-1   Att 42,683   Position 6th
Trailing to Forssell's goal, then having come from behind through a dubious penalty (for Cunningham's challenge on Sinama-Pongolle) and Kewell's header, Liverpool seal victory with an outstanding finish from Heskey, who hooks a volley over his shoulder in spectacular style.

Kirkland — Diao, Biscan, Hyypia, Traore (Riise 67) — Diouf (Smicer 55), Gerrard, Hamann, Kewell — Heskey, Sinama-Pongolle (Murphy 79) *Subs not used* Dudek, Le Tallec *Booked* Diao, Hamann
Scorers Gerrard 34 (pen), Kewell 69, Heskey 78
Referee **N Barry**

Wednesday December 3
BOLTON WANDERERS (h)
Carling Cup, 4th rnd
Lost 2-3   HT 0-1   Att 33,185
Gerrard Houllier lays into his team in a rare public attack as the holders are eliminated by rapidly improving Bolton. Twice behind, Liverpool seem to have forced extra time with Smicer's late equaliser, only for Diao to bring down Davies with a reckless tackle. Djorkaeff wins the tie from the spot.

Dudek — Otsemobor, Biscan, Traore (Gerrard 67), Riise — Diao — Murphy, Smicer, Diouf (Kewell 59) — Heskey, Le Tallec (Sinama-Pongolle 60) *Subs not used* Kirkland, Cheyrou
Scorers Murphy 66, Smicer 88
Referee **M Riley**

Saturday December 6
NEWCASTLE UNITED (a)
Drew 1-1   HT 1-0   Att 52,151   Position 5th
Kirkland — Otsemobor, Biscan, Hyypia, Riise — Heskey, Gerrard, Hamann, Murphy, Diouf — Sinama-Pongolle (Smicer 57) *Subs not used* Diao, Le Tallec, Traore, Luzi
Booked Diouf, Kirkland, Hamann, Otsemobor
Scorer Murphy 6
Report page 222

Saturday December 13
SOUTHAMPTON (h)
Lost 1-2   HT 0-1   Att 41,762   Position 9th
Gerrard Houllier has been told by his chairman that Champions League qualification is a "minimum requirement", but Liverpool find themselves in ninth place, booed off after a fourth home league defeat. Ormerod puts Southampton on the way to victory after 75 seconds and Michael Svensson heads a second before Heskey's reply.

Kirkland — Otsemobor, Biscan, Hyypia, Riise — Murphy, Gerrard, Hamann (Sinama-Pongolle 57), Diouf (Le Tallec 57) — Heskey, Smicer *Subs not used* Luzi, Diao, Cheyrou
Scorer Heskey 75
Referee **P Durkin**

THE TIMES

Thursday January 8 2004

MATCH OF THE SEASON

Chelsea 0 Liverpool 1
Stamford Bridge, Wednesday January 7 2004
Matt Dickinson

FORCEFULLY CRITICISED AT THE CLUB'S annual meeting on Monday evening, Gerard Houllier heard his name sung by many Liverpool fans at Stamford Bridge last night as his side secured a rugged and important Barclaycard Premiership victory.

Claudio Ranieri will advise him not to listen to a fickle public because it was not so long ago that he was the darling at Chelsea. Last night, the Italian's press conference had to be delayed because of an unusually long debrief with Roman Abramovich, the Chelsea owner, after a third defeat in five league matches. "Don't worry, I'll be here tomorrow," Ranieri replied to questions about his own position. "He [Abramovich] is not happy, but he's patient."

Wild fluctuations can be expected for both managers over the next five months but, last night, Houllier could savour his team's most significant conquest of the season. They had come to fight and frustrate and they did it right up to El-Hadji Diouf's late dismissal for tangling with Adrian Mutu. "Liverpool had never won here in the Premiership, so we had to take what we could," Houllier said. "You can dream, but sometimes we have to be realistic."

It was rarely pretty, but Houllier has long since abandoned the ambitions of style with which he started the season and reverted to the prosaic virtues on which he built his regime at Anfield. Liverpool are still 13 points behind Chelsea, but tenacity brought them superiority for 90 minutes and they could claim to have contributed by far the best move of the game. It brought a rare goal for Bruno Cheyrou, but the plaudits should go to Emile Heskey, the man of the match, who appears to have been reinvigorated now that his club is intent on replacing him. All this and with Michael Owen on the bench for the first time in six weeks.

Steven Gerrard should return before long and Diouf's harsh dismissal for a second booking will have no impact because the Senegal forward is due to disappear to Tunisia for the African Nations Cup next week. Fourth place might be a lowly ambition for a club of Liverpool's former glories, but at least now it is looking within their capabilities.

For Chelsea, defeat left them seven points behind Manchester United and facing what suddenly looks a treacherous trip to Leicester City on Sunday. A few months ago, victory at the Walkers Stadium would have been regarded as a formality, but an injury to Damien Duff and Mutu's failure to score for more than two months are among the causes of recent inconsistencies.

Having forced United and Arsenal to raise their standards, Chelsea can hardly afford to drop their own, but seven points from their past six games is not title-winning form. "We don't need to buy

Cheyrou slides in to convert Heskey's cross and secure a battling victory

new players this month, just get through this bad run," Ranieri said. "I said 'well done' to the players afterwards because, even if it wasn't good, they give their maximum."

Before Cheyrou's unexpected strike, in the 33rd minute, and for much of what followed the solitary goal, it had been a wretched game by any reckoning. Hernan Crespo was forced off after only 12 minutes with a calf strain, but the striker was not suffering as much as the supporters inside Stamford Bridge. "He told me he was fit to play," Ranieri said of Crespo. "Now he could be out for weeks."

December defeats to Bolton Wanderers and Charlton Athletic had left visible cracks in Chelsea's confidence, while Liverpool's principal tactic was suffocation. Heskey was deployed as a lone striker and he was tracking back so often, and so diligently, that he was often a sixth member of the midfield. Harrying Chelsea was the intention and not only did it succeed in frustrating Ranieri's men but, with a swift counter-attack, Liverpool also took a half-time lead. Cheyrou was the scorer but it was as much a goal for Heskey, who, as John Terry must have been disappointed to discover, was having one of those nights when he was punching his weight.

First to reach a long clearance, Heskey chested the ball down to Cheyrou and then set off on a gallop down the right flank. The Frenchman found him and embarked on his own charge forward. The exchange of measured passes was completed when Heskey whipped over a cross beyond Terry which Cheyrou met with an emphatic, sliding

Friday December 26
BOLTON WANDERERS (h)
Won 3-1   HT 1-0   Att 42,987   Position 9th
A hat-trick of headers earns Gerard Houllier some breathing space, but Liverpool lose Kirkland to a broken finger. Bolton's recent heroics cannot save them from an angry outburst from Sam Allardyce, who replaces his three stars — Campo, Djorkaeff and Okocha — in a pointed triple substitution.

Kirkland — Otsemobor, Biscan, Hyypia, Riise — Murphy, Gerrard, Hamann, Smicer (Le Tallec 80) — Sinama-Pongolle (Heskey 66), Kewell (Diouf 66) *Subs not used* Dudek, Henchoz
Scorers **Hyypia 30, Sinama-Pongolle 47, Smicer 54**
Referee **J Winter**

Sunday December 28
MANCHESTER CITY (a)
Drew 2-2   HT 0-1   Att 47,201   Position 6th
Dudek — Otsemobor (Henchoz 28), Biscan, Hyypia, Riise — Murphy, Hamann, Gerrard (Diouf 60) — Smicer (Sinama-Pongolle 77) — Kewell, Heskey *Subs not used* Luzi, Cheyrou *Booked* Kewell, Biscan
Scorers **Smicer 66, Hamann 80**
Report page 190

Sunday January 4 2004
YEOVIL TOWN (a)
FA Cup, 3rd rnd
Won 2-0   HT 0-0   Att 9,348
Probably the country's most famous Cup giantkillers give an excellent first-half performance but are beaten by a goal from Heskey and, controversially, a penalty earned when Kewell appears to dive over Rodriques's tackle. "They respected us enough . . . to try and cheat," Gary Johnson, the Yeovil manager, says.

Dudek — Henchoz, Biscan, Hyypia, Riise — Diouf (Le Tallec 88), Hamann, Murphy, Smicer (Cheyrou 82) — Kewell, Sinama-Pongolle (Heskey 52) *Subs not used* Traore, Luzi *Booked* Diouf, Le Tallec, Smicer
Scorers **Heskey 70, Murphy 77 (pen)**
Referee **N Barry**

Wednesday January 7
CHELSEA (a)
Won 1-0   HT 1-0   Att 41,420   Position 5th
Dudek (Luzi 77) — Henchoz, Biscan, Hyypia, Traore — Diouf, Hamann, Murphy, Kewell — Cheyrou (Riise 77) — Heskey *Subs not used* Owen, Smicer, Le Tallec *Booked* Diouf, Heskey *Sent off* Diouf 87
Scorer **Cheyrou 33**
Report page 127

Saturday January 10
ASTON VILLA (h)
Won 1-0   HT 1-0   Att 43,771   Position 5th
After eight games out and with his future unsure ("I need to make sure my new contract is right before I sign it," he says), Owen returns — still as their top scorer — and hits the bar from two yards, but Liverpool triumph nonetheless. After their fluke winner against Portsmouth, luck deserts Villa as Delaney turns Heskey's header into his own net.

Jones — Henchoz, Biscan, Hyypia, Riise — Hamann — Diouf (Cheyrou 83), Murphy, Kewell — Owen (Sinama-Pongolle 73), Heskey *Subs not used* Traore, Le Tallec, Luzi *Booked* Kewell, Diouf, Hamann
Scorer **Delaney 36 (og)**
Referee **G Barber**

Saturday January 17
TOTTENHAM HOTSPUR (a)
Lost 1-2   **HT 0-1**   Att **36,104**   Position **5th**
Jones — Henchoz, Biscan (Finnan 66), Hyypia, Traore
(Riise 61) — Cheyrou, Murphy, Hamann, Kewell — Heskey,
Owen *Subs not used* Dudek, Le Tallec, Carragher *Booked*
Hamann
Scorer **Kewell 75**
Report page 255

Wednesday January 21
WOLVERHAMPTON WANDERERS (a)
Drew 1-1   **HT 1-0**   Att **29,380**   Position **5th**
Dudek — Finnan, Biscan (Henchoz ht), Hyypia, Carragher
— Heskey, Gerrard, Hamann, Kewell — Cheyrou
(Murphy 76) — Owen *Subs not used* Jones, Riise,
Le Tallec *Booked* Carragher
Scorer **Cheyrou 42**
Report page 265

Saturday January 24
NEWCASTLE UNITED (h)
FA Cup, 4th rnd
Won 2-1   **HT 1-1**   Att **41,365**
Sir Bobby Robson acknowledges that he may never get
his hands on the FA Cup again after losing an excellent
heavyweight contest to Cheyrou's double, Robert having
lashed in a 78mph equaliser as early as the fourth
minute. The Newcastle manager has not won at Anfield
now in 30 attempts.

Dudek — Finnan, Henchoz, Hyypia, Carragher — Heskey
(Le Tallec ht), Gerrard, Hamann, Kewell — Cheyrou, Owen
Subs not used Jones, Murphy, Riise, Biscan *Booked*
Henchoz
Scorer **Cheyrou 2, 61**
Referee **G Poll**

Saturday January 31
EVERTON (h)
Drew 0-0   **HT 0-0**   Att **44,056**   Position **5th**
Forget the scoreline, the 170th Merseyside derby is
an action-packed thriller in which Martyn pips his
opposite number to the man-of-the-match award, his
two saves from Gerrard the pick of the bunch.
Ferguson and Carragher are lucky not to concede
penalties and Hyypia escapes a red card after bringing
down Radzinski.

Dudek — Finnan, Henchoz, Hyypia, Carragher — Le Tallec,
Gerrard, Hamann, Kewell — Owen, Cheyrou *Subs not
used* Luzi, Murphy, Riise, Traore, Biscan
Referee **S Bennett**

Saturday February 7
BOLTON WANDERERS (a)
Drew 2-2   **HT 0-1**   Att **27,552**   Position **6th**
Dudek — Finnan, Henchoz, Hyypia, Carragher — Le Tallec
(Murphy 83), Gerrard, Hamann, Kewell — Owen, Cheyrou
(Sinama-Pongolle 65) *Subs not used* Luzi, Riise, Biscan
Booked Kewell, Finnan
Scorers **Hyypia 51, Gerrard 69**
Report page 107

Houllier and Ranieri — both destined for the axe — are all smiles

finish past Carlo Cudicini. Cheyrou has struggled to justify his
£4 million fee, never mind the comparisons with Zinedine Zidane
made by Houllier. This was his first league start since the opening-
day defeat to Chelsea, but maybe his first Premiership goal will mark
a change of fortune for a player who has looked too effete.

His goal was a fine move, one of the few. Glen Johnson had made
a few incursions down the right flank but Joe Cole could rarely
wriggle free of the red shirts swarming through midfield and there
was little width even when he was replaced by Jesper Gronkjaer.
Liverpool were so resilient that they could even withstand the loss of
Jerzy Dudek. Liverpool were forced to give Patrice Luzi his debut in
goal 13 minutes from time but, when he was beaten, Mutu's header
hit the crossbar.

CHELSEA (4-3-1-2): C Cudicini — G Johnson, W Gallas, J Terry, W Bridge — F Lampard, C Makelele,
Geremi — J Cole (sub: J Gronkjaer, 62min) — A Mutu, H Crespo (sub: E Gudjohnsen, 12). **Substitutes
not used:** N Sullivan, C Babayaro, M Desailly.
LIVERPOOL (4-4-1-1): J Dudek (sub: P Luzi, 77) — S Henchoz, I Biscan, S Hyypia, D Traore — E-H Diouf,
D Hamann, D Murphy, H Kewell — B Cheyrou (sub: J A Riise, 77) — E Heskey. **Substitutes not used:**
M Owen, V Smicer, A Le Tallec. **Booked:** Heskey, Diouf. **Sent off:** Diouf.

STATS AND FACTS

● Liverpool finished fourth in the Premiership and qualified for the Champions League, yet they were still closer in points to the bottom of the table than the top.

● For the third time in four seasons, Liverpool won 1-0 away to Manchester United in the Premiership with a Danny Murphy goal.

● For the third successive season, Emile Heskey scored the winning goal at home to Leicester City, his former club.

● In their past 64 league games Liverpool have gained 92 points (1.44 points per game). In their previous 27 league matches they picked up 70 points (2.59 points per game).

● Liverpool were taken to a replay for only the second time in 22 FA Cup ties when Portsmouth drew at Anfield.

● Gerard Houllier's defence kept 12 clean sheets in the 22 Premiership matches in which Jamie Carragher appeared, but

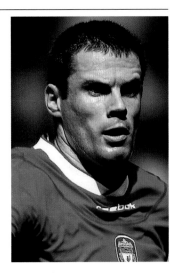

just three in the 16 games when he was not in the side.

● For the second time since 1972 and the first since 1981, neither Manchester United nor Liverpool finished in the top two.

● The away match against Manchester United in April was the first time in 23 fixtures between the sides that the match was not shown live on television in Britain.

Bill Edgar

GOALSCORERS

	Prem	FAC	CC	Euro	Total
M Baros	1	-	-	1	2
B Cheyrou	2	2	-	-	4
S Gerrard	4 (1p)	-	-	2	6 (1p)
D Hamann	2	-	-	1	3
E Heskey	7	1	2	2	12
S Hyypia	4	-	-	1	5
H Kewell	7	-	1	3	11
A Le Tallec	-	-	-	1	1
D Murphy	5 (3p)	1 (p)	2 (1p)	-	8 (5p)
M Owen	16 (4p)	1	-	2	19 (4p)
F Sinama-Pongolle	2	-	-	-	2
V Smicer	3	-	1	-	4
D Traore	-	-	-	1	1
Own goals	2	-	-	-	2

Wednesday February 11
MANCHESTER CITY (h)
Won 2-1 HT 1-0 Att **43,257** Position **4th**
Liverpool move up to fourth, their highest position of the season, when Gerrard punishes a handling error by James just 90 seconds after Wright-Phillips equalises for Manchester City. Owen had given Liverpool an early lead with his first goal since October 25.

Dudek — Finnan, Henchoz, Hyypia, Carragher — Le Tallec (Murphy 68), Gerrard, Hamann, Cheyrou (Biscan 85) — Kewell (Heskey 59), Owen *Subs not used* Kirkland, Sinama-Pongolle
Scorers **Owen 3, Gerrard 51**
Referee **M Riley**

Sunday February 15
PORTSMOUTH (h)
FA Cup, 5th rnd
Drew 1-1 HT 1-0 Att **34,669**
The weekend papers are full of stories suggesting that Owen's future may lie away from Anfield if they fail to reach the Champions League, and he shows his worth again with a goal after 68 seconds. Taylor, though, responds for a resilient Portsmouth six minutes after his arrival as a substitute.

Dudek — Finnan, Henchoz, Hyypia, Carragher — Gerrard, Hamann — Heskey, Cheyrou (Sinama-Pongolle 82), Kewell (Le Tallec 84) — Owen *Subs not used* Biscan, Murphy, Kirkland *Booked* Sinama-Pongolle
Scorer **Owen 2**
Referee **M Halsey**

Sunday February 22
PORTSMOUTH (a)
FA Cup, 5th rnd replay
Lost 0-1 HT 0-0 Att **19,529**
Kirkland — Finnan, Henchoz, Hyypia, Carragher — Le Tallec (Murphy 59), Gerrard, Hamann, Cheyrou (Sinama-Pongolle 82), Heskey (Baros ht) — Owen *Subs not used* Dudek, Biscan
Report page 236

Thursday February 26
LEVSKI SOFIA (h)
Uefa Cup, 3rd rnd, 1st leg
Won 2-0 HT 0-0 Att **39,149**
A match Gerard Houllier dare not lose after Liverpool's FA Cup exit — and his team do not let him down. Owen, still short of confidence, misses three chances, but the Bulgarians finally crack under pressure, conceding twice in three minutes.

Kirkland — Finnan, Henchoz, Hyypia, Carragher — Murphy, Hamann, Gerrard, Kewell (Diouf 85) — Baros (Cheyrou 90), Owen *Subs not used* Dudek, Le Tallec, Traore, Biscan, Welsh
Scorers **Gerrard 67, Kewell 70**
Referee **R Temmink (the Netherlands)**

Sunday February 29
LEEDS UNITED (a)
Drew 2-2 HT 2-2 Att **39,932** Position **6th**
Kirkland — Finnan, Henchoz, Hyypia, Carragher — Murphy, Hamann, Gerrard, Kewell — Owen, Baros (Heskey 80) *Subs not used* Dudek, Diouf, Biscan, Cheyrou *Booked* Henchoz
Scorers **Kewell 21, Baros 42**
Report page 160

Wednesday March 3
LEVSKI SOFIA (a)
Uefa Cup, 3rd rnd, 2nd leg
Won 4-2 (won 6-2 on agg) HT **3-2** Att **40,281**
Ahead 2-0 within 11 minutes, pulled back to 2-2,
Liverpool eventually romp to a handsome aggregate
victory in a clear display of unity after the death threats
to their manager, which are revealed on the eve of the
match.

Kirkland — Finnan (Biscan 58), Henchoz, Hyypia,
Carragher — Murphy, Hamann, Gerrard, Kewell
(Le Tallec 80) — Cheyrou (Baros 69) — Owen *Subs not
used* Dudek, Heskey, Diouf, Traore *Booked* Henchoz
Scorers **Gerrard 7, Owen 11, Hamann 44, Hyypia 67**
Referee **P Frojdfeldt (Sweden)**

Thursday March 11
MARSEILLES (h)
Uefa Cup, 4th rnd, 1st leg
Drew 1-1 HT **0-0** Att **41,270**
Gerrard is yet again the pick of Liverpool's players and
he creates a goal for Baros, but Drogba's 78th-minute
equaliser leaves Marseilles — for whom Barthez makes
two good late saves — favourites to progress.

Kirkland — Finnan (Biscan 89), Henchoz, Hyypia,
Carragher — Murphy (Heskey 82), Hamann, Gerrard,
Kewell — Owen, Baros *Subs not used* Dudek, Riise,
Cheyrou, Diouf, Sinama-Pongolle
Scorer **Baros 55**
Referee **Y Baskakov (Russia)**

Sunday March 14
SOUTHAMPTON (a)
Lost 0-2 HT **0-0** Att **32,056**   Position **8th**
Dudek — Henchoz (Riise 74), Biscan, Hyypia, Carragher —
Diouf (Heskey 60), Hamann, Gerrard, Kewell — Owen,
Baros *Subs not used* Luzi, Traore, Murphy *Booked*
Hamann
Report page 246

Wednesday March 17
PORTSMOUTH (h)
Won 3-0 HT **2-0** Att **34,663**   Position **5th**
Liverpool gain a measure of revenge for their Cup
defeat, with Owen to the fore. His cross is met with a
sensational volley from Hamann and Owen adds two
goals of his own — the second a header — as
Portsmouth's away-day misery continues.

Dudek — Carragher, Biscan, Hyypia, Riise — Murphy,
Gerrard (Cheyrou 74), Hamann, Kewell (Diouf 80) —
Heskey, Owen *Subs not used* Henchoz, Baros, Luzi
Scorers **Hamann 6, Owen 28, 58**
Referee **B Knight**

Saturday March 20
WOLVERHAMPTON WANDERERS (h)
Won 1-0 HT **0-0** Att **43,795**   Position **4th**
For all the talk of crisis, Liverpool are back up to fourth
place, though they could hardly have left it later to beat
Wolves, for whom Hyypia's towering header from
Gerrard's corner must have felt like a dagger through the
heart. It gets worse for them, though, as Leeds relegate
them to bottom position two days later.

Dudek — Carragher, Biscan, Hyypia, Riise — Murphy
(Sinama-Pongolle 83), Hamann, Gerrard, Kewell
(Diouf 70) — Heskey (Baros 70), Owen *Subs not used*
Henchoz, Luzi
Scorer **Hyypia 90**
Referee **R Styles**

THE PLAYERS

MILAN BAROS (forward) **Born**
October 28, 1981, Ostrava, Czech
Republic **Ht** 6ft 0in **Wt** 12st 0lb
Signed from Banik Ostrava, December
2001, £3.4m

IGOR BISCAN (defender) **Born** May 4,
1978, Zagreb **Ht** 6ft 3in **Wt** 12st 8lb
Signed from Dynamo Zagreb,
December 2000, £3.5m

JAMIE CARRAGHER (defender) **Born**
January 28, 1978, Bootle **Ht** 6ft 1in
Wt 12st 10lb **Signed from** trainee,
October 1996

BRUNO CHEYROU (midfield) **Born** May
10, 1978, Suresnes, France **Ht** 6ft 1in
Wt 12st 6lb **Signed from** Lille, July
2002, £3.7m

SALIF DIAO (midfield) **Born**
February 10, 1977, Kadougou,
Senegal **Ht** 6ft 0in **Wt** 11st 7lb
Signed from Sedan, August 2002,
£5m

EL-HADJI DIOUF (midfield) **Born**
January 15, 1981, Dakar, Senegal
Ht 5ft 10in **Wt** 11st 11lb **Signed from**
Lens, June 2002, £10m

JERZY DUDEK (goalkeeper) **Born**
March 23, 1973, Rybnik, Poland

Ht 6ft 1in **Wt** 12st 7lb **Signed from**
Feyenoord, August 2001, £4.85m

STEVE FINNAN (defender) **Born** April
20, 1976, Limerick **Ht** 5ft 10in
Wt 11st 6lb **Signed from** Fulham, July
2003, £3.5m

STEVEN GERRARD (midfield) **Born** May
30, 1980, Huyton **Ht** 6ft 1in
Wt 12st 6lb **Signed from** trainee,
February 1998

DIETMAR HAMANN (midfield) **Born**
August 27, 1973, Waldsasson,
Germany **Ht** 6ft 2in **Wt** 12st 9lb
Signed from Newcastle United, July
1999, £8m

STEPHANE HENCHOZ (defender) **Born**
September 7, 1974, Billens,
Switzerland **Ht** 6ft 2in **Wt** 12st 8lb
Signed from Blackburn Rovers, July
1999, £3.75m

EMILE HESKEY (forward) **Born** January
11, 1978, Leicester **Ht** 6ft 2in
Wt 13st 12lb **Signed from** Leicester
City, March 2000, £11m

SAMI HYYPIA (defender) **Born** October
7, 1973, Porvoo, Finland **Ht** 6ft 3in
Wt 13st 5lb **Signed from** Willem II, the
Netherlands, £2.6m

PAUL JONES (goalkeeper) **Born** April 18, 1967, Chirk **Ht** 6ft 2in **Wt** 14st 8lb **Signed from** Southampton (loan), January 2004

HARRY KEWELL (forward) **Born** September 22, 1978, Sydney **Ht** 5ft 11in **Wt** 12st 4lb **Signed from** Leeds United, July 2003, £5m

CHRIS KIRKLAND (goalkeeper) **Born** May 2, 1981, Leicester **Ht** 6ft 6in **Wt** 11st 7lb **Signed from** Coventry City, August 2001, £6m

ANTHONY LE TALLEC (midfield) **Born** October 3, 1984, Hennebont, France **Ht** 6ft 1in **Wt** 11st 7lb **Signed from** Le Havre, July 2002, £6m (combined fee with Florent Sinama-Pongolle)

PATRICE LUZI (goalkeeper) **Born** July 8, 1980, Ajaccio, France **Ht** 6ft 3in **Wt** 13st 8lb **Signed from** AS Monaco, September 2003, free

DANNY MURPHY (midfield) **Born** March 18, 1977, Chester **Ht** 5ft 9in **Wt** 12st 8lb **Signed from** Crewe Alexandra, July 1997, £1.5m

JON OTSEMOBOR (defender) **Born** March 23, 1983, Liverpool **Ht** 5ft 10in **Wt** 12st 0lb **Signed from** trainee, July 2002

MICHAEL OWEN (forward) **Born** December 14, 1979, Chester **Ht** 5ft 8in **Wt** 10st 9lb **Signed from** trainee, December 1996

JOHN ARNE RIISE (defender) **Born** September 24, 1980, Molde, Norway **Ht** 6ft 1in **Wt** 12st 6lb **Signed from** AS Monaco, July 2001, £4m

FLORENT SINAMA-PONGOLLE (forward) **Born** October 20, 1984, Saint Pierre, France **Ht** 5ft 10in **Wt** 10st 12lb **Signed from** Le Havre, July 2002, £6m (combined fee with Anthony Le Tallec)

VLADIMIR SMICER (midfield) **Born** May 24, 1973, Decin, Czech Republic **Ht** 5ft 10in **Wt** 11st 13lb **Signed from** Lens, July 1999, £3.75m

DJIMI TRAORE (defender) **Born** March 1, 1980, Paris **Ht** 6ft 3in **Wt** 12st 8lb **Signed from** Laval, France, February 1999, £550,000

JOHN WELSH (defender) **Born** January 1, 1984, Liverpool **Ht** 5ft 7in **Wt** 11st 6lb **Signed from** trainee, July 2002

Thursday March 25
MARSEILLES (a)
Uefa Cup, 4th rnd, 2nd leg
Lost 1-2 (lost 2-3 on agg)   HT 1-1   Att 50,000
Liverpool's hopes of punishing Marseilles for their Anfield celebrations are going to plan when Heskey puts them ahead, but the dismissal of Biscan for holding Marlet back by the shorts well outside the area proves crucial. Drogba converts the erroneously awarded penalty and Meite's header seals their fate.

Dudek — Carragher, Biscan, Hyypia, Riise — Hamann — Gerrard, Kewell (Sinama-Pongolle 82), Murphy (Cheyrou 69) — Heskey, Owen (Baros 62) *Subs not used* Henchoz, Traore, Diouf, Luzi *Booked* Carragher *Sent off* Biscan 36
Referee A Dauden Ibanez (Spain)

Sunday March 28
LEICESTER CITY (a)
Drew 0-0   HT 0-0   Att 32,013   Position 4th
Dudek — Carragher, Biscan, Hyypia, Traore — Hamann — Gerrard, Cheyrou (Murphy 71), Kewell — Baros (Sinama-Pongolle 85), Heskey *Subs not used* Luzi, Henchoz, Diouf *Booked* Carragher, Hamann, Baros
Report page 171

Sunday April 4
BLACKBURN ROVERS (h)
Won 4-0   HT 3-0   Att 41,559   Position 4th
The game is over within 24 minutes as rampant Liverpool tear Blackburn apart to reclaim fourth place and leave Graeme Souness looking anxiously over his shoulders. "We were properly bashed up by a very good side," Souness says of a team led brilliantly from the front by Heskey. "They were excellent."

Dudek — Carragher, Biscan, Hyypia, Riise — Diouf (Murphy 71), Hamann, Gerrard, Kewell — Heskey (Sinama-Pongolle 85), Owen (Baros 76) *Subs not used* Luzi, Henchoz
Scorers Owen 7, 24, Todd 22 (og), Heskey 79
Referee J Winter

Friday April 9
ARSENAL (a)
Lost 2-4   HT 2-1   Att 38,119   Position 4th
Dudek — Carragher, Biscan, Hyypia, Riise — Diouf (Murphy 84), Hamann, Gerrard, Kewell — Heskey (Baros 65), Owen *Subs not used* Henchoz, Cheyrou, Luzi *Booked* Diouf
Scorers Hyypia 5, Owen 42
Report page 69

Monday April 12
CHARLTON ATHLETIC (h)
Lost 0-1   HT 0-0   Att 40,003   Position 4th
Charlton's first victory at Anfield for more than 50 years deals a sizeable blow to Liverpool's Champions League hopes. The controversial award of a corner enables Bartlett to head the winner, a goalline clearance by Powell, plus Kiely's excellent save from Smicer, ensuring victory.

Dudek — Carragher, Henchoz, Hyypia, Riise — Diouf (Smicer 58), Hamann, Gerrard, Kewell — Heskey (Baros 58), Owen *Subs not used* Murphy, Cheyrou, Luzi *Booked* Gerrard
Referee P Dowd

PLAYER OF THE SEASON
Steven Gerrard

So, finally, Steven Gerrard stopped growing and became a man. He became the captain, he became a father and he became Liverpool. To cap it all, he even became Sir Alex Ferguson's favourite player, one that the Manchester United manager compared to Roy Keane at his peak. Gerrard turned from promising Scouser to awesome athlete. That last, desperate push for a Champions League place was led by the sheer willpower of Gerrard. He knew calamity would loom should Liverpool finish outside the top four and so he found more reserves of energy, more inch-perfect passes and more determination. If it was good, it was Gerrard who made it happen.
Alyson Rudd

Saturday April 17
FULHAM (h)
Drew 0-0   HT **0-0**   Att **42,042**   Position **4th**
Chris Coleman omits Knight and Davis for breaking a curfew and is rewarded by another gritty Fulham performance as Liverpool's April malaise continues. Gerrard, taking over duties from Owen, has a penalty saved and Kewell and Heskey hit the post, but Fulham create three good chances of their own and deserve a point.

Dudek — Carragher, Henchoz, Hyypia, Riise — Smicer (Diouf 76), Hamann, Gerrard, Kewell (Heskey 76) — Cheyrou (Baros 59), Owen *Subs not used* Murphy, Luzi
Referee **S Bennett**

Saturday April 24
MANCHESTER UNITED (a)
Won 1-0   HT **0-0**   Att **67,647**   Position **4th**
Dudek — Carragher, Henchoz, Hyypia, Riise — Finnan (Smicer 60), Hamann, Gerrard, Murphy — Kewell (Cheyrou 81) — Owen (Heskey 84) *Subs not used* Baros, Luzi *Booked* Gerrard, Murphy
Scorer **Murphy 63 (pen)**
Report page 206

Sunday May 2
MIDDLESBROUGH (h)
Won 2-0   HT **0-0**   Att **42,031**   Position **4th**
Another penalty by Murphy puts Liverpool on the way to another vital win as they maintain their grip on fourth place. An excellent contest is tipped their way when Riggott is adjudged to have brought down Owen — "very harsh", Steve McClaren says of the decision — and Heskey gets the second to end Middlesbrough's hopes.

Dudek — Carragher, Henchoz (Finnan ht), Hyypia, Riise — Smicer (Heskey ht), Hamann, Gerrard, Murphy — Owen, Kewell *Subs not used* Cheyrou, Baros, Luzi *Booked* Gerrard
Scorers **Murphy 50 (pen), Heskey 53**
Referee **A D'Urso**

Saturday May 8
BIRMINGHAM CITY (a)
Won 3-0   HT **1-0**   Att **29,533**   Position **4th**
Dudek — Finnan, Carragher, Hyypia, Riise — Murphy, Hamann, Gerrard, Kewell — Heskey, Owen *Subs not used* Baros, Sinama-Pongolle, Biscan, Cheyrou, Luzi
Scorers **Owen 29, Heskey 51, Gerrard 86**
Report page 90

Saturday May 15
NEWCASTLE UNITED (h)
Drew 1-1   HT **0-1**   Att **44,172**   Position **4th**
Newcastle's failure to beat Southampton in midweek means that Liverpool are already assured of a Champions League place, but Sir Bobby Robson's side still need to do better than Aston Villa manage against Manchester United to qualify for the Uefa Cup and, with Villa losing, they get the point they require. Liverpool, meanwhile, are still weighing up the merits of two rival investment bids, from the Prime Minister of Thailand and Steve Morgan, a wealthy fan.

Dudek — Finnan, Carragher, Hyypia, Riise — Murphy, Hamann, Gerrard, Kewell — Heskey, Owen *Subs not used* Henchoz, Baros, Sinama-Pongolle, Cheyrou, Harrison *Booked* Kewell
Scorer **Owen 67**
Referee **M Riley**

PREMIERSHIP

	P	W	D	L	F	A	GD	Pts
Arsenal	38	26	12	0	73	26	47	**90**
Chelsea	38	24	7	7	67	30	37	**79**
Man Utd	38	23	6	9	64	35	29	**75**
Liverpool	38	16	12	10	55	37	18	**60**
Newcastle	38	13	17	8	52	40	12	**56**
Aston Villa	38	15	11	12	48	44	4	**56**
Charlton	38	14	11	13	51	51	0	**53**
Bolton	38	14	11	13	48	56	-8	**53**
Fulham	38	14	10	14	52	46	6	**52**
Birmingham	38	12	14	12	43	48	-5	**50**
Middlesbro	38	13	9	16	44	52	-8	**48**
Southampton	38	12	11	15	44	45	-1	**47**
Portsmouth	38	12	9	17	47	54	-7	**45**
Tottenham	38	13	6	19	47	57	-10	**45**
Blackburn	38	12	8	18	51	59	-8	**44**
Man City	38	9	14	15	55	54	1	**41**
Everton	38	9	12	17	45	57	-12	**39**
Leicester	38	6	15	17	48	65	-17	**33**
Leeds	38	8	9	21	40	79	-39	**33**
Wolves	38	7	12	19	38	77	-39	**33**

FA CUP
Fifth round

CARLING CUP
Fourth round

UEFA CUP
Second round

In with a shout: David James was one of Kevin Keegan's signings that paid dividends as City flirted with the nightmare scenario of the drop

Thursday August 14 2003
TNS LLANSANTFFRAID (h)
Uefa Cup, 1st qualifying rnd, 1st leg
Won 5-0 HT 1-0 Att 34,103
Sinclair has the honour of scoring the first goal in a competitive match at the City of Manchester Stadium as City return to the continental stage for the first time since 1979 with their biggest European win.

Seaman — Sun, Sommeil, Distin, Tarnat (Tiatto 75) — Wright-Phillips, Bosvelt (Barton 64), Berkovic, Sinclair — Anelka, Fowler (Wanchope 71) *Subs not used* Dunne, Wiekens, Huckerby, Weaver
Scorers **Sinclair 14, Wright-Phillips 51, Sun 60, Sommeil 74, Anelka 87**
Referee **A Tiumin (Russia)**

Sunday August 17
CHARLTON ATHLETIC (a)
Won 3-0 HT 2-0 Att 25,780 Position 3rd
Seaman — Sun, Sommeil, Distin, Tarnat — Wright-Phillips, Barton, Sibierski, Sinclair (Tiatto 89) — Anelka, Fowler (Wanchope 76) *Subs not used* Weaver, Berkovic, Dunne *Booked* Sibierski
Scorers **Anelka 13 (pen), Sibierski 23, Sun 83**
Report page 112

Saturday August 23
PORTSMOUTH (h)
Drew 1-1 HT 0-1 Att 46,287 Position 4th
Portsmouth are within seven seconds of making it two wins out of two on their return when Sommeil's header rescues a point for City, who fall behind when Yakubu rounds Seaman and finishes coolly. Sommeil's earlier elbowing offence on Pericard had gone undetected.

Seaman — Sun, Sommeil, Distin, Tarnat — Wright-Phillips, Barton, Sibierski (Berkovic 64), Sinclair — Anelka, Fowler (Wanchope ht) *Subs not used* Wiekens, Tiatto, Weaver *Booked* Tarnat, Barton
Scorer **Sommeil 90**
Referee **M Messias**

Monday August 25
BLACKBURN ROVERS (a)
Won 3-2 HT 1-1 Att 23,361 Position 1st
Seaman — Sun, Sommeil, Distin, Tarnat — Wright-Phillips, Barton, Bosvelt, Sibierski, Sinclair — Anelka *Subs not used* Macken, Berkovic, Tiatto, Dunne, Weaver *Booked* Distin
Scorers **Tarnat 4, Barton 59, Anelka 87**
Report page 92

Thursday August 28
TNS LLANSANTFFRAID (a)
Uefa Cup, 1st qualifying rnd, 2nd leg
Won 2-0 (won 7-0 on agg) HT 1-0 Att 10,123
City take a large contingent of reserves to the Millennium Stadium in Cardiff and a largely reserve side complete an emphatic victory over the Welsh part-timers.

Weaver — Dunne, Wiekens, Bischoff — Flood, Bosvelt (Whelan 73), Negouai, Tiatto — Berkovic (Barton 80) — Macken (Wright-Phillips 58), Huckerby *Subs not used* Distin, Sun, Sinclair, Stuhr-Ellegaard
Scorers **Negouai 43, Huckerby 81**
Referee **Z Szabo (Hungary)**

AFTER THE LAST GAME OF THE SEASON, a 5-1 home demolition of Everton, Kevin Keegan, the Manchester City manager, had to be persuaded by his chairman, John Wardle, to join the players for their end-of-season lap of honour. Keegan said that he felt a fraud after spending £50 million or so on a team that had finished fifth from bottom of the Premiership and endured relegation worries since February. Keegan, however, was astonished by the reception from the 40,000 or so fans who had stayed behind after the game.

"They are the greatest thing about this club and the level of support we have enjoyed throughout a very poor season has been amazing," he said. "Thirty thousand of them bought season-tickets for next year without even knowing what division we would be in. What we've done to deserve this is beyond me."

Even Wardle, a lifelong City fan, was nonplussed. "You wonder what it would be like if we won something," he said. "It was typical City, the tag we are trying to get rid of. We got cheered to the rafters even though we've had such a bad season."

Both men seem to have forgotten that although City fans would love to end their 28-year trophy drought, they have become inured to failure and take consolation in the smallest of morsels. The 2003-04 season offered two very tasty morsels indeed.

First was the astonishing 4-3 FA Cup replay win over Tottenham Hotspur, achieved despite being 3-0 and one man down at half-time at White Hart Lane. Then, and most important, was the 4-1 drubbing of Manchester United at the City of Manchester Stadium. Keegan can perhaps be forgiven for underestimating such a result, but surely Wardle should realise how much it meant for City fans. If City had lost that game 4-1 there can be little doubt that the end-of-season revelries would have been a good deal more subdued.

Even then, most supporters would take refuge in the fact that, while their club underperformed, they enjoyed little luck during the campaign. Although they only won five league games at home all season (only relegated Leicester City won fewer), just five were lost, a record bettered only by five of the top six sides.

Often, City would dominate games territorially without making their superiority pay. However, as the season ground on and wins continued to elude them, so performances edged slowly from adequate to abject. Two consecutive home games in April, against Wolverhampton Wanderers (3-3) and Southampton (1-3), saw the bottom of the barrel left with inch-deep gouges. Only a minor players' revolt that ensured extra training and the reintroduction

HONOURS BOARD

FOOTBALL LEAGUE
Champions 1937, 1968
Runners-up 1904, 1921, 1977
FA CUP
Winners 1904, 1934, 1956, 1969
Runners-up 1926, 1933, 1955, 1981
LEAGUE CUP
Winners 1970, 1976
Runners-up 1974
CUP WINNERS' CUP
Winners 1970

Record attendance 84,569 (v Stoke
City, FA Cup 6th rnd, March 3, 1934)
Current capacity 48,000
Record victory 10-1 (v Swindon
Town, FA Cup 4th rnd, January 29,
1930 and
v Huddersfield Town, second division,
November 7, 1987)
Record defeat 1-9 (v Everton, first
division September 3, 1906)

into the attack of Paulo Wanchope in place of the moribund Robbie Fowler saw the team edge clear of relegation.

In contrast, the season could hardly have begun any more brightly. After comprehensive home wins against Aston Villa (4-1) and Bolton Wanderers (6-2), City's form reached new heights in a 2-0 win away to Southampton on November 1, a result that left them settled in the top six. Their football was fluent and sharp and the match was won more easily than the scoreline suggests. Furthermore, two comfortable ties had seen them reach the second round of the Uefa Cup with what looked a winnable tie against the Polish minnows, Groclin Dyskobolia. Unfortunately, Groclin eased out an anaemic City on away goals and the win away to Southampton proved to be the last in the league until February 21 2004.

What happened? After all, in the summer Keegan had brought in proven experience in Steve McManaman (from Real Madrid), Trevor Sinclair (from West Ham United), David Seaman (from Arsenal), Michael Tarnat (from Bayern Munich) and Paul Bosvelt (from Feyenoord). Not only were they proven winners but their experience in European football would surely prove invaluable. And reuniting McManaman with his old partner and great mate, Fowler, would surely ignite the latter's goalscoring fire.

Unfortunately, only Bosvelt — and then not until the final few games of the season — proved committed to the cause. Seaman's indecision cost at least eight goals before he retired and David James was brought in during the January transfer window. McManaman was, apart from his debut against Villa and the

Sunday August 31
ARSENAL (h)
Lost 1-2 **HT 1-0** Att **46,436** Position **4th**
Lauren puts through his own net and Arsenal hit more bad passes in the first half than they would expect to in a season, but they maintain the Premiership's only 100 per cent record through Wiltord and — partly with the aid of Seaman's error against his former club — Ljungberg.

Seaman — Sun, Sommeil, Distin, Tarnat — Wright-Phillips (Berkovic 80), Barton, Bosvelt (Fowler 80), Sinclair — Sibierski (Tiatto 68) — Anelka *Subs not used* Weaver, Dunne *Booked* Sommeil, Tarnat, Tiatto, Barton
Scorer Lauren 10 (og)
Referee G Poll

Sunday September 14
ASTON VILLA (h)
Won 4-1 **HT 0-1** Att **46,687** Position **3rd**
Angel gives Villa an interval lead, but they are overrun in the second half, contributing to their own downfall by conceding two penalties, both converted by Anelka, who completes a hat-trick. Tarnat adds another thunderbolt.

Seaman — Sun, Sommeil, Distin, Tarnat — Wright-Phillips, Barton (Sibierski 73), McManaman, Sinclair — Anelka, Wanchope (Reyna 82) *Subs not used* Weaver, Fowler, Dunne
Scorers Anelka 48 (pen), 68 (pen), 83, Tarnat 50
Referee M Halsey

Saturday September 20
FULHAM (a)
Drew 2-2 **HT 0-0** Att **16,124** Position **5th**
Seaman — Sun, Sommeil, Distin, Tiatto — Wright-Phillips (Bosvelt 77), Barton, McManaman (Fowler 84), Sinclair — Anelka (Sibierski 67), Wanchope *Subs not used* Weaver, Dunne *Booked* Sun, Sommeil, Wright-Phillips, Anelka, Barton
Scorers Anelka 46, Wanchope 90
Report page 144

Wednesday September 24
LOKEREN (h)
Uefa Cup, 1st rnd, 1st leg
Won 3-2 **HT 1-2** Att **29,067**
Kevin Keegan is angry with the fans who boo his team off at half-time and target Seaman, who is partly at fault with both Lokeren goals. But Fowler gets off the mark for the season and Anelka's penalty, for Van Hoey's foul on Sun, gives City a precious advantage to take to Belgium.

Seaman — Sun, Sommeil, Distin, Tiatto (Dunne 69) — Sibierski, Bosvelt (Wright-Phillips 65), Reyna, McManaman — Anelka, Fowler *Subs not used* Weaver, Barton, Sinclair, Berkovic, Jordan
Scorers Sibierski 8, Fowler 77, Anelka 80 (pen)
Referee G Gilewski (Poland)

Sunday September 28
TOTTENHAM HOTSPUR (h)
Drew 0-0 **HT 0-0** Att **46,842** Position **5th**
Martin O'Neill is now the newspapers' favourite to succeed Glenn Hoddle at Tottenham, who use up several large slices of luck to escape with a point. Wanchope misses the best of City's numerous chances.

Seaman — Sun, Sommeil, Distin, Tarnat — Wright-Phillips, Bosvelt, McManaman (Reyna 85), Sinclair (Sibierski 72) — Anelka, Wanchope (Fowler 76) *Subs not used* Bischoff, Weaver *Booked* Sun, Tarnat
Referee N Barry

Saturday October 4
WOLVERHAMPTON WANDERERS (a)
Lost 0-1 **HT 0-0** Att **29,386** Position **6th**
Seaman — Sun, Sommeil, Distin, Tarnat — Wright-Phillips, Bosvelt, Reyna, Sibierski (Sinclair 63) — Anelka (Fowler 79), Wanchope *Subs not used* Weaver, Wiekens, Barton *Booked* Distin, Sinclair
Report page 261

Wednesday October 15
LOKEREN (a)
Uefa Cup, 1st rnd, 2nd leg
Won 1-0 (won 4-2 on agg) **HT 1-0** Att **10,000**
Wanchope makes the most of slight contact by Coulibaly
to win the penalty that settles a very poor contest.

Seaman — Sun, Sommeil, Distin, Tarnat — Wright-Phillips,
Bosvelt, McManaman, Sinclair (Barton 89) — Anelka,
Wanchope (Reyna 78) *Subs not used* Weaver, Wiekens,
Berkovic, Sibierski, Fowler *Booked* Sinclair
Scorer **Anelka 19 (pen)**
Referee **D Ledentu (France)**

Saturday October 18
BOLTON WANDERERS (h)
Won 6-2 **HT 1-1** Att **47,101** Position **4th**
Bolton take the lead: big mistake. They are condemned
to their heaviest league defeat for almost eight years as
City hit them for six. City are 4-2 up when Wright-Phillips
is sent off for a reckless challenge on Charlton.

Seaman — Sun, Sommeil, Distin, Tarnat — Wright-Phillips,
Barton (Dunne 75), Reyna, McManaman (Sibierski 57)
— Anelka, Fowler (Tiatto 67) *Subs not used*
Stuhr-Ellegaard, Wanchope *Booked* Wright-Phillips
Sent off Wright-Phillips 62
Scorers **Wright-Phillips 27, 56, Distin 48,
Anelka 58, 72, Reyna 84**
Referee **S Bennett**

Saturday October 25
CHELSEA (a)
Lost 0-1 **HT 0-1** Att **41,040** Position **7th**
Seaman — Sun, Sommeil, Distin, Tarnat — Wright-Phillips,
Barton, Reyna (Sibierski 80), Sinclair — Anelka, Fowler
(Wanchope 73) *Subs not used* Stuhr-Ellegaard, Dunne,
Bosvelt
Report page 124

Tuesday October 28
QUEENS PARK RANGERS (a)
Carling Cup, 3rd rnd
Won 3-0 **HT 1-0** Att **16,773** Watched by his
stepfather, Ian Wright, who is involved in
a heated row with two fans later arrested for alleged
racial abuse, Wright-Phillips scores the first two goals in a
reasonably comfortable passage for City.

Seaman — Sun, Distin, Dunne, Tarnat — Wright-Phillips,
Bosvelt, Barton, Sinclair (Berkovic 85) — Anelka
(Macken 72), Fowler (Sibierski 85) *Subs not used*
Stuhr-Ellegaard, Wiekens *Booked* Bosvelt
Scorers **Wright-Phillips 22, 77, Macken 79**
Referee **S Dunn**

Saturday November 1
SOUTHAMPTON (a)
Won 2-0 **HT 1-0** Att **31,952** Position **5th**
Seaman — Sun, Dunne, Distin, Tarnat — Sinclair, Reyna,
Barton, McManaman — Fowler (Sibierski 82), Wanchope
Subs not used Stuhr-Ellegaard, Sommeil, Bosvelt,
Macken *Booked* Dunne
Scorers **Fowler 4, Wanchope 85**
Report page 242

Thursday November 6
GROCLIN DYSKOBOLIA (h)
Uefa Cup, 2nd rnd, 1st leg
Drew 1-1 **HT 1-0** Att **32,506**
Ahead within six minutes when Anelka chips Liberda, City
have enough chances to make the tie safe and are
rocked when Mila converts a 65th-minute free kick.

Seaman — Sun, Dunne, Distin, Tarnat — Wright-Phillips,
Reyna (Bosvelt 25), Barton, McManaman (Tiatto 64) —
Anelka, Fowler (Wanchope 69) *Subs not used*
Stuhr-Ellegaard, Sibierski, Sommeil, Macken *Booked*
Tarnat
Scorer **Anelka 6**
Referee **G Kasnaferis (Greece)**

**Fowler squeezes the ball past Howard to put City ahead after three
minutes of a pulsating first derby at the City of Manchester Stadium**

consummate performance against Southampton, appalling, Sinclair
forgot how to get past defenders and Tarnat was lackadaisical.

To many observers, the problem with City's underperformance
lies squarely with those expensive (in terms of wages) signings who
just saw City as a last money-spinning opportunity before
retirement. Others blame Keegan for being unable to motivate his
team. While there is an element of truth in both arguments, the
latter perhaps holds more water. City's best players — other than
James — were three relative youngsters, Richard Dunne, Joey
Barton and Shaun Wright-Phillips. Keegan is at his best working
with younger, more impressionable players. One only has to be
reminded of his record as the coach of England to understand that
his boundless enthusiasm does not work wonders on experienced,
successful players.

The 2003-04 season was poor, let there be no doubt about that.
However, City fans are, in the words of a *Manchester Evening News*
pundit, "as blind as bats and daft as brushes" and will point to City
winning the last two games in their magnificent new stadium as
laying to rest their home problems and as reasons to be cheerful for
the new season. They will also still be luxuriating in the spanking of
United and savouring that rarest of City feats — a successful battle
against relegation.

THE MANAGER

Kevin Keegan

Kevin Keegan must take much of the blame for a disappointing campaign. He exhibited poor judgment in the transfer market, then compounded his errors by showing loyalty to players who were clearly not interested in playing for City. His inability to coax his experienced squad out of a rut was even more worrying. The vast majority of City fans still believe in him, but whether this loyalty will endure another bad season is doubtful in the extreme.

Paul Connolly

APPEARANCES

	Prem	FAC	CC	Euro	Total
N Anelka	31 (1)	4	2	5	42 (1)
A Arason	-	2	-	-	2
J Barton	24 (4)	3 (1)	2	2 (3)	31 (8)
E Berkovic	1 (3)	-	0 (1)	2	3 (4)
M Bischoff	-	-	-	1	1
P Bosvelt	22 (3)	4	1	4 (1)	31 (4)
S Distin	38	5	2	5	50
R Dunne	28 (1)	5	2	3 (1)	38 (2)
S Elliott	0 (2)	-	-	-	0 (2)
W Flood	-	-	-	1	1
R Fowler	23 (8)	4	2	4	33 (8)
D Huckerby	-	-	-	1	1
D James	17	-	-	-	17
S Jordan	0 (2)	-	-	-	0 (2)
J Macken	7 (8)	1 (2)	0 (1)	1 (1)	9 (12)
S McManaman	20 (2)	2 (1)	0 (1)	4	26 (4)
C Negouai	-	-	-	1	1
C Reyna	19 (4)	3	1	2 (2)	25 (6)
D Seaman	19	1	1	5	26
A Sibierski	18 (15)	3 (2)	0 (1)	1	22 (18)
T Sinclair	20 (9)	3 (1)	2	3	28 (10)
D Sommeil	18	2	1	4	25
K Stuhr-Ellegaard	2 (2)	2	1	-	5 (2)
Sun Jihai	29 (4)	3	1	5	38 (4)
M Tarnat	32	4	2	3	41
D Tiatto	1 (4)	-	-	2 (2)	3 (6)
D van Buyten	5	1	-	-	6
P Wanchope	12 (10)	-	-	1 (3)	13 (13)
N Weaver	-	-	-	1	1
G Whelan	-	-	-	0 (1)	0 (1)
G Wiekens	-	-	-	1	1
S Wright-Phillips	32 (2)	3 (1)	2	4 (2)	41 (5)

Sunday November 9
LEICESTER CITY (h)
Lost 0-3 HT 0-1 Att **46,966** Position **6th**
With Seaman hamstrung, Stuhr-Ellegaard makes his debut in goal for City and is on the wrong end of a drubbing as Leicester, with five defeats out of five away from home, turn the formbook upside down. Their second goal is a penalty, conceded by Distin for shoving Dickov in the face off the ball.

Stuhr-Ellegaard — Sun, Dunne, Distin, Tarnat — McManaman, Barton (Bosvelt 60), Sibierski, Berkovic — Anelka, Wanchope (Fowler 60) *Subs not used* Weaver, Sommeil, Macken *Booked* Distin, Bosvelt
Referee **M Riley**

Saturday November 22
NEWCASTLE UNITED (a)
Lost 0-3 HT 0-0 Att **52,159** Position **8th**
Seaman — Sun, Dunne, Distin, Tarnat — McManaman, Bosvelt (Berkovic 72; Sibierski 88), Barton, Sinclair — Anelka, Fowler (Macken 72) *Subs not used* Stuhr-Ellegaard, Sommeil *Booked* Distin, Tarnat
Report page 221

Thursday November 27
GROCLIN DYSKOBOLIA (a)
Uefa Cup, 2nd rnd, 2nd leg
Drew 0-0 (agg 1-1; lose on away goals)
HT 0-0 Att **5,500**
"We got in through the back door [the fair-play league] and we go out through the back door." Kevin Keegan sums up a miserable night for City, who need two goalline clearances to keep them in the game, but then see Anelka and Fowler miss glorious chances to win the tie. Both are summarily substituted, but to no avail.

Seaman — Sun, Dunne, Sommeil, Distin — Wright-Phillips (Reyna 79), Barton, McManaman, Distin — Anelka (Macken 75), Fowler (Wanchope 75) *Subs not used* Stuhr-Ellegaard, Wiekens, Sibierski, Bosvelt *Booked* Fowler, Dunne
Referee **P Frojdfeldt (Sweden)**

Sunday November 30
MIDDLESBROUGH (h)
Lost 0-1 HT 0-1 Att **46,824** Position **9th**
Middlesbrough somehow win without managing a shot on target, Sun doing the job for them with a decisive own goal — "winning ugly", Steve McClaren calls it. Denied a clear penalty when Mills holds Wanchope back by the shirt, and with Fowler missing another great chance, City lurch from one calamity to another.

Stuhr-Ellegaard — Sun (Fowler 66), Dunne, Sommeil, Distin — Wright-Phillips, Barton (Sibierski 74), Reyna, Sinclair — Anelka, Wanchope *Subs not used* K Schmeichel, Wiekens, McManaman
Referee **M Riley**

Wednesday December 3
TOTTENHAM HOTSPUR (a)
Carling Cup, 4th rnd
Lost 1-3 HT 0-2 Att **31,727**
Stuhr-Ellegaard — Sommeil, Distin, Dunne, Tarnat (McManaman 71) — Wright-Phillips, Barton, Reyna, Sinclair — Anelka, Fowler *Subs not used* K Schmeichel, Wiekens, Sibierski, Macken *Booked* Wright-Phillips, Anelka
Scorer **Fowler 80**
Report page 253

Sunday December 7
EVERTON (a)
Drew 0-0 HT 0-0 Att **37,871** Position **10th**
Seaman (Stuhr-Ellegaard 53) — Sun, Dunne, Sommeil, Distin — Wright-Phillips (Wanchope 77), Barton, McManaman, Sinclair — Anelka, Fowler *Subs not used* Reyna, Berkovic, Sibierski *Booked* Barton
Report page 137

Saturday December 13
MANCHESTER UNITED (a)
Lost 1-3   HT 0-2   Att 67,645   Position 12th
Seaman — Sun, Dunne, Sommeil, Distin — Wright-Phillips, Barton, McManaman, Sinclair (Wanchope 80) — Anelka, Fowler *Subs not used* Stuhr-Ellegaard, Reyna, Sibierski, Berkovic *Booked* Sun, Barton
Scorer **Wright-Phillips 52**
Report page 200

Monday December 22
LEEDS UNITED (h)
Drew 1-1   HT 0-1   Att 47,126   Position 11th
Eddie Gray is absent, attending his daughter's wedding, and Kevin Blackwell, deputising for the Leeds caretaker manager, sees them take the lead when Sommeil's blunder lets in Viduka. But though Kevin Keegan is booed for his triple substitution, Sibierski, one of the new arrivals, heads City's equaliser.

Seaman — Sun, Dunne, Sommeil, Distin — Wright-Phillips, Barton (Sibierski 71), Reyna, McManaman (Macken 71) — Fowler (Wanchope 71), Anelka *Subs not used* Stuhr-Ellegaard, Tarnat
Scorer **Sibierski 82**
Referee **G Barber**

Friday December 26
BIRMINGHAM CITY (a)
Lost 1-2   HT 1-0   Att 29,520   Position 13th
Seaman — Sun, Dunne, Sommeil, Distin — Wright-Phillips, Barton, Reyna, McManaman (Sinclair 70) — Fowler (Sibierski 70), Anelka *Subs not used* Macken, Tarnat, Stuhr-Ellegaard *Booked* Sun
Scorer **Fowler 14**
Report page 85

Sunday December 28
LIVERPOOL (h)
Drew 2-2   HT 1-0   Att 47,201   Position 13th
With the City of Manchester Stadium staging an Anfield old boys' reunion, it is pre-ordained that Anelka, with the penalty that gives City the lead, and Fowler, with a dramatic stoppage-time equaliser, should take centre stage. Hamann threatens to win it for Liverpool by beating Seaman from 25 yards to make it 2-1.

Seaman — Sommeil, Dunne, Distin, Tarnat (Sinclair 71) — Wright-Phillips, Bosvelt (Macken 84), Reyna, McManaman (Sibierski 79) — Fowler, Anelka *Subs not used* Stuhr-Ellegaard, Wiekens *Booked* Sommeil
Scorers **Anelka 30 (pen), Fowler 90**
Referee **M Riley**

Saturday January 3 2004
LEICESTER CITY (h)
FA Cup, 3rd rnd
Drew 2-2   HT 1-1   Att 30,617
Twice behind, City's season is saved from complete collapse by Anelka, who converts his seventh penalty of the season and heads in Fowler's corner after Dickov, their former player, threatens to inspire Leicester's second win at the ground this season.

Seaman — Sommeil, Dunne, Distin — Wright-Phillips (Sinclair 81), Reyna, Bosvelt (Barton 80), Sun — McManaman (Sibierski ht) — Fowler, Anelka *Subs not used* Macken, Stuhr-Ellegaard *Booked* Sommeil
Scorer **Anelka 27 (pen), 69**
Referee **G Poll**

MATCH OF THE SEASON

Manchester City 4 Aston Villa 1
City of Manchester Stadium, Sunday September 14 2003
David McVay

KEVIN KEEGAN HAS ADMITTED that he is embarrassed by the riches he has at his disposal in his squad. Goodness knows how he might react if a Russian oil mogul suddenly grew tired of the "black gold" and developed a passion for the Blue Moon.

A historic first victory at the City of Manchester Stadium, Eastlands, or whatever the club's new home ultimately will be known as, lifted City above Chelsea to third position in the table yesterday. The power of the pound may attract attention and some of the game's leading lights to Stamford Bridge, but Keegan's typically cavalier sides remain as appealing and unpredictable as ever. City's presence in the top three is heartening news for both the Premiership and football neutrals and, who knows, they may even have the resilience not to falter in the longer term.

Aston Villa, at least for the first 45 minutes, contributed to an enthralling game and, having secured just one away win in the league last season, appeared ready to equal that unenviable record in mid-September. However, the West Midlands team, ahead through Juan Pablo Angel's 31st-minute header, were swept away by a hat-trick from Nicolas Anelka and an assured debut by Steve McManaman, his former Real Madrid colleague, as the stadium, in the words of Keegan, "finally came alive".

McManaman returned after a four-year absence from the Premiership to provide the catalyst that galvanised City's ambition. His influence was laced with class and authority, befitting a player whose creative craft has been largely ignored by the present England regime. It is nearly two years since he last appeared for his country, and while his potency curiously diminishes every time he pulls on the white shirt, it is a measure of the low esteem in which Sven-Goran Eriksson holds him that Emile Heskey has been preferred down the left wing by the England head coach.

"Anelka was man of the match, but McManaman was my man of the match," Keegan, who had no hesitation selecting the 31-year-old McManaman during his period as England coach, said. "He was involved in everything good that we did; he was safe when he had to be safe and inventive when the time was right. His workrate and fitness, considering he has hardly played for Real Madrid in pre-season, speaks volumes for him."

It was McManaman's guile on the edge of the area, drifting past two defenders and flicking the ball up for Mark Delaney to handle, that elicited the equaliser in the 48th minute, Anelka finishing with the spot kick. Two minutes later, City seized the moment and the advantage when Michael Tarnat struck a 20-yard free kick that Thomas Sorensen, the Villa goalkeeper, may reproach himself for

Delaney is at full stretch to curb the threat of a rampant Anelka

not tipping over. "With the players we have here now, we have the potential to do something really special," Keegan said. "Whether we can fulfil that is the real test." Sorensen could not resist City's third, in the 68th minute. Peter Whittingham took the legs of Sun Jihai in the penalty area after Shaun Wright-Phillips's clever back-heel had released the full back and Anelka smashed away his fourth league goal of the season. His fifth came six minutes from time, Tarnat intercepting a counter-attack on the halfway line before Anelka ran on with purpose to finish from 18 yards out with a low shot.

So has the Incredible Sulk of Arsenal and Real Madrid finally grown up? "Some of the things he does in training and on the football pitch, I haven't seen very often," Keegan said. "I was 27 before I knew what this game was all about. Anelka is still only young. You may think I'm joking because he seems to have been about for ever, but he is just 24 and, if he can learn more in the next three years when he reaches what should be his peak, he could be one of the best in the world, and there are some good ones out there."

MANCHESTER CITY (4-4-2): D Seaman — Sun Jihai, D Sommeil, S Distin, M Tarnat — S Wright-Phillips, J Barton (sub: A Sibierski, 73min), S McManaman, T Sinclair — P Wanchope (sub: C Reyna, 82), N Anelka. **Substitutes not used:** N Weaver, R Fowler, R Dunne.
ASTON VILLA (4-4-2): T Sorensen — M Delaney, O Mellberg (sub: Alpay, 37), R Johnsen (sub: M Hadji, 66), J Samuel — L Hendrie, G McCann, T Hitzlsperger, P Whittingham — J P Angel (sub: D Dublin, 76), M Allback. **Substitutes not used:** S Postma, M Kinsella. **Booked:** Johnsen.

Wednesday January 7
CHARLTON ATHLETIC (h)
Drew 1-1   HT 1-0   Att 44,307   Position 14th
City's winless run is up to 13 matches when Dunne is harshly penalised for handball, allowing Di Canio to equalise after Seaman parries his spot kick. Fowler had given them the lead against a Charlton side still smarting from their FA Cup defeat to Gillingham.

Seaman — Sommeil, Dunne, Distin, Tarnat — Sinclair, Reyna (Barton 20), Bosvelt, Sibierski (Wright-Phillips 74) — Fowler (Macken 71), Anelka *Subs not used* Stuhr-Ellegaard, Sun
Scorer **Fowler 39**
Referee **P Walton**

Saturday January 10
PORTSMOUTH (a)
Lost 2-4   HT 2-1   Att 20,120   Position 15th
Seaman (Stuhr-Ellegaard 13) — Sommeil, Dunne, Distin, Tarnat — Sinclair, Barton, Bosvelt, Sibierski — Fowler, Anelka *Subs not used* Wiekens, Macken, McManaman, Tiatto *Booked* Fowler, Dunne
Scorers **Anelka 21, Sibierski 45**
Report page 234

Wednesday January 14
LEICESTER CITY (a)
FA Cup, 3rd rnd replay
Won 3-1   HT 1-0   Att 18,916
Stuhr-Ellegaard — Sommeil, Dunne, Distin, Tarnat — Sinclair, Barton, Bosvelt, Sibierski — Anelka, Macken
Subs not used K Schmeichel, Sun, Wiekens, McManaman, Wright-Phillips
Scorers **Sibierski 12, Anelka 90, Macken 90**
Report page 169

Saturday January 17
BLACKBURN ROVERS (h)
Drew 1-1   HT 0-0   Att 47,090   Position 15th
James, who replaced Seaman between the posts for England, now does the same at club level, having been recruited from West Ham United after the veteran's decision to retire. The first goal James concedes costs City a point, Flitcroft sliding in to cancel out the opener, curled round the wall by Anelka.

James — Sun, Dunne, Distin, Tarnat — Sinclair (Tiatto 77), Barton, Bosvelt, Sibierski — Macken (Wright-Phillips 71), Anelka *Subs not used* Sommeil, McManaman, Stuhr-Ellegaard *Booked* Sun, Bosvelt
Scorer **Anelka 50**
Referee **M Dean**

Sunday January 25
TOTTENHAM HOTSPUR (h)
FA Cup, 4th rnd
Drew 1-1   HT 1-0   Att 28,840
The rows of empty seats at the City of Manchester Stadium make for worrying viewing, a crowd 18,000 down on the league norm seeing Anelka's opener cancelled out by Doherty, who heads in when Stuhr-Ellegaard — deputising for the ineligible James — flaps at a corner.

Stuhr-Ellegaard — Sun, Dunne, Distin, Tarnat — Sinclair, Bosvelt, Reyna, Sibierski (Wright-Phillips 69) — Fowler (Macken 69), Anelka *Subs not used* Sommeil, McManaman, Arason *Booked* Bosvelt, Reyna
Scorer **Anelka 11**
Referee **S Dunn**

Sunday February 1
ARSENAL (a)
Lost 1-2   HT 0-1   Att 38,103   Position 15th
James — Sun, Dunne, Distin, Tarnat — Wright-Phillips, Bosvelt (Fowler 77), Barton, Reyna (McManaman 77), Sinclair — Anelka *Subs not used* Sibierski, Macken, Arason *Booked* Sinclair, Barton *Sent off* Anelka 90
Scorer **Anelka 89**
Report page 66

Wednesday February 4
TOTTENHAM HOTSPUR (a)
FA Cup, 4th rnd replay
Won 4-3   HT 0-3   Att 30,400
Arason — Sun, Dunne, Distin, Tarnat — Wright-Phillips, Barton, Bosvelt (Sibierski 80), Sinclair (McManaman 80) — Anelka (Macken 27), Fowler *Subs not used* Stuhr-Ellegaard, Jordan *Booked* Sun, Bosvelt, Barton *Sent off* Barton 45
Scorers **Distin 48, Bosvelt 61, Wright-Phillips 80, Macken 90**
Report page 255

Sunday February 8
BIRMINGHAM CITY (h)
Drew 0-0   HT 0-0   Att 46,967   Position 16th
Four days after their sensational Cup comeback against Spurs, City are shut out by a Birmingham side for whom Taylor is in inspired form. The goalkeeper makes a handful of world-class saves, the pick of them thwarting Sibierski.

James — Dunne (Sun 55), Van Buyten, Distin — Wright-Phillips, Bosvelt (Barton 70), Reyna (McManaman 70), Tarnat — Sibierski — Macken, Fowler *Subs not used* Jordan, Arason
Referee **P Durkin**

Wednesday February 11
LIVERPOOL (a)
Lost 1-2   HT 0-1   Att 43,257   Position 16th
James — Dunne, Van Buyten, Distin — Wright-Phillips, Bosvelt, Reyna (Barton 68), Tarnat — McManaman — Macken (Sibierski 77), Fowler *Subs not used* Arason, Sun, Elliott
Scorer **Wright-Phillips 50**
Report page 181

Saturday February 14
MANCHESTER UNITED (a)
FA Cup, 5th rnd
Lost 2-4   HT 0-1   Att 67,228
Arason — Dunne, Van Buyten, Distin — Wright-Phillips, Reyna, Barton, McManaman, Tarnat — Sibierski — Fowler *Subs not used* Wiekens, Bosvelt, Elliott, Macken, Stuhr-Ellegaard *Booked* Tarnat, Barton
Scorers **Tarnat 78, Fowler 86**
Report page 203

Saturday February 21
BOLTON WANDERERS (a)
Won 3-1   HT 2-1   Att 27,301   Position 14th
James — Wright-Phillips, Dunne, Distin, Tarnat — Sinclair, Reyna, Sibierski, McManaman (Jordan 90) — Fowler (Elliott 88), Macken (Sun 74) *Subs not used* Arason, Negouai *Booked* Dunne, McManaman
Scorers **Fowler 27, 31, Charlton 50 (og)**
Report page 108

Saturday February 28
CHELSEA (h)
Lost 0-1   HT 0-0   Att 47,304   Position 16th
With Manchester United dropping points away to Fulham, Chelsea are up to second place thanks to Gudjohnsen's late breakaway winner. "We're the unluckiest team in the world at the moment," Kevin Keegan says after seeing City dominate the second half, Fowler going close three times in three minutes.

James — Dunne, Van Buyten, Distin — Wright-Phillips, Reyna, McManaman, Tarnat — Sibierski — Fowler, Macken (Sinclair 71) *Subs not used* Arason, Sun, Barton, Bosvelt
Referee **R Styles**

THE PLAYERS

NICOLAS ANELKA (forward) **Born** March 14, 1979, Versailles **Ht** 6ft 1in **Wt** 12st 2lb **Signed from** Paris Saint-Germain, July 2002, £13m

ARNI ARASON (goalkeeper) **Born** May 7, 1975, Reykjavik **Ht** 6ft 2in **Wt** 13st 4lb **Signed from** Rosenborg, January 2004, free

JOEY BARTON (midfield) **Born** September 2, 1982, Huyton **Ht** 5ft 9in **Wt** 11st 0lb **Signed from** trainee, August 2001

EYAL BERKOVIC (see Portsmouth)

MIKKEL BISCHOFF (defender) **Born** February 3, 1982, Denmark **Ht** 6ft 3in **Wt** 13st 4lb **Signed from** AB Copenhagen, July 2002, £750,000

PAUL BOSVELT (midfield) **Born** March 26, 1970, Doetinchem, the Netherlands **Ht** 6ft 1in **Wt** 12st 4lb **Signed from** Feyenoord, July 2003, undisclosed

SYLVAIN DISTIN (defender) **Born** December 16, 1977, Paris **Ht** 6ft 4in **Wt** 13st 6lb **Signed from** Newcastle United, May 2002, £4m

RICHARD DUNNE (defender) **Born** September 21, 1979, Dublin **Ht** 6ft 2in **Wt** 14st 0lb **Signed from** Everton, October 2000, £3m

STEPHEN ELLIOTT (forward) **Born** January 6, 1984, Dublin **Ht** 5ft 9in **Wt** 11st 9lb **Signed from** trainee, February 2004

WILLO FLOOD (midfield) **Born** April 10, 1985, Dublin **Ht** 5ft 7in **Wt** 10st 7lb **Signed from** trainee, August 2003

ROBBIE FOWLER (forward) **Born** April 9, 1975, Toxteth **Ht** 5ft 8in **Wt** 11st 6lb **Signed from** Leeds United, January 2003, £6m

DARREN HUCKERBY (forward) **Born** April 23, 1976, Nottingham **Ht** 5ft 10in **Wt** 11st 12lb **Signed from** Leeds United, December 2000, £2.25m

DAVID JAMES (goalkeeper) **Born** August 1, 1970, Welwyn **Ht** 6ft 5in **Wt** 14st 2lb **Signed from** West Ham United, January 2004, £2m

STEPHEN JORDAN (midfield) **Born** March 6, 1982, Warrington **Ht** 6ft 0in **Wt** 11st 13lb **Signed from** trainee, June 2000

JON MACKEN (forward) **Born** September 7, 1977, Manchester **Ht** 5ft 10in **Wt** 12st 8lb **Signed from** Preston North End, March 2002, £4m

STEVE McMANAMAN (midfield) **Born** February 11, 1972, Liverpool **Ht** 6ft 0in **Wt** 10st 6lb **Signed from** Real Madrid, August 2003, free

CHRISTIAN NEGOUAI (midfield) **Born** January 20, 1975, Martinique **Ht** 6ft 4in **Wt** 14st 0lb **Signed from** Charleroi, November 2001, £1.5m

CLAUDIO REYNA (midfield) **Born** July 20, 1973, Springfield, New Jersey **Ht** 5ft 9in **Wt** 11st 5lb **Signed from** Sunderland, August 2003, £2.5m

DAVID SEAMAN (goalkeeper) **Born** September 19, 1963, Rotherham **Ht** 6ft 3in **Wt** 13st 0lb **Signed from** Arsenal, June 2003, free

TREVOR SINCLAIR (midfield) **Born** March 2, 1973, Dulwich **Ht** 5ft 10in **Wt** 12st 5lb **Signed from** West Ham United, July 2003, £2.5m

DAVID SOMMEIL (defender) **Born** August 10, 1974, Guadeloupe **Ht** 5ft 11in **Wt** 11st 6lb **Signed from** Bordeaux, January 2003, £3.5m

ANTOINE SIBIERSKI (midfield) **Born** August 5, 1974, Lille **Ht** 6ft 2in **Wt** 12st 6lb **Signed from** RC Lens, August 2003, £700,000

KEVIN STUHR-ELLEGAARD (goalkeeper) **Born** May 23, 1983, Copenhagen **Ht** 6ft 5in **Wt** 14st 13lb **Signed from** Farum BK, Denmark, £750,000

SUN JIHAI (defender) **Born** September 30, 1977, Dalian, China **Ht** 5ft 10in **Wt** 10st 12lb **Signed from** Crystal Palace, February 2002, £2m

MICHAEL TARNAT (defender) **Born** October 27, 1969, Hilden, Germany **Ht** 6ft 1in **Wt** 12st 6lb **Signed from** Bayern Munich, June 2003, free

DANNY TIATTO (midfield) **Born** May 22, 1973, Melbourne **Ht** 5ft 7in **Wt** 12st 0lb **Signed from** FC Baden, Switzerland, July 1998, £300,000

DANIEL VAN BUYTEN (defender) **Born** February 7, 1978, Chimay, Belgium **Ht** 6ft 4in **Wt** 13st 6lb **Signed from** Marseilles (loan), January 2004

PAULO WANCHOPE (forward) **Born** July 31, 1976, Heredia, Costa Rica **Ht** 6ft 4in **Wt** 12st 5lb **Signed from** West Ham United, August 2000, £3.65m

NICKY WEAVER (goalkeeper) **Born** March 2, 1979, Sheffield **Ht** 6ft 4in **Wt** 13st 6lb **Signed from** Mansfield Town, May 1997, £200,000

GLENN WHELAN (midfield) **Born** January 13, 1984, Dublin **Ht** 5ft 10in **Wt** 11st 13lb **Signed from** trainee, August 2001

GERARD WIEKENS (defender) **Born** February 25, 1973, Tolhuiswyk, Holland **Ht** 6ft 0in **Wt** 13st 4lb **Signed from** SC Veendam, the Netherlands, July 1997, £500,000

SHAUN WRIGHT-PHILLIPS (midfield) **Born** October 25, 1981, Greenwich **Ht** 5ft 6in **Wt** 10st 1lb **Signed from** trainee, October 1998

● City's 4-1 win against Manchester United ended a run of 11 games without a victory at their new home.

● City have not beaten Chelsea in 12 attempts . . .

● . . . and have won just one of their past 17 matches against Middlesbrough.

● City dropped to sixteenth

place from ninth in 2002-03, yet their goal difference improved by eight.

● City have won one of their past ten home games at home to Spurs.

● City have not won any of their past 25 games away to Manchester United.

Bill Edgar

GOALSCORERS

	Prem	FAC	CC	Euro	Total
N Anelka	17 (4p)	4 (1p)	-	4 (2p)	25 (7p)
J Barton	1	-	-	-	1
P Bosvelt	-	1	-	-	1
S Distin	2	1	-	-	3
R Fowler	7	1	1	1	10
D Huckerby	-	-	-	1	1
J Macken	1	2	1	-	4
C Negouai	-	-	-	1	1
C Reyna	1	-	-	-	1
A Sibierski	5	1	-	1	7
T Sinclair	1	-	-	1	2
D Sommeil	1	-	-	1	2
Sun Jihai	1	-	-	1	2
M Tarnat	3	1	-	-	4
P Wanchope	6	-	-	-	6
S Wright-Phillips	7	1	2	1	11
Own goals	2	-	-	-	2

Sunday March 14
MANCHESTER UNITED (h)
Won 4-1   HT 2-1   Att 47,284   Position 15th
Knocked out of Europe by FC Porto, Manchester United are now surely out of the title race too, 12 points behind Arsenal after this humiliating defeat. They are unlucky to be behind at half-time, hitting the woodwork twice through Ronaldo, but are well-beaten by the end, Wright-Phillips having the last word for a delirious Manchester City.

James — Dunne, Van Buyten, Distin — Wright-Phillips, Reyna (Bosvelt ht), McManaman (Sinclair ht), Tarnat — Sibierski (Sun 84) — Fowler, Macken *Subs not used* Arason, Wanchope *Booked* Distin
Scorers **Fowler 3, Macken 32, Sinclair 73, Wright-Phillips 90**
Referee **S Bennett**

Monday March 22
LEEDS UNITED (a)
Lost 1-2   HT 1-1   Att 36,998   Position 16th
James — Dunne, Van Buyten, Distin — Wright-Phillips, Barton, Bosvelt (Sun 82) Tarnat — Sibierski — Anelka, Fowler *Subs not used* Arason, Wanchope, Macken, Sinclair *Booked* Sun *Sent off* Van Buyten 75
Scorer **Anelka 44**
Report page 160

Saturday March 27
FULHAM (h)
Drew 0-0   HT 0-0   Att 46,522   Position 15th
Kevin Keegan is absent, nursing a bad back under doctor's orders, and the City manager misses a dismal game notable only for two rejected penalty appeals, one to each side. Chris Coleman, happier with Fulham's performance, insists that City are too good to go down.

James — Sun, Dunne, Distin, Tarnat — Wright-Phillips, Reyna, Bosvelt, Sibierski (Sinclair 73) — Fowler (Macken 64), Anelka (Wanchope 64) *Subs not used* Arason, Barton *Booked* Distin
Referee **J Winter**

Sunday April 4
ASTON VILLA (a)
Drew 1-1   HT 0-1   Att 37,602   Position 15th
James — Sun, Dunne, Distin, Tarnat — Wright-Phillips, Reyna (Sinclair 73), Bosvelt, McManaman — Macken (Fowler 67), Wanchope (Anelka 67) *Subs not used* Barton, Arason *Booked* Dunne, Sun
Scorer **Distin 82**
Report page 79

Saturday April 10
WOLVERHAMPTON WANDERERS (h)
Drew 3-3   HT 2-2   Att 47,248   Position 15th
Wolves blow perhaps their last chance of closing the gap at the bottom. Ahead 2-0, they let the advantage slip and then miss a penalty, James saving from Cameron. Dave Jones's side regain the lead through Camara, only to concede a last-minute equaliser in a rollercoaster match.

James — Sun, Dunne, Distin, Tarnat — Wright-Phillips, Bosvelt (Barton 72), Sibierski, McManaman — Anelka, Fowler (Wanchope 72) *Subs not used* Arason, Macken, Sinclair
Scorers **Anelka 25, Sibierski 39, Wright-Phillips 90**
Referee **J Winter**

Monday April 12
TOTTENHAM HOTSPUR (a)
Drew 1-1   HT 1-0   Att 35,282   Position 15th
James — Sun (Sinclair 73), Dunne, Distin, Tarnat — Wright-Phillips, Bosvelt, Sibierski, McManaman — Anelka, Fowler (Wanchope 64) *Subs not used* Arason, Macken, Barton *Booked* Fowler
Scorer **Anelka 25**
Report page 257

PLAYER OF THE SEASON
Shaun Wright-Phillips

There really was no contest for this accolade — Wright-Phillips was by far and away City's best player in 2003-04. Nicolas Anelka may have scored more goals but he squandered several easy chances in important games and his attitude was sometimes questionable. Wright-Phillips was indefatigable in attack and defence and gave many international full backs (Ashley Cole, of Arsenal, and Wayne Bridge, of Chelsea, spring readily to mind) a torrid time — quite why he didn't make Sven-Goran Eriksson's squad for the European Championship is a mystery. Best moment? His brilliant solo fourth goal and ragdoll celebration (the poor chap was so exhausted he could barely stand up) against Manchester United.
Paul Connolly

Saturday April 17
SOUTHAMPTON (h)
Lost 1-3   HT 0-1   Att 47,152   Position 17th
Kevin Keegan returns to the dugout after four games on the injured list, just in time to see City slip to seventeenth, only two points above the drop zone. Beattie and Phillips score with headers before Anelka — guilty of a bad miss at 0-0 — replies, but Phillips kills them off as Southampton cruise to victory.

James — Sun, Dunne, Distin, Tarnat — Wright-Phillips, Bosvelt (Reyna 60), Sibierski, McManaman (Sinclair 11) — Anelka, Fowler (Wanchope 60) *Subs not used* Arason, Macken *Booked* Dunne
Scorer **Anelka 78**
Referee **G Barber**

Saturday April 24
LEICESTER CITY (a)
Drew 1-1   HT 1-0   Att 31,457   Position 17th
James — Sun, Dunne, Distin, Tarnat — Wright-Phillips, Bosvelt, Barton, Sinclair — Wanchope, Anelka (Sibierski 90) *Subs not used* Reyna, Macken, Arason, Jordan *Booked* Barton, Tarnat, Wanchope
Scorer **Tarnat 45**
Report page 172

Saturday May 1
NEWCASTLE UNITED (h)
Won 1-0   HT 0-0   Att 47,226   Position 17th
The match of the day, affecting both relegation and Uefa Cup places, deservedly goes the way of the strugglers thanks to Wanchope's deft header. Nothing is resolved as far as Newcastle are concerned, but City's victory sends Leicester City down and all but condemns Wolves. Leeds United's fate may be sealed the next day.

James — Sun, Dunne, Distin, Tarnat — Wright-Phillips, Barton, Bosvelt, Sinclair (Reyna 72) — Wanchope (Macken 90), Anelka *Subs not used* Sibierski, Fowler, Arason *Booked* Bosvelt
Scorer **Wanchope 59**
Referee **M Halsey**

Saturday May 8
MIDDLESBROUGH (a)
Lost 1-2   HT 1-2   Att 34,734   Position 17th
James — Sun, Dunne, Distin, Tarnat — Wright-Phillips, Bosvelt (Sibierski 61), Reyna, Barton — Anelka (Macken 74), Wanchope (Elliott 74) *Subs not used* Arason, Jordan *Booked* Tarnat
Scorer **Wanchope 35**
Report page 216

Saturday May 15
EVERTON (h)
Won 5-1   HT 3-0   Att 47,284   Position 16th
The pressure off, City relax and inflict a heavy beating on a poor Everton side, who finish one place outside the relegation zone. Kevin Keegan then announces he will quit — but only after he has completed the two years left on his contract.

James — Sun, Dunne, Distin, Tarnat — Wright-Phillips, Bosvelt, Barton (Sibierski 85), Reyna (Jordan 82) — Wanchope (Macken 79), Anelka *Subs not used* Fowler, Arason *Booked* Barton
Scorers **Wanchope 16, 30, Anelka 41, Sibierski 89, Wright-Phillips 90**
Referee **S Dunn**

MANCHESTER UNITED

PREMIERSHIP

	P	W	D	L	F	A	GD	Pts
Arsenal	38	26	12	0	73	26	47	90
Chelsea	38	24	7	7	67	30	37	79
Man Utd	38	23	6	9	64	35	29	75
Liverpool	38	16	12	10	55	37	18	60
Newcastle	38	13	17	8	52	40	12	56
Aston Villa	38	15	11	12	48	44	4	56
Charlton	38	14	11	13	51	51	0	53
Bolton	38	14	11	13	48	56	-8	53
Fulham	38	14	10	14	52	46	6	52
Birmingham	38	12	14	12	43	48	-5	50
Middlesbro	38	13	9	16	44	52	-8	48
Southampton	38	12	11	15	44	45	-1	47
Portsmouth	38	12	9	17	47	54	-7	45
Tottenham	38	13	6	19	47	57	-10	45
Blackburn	38	12	8	18	51	59	-8	44
Man City	38	9	14	15	55	54	1	41
Everton	38	9	12	17	45	57	-12	39
Leicester	38	6	15	17	48	65	-17	33
Leeds	38	8	9	21	40	79	-39	33
Wolves	38	7	12	19	38	77	-39	33

FA CUP
Winners

CARLING CUP
Fourth round

CHAMPIONS LEAGUE
First knockout round

Time to go?: the future of Sir Alex Ferguson as Manchester United manager was the subject of feverish debate during the season

Sunday August 10 2003
ARSENAL
Community Shield (Cardiff)
Drew 1-1 (won 4-3 on pens)   HT 1-1   Att 59,293
The big guns lock horns in pitch-side temperatures of
41C and it is United who triumph in the heat of a penalty
shoot-out. Howard's saves from Van Bronckhorst and
Pires proving decisive. Silvestre and Henry trade early
goals, but Arsenal reach an unwanted landmark when
Jeffers becomes the 50th player sent off under Arsene
Wenger after kicking out at Phil Neville.

Howard — P Neville (Forlan 79), Ferdinand, Silvestre,
Fortune (O'Shea 69) — Solskjaer, Keane, Butt
(Djemba-Djemba 60), Scholes — Van Nistelrooy, Giggs
Subs not used Bellion, Carroll, Richardson, Fletcher
Booked P Neville, Fortune, Scholes
Scorer **Silvestre 15**
Referee **S Bennett**

Saturday August 16
BOLTON WANDERERS (h)
Won 4-0   HT 1-0   Att 67,647   Position 2nd
A handsome win, a Premiership and club record for Van
Nistelrooy, who scores for the ninth successive league
match, and a double for Giggs — the first a
Beckham-esque free kick — are all overshadowed by
Ronaldo's debut, the substitute stealing the show and
helping to put Bolton on the bottom of the first table.

Howard — P Neville, Ferdinand, Silvestre, Fortune —
Keane, Butt (Ronaldo 61) — Solskjaer
(Djemba-Djemba 67), Giggs (Forlan 80), Scholes —
Van Nistelrooy *Subs not used* O'Shea, Carroll
Scorers **Giggs 35, 74, Scholes 77, Van Nistelrooy 87**
Referee **P Durkin**

Saturday August 23
NEWCASTLE UNITED (a)
Won 2-1   HT 0-1   Att 52,165   Position 1st
Howard — P Neville, Ferdinand, Silvestre, O'Shea —
Solskjaer (Ronaldo 77), Keane, Djemba-Djemba, Scholes
— Giggs (Forlan 90) — Van Nistelrooy *Subs not used*
Carroll, Kleberson, Fletcher *Booked* Solskjaer,
Van Nistelrooy
Scorers **Van Nistelrooy 51, Scholes 59**
Report page 218

Wednesday August 27
WOLVERHAMPTON WANDERERS (h)
Won 1-0   HT 1-0   Att 67,648   Position 2nd
Sir Alex Ferguson admits he made "too many changes"
after United struggle to overcome the bottom side, who
could have caused a huge upset had Camara not fluffed
two first-half chances on his full Wolves debut.

Howard — G Neville, Keane, O'Shea, P Neville — Solskjaer
(Bellion 85), Kleberson (Scholes 67), Djemba-Djemba,
Ronaldo (Giggs 67) — Forlan — Van Nistelrooy *Subs not
used* Carroll, Fletcher *Booked* O'Shea, G Neville
Scorer **O'Shea 10**
Referee **G Poll**

Sunday August 31
SOUTHAMPTON (a)
Lost 0-1   HT 0-0   Att 32,066   Position 2nd
Howard — G Neville, O'Shea, Silvestre, P Neville
(Fortune 89) — Kleberson (Ronaldo 67), Keane,
Djemba-Djemba (Butt 77), Giggs — Van Nistelrooy,
Forlan *Subs not used* Carroll, Bellion
Report page 240

IT WAS THE SEASON MANCHESTER UNITED took the title
from Arsenal. Unfortunately the title in question was the "boring,
boring" one. Sure, United finished third in the league with 75 points
— enough to have won them the Premiership in four other seasons
since its inception. They won the FA Cup for a record-extending
eleventh time. Were it not for a visually impaired Russian linesman
at Old Trafford ruling out Paul Scholes's second goal, they would
have knocked FC Porto, the eventual winners, out of the European
Cup. And in three matches against Arsenal (one win, two draws, one
crossbar dented by Ruud van Nistelrooy's penalty), they made
Arsene Wenger's "immortal" team look decidedly human.

But forget for a moment about always looking on the bright side
of life. United were boring and well beaten, hoist by their own high
standards of the past decade. They finished an unheard-of 15 points
behind Arsenal and for the first time in 14 seasons were out of the
title race before the Easter bunny appeared, never mind the fat lady
sang. They suffered more Premiership defeats (nine) than ever
before, the 4-1 thrashing away to Manchester City and the debacle
away to rock-bottom Wolverhampton Wanderers competing to be
remembered as United's most embarrassing Premiership result. And
for the first time in eight years United were not in the last eight of
the European Cup — perhaps that Russian linesman was only
performing a mercy killing to avoid worse pain later.

United's biggest achievement was to stop somebody else winning
everything. The FA Cup semi-final at Villa Park, which spoilt
Arsenal's bid to emulate United's unique treble, was the high point
for both team and fans, far more so than victory in the final over the
toothless lions of Millwall. Sir Alex Ferguson once said that his
greatest achievement was to "knock Liverpool off their f***ing
perch". But in 2003-04, United came closer to matching the dead
parrot Liverpool teams of the past decade: capable of winning the
odd cup or "beating anybody on their day", but not up to sustaining
a title challenge.

Where did it go wrong, after the exhilarating championship
triumph of 2003? Most assessments tend to round up the usual
suspects, from the manager's legal dispute with John Magnier and
J. P. McManus (now major United shareholders), through the fallout
from David Beckham's departure, to the Rio Ferdinand drugs test
fiasco.

But these extraneous factors look more like excuses than
explanations for United's failings. Whatever was going on in the
pages of the newspapers, the United boardroom or Ferdinand's
head, the underlying problem was on the pitch, where the

HONOURS BOARD

FOOTBALL LEAGUE
Champions 1908, 1911, 1952, 1956, 1957, 1965, 1967
Runners-up 1947, 1948, 1949, 1951, 1959, 1964, 1968, 1980, 1988, 1992
PREMIERSHIP
Champions 1993, 1994, 1996, 1997, 1999, 2000, 2001, 2003
Runners-up 1995, 1998
FA CUP
Winners 1909, 1948, 1963, 1977, 1983, 1985, 1990, 1994, 1996, 1999, 2004
Runners-up 1957, 1958, 1976, 1979, 1995
LEAGUE CUP
Winners 1992

Runners-up 1983, 1991, 1994, 2003
EUROPEAN CUP
Winners 1968, 1999
CUP WINNERS' CUP
Winners 1991

Record attendance (club match) 70,504 (v Aston Villa, first division, December 27, 1920) **Current capacity** 68,210
Record victory 10-0 (v Anderlecht, European Cup preliminary round, 2nd leg, September 26, 1956)
Record defeat 0-7 (v Blackburn Rovers, first division, April 10, 1926)

the multimillion-pound teams Ferguson put out were simply not good enough. That cannot be put down to the absence of Beckham, whose contribution to the previous season's title win was minimal at most. Nor is it good enough to blame it on the loss of Rio.

"The Ferdinand business killed us," Ferguson said. If so, United must have already been living on borrowed time. Like Beckham, Ferdinand's reputation as a United player seems to have grown since he stopped playing for them.

Before his eight-month suspension for missing a drugs test, the central defender had looked anything but a £30 million player, prone to costly mistakes at key moments. Ferdinand's biggest blunder, however, was starting his ban early (in the naive hope that the FA might let him have his ball back in time for the European Championship), weeks before the more talented but ring-rusty Wes Brown was ready to fill his boots.

With hindsight, the shocking thing is not that United slumped after Ferdinand started his suspension. It is that Ferguson's side were four points clear at the top beforehand. As the typically blunt Scholes said: "We said earlier in the season we weren't playing very well but, hopefully, by February and March we would start to go on a good run. But for some reason that never materialised."

The fact that they had won so many games probably said more

Saturday September 13
CHARLTON ATHLETIC (a)
Won 2-0   HT 0-0   Att 26,078   Position 2nd
Howard — G Neville, Ferdinand, O'Shea, Fortune (Silvestre 83) — P Neville, Keane (Solskjaer 60), Butt, Ronaldo — Giggs — Van Nistelrooy *Subs not used* Carroll, Djemba-Djemba, Forlan *Booked* P Neville, Butt
Scorer **Van Nistelrooy 62, 81**
Report page 113

Tuesday September 16
PANATHINAIKOS (h)
Champions League
Won 5-0   HT 4-0   Att 66,520
United equal their record Champions League victory with a first-half rout of the travel-sick Greeks, but lose Solskjaer to injury after he punishes a dreadful goalkeeping error with the third goal.

Howard — G Neville, Ferdinand, Silvestre, O'Shea (Fletcher 57) — Solskjaer (Bellion 45), P Neville, Butt (Djemba-Djemba 57), Fortune — Giggs — Van Nistelrooy *Subs not used* Keane, Ronaldo, Forlan, Carroll
Scorers **Silvestre 13, Fortune 15, Solskjaer 33, Butt 40, Djemba-Djemba 83**
Referee **A Sars (France)**

Sunday September 21
ARSENAL (h)
Drew 0-0   HT 0-0   Att 67,639   Position 3rd
This summit meeting is strangely uneventful until Vieira kicks out at Van Nistelrooy to incur a second booking and a red card — and mayhem is not far behind. The Dutchman hits the bar with a last-minute penalty and the "Battle of Old Trafford" is sparked with Arsenal's excesses on the final whistle. The FA gets ready to throw the book at the league leaders.

Howard — G Neville, Ferdinand, Silvestre, O'Shea (Forlan 76) — Ronaldo, Keane, P Neville, Fortune — Giggs, Van Nistelrooy *Subs not used* Butt, Djemba-Djemba, Fletcher, Carroll *Booked* Fortune, Keane, Van Nistelrooy, Ronaldo
Referee **S Bennett**

Saturday September 27
LEICESTER CITY (a)
Won 4-1   HT 3-0   Att 32,044   Position 2nd
Howard — G Neville, Ferdinand, O'Shea — Fletcher, Keane (Djemba-Djemba ht) — P Neville, Giggs (Butt 62) — Scholes (Forlan 56) — Van Nistelrooy *Subs not used* Ronaldo, Carroll
Scorers **Keane 15, Van Nistelrooy 16, 45, 52**
Report page 165

Wednesday October 1
VfB STUTTGART (a)
Champions League
Lost 1-2   HT 0-0   Att 53,000
United are toppled by the Bundesliga leaders, who score twice in two minutes, through Szabics and Kuranyi, before Ronaldo collapses under a challenge from Hildebrand to earn a penalty that Van Nistelrooy converts. Howard saves a later spot kick from Meira.

Howard — G Neville, Ferdinand (Forlan 82), Silvestre, O'Shea (Fortune 65) — Scholes, Keane, P Neville, Ronaldo (Fletcher 90) — Giggs — Van Nistelrooy *Subs not used* Carroll, Butt, Djemba-Djemba, Bellion *Booked* G Neville
Scorer **Van Nistelrooy 67 (pen)**
Referee **M Bolognino (Italy)**

Saturday October 4
BIRMINGHAM CITY (h)
Won 3-0   HT 1-0   Att 67,633   Position 2nd
Steve Bruce takes his unbeaten side, boasting the best defensive record in the Premiership, to Old Trafford, but Birmingham's fate is sealed once Taylor is sent off for bringing down Scholes and Van Nistelrooy beats Bennett, the replacement goalkeeper, from the spot. Two days later, news breaks of Ferdinand's apparent failure to take a drugs test.

Howard — G Neville, Ferdinand, Silvestre, Fortune — Fletcher, Keane (Forlan 66), P Neville (Butt 71), Giggs — Scholes — Van Nistelrooy *Subs not used* Carroll, Ronaldo, O'Shea
Scorers **Van Nistelrooy 36 (pen), Scholes 57, Giggs 82**
Referee **M Dean**

Saturday October 18
LEEDS UNITED (a)
Won 1-0   HT 0-0   Att 40,153   Position 2nd
Howard — G Neville, Ferdinand, Silvestre, Fortune (O'Shea 40) — Fletcher (Forlan 60), Keane, P Neville, Ronaldo (Butt 90) — Scholes — Van Nistelrooy *Subs not used* Djemba-Djemba, Carroll *Booked* Ronaldo
Scorer **Keane 81**
Report page 156

Wednesday October 22
RANGERS (a)
Champions League
Won 1-0   HT 1-0   Att 48,730
First blood to United in the new "Battle of Britain", and via an unlikely source, Phil Neville finishing a fine run with only his eighth goal in 320 appearances. It is a deserved win, Sir Alex Ferguson's 50th in the Champions League.

Howard — G Neville, Ferdinand, Silvestre, O'Shea — P Neville (Butt 86), Keane, Fortune (Djemba-Djemba 90), Scholes — Giggs, Van Nistelrooy *Subs not used* Fletcher, Ronaldo, Bellion, Forlan, Carroll *Booked* Scholes, O'Shea
Scorer **P Neville 5**
Referee **A Frisk (Sweden)**

Saturday October 25
FULHAM (h)
Lost 1-3   HT 1-1   Att 67,727   Position 3rd
Sir Alex Ferguson begins a two-match touchline ban by watching from the directors' box as his side lose at home for the first time in more than a year. It is no fluke, either, an outstanding Fulham performance earning their first Old Trafford victory for 40 years — and all in front of a record Premiership attendance.

Howard — G Neville, Ferdinand, Silvestre (Fortune ht), O'Shea — Giggs, Djemba-Djemba (Bellion 80), Butt, Ronaldo (Forlan 69) — Van Nistelrooy, Forlan *Subs not used* Carroll, Fletcher *Booked* Fortune, Giggs, Djemba-Djemba, Forlan
Scorer **Forlan 45**
Referee **M Riley**

Tuesday October 28
LEEDS UNITED (a)
Carling Cup, 3rd rnd
Won 3-2 (aet; 1-1 after 90min)   HT 0-0   Att 37,546
Carroll — P Neville, G Neville, O'Shea, Fortune — Fletcher (Johnson 112), Djemba-Djemba, Butt, Richardson (Eagles 65) — Forlan, Bellion *Subs not used* Howard, Pugh, Lynch *Booked* G Neville, P Neville
Scorers **Bellion 78, Forlan 108, Djemba-Djemba 117**
Report page 156

Before his season turned sour, Ferdinand celebrates the victory at Ibrox

about the quality of the Premiership than about United. Even when they were winning, United were as dull as a December day in Manchester. Roy Keane struggled to stay the right side of over-the-hill, Ryan Giggs seemed to be undergoing a turning-thirty identity crisis, even Ruud van Nistelrooy appeared listless in the second half of the season. With the exception of Tim Howard and Louis Saha, the latter a mid-season arrival, none of the players whom Ferguson bought with his Beckham windfall really rose to the challenge.

Slip the red-tinted glasses back on, however, and it is just possible to see 2003-04 as a seedling year for a future crop of United winners. Cristiano Ronaldo, 19, and Darren Fletcher, 20, had grown into their roles by the FA Cup Final and Ferguson could point to half a dozen others under the age of 25 who he sees as the nucleus of a first team to come. Shades of 1995, "you win nothing with kids" and all that? Perhaps, although there is little sign as yet of an Eric Cantona to make men of these boys.

Here, however, is an historical footnote. Thirty years ago, at the end of season 1973-74, Manchester United were relegated to the old second division — and Leeds United took the championship. A poor season, as every football fan understands, is a relative concept.

THE MANAGER ## Sir Alex Ferguson

Many pundits took rather too obvious pleasure in comparing Sir Alex Ferguson to a once-great third-term prime minister now in terminal decline and denial, threatening to go on and on and on while his empire crumbled around him. Distracted and coach-less, he certainly did not look like the manager who won the 2003 championship by sheer willpower. But there is no sign yet of men in grey suits willing to tell him to go. Ferguson may no longer look like the Premiership's irresistible force, but he still appears to be the immovable object of Old Trafford. Were he to confound the critics again and make another winning comeback, it would be his most remarkable achievement.

Mick Hume

APPEARANCES

	Prem	FAC	CC	Euro	Total
P Bardsley	-	0 (1)	1	-	1 (1)
D Bellion	4 (10)	1 (1)	2	0 (4)	7 (15)
W Brown	15 (2)	5 (1)	-	2	22 (3)
N Butt	12 (9)	3 (2)	2	4 (1)	22* (12)
R Carroll	6	2 (1)	2	1	11 (1)
E Djemba-Djemba	10 (5)	0 (1)	1	1 (3)	12 (10†)
C Eagles	-	-	0 (2)	-	0 (2)
R Ferdinand	20	-	-	6	27*
D Fletcher	17 (5)	4 (1)	2	3 (3)	26 (9)
D Forlan	10 (14)	2	1	2 (2)	15 (17†)
Q Fortune	18 (5)	3	1	6 (1)	29* (6)
R Giggs	29 (4)	5	-	8	43* (4)
T Howard	32	4	-	7	44*
E Johnson	-	-	0 (1)	-	0 (1)
R Keane	25 (3)	4 (1)	-	4	34* (4)
Kleberson	10 (2)	1	1	1 (1)	13 (3)
D Nardiello	-	-	0 (1)	-	0 (1)
G Neville	30	4	1	7	42
P Neville	29 (2)	2 (1)	1	7	40* (3)
J O'Shea	32 (1)	6	2	6 (1)	46 (3†)
D Pugh	-	0 (1)	1	-	1 (1)
K Richardson	-	0 (1)	2	-	2 (1)
C Ronaldo	15 (14)	5	1	3 (2)	24 (16)
L Saha	9 (3)	-	-	1 (1)	10 (4)
P Scholes	24 (4)	6	-	5	36* (4)
M Silvestre	33 (1)	5	-	6	45* (1)
O G Solskjaer	7 (6)	1 (2)	-	1 (1)	10* (9)
P Tierney	-	-	1	-	1
R van Nistelrooy	31 (1)	3 (1)	-	7	42* (2)

(* denotes appearance and † denotes substitute appearance in Community Shield)

Saturday November 1
PORTSMOUTH (h)
Won 3-0   HT 1-0   Att 67,639   Position 3rd
Only Forlan's goal separates well-matched sides before a double substitution works wonders for United, Ronaldo bending in a free kick for his first goal for the club and Keane curling a left-foot shot from the edge of the area. Portsmouth deserve better than a second successive 3-0 league defeat.

Howard — G Neville, Ferdinand, O'Shea, Fortune — Fletcher, Djemba-Djemba (Keane 75), Butt, Giggs (Bellion 79) — Van Nistelrooy, Forlan (Ronaldo 75) *Subs not used* Carroll, P Neville
Scorers **Forlan 37, Ronaldo 80, Keane 82**
Referee **N Barry**

Tuesday November 4
RANGERS (h)
Champions League
Won 3-0   HT 2-0   Att 66,707
Van Nistelrooy, whose so-called "drought" stretches to four games, scores twice, albeit with a lucky rebound and a tap-in, Forlan's superb volley having put United on the way to a second victory over the Scottish champions.

Howard — G Neville, Ferdinand, Silvestre, Fortune — Ronaldo, Keane, P Neville, Giggs (Kleberson 67) — Van Nistelrooy (Fletcher 77), Forlan (Bellion 67) *Subs not used* Carroll, Butt, Djemba-Djemba, O'Shea
Scorers **Forlan 6, Van Nistelrooy 43, 60**
Referee **P Collina (Italy)**

Sunday November 9
LIVERPOOL (a)
Won 2-1   HT 0-0   Att 44,159   Position 3rd
Howard — G Neville, Ferdinand, Silvestre, O'Shea — Giggs, Keane, P Neville, Fortune (Fletcher 82) — Van Nistelrooy, Forlan *Subs not used* Butt, Djemba-Djemba, Ronaldo, Carroll *Booked* P Neville, Van Nistelrooy
Scorer **Giggs 59, 70**
Report page 177

Saturday November 22
BLACKBURN ROVERS (h)
Won 2-1   HT 2-0   Att 67,748   Position 3rd
Van Nistelrooy follows up his midweek hat-trick against Scotland with the opener, then sets up Kleberson's first United goal. Another record Premiership crowd fills Old Trafford 90 minutes after England's rugby World Cup final win. Emerton is the only Aussie with something to smile about after he replies for Blackburn.

Howard — G Neville, Ferdinand, Silvestre, O'Shea — Keane, P Neville — Bellion (Ronaldo 73), Kleberson, Fortune (Giggs 85) — Van Nistelrooy (Forlan 89) *Subs not used* Butt, Carroll
Scorers **Van Nistelrooy 24, Kleberson 38**
Referee **M Halsey**

Wednesday November 26
PANATHINAIKOS (a)
Champions League
Won 1-0   HT 0-0   Att 6,890
Needing a point to qualify, a depleted United side get all three in a desperately dull match against a side already eliminated, Forlan providing the decisive moment after being put through by Bellion.

Howard — O'Shea, Ferdinand, Silvestre, Fortune — Ronaldo, Fletcher (Bellion 75), Butt, Kleberson, Giggs — Forlan *Subs not used* Carroll, G Neville, P Neville, Van Nistelrooy, Pugh, Tierney *Booked* Ferdinand
Scorer **Forlan 85**
Referee **J Wegereef (the Netherlands)**

Sunday November 30
CHELSEA (a)
Lost 0-1   HT 0-1   Att 41,932   Position 3rd
Howard — G Neville, Ferdinand, Silvestre, O'Shea — Giggs,
P Neville (Kleberson 77), Keane, Fortune
(Ronaldo 72) — Van Nistelrooy, Forlan *Subs not used*
Carroll, Butt, Bellion *Booked* Keane
Report page 126

Wednesday December 3
WEST BROMWICH ALBION (a)
Carling Cup, 4th rnd
Lost 0-2   HT 0-1   Att 25,282
United's novices are well beaten by the first-division
leaders, for whom Haas and Dobie are on target.
Carroll saves Koumas's penalty in between as United
suffer their first defeat to non-Premiership opposition
for six years.
Carroll — Bardsley, O'Shea, Tierney, Pugh — Ronaldo
(Eagles 77), Fletcher, Butt, Kleberson (Nardiello 77),
Richardson — Bellion *Subs not used* Jones, Wood,
Williams *Booked* Bardsley
Referee **J Winter**

Saturday December 6
ASTON VILLA (h)
Won 4-0   HT 2-0   Att 67,621   Position 3rd
Sir Alex Ferguson has had treatment for a heart murmur
during the week, but there is no added stress as
Van Nistelrooy scores twice before making way for Forlan,
who does the same in stoppage time. Villa go down with
barely a whimper.
Howard — G Neville, Ferdinand, Silvestre, Fortune —
Ronaldo, P Neville (Scholes 59), Keane, Giggs
(Bellion 59) — Kleberson — Van Nistelrooy (Forlan 72)
Subs not used Carroll, O'Shea
Scorers **Van Nistelrooy 16, 45, Forlan 90, 90**
Referee **S Dunn**

Tuesday December 9
VfB STUTTGART (h)
Champions League
Won 2-0   HT 1-0   Att 67,141
United get the win they need to finish top of group E.
Van Nistelrooy heads in a cross from Giggs for his 28th
European goal in 30 matches, equalling Denis Law's club
record, and returns the compliment to the Welshman in
the second half.
Carroll — G Neville, Ferdinand, Silvestre, O'Shea —
Fletcher, P Neville, Scholes (Djemba-Djemba 79), Fortune
— Giggs (Bellion 71) — Van Nistelrooy (Forlan 71) *Subs
not used* Howard, Keane, Butt, Kleberson *Booked*
Fortune, Scholes
Scorers **Van Nistelrooy 45, Giggs 58**
Referee **E Poulat (France)**

Saturday December 13
MANCHESTER CITY (h)
Won 3-1   HT 2-0   Att 67,645   Position 1st
A hat-trick of headers in the midday kick-off puts United
back on top and they stay there with Chelsea's home
defeat by Bolton. United deserve their victory, but are
grateful to three fine saves by Howard from Fowler,
Anelka and McManaman, plus a goalline clearance by
Scholes.
Howard — G Neville, Ferdinand, Silvestre, O'Shea —
Kleberson (Ronaldo 73), Keane, P Neville, Giggs —
Scholes — Van Nistelrooy *Subs not used* Carroll, Butt,
Fortune, Forlan
Scorers **Scholes 7, 73, Van Nistelrooy 34**
Referee **M Halsey**

MATCH OF THE SEASON

Everton 3 Manchester United 4
Goodison Park, Saturday February 7 2004
Oilver Kay

FOOTBALL, BLOODY HELL. THOSE were the immortal words
uttered by a breathless Sir Alex Ferguson — then plain old Alex
Ferguson — when someone shoved a microphone under his nose
within seconds of his team's dramatic European Cup final triumph
over Bayern Munich in May 1999, but rarely in recent times has it
been football that has reduced the Manchester United manager to
such banalities. Drug tests, bloody hell, perhaps, or stud fees, bloody
hell, but not football.

Off-the-field issues continue to dominate the agenda at Old
Trafford, where Ferguson's position remains under genuine threat
from the club's biggest shareholders, but, for 90 pulsating minutes
on Saturday, it was all about the game.

Yes, there was also controversy — with three United players
reported to the police by Everton fans for their reaction to the
89th-minute winner by Ruud van Nistelrooy, who had earlier scored
his hundredth goal for the club — but, if one can overlook those
various issues, if only for a moment, this was one hell of a game.

In recent times, United have been characterised by organisation
and hard work rather than the flowing football on which their
reputation is based, but on Saturday it was the exact opposite. For
the first 45 minutes, as they coasted into a 3-0 lead, they were
magnificent — "probably our best performance away from home in
years", according to Ferguson — but their chaotic defending was
fully exploited in the second half by Everton, who, astonishingly,
restored parity before Van Nistelrooy had the final say.

To fight back from three goals down, as Everton did, requires guts,
which Manchester City showed in abundance away to Tottenham
Hotspur last Wednesday, but to concede three goals in 26 minutes
and then to muster the energy for one last push requires an
indomitable spirit of the type that is unique to United.

"When you're 3-0 up at half-time and end up drawing, it's a
massive disappointment, so to bounce back and win in the end was
great," Van Nistelrooy said. "Your lead is getting cut from 3-0 to 3-1
to 3-2 and you think: 'Oh God, it's happening to us.' At 3-3 we
couldn't believe it, but to get over that disappointment and show the
character to bounce back and win says something about us."

What it also says is that United have the firepower to compensate
for a defence that is leaking goals at an alarming rate. They have
conceded five goals in their past two games, having been pegged
back from 2-0 up against Southampton and 3-0 up away to Everton,
but have won on both occasions.

Ferguson should be worried by the form of Wes Brown, who has
lacked confidence on his return from injury, but Van Nistelrooy and

David Unsworth is reduced to the role of spectator as Ruud van Nistelrooy cracks the ball home to put United 2-0 ahead at Goodison

Louis Saha have glossed over the cracks left by Rio Ferdinand's suspension.

Van Nistelrooy has never complained about having to carry the goalscoring burden for United over his first two seasons at the club, but he looks delighted with the early success of his partnership with Saha, who scored two of the goals that seemed to have put the game beyond Everton on Saturday. "To have scored six in your first two games together is very rare for a new partnership," Van Nistelrooy said. In truth, they could each have claimed a hat-trick in the first half, so often did United cut their way through an inept home defence. Saha scored the first on nine minutes, after beating the offside trap, but Van Nistelrooy missed a clear opportunity either side of his 24th-minute goal, again courtesy of some sluggish defending, before Saha appeared to put the game beyond doubt five minutes later with a crisp right-foot shot.

David Moyes made a triple substitution at half-time, more out of desperation than expectation, but, as much as Wayne Rooney impressed after his belated introduction, it was the less-heralded Gary Naysmith who made the greater impact.

His excellent set-piece delivery, to which United's defence had no answer, yielded a far-post header from David Unsworth and an own goal from John O'Shea before Kevin Kilbane, to the astonishment of

Sunday December 21
TOTTENHAM HOTSPUR (a)
Won 2-1   HT 2-0   Att 35,910   Position 1st
Howard — G Neville, Ferdinand, Silvestre, O'Shea — Fletcher (Ronaldo 79), Keane (Butt 83), P Neville, Giggs — Scholes — Van Nistelrooy *Subs not used* Carroll, Forlan, Fortune *Booked* Scholes, Giggs
Scorers **O'Shea 15, Van Nistelrooy 25**
Report page 254

Friday December 26
EVERTON (h)
Won 3-2   HT 2-1   Att 67,642   Position 1st
A handful of stars are rested, but United stay top with a deserved if narrow victory. Ronaldo is Everton's tormentor-in-chief — Rooney is cautioned for a scything tackle on the winger — as Bellion's first Premiership goal makes it 3-1 before Ferguson's headed riposte in the last minute.

Howard — G Neville, Ferdinand, Silvestre (Djemba-Djemba 72), O'Shea (Scholes 50) — Butt — Bellion, Kleberson, Fortune, Ronaldo — Forlan *Subs not used* Carroll, Van Nistelrooy, Giggs
Scorers **Butt 9, Kleberson 44, Bellion 68**
Referee **M Dean**

Sunday December 28
MIDDLESBROUGH (a)
Won 1-0   HT 1-0   Att 34,738   Position 1st
Howard — G Neville, Ferdinand, Silvestre, Fortune — Fletcher, Keane, P Neville, Giggs — Scholes — Van Nistelrooy (Butt 84) *Subs not used* Carroll, Kleberson, Brown, Forlan *Booked* P Neville, Fletcher
Sent off Fletcher 65
Scorer **Mills 14 (og)**
Report page 212

Sunday January 4 2004
ASTON VILLA (a)
FA Cup, 3rd rnd
Won 2-1   HT 0-1   Att 40,371
Howard — G Neville, Brown, Silvestre, O'Shea (Keane 55) — Kleberson (Fletcher 84), Butt, Scholes, Fortune (Van Nistelrooy 55) — Forlan, Giggs *Subs not used* Bellion, Carroll *Booked* Silvestre
Scorer **Scholes 64, 68**
Report page 77

Wednesday January 7
BOLTON WANDERERS (a)
Won 2-1   HT 2-0   Att 27,668   Position 1st
Howard — G Neville, Ferdinand, Silvestre, O'Shea — Fletcher, P Neville, Keane (Butt 81), Scholes — Giggs (Fortune 83) — Van Nistelrooy *Subs not used* Kleberson, Forlan, Carroll
Scorers **Scholes 24, Van Nistelrooy 39**
Report page 106

Sunday January 11
NEWCASTLE UNITED (h)
Drew 0-0   HT 0-0   Att 67,622   Position 1st
With weekend reports hinting at irregularities in some of their transfer dealings — the club denies any wrongdoing — Manchester United have to be content with a point. It might have been none had Paul Durkin not failed to penalise Howard's trip on Shearer, the referee bravely admitting to his mistake in not awarding a penalty.

Howard — G Neville (Bellion 80), Ferdinand, Silvestre, O'Shea — Kleberson, Keane, P Neville (Fortune 68), Scholes — Giggs (Forlan ht) — Van Nistelrooy *Subs not used* Carroll, Butt *Booked* P Neville, G Neville
Referee **P Durkin**

Saturday January 17
WOLVERHAMPTON WANDERERS (a)
Lost 0-1   HT 0-0   Att 29,396   Position 1st
Howard — O'Shea, Ferdinand (Brown 50), Silvestre, Fortune — Fletcher (Bellion 65), Keane, P Neville (Forlan 68), Ronaldo — Scholes — Van Nistelrooy *Subs not used* Butt, Carroll
Report page 265

Sunday January 25
NORTHAMPTON TOWN (a)
FA Cup, 4th rnd
Won 3-0   HT 1-0   Att 7,356
Prospects of a huge upset increase when Harper saves Forlan's penalty, but after the build-up features endless replays of George's "Six of the Best" against the same opponents in 1970, three of the scruffiest goals imaginable see off the third-division side.

Carroll — O'Shea, Brown, Silvestre (Bardsley 72), Fortune (Pugh 88) — Ronaldo, Butt, Fletcher, Scholes (Richardson 72) — Bellion, Forlan *Subs not used* Howard, Keane *Booked* Bardsley
Scorers **Silvestre 34, Hargreaves 47 (og), Forlan 68**
Referee **S Bennett**

Saturday January 31
SOUTHAMPTON (h)
Won 3-2   HT 2-1   Att 67,758   Position 1st
Saha is off the mark at the first attempt, though his debut free kick owes everything to a deflection off Phillips. It starts a rollercoaster afternoon in front of a record Premiership crowd during which Southampton, having fought back from 2-0 down to 2-2, are finally undone by a controversial goal from Van Nistelrooy that reopens the old offside debate about interfering with play.

Howard — O'Shea, Brown, Silvestre, Fortune — Ronaldo (Butt 90), Keane, P Neville, Scholes — Van Nistelrooy, Saha (Fletcher 71) *Subs not used* Kleberson, Forlan, Carroll
Scorers **Saha 18, Scholes 37, Van Nistelrooy 61**
Referee **G Barber**

Saturday February 7
EVERTON (a)
Won 4-3   HT 3-0   Att 40,190   Position 2nd
Howard — G Neville, Brown, Silvestre, O'Shea — Fletcher (Ronaldo 80), Keane, Scholes, Giggs — Van Nistelrooy, Saha (Fortune 73) *Subs not used* Butt, Kleberson, Carroll
Scorers **Saha 9, 29, Van Nistelrooy 24, 89**
Report page 140

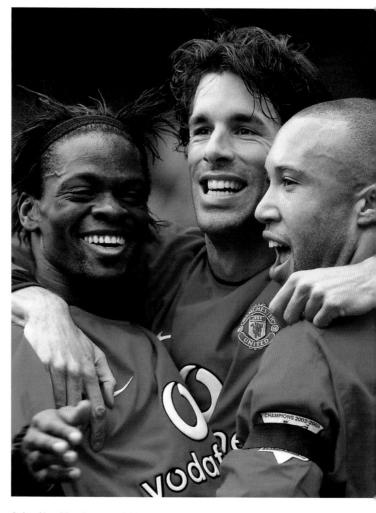

Saha, Van Nistelrooy and Silvestre are united by victory over Everton

all at Goodison Park, headed an equaliser on 75 minutes. At that point, Everton looked the more likely winners, but United regained the initiative after the introduction of Cristiano Ronaldo, whose perfect cross allowed Van Nistelrooy to head home with only one minute remaining.

The ensuing celebrations will be scrutinised by Everton, the police and the FA, after home fans accused Gary Neville, Roy Keane and Ronaldo of making offensive gestures, but, if ever such actions can be understood, if not excused, it is after a game as dramatic as this. Football, bloody hell.

EVERTON (4-4-2): N Martyn — T Hibbert, A Stubbs, D Unsworth, A Pistone (sub: G Naysmith, 46min) — S Watson (sub: W Rooney, 46), T Gravesen, L Carsley, K Kilbane — F Jeffers (sub: T Radzinski, 46), D Ferguson. **Substitutes not used:** T Linderoth, S Simonsen. **Booked:** Gravesen.
MANCHESTER UNITED (4-4-2): T Howard — G Neville, W Brown, M Silvestre, J O'Shea — D Fletcher (sub: C Ronaldo, 80), R Keane, P Scholes, R Giggs — R van Nistelrooy, L Saha (sub: Q Fortune, 73). **Substitutes not used:** N Butt, Kleberson, R Carroll.

STATS AND FACTS

● Manchester United have not lost any of the 14 games in which either Phil or Gary Neville has scored.

● Danny Murphy, of Liverpool, was the first player to convert a Premiership penalty at Old Trafford since Ruel Fox did so for Norwich City in late 1993. Three penalties were awarded against United in the league at the ground in between and all were missed.

● United became the eighth team in nine years to fail to win the title after leading the table on Christmas Day.

● No wonder it is one of their favourite venues: United won three times at Villa Park during the season, all in 2004. They beat Aston Villa in the league and FA Cup and Arsenal in an FA Cup semi-final.

● United are unbeaten in their past 16 domestic semi-finals,

11 in the FA Cup and five in the League Cup.

● The goalless match at home to Newcastle United in January was their first draw against a side other than Arsenal in 43 matches in all competitions.

● There have been only three winning margins of at least three goals in the FA Cup Final since 1974 — all by Manchester United. They beat Millwall 3-0 last season, Chelsea 4-0 in 1994 and Brighton 4-0 in a replay in 1983.

● Roy Keane appeared in his sixth FA Cup Final, a postwar record. He played for Nottingham Forest in the 1991 Final and for United in 1994, 1995, 1996 and 1999.

● None of United's past 95 away league games have finished goalless.

Bill Edgar

GOALSCORERS

	Prem	FAC	CC	Euro	Total
D Bellion	2	-	1	-	3
N Butt	1	-	-	1	2
E Djemba-Djemba	-	-	1	1	2
D Forlan	4	1	1	2	8
Q Fortune	-	-	-	2	2
R Giggs	7	-	-	1	8
R Keane	3	-	-	-	3
Kleberson	2	-	-	-	2
G Neville	2	-	-	-	2
P Neville	-	-	-	1	1
J O'Shea	2	-	-	-	2
C Ronaldo	4	2	-	-	6
L Saha	7	-	-	-	7
P Scholes	9	4	-	1	14
M Silvestre	-	1	-	1	3*
O G Solskjaer	-	-	-	1	1
R van Nistelrooy	20 (1p)	6 (1p)	-	4 (1p)	30 (3p)
Own goals	1	1	-	-	2
(† Total includes goal in Community Shield)					

Wednesday February 11
MIDDLESBROUGH (h)
Lost 2-3   HT 1-2   Att 67,346   Position 2nd
Off the pitch, John Magnier and J. P. McManus have increased their stake in the club. On it, United are hit by two headers from Juninho, the smallest player on the field, and Job's late winner for Middlesbrough. Forlan heads against the bar in stoppage time. "We can't afford to lose another game," Sir Alex Ferguson says.

Howard — O'Shea, Brown (P Neville ht), Silvestre, Fortune — Kleberson, Butt (Forlan 87), Scholes, Giggs — Van Nistelrooy, Saha *Subs not used* Fletcher, Carroll *Booked* Silvestre
Scorers **Van Nistelrooy 45, Giggs 63**
Referee **P Durkin**

Saturday February 14
MANCHESTER CITY (h)
FA Cup, 5th rnd
Won 4-2   HT 1-0   Att 67,228
The day begins with reports of a peace deal between Sir Alex Ferguson and the "Coolmore Mafia" and ends with United in the quarter-finals, but they get there without Gary Neville, who is booked for diving and immediately sent off for butting McManaman.

Howard — G Neville, O'Shea, Silvestre, Fortune — Ronaldo, Keane, P Neville (Brown 90), Scholes — Giggs (Butt 88) — Van Nistelrooy *Subs not used* Fletcher, Forlan, Carroll *Booked* G Neville *Sent off* G Neville 39
Scorers **Scholes 34, Van Nistelrooy 71, 80, Ronaldo 73**
Referee **J Winter**

Saturday February 21
LEEDS UNITED (h)
Drew 1-1   HT 0-0   Att 67,744   Position 2nd
After an immaculately observed silence in memory of John Charles, who died this morning at 72, Leeds — with Carson making his debut in goal in place of the suspended Robinson — do their "Gentle Giant" proud when Smith cancels out Scholes's opener.

Howard — G Neville, O'Shea, Silvestre (Brown 25), Fortune — P Neville (Solskjaer 71), Butt — Scholes, Kleberson (Keane 58), Giggs — Van Nistelrooy *Subs not used* Ronaldo, Carroll *Booked* G Neville
Scorer **Scholes 64**
Referee **M Halsey**

Wednesday February 25
FC PORTO (a)
European Cup, 1st knockout rnd, 1st leg
Lost 1-2   HT 1-1   Att 49,977
Beaten by McCarthy's double after taking an early lead, United must also go into the second leg without Keane. Their captain is sent off for the eleventh time in his club career after putting his studs in on the FC Porto goalkeeper and their own manager admits that United are lucky to get away with a one-goal defeat.

Howard — P Neville (O'Shea 70), G Neville, Brown, Fortune — Scholes, Keane, Butt, Giggs — Van Nistelrooy, Saha (Ronaldo 76) *Subs not used* Djemba-Djemba, Kleberson, Bellion, Forlan, Carroll *Booked* Fortune, Butt *Sent off* Keane 87
Scorer **Fortune 14**
Referee **H Fandel (Germany)**

Saturday February 28
FULHAM (a)
Drew 1-1   HT 1-0   Att 18,306   Position 3rd
Carroll — O'Shea, Brown, Keane, Fortune — Fletcher (Giggs 72), P Neville, Scholes, Ronaldo — Forlan (Van Nistelrooy 72), Saha *Subs not used* Howard, Bellion, Djemba-Djemba *Booked* Van Nistelrooy, Forlan, Brown
Scorer **Saha 14**
Report page 150

Saturday March 6
FULHAM (h)
FA Cup, 6th rnd
Won 2-1   HT 1-1   Att 67,614
On the ground where they won 3-1 in the league, Fulham take the lead again from the spot — the first penalty by a visiting player in a domestic match at Old Trafford for 11 years — but the returning Van Nistelrooy scores twice to mark Walter Smith's debut in the United dugout as Sir Alex Ferguson's No 2 with victory.

Howard — P Neville, Keane (Djemba-Djemba 75), Brown, O'Shea — Ronaldo (Solskjaer 88), Fletcher, Butt, Scholes, Giggs — Van Nistelrooy *Subs not used* Kleberson, Forlan, Carroll *Booked* P Neville, Keane
Scorer **Van Nistelrooy 25, 62**
Referee **R Styles**

Tuesday March 9
FC PORTO (h)
European Cup, 1st knockout rnd, 2nd leg
Drew 1-1 (lost 2-3 on agg)   HT 1-0   Att 67,029
United's season threatens to disintegrate as they fail to reach the quarter-finals for the first time in eight years. Scholes, having scored with a header, has a second goal wrongly disallowed for offside and the error comes home to roost when Howard parries McCarthy's last-minute free kick only as far as Costinha.

Howard — P Neville, G Neville, Brown, O'Shea — Djemba-Djemba (Saha ht), Butt — Fletcher (Ronaldo 75; Solskjaer 83), Scholes, Giggs — Van Nistelrooy *Subs not used* Carroll, Bellion, Kleberson, Forlan *Booked* P Neville, Scholes
Scorer **Scholes 32**
Referee **V Ivanov (Russia)**

Sunday March 14
MANCHESTER CITY (a)
Lost 1-4   HT 1-2   Att 47,284   Position 3rd
Howard — P Neville, Brown, Silvestre, O'Shea — Fletcher, Butt, Scholes, Ronaldo (Solskjaer 73) — Giggs (Forlan 78) — Van Nistelrooy *Subs not used* Carroll, Bellion, Lynch *Booked* Butt, Scholes
Scorer **Scholes 35**
Report page 193

Saturday March 20
TOTTENHAM HOTSPUR (h)
Won 3-0   HT 1-0   Att 67,634   Position 3rd
Two days after Ferdinand's eight-month ban is upheld on appeal, Sir Alex Ferguson denies that "the empire is crumbling" and there are no obvious signs that it is as two goals in the last two minutes put the gloss on this traditional cruise, Tottenham's ninth successive defeat at Old Trafford.

Carroll — P Neville, Brown, Silvestre, O'Shea — Solskjaer (Ronaldo 74), Keane, Scholes (Bellion 90), Giggs — Forlan (Butt 81), Van Nistelrooy *Subs not used* Howard, Fletcher *Booked* Giggs
Scorers **Giggs 30, Ronaldo 89, Bellion 90**
Referee **D Gallagher**

Sunday March 28
ARSENAL (a)
Drew 1-1   HT 0-0   Att 38,184   Position 3rd
Carroll — G Neville, Brown, Silvestre, O'Shea — Fletcher (Solskjaer 72), Djemba-Djemba (Saha 59), Keane, Giggs — Scholes — Van Nistelrooy *Subs not used* Howard, P Neville, Butt *Booked* Scholes
Scorer **Saha 86**
Report page 68

THE PLAYERS

PHILLIP BARDSLEY (defender) **Born** June 28, 1985, Salford **Signed from** trainee, July 2003

DAVID BELLION (forward) **Born** November 27, 1982, Paris **Ht** 6ft 0in **Wt** 11st 5lb **Signed from** Sunderland, July 2003, £2m

WES BROWN (defender) **Born** October 13, 1979, Manchester **Ht** 6ft 1in **Wt** 12st 4lb **Signed from** trainee, November 1996

NICKY BUTT (midfield) **Born** January 21, 1975, Manchester **Ht** 5ft 10in **Wt** 11st 3lb **Signed from** trainee, January 1993

ROY CARROLL (goalkeeper) **Born** September 30, 1977, Enniskillen **Ht** 6ft 2in **Wt** 12st 9lb **Signed from** Wigan Athletic, July 2001, £2.5m

ERIC DJEMBA-DJEMBA (midfield) **Born** May 4, 1981, Douala, Cameroon **Ht** 5ft 9in **Wt** 11st 11lb **Signed from** Nantes, July 2003, £3.5m

CHRISTOPHER EAGLES (midfield) **Born** November 19, 1985, Hemel Hempstead **Ht** 5ft 10in **Signed from** trainee, July 2003

RIO FERDINAND (defender) **Born** November 8, 1980, Peckham **Ht** 6ft 2in **Wt** 12st 1lb **Signed from** Leeds United, July 2002, £30m

DARREN FLETCHER (midfield) **Born** February 1, 1984, Edinburgh **Ht** 6ft 0in **Wt** 13st 1lb **Signed from** trainee, August 2000

DIEGO FORLAN (forward) **Born** May 19, 1979, Montevideo **Ht** 5ft 8in **Wt** 11st 1lb **Signed from** Independiente, January 2002, £7.5m

QUINTON FORTUNE (midfield) **Born** May 21, 1977, Cape Town **Ht** 5ft 11in **Wt** 11st 1lb **Signed from** Atletico Madrid, August 1999, £1.5m

RYAN GIGGS (forward) **Born** November 29, 1973, Cardiff **Ht** 5ft 11in **Wt** 10st 9lb **Signed from** trainee, December 1990

TIM HOWARD (goalkeeper) **Born** June 3, 1979, North Brunswick, New Jersey **Ht** 6ft 2in **Wt** 13st 8lb **Signed from** NY/NJ MetroStars, July 2003, £2.3m

EDDIE JOHNSON (forward) **Born** September 20, 1984, Chester **Ht** 5ft 10in **Wt** 13st 5lb **Signed from** trainee, July 2001

ROY KEANE (midfield) **Born** August 10, 1971, Cork **Ht** 5ft 10in **Wt** 12st 10lb **Signed from** Nottingham Forest, July 1993, £3.75m

KLEBERSON (midfield) **Born** June 19, 1979, Urai, Brazil **Ht** 5ft 9in **Wt** 10st 3lb **Signed from** Paranaense, August 2003, £5.9m

DANNY NARDIELLO (forward) **Born** October 22, 1982, Coventry **Ht** 5ft 11in **Wt** 11st 4lb **Signed from** trainee, November 1999

GARY NEVILLE (defender) **Born** February 18, 1975, Bury **Ht** 5ft 11in **Wt** 12st 8lb **Signed from** trainee, January 1993

PHIL NEVILLE (defender) **Born** January 21, 1977, Bury **Ht** 5ft 11in **Wt** 12st 0lb **Signed from** trainee, June 1994

JOHN O'SHEA (defender) **Born** April 30, 1981, Waterford **Ht** 6ft 3in **Wt** 11st 12lb **Signed from** Waterford United, September 1998

DANNY PUGH (midfield) **Born** October 19, 1982, Manchester **Ht** 6ft 0in **Wt** 12st 7lb **Signed from** trainee, August 2002

KIERAN RICHARDSON (midfield) **Born** October 21, 1984, London **Ht** 5ft 11in **Wt** 11st 5lb **Signed from** West Ham United, July 2002, undisclosed

CRISTIANO RONALDO (midfield) **Born** February 5, 1985, Madeira **Ht** 6ft 1in **Wt** 11st 7lb **Signed from** Sporting Lisbon, August 2003, £12.2m

LOUIS SAHA (forward) **Born** August 8, 1978, Paris **Ht** 5ft 11in **Wt** 11st 10lb **Signed from** Fulham, January 2004, £12.8m

PAUL SCHOLES (midfield) **Born** November 16, 1974, Salford **Ht** 5ft 7in **Wt** 11st 10lb **Signed from** trainee, January 1993

MIKAEL SILVESTRE (defender) **Born** August 9, 1977, Tours, France **Ht** 6ft 0in **Wt** 13st 1lb **Signed from** Inter Milan, September 1999, £4m

OLE GUNNAR SOLSKJAER (forward) **Born** February 26, 1973, Kristiansund, Norway **Ht** 5ft 10in **Wt** 11st 10lb **Signed from** Molde, July 1996, £1.5m

PAUL TIERNEY (midfield) **Born** September 15, 1982, Salford **Ht** 5ft 10in **Wt** 12st 10in **Signed from** trainee, August 2000

RUUD VAN NISTELROOY (forward) **Born** July 1, 1976, Oss, the Netherlands **Ht** 6ft 2in **Wt** 12st 13lb **Signed from** PSV Eindhoven, July 2001, £19m

---

Saturday April 3
ARSENAL
FA Cup, semi-final (Villa Park)
Won 1-0   HT 1-0   Att 39,939
Report and details page 328

Saturday April 10
BIRMINGHAM CITY (a)
Won 2-1   HT 0-1   Att 29,548   Position 3rd
Carroll — G Neville, Brown, Silvestre, O'Shea — Fletcher, Djemba-Djemba (Forlan 74), Scholes, Solskjaer (Ronaldo 55) — Saha, Giggs (P Neville 89) *Subs not used* Butt, Howard
Scorers **Ronaldo 60, Saha 78**
Report page 89

Tuesday April 13
LEICESTER CITY (h)
Won 1-0   HT 0-0   Att 67,749   Position 3rd
Leicester are pushed nearer the precipice by the unlikely figure of Gary Neville, who scores his first league goal for more than three years. Leicester shade the first half, Bent missing their best chance, but they are now six points adrift of safety with only five games to go.

Carroll — G Neville, Brown, Silvestre, O'Shea — Bellion (Djemba-Djemba 83), Scholes, Butt, Ronaldo — Forlan (Fletcher 57), Saha *Subs not used* Giggs, Solskjaer, Howard
Scorer **G Neville 56**
Referee **M Halsey**

Saturday April 17
PORTSMOUTH (a)
Lost 0-1   HT 0-1   Att 20,140   Position 3rd
Carroll — G Neville, Brown, Silvestre, O'Shea (Fletcher 74) — Solskjaer, Djemba-Djemba (Ronaldo 58), Butt (Bellion 89), Scholes, Giggs — Saha *Subs not used* Howard, Pugh *Booked* G Neville
Report page 237

Tuesday April 20
CHARLTON ATHLETIC (h)
Won 2-0   HT 1-0   Att 67,477   Position 3rd
There is extra security after reports that terrorists may target Old Trafford, where the newly prolific Gary Neville seals a convincing victory over Charlton after a long run and exchange of passes with Saha, who had put United ahead. Charlton fail to test the recalled Howard in the United goal.

Howard — G Neville, Brown, Silvestre, P Neville — Fletcher (Ronaldo 83), Djemba-Djemba, Butt (Keane 74), Bellion — Van Nistelrooy, Saha (Giggs 66) *Subs not used* Carroll, O'Shea
Scorers **Saha 28, G Neville 65**
Referee **S Dunn**

PLAYER OF THE YEAR
Cristiano Ronaldo

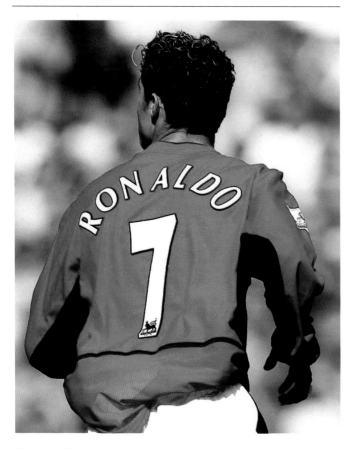

Written off as a show-pony soon after his summer arrival from Sporting Lisbon, by the time the season ended, Cristiano Ronaldo looked more like a thoroughbred classic-winner in the making. In the FA Cup Final he combined his tricks with an attacking style that would have embarrassed better defences than Millwall's. And far from fitting the stereotype of a diving fancy Dan, he has the guts to get back up and run at the opposition time and again. Sir Alex Ferguson has already paid Ronaldo the high compliment of comparing him to Cantona. Like King Eric, Prince Cristiano seems to have everything it takes to be a folk hero at Old Trafford — the skill, the arrogance, and the fact that fans of every other club already hate his guts.

Mick Hume

Saturday April 24
LIVERPOOL (h)
Lost 0-1   HT 0-0   Att **67,647**   Position **3rd**
After recent misses by Owen and Gerrard, Murphy takes responsibility from the spot for Liverpool after Gary Neville brings down Gerrard, and makes no mistake to settle an unusually tepid encounter. United can hardly go closer to replying than when a shot by Giggs rebounds clear off both posts.

Howard — G Neville, Brown, Silvestre, O'Shea (Solskjaer 65) — Fletcher, Keane, P Neville (Bellion 82), Ronaldo — Giggs — Saha Subs not used Butt, Djemba-Djemba, Carroll Booked Ronaldo, Silvestre
Referee **M Riley**

Saturday May 1
BLACKBURN ROVERS (a)
Lost 0-1   HT 0-0   Att **29,616**   Position **3rd**
Howard — G Neville, Brown, Silvestre, O'Shea — Butt (Bellion 69), Djemba-Djemba (Fletcher 80), P Neville — Kleberson (Forlan 77) — Solskjaer, Giggs Subs not used Spector, Carroll Booked Solskjaer
Report page 100

Saturday May 8
CHELSEA (h)
Drew 1-1   HT 0-1   Att **67,609**   Position **3rd**
Sir Alex Ferguson has already conceded second place in the Premiership to Chelsea and this result confirms it. Van Nistelrooy has a second-half penalty saved, but then pounces on a mistake by Cudicini to cancel out Gronkjaer's fine opener for Chelsea, who have Huth dismissed for two fouls. With the Cup Final looming, Scholes is lucky not to suffer the same fate before he is withdrawn early.

Howard — G Neville, Brown, Silvestre, O'Shea — Fletcher, P Neville (Kleberson 78), Scholes (Saha 37) — Ronaldo (Solskjaer 87), Giggs — Van Nistelrooy Subs not used Butt, Carroll Booked P Neville, Scholes, Kleberson
Scorer **Van Nistelrooy 77**
Referee **S Bennett**

Saturday May 15
ASTON VILLA (a)
Won 2-0   HT 2-0   Att **42,573**   Position **3rd**
Howard — G Neville, Brown, Silvestre, O'Shea (Djemba-Djemba 73) — Ronaldo, Fletcher, P Neville, Scholes, Giggs — Van Nistelrooy (Saha 61) Subs not used Carroll, Kleberson, Solskjaer Booked Fletcher, Scholes, Ronaldo Sent off Fletcher 75, Ronaldo 85
Scorers **Ronaldo 4, Van Nistelrooy 10**
Report page 80

Saturday May 22
MILLWALL
FA Cup, Final (Cardiff)
Won 3-0   HT 1-0   Att **71,350**
Report and details page 328

MIDDLESBROUGH

PREMIERSHIP

	P	W	D	L	F	A	GD	Pts
Arsenal	38	26	12	0	73	26	47	**90**
Chelsea	38	24	7	7	67	30	37	**79**
Man Utd	38	23	6	9	64	35	29	**75**
Liverpool	38	16	12	10	55	37	18	**60**
Newcastle	38	13	17	8	52	40	12	**56**
Aston Villa	38	15	11	12	48	44	4	**56**
Charlton	38	14	11	13	51	51	0	**53**
Bolton	38	14	11	13	48	56	-8	**53**
Fulham	38	14	10	14	52	46	6	**52**
Birmingham	38	12	14	12	43	48	-5	**50**
Middlesbro	38	13	9	16	44	52	-8	**48**
Southampton	38	12	11	15	44	45	-1	**47**
Portsmouth	38	12	9	17	47	54	-7	**45**
Tottenham	38	13	6	19	47	57	-10	**45**
Blackburn	38	12	8	18	51	59	-8	**44**
Man City	38	9	14	15	55	54	1	**41**
Everton	38	9	12	17	45	57	-12	**39**
Leicester	38	6	15	17	48	65	-17	**33**
Leeds	38	8	9	21	40	79	-39	**33**
Wolves	38	7	12	19	38	77	-39	**33**

FA CUP
Fourth round

CARLING CUP
Winners

Chair man: Steve Gibson is at the centre of all the celebrations as Middlesbrough's long, long wait for a trophy is finally ended in Cardiff

THE GAMES

Shaun Keogh

Saturday August 16 2003
FULHAM (a)
Lost 2-3 HT 1-1 Att 14,546 Position 15th
Schwarzer — Parnaby, Riggott, Southgate, Wright —
Boateng (Cooper 78), Doriva — Greening, Marinelli
(Job 55), Juninho (Nemeth 72) — Christie *Subs not used*
Nash, Downing *Booked* Southgate
Scorers **Marinelli 10, Nemeth 81**
Report page 144

Sunday August 24
ARSENAL (h)
Lost 0-4 HT 0-3 Att 29,450 Position 19th
"The gulf was enormous," Steve McClaren admits after
this thrashing, watched by a nationwide TV audience and
by Mills and Mendieta, Middlesbrough's new loan
signings, from the stands. Henry sparks Arsenal into life
with an early tap-in and sets up the second for Gilberto
before Wiltord's double completes a rout.

Schwarzer — Riggott (Davies 66), Southgate, Cooper —
Parnaby, Boateng, Doriva, Wright — Juninho — Christie,
Nemeth (Downing 84) *Subs not used* Nash, Stockdale,
Wilson *Booked* Cooper
Referee **D Gallagher**

Tuesday August 26
LEICESTER CITY (a)
Drew 0-0 HT 0-0 Att 30,823 Position 18th
Schwarzer — Parnaby, Davies, Southgate, Cooper
(Stockdale ht) — Mendieta, Boateng, Juninho, Greening —
Job (Ricketts 80), Nemeth (Christie 80) *Subs not used*
Nash, Doriva *Booked* Parnaby, Boateng
Report page 164

Saturday August 30
LEEDS UNITED (h)
Lost 2-3 HT 0-1 Att 30,414 Position 19th
A result that leaves Mills not knowing whether to laugh
or cry as he makes his Middlesbrough debut against the
club that has loaned him out. Ahead 1-0, then 2-1 down,
Leeds equalise through Camara with 13 minutes to go
and steal the points when Viduka punishes a late slip by
Davies with his 50th Premiership goal.

Schwarzer — Mills, Davies, Southgate, Parnaby
(Stockdale 52) — Mendieta, Boateng, Greening —
Juninho — Job (Christie 82), Nemeth (Ricketts 88) *Subs
not used* Doriva, Nash *Booked* Juninho, Mendieta
Scorers **Nemeth 60, Juninho 63**
Referee **N Barry**

Saturday September 13
BOLTON WANDERERS (a)
Lost 0-2 HT 0-1 Att 26,419 Position 19th
Schwarzer — Parnaby, Davies, Southgate, Cooper —
Mendieta, Boateng, Greening, Zenden — Juninho (Job 58)
— Nemeth (Ricketts ht) *Subs not used* Doriva, Nash,
Stockdale *Booked* Cooper, Mills, Zenden
Report page 102

IT IS SAID THAT GLOBAL WARMING is such a slow process
that it is impossible to notice its effects unless one studies the
statistics over a long period. This is also the only way of measuring
the progress of Middlesbrough Football Club over the past 100 years
and more. Season by season, nothing much seems to happen and
then suddenly, with the capturing of the Carling Cup in February, all
of the players assembled by Steve McClaren appeared to vindicate
his judgment in putting together what is — on paper at least — a
talented squad.

This was a truly historic season for the Boro. Winning the Carling
Cup aside, it was also the third season in succession that the club
had not been involved in the fight against relegation, thereby further
establishing them in the mid-table comfort zone of the Premiership.

It did not start all that well, though; losing five of the first nine
games left the team third from bottom of the table. The first home
game of the season, against a rampant Arsenal, saw Middlesbrough
on the wrong end of a 4-0 thrashing. Luckily, the newspapers were
more concerned with a farcical incident in which a home fan had
been thrown out of the ground for having the temerity to fall asleep
during this dreadful display. This writer was always under the
impression that the club stewards are there to stop idiotic behaviour,
not to provide examples of it.

These early losses were made worse by the fact that
Middlesbrough deserved to win two of those matches. After
forfeiting the lead at home against a demoralised Leeds United,
Middlesbrough capitulated 3-2, and after a 2-1 home defeat against
Chelsea, even Damien Duff was forced to admit: "I wouldn't say we
deserved it and in the end we were lucky."

Middlesbrough's season traditionally falls apart as the close of the
year approaches, but this season that particular curse was lifted.
From the end of October, the team embarked upon an eight-match
unbeaten league run and in between won three Carling Cup games
to earn themselves a two-legged semi-final against Arsenal.

In the previous season, their dreadful away record of only three
wins was held up as a principal factor in the team finishing so
woefully short of challenging for one of the European places. Even
though the balance has been redressed somewhat this time, with five
away wins, Middlesbrough are still a long way short of having the
right combination of players to compete with the top ten in the
Premiership.

In years gone by, this would have been an acceptable state of
affairs for a club such as Boro, who have spent 12 of the past 30 years
outside of the top division. However, when it is noted that clubs of a

Still Boro's greatest player, wonderful Wilf Mannion

similarly unspectacular recent past — such as Birmingham City, Fulham and Bolton Wanderers — finished the season above them, then questions surely have to be asked.

The highlight of Middlesbrough's league campaign came in February with a fantastic 3-2 win over Manchester United at Old Trafford. Coming soon after winning both legs of the Carling Cup semi-final against Arsenal (understrength though they were), it instilled confidence in the fans that great things could be achieved this season and a couple of weeks later the club did indeed lift its first trophy. But, save for a thrilling 5-3 win against Birmingham in March, the fans would have done well to savour the winning of the Carling Cup and quit while they were ahead rather than returning to Teesside.

Middlesbrough's season was effectively over from the moment that the final whistle blew in Cardiff. From their remaining 13 games, when the team should have been on a high, they took 17 points from a possible 39, including defeats to Wolverhampton Wanderers and a final-day humiliation away to Portsmouth.

Granted, the home win against Birmingham and a 0-0 draw, which felt like a win, against Chelsea at Stamford Bridge did maintain the feel-good factor, but it was the killer instinct that was lacking to capitalise on the success against Bolton at the Millennium Stadium.

Even though this was the club's most successful season they have still, in some respects, underachieved. If the club cannot finish in the top half of the table with players such as Mendieta, Boudewijn

Sunday September 21
EVERTON (h)
Won 1-0   HT 1-0   Att 28,113   Position 17th
The incident is overshadowed by the "Battle of Old Trafford" the same afternoon, but Steve McClaren and David Moyes are involved in an angry touchline dispute when Everton appear to break the unwritten code about returning the ball to the opposition after an injury. Job's early goal gives Middlesbrough their first win of the season.
Schwarzer — Mills, Southgate, Cooper, Queudrue — Greening (Ricketts 76), Boateng, Doriva, Zenden — Christie (Nemeth 85), Job (Riggott 81) *Subs not used* Nash, Juninho *Booked* Greening, Mills
Scorer **Job 6**
Referee **A Wiley**

Wednesday September 24
BRIGHTON & HOVE ALBION (h)
Carling Cup, 2nd rnd
Won 1-0 (aet)   HT 0-0   Att 10,435
No squad rotation for Middlesbrough, who turn out a full-strength side but still need extra time to end Brighton's resistance, the second-division side falling to a cute back-heeled finish from Christie.
Schwarzer — Mills, Southgate (Riggott 18), Cooper, Queudrue — Greening, Boateng, Doriva, Downing (Christie 65) — Nemeth, Ricketts (Juninho 65) *Subs not used* Nash, Stockdale *Booked* Ricketts
Scorer **Christie 94**
Referee **G Cain**

Saturday September 27
SOUTHAMPTON (a)
Won 1-0   HT 1-0   Att 30,772   Position 12th
Schwarzer — Mills, Riggott, Cooper, Queudrue — Greening, Boateng, Doriva, Zenden — Christie (Ricketts 86), Job (Nemeth 76) *Subs not used* Jones, Davies, Juninho *Booked* Riggott, Cooper, Mills
Scorer **Christie 13**
Report page 241

Sunday October 5
CHELSEA (h)
Lost 1-2   HT 0-1   Att 29,170   Position 17th
Claudio Ranieri reacts to defeat by Besiktas, Chelsea's first of the season, by making seven changes and enjoys liberal good fortune. Middlesbrough, with Mendieta outstanding, create the better chances after Nemeth cancels out Gudjohnsen's opener, but Crespo heads a late winner from Duff's cross.
Schwarzer — Mills, Riggott, Cooper, Queudrue — Mendieta, Boateng, Doriva (Juninho 89), Greening — Nemeth (Downing 87), Christie (Ricketts 83) *Subs not used* Jones, Davies *Booked* Christie
Scorer **Nemeth 46**
Referee **M Halsey**

Saturday October 18
NEWCASTLE UNITED (h)
Lost 0-1   HT 0-1   Att 34,081   Position 18th
Middlesbrough's luck is out again at home, this time as Newcastle score against the run of play through Ameobi and then hang on through Given's brilliance in goal. Sir Bobby Robson's side leap seven places to eleventh.
Schwarzer — Mills, Southgate, Cooper, Queudrue — Mendieta, Boateng, Doriva (Juninho 69), Zenden (Greening 69) — Christie, Nemeth (Maccarone 69) *Subs not used* Nash, Riggott *Booked* Doriva, Mills
Referee **A Wiley**

Sunday October 26
TOTTENHAM HOTSPUR (a)
Drew 0-0   HT 0-0   Att 32,643   Position 17th
Schwarzer – Davies, Southgate, Cooper, Queudrue –
Mendieta, Boateng, Doriva, Zenden (Greening 90) –
Christie (Maccarone 79), Nemeth (Juninho 79) *Subs not
used* Nash, Riggott *Booked* Doriva, Mendieta
Report page 252

Wednesday October 29
WIGAN ATHLETIC (a)
Carling Cup, 3rd rnd
Won 2-1   HT 1-0   Att 8,046
A goal from Maccarone, on his way back to full fitness,
and Mendieta's first for the club see the first-division
high-flyers downed at the JJB Stadium, a regular
graveyard for Premiership clubs in cups. Wigan, though,
hit the woodwork twice before Bullard's goal ensures a
tense finale.

Schwarzer – Mills, Riggott, Southgate, Queudrue –
Mendieta (Zenden 72), Boateng, Juninho, Greening –
Maccarone (Nemeth 86), Ricketts (Doriva 56) *Subs not
used* Nash, Davies
Scorers **Maccarone 36, Mendieta 66**
Referee **U Rennie**

Saturday November 1
WOLVERHAMPTON WANDERERS (h)
Won 2-0   HT 0-0   Att 30,305   Position 14th
Lucky to stay on the pitch after kicking out at Rae,
Mendieta thunders a 25-yard free kick into the top
corner to help to bring an end to Wolves' six-match
unbeaten run. Trouble in the tunnel follows Rae's
dismissal for two bookable offences, with the behaviour
of Mills under particular scrutiny.

Schwarzer – Mills, Southgate, Cooper, Queudrue –
Mendieta, Boateng, Doriva (Juninho 63), Zenden –
Nemeth (Christie ht), Maccarone (Greening 75) *Subs not
used* Davies, Nash *Booked* Mendieta, Mills
Scorers **Mendieta 73, Juninho 83**
Referee **S Dunn**

Saturday November 8
ASTON VILLA (a)
Won 2-0   HT 1-0   Att 29,898   Position 12th
Nash – Mills, Southgate, Cooper, Queudrue – Mendieta,
Boateng, Doriva, Zenden – Juninho (Greening 79) –
Ricketts (Maccarone 74) *Subs not used* Turnbull, Riggott,
Nemeth
Scorers **Zenden 30, Ricketts 49 (pen)**
Report page 74

Saturday November 22
LIVERPOOL (h)
Drew 0-0   HT 0-0   Att 34,268   Position 12th
Fifteen points off the pace with November not yet out,
Gerrard concedes that fourth place is the limit of
Liverpool's Premiership ambitions after this dull draw.
Sinama-Pongolle volleys the best chance over
Schwarzer's bar and is unlucky not to earn a penalty
after Queudrue's challenge from behind.

Schwarzer – Davies, Southgate, Cooper, Queudrue –
Mendieta, Boateng, Doriva, Zenden – Juninho – Ricketts
(Nemeth 70) *Subs not used* Nash, Riggott, Maccarone,
Greening *Booked* Doriva, Queudrue
Referee **P Dowd**

Christie and Job celebrate after the latter's early goal proved enough to
beat Everton and provide an early-season victory at the Riverside

Zenden, Gareth Southgate, Ugo Ehiogu and Juninho in the team, it
either demonstrates how strong the Premiership now is, or it means
that McClaren and his management team need to spend a long time
puzzling over why the league campaign finished with such a
whimper.

   Some of the key contributors to the cause through the season —
and who played a huge part in winning the trophy — were not even
Middlesbrough players. Mendieta, Danny Mills and Zenden played
the entire season on loan. They could go down in history as being
key members of the club's first trophy-winning team without ever
becoming permanent Boro players, a bizarre circumstance. Perhaps
fans can draw some comfort that in future times, quiz compilers will
be asking who were the only team to beat Arsenal twice during their
unbeaten league season.

   If Middlesbrough do continue their progress in line with the
speed of global warming, it may well be another 128 years before
they emulate this season. But no matter; this was a year in which the
shackles of those decades of mediocrity were thrown to the depths
of the Tees — and the people of Teesside will be happy to dine out
on that for a few years yet to come.

THE MANAGER — Steve McClaren

Even though their Premiership season fizzled out like a damp firework, Steve McClaren's only serious error of judgment during his tenure has been the club-record signing of Massimo Maccarone for more than £8 million two years ago. The Italian is a talented player, but given his form and the transfer climate, Middlesbrough would be fortunate to recoup £2 million for him. With European football

coming to the Riverside Stadium, McClaren has the opportunity and funds to show his worth as a potential future manager of England.
Shaun Keogh

APPEARANCES

	Prem	FAC	CC	Total
G Boateng	35	2	6	43
M Christie	7 (3)	-	0 (1)	7 (4)
C Cooper	17 (2)	-	2	19 (2)
A Davies	8 (2)	-	-	8 (2)
Doriva	19 (2)	-	4 (1)	23 (3)
S Downing	7 (13)	2	1 (1)	10 (14)
U Ehiogu	16	1	2	19
J Greening	17 (8)	-	4	21 (8)
J-D Job	19 (5)	2	1 (2)	22 (7)
B Jones	1	1	-	2
Juninho	26 (5)	0 (1)	5 (1)	31 (7)
M Maccarone	13 (10)	0 (2)	5	18 (12)
C Marinelli	1	-	-	1
G Mendieta	30 (1)	1	6	37 (1)
D Mills	28	2	7	37
J Morrison	0 (1)	0 (1)	-	0 (2)
C Nash	1	-	-	1
S Nemeth	17 (15)	1 (1)	2 (2)	20 (18)
S Parnaby	8 (5)	1	0 (2)	9 (7)
F Queudrue	31	2	7	40
M Ricketts	7 (16)	2	3 (2)	12 (18)
C Riggott	14 (3)	1 (1)	4 (1)	19 (5)
M Schwarzer	36	1	7	44
G Southgate	27	1	6	34
R Stockdale	0 (2)	-	-	0 (2)
A Wright	2	-	-	2
B Zenden	31	2	5 (1)	38 (1)

Sunday November 30
MANCHESTER CITY (a)
Won 1-0   HT 1-0   Att 46,824   Position 10th
Schwarzer — Mills, Southgate, Cooper, Queudrue — Mendieta, Boateng (Nemeth 73), Doriva (Greening 35), Zenden — Juninho — Ricketts (Riggott 82) *Subs not used* Nash, Maccarone
Scorer **Sun 30 (og)**
Report page 189

Wednesday December 3
EVERTON (h)
Carling Cup, 4th rnd
Drew 0-0 (aet; won 5-4 on pens)   HT 0-0   Att 18,568
The draw for the quarter-finals has already been made when the penalty shoot-out is settled by the only miss in ten, Schwarzer saving with his trailing leg from Osman. Mendieta goes closest to winning the tie in 120 goalless minutes, twice being denied by Martyn.

Schwarzer — Mills, Riggott, Southgate, Queudrue — Mendieta, Boateng, Greening, Zenden — Maccarone, Nemeth (Ricketts 77) *Subs not used* Nash, Ehiogu, Davies, Cooper
Referee **M Halsey**

Saturday December 6
PORTSMOUTH (h)
Drew 0-0   HT 0-0   Att 28,031   Position 9th
Portsmouth are happy with a point after their poor recent run and Middlesbrough extend their sequence of league games without conceding a goal to six, but excitement is in short supply. Mills goes nearest to scoring, hitting the bar from eight yards before Stone is dismissed for two cautions.

Schwarzer — Mills, Southgate, Cooper, Queudrue — Mendieta, Boateng, Greening, Zenden — Juninho (Nemeth 68) — Ricketts (Maccarone 68) *Subs not used* Nash, Riggott, Davies *Booked* Greening, Nemeth
Referee **S Bennett**

Saturday December 13
CHARLTON ATHLETIC (h)
Drew 0-0   HT 0-0   Att 26,721   Position 11th
Perhaps the season's most predictable goalless draw, a fourth in a row at home for Middlesbrough, for whom it is also a club-record seventh successive clean sheet. Mills leaves his mark, though, his studs causing a nasty gash above Di Canio's eye after a tangle on the byline.

Schwarzer — Mills, Riggott, Southgate, Queudrue — Greening (Downing 77), Boateng, Mendieta, Zenden — Nemeth, Maccarone (Ricketts 73) *Subs not used* Nash, Ehiogu, Davies *Booked* Ricketts
Referee **H Webb**

Wednesday December 17
TOTTENHAM HOTSPUR (a)
Carling Cup, quarter-final
Drew 1-1 (aet; 1-1 after 90min; won 5-4 on pens)   HT 0-1   Att 25,307
Schwarzer — Mills, Southgate, Cooper (Nemeth 79), Queudrue — Mendieta, Boateng, Zenden, Juninho — Ricketts, Maccarone (Downing ht) *Subs not used* Jones, Davies, Riggott *Booked* Mills
Scorer **Ricketts 86**
Report page 254

Friday December 26
BLACKBURN ROVERS (a)
Drew 2-2   **HT 1-1**   Att 25,452   Position **11th**
Schwarzer – Davies, Southgate, Cooper, Queudrue –
Mendieta, Boateng, Zenden, Downing – Juninho
(Greening 73), Ricketts *Subs not used* Ehiogu, Riggott,
Maccarone, Jones *Booked* Boateng
Scorer **Juninho 31, 51**
Report page 96

Sunday December 28
MANCHESTER UNITED (h)
Lost 0-1   **HT 0-1**   Att 34,738   Position **15th**
The champions end the year in pole position again after
Mills diverts Fortune's shot past Schwarzer, the first goal
conceded at the Riverside in more than nine hours. The
bookings that lead to Fletcher's dismissal anger Sir Alex
Ferguson.

Schwarzer – Mills, Ehiogu, Southgate, Queudrue
(Parnaby 19; Downing 74) – Mendieta, Boateng, Zenden,
Greening (Maccarone 74) – Juninho, Ricketts *Subs not
used* Jones, Riggott *Booked* Boateng, Juninho, Mills
Referee **M Messias**

Saturday January 3 2004
NOTTS COUNTY (h)
FA Cup, 3rd rnd
Won 2-0   **HT 1-0**   Att 15,061
Already ahead when Richardson deflects Job's cross in
for an own goal, Middlesbrough's passage is assured
once Barness is sent off for a 33rd-minute trip on
Ricketts. Zenden's volley helps to entertain a crowd
20,000 down on the last home fixture.

Jones – Mills, Ehiogu (Riggott 80), Southgate, Queudrue
– Nemeth, Boateng, Zenden, Job
(Maccarone 63), Ricketts (Morrison 63) *Subs not used*
Turnbull, Parnaby *Booked* Queudrue
Scorers **Richardson 25 (og), Zenden 64**
Referee **M Halsey**

Wednesday January 7
FULHAM (h)
Won 2-1   **HT 1-0**   Att 27,869   Position **12th**
Saha says he is "disgusted and virtually destroyed" by
Fulham's decision to block his proposed move to Old
Trafford and Chris Coleman's side are nearly destroyed
by Middlesbrough, who could have doubled their two-goal
lead and more before Hayles's last-minute consolation
goal.

Jones – Mills, Ehiogu, Southgate, Queudrue – Zenden,
Boateng, Downing – Juninho – Nemeth, Job *Subs not
used* Turnbull, Riggott, Maccarone, Doriva, Parnaby
Booked Ehiogu
Scorers **Job 15, Nemeth 67**
Referee **P Durkin**

Saturday January 10
ARSENAL (a)
Lost 1-4   **HT 0-2**   Att 38,117   Position **14th**
Schwarzer – Mills, Ehiogu (Riggott ht), Southgate,
Queudrue – Nemeth, Boateng, Doriva (Juninho 62),
Zenden, Downing – Job (Maccarone 62) *Subs not used*
Parnaby, Jones *Booked* Doriva
Scorer **Maccarone 86 (pen)**
Report page 65

THE ✶ TIMES   Thursday February 12 2004

MATCH OF THE SEASON

Manchester United 2 Middlesbrough 3
Old Trafford, Wednesday February 11 2004
Oliver Kay

ONLY TIME WILL TELL HOW much Manchester United
surrendered off the pitch yesterday as they resigned themselves to
allowing rebel factions into the boardroom, but the impact of their
capitulation on it last night was immediately evident. A careless
defeat, littered with wretched defending, kept Sir Alex Ferguson's
team five points adrift of Arsenal at the top of the Barclaycard
Premiership and, if they continue to play like this, that gap will only
grow between now and May.

The cracks that have been appearing in United's title challenge in
recent weeks were ruthlessly exploited by a Middlesbrough team
whose usual solidity in defence combined with an unexpected killer
instinct in attack. As impressively as Steve McClaren's team
performed, however, they were given far too much assistance by the
home defence, which allowed Juninho, the smallest man on the
pitch, to head Middlesbrough into a two-goal lead. Having fought
back to 2-2, United then afforded Joseph-Desire Job time and space
to hit the decisive goal with ten minutes left.

In three Premiership matches since Rio Ferdinand began his
eight-month suspension for missing a drugs test, the United defence
has leaked no fewer than eight goals. On the previous two occasions
the goals of Ruud van Nistelrooy and Louis Saha ensured that no
points were dropped, but last night they gave themselves far too
much to do.

Whether they have given themselves too much to do in the title
race remains to be seen, but a fifth league defeat of the season has
seriously damaged their hopes. "We can't afford to lose another
game," Ferguson said. "We've been here before. We don't enjoy that
and we know it's not a healthy position to be in. There's plenty of
time to do something about it, but we've been slack in defence and, if
we keep doing that, we can say goodbye to the league."

Ferguson referred to the "soft" goals his team conceded, but
Middlesbrough deserved credit for the way they controlled midfield
and attacked with penetration, in addition to standing firm when put
under pressure in the second half. Although they conceded two
goals, to Van Nistelrooy on the stroke of half-time and to Ryan
Giggs in the 63rd minute, they defended magnificently, with Gareth
Southgate in particular suggesting that United should have followed
up their longstanding interest in him during the transfer window.

To portray this as backs against the wall, however, would be a
gross injustice to Middlesbrough, who were the better team for all
but the period immediately after half-time. "I always thought that, if
we passed the ball well, we would create chances," McClaren, the
manager, said as he reflected on his team's second victory at Old

Doriva gets away from Saha in Middlesbrough's epic win at Old Trafford

Trafford in three visits. Middlesbrough could have scored three times before they took a well-deserved lead in the 34th minute. Franck Queudrue, given far too much space 30 yards from goal, struck a fierce shot that Tim Howard did well to push on to the crossbar. As the ball ran loose, the United defence again stood and watched as Juninho stooped to head past Howard. Four minutes later, almost unbelievably, Juninho was celebrating a second headed goal. A short corner on the right was played to Stewart Downing, whose cross was glanced past Howard.

The expected backlash did not occur immediately, but Van Nistelrooy displayed none of the hesitancy of his team-mates when reducing the arrears in first-half stoppage time. Giggs sent a pass into the area and, after Saha chested the ball forward, it was taken off his toe by Van Nistelrooy, who smashed it past Mark Schwarzer. Eighteen minutes into the second half it was 2-2 as Giggs, profiting from an unfortunate slip by Danny Mills, scored at the far post after Van Nistelrooy flicked on Phil Neville's cross.

Shortly afterwards, Southgate produced a stupendous block to deny John O'Shea, but with Old Trafford expecting a United goal, Middlesbrough broke forward to score their third, Job turning and shooting past Howard from the edge of the penalty area. There was time for Diego Forlan to head against the crossbar from six yards.

MANCHESTER UNITED (4-4-2): T Howard — J O'Shea, W Brown (sub: P Neville, 46min), M Silvestre, Q Fortune — Kleberson (sub: C Ronaldo, 63), N Butt (sub: D Forlan, 87), P Scholes, R Giggs — R van Nistelrooy, L Saha. **Substitutes not used:** D Fletcher, R Carroll. **Booked:** Silvestre.
MIDDLESBROUGH (4-4-1-1): M Schwarzer — D Mills, C Riggott, G Southgate, F Queudrue — G Mendieta (sub: S Parnaby, 73), Doriva, B Zenden, S Downing — Juninho (sub: C Cooper, 90) — J-D Job. **Substitutes not used:** S Nemeth, M Maccarone, B Jones. **Booked:** Mills.

Saturday January 17
LEICESTER CITY (h)
Drew 3-3   HT 1-0   Att 27,125   Position 13th
"If you don't win games like that, you're relegated," Micky Adams says when the dust settles on an extraordinary match. Leicester are already behind when Walker saves Job's penalty, but then go 3-1 in front before Middlesbrough score twice in stoppage time — the equaliser coming via Curtis's own goal — to snatch the unlikeliest of draws.

Schwarzer — Mills, Riggott, Cooper (Davies 32), Queudrue — Nemeth, Boateng, Zenden (Mendieta 61), Downing — Juninho — Job (Maccarone 61) *Subs not used* Jones, Doriva *Booked* Zenden, Maccarone
Scorers **Juninho 8, Maccarone 90, Curtis 90 (og)**
Referee **B Knight**

Tuesday January 20
ARSENAL (a)
Carling Cup, semi-final, 1st leg
Won 1-0   HT 0-0   Att 31,070
Report and details page 332

Saturday January 24
ARSENAL (a)
FA Cup, 4th rnd
Lost 1-4   HT 1-2   Att 37,256
Schwarzer — Mills, Riggott, Queudrue, Parnaby — Mendieta, Boateng, Zenden, Downing (Nemeth 73) — Job (Juninho 73), Ricketts (Maccarone 73) *Subs not used* Davies, Jones *Booked* Parnaby, Riggott, Boateng, Zenden *Sent off* Boateng 86
Scorer **Job 23**
Report page 66

Saturday January 31
LEEDS UNITED (a)
Won 3-0   HT 0-0   Att 35,970   Position 12th
Schwarzer — Davies (Parnaby 54), Riggott, Southgate, Queudrue — Mendieta, Boateng, Doriva, Zenden — Juninho (Ricketts 85) — Maccarone (Job 74) *Subs not used* Jones, Downing *Booked* Queudrue
Scorers **Zenden 53, Job 77, Ricketts 89 (pen)**
Report page 159

Tuesday February 3
ARSENAL (h)
Carling Cup, semi-final, 2nd leg
Won 2-1 (won 3-1 on agg)   HT 0-0   Att 28,781
Report and details page 333

Saturday February 7
BLACKBURN ROVERS (h)
Lost 0-1   HT 0-1   Att 28,307   Position 13th
The Carling Cup finalists are brought down to earth by Stead, a £1.2m transfer window signing from Huddersfield Town, who coolly grabs the only goal on his debut for Blackburn, Graeme Souness having seemingly lost patience with Cole and Yorke. Friedel makes brilliant saves from Juninho and Southgate to seal victory.

Schwarzer — Mills, Riggott, Southgate, Queudrue — Mendieta (Nemeth 65), Parnaby (Downing ht), Doriva, Zenden — Maccarone (Job ht), Juninho *Subs not used* Jones, Cooper
Referee **R Styles**

Wednesday February 11
MANCHESTER UNITED (a)
Won 3-2   **HT 2-1**   **Att 67,346**   Position **13th**
Schwarzer — Mills, Riggott, Southgate, Queudrue —
Mendieta (Parnaby 73), Doriva, Zenden, Downing —
Juninho (Cooper 90) — Job *Subs not used* Nemeth,
Maccarone, Jones *Booked* Mills
Scorers **Juninho 34, 38, Job 80**
Report page 203

Saturday February 21
NEWCASTLE UNITED (a)
Lost 1-2   **HT 1-0**   **Att 52,156**   Position **13th**
Schwarzer — Mills, Ehiogu, Southgate, Parnaby
(Downing 85) — Mendieta, Boateng, Doriva (Ricketts 85),
Zenden — Juninho — Job *Subs not used* Jones,
Maccarone, Riggott *Booked* Doriva, Job, Mills
Scorer **Zenden 33**
Report page 224

Sunday February 29
BOLTON WANDERERS
Carling Cup, final (Cardiff)
Won 2-1   **HT 2-1**   **Att 72,634**
Report and details page 334

Wednesday March 3
BIRMINGHAM CITY (a)
Lost 1-3   **HT 0-1**   **Att 29,369**   Position **13th**
Schwarzer — Mills, Ehiogu, Southgate, Queudrue —
Greening (Nemeth 63), Boateng, Zenden, Downing
(Doriva ht) — Job (Maccarone ht), Ricketts *Subs not used*
Jones, Riggott *Booked* Boateng, Ricketts, Mills, Zenden,
Ehiogu *Sent off* Zenden 87
Scorer **Nemeth 75**
Report page 88

Tuesday March 9
TOTTENHAM HOTSPUR (h)
Won 1-0   **HT 0-0**   **Att 31,789**   Position **11th**
After their previous four games had produced 28 goals,
Spurs return to "sensible" football — and lose to
Nemeth's second-half strike. Keller had earlier kept out
Maccarone's penalty, while Schwarzer saves Anderton's
spectacular volley in the first half.

Schwarzer — Davies (Parnaby ht), Ehiogu, Southgate,
Queudrue — Mendieta, Boateng, Doriva (Maccarone ht),
Zenden — Juninho — Job (Nemeth 68) *Subs not used*
Jones, Riggott
Scorer **Nemeth 73**
Referee **M Halsey**

Saturday March 13
CHARLTON ATHLETIC (a)
Lost 0-1   **HT 0-1**   **Att 26,270**   Position **11th**
Schwarzer — Parnaby, Ehiogu, Southgate, Queudrue —
Mendieta (Greening 69), Boateng, Doriva (Nemeth ht),
Zenden — Juninho — Job (Maccarone ht) *Subs not used*
Jones, Riggott
Report page 118

THE PLAYERS

GEORGE BOATENG (midfield) **Born**
September 5, 1975, Nkawkaw, Ghana
Ht 5ft 9in **Wt** 10st 12lb **Signed from**
Aston Villa, August 2002, £5m

MALCOLM CHRISTIE (forward) **Born**
April 11, 1979, Stamford **Ht** 6ft 0in
Wt 12st 3lb **Signed from** Derby
County, January 2003, £3m

COLIN COOPER (defender) **Born**
February 28, 1967, Sedgefield
Ht 5ft 10in **Wt** 11st 9lb **Signed from**
Nottingham Forest, August 1998,
£2.5m

ANDREW DAVIES (defender) **Born**
December 17, 1984,
Stockton-on-Tees **Ht** 6ft 2in
Wt 12st 13lb **Signed from** trainee,
October 2002

DORIVA (midfield) **Born** May 28,
1972, Maranhao, Brazil **Ht** 5ft 9in
Wt 12st 4lb **Signed from** Celta Vigo
(initial loan), January 2003, free

STEWART DOWNING (midfield) **Born**
July 22, 1984, Middlesbrough
Ht 5ft 11in **Wt** 10st 6lb **Signed from**
trainee, September 2001

UGO EHIOGU (defender) **Born**
November 3, 1972, Hackney
Ht 6ft 2in **Wt** 14st 2lb **Signed from**
Aston Villa, October 2000, £8m

JONATHAN GREENING (midfield)
Born January 2, 1979, Scarborough
Ht 6ft 0in **Wt** 11st 0lb
Signed from Manchester United,
August 2001, £2m

JOSEPH-DESIRE JOB (forward) **Born**
December 1, 1977, Lyons **Ht** 5ft 10in
Wt 11st 0lb **Signed from** Lens, August
2000, £3m

BRADLEY JONES (goalkeeper) **Born**
February 19, 1982, Armadale,
Australia **Ht** 6ft 3in **Wt** 12st 0lb
Signed from trainee, August 2000

JUNINHO (midfield) **Born** February 22,
1973, Sao Paulo **Ht** 5ft 5in
Wt 9st 2lb **Signed from** Atletico
Madrid, August 2002, £6m

MASSIMO MACCARONE (forward)
Born September 6, 1979, Galliate,
Italy **Ht** 5ft 11in **Wt** 11st 9lb
Signed from Empoli, July 2002,
£8.15m

CARLOS MARINELLI (midfield) **Born**
March 14, 1982, Buenos Aires
Ht 5ft 8in **Wt** 11st 8lb **Signed from**
Boca Juniors, October 1999, £1.5m

GAIZKA MENDIETA (midfield) **Born**
March 27, 1974, Bilbao **Ht** 5ft 8in

Wt 10st 12lb **Signed from** Lazio
(loan), August 2003

DANNY MILLS (defender) **Born** May
18, 1977, Norwich **Ht** 5ft 11in
Wt 11st 9lb **Signed from** Leeds
United (loan) August 2003

JAMES MORRISON (midfield) **Born**
May 25, 1986, Darlington **Ht** 5ft 10in
Wt 10st 1lb **Signed from** trainee,
January 2004

CARLO NASH (goalkeeper) **Born**
September 13, 1973, Bolton
Ht 6ft 5in **Wt** 14st 1lb **Signed from**
Stockport County, January 2001,
£100,000

SZILARD NEMETH (forward) **Born**
September 14, 1972, Komarno,
Slovakia **Ht** 5ft 10in **Wt** 10st 10lb
Signed from Inter Bratislava, July
2001, free

STUART PARNABY (defender) **Born**
July 19, 1982, Durham **Ht** 5ft 10in
Wt 11st 0lb **Signed from** trainee,
August 2000

FRANCK QUEUDRUE (defender) **Born**
August 27, 1978, Paris **Ht** 6ft 0in
Wt 12st 2lb **Signed from** Lens,
October 2001, £2.5m

MICHAEL RICKETTS (forward) **Born**
December 4, 1978, Birmingham
Ht 6ft 2in **Wt** 11st 12lb **Signed from**
Bolton Wanderers, January 2003,
£3.5m

CHRIS RIGGOTT (defender) **Born**
September 1, 1980, Derby **Ht** 6ft 0in
Wt 12st 3lb **Signed from** Derby
County, January 2000, £2m

MARK SCHWARZER (goalkeeper)
Born October 6, 1972, Sydney
Ht 6ft 5in **Wt** 13st 6lb **Signed from**
Bradford City, February 1997, £1.5m

GARETH SOUTHGATE (defender)
Born September 3, 1970, Watford
Ht 6ft 0in **Wt** 12st 8lb **Signed from**
Aston Villa, July 2001, £6.5m

ROBBIE STOCKDALE (defender) **Born**
November 30, 1979, Redcar
Ht 5ft 11in **Wt** 11st 3lb **Signed from**
trainee, July 1998

ALAN WRIGHT (defender) **Born**
September 28, 1971,
Ashton-under-Lyne **Ht** 5ft 4in
Wt 9st 4lb **Signed from** Aston Villa,
July 2003, free

BOUDEWIJN ZENDEN (midfield) **Born**
August 15, 1976, Maastricht **Ht** 5ft 8in
Wt 11st 0lb **Signed from** Chelsea
(loan), August 2003

STATS AND FACTS

● In December and January, Middlesbrough had a run of seven successive matches that were played either at their own Riverside Stadium (four games) or in North London against Arsenal at Highbury (three).

● Middlesbrough have won just one of their past 15 meetings with Chelsea, their Wembley nemesis in 1997 and 1998.

● However, they have lost once to Tottenham Hotspur in their past 12 meetings.

● Middlesbrough's Carling Cup semi-final win at Highbury ended a run of seven successive defeats by Arsenal.

● The past eight meetings between Charlton Athletic and Middlesbrough have produced just five goals.

● In January, Juninho became the third Brazilian to score for Middlesbrough against Arsenal at Highbury in the past three years. The others were Edu and Silvinho, with own goals.

Bill Edgar

GOALSCORERS

	Prem	FAC	CC	Total
M Christie	1	-	1	2
J Greening	1	-	-	1
J-D Job	6	1	1	8
Juninho	8	-	1	9
M Maccarone	6 (1p)	-	1	7 (1p)
C Marinelli	1	-	-	1
G Mendieta	2	-	1	3
S Nemeth	9	-	-	9
M Ricketts	2 (2p)	-	1	3 (2p)
G Southgate	1	-	-	1
B Zenden	4	1	2 (1p)	7 (1p)
Own goals	3	1	1	5

Saturday March 20
BIRMINGHAM CITY (h)
Won 5-3   HT 4-2   Att 30,244   Position 10th
It is not often that a goalkeeper is beaten three times and earns the man-of-the-match award, but Schwarzer emerges as the clear hero from the highest-scoring game in Riverside Stadium history. He makes five outstanding saves in the first half alone as Middlesbrough three times open a two-goal lead, but they need a fifth in the last minute finally to see off Birmingham.

Schwarzer — Mills, Ehiogu, Southgate, Queudrue — Mendieta, Doriva, Greening — Juninho (Nemeth 76) — Job (Downing 64), Maccarone (Ricketts 75) *Subs not used* Jones, Parnaby *Booked* Greening, Queudrue
Scorers **Mendieta 5, Maccarone 21, 45, Southgate 30, Nemeth 90**
Referee **U Rennie**

Saturday March 27
EVERTON (a)
Drew 1-1   HT 0-0   Att 38,210   Position 11th
Schwarzer — Mills (Nemeth 80), Riggott, Southgate, Queudrue — Mendieta, Boateng, Zenden — Juninho — Job, Maccarone (Doriva 58; Parnaby 64) *Subs not used* Ricketts, Jones *Booked* Boateng, Zenden
Scorer **Job 83**
Report page 141

Saturday April 3
BOLTON WANDERERS (h)
Won 2-0   HT 1-0   Att 30,107   Position 11th
The resumption of hostilities between the Carling Cup finalists ends in victory for Middlesbrough again. Sent on their way by Hunt's sliced own goal, they deserve to win by a wider margin but have to settle for a second by Greening. "The players and fans are enjoying our football," Steve McClaren says.

Schwarzer — Mills, Ehiogu, Riggott, Zenden — Mendieta, Boateng, Greening — Juninho (Ricketts 79) — Job (Nemeth ht), Maccarone (Downing 70) *Subs not used* Jones, Bates *Booked* Greening, Ehiogu
Scorers **Nolan 8 (og), Greening 51**
Referee **N Barry**

Saturday April 10
CHELSEA (a)
Drew 0-0   HT 0-0   Att 40,873   Position 11th
Schwarzer — Parnaby, Ehiogu, Cooper, Queudrue — Mendieta, Boateng, Greening — Nemeth (Ricketts 68), Maccarone (Downing 75) *Subs not used* Turnbull, Ricardinho, Bates *Booked* Boateng
Report page 131

Monday April 12
SOUTHAMPTON (h)
Won 3-1   HT 2-0   Att 30,768   Position 9th
Steve McClaren has challenged his side to beat the club's highest top-division finish of ninth, the position they occupy after this decisive win. Juninho is the architect and Southampton are well beaten before Beattie's reply, Niemi preventing a much heavier defeat.

Schwarzer — Mills, Ehiogu, Cooper, Queudrue — Mendieta (Greening 86), Boateng, Zenden — Juninho (Ricketts 88) — Maccarone, Nemeth (Downing 81) *Subs not used* Jones, Bates
Scorers **Juninho 23, Nemeth 32, Maccarone 49**
Referee **D Gallagher**

PLAYER OF THE SEASON

Mark Schwarzer

It is all too easy to take good goalkeepers for granted — it is their job to make sometimes spectacular saves that bring gasps from the crowd, but which are promptly forgotten minutes later when a cross is fumbled and grumbles echo around the stadium. The difference between Mark Schwarzer and some of his fellow goalkeepers is the way that he reacts to such adversity. In the Carling Cup final, rather than go to pieces after his awful error handed Bolton a lifeline, Schwarzer turned in a breathtaking performance to keep Middlesbrough in the game. Other creditable performances, notably in the 5-3 win against Birmingham City, exemplify what an important part the captain of Australia played for his club this season.

Shaun Keogh

Saturday April 17
WOLVERHAMPTON WANDERERS (a)
Lost 0-2 HT 0-1 Att **27,975** Position **11th**
Schwarzer — Mills, Ehiogu, Riggott, Queudrue (Ricketts 74) — Mendieta, Boateng, Zenden — Juninho — Maccarone, Nemeth (Job 60) Subs not used Greening, Jones, Cooper Booked Queudrue, Riggott
Report page 268

Saturday April 24
ASTON VILLA (h)
Lost 1-2 HT 1-1 Att **31,322** Position **12th**
A superb display by Sorensen, who make outstanding saves from Job — before he gives Middlesbrough the lead — and Mendieta, earns Villa victory, although it is Crouch who taps in the late winner. They are forced to play for 33 minutes with ten men after Solano, not helped by Boateng's theatrics, is sent off for violent conduct.
Schwarzer — Mills (Nemeth 83), Ehiogu, Riggott, Queudrue (Downing 87) — Mendieta, Boateng, Zenden — Juninho — Maccarone, Job Subs not used Greening, Cooper, Jones
Scorer **Job 41**
Referee **G Barber**

Sunday May 2
LIVERPOOL (a)
Lost 0-2 HT 0-0 Att **42,031** Position **12th**
Schwarzer — Mills, Ehiogu, Riggott (Downing 64), Queudrue — Mendieta, Boateng, Greening, Zenden — Job (Ricketts 83), Maccarone (Nemeth 64) Subs not used Bates, Jones Booked Mills
Report page 184

Saturday May 8
MANCHESTER CITY (h)
Won 2-1 HT 2-1 Att **34,734** Position **11th**
"Probably our worst performance of the season," Ehiogu says, but Middlesbrough win nonetheless when Maccarone's mis-hit cross and Nemeth's goal account for Manchester City, for whom Wanchope replies. Kevin Keegan, grateful that his team's status is already assured, reiterates that he will not walk away from his job as manager.
Schwarzer — Mills, Ehiogu, Queudrue, Zenden — Mendieta, Boateng, Greening — Nemeth — Job, Maccarone (Downing 63) Subs not used Nash, Ricketts, Morrison, Bates Booked Nemeth
Scorers **Maccarone 8, Nemeth 32**
Referee **M Riley**

Saturday May 15
PORTSMOUTH (a)
Lost 1-5 HT 1-3 Att **20,134** Position **11th**
Schwarzer — Mills, Ehiogu, Queudrue, Zenden — Mendieta, Boateng, Greening, Downing (Morrison 63) — Job, Nemeth (Ricketts 63) Subs not used Nash, Wilson, Bates
Scorer **Zenden 27**
Report page 238

NEWCASTLE UNITED

PREMIERSHIP

	P	W	D	L	F	A	GD	Pts
Arsenal	38	26	12	0	73	26	47	**90**
Chelsea	38	24	7	7	67	30	37	**79**
Man Utd	38	23	6	9	64	35	29	**75**
Liverpool	38	16	12	10	55	37	18	**60**
Newcastle	38	13	17	8	52	40	12	**56**
Aston Villa	38	15	11	12	48	44	4	**56**
Charlton	38	14	11	13	51	51	0	**53**
Bolton	38	14	11	13	48	56	-8	**53**
Fulham	38	14	10	14	52	46	6	**52**
Birmingham	38	12	14	12	43	48	-5	**50**
Middlesbro	38	13	9	16	44	52	-8	**48**
Southampton	38	12	11	15	44	45	-1	**47**
Portsmouth	38	12	9	17	47	54	-7	**45**
Tottenham	38	13	6	19	47	57	-10	**45**
Blackburn	38	12	8	18	51	59	-8	**44**
Man City	38	9	14	15	55	54	1	**41**
Everton	38	9	12	17	45	57	-12	**39**
Leicester	38	6	15	17	48	65	-17	**33**
Leeds	38	8	9	21	40	79	-39	**33**
Wolves	38	7	12	19	38	77	-39	**33**

FA CUP
Fourth round

CARLING CUP
Third round

UEFA CUP
Semi-finals

Spot of trouble: the faces say it all as Newcastle go out of the Champions League in a penalty shoot-out against Partizan Belgrade

THE GAMES

Wednesday August 13 2003
PARTIZAN BELGRADE (a)
Champions League, 3rd qualifying rnd, 1st leg
Won 1-0   **HT 1-0**   Att **32,500**
Most English eyes are on Chelsea after their
big-spending summer, but Solano's goal gets Newcastle's
European campaign off to a superb start, even if five
bookings – Partizan also have four players cautioned –
means an automatic Uefa fine.

Given – Griffin, O'Brien, Woodgate, Bernard – Solano
(Jenas 88), Dyer, Speed, Robert (Ameobi 65) – Shearer,
Bellamy *Subs not used* Harper, Elliott, Hughes, Bramble,
Chopra *Booked* O'Brien, Bernard, Shearer, Bellamy,
Ameobi
Scorer **Solano 39**
Referee **V Hrinak (Slovakia)**

Sunday August 17
LEEDS UNITED (a)
Drew 2-2   **HT 1-1**   Att **36,766**   Position **11th**
Given – Hughes, O'Brien, Woodgate, Bernard (Jenas 73)
– Bowyer (Ameobi 73), Dyer, Speed, Robert (Solano 84)
– Shearer, Bellamy *Subs not used* Harper, Griffin *Booked*
Woodgate, Bellamy
Scorer **Shearer 20 (pen), 88**
Report page 154

Saturday August 23
MANCHESTER UNITED (h)
Lost 1-2   **HT 1-0**   Att **52,165**   Position **15th**
Sir Alex Ferguson watches his team win from behind
from Sir Bobby Robson's office after being sent from the
touchline for his furious protest to Jeff Winter, the fourth
official, after Uriah Rennie's failure to punish O'Brien's
seeming professional foul on Giggs. Scholes chests in
the winner from close range.

Given – Griffin, Bramble, O'Brien, Hughes – Bowyer
(Jenas 72), Dyer, Speed, Robert (Viana 72) – Shearer,
Ameobi (Chopra 72) *Subs not used* Harper, Bernard
Booked Griffin, Bramble
Scorer **Shearer 26**
Referee **U Rennie**

Wednesday August 27
PARTIZAN BELGRADE (h)
Champions League, 3rd qualifying rnd, 2nd leg
Lost 0-1 (aet; 1-1 on agg; lost 3-4 on pens)
HT 0-0 Att **37,293**
Defeat, and consequent demotion from the Champions
League to the Uefa Cup, is a potential £10m calamity for
Newcastle, who concede a 50th-minute goal to Iliev and
blow the penalty shoot-out when Shearer, Dyer and
Woodgate miss the first three spot kicks. Hughes's
failure is the final straw.

Given – Hughes, O'Brien, Woodgate, Bernard – Solano
(LuaLua 106), Dyer, Speed (Jenas 91), Viana (Robert 86)
– Shearer, Ameobi *Subs not used* Griffin, Harper,
Bramble, Chopra *Booked* O'Brien
Referee **J Wegereef (the Netherlands)**

"WHAT'S IN FRONT OF US IS HUGE," Alan Shearer told George
Caulkin, of *The Times*, on the eve of the Uefa Cup semi-final second
leg away to Marseilles. "There can't be any middle ground now,
there can't be anything in between. It's either great or nothing."
Well, taking the Newcastle United captain at face value, "nothing"
was what it turned out to be. A season that had opened with such
bright promise petered out beneath the Stade Velodrome
floodlights, although in reality the decisive points had been passed
much earlier.

The successful teams always strengthen when they are ahead and
Newcastle's decision to not spend after 2002-03's stirring third-
place finish never looked anything other than perverse. Subsequent
decisions to sell or loan out players who could have made a
difference in Marseilles compounded the error, seriously calling Sir
Bobby Robson's judgment into question for the first time.

The manager defended the cut-price sale of Nolberto Solano to
the team that almost pipped Newcastle for a place in Europe as
"good business". By that rationale, United consider the cost of failing
to qualify for the Champions League and inability to compete for a
place in the Uefa Cup final to be less than £1.5 million.

It might be stretching the point to claim that Solano was the
difference between fifth and fourth place, or between winning and
losing against Marseilles, but his replacements have been woefully
inadequate. Since he joined Newcastle, the only Premiership players
to have created more goals than the Peruvian are David Beckham
and Ryan Giggs — a rare case of statistics accurately representing a
player's worth. The plucky Darren Ambrose is a trier but is clearly
not yet in Solano's class and Lee Bowyer bears only scant relation to
the player of the same name who used to turn out for Leeds United.

Defeat by Partizan Belgrade ended United's Champions League
campaign before it had even begun and when it has been almost 40
years since the last trophy, turning out weakened teams in Carling
Cup matches is to invite defeat. Which is exactly what happened
when West Bromwich Albion visited St James' Park.

The results after the Marseilles defeat did not help. Fifth place was
secured, if fans are honest, by dint of some harsh refereeing at Villa
Park, where the home team were denied two goals that might have
earned them a point against Manchester United, rather than
anything the team had merited from displays away to Liverpool and,
particularly, at home to Wolverhampton Wanderers. The booing
meted out to the team that day was regrettable, but for many who
pay increasingly inflated sums to a club all too adept at treating their
loyalty with something approaching contempt, it was entirely

HONOURS BOARD

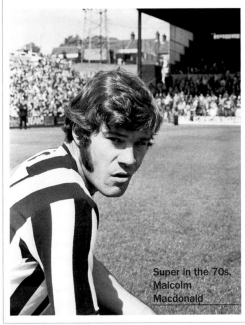

Super in the 70s, Malcolm Macdonald

understandable. After the dreadful start to the season, a decent European run and a top-five finish might well have been enough for most Newcastle fans. But, yet again, the club clawed their way to within touching distance of something better, only for hopes to be dashed by some careless and, seemingly, passionless performances — particularly away from home — when the pressure was on.

To what extent the club's problems off the field affected morale and performance is difficult to say, but the fact that Kieron Dyer and Titus Bramble were in the thick of a raft of unwanted headlines after the word "roasting" acquired a whole new meaning cannot have helped.

It was strongly rumoured that an incandescent Robson all but resigned when learning that members of his squad had even been in the position to be accused of such impropriety, whether guilty or not, and that senior squad members were understandably disgusted. Subsequent reports have painted a picture of a divided dressing-room, older professionals such as Shearer and Gary Speed distancing themselves from the younger and wilder element.

Few non-playing United employees emerged with any credit from the season either. Bowyer's six-game European ban was doubled because someone at United forgot to send the correct form to Uefa. Lomana LuaLua was bizarrely allowed to play against Newcastle while on loan to Portsmouth, scoring a late goal that cost United two points, while Nikos Dabizas, the popular defender, was denied the opportunity of a final run-out at St James' for Leicester City. Inconsistency compounded ineptitude as the club lurched from one

Saturday August 30
BIRMINGHAM CITY (h)
Lost 0-1 **HT 0-0** Att **52,006** Position **18th**
"The most horrendous week I've had in football" — Sir Bobby Robson's verdict after a third successive home defeat for Newcastle is inflicted by Dunn, who reacts quickest when Given parries his penalty. Birmingham are the only senior side in England yet to concede a goal.

Given — Griffin, O'Brien, Bramble, Speed — Solano (Bowyer 66), Dyer, Jenas, Viana (Robert 66) — Shearer, Ameobi (Chopra 66) *Subs not used* Harper, Hughes *Booked* Speed, Jenas
Referee **M Messias**

Saturday September 13
EVERTON (a)
Drew 2-2 **HT 0-0** Att **40,228** Position **17th**
Given — Griffin, O'Brien, Bramble, Bernard — Bowyer, Dyer, Speed (Jenas 71), Robert — Shearer, Bellamy *Subs not used* Hughes, Ameobi, Caig, Viana *Booked* Griffin, Bernard, Robert, Bellamy, Jenas *Sent off* Robert 40
Scorer **Shearer 59 (pen), 82 (pen)**
Report page 135

Saturday September 20
BOLTON WANDERERS (h)
Drew 0-0 **HT 0-0** Att **52,014** Position **18th**
Close shaves for Speed, Bramble — who hits the bar — and Dyer consign Newcastle to their first goalless draw in 80 matches. Okocha forces the save of the game from Given as Bolton keep a third successive clean sheet.

Given — Griffin, Bramble, Woodgate, Bernard — Solano (Ameobi 79), Dyer, Speed (Jenas 78), Robert — Shearer, Bellamy *Subs not used* Hughes, Caig, Bowyer *Booked* Dyer
Referee **G Barber**

Wednesday September 24
NAC BREDA (h)
Uefa Cup, 1st rnd, 1st leg
Won 5-0 **HT 2-0** Att **36,007**
Newcastle's first home victory, at the fifth time of asking, is delivered in style, Bellamy getting off the mark for the season with the first two goals.

Given — Hughes, O'Brien, Bramble, Bernard (Viana 84) — Dyer (Ambrose 79), Jenas, Speed, Robert — Shearer, Bellamy (Ameobi 79) *Subs not used* Griffin, LuaLua, Caig, Caldwell
Scorers **Bellamy 31, 37, Bramble 59, Shearer 77, Ambrose 89**
Referee **N Ibanov (Russia)**

Friday September 26
ARSENAL (a)
Lost 2-3 **HT 1-1** Att **38,112** Position **19th**
Given — Hughes, Bramble, O'Brien, Bernard — Dyer, Bowyer (Speed 72), Jenas (Ameobi 89), Robert (Ambrose 81) — Shearer, Bellamy *Subs not used* Griffin, Caig *Booked* Robert
Scorers **Robert 26, Bernard 71**
Report page 61

Saturday October 4
SOUTHAMPTON (h)
Won 1-0 **HT 1-0** Att **52,157** Position **18th**
A difficult week for Sir Bobby Robson, in which he is forced to deny rumours that he has resigned, ends on a brighter note when Shearer's 250th league goal, against his first professional club, earns Newcastle's first Premiership win. Jones, dropped as Southampton goalkeeper in favour of Niemi, says he wants a move.

Given — Hughes, Bramble, O'Brien, Bernard — Dyer, Jenas, Speed, Bowyer — Shearer, Bellamy *Subs not used* Griffin, Harper, Ambrose, Ameobi, Viana *Booked* O'Brien, Bramble, Bowyer
Scorer **Shearer 44**
Referee **P Dowd**

Wednesday October 15
NAC BREDA (a)
Uefa Cup, 1st rnd, 2nd leg
Won 1-0 (won 6-0 on agg) HT 0-0 Att 15,564
Sir Bobby Robson's 100th win as Newcastle manager is
achieved with Robert's simple late finish from Jenas's
pass. A routine night is spoilt only by reports of 90
pre-match arrests after rival fans clash.

Harper — Griffin, O'Brien, Bramble (Caldwell 78), Bernard
— Solano (Ambrose 78), Dyer (LuaLua 84), Jenas, Robert
— Ameobi, Viana *Subs not used* Given, Shearer, Speed,
Hughes *Booked* Bramble, Bernard
Scorer **Robert 86**
Referee **E Bernsten (Norway)**

Saturday October 18
MIDDLESBROUGH (a)
Won 1-0 HT 1-0 Att 34,081 Position 11th
Given — Hughes, Bramble, O'Brien, Bernard — Dyer,
Jenas, Speed, Bowyer (Robert 77) — Shearer, Ameobi
Subs not used Harper, Griffin, LuaLua, Viana *Booked*
O'Brien, Speed, Bramble
Scorer **Ameobi 21**
Report page 209

Tuesday October 21
FULHAM (a)
Won 3-2 HT 1-2 Att 16,506 Position 10th
Given — Hughes, Bramble, O'Brien, Bernard — Bowyer,
Jenas, Speed, Robert (Ambrose 87) — Shearer, Ameobi
Subs not used Harper, LuaLua, Caldwell, Viana *Booked*
Speed, Bowyer
Scorers **Robert 16, Shearer 51 (pen), 56**
Report page 145

Saturday October 25
PORTSMOUTH (h)
Won 3-0 HT 2-0 Att 52,161 Position 8th
Newcastle claim their fifth successive win after 90
minutes of one-way traffic, Speed putting them on their
way from distance and Shearer converting his fifth
penalty of the season after Stefanovic handles. "There
are no positives for us," Harry Redknapp says of
Portsmouth's "poorest performance of the season".

Given — Hughes, O'Brien, Bramble, Bernard — Bowyer
(Ambrose 80), Jenas, Speed, Robert (Viana 80) —
Shearer, Ameobi (LuaLua 80) *Subs not used* Harper,
Caldwell
Scorers **Speed 17, Shearer 28 (pen), Ameobi 61**
Referee **P Durkin**

Wednesday October 29
WEST BROMWICH ALBION (h)
Carling Cup, 3rd rnd
Lost 1-2 (aet; 1-1 after 90min) HT 0-1 Att 46,932
The shock of the night. Ameobi's own goal puts the
first-division leaders in front and, after Robert forces
extra time, Hughes earns Albion a tie against Manchester
United with his first goal for two months.

Harper — Griffin, Caldwell, Bramble, Bernard — Solano
(Ambrose 84), Jenas, Viana (Speed ht), Robert
(Shearer 99) — Ameobi, LuaLua *Subs not used* Given,
Hughes *Booked* Bramble, LuaLua
Scorer **Robert 65**
Referee **N Barry**

Bernard and Jenas join Robert in celebrating his equaliser at Highbury

crisis of its own making to the next. In Robson's considerable favour,
he never tried to hide behind the excuse that injuries provided.

Assuming Robson's first-choice XI includes Jonathan Woodgate,
Craig Bellamy and Dyer, then he was only able to play it five times
all season. When other casualties are taken into account, perhaps
fifth place starts to look like some sort of achievement.

Dyer himself admitted before the final game of the season that the
"young guns" had let the rest down. "We'd started to believe our
own hype," he said. "We believed the nice things that were being
said and written about us after two years of steady improvement and
thought we just needed to turn up to get fourth place." Singling out
Shearer, Speed, Bellamy, the incomparable Shay Given and Olivier
Bernard as the only players who had pulled their weight, Dyer
concluded that "the rest of us have, quite simply, not been good
enough. We need to take a long hard look at ourselves."

If Dyer and his fellow underachievers do not turn that introspec-
tion into improvement, Newcastle are in trouble. It is not just the
presence of Woodgate and Bowyer that gives Newcastle the look of
Leeds two years ago. Just as worrying is the prospect that the club is
on the verge of becoming the Tottenham Hotspur of the North.

The gap to the top three seems unbridgeable and if United cannot
compete with Liverpool, then a slow and painful period of mediocrity beckons. Application, passion and commitment from those
wearing the black and white has never been more urgently required.

THE MANAGER — Sir Bobby Robson

While he remains immensely popular, Robson's management is under intense scrutiny. When what appear to be personality differences are allowed to influence team selection (the departures of Nolberto Solano and Lomana LuaLua followed alleged disagreements with Robson over availability for internationals), then a turning point has surely been reached. Robson faces several pressing challenges. He must continue to build for the future, but has urgently to shore up the team for the present and unite a divided dressing-room. It is a Herculean task. No United fan seriously wants him to leave before winning something, but he is not immortal.

Angus Batey

APPEARANCES

	Prem	FAC	CC	Euro	Total
D Ambrose	10 (14)	0 (1)	0 (1)	6 (5)	16 (21)
F Ameobi	18 (8)	0 (1)	1	8 (5)	27 (14)
C Bellamy	13 (3)	-	-	7 (1)	20 (4)
O Bernard	35	2	1	13	51
L Bowyer	17 (7)	-	-	0 (1)	17 (8)
T Bramble	27 (2)	1	1	11	40 (2)
M Bridges	0 (6)	-	-	1 (2)	1 (8)
M Brittain	0 (1)	-	-	0 (1)	0 (2)
S Caldwell	3 (2)	-	1	0 (1)	4 (3)
M Chopra	1 (5)	-	-	-	1 (5)
K Dyer	25	2	-	6 (1)	33 (1)
S Given	38	2	-	13	53
A Griffin	5	-	1	2	8
S Harper	-	-	1	1	2
A Hughes	34	2	-	11	47
J Jenas	26 (5)	2	1	10 (2)	39 (7)
L LuaLua	2 (5)	0 (1)	1	0 (2)	3 (8)
A O'Brien	27 (1)	1	-	12 (1)	40 (2)
L Robert	31 (4)	2	1	12 (2)	46 (6)
A Shearer	37	2	0 (1)	12	51 (1)
N Solano	8 (4)	2	1	4 (1)	15 (5)
G Speed	37 (1)	2	0 (1)	13	52 (2)
S Taylor	1	-	-	0 (1)	1 (1)
H Viana	5 (11)	0 (1)	1	5 (4)	11 (16)
J Woodgate	18	2	-	7	27

Saturday November 1
ASTON VILLA (h)
Drew 1-1   HT 1-1   Att 51,975   Position 7th
Villa need Sorensen's second-half penalty save from Shearer to record their fourth successive league draw after Dublin, up from centre half for a corner, and Robert, with a fine volley, score before the break. Villa's ten men hold on after McCann's dismissal for two bookings with 20 minutes left.

Given — Hughes, Caldwell, Bramble, Bernard — Bowyer, Jenas, Speed, Robert — Shearer, Ameobi *Subs not used* Solano, Harper, Ambrose, LuaLua, Dabizas *Booked* Speed, Bowyer
Scorer **Robert 45**
Referee **M Messias**

Thursday November 6
FC BASLE (a)
Uefa Cup, 2nd rnd, 1st leg
Won 3-2   HT 2-2   Att 30,000
Twice behind in the first half, Newcastle recover each time and go on to inflict a first defeat on Basle since April when Ameobi scores from Solano's pass.

Given — Hughes, O'Brien, Bramble, Bernard — Solano (Ambrose 86), Jenas, Speed, Robert (Viana 90) — Shearer, Ameobi *Subs not used* Harper, LuaLua, Chopra, Caldwell, Dabizas
Scorers **Robert 14, Bramble 37, Ameobi 75**
Referee **T Ovrebo (Norway)**

Sunday November 9
CHELSEA (a)
Lost 0-5   HT 0-3   Att 41,332   Position 10th
Given — Hughes, O'Brien, Bramble, Bernard — Bowyer, Jenas, Speed, Robert (LuaLua 77) — Ameobi, Viana (Caldwell 43) *Subs not used* Solano, Harper, Chopra
Sent off O'Brien 42
Report page 125

Saturday November 22
MANCHESTER CITY (h)
Won 3-0   HT 0-0   Att 52,159   Position 6th
Newcastle Falcons' Jonny Wilkinson may have won the rugby World Cup for England this morning, but Shearer is still King of Tyneside after his double — a thumping header and a scrambled second — rounds off victory. "He's the complete player," Kevin Keegan says of his former star striker.

Given — Hughes, Bramble, Woodgate, Bernard — Dyer (Bowyer 86), Jenas, Speed, Robert (Ambrose 88) — Shearer, Ameobi (LuaLua 89) *Subs not used* Harper, Caldwell *Booked* Bowyer
Scorers **Ameobi 57, Shearer 77, 85**
Referee **N Barry**

Thursday November 27
FC BASLE (h)
Uefa Cup, 2nd rnd, 2nd leg
Won 1-0 (won 4-2 on agg)   HT 1-0   Att 40,395
The gift of an own goal eases Newcastle's nerves, but they ride their luck in the second half as the Swiss team have a goal disallowed for offside, are denied a penalty for Given's foul on Cantaluppi and finally hit the woodwork.

Given — Hughes, Bramble, O'Brien, Bernard — Dyer (Solano 78), Jenas, Speed, Robert (Ambrose 78) — Shearer, Ameobi *Subs not used* Harper, LuaLua, Woodgate, Caldwell, Viana *Booked* Shearer
Scorer **Smiljanic 14 (og)**
Referee **K E Fisker (Denmark)**

Saturday November 29
WOLVERHAMPTON WANDERERS (a)
Drew 1-1   **HT 1-1**   Att **29,344**   Position **6th**
Given — Hughes, Woodgate, Bramble, Bernard — Dyer,
Jenas, Speed, Bowyer (Solano 78) — Shearer, LuaLua
(Ameobi 78) *Subs not used* Harper, Caldwell, Viana
Booked Bernard
Scorer **Shearer 31**
Report page 263

Saturday December 6
LIVERPOOL (h)
Drew 1-1   **HT 0-1**   Att **52,151**   Position **7th**
Tord Grip is reported as saying in the morning
newspapers that England would love to have Shearer at
Euro 2004 and, typically, the now-retired international
striker scores Newcastle's equaliser from the spot. An
excellent lunchtime contest between the favourites for
fourth place has a frantic finale, including goalline
clearances at each end.

Given — Hughes (Solano ht), Woodgate, Bramble, Bernard
— Dyer, Jenas, Speed, Robert — Shearer, Ameobi *Subs
not used* Harper, O'Brien, Ambrose, LuaLua *Booked*
Bramble
Scorer **Shearer 63 (pen)**
Referee **G Poll**

Saturday December 13
TOTTENHAM HOTSPUR (h)
Won 4-0   **HT 1-0**   Att **52,139**   Position **5th**
Robert, who almost misses the game through illness,
leaves Spurs feeling groggy with two stunning long-range,
left-foot volleys before Shearer strikes twice from much
closer distance. His second sparks a furious
finger-jabbing exchange between Keller and Richards as
Spurs implode.

Given — Hughes, Woodgate (O'Brien ht), Bramble, Bernard
— Dyer, Jenas, Speed (Solano 80), Robert (Ambrose 79)
— Shearer, Ameobi *Subs not used* Harper, LuaLua
Booked Jenas, Ambrose
Scorers **Robert 35, 55, Shearer 59, 66**
Referee **A Wiley**

Saturday December 20
CHARLTON ATHLETIC (a)
Drew 0-0   **HT 0-0**   Att **26,508**   Position **5th**
Given — Solano, O'Brien, Hughes, Bernard — Dyer,
Jenas, Speed, Robert (Ambrose 87) — Shearer,
Ameobi (LuaLua 77) *Subs not used* Harper, Caldwell,
Viana
Report page 116

Friday December 26
LEICESTER CITY (a)
Drew 1-1   **HT 0-0**   Att **32,148**   Position **6th**
Given — Hughes (Ambrose 85), O'Brien, Bramble,
Bernard — Solano, Jenas, Speed, Robert — Shearer,
LuaLua (Chopra 85) *Subs not used* Harper, Woodgate,
Viana
Scorer **Ambrose 90**
Report page 168

MATCH OF THE SEASON

Newcastle United 2 Chelsea 1
St James' Park, Sunday April 25 2004
George Caulkin

THEY THINK IT'S ALL OVER — it was an age ago. The last rites had been said for Chelsea's lingering challenge for the championship when Arsenal had trounced Liverpool and turned a Good Friday distinctly bad for Claudio Ranieri, but St James' Park was the scene of the burial yesterday. And yet it was never sombre; the hosts were disrespectful, the guests misbehaved and the atmosphere remained consistently raucous.

As Chelsea raged against the dying of the light, Newcastle United energised their push for fourth place in the Barclaycard Premiership with a performance crammed full of vim, desire and two sublime goals from Shola Ameobi and Alan Shearer. The drama was compelling and if anticlimax hung over Tyneside last night, it was only because a home victory came at a considerable cost. Jonathan Woodgate is likely to miss the rest of the season.

Woodgate limped from the field in the 78th minute after pulling a thigh muscle fending Jimmy Floyd Hasselbaink away from the ball. According to Sir Bobby Robson, the injury could be felt for "three, four or even six weeks" and with Craig Bellamy, Kieron Dyer and Jermaine Jenas also absent, the timing was cruel. England may also suffer. "Other teams will be laughing at us," the manager said.

Chelsea can now expect similar treatment. Having wallowed in Roman Abramovich's largesse and treated Ranieri with contempt, the denizens of Stamford Bridge will not be offered sympathy having failed to derail the Arsenal bandwagon, but they tried manfully here. "I'm not going to congratulate Arsenal again, because I did that four matches ago," Ranieri said. "They were champions then." The Italian also insisted that he was "not disappointed, but unhappy" with the result. "I've always said to my players that if they give their maximum and try their best, they don't have to worry about anything else," he said. "They're very focused." They also hit the woodwork in the final moments.

Chelsea must recharge again to ward off Manchester United from second place, but Marcel Desailly apart, there was no slackness against Newcastle. They lost from a winning position earned by Joe Cole, but they fought for everything, if sometimes too literally; Robert Huth, the substitute, was guilty of a dreadful tackle that almost separated Shearer from his. "I've checked downstairs and I've still got two," the former England captain said.

Shearer had the last laugh, because the goal with which he won the game — his 28th of the season — was supreme. "It has to be one of his best," Robson said. "It was a stunning shot and right off his lace-holes." Robson described the match as "epic, enthralling and fantastic", praising the "remarkable effort" from his team. Yet

The familiar salute goes up after Shearer had blasted the winning goal

Newcastle began hesitantly. A lightning exchange of passes with Frank Lampard inside five minutes took Cole down the spine of the pitch, squeezing between Woodgate and Andy O'Brien to claim his first league goal for Chelsea. "We allowed Cole to walk it in," Robson said. "It wasn't a dribble, it was drivel."

Buoyed by the knowledge that Newcastle would strain for an equaliser, Chelsea scented the possibility of mischief. In spite of being moored on Chelsea's left flank, Cole was seldom marooned, producing one of his more engaged performances. By rights, the lead should have been doubled when he tracked into the penalty area, caused O'Brien to lose his footing by checking his run and slid his shot narrowly off target. In attack, Eidur Gudjohnsen had his moments, while Hernan Crespo spurned his.

Newcastle's return to parity was timed to perfection, because it robbed Chelsea of a momentum that they were to scratch around for

Sunday December 28
BLACKBURN ROVERS (h)
Lost 0-1   HT 0-0   Att **51,648**   Position **7th**
Sir Bobby Robson insists that Gallagher uses his hand to bundle in Blackburn's winner and television evidence is on his side, but Rovers' joy is cut short when Ferguson suffers a broken kneecap in an innocuous but grisly collision with Speed and is ruled out of the rest of the season.

Given — Hughes, O'Brien, Bramble, Bernard — Solano (Ambrose 70), Jenas, Speed (Viana 80), Robert — Shearer, Chopra (LuaLua 70) *Subs not used* Harper, Woodgate
Referee **M Halsey**

Saturday January 3 2004
SOUTHAMPTON (a)
FA Cup, 3rd rnd
Won 3-0   HT 2-0   Att **28,456**
Given — Hughes, Woodgate, Bramble, Bernard — Solano (Ambrose 82), Jenas, Speed, Robert (Viana 87) — Shearer, Dyer (LuaLua 82) *Subs not used* Harper, O'Brien
Scorers **Dyer 24, 67, Robert 39**
Report page 245

Wednesday January 7
LEEDS UNITED (h)
Won 1-0   HT 1-0   Att **52,130**   Position **6th**
With Smith banned earlier in the day after his Elland Road bottle-throwing episode, Leeds are behind within four minutes and rarely threaten a reply. Robinson prevents a heavier defeat after he escapes a red card for bringing down Dyer outside the area.

Given — Hughes, Woodgate, Bramble, Bernard — Solano (Ambrose 81), Jenas, Speed, Robert (Viana 79) — Shearer, Dyer *Subs not used* Harper, O'Brien, LuaLua
Scorer **Shearer 4**
Referee **P Dowd**

Sunday January 11
MANCHESTER UNITED (a)
Drew 0-0   HT 0-0   Att **67,622**   Position **7th**
Given — Hughes, Woodgate, O'Brien, Bernard — Solano (Ambrose 82), Jenas, Speed, Robert — Shearer, Dyer *Subs not used* Harper, Griffin, Chopra, Viana
Report page 202

Monday January 19
FULHAM (h)
Won 3-1   HT 2-0   Att **50,104**   Position **5th**
The day after Fulham concede defeat in their battle to keep Saha out of Manchester United's clutches, a compatriot steals the show at St James' Park, Robert twisting spectacularly in mid-air to backheel Newcastle's third goal.

Given — Hughes, Woodgate, O'Brien, Bernard — Solano (Ambrose 84), Jenas, Speed, Robert (Viana 84) — Shearer (Ameobi 84), Dyer *Subs not used* Harper, Bramble
Scorers **O'Brien 4, Speed 41, Robert 54**
Referee **N Barry**

Saturday January 24
LIVERPOOL (a)
FA Cup, 4th rnd
Lost 1-2   HT 1-1   Att 41,365
Given — Hughes, Woodgate, O'Brien, Bernard — Solano
(Ameobi 68), Jenas, Speed, Robert — Shearer, Dyer *Subs
not used* Harper, Ambrose, Bramble, Viana
Scorer **Robert 4**
Report page 180

Saturday January 31
BIRMINGHAM CITY (a)
Drew 1-1   HT 1-0   Att 29,513   Position 6th
Given — Hughes, Woodgate, O'Brien, Bernard — Ambrose
(Bellamy 75), Jenas, Speed, Robert (Viana 88) —
Shearer, Dyer *Subs not used* Griffin, Harper, Ameobi
Booked Woodgate, Bernard, Bellamy, Viana
Scorer **Speed 35**
Report page 87

Saturday February 7
LEICESTER CITY (h)
Won 3-1   HT 2-0   Att 52,125   Position 4th
Newcastle mark Speed's achievement of becoming the
first player to make 400 Premiership appearances by
climbing to their highest position of the season. Taggart
endures a nightmare return to the Leicester defence
after injury, deflecting in Ameobi's opener and then
slicing an embarrassing own goal.

Given — Hughes, Woodgate, O'Brien, Bernard — Dyer
(Ambrose 69), Jenas, Speed, Viana — Shearer
(Bridges 79), Ameobi (Bellamy 79) *Subs not used* Harper,
Bramble *Booked* Ambrose
Scorers **Ameobi 30, Taggart 37 (og), Jenas 59**
Referee **S Dunn**

Wednesday February 11
BLACKBURN ROVERS (a)
Drew 1-1   HT 0-0   Att 23,459   Position 5th
Given — Hughes, O'Brien, Bramble, Bernard — Dyer,
Jenas, Speed, Robert — Shearer, Bellamy *Subs not used*
Elliott, Ambrose, Ameobi, Viana, Harper
Scorer **Bellamy 52**
Report page 98

Saturday February 21
MIDDLESBROUGH (h)
Won 2-1   HT 0-1   Att 52,156   Position 4th
Next stop Cardiff for Middlesbrough, who take the lead
but lose out when Ehiogu's awful error lets in Bellamy
and then when Southgate's trip on Ambrose allows
Shearer to hit the winner from the spot. There is still
time for Ricketts to have a header dubiously disallowed
for offside.

Given — Hughes, O'Brien, Bramble, Bernard — Ambrose
(Bowyer 85), Dyer, Speed, Robert — Shearer, Bellamy
Subs not used Harper, Elliott, Ameobi, Viana
Scorers **Bellamy 63, Shearer 83 (pen)**
Referee **G Poll**

After a swift turn past Desailly, Ameobi drills a shot past Ambrosio

thereafter. Coming two minutes before half-time, Ameobi's
intervention — chesting down a flighted cross from Darren
Ambrose, turning Desailly from 17 yards and shooting accurately —
was like Shearer's, in that it was of a sufficiently startling nature to
suck the breath from Chelsea lungs.

They were still gasping after the interval when Shearer collected a
ball from Olivier Bernard in the left-hand channel, stepped around
Desailly and launched himself at a shot that could not have been
stopped, even without its vicious swerve.

The balance of the match swung appealingly but Chelsea's
desperation finally translated into possession. Hasselbaink blasted a
shot above the crossbar, Lampard powered a header down and wide,
Huth careered upfield to do the same and, in the 94th minute, John
Terry smacked the ball against the left post. "You can have all the
spirit in the world, but you also need luck," Ranieri observed.

NEWCASTLE UNITED (4-4-2): S Given — A Hughes, A O'Brien, J Woodgate (sub: T Bramble, 78min),
O Bernard — D Ambrose, H Viana, G Speed, L Robert — A Shearer, F Ameobi (sub: M Bridges, 85).
Substitutes not used: S Harper, M Chopra, M Brittain. **Booked:** Viana.
CHELSEA (4-4-2): M Ambrosio — M Melchiot, M Desailly (sub: R Huth, 72), J Terry, W Bridge — Geremi,
F Lampard, C Makelele, J Cole — H Crespo (sub: J F Hasselbaink, 72), E Gudjohnsen. **Substitutes not
used:** N Sullivan, A Nicolas, F Oliveira. **Booked:** Huth.

STATS AND FACTS

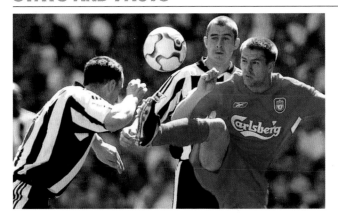

- Sir Bobby Robson's team recorded the highest proportion of away draws ever in the top flight (12 from 19 matches). Norwich City drew 13 away in 1978-79, but from 21 games.

- Last season, Newcastle gained three points from their first six games; in 2002-03 they collected four points from the first five matches; in 1999-2000 they won one point from the first seven; and in 1998-99 they picked up two points from the first four.

- In the past four and a half years, Alan Shearer has scored 25 doubles, but just one hat-trick.

- In April, Newcastle recorded successive goalless draws for the first time since May 1997 (away to Aston Villa and at home to Marseilles).

- Newcastle's recent record at Old Trafford is abysmal — they have not won in their past 23 games away to Manchester United . . .

- . . . and they have won none of their past ten games away to Liverpool.

Bill Edgar

GOALSCORERS

	Prem	FAC	CC	Euro	Total
D Ambrose	2	-	-	1	3
F Ameobi	7	-	-	3	10
C Bellamy	4	-	-	5	9
O Bernard	1	-	-	-	1
L Bowyer	2	-	-	-	2
T Bramble	-	-	-	3	3
K Dyer	1	2	-	-	3
J Jenas	2	-	-	1	3
A O'Brien	1	-	-	-	1
L Robert	6	2	1	3	12
A Shearer	22 (7p)	-	-	6	28 (7p)
N Solano	-	-	-	1	1
G Speed	3	-	-	1	4
Own goals	1	-	-	1	2

Thursday February 26
VALERENGA (a)
Uefa Cup, 3rd rnd, 1st leg
Drew 1-1   HT 1-0   Att 17,039
Shearer is "disappointed, angry and surprised" to be omitted as Sir Bobby Robson keeps one eye on the fourth round and the other on fourth place in the Premiership. Bellamy's goal is cancelled out by Normann, a former team-mate at Coventry City.

Given — Hughes, O'Brien, Bramble, Bernard — Ambrose (Dyer 51), Jenas, Speed, Viana (Robert 74) — Ameobi (Bridges 74), Bellamy *Subs not used* Harper, Elliott, Shearer, Taylor *Booked* Bernard
Scorer **Bellamy 39**
Referee **G Gilewski (Poland)**

Sunday February 29
PORTSMOUTH (a)
Drew 1-1   HT 1-0   Att 20,140   Position 4th
Given — Hughes, O'Brien, Bramble, Bernard — Bowyer (Bridges 83), Dyer (Jenas 40), Speed, Robert (Viana 78) — Shearer, Bellamy *Subs not used* Harper, Woodgate
Booked Bramble, Bernard
Scorer **Bellamy 34**
Report page 236

Wednesday March 3
VALERENGA (h)
Uefa Cup, 3rd rnd, 2nd leg
Won 3-1 (won 4-2 on agg)   HT 1-1   Att 38,531
Helped by a couple of errors from the Norwegians' goalkeeper, Newcastle ease through untroubled, but they fail to impress. "We won't get away with a performance like that in the next round," Sir Bobby Robson says.

Given — O'Brien, Woodgate, Bramble, Hughes — Bridges (Brittain 76), Jenas, Speed, Robert — Shearer, Bellamy (Ameobi ht) *Subs not used* Elliott, Harper, Viana, Orr, Taylor *Booked* Hughes, Bramble
Scorers **Shearer 19, Ameobi 47, 89**
Referee **E Braamhaar (the Netherlands)**

Thursday March 11
REAL MALLORCA (h)
Uefa Cup, 4th rnd, 1st leg
Won 4-1   HT 0-0   Att 38,012
On the day of the Madrid bombings, Uefa rejects an appeal for a postponement by the Spanish clubs involved in European competitions. Four Newcastle goals in 14 minutes settle this match, and the tie.

Given — Hughes, O'Brien, Bramble, Bernard — Dyer (Ambrose 86), Jenas, Speed, Robert — Shearer, Bellamy *Subs not used* Elliott, Bridges, Ameobi, Caig, Woodgate, Viana *Booked* Dyer
Scorers **Bellamy 67, Shearer 71, Robert 74, Bramble 84**
Referee **A Hamer (Luxembourg)**

Sunday March 14
TOTTENHAM HOTSPUR (a)
Lost 0-1   HT 0-0   Att 36,083   Position 5th
Given — Hughes (Ameobi 89), O'Brien, Woodgate, Bernard — Bowyer (Ambrose 76), Jenas, Speed, Robert — Shearer, Bellamy *Subs not used* Harper, Elliott, Viana
Report page 256

Saturday March 20
CHARLTON ATHLETIC (h)
Won 3-1   **HT 2-0**   Att **51,847**   Position **5th**
The battle for fourth place is getting serious and Newcastle leapfrog Charlton thanks in part to a highly controversial penalty, when Robert tumbles over Perry's leg. Shearer, having scored within a minute, gets a second after Kiely pushes his spot kick on to a post. Charlton, who hit wood twice in the second half, are furious.

Given — Hughes (Bramble ht), O'Brien, Woodgate, Bernard — Ambrose (Bowyer 79), Jenas, Speed, Robert — Shearer, Ameobi *Subs not used* Harper, Chopra, Viana
Scorers **Shearer 1, 77, Jenas 35**
Referee **M Riley**

Thursday March 25
REAL MALLORCA (a)
Uefa Cup, 4th rnd, 2nd leg
Won 3-0 (won 7-1 on agg)   **HT 0-0**   Att **11,500**
Bellamy is in trouble before the match, with reports of disputes with backroom staff and fans, but there are no such problems on the pitch, where his goal is the filling in a Shearer sandwich.

Given — O'Brien (Taylor 80), Woodgate, Bramble, Bernard — Ambrose, Jenas, Speed (Bellamy 77), Robert (Viana 66) — Shearer, Ameobi *Subs not used* Harper, Elliott, Chopra, Orr *Booked* Jenas, Ameobi
Scorers **Shearer 46, 89, Bellamy 78**
Referee **K Plautz (Austria)**

Sunday March 28
BOLTON WANDERERS (a)
Lost 0-1   **HT 0-1**   Att **27,360**   Position **5th**
Given — Taylor, Woodgate, Bramble, Bernard — Bowyer (Ambrose 70), Jenas (Viana 70), Speed, Robert (Ameobi 70) — Shearer, Bellamy *Subs not used* Elliott, Harper *Booked* Woodgate, Bramble
Report page 109

Saturday April 3
EVERTON (h)
Won 4-2   **HT 2-1**   Att **42,155**   Position **4th**
Shearer's double, the second his 26th goal of the season, keeps Newcastle on course for the Champions League as Everton — without the suspended Ferguson and Rooney — make too many mistakes in central defence. Everton are unlucky, though, to hit the bar and have Watson's header disallowed, both at 3-1 down.

Given — Hughes, Woodgate, Bramble, Bernard — Ambrose (Bowyer 75), Dyer, Speed, Robert (Ameobi 84) — Shearer, Bellamy *Subs not used* Harper, Taylor, Viana
Scorers **Bellamy 5, Dyer 21, Shearer 52, 90**
Referee **D Gallagher**

Thursday April 8
PSV EINDHOVEN (a)
Uefa Cup, quarter-final, 1st leg
Drew 1-1   **HT 1-1**   Att **35,000**
Sir Bobby Robson is feted on his return to Eindhoven, but the locals are less enamoured with his team after Bramble's off-the-ball elbow on Van der Schaaf. Jenas's equalising header on the stroke of half-time gives Newcastle the slight advantage.

Given — Hughes, Woodgate, Bramble, Bernard — Ambrose, Jenas, Speed, Robert — Shearer (Ameobi 90), Bellamy *Subs not used* Harper, Elliott, O'Brien, Bridges, Viana, Brittain *Booked* Jenas
Scorer **Jenas 45**
Referee **G Veissiere (France)**

THE PLAYERS

DARREN AMBROSE (midfield) **Born** February 29, 1984, Harlow **Ht** 6ft 0in **Wt** 11st 0lb **Signed from** Ipswich Town, March 2003, £1m

SHOLA AMEOBI (forward) **Born** October 12, 1981, Zaria, Nigeria **Ht** 6ft 2in **Wt** 12st 0lb **Signed from** trainee, October 1998

CRAIG BELLAMY (forward) **Born** July 13, 1979, Cardiff **Ht** 5ft 9in **Wt** 10st 12lb **Signed from** Coventry City, July 2001, £6m

OLIVIER BERNARD (defender) **Born** October 14, 1979, Paris **Ht** 5ft 9in **Wt** 10st 10lb **Signed from** Lyons, October 2000, free

LEE BOWYER (midfield) **Born** January 3, 1977, Canning Town **Ht** 5ft 9in **Wt** 9st 11lb **Signed from** West Ham United, January 2003, nominal

TITUS BRAMBLE (defender) **Born** July 31, 1981, Ipswich **Ht** 6ft 1in **Wt** 13st 10lb **Signed from** Ipswich Town, July 2002, £5m

MICHAEL BRIDGES (forward) **Born** August 5, 1978, North Shields

Ht 6ft 1in **Wt** 12st 6lb **Signed from** Leeds United, February 2004, loan

MARTIN BRITTAIN (midfield) **Born** December 29, 1984, Cramlington **Ht** 5ft 8in **Wt** 10st 7lb **Signed from** trainee, March 2004

STEVE CALDWELL (defender) **Born** September 12, 1980, Stirling **Ht** 6ft 3in **Wt** 11st 5lb **Signed from** trainee, June 1997

MICHAEL CHOPRA (forward) **Born** December 23, 1983, Newcastle **Ht** 5ft 8in **Wt** 10st 4lb **Signed from** trainee, January 2002

KIERON DYER (midfield) **Born** December 29, 1978, Ipswich **Ht** 5ft 8in **Wt** 10st 1lb **Signed from** Ipswich Town, July 1997, £6m

SHAY GIVEN (goalkeeper) **Born** April 20, 1976, Lifford, Co Donegal **Ht** 6ft 1in **Wt** 13st 4lb **Signed from** Blackburn Rovers, July 1997, £1.5m

ANDY GRIFFIN (defender) **Born** March 7, 1979, Billinge **Ht** 5ft 9in **Wt** 10st 10lb **Signed from** Stoke City, January 1998, £1.5m

STEVE HARPER (goalkeeper) **Born** March 14, 1975, Easington **Ht** 6ft 2in **Wt** 13st 0lb **Signed from** Seaham Red Star, July 1993, free

AARON HUGHES (defender) **Born** November 8, 1979, Cookstown **Ht** 6ft 0in **Wt** 11st 2lb **Signed from** trainee, March 1997

JERMAINE JENAS (midfield) **Born** February 18, 1983, Nottingham **Ht** 5ft 11in **Wt** 11st 8lb **Signed from** Nottingham Forest, February 2002, £5m

LOMANA LUALUA (forward) **Born** December 28, 1980, Kinshasa, Zaire **Ht** 5ft 10in **Wt** 11st 6lb **Signed from** Colchester United, September 2000, £2.25m

ANDY O'BRIEN (defender) **Born** June 29, 1979, Harrogate **Ht** 6ft 3in **Wt** 11st 9lb **Signed from** Bradford City, March 2001, £2m

LAURENT ROBERT (midfield) **Born** May 21, 1975, Saint-Benoit, France **Ht** 5ft 9in **Wt** 10st 12lb **Signed from** Paris Saint-Germain, August 2001, £10.5m

ALAN SHEARER (forward) **Born** August 13, 1970, Newcastle **Ht** 6ft 0in **Wt** 12st 6lb **Signed from** Blackburn Rovers, July 1996, £15m

NOLBERTO SOLANO (see Aston Villa)

GARY SPEED (midfield) **Born** September 8, 1969, Deeside **Ht** 5ft 10in **Wt** 12st 11lb **Signed from** Everton, February 1998, £5.5m

STEVEN TAYLOR (midfield) **Born** January 23, 1986, Greenwich **Ht** 6ft 2in **Wt** 12st 11lb **Signed from** trainee, July 2002

HUGO VIANA (midfield) **Born** January 15, 1983, Barcelos, Portugal **Ht** 5ft 11in **Wt** 11st 7lb **Signed from** Sporting Lisbon, June 2002, £850,000

JONATHAN WOODGATE (defender) **Born** January 22, 1980, Middlesbrough **Ht** 6ft 0in **Wt** 12st 9lb **Signed from** Leeds United, January 2003, £9m

Sunday April 11
ARSENAL (h)
Drew 0-0   HT 0-0   Att 52,141   Position 5th
A rare blank for Arsenal but a reasonably entertaining goalless draw on a difficult surface which Arsene Wenger blames for costing Henry a goal. "No one will beat them," Sir Bobby Robson says as the undefeated leaders move one point nearer their thirteenth title.

Given — Hughes, Woodgate, O'Brien, Bernard — Ambrose (Bowyer 76), Jenas, Speed, Robert (Viana 77) — Shearer, Bellamy Subs not used Harper, Bramble, Ameobi
Referee **P Durkin**

Wednesday April 14
PSV EINDHOVEN (h)
Uefa Cup, quarter-final, 2nd leg
Won 2-1 (won 3-2 on agg)   HT 1-0   Att 50,083
Newcastle reach their second European semi-final with two headers by two stalwarts from two corners, either side of Kezman's penalty after Bernard brings down Park. Given seals their passage with a late save from Bouma's free kick.

Given — Hughes, Woodgate, Bramble (O'Brien 77), Bernard — Ambrose (Ameobi 81), Jenas, Speed, Robert (Viana 90) — Shearer, Bellamy Subs not used Elliott, Dyer, Harper, Bridges
Scorers **Shearer 9, Speed 66**
Referee **M E Mejuto Gonzalez (Spain)**

Sunday April 18
ASTON VILLA (a)
Drew 0-0   HT 0-0   Att 40,786   Position 5th
Given — Hughes, Woodgate, O'Brien, Bernard — Dyer, Jenas (Viana 36), Speed, Robert (Bowyer 36) — Shearer, Bellamy (Bridges 52) Subs not used Elliott, Harper Booked Given, Speed, Shearer, Bridges Sent off O'Brien 10
Report page 80

Thursday April 22
MARSEILLES (h)
Uefa Cup, semi-final, 1st leg
Drew 0-0   HT 0-0   Att 52,004
With Jenas, Bellamy, Dyer and Bowyer among those injured, Newcastle do not feel too disheartened by a goalless draw against a talented side who have already eliminated Liverpool and Inter Milan. Speed misses their best chance, but Drogba goes closest when he hits the inside of Given's post.

Given — Hughes, Woodgate, O'Brien, Bramble — Ambrose, Viana, Speed, Robert — Shearer, Ameobi (Bridges 78) Subs not used Harper, Elliott, Bramble, Chopra, Brittain, Orr
Referee **V Ivanov (Russia)**

Sunday April 25
CHELSEA (h)
Won 2-1   HT 1-1   Att 52,016   Position 5th
Shearer opens the door for Arsenal to secure the championship later in the day with a superb 25-yard shot into the top corner that earns victory over Chelsea, who had taken the lead through Joe Cole, but a thigh injury suffered by Woodgate spoils the occasion for Sir Bobby Robson — and Sven-Goran Eriksson.

Given — Hughes, Woodgate (Bramble 78), O'Brien, Bernard — Ambrose, Viana, Speed, Robert — Shearer, Ameobi (Bridges 86) Subs not used Harper, Chopra, Brittain Booked Viana
Scorers **Ameobi 44, Shearer 48**
Referee **R Styles**

PLAYER OF THE SEASON
Alan Shearer

While almost all around him seemed to fall apart, the Newcastle captain was a colossus. His goal tally is remarkable for anyone, let alone a man approaching the end of his career whose body has spent as much time under the surgeon's scalpel. That he failed again in what at times looked like a personal quest for silverware will have hurt the player as much as it did the supporters. Shearer's imminent retirement poses several difficult questions: United have either to replace him, which will be all but impossible, or find a way of playing that does not rely on him. But arguably the greatest No 9 in Newcastle's illustrious history will continue to strive, for one last season, for that elusive trophy.

Angus Batey

Saturday May 1
MANCHESTER CITY (a)
Lost 0-1   HT 0-0   Att **47,226**   Position **5th**
Given — Hughes, O'Brien, Bramble, Bernard — Ambrose (Chopra 85), Viana, Speed, Robert (Brittain 76) — Shearer, Ameobi (Bridges 85) *Subs not used* Taylor, Harper *Booked* Speed
Report page 194

Thursday May 6
MARSEILLES (a)
Uefa Cup, semi-final, 2nd leg
Lost 0-2 (lost 0-2 on agg)   HT 0-1   Att **57,500**
Deprived by injury of three potential match-winners, Newcastle have no answer to the finishing of Drogba, who scores in the 18th and 82nd minutes, and the all-round polish of the French side, who deserve their place in the Gothenburg final against Valencia. Will Sir Bobby Robson ever get a better chance of ending Newcastle's trophy drought?

Given — Hughes, O'Brien, Bramble, Bernard — Ambrose, Viana (Bowyer 65), Speed, Robert — Shearer, Ameobi *Subs not used* Harper, Elliott, Bridges, Chopra, Caldwell, Brittain *Booked* O'Brien, Viana, Bowyer
Referee **M Lubos (Slovakia)**

Sunday May 9
WOLVERHAMPTON WANDERERS (h)
Drew 1-1   HT 1-0   Att **52,139**   Position **6th**
Newcastle are booed off and left needing to win both their remaining matches to pip Liverpool for fourth place. Bowyer scores his first goal since October 2002 and Ameobi hits a post, but Jones's penalty save from Shearer seven minutes from time could prove costly. Wolves' mathematical lifeline is severed.

Given — Hughes, Caldwell, Bramble, Bernard — Ambrose (Chopra 80), Bowyer, Speed, Robert (Viana 80) — Shearer, Ameobi *Subs not used* Harper, Griffin, Bridges *Booked* Bowyer
Scorer **Bowyer 38**
Referee **M Messias**

Wednesday May 12
SOUTHAMPTON (a)
Drew 3-3   HT 2-2   Att **31,815**   Position **6th**
Given — Hughes, Caldwell, Bramble (Bridges 90), Bernard — Ambrose, Bowyer, Speed, Dyer (Robert 74) — Shearer, Ameobi *Subs not used* Harper, Griffin, Viana *Booked* Bramble, Caldwell
Scorers **Ameobi 7, Bowyer 35, Ambrose 90**
Report page 248

Saturday May 15
LIVERPOOL (a)
Drew 1-1   HT 1-0   Att **44,172**   Position **5th**
Given — Griffin (Caldwell 79), O'Brien, Bramble, Hughes — Ambrose (Robert 82), Bowyer, Speed, Dyer — Shearer, Ameobi (Bellamy 40) *Subs not used* Harper, Viana *Booked* Ambrose
Scorer **Ameobi 25**
Report page 184

PORTSMOUTH

PREMIERSHIP

	P	W	D	L	F	A	GD	Pts
Arsenal	38	26	12	0	73	26	47	**90**
Chelsea	38	24	7	7	67	30	37	**79**
Man Utd	38	23	6	9	64	35	29	**75**
Liverpool	38	16	12	10	55	37	18	**60**
Newcastle	38	13	17	8	52	40	12	**56**
Aston Villa	38	15	11	12	48	44	4	**56**
Charlton	38	14	11	13	51	51	0	**53**
Bolton	38	14	11	13	48	56	-8	**53**
Fulham	38	14	10	14	52	46	6	**52**
Birmingham	38	12	14	12	43	48	-5	**50**
Middlesbro	38	13	9	16	44	52	-8	**48**
Southampton	38	12	11	15	44	45	-1	**47**
Portsmouth	38	12	9	17	47	54	-7	**45**
Tottenham	38	13	6	19	47	57	-10	**45**
Blackburn	38	12	8	18	51	59	-8	**44**
Man City	38	9	14	15	55	54	1	**41**
Everton	38	9	12	17	45	57	-12	**39**
Leicester	38	6	15	17	48	65	-17	**33**
Leeds	38	8	9	21	40	79	-39	**33**
Wolves	38	7	12	19	38	77	-39	**33**

FA CUP
Sixth round

CARLING CUP
Fourth round

Pulling power: Yakubu Ayegbeni proved too much of a handful for the Southampton defence in Pompey's Fratton derby triumph

THE GAMES

Saturday August 16 2003
ASTON VILLA (h)
Won 2-1   HT 1-0   Att 20,101   Position 5th
Back in the top flight after 16 years, Portsmouth lead the table between lunch and tea after winning a 12.30 kick-off. Sheringham gets the opener on his debut, but they are hanging on after Villa, now under David O'Leary's control, win and convert a penalty via Barry, who is then sent off for aiming a verbal volley at a linesman.

Hislop – Zivkovic, Foxe, Stefanovic, De Zeeuw – Stone, Faye (Schemmel 88), Quashie, Berger – Yakubu (Pericard 76), Sheringham *Subs not used* Wapenaar, O'Neil, Burton *Booked* Stefanovic, Faye
Scorers **Sheringham 42, Berger 63**
Referee **G Barber**

Saturday August 23
MANCHESTER CITY (a)
Drew 1-1   HT 1-0   Att 46,287   Position 5th
Hislop – Schemmel, Stefanovic, De Zeeuw, Zivkovic – Stone, Faye, Quashie, Berger (Harper 83) – Yakubu (Pericard 74), Sheringham *Subs not used* Primus, O'Neil, Wapenaar *Booked* Zivkovic, Faye, Pericard
Scorer **Yakubu 24**
Report page 186

Tuesday August 26
BOLTON WANDERERS (h)
Won 4-0   HT 0-0   Att 20,113   Position 1st
Delirium at Fratton Park as Portsmouth head the top division for the first time since 1951, Sheringham's hat-trick – launched by a bullet header, completed by a penalty – condemning Bolton to a second successive 4-0 away defeat which leaves Sam Allardyce "extremely embarrassed".

Hislop – Schemmel (Primus 81), Stefanovic, De Zeeuw, Zivkovic – Stone, Faye, Quashie, Berger – Yakubu (Pericard 84), Sheringham *Subs not used* O'Neil, Wapenaar, Harper *Booked* Zivkovic, Quashie
Scorers **Stone 48, Sheringham 57, 88, 90 (pen)**
Referee **D Gallagher**

Saturday August 30
WOLVERHAMPTON WANDERERS (a)
Drew 0-0   HT 0-0   Att 28,860   Position 3rd
Hislop – Schemmel, Stefanovic, De Zeeuw, Zivkovic – Stone (Smertin 68), Faye, Quashie, Berger – Yakubu (Pericard 86), Sheringham *Subs not used* Wapenaar, Primus, Harper *Booked* Zivkovic, Stone, Quashie, Yakubu, Schemmel
Report page 260

Saturday September 13
ARSENAL (a)
Drew 1-1   HT 1-1   Att 38,052   Position 4th
Hislop – Schemmel, Stefanovic, De Zeeuw, Zivkovic – Stone, Faye, Quashie, Berger (Smertin 35) – Yakubu (Roberts 72), Sheringham (Sherwood 90) *Subs not used* Foxe, Wapenaar *Booked* Stefanovic, De Zeeuw, Schemmel
Scorer **Sheringham 26**
Report page 61

THEY ARE A HAPPY BUNCH, THE supporters of Portsmouth Football Club. How they sang when they topped the Premiership for all of an hour and a half last August (it was an early kick-off); how excited they were when Arsenal were outplayed at Highbury, only forcing a draw when an outrageous dive by Robert Pires gave them a penalty; and how joyfully they jeered poor old Peter Reid when they walloped Leeds United 6-1. Six-one! Even when they dipped into the bottom three, the *Pompey Chimes* kept on ringing.

In March the ecstasy was positively indecent when they beat Southampton 1-0, and when Thierry Henry led Arsenal to a fabulous 5-1 FA Cup victory at Fratton Park they cheered him so long and loud you would have thought he had been signed by Harry Redknapp on a free. In fact, according to an obscure website, Portsmouth fans have been voted the best in the country.

It is not just about defying the pundits, every single one of whom had consigned the club to relegation before a ball had been kicked, or indeed about finishing a respectable thirteenth — the club's highest position for 48 years — that made them so cheerful. It is more than that. The atmosphere at the club has changed. The ground may be as down-at-heel as ever — the South Stand was built in 1925 — but instead of the sour, disappointed, cynical mood of the Nineties (and most of the Eighties, Seventies, Sixties and Fifties), there is a ring of confidence about the place.

Just think, two years ago Portsmouth fans were told to expect mid-table mediocrity and got just that: fifteenth in the Nationwide League first division. Mind you, that was one of the better seasons. You have to hand it to the management team of Peter Storrie, the chief executive, Redknapp, the manager, and his trusty aides, Jim Smith and Kevin Bond. They have started to run the place like a proper business for the first time since Milan Mandaric, the chairman, bought Portsmouth out of administration for about £5 million in 1999.

Now it is fun. How exotic is it that unglamorous Portsmouth have more than 20 foreign players on the books? They used to think that Alan Biley, with his outrageous mullet, was pretty spectacular back in the Eighties, but Fratton has never seen anything quite as outrageously exuberant as Lomana LuaLua's celebratory triple somersaults, the panache of Patrik Berger, the potential brilliance of Yakubu Ayegbeni, the sheer professionalism of Amdy Faye, Steve Stone and Alexei Smertin. And was that really the great Teddy Sheringham scoring a hat-trick against Bolton Wanderers in August?

Redknapp was entitled to grumble about injuries at the start of

HONOURS BOARD

Spot the legends from Pompey's postwar heyday

FOOTBALL LEAGUE
Champions 1949, 1950
FA CUP
Winners 1939
Runners-up 1929, 1934

Record attendance 51,385 (v Derby County, FA Cup 6th rnd, February 26, 1949) **Current capacity** 20,140
Record victory 9-1 (v Notts County, second division, April 9, 1927)
Record defeat 0-10 (v Leicester City, first division, October 20, 1928)

the season: the two key strikers, Svetoslav Todorov, who scored 26 goals in the promotion season, and Vincent Pericard only played for a few minutes all season. Everyone got twitchy come January, when a dozen players were out of action and the onus in attack was left to a tiring Sheringham and an overworked Yakubu. But, come January, Redknapp performed his popular phone trick, contacted most of the clubs in Europe and brought in Eyal Berkovic, LuaLua and half a dozen others. All but one on loans and frees, naturally.

It took a while to gel, but they had a nice run to the sixth round of the FA Cup, beating Liverpool on the way, plus eventually, after 16 attempts, the first away win of the season, over Blackburn Rovers, and in April a famous league victory over Manchester United. Now the fans are waiting for delivery on the new stadium that Mandaric promised in 1999 and which looks, at last, to be working its way through the city's planning department. The players deserve a training ground fit for professionals and not the one they use now, which is owned by Southampton University.

There was only one cloud. But it was a big one and it is one that is bound to build up again.

In the last week of the season, a coruscating row broke out between Mandaric and Redknapp. Mandaric, who has spent £20 million or so in five years, appeared to complain about Redknapp's wheeler-dealing and the leap in the wage bill to about £19 million. He did not seem to acknowledge that the finances were better than they have been for years — £23.5 million from the Premier League and Sky TV — and even with Portsmouth's tiny

Saturday September 20
BLACKBURN ROVERS (h)
Lost 1-2   HT 0-2   Att 20,024   Position 8th
Neill, the villain of Blackburn's defeat at Anfield a week earlier for the tackle that left Carragher nursing a broken leg, puts his ability to better use with their opening goal as Portsmouth are beaten for the first time this season despite plenty of second-half pressure after De Zeeuw's powerful header.

Hislop — Schemmel, De Zeeuw, Stefanovic, Zivkovic — Stone, Faye, Sherwood (Roberts 54), Quashie (Pericard 83) — Yakubu, Sheringham *Subs not used* Wapenaar, Foxe, Smertin *Booked* Quashie, Schemmel
Scorer De Zeeuw 57
Referee P Durkin

Tuesday September 23
NORTHAMPTON TOWN (h)
Carling Cup, 2nd rnd
Won 5-2   HT 3-0   Att 11,130
Harry Redknapp follows the Carling Cup trend by making eight changes, but once Northampton are reduced to ten men by Reid's tenth-minute dismissal for a professional foul on Roberts, Portsmouth are on cruise control. Taylor marks his return after six months on the sidelines with the third goal.

Wapenaar — Schemmel (Stone 64), Primus, Foxe, Taylor — O'Neil, Sherwood, Smertin, Pericard — Roberts, Sheringham *Subs not used* Srnicek, De Zeeuw, Stefanovic, Yakubu
Scorers Sherwood 13, 83, Roberts 17, 60, Taylor 41
Referee D Crick

Saturday September 27
BIRMINGHAM CITY (a)
Lost 0-2   HT 0-1   Att 29,057   Position 8th
Hislop — Schemmel, De Zeeuw, Stefanovic, Zivkovic — Stone, Faye (Sherwood 65), Smertin, Taylor (Roberts 55) — Yakubu, Sheringham *Subs not used* Wapenaar, Foxe, Primus *Booked* Faye, Sheringham, Sherwood
Report page 83

Saturday October 4
CHARLTON ATHLETIC (h)
Lost 1-2   HT 1-0   Att 20,106   Position 10th
"It could be a long, hard winter," Steve Stone says after Portsmouth's third successive defeat. A double substitution works wonders for Charlton, Fortune cancelling out Sheringham's opener — which just crosses the line before Parker clears — and Di Canio's corner finding Bartlett for a last-gasp winner.

Hislop — Schemmel, De Zeeuw, Stefanovic, Zivkovic — Stone, Smertin (Sherwood 29), Faye, Berger (Taylor 85) — Yakubu (Roberts 76), Sheringham *Subs not used* Wapenaar, Foxe *Booked* De Zeeuw, Sheringham, Sherwood
Scorer Sheringham 34
Referee G Poll

Saturday October 18
LIVERPOOL (h)
Won 1-0   HT 1-0   Att 20,123   Position 8th
Berger, inevitably, gets the winner against his former club, though Heskey has already hit a post before he scores in the fourth minute. Biscan and Yakubu also strike the woodwork in the second half as Liverpool suffer a third straight league defeat and Portsmouth end their own poor run.

Hislop — Schemmel, De Zeeuw, Stefanovic (Foxe 35), Zivkovic — Stone, Faye, Quashie (Sherwood 90), Berger — Yakubu, Sheringham *Subs not used* Wapenaar, Taylor, Roberts *Booked* Zivkovic, Faye
Scorer Berger 4
Referee S Dunn

Saturday October 25
NEWCASTLE UNITED (a)
Lost 0-3   HT 0-2   Att 52,161   Position 11th
Hislop — Schemmel (Taylor 51), De Zeeuw, Stefanovic,
Zivkovic (Foxe 73) — Stone, Faye (Sherwood 76),
Quashie, Berger — Yakubu, Sheringham *Subs not used*
Wapenaar, Roberts *Booked* Zivkovic, Sheringham
Report page 220

Wednesday October 29
NOTTINGHAM FOREST (a)
Carling Cup, 3rd rnd
Won 4-2 (aet; 2-2 after 90min)   HT 0-1   Att 20,078
Portsmouth get their first away win of the season, but it
is a struggle. A double by Bopp forces them into extra
time, when a second goal by Yakubu, a half-time
substitute, and one from Roberts finally see off the
first-division side.

Wapenaar — De Zeeuw, Foxe, Stefanovic (Yakubu ht) —
Schemmel, Stone, Sherwood, Quashie (Berger ht), Taylor
— Sheringham (O'Neil 110) — Roberts *Subs not used*
Srnicek, Primus *Booked* Quashie
**Scorers Walker 57 (og), Yakubu 64, 108,
Roberts 101**
Referee **H Webb**

Saturday November 1
MANCHESTER UNITED (a)
Lost 0-3   HT 0-1   Att 67,639   Position 11th
Hislop — Zivkovic (Roberts 79), Foxe, Stefanovic,
De Zeeuw — Stone, Sherwood (Taylor 68), Quashie,
Berger — Yakubu, Sheringham *Subs not used*
Wapenaar, Schemmel, O'Neil *Booked* De Zeeuw,
Quashie, Sherwood
Report page 199

Saturday November 8
LEEDS UNITED (h)
Won 6-1   HT 2-1   Att 20,112   Position 11th
Peter Reid says that he will not walk away from his job,
but newspaper reports the next day say that the Leeds
manager will be sacked within 48 hours after they suffer
their heaviest defeat in the top flight since 1959. O'Neil
marks his Premiership debut with two goals for a
rampant Portsmouth.

Hislop — Schemmel, Foxe, Stefanovic, De Zeeuw —
Stone (Taylor 83), Sherwood, O'Neil, Berger — Yakubu,
Sheringham *Subs not used* Wapenaar, Zivkovic, Primus,
Roberts *Booked* De Zeeuw
**Scorers Stefanovic 17, O'Neil 45, 71, Foxe 63,
Berger 75, Yakubu 86**
Referee **C Foy**

Monday November 24
FULHAM (a)
Lost 0-2   HT 0-2   Att 15,624   Position 11th
Wapenaar — Schemmel, Foxe (Taylor 60), Stefanovic,
De Zeeuw — Stone (Burton 72), O'Neil (Smertin 60),
Sherwood, Berger — Yakubu, Sheringham *Subs not used*
Srnicek, Zivkovic *Booked* Stone, Schemmel, Sherwood
Sent off Berger 82
Report page 146

Joy at Fratton as Stone scores the winner against Manchester United

capacity — 20,140 — gate receipts were at an all-time high.
Mandaric was reported to want to sack Redknapp's deputy, Smith,
and shift Bond, the assistant coach.

The vituperation between the two, which was aired on television
and radio, threatened to ruin the season. It did seem odd to celebrate
a good season with threats of sackings and resignations, though
Mandaric professed himself unimpressed with the team's progress
and expressed an enthusiasm for a youth academy, a vision he had
not shared publicly before. He said of Redknapp: "Our philosophies
are different. Right or wrong, he's not interested in coaching while I
believe you have to have a coaching structure and youth system. All
I can say for the moment is that we shall be watching each other. I'm
not sure Harry wants to work my way."

The players responded with rather more composure than their
owners and elders by trouncing Middlesbrough 5-1 in the final game
of the season, when Yakubu, confirming his emergence as a striker
of exceptional potential, helped himself to no fewer than four of the
goals.

The supporters made what they felt clear with prolonged and
orchestrated chants for the main protagonists, building up to a
climactic "We want Milan, with Harry and Jim". Yes, they are happy
fans, but they want to stay that way.

It will be a brave chairman who ignores their message.

THE MANAGER
Harry Redknapp

On a local radio station in May, as Portsmouth zoomed out of the relegation zone with 21 points from ten games, the question was asked: should Harry Redknapp be the manager of England? The fact that the question was even posed illustrates the admiration the supporters have for him after two tremendous seasons. His style may upset the purists and very possibly not land him the England job, but it works for Portsmouth.

Richard Holledge

APPEARANCES

	Prem	FAC	CC	Total
P Berger	20	1	1 (1)	22 (1)
E Berkovic	10 (1)	4	-	14 (1)
D Burton	0 (1)	1	-	1 (1)
J Curtis	5 (1)	-	-	5 (1)
A De Zeeuw	36	4	2	42
R Duffy	0 (1)	-	-	0 (1)
A Faye	27	2 (1)	1	30 (1)
H Foxe	8 (2)	-	2 (1)	10 (3)
K Harper	0 (7)	2	-	2 (7)
S Hislop	30	4	-	34
R Hughes	8 (3)	2 (2)	-	10 (5)
L LuaLua	10 (5)	-	-	10 (5)
I Mornar	3 (5)	2	-	5 (5)
S Olszar	-	0 (1)	-	0 (1)
G O'Neil	3	-	1 (1)	4 (1)
P Pasanen	11 (1)	4	-	15 (1)
V Pericard	0 (6)	-	1	1 (6)
L Primus	19 (2)	4	1	24 (2)
N Quashie	17 (4)	3	1	21 (4)
J Roberts	4 (6)	-	2	6 (6)
C Robinson	0 (1)	0 (2)	-	0 (3)
S Schemmel	12 (2)	1 (1)	2	15 (3)
E Sheringham	25 (7)	2 (1)	3	30 (8)
T Sherwood	7 (6)	-	2 (1)	9 (7)
A Smertin	23 (3)	5	2	30 (3)
P Srnicek	3	-	1	4
D Stefanovic	32	4	2	38
S Stone	29 (3)	0 (1)	2 (1)	31 (5)
M Taylor	18 (12)	4 (1)	3	25 (13)
S Todorov	1	-	-	1
H Wapenaar	5	1	2	8
Yakubu Ayegbeni	35 (2)	4	1 (1)	40 (3)
B Zivkovic	17 (1)	1	1	19 (1)

Saturday November 29
LEICESTER CITY (h)
Lost 0-2   HT 0-1   Att **20,061**   Position **13th**
Ferdinand confirms his plans to retire at the end of the season, but not before another signature goal from the veteran striker sends Leicester on the way to victory and twelfth place. Ferdinand's free kick takes a slight deflection off Smertin, Bent doubling the lead from Izzet's free kick.

Wapenaar — Zivkovic, Foxe (Taylor 63), Stefanovic, De Zeeuw — Stone, Smertin, Sherwood, Berger — Yakubu, Sheringham *Subs not used* Srnicek, Primus, Schemmel, Burton *Booked* De Zeeuw, Berger, Yakubu, Sheringham, Smertin
Referee **M Dean**

Tuesday December 2
SOUTHAMPTON (a)
Carling Cup, 4th rnd
Lost 0-2   HT 0-1   Att **29,201**
Srnicek — Zivkovic (Foxe 83), Stefanovic, De Zeeuw, Taylor — Stone, Faye (Sherwood 74), Smertin, Berger — Yakubu, Sheringham *Subs not used* Wapenaar, Primus, Schemmel *Booked* Smertin *Sent off* De Zeeuw 90
Report page 243

Saturday December 6
MIDDLESBROUGH (a)
Drew 0-0   HT 0-0   Att **28,031**   Position **16th**
Srnicek — Zivkovic, Foxe, De Zeeuw, Taylor — Stone, Faye (Quashie 67), Smertin, Berger (Sherwood 90) — Yakubu, Sheringham (Primus 81) *Subs not used* Wapenaar, Burton *Booked* Foxe, Stone, Berger *Sent off* Stone 78
Report page 211

Saturday December 13
EVERTON (h)
Lost 1-2   HT 1-2   Att **20,101**   Position **17th**
If scoring the winner is not enough, Rooney makes sure that he steals the headlines by walking off the pitch after pushing Stone to the ground in the mistaken belief that he is about to be shown a red card. Team-mates usher him back on as Everton complete the win that sees Portsmouth slip into the bottom three 24 hours later.

Srnicek — Zivkovic, Foxe, Stefanovic, Taylor — Stone, Faye, Smertin — Sheringham (Pericard 79) — Yakubu, Roberts *Subs not used* Wapenaar, Primus, Sherwood, O'Neil *Booked* Taylor
Scorer **Roberts 15**
Referee **U Rennie**

Sunday December 21
SOUTHAMPTON (a)
Lost 0-3   HT 0-1   Att **31,697**   Position **18th**
Wapenaar — Foxe, Stefanovic, Taylor — Schemmel (Zivkovic 56), Smertin, Sherwood, Hughes (Yakubu 60), Taylor — Roberts, Sheringham *Subs not used* Srnicek, Burton, Robinson *Booked* Foxe, Schemmel, Sherwood
Report page 244

Friday December 26
TOTTENHAM HOTSPUR (h)
Won 2-0   HT 0-0   Att 20,078   Position 15th
Portsmouth's joy at the win that takes them out of the relegation zone — courtesy of two free kicks by Berger, the second deflected by Postiga — is soured by Sherwood's suspected broken leg. It is Spurs' fourth successive defeat since David Pleat was confirmed acting manager until the end of the season.

Wapenaar — Primus, De Zeeuw, Stefanovic, Zivkovic — Stone, Smertin (Taylor 90), Sherwood (Hughes 78), Berger — Yakubu (Roberts 84), Sheringham *Subs not used* Srnicek, Schemmel *Booked* Sherwood
Scorer **Berger 52, 68**
Referee **S Dunn**

Sunday December 28
CHELSEA (a)
Lost 0-3   HT 0-0   Att 41,552   Position 16th
Wapenaar — Primus, De Zeeuw, Stefanovic, Zivkovic — Stone (Schemmel 53), O'Neil (Taylor 84), Hughes, Berger, Yakubu (Robinson 84) — Roberts *Subs not used* Srnicek, Sheringham
Report page 127

Saturday January 3 2004
BLACKPOOL (h)
FA Cup, 3rd rnd
Won 2-1   HT 1-1   Att 13,479
With three rookies on the bench, Harry Redknapp's injury-hit squad are spared a replay when Yakubu pounces in the last minute to see off the second-division side, who cancel out Schemmel's opener just before half-time. It is Portsmouth's first FA Cup win for five years.

Wapenaar — Zivkovic, De Zeeuw, Stefanovic — Schemmel, Hughes, Smertin, Taylor — Sheringham — Yakubu (Robinson 90), Burton *Subs not used* Srnicek, Pulis, Hunt, Cooper *Booked* Yakubu, Hughes
Scorers **Schemmel 36, Yakubu 90**
Referee **S Dunn**

Tuesday January 6
ASTON VILLA (a)
Lost 1-2   HT 0-1   Att 28,625   Position 16th
Srnicek — Primus, Pasanen, De Zeeuw — Zivkovic (Harper 87), Smertin (Sheringham 87), Hughes, Berger, Taylor — Yakubu, Roberts *Subs not used* Robinson, Burton, Knight *Booked* Hughes
Scorer **Yakubu 49**
Report page 77

Saturday January 10
MANCHESTER CITY (h)
Won 4-2   HT 1-2   Att 20,120   Position 17th
Seaman lasts just an unlucky 13 minutes before injuring his shoulder (he announces his retirement three days later). Six goals follow, four past Stuhr-Ellegaard, Seaman's replacement, in a game in which City also hit the woodwork three times. The plane carrying City's directors home is forced to make an emergency landing in Hampshire.

Hislop — Primus, Pasanen, De Zeeuw, Stefanovic — Smertin, Hughes, Berger — Sheringham, Berkovic (Harper 76) — Yakubu *Subs not used* Wapenaar, Taylor, Schemmel, Roberts
Scorers **Stefanovic 19, Yakubu 52, 77, Sheringham 58**
Referee **M Messias**

MATCH OF THE SEASON

Portsmouth 1 Southampton 0
Fratton Park, Sunday March 21 2004
Nick Szczepanik

AS PAUL STURROCK, THE SOUTHAMPTON manager, said afterwards, only one of the teams desperately wanted to win, and the result reflected as much. Portsmouth put everything they had into yesterday's derby and were rewarded with a first league victory over their traditional rivals since January 1988, and their first against them at Fratton Park since September 1963. Overcoming a strangely passive Southampton sent their supporters into ecstasy and brought three points that kept alive their hopes of staying in the Premiership.

Portsmouth needed a victory by three clear goals to move above Leicester City and out of the bottom three, but they were happy to settle for a single goal, scored from close range after 68 minutes by Yakubu Ayegbeni, the Nigeria forward.

"It was a massive game," Harry Redknapp, the Portsmouth manager, said. "In the last ten minutes it was all hands to the pump, but overall we were the better team and deserved to win. We would have been in desperate trouble if we had lost and it would have knocked everyone flat. And it was beating Southampton, which was very important for the fans." Not to mention the club's future in the Premiership. "You're probably looking at winning three home games and one away, but it's difficult to know," Redknapp said. "It may take three wins; it may take six. It's probably going right down to the wire."

At least his team has plenty to play for, the absence of which looked to be Southampton's problem. Their supporters, at the open Milton End, had to endure a pre-match hailstorm as well as intermittent showers and their team's unconvincing performance cannot have done much to improve their spirits. Sturrock has a lot to do to steady a downward drift that was briefly arrested by last weekend's fortunate victory over Liverpool. "I'm obviously very disappointed and gutted for the fans," Sturrock said. "The two games have given me a lot of food for thought. Our mental approach has to be completely different, especially at the beginning of matches. We seemed flat and negative, but there was an urgency about Portsmouth. I don't know if we think we're in a comfort zone and can saunter through the rest of the season. There will be changes next week."

Redknapp had problems even before the kick-off, when Eyal Berkovic withdrew with a virus during the warm-up and had to be replaced in the team by Matthew Taylor. That had the effect of reducing the number of changes to the team beaten 3-0 by Liverpool in midweek from five to four, but Southampton also had to make a late alteration, replacing Michael Svensson, who had injured a calf, with Stephen Crainey.

Portsmouth opened the first half with a series of wind-assisted

Taylor gets in a shot at the Southampton goal as Lundekvam moves in

high balls into the Southampton penalty area, but the chances they made were not converted. Yakubu shot tamely at Antti Niemi then curled a shot wide, while Teddy Sheringham slipped after Danny Higginbotham had missed Arjan de Zeeuw's long pass and could only shoot straight at Niemi.

Portsmouth continued to look more threatening after the interval. Their pressure told when Alexei Smertin played the ball down the right to Steve Stone and his low cross was swept in by Yakubu.

Finally, Southampton showed some urgency. Rory Delap fired in a low shot that rebounded to Kevin Phillips, but Shaka Hislop clawed away his angled effort and dived at the former England forward's feet minutes later. Taylor nearly made it 2-0 with a dipping volley five minutes from time, palmed over by Niemi, but Southampton went even closer in injury time. Phillips's volley hit the inside of a post and bounced clear, then Claus Lundekvam's firm header was held on the goalline by Hislop.

PORTSMOUTH (4-4-2): S Hislop — P Pasanen, L Primus, A De Zeeuw, D Stefanovic — S Stone, A Smertin, A Faye, M Taylor — E Sheringham, Yakubu Ayegbeni (sub: L LuaLua, 83min). **Substitutes not used:** H Wapenaar, R Hughes, J Curtis, I Mornar.
SOUTHAMPTON (4-4-2): A Niemi — J Dodd, C Lundekvam, D Higginbotham, S Crainey (sub: F Fernandes, 80) — R Delap, P Telfer, A Svensson (sub: D Prutton, 60), N McCann (sub: M Pahars, 73) — K Phillips, J Beattie. **Substitutes not used:** P Smith, F Hall. **Booked:** Higginbotham, Prutton.

Saturday January 17
BOLTON WANDERERS (a)
Lost 0-1   HT 0-0   Att 26,558   Position 17th
Hislop — Primus (Harper 77), Pasanen, De Zeeuw, Stefanovic — Smertin, Hughes (Taylor 77), Berger — Berkovic — Yakubu, Sheringham *Subs not used* Wapenaar, Robinson, Pulis *Booked* Hughes *Sent off* Stefanovic 90
Report page 107

Saturday January 24
SCUNTHORPE UNITED (h)
FA Cup, 4th rnd
Won 2-1   HT 1-0   Att 17,508
Deprived of most of their strike force by injury, Portsmouth find a match-winner in Taylor, who scores twice — a tap-in after Berkovic's effort is parried and a shot squeezed inside the post — before Parton replies at the death for the third-division side.

Hislop — Primus, Pasanen, Stefanovic — Harper (Robinson 88), Hughes, Smertin (Schemmel 58), Berkovic, Taylor — Berger (Faye 58) — Sheringham *Subs not used* Wapenaar, De Zeeuw *Booked* Stefanovic
Scorer **Taylor 35, 66**
Referee **G Barber**

Saturday January 31
WOLVERHAMPTON WANDERERS (h)
Drew 0-0   HT 0-0   Att 20,112   Position 17th
A huge relegation battle finishes in a repeat of the scoreline at Molineux, but how? Portsmouth hit the Wolves woodwork on no fewer than four occasions. Yakubu is a half-time substitute, having arrived late after being sent home from the African Nations Cup by Nigeria for allegedly breaking a curfew.

Hislop — Primus, Pasanen, De Zeeuw, Taylor — Smertin (Quashie 88), Faye, Berkovic (Stone 75), Berger — Sheringham, Mornar (Yakubu ht) *Subs not used* Wapenaar, Hughes
Referee **H Webb**

Saturday February 7
TOTTENHAM HOTSPUR (a)
Lost 3-4   HT 1-2   Att 36,107   Position 17th
Hislop — Curtis, Primus, De Zeeuw, Taylor — Smertin, Berkovic (Stone 84), Faye (LuaLua 64), Quashie — Yakubu, Sheringham (Mornar ht) *Subs not used* Wapenaar, Berger *Booked* Faye
Scorers **Berkovic 39, LuaLua 73, Mornar 84**
Report page 256

Wednesday February 11
CHELSEA (h)
Lost 0-2   HT 0-1   Att 20,140   Position 17th
Chelsea ride their luck and are now only one point behind Manchester United in second place. In between Parker's first goal for Claudio Ranieri's team and Crespo chesting in when Hasselbaink's chip rebounds off the bar, Portsmouth go close several times, especially when Berger hits a post after a great run.

Hislop — Primus, Pasanen, De Zeeuw, Stefanovic — Quashie, Berkovic (Taylor 83), Faye, Berger (LuaLua 56) — Mornar, Yakubu *Subs not used* Wapenaar, Curtis, Hughes *Booked* Stefanovic
Referee **G Poll**

Sunday February 15
LIVERPOOL (a)
FA Cup, 5th rnd
Drew 1-1   HT 0-1   Att 34,669
Hislop — Pasanen, Primus, De Zeeuw, Stefanovic — Smertin, Faye, Quashie — Berkovic (Taylor 71) — Mornar (Olszar 57), Yakubu *Subs not used* Schemmel, Hughes, Wapenaar *Booked* Pasanen, Smertin
Scorer **Taylor 77**
Report page 181

Sunday February 22
LIVERPOOL (h)
FA Cup, 5th rnd replay
Won 1-0 HT 0-0 Att 19,529
"I know I'm going to get slaughtered," Gerard Houllier admits after his Liverpool side fall to a side deprived of 13 first-team players. Owen's desperately weak penalty is saved on the hour and Hughes, a half-time substitute, settles the tie 11 minutes later, completing a sweet move to earn a quarter-final against Arsenal.

Hislop — Pasanen, Primus, De Zeeuw, Stefanovic (Hughes ht) — Harper, Berkovic, Smertin, Quashie, Taylor — Yakubu *Subs not used* Wapenaar, O'Neil, Olszar, Cooper *Booked* Quashie, Yakubu, Smertin, Hughes
Scorer **Hughes 71**
Referee **M Messias**

Sunday February 29
NEWCASTLE UNITED (h)
Drew 1-1 HT 0-1 Att 20,140 Position 17th
Sir Bobby Robson is forced to defend Newcastle's transfer policy after LuaLua scores the late, low equaliser that takes the club he has joined on loan out of the bottom three at the expense of his permanent employers — a goal that could have huge repercussions when the Champions League positions are finalised.

Hislop — Pasanen, Primus, De Zeeuw, Taylor — Smertin, Faye (Mornar 72), Quashie — Berkovic (Harper 90) — LuaLua, Yakubu *Subs not used* Wapenaar, Curtis, Hughes *Booked* Faye, Berkovic
Scorer **LuaLua 89**
Referee **A D'Urso**

Saturday March 6
ARSENAL (h)
FA Cup, 6th rnd
Lost 1-5 HT 0-3 Att 20,137
Just how good are Arsenal? Given a standing ovation by mesmerised Portsmouth fans, they are now only 7-1 for the Treble after a brilliant, goal-laden display in which Ljungberg and the imperious Henry score twice. "They could win everything — including the Boat Race," Harry Redknapp says.

Hislop — Pasanen, Primus, De Zeeuw, Taylor — Smertin, Faye, Quashie (Hughes 70) — Berkovic (Stone ht) — Yakubu, Mornar (Sheringham 77) *Subs not used* Wapenaar, Harper
Scorer **Sheringham 90**
Referee **J Winter**

Saturday March 13
EVERTON (a)
Lost 0-1 HT 0-0 Att 40,105 Position 18th
Hislop — Pasanen, Primus, De Zeeuw, Stefanovic (Sheringham 80), Faye, Hughes, LuaLua (Taylor ht) — Berkovic (Mornar 67) — Yakubu *Subs not used* Wapenaar, Todorov *Booked* Berkovic, Pasanen
Report page 140

Wednesday March 17
LIVERPOOL (a)
Lost 0-3 HT 0-2 Att 34,663 Position 18th
Hislop — Curtis, Primus, De Zeeuw, Stefanovic — Smertin (Stone ht), Faye, Hughes — Mornar, LuaLua — Todorov (Taylor ht) *Subs not used* Pasanen, Sheringham, Wapenaar *Booked* Stefanovic
Report page 182

THE PLAYERS

PATRIK BERGER (midfield) **Born** November 10, 1973, Prague **Ht** 6ft 1in **Wt** 12st 6lb **Signed from** Liverpool, June 2003, free

EYAL BERKOVIC (midfield) **Born** April 2, 1972, Haifa **Ht** 5ft 7in **Wt** 10st 2lb **Signed from** Manchester City, January 2004, free

DEON BURTON (forward) **Born** October 25, 1976, Ashford **Ht** 5ft 8in **Wt** 10st 1lb **Signed from** Derby County (initial loan), August 2002, £250,000

JOHN CURTIS (defender) **Born** September 3, 1978, Nuneaton **Ht** 5ft 10in **Wt** 11st 9lb **Signed from** Leicester City, February 2004, free

ARJAN DE ZEEUW (defender) **Born** April 16, 1970, Castricum, the Netherlands **Ht** 6ft 1in **Wt** 13st 11lb **Signed from** Wigan Athletic, June 2002, free

RICHARD DUFFY (defender) **Born** August 30, 1985, Swansea **Ht** 5ft 9in **Wt** 10st 3lb **Signed from** Swansea City, January 2004, nominal

AMDY FAYE (midfield) **Born** March 12, 1977, Dakar **Ht** 6ft 0in **Wt** 12st 4lb **Signed from** Auxerre, August 2003, £1.5m

KEVIN HARPER (midfield) **Born** January 15, 1976, Oldham **Ht** 5ft 6in **Wt** 10st 9lb **Signed from** Derby County, March 2000, £300,000

SHAKA HISLOP (goalkeeper) **Born** February 12, 1969, London **Ht** 6ft 4in **Wt** 14st 4lb **Signed from** West Ham United, July 2002, free

RICHARD HUGHES (midfield) **Born** June 25, 1979, Glasgow **Ht** 6ft 0in **Wt** 13st 0lb **Signed from** Bournemouth, June 2002, £50,000

HAYDEN FOXE (defender) **Born** June 23, 1977, Sydney **Ht** 6ft 2in **Wt** 12st 1lb **Signed from** West Ham United, May 2002, £400,000

LOMANA LUALUA (forward) **Born** December 28, 1980, Kinshasa, Zaire **Ht** 5ft 8in **Wt** 12st 2lb **Signed from** Newcastle United (loan), February 2004

IVICA MORNAR (forward) **Born** December 1, 1974, Split **Ht** 6ft 0in **Wt** 12st 4lb **Signed from** Anderlecht, January 2004, £500,000

SEBASTIEN OLSZAR (forward) **Born** October 12, 1981, Poland **Ht** 5ft 11in **Wt** 11st 2lb **Signed from** Admira Wacker (loan), February 2004

GARY O'NEIL (midfield) **Born** May 18, 1983, London **Ht** 5ft 8in **Wt** 9st 8lb **Signed from** trainee, August 1999

PETRI PASANEN (defender) **Born** September 24, 1980, Lahti, Finland **Ht** 6ft 1in **Wt** 12st 1lb **Signed from** Ajax (loan), January 2004

VINCENT PERICARD (forward) **Born** October 3, 1982, Efko, Cameroon **Ht** 6ft 1in **Wt** 13st 5lb **Signed from** Juventus (initial loan), July 2003, £400,000

LINVOY PRIMUS (defender) **Born** September 14, 1973, Forest Gate **Ht** 5ft 10in **Wt** 12st 0lb **Signed from** Reading, June 2000, free

NIGEL QUASHIE (midfield) **Born** July 20, 1978, Nunhead **Ht** 5ft 9in **Wt** 11st 0lb **Signed from** Nottingham Forest, August 2000, £600,000

JASON ROBERTS (forward) **Born** January 25, 1978, Park Royal **Ht** 6ft 1in **Wt** 14st 0lb **Signed from** West Bromwich Albion (loan), September 2003

CARL ROBINSON (midfield) **Born** October 13, 1976, Llandrudod **Ht** 5ft 10in **Wt** 12st 10lb **Signed from** Wolverhampton Wanderers, July 2002, free

SEBASTIEN SCHEMMEL (defender) **Born** June 2, 1975, Nancy **Ht** 5ft 10in **Wt** 12st 0lb **Signed from** West Ham United, August 2003, free

TEDDY SHERINGHAM (forward) **Born** April 2, 1966, Highams Park **Ht** 6ft 0in **Wt** 12st 5lb **Signed from** Tottenham Hotspur, June 2003, free

TIM SHERWOOD (midfield) **Born** February 2, 1969, St Albans **Ht** 6ft 0in **Wt** 12st 8lb **Signed from** Tottenham Hotspur, January 2003, free

ALEXEI SMERTIN (midfield) **Born** May 1, 1975, Barnaul, Russia **Ht** 5ft 9in **Wt** 10st 0lb **Signed from** Chelsea (loan), August 2003

PAVEL SRNICEK (goalkeeper) **Born** March 10, 1968, Ostrava **Ht** 6ft 2in **Wt** 14st 9lb **Signed from** Brescia, September 2003, free

DEJAN STEFANOVIC (defender) **Born** October 28, 1974, Nis, Yugoslavia **Ht** 5ft 11in **Wt** 13st 1lb **Signed from** Vitesse Arnhem, July 2003, £1.9m

STEVE STONE (midfield) **Born** August 20, 1971, Gateshead **Ht** 5ft 9in **Wt** 11st 3lb **Signed from** Aston Villa (initial loan), October 2002, free

MATTHEW TAYLOR (defender) **Born** September 10, 1979, Oxford **Ht** 5ft 10in **Wt** 11st 8lb **Signed from** Luton Town, June 2002, £400,000

SVETOSLAV TODOROV (forward) **Born** August 30, 1978, Dobrich, Bulgaria **Ht** 5ft 11in **Wt** 11st 6lb **Signed from** West Ham United, March 2002, £750,000

HARALD WAPENAAR (goalkeeper) **Born** April 10, 1970, Vlaadingen, the Netherlands **Ht** 6ft 4in **Wt** 12st 0lb **Signed from** FC Utrecht, July 2003, free

YAKUBU AYEGBENI (forward) **Born** November 22, 1982, Benin City, Nigeria **Ht** 6ft 0in **Wt** 13st 0lb **Signed from** Maccabi Haifa (initial loan), January 2003, undisclosed

BORIS ZIVKOVIC (defender) **Born** November 15, 1975, Zivinice, Yugoslavia **Ht** 6ft 0in **Wt** 11st 11lb **Signed from** Bayer Leverkusen, June 2003, free

STATS AND FACTS

● Lomana LuaLua and Yakubu Ayegbeni rejected the chance to play in big cup matches abroad this season to stay with Portsmouth. LuaLua, bitter over his treatment by Newcastle United, rejected the club's attempt to recall him from his loan to play in the Uefa Cup semi-final, second leg away to Marseilles; Yakubu, angry that Nigeria had sent him home from the African Nations Cup in January, turned down their invitation to rejoin the squad in Tunisia for the quarter-finals.

● Portsmouth were the fifth successive first-division champions to avoid an immediate relegation from the Premiership: Sunderland finished 7th, Charlton Athletic 9th, Fulham 13th, Manchester City 9th and Portsmouth 13th in their first seasons back in the top flight.

● Portsmouth were one of two Premiership sides with an average attendance below 24,000 (the other was Fulham). When they were last in the top flight, in 1987-88, 16 clubs had average attendances below 22,000.

● Portsmouth recorded their first win in 16 games against Manchester United in April.

● The past six games against Blackburn Rovers at Fratton Park have not produced a home win.

● Portsmouth have not won any of their past 19 games away to Newcastle United.

Bill Edgar

GOALSCORERS

	Prem	FAC	CC	Total
P Berger	5	-	-	5
E Berkovic	1	-	-	1
A De Zeeuw	1	-	-	1
H Foxe	1	-	-	1
R Hughes	-	1	-	1
L LuaLua	4	-	-	4
I Mornar	1	-	-	1
G O'Neil	2	-	-	2
N Quashie	1	-	-	1
J Roberts	1	-	3	4
S Schemmel	-	1	-	1
E Sheringham	9 (1p)	1	-	10 (1p)
T Sherwood	-	-	2	2
D Stefanovic	3	-	-	3
S Stone	2	-	-	2
M Taylor	-	3	1	4
Yakubu Ayegbeni	16 (1p)	1	2	19 (1p)
Own goals	-	-	1	1

Sunday March 21
SOUTHAMPTON (h)
Won 1-0   HT **0-0**   Att **20,140**   Position **18th**
After two defeats against their neighbours, Portsmouth secure a vital three points thanks to Yakubu, who turns in Stone's cross to send Fratton Park into a frenzy. The same player had missed two good chances and Portsmouth get the stroke of luck they need when Phillips's acrobatic volley rebounds off the inside of a post.

Hislop — Pasanen, Primus, De Zeeuw, Stefanovic — Stone, Smertin, Faye, Taylor — Sheringham, Yakubu (LuaLua 83) *Subs not used* Wapenaar, Hughes, Curtis, Mornar
Scorer **Yakubu 68**
Referee **M Halsey**

Saturday March 27
BLACKBURN ROVERS (a)
Won 2-1   HT **1-1**   Att **22,855**   Position **17th**
Hislop — Pasanen, Primus, De Zeeuw, Stefanovic — Stone, Smertin, Faye, Taylor (Hughes 88) — Sheringham (LuaLua 70), Yakubu *Subs not used* Mornar, Berkovic, Wapenaar
Scorers **Sheringham 17, Yakubu 82**
Report page 99

Saturday April 10
CHARLTON ATHLETIC (a)
Drew 1-1   HT **0-1**   Att **26,385**   Position **17th**
Hislop — Pasanen (Berkovic ht), Primus, De Zeeuw, Stefanovic — Stone, Faye, Smertin, Taylor — Sheringham (LuaLua 58), Yakubu *Subs not used* Wapenaar, Quashie, Curtis *Booked* De Zeeuw
Scorer **Yakubu 65**
Report page 119

Monday April 12
BIRMINGHAM CITY (h)
Won 3-1   HT **1-0**   Att **20,104**   Position **17th**
Controversy surrounds Portsmouth's third win in four games when Maik Taylor, the Birmingham goalkeeper, is sent off for handling outside the box, even though Yakubu goes on to put the ball in the net. Stefanovic beats Bennett, Taylor's replacement, from the free kick, Yakubu completing victory from the spot after Cunningham is penalised for handball.

Hislop — Primus (Pasanen 58), De Zeeuw, Stefanovic — Stone, Berkovic (Quashie 74), Faye (Harper 81), Smertin, Taylor — Yakubu, LuaLua *Subs not used* Wapenaar, Sheringham *Booked* Quashie
Scorers **Stefanovic 45, LuaLua 62, Yakubu 73 (pen)**
Referee **B Knight**

Saturday April 17
MANCHESTER UNITED (h)
Won 1-0   HT **1-0**   Att **20,140**   Position **16th**
Stone marks his 50th game for Portsmouth with the goal that makes it 13 points out of 15 and gives them every chance of avoiding the drop. United should get the chance to level from the penalty spot, but the officials miss Taylor deflecting Gary Neville's shot over the bar with his hand.

Hislop — Primus, De Zeeuw, Stefanovic, Taylor — Smertin, Faye, Stone, Berkovic (Quashie ht) — Yakubu, LuaLua (Sheringham 79) *Subs not used* Curtis, Harper, Wapenaar *Booked* Taylor, Sheringham
Scorer **Stone 36**
Referee **N Barry**

PLAYER OF THE SEASON
Yakubu Ayegbeni

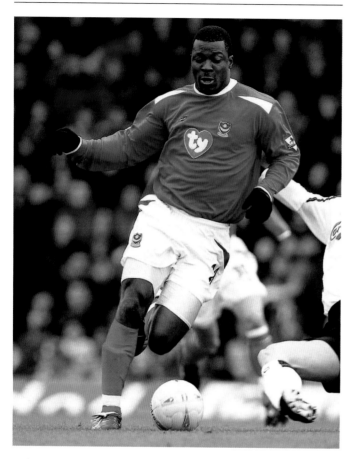

The vast majority of fans voted for Arjan de Zeeuw, the indomitable central defender, and the rest kept praying that Chelsea would forget that Alexei Smertin was still on their books. But the scoring spree at the end of the season by Yakubu Ayegbeni made the difference. Until March 21, when he scored the winner against Southampton, he had the distinction of being offside 56 times and missing the target 61 times. He then scored 11 in the final ten games. Whether it was the coaching of Luther Blissett or having Lomana LuaLua disrupting defences alongside him — or both — he has proved his potential. He is only 21, strong, has two good feet and is showing the confidence — almost the arrogance — of a true star.

Richard Holledge

Sunday April 25
LEEDS UNITED (a)
Won 2-1   **HT 1-0**   Att **39,273**   Position **14th**
Hislop — Primus, De Zeeuw, Stefanovic, Taylor — Stone (Harper 80), Smertin, Faye, Quashie — Yakubu, LuaLua (Sheringham 74) *Subs not used* Wapenaar, Curtis, Berkovic *Booked* De Zeeuw, Smertin
Scorers **Yakubu 9, LuaLua 51**
Report page 162

Saturday May 1
FULHAM (h)
Drew 1-1   **HT 0-0**   Att **20,065**   Position **14th**
Their real fears were banished some weeks ago, but Portsmouth are now mathematically safe after Yakubu — pouncing on Van der Sar's handling error — and McBride trade late goals. Fulham "will keep battling until the end" for a Uefa Cup place, Chris Coleman says.
Hislop — Primus (Duffy 22), De Zeeuw, Stefanovic, Taylor — Stone, Smertin, Faye, Quashie — LuaLua, Yakubu (Sheringham 90) *Subs not used* Wapenaar, Berkovic, Harper *Booked* Faye
Scorer **Yakubu 80**
Referee **S Dunn**

Tuesday May 4
ARSENAL (h)
Drew 1-1   **HT 1-0**   Att **20,140**   Position **14th**
Just two more games to go now for Arsenal if they are to complete the league season unbeaten. They hit the woodwork twice either side of a first Premiership goal by Reyes, but hold their breath when Yakubu, who had given Portsmouth the lead, shoots too close to Lehmann when clean through.
Hislop — Curtis, De Zeeuw, Stefanovic, Taylor — Stone, Faye, Quashie, Hughes — LuaLua, Yakubu (Mornar 81) *Subs not used* Wapenaar, Duffy, Sheringham, Harper
Scorer **Yakubu 30**
Referee **M Riley**

Saturday May 8
LEICESTER CITY (a)
Lost 1-3   **HT 0-2**   Att **31,536**   Position **14th**
Hislop — Curtis, De Zeeuw, Stefanovic, Taylor — Faye (Mornar 57) — Stone (Sheringham 69), Smertin, Quashie — Yakubu, LuaLua *Subs not used* Wapenaar, Hughes, Duffy *Booked* Hislop, LuaLua
Scorer **Quashie 66**
Report page 172

Saturday May 15
MIDDLESBROUGH (h)
Won 5-1   **HT 3-1**   Att **20,134**   Position **13th**
After an extraordinary 48 hours at Fratton Park — with Milan Mandaric and Harry Redknapp involved in a vitriolic slanging match over the future of Jim Smith, Redknapp's No 2 — comes an extraordinary finale to the season, Yakubu hitting four against a nonplussed Middlesbrough and Sheringham signing off from the home club with a goal.
Hislop — Pasanen (Curtis ht), De Zeeuw, Stefanovic, Taylor — Stone, Smertin, Berkovic, Quashie (Hughes 81) — Yakubu, LuaLua (Sheringham 68) *Subs not used* Wapenaar, Mornar
Scorers **Yakubu 4, 14 (pen), 31, 83, Sheringham 80**
Referee **M Halsey**

SOUTHAMPTON

PREMIERSHIP

	P	W	D	L	F	A	GD	Pts
Arsenal	38	26	12	0	73	26	47	**90**
Chelsea	38	24	7	7	67	30	37	**79**
Man Utd	38	23	6	9	64	35	29	**75**
Liverpool	38	16	12	10	55	37	18	**60**
Newcastle	38	13	17	8	52	40	12	**56**
Aston Villa	38	15	11	12	48	44	4	**56**
Charlton	38	14	11	13	51	51	0	**53**
Bolton	38	14	11	13	48	56	-8	**53**
Fulham	38	14	10	14	52	46	6	**52**
Birmingham	38	12	14	12	43	48	-5	**50**
Middlesbro	38	13	9	16	44	52	-8	**48**
Southampton	38	12	11	15	44	45	-1	**47**
Portsmouth	38	12	9	17	47	54	-7	**45**
Tottenham	38	13	6	19	47	57	-10	**45**
Blackburn	38	12	8	18	51	59	-8	**44**
Man City	38	9	14	15	55	54	1	**41**
Everton	38	9	12	17	45	57	-12	**39**
Leicester	38	6	15	17	48	65	-17	**33**
Leeds	38	8	9	21	40	79	-39	**33**
Wolves	38	7	12	19	38	77	-39	**33**

FA CUP
Third round

CARLING CUP
Quarter-finals

UEFA CUP
First round

Phillips electric: ecstasy at St Mary's after the striker's goal wrapped up victory over Liverpool in Paul Sturrock's first match

THE GAMES

Saturday August 16 2003
LEICESTER CITY (a)
Drew 2-2 HT 0-2 Att 31,621 Position 8th
Jones — Dodd, Lundekvam (Higginbotham 13),
M Svensson, Le Saux — Telfer (Fernandes 68), Oakley,
Delap, McCann — Beattie, A Svensson (Phillips ht) *Subs
not used* Blayney, Prutton *Booked* McCann
Scorers **Phillips 76, Beattie 80**
Report page 164

Saturday August 23
BIRMINGHAM CITY (h)
Drew 0-0 HT 0-0 Att 31,656 Position 12th
Both sides hit the woodwork, through Beattie and
Clemence, Le Saux clears off the line from John and
Jones makes a late save from Morrison. With Dunn
also being denied a penalty after Le Saux's trip,
Birmingham will feel more aggrieved by this goalless
stalemate.

Jones — Dodd, Lundekvam, M Svensson, Le Saux —
Fernandes (Telfer 89), Oakley, Delap (A Svensson 64),
McCann (Tessem 75) — Beattie, Phillips *Subs not used*
Blayney, Higginbotham *Booked* Lundekvam, Le Saux,
Fernandes
Referee **G Barber**

Tuesday August 26
LEEDS UNITED (a)
Drew 0-0 HT 0-0 Att 34,721 Position 10th
Jones — Dodd, Lundekvam, M Svensson, Le Saux —
Fernandes, Oakley, Delap (Telfer 9), Prutton
(McCann 78) — Beattie, Phillips (Ormerod 85) *Subs not
used* Blayney, Higginbotham *Booked* Le Saux, Oakley,
Fernandes
Report page 154

Sunday August 31
MANCHESTER UNITED (h)
Won 1-0 HT 0-0 Att 32,066 Position 8th
Beckham's book serialisation is causing Sir Alex
Ferguson some embarrassment and Beattie adds to it
by heading the late winner — after Howard flaps at
Le Saux's corner — that gives Southampton their first
win of the season and ends United's 21-match
unbeaten league run.

Jones — Dodd, Lundekvam, M Svensson, Le Saux —
Fernandes (A Svensson 86), Oakley, Telfer, McCann
(Marsden 62) — Beattie, Phillips (Ormerod 77) *Subs not
used* Niemi, Higginbotham *Booked* McCann
Scorer **Beattie 88**
Referee **M Halsey**

Saturday September 13
WOLVERHAMPTON WANDERERS (h)
Won 2-0 HT 1-0 Att 31,711 Position 5th
Dave Jones's return to Southampton with Wolves ends in
a controversial defeat after Uriah Rennie somehow
interprets Phillips's fall into the area, after being caught
by Irwin three yards outside it, as worthy of a penalty.
Beattie converts from the spot and adds a second when
his fierce drive goes though Oakes's hands.

Jones — Dodd, Lundekvam, M Svensson, Le Saux —
Fernandes (A Svensson 90), Oakley, Telfer, Marsden
(McCann 89) — Beattie, Phillips *Subs not used* Niemi,
Higginbotham, Ormerod *Booked* Le Saux, Telfer,
Beattie
Scorer **Beattie 37 (pen), 52**
Referee **U Rennie**

THERE IS NO GETTING AWAY FROM it, Southampton are a
mid-table club. The team finished twelfth in the Premiership last
season, a slight dip after three years occupying eighth, eleventh and
tenth spots. Average attendances, despite full houses, ranked the
club eleventh in the Premiership attendance table. Even the Fair
Play League failed to show whether they were sinners or saints, with
Southampton at a respectable eleventh.

With the club also mid-table in terms of financial turnover, the
neat argument would be that you achieve what your income allows,
which, by and large, is exactly what Premiership football is about
these days. So, on that basis, Southampton fans were expecting too
much when looking to improve on the previous season's eighth
place and qualification for the Uefa Cup. To achieve that with an
Alan Curbishley or a Steve Bruce in charge, everything had to go
right. To attempt it with three managers in one season was asking
too much.

Yet with several teams in the top half of the table unable to show
any consistent quality, they went into the last five games with faint
hopes of another Uefa Cup place, boosted by away wins to
Wolverhampton and Manchester City. Then came a home defeat to
Bolton Wanderers — and Southampton did not win another game.

"It wouldn't be like us to finish with a positive goal difference,"
one fan said at the Bolton game. He was right, the 2-1 defeat away to
Charlton Athletic on the final day tipping Southampton's difference
into minus figures for the first time. It was a sad end to a season that
initially promised much more. On Christmas Day, Southampton
were fourth, having just thrashed Portsmouth 3-0. It turned out to
be much the best present of the lot.

As in the previous campaign, the team started well, then
blundered through winter and slumbered through spring. In
2002-03, Southampton earned just 15 points from the last 15 games:
this season, 21 points from the last 21.

Only three teams scored fewer goals, with James Beattie and
Kevin Phillips accounting for two-thirds of Southampton's
Barclaycard Premiership goals between them. Claus Lundekvam
and Michael Svensson, the central defenders, scored as many
goals as the entire midfield put together. John Cleese could have
been talking about the talented but ultimately wasteful midfield duo
of Fabrice Fernandes and Anders Svensson when he said: "It's not
the despair. I can cope with the despair — it's the hope I can't cope
with".

A poll of fans on the website of the London suppporters' club
showed that 58 per cent were disappointed with the season. Still,

HONOURS BOARD

FOOTBALL LEAGUE
Runners-up 1984
FA CUP
Winners 1976
Runners-up 1900, 1902, 2003
LEAGUE CUP
Runners-up 1979

Record attendance 32,151 (v Arsenal, Premiership, December 29, 2003) **Current capacity** 32,689
Record victory 9-3 (v Wolverhampton Wanderers, second division, September 18, 1965)
Record defeat 0-8 (v Tottenham Hotspur, second division, March 28, 1936 and v Everton, first division, November 20, 1971)

Southampton finished above Portsmouth and Tottenham Hotspur, a modest but still hugely satisfying state of affairs to most. And it was not a dull season, despite the bizarre argument of Jason Cowley, Editor of *Observer Sports Monthly*, who claimed that Leeds United's rollercoaster ride of recent seasons was at least preferable to following Southampton: try to find a Leeds fan who would agree.

After a decade of being tagged "Struggling Southampton", sharing top table with the Premiership's "a-place-in-Europe-is-achievable" also-rans produced many a feast. There was the double over Liverpool, two cracking games against Charlton Athletic (honours shared) and the 1-1 home draw against Aston Villa in the most open game of the season, a real throwback to football of yore.

Sky TV viewers will also recall the devil-may-care 3-3 draw against Newcastle United in the final week of the season that handed Liverpool that fourth Champions League place. Beating Manchester United at home was nothing special when Portsmouth and Wolves did the same and, predictably, Southampton lost home and away to Chelsea and Arsenal.

But there were so many mitigating factors — not least those three managers — that twelfth place was considered by many to be an achievement. Gordon Strachan's decision to leave at the end of the season, then go sooner, totally disrupted the campaign. The prospect of Glenn Hoddle returning angered the fans before the board plucked Paul Sturrock from Plymouth Argyle to replace Steve Wigley, the caretaker manager. For a club that has now appointed nine managers in ten seasons, surviving another change without falling apart has to be seen as a positive. And there were

Saturday September 20
TOTTENHAM HOTSPUR (a)
Won 3-1   HT 2-0   Att 35,784   Position 4th
Jones — Dodd, Lundekvam, M Svensson, Le Saux — Fernandes (A Svensson 71), Oakley, Telfer, Marsden (Prutton 84) — Beattie, Phillips *Subs not used* Niemi, Higginbotham, Ormerod *Booked* Marsden
Scorers **Beattie 3, 43, Gardner 60 (og)**
Report page 251

Wednesday September 24
STEAUA BUCHAREST (h)
Uefa Cup, 1st rnd, 1st leg
Drew 1-1   HT 0-1   Att 30,557
As Gordon Strachan had feared when he called Steaua the hardest opponents his team could have been paired with, Southampton have to be content with a draw in their first European match for 19 years. Replying to Raducanu's brave header, Phillips gives them hope with his first goal at St Mary's.

Jones — Dodd (Delap 84), Lundekvam, M Svensson, Le Saux — Fernandes (Telfer 85), Oakley, A Svensson, Marsden (McCann 67) — Beattie, Phillips *Subs not used* Niemi, Higginbotham, Tessem, Ormerod
Scorer **Phillips 52**
Referee **T Skjerven (Norway)**

Saturday September 27
MIDDLESBROUGH (h)
Lost 0-1   HT 0-1   Att 30,772   Position 5th
A "home banker" goes awry as Southampton suffer their first defeat of the season, beaten by Christie's early goal. Marsden is fortunate not to see red after raising his hands to Mills, but Phillips is not so lucky, sent off in the last minute for kicking out at Queudrue, who had been standing on his calf.

Jones — Dodd (A Svensson 54), Lundekvam, M Svensson, Le Saux — Fernandes (Ormerod 76), Oakley, Telfer, Marsden (McCann 39) — Beattie, Phillips *Subs not used* Niemi, Higginbotham *Booked* M Svensson, Oakley, A Svensson, Marsden *Sent off* Phillips 90
Referee **B Knight**

Saturday October 4
NEWCASTLE UNITED (a)
Lost 0-1   HT 0-1   Att 52,127   Position 7th
Niemi — Dodd (Prutton 81), Lundekvam, M Svensson, Higginbotham — Fernandes (Ormerod 81), Telfer, Marsden, McCann (A Svensson 20) — Beattie, Phillips *Subs not used* Jones, Hall *Booked* M Svensson, A Svensson
Report page 219

Wednesday October 15
STEAUA BUCHAREST (a)
Uefa Cup, 1st rnd, 2nd leg
Lost 0-1 (lost 1-2 on agg)   HT 0-0   Att 25,000
Southampton's journey into Europe lasts just one stop. They create enough chances to beat the Romanians, Phillips missing the best of them just before half-time, before Raducanu ends their hopes with an 82nd-minute winner. "It was our best performance of the year," Gordon Strachan insists.

Niemi — Dodd, Lundekvam, M Svensson, Higginbotham — Telfer, Delap, A Svensson, Fernandes — Beattie (Tessem 86), Phillips *Subs not used* Jones, Hall, Prutton, Griffit, Folly, Ormerod *Booked* Delap, Beattie
Referee **S Johannesson (Sweden)**

Sunday October 19
EVERTON (a)
Drew 0-0   HT 0-0   Att 35,775   Position 7th
Niemi — Dodd, Lundekvam, M Svensson, Higginbotham —
Telfer, Delap, A Svensson, Fernandes (Prutton 54) —
Beattie, Ormerod *Subs not used* Hall, Tessem, Griffit,
Jones *Booked* M Svensson, A Svensson
Report page 136

Saturday October 25
BLACKBURN ROVERS (h)
Won 2-0   HT 0-0   Att 31,620   Position 6th
A desperate first half is followed by a livelier second,
with goals from Beattie and Griffit — a fine finish on his
Premiership debut — sandwiching a free-for-all, after
which Cole is dismissed. It's jackets off and an invitation
outside at the final whistle, too, as Graeme Souness and
Dennis Rofe tangle on the touchline.

Niemi — Dodd, Lundekvam, M Svensson, Le Saux —
Telfer, Delap, A Svensson, McCann — Beattie
(Marsden 90), Tessem (Griffit 82) *Subs not used* Jones,
Fernandes, Higginbotham
Scorers **Beattie 59, Griffit 87**
Referee **S Bennett**

Tuesday October 28
BRISTOL CITY (a)
Carling Cup, 3rd rnd
Won 3-0   HT 1-0   Att 17,408
Unlike many of his counterparts, Gordon Strachan fields
a full-strength side in the Carling Cup and Southampton
ease through untroubled, despite losing the injured
Niemi at half-time. Beattie's goal is his eighth of the
season, Ormerod's his first.

Niemi (Jones ht) — Dodd, Lundekvam, M Svensson,
Le Saux — Fernandes (McCann 71), Delap (Telfer 62),
A Svensson, Marsden — Beattie, Ormerod *Subs not used*
Higginbotham, Griffit *Booked* Lundekvam
Scorers **Beattie 31, Ormerod 67, Le Saux 89**
Referee **P Walton**

Saturday November 1
MANCHESTER CITY (h)
Lost 0-2   HT 0-1   Att 31,952   Position 8th
A difficult weekend for Kevin Keegan — who is forced to
deny rumours of a bust-up with Anelka (officially absent
with a calf strain) before pictures of Fowler apparently
smoking and drinking in a nightclub are published in a
newspaper — is eased by victory. Gordon Strachan,
Keegan's opposite number, is incandescent over
Southampton's limp performance.

Jones — Dodd (Telfer 73), Lundekvam, M Svensson,
Le Saux — Fernandes (McCann 57), Delap, A Svensson,
Marsden — Beattie, Phillips (Ormerod 73) *Subs not used*
Blayney, Higginbotham *Booked* Marsden
Referee **A Wiley**

Beattie finds Carragher in his way in the win over Liverpool at St Mary's

many other positives from the end of the season for fans to hang on
to, not least from the old-fashioned philosophy of promoting players
from the youth ranks.

The club's under-17 and under-19 teams won their respective
leagues, prompting a flurry of debuts in the final matches as injuries
played havoc with the first-team squad. Not one of the back four
that started the season at the Walkers Stadium finished it at The
Valley, when Antti Niemi, the player of the season, was also injured.
It meant that Martin Cranie, the under-19 full back, and Alan
Blayney, the goalkeeper, made debuts, while another from the youth
ranks, Dexter Blackstock, made the bench. Yoann Folly and Leandre Griffit, the French teenagers, broke through into the first team.

Rupert Lowe, the chairman, has, to date, been rightly praised for
his astute handling of the club's finances, especially as the failings of
other clubs became apparent. But he refuses to commit to a stadium
extension and the success of his appointment of a manager from the
second division will take time to evaluate.

There is no apparent slowdown in support, as Southampton fans
have long learnt to be stoical and were grateful for trips to Cardiff
and Bucharest in the past two seasons. Staying in the top flight for
the past 26 years has proved hard enough — four years of stability
with cherries on the cake has been a bonus. But the prospect of
turning into another Spurs, or slipping below Portsmouth, would not
be tolerated.

THE MANAGER

Paul Sturrock

After Gordon Strachan walked out, claiming that he needed a rest, Steve Wigley steadied the ship before Glenn Hoddle was mooted — and rejected by the fans — and Paul Sturrock became the "safe pair of hands". Still Southampton did not collapse, a testimony to a squad more versed in changes of tactics than the England midfield. The appointment of Sturrock, the former Plymouth Argyle manager, was lauded by the League Managers Association, which is concerned that the rash of foreign appointments is foiling British talent. Southampton fans could not give two hoots: if another Scotsman brings on the squad the way that Strachan did, it will mean a top-six finish.

Steve Keenan

APPEARANCES

	Prem	FAC	CC	Euro	Total
C Baird	1 (3)	-	-	-	1 (3)
J Beattie	32 (5)	1	2	2	37 (5)
A Blayney	2	-	-	-	2
S Crainey	5	-	-	-	5
M Cranie	1	-	-	-	1
R Delap	26 (1)	-	3	1 (1)	30 (2)
A Delgado	0 (4)	-	1 (1)	-	1 (5)
J Dodd	27 (1)	1	3	2	33 (1)
F Fernandes	21 (6)	-	2	2	25 (6)
Y Folly	9	-	-	-	9
F Hall	7 (4)	-	1	-	8 (4)
D Higginbotham	24 (3)	1	2	1	28 (3)
L Griffit	2 (3)	-	-	-	2 (3)
P Jones	8	-	0 (1)	1	9 (1)
D Kenton	3 (4)	-	-	-	3 (4)
G Le Saux	19	-	1	1	21
C Lundekvam	31	1	2	2	36
C Marsden	9 (4)	-	2 (1)	1	12 (5)
N McCann	9 (9)	-	0 (2)	0 (1)	9 (12)
A Niemi	28	1	3	1	33
M Oakley	7	-	-	1	8
B Ormerod	14 (8)	0 (1)	3	-	17 (9)
M Pahars	6 (8)	1	1	-	8 (8)
K Phillips	28 (6)	1	-	2	31 (6)
D Prutton	22 (5)	1	1 (1)	-	24 (6)
A Svensson	17 (13)	1	1	2	21 (13)
M Svensson	26	1	3	2	32
P Telfer	33 (4)	1	2 (1)	1 (1)	37 (6)
J Tessem	1 (2)	-	-	0 (1)	1 (3)

Saturday November 8
BOLTON WANDERERS (a)
Drew 0-0 HT 0-0 Att 25,619 Position 9th
Niemi — Dodd, Lundekvam, M Svensson, Le Saux — Telfer, A Svensson, Delap, Marsden — Beattie, Phillips (Higginbotham 85) Subs not used Jones, Prutton, Griffit, Ormerod Booked Dodd, M Svensson Sent off M Svensson 85
Report page 104

Saturday November 22
CHELSEA (h)
Lost 0-1 HT 0-0 Att 32,149 Position 10th
Chelsea's seventh successive win in all competitions comes via a rare goal from Melchiot, but Phillips misses a sitter with his head from six yards as time runs out in a downpour. Gordon Strachan is now certain to take over at Leeds, according to newspaper reports and bookmakers, but the Southampton manager refuses to talk after this defeat.
Niemi — Telfer, Lundekvam, Higginbotham, Le Saux — Fernandes, Delap, Marsden (A Svensson 70), Griffit (Prutton 70) — Ormerod (Delgado 70), Phillips Subs not used Jones, Hall
Referee **D Gallagher**

Saturday November 29
ASTON VILLA (a)
Lost 0-1 HT 0-1 Att 31,285 Position 11th
Niemi — Telfer, Lundekvam, M Svensson, Higginbotham — A Svensson (Marsden ht), Prutton, Delap (Dodd ht), McCann (Pahars 70) — Beattie, Phillips Subs not used Jones, Delgado Booked Marsden
Report page 75

Tuesday December 2
PORTSMOUTH (h)
Carling Cup, 4th rnd
Won 2-0 HT 1-0 Att 29,201
Some Portsmouth fans ignore pre-match appeals to show respect by forcing an early end to a minute's silence for Ted Bates, and neutrals may therefore have been pleased that Beattie's double — the second a penalty after De Zeeuw is sent off for bringing him down — give Southampton victory in the first meeting between the South Coast rivals for seven years.
Niemi — Dodd, Lundekvam, M Svensson, Higginbotham — Fernandes, Delap, Telfer, Marsden (Prutton 75) — Beattie, Ormerod (Delgado 84) Subs not used Blayney, A Svensson, Pahars
Scorer Beattie 33, 90 (pen)
Referee **G Poll**

Sunday December 7
CHARLTON ATHLETIC (h)
Won 3-2 HT 2-0 Att 30,513 Position 8th
Sven-Goran Eriksson sees Parker enhance his England credentials with two spectacular long-range goals in a televised thriller, but having fought back from 2-0 down, Charlton leave with nothing when Ormerod poaches his second goal of the game four minutes from time. There are chances galore at both ends.
Niemi — Dodd, Lundekvam, M Svensson, Higginbotham — Telfer, Prutton, Delap — Ormerod, Beattie, Pahars (Phillips 77) Subs not used Jones, Fernandes, Hall, Delgado
Scorers M Svensson 6, Ormerod 45, 86
Referee **P Walton**

Saturday December 13
LIVERPOOL (a)
Won 2-1   HT **1-0**   Att **41,762**   Position **6th**
Niemi — Dodd, Lundekvam (Marsden 41), M Svensson,
Higginbotham — Telfer, Prutton, Delap, Pahars
(Fernandes 63) — Ormerod, Beattie (Delgado 81) *Subs
not used* Jones, Phillips
Scorers **Ormerod 2, M Svensson 64**
Report page 178

Tuesday December 16
BOLTON WANDERERS (a)
Carling Cup, quarter-final
Lost 0-1 (aet)   HT **0-0**   Att **13,957**
Niemi — Dodd, Hall, M Svensson, Higginbotham — Telfer,
Prutton, Delap, Pahars (McCann 68) — Delgado
(Marsden 65), Ormerod *Subs not used* Jones, Kenton,
Fernandes *Booked* Ormerod
Report page 105

Sunday December 21
PORTSMOUTH (h)
Won 3-0   HT **1-0**   Att **31,697**   Position **4th**
With one point from five games, two defeats against
the old enemy and his team in the relegation zone,
Harry Redknapp "cancels Christmas" for Portsmouth
after an emphatic defeat. Dodd opens the scoring direct
from a corner and Pahars curls in a beauty before
Beattie's near-post header completes Southampton's
stroll.
Niemi — Dodd, Lundekvam, M Svensson, Higginbotham —
Telfer, Marsden (Baird 90), Prutton, Pahars (McCann 80)
— Beattie, Ormerod (Phillips 80) *Subs not used* Jones,
A Svensson
Scorers **Dodd 34, Pahars 67, Beattie 90**
Referee **J Winter**

Friday December 26
FULHAM (a)
Lost 0-2   HT **0-1**   Att **16,767**   Position **7th**
Niemi — Dodd, Lundekvam, M Svensson, Higginbotham —
Telfer, Prutton, Marsden, McCann (Delgado 77) — Beattie,
Ormerod (Phillips 51) *Subs not used* Blayney,
A Svensson, Baird *Booked* M Svensson, Prutton
Report page 147

Monday December 29
ARSENAL (h)
Lost 0-1   HT **0-1**   Att **32,151**   Position **8th**
Arsenal reach the halfway stage of their league campaign
still unbeaten, defeating a badly depleted Southampton
easily despite the narrowness of the scoreline. Pires gets
the only goal, from Henry's perfect pass, Niemi preventing
a heavier defeat. Lehmann is reported for throwing the
ball at Phillips at the final whistle.
Niemi — Baird (Kenton 59), Hall, M Svensson,
Higginbotham — Telfer (McCann 78), Delap, Prutton,
Griffit (Ormerod 58) — Beattie, Phillips *Subs not used*
Jones, Marsden *Booked* McCann
Referee **S Dunn**

MATCH OF THE SEASON

Southampton 3 Portsmouth 0
St Mary's Stadium, Sunday December 21 2003
Nick Szczepanik

IN ITS PREMIERSHIP CONTEXT, this was an excellent result for Southampton, taking them up to fourth place in the table, and a disappointing one for Portsmouth, keeping them firmly in the relegation zone. But add in that it was the first league game between the South Coast rivals for almost 16 years and the elation of the winners and the despair of the losers were magnified.

Among the supporters, that is. Gordon Strachan, the Southampton manager, was more satisfied with the points than local bragging rights. "It's manna from heaven for a middle-of-the-league club to pick up nine points from three games," he said. "It's not the derby, it's three points."

Hang on — what did he mean, "middle-of-the-league club"? What about being in a Champions League place, with the possibility of European football? "Six, seven, eight clubs have been in this position this season and that'll happen until we get to April," he said. "If we get to April and we're still there, that's a different matter."

Portsmouth have different concerns. Their supporters must almost be wondering whether it was worth waiting so long to resume top-flight hostilities with their neighbours. While the Carling Cup tie that Southampton won 2-0 this month was in the balance until a late second goal, Portsmouth were never in this game and, unless their team improve substantially, especially on their travels, they will soon be out of this division.

In mitigation, Portsmouth had more than half a team injured or suspended. "I came here with no team — six missing from my best XI," Harry Redknapp, the Portsmouth manager, said. "Take six out of Gordon's team today and see how they cope. But we've just got to keep going. We've got a massive game on Friday [against Tottenham Hotspur] and we've got to win."

Windy conditions and the derby atmosphere did little for the standard of the early play. Not surprisingly, when the breakthrough came after 34 minutes, it owed little to flowing football and everything to defensive uncertainty and the elements. Harald Wapenaar, the Portsmouth goalkeeper, had failed to command his penalty area on a number of occasions as Jason Dodd curled in free kicks and he was stranded as the long-serving Southampton captain delivered an inswinging, wind-assisted corner from the left. Although Sebastien Schemmel was stationed on the far post, his attempt to nod the ball clear sent it against the underside of the crossbar, back against his own head and in.

Dodd has only recently taken over the role of the team's dead-ball specialist and has been a great success. "It could be one of my better decisions, asking Doddy to take free kicks and corners," Strachan

Beattie gets the better of Sherwood in an emphatic derby victory

said. "People think it's easy but it's not, as we've proved over two years. You have to be brave, to be focused and to take responsibility when you're taking corner kicks with 30,000 people watching you. Some people can't handle it."

Marian Pahars's strike to double the lead after 67 minutes was of considerably higher quality. Receiving the ball 25 yards out, he drifted left, cut back inside Boris Zivkovic and Alexei Smertin and hit a swerving shot beyond Wapenaar. The Southampton supporters also acclaimed the return to the goalscoring charts of a favourite who has started the past four games after being sidelined for more than a year with a series of injuries. "It was a terrible year," Pahars said. "But I hope it's all over now and I can score more."

If a one-goal deficit gave a team as short of goals as Portsmouth a mountain to climb, then two was an entire alpine range and, with virtually the final touch of the match, James Beattie rubbed it in by diving in front of Linvoy Primus to head home Dodd's cross from the right. By then, the Southampton supporters were in two minds, taunting the Portsmouth fans with "We'll never play you again", followed by "Can we play you every week?" Looking at the table, Portsmouth would settle for playing Southampton next season.

SOUTHAMPTON (4-4-2): A Niemi — J Dodd, C Lundekvam, M Svensson, D Higginbotham — P Telfer, C Marsden (sub: C Baird, 90min), D Prutton, M Pahars (sub: N McCann, 80) — B Ormerod (sub: K Phillips, 80), J Beattie. **Substitutes not used:** P Jones, A Svensson.
PORTSMOUTH (3-5-2): H Wapenaar — L Primus, H Foxe, D Stefanovic — S Schemmel (sub: B Zivkovic, 56), R Hughes (sub: Yakubu Ayegbeni, 60), T Sherwood, A Smertin, M Taylor — E Sheringham, J Roberts. **Substitutes not used:** P Srnicek, D Burton, C Robinson. **Booked:** Schemmel, Sherwood, Foxe.

Saturday January 3 2004
NEWCASTLE UNITED (h)
FA Cup, 3rd rnd
Lost 0-3   HT 0-2   Att 28,456
Stung by pre-match criticism from their own chairman, Newcastle take it out on last season's beaten finalists, who are outplayed from first to last. Dyer, returning as Shearer's strike partner, scores the first and third goals, his second an outstanding effort after a long run. "This will hurt me long into the night," Gordon Strachan says.

Niemi — Dodd, Lundekvam, M Svensson, Higginbotham — Telfer, Prutton, A Svensson, Pahars (Ormerod 66) — Beattie, Phillips *Subs not used* Jones, Fernandes, Marsden, Kenton *Booked* Prutton
Referee **M Dean**

Wednesday January 7
LEICESTER CITY (h)
Drew 0-0   HT 0-0   Att 31,053   Position 8th
Southampton make it four games without a goal in a dire encounter. Izzet and Ferdinand go close for Leicester — who have Dabizas in defence after his free transfer from Newcastle — in the first half, but the match peters out completely after the break. (Two days later, Gordon Strachan announces that he will not seek a new contract at the end of the season.)

Niemi — Dodd, Lundekvam (Delap 42), M Svensson, Higginbotham — Telfer, A Svensson, Prutton, Fernandes (McCann 77) — Beattie, Phillips (Delgado 83) *Subs not used* Jones, Ormerod *Booked* M Svensson, Higginbotham
Referee **H Webb**

Saturday January 10
BIRMINGHAM CITY (a)
Lost 1-2   HT 1-1   Att 29,071   Position 9th
Niemi — Dodd, Hall, M Svensson, Higginbotham — Prutton, A Svensson, Delap (Pahars 85), Fernandes (McCann 71) — Ormerod (Phillips 72), Beattie *Subs not used* Blayney, Kenton *Booked* Delap *Sent off* Prutton 69
Scorer **Ormerod 6**
Report page 86

Saturday January 17
LEEDS UNITED (h)
Won 2-1   HT 2-0   Att 31,976   Position 8th
Two days before the deadline to find new backers and still £80m in debt, Leeds find themselves bottom of the table after an unlucky defeat. Southampton put Beattie on the bench, but goals from Ormerod and Phillips — his first in the league since the opening day — make Kilgallon's first senior goal redundant, though Michael Svensson later hits his own post.

Niemi — Dodd, M Svensson, Hall (Kenton 81), Higginbotham — Fernandes (Telfer 86), Prutton, Delap, A Svensson — Phillips (Beattie 86), Ormerod *Subs not used* Blayney, Pahars *Booked* A Svensson
Scorers **Ormerod 36, Phillips 43**
Referee **A Wiley**

Saturday January 31
MANCHESTER UNITED (a)
Lost 2-3   HT 1-2   Att 67,758   Position 10th
Niemi — Dodd, Hall, Higginbotham, Le Saux (Kenton 80) — Telfer, Delap, A Svensson, Fernandes (Pahars 67) — Phillips, Ormerod (Beattie 67) *Subs not used* Folly, Smith *Booked* Ormerod
Scorer **Phillips 38, 53**
Report page 202

Saturday February 7
FULHAM (h)
Drew 0-0   HT 0-0   Att 31,820   Position 10th
Van der Sar is the outstanding performer in a decidedly
uneventful match and even the Fulham goalkeeper
admits that the visiting side do not deserve a draw after
Pearce, sliding in to clear, gets away with a clear
handball which Andy D'Urso, the referee, fails to detect.

Niemi — Dodd, M Svensson, Higginbotham, Le Saux —
Telfer, A Svensson, Delap — Phillips, Ormerod
(Beattie 75), Pahars *Subs not used* Smith, Hall, Baird,
Fernandes *Booked* Phillips
Referee **A D'Urso**

Tuesday February 10
ARSENAL (a)
Lost 0-2   HT 0-1   Att 38,007   Position 11th
Niemi — Kenton, M Svensson, Higginbotham, Crainey —
Telfer, A Svensson (Baird 26; Beattie 81), Delap, Le Saux
(Pahars 83) — Ormerod, Phillips *Subs not used* Smith,
Hall *Booked* M Svensson, Niemi, Baird
Report page 66

Saturday February 21
EVERTON (h)
Drew 3-3   HT 0-2   Att 31,875   Position 12th
With Gordon Strachan having departed eight days earlier,
three months before he had planned — and with fans
reacting furiously to the prospect of Glenn Hoddle
returning as manager — there is a welcome return to
matters on the field and a terrific match against Everton
in which Southampton, 2-0 and 3-1 down, grab a point
with a 25-yard curler from Fernandes as stoppage time
begins.

Niemi — Dodd, Lundekvam (Fernandes ht), M Svensson,
Higginbotham — Telfer (Pahars 88), Prutton, Delap,
Le Saux — Ormerod (Beattie ht), Phillips *Subs not used*
Smith, Crainey *Booked* Le Saux
Scorers **Phillips 58, Beattie 82 (pen), Fernandes 90**
Referee **P Dowd**

Saturday February 28
BLACKBURN ROVERS (a)
Drew 1-1   HT 1-0   Att 21,970   Position 12th
Niemi — Dodd, Lundekvam, M Svensson, Le Saux —
Fernandes (McCann 62), Telfer, Delap, Prutton — Beattie,
Phillips (Pahars 87) *Subs not used* Higginbotham,
Ormerod, Smith *Booked* Dodd
Scorer **Phillips 5**
Report page 98

Sunday March 14
LIVERPOOL (h)
Won 2-0   HT 0-0   Att 32,056   Position 11th
Paul Sturrock's first game in charge brings a huge
change in luck for Southampton. While Owen hits a
post from two yards and has a weak penalty saved —
his tenth miss in 23 spot kicks — Southampton score
twice against the run of play, Beattie from an offside
position and Phillips only with the aid of a deflection off
Riise.

Niemi — Dodd, Lundekvam, M Svensson, Le Saux
(Higginbotham 44) — Telfer, Delap, Prutton, McCann
(A Svensson 68) — Beattie, Phillips (Tessem 90) *Subs
not used* Smith, Pahars *Booked* Lundekvam, Telfer,
McCann
Scorers **Beattie 51, Phillips 85**
Referee **D Gallagher**

THE PLAYERS

CHRIS BAIRD (defender) **Born**
February 25, 1982, Ballymena
Ht 6ft 1in **Wt** 12st 0lb **Signed from**
trainee, August 2001

JAMES BEATTIE (forward) **Born**
February 27, 1978, Lancaster
Ht 6ft 1in **Wt** 13st 3lb **Signed from**
Blackburn Rovers, July 1998, £1m

ALAN BLAYNEY (goalkeeper) **Born**
October 9, 1981, Belfast **Ht** 6ft 2in
Wt 13st 12lb **Signed from** trainee,
August 2002

STEPHEN CRAINEY (defender) **Born**
June 22, 1981, Glasgow **Ht** 5ft 9in
Wt 9st 11lb **Signed from** Celtic (loan),
February 2004

MARTIN CRANIE (defender) **Born**
September 26, 1986, Yeovil **Ht** 6ft 0in
Wt 12st 4lb **Signed from** trainee,
May 2004

RORY DELAP (midfield) **Born** July 6,
1976, Sutton Coldfield **Ht** 6ft 0in
Wt 11st 11lb **Signed from** Derby
County, July 2001, £4m

AGUSTIN DELGADO (forward) **Born**
December 23, 1974, Ibarra, Ecuador
Ht 6ft 3in **Wt** 14st 2lb **Signed from**
Necaxa, Mexico, November 2001,
£3.2m

JASON DODD (defender) **Born**
November 2, 1970, Bath **Ht** 5ft 11in
Wt 12st 3lb **Signed from** Bath City,
April 1989, £50,000

FABRICE FERNANDES (midfield)
Born October 29, 1979, Aubervilliers,
France **Ht** 5ft 8in **Wt** 11st 7lb
Signed from Rennes, December 2001,
£1.1m

YOANN FOLLY (midfield) **Born** June 6,
1985, Togo **Signed from** Saint Etienne,
July 2003, £250,000

LEANDRE GRIFFIT (midfield) **Born** May
21, 1984, Maubeuge, France **Ht** 5ft 8in
Wt 11st 0lb **Signed from** Amiens, July
2003, free

FITZ HALL (defender) **Born**
December 20, 1980, Walthamstow
Ht 6ft 4in **Wt** 13st 0lb **Signed from**
Oldham Athletic, July 2003, £250,000

DANNY HIGGINBOTHAM (defender)
Born December 29, 1978,
Manchester **Ht** 6ft 2in **Wt** 12st 6lb
Signed from Derby County, January
2003, £1.5m

PAUL JONES
(see Wolverhampton Wanderers)

DARREN KENTON (defender) **Born**
September 13, 1978, Wandsworth
Ht 5ft 10in **Wt** 11st 2lb **Signed from**
Norwich City, May 2003, free

GRAEME LE SAUX (defender) **Born**
October 17, 1968, Jersey **Ht** 5ft 10in
Wt 12st 2lb **Signed from** Chelsea, July
2003, undisclosed

CLAUS LUNDEKVAM (defender) **Born**
February 22, 1973, Austevoll,
Norway **Ht** 6ft 3in **Wt** 12st 10lb
Signed from SK Brann, September
1996, £400,000

CHRIS MARSDEN (midfield) **Born**
January 3, 1969, Sheffield **Ht** 6ft 0in
Wt 10st 12lb **Signed from**
Birmingham City, February 1999,
£800,000

NEIL McCANN (midfield) **Born**
November 8, 1974, Greenock
Ht 5ft 10in **Wt** 10st 8lb **Signed from**
Rangers, August 2003, £1.5m

ANTTI NIEMI (goalkeeper) **Born** May
31, 1971, Oulu, Finland **Ht** 6ft 1in
Wt 14st 0lb **Signed from** Heart of
Midlothian, August 2002, £2m

MATTHEW OAKLEY (midfield) **Born**
August 17, 1977, Peterborough
Ht 5ft 10in **Wt** 11st 0lb **Signed from**
trainee, July 1995

BRETT ORMEROD (forward) **Born**
October 18, 1976, Blackburn
Ht 5ft 11in **Wt** 11st 4lb **Signed from**
Blackpool, December 2001, £1.75m

MARIAN PAHARS (forward) **Born**
August 5, 1976, Riga, Latvia **Ht** 5ft 8in
Wt 10st 9lb **Signed from** Skonto Riga,
March 1999, £800,000

KEVIN PHILLIPS (forward) **Born** July
25, 1973, Hitchin **Ht** 5ft 7in
Wt 11st 0lb **Signed from** Sunderland,
August 2003, £3.25m

DAVID PRUTTON (midfield) **Born**
September 12, 1981, Hull **Ht** 5ft 10in
Wt 11st 10lb **Signed from**
Nottingham Forest, January 2003,
£2.5m

ANDERS SVENSSON (midfield) **Born**
July 17, 1976, Gothenburg
Ht 5ft 10in **Wt** 12st 1lb **Signed from**
IF Elfsborg, Sweden, June 2001,
£750,000

MICHAEL SVENSSON (defender) **Born**
November 25, 1975, Sweden
Ht 6ft 2in **Wt** 13st 3lb **Signed from**
Troyes, June 2002, £2m

PAUL TELFER (defender) **Born**
October 21, 1971, Edinburgh
Ht 5ft 9in **Wt** 11st 6lb **Signed from**
Coventry City, November 2001, free

JO TESSEM (midfield) **Born** February
28, 1972, Orlandet, Norway **Ht** 6ft 3in
Wt 13st 5lb **Signed from** Molde,
November 1999, £600,000

STATS AND FACTS

- Only James Beattie and Kevin Phillips scored in Southampton's first 11 games this season

- In December, Southampton recorded only their third away win against Liverpool in 40 attempts.

- Southampton have still not finished below Portsmouth in the league since the 1959-60 season, when Portsmouth were in the old second division and Southampton were promoted from the old third division.

- Paul Sturrock has become Southampton's third Scottish manager in seven years, after Gordon Strachan and Graeme Souness.

- Southampton are unbeaten in 11 matches against Wolverhampton Wanderers.

- They have lost just once in their past 19 matches at home to Blackburn Rovers and also once in their past 19 at home to Charlton Athletic.

Bill Edgar

GOALSCORERS

	Prem	FAC	CC	Euro	Total
J Beattie	14 (2p)	-	3 (1p)	-	17 (3p)
R Delap	1	-	-	-	1
J Dodd	1	-	-	-	1
F Fernandes	1	-	-	-	1
L Griffit	2	-	-	-	2
G Le Saux	-	-	1	-	1
C Lundekvam	1	-	-	-	1
B Ormerod	5	-	1	-	6
M Pahars	2	-	-	-	2
K Phillips	12	-	-	1	13
D Prutton	1	-	-	-	1
M Svensson	2	-	-	-	2
Own goals	2	-	-	-	2

Sunday March 21
PORTSMOUTH (a)
Lost 0-1   HT 0-0   Att 20,140   Position 12th
Niemi — Dodd, Lundekvam, Higginbotham, Crainey (Fernandes 80) — Delap, Telfer, A Svensson (Prutton 60), McCann (Pahars 73) — Phillips, Beattie *Subs not used* Smith, Hall *Booked* Higginbotham, Prutton
Report page 237

Saturday March 27
TOTTENHAM HOTSPUR (h)
Won 1-0   HT 0-0   Att 31,973   Position 10th
A mid-table encounter is settled by Delap's spectacular bicycle kick, a sensational way to end a two-year goal drought and inflict defeat on Tottenham. As Paul Sturrock celebrates a second win in three games, speculation is rife that Claudio Ranieri will take charge at White Hart Lane in the summer.

Niemi — Telfer, Lundekvam, Higginbotham, Dodd — Fernandes (A Svensson 76), Folly, Delap, Prutton — Phillips (Ormerod 76), Beattie *Subs not used* Smith, Hall, Pahars
Scorer **Delap 64**
Referee **C Foy**

Saturday April 3
WOLVERHAMPTON WANDERERS (a)
Won 4-1   HT 1-0   Att 29,106   Position 9th
Niemi — Telfer, Lundekvam, Higginbotham, Dodd (Hall 52) — Fernandes (A Svensson 84), Delap, Folly, Prutton — Phillips, Beattie *Subs not used* Smith, Griffit, Ormerod *Booked* Prutton
Scorers **Beattie 25, Lundekvam 58, Phillips 89, 90**
Report page 267

Monday April 12
MIDDLESBROUGH (a)
Lost 1-3   HT 0-2   Att 30,768   Position 11th
Niemi — Telfer, Lundekvam, Higginbotham, Crainey — Fernandes (Pahars 57), Folly, Delap (A Svensson 81), Prutton — Phillips, Beattie *Subs not used* Smith, Hall, Ormerod
Scorer **Beattie 70**
Report page 215

Saturday April 17
MANCHESTER CITY (a)
Won 3-1   HT 1-0   Att 47,152   Position 9th
Niemi — Telfer, Lundekvam, Higginbotham, Le Saux — Prutton, Delap, Folly, Pahars (A Svensson 84) — Beattie (Hall 89), Phillips *Subs not used* Smith, Fernandes, Ormerod *Booked* Beattie
Scorers **Beattie 34, Phillips 55, 81**
Report page 194

Saturday April 24
BOLTON WANDERERS (h)
Lost 1-2   HT 1-0   Att 31,712   Position 11th
Before the match, Bolton make a statement that most fans never thought they would hear — "Negotiations to sign Rivaldo are going well" — and after it they bask in a victory secured by a less famous forward, Davies punishing his old club, who lead through Pahars, by helping to set up Nolan's equaliser and heading the winner a minute later.

Niemi — Telfer, Lundekvam, Higginbotham, Le Saux (Hall 10) — Prutton, Delap (A Svensson 49), Folly, Pahars (Fernandes 79) — Beattie, Phillips *Subs not used* Smith, Ormerod *Booked* Telfer, A Svensson, Phillips, Folly
Scorer **Pahars 21**
Referee **S Dunn**

PLAYER OF THE SEASON
Antti Niemi

Antti Niemi got better and better as the season went on and many commentators now regard him as the best goalkeeper in the Premiership. Signed from Heart of Midlothian two years ago, his £2 million fee looks a steal. A superb shot-stopper, he also has a commanding aerial presence that Paul Jones, his rival at the beginning of the season, always lacked. Several fans' polls unanimously voted him player of the year and Niemi even showed his outfield prowess away to Fulham. With the team 2-1 down and time ticking away, he came up for a corner. The ball dropped, he chested it down and struck the bar with a volley. Michael Svensson nodded home the rebound for the equaliser.
Steve Keenan

Saturday May 1
CHELSEA (a)
Lost 0-4 HT **0-0** Att **41,321** Position **11th**
Niemi — Kenton (Hall 78), Lundekvam, Higginbotham — Telfer, Prutton, Folly, A Svensson (Ormerod 69), Cranie (Fernandes 63) — Beattie, Phillips *Subs not used* Blayney, Crainey
Report page 132

Saturday May 8
ASTON VILLA (h)
Drew 1-1 HT **1-1** Att **32,054** Position **12th**
Villa are now out of the running for the Champions League. They take the lead in mysterious circumstances when a penalty is awarded without a single appeal, Howard Webb apparently spotting a push by Higginbotham, but luck evens itself out almost immediately as Phillips, a yard offside, gets the equaliser on the stroke of half-time.

Niemi — Telfer, Lundekvam, Hall, Higginbotham — Fernandes, Prutton, Folly, A Svensson — Beattie, Phillips *Subs not used* Blayney, Griffit, Blackstock, Kenton, Ormerod *Booked* A Svensson
Scorer **Phillips 45**
Referee **H Webb**

Wednesday May 12
NEWCASTLE UNITED (h)
Drew 3-3 HT **2-2** Att **31,815** Position **6th**
Newcastle's Champions League hopes are ended after an extraordinary match that might easily have produced double the six goals shared with Southampton. Liverpool are the beneficiaries as they are assured of fourth place, leaving Newcastle — twice ahead, but needing a stoppage-time equaliser to claim a point — facing the prospect of not even qualifying for the Uefa Cup.

Blayney — Telfer, Lundekvam (Kenton 36), Hall, Crainey — Fernandes (Griffit 82), Prutton, Folly, A Svensson — Beattie, Ormerod (Phillips 74) *Subs not used* Poke, Blackstock *Booked* Beattie
Scorers **Beattie 19, Bramble 39 (og), Griffit 88**
Referee **G Poll**

Saturday May 15
CHARLTON ATHLETIC (a)
Lost 1-2 HT **0-1** Att **26,614** Position **12th**
Blayney — Telfer, Hall, Kenton, Crainey — Fernandes (Griffit 85), Prutton, Folly, A Svensson (Baird 14) — Beattie, Ormerod *Subs not used* Poke, Cranie, Blackstock *Booked* Prutton
Scorer **Prutton 64**
Report page 120

TOTTENHAM HOTSPUR

PREMIERSHIP

	P	W	D	L	F	A	GD	Pts
Arsenal	38	26	12	0	73	26	47	**90**
Chelsea	38	24	7	7	67	30	37	**79**
Man Utd	38	23	6	9	64	35	29	**75**
Liverpool	38	16	12	10	55	37	18	**60**
Newcastle	38	13	17	8	52	40	12	**56**
Aston Villa	38	15	11	12	48	44	4	**56**
Charlton	38	14	11	13	51	51	0	**53**
Bolton	38	14	11	13	48	56	-8	**53**
Fulham	38	14	10	14	52	46	6	**52**
Birmingham	38	12	14	12	43	48	-5	**50**
Middlesbro	38	13	9	16	44	52	-8	**48**
Southampton	38	12	11	15	44	45	-1	**47**
Portsmouth	38	12	9	17	47	54	-7	**45**
Tottenham	38	13	6	19	47	57	-10	**45**
Blackburn	38	12	8	18	51	59	-8	**44**
Man City	38	9	14	15	55	54	1	**41**
Everton	38	9	12	17	45	57	-12	**39**
Leicester	38	6	15	17	48	65	-17	**33**
Leeds	38	8	9	21	40	79	-39	**33**
Wolves	38	7	12	19	38	77	-39	**33**

FA CUP
Fourth round

CARLING CUP
Quarter-finals

New balls, please: Jacques Santini
is the latest man charged with the
task of reviving the fortunes of
Spurs after a dreadful 2003-04

THE GAMES

Saturday August 16 2003
BIRMINGHAM CITY (a)
Lost 0-1   **HT 0-1**   Att **29,358**   Position **18th**
Keller — Doherty, Bunjevcevic, Gardner — Carr,
Davies, Redknapp, Ricketts, Taricco (Marney 70) —
Keane, Postiga (Zamora 57) *Subs not used* Sullivan,
Acimovic, Kelly *Booked* Gardner, Carr, Davies, Ricketts,
Marney
Report page 82

Saturday August 23
LEEDS UNITED (h)
Won 2-1   **HT 1-1**   Att **34,354**   Position **10th**
Aaron Lennon becomes the youngest Premiership player,
at 16 years 128 days, and a relatively seasoned
team-mate, Smith, gives Leeds the lead from distance,
but exceptional finishing by Taricco and Kanoute, who
score with a 25-yard rocket and an over-the-shoulder
shot respectively, claim the points for Spurs.
Keller — King, Richards, Gardner — Carr, Davies,
Redknapp, Ricketts, Taricco (Marney 86) — Zamora
(Kanoute 62), Postiga *Subs not used* Sullivan, Acimovic,
Bunjevcevic *Booked* Postiga
Scorers **Taricco 41, Kanoute 71**
Referee **S Dunn**

Wednesday August 27
LIVERPOOL (a)
Drew 0-0   **HT 0-0**   Att **43,778**   Position **10th**
Keller — King, Richards, Gardner — Carr, Davies,
Redknapp, Ricketts, Taricco — Zamora (Kanoute 66),
Postiga (Anderton 86) *Subs not used* Bunjevcevic,
Marney, Sullivan *Booked* Gardner, Carr, Redknapp,
King, Richards
Report page 174

Saturday August 30
FULHAM (h)
Lost 0-3   **HT 0-1**   Att **33,421**   Position **14th**
After their fine performance at Anfield, Spurs collapse
alarmingly back at home, allowing Fulham to coast to
their first win at White Hart Lane since 1948. Hayles
punishes poor defending with the first two goals and
sets up Boa Morte for the third. "They were better than
us all over the pitch," Glenn Hoddle admits.
Keller — King (Zamora ht), Richards, Gardner — Carr,
Davies (Anderton 58), Redknapp, Ricketts, Taricco —
Kanoute, Postiga *Subs not used* Burch, Bunjevcevic,
Marney
Referee **J Winter**

Saturday September 13
CHELSEA (a)
Lost 2-4   **HT 1-2**   Att **41,165**   Position **16th**
Keller — King (Bunjevcevic 40), Richards, Gardner —
Carr, Anderton (Dalmat 60), Redknapp, Ricketts, Taricco
(Konchesky 68) — Kanoute, Zamora *Subs not used*
Burch, Postiga *Booked* Redknapp, Taricco, Zamora,
Dalmat
Scorer **Kanoute 25, 87**
Report page 123

VIVE LA REVOLUTION! A SEASON that seemed wasted finally
found meaning on June 3, when none other than the France coach
was unveiled as the man to lead Tottenham Hotspur into a new era.
Jacques Santini's appointment as head coach provoked a collective
gasp of disbelief and vindicated a 256-day delay in naming a
successor to Glenn Hoddle. After all, what are another few months
when you have been waiting for success as long as Spurs?

The biggest frustration of the wilderness years has been seeing
teams with recent Nationwide League experience, such as
Birmingham City and Bolton Wanderers, accelerate past a Spurs
side stuck in the Premiership's middle lane. And yet the club's aura
remains. How else could Frank Arnesen be lured as sporting
director from PSV Eindhoven? The Dane's record of identifying and
nurturing young talent, including Ruud van Nistelrooy and Ronaldo, provides even more cause for optimism than Santini's arrival.

Reaching an end to the "who will replace Hoddle?" guessing game
was in itself cause for celebration. Speculation over the identity of
the mysterious Man With No Name made it easy to forget there
were matches to be played, which was often a blessing because the
on-field fare left everyone eager to draw the curtain on the season
and wait for another new dawn.

The sun set on Hoddle's regime after six matches in which it was
clear that the side was performing at a level far below the sum of its
parts. Southampton revelled in finishing off their former manager
with a 3-1 victory and Enic, Spurs' owning company, acted swiftly,
just as it had in dismissing George Graham. It was to Enic's
embarrassment that Hoddle lasted fewer matches than his
unpopular predecessor and explains why its second managerial
appointment was not so impetuous.

David Pleat, the director of football, began his third stint as
caretaker manager with a six-game unbeaten run comprising two
Nationwide League teams and mediocre Premiership opposition.
The only goal conceded during that period trickled through the
arms and legs of Kasey Keller, whose uncertainty regularly
permeated through the defence. Little wonder that Spurs pursued
Paul Robinson, the Leeds United goalkeeper, in January, eventually
getting their man in May.

It is, however, a brave soul who joins Spurs in these troubled times
and few emerge with their reputations intact. Three young forwards
arrived before the season, an indulgence given the frail midfield, and
all had difficult times. Helder Postiga was soon being compared to
Sergei Rebrov for all the wrong reasons. Spurs once blazed a trail in
signing overseas players, but they now seem adept at stunting their

HONOURS BOARD

FOOTBALL LEAGUE
Champions 1951, 1961
Runners-up 1922, 1952, 1957, 1963
FA CUP
Winners 1901, 1921, 1961, 1962, 1967,
1981, 1982, 1991
Runners-up 1987
LEAGUE CUP
Winners 1971, 1973, 1999
Runners-up 1982, 2002
CUP WINNERS' CUP
Winners 1963

FAIRS CUP/UEFA CUP
Winners 1972, 1984
Runners-up 1974

Record attendance 75,038
(v Sunderland, FA Cup 6th rnd,
March 5, 1938)
Current capacity 36,236
Record victory 13-2 (v Crewe Alexandra,
FA Cup 4th rnd, February 3, 1960)
Record defeat 0-8 (v Cologne, Intertoto
Cup, July 22, 1995)

careers. While his previous club, FC Porto, headed for European Cup glory, the Portugal striker found himself in Spurs' reserve team after struggling to adapt to the pace of the Premiership. Postiga and Bobby Zamora failed to register a league goal before January, neither helped by the sheer number of forwards at the club. Perhaps Postiga was taking out his frustration on England in June.

Frederic Kanoute thrived on the competition, scoring the winner against Leeds United on his debut and the goal of the season against Everton, but his decision to represent Mali in the African Nations Cup provoked an overreaction from the club that unsettled both parties. The club's protestations implied a lack of faith in the striker's replacements, whose confidence was low enough. Kanoute struck a hat-trick against Crystal Palace in his penultimate match before leaving for Tunisia. He did not score again on his return.

Whether the dispute prompted Spurs to sign Jermain Defoe in January is unclear, but the transfer certainly provided a timely fillip. Daniel Levy, the executive chairman, increased the supporters' confusion before the deal. "The potential manager is aware of the targets we are looking at," he said. "There have been discussions with him, but there is no guarantee he will be here in the summer."

The manager-in-waiting may have sought a careers adviser in February, when four matches yielded 28 goals, beginning with *that* 4-3 defeat to Manchester City in the FA Cup. The mayhem continued as the goals threatened to outnumber the names being linked to the managerial vacancy. Pleat eventually stemmed the tide

Saturday September 20
SOUTHAMPTON (h)
Lost 1-3 HT **0-2** Att **35,784** Position **17th**
With an impeccable sense of timing, Southampton, enjoying their best start to a Premiership campaign, register a thumping win — Beattie scoring twice and Phillips forcing Gardner into an own goal — against the club that Glenn Hoddle left them for. Victory probably tastes even sweeter when the Tottenham manager is dismissed the next day.

Keller — Richards, Bunjevcevic (Postiga 64), Gardner — Carr, Dalmat (Anderton ht), Redknapp, Ricketts, Taricco — Kanoute, Zamora (Keane ht) *Subs not used* Burch, Doherty *Booked* Redknapp
Scorer **Kanoute 62**
Referee **A D'Urso**

Wednesday September 24
COVENTRY CITY (a)
Carling Cup, 2nd rnd
Won 3-0 HT **2-0** Att **15,474**
With David Pleat now in temporary charge, Spurs respond to Glenn Hoddle's departure with an emphatic victory capped by Ricketts's spectacular 25-yard goal, his first for the club. Pleat insists that no decisions have been taken regarding a full-time successor, but could he be in the running himself?

Keller — Carr, Richards, Gardner, Taricco — Anderton, Bunjevcevic, Poyet, Blondel (Ricketts 63) — Keane (Postiga 80), Kanoute *Subs not used* Dalmat, Doherty, Burch *Booked* Carr, Gardner
Scorers **Kanoute 13, Keane 23, Ricketts 85**
Referee **M Jones**

Sunday September 28
MANCHESTER CITY (a)
Drew 0-0 HT **0-0** Att **46,842** Position **17th**
Keller — Carr, Richards, Gardner, Taricco — Anderton, Bunjevcevic (Ricketts 62), Poyet, Konchesky (Dalmat 76) — Keane, Kanoute *Subs not used* Doherty, Postiga, Burch *Booked* Gardner
Report page 187

Saturday October 4
EVERTON (h)
Won 3-0 HT **1-0** Att **36,137** Position **13th**
David Pleat's first home game in charge produces a fine win, a third clean sheet and a candidate for goal of the season from Kanoute, who thrashes a dipping volley into the top corner of Everton's goal from 35 yards, the first of three in six minutes for Spurs. Pleat, though, refuses to rule himself in or out of the job full-time.

Keller — Carr, Richards, Gardner, Taricco (Dalmat 72) — Ricketts, Anderton, Poyet, Konchesky — Keane, Kanoute (Postiga 77) *Subs not used* Burch, Bunjevcevic, Zamora *Booked* Gardner, Konchesky
Scorers **Kanoute 43, Poyet 46, Keane 49**
Referee **D Gallagher**

Sunday October 19
LEICESTER CITY (a)
Won 2-1 HT **0-1** Att **31,521** Position **11th**
Keller — Carr, Doherty, Richards, Taricco — Ricketts (Dalmat ht), Poyet (Mabizela 74), Anderton, Konchesky (Zamora 66) — Kanoute, Keane *Subs not used* Burch, Bunjevcevic *Booked* Doherty, Anderton, Mabizela
Scorers **Mabizela 79, Kanoute 90**
Report page 166

Saturday October 26
MIDDLESBROUGH (h)
Drew 0-0   HT 0-0   Att 32,643   Position 12th
Boateng puts the best chance of a dull match over the
bar in the second half, but a point is enough to take
Middlesbrough out of the bottom three and extend
Spurs' unbeaten run under David Pleat — the home side
shade the first half — to five matches, with four clean
sheets.

Keller — Carr, Gardner, Richards, Taricco — Dalmat,
Poyet (King 69), Anderton, Konchesky (Ricketts 84) —
Zamora (Postiga 65), Keane *Subs not used* Burch,
Mabizela *Booked* Gardner, Taricco, Anderton
Referee **M Dean**

Wednesday October 29
WEST HAM UNITED (h)
Carling Cup, 3rd rnd
Won 1-0 (aet)   HT 0-0   Att 36,053
Zamora's first goal for Spurs, early in extra time, settles
a tight tie against the club he supported as a boy, but it
is not all good news: Ziege suffers a cruel knee ligament
injury on his return after ten months out and there are
90 arrests — as well as three pubs badly damaged — in
trouble before and after the match.

Keller — Carr, Gardner, Doherty, Ziege (Blondel 61) —
Ricketts (Postiga 77), Dalmat (Mabizela 58), King,
Konchesky — Keane, Zamora *Subs not used* Burch,
Bunjevcevic *Booked* Mabizela
Scorer **Zamora 91**
Referee **G Barber**

Saturday November 1
BOLTON WANDERERS (h)
Lost 0-1   HT 0-0   Att 35,191   Position 12th
David Pleat's first defeat as caretaker manager is
inflicted by Nolan's goal after Keller parries Okocha's
shot, and it is the brilliant Nigerian who continues to
torment Spurs, hitting the bar three times —
Giannakopoulos also strikes the woodwork — from
outside the box. Okocha later reveals that Glenn Hoddle
had rejected the chance to sign him.

Keller — Carr, Doherty, Richards, Taricco (Blondel 64) —
Anderton, King (Mabizela 86), Poyet (Postiga ht),
Konchesky — Keane, Zamora *Subs not used* Burch,
Bunjevcevic *Booked* Carr, Konchesky, Blondel
Referee **U Rennie**

Saturday November 8
ARSENAL (a)
Lost 1-2   HT 1-0   Att 38,101   Position 13th
Keller — Carr, Richards, Gardner, Taricco — Anderton,
King, Dalmat (Ricketts 82), Konchesky (Mabizela 72) —
Keane, Postiga (Zamora 82) *Subs not used* Doherty,
Burch *Booked* Taricco, Richards, Anderton,
Konchesky
Scorer **Anderton 5**
Report page 63

Kanoute tucks away the first goal of his FA Cup hat-trick against Palace

of goals conceded by plugging one hole in the dyke; another sprang
up. The five matches that followed February contained four one-nils
and one Spurs goal. The mercurial Robbie Keane lapsed into his
third barren spell of the season, but the midfield did little to help
him. Jamie Redknapp was still conspicuous by his absence through
injury, highlighting how farcical was his appointment as captain.

Spurs had the firepower but lacked someone to call the shots on
the field and off. The Man With No Name was still on the horizon,
waiting to ride in and clean up the town, or what was left after Enic
had blown much of it away. Despite the turmoil, Spurs finished with
two victories and a pair of clean sheets. Was it coincidental that
Ledley King reverted from midfield to centre back in both?
Successful teams are built from the back, but Pleat realised it too
late, making do with Gary Doherty while Spurs' best defender tried
to compensate for deficiencies elsewhere.

Defeating Wolverhampton Wanderers on the last day averted the
club's first bottom-six finish in the Premiership, but the final
indignity came at White Hart Lane when Arsenal clinched the title.
The lilywhite half of North London could only dream that their
Arsene Wenger was on the way, but few thought the Gallic example
would be so closely followed until Santini's appointment. After a
season in which Spurs kept everyone in the dark, it would be cruel if
another new dawn proved to be a false one.

THE MANAGER — David Pleat

Spurs began looking for a new manager shortly after the start of the season, but by the end of the campaign it was clear that the director of football also had to be replaced. David Pleat moved from the bunker of the boardroom into the firing line as caretaker manager and was left in an untenable position by his failure to inspire any improvement. Settling on his preferred first team would have been a start. Rohan Ricketts and Stephane Dalmat were handled erratically, Ledley King was deployed incorrectly and the forwards were rotated with desperation. Sadness surrounded Hoddle's departure, but no tears were shed when Pleat left.

Phil Myers

APPEARANCES

	Prem	FAC	CC	Total
D Anderton	16 (4)	1	3	20 (4)
J Blondel	0 (1)	-	1 (1)	1 (2)
M Brown	17	2	-	19
G Bunjevcevic	3 (4)	-	1	4 (4)
S Carr	32	3	4	39
S Dalmat	12 (10)	2 (1)	1 (2)	15 (13)
S Davies	17	2 (1)	-	19 (1)
J Defoe	14 (1)	-	-	14 (1)
G Doherty	16 (1)	2	2 (1)	20 (2)
A Gardner	33	3	4	40
J Jackson	9 (2)	1 (2)	-	10 (4)
F Kanoute	19 (8)	1	2 (1)	22 (9)
R Keane	31 (3)	3	4	38 (3)
K Keller	38	3	4	45
S Kelly	7 (4)	-	-	7 (4)
L King	28 (1)	3	3	34 (1)
P Konchesky	10 (2)	-	2 (1)	12 (3)
M Mabizela	0 (6)	-	0 (1)	0 (7)
D Marney	1 (2)	-	-	1 (2)
H Postiga	9 (10)	2	1 (2)	12 (12)
G Poyet	12 (8)	1 (1)	2 (1)	15 (10)
J Redknapp	14 (3)	-	-	14 (3)
D Richards	23	1	2	26
R Ricketts	12 (12)	-	3 (1)	15 (13)
M Taricco	31 (1)	2	3	36 (1)
M Yeates	1	-	-	1
R Zamora	6 (10)	0 (1)	1	7 (11)
C Ziege	7 (1)	1	1	9 (1)

Sunday November 23
ASTON VILLA (h)
Won 2-1   HT 0-0   Att 33,140   Position 12th
"Nobody is too good to go down," David O'Leary admits as Villa slip into the bottom three. They take the lead against Spurs though Allback's header but then concede two goals in three minutes, Ricketts shooting through Zamora's legs and Keane finding the opposite corner to make amends for Postiga's earlier misses.
Keller — Carr, Richards, Gardner, Taricco — Anderton, King, Dalmat, Konchesky (Ricketts 56) — Keane, Postiga (Zamora 72) *Subs not used* Burch, Doherty, Poyet
Scorers **Ricketts 78, Keane 81**
Referee **J Winter**

Saturday November 29
BLACKBURN ROVERS (a)
Lost 0-1   HT 0-0   Att 22,802   Position 15th
Keller — Carr, Richards, Gardner, Taricco — Dalmat (Mabizela 66), Anderton, King, Konchesky (Ricketts 82) — Keane, Postiga (Zamora 66) *Subs not used* Doherty, Burch *Booked* Gardner
Report page 95

Wednesday December 3
MANCHESTER CITY (h)
Carling Cup, 4th rnd
Won 3-1   HT 2-0   Att 31,727
Spurs complete a miserable seven days for Kevin Keegan's side after their Uefa Cup elimination, Postiga breaking his duck at the fourteenth attempt with the second goal, presented to him by Sinclair, and Kanoute killing Manchester City off after Fowler punishes Doherty's blunder to given the visiting side some hope.
Keller — Carr, Doherty, Gardner, Taricco — Anderton, King, Poyet (Dalmat 85), Ricketts (Konchesky 69) — Keane, Postiga (Kanoute 77) *Subs not used* Burch, Mabizela *Booked* Postiga
Scorers **Anderton 9, Postiga 30, Kanoute 90**
Referee **P Durkin**

Saturday December 6
WOLVERHAMPTON WANDERERS (h)
Won 5-2   HT 1-1   Att 34,825   Position 11th
Keane's goal celebrations are muted and he confesses to mixed emotions after his hat-trick sends his first professional club back to the bottom of the table. Wolves fight back to 1-1 and 2-4, but are finished off by Kanoute and Dalmat, whose last-minute goal is probably the pick of the bunch.
Keller — Carr, Richards, Gardner, Taricco — Anderton, King, Poyet (Dalmat 76), Ricketts (Konchesky 67) — Keane, Kanoute *Subs not used* Burch, Postiga, Mabizela *Booked* Richards, Anderton
Scorers **Keane 29, 75, 83, Kanoute 50, Dalmat 90**
Referee **U Rennie**

Saturday December 13
NEWCASTLE UNITED (a)
Lost 0-4   HT 0-1   Att 52,139   Position 13th
Keller — Carr, Richards, Gardner, Taricco — Anderton, King, Poyet (Mabizela 54), Konchesky (Dalmat 80) — Keane, Kanoute (Postiga 62) *Subs not used* Burch, Doherty *Booked* Gardner, Carr
Report page 222

Wednesday December 17
MIDDLESBROUGH (h)
Carling Cup, quarter-final
Drew 1-1 (aet; 1-1 after 90min; lost 4-5 on pens)
HT 1-0   Att 25,307
Having gone 669 minutes without conceding a goal, Middlesbrough are behind after just 65 seconds, but once Michael Ricketts equalises four minutes from time only Keller's brilliance in the Spurs goal takes the game into extra time and then a shoot-out. Mendieta squanders a chance to seal it after Poyet's failure, but Queudrue does not make the same mistake after Taricco's miss in sudden death.

Keller — Carr, Richards (Doherty ht), Gardner, Taricco — Ricketts (Dalmat 95), Anderton (Poyet 77), King, Konchesky — Keane, Kanoute *Subs not used* Burch, Postiga
Scorer **Anderton 2**
Referee **M Dean**

Sunday December 21
MANCHESTER UNITED (h)
Lost 1-2   HT 0-2   Att 35,910   Position 15th
All eyes are on Ferdinand, two days after his eight-month ban for missing a drugs test is announced, and his composed display helps United to victory. O'Shea, from a corner, and Van Nistelrooy, with the aid of a deflection off Gardner, take the champions back to the top of the table for Christmas.

Keller — Carr, Richards, Gardner, Taricco (Ricketts 64) — Dalmat (Postiga 77), Anderton (Poyet 19), King, Konchesky — Kanoute, Keane *Subs not used* Hirschfeld, Doherty *Booked* Taricco, Konchesky
Scorer **Poyet 63**
Referee **R Styles**

Friday December 26
PORTSMOUTH (a)
Lost 0-2   HT 0-0   Att 20,078   Position 17th
Keller — Carr, Richards, Gardner, Taricco — Dalmat (Ricketts 67), King, Poyet (Postiga 61), Jackson — Keane, Kanoute (Zamora 86) *Subs not used* Burch, Doherty *Booked* Taricco
Report page 234

Sunday December 28
CHARLTON ATHLETIC (h)
Lost 0-1   HT 0-0   Att 34,534   Position 18th
Spurs slide into the bottom three, losing to a side managed by the man many think will take over at White Hart Lane. On the back foot in the first half, Charlton take the points when Cole, on loan from Chelsea, heads his first goal for the club, Kiely just saving from Keane and Kanoute. "We need to win quickly," David Pleat admits.

Keller — Kelly, Richards, Gardner, Taricco (Mabizela 90) — Ricketts (Zamora 71), King, Poyet (Postiga 80), Jackson — Keane, Kanoute *Subs not used* Hirschfeld, Doherty *Booked* Gardner
Referee **P Durkin**

Saturday January 3 2004
CRYSTAL PALACE (h)
FA Cup, 3rd rnd
Won 3-0   HT 2-0   Att 32,340
Kanoute, who most reports predict will be omitted over his decision to play for Mali in the forthcoming African Nations Cup, starts for Spurs — and scores three times, the second after a magnificent run by Dalmat. Poyet is sent off for butting Freedman in retaliation, Butterfield also seeing red for a foul on Zamora, though with the Palace man it is a case of mistaken identity.

Keller — Carr, Doherty, Gardner, Taricco — Dalmat, King (Davies 61), Poyet, Jackson (Zamora 72) — Keane, Kanoute *Subs not used* Hirschfeld, Postiga, Kelly *Booked* Doherty, Jackson *Sent off* Poyet 79
Scorer **Kanoute 15, 20, 48**
Referee **A D'Urso**

MATCH OF THE SEASON

Tottenham Hotspur 1 Newcastle United 0
White Hart Lane, Sunday March 14 2004
Alyson Rudd

YOU COULD SEE THE TOTTENHAM Hotspur fans nodding their heads in agreement. Oh yes, a good, old fashioned 1-0 will do very nicely, thank you — and it was entertaining to boot. After a rollercoaster run of bizarre games in the FA Cup and the Premiership, Spurs needed to calm down. This was their first clean sheet at home since October in the league and the relief was palpable when Andy O'Brien put the ball into his own net four minutes from the end. It was a hard-earned victory. Newcastle United were, in bursts, extremely impressive and arrived in North London with a run of seven consecutive draws away from St James' Park. In terms of chances created and possession, Sir Bobby Robson's team deserved yet another one.

"I think that fourth place is wide open for a lot of teams," David Pleat, the Tottenham caretaker manager, said. The title race may not go to the wire, but it would be reckless for anyone to maintain that the battle for fourth spot is between only Newcastle and Liverpool. And as for Tottenham, on this form a Uefa Cup spot is not unrealistic. "Nothing is out of the question," Pleat said, "we're just like Arsenal, focused on the next game."

There were two shocks in store for the fans. Not only did Spurs keep a clean sheet, they began with a daring attacking formation, with Robbie Keane given a free role behind Frederic Kanoute and Jermain Defoe. "It was an interesting triangle," Robson said. But it was a shape that his team had little difficulty coping with. "We didn't change the way we play," Robson said and that approach looked as if it would pay dividends — until Pleat gave up on his fancy geometry, took off Kanoute and reverted to 4-4-2.

It was Stephane Dalmat who, having evaded the challenge of Jonathan Woodgate, crossed the ball into the penalty area in the 86th minute. O'Brien, who had been so composed at the heart of the defence, slid in to clear but instead forced the ball over the line.

It must have felt particularly cruel because Robson was convinced that his team had earned a penalty in the first half. Mauricio Taricco appeared to have brought down Aaron Hughes and there was no need for Hughes to have dived at that juncture. But Howard Webb, the referee, waved away the heated appeals. Robson was also convinced that Craig Bellamy should have won a penalty for having his shirt tugged by Anthony Gardner, but TV replays showed that the referee was correct not to penalise the Tottenham defender.

Pleat praised the referee for issuing no bookings in what he termed "a committed game on a wet pitch". Despite the constant stream of swirling rain, the calibre of football was excellent. Tottenham, without Dean Richards, who has been error prone of late, dealt

Taricco struggles to escape the attentions of Bellamy in Spurs' fine win

competently with the pressure. Gary Doherty, in particular, was there when it mattered.

In the first half, Kasey Keller dropped the ball, leaving Alan Shearer in possession, but Shearer could not muscle his way past Doherty. It was Doherty, too, who spared Keller's blushes when stranded and Bellamy was loitering to take advantage. Doherty has been used as a centre forward in his Spurs career, not a position he prefers, and he made that plain enough when, finding himself in space after a corner by Michael Brown, he put a good opportunity wide.

The visiting team's defence were also called upon to perform heroics and Woodgate did well to hook the ball off the line while under pressure from Keane. "Fortune favours the brave," Pleat said. "In the end, we were dangerous on the break and got the goal." Tottenham's cause was aided by the return of Jamie Redknapp, who had not played since September because of a knee injury.

Where Glenn Hoddle had been forced to endure too many crucial players injured, Pleat is seeing the injury list depleted daily. The fact that he played three strikers was not so much tactical as not wanting to look a gift horse in the mouth, with so much talent available.

TOTTENHAM HOTSPUR (4-3-1-2): K Keller — S Carr, G Doherty, A Gardner, M Taricco — M Brown, L King, C Ziege (sub: S Dalmat, 80min) — R Keane — F Kanoute (sub: J Redknapp, 70), J Defoe. **Substitutes not used:** L Hirschfeld, H Postiga, S Kelly.
NEWCASTLE UNITED (4-4-2): S Given — A Hughes (sub: F Ameobi, 89), A O'Brien, J Woodgate, O Bernard — L Bowyer (sub: D Ambrose, 76), J Jenas, G Speed, L Robert — A Shearer, C Bellamy. **Substitutes not used:** S Harper, R Elliott, H Viana.

Wednesday January 7
BIRMINGHAM CITY (h)
Won 4-1   HT 3-0   Att 30,016   Position 16th
After four successive league defeats, Spurs leap out of the bottom three with their biggest win of the season. Birmingham are destroyed by the flying Dalmat, Steve Bruce trying three different players at left back in an attempt to counter him. Dalmat scores twice as well as conceding the penalty from which Savage replies.

Keller — Carr, Doherty, King, Jackson — Dalmat (Ricketts 79), Anderton (Kelly 86), Poyet, Davies — Kanoute (Postiga 79), Keane Subs not used Hirschfeld, Bunjevcevic
Scorers **Dalmat 10, 24, Davies 39, Keane 79**
Referee **B Knight**

Saturday January 10
LEEDS UNITED (a)
Won 1-0   HT 0-0   Att 35,365   Position 13th
Keller — Carr, Doherty, Gardner, Taricco — Dalmat, King, Anderton (Poyet 88), Davies — Kanoute, Keane Subs not used Hirschfeld, Postiga, Jackson, Kelly Booked Taricco
Scorer **Keane 56**
Report page 159

Saturday January 17
LIVERPOOL (h)
Won 2-1   HT 1-0   Att 36,104   Position 12th
Spurs' fourth win in four games — and Liverpool's first defeat of 2004 — is a tale of two penalties. Biscan is penalised for bringing down Keane, who opens the scoring from the spot, but, after Postiga's overdue first Premiership goal makes it 2-0 and Kewell halves the deficit, Doherty escapes detection for a handling offence.

Keller — Carr, Doherty, Gardner, Taricco — Dalmat (Jackson ht), Anderton, Brown, Davies — Postiga (Zamora 78), Keane Subs not used Hirschfeld, Bunjevcevic, Kelly Booked Carr
Scorers **Keane 25 (pen), Postiga 54**
Referee **U Rennie**

Sunday January 25
MANCHESTER CITY (a)
FA Cup, 4th rnd
Drew 1-1   HT 0-1   Att 34,000
Keller — Carr, Doherty, Gardner, Taricco (Jackson ht) — Anderton (Dalmat ht), Brown, King, Davies — Postiga, Keane Subs not used Bunjevcevic, Zamora, Hirschfeld Booked Carr, Anderton
Scorer **Doherty 57**
Report page 191

Saturday January 31
FULHAM (a)
Lost 1-2   HT 1-1   Att 17,024   Position 13th
Keller — Carr, Doherty, Gardner, Ziege — Dalmat, King, Brown, Davies — Keane, Postiga (Zamora 78) Subs not used Burch, Bunjevcevic, Jackson, Kelly Booked Ziege
Scorer **Keane 18 (pen)**
Report page 149

Wednesday February 4
MANCHESTER CITY (h)
FA Cup, 4th rnd replay
Lost 3-4   HT 3-0   Att 30,400
Trailing 3-0 and down to ten men after Barton's dismissal as the players leave the field at half-time, Manchester City find the stage set for one of the greatest Cup comebacks of all time. Distin, Bosvelt and, amid mounting disbelief, Wright-Phillips drag them level, then Macken's far-post header completes an extraordinary turnaround in the last minute.

Keller — Carr, Richards, Gardner, Ziege (Jackson 60) — Dalmat, Brown, King, Davies — Keane, Postiga (Poyet 9) Subs not used Burch, Yeates, Kelly
Scorers **King 2, Keane 19, Ziege 43**
Referee **R Styles**

Saturday February 7
PORTSMOUTH (h)
Won 4-3   HT 2-1   Att 36,107   Position 12th
Another game, another seven-goal thriller, but this time Spurs come out on top. Defoe takes just 13 minutes of his debut after a £7m move from West Ham United to put them ahead and they take the lead on three occasions, but Portsmouth fight back each time — all three scorers registering their first goals for the club — before Poyet has the final word.

Keller — Carr, Richards, Gardner, Jackson — Dalmat (Ricketts 71), Brown, King, Davies — Keane, Defoe (Poyet 81) *Subs not used* Burch, Doherty, Yeates
Booked Dalmat
Scorers **Defoe 13, Keane 42, 79, Poyet 89**
Referee **P Walton**

Wednesday February 11
CHARLTON ATHLETIC (a)
Won 4-2   HT 2-0   Att 26,660   Position 11th
Keller — Carr, Doherty, Richards, Taricco — Davies, King, Brown, Jackson — Keane, Defoe (Poyet 86) *Subs not used* Burch, Bunjevcevic, Dalmat, Barnard
Scorers **Davies 10, Defoe 43, King 46, Jackson 85**
Report page 118

Sunday February 22
LEICESTER CITY (h)
Drew 4-4   HT 3-1   Att 35,218   Position 10th
More White Hart Lane madness. Spurs' past four fixtures have now produced no fewer than 28 goals and here they not only score four, but three of Leicester's marksmen are present (Doherty concedes an awful own goal) or former Spurs players. Ahead 3-1 and facing ten men for the last 20 minutes, Spurs somehow need a late equaliser from Defoe to rescue a point.

Keller — Carr, Doherty, Richards, Taricco — Davies, Brown (Kanoute 79), King, Jackson (Anderton 61) — Defoe, Keane *Subs not used* Burch, Dalmat, Poyet
Booked Taricco
Scorers **Brown 7, Defoe 13, 89, Keane 28**
Referee **N Barry**

Tuesday March 9
MIDDLESBROUGH (a)
Lost 0-1   HT 0-0   Att 31,789   Position 10th
Keller — Carr, Richards, Gardner, Taricco — Anderton (Postiga 86), Brown (Poyet 80), King, Jackson (Dalmat 65) — Keane, Defoe *Subs not used* Burch, Doherty *Booked* Carr, Brown
Report page 214

Sunday March 14
NEWCASTLE UNITED (h)
Won 1-0   HT 0-0   Att 36,083   Position 10th
Newcastle's eighth successive away league draw is only four minutes away when O'Brien crashes Dalmat's teasing low cross high into his own net. Spurs' luck is certainly in: Taricco escapes conceding a first-half penalty for what appears to be a clear trip on Hughes.

Keller — Carr, Doherty, Gardner, Taricco — Brown, King, Ziege (Dalmat 80) — Keane — Kanoute (Redknapp 70), Defoe *Subs not used* Hirschfeld, Postiga, Kelly
Scorer **O'Brien 86 (og)**
Referee **H Webb**

THE PLAYERS

DARREN ANDERTON (midfield)
Born March 3, 1972, Southampton
Ht 6ft 1in **Wt** 12st 5lb **Signed from** Portsmouth, June 1992, £1.75m

JONATHAN BLONDEL (midfield)
Born May 3, 1984, Ypres, Belgium
Ht 5ft 8in **Wt** 10st 9lb **Signed from** Excelsior Mouscron, July 2002, undisclosed

MICHAEL BROWN (midfield) **Born** January 25, 1977, Hartlepool
Ht 5ft 9in **Wt** 11st 13lb **Signed from** Sheffield United, January 2004, £500,000

GORAN BUNJEVCEVIC (midfield)
Born February 17, 1973, Karlovac, Yugoslavia **Ht** 6ft 2in **Wt** 11st 11lb
Signed from Red Star Belgrade, July 2001, £1.4m

STEPHEN CARR (defender) **Born** August 29, 1976, Dublin **Ht** 5ft 9in **Wt** 12st 4lb **Signed from** trainee, September 1993

STEPHANE DALMAT (midfield) **Born** February 16, 1979, Joue-les-Tours, France **Ht** 6ft 1in **Wt** 12st 6lb
Signed from Inter Milan (loan), August 2003

SIMON DAVIES (midfield) **Born** October 23, 1979, Haverfordwest
Ht 5ft 10in **Wt** 11st 4lb **Signed from** Peterborough United, January 2000, £700,000

JERMAIN DEFOE (forward) **Born** October 7, 1982, Beckton
Ht 5ft 7in **Wt** 10st 4lb
Signed from West Ham United, February 2004, £7m

GARY DOHERTY (defender) **Born** January 31, 1980, Donegal **Ht** 6ft 1in **Wt** 13st 6lb **Signed from** Luton Town, April 2000, £1m

ANTHONY GARDNER (defender) **Born** September 10, 1980, Stafford
Ht 6ft 5in **Wt** 13st 8lb **Signed from** Port Vale, January 2000, £1m

JOHNNIE JACKSON (midfield) **Born** August 15, 1982, Camden **Ht** 6ft 1in **Wt** 10st 0lb **Signed from** trainee, August 1999

FREDERIC KANOUTE (forward) **Born** September 2, 1977, Sainte-Foy, France **Ht** 6ft 4in **Wt** 13st 8lb
Signed from West Ham United, August 2003, £3.5m

ROBBIE KEANE (forward) **Born** July 8, 1980, Dublin **Ht** 5ft 9in **Wt** 11st 10lb
Signed from Leeds United, August 2002, £7m

KASEY KELLER (goalkeeper) **Born** November 29, 1969, Washington

Ht 6ft 1in **Wt** 13st 12lb **Signed from** Rayo Vallecano, August 2001, free

STEPHEN KELLY (defender) **Born** September 6, 1983, Dublin
Ht 6ft 0in **Wt** 12st 12lb **Signed from** trainee, August 2000

LEDLEY KING (defender) **Born** December 10, 1980, Bow **Ht** 6ft 2in **Wt** 14st 5lb **Signed from** trainee, July 1998

PAUL KONCHESKY (midfield) **Born** May 15, 1981, Barking **Ht** 5ft 10in **Wt** 10st 12lb **Signed from** Charlton Athletic (loan), September 2003

MBULELO MABIZELA (defender) **Born** September 16, 1980, Pietermaritzburg **Ht** 5ft 10in **Wt** 12st 6lb **Signed from** Orlando Pirates, August 2003, undisclosed

DEAN MARNEY (midfield) **Born** January 31, 1984, Barking **Ht** 6ft 0in **Wt** 11st 5lb **Signed from** trainee, August 2002

HELDER POSTIGA (forward) **Born** August 2, 1982, Vila do Conde, Portugal **Ht** 5ft 11in **Wt** 12st 4lb
Signed from FC Porto, July 2003, £6.25m

GUSTAVO POYET (midfield) **Born** November 15, 1967, Montevideo
Ht 6ft 1in **Wt** 13st 0lb **Signed from** Chelsea, July 2001, £2m

JAMIE REDKNAPP (midfield) **Born** June 25, 1973, Barton-on-Sea
Ht 6ft 0in **Wt** 13st 4lb **Signed from** Liverpool, April 2002, free

DEAN RICHARDS (defender) **Born** June 9, 1974, Bradford **Ht** 6ft 2in **Wt** 13st 12lb **Signed from** Southampton, September 2001, £8.1m

ROHAN RICKETTS (midfield) **Born** December 22, 1982, Clapham
Ht 5ft 11in **Wt** 10st 13lb **Signed from** Arsenal, July 2002, free

MAURICIO TARICCO (defender) **Born** March 10, 1973, Buenos Aires
Ht 5ft 9in **Wt** 11st 7lb
Signed from Ipswich Town, December 1998, £1.8m

MARK YEATES (forward) **Born** January 11, 1985, Dublin **Signed from** trainee, August 2002

BOBBY ZAMORA (forward) **Born** January 16, 1981, Barking **Ht** 6ft 1in **Wt** 11st 11lb **Signed from** Brighton & Hove Albion, July 2003, £1.5m

CHRISTIAN ZIEGE (defender) **Born** February 1, 1972, Berlin **Ht** 6ft 2in **Wt** 12st 13lb **Signed from** Liverpool, August 2001, £4m

STATS AND FACTS

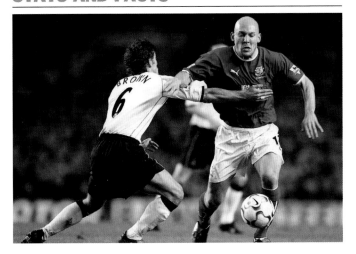

● Tottenham have won just one of their past 14 matches in the North.

● It is now 28 league meetings since Spurs beat Chelsea.

● Tottenham have lost only two of their past 15 home games against Arsenal . . .

● . . . but have won just one of their past 18 games away to Aston Villa.

● Tottenham have lost just two of their past 21 meetings with Wolverhampton Wanderers.

● All four goals were scored by defenders when Everton beat Tottenham Hotspur 3-1 on Good Friday: David Unsworth, Gary Naysmith and Joseph Yobo for Everton and Stephen Carr for Tottenham.

Bill Edgar

GOALSCORERS

	Prem	FAC	CC	Total
D Anderton	1	-	2	3
M Brown	1	-	-	1
S Carr	1	-	-	1
S Dalmat	3	-	-	3
S Davies	2	-	-	2
J Defoe	7	-	-	7
G Doherty	-	1	-	1
J Jackson	1	-	-	1
F Kanoute	7	3	2	12
R Keane	14 (3p)	1	1	16 (3p)
L King	1	1	-	2
M Mabizela	1	-	-	1
H Postiga	1	-	1	2
G Poyet	3	-	-	3
J Redknapp	1	-	-	1
R Ricketts	1	-	1	2
M Taricco	1	-	-	1
R Zamora	-	-	1	1
C Ziege	-	1	-	1
Own goals	1	-	-	1

Saturday March 20
MANCHESTER UNITED (a)
Lost 0-3 HT 0-1 Att 67,634 Position **11th**
Keller — Carr, Doherty, Gardner, Taricco (Dalmat ht) — Marney (Redknapp 66), Brown, King, Ziege — Keane, Defoe (Kanoute 79) *Subs not used* Hirschfeld, Kelly *Booked* Carr
Report page 204

Saturday March 27
SOUTHAMPTON (a)
Lost 0-1 HT 0-0 Att 31,973 Position **12th**
Keller — Carr, Doherty, Gardner, Ziege (Kelly 47) — Kanoute, Brown (Dalmat 76), Jackson (Redknapp ht) — Keane, Defoe *Subs not used* Hirschfeld, Postiga *Booked* Doherty, Ziege
Report page 247

Saturday April 3
CHELSEA (h)
Lost 0-1 HT 0-1 Att 36,101 Position **12th**
Chelsea prepare for their European Cup summit meeting with Arsenal by recording their traditional victory over Spurs, Hasselbaink's simple finish from Duff's cross earning their sixth straight Premiership away win. Spurs, who have now failed to beat them in 28 league games, rue the officials' failure to spot Terry stopping Brown's shot with his hand.

Keller — Carr, Doherty, Gardner, Taricco (Kelly 60) — Brown, Redknapp (Jackson 66), King, Ziege (Kanoute ht) — Keane, Defoe *Subs not used* Hirschfeld, Poyet *Booked* Carr, Taricco
Referee **S Bennett**

Friday April 9
EVERTON (a)
Lost 1-3 HT 0-3 Att 38,086 Position **13th**
Keller — Carr, Doherty, Gardner, Kelly — Davies (Ricketts 73), Brown, Redknapp (Bunjevcevic 73), Ziege (Kanoute ht) — Keane, Defoe *Subs not used* Jackson, Hirschfeld *Booked* Redknapp, Doherty, Carr *Sent off* Carr 77
Scorer **Carr 75**
Report page 141

Monday April 12
MANCHESTER CITY (h)
Drew 1-1 HT 0-1 Att 35,282 Position **13th**
City's fourth successive draw under the temporary stewardship of Arthur Cox, Spurs' first point after four successive defeats: both sides emerge reasonably content and unscathed after Defoe cancels out Anelka's opener. Chances to win are wasted at either end, none more so than by Fowler, who misses from six yards.

Keller — Carr (Kelly 31), Doherty, Gardner, Taricco (Bunjevcevic 63) — Brown, Redknapp, Poyet (Keane 72), Davies — Kanoute, Defoe *Subs not used* Hirschfeld, Ricketts *Booked* Poyet
Scorer **Defoe 52**
Referee **C Foy**

PLAYER OF THE SEASON
Jermain Defoe

Jermain Defoe took 13 minutes to prove himself at White Hart Lane. After a short run into the Portsmouth penalty area on his debut, the trigger was cocked and a low shot fired just inside the far post. Several subsequent efforts confirmed that the striker does not just "know where the goal is", he knows where its corners are. The immediate impact evoked memories of Jurgen Klinsmann's arrival ten years earlier and Defoe is a worthy heir to the German's No 18 shirt. He also brushed aside disciplinary concerns raised by his three red cards for West Ham United earlier in the season. It is, however, both a tribute to Defoe's marksmanship and an indictment of his team-mates that the accolade was earned by a player signed in January.

Phil Myers

Saturday April 17
BOLTON WANDERERS (a)
Lost 0-2   HT 0-1   Att 26,440   Position 14th
Keller — Kelly, Doherty, Gardner, King — Brown, Redknapp (Keane 63), Poyet (Taricco ht), Davies (Ricketts 81) — Kanoute, Defoe *Subs not used* Hirschfeld, Bunjevcevic *Booked* Davies, Taricco
Report page 109

Sunday April 25
ARSENAL (h)
Drew 2-2   HT 0-2   Att 36,097   Position 16th
Chelsea's defeat away to Newcastle earlier in the day leaves Arsenal needing only a draw to secure the title, and that is what they get. Vieira finishes a devastating counter-attack and Pires doubles their lead, but though Spurs' nightmare comes true, they at least restore a measure of pride through Redknapp's long-range goal and a last-ditch penalty by Keane, after Lehmann is penalised for roughing him up at a corner.
Keller — Kelly (Poyet 79), Gardner, King, Taricco (Bunjevcevic 90) — Davies, Redknapp, Brown, Jackson (Defoe ht) — Keane, Kanoute *Subs not used* Hirschfeld, Ricketts *Booked* Redknapp, Keane
Scorers Redknapp 62, Keane 90 (pen)
Referee **M Halsey**

Sunday May 2
ASTON VILLA (a)
Lost 0-1   HT 0-1   Att 42,573   Position 16th
Keller — Kelly (Ricketts 71), Richards, Gardner, Taricco — Davies, Redknapp, Brown — Keane — Kanoute (Doherty 79), Defoe *Subs not used* Bunjevcevic, Mabizela, Hirschfeld *Booked* Defoe
Report page 80

Saturday May 8
BLACKBURN ROVERS (h)
Won 1-0   HT 1-0   Att 35,698   Position 15th
Spurs' first victory in nine games cannot prevent a chorus of "stand up if you want Pleat out" from disgruntled fans. Defoe's blistering finish gives Enckelman no chance on his debut in the Blackburn goal, Stead wasting their best chance of an equaliser as their four-match winning streak ends.
Keller — Kelly, King, Gardner, Taricco (Ziege 13) — Davies, Redknapp (Poyet 88), Brown, Ricketts (Kanoute 64) — Keane, Defoe *Subs not used* Hirschfeld, Doherty
Scorer Defoe 18
Referee **A D'Urso**

Saturday May 15
WOLVERHAMPTON WANDERERS (a)
Won 2-0   HT 1-0   Att 29,389   Position 14th
Keller — Kelly, King, Gardner, Ziege — Yeates, Redknapp, Brown, Ricketts (Kanoute 72) — Keane (Poyet 88), Defoe *Subs not used* Burch, Doherty, Mabizela *Booked* Redknapp
Scorers Keane 34, Defoe 57
Report page 268

WOLVERHAMPTON WANDERERS

PREMIERSHIP

	P	W	D	L	F	A	GD	Pts
Arsenal	38	26	12	0	73	26	47	**90**
Chelsea	38	24	7	7	67	30	37	**79**
Man Utd	38	23	6	9	64	35	29	**75**
Liverpool	38	16	12	10	55	37	18	**60**
Newcastle	38	13	17	8	52	40	12	**56**
Aston Villa	38	15	11	12	48	44	4	**56**
Charlton	38	14	11	13	51	51	0	**53**
Bolton	38	14	11	13	48	56	-8	**53**
Fulham	38	14	10	14	52	46	6	**52**
Birmingham	38	12	14	12	43	48	-5	**50**
Middlesbro	38	13	9	16	44	52	-8	**48**
Southampton	38	12	11	15	44	45	-1	**47**
Portsmouth	38	12	9	17	47	54	-7	**45**
Tottenham	38	13	6	19	47	57	-10	**45**
Blackburn	38	12	8	18	51	59	-8	**44**
Man City	38	9	14	15	55	54	1	**41**
Everton	38	9	12	17	45	57	-12	**39**
Leicester	38	6	15	17	48	65	-17	**33**
Leeds	38	8	9	21	40	79	-39	**33**
Wolves	38	7	12	19	38	77	-39	**33**

FA CUP
Fourth round

CARLING CUP
Fourth round

Golden handshake: Sir Bobby Robson greets Dave Jones — by the end of 2003-04 Wolves were saying goodbye to the Premiership

THE GAMES

Saturday August 16 2003
BLACKBURN ROVERS (a)
Lost 1-5   **HT 0-2**   Att **26,270**   Position **19th**
Murray — Irwin, Craddock, Butler, Naylor — Newton
(Camara 85), Ince, Cameron, Silas (Blake 60) — Iversen,
Sturridge (Luzhny 71) *Subs not used* Rae, Oakes *Booked*
Blake
Scorer **Iversen 71**
Report page 92

Saturday August 23
CHARLTON ATHLETIC (h)
Lost 0-4   **HT 0-4**   Att **27,327**   Position **20th**
Wolves' desperate start to the season continues as they
are torn apart in the first half by a Charlton side giving
debuts to Di Canio and Cole, the latter on loan from
Chelsea. A straight red for Parker — subsequently
rescinded — for a tackle on Cooper, having earlier set up
both of Bartlett's goals, is the only blemish for Alan
Curbishley.

Oakes — Irwin, Craddock, Butler, Naylor — Newton, Ince,
Cameron (Rae ht), Silas (Cooper ht) — Iversen
(Sturridge 62), Blake *Subs not used* Murray, Luzhny
Booked Ince, Iversen
Referee **P Dowd**

Wednesday August 27
MANCHESTER UNITED (a)
Lost 0-1   **HT 0-1**   Att **67,648**   Position **20th**
Oakes — Irwin, Craddock, Butler, Naylor — Newton
(Silas 74), Rae, Ince, Cameron, Camara — Blake *Subs
not used* Murray, Iversen, Okoronkwo, Clingan *Booked*
Butler, Blake
Report page 196

Saturday August 30
PORTSMOUTH (h)
Drew 0-0   **HT 0-0**   Att **28,860**   Position **20th**
Dave Jones's relief as his side pick up their first point
contrasts with Harry Redknapp's anger after he is sent to
the stand for comments to the fourth official about the
referee, who books eight players (Portsmouth edge that
contest 5-3). The visiting side go closest, Butler clearing
off the line from Sheringham.

Oakes — Irwin, Craddock, Butler, Naylor — Newton, Ince,
Rae (Gudjonsson 80), Cameron — Blake, Camara *Subs
not used* Murray, Iversen, Silas, Okoronkwo *Booked*
Butler, Ince, Rae
Referee **A D'Urso**

Saturday September 13
SOUTHAMPTON (a)
Lost 0-2   **HT 0-1**   Att **31,711**   Position **20th**
Oakes — Irwin, Craddock, Butler, Naylor — Newton
(Silas 77), Rae (Iversen 83), Ince, Cameron
(Gudjonsson 64), Kennedy — Blake *Subs not used*
Murray, Luzhny *Booked* Craddock, Naylor, Ince,
Cameron, Rae
Report page 240

THE TROUBLE WITH PLAYING the game of Premiership
catch-up is that from the moment you manage to achieve a level of
parity with your rivals, you have to run faster than them for the
remainder of the season. Wolves had a brave stab at catching up,
coming from 3-0 down to beat Leicester City in October, beating
Manchester United in January and finishing the season with Henri
Camara's goals justifying his decision to play in fluorescent orange
boots, but their doom was shaped very early on.

Even with the heady memories of the Nationwide League first
division play-offs final victory over Sheffield United still fresh, a
19-year exile from the elite joyously closed off, Wolves made it clear
through a close season of bemusingly understated transfer activity
that they would stagger into the Premiership. While the
automatically promoted clubs had the extra weeks to start shopping,
either through quality (Portsmouth) or quantity (Leicester), Dave
Jones, the manager, actually started Wolves' inaugural campaign in
the Premiership with a side inferior to the one that left the first
division.

Citing injuries to key players sounds like an excuse, but the form
in which Mark Kennedy, Joleon Lescott, Kenny Miller and Matt
Murray finished the 2002-03 season made their absences keenly felt
as the team attempted to settle at the new level. The replacements
were simply not as good and neither did they possess the heart or
momentum with which Wolves had gloriously swept to promotion
in the second half of 2002-03. The new, lighter team managed one
goal (and that a consolation in a 5-1 bludgeoning away to Blackburn
Rovers) and one point from the first six games. Thank you and good
night.

Against that backdrop, keeping hopes of salvation alive into May
smacked of heroism for a squad that could at best have hoped to aim
for mid-table. This is why so many Wolves supporters felt proud
even as relegation was confirmed. This was much, much better than
another season of thwarted play-off ambition.

Time will tell whether Lescott, a pacy and tenacious central
defender, and Murray, a commanding giant of a goalkeeper, are
good Premiership players. The loss, through season-long injuries, of
the two England Under-21 internationals meant that Jones relied
upon Michael Oakes and Paul Jones in goal and a variety of flawed
partners alongside Paul Butler in the centre of defence. Butler
makes up in heart and timing what he lacks in pace and produced
some exceptional performances, but it would have been prudent to
play someone quick alongside him.

With Oleg Luzhny as an alternative, Jody Craddock got the vote

HONOURS BOARD

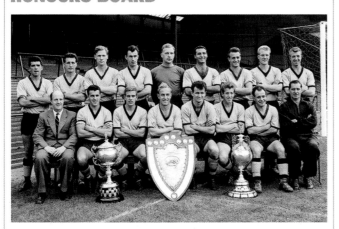

FOOTBALL LEAGUE
Champions 1954, 1958, 1959
Runners-up 1938, 1939, 1950, 1955, 1960
FA CUP
Winners 1893, 1908, 1949, 1960
Runners-up 1889, 1896, 1921, 1939
LEAGUE CUP
Winners 1974, 1980

FAIRS CUP/UEFA CUP
Runners-up 1972

Record attendance 61,315 (v Liverpool, FA Cup 5th rnd, February 11, 1939)
Current capacity 29,396
Record victory 14-0 (v Crosswell's Brewery, FA Cup 2nd rnd, November 13, 1886)
Record defeat 1-10 (v Newton Heath, first division, October 15, 1892)

for the majority of the season and was culpable for too many soft goals. With Denis Irwin delaying his retirement, it meant that the back four was prey to any attack with speed.

Which, in the Premiership, tends to be everyone. Mark Clyde, the club's young player of the year, showed great promise when he came in, but Lee Naylor, the longest-serving player, was punished for his lapses of concentration, though he never played with anything less than total commitment and his attacking combination with Kennedy gave Wolves thrust down the left. Only as a last throw of the dice did Jones give Isaac Okoronkwo a run in the team and the Nigeria central defender at last brought pace to the defence. Wolves lost only two of their last seven matches.

If the defence are cast as the whipping boys — and only Leeds United conceded more goals — then the midfield took the honours. Alex Rae scored *The Premiership's* goal of the month for September, a 30-yard volley into the top corner, as Wolves came within seconds of winning away to Bolton Wanderers, and added another six vital goals by the first week of January. Colin Cameron scored as Manchester City (1-0) and Leicester (4-3) were beaten at Molineux, where Jones's team became impregnable for the middle four months of the season. Paul Ince snarled away with the best of them, he and Rae coming out on top against Manchester United and Liverpool, when Miller reminded everyone of his capabilities.

Four points from those two games in January proved the high point of the season, however. Catching up was emotionally and

---

Saturday September 20
CHELSEA (h)
Lost 0-5   HT 0-2   Att 29,208   Position 20th
Another seven Chelsea changes, another five goals shipped by Wolves. The floodgates eventually open after Lampard breaks through and Crespo proves a lethal late substitute with a double, Hasselbaink and Duff — his first goal in blue — scoring in between. Wolves are stuck on the bottom, Chelsea go top for a day.

Oakes — Irwin, Craddock, Butler, Naylor — Newton (Cameron 59), Gudjonsson (Silas 79), Ince, Kennedy, Camara — Iversen *Subs not used* Murray, Luzhny, Rae
Booked Butler, Ince
Referee **M Messias**

Tuesday September 23
DARLINGTON (h)
Carling Cup, 2nd rnd
Won 2-0   HT 1-0   Att 10,232
After five games without a goal, Wolves end their drought with Rae's low 25-yard shot and go on to record a much-needed victory, albeit against third-division opposition. Gudjonsson capitalises on a goalkeeping error with their second.

Murray (Oakes ht) — Luzhny, Craddock, Okoronkwo, Naylor — Gudjonsson (Newton 81), Rae, Cameron, Silas, Kennedy (Clarke 89) — Iversen *Subs not used* Ingimarsson, Clingan
Scorers **Rae 37, Gudjonsson 53**
Referee **K Hill**

Saturday September 27
BOLTON WANDERERS (a)
Drew 1-1   HT 1-0   Att 27,043   Position 20th
Oakes — Irwin, Craddock, Butler, Naylor — Newton (Kachloul 86), Rae, Cameron, Ince, Kennedy (Miller ht) *Subs not used* Murray, Gudjonsson, Okoronkwo
Scorer **Rae 30**
Report page 103

Saturday October 4
MANCHESTER CITY (h)
Won 1-0   HT 0-0   Att 29,386   Position 20th
A poor game it may be, but nobody at Wolves cares too much after Seaman's initial fumble is followed by Cameron's far-post header and an overdue first league win of the season, ensured when Wanchope heads against a post and Oakes makes a splendid late save from Sun's header. Wolves are now level on points with Leicester City.

Oakes — Irwin, Craddock, Butler, Naylor — Miller (Newton 89), Rae, Ince, Cameron, Camara (Kachloul 78) — Blake *Subs not used* Murray, Okoronkwo, Sturridge
Booked Ince, Rae, Miller
Scorer **Cameron 75**
Referee **J Winter**

Saturday October 18
FULHAM (a)
Drew 0-0   HT 0-0   Att 17,031   Position 19th
Oakes — Irwin, Craddock, Butler, Naylor — Miller
(Kennedy 59), Rae, Gudjonsson, Cameron, Camara —
Blake *Subs not used* Murray, Ingimarsson, Sturridge,
Kachloul *Booked* Naylor, Miller
Report page 145

Saturday October 25
LEICESTER CITY (h)
Won 4-3   HT 0-3   Att 28,578   Position 15th
One of the comebacks of this or any other season sees
Wolves, having scored three times in nine league
matches, rattle in four in 34 crazy second-half minutes
to turn a 3-0 interval deficit into a 4-3 win that lifts them
to the giddy heights of fifteenth place. Micky Adams is
almost speechless after his Leicester side waste the
lead given them by Ferdinand, who scores twice with
headers from corners and then tees up Scimeca.

Oakes — Irwin, Craddock, Butler, Naylor — Miller
(Kachloul ht), Rae, Gudjonsson (Newton 22), Cameron,
Camara — Blake *Subs not used* Murray, Iversen, Luzhny
Scorers **Cameron 52, 60 (pen), Rae 68, Camara 86**
Referee **P Walton**

Tuesday October 28
BURNLEY (h)
Carling Cup, 3rd rnd
Won 2-0   HT 0-0   Att 18,548
Wolves' unbeaten run now extends to six games. Miller,
celebrating the birth of his first child, Coby, the day
before, puts them ahead against Burnley and Craddock's
header polishes off the first-division side.

Oakes — Luzhny, Craddock, Butler, Naylor — Silas, Ince
(Rae ht), Gudjonsson — Miller, Iversen (Clarke 81),
Camara *Subs not used* Blake, Okoronkwo, Ikeme *Booked*
Gudjonsson
Scorers **Miller 48, Craddock 81**
Referee **C Foy**

Saturday November 1
MIDDLESBROUGH (a)
Lost 0-2   HT 0-0   Att 30,305   Position 17th
Oakes — Irwin, Craddock, Butler, Naylor — Miller
(Kennedy 63), Rae, Ince, Gudjonsson (Silas 79), Camara
— Iversen *Subs not used* Clingan, Clyde, Ikeme *Booked*
Rae, Gudjonsson *Sent off* Rae 89
Report page 210

Saturday November 8
BIRMINGHAM CITY (h)
Drew 1-1   HT 0-0   Att 28,831   Position 17th
Birmingham are grateful for a point in their first
top flight Molineux derby for 20 years after Iversen, who
scrambles an equaliser at the far post, misses a
gilt-edged chance to win it for Wolves with just ten
seconds left to play. Forssell gives Birmingham the lead
just after half-time.

Oakes — Irwin (Clyde 87), Craddock, Butler, Naylor —
Camara, Ince, Rae, Kennedy — Iversen, Miller
(Newton 57) *Subs not used* Gudjonsson, Sturridge,
Ikeme *Booked* Irwin, Ince
Scorer **Iversen 66**
Referee **G Barber**

Naylor forces his way ahead of Scowcroft in the epic win over Leicester

physically exhausting and a thin squad was never going to last the
season. Jones the manager, belatedly given some cash, paid £2.25 million to bring in Jones the goalkeeper and, from Newcastle United,
Carl Cort. While they took their time to settle, results slipped away.

Particularly crushing was a 4-1 reverse away to Leeds, when
victory would have lifted Wolves out of the bottom three with the
easiest run-in of the main relegation candidates to follow. A point
away to Leicester felt like an opportunity missed and going the
whole season without an away win tells its own story. Morale
inevitably took a pounding and heavy defeats at Molineux — by
Aston Villa and Southampton — also followed.

So it came to pass that, as ever, the team that is bottom of the
Premiership at Christmas must go. Sir Jack Hayward stepped down
as chairman in December; the anticipated new investment, however,
was not swift in arriving. It is questionable how many of Jones's
signings in the past year would have been made if he had been
armed with a reasonable transfer budget; perhaps only Camara, who
scored six goals in the final nine games. At least such a spirited finale
— please do not mention Shaun Wright-Phillips's late, late equaliser
away to Manchester City or Uriah Rennie's refereeing performance
at home to Bolton — gave Wolves fans their pride back.

THE MANAGER — Dave Jones

Dave Jones, allowed to spend around half of what West Bromwich Albion paid out 12 months earlier, may well be the only manager to have improved his reputation by leading his team to relegation from the Premiership. Jones may have thought that if he could keep his squad in with a chance of staying up until May, then what could he have achieved with a decent transfer budget? He will never know, but both the board and the supporters stuck with him until the end as the team gave nothing less than their all and played some cracking stuff going forward.

Peter Lansley

APPEARANCES

	Prem	FAC	CC	Total
K Andrews	1	1	1	3
N Blake	10 (3)	-	1	11 (3)
P Butler	37	2	2	41
H Camara	29 (1)	-	2	31 (1)
C Cameron	25 (5)	2	1	28 (5)
L Clarke	-	0 (1)	0 (2)	0 (3)
M Clyde	6 (3)	3	-	9 (3)
K Cooper	0 (1)	-	-	0 (1)
C Cort	13 (3)	-	-	13 (3)
J Craddock	31 (1)	2 (1)	3	36 (2)
I Ganea	6 (10)	2 (1)	-	8 (11)
J Gudjonsson	5 (6)	1 (1)	3	9 (7)
P Ince	32	1	2	35
D Irwin	30 (2)	1	-	31 (2)
S Iversen	11 (5)	1 (1)	2	14 (6)
P Jones	16	-	-	16
H Kachloul	0 (4)	-	-	0 (4)
M Kennedy	28 (3)	3	1 (1)	32 (4)
O Luzhny	4 (2)	2	2	8 (2)
A Marshall	-	-	1	1
K Miller	17 (8)	3	2	22 (8)
M Murray	1	-	1	2
L Naylor	37 (1)	2	3	42 (1)
S Newton	20 (8)	2	0 (2)	22 (10)
M Oakes	21	3	1 (1)	25 (1)
I Okoronkwo	7	-	1	8
A Rae	27 (6)	1	2 (1)	30 (7)
Silas	2 (7)	1 (2)	2	5 (9)
D Sturridge	2 (3)	-	0 (1)	2 (4)

Saturday November 22
EVERTON (a)
Lost 0-2   HT 0-2   Att 40,190   Position 19th
Oakes — Craddock, Butler, Naylor — Newton (Miller ht), Ince, Rae (Gudjonsson 65), Kennedy — Iversen (Blake ht), Camara *Subs not used* Clyde, Marshall
Booked Craddock, Blake
Report page 137

Saturday November 29
NEWCASTLE UNITED (h)
Drew 1-1   HT 1-1   Att 29,344   Position 19th
Both sides hit the woodwork, both are denied penalties and both take a point after goals within four first-half minutes. But the match will be best remembered for the female Wolves fan who suffers nasty injuries when a firework from the pre-match entertainment shoots into the crowd and hits her in the face.

Oakes — Irwin, Craddock, Butler, Naylor — Rae, Andrews, Gudjonsson — Kennedy (Miller 76), Blake *Subs not used* Newton, Silas, Cooper, Marshall *Booked* Butler, Naylor
Scorer **Blake 27**
Referee **S Bennett**

Tuesday December 2
ARSENAL (a)
Carling Cup, 4th rnd
Lost 1-5   HT 0-1   Att 28,161
Marshall — Gudjonsson, Craddock, Butler, Naylor — Miller (Kennedy 60), Rae, Ince, Andrews (Sturridge 68), Camara (Newton 73) — Blake *Subs not used* Oakes, Silas *Booked* Blake, Gudjonsson
Scorer **Rae 81**
Report page 64

Saturday December 6
TOTTENHAM HOTSPUR (a)
Lost 2-5   HT 1-1   Att 34,825   Position 20th
Oakes — Irwin, Craddock, Butler, Naylor — Rae (Miller 86), Ince, Cameron, Kennedy — Camara, Blake (Sturridge 57) *Subs not used* Marshall, Luzhny, Gudjonsson
Scorers **Ince 30, Rae 84**
Report page 253

Sunday December 14
ASTON VILLA (a)
Lost 2-3   HT 1-2   Att 36,964   Position 20th
Oakes — Luzhny, Craddock, Butler, Irwin (Naylor 83) — Rae, Ince, Cameron (Silas 59), Kennedy — Camara, Sturridge (Miller 59) *Subs not used* Gudjonsson, Marshall *Booked* Ince, Camara, Luzhny, Rae
Scorers **Rae 36, Kennedy 80**
Report page 75

ARSENAL (a)

Lost 0-3   HT 0-2   Att 38,003   Position 20th
Oakes — Luzhny, Craddock, Butler, Naylor — Camara (Sturridge 85), Rae, Ince, Cameron, Kennedy — Miller (Newton 75) *Subs not used* Iversen, Clyde, Marshall
Booked Butler, Naylor, Ince, Luzhny, Rae
Report page 65

Sunday December 28
LEEDS UNITED (h)

Won 3-1   HT 1-1   Att 29,139   Position 20th
Starting the day six points behind Leeds at the bottom, this is a match Wolves have to win if they are not to be cut adrift and they do so from behind after Duberry, without a goal for more than three years, gets his second in a month. Smith slices Camara's corner into his own net and Iversen's double brings Leeds's five-match unbeaten run to a shuddering halt. They also have Matteo sent off for two fouls.

Oakes — Luzhny, Craddock, Butler, Naylor — Newton (Kachloul 82), Ince, Cameron, Camara — Iversen, Miller *Subs not used* Marshall, Silas, Gudjonsson, Clyde
Booked Naylor
Scorers **Smith 18 (og), Iversen 48, 90**
Referee **A D'Urso**

Saturday January 3 2004
KIDDERMINSTER HARRIERS (a)

FA Cup, 3rd rnd
Drew 1-1   HT 0-0   Att 6,005
Williams, the "flying postman", delivers what appears to be the knockout blow when he puts Harriers ahead two minutes after his arrival as a substitute, but Rae spares Wolves an embarrassing defeat to their near neighbours, who are struggling to avoid a return to the Nationwide Conference, with a late equaliser.

Oakes — Irwin, Clyde, Craddock, Naylor — Newton, Rae, Cameron, Kennedy (Silas 77) — Miller (Ganea 72), Iversen *Subs not used* Luzhny, Gudjonsson, Ikeme *Booked* Irwin, Craddock, Cameron
Scorer **Rae 89**
Referee **C Foy**

Wednesday January 7
BLACKBURN ROVERS (h)

Drew 2-2   HT 0-1   Att 27,393   Position 20th
With Dave Jones sidelined with flu, Stuart Gray takes charge of Wolves and sees them go behind to the 250th goal of Cole's club career. Blackburn are then breached by Butler and the newly prolific Rae, but Yorke heads an equaliser and then misses a chance to secure all three points.

Oakes — Irwin, Craddock, Butler, Naylor — Newton (Gudjonsson 83), Rae, Cameron, Kennedy — Iversen (Blake 32), Camara *Subs not used* Miller, Clyde, Ikeme *Booked* Cameron
Scorers **Butler 63, Rae 72**
Referee **N Barry**

Saturday January 10
CHARLTON ATHLETIC (a)

Lost 0-2   HT 0-1   Att 26,148   Position 20th
Oakes — Irwin, Craddock, Clyde, Naylor (Luzhny ht) — Newton (Ganea 82), Ince, Rae, Camara — Blake, Cameron (Kennedy 69) *Subs not used* Ikeme, Gudjonsson *Booked* Ince, Cameron, Rae
Report page 117

THE TIMES

MATCH OF THE SEASON

Wolverhampton Wanderers 1 Manchester United 0
Molineux, Saturday January 17 2004
Tom Dart

THERE is *Schadenfreude* in discovering that even the famous and brilliant are vulnerable to embarrassment. For Wolverhampton Wanderers fans it must have seemed like meeting a Hollywood star and noticing that his flies are undone. Any awe was soon dispelled by the realisation that Manchester United's players are not invulnerable gods.

The defiance that United displayed over Rio Ferdinand, who starts his ban for failing to take a drugs test tomorrow, pending an appeal, did not manifest itself on the pitch. Instead they were humbled and, after their second poor performance in a week, their Barclaycard Premiership title credentials are now, like Ferdinand's situation, shrouded in uncertainty.

Like Ferdinand in September, United were guilty on Saturday of failing to enact what should have been a routine procedure: arrive in the Black Country, perform as required against the bottom team, collect three points. One of the most unexpected results of this or any other Premiership season was a big outcome, too, for those who felt the league was becoming too predictable at both ends of the table.

At the final whistle, delirium swirled round Molineux in place of the mist that had hugged the surroundings before kick-off. The stadium announcer kept repeating the final score as if he would never get the chance to say the words again. Molineux wanted to party like there was no tomorrow, yet the result raised the possibility of a brighter dawn. Would this prove to be the highlight of Wolves' season, or will that come in May if Premiership survival is secured?

This was a triumph of containment, of motivation above talent. That it is possible to tame United by sheer determination will be noted in Northampton, where United travel for the FA Cup on Sunday, and discussed in Dubai, where the squad is spending a five-night break. The game had the feel of a cup-tie, as Dave Jones, the Wolves manager, implied when he described the result as "a giant-killing". Of course, the extent of the tremors caused by this seismic outcome is also a reflection of Wolves' Premiership inadequacies so far. "Psychologically, it's a massive boost," Jones said. "We've got to push on. It's no good thinking we are home and dry because we are a long, long way away from it." Next up for Wolves are Liverpool on Wednesday. "I feel like we're playing in the Champions League this week," Jones said.

Ferdinand suffered an injury early in the first half and limped on until he was finally removed five minutes into the second period, to the jeers of the home fans. His reluctance to go off, and United's hesitation in substituting him, suggested both the fear that he may not make another appearance for some time, as well as a lack of

Kennedy and Naylor join forces to get the better of Fletcher on the day that Molineux was given a reminder of the Old Gold glory days

trust in his replacement. It would be too facile to blame defeat on Wes Brown and it is too early to say that Brown will prove an inadequate replacement for Ferdinand. Brown's treacherous studs, rather than any lack of ability, were culpable on Saturday. He slipped to allow Kenny Miller a clear run on goal in the second half.

The United defence had contained Miller comfortably but suddenly he exploded like a firework, striding past Brown then sliding his shot past Howard with an assertiveness that his travails had hitherto hardly merited. It had the hint of destiny about it, as if he knew this was his moment, and Howard deferred, making a feeble attempt to push the ball away. Miller left clutching a video of the game and promising to wear it out with replays of his first Premiership goal.

As United pressed for an equaliser, it was possible to pinpoint essential defensive contributions from Denis Irwin, Lee Naylor and Michael Oakes, but at times it seemed like the Wolves goal was protected by a shield of sheer energy, a demented Old Gold blur.

WOLVERHAMPTON WANDERERS (4-4-1-1): M Oakes — D Irwin, P Butler, J Craddock, L Naylor — S Newton, P Ince, A Rae, M Kennedy — K Miller— S Iversen (sub: I Ganea, 80min). **Substitutes not used:** C Cameron, M Clyde, H Kachloul, C Ikeme. **Booked:** Butler, Ganea.
MANCHESTER UNITED (4-4-1-1): T Howard — J O'Shea, R Ferdinand (sub: W Brown, 50), M Silvestre, Q Fortune — D Fletcher (sub: D Bellion, 65), R Keane, P Neville (sub: D Forlan, 68), C Ronaldo — P Scholes — R van Nistelrooy. **Substitutes not used:** N Butt, R Carroll.

Tuesday January 13
KIDDERMINSTER HARRIERS (h)
FA Cup, 3rd rnd replay
Won 2-0   HT 1-0   Att 25,808
With Manchester United and Liverpool due at Molineux in the next eight days, Wolves make worryingly hard work of this replay. Miller is their match-winner with a far-post header and a lucky intended cross that a linesman rules has crossed the line via a post, replays suggesting that the official got it wrong.

Oakes — Clyde, Craddock, Butler, Luzhny — Newton, Gudjonsson, Andrews, Kennedy (Silas 90) — Ganea (Iversen 82), Miller Subs not used Ikeme, Rae, Cameron Booked Butler, Clyde, Oakes, Andrews
Scorer **Miller 35, 65**
Referee **M Messias**

Saturday January 17
MANCHESTER UNITED (h)
Won 1-0   HT 0-0   Att 29,396   Position 19th
The biggest shock of the league season by some distance as bottom beats top. Ferdinand's last match before beginning his eight-month ban is curtailed by injury and Miller glides past Brown, Ferdinand's replacement in the United defence, to score the only goal, his first in the Premiership. Ince also hits a post from distance, but Wolves need Oakes to make good saves from Scholes and Bellion.

Oakes — Irwin, Craddock, Butler, Naylor — Newton, Ince, Rae, Kennedy — Miller — Iversen (Ganea 80) Subs not used Cameron, Clyde, Kachloul, Ikeme Booked Butler, Ganea
Scorer **Miller 67**
Referee **A D'Urso**

Wednesday January 21
LIVERPOOL (h)
Drew 1-1   HT 0-1   Att 29,380   Position 19th
Miller, the man who downed Manchester United, is on the spot again, this time to volley a last-minute equaliser and take a valuable point off Liverpool. Cheyrou springs the offside trap to earn the lead and Murphy hits a post, but Iversen is guilty of a dreadful miss and Wolves deserve a draw despite the lateness of their goal.

Oakes — Irwin, Craddock, Butler, Naylor — Newton (Cameron 21), Ince, Rae, Kennedy (Silas 72) — Iversen (Ganea 82), Miller Subs not used Clyde, Ikeme Booked Ince, Rae
Scorer **Miller 90**
Referee **B Knight**

Sunday January 25
WEST HAM UNITED (h)
FA Cup, 4th rnd
Lost 1-3   HT 1-3   Att 24,413
"This was probably a game too far for some of my players," Dave Jones says as Wolves' first home defeat in 14 games costs them their place in the FA Cup, beaten by the first-division promotion hopefuls. Ganea scores his first for Wolves to halve the deficit, but Connolly's goal against his old club earns West Ham their winning margin.

Oakes — Luzhny (Craddock ht), Clyde, Butler, Naylor — Silas (Gudjonsson 66), Ince, Cameron, Kennedy — Ganea, Miller (Clarke 59) Subs not used Ikeme, Iversen
Scorer **Ganea 23**
Referee **M Halsey**

Saturday January 31
PORTSMOUTH (a)
Drew 0-0   HT 0-0   Att 20,112   Position 19th
Jones — Irwin, Butler, Craddock, Naylor — Cameron, Rae, Ince, Kennedy — Cort (Iversen 67), Miller (Ganea 90) Subs not used Oakes, Silas, Clyde Booked Naylor
Report page 235

Saturday February 7
ARSENAL (h)
Lost 1-3   **HT 1-1**   Att **29,392**   Position **19th**
Arsenal make it a club record 24 league matches unbeaten from the start of a season. Ganea cancels out a superb finish by Bergkamp, the Dutchman scoring with the outside of his boot, but Wolves are then hit by two goals in five second-half minutes from Henry and Toure and finish well beaten.

Jones — Irwin, Craddock, Butler, Naylor — Miller, Rae, Cameron, Kennedy — Cort (Iversen 76), Ganea *Subs not used* Oakes, Silas, Gudjonsson, Clyde *Booked* Irwin, Kennedy, Ganea
Scorer **Ganea 26**
Referee **P Dowd**

Tuesday February 10
LEEDS UNITED (a)
Lost 1-4   **HT 1-2**   Att **36,867**   Position **20th**
Jones — Irwin, Craddock, Butler, Naylor — Miller (Silas 62), Rae, Cameron, Kennedy — Ganea, Cort (Iversen 77) *Subs not used* Oakes, Clyde, Gudjonsson *Booked* Irwin, Cameron
Scorer **Ganea 21**
Report page 159

Saturday February 21
FULHAM (h)
Won 2-1   **HT 1-0**   Att **28,424**   Position **18th**
Wolves refuse to go quietly, moving up two places to eighteenth after Ince, cleverly set up by Clyde and Rae, then Cort, punishing an error by Bocanegra, score the goals that defeat Fulham, for whom Malbranque replies with six minutes left. "I'll have to start growling at them soon," Chris Coleman says of his out-of-sorts Fulham side.

Jones — Clyde, Craddock, Butler, Naylor — Camara, Ince, Rae, Kennedy — Miller (Ganea 78), Cort (Cameron 89) *Subs not used* Oakes, Iversen, Luzhny *Booked* Ince
Scorers **Ince 20, Cort 51**
Referee **H Webb**

Saturday February 28
LEICESTER CITY (a)
Drew 0-0   **HT 0-0**   Att **31,768**   Position **17th**
Jones — Irwin (Clyde 65), Craddock, Butler, Naylor — Camara (Newton 82), Ince, Rae, Kennedy — Miller (Ganea 65), Cort *Subs not used* Oakes, Iversen *Booked* Rae
Report page 170

Sunday March 14
ASTON VILLA (h)
Lost 0-4   **HT 0-3**   Att **29,386**   Position **19th**
Trailing 3-0 inside 25 minutes, a wretched Wolves performance is punished by a comprehensive derby defeat. Angel's second goal, after the break, is the best of the four and makes him the first Villa player to score 20 in a season since 1997. Sorensen saves Ganea's penalty just before half-time.

Jones — Irwin (Clyde 65), Butler, Craddock, Naylor — Camara, Ince, Rae, Kennedy — Ganea, Cort (Iversen 65) *Subs not used* Oakes, Newton, Miller *Booked* Ganea
Referee **P Durkin**

THE PLAYERS

KEITH ANDREWS (midfield) **Born** August 13, 1980, Dublin **Ht** 5ft 8in **Wt** 12st 4lb **Signed from** trainee, August 1999

NATHAN BLAKE (forward) **Born** January 27, 1972, Cardiff **Ht** 5ft 11in **Wt** 13st 12lb **Signed from** Blackburn Rovers, September 2001, £1.5m

PAUL BUTLER (defender) **Born** November 2, 1972, Manchester **Ht** 6ft 2in **Wt** 13st 0lb **Signed from** Sunderland (initial loan), January 2001, £1m

HENRI CAMARA (forward) **Born** May 10, 1977, Dakar **Ht** 5ft 9in **Wt** 10st 8lb **Signed from** Sedan, August 2003, £1.5m

COLIN CAMERON (midfield) **Born** October 23, 1972, Kirkcaldy **Ht** 5ft 5in **Wt** 9st 7lb **Signed from** Heart of Midlothian, August 2001, £1.75m

LEON CLARKE (forward) **Born** February 2, 1985, Birmingham **Ht** 6ft 2in **Wt** 14st 2lb **Signed from** trainee, July 2003

MARK CLYDE (defender) **Born** December 27, 1982, Limavady, Northern Ireland **Ht** 6ft 2in **Wt** 13st 0lb **Signed from** trainee, August 2000

KEVIN COOPER (midfield) **Born** February 8, 1975, Derby **Ht** 5ft 7in **Wt** 10st 7lb **Signed from** Wimbledon, March 2002, £1m

CARL CORT (forward) **Born** November 1, 1977, Southwark **Ht** 6ft 4in **Wt** 12st 7lb **Signed from** Newcastle United, January 2004, £2m

JODY CRADDOCK (defender) **Born** July 25, 1975, Redditch **Ht** 6ft 2in **Wt** 12st 4lb **Signed from** Sunderland, July 2003, £1.75m

IOAN GANEA (forward) **Born** August 10, 1973, Fagaras, Romania **Ht** 5ft 9in **Wt** 13st 3lb **Signed from** Bursaspor, December 2003, free

JOEY GUDJONSSON (midfield) **Born** May 25, 1980, Akranes, Iceland **Ht** 5ft 6in **Wt** 11st 5lb **Signed from** Real Betis (loan), January 2003

PAUL INCE (midfield) **Born** October 21, 1967 **Ht** 5ft 11in **Wt** 12st 2lb **Signed from** Middlesbrough, August 2002, free

DENIS IRWIN (defender) **Born** October 31, 1965, Cork **Ht** 5ft 8in **Wt** 10st 11lb **Signed from** Manchester United, July 2002, free

STEFFEN IVERSEN (forward) **Born** October 11, 1976, Oslo **Ht** 6ft 1in **Wt** 12st 7lb **Signed from** Tottenham Hotspur, August 2003, free

PAUL JONES (goalkeeper) **Born** April 18, 1967, Chirk **Ht** 6ft 2in **Wt** 14st 8lb **Signed from** Southampton, January 2004, £250,000

HASSAN KACHLOUL (midfield) **Born** February 19, 1973, Agadir, Morocco **Ht** 6ft 1in **Wt** 12st 2lb **Signed from** Aston Villa (loan), September 2003

MARK KENNEDY (midfield) **Born** May 15, 1976, Dublin **Ht** 5ft 11in **Wt** 11st 9lb **Signed from** Manchester City, July 2001, £2m

OLEG LUZHNY Born August 5, 1968, Kiev **Ht** 6ft 0in **Wt** 12st 2lb **Signed from** Arsenal, July 2003, free

ANDY MARSHALL (goalkeeper) **Born** April 14, 1975, Bury **Ht** 6ft 2in **Wt** 13st 7lb **Signed from** Ipswich Town (loan), November 2003

KENNY MILLER (forward) **Born** December 23, 1979, Edinburgh **Ht** 5ft 9in **Wt** 10st 9lb **Signed from** Rangers (initial loan), December 2001, £3m

MATTHEW MURRAY (goalkeeper) **Born** May 2, 1981, Solihull **Ht** 6ft 4in **Wt** 13st 10lb **Signed from** trainee, August 1997

LEE NAYLOR (defender) **Born** March 19, 1980, Walsall **Ht** 5ft 10in **Wt** 11st 3lb **Signed from** trainee, August 1997

MICHAEL OAKES (goalkeeper) **Born** October 30, 1973, Northwich **Ht** 6ft 2in **Wt** 14st 6lb **Signed from** Aston Villa, October 1999, £500,000

ISAAC OKORONKWO (defender) **Born** May 1, 1978, Abia, Nigeria **Ht** 6ft 0in **Wt** 11st 10lb **Signed from** Shakhtar Donetsk, July 2003, free

SHAUN NEWTON (midfield) **Born** August 20, 1975, Camberwell **Ht** 5ft 8in **Wt** 11st 7lb **Signed from** Charlton Athletic, August 2001, £850,000

ALEX RAE (midfield) **Born** August 30, 1969, Glasgow **Ht** 5ft 10in **Wt** 11st 9lb **Signed from** Sunderland, September 2001, £1.2m

JORGE MANUEL SILAS (forward) **Born** September 1, 1976, Lisbon **Ht** 5ft 10in **Wt** 11st 3lb **Signed from** Uniao Leiria, July 2003, £1m

DEAN STURRIDGE (forward) **Born** July 27, 1973, Birmingham **Ht** 5ft 8in **Wt** 12st 12lb **Signed from** Leicester City (initial loan), December 2001, £350,000

STATS AND FACTS

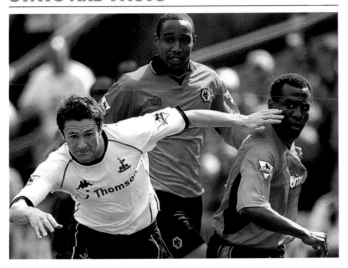

● When Wolves beat Leicester City 4-3 in October it was the first time they had scored more than one goal in 31 top-flight games.

● Wolves became only the second team in 11 years to go a season without an away victory in the Premiership. The other was Coventry City in 1999-2000.

● In 21 matches away to Middlesbrough, Wolves have failed to register a win . . .

● . . . and they have also not won in 11 away matches against Tottenham Hotspur.

● Filbert Street or the Walkers Stadium, it's all the same to Wolves. They have won none of their past 16 games away to Leicester City.

● They may once have dominated the region, but Wolves have drawn two and lost the other 12 of their past 14 meetings with Aston Villa.

Bill Edgar

GOALSCORERS

	Prem	FAC	CC	Total
N Blake	1	-	-	1
P Butler	1	-	-	1
H Camara	6	-	-	6
C Cameron	5 (1p)	-	-	5 (1p)
C Cort	5	-	-	5
J Craddock	1	-	1	2
I Ganea	3	1	-	4
J Gudjonsson	-	-	1	1
P Ince	2	-	-	2
S Iversen	4	-	-	4
M Kennedy	2	-	-	2
K Miller	2	2	1	5
A Rae	5	1	2	8
Own goals	1	-	-	1

Saturday March 20
LIVERPOOL (a)
Lost 0-1   HT 0-0   Att 43,795   Position 19th
Jones — Clyde, Craddock, Butler, Naylor — Camara, Ince, Rae, Kennedy (Cort 81) — Miller, Ganea (Newton 70) *Subs not used* Oakes, Cameron, Irwin
Booked Newton
Report page 182

Saturday March 27
CHELSEA (a)
Lost 2-5   HT 1-1   Att 41,215   Position 20th
Jones — Clyde, Craddock, Butler, Naylor — Miller (Cort 84), Ince, Rae (Cameron 84), Kennedy (Newton 73) — Camara, Ganea *Subs not used* Oakes, Irwin *Booked* Rae, Ganea
Scorers **Camara 23, Craddock 57**
Report page 130

Saturday April 3
SOUTHAMPTON (h)
Lost 1-4   HT 0-1   Att 29,106   Position 20th
Time is now running out for the bottom club, who do what no other side has done in 296 games spread over seven years — they let Lundekvam score. The Southampton defender puts his side 2-0 up and, though Camara replies, Phillips strikes twice in the last two minutes to inflict a fourth successive defeat on a team now leaking goals at an alarming rate.

Jones — Irwin (Cameron 81), Craddock, Butler, Naylor — Camara, Ince, Rae, Kennedy — Miller (Newton 60), Ganea (Cort ht) *Subs not used* Oakes, Luzhny *Booked* Butler, Camara
Scorer **Camara 72**
Referee **M Halsey**

Saturday April 10
MANCHESTER CITY (a)
Drew 3-3   HT 2-2   Att 47,248   Position 20th
Jones — Clyde (Irwin ht), Okoronkwo, Butler, Naylor — Newton (Gudjonsson 66), Ince, Cameron, Kennedy — Camara (Miller 90), Cort *Subs not used* Oakes, Ganea *Booked* Okoronkwo
Scorers **Kennedy 13, Cort 23, Camara 78**
Report page 193

Monday April 12
BOLTON WANDERERS (h)
Lost 1-2   HT 1-1   Att 28,695   Position 20th
The game is almost up for Wolves and Dave Jones cannot contain his anger after Davies runs clear two minutes into stoppage time to grab Bolton's winner, the manager launching a blistering post-match attack on Uriah Rennie, who had turned down two convincing penalty appeals. Bolton, ending their own poor run, are now probably safe.

Jones — Irwin (Miller 83), Okoronkwo, Butler, Naylor — Newton, Ince, Cameron, Kennedy — Camara, Cort *Subs not used* Oakes, Craddock, Ganea, Gudjonsson *Booked* Irwin, Okoronkwo, Cort
Scorer **Camara 44**
Referee **U Rennie**

PLAYER OF THE SEASON
Alex Rae

Henri Camara's brilliant pace and late flurry of goals earned him the supporters' player-of-the-year award, but for the bulk of the season, Alex Rae was Wolves' best performer. Throwing his body into tackles where others fear to proffer a foot, Rae maintained an admirable composure on the ball and, when playing with Colin Cameron and Paul Ince, got forward to score eight goals in 16 games. His immense contribution, even at the age of 34, earned him a dream move back home to Rangers, where he had started his career, when his contract at Molineux expired.

Peter Lansley

Saturday April 17
MIDDLESBROUGH (h)
Won 2-0   **HT 1-0**   Att **27,975**   Position **20th**
Wolves live to fight another day. After Ehiogu and — dismally — Nemeth miss headers, Cort meets Clyde's cross to put the home side in front and Camara makes it four goals in five games with a spectacular over-the-shoulder volley. Wolves can even afford to waste a late penalty, Schwarzer saving from Camara.

Jones — Clyde (Irwin 62), Okoronkwo, Butler, Naylor — Newton (Rae 86), Ince, Cameron, Kennedy — Cort, Camara *Subs not used* Oakes, Miller, Ganea *Booked* Ince
Scorers **Cort 28, Camara 62**
Referee **A D'Urso**

Sunday April 25
BIRMINGHAM CITY (a)
Drew 2-2   **HT 1-2**   Att **29,494**   Position **20th**
Jones — Luzhny (Ganea 59), Okoronkwo, Butler, Naylor — Newton, Ince, Cameron (Miller 87), Kennedy (Rae 82) — Cort, Camara *Subs not used* Oakes, Craddock
Scorers **Cameron 6, Cort 75**
Report page 90

Saturday May 1
EVERTON (h)
Won 2-1   **HT 0-1**   Att **29,395**   Position **19th**
The mathematics say they are not down yet, but Wolves' fate is sealed despite this victory, Manchester City's win against Newcastle United effectively sending them down. Everton take the lead through Osman on his first Premiership start, but either side of a bad lunge by Rooney that catches Jones on the head — for which the striker is lucky only to be cautioned — Camara and Cort win the game.

Jones — Irwin (Ganea 77), Okoronkwo, Butler, Naylor — Newton, Ince, Cameron (Rae 73), Kennedy — Camara, Cort *Subs not used* Oakes, Iversen, Luzhny
Scorers **Camara 55, Cort 84**
Referee **M Riley**

Sunday May 9
NEWCASTLE UNITED (a)
Drew 1-1   **HT 0-1**   Att **52,139**   Position **19th**
Jones — Irwin (Ganea 65), Okoronkwo, Butler, Naylor (Rae 32) — Newton, Ince, Cameron (Gudjonsson 90), Kennedy — Camara, Cort *Subs not used* Oakes, Lowe *Booked* Ince, Cameron
Scorer **Ganea 70**
Report page 228

Saturday May 15
TOTTENHAM HOTSPUR (h)
Lost 0-2   **HT 0-1**   Att **29,389**   Position **20th**
Wolves' Premiership farewell — and Irwin's last hurrah after 958 senior games — ends in defeat and, with the sending-off of Ince for two yellow cards, disrepute. David Pleat refuses to answer questions about his future or the identity of Spurs' next manager after goals from Keane and Defoe give them a winning end to a poor season.

Jones — Irwin (Craddock 89), Okoronkwo, Butler, Naylor (Rae 71) — Newton (Ganea 60), Ince, Cameron, Kennedy — Camara, Cort *Subs not used* Oakes, Iversen *Booked* Ince *Sent off* Ince 67
Referee **S Bennett**

NATIONWIDE LEAGUE

FIRST DIVISION

CHAMPIONS
Norwich City
RUNNERS-UP
West Bromwich Albion

PROMOTED VIA PLAY-OFFS
Crystal Palace

RELEGATED
Walsall
Bradford City
Wimbledon

PFA TEAM OF THE SEASON
Robert Green (Norwich City)

Phil Jagielka (Sheffield United)
Danny Gabbidon (Cardiff City)
Malky Mackay (Norwich City)
Julio Arca (Sunderland)

Tim Cahill (Millwall)
Jason Koumas (West Brom Albion)
Michael Carrick (West Ham)
Andy Reid (Nottingham Forest)

Robert Earnshaw (Cardiff City)
Andrew Johnson (Crystal Palace)

Chirpy Canary: the smile on the face of Iwan Roberts says it all as Norwich City — the first division champions — salute their fans at Carrow Road

Saturday August 9 2003

Bradford 2 Norwich 2; Burnley 2 C Palace 3; Derby 0 Stoke 3; Ipswich 1 Reading 1; Millwall 2 Wigan 0; Nott'm Forest 2 Sunderland 0; Preston 1 West Ham 2; Rotherham 0 Cardiff 0; Sheffield Utd 0 Gillingham 0; Walsall 4 West Brom 1; Wimbledon 3 Crewe 1

Saturday August 16

Cardiff 0 Bradford 2; Coventry 0 Walsall 0; Crewe 1 Ipswich 0; C Palace 1 Watford 0; Gillingham 0 Derby 0; Norwich 2 Rotherham 0; Reading 3 Nott'm Forest 0; Stoke 2 Wimbledon 1; Sunderland 0 Millwall 1; West Brom 4 Burnley 1; West Ham 0 Sheffield Utd 0; Wigan 1 Preston 1

Saturday August 23

Bradford 0 Gillingham 1; Burnley 0 Wigan 2; Derby 2 Reading 3; Ipswich 1 Coventry 1; Millwall 1 Crewe 1; Nott'm Forest 1 Cardiff 2; Preston 0 Sunderland 2; Rotherham 1 West Ham 0; Sheffield Utd 1 Norwich 0; Walsall 1 Stoke 1; Watford 0 West Brom 1; Wimbledon 1 C Palace 3

Monday August 25

Cardiff 4 Derby 1; Crewe 1 Walsall 0; Gillingham 0 Burnley 3; Reading 0 Rotherham 0; Sunderland 2 Watford 0; West Brom 1 Preston 0

Tuesday August 26

C Palace 1 Sheffield Utd 2; Norwich 3 Wimbledon 2; Stoke 0 Millwall 0; West Ham 1 Bradford 0; Wigan 1 Ipswich 0

Wednesday August 27

Coventry 1 Nott'm Forest 3

Saturday August 30

Bradford 0 Sunderland 4; Burnley 1 Crewe 0; Derby 0 West Brom 1; Ipswich 1 West Ham 2; Millwall 1 C Palace 1; Nott'm Forest 2 Norwich 0; Preston 0 Stoke 0; Rotherham 0 Wigan 3; Sheffield Utd 2 Coventry 1; Walsall 1 Cardiff 1; Watford 2 Gillingham 2; Wimbledon 0 Reading 3

Saturday September 6

Gillingham 4 Millwall 3; Stoke 1 Burnley 2

Saturday September 13

Bradford 2 Preston 1; Cardiff 5 Gillingham 0; Coventry 4 Stoke 2; Norwich 2 Burnley 0; Nott'm Forest 3 Sheffield Utd 1; Rotherham 0 Crewe 2; Sunderland 2 C Palace 1; Walsall 0 Derby 1; Watford 3 Millwall 1; West Brom 4 Ipswich 0; West Ham 1 Reading 0; Wimbledon 2 Wigan 4

Tuesday September 16

Burnley 0 Nott'm Forest 3; Crewe 0 West Ham 3; C Palace 1 Gillingham 1 Norwich 2; Ipswich 2 Walsall 1; Millwall 2 Wimbledon 0; Preston 4 Coventry 2; Reading 2 Cardiff 1; Sheffield Utd 5 Rotherham 0; Stoke 3 Sunderland 1; Wigan 1 West Brom 0

Wednesday September 17

Derby 3 Watford 2

AT CARROW ROAD AT THE START of last season, they were mulling over some old bones. Fortunately for Norwich City, they were not the variety found at Elland Road, where sufficient skeletons popped out of the cupboard to keep the entire cast and family friends of *101 Dalmatians* nourished for years.

The East Anglian bones were more refined — there was a hint of class and it was an educational process, too — and it was eventually reflected in Norwich's edifying progress to the first-division championship. To increase the capacity of Carrow Road and further the club's development, Norwich had to fund an archaeological dig on a site of historical importance that was located where the foundations for a new stand were to be laid. The £300,000 it cost represented something of a gamble, the first of several that paid off handsomely during a season of Norfolk nirvana.

On the face of it, recruiting Peter Crouch and Darren Huckerby, on loan from Aston Villa and Manchester City respectively, was not the most inspirational of moves by Nigel Worthington, the Norwich manager. Yet the two Premiership lightweights galvanised the squad to such an extent that aspirations altered dramatically before Christmas.

Two years previously, Norwich had squeezed into the play-offs only to lose to Birmingham City on penalties in Cardiff. Now, far from being satisfied with a meagre sixth position, all eyes and ambitions were trained on the top. Crouch departed and for a while the board's resolve was tested as Huckerby returned to City and was the subject of a bid by West Bromwich Albion.

However, it was another virtuoso performance from the Nottingham-born forward that tipped the balance in his favour, a goal and a thrilling contribution in a 4-1 home defeat of Cardiff in mid-December.

It might have been a swansong — until Norwich stumped up £750,000, a calculated risk since they needed the income from Premiership football to pay his reported weekly salary of around £30,000. Yet the sense of purpose was restored. A 2-0 victory away to Ipswich Town, their arch-rivals, lifted Norwich to the top of the table and a sequence of only four defeats in the remaining 24 league games kept them there and secured the title and a return to the Premiership after nine seasons away.

For West Bromwich, the absence was just one season. Gary Megson's side began inauspiciously with a 4-1 defeat away to Walsall on a hot August afternoon. Their penultimate match, away to Stoke City, brought a replica trouncing. Mercifully for their fans, in between a more resilient Albion emerged. True, the "boing,

Koumas takes charge in West Brom's crucial win away to Sunderland

boing" goal celebrations were often restricted to one a game and watching paint dry sometimes became a serious alternative to afternoons at The Hawthorns, but Megson, impervious to the criticism, can rightly bask in the achievement.

As can Iain Dowie, the Crystal Palace manager. When he took charge in December, Palace were nineteenth and a talented but unfulfilled squad flirted with relegation. A 1-0 home defeat to Millwall on Boxing Day did not augur well, yet the former Northern Ireland forward traded a few home truths and then allowed his players to trade punches as part of an unorthodox training regime.

The pugilists came out fighting, too, sneaking sixth position thanks chiefly to Brian Deane, the West Ham United forward, whose header denied Wigan Athletic the last play-off place in injury time on the final day of the season. And how did Dowie and Palace repay that selfless act? By beating West Ham in the final. Flaming ingrates, as Alf Garnett might have put it.

Many thought — or hoped, given their style of football — that Nottingham Forest would be in the shake-up at the top of the table. Paul Hart, the manager, had fashioned a side brimming with talent that reached the play-offs the previous season, but the naivety of youth could not sustain another challenge. After a run that brought them just two wins in 22 games, Hart was dismissed in February. Joe Kinnear replaced him and steered Forest to safety. Bryan Robson was hopeful of similar results with Bradford City. His first game in charge in November certainly nourished the ambition. On a bitterly cold Friday night, West Yorkshire welcomed Robson and Bradford, after being two goals down, recovered to beat Millwall 3-2.

It could not last given the club's financial state and it did not. Bradford were relegated along with Wimbledon and Walsall, where, curiously, Colin Lee was sacked with just a handful of games left.

Saturday September 20
Burnley 4 Bradford 0; Crewe 3 Nott'm Forest 1; C Palace 2 West Brom 2; Derby 2 Sunderland 1; Gillingham 2 West Ham 0; Ipswich 4 Wimbledon 1; Millwall 2 Walsall 1; Preston 4 Rotherham 1; Reading 1 Coventry 2; Sheffield Utd 5 Cardiff 3; Stoke 1 Norwich 1; Wigan 1 Watford 0

Saturday September 27
Bradford 1 Sheffield Utd 2; Cardiff 3 Crewe 0; Coventry 1 Wigan 1; Norwich 2 C Palace 1; Nott'm Forest 1 Derby 1; Rotherham 2 Rotherham 1; Sunderland 2 Reading 0; Walsall 2 Preston 1; Watford 2 Ipswich 2; West Brom 1 Stoke 0; Wimbledon 2 Burnley 2

Sunday September 28
West Ham 1 Millwall 1

Monday September 29
Walsall 2 Gillingham 1

Tuesday September 30
Bradford 1 Derby 2; Cardiff 0 Wigan 0; Norwich 2 Reading 1; Rotherham 3 Stoke 0; Sunderland 3 Ipswich 2; West Brom 2 Millwall 1; Watford 1 Burnley 1; Wimbledon 1 Sheffield Utd 2

Wednesday October 1
Coventry 2 Crewe 0; Nott'm Forest 0 Preston 1; West Ham 3 C Palace 0

Saturday October 4
Burnley 3 Walsall 1; Crewe 0 Watford 1; C Palace 2 Cardiff 1; Derby 0 West Ham 1; Gillingham 0 West Brom 2; Ipswich 2 Rotherham 1; Millwall 2 Coventry 1; Preston 1 Wimbledon 0; Reading 2 Bradford 2; Stoke 2 Nott'm Forest 1; Sheffield Utd 0 Sunderland 1; Wigan 1 Norwich 1

Saturday October 11
Bradford 0 Ipswich 1; Derby 2 Wigan 2; Rotherham 0 Millwall 0

Tuesday October 14
Crewe 2 Bradford 2; C Palace 1 Derby 1; Ipswich 6 Burnley 1; Millwall 0 Preston 1; Nott'm Forest 2 Rotherham 2; Reading 2 Gillingham 1; Sunderland 0 Cardiff 0; Watford 1 Walsall 1; West Brom 0 Sheffield Utd 2; Wigan 2 Stoke 1

Wednesday October 15
Coventry 1 Wimbledon 0; West Ham 1 Norwich 1

Saturday October 18
Coventry 1 Cardiff 3; Crewe 3 Derby 0; C Palace 1 Rotherham 1; Ipswich 1 Stoke 0; Millwall 2 Sheffield Utd 0; Nott'm Forest 6 Wimbledon 0; Reading 3 Preston 2; Sunderland 1 Walsall 0; Watford 1 Bradford 0; West Brom 1 Norwich 0; West Ham 2 Burnley 2; Wigan 1 Gillingham 0

Tuesday October 21
Crewe 2 Preston 1; C Palace 3 Ipswich 4; Norwich 2 Derby 1; Reading 0 Walsall 1; Sunderland 0 Rotherham 0; Watford 1 Coventry 1; West Brom 0 Wimbledon 1; Wigan 1 Sheffield Utd 1

Wednesday October 22
West Ham 1 Nott'm Forest 1

Friday October 24
Sheffield Utd 1 Reading 2

Saturday October 25
Bradford 1 Nott'm Forest 2; Burnley 1 Millwall 1; Cardiff 0 West Ham 0; Derby 1 Coventry 3; Gillingham 1 C Palace 0; Norwich 1 Sunderland 0; Preston 1 Ipswich 1; Rotherham 0 West Brom 3; Stoke 1 Crewe 1; Walsall 2 Wigan 0; Wimbledon 1 Watford 3

FINAL TABLE

		HOME					AWAY						
Team	P	W	D	L	F	A	W	D	L	F	A	P	GD
NORWICH	46	18	3	2	44	15	10	7	6	35	24	94	40
WEST BROM	46	14	5	4	34	16	11	6	6	30	26	86	22
SUNDERLAND	46	13	8	2	33	15	9	5	9	29	30	79	17
WEST HAM	46	12	7	4	42	20	7	10	6	25	25	74	22
IPSWICH	46	12	3	8	49	36	9	7	7	35	36	73	12
CRYSTAL PALACE	46	10	8	5	34	25	11	2	10	38	36	73	11
WIGAN	46	11	8	4	29	16	7	9	7	31	29	71	15
SHEFFIELD UTD	46	11	6	6	37	25	9	5	9	28	31	71	9
READING	46	11	6	6	29	25	9	4	10	26	32	70	-2
MILLWALL	46	11	8	4	28	15	7	7	9	27	33	69	7
STOKE	46	11	7	5	35	24	7	5	11	23	31	66	3
COVENTRY	46	9	9	5	34	22	8	5	10	33	32	65	13
CARDIFF	46	10	6	7	40	25	7	8	8	28	33	65	10
NOTT'M FOREST	46	8	9	6	33	25	7	6	10	28	33	60	3
PRESTON	46	11	7	5	43	29	4	7	12	26	42	59	-2
WATFORD	46	9	8	6	31	28	6	4	13	23	40	57	-14
ROTHERHAM	46	8	8	7	31	27	5	7	11	22	34	54	-8
CREWE	46	11	3	9	33	26	3	8	12	24	40	53	-9
BURNLEY	46	9	6	8	37	32	4	8	11	23	45	53	-17
DERBY	46	11	5	7	39	33	2	8	13	14	34	52	-14
GILLINGHAM	46	10	1	12	28	34	4	8	11	20	33	51	-19
WALSALL	46	8	7	8	29	31	5	5	13	16	34	51	-20
BRADFORD	46	6	3	14	23	35	4	3	16	15	34	36	-31
WIMBLEDON	46	3	4	16	21	40	5	1	17	20	49	29	-48

LEADING SCORERS

		League	FAC	CC	Total
Andy Johnson	Crystal Palace	27+1	0	4	32
Marlon Harewood	West Ham United	25	1	0	26
Robert Earnshaw	Cardiff City	21	0	5	26
Robert Blake	Burnley	19	2	1	22
Leon McKenzie	Norwich City	19	0	0	22
Dean Ashton	Crewe Alexandra	19	0	1	20
Gary McSheffrey	Coventry City	19	1	0	20
Nathan Ellington	Wigan Athletic	18	0	1	19
Ricardo Fuller	Preston North End	17	2	0	19
Shefki Kuqi	Ipswich Town	16	1	0	17
Onandi Lowe	Coventry City	16	0	1	17

Figures after the + sign indicate play-off goals
Harewood's total includes 12 league goals for Nottingham Forest
McKenzie's total includes 10 league and
3 LDV Vans Trophy goals for Peterborough United
McSheffrey's total includes 8 league goals for Luton Town
Kuqi's total includes 5 league goals for Sheffield Wednesday
Lowe's total includes 15 league and
1 Carling Cup goal for Rushden & Diamonds

FIRST DIVISION RESULTS

HOME \ AWAY	BRADFORD CITY	BURNLEY	CARDIFF CITY	COVENTRY CITY	CREWE ALEXANDRA	CRYSTAL PALACE	DERBY COUNTY	GILLINGHAM	IPSWICH TOWN	MILLWALL	NORWICH CITY	NOTTINGHAM FOREST	PRESTON NORTH END	READING	ROTHERHAM UNITED	SHEFFIELD UNITED	STOKE CITY	SUNDERLAND	WALSALL	WATFORD	WEST BROMWICH ALBION	WEST HAM UNITED	WIGAN ATHLETIC	WIMBLEDON
BRADFORD CITY		1-2	0-1	1-0	2-1	1-2	1-2	0-1	0-1	3-2	2-2	1-2	2-1	2-1	0-2	1-2	0-2	0-4	1-1	2-0	0-1	1-2	0-0	2-3
BURNLEY	4-0		1-1	1-2	1-0	2-3	1-0	1-0	4-2	1-1	3-5	0-3	1-1	3-0	1-1	3-2	0-1	1-2	3-1	2-3	1-1	1-1	0-2	2-0
CARDIFF CITY	0-2	2-0		0-1	3-0	0-2	4-1	5-0	2-3	1-3	2-1	0-0	2-2	2-3	3-2	2-1	3-1	4-0	0-1	3-0	1-1	0-0	0-0	1-1
COVENTRY CITY	0-0	4-0	1-3		2-0	2-1	2-0	2-2	1-1	4-0	0-2	1-3	4-1	1-2	1-1	0-1	4-2	1-1	0-0	0-0	1-0	1-1	1-1	1-0
CREWE ALEXANDRA	2-2	3-1	0-1	3-1		2-3	3-0	1-1	1-0	1-2	1-3	3-1	2-1	1-0	0-0	0-1	2-0	3-0	1-0	0-1	1-2	0-3	2-3	1-0
CRYSTAL PALACE	0-1	0-0	2-1	1-1	1-3		1-1	1-0	3-4	0-1	1-0	1-0	1-1	2-2	1-1	1-2	6-3	3-0	1-0	1-0	2-2	1-0	1-3	3-1
DERBY COUNTY	3-2	2-0	2-2	1-3	0-0	2-1		2-1	2-2	2-0	0-4	4-2	5-1	2-3	1-0	2-0	0-3	1-1	0-1	3-2	0-1	0-1	2-2	3-1
GILLINGHAM	1-0	0-3	1-2	2-5	2-0	1-0	0-0		1-2	4-3	1-2	2-1	0-1	0-1	2-0	0-3	3-1	1-3	3-0	1-0	0-2	2-0	0-3	1-2
IPSWICH TOWN	3-1	6-1	1-1	1-1	6-4	1-3	2-1	3-4		1-3	0-2	1-2	2-0	1-1	2-1	3-0	1-0	1-0	2-1	4-1	2-3	1-2	1-3	4-1
MILLWALL	1-0	2-0	0-0	2-1	1-1	1-1	0-0	1-2	0-0		0-0	1-0	0-1	2-1	2-0	1-1	2-1	2-1	1-2	1-1	1-1	4-1	2-0	2-0
NORWICH CITY	0-1	2-0	4-1	1-1	1-0	2-1	2-1	3-0	3-1	3-1		1-0	3-2	2-1	2-0	1-0	1-0	5-0	1-2	0-0	1-1	2-0	3-2	
NOTTINGHAM FOREST	2-1	1-1	1-2	0-1	2-0	3-2	1-1	0-0	1-1	2-2	2-0		0-1	0-1	2-2	3-1	0-0	3-3	1-1	0-3	0-2	1-0	6-0	
PRESTON NORTH END	1-0	5-3	2-2	4-2	0-0	4-1	3-0	0-0	1-1	1-2	0-0	2-2		2-1	4-1	3-3	1-0	0-2	1-2	2-1	3-0	1-2	2-4	1-0
READING	2-2	2-2	2-1	1-2	1-1	0-3	3-1	2-1	1-1	1-0	0-1	3-0	3-2		0-0	2-1	0-0	0-2	0-1	2-1	1-0	2-0	1-0	0-3
ROTHERHAM UNITED	1-2	3-0	0-0	2-0	0-2	1-2	0-0	1-1	1-3	0-0	4-4	1-1	1-0	5-1		1-1	3-0	0-2	2-0	1-1	0-3	1-0	0-3	3-1
SHEFFIELD UNITED	2-0	1-0	5-3	2-1	2-0	0-3	1-1	0-0	1-1	2-1	1-0	1-2	2-0	1-2	5-0		0-1	0-1	2-0	2-2	1-2	3-3	1-1	2-1
STOKE CITY	1-0	1-2	2-3	1-0	1-1	0-1	2-1	0-0	2-0	0-0	1-1	2-1	3-0	0-2	2-2	3-1		3-2	3-1	4-1	0-2	1-1	2-1	
SUNDERLAND	3-0	1-1	0-0	0-0	1-1	2-1	2-1	2-1	3-2	0-1	1-0	0-3	3-3	2-0	0-0	3-0	1-1		1-0	2-0	0-1	2-0	1-1	2-1
WALSALL	1-0	0-1	1-1	1-6	1-1	0-0	0-1	2-1	1-3	1-1	1-3	4-1	2-1	1-1	3-2	0-1	1-1	1-3		0-1	4-1	1-1	2-0	1-0
WATFORD	1-0	1-1	2-1	1-1	2-1	1-5	2-1	2-2	1-2	3-1	1-2	1-1	1-0	1-0	0-2	1-3	2-2	1-1			0-1	0-0	1-1	4-0
WEST BROMWICH ALBION	2-0	4-1	2-1	3-0	2-2	2-0	1-1	1-0	4-1	2-1	1-0	0-2	1-0	0-0	0-1	2-0	1-0	0-0	2-0	3-1		1-1	2-1	0-1
WEST HAM UNITED	1-0	2-2	1-0	2-0	4-2	3-0	0-0	2-1	1-2	1-1	1-1	1-2	1-0	2-1	0-0	0-1	3-2	0-0	4-0	3-4	1-1		2-1	0-1
WIGAN ATHLETIC	1-0	0-0	3-0	2-1	2-3	5-0	2-0	1-0	1-0	0-0	1-1	2-2	1-0	0-2	1-2	1-1	2-1	0-0	1-0	1-0	1-0	1-1		0-1
WIMBLEDON	2-1	2-2	0-1	0-3	3-1	1-3	1-0	1-2	1-2	0-1	0-1	0-0	3-3	0-3	1-2	1-2	0-1	1-2	0-1	1-3	0-0	1-1	2-4	

PLAYER OF THE SEASON
Darren Huckerby   Norwich City

Jason Koumas, of West Bromwich Albion and Wales, may have been the most talented player at this level, but Huckerby's contribution has been remarkable in many respects. A lack of consistency and a reputation for movement resembling a headless chicken by a player not noted for his mental agility have often betrayed him, but at Carrow Road he translated that turn of pace into match-winning performances on a regular basis. He scored 14 goals but created many more. Ultimately, the club followed in Huckerby's often unguided footsteps and threw caution to the wind by purchasing him. A fruitful mutual admiration society.

David McVay

Tuesday October 28
Cardiff 3 Watford 0

Saturday November 1
Burnley 1 Cardiff 1; Coventry 1 West Ham 1; Crewe 1 Reading 0; Ipswich 3 Gillingham 4; Millwall 1 Nott'm Forest 0; Preston 3 Derby 0; Stoke 2 Sheffield Utd 2; Walsall 1 Norwich 3; Watford 1 Rotherham 0; West Brom 0 Sunderland 0; Wigan 5 C Palace 0; Wimbledon 2 Bradford 1

Tuesday November 4
Gillingham 1 Sunderland 3; Preston 2 Watford 1; Sheffield Utd 2 Crewe 0; Walsall 4 Nott'm Forest 1

Wednesday November 5
Coventry 0 Bradford 0

Saturday November 8
Bradford 1 Walsall 1; Cardiff 3 Stoke 1; C Palace 1 Preston 1; Derby 2 Ipswich 2; Gillingham 2 Crewe 0; Norwich 3 Millwall 1; Nott'm Forest 1 Watford 1; Reading 1 Wigan 0; Rotherham 3 Wimbledon 1; Sheffield Utd 1 Burnley 0; Sunderland 0 Coventry 0; West Ham 3 West Brom 4

Saturday November 15
Derby 2 Burnley 0; Gillingham 1 Wimbledon 2; Norwich 1 Watford 2; Reading 1 Millwall 0

Saturday November 22
Burnley 1 Rotherham 1; Coventry 2 Gillingham 2; Crewe 3 Sunderland 0; Ipswich 3 Sheffield Utd 0; Millwall 0 Derby 0; Preston 0 Norwich 0; Stoke 1 Bradford 0; Walsall 0 C Palace 0; Watford 0 West Ham 0; West Brom 0 Reading 0; Wigan 2 Nott'm Forest 2; Wimbledon 0 Cardiff 1

Tuesday November 25
Burnley 3 Reading 0; Cardiff 1 West Brom 1; Norwich 1 Coventry 1; Stoke 0 C Palace 1; Wimbledon 1 West Ham 1

Saturday November 29
Bradford 3 Millwall 2; Cardiff 2 Ipswich 3; C Palace 1 Coventry 1; Derby 3 Wimbledon 1; Gillingham 3 Stoke 1; Norwich 1 Crewe 0; Nott'm Forest 0 West Brom 3; Reading 2 Watford 1; Rotherham 2 Walsall 0; Sheffield Utd 2 Preston 0; Sunderland 1 Burnley 1; West Ham 4 Wigan 0

Tuesday December 2
Rotherham 2 Coventry 0; Sunderland 1 Wigan 1

Wednesday December 3
Nott'm Forest 1 Ipswich 1

Saturday December 6
Burnley 3 Sheffield Utd 2; Crewe 1 Gillingham 1; Ipswich 2 Derby 1; Millwall 0 Norwich 0; Preston 4 C Palace 1; Stoke 2 Cardiff 3; Walsall 1 Bradford 0; Watford 1 Nott'm Forest 1; West Brom 1 West Ham 1; Wigan 0 Reading 2; Wimbledon 1 Rotherham 2

Monday December 8
Coventry 1 Sunderland 1

Tuesday December 9
Bradford 0 West Brom 1; Cardiff 2 Preston 2; C Palace 1 Crewe 3; Sheffield Utd 2 Walsall 0; West Ham 0 Stoke 1

Saturday December 13
Burnley 1 Coventry 2; C Palace 1 Nott'm Forest 0; Gillingham 0 Preston 1; Millwall 0 Ipswich 0; Norwich 4 Cardiff 1; Rotherham 0 Derby 0; Sheffield Utd 2 Watford 2; Stoke 3 Reading 0; West Brom 2 Crewe 2; West Ham 3 Sunderland 2; Wigan 1 Bradford 0; Wimbledon 0 Walsall 1

Saturday December 20
Bradford 0 Rotherham 2; Cardiff 1 Millwall 3; Coventry 1 West Brom 0; Crewe 2 Wigan 3; Preston 5 Burnley 3; Reading 0 C Palace 3; Sunderland 2 Wimbledon 1; Walsall 1 West Ham 1; Watford 1 Stoke 3

Sunday December 21
Ipswich 0 Norwich 2

Friday December 26
Cardiff 0 Walsall 1; Coventry 0 Sheffield Utd 1; Crewe 3 Burnley 1; C Palace 0 Millwall 1; Gillingham 1 Watford 0; Norwich 1 Nott'm Forest 0; Reading 0 Wimbledon 3; Stoke 1 Preston 1; Sunderland 3 Bradford 0; West Brom 1 Derby 1; West Ham 1 Ipswich 2; Wigan 1 Rotherham 2

Sunday December 28
Bradford 1 Coventry 0; Burnley 0 Stoke 1; Derby 0 Norwich 4; Ipswich 1 C Palace 3; Millwall 1 Gillingham 2; Nott'm Forest 0 West Ham 2; Preston 0 Crewe 0; Rotherham 0 Sunderland 2; Sheffield Utd 1 Wigan 1; Walsall 1 Reading 1; Watford 2 Cardiff 1

Tuesday December 30
Wimbledon 0 West Brom 0

Friday January 9 2004
West Brom 2 Walsall 0

Saturday January 10
Cardiff 3 Rotherham 2; Coventry 0 Watford 0; Crewe 1 Wimbledon 0; C Palace 0 Burnley 0; Gillingham 0 Sheffield Utd 3; Norwich 0 Bradford 1; Reading 1 Ipswich 1; Stoke 2 Derby 1; Sunderland 1 Nott'm Forest 0; West Ham 1 Preston 2; Wigan 0 Millwall 0

Saturday January 17
Bradford 0 Cardiff 1; Burnley 1 West Brom 1; Derby 2 Gillingham 1; Ipswich 6 Crewe 4; Millwall 2 Sunderland 1; Nott'm Forest 0 Reading 1; Preston 2 Wigan 4; Rotherham 4 Norwich 4; Sheffield Utd 3 West Ham 3; Walsall 1 Coventry 6; Watford 1 C Palace 5; Wimbledon 0 Stoke 1

Saturday January 24
Bradford 1 C Palace 2

Wednesday January 28
Derby 2 Sheffield Utd 0

Saturday January 31
Cardiff 0 Nott'm Forest 0; Coventry 1 Ipswich 1; Crewe 1 Millwall 2; C Palace 3 Wimbledon 1; Gillingham 1 Bradford 0; Norwich 1 Sheffield Utd 0; Reading 3 Derby 1; Stoke 3 Walsall 2; West Brom 3 Watford 1; West Ham 2 Rotherham 1; Wigan 0 Burnley 0

Saturday February 7
Bradford 1 West Ham 2; Burnley 1 Gillingham 0; Derby 2 Cardiff 2; Ipswich 1 Wigan 3; Millwall 1 Stoke 1; Nott'm Forest 0 Coventry 1; Preston 3 West Brom 0; Rotherham 5 Reading 1; Sheffield Utd 0 C Palace 3; Walsall 1 Crewe 1; Watford 2 Sunderland 2; Wimbledon 0 Norwich 1

Saturday February 14
Coventry 0 Norwich 2; C Palace 6 Stoke 3; Ipswich 3 Bradford 1; Nott'm Forest 3 Walsall 3; Watford 2 Preston 0; West Brom 2 Cardiff 1; Wigan 2 Derby 0

Saturday February 21
Bradford 2 Crewe 1; Burnley 4 Ipswich 2; Cardiff 4 Sunderland 0; Derby 2 C Palace 1; Gillingham 0 Reading 1; Norwich 1 West Ham 1; Preston 1 Millwall 2; Rotherham 1 Nott'm Forest 1; Sheffield Utd 1 West Brom 2; Stoke 2 Wigan 1; Walsall 0 Watford 1; Wimbledon 0 Coventry 3

Tuesday February 24
Crewe 0 Sheffield Utd 1; Millwall 2 Rotherham 1; Reading 2 Burnley 2

MATCH OF THE SEASON

Rotherham United 4 Norwich City 4
Millmoor, Saturday January 17 2004
Ron Lewis

MATCHES OFTEN TURN ON key refereeing decisions. The penalty given against Shaun Barker, the Rotherham United right back, for a challenge on Darren Huckerby, as the Norwich City forward ran towards the byline just before half-time, turned an entertaining match into a thriller. It led to a brawl by the players' tunnel and to Ronnie Moore and Guy Branston, the Rotherham manager and defender respectively, being sent off in the dressing-room. However, the home side still had enough fight left to come within moments of inflicting the first division leaders' third successive defeat.

The assertion by Nigel Worthington, the Norwich manager, that Huckerby "had his legs taken away" merely showed that he cannot have had a view of the 44th-minute incident at all, or that he hoped nobody else had. Barker did seem to lean on Huckerby, putting it into a "probably was" file. Certainly, Michael Jones, the referee, who had an excellent game, particularly during a tense second half, did not hesitate in awarding the penalty and Huckerby slotted it home.

The decision, though, infuriated the Rotherham players and supporters, who had only moments before seen Martin Butler level the score at 2-2 with a bullet header from a cross by Chris Sedgwick, the second goal of a hat-trick. Moore was furious enough to chase Huckerby at half-time to remonstrate with him at the mouth of the tunnel. "I spoke to Huckerby and said, 'I hope you're pleased at yourself, diving in the box', and he said, 'have a look at the video'," Moore said. "That's all I said. I didn't see what went on after that as I was halfway down the tunnel."

"A lot of pushing and shoving," was what Worthington said that he saw, as he held back Huckerby from the melee, which threatened to spill over into the crowd after the concertina tunnel had been forced back. Worthington also said that there was no truth in the accusation that Leon McKenzie, his striker, had spat in the face of Branston, leading to the defender "putting his hand in McKenzie's face", in Moore's words.

"The fourth official has reported Guy for violent conduct and sent him off," Moore said. "I would love to know what he sent me off for, because I haven't got a clue." Huckerby declined to share his thoughts on the incidents afterwards and he might have been better served had he kept his mouth shut rather than engaging in a pointless and rather ugly slanging match with a Rotherham supporter as he left the ground.

Having begun the first half well, Rotherham took the lead when Butler guided in his first goal after 28 minutes, only to fall behind five minutes later, Iwan Roberts firing in after Gary Holt's clever

Butler, Rotherham's hero in the high-scoring draw against Norwich, slips the first of his three goals past Green during a controversial encounter

header and McKenzie tapping in Huckerby's cross after Mike Pollitt had done well to stop his initial header. Rotherham battled for everything in the second half and got their reward when Butler won a challenge with Robert Green, the goalkeeper, for a cross by John Mullin. But the home side could not hold on and Damien Francis banged in the equalising goal from a corner in the final minute of normal time.

Millmoor is not spoken about as a hotbed of football, largely because, well, Rotherham play there. Their home defeat by Northampton Town in midweek was scarcely given credit as an upset. But while Moore may have Rotherham overachieving as a club, they are underachieving as a team and, on this form, look better than their league position. Despite being without a win in 2004, Norwich still sit two points clear at the top of the table and do not lack the fighting qualities needed to gain promotion.

ROTHERHAM UNITED (4-4-2): M Pollitt — S Barker, C Swailes, G Branston, P Hurst — C Sedgwick, D Garner, J Mullin, A Monkhouse (sub: S Minto, 46min) — D Byfield, M Butler. **Substitutes not used:** G Montgomery, R Barker, S Talbot, P Warne. **Booked:** Butler, Sedgwick. **Sent off:** Branston.
NORWICH CITY (4-3-3): R Green — M Edworthy (sub: M Rivers, 86), C Fleming, M Mackay, A Drury — G Holt, D Francis, P McVeigh (sub: I Henderson, 77) — L McKenzie, I Roberts, D Huckerby. **Substitutes not used:** P Crichton, P Mulryne, J Brennan.

Wednesday February 25
Nott'm Forest 0 Gillingham 0

Saturday February 28
Coventry 2 Derby 0; C Palace 1 Gillingham 0; Ipswich 2 Preston 0; Millwall 2 Burnley 0; Nott'm Forest 2 Bradford 1; Reading 2 Sheffield Utd 1; Watford 4 Wimbledon 0; West Brom 0 Rotherham 1; West Ham 1 Cardiff 0; Wigan 1 Walsall 0

Tuesday March 2
Burnley 1 West Ham 1; Cardiff 0 Coventry 1; Norwich 0 West Brom 0; Preston 2 Reading 1; Sheffield Utd 2 Millwall 1; Stoke 2 Ipswich 0; Wimbledon 0 Nott'm Forest 1

Wednesday March 3
Derby 0 Crewe 0; Walsall 1 Sunderland 3

Saturday March 6
Burnley 1 Preston 1; C Palace 2 Reading 2; Gillingham 2 Nott'm Forest 1; Rotherham 1 Bradford 2; Stoke 3 Watford 1; West Brom 3 Coventry 0; West Ham 0 Walsall 0; Wigan 2 Crewe 3

Sunday March 7
Norwich 3 Ipswich 1

Tuesday March 9
Bradford 2 Watford 0; West Ham 5 Wimbledon 0

Wednesday March 10
Sunderland 3 Preston 3

Saturday March 13
Bradford 0 Wigan 0; Cardiff 2 Norwich 1; Coventry 4 Burnley 0; Crewe 1 West Brom 2; Derby 1 Rotherham 0; Ipswich 1 Millwall 3; Nott'm Forest 3 C Palace 2; Preston 0 Gillingham 0; Reading 0 Stoke 0; Sunderland 2 West Ham 0; Walsall 1 Wimbledon 0; Watford 0 Sheffield Utd 2

Tuesday March 16
Cardiff 2 Reading 3; Norwich 3 Gillingham 0; Rotherham 1 Sheffield Utd 1; Sunderland 1 Stoke 1; Walsall 1 Ipswich 3; Watford 2 Derby 1; West Brom 2 Wigan 1

Wednesday March 17
Coventry 4 Preston 1; Nott'm Forest 1 Burnley 1; West Ham 4 Crewe 2

Saturday March 20
Crewe 0 Cardiff 1; C Palace 1 Norwich 0; Derby 4 Nott'm Forest 2; Gillingham 2 Rotherham 0; Ipswich 4 Watford 1; Preston 1 Walsall 2; Reading 0 Sunderland 2; Sheffield Utd 2 Bradford 0; Wigan 2 Coventry 1

Sunday March 21
Millwall 4 West Ham 1

Tuesday March 23
Crewe 2 Stoke 0; Sheffield Utd 1 Derby 1; Sunderland 2 Gillingham 1

Wednesday March 24
Wimbledon 0 Millwall 1

Saturday March 27
Bradford 1 Burnley 2; Cardiff 2 Sheffield Utd 1; Coventry 1 Reading 2; Norwich 1 Stoke 0; Nott'm Forest 2 Crewe 0; Rotherham 1 Preston 0; Sunderland 2 Derby 1; Walsall 1 Millwall 1; Watford 1 Wigan 1; West Brom 2 C Palace 0; West Ham 2 Gillingham 1; Wimbledon 1 Ipswich 2

Saturday April 3
Burnley 3 Norwich 5; Crewe 0 Rotherham 0; Derby 0 Walsall 1; Gillingham 1 Cardiff 2; Preston 1 Bradford 0; Reading 2 West Ham 0; Sheffield Utd 1 Nott'm Forest 2; Stoke 1 Coventry 0; Wigan 0 Wimbledon 1

GOING UP ON A DOWNER

Malcolm Boyden

THERE IS AN AWKWARD atmosphere at the inaugural meeting of the Christian branch of the West Bromwich Albion Supporters Club. Two fans are involved in a nail-biting play-off as the evening culminates in a quick-fire quiz. The Reverend Ken Hipkiss, Albion Chaplain and chairman of the branch, nervously prepares a tie-break question. "Which way do the stripes go on a Baggies shirt?" he asks the contestents. "Up or down?"

For the dearly beloved who have gathered at the Bethel Christian Fellowship Church in Oldbury, it is the dilemma of the decade. For a club that has adopted the "boing" as its signature chant, a quirky little ditty during which fans bounce up and down, the topsy-turvy nature of Albion's recent past is the only topic of conversation.

On the one hand, confused Baggies relish the prospect of Premiership football. Bouncing back at the first time of asking was a tremendous achievement by Gary Megson, the manager and Lord of the Manor of West Bromwich. Even when you are boinging, it is easier to go down than come back up. Just ask Ian "The Belly" Kitson, a 20st factory worker from Darlaston who has become famous on the Birmingham Road End for his bare-belly boinging. But this time, promotion was different. If it is possible to go up on a low, Albion achieved it in 2003-04.

Before the season started, Megson warned his players that only automatic promotion would do. Expectation among the fans was at an all-time high. So, when the mission was successfully accomplished, why was there such an air of discontent among The Hawthorns faithful? What was so different about going up in 2004 compared with the emotionally charged promotion campaigns of days gone by?

For a start, there was the reality of what lies ahead. Albion are all too aware of the pitfalls of the Premiership. There are no promises in this "promised land".

If you stand on the corner of The Hawthorns, where the recently demolished Woodman pub stood for more than a century, you can faintly detect the ghostly grumbles of disgruntled Baggies fans from promotions past. "You're all doomed," they warn, "The Premier League is bent. One penalty all season, referees against you every game, you're not on *The Premiership* until after midnight and you're down by Christmas."

Then there is the way that this promotion was achieved. Albion secured their passage with four matches remaining — then lost the last three. After Lord Megson's parade in Oldbury, the fans came crashing to earth with a "Belly" flop, leaving a ginger ale taste in the

Wembley 1993 and Ossie Ardiles's side, roared on by thousands of West Brom fans, celebrate an old-fashioned promotion

Joy on the field last season, but many fans had their doubts

doom in The Woodman would mutter into the dregs of their Bathams Best Bitter. So overhauling their arch-rivals, Wolverhampton Wanderers, for the second automatic promotion place was enough to make the editors of *Grorty Dick*, the club's fanzine, reconsider their publication's Latin motto, *Semper Te Fallant*, which translates as "They always let you down".

Even the ghosts of The Woodman — who have seen it all from W. G. Richardson to Cyrille Regis and Ronnie Allen to Jeff Astle — were taken aback by the ecstasy that followed the last game of the season, at home to Crystal Palace. "How did that happen?" they questioned with begrudging contentment.

Other promotion seasons have been greeted with equal amounts of elation. In 1993, the Baggies came out of the second division with a Wembley play-off final win over Port Vale. It was a victory that changed the course of Albion's history, heralding the rebirth of a club in crisis. The Baggies had not played at Wembley for nearly 25 years and the fans, many of whom had never seen their heroes perform in the shadow of the twin towers, turned the day into an unforgettable jamboree.

In 1976, when "the Messiah", Johnny Giles, led the club back into the old first division, there was also a real sense of jubilation. In those days you did not go into the top flight just to make up the numbers. At the very least, a lengthy spell among the elite was expected. The more ambitious even suggested instant honours — a concept that seems laughable in today's world of Old Trafford vol-au-vents and Thierry Henry.

This time around, the party had fizzled out before it even started. On the final day of the season, a little Scottish woman was struggling to blow up her yellow and green balloons in the Birmingham Road End. With one last puff, she turned to watch her heroes traipse off the field after receiving their runners-up medals. She summed up the mood perfectly. "We should be the ones receiving the medals for having to sit through it every week," she declared, palming her last balloon towards a now empty field of fading dreams.

She will still be boinging shoulder to shoulder with "The Belly" as Albion attempt to confound the Woodman ghosts and survive in the Premiership. Maybe the Christian branch of the West Bromwich Albion Supporters Club might like to have a word with him upstairs. After all, in the words *The Lord's My Shepherd* — Albion's other traditional anthem — "In pastures green, he leadeth me ..."

He might well have to.

mouths of those beginning to get a penchant for champagne. Even "The Belly" himself was missing from the run-in, banned after revealing a little too much flesh in the match away to Stoke City.

Ultimately, Albion did what they had to do to. The players were given a task and stuck to it rigidly. It was effective, not attractive. It was premeditated, not pretty. It was disciplined, not delectable. It was organised and definitely not awesome.

But the last day of the season — a 2-0 home defeat by Nottingham Forest — was the ultimate anticlimax. "The Premier League? You're having a laugh," the visiting supporters taunted. What was left of the home crowd then had to fake elation for a muted medal ceremony.

Of course, there was some euphoria. Albion's last-minute victory away to Sunderland, which virtually guaranteed them promotion, should be included in every football tactics manual as a masterclass in how not to lose a vital game. The bubbly flowed the following weekend after a narrow home win over Bradford City, but like the team, it soon went flat.

The atmosphere was in stark contrast to two years ago when Albion last won promotion, a feat some ardent Baggies still consider to be the "creme de la creme". At the start of the 2001-02 season, the Albion expect-o-meter had peaked at zero. After 16 years in the wilderness, supporters had resigned themselves to a lifetime in the lower echelons. "We'll never get back into the Premiership, not in my lifetime," the merchants of

PLAY-OFFS

Semi-finals: First legs
CRYSTAL PALACE (0) **3**
Shippperley 52, Butterfield 64, Johnson 87
25,287

Friday May 14
SUNDERLAND (0) **2**
Stewart 51 (pen), Kyle 85

IPSWICH TOWN (0) **1**
Bent 57

Saturday May 15
WEST HAM UNITED (0) **0**
28,435

Second legs
SUNDERLAND (2) **2**
Kyle 42, Stewart 45
34,536

Monday May 17
CRYSTAL PALACE (0) **1**
Powell 90

(aet; 4-4 on agg; C Palace won 5-4 on pens)

WEST HAM UNITED (0) **2**
Etherington 50, Dailly 71

Tuesday May 18
IPSWICH TOWN (0) **0**
34,002

(West Ham United won 2-1 on agg)

THE FINAL
CRYSTAL PALACE (0) **1**
Shipperley 62

Saturday May 29, Millennium Stadium
WEST HAM UNITED (0) **0**
72,523

Crystal Palace were in danger of relegation when Iain Dowie took over as manager in December and they will be among the candidates to go down again — the difference is that any demotion would be from the Barclays Premiership thanks to this deserved victory over West Ham United. Neil Shipperley, the Palace captain, got the goal worth an estimated £30 million to the club when Stephen Bywater could only parry Andy Johnson's shot. West Ham failed to play to their potential and rarely threatened an equaliser.

CRYSTAL PALACE (4-4-2): N Vaesen — D Butterfield (sub: D Powell, 70min), M Leigertwood, A Popovic, D Granville — W Routledge, A Riihilahti, M Hughes, S Derry — A Johnson, N Shipperley. **Substitutes not used:** C Berthelin, T Black, B Watson, D Freedman. **Booked:** Derry, Hughes, Routledge.
WEST HAM UNITED (4-4-2): S Bywater — T Repka, C Dailly, A Melville, H Mullins — M Harewood (sub: N Reo-Coker, 69), M Carrick, S Lomas, M Etherington — R Zamora (sub: B Deane, 68), D Connolly (sub: D Hutchison, 74). **Substitutes not used:** P Srnicek, R Brevett. **Booked:** Repka, Harewood, Mullins, Etherington.
Referee: G Poll.

Sunday April 4
Ipswich 2 West Brom 3

Tuesday April 6
Gillingham 0 Wigan 3; Rotherham 1 C Palace 2; Wimbledon 1 Sunderland 2

Wednesday April 7
Millwall 0 Cardiff 0

Friday April 9
Norwich 2 Wigan 0; Sunderland 3 Sheffield Utd 0

Saturday April 10
Bradford 2 Reading 1; Cardiff 0 C Palace 2; Coventry 4 Millwall 0; Nott'm Forest 0 Stoke 0; Rotherham 1 Ipswich 3; Walsall 0 Burnley 1; Watford 2 Crewe 1; West Brom 1 Gillingham 0; West Ham 0 Derby 0; Wimbledon 3 Preston 3

Monday April 12
Burnley 2 Watford 3; Crewe 3 Coventry 1; C Palace 1 West Ham 0; Derby 3 Bradford 2; Gillingham 3 Walsall 0; Ipswich 1 Sunderland 0; Millwall 1 West Brom 1; Preston 2 Nott'm Forest 2; Reading 0 Norwich 1; Sheffield Utd 2 Wimbledon 1; Stoke 0 Rotherham 2

Tuesday April 13
Wigan 3 Cardiff 0

Saturday April 17
Bradford 2 Wimbledon 3; Cardiff 2 Burnley 0; C Palace 1 Wigan 1; Derby 5 Preston 1; Gillingham 2 Ipswich 2; Norwich 5 Walsall 0; Nott'm Forest 2 Millwall 2; Reading 1 Crewe 1; Rotherham 1 Watford 1; Sheffield Utd 0 Stoke 1; West Ham 2 Coventry 0

Sunday April 18
Sunderland 0 West Brom 1

Tuesday April 20
Burnley 2 Wimbledon 0; Millwall 1 Watford 2

Wednesday April 21
C Palace 3 Sunderland 0

Saturday April 24
Burnley 1 Derby 0; Coventry 1 Rotherham 1; Crewe 2 C Palace 3; Ipswich 1 Nott'm Forest 2; Millwall 0 Reading 1; Preston 2 Cardiff 2; Stoke 0 West Ham 2; Walsall 0 Sheffield Utd 1; Watford 1 Norwich 2; West Brom 2 Bradford 0; Wigan 0 Sunderland 0; Wimbledon 1 Gillingham 2

Friday April 30
Sheffield Utd 1 Ipswich 1

Saturday May 1
Bradford 0 Stoke 2; Cardiff 1 Wimbledon 1; C Palace 1 Walsall 0; Derby 2 Millwall 0; Gillingham 2 Coventry 5; Norwich 3 Preston 2; Nott'm Forest 1 Wigan 0; Reading 1 West Brom 0; Rotherham 3 Burnley 0; Sunderland 1 Crewe 1; West Ham 4 Watford 0

Tuesday May 4
Stoke 4 West Brom 1; Sunderland 1 Norwich 0

Sunday May 9
Burnley 1 Sunderland 2; Coventry 2 C Palace 1; Crewe 1 Norwich 3; Ipswich 1 Cardiff 1; Millwall 1 Bradford 0; Preston 3 Sheffield Utd 3; Stoke 0 Gillingham 0; Walsall 3 Rotherham 2; Watford 1 Reading 0; West Brom 0 Nott'm Forest 2; Wigan 1 West Ham 1; Wimbledon 1 Derby 0

NATIONWIDE LEAGUE

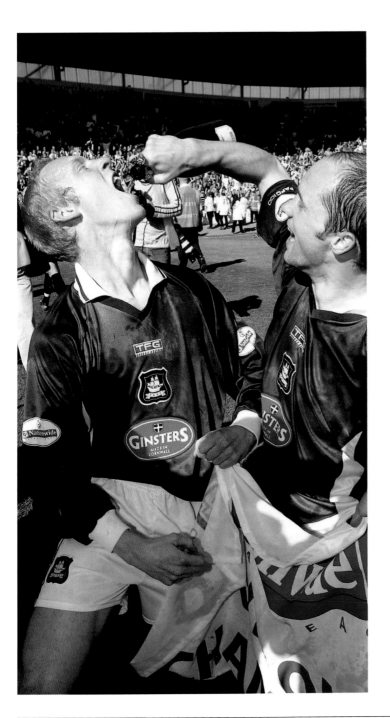

SECOND DIVISION

CHAMPIONS
Plymouth Argyle
RUNNERS-UP
Queens Park Rangers

PROMOTED VIA PLAY-OFFS
Brighton & Hove Albion

RELEGATED
Grimsby Town
Rushden & Diamonds
Notts County
Wycombe Wanderers

PFA TEAM OF THE SEASON
Steve Phillips (Bristol City)

Graham Coughlan (Plymouth Arg)
Danny Cullip (Brighton)
Louis Carey (Bristol City)
Gino Padula (QPR)

Brian Tinnion (Bristol City)
Richard Wellens (Blackpool)
David Friio (Plymouth Arg)
Carlos Edwards (Wrexham)

Scott Taylor (Blackpool)
Leon Knight (Brighton)

Pour relations: Nathan Lowndes
(left) and Marino Keith join the
Home Park party to mark Plymouth
Argyle's championship triumph

THE GAMES

THE REVIEW
Nick Szczepanik

Saturday August 9 2003
Barnsley 1 Colchester 0; Bristol City 5 Notts Co 0;
Luton 3 Rushden 1; Oldham 1 Brighton 3;
Peterborough 3 Hartlepool 4; Plymouth 2 Grimsby 2;
Port Vale 2 Bournemouth 1; QPR 5 Blackpool 0;
Swindon 2 Sheffield Weds 3; Tranmere 4 Brentford 1;
Wrexham 0 Chesterfield 0; Wycombe 1 Stockport 0

Friday August 15
Colchester 0 Swindon 1

Saturday August 16
Blackpool 3 Wycombe 2; Bournemouth 2 Barnsley 2;
Brentford 0 Peterborough 3; Chesterfield 1 Bristol City 1;
Grimsby 1 Port Vale 2; Hartlepool 0 Tranmere 0;
Notts Co 0 Wrexham 1; Rushden 2 Plymouth 1;
Sheffield Weds 2 Oldham 2; Stockport 1 Luton 2

Monday August 18
Brighton 2 QPR 1

Saturday August 23
Barnsley 1 Brighton 0; Bristol City 1 Hartlepool 1;
Luton 1 Grimsby 2; Oldham 2 Blackpool 3;
Peterborough 0 Sheffield Weds 1; Plymouth 3 Stockport
1; Port Vale 4 Colchester 3; QPR 1 Bournemouth 0;
Swindon 4 Notts Co 0; Tranmere 1 Rushden 2;
Wrexham 1 Brentford 0; Wycombe 3 Chesterfield 3

Monday August 25
Blackpool 0 Barnsley 2; Bournemouth 2 Swindon 2;
Brentford 2 Oldham 1; Brighton 2 Luton 0; Chesterfield
1 Plymouth 0; Grimsby 3 Wycombe 1; Hartlepool 2 Port
Vale 0; Notts Co 0 Peterborough 1; Rushden 3 QPR 3;
Sheffield Weds 2 Wrexham 3; Stockport 1 Tranmere 1

Tuesday August 26
Colchester 2 Bristol City 1

Saturday August 30
Barnsley 1 Notts Co 1; Bristol City 1 Grimsby 0; Luton 3
Hartlepool 2; Oldham 3 Rushden 2; Peterborough 1
Stockport 2; Plymouth 3 Brighton 3; Port Vale 1
Brentford 0; QPR 3 Chesterfield 0; Swindon 3 Blackpool
2; Tranmere 1 Colchester 1; Wrexham 0 Bournemouth 1

Monday September 1
Wycombe 1 Sheffield Weds 2

Saturday September 6
Bournemouth 0 Bristol City 0; Brentford 1 Plymouth 3;
Brighton 2 Swindon 2; Chesterfield 0 Barnsley 2;
Colchester 2 QPR 2; Grimsby 1 Peterborough 1;
Hartlepool 0 Oldham 0; Notts Co 1 Luton 1; Rushden 2
Wycombe 0; Sheffield Weds 3 Tranmere 0; Stockport 2
Port Vale 2

Friday September 12
Hartlepool 8 Grimsby 1

Saturday September 13
Blackpool 1 Bournemouth 2; Chesterfield 0 Notts Co 1;
Colchester 1 Brighton 0; Oldham 1 Bristol City 1;
Plymouth 2 Luton 1; Port Vale 3 Barnsley 1; QPR 0
Wycombe 0; Rushden 0 Brentford 1; Sheffield Weds 2
Stockport 2; Swindon 1 Wrexham 0; Tranmere 0
Peterborough 0

Tuesday September 16
Barnsley 1 Oldham 1; Bournemouth 1 Sheffield Weds 0;
Brentford 0 Blackpool 0; Brighton 1 Chesterfield 0;
Bristol City 2 Tranmere 0; Grimsby 1 Swindon 2; Luton 2
Port Vale 0; Notts Co 1 Rushden 3; Peterborough 2
Plymouth 2; Stockport 1 Hartlepool 2; Wrexham 0
QPR 2; Wycombe 1 Colchester 2

EVERY SILVER LINING has a black cloud — just ask Plymouth Argyle. Underachievers for most of their recent history, they are back in the top half of the senior football pyramid for the first time since 1992 after winning the second division championship and are now, in theory, only 46 games away from a first appearance in the top flight. Unfortunately, even before Argyle had won promotion, they had lost their manager, Paul Sturrock, who was lured away by Southampton in March.

Sturrock had arrived in October 2000 and revitalised an ailing squad, taking the third-division title within two years and building a side without stars, but with strong contributions from all areas. Last season the team's 85 goals, the highest total in the division, were spread around between 14 players, but only two broke into double figures and only one of them, Micky Evans, was a forward. It was a formula that survived the departure of its architect during the promotion run-in, as Sturrock's backroom staff kept the team on course until a successor was appointed.

That appointment was delayed until April 20, producing a pub quiz question of the future: which manager won a championship in his first match? The answer is Bobby Williamson, who took over four days before Plymouth clinched the title by beating Queens Park Rangers 2-0 at Home Park.

If Argyle are without top-level pedigree, then QPR, the runners-up, will feel they are a step closer to being back where they belong. The losing play-off finalists in 2003, they avoided the end-of-season lottery this time by finishing a point ahead of third-placed Bristol City. Ian Holloway, their manager and former midfield player, was one of the characters of the season, with his post-match comparisons of margins of victory to various types of female companionship, his visit to anger-management courses and his decision to allow supporters to attend pre-match team talks. The players, including Marc Bircham, a proud Rangers fan whose blue and white dyed hair proclaimed his allegiance, and Kevin Gallen, the top scorer with 17 goals, were happy to go along with it all — even the ballet sessions.

For long periods, it seemed that Bristol City might catch them, especially when they embarked on a run of 11 successive victories between December 20 and February 21. However, they won only one of the next seven games, fell agonisingly short of QPR and had to settle for the play-offs. Although they edged past Hartlepool United, who were looking for a second successive promotion, in the semi-finals, they lost Lee Peacock, their top scorer, to injury. That proved costly as they were beaten in a close final at the Millennium

QPR striker Paul Furlong is thwarted by Rhys Evans, of Bristol City

Stadium by a stubborn Brighton & Hove Albion side, who won 1-0 thanks to a late penalty from Leon Knight, the division's top scorer with 26 goals.

Brighton seem intent on redefining the term yo-yo club. Third division champions in 2001 and second division champions a year later, they found the first division a promotion too far in the 2002-03 season. However, they recovered well from relegation and the departure of Steve Coppell, the manager, to Reading in the autumn. His replacement, Mark McGhee, brought players through from the youth team to refresh the side and his team took fourth place, thanks largely to their record at the idiosyncratic Withdean Stadium, an unnerving venue for visiting teams. Replacing Bobby Zamora, who had been sold to Tottenham Hotspur in the summer, with Knight — only 5ft 4in — maintained the flow of goals, while the defence kept clean sheets in seven of their last eight games.

The other teams relegated from the first division with Brighton fared less well. Grimsby Town suffered a second successive drop thanks to a late goal by Chesterfield on the final day of the season, but perhaps even more surprising was the poor showing of Sheffield Wednesday. With their vast and loyal following, they had been expected to stage a recovery under Chris Turner, their former goalkeeper, but seldom threatened to rise above mid-table.

The outstanding individual performance of the season was also one of the briefest. James Hayter, of Bournemouth, took the field as a substitute against Wrexham at Dean Court on February 24 after 84 minutes and left it clutching the match ball after scoring what was hailed as the fastest hat-trick in the history of League football, between the 86th and 88th minutes. Too bad his parents had left early to get the ferry back to their home on the Isle of Wight and missed the whole thing. Every silver lining ...

Saturday September 20
Barnsley 1 Swindon 1; Bournemouth 2 Rushden 1; Brentford 2 Hartlepool 1; Brighton 2 Sheffield Weds 0; Bristol City 0 Port Vale 1; Grimsby 4 Chesterfield 0; Luton 1 QPR 1; Notts Co 2 Tranmere 2; Peterborough 1 Colchester 2; Stockport 1 Blackpool 3; Wrexham 2 Plymouth 2; Wycombe 2 Oldham 5

Saturday September 27
Blackpool 2 Notts Co 1; Chesterfield 1 Brentford 2; Colchester 1 Bournemouth 0; Hartlepool 0 Brighton 0; Oldham 3 Luton 0; Plymouth 2 Barnsley 0; Port Vale 1 Wycombe 1; QPR 1 Bristol City 1; Rushden 2 Stockport 2; Sheffield Weds 0 Grimsby 0; Swindon 2 Peterborough 0; Tranmere 1 Wrexham 2

Tuesday September 30
Blackpool 0 Grimsby 1; Chesterfield 1 Bournemouth 1; Colchester 1 Brentford 1; Hartlepool 2 Wrexham 0; Oldham 2 Stockport 0; Plymouth 0 Bristol City 1; Port Vale 3 Peterborough 0; QPR 4 Barnsley 0; Rushden 1 Brighton 3; Tranmere 2 Wycombe 1

Wednesday October 1
Sheffield Weds 2 Notts Co 1; Swindon 2 Luton 2

Saturday October 4
Barnsley 2 Rushden 0; Bournemouth 2 Hartlepool 2; Brentford 0 Sheffield Weds 3; Brighton 3 Blackpool 0; Bristol City 2 Swindon 1; Grimsby 0 QPR 1; Notts Co 3 Colchester 0; Peterborough 2 Oldham 2; Stockport 0 Chesterfield 0; Wycombe 0 Plymouth 0; Wrexham 2 Port Vale 1

Monday October 6
Luton 3 Tranmere 1

Friday October 10
Bristol City 1 Peterborough 1; Hartlepool 1 Sheffield Weds 1

Saturday October 11
Brighton 3 Grimsby 0; Colchester 1 Blackpool 1; Luton 3 Wycombe 1; Notts Co 0 Bournemouth 0; Oldham 2 Port Vale 1; Plymouth 6 Tranmere 0; Rushden 2 Chesterfield 1; Swindon 1 Stockport 2

Saturday October 18
Blackpool 4 Hartlepool 0; Bournemouth 1 Brighton 0; Brentford 4 Luton 2; Chesterfield 3 Swindon 0; Grimsby 2 Colchester 0; Peterborough 0 QPR 0; Port Vale 1 Plymouth 5; Sheffield Weds 0 Rushden 0; Stockport 2 Notts Co 2; Tranmere 2 Oldham 1; Wrexham 0 Bristol City 0; Wycombe 1 Barnsley 2

Tuesday October 21
Blackpool 2 Rushden 3; Bournemouth 6 Luton 3; Brentford 4 Brighton 0; Chesterfield 1 Hartlepool 2; Grimsby 2 Notts Co 0; Peterborough 2 Barnsley 3; Port Vale 2 QPR 0; Stockport 1 Colchester 3; Tranmere 1 Swindon 0; Wycombe 3 Bristol City 0; Wrexham 4 Oldham 0

Wednesday October 22
Sheffield Weds 1 Plymouth 3

Saturday October 25
Barnsley 0 Grimsby 0; Brighton 0 Stockport 1; Bristol City 1 Sheffield Weds 1; Colchester 1 Chesterfield 0; Hartlepool 1 Wycombe 1; Luton 1 Peterborough 1; Notts Co 2 Brentford 0; Oldham 1 Bournemouth 1; Plymouth 1 Blackpool 0; QPR 1 Tranmere 1; Rushden 2 Wrexham 3; Swindon 0 Port Vale 0

Tuesday October 28
Barnsley 2 Wrexham 1

FINAL TABLE

	P	HOME					AWAY					P	GD
		W	D	L	F	A	W	D	L	F	A		
PLYMOUTH	46	17	5	1	52	13	9	7	7	33	28	90	44
QPR	46	16	7	0	47	12	6	10	7	33	33	83	35
BRISTOL CITY	46	15	6	2	34	12	8	7	8	24	25	82	21
BRIGHTON	46	17	4	2	39	11	5	7	11	25	32	77	21
SWINDON	46	12	7	4	41	23	8	6	9	35	35	73	18
HARTLEPOOL	46	10	8	5	39	24	10	5	8	37	37	73	15
PORT VALE	46	15	6	2	45	28	6	4	13	28	35	73	10
TRANMERE	46	13	7	3	36	18	4	9	10	23	38	67	3
BOURNEMOUTH	46	11	8	4	35	25	6	7	10	21	26	66	5
LUTON	46	14	6	3	44	27	3	9	11	25	39	66	3
COLCHESTER	46	11	8	4	33	23	6	5	12	19	33	64	-4
BARNSLEY	46	7	12	4	25	19	8	5	10	29	39	62	-4
WREXHAM	46	9	6	8	27	21	8	3	12	23	39	60	-10
BLACKPOOL	46	9	5	9	31	28	7	6	10	27	37	59	-7
OLDHAM	46	9	8	6	37	25	3	13	7	29	35	57	6
SHEFFIELD WEDS	46	7	9	7	25	26	6	5	12	23	38	53	-16
BRENTFORD	46	9	5	9	34	38	6	12	18	31	53	53	-17
PETERBOROUGH	46	5	8	10	36	33	7	8	8	22	25	52	0
STOCKPORT	46	6	8	9	31	36	5	11	7	31	34	52	-8
CHESTERFIELD	46	9	7	7	34	31	3	8	12	15	40	51	-22
GRIMSBY	46	10	5	8	36	26	3	6	14	19	55	50	-26
RUSHDEN & D	46	9	5	9	37	34	4	4	15	23	40	48	-14
NOTTS CO	46	6	9	8	32	27	4	3	16	18	51	42	-28
WYCOMBE	46	5	7	11	31	39	1	12	10	19	36	37	-25

LEADING SCORERS

		League	FAC	CC	Total
Leon Knight	Brighton	25+1	0	0	27
Steve McPhee	Port Vale	25	1	0	27
Scott Taylor	Blackpool	16	6	3	27
Sam Parkin	Swindon Town	19+1	0	3	23
Paul Heffernan	Notts County	20	1	0	21
Tommy Mooney	Swindon Town	19	0	1	20
Eugene Dadi	Tranmere Rovers	16	2	1	19
Kevin Gallen	QPR	17	0	0	17
Scott McGleish	Colchester United	10	1	0	17

Figures after the + sign indicate play-off goals

Knight's total includes 1 LDV Vans Trophy goal

McPhee's total includes 1 LDV Vans Trophy goal

Taylor's total includes 2 LDV Vans Trophy goals

McGleish's total includes 6 LDV Vans Trophy goals

SECOND DIVISION RESULTS

HOME \ AWAY	BARNSLEY	BLACKPOOL	BOURNEMOUTH	BRENTFORD	BRIGHTON & HOVE ALB	BRISTOL CITY	CHESTERFIELD	COLCHESTER UNITED	GRIMSBY TOWN	HARTLEPOOL UNITED	LUTON TOWN	NOTTS COUNTY	OLDHAM ATHLETIC	PETERBOROUGH UNITED	PLYMOUTH ARGYLE	PORT VALE	QUEENS PARK RANGERS	RUSHDEN & DIAMONDS	SHEFFIELD WEDNESDAY	STOCKPORT COUNTY	SWINDON TOWN	TRANMERE ROVERS	WREXHAM	WYCOMBE WANDERERS
BARNSLEY		3-0	1-1	0-2	1-0	0-1	0-1	1-0	0-0	2-2	0-0	1-1	1-1	0-1	1-0	0-0	3-3	2-0	1-1	3-3	1-1	2-0	2-1	0-0
BLACKPOOL	0-2		1-2	1-1	3-1	1-0	1-0	0-0	0-1	4-0	0-1	2-1	1-1	1-4	0-1	2-1	0-1	2-3	4-1	1-1	2-2	2-1	0-1	3-2
BOURNEMOUTH	2-2	1-2		1-0	1-0	0-0	2-2	1-1	0-0	2-2	6-3	1-0	1-0	1-2	0-2	2-1	1-0	2-1	1-0	0-0	2-2	1-5	6-0	1-0
BRENTFORD	2-1	0-0	1-0		4-0	1-2	1-1	3-2	1-3	2-1	4-2	2-3	2-1	0-3	1-3	3-2	1-1	3-2	0-3	0-2	0-2	2-2	0-1	1-1
BRIGHTON & HOVE ALBION	1-0	3-0	3-0	1-0		1-4	1-0	2-1	3-0	2-0	2-0	1-0	0-0	1-0	2-1	1-1	2-1	0-0	2-0	0-1	2-2	3-0	2-0	4-0
BRISTOL CITY	2-1	2-1	2-0	3-1	0-0		4-0	1-0	1-0	1-1	1-1	5-0	0-2	1-1	1-0	0-1	1-0	1-0	1-1	1-0	2-1	2-0	1-0	1-1
CHESTERFIELD	0-2	1-0	1-1	1-2	0-2	1-1		1-2	4-4	1-2	1-0	0-1	1-1	2-1	1-1	1-0	4-2	2-0	3-1	0-3	3-0	2-2	2-1	2-2
COLCHESTER UNITED	1-1	1-1	1-0	1-1	1-0	2-1	1-0		2-0	1-2	1-1	4-1	2-1	0-0	0-2	1-4	2-2	2-0	3-1	2-1	0-1	1-1	3-1	1-1
GRIMSBY TOWN	6-1	0-2	1-1	1-0	2-1	1-2	4-0	2-0		0-2	3-2	2-0	3-3	1-1	0-0	1-2	0-1	1-0	2-0	1-1	1-2	0-1	1-3	3-1
HARTLEPOOL UNITED	1-2	1-1	2-1	1-2	0-0	1-2	2-0	0-0	8-1		4-3	4-0	0-0	1-0	1-3	2-0	1-4	2-1	1-1	2-2	2-0	0-0	2-0	1-1
LUTON TOWN	0-1	3-2	1-1	4-1	2-0	3-2	1-0	1-0	1-2	3-2		2-0	1-1	1-1	1-1	2-0	1-1	3-1	3-2	2-2	0-3	3-1	3-2	3-1
NOTTS COUNTY	1-1	4-1	0-1	2-0	1-2	1-2	1-1	3-0	3-1	1-0	1-1		1-1	0-1	0-2	3-3	1-3	0-0	4-1	1-2	2-2	0-1	1-1	
OLDHAM ATHLETIC	1-1	2-3	1-1	1-1	1-3	1-1	2-0	0-0	6-0	0-2	3-0	0-1		1-1	4-1	2-1	2-1	3-2	1-0	2-0	0-1	1-1	1-1	2-3
PETERBOROUGH UNITED	2-3	0-1	0-1	0-0	2-2	0-1	0-2	1-2	0-0	3-4	1-2	5-2	2-2		2-2	3-1	0-0	3-1	0-1	1-2	4-2	0-0	6-1	1-1
PLYMOUTH ARGYLE	2-0	1-0	0-0	2-0	3-3	0-1	7-0	2-0	2-2	2-0	2-1	3-0	2-2	2-0		2-1	2-0	3-0	2-0	3-1	2-1	6-0	0-0	2-1
PORT VALE	3-1	2-1	2-1	1-0	1-1	2-1	1-1	4-3	5-1	2-5	1-0	1-0	3-0	1-5			2-0	1-1	3-0	2-2	3-3	2-1	1-0	1-1
QUEENS PARK RANGERS	4-0	5-0	1-0	1-0	2-1	1-1	3-0	2-0	3-0	4-1	1-1	3-2	1-1	1-1	3-0	3-2		1-0	3-0	1-1	1-0	1-1	2-0	0-0
RUSHDEN & DIAMONDS	2-3	0-0	0-3	0-1	1-3	1-1	2-1	4-0	3-1	0-2	2-2	2-1	4-1	0-1	2-1	0-2	3-3		1-2	2-2	2-0	2-1	2-3	2-0
SHEFFIELD WEDNESDAY	2-1	0-1	0-2	1-1	1-1	1-0	0-0	0-1	0-0	1-0	0-0	2-1	2-2	2-0	1-3	2-3	1-3	0-0		2-2	1-1	2-0	2-3	1-1
STOCKPORT COUNTY	2-3	1-3	3-2	1-1	1-1	2-0	0-0	1-3	2-1	1-2	1-2	2-2	1-1	2-0	2-2	1-2	1-2	0-2	2-1		2-4	1-1	0-1	2-0
SWINDON TOWN	1-1	2-2	2-1	2-1	2-1	1-1	2-0	2-0	2-0	1-1	2-2	4-0	1-2	2-0	2-3	0-0	1-1	4-2	2-3	1-2		2-0	1-0	2-0
TRANMERE ROVERS	2-0	1-1	1-1	4-1	1-0	1-0	2-3	1-1	2-1	0-0	1-0	4-1	0-0	3-0	1-0	0-0	1-2	2-2	3-2	1-0	1-2		1-2	2-1
WREXHAM	1-0	4-2	0-1	1-0	0-2	0-0	0-0	0-1	3-0	1-2	2-1	1-0	4-0	2-0	2-2	2-1	0-2	1-1	1-2	0-0	3-2	0-1		0-0
WYCOMBE WANDERERS	1-2	0-3	2-0	1-2	1-1	3-0	3-3	1-2	4-1	3-4	0-0	1-1	2-5	1-2	0-0	1-1	2-2	0-2	1-2	1-1	0-3	1-2	1-1	

PLAYER OF THE SEASON
David Friio   Plymouth Argyle

A player is often best judged by the respect he has among his peers and Steve Fletcher, of Bournemouth, unhesitatingly described Friio as "the Frank Lampard of the second division". The French midfield player, who joined Plymouth Argyle from Valence in December 2000, was the club's top scorer, with 15 league and cup goals, including five in four games in October and a hat-trick in a 7-0 win over Chesterfield, but it was his silky passing that drew most admiration.

Nick Szczepanik

Friday October 31
Wrexham 0 Colchester 1

Saturday November 1
Brentford 2 Barnsley 1; Bristol City 1 Luton 1; Chesterfield 1 Port Vale 0; Notts Co 1 Hartlepool 0; Peterborough 2 Brighton 2; Plymouth 2 Oldham 2; Rushden 3 Grimsby 1; Sheffield Weds 0 Blackpool 1; Stockport 1 QPR 2; Swindon 2 Wycombe 0; Tranmere 1 Bournemouth 1

Tuesday November 11
Blackpool 0 Wrexham 1; QPR 1 Brentford 0

Saturday November 15
Barnsley 2 Tranmere 0; Blackpool 1 Chesterfield 0; Bournemouth 1 Peterborough 2; Brighton 1 Bristol City 4; Colchester 3 Sheffield Weds 1; Grimsby 1 Stockport 1; Hartlepool 2 Rushden 1; Luton 3 Wrexham 2; Oldham 0 Swindon 1; Port Vale 1 Notts Co 0; QPR 3 Plymouth 0; Wycombe 1 Brentford 2

Saturday November 22
Brentford 1 Grimsby 3; Bristol City 2 Barnsley 1; Chesterfield 1 Oldham 1; Notts Co 1 Brighton 2; Peterborough 0 Blackpool 1; Plymouth 2 Hartlepool 0; Rushden 4 Colchester 0; Sheffield Weds 0 Luton 0; Stockport 3 Bournemouth 2; Swindon 1 QPR 1; Tranmere 1 Port Vale 0; Wrexham 0 Wycombe 0

Saturday November 29
Barnsley 3 Stockport 3; Blackpool 1 Bristol City 0; Bournemouth 1 Brentford 0; Brighton 2 Wrexham 0; Colchester 0 Plymouth 2; Grimsby 0 Tranmere 1; Hartlepool 2 Swindon 0; Luton 1 Chesterfield 0; Oldham 0 Notts Co 1; Port Vale 1 Rushden 1; QPR 3 Sheffield Weds 0; Wycombe 1 Peterborough 2

Friday December 12
Brighton 1 Port Vale 1

Saturday December 13
Barnsley 1 Sheffield Weds 1; Blackpool 0 Luton 1; Bournemouth 0 Grimsby 0; Chesterfield 2 Tranmere 2; Colchester 2 Oldham 1; Notts Co 1 Wycombe 1; QPR 4 Hartlepool 1; Rushden 1 Bristol City 1; Stockport 1 Brentford 1; Swindon 2 Plymouth 3; Wrexham 2 Peterborough 0

Saturday December 20
Brentford 0 Swindon 2; Bristol City 1 Stockport 0; Hartlepool 0 Colchester 0; Luton 0 Barnsley 1; Oldham 2 QPR 1; Peterborough 3 Rushden 1; Plymouth 3 Notts Co 0; Sheffield Weds 0 Chesterfield 0; Tranmere 1 Brighton 0; Wycombe 2 Bournemouth 0

Friday December 26
Blackpool 2 Tranmere 1; Bournemouth 0 Plymouth 2; Brentford 1 Bristol City 2; Brighton 4 Wycombe 0; Chesterfield 2 Peterborough 1; Colchester 1 Luton 1; Grimsby 3 Oldham 3; Hartlepool 1 Barnsley 2; Notts Co 3 QPR 3; Rushden 2 Swindon 0; Sheffield Weds 2 Port Vale 3; Stockport 0 Wrexham 1

Sunday December 28
Barnsley 0 Chesterfield 1; Bristol City 2 Bournemouth 0; Luton 2 Notts Co 0; Oldham 0 Hartlepool 2; Peterborough 0 Grimsby 0; Plymouth 2 Brentford 0; Port Vale 2 Stockport 2; QPR 2 Colchester 0; Swindon 2 Brighton 1; Tranmere 2 Sheffield Weds 2; Wrexham 4 Blackpool 2; Wycombe 0 Rushden 2

Saturday January 3 2004
Oldham 1 Brentford 1; Plymouth 7 Chesterfield 0; QPR 1 Rushden 0; Swindon 2 Bournemouth 1; Wrexham 1 Sheffield Weds 2; Wycombe 4 Grimsby 1

Tuesday January 6
Peterborough 5 Notts Co 2

Saturday January 10
Blackpool 0 QPR 1; Bournemouth 2 Port Vale 1;
Brentford 2 Tranmere 2; Brighton 0 Oldham 0;
Chesterfield 2 Wrexham 1; Colchester 1 Barnsley 1;
Grimsby 0 Plymouth 0; Hartlepool 1 Peterborough 0;
Notts Co 1 Bristol City 2; Rushden 2 Luton 2;
Sheffield Weds 1 Swindon 1; Stockport 2 Wycombe 0

Wednesday January 14
Port Vale 2 Blackpool 1

Saturday January 17
Barnsley 1 Bournemouth 1; Bristol City 4 Chesterfield 0;
Luton 2 Stockport 2; Oldham 1 Sheffield Weds 0;
Peterborough 0 Brentford 0; Plymouth 3 Rushden 0;
Port Vale 5 Grimsby 1; QPR 2 Brighton 1; Swindon 2
Colchester 0; Tranmere 0 Hartlepool 0; Wrexham 0
Notts Co 1; Wycombe 0 Blackpool 3

Tuesday January 20
Grimsby 1 Wrexham 3

Saturday January 24
Blackpool 1 Oldham 1; Bournemouth 1 QPR 0;
Brentford 0 Wrexham 1; Brighton 1 Barnsley 0;
Chesterfield 2 Wycombe 2; Hartlepool 1 Bristol City 2;
Notts Co 1 Swindon 2; Sheffield Weds 2
Peterborough 0; Stockport 0 Plymouth 2

Tuesday January 27
Barnsley 3 Blackpool 0; Bristol City 1 Colchester 0;
Port Vale 2 Hartlepool 5; Tranmere 3 Stockport 2

Friday January 30
Sheffield Weds 1 Wycombe 1

Saturday January 31
Blackpool 2 Swindon 2; Brentford 3 Port Vale 2;
Brighton 2 Plymouth 1; Chesterfield 4 QPR 2;
Colchester 1 Tranmere 1; Notts Co 1 Barnsley 1;
Rushden 4 Oldham 1; Stockport 2 Peterborough 2

Saturday February 7
Barnsley 2 Hartlepool 2; Bristol City 3 Brentford 1;
Luton 1 Colchester 0; Peterborough 0 Chesterfield 2;
Plymouth 0 Bournemouth 0; Port Vale 3
Sheffield Weds 0; QPR 3 Notts Co 2; Swindon 4
Rushden 2; Tranmere 1 Blackpool 1; Wrexham 0
Stockport 0; Wycombe 1 Brighton 1

Sunday February 8
Oldham 6 Grimsby 0

Tuesday February 10
Luton 2 Brighton 0

Saturday February 14
Bournemouth 1 Notts Co 0; Brentford 1 QPR 1;
Chesterfield 2 Rushden 0; Grimsby 2 Brighton 1;
Peterborough 0 Bristol City 1; Port Vale 1 Oldham 0;
Sheffield Weds 1 Hartlepool 0; Stockport 2 Swindon 4;
Wrexham 1 Barnsley 0; Wycombe 0 Luton 0

Tuesday February 17
Grimsby 1 Bristol City 2; Tranmere 3 Plymouth 0

Friday February 20
Hartlepool 1 Blackpool 1; QPR 1 Peterborough 1

MATCH OF THE SEASON

Bristol City 1 Queens Park Rangers 0
Ashton Gate, Saturday April 3 2004
Tom Dart

IT'S ALL GONE QUIET for Bristol City. Danny Wilson, the manager, has banned his squad from talking to the media. If the odd player does speak, he will not be allowed to comment on the issue that everybody wants to discuss: promotion from the Nationwide League second division. "Whoever has the most focus will get the rewards at the end," Wilson said. "I think we're very focused at the moment and I don't want any distractions."

City do appear to be easily befuddled. They went on an 11-match winning streak in mid-season, then suddenly displayed all the focus of Mr Magoo, with one victory in seven matches before Saturday. Five of their final six games are against promotion hopefuls, so Wilson's players will bottle up their thoughts and try to avoid bottling it on the pitch. By contrast, Ian Holloway, the Queens Park Rangers manager, has found that unfettering his emotions in the right way can lift tension.

The anger-management classes that Holloway has taken for a BBC programme seem to be working. He has released his frustrations through painting and singing. "I felt calm out there; it didn't look like my lads felt the same way," he said. "I had a little laugh and joke with the City fans today. They've got that little song about me, 'Cheer up Holloway', and I have cheered up, to be perfectly honest. I'm still very chirpy — you can ask my good lady. I've learnt a lot over the past few months."

Holloway was far more interesting after the match than his team were during it. "I was quite bored with the whole game," he said. "Being a Bristolian, I wanted my team to do me proud and unfortunately I don't think they did. But there you go, that's life. I'm not going to take it personally, like I would have done in the past."

Two returning old boys were the key protagonists. Scott Murray, the winger re-signed from Reading, supplied the cross for Christian Roberts to score; Tony Thorpe, back at Ashton Gate but now in blue-and-white hoops, was clean through late on but his shot was saved. QPR stay second in the table and if they win their game in hand, away to Tranmere Rovers on Tuesday, they will be three points clear of City with a far superior goal difference. "If is a big word," Holloway said. The presence of Audley Harrison in the crowd was a reminder of what Holloway and Wilson already know. As the boxing cliche has it, talking the talk at this stage of the campaign is one thing; walking the walk is another.

BRISTOL CITY (4-4-2): S Phillips — L Carey, D Coles, A Butler, M Hill — S Murray, T Doherty, B Tinnion (sub: L Wilkshire, 68min), M Bell — L Peacock, C Roberts (sub: L Miller, 81). **Substitutes not used:** J Burnell, C Fortune, A Rougier. **Booked:** Doherty.
QUEENS PARK RANGERS (4-4-2): L Camp — M Bignot, C Carlisle, A Gnohere, M Rose — M Rowlands, R Johnson (sub: S Palmer, 64), M Bean (sub: J Cureton, 46), K McLeod (sub: A Thorpe, 74) — P Furlong, K Gallen. **Substitutes not used:** C Day, R Edghill.

Bristol City's Lee Peacock shields the ball from Clarke Carlisle, of QPR

Saturday February 21
Barnsley 0 Wycombe 0; Brighton 3 Bournemouth 0;
Bristol City 1 Wrexham 0; Colchester 2 Grimsby 0;
Luton 4 Brentford 1; Notts Co 4 Stockport 1; Oldham 1
Tranmere 1; Plymouth 2 Port Vale 1; Rushden 1
Sheffield Weds 2; Swindon 2 Chesterfield 0

Tuesday February 24
Bournemouth 6 Wrexham 0; Colchester 1 Port Vale 4;
Grimsby 3 Luton 2; Rushden 2 Tranmere 1

Saturday February 28
Blackpool 0 Plymouth 1; Bournemouth 1 Oldham 0;
Brentford 2 Notts Co 3; Grimsby 6 Barnsley 1;
Peterborough 1 Luton 2; Sheffield Weds 1 Bristol City 0;
Stockport 1 Brighton 1; Wrexham 1 Rushden 1;
Wycombe 3 Hartlepool 4

Tuesday March 2
Barnsley 0 Peterborough 1; Brighton 1 Brentford 0;
Bristol City 1 Wycombe 1; Colchester 2 Stockport 1;
Hartlepool 2 Chesterfield 0; Notts Co 3 Grimsby 1;
Plymouth 2 Sheffield Weds 0; QPR 3 Port Vale 2;
Rushden 0 Blackpool 0

Wednesday March 3
Swindon 2 Tranmere 0

Saturday March 6
Barnsley 0 Luton 0; Blackpool 2 Port Vale 1;
Bournemouth 1 Wycombe 0; Colchester 1 Hartlepool 2;
Notts Co 0 Plymouth 0; QPR 1 Oldham 1; Rushden 0
Peterborough 1; Stockport 2 Bristol City 0; Swindon 2
Brentford 1; Wrexham 3 Grimsby 0

Sunday March 7
Chesterfield 3 Sheffield Weds 1

Wednesday March 10
Brighton 3 Tranmere 0

Friday March 12
Bristol City 1 Rushden 0

Saturday March 13
Brentford 0 Stockport 2; Grimsby 1 Bournemouth 1;
Hartlepool 1 QPR 4; Luton 3 Blackpool 2; Oldham 0
Colchester 0; Peterborough 6 Wrexham 1; Plymouth 2
Swindon 1; Port Vale 1 Brighton 1; Sheffield Weds 2
Barnsley 1; Tranmere 2 Chesterfield 3; Wycombe 1
Notts Co 1

Tuesday March 16
Blackpool 1 Brentford 1; Chesterfield 0 Brighton 2;
Colchester 1 Wycombe 1; Hartlepool 2 Stockport 2;
Oldham 1 Barnsley 1; Plymouth 2 Peterborough 0;
Port Vale 1 Luton 0; QPR 2 Wrexham 0; Rushden 2
Notts Co 1

Wednesday March 17
Sheffield Weds 0 Bournemouth 2; Swindon 2 Grimsby 0

Saturday March 20
Barnsley 0 Port Vale 0; Brentford 3 Rushden 2;
Brighton 2 Colchester 1; Bristol City 0 Oldham 2;
Grimsby 0 Hartlepool 2; Luton 1 Plymouth 1; Notts Co 1
Chesterfield 1; Peterborough 0 Tranmere 0; Stockport 1
Sheffield Weds 0; Wrexham 3 Swindon 2; Wycombe 2
QPR 2

Tuesday March 23
Chesterfield 1 Colchester 2

Wednesday March 24
Bournemouth 1 Blackpool 2; Tranmere 1 Bristol City 0

FAR CORNERS OF THE EMPIRE

David McVay

CUE THE FAMILIAR THEME tune. Now for the introduction in hushed tones. You are now entering football's equivalent of the twilight zone. Your journey will take you to the far reaches of the game's galaxy and the darkest reaches of your imagination, where men are men and sheep are, OK, sheep. Do not be afraid, but do not linger. You may find that you feel at home. And that is dangerous.

The plagiarism, with apologies to *The Twilight Zone*, the cult American sci-fi series of the 1960s, is entirely intentional. There was another similar series that attempted to explain events beyond our understanding called *The Outer Limits*, a fitting description of a variety of geographically-challenged football outposts at the extremities of the compass points in England.

From Carlisle and Workington in the far North West to Plymouth and Torquay in Devon and then East as far as the dry land will take you to Boston and up the coast a bit to Hull, the black holes that suck in players but seldom radiate success are abundant.

Everything is relative, of course, and Plymouth Argyle, Torquay United and Hull City experienced the euphoria of promotion from the Nationwide League second and third divisions last season. In doing so they generated a rare passion and, in the case of Hull, average attendances of more than 16,000. But is the upwardly mobile venture an enduring one?

Explaining why clubs on the peripheral routes of the country's main trunk roads seldom sustain progress is almost as difficult and tortuous as the trip that leads to their grounds. As someone born in Workington, farmed out to Torquay United for a month and who then ended an uneventful career at Boston United, I may be able to shed some light on the issue. In 1977 Ronnie Fenton, then the Notts County manager, sent me to Torquay on loan. If the Faeroe Isles had been a little more advanced in its football back then, he would certainly have bought me a one-way ticket just to get me out of his sight.

As every lower-division supporter knows, the travel was horrendous. If I had kept a diary for one week, a couple of its entries might have read thus: Monday: training in the morning, preparing for game away to Huddersfield tomorrow night. Light lunch then set off north at 1.30pm. Arrive Huddersfield 7pm. Evening meal. Bed. Tuesday: morning, training. Draw 1-1 at Leeds Road. Fish and chips on the coach after game. Drop off three players at Gordano Services on the M5, Bristol. Birds are twittering as we alight coach at Plainmoor. Drive back to digs. It is 6.35am. Morning Milkie. Bed.

Even with the advent of better vehicles, more motorways and an allegedly streamlined transport infrastructure, the journeys north and south from Carlisle to Plymouth remain tests of stamina. "The miles we put in are unbelievable," Graham Coughlan, the Dublin-born Plymouth defender, said. "I knew Plymouth was down south, but I didn't know how far down. At times I think we'd be better off playing in the French League."

Often clubs tend to attract the wrong sort of player, one looking for a "cushy little number" among either the palm trees of Torquay or the more pastoral pleasures of Carlisle. In Torquay in particular, many old lags spotted the potential of climbing aboard what was known as the Devon Express. A couple of seasons at Home Park and Plainmoor before retirement behind the bar of a local hostelry or a guest house.

It is the consequence not only of the travel, which deters many professionals, but the fact that many of these outposts have been regarded by players as sleepy hollows with a *laissez-faire* ethic to the fore.

Inevitably, the core support that is so vital to development dwindles. "My cry for years has been, 'where are the people'?" Mike Bateson, the Torquay chairman, said. "It's the nature of a seaside town — a lot of migrant workers. The ones that do stay haven't got the loyalty to us. Seaside towns also attract a lot of retired people from outside the area."

They have a feast of fans in Hull and Plymouth. Success, though, has been strictly rationed. Plymouth have never appeared in the top flight, yet the city has a

Will Hull's impressive KC Stadium ever stage top-flight football? Plymouth, meanwhile, are dreaming of higher things

population of around 250,000 — nearly twice that of Middlesbrough and Blackburn and bigger than Southampton, Portsmouth and Wolverhampton. With a catchment area in the East Riding in excess of half a million residents, Hull remains the most populated city in Europe never to have secured a promotion to the highest echelons in the game.

Carlisle United, on the other hand, did enjoy a fleeting moment of fame in 1974 when Chris Balderstone captained his side briefly to the top of the first division before relegation saw them restored to the second division after a famous season in Cumbria.

Having lost their league status last May, John Courtenay, the Carlisle chairman, is optimistic of a swift return. "Whatever happens we will be full-time," Courtenay said. "We are getting gates over 8,000 at home and we took 3,600 to Rochdale with us. The supporters deserve it. They will come back next season no matter what. And so will we."

In keeping with tradition, however, the fix usually is merely short term, which in itself exacerbates the already inherent problems of location for the likes of Plymouth, Hull and Torquay.

Once the good times grind to a halt, it is not only the players and spectators who head swiftly for the exit. Observe the list of managers at those three clubs, and most likely the directors, too. Ambition is the driving force of professional sport and nowhere is it more exposed and apparent than in the ruthless world of football management.

Howard Wilkinson learnt his trade at York Street with Boston; Graham Taylor honed his skills at Sincil Bank with Lincoln City. Did either ever imagine they would stay for ever? Did Paul Sturrock ponder very long when the chance to bail out of Plymouth for the bright lights of Southampton in the Premiership beckoned? A negative in both cases.

Football outposts are the stepping stones to greater things and the comfy sofas to soften the blow of failure or imminent retirement for most players. Occasionally the natural order of things is interrupted, but sadly, the historical precedents tend to point to this being a brief encounter. If we were meant to fly, nature would have given us wings. If clubs such as Hull and Plymouth were meant to fly higher, nature would have located them more favourably and not in isolation.

I still have fond memories of Torquay. A month of sun, palm trees and fresh seaside air. Just the tonic to revive me before I returned to Meadow Lane shortly after Fenton had been sacked.

Back in Torquay, however, normal service was restored in the twilight zone.

PLAY-OFFS

Semi-finals: First legs
HARTLEPOOL UTD (0) **1**
Porter 74
7,211

Saturday May 15
BRISTOL CITY (1) **1**
Rougier 5

Sunday May 16
SWINDON TOWN (0) **0**
14,034

BRIGHTON (0) **1**
Carpenter 71

Second legs
BRISTOL CITY (0) **2**
Goodfellow 88, Roberts 90
18,434

Wednesday May 19
HARTLEPOOL UTD (0) **1**
Sweeney 63

(Bristol City won 3-2 on agg)

BRIGHTON (0) **1**
Virgo 120
6,876

Thursday May 20
SWINDON TOWN (0) **2**
Parkin 81, Fallon 97

(aet; 2-2 on agg; Brighton win 4-3 on pens)

THE FINAL

BRIGHTON (0) **1**
Knight 84 (pen)

Sunday May 30, Millennium Stadium
BRISTOL CITY (0) **0**
65,167

IF IT'S MAY, IT MUST BE time for Brighton & Hove Albion to change divisions. They won their third promotion in four seasons by beating Bristol City in Cardiff, bouncing back from relegation at the first attempt. A penalty converted by Leon Knight six minutes from time, after Chris Iwelumo was tripped by Danny Coles, decided an increasingly tense encounter. It also gives Brighton a problem that they narrowly failed to solve the previous season — trying to compete in the first division on a maximum gate of 7,000 at their temporary Withdean Stadium. Pictured above, Christian Roberts, the City striker, is consoled by Richard Carpenter.

BRIGHTON & HOVE ALBION (4-4-2): B Roberts — A Virgo, D Cullip, G Butters, D Harding — G Hart, C Oatway, R Carpenter (sub: P Reid, 62min), N Jones (sub: J Piercy, 78) — L Knight, C Iwelumo. **Substitutes not used:** M Kuipers, K Mayo, A Hinshelwood. **Booked:** Virgo.

BRISTOL CITY (4-4-2): S Phillips — L Carey, A Butler (sub: M Goodfellow, 88), D Coles, M Hill — A Rougier, T Doherty, B Tinnion (sub: L Wilkshire, 82), C Woodman — L Miller (sub: S Murray, 62), C Roberts. **Substitutes not used:** M Stowell, J Burnell.
Referee: R Beeby.

Saturday March 27
Blackpool 1 Stockport 1; Chesterfield 4 Grimsby 4; Colchester 0 Peterborough 0; Hartlepool 1 Brentford 2; Oldham 2 Wycombe 3; Plymouth 0 Wrexham 0; Port Vale 2 Bristol City 1; QPR 1 Luton 1; Rushden 0 Bournemouth 3; Sheffield Weds 2 Brighton 1; Swindon 1 Barnsley 1; Tranmere 4 Notts Co 0

Tuesday March 30
Blackpool 0 Colchester 0; Port Vale 3 Swindon 3

Saturday April 3
Barnsley 1 Plymouth 0; Bournemouth 1 Colchester 1; Brentford 1 Chesterfield 1; Brighton 2 Hartlepool 0; Bristol City 1 QPR 0; Grimsby 2 Sheffield Weds 0; Luton 1 Oldham 1; Notts Co 4 Blackpool 1; Peterborough 4 Swindon 2; Stockport 2 Rushden 1; Wrexham 0 Tranmere 1; Wycombe 2 Port Vale 1

Tuesday April 6
Hartlepool 4 Luton 3; Tranmere 0 QPR 0

Saturday April 10
Blackpool 3 Brighton 1; Chesterfield 0 Stockport 3; Colchester 4 Notts Co 1; Hartlepool 2 Bournemouth 1; Oldham 1 Peterborough 1; Plymouth 2 Wycombe 1; Port Vale 1 Wrexham 0; QPR 3 Grimsby 0; Rushden 2 Barnsley 3; Sheffield Weds 1 Brentford 1; Swindon 1 Bristol City 1; Tranmere 1 Luton 0

Monday April 12
Barnsley 3 QPR 3; Bournemouth 2 Chesterfield 2; Brentford 3 Colchester 2; Brighton 0 Rushden 0; Grimsby 0 Blackpool 2; Luton 0 Swindon 3; Notts Co 0 Sheffield Weds 0; Peterborough 3 Port Vale 1; Stockport 1 Oldham 1; Wrexham 1 Hartlepool 2; Wycombe 1 Tranmere 2

Tuesday April 13
Bristol City 1 Plymouth 0

Saturday April 17
Barnsley 0 Brentford 2; Blackpool 4 Sheffield Weds 1; Bournemouth 1 Tranmere 5; Brighton 1 Peterborough 0; Colchester 3 Wrexham 0; Grimsby 1 Rushden 0; Hartlepool 4 Notts Co 0; Luton 3 Bristol City 2; Oldham 4 Plymouth 1; Port Vale 1 Chesterfield 1; QPR 1 Stockport 1; Wycombe 0 Swindon 3

Tuesday April 20
Luton 1 Bournemouth 1; Oldham 1 Wrexham 1

Saturday April 24
Brentford 1 Wycombe 1; Bristol City 0 Brighton 0; Chesterfield 1 Blackpool 0; Notts Co 1 Port Vale 2; Peterborough 0 Bournemouth 1; Plymouth 2 QPR 0; Rushden 0 Hartlepool 2; Sheffield Weds 0 Colchester 1; Stockport 2 Grimsby 1; Swindon 1 Oldham 2; Tranmere 2 Barnsley 0; Wrexham 2 Luton 1

Saturday May 1
Blackpool 1 Peterborough 4; Bournemouth 0 Stockport 0; Brighton 1 Notts Co 0; Colchester 2 Rushden 0; Grimsby 1 Brentford 0; Hartlepool 1 Plymouth 3; Luton 3 Sheffield Weds 2; Oldham 2 Chesterfield 0; Port Vale 2 Tranmere 1; QPR 1 Swindon 0; Wycombe 1 Wrexham 1

Sunday May 2
Barnsley 0 Bristol City 1

Saturday May 8
Brentford 1 Bournemouth 0; Bristol City 2 Blackpool 1; Chesterfield 1 Luton 0; Peterborough 1 Wycombe 1; Plymouth 2 Colchester 0; Rushden 0 Port Vale 2; Sheffield Weds 1 QPR 3; Stockport 2 Barnsley 3; Swindon 1 Hartlepool 1; Tranmere 2 Grimsby 1; Wrexham 0 Brighton 2

NATIONWIDE LEAGUE

THIRD DIVISION

CHAMPIONS
Doncaster Rovers
RUNNERS-UP
Hull City

ALSO PROMOTED
Torquay United

PROMOTED VIA PLAY-OFFS
Huddersfield Town

RELEGATED
Carlisle United
York City

PFA TEAM OF THE SEASON
Chris Weale (Yeovil Town)

Nathan Stanton (Scunthorpe Utd)
Efe Sodje (Huddersfield Town)
Andy Crosby (Oxford Utd)
Andy Dawson (Hull City)

Peter Beagrie (Scunthorpe Utd)
Alex Russell (Torquay Utd)
Liam Lawrence (Mansfield Town)
Michael McIndoe (Doncaster R)

David Graham (Torquay Utd)
Lee Trundle (Swansea City)

Don it again: just a year after
returning to the Football League,
Doncaster Rovers celebrate in style
after winning the third division title

Saturday August 9 2003
Carlisle 1 York 2; Hudd'field 2 Cambridge 2; Hull 4 Darlington 1; Kidder'ster 2 Mansfield 1; L Orient 1 Doncaster 3; Lincoln 0 Oxford 1; Macc'field 0 Boston 0; North'ton 0 Torquay 1; Rochdale 1 Yeovil 3; Scunthorpe 1 Bristol Rov 2; Southend 2 Cheltenham 0; Swansea 4 Bury 2

Saturday August 16
Boston 2 Hudd'field 2; Bristol Rov 0 Rochdale 0; Bury 2 Scunthorpe 3; Cambridge 3 Macc'field 1; Cheltenham 3 Swansea 4; Darlington 0 Kidder'ster 2; Doncaster 2 Southend 0; Mansfield 1 L Orient 1; Oxford 2 Hull 1; Torquay 1 Lincoln 0; Yeovil 3 Carlisle 0; York 1 North'ton 0

Friday August 22
North'ton 1 Darlington 0; Swansea 3 Boston 0

Saturday August 23
Carlisle 0 Bristol Rov 2; Hudd'field 0 York 1; Hull 3 Cheltenham 3; Kidder'ster 0 Bury 2; L Orient 2 Yeovil 0; Lincoln 0 Doncaster 0; Macc'field 1 Torquay 1; Rochdale 2 Cambridge 2; Scunthorpe 1 Oxford 1; Southend 0 Mansfield 3

Monday August 25
Boston 1 Carlisle 0; Bristol Rov 2 Macc'field 2; Bury 2 Lincoln 1; Cambridge 0 Hull 2; Cheltenham 2 Kidder'ster 1; Darlington 2 L Orient 1; Doncaster 1 Hudd'field 1; Oxford 3 Swansea 0; Torquay 1 Rochdale 3; Yeovil 0 North'ton 2

Tuesday August 26
Mansfield 5 Scunthorpe 0; York 2 Southend 0

Saturday August 30
Carlisle 0; Hudd'field 2 Bristol Rov 1; Hull 2 Boston 1; Kidder'ster 1 Oxford 1; L Orient 1 Cheltenham 4; Lincoln 3 York 0; Macc'field 4 Yeovil 1; North'ton 1 Doncaster 0; Rochdale 4 Darlington 2; Scunthorpe 2 Torquay 1; Southend 1 Bury 0; Swansea 4 Mansfield 1

Friday September 5
Cambridge 0 Lincoln 0; Cheltenham 4 North'ton 3

Saturday September 6
Boston 1 Scunthorpe 1; Bristol Rov 1 Kidder'ster 0; Bury 2 Hudd'field 1; Darlington 2 Carlisle 0; Mansfield 3 Macc'field 1; Oxford 2 Southend 0; Torquay 2 L Orient 1; Yeovil 2 Swansea 0; York 1 Rochdale 2

Monday September 8
Doncaster 0 Hull 0

Saturday September 13
Bristol Rov 2 Boston 0; Bury 1 Cheltenham 1; Cambridge 1 Torquay 1; Carlisle 3 Rochdale 2; Darlington 2 Doncaster 1; Hudd'field 3 North'ton 3; Hull 3 Southend 2; Lincoln 0 L Orient 0; Macc'field 1 Kidder'ster 1; Oxford 1 Mansfield 1; Scunthorpe 2 Swansea 2; Yeovil 3 York 0

Tuesday September 16
Cheltenham 0 Oxford 0; Doncaster 0 Yeovil 1; Kidder'ster 0 Scunthorpe 2; Mansfield 5 Bury 3; North'ton 0 Southend 0 Lincoln 0; Swansea 3 Macc'field 0; Torquay 2 Bristol Rov 1; York 1 Darlington 1

Tuesday September 16
L Orient 1 Hull 1; Rochdale 1 Hudd'field 1

Wednesday September 17
Boston 1 Cambridge 2

Saturday September 20
Boston 1 Bury 0; Cheltenham 0 Cambridge 3; Doncaster 2 Oxford 0; Kidder'ster 1 Lincoln 2; L Orient 1 Scunthorpe 1; Mansfield 0 Yeovil 1; North'ton 0 Macc'field 0; Rochdale 0 Hull 2; Southend 2 Carlisle 2; Swansea 2 Hudd'field 0; Torquay 2 Darlington 2; York 2 Bristol Rov 1

THINK MANAGERS SACKED IN 2003-04, think of a certain Italian and the endless Stamford Bridge soap opera. But for sheer number of desks cleared, the Nationwide League third division was the place to be. Or not to be, as it turned out for 16 unlucky bosses.

The pressure of the Premiership? Only four top-flight managers were fired, all rich men. Down in the basement, managers have the career longevity of your average manufactured boy band. Few are wealthy. Few will find another job in the League. By the end of the season, every club below Yeovil Town in the table except York City, the bottom side, had replaced their manager.

In no division are results less predictable. In no division is confidence so often more important than tactics or talent. The mid-term renaissances of Carlisle United, Northampton Town, Boston United and Cambridge United under new management testify that boardroom brutality frequently works.

Sport's most prolonged game of Russian roulette finally ended terminally for those expert bullet-dodgers, Carlisle United. They had finished outside the bottom three only once in the previous six years. This time they could not resist the siren call of the Nationwide Conference. Still, it was close — Carlisle had accumulated an embarrassing five points by mid-December but picked up another 40 thereafter. Their triumph in the second half of the campaign was turning the certainty of relegation into a mere probability.

The traditional last-day miracle was brought forward two weeks. Needing a win to preserve any hope, Carlisle were 2-0 up away to Mansfield Town. The home side equalised but the Cumbrians reclaimed the lead and preserved it with an injury-time penalty save by Matt Glennon. It was like Houdini escaping the straitjacket only to find he was still trapped in a tank with the water level rising.

York were firm pre-season favourites for relegation: a weak squad led by a rookie player-manager, Chris Brass. Even so, they won their first four league games. Unfortunately for them, in 2004 they went downhill faster than a skier with a jet pack: no victories in their final 20 fixtures. Yet after relegation was confirmed with a home defeat to Leyton Orient in their penultimate match, York's fans massed beneath the directors' box and chanted, loud and proud. They could see the wider perspective. At least, thanks to the hard work of their Supporters Trust, there was still a club for them to cherish. Carlisle were relegated on the same afternoon as York when a late equaliser by Cheltenham Town saw them succumb to mathematical certainty.

There was still last-day drama, but at the table's bright and shiny end. Torquay United tiptoed past Huddersfield Town into third place with a fortuitous 2-1 win away to Southend United. That

Ian Ashbee, right, was one of the mainstays of Hull City's success

would have been irrelevant had the Yorkshire club beaten mid-table Cheltenham, but they squandered a lead late on because of a careless backpass.

So Leroy Rosenior's side celebrated a first automatic promotion for 38 years — deserved reward for a team with a smart young head coach that played beguilingly. Huddersfield dried their tears and effected an instant return to the second division anyway, edging past Lincoln City in the play-offs, then defeating Mansfield on penalties at the Millennium Stadium in a desperately close game.

Mansfield had dispatched Northampton via spot-kicks in the semi-finals: no mean task, since Northampton were in form. Lincoln missed out in the play-offs, but more important was that their like-able manager, Keith Alexander, was able to resume dug-out duties just a couple of months after suffering a ruptured cerebral aneurism.

Despite the four promotion places on offer, some teams continue to make elevating themselves out of the division look like the toughest task in sport. Step forward, or rather, sideways, Bristol Rovers, Rochdale, Leyton Orient and Southend United. Step upwards Doncaster Rovers, back in the League after a five-year absence and in no mood to waste time. They sliced through the division like a speedboat through calm waters. Dave Penney, their manager, bought wisely and built a tough, direct, determined team whose biggest virtue was a momentum that increased inexorably as the season wore on.

They were deserving champions; Hull City were comfortable runners-up, finally producing a side worthy of their stadium and fan base. Hull's average attendance of 16,847 would have been the tenth-best in the first division. It only took them the small matter of eight seasons to escape the League's twilight zone. Oh, and they went through five managers in that period; but then that's not so surprising.

Saturday September 27
Bristol Rov 2 Cheltenham 0; Bury 1 Doncaster 3; Cambridge 1 Mansfield 2; Carlisle 1 Swansea 2; Darlington 3 Boston 0; Hudd'field 3 L Orient 0; Lincoln 1 Rochdale 1; Hull 6 Kidder'ster 1; Macc'field 0 York 0; Oxford 3 North'ton 0; Scunthorpe 1 Southend 1; Yeovil 0 Torquay 2

Tuesday September 30
Bristol Rov 1 Mansfield 3; Bury 2 York 0; Cambridge 3 Doncaster 3; Carlisle 0 L Orient 1; Darlington 0 Southend 0; Hudd'field 1 Kidder'ster 0; Hull 1 Swansea 0; Lincoln 0 North'ton 0; Macc'field 2 Rochdale 1; Scunthorpe 5 Cheltenham 2; Yeovil 2 Boston 0

Wednesday October 1
Oxford 1 Torquay 0

Saturday October 4
Boston 1 Oxford 1; Cheltenham 3 Yeovil 1; Doncaster 5 Bristol Rov 1; Kidder'ster 2 Carlisle 1; L Orient 2 Macc'field 0; Mansfield 3 Darlington 0; North'ton 1 Hull 5; Rochdale 2 Scunthorpe 0; Southend 1 Hudd'field 2; Swansea 2 Lincoln 2; Torquay 3 Bury 1; York 2 Cambridge 0

Saturday October 11
Boston 3 Cheltenham 1; Cambridge 1 Bury 2; Darlington 0 Bristol Rov 4; Hudd'field 1 Torquay 0; Kidder'ster 1 Southend 2; L Orient 1 Swansea 2; Macc'field 1 Doncaster 3; Mansfield 2 York 0; Oxford 1 Yeovil 0; Rochdale 1 North'ton 1; Scunthorpe 1 Lincoln 3

Sunday October 12
Hull 2 Carlisle 1

Friday October 17
North'ton 1 Scunthorpe 1

Saturday October 18
Bristol Rov 0 Cambridge 2; Bury 0 Oxford 4; Carlisle 0 Macc'field 1; Cheltenham 0 Rochdale 2; Doncaster 4 Mansfield 2; Lincoln 3 Hudd'field 1; Southend 1 L Orient 2; Swansea 0 Kidder'ster 0; Torquay 1 Hull 1; Yeovil 1 Darlington 0; York 1 Boston 1

Tuesday October 21
Bristol Rov 1 L Orient 1; Bury 0 Hull 0; Carlisle 1 Scunthorpe 4; Cheltenham 2 Darlington 1; Doncaster 2 Rochdale 1; Lincoln 3 Macc'field 2; North'ton 0 Kidder'ster 1; Southend 0 Boston 2; Swansea 0 Cambridge 2; Torquay 1 Mansfield 0; Yeovil 2 Hudd'field 1; York 2 Oxford 2

Saturday October 25
Boston 4 Torquay 0; Cambridge 1 Yeovil 4; Darlington 1 Bury 3; Hudd'field 2 Carlisle 1; Kidder'ster 0 Doncaster 2; Hull 3 Lincoln 0; L Orient 1 North'ton 1; Macc'field 1 Southend 2; Mansfield 4 Cheltenham 0; Oxford 0 Bristol Rov 0; Rochdale 0 Swansea 1; Scunthorpe 0 York 0

Saturday November 1
Bury 2 Yeovil 1; Cheltenham 1 York 1; Doncaster 1 Torquay 0; Hull 2 Macc'field 0; Kidder'ster 2 Cambridge 2; L Orient 2 Rochdale 1; Lincoln 2 Carlisle 0; Mansfield 2 Boston 1; Oxford 3 Darlington 1; Scunthorpe 6 Hudd'field 2; Southend 0 North'ton 1; Swansea 0 Bristol Rov 0

Saturday November 15
Boston 3 L Orient 0; Bristol Rov 1 Bury 2; Cambridge 1 Oxford 1; Carlisle 0 Mansfield 2; Darlington 0 Lincoln 0; Hudd'field 3 Hull 1; Macc'field 2 Scunthorpe 2; Rochdale 0 Kidder'ster 1; Torquay 3 Cheltenham 1; Yeovil 4 Southend 0; York 1 Doncaster 0

Monday November 17
North'ton 2 Swansea 1

Saturday November 22
Bury 1 North'ton 0; Cheltenham 2 Carlisle 1; Doncaster 3 Boston 0; Hull 0 Yeovil 0; Kidder'ster 1 Torquay 2; L Orient 2 York 1; Lincoln 3 Bristol Rov 1; Mansfield 3 Hudd'field 3; Oxford 3 Macc'field 1; Scunthorpe 4 Cambridge 0; Southend 4 Rochdale 0; Swansea 1 Darlington 0

FINAL TABLE

	P	W	D	L	F	A	W	D	L	F	A	P	GD
			HOME						**AWAY**				
DONCASTER	46	17	4	2	47	13	10	7	6	32	24	92	42
HULL	46	16	4	3	50	21	9	9	5	32	23	88	38
TORQUAY	46	15	6	2	44	18	8	6	9	24	26	81	24
HUDDERSFIELD	46	16	4	3	42	18	7	8	8	26	34	81	16
MANSFIELD	46	13	5	5	44	25	9	4	10	32	37	75	14
NORTHAMPTON	46	13	4	6	30	23	9	5	9	28	28	75	7
LINCOLN	46	9	11	3	36	23	10	6	7	32	24	74	21
YEOVIL	46	14	3	6	40	19	9	2	12	30	38	74	13
OXFORD	46	14	8	1	34	13	4	9	10	21	31	71	11
SWANSEA	46	9	8	6	36	26	6	6	11	22	35	59	-3
BOSTON	46	11	7	5	35	21	5	4	14	15	33	59	-4
BURY	46	10	7	6	29	26	5	4	14	25	38	56	-10
CAMBRIDGE	46	6	7	10	26	32	8	7	8	29	35	56	-12
CHELTENHAM	46	11	4	8	37	38	3	10	10	20	33	56	-14
BRISTOL ROVERS	46	9	7	7	29	26	5	6	12	21	35	55	-11
KIDDERMINSTER	46	9	5	9	28	29	5	8	10	17	30	55	-14
SOUTHEND	46	8	4	11	27	29	6	8	9	24	34	54	-12
DARLINGTON	46	10	4	9	30	28	4	7	12	23	33	53	-8
LEYTON ORIENT	46	8	9	6	28	28	5	5	13	20	38	53	-17
MACCLESFIELD	46	8	9	6	28	25	5	4	14	26	44	52	-15
ROCHDALE	46	7	8	8	28	26	5	6	12	21	32	50	-9
SCUNTHORPE	46	7	10	6	36	27	4	6	13	33	45	49	-3
CARLISLE	46	8	5	10	23	27	4	4	15	23	42	45	-23
YORK	46	7	6	10	22	29	3	8	12	13	37	44	-31

LEADING SCORERS

		League	FAC	CC	Total
Steve MacLean	Scunthorpe United	23	0	1	25
Leon Constantine	Southend United	21	0	0	25
David Graham	Torquay United	22	0	1	23
Liam Lawrence	Mansfield Town	18	3	0	21
Lee Trundle	Swansea City	16	5	0	21
Gregg Blundell	Doncaster Rovers	18	0	2	20
Gary Fletcher	Lincoln City	16+1	0	0	19
Matthew Tipton	Macclesfield Town	16	3	0	19
Ben Burgess	Hull City	18	0	0	18
Gary Alexander	Leyton Orient	15	1	0	16

Figures after the + sign indicate play-off goals

MacLean's total includes 1 LDV Vans Trophy goal

Constantine's total includes 4 LDV Vans Trophy goals

Fletcher's total includes 2 LDV Vans Trophy goals

THIRD DIVISION RESULTS

HOME \ AWAY	BOSTON UNITED	BRISTOL ROVERS	BURY	CAMBRIDGE UNITED	CARLISLE UNITED	CHELTENHAM TOWN	DARLINGTON	DONCASTER ROVERS	HUDDERSFIELD TOWN	HULL CITY	KIDDERMINSTER HARRIERS	LEYTON ORIENT	LINCOLN CITY	MACCLESFIELD TOWN	MANSFIELD TOWN	NORTHAMPTON TOWN	OXFORD UNITED	ROCHDALE	SCUNTHORPE UNITED	SOUTHEND UNITED	SWANSEA CITY	TORQUAY UNITED	YEOVIL TOWN	YORK CITY
BOSTON UNITED	–	1-0	1-0	1-2	1-0	3-1	1-0	0-0	2-2	1-2	2-2	3-0	0-1	3-1	1-2	1-1	1-1	2-0	1-1	0-2	1-1	4-0	3-2	2-0
BRISTOL ROVERS	2-0	–	1-2	0-2	1-0	2-0	0-3	1-2	1-1	2-1	1-0	1-1	3-1	2-2	1-3	1-2	1-1	0-0	1-0	1-1	2-1	2-2	0-1	3-0
BURY	1-3	0-0	–	1-0	1-3	1-1	1-1	1-3	2-1	0-0	0-0	1-1	2-1	2-0	3-0	1-0	0-4	1-2	2-3	1-1	2-0	2-1	2-1	2-0
CAMBRIDGE UNITED	0-1	3-1	1-2	–	2-2	2-1	1-0	3-3	1-2	0-2	0-0	1-4	0-0	3-1	1-2	0-1	1-1	0-0	3-2	0-1	0-1	1-1	1-4	2-0
CARLISLE UNITED	2-1	0-2	2-1	0-0	–	1-1	1-1	0-1	1-0	1-1	1-0	0-1	0-2	0-1	0-2	1-1	2-0	3-2	1-4	1-2	1-2	2-0	2-0	1-2
CHELTENHAM TOWN	1-0	1-2	1-2	0-3	2-1	–	2-1	1-3	1-1	0-2	2-1	1-0	3-2	3-2	4-2	4-3	0-0	0-2	2-1	1-1	3-4	1-3	3-1	1-1
DARLINGTON	3-0	0-4	1-3	3-4	2-0	2-1	–	2-1	0-1	0-1	0-2	2-1	0-0	1-0	1-2	2-0	1-0	2-2	0-0	1-2	1-1	3-2	3-0	
DONCASTER ROVERS	3-0	5-1	3-1	2-0	1-0	1-1	1-1	–	1-1	0-0	5-0	5-0	0-2	1-0	4-2	1-0	2-0	2-1	1-0	2-0	3-1	1-0	0-1	3-1
HUDDERSFIELD TOWN	2-0	2-1	1-0	2-2	2-1	0-0	0-2	3-1	–	3-1	1-0	3-0	2-1	4-0	1-3	3-0	1-1	1-1	3-2	1-0	3-0	1-0	3-1	0-1
HULL CITY	2-1	3-0	2-0	2-0	2-1	3-3	4-1	3-1	0-0	–	6-1	3-0	3-0	2-2	0-1	2-3	4-2	1-0	2-1	3-2	1-0	0-1	0-0	2-1
KIDDERMINSTER HARRIERS	2-0	1-0	0-2	2-2	2-1	0-0	1-1	0-2	2-1	1-1	–	2-1	1-2	1-4	2-1	2-1	1-1	0-1	0-2	1-2	2-0	1-2	0-1	4-1
LEYTON ORIENT	1-3	1-1	2-0	0-1	1-1	1-4	1-0	1-3	1-1	1-1	1-1	–	0-2	2-0	3-1	1-1	1-0	2-1	1-1	2-1	1-2	0-0	2-0	2-2
LINCOLN CITY	1-1	3-1	2-1	2-2	2-0	0-0	1-1	0-0	3-1	2-0	1-1	0-0	–	3-2	4-1	0-0	0-1	1-1	1-2	2-2	1-1	1-3	2-3	3-0
MACCLESFIELD TOWN	0-0	2-1	1-0	0-1	1-1	1-2	0-1	1-3	4-0	1-1	1-1	1-0	1-1	–	1-2	3-1	2-1	2-2	1-2	2-1	1-1	1-1	4-1	0-0
MANSFIELD TOWN	2-1	0-0	5-3	1-1	2-3	4-0	3-1	1-2	3-3	1-0	1-0	1-1	3-2		–	1-2	3-1	1-0	5-0	1-0	1-1	2-1	0-1	2-0
NORTHAMPTON TOWN	2-0	2-0	3-2	1-2	2-0	1-0	1-0	1-0	0-1	1-5	0-1	1-0	1-1	0-0	0-3	–	2-1	3-1	1-1	2-2	2-1	0-2	2-0	2-1
OXFORD UNITED	0-0	0-0	1-1	2-2	3-1	1-1	3-1	0-0	0-1	2-1	2-1	2-1	0-0	3-1	1-1	3-0	–	2-0	3-2	2-0	3-0	1-0	1-0	0-0
ROCHDALE	1-0	2-2	0-0	2-2	2-0	0-0	4-2	1-1	1-1	0-2	0-1	3-0	0-3	1-2	3-0	1-1	1-2	–	2-0	1-1	0-1	1-0	1-3	1-2
SCUNTHORPE UNITED	0-1	1-2	0-0	4-0	2-3	5-2	0-1	2-2	6-2	1-1	0-2	1-1	1-3	1-0	0-0	1-0	1-1	2-2	–	1-1	2-2	2-1	3-0	0-0
SOUTHEND UNITED	0-2	0-1	1-0	1-0	2-2	2-0	3-2	0-2	1-2	2-2	3-0	1-2	0-2	1-0	0-3	0-1	0-1	4-0	4-2	–	1-1	1-2	1-0	0-0
SWANSEA CITY	3-0	0-0	4-2	0-2	1-2	0-0	1-0	1-1	2-0	2-3	0-0	2-1	2-2	3-0	4-1	0-2	0-0	1-1	4-2	2-3	–	1-2	3-2	0-0
TORQUAY UNITED	2-0	2-1	3-1	3-0	4-1	3-1	2-2	2-1	0-1	1-1	1-1	2-1	1-0	4-1	1-0	3-1	3-0	1-3	1-0	3-0	0-0	–	2-2	1-1
YEOVIL TOWN	2-0	4-0	2-1	4-1	3-0	0-0	1-0	0-1	2-1	1-2	1-2	1-2	3-1	2-2	2-1	0-2	1-0	1-0	2-1	4-0	2-0	0-2	–	3-0
YORK CITY	1-1	2-1	1-1	2-0	2-0	0-2	1-1	1-0	0-2	0-2	1-0	1-2	1-4	0-2	1-2	1-0	2-2	1-2	1-3	2-0	0-0	0-0	1-2	–

PLAYER OF THE SEASON
David Graham Torquay United

Coveted by several clubs, David Graham decided to leave Torquay United in the summer for Coca-Cola League Championship football with Wigan Athletic. How times change: Leeds United also made a bid but could not match the personal terms Wigan offered. Signed for £215,000, Wigan may well have a bargain in the 25-year-old Scot, who arrived at Plainmoor in March 2001 and played a key role in the Devon side escaping relegation to the Nationwide Conference. Last season the former Rangers trainee struck 23 goals, 22 of them in the League and many of them spectacular. Deceptively quick, intelligent and unafraid to take on defenders, Graham is one of those rare forwards who are both predators and creators of chances.

Tom Dart

Saturday November 29
Boston 2 Kidder'ster 2; Bristol Rov 2 Hull 1; Cambridge 1 L Orient 4; Carlisle 0 Doncaster 1; Darlington 2 Scunthorpe 2; Hudd'field 0 Cheltenham 0; Macc'field 1 Bury 0; North'ton 0 Mansfield 3; Rochdale 1 Oxford 2; Torquay 3 Southend 0; Yeovil 3 Lincoln 1; York 0 Swansea 0

Saturday December 6
Darlington 3 York 0; Hull 2 Bury 0

Saturday December 13
Boston 1 North'ton 1; Bristol Rov 0 Yeovil 1; Bury 1 Rochdale 2; Cambridge 1 Darlington 0; Cheltenham 1 Doncaster 3; Kidder'ster 2 L Orient 1; Macc'field 4 Hudd'field 0; Mansfield 1 Lincoln 2; Oxford 2 Carlisle 1; Scunthorpe 1 Hull 1; Swansea 2 Southend 3; Torquay 1 York 1

Friday December 19
Doncaster 3 Swansea 1; North'ton 1 Cambridge 2

Saturday December 20
Carlisle 2 Torquay 0; Darlington 0 Macc'field 1; Hudd'field 1 Oxford 1; Hull 0 Mansfield 1; L Orient 2 Bury 0; Rochdale 1 Boston 0; Southend 0 Bristol Rov 1; Yeovil 2 Scunthorpe 1

Sunday December 21
York 1 Kidder'ster 0

Friday December 26
Boston 0 Lincoln 1; Bristol Rov 1 North'ton 2; Bury 1 Carlisle 3; Cambridge 0 Southend 1; Cheltenham 3 Macc'field 2; Darlington 0 Hudd'field 1; Doncaster 1 Scunthorpe 0; Mansfield 1 Rochdale 0; Oxford 2 L Orient 1; Torquay 0 Swansea 0; Yeovil 1 Kidder'ster 2; York 0 Hull 2

Sunday December 28
Carlisle 1 Darlington 1; Hudd'field 1 Bury 0; Hull 3 Doncaster 1; Kidder'ster 1 Bristol Rov 0; L Orient 0 Torquay 0; Lincoln 2 Cambridge 2; Macc'field 1 Mansfield 1; North'ton 1 Cheltenham 0; Rochdale 1 York 2; Scunthorpe 0 Boston 1; Southend 0 Oxford 1; Swansea 3 Yeovil 2

Saturday January 3 2004
Carlisle 2 Boston 1; Hudd'field 3 Doncaster 1; Hull 2 Cambridge 0; L Orient 1 Darlington 0; Lincoln 2 Bury 1; Rochdale 1 Torquay 0

Tuesday January 6
Swansea 0 Oxford 0

Friday January 9
Cheltenham 1 Southend 1

Saturday January 10
Boston 3 Macc'field 1; Bristol Rov 1 Scunthorpe 0; Bury 2 Swansea 0; Cambridge 1 Hudd'field 2; Darlington 0 Hull 1; Doncaster 5 L Orient 0; Mansfield 1 Kidder'ster 0; Oxford 0 Lincoln 0; Torquay 3 North'ton 1; Yeovil 1 Rochdale 0; York 2 Carlisle 0

Tuesday January 13
Lincoln 0 Cheltenham 0; Macc'field 2 Bristol Rov 1

Saturday January 17
Carlisle 2 Yeovil 0; Hudd'field 2 Boston 0; Hull 4 Oxford 2; Kidder'ster 1 Darlington 1; L Orient 3 Mansfield 1; Lincoln 1 Torquay 3; Macc'field 0 Cambridge 1; North'ton 2 York 1; Rochdale 2 Bristol Rov 2; Scunthorpe 0 Bury 0; Southend 0 Doncaster 2; Swansea 0 Cheltenham 0

Friday January 23
Doncaster 0 Lincoln 2

Saturday January 24
Bristol Rov 1 Carlisle 0; Bury 0 Kidder'ster 0; Cambridge 0 Rochdale 0; Cheltenham 0 Hull 2; Mansfield 1 Southend 0; Torquay 4 Macc'field 1; Yeovil 1 L Orient 2

Sunday January 25
York 0 Hudd'field 2

Tuesday January 27
Scunthorpe 0 Mansfield 0; Southend 0 York 0

Friday January 30
Doncaster 1 North'ton 0

THE ☙ TIMES   Monday April 12 2004

Saturday January 31
Cheltenham 1 L Orient 0; Darlington 1 Rochdale 0;
Oxford 2 Kidder'ster 1; Yeovil 2 Macc'field 2

Tuesday February 3
North'ton 2 Yeovil 0

Saturday February 7
Carlisle 2 Bury 1; Hudd'field 0 Darlington 2; Hull 2
York 1; Kidder'ster 0 Yeovil 1; L Orient 1 Oxford 0;
Lincoln 1 Boston 1; Macc'field 1 Cheltenham 2;
North'ton 2 Bristol Rov 0; Rochdale 3 Mansfield 0;
Scunthorpe 2 Doncaster 0; Southend 1 Cambridge 0;
Swansea 1 Torquay 2

Tuesday February 10
Kidder'ster 0 Cheltenham 0

Wednesday February 11
Oxford 3 Scunthorpe 2

Saturday February 14
Bristol Rov 0 Darlington 3; Bury 1 Cambridge 0; Carlisle 1
Hull 1; Cheltenham 1 Boston 0; Doncaster 1
Macc'field 0; Lincoln 1 Scunthorpe 1; North'ton 3
Rochdale 1; Southend 3 Kidder'ster 0; Torquay 0
Hudd'field 1; Yeovil 1 Oxford 0; York 1 Mansfield 2

Tuesday February 17
Bristol Rov 1 Hudd'field 1; Cambridge 2 Carlisle 2;
Darlington 1 North'ton 3; York 1 Lincoln 4

Wednesday February 18
Boston 1 Swansea 1

Saturday February 21
Boston 2 York 0; Cambridge 3 Bristol Rov 1; Darlington 3
Yeovil 2; Hudd'field 2 Lincoln 1; Hull 0 Torquay 1;
Kidder'ster 2 Swansea 0; L Orient 2 Southend 1;
Macc'field 1 Carlisle 1; Mansfield 1 Doncaster 2;
Oxford 1 Bury 1; Rochdale 0 Cheltenham 0;
Scunthorpe 1 North'ton 0

Tuesday February 24
Bury 1 Southend 1; Swansea 2 L Orient 1; Torquay 1
Scunthorpe 0

Friday February 27
Doncaster 5 Kidder'ster 0

Saturday February 28
Bristol Rov 1 Oxford 1; Bury 1 Darlington 1;
Cheltenham 4 Mansfield 2; Lincoln 2 Hull 0; North'ton 1
L Orient 0; Southend 1 Macc'field 0; Torquay 2 Boston 0;
Yeovil 4 Cambridge 1

Tuesday March 2
Cambridge 0 Swansea 1; Hudd'field 3 Yeovil 1;
Kidder'ster 2 North'ton 1; L Orient 1 Bristol Rov 1

Wednesday March 3
Boston 0 Southend 2; Oxford 0 York 0

Friday March 5
Swansea 1 Doncaster 1

Saturday March 6
Boston 2 Rochdale 0; Bristol Rov 1 Southend 1; Bury 1
L Orient 1; Cambridge 0 North'ton 1; Cheltenham 3
Lincoln 2; Kidder'ster 4 York 1; Macc'field 0
Darlington 1; Mansfield 1 Hull 0; Oxford 0 Hudd'field 1;
Scunthorpe 3 Yeovil 0; Torquay 4 Carlisle 1

Tuesday March 9
Carlisle 1 Hudd'field 0; Darlington 2 Cheltenham 1;
Swansea 1 Rochdale 1; York 1 Scunthorpe 3

Saturday March 13
Carlisle 2 Oxford 0; Darlington 3 Cambridge 4;
Doncaster 1 Cheltenham 1; Hudd'field 4 Macc'field 0;
Hull 2 Scunthorpe 1; L Orient 1 Kidder'ster 1; Lincoln 4
Mansfield 1; North'ton 2 Boston 0; Rochdale 0 Bury 0;
Southend 1 Swansea 1; Yeovil 4 Bristol Rov 1; York 0
Torquay 0

Tuesday March 16
Bristol Rov 2 Torquay 2; Bury 3 Mansfield 0;
Cambridge 0 Boston 1; Carlisle 1 North'ton 1;
Hudd'field 1 Rochdale 1; Hull 3 L Orient 0; Lincoln 2
Southend 2; Macc'field 2 Swansea 1; Scunthorpe 0
Kidder'ster 2; Yeovil 0 Doncaster 1

Wednesday March 17
Oxford 1 Cheltenham 0

MATCH OF THE SEASON

Carlisle United 1 Kidderminster Harriers 0
Brunton Park, Saturday April 10 2004
Jason Mellor

FORGET ARSENE WENGER OR even Claudio Ranieri. There is, potentially, a far more worthy recipient of the manager-of-the-season award.

Sadly, in this Premiership-obsessed world, there is little chance that someone such as Paul Simpson will ever claim such an accolade. However, if he manages to pull off the kind of unlikely recovery he is on the verge of with Carlisle United, those renowned escapologists, it would be difficult to mount any kind of compelling case to the contrary.

That, at 37, Simpson remains a central performer for his home-town club, and was by some distance their finest player on show here, only adds to the magnitude of his achievement since taking over the managerial reins six months ago. Shortly before Christmas, Carlisle were a club in disarray. They were dead and buried, 15 points adrift of safety and heading for the Nationwide Conference, an opportunity to enhance their reputation for last-day-of-the-season extrications a distant dream.

However, Craig Farrell's fifth goal in seven games, scuffed into the bottom corner from a cross by the impressive Brendan McGill, secured a victory which sees Carlisle having gathered 35 points from the past 20 games. They remain bottom of the Nationwide League third division, but are now within just four points of safety; another chapter in their recent history of improbable escapes is ready to be written.

That they have recovered to such a position is largely down to Simpson, one of football's nice guys, who has used his contacts to assemble a squad which, had it been together all season, would be comfortably in mid-table by now. However it isn't and there remain five games to secure League status. "I felt my 37 years climbing up the stairs to do the post-match press conference, but wins like that help aching limbs," Simpson, a Brunton Park regular as a child growing up in the city, said.

Any thought of personal accolades that might come his way should Carlisle stay up politely sidestepped, he added: "We've worked so hard to get ourselves into a position where we can get out of the bottom two, but this win will mean a lot less if we don't go down to Orient on Monday and get something."

Carlisle have hit form at exactly the right time, when their relegation rivals are becoming increasingly nervous at the run being put together by a side that had supposedly made one of the two relegation spots its own.

Victory would have been more handsome but for twice striking the woodwork, in addition to some heroic interventions from John

Brendan McGill is halted by a last-ditch tackle as Carlisle go for goal

Danby in the Kidderminster Harriers goal. The side, managed by Jan Molby, are still not safe from the threat of Conference football next season.

The Dane admitted: "Carlisle are in a situation where they have to gamble and go for wins because draws are no good and, to be honest, they would have won by more had it not been for our keeper."

CARLISLE UNITED (4-3-1-2): M Glennon — B Shelley, K Gray (sub: P Arnison, 66min), L Andrews, P Murphy — B McGill, M Boyd, P Simpson — C Farrell — A Preece (sub: K Langmead, 77), P Duffield. **Substitutes not used:** P Keen, R Foran, A Rundle.
KIDDERMINSTER HARRIERS (4-3-3): J Danby — C Hinton, M Gadsby, W Hatswell, S Stamps (sub: S Burton, 62) — M Yates, A Murray, L Jenkins (sub: S Parrish, 79) — S Brown, J Williams, L Clarke (sub: J Christiansen, 59). **Substitutes not used:** S Brock, I Foster. **Booked:** Williams.

Saturday March 20
Boston 1 Bristol Rov 0; Cheltenham 1 Bury 2; Doncaster 1 Darlington 1; Kidder'ster 1 Macc'field 4; L Orient 0 Lincoln 2; Rochdale 2 Carlisle 0; Swansea 4 Scunthorpe 2; Torquay 3 Cambridge 0

Tuesday March 23
Mansfield 1 Swansea 1; Scunthorpe 2 Carlisle 3

Saturday March 27
Bristol Rov 3 York 0; Bury 1 Boston 3; Cambridge 2 Cheltenham 1; Carlisle 1 Southend 2; Darlington 1 Torquay 1; Hudd'field 3 Swansea 0; Hull 1 Rochdale 0; Lincoln 1 Kidder'ster 1; Macc'field 0 North'ton 4; Oxford 0 Doncaster 0; Scunthorpe 2 L Orient 1; Yeovil 1 Mansfield 1

Tuesday March 30
Macc'field 0 Lincoln 0; Mansfield 2 Torquay 1; Rochdale 1 Doncaster 1

Wednesday March 31
Boston 1 Hull 2

Friday April 2
Southend 4 Scunthorpe 2

Saturday April 3
Boston 1 Darlington 0; Cheltenham 1 Bristol Rov 2; Doncaster 3 Bury 1; Kidder'ster 1 Hull 1; L Orient 1 Hudd'field 1; Mansfield 1 Cambridge 1; North'ton 2 Oxford 1; Rochdale 0 Lincoln 3; Swansea 1 Carlisle 2; Torquay 2 Yeovil 2

Sunday April 4
York 0 Macc'field 2

Tuesday April 6
Mansfield 3 Oxford 1

Friday April 9
Bury 2 Torquay 1; Cambridge 2 York 0; Oxford 0 Boston 0

Saturday April 10
Bristol Rov 1 Doncaster 2; Carlisle 1 Kidder'ster 0; Darlington 1 Mansfield 0; Hudd'field 1 Southend 0; Hull 2 North'ton 3; Lincoln 2 Swansea 1; Macc'field 1 L Orient 0; Scunthorpe 2 Rochdale 0; Yeovil 0 Cheltenham 0

Monday April 12
Boston 3 Yeovil 2; Cheltenham 2 Scunthorpe 1; Doncaster 2 Cambridge 0; Kidder'ster 2 Hudd'field 1; L Orient 1 Carlisle 1; Mansfield 0 Bristol Rov 0; North'ton 1 Lincoln 0; Rochdale 1 Macc'field 2; Southend 3 Darlington 2; Swansea 2 Hull 3; Torquay 3 Oxford 0

Tuesday April 13
York 1 Bury 1

Saturday April 17
Boston 1 Mansfield 2; Bristol Rov 2 Swansea 1; Cambridge 0 Kidder'ster 0; Carlisle 0 Lincoln 2; Darlington 2 Oxford 0; Hudd'field 3 Scunthorpe 2; Macc'field 1 Hull 1; North'ton 2 Southend 2; Rochdale 3 L Orient 0; Torquay 1 Doncaster 0; Yeovil 2 Bury 1; York 0 Cheltenham 2

Tuesday April 20
North'ton 0 Hudd'field 1; Southend 2 Hull 2; York 1 Yeovil 2

Saturday April 24
Bury 0 Bristol Rov 0; Cheltenham 1 Torquay 3; Doncaster 3 York 1; Hull 0 Hudd'field 0; Kidder'ster 0 Rochdale 1; L Orient 1 Boston 3; Lincoln 1 Darlington 1; Mansfield 2 Carlisle 3; Oxford 2 Cambridge 2; Scunthorpe 1 Macc'field 0; Southend 0 Yeovil 2; Swansea 0 North'ton 2

Saturday May 1
Boston 0 Doncaster 0; Bristol Rov 3 Lincoln 1; Cambridge 3 Scunthorpe 2; Carlisle 1 Cheltenham 1; Darlington 1 Swansea 2; Hudd'field 1 Mansfield 3; Macc'field 2 Oxford 1; North'ton 3 Bury 2; Rochdale 1 Southend 1; Torquay 1 Kidder'ster 2; Yeovil 1 Hull 1; York 1 L Orient 2

Saturday May 8
Bury 2 Macc'field 0; Cheltenham 1 Hudd'field 1; Doncaster 1 Carlisle 0; Hull 3 Bristol Rov 0; Kidder'ster 2 Boston 0; L Orient 0 Cambridge 1; Lincoln 2 Yeovil 3; Mansfield 1 North'ton 2; Oxford 2 Rochdale 0; Scunthorpe 0 Darlington 1; Southend 1 Torquay 2; Swansea 0 York 0

A LEAGUE OF OUR OWN

Mark Hodkinson

TUESDAY, MARCH 6, 1962, Lancashire, England. Solemn faces. Blokes in overcoats staring at their shoes. A few drops of rain coming down. Then the announcement: sad to say, it's over, finished. Thanks for your support. Please make your way home.

Vincent Studholme is now 76. He has never forgotten the day his beloved Accrington Stanley left the Football League. "You can't describe it," he said. "It's an emptiness. I don't think I've ever got used to it. The town dies when it loses its football club."

We're with him, those of us that support lower-division clubs. We're are all big softies really, proper football fans, so when he talks like this, sitting in his favourite armchair, eyes a bit watery, we want to hug him, tell him we understand.

Of course, Accrington had acute problems that precipitated their darkest day. They were hugely in debt. Thankfully the club survived and has moved slowly towards regaining its League status. Still, whether through bankruptcy or relegation, the outcome is the same — an exit from the most prestigious sporting fraternity in the world. Worth crying about, then.

This season, my club, Rochdale, came perilously close to this very catastrophe (no other word will do). As the campaign drew to a close, defeat upon defeat, I had my first sleepless night caused wholly by football. We had lost in mid-April, at home, to our fellow relegation-strugglers, Macclesfield Town: we looked doomed. I'm not sure where the pain was centred but it bloody hurt. My insides all mixed up, head aching, wanting to punch something, run somewhere, shout, cry, or march up to Spotland and wail at the wall, any wall.

Until this point, I had dealt with our impending fate in two distinct ways. Firstly, I pretended the relegation places were already pre-booked. York City and Carlisle United were still below us, we had a squad too good to go down — the usual flannel.

Then I embraced the new football orthodoxy. Hey,

what's the big deal? The Nationwide Conference is practically the fourth division of the Football League. No one can tell the two divisions apart any more. Come on lad, get a grip.

On that long night's journey into day, none of this helped. Not one bit.

Head like a tipped-over beehive, I realised how much it meant that my club belonged to this largely abstract entity, the Football League. It also mattered deeply that we had had continuous membership since joining 83 years earlier. I know, you don't have to tell me: we've been rubbish a good deal of that time, never done much, but, come on, 83 years. Still there, still kicking.

Other Dale fans had prepared for the worst. Football League clubs always bounce back from the Conference, they said — reinvigorated, tough as new boots. We'll be the Manchester United of the division, imagine that.

Spotland, the non-League Wembley. No, no, I don't want this. I want every single one of my Rochdale programmes to have on the front, proud as punch, "Nationwide League", or whatever they choose to call it in the years to come. I want to remain in the League and relish all it confers on the club, the town, my support.

Poor Carlisle, poor York. They didn't quite catch us up at the end and were relegated. Two clubs with long traditions, great fans. They don't deserve it. At least their places are being taken by ex-League clubs. So, welcome back Chester City and Shrewsbury Town, you have been missed.

Strange how the top six sides in this season's Conference were all ex-League clubs. And that every club going down has come back up within a few seasons, quite often the first. Where is the evidence of this supposed parity between the divisions? When new clubs do enter the League they have the obligatory decent first season but thereafter do little to enrich it. Macclesfield and Boston United, both recent arrivals, were two of the three worst-supported teams in the League last season and 12 of the 13 lowest attendances were recorded at their grounds, along with their fellow newcomers, Kidderminster Harriers.

If all this sounds embittered, it's supposed to. I am

Defeat to Macclesfield, left, had Rochdale in despair, but fans can now welcome Chester, right, back into the League fold

bitter. Six pints, please. I can't do with the homilies about how nice it is that the League receives new clubs, how it keeps everything fresh. This blather is uttered routinely by fans (usually passive, the one-match-a-season wallahs) of Premiership clubs. Look, pal, if someone was about to usurp your club, take your place, spoil your fun, you wouldn't be quite so chipper. You'd be at the barricades.

There is also the insinuation that because we're only Rochdale or York or Carlisle, it doesn't matter quite so much. It's all a bit quaint down there at the other end of the League, isn't it? Not like supporting an Arsenal or a Manchester United where it really, really matters because it says so on the telly, the radio, in the papers, day after day.

This is to overlook perhaps the most vital constituent of the League: that it does matter, all the way down, top to bottom. Passion remains outside the claim of wealth and status. It belongs to us all and England is unique in its depth of support. Nowhere else is a country criss-crossed by regional pockets of ardent, do-or-die loyalty to home-town clubs. The average attendance in the third division last season was 5,389. In Italy and Germany, clubs of comparative size can expect turnouts of about 1,200 and 800 respectively: not the same thing at all.

As someone with an undeniable vested interest in the machinery of the League's administration, I'm often teased, "You hate non-League football, don't you?" But I don't. I could cheerfully succumb to a Saturday afternoon watching Quorn take on Biddulph Victoria in the Trafford Factory Midland Alliance, or Frimley Green against Chipstead in the (deep breath, please) Seagrave Haulage Combined Counties League premier division. Freshly cut grass, stands the size of bus shelters, honest endeavour — all good fun. It's the other lot I can't abide, the interlopers-to-be, those buggers a bit too close to the top of the pyramid.

Bitter, for sure, but not peevish. Once they're with us — the Yeovils, the Kidderminsters et al — I don't draw a real distinction between them and the clubs they've replaced. They're in the Football League now, respect due, and a game against them is as valid as any other. All the same, a victory over them is usually that little bit sweeter and leads to some playful chants implying they're not worthy of football's highest caste.

This might be what it's all about really: looking down on someone, feeling good about where you are and where you're not. Nothing shameful, here. It's the whole point, the very principle of sport. If you can't be the best you can be better than someone else. Ask Vincent.

PLAY-OFFS

Semi-finals: First legs

Saturday May 15

LINCOLN CITY (0) **1**
Fletcher 51
9,202

HUDDERSFIELD TOWN (1) **2**
Onuora 5, Mirfin 72

Sunday May 16

NORTHAMPTON TOWN (0) **0**
6,960

MANSFIELD TOWN (1) **2**
Day 40, Mendes 67

Second legs

Wednesday May 19

HUDDERSFIELD TOWN (0) **2**
Schofield 60 (pen), Edwards 83
19,467

LINCOLN CITY (2) **2**
Butcher 38, Bailey 39

(Huddersfield won 4-3 on agg)

Thursday May 20

MANSFIELD TOWN (0) **1**
Curtis 68
9,243

NORTHAMPTON TOWN (2) **2**
Richards 36, Hargreaves 42, Smith 46

(aet; 3-3 on agg; Mansfield won 5-4 on pens)

THE FINAL

Monday May 31, Millennium Stadium

HUDDERSFIELD TOWN (0) **0**
37,298

MANSFIELD TOWN (0) **0**

(aet; Huddersfield won 4-1 on pens)

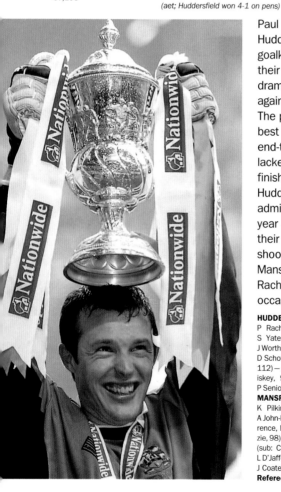

Paul Rachubka, the Huddersfield Town goalkeeper, celebrates their success in a dramatic contest against Mansfield Town. The play-offs saved the best until last as an end-to-end match lacked only cool finishing, but it was Huddersfield — in administration only a year earlier — who found their touch in the shoot-out, when Mansfield could beat Rachubka on only one occasion.

HUDDERSFIELD TOWN (3-5-2): P Rachubka — D Mirfin, E Sodje, S Yates — A Holdsworth, A Carss, J Worthington (sub: L Fowler, 85min), D Schofield, A Lloyd (sub: R Edwards, 112) — A Booth, P Abbott (sub: J McAliskey, 91). **Substitutes not used:** P Senior, N Brown. **Booked:** Sodje.
MANSFIELD TOWN (4-4-2): K Pilkington — B Hassell, R Day, A John-Baptiste, A Eaton — L Lawrence, L Williamson (sub: N MacKenzie, 98), T Curtis, W Corden — C Disley (sub: C Larkin, 60), J Mendes (sub: L D'Jaffo, 69). **Substitutes not used:** J Coates, D Artell. **Booked:** Eaton. **Referee:** M Clattenburg.

IN THE FIRING LINE
MANAGERIAL COMINGS AND GOINGS 2003-04

AUGUST 2003

24 West Ham sack Glenn Roeder three games into the season. Trevor Brooking takes the reins again.

29 Four defeats out of four cost Roddy Collins the Carlisle job. Paul Simpson takes over on October 9.

SEPTEMBER

10 Alan Pardew resigns from Reading and, after much bitterness and High Court action, takes over at Upton Park on October 18. Steve Coppell replaces Pardew at the Madejski Stadium on October 9.

19 Stockport sack Carlton Palmer. Sammy McIlroy, two days after quitting Northern Ireland, is appointed on October 15.

21 Officially by mutual consent but in reality sacked, Glenn Hoddle leaves Spurs. David Pleat begins an eight-month role as caretaker before Jacques Santini is unveiled on June 3.

27 Tranmere dismiss Ray Mathias (Brian Little succeeds him on October 12). Paul Brush is sacked over the phone by Leyton Orient, heralding the Martin Ling dynasty.

29 Northampton sack Martin Wilkinson, to be replaced by Colin Calderwood on October 9.

30 Lawrie Sanchez pays for Wycombe's poor start. Tony Adams starts his managerial career on November 10.

OCTOBER

9 Steve Coppell resigns from Brighton to take over at Reading.

15 Mark McGhee departs Millwall,

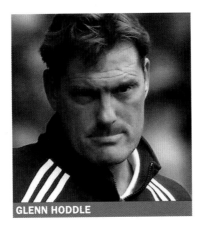

GLENN HODDLE

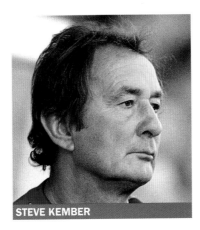

STEVE KEMBER

turning up at Brighton two weeks later. Dennis Wise is sent off in his first game as Millwall caretaker manager, but gets the job full-time on November 11.

18 Bobby Gould resigns from Cheltenham (John Ward takes over on November 6) and Ian Britton leaves Kidderminster the same day, paving the way for Jan Molby's return.

25 Dave Askey moves into the Macclesfield hot seat after David Moss is dismissed.

30 David Hodgson returns to Darlington for a third spell after Mick Tait's caretaker role ends.

NOVEMBER

3 A 5-0 televised defeat to Wigan costs Steve Kember the Crystal Palace job. They are nineteenth when Iain Dowie takes over on December 22. Southend sack Steve Wignall, Steve Tilson getting the job until the end of the season.

8 Nicky Law's dismissal by Bradford paves the way for Bryan Robson's return to management.

10 Bottom and £78m in debt, Leeds sack Peter Reid after 20 league games in charge. Eddie Gray's caretaker role ends on May 10, when Kevin Blackwell takes charge.

DECEMBER

16 Bury sack Andy Preece. Graham Barrow takes temporary charge.

19 Iain Dowie resigns from Oldham and heads for Crystal Palace. Brian Talbot takes over at Boundary Park on March 10.

31 Steve Parkin succeeds Alan Buckley, sacked by Rochdale.

JANUARY 2004

7 Billy Dearden is the first casualty of the new year, Gary Mills taking over at Notts County.

12 A month after taking leave to look after his seriously ill wife, Gary McAllister officially resigns from Coventry. Eric Black is appointed until the end of the season.

19 Bristol Rovers sack Ray Graydon. Ian Atkins takes charge more than four months later.

FEBRUARY

7 Nottingham Forest, 22nd, sack Paul Hart and bring in Joe Kinnear.
9 Grimsby sack Paul Groves, though he will stay on as a player. Nicky Law is appointed until the end of the season on March 4.
12 Brian Horton leaves Port Vale by mutual consent. Martin Foyle moves from dressing-room to manager's office the next day.
13 Having announced his intention to leave Southampton at the end of the season, Gordon Strachan goes early "by mutual agreement". Steve Wigley takes temporary charge. Boston sack Neil Thompson to set up Steve Evans's return.

MARCH

4 Paul Sturrock resigns from Plymouth to replace Strachan at Southampton. Bobby Williamson, formerly of Hibernian, replaces Sturrock on April 20 and wins the title in his first game in charge. Barnsley sack Gudjon Thordarsson and replace him with Paul Hart.
8 Brian Talbot quits Rushden and takes over at Oldham two days later. Ernie Tippet succeeds Talbot.
14 Brentford sack Wally Downes and grab Martin Allen from Barnet.
18 Cambridge sack John Taylor and appoint Claude Le Roy, the former Senegal and Cameroon coach. Swansea oust Brian Flynn, who is succeeded by Kenny Jackett.

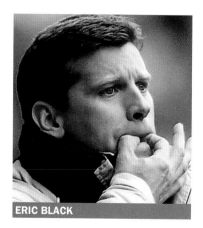

ERIC BLACK

LIVERPOOL

RAFAEL BENITEZ

20 Ian Atkins is suspended by Oxford, then sacked, after Bristol Rovers announce that he is to take over in the summer. Graham Rix returns to management as Atkins's successor.
25 Scunthorpe sack Brian Laws, but he is reinstated on April 14 after boardroom changes.
31 Dave Askey, the Macclesfield caretaker manager, is demoted again, Brian Horton taking charge.

APRIL

16 Colin Lee, allowed to speak to Plymouth about their vacancy, is then sacked by Walsall, who give Paul Merson the task of avoiding relegation.

MAY

3 Eric Black is sacked by Coventry after he demands to know if there is any truth in rumours that Peter Reid is to replace him. Three days later, Peter Reid replaces him. Stan Ternent is dismissed by Burnley after six years in charge, Steve Cotterill taking over.
6 Steve McMahon's 4½-year Blackpool reign ends. Colin Hendry takes over on June 7.
24 Six years, six trophies, Champions League qualification ... that cannot stop Liverpool parting company with Gerard Houllier. Rafael Benitez arrives on June 16.
28 Relegated Grimsby sack Nicky Law, recruiting Russell Slade from Scarborough.
31 The longest goodbye of all: Claudio Ranieri, Chelsea's "dead man walking", exits. Two days later, Jose Mourinho enters.

JUNE

4 Two successive failures in the play-offs cost Danny Wilson his job at Bristol City. Brian Tinnion, a City stalwart, takes over.
16 ... and finally, Bryan Robson resigns from relegated Bradford. Colin Todd replaces him with the club seemingly on the brink of going out of business.

SCOTTISH FOOTBALL

BANK OF SCOTLAND PREMIERLEAGUE
Celtic

RUNNERS-UP
Rangers

TENNENT'S SCOTTISH CUP
Celtic

RUNNERS-UP
Dunfermline Athletic

CIS INSURANCE CUP
Livingston

RUNNERS-UP
Hibernian

BELL'S SCOTTISH LEAGUE FIRST DIVISION
Inverness Caledonian Thistle

RUNNERS-UP
Clyde

SECOND DIVISION
Airdrie United

RUNNERS-UP
Hamilton Academical

THIRD DIVISION
Stranraer

RUNNERS-UP
Stirling Albion

Son shines in Paradise: the great Henrik Larsson is accompanied by Jordan, 7, as he bids a final fond farewell to the Celtic faithful

THE GAMES

Saturday August 9 2003

Dundee United 1 Hibernian 2; Hearts 2 Aberdeen 0;
Motherwell 0 Dundee 3; Partick Thistle 1 Livingston 1;
Dunfermline 0 Celtic 0; Rangers 4 Kilmarnock 0

Saturday August 16

Kilmarnock 2 Partick Thistle 1; Livingston 1
Motherwell 0; Celtic 5 Dundee United 0; Aberdeen 2
Rangers 3

Sunday August 17

Dundee 0 Dunfermline 2; Hibernian 1 Hearts 0

Saturday August 23

Aberdeen 1 Dunfermline 2; Dundee 2 Livingston 1;
Hearts 3 Dundee United 0; Motherwell 2 Kilmarnock 1;
Rangers 5 Hibernian 2; Partick Thistle 1 Celtic 2

Saturday August 30

Celtic 5 Livingston 1; Hibernian 1 Aberdeen 1;
Motherwell 2 Partick Thistle 2

Sunday August 31

Dundee United 1 Rangers 3; Hearts 1 Dunfermline 0;
Kilmarnock 1 Dundee 1

Saturday September 13

Aberdeen 2 Partick Thistle 1; Hibernian 0 Motherwell 2;
Kilmarnock 0 Hearts 2; Livingston 0 Dundee United 0;
Rangers 4 Dunfermline 0; Dundee 0 Celtic 1

Saturday September 20

Celtic 3 Motherwell 0; Dundee 2 Aberdeen 0;
Dunfermline 0 Hibernian 0; Livingston 1 Kilmarnock 2;
Partick Thistle 0 Dundee United 2

Sunday September 21

Hearts 0 Rangers 4

Saturday September 27

Aberdeen 0 Livingston 3; Dundee United 1 Kilmarnock 1;
Dunfermline 2 Partick Thistle 1; Motherwell 1 Hearts 1;
Rangers 3 Dundee 1; Hibernian 1 Celtic 2

Saturday October 4

Dundee Utd 0 Motherwell 2; Hearts 2 Dundee 2;
Kilmarnock 1 Aberdeen 3; Livingston 0 Dunfermline 0;
Partick Thistle 0 Hibernian 1; Rangers 0 Celtic 1

Saturday October 18

Aberdeen 0 Dundee Utd 1; Celtic 5 Hearts 0; Dundee 1
Partick Thistle 0; Dunfermline 2 Kilmarnock 3;
Hibernian 0 Livingston 2

Sunday October 19

Motherwell 1 Rangers 1

Saturday October 25

Celtic 4 Aberdeen 0; Hibernian 3 Kilmarnock 1;
Partick Thistle 1 Hearts 4; Livingston 0 Rangers 0

IT WAS DUBBED "THE LONG GOODBYE". Henrik Larsson's departure from Celtic was so emotional and drawn-out that there were more tears than Halle Berry on Oscars night. The man known as The Magnificent Seven had ridden off into the sunset — and there will be no return.

Some of Larsson's team-mates had ventured that his iconic No 7 shirt be "retired", but Martin O'Neill did not subscribe to that wish. The Celtic manager may have lost his leading man, but as he reviewed a successful 2003-04 campaign, he knew that he had a supporting cast who looked capable of delivering a follow-up.

Just like *The Return of the King*, Celtic monopolised almost every award ceremony. Even if they missed out on the treble, there was still a trilogy of their own to eulogise: a third Bank of Scotland Premierleague title in four seasons under O'Neill — with a gap so large over Rangers, 17 points, it required Glasgow's giant IMAX screen to get both in the picture — as well as a record 32nd triumph in the Scottish Cup.

The prolific Larsson may have been top scorer yet again, but he was muscled out of the personal awards by his team-mates: Jackie McNamara received the Footballer of the Year trophy while Chris Sutton won the accolade from the players' union.

However, if Celtic swept the board with true blockbuster gluttony, the tales of intrigue and drama that cloaked much of the season came from the smaller productions. Dundee and Livingston went into administration, prompting fears for their futures: both survived, the latter defying the odds to win their first trophy by beating Hibernian in the CIS Insurance Cup final, while Dundee displayed the zeal of a reformed addict as they mapped out a frugal way ahead after revealing a debt of £20 million.

Over at Ibrox, the empire was crumbling. Alex McLeish's side, treble-winners a year earlier, finished the season without a trophy. Rangers' season effectively ended in March, when Celtic knocked them out of the Scottish Cup. There were plenty of other zeroes: the £80 million worth of debt and the trio of signings brought in by McLeish last summer: Nuno Capucho, Emerson and Egil Ostenstad, who were all paid to leave with time left on their contracts.

Capucho's arrival last July may have been perceived as an expensive way to rub salt into Celtic's wounds — he had been purchased from FC Porto just weeks after Jose Mourinho's team had beaten Celtic in the Uefa Cup final. However, so calamitous was the Portugal forward that the abiding memory of his stay in Glasgow will be his arrival as a substitute during his last Old Firm derby and receiving raucous applause — from 53,000 mocking Celtic fans.

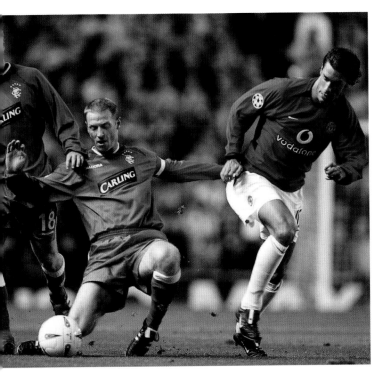

Rangers' tussles with Manchester United were disappointingly one-sided

Rangers began the season with such high hopes. However, the exit of Barry Ferguson, their talismanic captain, to Blackburn Rovers at the end of August robbed them of an influential personality. Christian Nerlinger supplied a match-winner against VfB Stuttgart on the opening night of the Champions League, but by the end of the season the German was back in his homeland, another whose contract had been terminated as Rangers' wretched season unravelled.

When Celtic went to Ibrox on October 4 they were trailing their rivals by two points and were without the suspended Bobo Balde. Sutton was asked to fill the void and there was no trace of vanity from the man who had underlined what a fine striker he is just days earlier by scoring against Lyons in the Champions League.

Sutton was a defensive rock while John Hartson scored to give Celtic a 1-0 success. They could have gone five points behind Rangers; instead they leapt one in front and never looked back.

Celtic then embarked on a run of 25 successive league victories, eclipsing the record of Jock Stein's side 35 years earlier and the Scottish benchmark of 23 achieved by Morton in 1963-64. They remained undefeated until after the title was wrapped up on April 18 with a 1-0 win away to Kilmarnock and then defeated Rangers in the final Old Firm encounter to complete a "green-and-whitewash" by winning all four league derbies, plus that Scottish Cup contest, and establishing a sequence of dominance not seen for 40 years.

Sunday October 26

Dundee Utd 1 Dundee 1

Saturday November 1

Aberdeen 0 Motherwell 3; Dundee 1 Hibernian 1; Dunfermline 2 Dundee Utd 0; Hearts 3 Livingston 1; Rangers 3 Partick Thistle 1; Kilmarnock 0 Celtic 5

Saturday November 8

Celtic 5 Dunfermline 0; Dundee 0 Motherwell 1; Hibernian 2 Dundee Utd 2; Livingston 2 Partick Thistle 0

Sunday November 9

Aberdeen 0 Hearts 1; Kilmarnock 2 Rangers 3

Saturday November 22

Dunfermline 2 Dundee 0; Motherwell 1 Livingston 1; Partick Thistle 2 Kilmarnock 4; Rangers 3 Aberdeen 0; Dundee Utd 1 Celtic 5

Sunday November 23

Hearts 2 Hibernian 0

Tuesday November 25

Motherwell 2 Dunfermline 2

Saturday November 29

Celtic 3 Partick Thistle 1; Dunfermline 2 Aberdeen 2; Kilmarnock 2 Motherwell 0; Livingston 1 Dundee 1

Sunday November 30

Dundee Utd 2 Hearts 1; Hibernian 0 Rangers 1

Saturday December 6

Dundee 1 Kilmarnock 2; Dunfermline 2 Hearts 1; Rangers 2 Dundee Utd 1; Livingston 0 Celtic 2

Sunday December 7

Aberdeen 3 Hibernian 1; Partick Thistle 1 Motherwell 0

Saturday December 13

Celtic 3 Dundee 2; Dundee Utd 2 Livingston 0; Hearts 2 Kilmarnock 1; Motherwell 0 Hibernian 1; Partick Thistle 0 Aberdeen 3

Sunday December 14

Dunfermline 2 Rangers 0

Saturday December 20

Aberdeen 2 Dundee 2; Kilmarnock 0 Livingston 3; Rangers 2 Hearts 1

Sunday December 21

Hibernian 1 Dunfermline 2; Motherwell 0 Celtic 2

Tuesday December 23

Dundee Utd 0 Partick Thistle 0

Saturday December 27

Celtic 6 Hibernian 0; Kilmarnock 0 Dundee Utd 2; Livingston 1 Aberdeen 1; Partick Thistle 4 Dunfermline 1; Hearts 0 Motherwell 0

Sunday December 28

Dundee 0 Rangers 2

Saturday January 3 2004

Aberdeen 3 Kilmarnock 1; Dunfermline 2 Livingston 2; Hibernian 3 Partick Thistle 2; Motherwell 3 Dundee Utd 1; Celtic 3 Rangers 0

Tuesday January 6
Dundee 1 Hearts 2

Saturday January 17
Dundee Utd 3 Aberdeen 2; Kilmarnock 1 Dunfermline 1;
Livingston 1 Hibernian 0; Partick Thistle 1 Dundee 2;
Rangers 1 Motherwell 0

Sunday January 18
Hearts 0 Celtic 1

Saturday January 24
Dunfermline 1 Motherwell 0; Hearts 2 Partick Thistle 0;
Kilmarnock 0 Hibernian 2; Rangers 1 Livingston 0;
Aberdeen 1 Celtic 3

Sunday January 25
Dundee 2 Dundee Utd 1

Saturday January 31
Celtic 5 Kilmarnock 1; Dundee Utd 1 Dunfermline 0;
Hibernian 1 Dundee 1

Sunday February 1
Partick Thistle 0 Rangers 1

Tuesday February 10
Dundee Utd 0 Hibernian 0

Wednesday February 11
Dunfermline 1 Celtic 4; Hearts 1 Aberdeen 0;
Motherwell 5 Dundee 3; Partick Thistle 5 Livingston 2;
Rangers 2 Kilmarnock 0

Saturday February 14
Celtic 2 Dundee Utd 1; Dundee 0 Dunfermline 1;
Kilmarnock 2 Partick Thistle 1; Livingston 3
Motherwell 1; Aberdeen 1 Rangers 1

Sunday February 15
Hibernian 1 Hearts 1

Saturday February 21
Aberdeen 2 Dunfermline 0; Dundee 1 Livingston 0;
Hearts 3 Dundee Utd 1; Motherwell 1 Kilmarnock 0;
Rangers 3 Hibernian 0

Sunday February 22
Partick Thistle 1 Celtic 4

Tuesday February 24
Livingston 2 Hearts 3; Motherwell 1 Aberdeen 0

Saturday February 28
Dunfermline 0 Hearts 0; Hibernian 0 Aberdeen 1;
Kilmarnock 4 Dundee 2; Motherwell 3 Partick Thistle 0

Sunday February 29
Celtic 5 Livingston 1; Dundee Utd 2 Rangers 0

Sunday March 7
Kilmarnock 1 Hearts 1

Tuesday March 9
Aberdeen 0 Partick Thistle 0

Saturday March 13
Dundee 1 Aberdeen 1; Hearts 1 Rangers 1;
Partick Thistle 1 Dundee Utd 1

Celtic made it a Double when they added the Scottish Cup to the title

Heart of Midlothian made it on to the list of honourable mentions onced more. Craig Levein's team again finished in third place, much closer to second than Rangers would like. Hearts' bright young manager defied budget cuts and the backdrop of supporter unrest about a move to Murrayfield to produce a side who defeated Rangers and drew twice with Celtic, as well as winning away to Bordeaux in the Uefa Cup. Levein has offered a glimpse of hope that the Edinburgh club can challenge the Glasgow duopoly. That will be aided by the club deciding to stay, for the time being, at Tynecastle, their spiritual home for more than a century, as well as a newly opened training complex and youth academy.

City rivals Hibernian missed out on their chance of a first trophy since 1991 when they did all the hard work by knocking Celtic and Rangers out of the CIS Insurance Cup but then lost to Livingston in the final, despite being backed by an army of almost 40,000 fans at Hampden Park. Bobby Williamson, the manager, departed for Plymouth Argyle but left behind an impressive collection of young talent for his successor, Tony Mowbray. That departure bug was contagious. Jimmy Calderwood left Dunfermline Athletic barely a week after they had contributed to an engrossing Scottish Cup final to take over from Steve Paterson at Aberdeen.

Inverness Caledonian Thistle translated their habitual cup heroics into league success by snatching the first-division championship from Clyde on a dramatic final day. Airdrie United relied on the evergreen Owen Coyle to win the second division, while Stranraer won the third thanks to their new manager, Neil Watt.

PLAYER OF THE SEASON
Henrik Larsson   Celtic

Great artists are rarely appreciated until after they have gone, which is why Henrik Larsson's work will now be seen from a different perspective in Scotland. The Swede's seven years at Celtic saw his contribution devalued the more prolific he became. The public and the media took his goals for granted and praise was reserved until his departure in May. As usual, he went out on a high with two goals in the Scottish Cup final to bring his total for the season to 41 and to 242 for Celtic. If the Bank of Scotland Premierleague is seen as painting by numbers, Larsson proved that he could could be as vivid on the larger canvas. He left with 35 goals in European competition for Celtic to put him seventh in the all-time European scorers list, in the company of Gerd Muller, Eusebio and Alfredo Di Stefano. That is the landscape on which Larsson should be judged.

Phil Gordon

LEADING SCORERS

		League	SFAC	CIS	Euro	Total
BANK OF SCOTLAND PREMIERLEAGUE						
Henrik Larsson	Celtic	30	5	0	6	41
Chris Sutton	Celtic	19	2	0	7	28
Nacho Novo	Dundee	19	1	1	4	25
James Grady	Partick Thistle	15	2	1	0	18
Derek Riordan	Hibernian	15	0	3	0	18
Stephen Crawford	Dunfermline	13	2	2	0	17
Mark de Vries	Hearts	13	0	1	2	16
Shota Arveladze	Rangers	12	2	0	1	15
Kris Boyd	Kilmarnock	15	0	0	0	15
David Clarkson	Motherwell	12	2	0	0	14
BELL'S LEAGUE FIRST DIVISION						
Paul Ritchie	Inverness CT	14	5	1	0	20
Alex Burke	Queen of the South	13	0	3	0	16
Ian Harty	Clyde	15	0	0	0	15
David Bingham	Inverness CT	13	2	0	0	15
Mixu Paatelainen	St Johnstone	11	0	2	0	13
SECOND DIVISION						
Gareth Hutchison	Berwick	22	3	0	0	25
Paul Tosh	Forfar	19	3	2	0	24
Brian McPhee	Hamilton	18	2	2	0	22
Peter Weatherson	Morton	15	1	1	0	17
Brian Carrigan	Hamilton	15	0	1	0	16
THIRD DIVISION						
Michael Moore	Stranraer	24	1	0	0	25
Scott McLean	Stirling	21	0	0	0	21
David Graham	Stranraer	19	0	0	0	19
Paul McManus	Albion	18	0	1	0	19
Martin Johnston	Peterhead	18	0	0	0	18
Martin Bavidge	Peterhead	16	2	0	0	18

Sunday March 14
Celtic 1 Motherwell 1

Wednesday March 17
Dundee 1 Celtic 2

Saturday March 20
Dundee Utd 4 Kilmarnock 1; Dunfermline 1 Partick Thistle 0; Rangers 4 Dundee 0

Sunday March 21
Aberdeen 1 Livingston 2; Hibernian 0 Celtic 4

Tuesday March 23
Rangers 4 Dunfermline 1

Wednesday March 24
Hibernian 3 Motherwell 3; Livingston 2 Dundee Utd 3

Saturday March 27
Dundee Utd 1 Motherwell 0; Hearts 3 Dundee 1; Kilmarnock 3 Aberdeen 1; Livingston 0 Dunfermline 0; Partick Thistle 1 Hibernian 1

Sunday March 28
Rangers 1 Celtic 2

Saturday April 3
Aberdeen 3 Dundee Utd 0; Celtic 2 Hearts 2; Dundee 2 Partick Thistle 1; Dunfermline 2 Kilmarnock 1; Hibernian 3 Livingston 1

Sunday April 4
Motherwell 0 Rangers 1

Wednesday April 7
Livingston 1 Kilmarnock 1; Motherwell 1 Hearts 1

Saturday April 10
Hibernian 3 Kilmarnock 0; Partick Thistle 1 Hearts 0

Sunday April 11
Dundee Utd 2 Dundee 2

Tuesday April 13
Dunfermline 1 Hibernian 1

Wednesday April 14
Livingston 1 Rangers 1

Thursday April 15
Motherwell 1 Dunfermline 0

Saturday April 17
Dundee 2 Hibernian 2; Dunfermline 1 Dundee Utd 1; Hearts 1 Livingston 1; Rangers 2 Partick Thistle 0

Sunday April 18
Aberdeen 0 Motherwell 2; Kilmarnock 0 Celtic 1

Wednesday April 21
Celtic 1 Aberdeen 2

Saturday April 24
Dundee Utd 3 Rangers 3; Dunfermline 3 Motherwell 0; Kilmarnock 2 Hibernian 0; Livingston 2 Aberdeen 0; Partick Thistle 0 Dundee 1

Sunday April 25

Hearts 1 Celtic 1

Saturday May 1

Dundee Utd 0 Hearts 2; Hibernian 1 Dundee 0;
Kilmarnock 4 Livingston 2; Partick Thistle 2 Aberdeen 0;
Rangers 4 Motherwell 0

Sunday May 2

Celtic 1 Dunfermline 2

Wednesday May 5

Hibernian 1 Partick Thistle 2

Saturday May 8

Aberdeen 0 Hibernian 1; Dundee 2 Kilmarnock 0;
Hearts 2 Dunfermline 1; Motherwell 0 Dundee Utd 1;
Celtic 1 Rangers 0

Sunday May 9

Livingston 2 Partick Thistle 2

Tuesday May 11

Dundee Utd 3 Dunfermline 2

Wednesday May 12

Dundee 2 Livingston 0; Kilmarnock 4 Aberdeen 0;
Motherwell 1 Celtic 1; Rangers 0 Hearts 1

Saturday May 15

Aberdeen 1 Dundee 2; Livingston 4 Hibernian 1;
Partick Thistle 2 Kilmarnock 2

Sunday May 16

Celtic 2 Dundee Utd 1; Dunfermline 2 Rangers 3;
Hearts 3 Motherwell 2

MATCH OF THE SEASON

Celtic 2 Heart of Midlothian 2
Celtic Park, Saturday April 3 2004
Phil Gordon

PAUL LAMBERT is 34, has money in the bank and a European Cup winner's medal in his cabinet at home. He doesn't need to be tearing about at five o'clock on a Saturday evening as if he was an eager young apprentice whose future depended on it. Yet he does. And the Celtic captain is not alone. His commitment is mirrored by everyone who shares the dressing-room that Martin O'Neill, the manager, has created — which is why the clock is still running on Celtic's remarkable run of being unbeaten at home since Ajax won there in August 2001.

After the amount of effort that the champions-elect have put into establishing such an overwhelming lead in the Bank of Scotland Premierleague title race this season, and with a Uefa Cup quarter-final against Villarreal approaching, Lambert and his team-mates would have been entitled to give up the ghost once Mark de Vries put Heart of Midlothian 2-0 in front with just 12 minutes left. The long, unbeaten league campaign was surely at an end. So too, possibly more painfully, was the impregnable record at Celtic Park. After 75 games, Hearts were about to succeed where others, notably Juventus, Barcelona and Bayern Munich, had failed.

When De Vries spun in the box then nutmegged Stanislav Varga to drill a left-foot finish beyond David Marshall and double the lead that Kevin McKenna had provided in the 21st minute, the silence around Celtic Park was overpowering. It was the end of an era.

Not quite. Cue the resurrection. There were only 150 seconds left when, finally, Chris Sutton breached the Hearts defence after Craig Gordon had saved his first shot. Celtic Park was in a ferment, but with 59,000 fans roaring them on, anything was possible. There was time for Henrik Larsson to have a header cleared off the line by Robbie Neilson and for De Vries to miss a sitter at the other end before Lambert began the move that brought the house down.

The former Scotland player chased to retrieve a ball that Hearts had thumped clear to the touchline and fended off a challenge before launching a deep, angled cross that Varga glanced into the path of Didier Agathe at the back post. The winger, for once, showed deft control before thrashing a left-foot shot into the roof of the net to complete the most astonishing comeback.

That stretched the unbeaten home record to 76 games. The number itself does not matter to Lambert, only the zero tolerance for failure. "We have guys in the dressing-room who are hungry to keep winning," Lambert said. "You can have all the ability in the world, but you must also have desire in abundance. We had created a record to be proud of and we didn't want to lose it.

"We want to win the league as quickly as possible. That is what we

Gordon saves at the feet of Sutton as Hearts battle to the bitter end

set out to do at the start of the season, win the title, not set records. What we have done here in the past few years has been phenomenal and we feel proud when players from the side that won the European Cup in 1967 — such as John Clark, our kit man — praise us, because they have earned the highest accolade. So has the manager, who won it twice." Lambert modestly left out his own name from that list, even though his Champions League success with Borussia Dortmund makes him one of the more recent Britons to achieve that rare honour.

"The crowd play a major part in our success," Lambert said. "They pulled us through when we were 2-0 down. The demand here is constant. The fans want us to win every single game, but if you can handle that, then you can be part of something special."

Levein would love to be able to recreate that environment. The shrewd young manager paid Celtic the sincerest form of flattery on Saturday by imitating them, with a physical presence and a non-stop work ethic as well as excellent finishing by McKenna and De Vries. Last April, his team had won at Tynecastle to inflict Celtic's last league defeat. This, for Levein, felt like a defeat. "Maybe in the cold light of day I will feel good about drawing 2-2 here, but not now," he said.

CELTIC (4-4-2): D Marshall — J McNamara, B Balde, S Varga, S McManus (sub: S Petrov, 63min) — D Agathe, P Lambert, S Pearson, A Thompson — H Larsson, C Sutton. **Substitutes not used:** M McGovern, C Beattie, J Smith. **Booked:** McNamara.

HEART OF MIDLOTHIAN (3-5-2): C Gordon — P Kisnorbo, S Pressley, S Severin — R Neilson, N McFarlane, P Hartley, N Jancyzk, A Maybury — G Weir (sub: C Berra, 90), K McKenna (sub: M de Vries, 73). **Substitutes not used:** T Moilanen, D Wyness, A Kirk. **Booked:** Maybury, McKenna.

BANK OF SCOTLAND PREMIERLEAGUE

	P	W	D	L	F	A	GD	Pts
Celtic	38	31	5	2	105	25	80	98
Rangers	38	25	6	7	76	33	43	81
Hearts	38	19	11	8	56	40	16	68
Dunfermline	38	14	11	13	45	52	-8	53
Dundee Utd	38	13	10	15	47	60	-13	49
Motherwell	38	12	10	16	42	49	-7	46
Dundee	38	12	10	16	48	57	-9	46
Hibernian	38	11	11	16	41	60	-19	44
Livingston	38	10	13	15	48	57	-9	43
Kilmarnock	38	12	6	20	51	74	-23	42
Aberdeen	38	9	7	22	39	63	-24	34
Partick	38	6	8	24	39	67	-28	26

BELL'S LEAGUE FIRST DIVISION

	P	W	D	L	F	A	GD	Pts
Inverness CT	36	21	7	8	67	33	34	70
Clyde	36	20	9	7	64	40	24	69
St Johnstone	36	15	12	9	59	45	14	57
Falkirk	36	15	10	11	43	37	6	55
Qn of the South	36	15	9	12	46	48	-2	54
Ross County	36	12	13	11	49	41	8	49
St Mirren	36	9	14	13	39	46	-7	41
Raith	36	8	10	18	37	57	-20	34
Ayr	36	6	13	17	37	58	-21	31
Brechin	36	6	9	21	37	73	-36	27

BELL'S LEAGUE SECOND DIVISION

	P	W	D	L	F	A	GD	Pts
Airdrie Utd	36	20	10	6	64	36	28	70
Hamilton	36	18	8	10	70	47	23	62
Dumbarton	36	18	6	12	56	41	15	60
Morton	36	16	11	9	66	58	8	59
Berwick	36	14	6	16	61	67	-6	48
Forfar	36	12	11	13	49	57	-8	47
Alloa	36	12	8	16	55	55	0	44
Arbroath	36	11	10	15	41	57	-16	43
East Fife	36	11	8	17	38	45	-7	41
Stenhousemuir	36	7	4	25	28	65	-37	25

BELL'S LEAGUE THIRD DIVISION

	P	W	D	L	F	A	GD	Pts
Stranraer	36	24	7	5	87	30	57	79
Stirling	36	23	8	5	78	27	51	77
Gretna	36	20	8	8	59	39	20	68
Peterhead	36	18	7	11	67	37	30	61
Cowdenbeath	36	15	10	11	46	39	7	55
Montrose	36	12	12	12	52	63	-11	48
Queen's Park	36	10	11	15	41	53	-12	41
Albion	36	12	4	20	66	75	-9	40
Elgin	36	6	7	23	48	93	-45	25
East Stirling	36	2	2	32	30	118	-88	8

HOW LOW CAN YOU GO?

Paul Connolly

THE GROUND IS WEE AND tucked behind a retail park in Falkirk. The entrance is in a street lined with grimy tenements where a flat can be bought for around £20,000. There's a small stand on one side of Firs Park and two sides of terracing. One end is backed by a 12ft wall, protecting shoppers from misdirected shots. Ian Ramsay, the chairman of East Stirlingshire Supporters' Club, said: "At least we save money on ball-boys at that end. If we could afford ball-boys in the first place, that is."

Even if you're a supporter of cash-strapped Leeds United who suffered the ignominies of relegation last season, or a Carlisle United fan who watched your club slip out of the Football League, spare a thought for the 100-odd hardcore support of East Stirlingshire, Britain's worst senior team in 2003-04.

They looked on as the club scraped just eight points from 36 games in the Bell's Scottish League third division, winning two games all season, losing 32 and failing to secure even one point away from home. The Shire also conceded 118 goals and finished with the sort of goal difference, minus 88, that would shame a pub team. Furthermore, they closed the season an astonishing 71 points behind Stranraer, the third-division champions. They managed to avoid becoming the worst senior team in British history only on the last day of the season with a 2-1 win over Elgin City (who were also their only previous victims, back in November), and only avoided relegation because there is no farther for them to fall, there being no lower national division in Scotland.

That said, pre-season, East Stirlingshire fans were hardly anticipating a season of champagne and glory. The previous campaign also saw them rack up just two wins, although seven draws ensured that their points total soared into double figures, just 15 behind Elgin, the second-bottom side.

I have had a soft spot for East Stirlingshire since I was 10, saw their name in the league table and liked the look of it (they were thirteenth in the second division even

then, so I can hardly be accused of glory-hunting). However, my lack of proximity to Falkirk, or indeed Scotland, meant that my first visit to Firs Park was in February 2003, when I saw the Shire battle out an enthralling 2-2 draw with their perennial benefactors, Elgin, a game that garnered them one of their 13 points in the 2002-03 season.

Even then it was clear that, results aside, the club was in trouble. A visit to the hopelessly misnamed merchandise shop — in essence an abandoned hut — proved fruitless. According to one of those on the terraces, it hadn't been open for a year or more and there was nothing to buy, a sure sign of a poorly run organisation.

I returned in December 2003 to research a feature as the Shire's appalling start to the 2003-04 season began to take shape with just one win in 15 games, a streak that would eventually extend to one in 35, with a 24-game losing run thrown in. There was a surprisingly convivial

Dennis Newall, the East Stirlingshire manager, tries to rally his troops during a season of almost unrelenting failure

atmosphere behind the scenes at the shabby little ground, although the granite-jawed chairman, Alan Mackin, would only speak to me off the record and was a stern presence throughout. The chief executive, Les Thomson, a club stalwart, was friendly if robustly straightforward. "If we stay here we'll die because there is no fan base," Thomson said. "This used to be a community club but the community's moved away — everything's been knocked down. Our fan base is down to about 100. If we lose one fan, who's going to replace that person? Who's going to come and support East Stirlingshire? We have to move or the club dies — it's really that simple. I know we have a loyal fan base and God knows they have to be right now, but do they want the club to die?"

Although one of the world's 100 oldest clubs, East Stirlingshire have rarely set Scottish football alight. Their honours list is limited to the 1932 second-division (now the first division) title and their two most notable products are Jimmy Smith, a centre forward who joined Rangers in 1928 and was capped by Scotland, and Sir Alex Ferguson, whose first foray into management was here in 1974 (tellingly, perhaps, East Stirling is the only club with which he has failed to win a trophy).

The present malaise can be traced back to the summer of 2002 when the new board, led by Mackin, took over the club and immediately imposed a £10 a week wage ceiling. Almost overnight a slew of the club's best players jumped ship and were replaced by youth-team players and journeymen from Scotland's junior (non-League) football system.

To say that the fans were peeved by Mackin's approach would be understating it — most seem to have been enraged, which is hardly surprising given some of the comments from Mackin. He was quoted by a local newspaper soon after the end of the season as saying: "As far as I am concerned I have done a great job at the club on the business side of things, but the results are a different matter," a statement of some insensitivity given that the board's penny-pinching approach has left the Shire with such a poor team.

The fans, who staged a protest after the game against Stirling Albion in May (the match was lost 3-1, although the attendance of 779 was the highest of the season), believe that Mackin, the major shareholder, is adhering to the manifesto by which he was elected — to sell the ground, pay the shareholders a dividend and let them decide what to do with it. The more the ground fetches, the more he stands to make.

Whenever profiteers, who have little respect for history or the community, close a club, few people continue to care beyond the immediate rumpus and hand-wringing. Life goes on and the people who really support the club find other ways to fill their time. It may be insignificant in the larger scheme of things, but every time it happens another little corner of football's soul is sucked dry.

TENNENT'S SCOTTISH CUP

Stilian Petrov, who scored Celtic's third goal, takes on Aaron Labonte in the Tennent's Scottish Cup final

Semi-finals (Hampden Park):   Saturday April 10
INVERNESS CT (1) **1**   **DUNFERMLINE ATHLETIC** (0) **1**
Ritchie 45   Brewster 67
13,255

                                                                    Sunday April 11
LIVINGSTON (0) **1**   **CELTIC** (1) **3**
McMenamin 79   Sutton 37, 65, Larsson 50
26,152

Replay (Pittodrie):   Tuesday April 20
DUNFERMLINE ATHLETIC (1) **3**   **INVERNESS CT** (1) **2**
Darren Young 25, Brewster 63, Nicholson 78   Ritchie 7, Bingham 90 (pen)
5,728

Final (Hampden Park):   Saturday May 22
DUNFERMLINE ATHLETIC (1) **1**   **CELTIC** (0) **3**
Skerla 40   Larsson 58, 71, Petrov 84
50,846

Within seconds of Celtic capturing a record 32nd Scottish Cup, Martin O'Neill was pondering how to replace the irreplaceable Henrik Larsson, whose two sublime second-half goals on his farewell took his tally for the club to 242 and earned his manager a Double to add to a first-season treble. "Is there another Larsson out there?" O'Neill mused. "I think you might have to go intergalactic to find him." Skerla had given Dunfermline the lead, but Larsson ended their hopes of a shock win.

DUNFERMLINE ATHLETIC (4-4-2): D Stillie — B Nicholson, A Skerla, A Labonte, R Byrne (sub: A Tod, 87min) — Derek Young, Darren Young, G Mason (sub: D Grondin, 81), G Dempsey (sub: L Bullen, 59) — S Crawford, C Brewster. **Substitutes not used:** S Thomson, B Mehmet. **Booked:** Brewster, Darren Young.
CELTIC (4-4-2): D Marshall — D Agathe, B Balde, S Varga, J McNamara — S Petrov, N Lennon, S Pearson (sub: R Wallace, 57), A Thompson — H Larsson, C Sutton. **Substitutes not used:** M McGovern, P Lambert, J Mjallby, C Beattie. **Booked:** Lennon.
Referee: S Dougal.

CIS INSURANCE CUP

Final (Hampden Park):   Sunday March 14
HIBERNIAN (0) **0**   **LIVINGSTON** (0) **2**
45,445   Lilley 50, McAllister 52

Livingston claimed the first silverware in their history when two goals in two second-half minutes accounted for the side that had knocked out Rangers and Celtic on route to the final.

HIBERNIAN (4-3-3): D Andersson — G Smith (sub: T McManus, 62min), C Murdock, M Doumbe, R Edge — G Caldwell, K Thomson, A Reid (sub: S Dobbie, 69) — S Brown, G O'Connor, D Riordan. **Substitutes not used:** A Brown, S Whittaker, K Nicol. **Booked:** Brown, Thomson.
LIVINGSTON (3-5-2): R McKenzie — O Rubio, M Andrews, E Dorardo — D McNamee (sub: S McLaughlin, 79), L Makel, S Lovell, B O'Brien (sub: J McGovern, 90), J McAllister — D Fernandez (sub: F Pasquinelli, 88), D Lilley. **Substitutes not used:** A Main, W Snowdon. **Booked:** McAllister, Dorado.
Referee: W Young.

NON-LEAGUE

NATIONWIDE CONFERENCE
Chester City

PROMOTED VIA PLAY-OFFS
Shrewsbury Town

DR MARTENS LEAGUE
Crawley Town

RYMAN LEAGUE
Canvey Island

UNIBOND LEAGUE
Hucknall Town

FA TROPHY
Hednesford Town

FA VASE
Winchester City

Cheshire cat: Daryl Clare is all smiles after Chester City secured the Conference title and a return to the Football League

FINAL TABLES

NATIONWIDE CONFERENCE

	P	W	D	L	F	A	Pts
Chester City	42	27	11	4	85	34	92
Hereford United	42	28	7	7	103	44	91
Shrewsbury Town	42	20	14	8	67	42	74
Barnet	42	19	14	9	60	46	71
Aldershot Town	42	20	10	12	80	67	70
Exeter City	42	19	12	11	71	57	69
Morecambe	42	20	7	15	66	66	67
Stevenage Bor	42	18	9	15	58	52	63
Woking	42	15	16	11	65	52	61
Accrington S	42	15	13	14	68	61	58
Gravesend	42	14	15	13	69	66	57
□ Telford United	42	15	10	17	49	51	55
Dagenham & Red	42	15	9	18	59	64	54
*Burton Albion	42	15	7	20	57	59	51
Scarborough	42	12	15	15	51	54	51
† Margate	42	14	9	19	56	64	51
Tamworth	42	13	10	19	49	68	49
Forest Green R	42	12	12	18	58	80	48
Halifax Town	42	12	8	22	43	65	44
Farnborough	42	10	9	23	53	74	39
Leigh RMI	42	7	8	27	46	97	29
Northwich Victoria	42	4	11	27	30	80	23

*Burton Albion deducted one point for fielding an ineligible player

† Margate relegated after rejecting ten-year ground-share

□ Telford Utd went into liquidation

PROMOTION PLAY-OFFS

SEMI-FINALS, FIRST LEGS

Thursday April 29

ALDERSHOT TOWN (1) **1**   **HEREFORD UNITED** (1) **1**
D'Sane 45 (pen)   Brown 7
6,379

BARNET (2) **2**   **SHREWSBURY TOWN** (0) **1**
Strevens 13 (pen)   Rodgers 43 (pen)
Clist 90   4,171

SECOND LEGS

Monday May 3

HEREFORD UNITED (0) **0**   **ALDERSHOT TOWN** (0) **0**
7,044

(aet; 1-1 on agg; Aldershot won 4-2 on penalties)

SHREWSBURY TOWN (1) **1**   **BARNET** (0) **0**
Rodgers 44 (pen)   7,021

(aet; 2-2 on agg; Shrewsbury won 5-3 on penalties)

FINAL

Sunday May 16   Britannia Stadium

ALDERSHOT TOWN (1) **1**   **SHREWSBURY TOWN** (1) **1**
McLean 35   Darby 43
19,216

(aet; 1-1 after 90min;
Shrewsbury won 3-0 on penalties)

THE REVIEW   Walter Gammie

A FOG OF POLITICS, BLOWN UP by the planned restructuring of the non-League game, frequently obscured a season of scintillating football. By the end, however, the way was cleared for the biggest shake-up since the Alliance Premier League, the present-day Nationwide Conference, was established in 1979. Conference North and South divisions will be introduced in 2004-05 above the Dr Martens League, UniBond League and Ryman League as the feeders into the national division.

The sticking point was a legal challenge by the Ryman League. The Dr Martens League and UniBond League had accepted that the new divisions would be better equipped to prepare clubs for a Conference increasingly dominated by those who are full-time after the introduction of the second promotion place to the Football League. The Ryman League wanted to retain the status quo. When its case was thrown out in February, clubs were again able to focus on securing their places in the new set-up. The last positions were decided by a series of play-offs that promise to become the norm. Two days later the FA, with commendable swiftness, announced who would play where in the new structure.

That did not end the uncertainty. Margate elected to yield their Conference place — they could have held on to it only by agreeing to a ten-year ground-share. Instead, they opted to drop to the Conference South in order to play at Hartsdown Park, whose delayed redevelopment missed a Conference deadline. Kettering Town were switched to the Conference North as Leigh RMI kept their place. That was followed by Telford United going into liquidation, thus giving a reprieve to Northwich Victoria, the only other club to have played in all 25 Conference seasons.

Telford had failed to find a buyer to take over the club after the collapse of the business empire of Andy Shaw, their chairman and the man behind the building of the New Bucks Head stadium. Supporters immediately announced the setting up of AFC Telford United, who were handed a place in the UniBond League first division. Meanwhile, their inspiration, AFC Wimbledon, completed their first step up the ladder by going unbeaten through the Seagrave Haulage Combined Counties League season to take a place in the Ryman League first division. Their forerunners, Aldershot Town, 12 years after Aldershot folded, were denied a return to the Football League only when losing a penalty shoot-out to Shrewsbury Town in the Conference promotion final.

The play-offs, in their second season, again supplied drama. They were cruel on Hereford United, who were left empty-handed after losing in a shoot-out to Aldershot in the semi-finals. They had

O'Connor, of Shrewsbury, tackles Aldershot's Antwi in the play-offs final

finished 21 points clear of Aldershot, 17 ahead of Shrewsbury and only one behind Chester City, the champions. They deserved better. No one, however, could deny Chester their return to the Football League after a four-year absence. Their strength of character reflected that of Mark Wright, their manager.

Shrewsbury's form was never entirely convincing but they held their nerve through the play-offs to follow Lincoln City in 1988 and Darlington in 1990 and reclaim their Football League place at the first attempt. Defeat in their last three matches ended Exeter City's play-off hopes, but they were never far from the headlines. Of all the political issues, nothing vexed the Conference more than the challenges posed by Exeter.

The last hurrah for the former feeder leagues provided a classic duel for the Dr Martens League. Weymouth, under the direction of a new board headed by Ian Ridley, enjoyed a welcome revival led by Steve Claridge, their high-profile player-manager. They could not, however, shake off Crawley Town. The Sussex club profited from the input of the Duly family, after a spell in administration in 1999, and their decision to appoint Francis Vines, an untried manager. The turning point was a meeting between the clubs before a record 4,522 crowd at Broadfield Stadium in March. Crawley won 2-1, took over at the top and went on to secure the title by 12 points.

Canvey Island, runners-up for the previous three seasons, romped to the Ryman League title, sealed on Good Friday. Hucknall Town won the UniBond League for the first time but had not applied for promotion. The capacity of their Watnall Road ground was insufficient for the Conference. Steve Burr, their manager, downcast at Nuneaton Borough after their final-day relegation from the Con-ference the previous season, was beaming again. By June, however, Burr was on his way to Northwich. He was replaced by Ernie Moss.

DR MARTENS LEAGUE
PREMIER DIVISION

	P	W	D	L	F	A	Pts
Crawley Town	42	25	9	8	77	43	84
Weymouth	42	20	12	10	76	47	72
Stafford Rangers	42	19	11	12	55	43	68
Nuneaton Bor	42	17	15	10	65	49	66
Worcester City	42	18	9	15	71	50	63
Hinckley United	42	15	14	13	55	46	59
Newport County	42	15	14	13	52	50	59
Cambridge City	42	14	15	13	54	53	57
Welling United	42	16	8	18	56	58	56
Weston-s-Mare	42	14	13	15	52	52	55
Eastbourne Boro	42	14	13	15	48	56	55
Havant and W	42	15	10	17	59	70	55
Moor Green	42	14	12	16	42	54	54
Merthyr Tydfil	42	13	14	15	60	66	53
Tiverton Town	42	12	15	15	63	64	51
Bath City	42	13	12	17	49	56	51
Dorchester Town	42	14	9	19	56	69	51
Chelmsford City	42	11	16	15	46	53	49
Dover Athletic	42	12	13	17	50	59	49
Hednesford Town	42	12	12	18	56	69	48
Chippenham Town	42	10	17	15	51	63	47
Grantham Town	42	10	15	17	45	67	45

EASTERN DIVISION

	P	W	D	L	F	A	Pts
King's Lynn	42	28	7	7	90	35	91
Histon	42	26	10	6	96	41	88
Tonbridge Angels	42	27	7	8	82	46	88
*Eastleigh	42	27	4	11	88	40	82
Folkestone I	42	20	15	7	91	45	75
Salisbury City	42	21	11	10	73	45	74
Stamford	42	20	11	11	63	45	71
Banbury United	42	19	10	13	65	57	67
Burgess Hill Town	42	19	7	16	67	54	64
Sittingbourne	42	18	8	16	61	55	62
Bashley	42	18	7	17	66	58	61
Ashford Town	42	15	9	18	51	53	54
Chatham Town	42	13	10	19	49	67	49
Fisher Athletic	42	13	10	19	61	81	49
Corby Town	42	12	9	21	44	75	45
Dartford	42	13	6	23	48	81	45
*Burnham	42	12	11	19	52	76	44
Hastings United	42	12	7	23	60	91	43
Newport IoW	42	11	7	24	42	69	40
Rothwell Town	42	9	11	22	30	47	38
Erith & Belvedere	42	7	10	25	45	84	31
Fleet Town	42	5	7	30	35	114	22

Eastleigh and Burnham deducted three points for fielding an ineligible player

WESTERN DIVISION

	P	W	D	L	F	A	Pts
Redditch United	40	25	9	6	75	30	84
Gloucester City	40	24	7	9	77	46	79
Cirencester Town	40	24	4	12	73	40	76
Halesowen Town	40	20	13	7	64	40	73
Rugby United	40	21	8	11	57	40	71
Team Bath	40	21	6	13	62	41	69
Solihull Borough	40	19	9	12	50	31	66
Sutton Coldfield	40	16	15	9	52	38	63
Bromsgrove R	40	16	11	13	60	48	59
Ilkeston Town	40	16	10	14	58	59	58
Clevedon Town	40	16	5	19	55	59	53
Gresley Rovers	40	15	7	18	52	60	52
Mangotsfield Utd	40	14	8	18	70	70	50
Evesham United	40	15	5	20	56	57	50
Taunton Town	40	14	8	18	50	55	50
Yate Town	40	11	9	20	51	79	42
Swindon S	40	10	9	21	41	69	39
Stourport Swifts	40	9	11	20	43	62	38
Bedworth United	40	8	12	20	39	61	36
Cinderford Town	40	7	9	24	50	94	30
Shepshed Dynamo	40	5	13	22	31	87	28

RYMAN LEAGUE
PREMIER DIVISION

	P	W	D	L	F	A	Pts
Canvey Island	46	32	8	6	106	42	104
Sutton Utd	46	25	10	11	94	56	85
Thurrock	46	24	11	11	87	45	83
Hendon	46	25	8	13	68	47	83
*Hornchurch	46	24	11	11	63	35	82
Grays Ath	46	22	15	9	82	39	81
Carshalton Ath	46	24	9	13	66	55	81
Hayes	46	21	11	14	56	46	74
Kettering Town	46	20	11	15	63	63	71
Bognor Regis Town	46	20	10	16	69	67	70
Bishop's Stortford	46	20	9	17	78	61	69
Maidenhead Utd	46	18	9	19	60	68	63
Ford Utd	46	16	14	16	69	63	62
Basingstoke Town	46	17	9	20	58	64	60
Bedford Town	46	14	13	19	62	63	55
Heybridge Swifts	46	14	11	21	57	78	53
Harrow Borough	46	12	14	20	47	63	50
Kingstonian	46	12	13	21	40	56	49
St Albans City	46	12	12	22	55	83	48
Hitchin Town	46	13	8	25	55	89	47
Northwood	46	12	9	25	65	95	45
Billericay Town	46	11	11	24	51	66	44
Braintree Town	46	11	6	29	41	88	39
Aylesbury Utd	46	5	14	27	41	101	29

Hornchurch deducted one point for fielding an ineligible player

NORTH DIVISION

	P	W	D	L	F	A	Pts
Yeading	46	32	7	7	112	54	103
Leyton	46	29	9	8	90	53	96
Cheshunt	46	27	10	9	119	54	91
Chesham Utd	46	24	9	13	104	60	81
Dunstable Town	46	23	9	14	86	61	78
Hemel Hempstead	46	22	12	12	75	72	78
Wealdstone	46	23	7	16	81	51	76
Arlesey Town	46	23	7	16	95	70	76
Boreham Wood	46	20	13	13	82	59	73
Harlow Town	46	20	10	16	75	51	70
Wingate & Finchley	46	19	13	14	68	63	70
East Thurrock Utd	46	19	11	16	62	54	68
Uxbridge	46	15	14	17	59	57	59
Aveley	46	15	14	17	67	71	59
Thame United	46	16	9	21	72	83	57
Waltham Forest	46	15	13	18	62	60	55
Wivenhoe Town	46	15	10	21	79	104	55
Barton Rovers	46	16	6	24	52	80	54
Oxford City	46	14	11	21	56	65	53
Berkhamsted Town	46	12	10	24	66	88	46
Great Wakering R	46	10	13	23	47	97	43
Tilbury	46	10	9	27	56	100	39
Barking & E Ham	46	8	7	31	37	100	31
Enfield	46	5	7	34	44	138	22

* Waltham Forest deducted three points for fielding an ineligible player

SOUTH DIVISION

	P	W	D	L	F	A	Pts
Lewes	46	29	7	10	113	61	94
Worthing	46	26	14	6	87	46	92
Windsor & Eton	46	26	13	7	75	39	91
Slough Town	46	28	6	12	103	63	90
Hampton & R	46	26	11	9	82	45	89
Staines Town	46	26	9	11	85	52	87
Dulwich Hamlet	46	23	15	8	77	57	84
Bromley	46	22	10	14	80	58	76
Walton & Hersham	46	20	14	12	76	55	74
Croydon Athletic	46	20	10	16	70	54	70
Tooting & Mitcham	46	20	9	17	82	68	69
Ashford Town (Mx)	46	18	13	15	69	62	67
Leatherhead	46	19	9	18	83	88	66
Bracknell Town	46	19	6	21	81	87	63
Horsham	46	16	11	19	71	69	59
Marlow	46	16	11	19	50	64	59
Whyteleafe	46	17	4	25	66	93	55
Banstead Athletic	46	15	8	23	56	73	53
Molesey	46	12	6	28	45	84	42
Metropolitan Police	46	9	14	23	58	84	41
Croydon	46	10	10	26	57	88	40
Egham Town	46	8	8	30	55	92	32
Corinthian-Casuals	46	6	6	34	48	110	24
Epsom & Ewell	46	5	8	33	40	117	23

MATCH OF THE SEASON

Aldershot 1 Shrewsbury Town 1 *(aet; Shrewsbury won 3-0 on pens)*
Britannia Stadium, Sunday May 16 2004
Mark Venables

TEN YEARS AFTER Jimmy Quinn suffered play-off heartbreak at Wembley, when Bolton Wanderers overcame a two-goal deficit to beat his Reading team to a place in the Premiership, the former Northern Ireland international finally tasted play-off success yesterday. After Scott Howie had saved Aldershot Town's first three spot kicks in the shoot-out, up stepped Trevor Challis to secure victory for Shrewsbury Town in the Nationwide Conference play-offs final at the Britannia Stadium and they returned to the Football League after a 12-month sojourn in the Conference.

Luke Rodgers blasted Shrewsbury's first penalty over the bar, but Howie settled their nerves by plunging to his left to palm away Tim Sills's effort, reaching out a hand to parry Chris Giles's powerful shot despite diving the wrong way and again hurling himself to his left to deny Jamie Gosling. In between, Jamie Tolley and Jake Sedgemore had scored for Shrewsbury, leaving Challis, deputising for the suspended Darren Moss, the honour of scoring the winning goal.

"I didn't show much emotion in the penalties, even after we missed the first one, because I've seen it all before," Quinn, the Shrewsbury manager, said. "There's a lot of pressure when you step up to take a penalty. Scott Howie took the video home of the penalties for the Aldershot v Hereford semi-final and studied it all week, which gave him a bit of an advantage."

Aldershot made the brighter start, with the lively front pair of Aaron McLean and Roscoe D'Sane tormenting the Shrewsbury rearguard, and it was just reward when McLean gave the Hampshire club the lead after 35 minutes, volleying home after Ray Warburton had headed a free kick from Adam Miller into his path.

Rather than inspire Aldershot, the goal appeared to stunt their attacking instincts and allowed Shrewsbury to gain the ascendancy. Martin O'Connor, the former Walsall midfield player, was the fulcrum of everything positive from Quinn's side. His aggressive tackling and strong running stifled the creativity of Jon Challinor and Gosling and his vision released the willing legs of Sam Aiston and Ryan Lowe.

There was an inevitability about the equaliser. Two minutes before half-time a corner from Tolley was headed back across the six-yard box by Darren Tinson and Duane Darby hit an unstoppable, rising half-volley past Nikki Bull.

The second half was a nervy, tetchy affair, with neither side coming close to scoring, and with both sets of players visibly wilting under the warm May sunshine the impasse was never truly threatened in extra time. As with both of the play-off semi-finals, the tie was settled on penalties. "When it goes to penalties, it's always a

PLAYER OF THE SEASON
Daryl Clare   Chester City

The pressure was on Daryl Clare. Mark Wright had signed the 25-year-old striker from Boston United in October 2002 to supply the cutting edge to a Chester City side built on rock-solid defending. A knee operation in the summer delayed Clare's start. He did not score until November 1 with a penalty away to Scarborough. A run of 14 goals in eight matches between December and February confirmed his return to his best. Come the end of the season, 29 goals in 30 matches, the Conference golden boot, promotion — Clare had delivered.

Walter Gammie

lottery, but we got here that way, so no complaints about the system," Terry Brown, the Aldershot manager, said.

The plaudits belong to Quinn. Brought to Gay Meadow to replace Kevin Ratcliffe, the former Northwich Victoria manager took over a team in turmoil. "We've spent some money to get the squad together and it has taken some time to gel … but we have achieved what we set out to do," Quinn said.

For Aldershot it is a sad culmination of their first season in non-League's top flight, but it is just 12 years since the club emerged from the ashes of the original Aldershot FC. They have gained four promotions, but the final leap into the Football League proved a step too far yesterday. "It really hurts," Brown said. "I told them to hold their heads up. They gave everything they had; they were treading water at the end. It was not meant to be this year, but my players and the management will have learnt an awful lot. There was nothing to choose between the sides; they were two nervous sides who can play better football, but the pressure was killing."

The challenge for Shrewsbury is to attempt to emulate Doncaster Rovers, who followed up victory in last season's promotion play-off final with the third-division championship.

ALDERSHOT TOWN (4-4-2): N Bull — S Downer (sub: D Hooper, 66min), R Warburton, C Giles, D Stirling — J Gosling, J Challinor, W Antwi, A Miller — R D'Sane (sub: L Charles, 86), A McLean (sub: T Sills, 60). **Substitutes not used:** R Barnard, J Chewins. **Booked:** Stirling.
SHREWSBURY TOWN (4-4-2): S Howie — J Sedgemore, D Tinson (sub: L Lawrence, 91), D Ridler, T Challis — R Lowe, M O'Connor (sub: K Street, 84), J Tolley, S Aiston — D Darby (sub: C Cramb, 93), L Rodgers. **Substitutes not used:** D Edwards, K Hart. **Booked:** Lowe, O'Connor, Ridler.

UNIBOND LEAGUE
PREMIER DIVISION

	P	W	D	L	F	A	Pts
*Hucknall Town	44	29	8	7	83	38	95
Droylsden	44	26	8	10	96	64	86
Barrow	44	22	14	8	82	52	80
Alfreton Town	44	23	9	12	73	43	78
Harrogate Town	44	24	5	15	79	63	77
Southport	44	20	10	14	71	52	70
Worksop Town	44	19	13	12	69	50	70
Lancaster City	44	20	9	15	62	49	69
Vauxhall Motors	44	19	10	15	78	75	67
Gainsborough Tr	44	17	13	14	70	52	64
Stalybridge Celtic	44	18	10	16	72	66	64
Altrincham	44	16	15	13	66	51	63
Runcorn	44	16	13	15	67	63	61
Ashton Utd	44	17	8	19	59	79	59
Whitby Town	44	14	11	19	55	70	53
Marine	44	13	12	19	62	74	51
Bradford P A	44	12	14	18	48	62	50
Spennymoor Utd	44	14	6	24	55	93	48
Burscough	44	10	15	19	47	67	45
Radcliffe Borough	44	12	6	26	74	99	42
Blyth Spartans	44	10	10	24	54	74	40
Frickley Athletic	44	11	7	26	51	83	40
Wakefield & Emley	44	8	6	30	45	99	30

*Hucknall Town were not eligible for promotion because of Nationwide Conference stadium criteria

FIRST DIVISION

	P	W	D	L	F	A	Pts
Hyde Utd	42	24	8	10	79	49	80
Matlock Town	42	23	7	12	78	51	76
Farsley Celtic	42	20	14	8	78	56	74
Lincoln Utd	42	20	11	11	73	53	71
Witton Albion	42	17	12	13	61	56	63
*Gateshead	42	21	4	17	65	68	63
Workington	42	17	11	14	70	58	62
Leek Town	42	16	13	13	56	47	61
Guiseley	42	16	12	14	66	54	60
Bamber Bridge	42	16	12	14	64	53	60
Bridlington Town	42	16	10	16	70	68	58
Prescot Cables	42	16	10	16	63	65	58
Bishop Auckland	42	14	13	15	61	64	55
*Ossett Town	42	15	10	17	62	73	52
Rossendale Utd	42	13	12	17	53	62	51
Colwyn Bay	42	14	9	19	56	82	51
North Ferriby Utd	42	13	11	18	64	70	50
Chorley	42	13	10	19	54	70	49
Stocksbridge PS	42	12	12	18	57	69	48
Belper Town	42	9	15	18	44	58	42
Kendal Town	42	11	7	24	53	79	40
Kidsgrove Athletic	42	10	9	23	45	67	39

* Gateshead (four points) and Ossett Town (three) penalised for breaching league rules

NEW CONFERENCE DIVISIONS

NORTH: Alfreton Town, Altrincham, Ashton United, Barrow, Bradford Park Avenue, Droylsden, Gainsborough Trinity, Harrogate Town, Hinckley United, Hucknall Town, Kettering Town, Lancaster City, Moor Green, Nuneaton Borough, Redditch United, Runcorn FC Halton, Southport, Stafford Rangers, Stalybridge Celtic, Vauxhall Motors, Worcester City, Worksop Town

SOUTH: Basingstoke Town, Bishop's Stortford, Bognor Regis Town, Cambridge City, Carshalton Athletic, Dorchester Town, Eastbourne Borough, Grays Athletic, Havant & Waterlooville, Hayes, Hornchurch, Lewes, Maidenhead United, Margate, Newport County, Redbridge, St Albans City, Sutton United, Thurrock, Welling United, Weston-super-Mare, Weymouth

HOPPING? OR JUST MAD . . .

TOM DART

PANINI. THESE DAYS, A posh toasted sandwich to accompany your grande latte. Previously, famous as the name of the company that makes football sticker albums. These playground essentials are habit-forming. They prepare the nascent fan for a lifetime of supporting: excitement and disappointment, hero-worship, obsession, banter, comparisons, chance; spending money and not always getting back what you hoped for. But hours of fruitless journeys to the newsagent would be forgotten at moments of glorious triumph, such as when you finally convinced your friend to swap his Darren Beckford for your Ian Olney, so completing your set of the 1993-94 Oldham Athletic squad. And then next season you'd do it all again — until you discovered girls.

Finishing a sticker album is not, it must be admitted, a profound and meaningful achievement, but it would have meant a lot at the time. Collecting is a way of showing your love of the game, of demonstrating your status as a serious fan, of codifying, quantifying and organising the game's myriad aspects. But what might the addicts do when they are too old to stick? They tick.

It's perhaps more socially acceptable to admit to a drug habit or a fondness for the music of Pat Benatar than to confess that you are a groundhopper. Groundhoppers are football tourists. Their fundamental, and quite possibly mental, aim is to watch matches at as many different grounds as possible.

Joining the 92 Club, whose members have been to every Premiership and Football League stadium? That's the equivalent of a trip to Sainsbury's for these people. Some have visited more than a thousand venues, metaphorically collecting them division by division, ticking them off their lists one by one.

Standing on the sidelines has never been so central as on March 20, 2004. This was the date of the Samsan Sports Central Midlands Football League Supreme Division Groundhoppers Day. Long title; long day. The league, towards the ground floor of the football pyramid,

decided to woo groundhoppers by attempting a British record. Five official, 90-minute matches in one day. Three fixtures on adjacent pitches; two, short drives away. The first kicked off at 11am, the last finished at 9.48pm. What we had here was a binge. We shovelled football into our faces and ate till we were sick.

It's a shame that Philip Larkin wrote poems about the likes of tombs and bad parenting rather than groundhopping. His fascination with the quirks that lurk in British life would have been well served by it. Not that hopping is a uniquely British pursuit; one man had come from Sweden. But the day felt essentially English: the grey Midlands backdrop, the burger stalls, the precise organisation, the match programmes and the commemorative certificates.

The eccentricity.

Groundhopping, like its buck-toothed sibling, train-spotting, breeds a nerdish fascination with trivial minutiae. Some hoppers have obsessive-compulsive rituals. Lore tells of the man who does not count scoreless draws as matches — if he sees one, he has to make another visit to the ground; of the partially sighted guy who watches games through a periscope; of the man who has to touch every corner of the playing surface; of the bloke who took flying lessons so he could photograph grounds from the air.

Transcribing their experiences is important for many hoppers. Notebooks out, they stood in front of Pelican FC's whiteboard, copying down the line-ups as if the names meant anything to them; would mean anything in the days, weeks and years to come. As if the day would somehow be devalued if they could not in future look back and tell their grandchildren who played at left back for Dinnington Town.

It is one thing to marvel at the art deco majesty of Highbury or admire the undulating sine curve stands at the City of Manchester Stadium. It is another to find intrigue and wonder at locations that are nothing more than pitches ringed with rusting white rails, or in stands with a smaller capacity than a bus shelter. Especially in such bad weather. Trees bowed and snapped, bark and twigs pirouetted across the pitch and slapped the skin.

During Dunkirk versus Retford United, the wind was so strong that a goalkeeper took a goal kick and the ball billowed up in the air then flew back over his head for a corner.

The matches' obscurity and the spectators' indifference produced passivity. What did we care which side won? The final whistle was not a prompt to applaud the teams but a signal to dash for the next site.

Their motives varied. Some simply like watching games; others enjoy the travelling. The extremists scour the fixture lists so they can go to as many matches in a week as possible. For a few, hopping gives them a chance to feel the solace that comes from being alone in a crowd, that curious sense of simultaneous togetherness and detachment.

This occasion was never going to attract the world's beautiful people, though if you have a thing for middle-aged men in raincoats, you'd have loved it. Of the 200-plus hoppers, perhaps five were women (they came with their partners). One man's relationship ended because his girlfriend was for some reason underwhelmed by being left to sit, bored and alone, in various clubhouses while he watched the games. Women, eh? Still, he regretted nothing. Girlfriends are easier to come by than British records.

Hopping is ultimately a restless, endless pursuit. Teams will get relegated or promoted, or move to new homes. Done Britain? Low-cost air fares mean that your long-held fantasy of visiting every top-flight ground in Finland can become blissful reality. And then you can set your sights on Slovakia; I hear that FC Spartak Trnava's stadium has interesting floodlights.

Perhaps this limitlessness is part of the appeal. Personal stagnation, loneliness or unfulfilment can be forgotten or evaded in the never-ending quest for new sensations, fresh sights and sounds, friendship or social solitude, the pleasure of the variation and repetition. What drives them is the same as any other fan: the way that following football so intensely and deeply can undulate your life according to the rhythms of the season and make the sport seem not like an interlude from the important stuff, but the keystone of your existence.

It's just that the hoppers prize novelty and variety above even the quality of the matches themselves — the backdrop above the main attraction. They hoard not mass-produced little stickers of their heroes but unique, three-dimensional experiences that, to them, are worth as much as vintage vinyl, rare books or tours of the great art galleries. Tick, tick, tick …

HOW THE DAY UNFOLDED
11am Lenton Lane, Nottingham: Greenwood Meadows 1, Radford 2 (attendance 302)
1pm Brian Wakefield Sports Ground, Lenton Lane: Pelican 1, Dinnington Town 2 (312)
3pm Ron Steel Sports Ground, Lenton Lane: Dunkirk 0, Retford United 1 (270)
5.30pm St Giles Park, Sandiacre: Sandiacre Town 2, Nettleham 0 (284)
8pm Asterdale Sports and Social Club, Spondon: Graham Street Prims 1, Blackwell Miners Welfare 0 (301).

FA VASE

Semi-finals: First legs   Saturday March 13
AFC SUDBURY (0) **3**   **COLNE** (2) **2**
Bennett 80, 83, Francis 90   Simpson 32, Gizon 41
1,109
BIDEFORD (1) **3**   **WINCHESTER CITY** (2) **3**
Pickard 44, Laight 60   Forbes 4, Webber 40
Gough 80   Mancey 50
1,983

Second legs   Saturday March 20
COLNE (0) **1**   **AFC SUDBURY** (0) **1**
Cooper 83   Banya 80
1,742   *(AFC Sudbury won 4-3 on agg)*
WINCHESTER CITY (2) **4**   **BIDEFORD** (0) **0**
Mancey 43, 49,   *1,818*
Forbes 45, 68 (pen)   *(Winchester City won 7-3 on agg)*

FINAL *(St Andrew's)*   Sunday May 16
AFC SUDBURY (0) **0**   **WINCHESTER CITY** (1) **2**
5,080   Forbes 17, Dyke 78 (pen)

Goalscorers Dyke and Forbes proudly show off the FA Vase

Andy Forbes, goalscoring phenomenon, opened the way for Winchester City's deserved victory in the FA Vase. Forbes calmly finished a one-two with Ian Mancey to register his 76th goal of the season. He missed the chance to make it 77 from the penalty spot because he had been forced off the field with a calf injury. Shaun Dyke converted the kick in his absence. For Sudbury, beaten the previous year by Brigg Town, it was a case of new manager (Gary Harvey), same old story.

AFC SUDBURY (3-5-2): D Greygoose — B Girling, C Tracey, S Wardley — D Head, S Hyde (sub: N Calver, 57min), L Norfolk, L Owen (sub: S Banya, 62), P Betson (sub: D Francis, 76) — G Bennett, A Claydon. **Substitutes not used:** B Nower, T Rayner. **Booked:** Hyde, Wardley. **Sent off:** Calver.
WINCHESTER CITY (3-5-2): S Arthur — D Goss, M Blake, T Redwood — S Dyke (sub: S Tate, 83), L Webber, G Green, D Smith (sub: L Green, 89), M Bicknell — A Forbes (sub: A Rogers, 70), I Mancey. **Substitutes not used:** S Lang, O Rastall. **Booked:** Mancey.
Referee: P Crossley.

FA TROPHY

SEMI-FINALS: First legs   Saturday March 27
ALDERSHOT TOWN (0) **0**   **HEDNESFORD TOWN** (1) **2**
3,500   Danks 25, Maguire 76
TELFORD UNITED (0) **0**   **CANVEY ISLAND** (0) **0**
3,061

Second legs   Saturday April 3
CANVEY ISLAND (0) **2**   **TELFORD UNITED** (1) **2**
Boylan 53, 105   Blackwood 41, Green 115
1,433
(aet; 2-2 on agg; Canvey Island won 4-2 on penalties)
HEDNESFORD TOWN (1) **1**   **ALDERSHOT TOWN** (0) **1**
Maguire 10   D'Sane 73 (pen)
2,084
(Hednesford won 3-1 on agg)

FINAL *(Villa Park)*   Sunday May 23
CANVEY ISLAND (0) **2**   **HEDNESFORD TOWN** (1) **3**
Boylan 46, Brindley 47 (og)   Maguire 27, Hines 53
6,635   Brindley 86

The veteran Brindley, right, celebrates Hednesford's triumph

It will go down as the Chris Brindley final. The old warhorse won a surprise victory for Hednesford Town with the sweetest of shots struck on the half-volley. Earlier he had been tormented by Lee Boylan, watching as the Canvey hot-shot headed his side level and within a minute helping Boylan's chip into his own net. Four days later Brindley stepped up from player-assistant to become manager as Barry Powell paid the price for Hednesford's terrible Dr Martens League season.

CANVEY ISLAND (3-5-2): D Potter — C Cowan, B Chenery, S Ward — J Kennedy, T Gooden (sub: K Dobinson, 89min), N Midgley (sub: O Berquez, 74), J Minton, C Duffy — N Gregory (sub: J McDougald, 80), L Boylan. **Substitutes not used:** D Theobald, A Harrison. **Booked:** Chenery.
HEDNESFORD TOWN (4-4-2): R Young — D Simkin, C Brindley, S Ryder (sub: L Barrow, 59), L Hines — A Maguire, J King, C Palmer, D Charie (sub: S Evans, 55) — S Anthrobus, M Danks (sub: S Piearce, 77). **Substitutes not used:** P Evans, D McGhee. **Booked:** Anthrobus, Danks.
Referee: M Dean.

FA CUP

WINNERS
Manchester United

RUNNERS-UP
Millwall

SEMI-FINALISTS
Arsenal
Sunderland

Red reign: a bloodless victory over
Millwall provided Manchester
United with their eleventh win in
their sixteenth final appearance

THE GAMES

        Rick Broadbent

EXTRA PRELIMINARY ROUND

Friday August 22

St Helens T 0 Trafford 2

Saturday August 23

Skelmersdale Utd 7 Glasshoughton Welfare 2; Brodsworth MW 0 Pickering T 1; Garforth T 0 Whickham 3; Holker OB 1 Penrith 0; Colne 2 Mossley 3; Norton & Stockton Ancients 0 Evenwood T 2; Ossett Alb 5 Alnwick T 2; Washington Nissan 1 Jarrow Roofing Boldon CA 2; Shotton Comrades 1 Newcastle Blue Star 4; Dunston Federation Brewery 1 Abbey Hey 0; Eccleshill Utd 1 Warrington T 2; Oldham T 3 Northallerton T 2; Fleetwood T 1 Darwen 0; Blackstones 1 Gedling T 4; Holbeach Utd 1 Staveley MW 1; Carlton T 0 Shirebrook T 3; Lincoln Moorlands 1 Arnold T 0; Nantwich T 1 Stratford T 2; Cradley T 2 Daventry T 0; Maldon T 4 Holmer Green 1; Stotfold 1 London Colney 2; Wroxham 4 Halstead T 1; Brentwood 0 Haringey Bor 2; Kingsbury T 1 Stowmarket T 2; Harpenden T 6 Woodbridge T 1; Needham Market 0 Norwich Utd 3; Romford 0 Bury T 2; Tiptree Utd 0 Cogenhoe Utd 1; Northampton Spencer 2 Desborough T 2; Broxbourne Bor V&E 0 Yaxley 2; Mildenhall T 2 Ilford 1; St Margaretsbury 0 Henley T 0; Bedford Utd & Valerio 1 Harefield Utd 0; Southend Manor 1 Buckingham T 1; Ruislip Manor 2 Ely C 2; Hadleigh Utd 0 Wootton Blue Cross 1; Brackley T 2 Hullbridge Sp 1; Royston T 0 Ford Sp Daventry 3; Great Yarmouth T 4 Southall T 1; St Leonards 1 Arundel 4; Thatcham T 6 Selsey 0; East Preston 2 Andover 3; Walton Casuals 5 Westfield 0; Brockenhurst 2 VCD Ath 3; Chichester C Utd 4 Tunbridge Wells 1; Sandhurst T 2 Camberley 5; Didcot T 2 Ramsgate 1; Saltdean Utd 0 Cray W 4; Bedfont 4 Littlehampton T 0; Horsham YMCA 3 Gosport Bor 3; Eastbourne Utd 1 Lordswood 0; Carterton T 1 Hungerford T 0; Lancing 0 Whitehawk 3; AFC Totton 3 Erith T 0; Reading T 1 Lymington & New Milton 2; Barnstaple T 2 Exmouth T 3; Highworth T 3 Shortwood Utd 1; Frome T 1 Tuffley Rov 0; Shepton Mallet 0 Falmouth T 1; Minehead 2 Liskeard Ath 0; Devizes T 0 Christchurch 4; Chard T 0 Paulton Rov 3

Sunday August 24

Wokingham T 2 Chertsey T 0; BAT Sp 3 Cobham 1

Replays

Tuesday August 26

Desborough T 4 Northampton Spencer 2; Ely C 0 Ruislip Manor 2; Gosport Bor 1 Horsham YMCA 0; Henley T 0 St Margaretsbury 3

Wednesday August 27

Buckingham T 4 Southend Manor 1 (aet); Staveley MW 3 Holbeach Utd 2

PRELIMINARY ROUND

Friday August 29

Whickham 2 Hebburn T 2

Saturday, August 30

Brigg T 2 Billingham T 2; Maine Road 2 Ashington 4; Harrogate Railway wo Hatfield Main; Armthorpe Welfare wo Louth Utd; Chadderton 1 Holker OB 2; Peterlee Newtown 1 Bridlington T 2; Mossley 1 Curzon Ashton 1; Bamber Bridge 3 Prescot Cables 1; Stocksbridge Park Steels 2 Squires Gate 1; Goole 2 Rossendale Utd 4; Witton Alb 4 Nelson 1; Thackley 0 Ossett T 1; Pontefract Collieries 0 Clitheroe 2; Blackpool Mechanics 1 Colwyn Bay 1; Crook T 2 Guiseley 3; Tow Law T 1 Salford C 1; South Shields 0 Bedlington Ter 0; Willington 0 Consett 5; Fleetwood T 3 Parkgate 0; Newcastle Blue Star 1 Dunston Federation Brewery 2; Billingham Synthonia 1 Chorley 1; Hyde Utd 6 Hallam 1; Liversedge 3 Gateshead 1; Guisborough T 1 Kendal 1; Tadcaster Alb 0 Winsford Utd 4; Great Harwood T 0 North Ferriby Utd 3; Cheadle T 1 Chester-le-Street T 2; Woodley Sp 1 Ramsbottom Utd 1; Durham C 0 Rossington Main 1; Horden CW 0 Brandon Utd 1; Esh Winning 1 Bacup Bor 3; Thornaby 5 Easington Colliery 1; Shildon 2 Workington 1;

AMID THE WAXWORKS, THE fish and chip shops and the tattoo parlours, something strange was happening. Football had gone to the seaside and Scarborough was buzzing with more than the odd stag party and a phalanx of pensioners dipping their toes in the water. This was no sad, decaying end-of-the-pier show. This was the FA Cup.

Scarborough's fourth-round tie against Chelsea was symptomatic of a season in which the old trophy regained much of its kudos. That game jolted us all from our pragmatism and faux gravitas and made us realise that Cup football was a hoot. Seeing Roman Abramovich's expensively-assembled collection of manicured nails and bouffant haircuts toil at the McCain Stadium was like watching Frank Sinatra play spoons in the back room at The Dog and Duck. Never mind "the bollocks", as Roy Keane would have the old trophy, this was the FA Cup as we used to know it, an amalgam of hope and pipe dreams, David and Goliath, Somme-like pitches and Freddie Starr loitering outside team hotels. It was, in short, fun.

Scarborough lost 1-0 and, even though they had a blatant penalty appeal waved away by a stony-hearted referee, they were happy enough. It had been a bumper day out by North Bay for all the family.

The minnows have always loved the FA Cup, but this was also the year when the big guns showed more than a snobbish disdain for the tournament. For Manchester United it was a silver lining, a cup of cheer in a sobering year. That they could afford to put out a weakened team away to Northampton Town in the fourth round was not down to lack of interest but the increasing cash chasm

Kidderminster and Wolves provided a cracking West Midlands derby

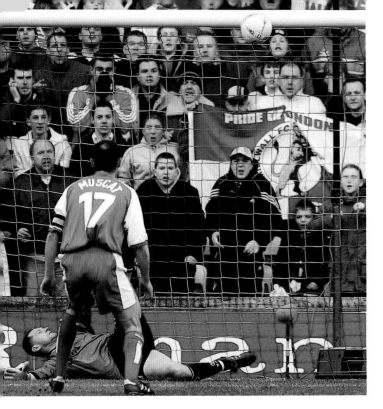

Tranmere's John Achterberg saves Kevin Muscat's quarter-final penalty

between the top of the Barclaycard Premiership and everybody else. Arsenal, too, wanted the trophy — they were, after all, chasing a third successive triumph and a fourth successive final — and the blossoming of Jose Antonio Reyes in a fifth-round tie against Chelsea, scoring his first goals in Britain to overhaul a half-time deficit, will live long in the memory. So, too, will the semi-final defeat by United that revealed intimations of mortality and dealt a psychological blow that Chelsea would take advantage of days later in the European Cup.

There was also one of the most incredible games of recent years to apply some Brasso to the silverware. Manchester City's comeback against Tottenham Hotspur was one of those inspiring, jaw-dropping moments that made you realise why you suffer countless games of dross. This was the sort of nugget every fan is searching for, a night when dreams and nightmares merged into a maddening rush.

Trailing 3-0 at half-time and reduced to ten men, City threw caution to the wind and won 4-3 thanks to Jon Macken's last-minute header. It was Roy of the Rovers with bells on. Blame it on the magic of the Cup or the emotional eccentricity of Kevin Keegan, but it was simply brilliant.

The trouble with the FA Cup in recent years has been the trend of prioritising. Despite bigger squads and a smaller top flight, clubs pool all their resources and aim for survival or European

Selby T 0 Washington 0; Maltby Main 1 West Auckland T 0; Sheffield 1 Jarrow Roofing Boldon CA 0; Evenwood T 3 Oldham T 5 (at West Auckland T FC); Hall Road Rangers 1 Trafford 1; Marske Utd 3 Winterton Rangers 0; Warrington T 1 Yorkshire Amateur 0; Prudhoe T 2 Morpeth T 0; Ossett Alb 2 Alsager T 1; Seaham Red Star 3 Murton 4; Atherton Collieries 0 Farsley Celtic 3; Gresley Rov 1 Buxton 1; Stamford 2 Bourne T 0; Shepshed Dynamo 0 Congleton T 1; Shirebrook T 2 Matlock T 1; Grosvenor Park 0 Glapwell 0; Quorn 0 Gedling T 1; Studley 3 Rushall Olympic 0; Oadby T 5 Stratford T 1; Corby T 2 Lincoln Utd 1; Bedworth Utd 0 Halesowen T 2; Belper T 1 Boston T 1; Mickleover Sp 3 Ludlow T 0; Chasetown 1 Sutton Coldfield T 2; Kidsgrove Ath 1 Rugby Utd 3; Borrowash Victoria 3 Biddulph Victoria 4; Racing Club Warwick 0 Stafford T 1; Rocester 1 Ilkeston T 1; Staveley MW 0 Sutton T 1; Pelsall Villa wo Atherstone Utd; Eastwood T 2 Deeping Rangers 2; Lincoln Moorlands 1 Leek T 2; Spalding Utd 3 Glossop North End 0; Stourport Swifts 1 Boldmere St Michaels 0; Cradley T 0 Bromsgrove Rov 4; Solihull Bor 3 Stone Dominoes 0; Leek CSOB 2 Redditch Utd 3; Barwell 3 Oldbury Utd 1; Newcastle T 3 Willenhall T 0; Stourbridge 0 Causeway Utd 2; Long Eaton Utd 0 Norton Utd 0; Haverhill Rov wo Gorleston; Burnham 1 Arlesey T 7; Burnham Ramblers 4 Potters Bar T 1; Dunstable T wo Saffron Walden T; Leighton T 3 Wootton Blue Cross 1; Mildenhall T wo Tring T; Sawbridgeworth T 2 AFC Wallingford 2; Newmarket T 5 Wembley 0; Chalfont St Peter 0 Chesham Utd 6; Boreham Wood 2 Desborough T 1; Ware 2 London Colney 2; Enfield T 2 Clacton T 1; Norwich Utd 2 Leyton 2; AFC Sudbury 4 Diss T 3; Histon 7 Yeading 0; Hampton & Richmond Bor 3 Great Wakering Rov 0; Harpenden T 1 St Margaretsbury 3; Haringey Bor 1 Dereham T 3; Barton Rov 2 Rothwell T 2; Stewarts & Lloyds 3 Fakenham T 0; Tilbury wo Milton Keynes C; Bedford Utd & Valerio 0 St Neots T 2; Beaconsfield SYCOB 1 Ipswich W 1; Wisbech T 1 Aveley 2; Stowmarket T 0 Waltham Forest 2; Stanway Rov 0 Staines T 1; Wivenhoe T 7 Bowers Utd 0; Cheshunt 2 Harlow T 3; Cogenhoe Utd 0 Maldon T 2; Wingate & Finchley 3 Bury T 2; Edgware T 2 Clapton 2; Stansted 0 Uxbridge 7 (at Uxbridge FC); Great Yarmouth T 0 Berkhamsted T 1; Raunds T 1 Hoddesdon T 0; Buckingham T 2 Ford Sp Daventry 0; Hertford T 2 Lowestoft T 4; Yaxley 2 Barking & East Ham Utd 1; Ruislip Manor 1 Soham T Rangers 4; Wroxham 6 Banbury Utd 1; Flackwell Heath 4 Concord Rangers 1; Long Buckby 1 King's Lynn 5; Hanwell T 2 East Thurrock Utd 2; Witham T 2 Marlow 0; Brook House 1 Wealdstone 4; Brackley T 4 Harwich & Parkeston 2; Greenwich Bor 1 Maidstone Utd 1; Hailsham T 0 Cowes Sp 1; Chessington & Hook Utd 2 Merstham 0; Leatherhead 3 Moneyfields 1; Windsor & Eton 0 Metropolitan Police 1; Walton & Hersham 0 Walton Casuals 2; Three Bridges 1 Redhill 1; Tonbridge Angels 4 BAT Sp 0; Fisher Ath 3 Bedfont 4; Blackfield & Langley 1 Thamesmead T 3; Abingdon Utd 3 Cove 2; Banstead Ath 0 Winchester C 2; Arundel 4 Hassocks 0; Tooting & Mitcham Utd 3 Ashford T (Middx) 1; Chipstead 1 Ringmer 2; Croydon 1 Hythe T 1; Abingdon T 3 Chichester C Utd 1; Whitchurch Utd 4 Withdean 2000 1; Worthing 7 Ash Utd 0; Fleet T 1 Epsom & Ewell 0; Slade Green 1 Hartley Wintney 2; Egham T 1 Thame Utd 8; Sidlesham 0 Sittingbourne 2; AFC Totton 3 AFC Newbury 1; Didcot T 4 Eastbourne T 1; Ashford T 3 Eastbourne Utd 0; Gosport Bor 2 Erith & Belvedere 4; Hastings Utd 1 Bracknell T 3; Southwick 1 Burgess Hill T 4; VCD Ath 2 Eastleigh 1; Beckenham T 2 Sandhurst T 5; Dulwich Hamlet 1 Folkestone Invicta 3; Dorking 5 Lewes 5; Hillingdon Bor 2 Corinthian-Casuals 0; Wick 0 Whyteleafe 5; Oxford C 6 Farnham T 1; Molesey 1 Godalming & Guildford 2; Croydon Ath 2 Herne Bay 1; Bromley 2 North Leigh 1; Whitehawk 0 Lymington & New Milton 2; Thatcham T 1 Alton T 2; Whitstable T 1 Raynes Park Vale 3; Peacehaven & Telscombe 2 Chessington Utd 1; Horsham 1 Newport IoW 2; Carterton T 1 Fareham T 2; Chatham T 2 Andover 4; Bideford 1 Swindon Supermarine 3; Backwell Utd 2 Fairford T 0; Bishop Sutton 1 Falmouth T 0; Bridport 2 Street 0; Cinderford T 1 Brislington 3; Melksham T 0 Mangotsfield Utd 4; Evesham Utd 3 Hallen 3; Taunton 1 Bournemouth 1; St Blazey 5 Willand Rov 0; Highworth T 4 Portland Utd 3; Westbury Utd 2 Keynsham T 2; Minehead 2 Welton Rov 2;

Bemerton Heath Harlequins 3 Torrington 2; Bristol Manor Farm 0 Gloucester C 5; Frome T 1 Clevedon T 1; Porthleven 0 Team Bath 4; Salisbury C 4 Odd Down 0; Elmore 1 Wimborne T 3; Downton 3 Exmouth T 4; Yate T 1 Cirencester T 2; Paulton Rov 2 Calne T 0; Bridgwater T 0 Corsham T 1; Dawlish T 1 Clevedon Utd 2

Sunday August 31

Bishop Auckland 8 Flixton 0; Skelmersdale Utd 3 Atherton LR 0; Pickering T 2 Whitley Bay 0; Bitton 3 Christchurch 4; Cray W 4 Pagham 0; Slough T 5 E Grinstead T 0 (at Windsor & Eton FC); Wokingham T 0 Deal T 1; Enfield 1 Hemel H T 1; Dartford 1 Bashley 0

Replays

Monday September 1

Curzon Ashton 2 Mossley 3 (aet)

Tuesday September 2

Billingham T 1 Brigg T 0 (at Thornaby FC); Colwyn Bay 3 Blackpool Mechanics 1; Salford C 4 Tow Law T 3; Hythe T 1 Croydon 1 (aet; Hythe T win 5-4 on pens); Hemel Hempstead T 2 Enfield 3; Clevedon T 2 Frome T 3 (aet); Welton Rov 2 Minehead 1; Bournemouth 0 Taunton T 5; Hallen 2 Evesham Utd 1 (aet); Chorley 3 Billingham Synthonia 1; Kendal T 2 Guisborough T 2 (aet; Guisborough T win 8-7 on pens); Ramsbottom Utd 3 Woodley Sp 0; Rossington Main 0 Durham C 1; Trafford 3 Hall Road Rangers 1; Buxton 4 Gresley Rov 0; Glapwell 2 Grosvenor Park 0; Boston T 0 Belper T 1; Ilkeston T 3 Rocester 1; AFC Wallingford 2 Sawbridgeworth T 0; London Colney 0 Ware 1 (aet); Leyton 2 Norwich Utd 1; Rothwell T 3 Barton Rov 0; Ipswich W 2 Beaconsfield SYCOB 1; Clapton 0 Edgware T 1; East Thurrock Utd 6 Hanwell T 3 (aet)

Wednesday September 3

Bedlington Terr 4 South Shields 1; Keynsham T 2 Westbury Utd 5; Hebburn T 1 Whickham 2; Washington 3 Selby T 3 (aet; Selby T win 5-4 on pens); Deeping Rangers 1 Eastwood T 2; Norton Utd 0 Long Eaton Utd 2; Maidstone Utd 1 Greenwich Bor 0; Redhill 0 Three Bridges 3 (at Dorking FC)

FIRST QUALIFYING ROUND

Friday September 12

Wealdstone 0 Uxbridge 1

Saturday September 13

Stocksbridge Park Steels 6 Prudhoe T 1; Mossley 1 Hyde Utd 6; Rossendale Utd 2 Harrogate Railway 1; Clitheroe 0 Brandon Utd 1; Maltby Main 4 Colwyn Bay 2; Winsford Utd 2 Marske Utd 2; Oldham T 3 Liversedge 2; Ossett Alb 0 Ossett T 0; Durham C 0 Shildon 2; Ashington 3 Ramsbottom Utd 1; Thornaby 1 Guisborough T 2; Armthorpe Welfare 0 Whickham 0; Bamber Bridge 2 Bacup Bor 0; Guiseley 1 Trafford 0; Bishop Auckland 0 Pickering T 1; Chester-le-Street T 2 Murton 0; Warrington T 6 North Ferriby Utd 1; Chorley 2 Selby T 1; Dunston Federation Brewery 2 Billingham T 1; Farsley Celtic 1 Sheffield 1; Bridlington T 5 Salford C 0; Skelmersdale Utd 2 Consett 0; Fleetwood T 3 Bedlington Terr 1; Stourport Swifts 0 Rugby Utd 3; Oadby T 0 Stamford 2; Barwell 2 Newcastle T 1; Glapwell 1 Gedling T 2; Shirebrook T 2 Stafford T 0; Studley 0 Bromsgrove Rov 1; Solihull Bor 0 Redditch Utd 3; Long Eaton Utd 2 Ilkeston T 2; Mickleover Sp 0 Eastwood T 0; Sutton Coldfield T 1 Causeway Utd 1; Pelsall Villa 0 Belper T 4; Corby T 1 Halesowen T 2; Spalding Utd 2 Sutton T 2; Congleton T 1 Leek T 0; Newmarket T 6 Brackley T 1; Hampton & Richmond Bor 1 Dunstable T 0; Harlow T 1 St Neots T 0; Waltham Forest 1 Rothwell T 3; Dereham T 1 Tilbury 4; Aveley 1 Lowestoft T 2; Leyton 4 Arlesey T 0; Edgware T 0 Enfield T 1; Ware 2 Buckingham T 2; Wingate & Finchley 3 Raunds T 1; Mildenhall T 1 Histon 6; AFC Wallingford 2 Ipswich W 0; Berkhamsted T 0 AFC Sudbury 9; Chesham Utd 2 Yaxley 0; Wroxham 2 Flackwell Heath 1; East Thurrock Utd 2 Staines T 1; Wivenhoe 2 Soham T Rangers 3; Boreham Wood 2 Maldon T 1; St Margaretsbury 2 Leighton T 2; Haverhill Rov 1 Burnham Ramblers 2; King's Lynn 2 Stewarts & Lloyds 2; Whitchurch Utd 0 Tooting & Mitcham Utd 3; Raynes Park Vale 0 Folkestone Invicta 2; Lymington & New Milton 1 Erith & Belvedere 0;

Paul Scholes's super strike secures Manchester United's semi-final win

qualification. It is why Sam Allardyce, the Bolton Wanderers manager, could profess to being glad when his team lost to lower-division opposition in the third round. Fans, too, have been suckered into the belief that qualifying for a tournament that you have little chance of winning or ensuring another year of domestic humdrum is the Holy Grail.

Now, Allardyce and Keane aside, there are signs that the FA Cup is beginning to matter. With over-hyped matches on our screens every night and over-analytical punditry preferred to tug-of-war contests between rival sets of fans, the Cup will never be what it was. But after the boom and bust of recent times, people are starting at least to remember what it used to be — a competition that cut through the cynicism and money and focused on pride and folklore.

It was sad, therefore, that the final itself was an appallingly one-sided contest. Millwall, the underdogs, were just happy to be there and, shorn of the injured Danny Dichio, opted for damage limitation rather than a shot at legend. Indeed, they did not even manage a shot on goal. We wanted have-a-go-heroes but got tepid surrender. Defeat was painless for Millwall and that hurt. It left even romantics wishing United and Arsenal had been kept apart in the semi-finals.

For the likes of Scarborough, Telford United and Accrington Stanley, the FA Cup was everything. It is also worth noting that at least one of the country's three top clubs — Arsenal, Chelsea and Manchester United — has made the final in each of the past dozen years. It could be argued that, far from not caring about this end-of-the-pier show, they actually care too much.

PLAYER OF THE SEASON
Tim Cahill   Millwall

Suggesting on the eve of the final that the present Manchester United side was the worst he had seen in years was the Australia midfield player's solitary mistake during a heady run. Seven years after his engineer father paid for his passage to London, Tim Cahill made his international debut, scored 12 league and cup goals for his club and was instrumental in Millwall's surge to the final. He scored in the third and sixth rounds before claiming the semi-final winner. A poor disciplinary record notwithstanding, his aggressive breaks and workrate suggested the 24-year-old could play at a higher level.

Rick Broadbent

TOP ATTENDANCES ROUND BY ROUND

Extra preliminary round	291	Great Yarmouth Town v Southall Town
Preliminary round	363	Ashford Town v Eastbourne United
First qualifying round	871	King's Lynn v Stewarts & Lloyds
Second qualifying round	1,352	Nuneaton Borough v Worcester City
Third qualifying round	1,416	Buxton v Radcliffe Borough
Fourth qualifying round	2,686	Exeter City v Gravesend & Northfleet
First round	11,219	Sheffield Weds v Salisbury City
Second round	11,722	Sheffield Weds v Scunthorpe United (replay)
Third round	40,816	Sunderland v Hartlepool United
Fourth round	41,365	Liverpool v Newcastle United
Fifth round	67,228	Manchester United v Manchester City
Sixth round	67,614	Manchester United v Fulham
Semi-finals	56,112	Sunderland v Millwall, at Old Trafford

MOST FA CUP WINS

11	Manchester United	
9	Arsenal	
8	Tottenham Hotspur	
7	Aston Villa	
6	Blackburn Rovers, Liverpool, Newcastle United	

5	Everton, Wanderers, West Bromwich Albion
4	Bolton Wanderers, Manchester City, Sheffield United, Wolverhampton Wanderers
3	Chelsea, Sheffield Wednesday, West Ham United

LEADING FA CUP GOALSCORERS 2003-04

9 Gary Barnes
(Shildon)
8 Dave Seal
(Mangotsfield United)
Danny Toronczak
(Ossett Albion)
7 Matt Bown (Paulton Rovers)

Freddy Eastwood
(Grays Athletic)
Alex Lawson
(Ashington)
6 Graeme Mitchell (Warrington Town), **Scott Taylor** (Blackpool), **Ruud van Nistelrooy** (Manchester United)

Cray W 4 Sandhurst T 1; Deal T 1 Leatherhead 2; Ashford T 1 Bromley 1; Tonbridge Angels 1 Lewes 1; Hillingdon Bor 1 Oxford C 1; Chessington & Hook Utd 1 Thamesmead T 4; Slough T 2 Godalming & Guildford 0; Metropolitan Police 2 Winchester C 3; Fareham T 1 Newport IoW 2; Hythe T 3 Alton T 1; Burgess Hill T 2 Abingdon Utd 1; Thame Utd 4 VCD Ath 2; Worthing 4 Walton Casuals 1; Sittingbourne 1 Whyteleafe 0; Andover 5 Arundel 0; Abingdon T 4 Ringmer 3; Bracknell 3 Hartley Wintney 2; Three Bridges 1 Fleet T 2; Croydon Ath 7 Bedfont 1; AFC Totton 1 Didcot T 3; Clevedon Utd 4 Frome T 1; Paulton Rov 2 Bemerton Hth H 0; Gloucester C 0 Team Bath 0; Christchurch 2 Westbury Utd 3; Mangotsfield Utd 4 Bridport 3; Cirencester T 2 Swindon Supermarine 1; Corsham T 1 Brislington 2; Salisbury C 4 Taunton T 1; Exmouth T 2 St Blazey 1; Hallen 1 Highworth T 2; Backwell Utd 1 Wimborne T 4; Welton Rov 3 Bishop Sutton 3

Sunday September 14
Witton Alb 7 Holker OB 0; Biddulph Victoria 1 Buxton 1; Enfield 4 Witham T 0; Dartford 3 Peacehaven & Telscombe 0; Maidstone Utd 4 Cowes Sp 0

Replays

Tuesday September 16
Ossett T 1 Ossett Alb 3; Billingham T 0 Dunston FB 1; Sheffield 1 Farsley C 3 (aet); Eastwood T 1 Mickleover Sp 0; Halesowen T 3 Corby T 2; Sutton T 0 Spalding Utd 5; Flackwell Heath 1 Wroxham 0; Leighton T 0 St Margaretsbury 1; Stewarts & Lloyds 0 King's Lynn 3; Bromley 1 Ashford T 0; Lewes 2 Tonbridge Angels 1; Oxford C 2 Hillingdon Bor 1

Wednesday September 17
Causeway Utd 0 Sutton Coldfield T 3; Team Bath 0 Gloucester C 2; St Blazey 2 Exmouth T 1 (aet; Exmouth win 4-3 on pens); Bishop Sutton 1 Welton Rov 0; Buckingham T 2 Ware 1; Whickham 2 Armthorpe Welfare 1; Buxton 3 Biddulph Victoria 1

SECOND QUALIFYING ROUND

Saturday September 27
Frickley Ath 0 Shildon 0; Whitby T 3 Winsford Utd 0; Runcorn FC Halton 3 Guiseley 0; Droylsden 2 Burscough 2; Pickering T 0 Ossett Alb 1; Vauxhall Motors 3 Southport 1; Dunston FB 1 Fleetwood T 1; Bridlington T 2 Farsley C 2; Stocksbridge PS 3 Brandon Utd 2; Ashton Utd 1 Hyde Utd 1; Blyth Spartans 3 Bamber Bridge 0; Marine 3 Rossendale Utd 1; Chester-le-Street T 0 Bradford PA 2; Maltby Main 2 Ashington 3; Barrow 2 Harrogate T 0; Lancaster C 2 Altrincham 0; Gainsborough Trinity 6 Skelmersdale Utd 0; Witton Alb 0 Wakefield & Emley 1; Guisborough T 2 Stalybridge C 2; Chorley 5 Whickham 0; Radcliffe Bor 2 Oldham T 1; Spennymoor Utd 0 Warrington T 2; Gedling T 1 Alfreton T 0; Newcastle T 2 Sutton Coldfield T 1; Cambridge C 3 Ilkeston T 1; Hednesford T 0 Bromsgrove Rov 2; Rothwell T 0 Bedford T 1; Stafford Rangers 1 Grantham T 2; Redditch Utd 1 Shirebrook T 1; Spalding Utd 1 Halesowen T 2; Stamford 0 Kettering T 3; Hucknall T 1 Congleton T 1; Soham T Rangers 0 Histon 2; Buxton 1 Belper T 0; Nuneaton Bor 1 Worcester C 0; Worksop T 2 King's Lynn 2; Rugby Utd 1 Eastwood T 3; Moor Green 1 Hinckley Utd 2; Basingstoke T 1 Cray W 0; Sutton Utd 0 Bishop's Stortford 0; Buckingham T 1 Thurrock 2; Bromley 3 Dartford 0; Sittingbourne 1 East Thurrock Utd 2; Boreham Wood 4 Burgess Hill T 0; Bracknell T 4 Tilbury 2; Hendon 4 Enfield 0; Canvey Island 6 Uxbridge 1; Hampton & Richmond Bor 2 Kingstonian 1; Heybridge Swifts 3 Worthing 3; Lowestoft T 2 Lewes 1; Hythe T 0 Maidstone Utd 4; Leyton 1 Leatherhead 0; Slough T 1 Welling Utd 1; Thame Utd 4 Thamesmead T 0; Abingdon T 1 Chesham Utd 2; Hornchurch 2 Billericay T 1; Newmarket T 3 Fleet T 0; Braintree T 3 Aylesbury Utd 2; St Albans C 2 Grays Ath 4; Hayes 4 Tooting & Mitcham Utd 2; Enfield T 0 Carshalton Ath 1; Hitchin T 0 Folkestone Invicta 0; Ford Utd 3 Didcot T 1; Croydon Ath 2 AFC Wallingford 0; Northwood 2 AFC Sudbury 4; Burnham Ramblers 1 St Margaretsbury 2; Eastbourne Bor 2 Chelmsford C 2; Harrow Bor 0 Flackwell Heath 0; Harlow T 0 Crawley T 4; Newport Co 3 Weymouth 2; Bognor Regis T 0 Havant & Waterlooville 4;

Newport IoW 2 Tiverton T 1; Weston-super-Mare 4 Dorchester T 1; Paulton Rov 4 Bishop Sutton 1; Mangotsfield Utd 3 Wimborne T 0; Brislington 0 Bath C 2; Salisbury C 1 Westbury Utd 1; Chippenham T 2 Winchester C 1; Gloucester C 2 Merthyr Tydfil 0; Lymington & New Milton 8 Clevedon Utd 2; Cirencester T 3 Andover 2; Exmouth T 0 Highworth T 1

Sunday September 28

Wingate & Finchley 1 Oxford C 2; Dover Ath 4 Maidenhead Utd 0

Replays

Wednesday October 1

Shildon 5 Frickley Ath 1; Burscough 1 Droylsden 2 (aet); Fleetwood T 1 Dunston FB 2; Farsley C 3 Bridlington T 0; Hyde Utd 1 Ashton Utd 2; Stalybridge C 3 Guisborough T 1; Shirebrook T 2 Redditch Utd 2 (aet; Shirebrook T win 4-1 on pens); Congleton T 3 Hucknall T 2; King's Lynn 1 Worksop T 4; Bishop's Stortford 1 Sutton Utd 1 (aet; Bishop's Stortford win 5-3 on pens); Worthing 2 Heybridge Swifts 0; Welling Utd 4 Slough T 1; Folkestone Invicta 3 Hitchin 1; Chelmsford C 0 Eastbourne Bor 2; Flackwell Heath 0 Harrow Bor 1; Westbury Utd 1 Salisbury C 2

THIRD QUALIFYING ROUND

Saturday October 11

Ashton Utd 2 Barrow 1; Farsley C 3 Worksop T 0; Shirebrook T 1 Shildon 3; Nuneaton Bor 1 Runcorn 1; Ashington 1 Grantham T 3; Gedling T 0 Stalybridge C 1; Eastwood T 1 Stocksbridge PS 1; Newcastle T 1 Ossett Alb 1; Marine 1 Dunston FB 2; Blyth Spartans 2 Halesowen 1; Bradford PA 1 Vauxhall Motors 1; Warrington T 0 Whitby T 0; Wakefield & E 0 Hinckley Utd 2; Droylsden 0 Gainsborough Trinity 2; Buxton 2 Radcliffe Bor 1; Chorley 1 Lancaster C 1; Congleton T 0 Bromsgrove Rov 2; Kettering T 2 St Margaretsbury 0; Folkestone Invicta 1 Welling Utd 1; Bromley 1 Thurrock 1; Histon 0 Newmarket T 0; Hornchurch 5 Carshalton Ath 0; Canvey Island 4 Dover Ath 3; Ford Utd 3 Worthing 2; Cambridge C 3 Lowestoft T 0; Maidstone Utd 1 Bishop's Stortford 1; Hayes 3 Boreham Wood 0; East Thurrock Utd 3 AFC Sudbury 2; Leyton 3 Bedford T 0; Grays Ath 3 Hendon 0; Braintree T 0 Eastbourne Bor 4; Crawley T 6 Croydon Ath 1; Basingstoke T 0 Bracknell T 0; Gloucester C 4 Chippenham T 1; Thame Utd 3 Bath C 0; Oxford C 0 Cirencester T 0; Havant & Waterlooville 3 Salisbury C 4; Newport IoW 2 Harrow Bor 1; Newport County 3 Mangotsfield Utd 6; Weston-super-Mare 1 Chesham Utd 1; Lymington & New Milton 2 Highworth T 0; Paulton Rov 2 Hampton & Richmond Bor 1

Replays

Tuesday October 14

Runcorn 2 Nuneaton Bor 2 (aet; Runcorn win 5-4 on pens); Stocksbridge PS 3 Eastwood T 1 (aet); Vauxhall M 1 Bradford PA 3; Lancaster C 1 Chorley 0; Welling Utd 2 Folkestone Invicta 2 (aet; Welling Utd win 5-3 on pens); Thurrock 3 Bromley 0; Newmarket T 0-1 Histon; Bishop's Stortford 3 Maidstone Utd 1; AFC Sudbury 1 East Thurrock Utd 1; (aet; East Thurrock Utd win 4-2 on pens); Bracknell T 1 Basingstoke T 0; Harrow Bor 2 Newport IoW 0; Chesham Utd 1 Weston-super-Mare 2

Wednesday October 15

Ossett Alb 4 Newcastle T 4 (aet; Ossett Alb win 3-0 on pens); Whitby T 2 Warrington T 1

FOURTH QUALIFYING ROUND

Saturday, October 25

Ossett Alb 0 Stalybridge C 1; Dunston FB 0 Lancaster C 1; Ashton Utd 1 Grantham T 2; Blyth Spartans 0 Chester C 1; Bromsgrove Rov 2 Whitby T 2; Burton Alb 6 Buxton 0; Morecambe 2 Shrewsbury T 4; Telford Utd 3 Tamworth 3; Scarborough 3 Hinckley Utd 1; Farsley C 1 Gainsborough Trinity 1; Accrington Stanley 2 Leigh RMI 0; Runcorn 0 Bradford PA 1; Shildon 6 Stocksbridge PS 0; Leyton 1 Histon 2; Eastbourne Bor 2 Stevenage Bor 2; Bracknell T 0 Barnet 3; Thame Utd 1 Farnborough T 2; Grays Ath 3 Margate 3; Welling Utd 2 Weston-super-Mare 3; Boreham Wood 1 Kettering T 0; Forest Green Rov 1 Aldershot T 3;

MATCH OF THE SEASON

Tottenham Hotspur 3 Manchester City 4
White Hart Lane, Wednesday February 4 2004
Tom Dart

IT WAS PURE KEVIN KEEGAN. Famously unpredictable, the Manchester City manager may feel tempted to resign now on the basis that nothing he could achieve will top this. You could call what City accomplished last night one of the greatest comebacks in the history of the FA Cup — and that would probably be selling it short.

Jon Macken's injury-time header won this fourth-round replay at White Hart Lane to crown an evening of scarcely believable drama, stun and appal Tottenham Hotspur's followers and bring Keegan back from the brink. Sure, matches such as these make the Cup special, but this transcended the venerable competition and was an affirmation of the emotional and theatrical power of the game itself.

Three goals down at half-time and reduced to ten men, City were dead and buried and the organist was warming up for the memorial service for Keegan's disintegrating managerial career. Keegan turned to his assistant and said: "I wonder where the nearest Job Centre is?" City seemed certain to extend their lamentable run to one win in 19 games. Instead they became awesome where they had been atrocious and bit back with superhuman energy.

This was an occasion to feel, to absorb, not one to analyse in minute detail, though David Pleat, the Tottenham acting manager, may feel differently. He is now the one questioning the character and motivation of his players. City have secured a Manchester derby against United a week on Saturday — a daunting task, but they will not care. This morning they must feel like they can do anything.

The opening recalled the clash between these sides in the Carling Cup in December, a 3-1 win for Tottenham in which they scored an early goal and went on to dominate the game. Last night, Ledley King lashed a marvellous shot into the roof of the net after one minute 46 seconds. Inside 20 minutes, City were two down courtesy of Robbie Keane's cute dinked finish. The ineligible Jermain Defoe was paraded before kick-off to rapturous applause. Optimism reigned at the Lane and was heightened when Nicolas Anelka, City's leading scorer, limped off to be replaced by Macken.

The tie was settled, theoretically at least, on the verge of half-time when Christian Ziege blasted in a wonderful free kick from outside the area. Keegan headed straight for the dressing-rooms. It did not lighten his mood to discover that only ten of his players would be taking the pitch for the second period. Joey Barton gave away an obvious free kick on the edge of the area and was booked for arguing about it. Ziege scored and Barton received a second yellow card for protesting to Rob Styles after the referee had blown for half-time.

"We're gonna win the Cup", the away supporters chanted as the second half began. Who could have imagined that what seemed like

Macken celebrates with the fans after completing City's comeback

trauma-induced delirium might yet turn out to be extraordinary prescience? Two minutes into the second half, Sylvain Distin pulled one back with a header. Then Paul Bosvelt's effort from distance took a deflection off Anthony Gardner and looped into the net. If City's first goal had given them hope, now they had belief.

Spurs were no longer coasting. Their potency melted into panic. This was now a Keegan event, closer to the famous, breakneck Newcastle United defeat by Liverpool than the helpless creative poverty of his final match in charge of England. He was on his feet, cajoling, urging, praying. This was a staggering affirmation of his attacking instincts and never-say-die spirit, no longer another sad example of the wilting under pressure that has blighted his managerial career.

Arni Arason made a superlative double save, then the unthinkable happened with 11 minutes to go. Shaun Wright-Phillips was put clean through and caressed the ball over Kasey Keller. Then came Macken and it was all the history of Keegan's past traumas, of goal-rich spectaculars that raised the pulse but dashed his hopes, rolled into one — but this time with a glorious finale.

TOTTENHAM HOTSPUR (4-4-2): K Keller — S Carr, A Gardner, D Richards, C Ziege (sub: J Jackson, 60min) — S Dalmat, M Brown, L King, S Davies — H Postiga (sub: G Poyet, 10), R Keane. **Substitutes not used:** R Burch, M Yeates, S Kelly.
MANCHESTER CITY (4-4-2): A Arason — Sun Jihai, R Dunne, S Distin, M Tarnat — S Wright-Phillips, J Barton, P Bosvelt (sub: A Sibierski, 80), T Sinclair (sub: S McManaman, 80) — N Anelka (sub: J Macken, 27), R Fowler. **Substitutes not used:** K Stuhr-Ellegaard, S Jordan. **Booked:** Barton, Bosvelt, Sun. **Sent off:** Barton.

Thurrock 2 Dagenham & R 1; Harrow Bor 1 Hereford Utd 6; Bishop's Stortford 2 Gloucester C 0; Salisbury C 5 Lymington & NM 1; Cambridge C 2 Ford Utd 3; Hornchurch 1 Paulton Rov 0; East Thurrock Utd 1 Woking 1; Cirencester T 2 Crawley T 4; Exeter C 0 Gravesend & Northfleet 0

Sunday October 26

Northwich Victoria 1 Halifax T 0; Mangotsfield Utd 1 Canvey Island 2

Replays

Tuesday October 28

Tamworth 2 Telford Utd 3 (aet); Gainsborough Trinity 3 Farsley C 0; Stevenage Bor 1 Eastbourne Bor 0; Margate 3 Grays Ath 3 (aet; Grays Ath win 3-1 on pens); Woking 2 East Thurrock Utd 0; Gravesend & Northfleet 3 Exeter C 3 (aet; Gravesend & Northfleet win 6-5 on pens)

Wednesday October 29

Whitby T 2 Bromsgrove Rov 1

FIRST ROUND

Saturday November 8

Lincoln C 3 Brighton 1; Peterborough Utd 2 Hereford Utd 0; Oldham Ath 3 Carlisle Utd 0; Cheltenham T 3 Hull C 1; Yeovil T 4 Wrexham 1; Macclesfield T 3 Boston Utd 0; Grays Ath 1 Aldershot T 2; Scarborough 1 Doncaster Rov 0; Barnet 2 Stalybridge Celtic 2; Blackpool 4 Boreham Wood 0; Wycombe W 4 Swindon T 1; Lancaster C 1 Cambridge Utd 2; Woking 3 Histon 1; Bournemouth 1 Bristol Rov 0; Stevenage Bor 2 Stockport Co 1; Grantham T 1 Leyton Orient 2; Thurrock 1 Luton T 1; Northampton T 3 Plymouth Argyle 1; Tranmere Rov 3 Chesterfield 2; Hornchurch 2 Darlington 0; Scunthorpe Utd 2 Shrewsbury T 1; Torquay Utd 1 Burton Alb 2; Accrington S 1 Huddersfield T 0; Grimsby T 1 QPR 0; Notts Co 7 Shildon 2; Brentford 7 Gainsborough Trinity 1; Kidderminster H 2 Northwich Victoria 1; Southend Utd 1 Canvey Island 1; York C 1 Barnsley 2; Port Vale 2 Ford Utd 2; Mansfield T 6 Bishop's Stortford 0; Sheffield Weds 4 Salisbury C 0; Farnborough T 0 Weston-super-Mare 1; Chester C 0 Gravesend & Northfleet 1; Telford Utd 3 Crawley T 2; Colchester Utd 1 Oxford Utd 0; Bradford PA 2 Bristol C 5; Bury 1 Rochdale 2; Swansea C 3 Rushden & Diamonds 0; Hartlepool Utd 4 Whitby T 0

Replays

Tuesday November 18

Stalybridge C 0 Barnet 2; Luton T 3 Thurrock 1

Wednesday November 19

Canvey Island 2 Southend Utd 3; Ford Utd 1 Port Vale 2 (aet)

SECOND ROUND

Friday December 5

Wycombe W 1 Mansfield T 1

Saturday December 6

Northampton T 4 Weston-super-Mare 1; Rochdale 0 Luton T 2; Colchester Utd 1 Aldershot T 0; Macclesfield T 1 Cambridge Utd 1; Peterborough Utd 3 Grimsby T 2; Bristol C 0 Barnsley 0; Oldham Ath 2 Blackpool 5; Gravesend & Northfleet 1 Notts Co 2; Telford Utd 3 Brentford 0; Woking 0 Kidderminster H 3; Hornchurch 0 Tranmere Rov 1; Bournemouth 1 Accrington S 1; Cheltenham T 3 Leyton Orient 1; Yeovil T 5 Barnet 1; Southend Utd 3 Lincoln C 0; Scunthorpe Utd 2 Sheffield Weds 2; Swansea C 2 Stevenage Bor 1

Sunday December 7

Burton Alb 0 Hartlepool Utd 1; Port Vale 0 Scarborough 1

Replays

Tuesday December 16

Cambridge Utd 2 Macclesfield T 2 (aet; Macclesfield T win 4-2 on pens); Barnsley 2 Bristol C 1; Mansfield T 3 Wycombe W 2; Sheffield Weds 0 Scunthorpe Utd 0 (aet; Scunthorpe Utd win 3-1 on pens)

Wednesday December 17

Accrington S 0 Bournemouth 0 (aet; Accrington S win 5-3 on pens)

A SEASIDE ROMANCE

Tom Dart

YOU'LL REMEMBER THE match, of course. Well, all right, you may not; but you'll remember the tie. Scarborough v Chelsea. FA Cup fourth round, January 24 2004. Perfect. Just perfect. Who better to host the London million-aires than a humble little Nation-wide Conference club? Where better than the nation's oldest seaside resort, a place devoted to pleasure? Fine old holiday towns such as Scarborough share some of the traits of the Cup. Their Victorian origins. The frothing ebb and flow of the tide and the clinking of coins back and forth in the arcades signify fun and profit. So, too, these days, does the Cup.

Scarborough, like the tournament, has a faded elegance that is a reminder of more stately, more prosperous days. True, early in the week of the match, the town centre was not exactly in the grip of Cup fever. It was more running a slight temperature with a ticklish cough. But the excitement slowly swelled on the chilly, sleepy streets as the town awoke from its usual winter hibernation and took pride in a football club that it had mostly taken for granted.

Scarborough had not enjoyed so much national attention since the Holbeck Hill Hotel subsided into the sea in 1993. As a place, it is a beguiling combination of natural appeal and gaudy man-made tackiness. Much the same was true of the media circus that was erected in the build-up. It was hard to tell whether the hype was an organic by-product of the fixture's appeal or a reflection of a desperate need to boost a venerable, ailing competition. Probably both.

The slightly dazed squad relished its temporary elevation to the A-list. Two days before the game, when the team held its big media morning in a clifftop restaurant, there were more journalists than at Chelsea's press conference when they hosted Lazio in the Champions League in October. Another point of contrast was that Claudio Ranieri and Juan Sebastian Veron did not stroll out of the room and go on a tour of the locality with some Page 3 girls in an open-top bus.

Romance is a word writ in bold type in the Bumper Book of Cup Cliches. It is said that when writing about the FA Cup, male journalists think about romance on average once every seven seconds. Appropriately, it descends from the Latin word meaning "in the Roman manner". Sadly, Roman Abramovich, the man whose millions instantly enriched Chelsea and doused the tie with extra resonance, did not make it. He preferred, it seems, to lounge in warmer climes on one of his yachts. Obviously the man's not a proper fan. *The Sun* sent a lookalike instead.

Even without Abramovich, money did not so much talk as holler at the top of its lungs. Live TV coverage meant that new sponsorship logos adorned the stadium, stretching out as far as the Sky could see. A couple of days before the game, men with cockney accents appeared in the town centre to peddle unofficial merchandise. *The Sun* signed a lucrative sponsorship deal with the club. A new men's magazine announced that in the unlikely event of a Scarborough goal, the players would line up and bare their bottoms, on which would be painted letters spelling out the publication's name.

Such bare-faced cheeks would have done the image of the club no favours, except with nudists; but who could blame them for having pound signs, as well as an upset, in their eyes? The £500,000 the club made will pay the wage bill for two years. The bonuses mattered to players who earned an average of £350 a week. Money is the root of all glamour and that Chelsea have it and Scarborough do not was a central reason why this tie seized the imagination like no other. Cup matches such as this are the sole cause to be grateful for the Grand Canyon-sized chasm between the Premiership and the other divisions. Even if, in the longer term, that gap is slowly suffocating the lower leagues, here it was a shot of adrenalin.

An added bonus was Scarborough's goalkeeping coach, a man whose deeds are stitched into the fabric of Cup folklore: Jim Montgomery, he of the impossible double-save in Sunderland's 1973 Wembley victory over Leeds United. Mention of Scarborough and goalkeepers generally brings to mind Jimmy Glass, their nemesis. It was Glass's famous late goal for Carlisle United that

Sand sculpture in Scarborough in Cup week while, at the match, a banner gently mocks the name of the McCain Stadium

relegated Scarborough into non-league football in 1999. Malcolm Reynolds, a banker, arrived in 2001 and saved it from debts, roughly equivalent to Jose Mourinho's monthly wage packet, that were threatening to kill off the club.

The dark days were forgotten as a 5,379 sell-out crowd crammed into the McCain Stadium on a beautiful sunny Saturday. The Theatre of Chips simmered with excitement. Could we be set for the greatest upset in the history of the FA Cup? *The Sun* had promised Leigh Walker, the Scarborough goalkeeper, a holiday — the longer he went unbeaten, the more glamorous the destination.

Fears that he would do well to bag a day-trip to Whitby were heightened when a long-range shot from Frank Lampard in the first minute bent like a plastic ruler and snapped back off the bar. Then John Terry headed in an easy goal in the tenth minute. Scarborough's worst fears were realised; Chelsea's affluence did not mean they were indifferent. The rest of the match was like a ride on a ghost train as an adult: more tame than you expect and hope, despite the odd screeching surprise.

Chelsea's threat diminished and Scarborough rarely looked like causing an upset — for which, in a perverse way, they deserved credit. They were too intent on playing delicate, passing football, too tidy and well-intentioned to be the prototype Cup giantkillers. And yet, and yet … In the final ten minutes, Colin Cryan put a free header straight at Carlo Cudicini. Then Mario Melchiot handled inside the area — but the referee, Barry Knight, did not award a penalty. The pre-game "what if?" melted into "if only". Afterwards, Scarborough's players did not know whether to be pleased that they had avoided humiliation or regretful that a replay at Stamford Bridge had been tantalisingly close.

Ten days later, Scarborough hosted Hereford United in the Conference and drew 3-3. The attendance was 1,459. Scarborough finished fifteenth and in late May, Russell Slade, the manager, took over at Grimsby Town and annoyed Reynolds by attempting to sign Scott Kerr, the club captain. Several players have left, including Mark Quayle, the scorer of the winner against Southend United in the previous round, who quit to pursue his dream of League football.

The newsmen are long gone; so, too, nearly all of the fairweather fans. But plans for a £2 million new stadium to the east of the town are advancing. The new season, inevitably, brings hope of promotion. There is money to invest and memories to cherish. For one afternoon, the humble little ground of Scarborough FC was transformed into a grand pleasure palace.

Saturday April 3 *(Villa Park)*

ARSENAL (0) **0**
39,939

MANCHESTER UNITED (1) **1**
Scholes 32

ARSENAL (4-4-2): J Lehmann — Lauren, S Campbell, K Toure, G Clichy — F Ljungberg, P Vieira, Edu (sub: Kanu, 76min), R Pires (sub: T Henry, 57) — D Bergkamp, J Aliadiere (sub: J A Reyes, 57). **Substitutes not used:** Keown, Stack. **Booked:** Lauren, Lehmann, Pires, Toure.
MANCHESTER UNITED (4-5-1): R Carroll — G Neville, W Brown, M Silvestre, J O'Shea — C Ronaldo (sub: D Bellion, 84min), D Fletcher, R Keane, P Scholes, R Giggs — O G Solskjaer (sub: P Neville, 75). **Substitutes not used:** N Butt, T Howard, E Djemba-Djemba. **Booked:** Scholes.
Referee: G Barber.

Sunday April 4 *(Old Trafford)*

MILLWALL (1) **1**
Cahill 26

SUNDERLAND (0) **0**
56,112

MILLWALL (4-3-1-2): A Marshall — K Muscat (sub: A Roberts, 42min), M Lawrence, D Ward, R Ryan (sub: M Elliott, 57) — P Ifill (sub: P Sweeney, 29), D Wise, D Livermore — T Cahill — D Dichio, N Harris. **Substitutes not used:** W Gueret, N Chadwick. **Booked:** Ifill, Wise.
SUNDERLAND (4-4-2): M Poom — S Wright (sub: S Thornton, 90), G Breen, P Babb (sub: M Piper, 78), G McCartney — J Oster, J McAteer, P Thirlwell, J Arca — K Kyle (sub: M Stewart, 62), T Smith. **Substitutes not used:** D Williams, T Myhre. **Booked:** McAteer, McCartney, Thirlwell. **Sent off:** McAteer (86).
Referee: P Durkin.

FINAL

MANCHESTER UNITED (1) **3**
Ronaldo 44, Van Nistelrooy 65 (pen), 81

Saturday May 22 *(Millennium Stadium)*

MILLWALL (0) **0**
71,530

An utterly predictable outcome, though that does not diminish Sir Alex Ferguson's celebrations of his fifth FA Cup triumph with United, his eighteenth Old Trafford trophy in all. The gulf in class between them and Millwall, the first-time finalists, is never remotely in danger of being crossed and only the margin of United's victory remains to be confirmed once Cristiano Ronaldo heads them into the lead just before half-time. The exemplary behaviour of Millwall's supporters is arguably the most pleasing aspect of (another) forgettable final.

MANCHESTER UNITED (4-3-2-1): T Howard (sub: R Carroll, 84min) — G Neville, W Brown, M Silvestre, J O'Shea — D Fletcher (sub: N Butt, 84), R Keane, P Scholes — C Ronaldo (sub: O G Solskjaer, 84), R Giggs — R van Nistelrooy. **Substitutes not used:** P Neville, E Djemba-Djemba.
MILLWALL (4-4-1-1): A Marshall — M Elliott, M Lawrence, D Ward, R Ryan (sub: B Cogan, 75) — P Ifill, D Wise (sub: C Weston, 89), D Livermore, P Sweeney — T Cahill — N Harris (sub: M McCammon, 75). **Substitutes not used:** A Dunne, W Gueret. **Booked:** Wise.
Referee: J Winter.

THIRD ROUND
Saturday January 3
Wimbledon 1 Stoke C 1; Cardiff C 0 Sheffield Utd 1; Mansfield T 0 Burnley 2; Crewe Alex 0 Telford Utd 1; Barnsley 0 Scunthorpe Utd 0; Portsmouth 2 Blackpool 1; Northampton T 1 Rotherham Utd 1; Manchester C 2 Leicester C 2; Southampton 0 Newcastle Utd 3; Birmingham C 4 Blackburn Rov 0; Nottingham F 1 West Bromwich Albion 0; Watford 2 Chelsea 2; Kidderminster H 1 Wolverhampton W 1; Gillingham 3 Charlton Ath 2; Swansea C 2 Macclesfield T 1; Tottenham Hotspur 3 Crystal Palace 0; Southend Utd 1 Scarborough 1; Sunderland 1 Hartlepool Utd 0; Tranmere Rov 1 Bolton W 1; Preston NE 3 Reading 3; Wigan Ath 1 West Ham Utd 2; Middlesbrough 2 Notts Co 0; Ipswich T 3 Derby Co 0; Coventry C 2 Peterborough Utd 1; Everton 3 Norwich C 1; Accrington S 0 Colchester Utd 0; Bradford C 1 Luton T 2; Millwall 3 Walsall 1

Sunday January 4
Fulham 2 Cheltenham T 1; Yeovil T 0 Liverpool 2; Leeds Utd 1 Arsenal 4; Aston Villa 1 Manchester Utd 2

Replays
Tuesday January 13
Stoke C 0 Wimbledon 1; Scunthorpe Utd 2 Barnsley 0; Rotherham Utd 1 Northampton T 2; Wolverhampton W 2 Kidderminster H 0; Bolton W 1 Tranmere Rov 2 (aet); Reading 1 Preston NE 2; Colchester Utd 2 Accrington S 1

Wednesday January 14
Leicester C 1 Manchester C 3; Chelsea 4 Watford 0; Scarborough 1 Southend Utd 0

FOURTH ROUND
Saturday January 24
Swansea C 2 Preston NE 1; Arsenal 4 Middlesbrough 1; Coventry C 1 Colchester Utd 1; Ipswich T 1 Sunderland 2; Luton T 0 Tranmere Rov 1; Liverpool 2 Newcastle Utd 1; Burnley 3 Gillingham 1; Nottingham F 0 Sheffield Utd 3; Portsmouth 2 Scunthorpe Utd 1; Telford Utd 0 Millwall 2; Scarborough 0 Chelsea 1; Birmingham C 1 Wimbledon 0

Sunday January 25
Manchester C 1 Tottenham Hotspur 1; Northampton T 0 Manchester Utd 3; Everton 1 Fulham 1; Wolverhampton W 1 West Ham Utd 3

Replays
Wednesday February 4
Tottenham Hotspur 3 Manchester C 4; Colchester Utd 3 Coventry C 1; Fulham 2 Everton 1 (aet)

FIFTH ROUND
Saturday February 14
Manchester Utd 4 Manchester City 2
Tranmere Rovers 2 Swansea City 1
Millwall 1 Burnley 0
Sunderland 1 Birmingham City 1
Fulham 0 West Ham Utd 0

Sunday February 15
Sheffield Utd 1 Colchester Utd 0
Arsenal 2 Chelsea 1
Liverpool 1 Portsmouth 1

Replays
Tuesday February 24
West Ham Utd 0 Fulham 3

Wednesday February 25
Birmingham City 0 Sunderland 2
Portsmouth 1 Liverpool 0

SIXTH ROUND
Saturday March 6
Manchester Utd 2 Fulham 1
Portsmouth 1 Arsenal 5

Sunday March 7
Millwall 0 Tranmere Rovers 0
Sunderland 1 Sheffield Utd 0

Replay
Tuesday, March 16
Tranmere Rovers 1 Millwall 2

CARLING CUP

WINNERS
Middlesbrough

RUNNERS-UP
Bolton Wanderers

SEMI-FINALISTS
Arsenal
Aston Villa

Knees-up: Juninho sinks to the ground in relief and jubilation as the referee's whistle confirms Middlesbrough's Cardiff triumph

THE GAMES

FIRST ROUND

Tuesday August 12

Barnsley 1 Blackpool 2
Bradford City 0 Darlington 0
(aet; Darlington win 5-3 on pens)
Bristol Rovers 0 Brighton & Hove Albion 1
Cambridge United 1 Gillingham 2
Cardiff City 4 Leyton Orient 1
Cheltenham Town 1 Queens Park Rangers 2
Chesterfield 0 Burnley 0
(aet; Burnley win 3-2 on pens)
Colchester United 2 Plymouth Argyle 1
Crewe Alexandra 2 Wrexham 0
Doncaster Rovers 3 Grimsby Town 2
Huddersfield Town 2 Derby County 1
Lincoln City 0 Stockport County 1
Luton Town 4 Yeovil Town 1
Macclesfield Town 1 Sheffield United 2
Millwall 0 Oxford United 1
Northampton Town 1 Norwich City 0
Port Vale 0 Nottingham Forest 0
(aet; Nottingham Forest win 3-2 on pens)
Preston North End 0 Notts County 0
(aet; Notts County win 7-6 on pens)
Rotherham United 2 York City 1
Scunthorpe United 2 Oldham Athletic 1
Southend United 2 Swindon Town 3
Torquay United 1 Crystal Palace 1
(aet; Crystal Palace win 3-1 on pens)
Tranmere Rovers 1 Bury 0
Walsall 2 Carlisle United 1
Watford 1 Bournemouth 0 *(aet)*
West Bromwich Albion 4 Brentford 0
Wigan Athletic 2 Hull City 0
Wycombe Wanderers 2 Wimbledon 0

August 13

Boston United 1 Reading 3
Bristol City 4 Swansea City 1 *(aet)*
Coventry City 2 Peterborough United 0
Ipswich Town 1 Kidderminster Harriers 0 *(aet)*
Mansfield Town 1 Sunderland 2
Sheffield Wednesday 2 Hartlepool United 2
(aet; Hartlepool win 5-4 on pens)
West Ham United 3 Rushden & Diamonds 1

August 19

Stoke City 2 Rochdale 1

SECOND ROUND

September 23

Blackpool 1 Birmingham City 0
Bristol City 1 Watford 0 *(aet)*
Cardiff City 2 West Ham United 3
Charlton Athletic 4 Luton Town 4
(aet; Charlton win 8-7 on pens)
Crystal Palace 2 Doncaster Rovers 1
Hartlepool United 1 West Bromwich Albion 2
Leicester City 1 Crewe Alexandra 0
Notts County 2 Ipswich Town 1
Portsmouth 5 Northampton Town 2
Rotherham United 1 Colchester United 0
Scunthorpe United 2 Burnley 3
Sheffield United 0 Queens Park Rangers 2
Stoke City 0 Gillingham 2
Sunderland 2 Huddersfield Town 4
Tranmere Rovers 0 Nottingham Forest 0
(aet; Nottingham Forest win 4-1 on pens)
Wigan Athletic 1 Fulham 0
Wolverhampton Wanderers 2 Darlington 0
Wycombe Wanderers 0 Aston Villa 5

THE IDEA OF A FINAL BETWEEN Bolton Wanderers and Middlesbrough may not have captured the imagination of those who hunger for glamour and big names, but Middlesbrough's 2-1 win over Bolton at the Millennium Stadium turned out to be the climax that the Carling Cup had merited. If the game was not of the very highest quality, then it was certainly eventful, as, indeed, most of the competition had been.

Take the third round, for example. On the one hand there was a seven-goal thriller at Ewood Park, where Liverpool beat Blackburn Rovers 4-3; a 4-2 win for Chelsea after Notts County had given them a scare at Stamford Bridge; and a 3-2 victory after extra time for Manchester United away to Leeds United, with Eric Djemba-Djemba scoring the decider in the 117th minute. On the other, Rotherham United took Arsenal to penalties after Darren Byfield's 90th-minute equaliser had sent the match at Highbury into extra time. The dismissal of Mike Pollitt, the Rotherham goalkeeper, brought on Gary Montgomery, 21, eventually to face a penalty shoot-out. It went to the 22nd kick — Montgomery, by the way, converted his with aplomb — before Arsenal finally won 9-8.

Arsenal were fielding a side that included a number of reserves and fringe first-team players and they did so again in the fourth round, but were still good enough to beat Wolverhampton Wanderers' full first XI 5-1. United put out a similar-strength team away to West Bromwich Albion but were beaten 2-0.

Portsmouth narrowly avoided a pile-up on the M27 on their way to Southampton, but they could not avoid defeat at St Mary's in the first derby between these intense South Coast rivals for seven years. Helder Postiga scored his first goal for Tottenham Hotspur in the 3-1 win over Manchester City and Liverpool were involved in another memorable tie, but this time it was Bolton who were celebrating after their 3-2 win at Anfield, thanks to a last-minute winner from the spot by Youri Djorkaeff.

In the fifth round, Arsenal's second string again proved their worth, winning 2-0 at The Hawthorns with goals from Kanu and Jeremie Aliadiere and the real possibility of a reserve team appearing in the final began to emerge. Yet while his youngsters continued to progress, it was hard to argue with Arsene Wenger's selection policy. After all, his side had just reached the semi-finals of the competition for the first time since his arrival at Highbury. Players such as Aliadiere were proving their quality while Francesc Fabregas Soler had become the club's youngest goalscorer in the match against Wolves.

However, the more games that Arsenal won, the closer came the

Humiliation for Wolves at the hands of Arsene Wenger's young hopefuls

prospect of empty seats in Cardiff, the last thing the competition required with a new sponsor.

In the end no one need have worried as Middlesbrough beat Arsenal in both legs of the semi-final. Juninho's goal at Highbury gave them a lead to take back to the Riverside, where a first goal in an Arsenal shirt by Jose Antonio Reyes — at the wrong end — settled matters in a 3-1 aggregate win. Ironically, the Arsenal side that lost the second leg was the strongest they had fielded.

But if that result was good for the competition, the other semi-final provided one of the matches of the season, Bolton beating Aston Villa 5-2 in the first leg at the Reebok Stadium. Wanderers had feared that Jay-Jay Okocha would be missing, playing for Nigeria in the African Nations Cup, but he delayed his departure and Bolton supporters — and the live television audience — were glad that he did as he topped and tailed the game with spectacular goals from free kicks. Villa had fought back from 3-0 down to 3-2 and won the second leg 2-0, but neither effort was enough.

So, instead of witnessing the best-attended reserve-team match in history, the Millennium Stadium was full to the brim with supporters of clubs whose chances for glory are fewer and farther between, but who enjoyed the day all the more for that — and for the first time in a leading cup final at the stadium there were no arrests and no ejections. The match itself, won 2-1 by Middlesbrough, exceeded expectations — disputed penalties awarded and not awarded, a tale of redemption as Mark Schwarzer handed Bolton a goal then rescued his team and his reputation with a series of saves, and in the end a first trophy in their 128-year history for Middlesbrough.

Another season like that and no one will be complaining.

September 24

Bolton Wanderers 3 Walsall 1
Coventry City 0 Tottenham Hotspur 3
Everton 3 Stockport County 0
Leeds United 2 Swindon Town 2
(aet; Leeds United win 4-3 on pens)
Middlesbrough 1 Brighton & Hove Albion 0 *(aet)*
Oxford United 1 Reading 3

THIRD ROUND

October 28

Arsenal 1 Rotherham United 1
(aet; Arsenal win 9-8 on pens)
Blackpool 1 Crystal Palace 3
Bolton Wanderers 2 Gillingham 0
Bristol City 0 Southampton 3
Leeds United 2 Manchester United 3 *(aet)*
Queens Park Rangers 0 Manchester City 3
Reading 1 Huddersfield Town 0
Wolverhampton Wanderers 2 Burnley 0

October 29

Aston Villa 1 Leicester City 0
Blackburn Rovers 3 Liverpool 4
Chelsea 4 Notts County 2
Everton 1 Charlton Athletic 0
Newcastle United 1 West Bromwich Albion 2 *(aet)*
Nottingham Forest 2 Portsmouth 4 *(aet)*
Tottenham Hotspur 1 West Ham United 0 *(aet)*
Wigan Athletic 1 Middlesbrough 2

FOURTH ROUND

December 2

Arsenal 5 Wolverhampton Wanderers 1
Southampton 2 Portsmouth 0

December 3

Aston Villa 3 Crystal Palace 0
Liverpool 2 Bolton Wanderers 3
Middlesbrough 0 Everton 0
(aet; Middlesbrough win 5-4 on pens)
Reading 0 Chelsea 1
Tottenham Hotspur 3 Manchester City 1
West Bromwich Albion 2 Manchester United 0

QUARTER-FINALS

December 16

Bolton Wanderers 1 Southampton 0 *(aet)*
West Bromwich Albion 0 Arsenal 2

December 17

Aston Villa 2 Chelsea 1
Tottenham Hotspur 1 Middlesbrough 1
(aet; Middlesbrough win 5-4 on pens)

Semi-finals and final details, pages 332-334

Tuesday January 20
ARSENAL (0) **0**   **MIDDLESBROUGH** (0) **1**
31,070   Juninho 53

Arsenal's first defeat in domestic competition of the season (the Community Shield apart) is inflicted by Juninho. Having hit the post and forced Graham Stack into a fine save, he makes no mistake at the third time of asking as Middlesbrough beat a team showing eight changes from the one that thumped them in the league ten days earlier.

ARSENAL (4-4-2): G Stack — K Toure, M Keown, P Cygan, G Clichy — R Parlour, Gilberto, Edu, D Bentley (sub: R Smith, 74min) — Kanu, Q Owusu-Abeyie (sub: J Thomas, 64). **Substitutes not used:** A Cole, C Holloway, O I Skulason.

MIDDLESBROUGH (4-4-1-1): M Schwarzer — D Mills, U Ehiogu, C Riggott, F Queudrue — S Parnaby, 81), G Boateng, Doriva, B Zenden — Juninho — M Maccarone (sub: J-D Job, 77) **Substitutes not used:**
B Jones, M Ricketts, S Downing. **Booked:** Juninho, Mills, Queudrue.
Referee: S Dunn.

Wednesday January 21
BOLTON WNDRS (3) **5**   **ASTON VILLA** (1) **2**
Okocha 2, 80, Nolan 9   Angel 20, 56
Giannakopoulos 17   16,302
N'Gotty 74

Jay-Jay Okocha's parting gifts to Bolton before leaving for the African Nations Cup are the opening and closing goals — both superb free kicks — on an extraordinary night that puts them within touching distance of Cardiff. "He is the best player the club has ever had, including Nat Lofthouse," Sam Allardyce, the Bolton manager, says.

BOLTON WANDERERS (4-1-3-2): J Jaaskelainen — N Hunt, E Thome, B N'Gotty, A Barness (sub: S Charlton, 63min) — I Campo — J-J Okocha, K Nolan, Y Djorkaeff (sub: I Ba, 84) — K Davies, S Giannakopoulos (sub: H Pedersen, 69). **Substitutes not used:** K Poole, J Moreno.

ASTON VILLA (4-4-2): T Sorensen — M Delaney, O Mellberg (sub: R Johnsen, 54), D Dublin, J Samuel — L Hendrie, G McCann, P Whittingham, G Barry (sub: T Hitzlsperger, 56) — D Vassell (sub: M Allback 78), J P Angel. **Substitutes not used:** S Postma, U De La Cruz. **Booked:** Hendrie, Barry, Vassell, Dublin.
Referee: P Durkin.

THE TIMES

MATCH OF THE SEASON

Aston Villa 2 Bolton Wanderers 0 (Bolton win 5-4 on aggregate)
Villa Park, Tuesday January 27 2004
Rick Broadbent

WHEN SAM ALLARDYCE started to mark outstanding team displays by eating sheep's testicles for his players' amusement, it suggested that he had the stomach for a fight. Three years on and Bolton Wanderers needed to employ all their manager's resilience and spirit last night to overcome Aston Villa and ensure their passage to next month's Carling Cup final.

Saddled by a 5-2 deficit from the first leg of this semi-final, Villa were given little chance but proceeded to ravage Bolton and might have achieved a remarkable turnaround had they not contributed to their own downfall through some schoolboy petulance. The sending-off of Gavin McCann in the first half proved the passion-killer at a time when the pot was boiling nicely, but Bolton still had to ride out a storm after a plethora of late penalty appeals and Jlloyd Samuel's 88th-minute strike.

"It felt like we were playing 12 men at the end," Allardyce said. "That's sweat underneath my shirt and champagne on top of it. What a waste. Champagne should go down the throat." Allardyce had every reason to be relieved after an intoxicating game that most had believed was effectively a dead rubber. Villa restored a modicum of pride, but these are trying times for a club struggling to shake off the shackles of mediocrity. It is a sign of their decline that they can gain solace from losing a semi-final to one of the Barclaycard Premiership's lesser lights. Even when they win, they lose.

Bolton survived to take Allardyce to his first cup final as a player or manager. Even those cynics who have dismissed his team as an eclectic bunch of mercenaries will not begrudge him his moment. "It was a hugely difficult night," he said. "We got through by some solid defending at the end and them going down to ten men. Emotions can run wild in games like these."

That was an accurate assessment after Villa Park, so often a drop-in centre for the terminally anxious, became a cauldron of febrile expectation. From the moment that Thomas Hitzlsperger curled a deft free kick into the corner after ten minutes, the fans believed that David O'Leary's dream was possible. Then it came crashing down and the miracle threatened to turn into a debacle.

McCann made an honest attempt to win the ball in the fortieth minute but caught Jussi Jaaskelainen, the Bolton goalkeeper. With Ivan Campo, the poodle-perm provocateur, leading histrionic protests, McCann lost his cool and slapped Emerson Thome. "If he has been sent off for striking a player, then I have no qualms with the referee," O'Leary, the Villa manager, said. "He's let himself down, but we restored our pride tonight. We played Bolton off the park with ten men."

Joy for Djorkaeff, despair for Whittingham and Hitzlsperger at the end

You could hardly blame McCann, given the example set by Roy Aitken, O'Leary's assistant, on the sideline. Aitken snarled at Nicky Hunt and gave Andy D'Urso, the fourth official, the third degree. Nevertheless, there were plus-points to be salvaged from the disappointment. "They let themselves down in the first leg and needed a performance," O'Leary said.

They gave him that, despite the gloomy portents. Interim losses of £16.5 million for the six months to December, announced yesterday, made for the most depressing preamble. The sight of Peter Crouch in the role of putative saviour did not send home spirits soaring, either. But Villa carved out chance after chance, Darius Vassell setting the tone by miscueing from three yards in the opening minutes. Crouch and Gareth Barry squandered further openings and, even after McCann exited, they continued to dominate. Had the second goal come earlier, who knows whether Bolton's nerves would have held out?

Samuel's late goal, which bounced off Campo's leg and into the top corner, made for a ripsnorting finale, but Bolton held on. For Villa, the damage was done a week ago.

ASTON VILLA (4-4-2): T Sorensen — M Delaney, O Mellberg, D Dublin, J Samuel — L Hendrie (sub: P Whittingham, 47min), G McCann, T Hitzlsperger, G Barry — D Vassell, P Crouch. **Substitutes not used:** S Postma, M Allback, L Ridgewell, R Johnsen. **Booked:** Samuel, McCann, Vassell. **Sent off:** McCann.
BOLTON WANDERERS (4-1-3-2): J Jaaskelainen — N Hunt, E Thome, B N'Gotty, S Charlton (sub: A Barness, 68) — I Campo — S Giannakopoulos, P Frandsen (sub: J Moreno, 88), I Ba — K Davies, Y Djorkaeff (sub: H Pedersen, 79). **Substitutes not used:** K Poole, R Vaz Te. **Booked:** Thome, Hunt, Davies.

SEMI-FINALS, SECOND LEGS

Tuesday January 27
ASTON VILLA (1) **2 BOLTON WNDRS** (0) **0**
Hitzlsperger 10   36,883
Samuel 88
(Bolton win 5-4 on agg)

The stars of the first leg, Jay-Jay Okocha and Juan Pablo Angel, are missing, but there is no shortage of drama as Sam Allardyce reaches his first final as a player or manager. Thomas Hitzlsperger's early free kick gives Villa hope in "mission impossible", but Gavin McCann's sending-off for slapping Emerson Thome effectively removes it, even though Jlloyd Samuel's late goal sets up a thrilling finale.

ASTON VILLA (4-4-2): T Sorensen — M Delaney, O Mellberg, D Dublin, J Samuel — L Hendrie (sub: P Whittingham, 47min), G McCann, T Hitzlsperger, G Barry — D Vassell, P Crouch. **Substitutes not used:** S Postma, M Allback, L Ridgewell, R Johnsen. **Booked:** Samuel, McCann, Vassell. **Sent off:** McCann (40).
BOLTON WANDERERS (4-1-3-2): J Jaaskelainen — N Hunt, E Thome, B N'Gotty, S Charlton (sub: A Barness, 68) — I Campo — S Giannakopoulos, P Frandsen (sub: J Moreno, 88), I Ba — K Davies, Y Djorkaeff (sub: H Pedersen, 79). **Substitutes not used:** K Poole, R Vaz Te. **Booked:** Thome, Hunt, Davies.
Referee: S Bennett.

Tuesday February 3
MIDDLESBROUGH (0) **2   ARSENAL** (0) **1**
Zenden 69   Edu 77
Reyes 85 (og)   28,781
(Middlesbrough win 3-1 on agg)

Middlesbrough are now one win away from ending their 128-year trophy drought after the dismissal of Martin Keown on the stroke of half-time (for a professional foul on Massimo Maccarone) eases their path to Cardiff. Bizarrely, Jose Antonio Reyes seals their triumph with an own goal after Edu's header had revived Arsenal's hopes.

MIDDLESBROUGH (4-4-1-1): M Schwarzer — D Mills, C Riggott, G Southgate, F Queudrue — G Mendieta, J Greening (sub: S Parnaby, 64min), Doriva, B Zenden — Juninho — M Maccarone (sub: J-D Job, 70). **Substitutes not used:** B Jones, M Ricketts, S Downing. **Booked:** Queudrue.
ARSENAL (4-4-2): G Stack — K Toure, M Keown, P Cygan, A Cole — R Parlour, P Vieira, Edu, G Clichy (sub: Q Owusu-Obeyie, 82) — J A Reyes, D Bentley. **Substitutes not used:** S Taylor, J Hoyte, O I Skulason, R Smith. **Booked:** Bentley. **Sent off:** Keown (45).
Referee: D Gallagher.

George Boateng and Danny Mills are at full stretch to stop the threat of Jay-Jay Okocha in an enthralling Carling Cup final

FINAL
Sunday February 29 *(Millennium Stadium)*

BOLTON WANDERERS (1) **1**   **MIDDLESBROUGH** (2) **2**
Davies 21   Job 2, Zenden 7 (pen)
72,634

Tense, compelling, controversial: the Carling Cup final is all of those and more, two of the country's less glamorous clubs combining to produce a memorable match that provides Middlesbrough with their first significant trophy after 128 years of striving, but Bolton with only heartache. The game looks over within seven minutes after Joseph-Desire Job and Boudewijn Zenden — the latter with a penalty more disputed for the manner in which it is scored (the Dutchman slips as he shoots and has technically kicked the ball twice) than in the award (Emerson Thome's foul on Job) — put Steve McClaren's team on top, but Kevin Davies's reply, after an awful blunder by Mark Schwarzer, sets up an absorbing contest. Middlesbrough create the clearer, more frequent chances, but Bolton's sense of injustice increases when Ugo Ehiogu's handling offence goes undetected in the frantic closing stages. With not a single arrest or ejection, the match is also officially the best-behaved sporting contest to be staged at the Millennium Stadium.

BOLTON WANDERERS (4-1-4-1): J Jaaskelainen — N Hunt (sub: S Giannakopoulos, 87min), E Thome, B N'Gotty, S Charlton — I Campo — K Nolan (sub: J Moreno, 78), P Frandsen (sub: H Pedersen, 64), J-J Okocha, Y Djorkaeff — K Davies. **Substitutes not used:** K Poole, A Barness. **Booked:** Campo, Frandsen.
MIDDLESBROUGH (4-4-1-1): M Schwarzer — D Mills, U Ehiogu, G Southgate, F Queudrue — G Mendieta, G Boateng, Doriva, B Zenden — Juninho — J-D Job (sub: M Ricketts, 66). **Substitutes not used:** B Jones, C Riggott, M Maccarone, S Downing.
Booked: Boateng, Ricketts.
Referee: M Riley.

PLAYER OF THE SEASON
Jay-Jay Okocha   Bolton Wanderers

The former African Player of the Year hit a rich vein of form in mid-season which, happily for Bolton, coincided with the later rounds of the Carling Cup and he scored his only goals for the club last season in the competition, all from free kicks. His second in the first leg of the semi-final against Aston Villa, a memorable and outrageously powerful effort that beat Thomas Sorensen at his near post, carried the stamp of true genius.
Nick Szczepanik

CARLING CUP LEADING GOALSCORERS

7	Juan Pablo Angel	Aston Villa
5	Robert Earnshaw	Cardiff City
4	Jeremie Aliadiere	Arsenal
	Jermain Defoe	West Ham United
	Nicky Forster	Reading
	Andy Johnson	Crystal Palace
3	James Beattie	Southampton
	Rob Hulse	West Bromwich Albion
	Mario Jardel	Bolton Wanderers
	Kevin Kyle	Sunderland
	Jay-Jay Okocha	Bolton Wanderers
	Scott Taylor	Blackpool

PREMIER LEAGUE
Arsenal
RUNNERS-UP
Charlton Athletic

NORTHERN DIVISION
Liverpool
RUNNERS-UP
Sunderland

SOUTHERN DIVISION
Bristol City
RUNNERS-UP
Southampton Saints

FA WOMEN'S CUP
Arsenal
RUNNERS-UP
Charlton Athletic

PREMIER LEAGUE CUP
Charlton Athletic
RUNNERS-UP
Fulham

Crest of a wave: Arsenal returned to prominence in 2003-04, winning the Cup and then securing the title in dramatic fashion

FINAL TABLES

FA NATIONWIDE PREMIER LEAGUE

NATIONAL DIVISION

	P	W	D	L	F	A	Pts
Arsenal	18	15	2	1	65	11	47
Charlton Athletic	18	15	1	2	52	17	46
Fulham	18	14	2	2	60	20	44
Leeds United	18	8	4	6	32	28	28
Doncaster	18	8	3	7	41	40	27
Everton	18	6	2	10	21	36	20
Birmingham City	18	4	5	9	17	31	17
Bristol Rovers	18	3	3	12	27	37	12
Aston Villa	18	1	4	13	18	63	7
Tranmere Rovers	18	1	4	13	13	63	7

NORTHERN DIVISION

	P	W	D	L	F	A	Pts
Liverpool	20	15	5	0	51	12	50
Sunderland	20	10	7	3	56	31	37
Stockport County	20	10	4	6	41	22	34
Oldham Curzon	20	9	7	4	39	22	34
Wolverhampton	20	6	9	5	27	22	27
Middlesbrough	20	7	5	8	25	28	26
Manchester City	20	7	3	10	35	45	24
Lincoln City	20	6	5	9	34	38	23
Sheffield Wed	20	6	4	10	30	45	22
Chesterfield	20	5	6	9	23	50	21
Bangor City	20	0	3	17	12	59	3

SOUTHERN DIVISION

	P	W	D	L	F	A	Pts
Bristol City	24	18	4	2	78	31	58
Southampton	24	18	3	3	54	18	57
AFC Wimbledon	24	17	2	5	57	38	53
Chelsea	24	13	6	5	60	38	45
Watford	24	9	5	10	34	38	32
Brighton	24	8	7	9	43	44	31
Langford	24	9	4	11	37	42	31
Millwall	24	8	6	10	35	38	30
Ipswich	24	8	5	11	39	44	29
Portsmouth	24	9	1	14	43	48	28
Enfield Town	24	4	4	16	17	54	16
Merthyr Tydfil	24	3	6	15	27	61	15
Barnet	24	2	7	15	31	61	11

FA NATIONWIDE PREMIER LEAGUE CUP

FIRST ROUND September 14

Arsenal 4 Ipswich T 0; Aston Villa 5 AFC Wimbledon 0; Barnet 2 Bangor C 4 (aet); Birmingham C 0 Fulham 4; Brighton 0 Charlton Ath 7; Enfield T 1 Lincoln C 5; Everton 3 Manchester C 0; Langford 1 Sheffield Weds 0; Leeds Utd 3 Bristol C 1; Liverpool 0 Bristol Rov 1; Middlesbrough 3 Chelsea 1; Oldham Curzon 4 Merthyr Tydfil 2; Southampton Saints 1 Doncaster Belles 3; Sunderland 3 Stockport Co 0; Watford 1 Tranmere Rov 7; Wolverhampton W 2 Portsmouth 1

SECOND ROUND October 12

Middlesbrough 1 Bristol Rov 5; Charlton Ath 10 Bangor C 1; Arsenal 4 Sunderland 2; Tranmere Rov 1 Doncaster Rov Belles 5; Fulham 9 Langford 0; Wolverhampton W 1 Lincoln C 1 (aet; Wolverhampton win 4-2 on pens); Leeds Utd 7 Everton 0; Aston Villa 2 Oldham Curzon 1

QUARTER-FINALS November 2

Bristol Rovers 4 Aston Villa 1
Wolverhampton Wanderers 0 Charlton Athletic 4
Arsenal 4 Doncaster Rovers Belles 0
Leeds United 2 Fulham 3

SEMI-FINALS December 14

Fulham 7 Bristol Rovers 0
Charlton Athletic 2 Arsenal 1

FINAL March 28

Charlton Athletic 1 Fulham 0

IT WAS THE KIND OF SEXY finish to a season that would have delighted Sepp Blatter. If the Fifa President had inadvertently brought the women's game its greatest blast of publicity of the year when he suggested that the sport might enjoy a higher profile if the players were to wear tighter shorts, then the fascinating title chase in England provided a more worthy conclusion to the domestic season.

Fixture congestion meant that Charlton Athletic completed their fixtures at the top of the FA Women's Premier League national division with Arsenal and Fulham, tied together two points behind them, still to play each other. So, after Arsenal had lifted the FA Women's Cup on May Bank Holiday Monday, defeating Charlton 3-0 at Loftus Road, Highbury provided the stage 12 days later for what amounted to a play-off for the championship. A win for either team would bring them the title; a draw would leave Charlton triumphant.

It was a fitting platform — Arsene Wenger's team had just celebrated their unbeaten league season by parading the Barclaycard Premiership trophy around Arsenal's home. With Vic Akers's side in fine form, having won 16 successive games in all competitions, perhaps it was no surprise that they prevailed, beating Fulham 3-1, but the destination of the title was in doubt until the last minute of the last game that Saturday night.

Lianne Sanderson and Julie Fleeting had put Arsenal two goals ahead, but when Rachel McArthur pulled one back for Fulham five minutes from time, all three teams were still in with a chance of winning the league. An equaliser would have had Charlton celebrating, but instead Ellen Maggs, the young England forward, gave the 5,000 Highbury crowd cause for double celebration with her stoppage-time finish.

Fleeting, the Scotland forward, played a pivotal role in the absorbing narrative of the 2003-04 season. Arsenal were well adrift of Charlton when she arrived, a casualty of the collapse of the Women's United Soccer Association, the American professional league, where she had been playing for San Diego Spirit. The powerful and pacy forward signed for Ross County in her homeland before arriving to bolster Arsenal's campaign in January. She proceeded to score 15 times in nine games as Arsenal, having finished the previous season without a trophy for the first time since 1996, seized a fourth Double in 11 years.

Her match-winning contribution to the Cup final was particularly dramatic. Only the day before, Fleeting had scored for her country against Germany, the world champions, in a 3-1 defeat before flying down to join her team-mates at their Hertfordshire retreat. Even

Another trophy for Highbury as Arsenal celebrate their title triumph

then, she had to stay up into the early hours of the morning having treatment on an injured shin.

Then, in pouring rain but in front of the live BBC cameras and a 12,244 crowd, she provided the main difference between the teams. Other players performed to a high level — Jayne Ludlow, the Wales midfield player who subsequently retained her Nationwide players' player of the year award, and Faye White, the captain, were as authoritative as ever — but Fleeting not only scored a superb hat-trick, she also worked the Charlton defence into submission.

So Charlton, after winning their first ten league games of the season, were left to collect runners-up medals in league and Cup, but at least they had the consolation of having won the Nationwide Premier League Cup final in March, when Emma Coss, the graceful defender, scored the only goal against Fulham. Keith Boanas was named as the manager of the year while Ann-Marie Heatherson was nominated as the Umbro young player of the year.

Fulham, treble-winners 12 months earlier in their first season in the top division, were left empty-handed and fearing for their future. Having downsized to join Arsenal, Charlton, Doncaster Rovers Belles and Leeds United in the semi-professional ranks, Marieanne Spacey, their manager, did well to keep the team in contention for honours, especially after the disappointment of bowing out of the quarter-finals of the Uefa Women's Cup by losing to FFC Frankfurt.

Aston Villa, after one season in the national division, and Tranmere Rovers were relegated. They will be replaced in the top flight by Liverpool, the northern division champions, and Bristol City, who pipped Southampton Saints to the southern division title. Football retained its status as the main female sport in England — 1.5 million girls aged between 7 and 15 played over the past year, while more than two million people watched the Cup final on television. Hosting the European Championship offers England an unprecedented opportunity to showcase the sport in the summer of 2005.

FIRST ROUND October 26

Crewe V 3 Chester-le-Street T 2 (aet); Manchester Utd 2 Newsham PH 0; Blackburn Rov 1 Newcastle Utd 0; Bolton W 1 E Durham 5; Blyth Sp 2 Bury G&L 4; Killingworth YPC 1 Hopwood 2; Bradford C 1 TNS Ladies 3; Scunthorpe Utd 1 Blackpool Wren Rov 2; Chester C 2 Barnsley 0; Shrewsbury T 1 Garswood Saints 2; Preston 5 Rotherham Utd 4; Darwen wo Ilkeston T; Doncaster P Rov 5 Leeds C Vixens 0; Loughborough Students 2 Luton T Belles 0; Derby Co 3 Leafield Ath 5; Nottingham F 3 Rushden & D 2; Leicester C 2 Bedford T Belles 1; Lichfield D 3 Coventry C 8; Cambridge Utd 1 Peterborough Utd 0; Birstall Utd 3 Stafford R 0; C Palace 1 Southwark T Utd 0; Reading 3 Stowmarket Sophtlogic 3 (aet; Reading win 4-2 on pens); Brook House 2 Reading Royals 3; Brentford 5 Gillingham 5 (aet; Gillingham won 8-7 on pens); L Orient 2 Woking 1; Dagenham & Red 2 Tottenham H 3; Crowborough Ath 4 Abbey Rgs 2 (aet); Redbridge Raiders 3 Chesham Utd 5; Colchester Utd 2 Barking 0; Lewes 1 Norwich C 0; London Colney 2 West Ham Utd 5; Caversham 0 Whitehawk 3; Denham Utd 2 QPR 4; Forest Green Rov 7 Rover Oxford 3; Bath C 3 Alphington 5; Newton Abbot 4 Plymouth Argyle 0; Team Bath 1 Cardiff C 5; Exeter C 1 Clevedon T 3; Yeovil T 0 Penzance 1; Plymouth Oak Villa 7 Swindon T 6

SECOND ROUND November 23

Darwen 3 Chester C 2; Bury G&L 0 Blackburn Rov 7; Garswood Saints 1 Manchester Utd 3; Hopwood 0 Crewe V 5; Blackpool Wren Rov 1 Doncaster Parklands Rov 0; E Durham 4 Preston 2 (aet); Nottingham F 2 TNS Ladies 0; Birstall Ath 1 Coventry C 5; Leafield Ath 2 Leicester C 0; Cambridge Utd 1 Loughborough Students 5; Whitehawk 1 West Ham Utd 1 (aet; West Ham win 4-3 on pens); Gillingham 4 Lewes 4 (aet; Gillingham win 4-2 on pens); C Palace 7 Crowborough Ath 1; L Orient 3 Colchester Utd 1; QPR 5 Tottenham H 4; Newton Abbot 2 Reading 2 (abandoned after 90min); Clevedon T 4 Plymouth Oak Villa 1; Cardiff C 5 Chesham Utd 3; Penzance 1 Forest Gr Rov 2 (aet); Alphington 0 Reading Royals 3. **November 16:** Reading 4 Newton Abbot 1

THIRD ROUND December 7

Stockport Co 2 Blackburn R 1; Leicester C 2 Sunderland Ladies 3; Nottingham F 3 Crewe Vags 1; Loughborough St 6 Blackpool Wren Rov 2; Lincoln C 3 Manchester C 1; Chesterfield 1 Manchester Utd 2; Darwen 2 Sheffield Weds 5; Wolverhampton W 2 Liverpool 1; Middlesbrough 2 Bangor C 0; QPR 0 Merthyr Tyd 2; Bristol C 0 Reading R 3; Portsmouth 3 Forest Green Rov 2; Chelsea 6 Gillingham 3; Barnet 2 Cardiff C 4; Enfield T 0 C Palace 0 (aet; C Palace win 4-2 on pens); Watford 1 Brighton 2; Coventry C 2 South'mpton Saints 3; Reading 0 AFC Wimbledon 3; West Ham Utd 1 Langford 1 (aet; Langford win 4-3 on pens); Clevedon T 1 Millwall Lionesses 3; L Orient 4 Ipswich T 2

FOURTH ROUND January 4

Reading Royals 2 Millwall Lionesses 1; Lincoln C 1 L Orient 3; Doncaster Belles 2 Leeds Utd 1; Middlesbrough 1 Southampton Saints 0 (aet); Chelsea 2 Manchester Utd 0; Birmingham C 1 Loughborough Students 0; Wolverhampton W 6 AFC Wimbledon 2; Charlton Ath 3 Portsmouth 0; Tranmere Rov 5 Brighton 3; Bristol Rov 1 Aston Villa 0; Arsenal 3 Stockport Co 0; Everton 2 Langford 1; Cardiff C 3 Merthyr Tydfil 1; Fulham 5 Sunderland Ladies 0; Nottingham F 3 Oldham Curzon 0; Sheffield Weds 1 C Palace 0

FIFTH ROUND January 25

Chelsea 3 Nottingham F 3 (aet; Nottingham F win 3-1 on pens); Doncaster Belles 4 Wolverhampton W 0; Charlton Ath 2 Fulham 1; Reading Royals 1 Bristol Rov 9; Tranmere Rov 1 Sheffield Weds 0; Middlesbrough 1 Arsenal 6; Cardiff C 2 Everton 1; L Orient 1 Birmingham C 6

QUARTER-FINALS February 8

Doncaster Rov Belles 0 Charlton Ath 1; Tranmere Rov 2 Birmingham C 3; Nottingham F 0 Bristol Rov 3; Arsenal 11 Cardiff City 1

SEMI-FINALS March 14

Birmingham C 0 Charlton Ath 1; Bristol Rov 0 Arsenal 2

FINAL May 3

Arsenal 3 Charlton Ath 0 (at Loftus Road)

Germany and Sweden will surely start next summer's European Championship, to be staged in the North West of England, as favourites.

England lost just two of their seven friendlies as they continued their preparations for Euro 2005, beating Australia, Scotland, Denmark and Iceland without conceding a goal. Ljungberg and Victoria Svensson, the Sweden forwards, were invited by Luciano Gaucci, the president of Perugia, to sign for the Serie A club, who then turned their attentions to Birgit Prinz, the top scorer in the 2003 World Cup finals with seven goals. All preferred to remain in the women's game.

IF IT WAS a golden goal that won Germany the 2003 Women's World Cup, it was a commercial own goal of gargantuan proportions that threatened to undermine the tournament just five days before it kicked off. Staged in the United States after the Sars epidemic ruled out China as the original venue, the organisers were rocking on their heels when it was announced that the Women's United Soccer Association, the world's only professional league, was to fold because of a lack of corporate sponsorship.

By the time that Nia Kunzer had headed Germany's winning goal eight minutes into the extra-time period of their 2-1 victory over Sweden in the final in Los Angeles, it had become clear that the health of the international game was not mortally endangered.

Professionalism may remain a distant horizon for

women's football, but the quality of play displayed by the world's top teams in these finals was indisputably high.

Disappointed that the host team, with Mia Hamm in her swansong tournament, were knocked out 1-0 in the semi-finals by Germany, a crowd of 26,137 watched Hanna Ljungberg give Sweden the lead before Maren Meinert equalised in a thrilling conclusion to the fourth World Cup finals in the Home Depot Centre.

Birgit Prinz, the player of the World Cup, and her Germany team-mates, above, celebrate

ENGLAND WOMEN RESULTS

September 3 2003
Turf Moor — Friendly
AUSTRALIA
Won 1-0
ENGLAND: R Brown, L Champ, C Stoney, M Phillip, R Unitt, K Moore (J Handley, ht), K Chapman, V Exley (R McArthur, 60), R Yankey, C Walker (K McDougall), K Smith (A Barr).
Scorer: Yankey 1
Att 4,349

September 11 2003
Darmstadt — Friendly
GERMANY
Lost 0-4
ENGLAND: P Cope, L Champ, C Stoney, M Phillip, R Unitt (C Yorston, 88), R Yankey, F Williams (V Exley, 82), K Chapman, K McDougall (K Smith, 72), S Smith (K Burke), C Walker (A Barr 81)

October 21 2003
Moscow — Friendly
RUSSIA
Drew 2-2
ENGLAND: R Brown (P Cope, ht), L Champ, F White (C Stoney, ht), M Phillip, R Unitt, J Handley, K Chapman, F Williams (V Exley, 68), R Yankey (S Smith, ht), K Smith (K McDougall, ht), A Barr (E Maggs, 81)
Scorers: Hanley 27, Barr 52
Att: 200

November 13 2003
Deepdale — Friendly
SCOTLAND
Won 5-0
ENGLAND: R Brown, L Champ (C Stoney, 66), R Unitt, K Chapman,
F White, M Phillip, J Handley (K Moore, 56), F Williams, A Barr, K Smith, R Yankey
Scorers: Barr 15, White 39, 49, Williams 44, Moore 86
Att: 6,700

February 19 2004
Fratton Park — Friendly
DENMARK
Won 2-0
ENGLAND: R Brown, L Champ, C Stoney, M Phillip, R Unitt, K Moore (J Handley, ht), K Chapman, V Exley (R McArthur, 60), R Yankey, C Walker (K McDougall), K Smith (A Barr).
Scorers: Cederkvist 73 (og), Smith 82 (pen)
Att: 8,101

April 22 2004
Madejski Stadium — Friendly
NIGERIA
Lost 0-2
ENGLAND: L Hall, C Stoney, F White, M Phillip, R Unitt, J Handley (A Barr, 59), K Chapman (R McArthur, 71), F Williams, K Smith, R Yankey (S Smith, 71), K Moore
Att: 4,089

May 14 2004
London Road — Friendly
ICELAND
Won 1-0
ENGLAND: L Hall, K Pealling (L Bassett, ht), C Stoney, M Phillip (A Asante, ht), R Unitt (L Champ, ht), K Moore (K Handley, ht), K Chapman (V Exley, ht), F Williams, K Smith, R Yankey (S Smith, ht), A Barr (C Walker, ht).
Scorer: Williams 42

CHAMPIONS LEAGUE

WINNERS
FC Porto

RUNNERS-UP
AS Monaco

SEMI-FINALISTS
Deportivo La Coruna
Chelsea

Carrying all before them: a year
after triumphing in the Uefa Cup,
the FC Porto players got their
hands on the biggest prize

THE GAMES

FIRST QUALIFYING ROUND

First legs, July 16

Glentoran 0 HJK Helsinki 0; Vardar 3 Barry Town 0; CS Grevenmacher 0 Leotar 0; HB Torshavn 0 FBK Kaunas 1; Omonia Nicosia 0 Irtysh Pavlodar 0; Sheriff Tiraspol 1 FC Flora Tallinn 0; Pyunik 1 KR Reykjavik 0; Sliema Wanderers 2 Skonto Riga 0; BATE Borisov 1 Bohemians 0; Dinamo Tbilisi 3 SK Tirana 0

Second legs, July 23

KR Reykjavik 1 Pyunik 1 (Pyunik win 2-1 on agg); Barry Town 1 Vardar 1 (Vardar win 4-2 on agg); Bohemians 3 BATE Borisov 0 (Bohemians win 3-1 on agg); FC Flora Tallinn 1 Sheriff Tiraspol 1 (Sheriff win 2-1 on agg); HJK Helsinki 1 Glentoran 0 (Glentoran win 1-0 on agg); SK Tirana 3 Dinamo Tbilisi 0 (aet; 3-3 on agg; Tirana win 4-2 on pens); Skonto Riga 3 Sliema Wanderers 1 (3-3 on agg; Sliema win on away goals); Leotar 2 CS Grevenmacher 0 (Leotar win 2-0 on agg); FBK Kaunas 4 HB Torshavn 1 (Kaunas win 5-1 on agg); Irtysh Pavlodar 1 Omonia Nicosia 0 (Nicosia win 2-1 on agg)

SECOND QUALIFYING ROUND

First legs, July 30

Bohemians 0 Rosenborg 1; MSK Zilina 1 Maccabi Tel Aviv 0; Maribor 1 Dinamo Zagreb 1; FBK Kaunas 0 Celtic 4; MTK Hungaria 3 HJK Helsinki 1; FC Copenhagen 4 Sliema Wanderers 1; Partizan Belgrade 1 Djurgardens IF 1; Rapid Bucharest 0 Anderlecht 0; Wisla Krakow 5 Omonia Nicosia 2; Sheriff Tiraspol 0 Shakhtar Donetsk 0; Leotar 1 Slavia Prague 2; SK Tirana 1 Graz AK 5; CSKA Moscow 1 Vardar 2; Pyunik 0 CSKA Sofia 2

Second legs August 6

Rosenborg 4 Bohemians 0 (Rosenborg win 5-0 on agg); Sliema Wanderers 0 FC Copenhagen 6 (Copenhagen win 10-1 on agg); Celtic 1 FBK Kaunas 0 (Celtic win 5-0 on agg); Dinamo Zagreb 2 Maribor 1 (Dinamo win 3-2 on agg); Djurgardens IF 2 Partizan Belgrade 2 (3-3 on agg; Partizan win on away goals); Anderlecht 3 Rapid Bucharest 2 (Anderlecht win 3-2 on agg); Graz AK 2 SK Tirana 1 (Graz win 7-2 on agg); CSKA Sofia 1 Pyunik 0 (CSKA win 3-0 on agg); Slavia Prague 2 Leotar 0 (Slavia win 4-1 on agg); Omonia Nicosia 2 Wisla Krakow 2 (Wisla win 7-4 on agg); Shakhtar Donetsk 2 Sheriff Tiraspol 0 (Shakhtar win 2-0 on agg); Vardar 1 CSKA Moscow 1 (Vardar win 3-2 on agg); HJK Helsinki 1 MTK Hungaria 0 (Hungaria win 3-2 on agg); Maccabi Tel Aviv 1 MSK Zilina 1 (Zilina win 2-1 on agg)

THIRD QUALIFYING ROUND

First legs, August 12

Celta Vigo 3 Slavia Prague 0; Graz AK 1 Ajax 1; Dinamo Kiev 3 Dinamo Zagreb 1

August 13

Lazio 0 Benfica 1; Rangers 1 FC Copenhagen 1; Rosenborg 0 Deportivo La Coruna 0; Austria Vienna 0 Marseilless 1; FC Bruges 2 Borussia Dortmund 1; Grasshoppers 1 AEK Athens 0; Partizan Belgrade 0 Newcastle United 1; Anderlecht 3 Wisla Krakow 1; Vardar 2 Sparta Prague 3; MTK Hungaria 0 Celtic 4; MSK Zilina 0 Chelsea 2; Galatasaray 3 CSKA Sofia 0; Shakhtar Donetsk 1 Lokomotiv Moscow 0

Second legs, August 26

Deportivo La Coruna 1 Rosenborg 0 (Deportivo win 1-0 on agg); Wisla Krakow 0 Anderlecht 1 (Anderlecht win 4-1 on agg); Chelsea 3 MSK Zilina 0 (Chelsea win 5-0 on agg); Sparta Prague 2 Vardar 2 (Sparta win 5-4 on agg)

August 27

Benfica 0 Lazio 1 (Lazio win 4-1 on agg); Marseilles 0 Austria Vienna 0 (Marseilles win 1-0 on agg); Newcastle United 0 Partizan Belgrade 1 (aet; 1-1 on agg; Partizan win 4-3 on pens); Slavia Prague 2 Celta Vigo 0 (Celta Vigo win 3-2 on agg); Celtic 1 MTK Hungaria 0 (Celtic win 5-0 on agg); Dinamo Zagreb 0 Dinamo Kiev 2 (Dinamo Kiev win 5-1 on agg); AEK Athens 3 Grasshoppers 1 (AEK win 3-2 on agg); Ajax 2 Graz AK 1 (Ajax win 3-2 on agg); Borussia Dortmund 2 FC Bruges 1 (aet; 3-3 on agg; Bruges win 4-2 on pens); FC Copenhagen 1 Rangers 2 (Rangers win 3-2 on agg); CSKA Sofia 0 Galatasaray 3 (Galatasaray win 6-0 on agg); Lokomotiv Moscow 3 Shakhtar Donetsk 1 (Lokomotiv win 3-2 on agg).

THE REVIEW   Russell Kempson

FOR MANY PURISTS, THE EUROPEAN Cup final between FC Porto and AS Monaco was little more than a sham. How dare the upstarts usurp the AC Milans, Manchester Uniteds and Real Madrids? How dare the have-nots dispossess the European elite of what they consider is rightfully theirs? The moment of crowning glory had been all but devalued.

For many romantics, the meeting of Iberian and Gallic influences in the magnificent Arena AufSchalke in Gelsenkirchen was a refreshing change from the norm. The big boys will be back, restoring the natural order, but fair play to the small fry. Not one iota did it detract from the most glittering of occasions.

While paying lip-service to the latter category, Lennart Johansson, the Uefa president, fell grumpily into the former. He is a fan of AIK Solna, the minor Swedish club, and can empathise with the underdogs. "I can dream," he said, "like so many other supporters in smaller countries. Impossible dreams, you might say." Yet Johansson still hankered for the main match-up: Bayern Munich versus Juventus or AC Milan against Manchester United. And he humbly admitted that it was probably a Uefa own goal — the scrapping of the second group stage — that had caused so many of the star names to fall by the wayside.

"A year ago, our main objective in reshaping the Champions League was to reduce the workload by four matches," Johansson said. "At the same time we were aware that, by creating a more even balance between group and knockout matches, we were opening the door to surprises. I have to admit that I did not expect so many." Johansson's dismay will have been echoed privately by the television moguls and commercial sponsors, whose largesse keeps the competition afloat. Porto v Monaco is not the sexiest of finales. Yet the introduction of an extra knockout phase produced an unpredictability that proved fascinating.

Few will forget the fightback of Deportivo La Coruna against Milan, the holders. Deportivo trailed 4-1 from the first leg but won 4-0 in the return at a disbelieving Riazor Stadium. Nor the recovery of Monaco from 4-2 down against Real, also in the quarter-finals, to 5-5 on aggregate and victory on away goals.

The all-Premiership clash, at the same stage, featuring Chelsea and Arsenal not only enthralled neutrals in England but many on the Continent, too. Arsenal appeared to have done the hard work by drawing 1-1 at Stamford Bridge, but they were undone by a thrilling Chelsea counter-offensive at Highbury, which was capped by a late winner from Wayne Bridge. That Arsenal had got so far, having taken only one point from their opening three matches in group B,

Porto's Carlos Alberto tries to shake off Monaco's dogged Patrick Evra

GROUP STAGE

Group A

September 17
Bayern Munich 2 Celtic 1
Lyons 1 Anderlecht 0

September 30
Anderlecht 1 Bayern Munich 1
Celtic 2 Lyons 0

October 21
Anderlecht 1 Celtic 0
Lyons 1 Bayern Munich 1

November 5
Celtic 3 Anderlecht 1
Bayern Munich 1 Lyons 2

November 25
Celtic 0 Bayern Munich 0
Anderlecht 1 Lyons 0

December 10
Lyons 3 Celtic 2
Bayern Munich 1 Anderlecht 0

	P	W	D	L	F	A	Pts
Lyons	6	3	1	2	7	7	10
Bayern Munich	6	2	3	1	6	5	9
Celtic	6	2	1	3	8	7	7
Anderlecht	6	2	1	3	4	6	7

Group B

September 17
Arsenal 0 Inter Milan 3
Dinamo Kiev 2 Lokomotiv Moscow 0

September 30
Lokomotiv Moscow 0 Arsenal 0
Inter Milan 2 Dinamo Kiev 1

October 21
Dinamo Kiev 2 Arsenal 1
Lokomotiv Moscow 3 Inter Milan 0

November 5
Inter Milan 1 Lokomotiv Moscow 1
Arsenal 1 Dinamo Kiev 0

November 25
Inter Milan 1 Arsenal 5
Lokomotiv Moscow 3 Dinamo Kiev 2

December 10
Dinamo Kiev 1 Inter Milan 1
Arsenal 2 Lokomotiv Moscow 0

	P	W	D	L	F	A	Pts
Arsenal	6	3	1	2	9	6	10
Lokomotiv Moscow	6	2	2	2	7	7	8
Inter Milan	6	2	2	2	8	11	8
Dinamo Kiev	6	2	1	3	8	8	7

Group C

September 17
AEK Athens 1 Deportivo La Coruna 1
PSV Eindhoven 1 AS Monaco 2

September 30
AS Monaco 4 AEK Athens 0
Deportivo La Coruna 2 PSV Eindhoven 0

October 21
Deportivo La Coruna 1 AS Monaco 0
AEK Athens 0 PSV Eindhoven 1

November 5
AS Monaco 8 Deportivo La Coruna 3
PSV Eindhoven 2 AEK Athens 0

November 25
Deportivo La Coruna 3 AEK Athens 0
AS Monaco 1 PSV Eindhoven 1

December 10
PSV Eindhoven 3 Deportivo La Coruna 2
AEK Athens 0 AS Monaco 0

	P	W	D	L	F	A	Pts
AS Monaco	6	3	2	1	15	6	11
Deportivo La Coruna	6	3	1	2	12	12	10
PSV Eindhoven	6	3	1	2	8	7	10
AEK Athens	6	0	2	4	1	11	2

owed much to a steely resolve in the face of elimination. The 5-1 win away to Inter Milan will hold a special place in the heart of every supporter. An easy win against Celta Vigo in the first knockout round augured well, but, as the business end beckoned, Arsenal wilted.

Chelsea's adventure had begun in the third qualifying round and they then sauntered to the top of group G by five points. The hiccup of a 2-0 home defeat against Besiktas was more than cancelled out by the glorious 4-0 success away to Lazio. VfB Stuttgart were edged out 1-0 on aggregate in the last 16 and, after Arsenal had been left dumbfounded, Monaco stood between Claudio Ranieri, the Chelsea head coach, and a place in the final. Ranieri tinkered calamitously in the first leg, with Chelsea losing 3-1 to ten-man Monaco, and his side then contrived to throw away a 2-0 lead at home. A month later, the head coach headed out of Stamford Bridge.

Manchester United plotted their usual course for the closing stages and they cruised through group E in comfort by amassing 15 points, the best total of the last-16 qualifiers. However, they never got to grips with the never-give-up Porto side of Jose Mourinho and paid dearly for allowing the last-gasp equaliser of Costinha at Old Trafford. Bayern Munich, another goliath, also disappeared, but at least they were beaten by Real Madrid, while Porto went on the defeat Lyons in the quarter-finals and Deportivo in the semi-finals.

In terms of drama the final was not the greatest game. Porto first subdued Monaco, whose coach, Didier Deschamps, was at a loss to explain his players' lethargy, and then cantered to a 3-0 victory. The Chelsea-bound Mourinho bade farewell and the Uefa grandees muttered darkly. Yet the European Cup had rediscovered its roots. The cartel had been blown apart, the relentless success of the giants replaced by rampant uncertainty and beguiling intrigue. Long may it continue.

Group D

September 17
Juventus 2 Galatasaray 1
Real Sociedad 1 Olympiakos 0

September 30
Olympiakos 1 Juventus 2
Galatasaray 1 Real Sociedad 2

October 21
Galatasaray 1 Olympiakos 0
Juventus 4 Real Sociedad 2

November 5
Olympiakos 3 Galatasaray 0
Real Sociedad 0 Juventus 0

November 25
Olympiakos 2 Real Sociedad 2

December 2
Galatasaray 2 Juventus 0

December 10
Real Sociedad 1 Galatasaray 1
Juventus 7 Olympiakos 0

	P	W	D	L	F	A	Pts
Juventus	6	4	1	1	15	6	13
Real Sociedad	6	2	3	1	8	8	9
Galatasaray	6	2	1	3	6	7	7
Olympiakos	6	1	1	4	5	13	4

Group E

September 16
Manchester United 5 Panathinaikos 0
Rangers 2 VfB Stuttgart 1

October 1
Stuttgart 2 Manchester United 1
Panathinaikos 1 Rangers 1

October 22
VfB Stuttgart 2 Panathinaikos 0
Rangers 0 Manchester United 1

November 4
Panathinaikos 1 VfB Stuttgart 3
Manchester United 3 Rangers 0

November 26
Panathinaikos 0 Manchester United 1
VfB Stuttgart 1 Rangers 0

December 9
Manchester United 2 VfB Stuttgart 0
Rangers 1 Panathinaikos 3

	P	W	D	L	F	A	Pts
Manchester Utd	6	5	0	1	13	2	15
VfB Stuttgart	6	4	0	2	9	6	12
Panathinaikos	6	1	1	4	5	13	4
Rangers	6	1	1	4	4	10	4

Group F

September 16
Partizan Belgrade 1 FC Porto 1
Real Madrid 4 Marseilles 2

October 1
Marseilles 3 Partizan Belgrade 0
FC Porto 1 Real Madrid 3

August 27
Marseilles 2 FC Porto 3
Real Madrid 1 Partizan Belgrade 0

November 4
FC Porto 1 Marseilles 0
Partizan Belgrade 0 Real Madrid 0

November 26
FC Porto 2 Partizan Belgrade 0
Marseilles 1 Real Madrid 0

December 9
Partizan Belgrade 1 Marseilles 1
Real Madrid 1 FC Porto 1

	P	W	D	L	F	A	Pts
Real Madrid	6	4	2	0	11	5	14
FC Porto	6	3	2	1	9	8	11
Marseilles	6	1	1	4	9	11	4
Partizan Belgrade	6	0	3	3	3	8	3

THE ~ TIMES

Wednesday April 7 2004

MATCH OF THE SEASON

Arsenal 1 Chelsea 2
Highbury, Tuesday April 6 2004
Matt Dickinson

CHELSEA'S dead man was not only walking but punching the air with triumphant delight at Highbury last night. Claudio Ranieri, for months a sacking waiting to happen, not merely tinkered but totally transformed the season when he led his team to an historic victory over Arsenal and into the European Cup semi-finals.

What odds the sack for Ranieri this morning? Longer, one suspects, than his chances of reaching the European Cup final in Gelsenkirchen on May 26. Chelsea will face AS Monaco in the semi-finals after Didier Deschamps, the former Chelsea player now managing in the principality, masterminded an entirely unexpected triumph over Real Madrid. "Chelsea will be favourites to beat Monaco by 80-20," Arsene Wenger, the Arsenal manager said.

"I was mad, happy, delirious for 30 seconds," Ranieri said of his emotions at the final whistle, although he would not go into his own future apart from to say that he was "still walking, still fighting". He would surely make it impossible for Roman Abramovich to dismiss him if he not only reached the European Cup final but also overtook Arsenal to win the Barclaycard Premiership. In this most extraordinary of seasons at Stamford Bridge, nothing should be ruled out.

A four-point advantage in the Premiership and a game in hand will feel like scant protection for Arsenal this morning after the most crushing reverse of Wenger's reign. The substitution of Thierry Henry nine minutes from time in the biggest game of the season spread a deep sense of unease around Highbury. It was a sure sign, if any was needed, that all was not right about Arsenal. Stunning confirmation came six minutes later when Wayne Bridge raced through to score the goal that knocked them out.

Henry appeared to have gone off with fatigue and it was a symptom of his team's collapse in the past few weeks. They have lost the physical power that drives their choreographed passing and last night Ranieri's men took full advantage with a late, sustained attacking burst that could have yielded more than Bridge's strike.

Perhaps the Arsenal players sensed that three games without a victory had broken up their rhythm. It took them at least 20 minutes of niggly fouls and raggedness to find it last night and they might have fallen behind in that jittery opening when Damien Duff swayed past Lauren and Sol Campbell and found himself eight yards out. The Irishman's right-foot miss not only shocked the Chelsea fans but also seemed to act as a jolt to Arsenal.

Robert Pires and Henry began to cast off their inhibitions and, for the next 25 minutes, they bore down on the visiting team's defence with familiar exuberance until the pressure finally told in the seconds before half-time. Lauren's deep cross from the right wing

Bridge, Chelsea's match-winner, attacks Ljungberg and Edu at Highbury

reached Henry at the far post and his knockdown was left by Fredrik Ljungberg for Jose Antonio Reyes to shoot home with his right foot. After a header from Pires into the side-netting and a shot high over the crossbar from Henry, it was Arsenal's first shot on target, but the pressure had been mounting on John Terry and William Gallas.

Ranieri's answer was to throw on Jesper Gronkjaer for Scott Parker, the first change from the Tinkerman, who had kept an unchanged team for only the second time this season. Even at a combined £33.8 million, Hernan Crespo and Adrian Mutu could not make the starting XI.

The pre-Abramovich pairing of Jimmy Floyd Hasselbaink and Eidur Gudjohnsen had not had much to work with in the first half, but Chelsea were first out after the interval in all respects and level within six minutes. Defending deep in their own area, Arsenal cleared as far as Claude Makelele, whose shot from 25 yards carried enough power, and flew through enough bodies, to disorient Jens Lehmann. The goalkeeper's parry was awkward, lacking in conviction, and bounced only as far as Frank Lampard, who scored with the rebound.

Not long after, the news came through that AS Monaco were leading Real Madrid 3-1 and Chelsea began to fancy a double upset. They were happy to wait for the counter-attack, which could have yielded a goal when Gronkjaer found room on the flank. The ball was crossed and laid back to Gudjohnsen, who failed to shoot immediately. He might have regretted that for the rest of his career — but it was he who slipped the ball through to Bridge for the dramatic and fully deserved winner.

ARSENAL (4-4-2): J Lehmann — Lauren, K Toure, S Campbell, A Cole — F Ljungberg, P Vieira, Edu, R Pires — J A Reyes, T Henry (sub: D Bergkamp, 81min). **Substitutes not used:** G Stack, M Keown, S Wiltord, Gilberto Silva, G Clichy, Kanu. **Booked:** Lauren.
CHELSEA (4-4-2): M Ambrosio — M Melchiot, W Gallas, J Terry, W Bridge — S Parker (sub: J Gronkjaer, 46), C Makelele, F Lampard, D Duff (sub: J Cole, 83) — E Gudjohnsen, J F Hasselbaink (sub: H Crespo, 83). **Substitutes not used:** N Sullivan, A Mutu, Geremi, R Huth. **Booked:** Gallas, Hasselbaink, Cole.

Group G

September 16
Besiktas 0 Lazio 2
Sparta Prague 0 Chelsea 1

October 1
Chelsea 0 Besiktas 2
Lazio 2 Sparta Prague 2

October 21
Sparta Prague 2 Besiktas 1

October 22
Chelsea 2 Lazio 1

November 4
Lazio 0 Chelsea 4
Besiktas 1 Sparta Prague 0

November 26
Lazio 1 Besiktas 1
Chelsea 0 Sparta Prague 0

December 9
Besiktas 0 Chelsea 2
Sparta Prague 1 Lazio 0

	P	W	D	L	F	A	Pts
Chelsea	6	4	1	1	9	3	13
Sparta Prague	6	2	2	2	5	5	8
Besiktas	6	2	1	3	5	7	7
Lazio	6	1	2	3	6	10	5

Group H

September 16
FC Bruges 1 Celta Vigo 1
AC Milan 1 Ajax 0

October 1
Ajax 2 FC Bruges 0
Celta Vigo 0 AC Milan 0

October 22
Ajax 1 Celta Vigo 0
AC Milan 0 FC Bruges 1

November 4
Celta Vigo 3 Ajax 2
FC Bruges 0 AC Milan 1

November 26
Celta Vigo 1 FC Bruges 1
Ajax 0 AC Milan 1

December 9
FC Bruges 2 Ajax 1
AC Milan 1 Celta Vigo 0

	P	W	D	L	F	A	Pts
AC Milan	6	3	1	2	4	3	10
Celta Vigo	6	2	3	1	7	6	9
FC Bruges	6	2	2	2	5	6	8
Ajax	6	2	0	4	6	7	6

FIRST KNOCKOUT ROUND

First legs, February 24
Bayern Munich 1 Real Madrid 1
Celta Vigo 2 Arsenal 3
Sparta Prague 0 AC Milan 0
Lokomotiv Moscow 2 AS Monaco 1

February 25
Deportivo La Coruna 1 Juventus 0
FC Porto 2 Manchester United 1
Real Sociedad 0 Lyons 1
VfB Stuttgart 0 Chelsea 1

Second legs, March 9
Chelsea 0 VfB Stuttgart 0
(Chelsea win 1-0 on agg)
Juventus 0 Deportivo La Coruna 1
(Deportivo La Coruna win 2-0 on agg)
Lyons 1 Real Sociedad 0
(Lyons win 2-0 on agg)
Manchester United 1 FC Porto 1
(FC Porto win 3-2 on agg)

March 10
AC Milan 4 Sparta Prague 1
(AC Milan win 4-1 on agg)
Arsenal 2 Celta Vigo 0
(Arsenal win 5-2 on agg)
AS Monaco 1 Lokomotiv Moscow 0
(2-2 on agg; AS Monaco win on away goals)
Real Madrid 1 Bayern Munich 0
(Real Madrid win 2-1 on agg)

EUROPE GOES RETRO

Gabriele Marcotti

This article first appeared in The Times *on May 24, two days before the European Cup final*

IF IT WEREN'T FOR THE fact that John Major is nowhere to be found and that the European Union has swelled to 25 nations, looking at this year's European Cup finalists, you could almost be forgiven for thinking you were back in the early 1990s: war in Iraq, Bush in the White House, Jonathan Ross all over the television and two sides from unfashionable countries contesting Europe's biggest footballing prize, just as Red Star Belgrade and Marseilles did in 1991.

There is something very retro about AS Monaco and FC Porto: the way they play football, which is highly reminiscent of Italian clubs in their heyday of the early 1990s. The respective young managers, Didier Deschamps and Jose Mourinho, are considered among the brightest in the game, despite neither having more than three years' experience at any level. Yet, far from being innovators, tactically speaking, both rely on tried-and-tested methods that are more effective than they are entertaining.

Deschamps's years in Serie A clearly left their mark as Monaco are, above all, a counter-attacking side. It just so happens that they break exceptionally well, perhaps better than any other club in the tournament. Ludovic Giuly from the right and the Patrice Evra-Jerome Rothen tandem on the left get the ball forward quickly and intelligently as soon as Monaco win possession and, with Fernando Morientes in a withdrawn role, they have a striker whose movement is second to none. Throw in a highly organised and disciplined back four and you have a solid outfit that knows how to capitalise on opponents' mistakes.

As for Porto, they mirror perfectly Mourinho's vision, the world view of a man who, since childhood, has been obsessed with coaching and tactics. He would name neighbourhood dogs after footballers and try to get them to line up in a 4-4-2 formation. Legend has it that, at 16,

he was on the books at Vitoria Setubal, scouting the opposition and submitting detailed tactical reports.

The swottish young Mourinho grew up to become a detail-obsessed coach, secure in his belief that most matches can be won on the tactical chalkboard. As recently as yesterday, he was quoted in a national newspaper as saying: "I want people to remember me as one of the all-time great managers."

Such naked ambition is usually frowned upon in footballing circles, but then Mourinho is unlike most of his colleagues. He has a passion that borders on religious fervour. Most of the time, his main tactical objective is to prevent the other team from playing. He did this effectively against Manchester United and Lyons and raised it to an art form against Deportivo La Coruna in the semi-finals, Porto winning by the flimsiest of scorelines: 1-0 on aggregate. Whenever a player gets booked for time-wasting after 23 minutes in a first leg, as Carlos Alberto, the striker, did, you know it's going to be a long, long night.

The key to Porto's success is the rough-and-tumble pairing of Costinha and Maniche, who sit in front of the back four and foil whatever creative intentions the opposition may have (when things get really tough, such as in the return leg against Deportivo, Mourinho adds a third holding midfield player in Pedro Mendes).

The task of scoring goals is left to the front three of Benni McCarthy, Carlos Alberto (or Derlei) and Deco, the playmaker. This sometimes leads to the somewhat comical situation where the forwards are in the opposing penalty box by themselves and the rest of the side basically stand around, making sure they maintain their positions. It's rarely pretty but it works, particularly away from home: Porto went nearly 11 months without losing on the road between May 2003 and April 2004.

The flip-side, alas, is that they don't score many goals. Since early March, despite playing in the goal-happy Portuguese league, they have scored more than one goal in only four out of 14 games. Those who enjoy wide-open, attacking football and end-to-end excitement are likely to be disappointed on Wednesday.

Thanks to Mourinho's tactical nous, Porto break up

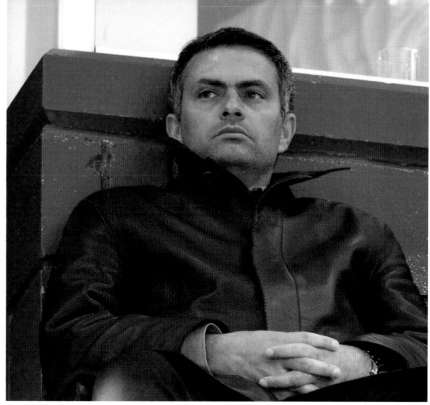

Faces of the future: Deschamps and Mourinho, the young coaches who made the most impact on the Champions League

play as well as any side in Europe. As for Monaco's counter-attacking, there isn't much counter-attacking to be done against teams who don't expose themselves. The David v Goliath element, which led many neutrals to back little Monaco to spoil Real Madrid's plans for global domination and Chelsea's rouble-fuelled assault on Europe, will be gone as well.

All this means that either Deschamps or Mourinho will have to reinvent themselves, at least for 90 minutes, if we are going to see something other than a tense, stifling tactical affair. In many ways, this will be a true test of either man's coaching mettle, whether they have the qualities required to handle the types of big jobs to which they have been linked.

The good news for both of them is that they have — at least for this year — the one intangible quality that every good manager needs: luck. Were it not for some eleventh-hour financial interventions (co-ordinated by Prince Albert, their biggest fan) and a good dose of understanding from the French FA, Monaco would be in the second division right now, trying to pay off their gargantuan debt. Were it not for a Portuguese referee who controversially sent off Dimitri Loskov, the Lokomotiv Moscow captain, after only 22 minutes in the

second leg of their first knockout round match, they might not have even made it to the quarter-finals. And were it not for Real Madrid's rock star-like penchant for self-destruction, they would have gone out in the quarter-finals.

Porto, too, benefited from some controversial refereeing decisions — just ask Sir Alex Ferguson or Jorge Andrade, the Deportivo defender — but they have made their own luck. They frustrate the opposition, dull them into submission and wait for one of the front three to do something special.

Whether the success of Porto and Monaco signals a return to the bad old days of overly tactical, conservative strategies aimed at stopping the other team from playing, remains to be seen. It is hard to argue, though, that the retro tactics have not worked well for Deschamps and Mourinho: both managers seem to overshadow their players, at least in terms of column inches.

Both would probably argue that the relative weakness of their squads left them with little choice and that, with more gifted players, things would have been different. Which only makes next season — when both are likely to have plenty of genuine talent at their disposal — all the more interesting.

QUARTER-FINALS

First legs, March 23

AC Milan 4 Deportivo La Coruna 1
FC Porto 2 Lyons 0

March 24

Chelsea 1 Arsenal 1
Real Madrid 4 AS Monaco 2

Second legs, April 6

Arsenal 1 Chelsea 2
(Chelsea win 2-1 on agg)
AS Monaco 3 Real Madrid 1
(5-5 on agg, AS Monaco win on away goals)

April 7

Deportivo La Coruna 4 AC Milan 0
(Deportivo La Coruna win 5-4 on agg)
Lyons 2 FC Porto 2
(FC Porto win 4-2 on agg)

SEMI-FINALS

First leg, April 20

AS Monaco 3 Chelsea 1

April 21

FC Porto 0 Deportivo La Coruna 0

Second leg, May 4

Deportivo La Coruna 0 FC Porto 1
(FC Porto win 1-0 on agg)

May 5

Chelsea 2 AS Monaco 2
(AS Monaco win 5-3 on agg)

PLAYER OF THE SEASON
Fernando Morientes   AS Monaco

The Real Madrid striker spent the season on loan with AS Monaco and played a key role in knocking Madrid out in an epic quarter-final. Morientes scored in both legs and also in the second leg of the semi-final success against Chelsea. However, the fairytale had no happy ending. Morientes may have finished as the leading scorer in the competition with nine goals, but he was rarely seen to any good effect in the final.

Russell Kempson

THE FINAL

Wednesday May 26 *Gelsenkirchen*
FC PORTO (1) **3**
Carlos Alberto 39,
Deco 71, Alenitchev 75

AS MONACO (0) **0**
52,000

Jose Mourinho sprinted from the pitch at the final whistle, having led his Porto team to victory, and hardly paused for breath before confirming that he would be managing in the Premiership next season, although he would not admit that Chelsea were his next port of call. Having lost Ludovic Giuly, their playmaker, Monaco were always going to struggle once Carlos Alberto had given Porto the lead and two goals in four second-half minutes killed them off.

FC PORTO (4-3-1-2): Vitor Baia — P Ferreira, J Costa, R Carvalho, N Valente — P Mendes, Costinha, Maniche — Deco (sub: Pedro Emanuel, 85min) — Carlos Alberto (sub: D Alenitchev, 60), Derlei (sub: B McCarthy, 78). **Substitutes not used:** Nuno, Ricardo Costa, E Jankauskas, J Bosingwa. **Booked:** Valente, Carlos Alberto, Costa.

AS MONACO (4-1-3-2): F Roma — H Ibarra, G Givet (sub: S Squillaci, 73), J Rodriguez, P Evra — A Zikos — E Cisse (sub: S Nonda, 64), L Bernardi, J Rothen — L Giuly (sub: D Prso, 23), F Morientes. **Substitutes not used:** T Sylva, J Plasil, E Adebayor, H El-Fakiri. **Booked:** Bernardi. **Referee:** K Milton Nielsen (Denmark).

LEADING GOALSCORERS		
Fernando Morientes	AS Monaco	9
Dado Prso	AS Monaco	7
Roy Makaay	Bayern Munich	6
Walter Pandiani	Deportivo La Coruna	6
Didier Drogba	Marseilles	5
Hakan Sukur	Galatasaray	5
Thierry Henry	Arsenal	5
Juninho Pernambucano	Lyons	5

UEFA CUP

WINNERS
Valencia

RUNNERS-UP
Marseilles

SEMI-FINALISTS
Newcastle United
Villarreal

Gripping stuff: Valencia's Francisco Rufete unsteadily holds the Uefa Cup aloft after the Spanish side's victory over Marseilles

THE GAMES

QUALIFYING ROUND

First legs, August 12

FK Sarajevo 1 FK Sartid 1; Valletta 0 Neuchatel Xamax 2; FC Haka 2 Hajduk Split 1

August 13

FK Ventspils 1 Wisla Plock 1

August 14

Manchester City 5 TNS Llansantffraid 0; AIK Solna 1 Fylkir 0; Zeljeznicar Sarajevo 1 Anorthosis Famagusta 0; Crvena Zvezda 5 FC Nistru Otaci 0; Groclin Dyskobolia 2 FK Atlantas 0; Hapoel Tel Aviv 1 Banants 1; Lens 3 Torpedo Kutaisi 0; Malmo FF 4 Portadown 0; Odense Boldklub 1 TVMK Tallinn 1; Olimpija 1 Shelbourne 0; Brondby 3 Dinamo Minsk 0; Coleraine 2 Uniao Leiria 1; Birkirkara 0 Ferencvaros 5; FC Vaduz 0 Dnipro 1; Liteks Lovetch 0 CSF Zimbru 0; Esbjerg 5 Santa Coloma 0; FC Nordsjaelland 4 Shirak 0; Molde 2 KI Klaksvik 0; NSI Runavik 3 SFK Lyn Oslo 0; Vllaznia Shkoder 0 Dundee 2; Cwmbran 0 Maccabi Haifa 3; Etzella Ettelbruck 1 Kamen Ingrad 2; Apoel Nicosia 2 Derry City 1; FC Karnten 2 Grindavik 1; Torpedo Moscow 5 Domagnano 0; Artmedia Petrzalka 1 F91 Dudelange 0; CMC Publikum 7 Belasica 2; MyPa 3 Young Boys 2; Cementarnica 55 0 Dospel Katowice 0; Dinamo Tirana 0 Lokeren 4; FK Ekranas 1 Debrecen 1; Levadia Maardu 1 Varteks 3; Matador Puchov 5 Sioni Bolnisi 0; Viktoria Zizkov 3 Zhenis Astana 0; Neman Belcard Grodno 1 Steaua Bucharest 1; FK Atyrau 1 Levski Sofia 4

Second legs, August 27

FK Atlantas 1 Groclin Dyskobolia 4 (Groclin win 6-1 on agg); Zhenis Astana 1 Viktoria Zizkov 3 (Zizkov win 6-1 on agg)

August 28

Uniao Leiria 5 Coleraine 0 (Uniao win 6-2 on agg); Dospel Katowice 1 Cementarnica 55 1 (1-1 on agg; Cementarnica win on away goals); Dundee 4 Vllaznia Shkoder 0 (Dundee win 6-0 on agg); Shelbourne 2 Olimpija 3 (Olimpija win 4-2 on agg); TNS Llansantffraid 0 Manchester City 2 (Manchester City win 7-0 on agg); Lokeren 3 Dinamo Tirana 0 (Lokeren win 7-1 on agg); Portadown 0 Malmo 2 (Malmo win 6-0 on agg); Derry City 0 Apoel Nicosia 3 (Apoel win 5-1 on agg); Domagnano 0 Torpedo Moscow 4 (Torpedo win 9-0 on agg); Hajduk Split 1 FC Haka 0 (2-2 on agg; Hajduk win on away goals); Neuchatel Xamax 2 Valletta 0 (Neuchatel win 4-0 on agg); Ferencvaros 1 Birkirkara 0 (Ferencvaros win 6-0 on agg); Fylkir 0 AIK Solna 0 (Solna win 1-0 on agg); KI Klaksvik 0 Molde 4 (Molde win 6-0 on agg); Kamen Ingrad 7 Etzella Ettelbruck 0 (Kamen win 9-1 on agg); Dinamo Minsk 0 Brondby 2 (Brondby win 5-0 on agg); Grindavik 1 FC Karnten 1 (Karnten win 3-2 on agg); Steaua Bucharest 0 Neman Belcard Grodno 0 (1-1 on agg; Steaua win on away goals); Young Boys 2 MyPa 2 (MyPa win 5-4 on agg); Santa Coloma 1 Esbjerg 4 (Esbjerd win 9-1 on agg); Anorthosis Famagusta 1 Zeljeznicar Sarajevo 3 (Zeljeznicar win 4-1 on agg); SFK Lyn Oslo 6 NSI Runavik 0 (Oslo win 9-1 on agg); Debrecen 2 FK Ekranas 1 (aet; Debrecen win 3-2 on agg); Maccabi Haifa 3 Cwmbran 0 (Maccabi win 6-0 on agg); Levski Sofia 2 FK Atyrau 1 (Levski win 6-1 on agg); TVMK Tallinn 0 Odense Boldklub 3 (Odense win 4-1 on agg); Varteks 3 Levadia Maardu 1 (Varteks win 6-3 on agg); Wisla Plock 2 FK Ventspils 2 (3-3 on agg; Ventspils win on away goals); F91 Dudelange 0 Artmedia Petrzalka 1 (Artmedia win 2-0 on agg); FC Nistru Otaci 2 Crvena Zvezda 3 (Crvena win 8-2 on agg); FK Metalurgs 1 Dinamo Bucharest 1 (Dinamo win 6-3 on agg); Torpedo Kutaisi 0 Lens 2 (Lens win 5-0 on agg); CSF Zimbru 2 Liteks Lovetch 0 (Zimbru win 2-0 on agg); Dnipro 1 FC Vaduz 0 (Dnipro win 2-0 on agg); Belasica 0 CMC Publikum 5 (Publikum win 12-2 on agg); FK Sartid 3 FK Sarajevo 0 (Sartid win 4-1 on agg); Banants 1 Hapoel Tel Aviv 2 (Hapoel win 3-2 on agg); Shirak 0 FC Nordsjaelland 2 (Nordsjaelland win 6-0 on agg); Sioni Bolnisi 0 Matador Puchov 0 (Matador win 6-0 on agg)

THE DEVALUATION OF THE Uefa Cup is complete. By incorporating a group stage into this season's competition, European football's governing body has done all that was left to turn the trophy bearing its name into an embarrassingly poor relation of the bloated Champions League. Dead rubbers between also-rans from Macedonia and Slovakia lie in prospect and yet, despite the persistent meddling, the competition seldom fails to provide an uplifting story or worthy winners.

This time it was Valencia, whose proud supporters had waited 24 years since last seeing their team win a European trophy. As an achievement, it may not match reaching consecutive European Cup finals in 2000 and 2001, but there is little doubt which event was enjoyed more by the supporters — or indeed the players, many of them earning success at the third attempt, having played in the teams beaten by Real Madrid and Bayern Munich.

In short, the Uefa Cup offers the prospect of gratification for those clubs lying just outside the elite. For Valencia, failing to qualify for the Champions League at the end of the 2002-03 season was said to spell financial disaster, just as it was for Liverpool in 2000 — but, 12 months and one trophy later, that loss of revenue was set against the priceless joy that only silverware can bring.

Ask the supporters of Newcastle United what winning the Uefa Cup would have meant to them. Demoted from the Champions League after a preliminary-round defeat by Partizan Belgrade, they beat NAC Breda, FC Basle, Valerenga, Real Mallorca and PSV Eindhoven to move within touching distance of their first European final in 35 years. However, after a goalless first leg in the semi-final against Marseilles, they were undone in the second match when Didier Drogba scored twice.

Drogba had also put paid to Liverpool's chances in the previous round, hitting a goal in each leg. A 3-2 aggregate defeat by Marseilles marked the end of a forgettable Uefa Cup campaign in which Liverpool never really got going, beating Olimpija Ljubljana, Steaua Bucharest and Levski Sofia before succumbing to Drogba. Nor did the other English participants light up the competition. Blackburn Rovers fell at the first hurdle to Genclerbirligi, of Turkey; Southampton lost to Steaua Bucharest in their first European tie since 1984; and Manchester City, conquerors of mighty TNS Llansantffraid in a qualifying round, beat Lokeren in the first round proper but were eliminated by Groclin, of Poland, in the second.

The Scots fared little better, with the exception of Celtic, who were aiming to go one better than the previous season, when they lost to FC Porto in the final. They produced one of the best European

Barcelona players at Celtic Park mourn victims of the Madrid bombings

performances by a British club in many years to beat Barcelona, with Alan Thompson scoring the only goal of the tie, but injuries caught up with Celtic in the quarter-finals, when they were beaten 3-1 on aggregate by Villarreal.

It was Villarreal who provided the opposition for Valencia in an all-Spanish semi-final and it was no surprise that the latter, by this time well on course for the Primera Liga title, progressed to the final, although the only goal of the tie came from a penalty, converted by Mista, their prolific centre forward.

And so to the final in Gothenburg, where Marseilles were holding their own until first-half stoppage time, when Fabien Barthez, the goalkeeper who had joined them on loan from Manchester United in January, was sent off for a professional foul on Mista. Valencia were awarded a penalty, which was coolly dispatched by Vicente. Twelve minutes after the interval, Mista scored the second goal with a delightful finish to round off an impressive counter-attack.

While the contest was ruined, in one sense, by Barthez's red card, no one could deny that Valencia were worthy winners. An extremely organised side, built on a robust defence and a combative midfield, they had been by far the strongest team in the Uefa Cup, a fact they underlined by winning the league by five points.

The task for Valencia will be to emulate FC Porto, the winners in 2003, and use the success as a platform from which to launch a serious challenge for the European Cup. That challenge will fall to Claudio Ranieri, who landed one of the most desirable coaching jobs in European football within days of his cruel dismissal by Chelsea. Ranieri replaces Rafael Benitez, from whom the Uefa Cup was a fitting farewell gift before his departure for Liverpool.

FIRST ROUND

First legs, September 24

Sporting Lisbon 2 Malmo 0; Villarreal 0 Trabzonspor 0; AS Roma 4 Vardar 0; Manchester City 3 Lokeren 2; Hearts 2 Zeljeznicar Sarajevo 0; Newcastle 5 NAC 0; Southampton 1 Steaua Bucharest 1; Auxerre 1 Neuchatel Xamax 0; Austria Vienna 1 Borussia Dortmund 2; AIK Solna 0 Valencia 1; PAOK Salonika 0 SFK Lyn Oslo 1; Ferencvaros 1 FC Copenhagen 1; Olimpija 1 Liverpool 1; Dundee 1 Perugia 2; Odense Boldklub 2 Crvena Zvezda 2; La Louviere 1 Benfica 1; Grasshoppers Zurich 1 Hajduk Split 1; Dinamo Bucharest 2 Shakhtar Donetsk 0; FK Ventspils 1 Rosenborg 4; Gaziantepspor 1 Hapoel Tel Aviv 0; Malatyaspor 0 FC Basle 2; Apoel Nicosia 1 Mallorca 2; Matador Puchov 1 Barcelona 1; FC Kaiserslautern 1 FK Teplice 2; FC Utrecht 2 MSK Zilina 0; Uniao Leiria 1 Molde 0; CSF Zimbru 1 Aris Salonika 1; Metalurg Donetsk 1 Parma 0; MyPa 0 Sochaux 1; SV Salzburg 0 Udinese 1; Spartak Moscow 2 Esbjerg 0; Valerenga 0 Graz AK 0; Varteks 1 Debrecen 3; Brondby 1 Viktoria Zizkov 0; Cementarnica 55 0 Lens 1; Dinamo Zagreb 3 MTK Hungaria 1; Hertha Berlin 0 Groclin Dyskobolia 0; Maccabi Haifa 2 CMC Publikum 1; Genclerbirligi 3 Blackburn Rovers 1; FK Sartid 1 Slavia Prague 2; Panionios 2 FC Nordsjaelland 1; CSKA Sofia 1 Torpedo Moscow 1; Hapoel Ramat Gan 0 Levski Sofia 1

September 25

Bordeaux 2 Artmedia Petrzalka 1; Feyenoord 2 FC Karnten 1; Wisla Krakow 2 NEC 1; Hamburg 2 Dnipro 1; Kamen Ingrad 0 Schalke 0

Second legs, October 15

Benfica 1 La Louviere 0 (Benfica win 2-1 on agg); Valencia 1 AIK Solna 0 (Valencia win 1-0 on agg); Barcelona 8 Matador Puchov 0 (Barcelona win 9-1 on agg); Blackburn Rovers 1 Genclerbirligi 1 (Genclerbirligi win 4-2 on agg); Liverpool 3 Olimpija 0 (Liverpool win 4-1 on agg); Real Mallorca 4 Apoel Nicosia 2 (Mallorca win 6-3 on agg); Lens 5 Cementarnica 55 0 (Lens win 6-0 on agg); Parma 3 Metalurg Donetsk 0 (Parma win 4-1); Udinese 1 SV Salzburg 2 (2-2 on agg; Salzburg win on away goals); Aris Salonika 2 CSF Zimbru 1 (Aris win 3-2 on agg); Lokeren 0 Manchester City 1 (Manchester City win 4-2 on agg); NEC 1 Wisla Krakow 2 (Wisla win 4-2 on agg); Perugia 0 Dundee 0 (Perugia win 2-1 on agg); Borussia Dortmund 1 Austria Vienna 0 (Dortmund win 3-1 on agg); MTK Hungaria 0 Dinamo Zagreb 0 (Dinamo win 3-1 on agg); Malmo 0 Sporting Lisbon 1 (Sporting win 3-0 on agg); Neuchatel Xamax 0 Auxerre 1 (Auxerre win 2-0 on agg); NAC 0 Newcastle United 1 (Newcastle win 6-0 on agg); Zeljeznicar Sarajevo 0 Hearts 0 (Hearts win 2-0 on agg); Crvena Zvezda 4 Odense Boldklub 3 (Crvena win 6-5 on agg); FC Copenhagen 2 Ferencvaros 1 (aet; 2-2 on agg; Copenhagen win 4-3 on pens); FC Basle 1 Malatyaspor 2 (aet; Basle win 3-2 on agg, silver goal); Sochaux 2 MyPa 0 (Sochaux win 3-0 on agg); SFK Lyn Oslo 0 PAOK Salonika 3 (PAOK win 3-1 on agg); Molde 3 Uniao Leiria 1 (Molde win 3-2 on agg); Trabzonspor 2 Villarreal 3 (Villarreal win 3-2 on agg); CMC Publikum 2 Maccabi Haifa 2 (Maccabi win 4-3 on agg); Artmedia Petrzalka 1 Bordeaux 1 (Bordeaux win 3-2 on agg); Steaua Bucharest 1 Southampton 1 (Steaua win 2-1 on agg); Rosenborg 6 FK Ventspils 0 (Rosenborg win 10-1 on agg); Debrecen 3 Varteks 2 (Debrecen win 6-3 on agg); Dnipro 3 Hamburg 0 (Dnipro win 4-2 on agg); Esbjerg 1 Spartak Moscow 1 (Spartak win 3-1 on agg); FC Nordsjaelland 0 Panionios 1 (Panionios win 3-1 on agg); Graz AK 1 Valerenga 1 (1-1 on agg; Valarenga win on away goals); MSK Zilina 0 FC Utrecht 4 (Utrecht win 6-0 on agg); Shakhtar Donetsk 2 Dinamo Bucharest 3 (Dinamo win 5-2 on agg); Slavia Prague 2 FK Sartid 1 (Slavia win 4-2 on agg); Vardar 1 AS Roma 1 (Roma win 5-1 on agg); Groclin Dyskobolia 1 Hertha Berlin 0 (Groclin win 1-0 on agg); Hajduk Split 0 Grasshoppers Zurich 0 (1-1 on agg; Hajduk win on away goals); Levski Sofia 4 Hapoel Ramat Gan 0 (Levski win 5-0 on agg); Hapoel Tel Aviv 0 Gaziantepspor 0 (Gaziantepspor win 1-0 on agg); Torpedo Moscow 1 CSKA Sofia 1 (aet; 2-2 on agg; Torpedo win 3-2 on pens)

October 16

FC Karnten 0 Feyenoord 1 (Feyenoord win 3-1 on agg); Schalke 1 Kamen Ingrad 0 (Schalke win 1-0 on agg); FK Teplice 1 FC Kaiserslautern 0 (Teplice win 3-1 on agg); Viktoria Zizkov 0 Brondby 1 (Brondby win 2-0 on agg)

SECOND ROUND

First legs, October 29

Rosenborg 0 Crvena Zvezda 0

November 6

Benfica 3 Molde 1; Valencia 0 Maccabi Haifa 0; Manchester City 1 Groclin Dyskobolia 1; Perugia 2 Aris Salonika 0; AS Roma 1 Hajduk Split 0; Feyenoord 0 FK Teplice 2; FC Basle 2 Newcastle United 3; SV Salzburg 0 Parma 4; Borussia Dortmund 2 Sochaux 2; PAOK Salonika 1 Debrecen 1; FC Copenhagen 1 Real Mallorca 2; Steaua Bucharest 1 Liverpool 1; Villarreal 2 Torpedo Moscow 0; Genclerbirligi 1 Sporting Lisbon 1; Panionios 0 Barcelona 3; Valerenga 0 Wisla Krakow 0; Bordeaux 0 Hearts 1; FC Utrecht 0 Auxerre 0; Schalke 2 Brondby 1; Dinamo Zagreb 0 Dnipro 2; Slavia Prague 2 Levski Sofia 2; Spartak Moscow 4 Dinamo Bucharest 0; Gaziantepspor 3 Lens 0

Second leg, November 27

Sporting Lisbon 0 Genclerbirligi 3 (Genclerbirligi win 4-1 on agg); Barcelona 2 Panionios 0 (Barcelona win 5-0 on agg); Liverpool 1 Steaua Bucharest 0 (Liverpool win 2-1 on agg); Real Mallorca 1 FC Copenhagen 1 (Mallorca win 3-2 on agg); Hajduk Split 1 AS Roma 1 (Roma win 2-1 on agg); Hearts 0 Bordeaux 2 (Bordeaux win 2-1 on agg); Newcastle United 1 FC Basle 1 (Newcastle win 4-2 on agg); Sochaux 4 Borussia Dortmund 0 (Sochaux win 6-2 on agg); Auxerre 4 FC Utrecht 0 (Auxerre win 4-0 on agg); Molde 0 Benfica 2 (Benfica win 5-1 on agg); Wisla Krakow 0 Valerenga 0 (aet; 0-0 on agg; Valarenga win 4-3 on pens); Aris Salonika 1 Perugia 1 (Perugia win 3-1 on agg); Crvena Zvezda 0 Rosenborg 1 (Rosenborg win 1-0 on agg); Dinamo Bucharest 3 Spartak Moscow 1 (Spartak win 5-3 on agg); Lens 1 Gaziantepspor 3 (Gaziantepspor win 6-1 on agg); Brondby 2 Schalke 1 (aet; 3-3 on agg; Brondby win 3-1 on pens); FK Teplice 1 Feyenoord Rotterdam 1 (Teplice win 3-1 on agg); Parma 5 SV Salzburg 0 (Parma win 9-0 on agg); Torpedo Moscow 1 Villarreal 0 (Villarreal win 2-1 on agg); Debrecen 0 PAOK Salonika 0 (1-1 on agg; Debrecen win on away goals); Groclin Dyskobolia 0 Manchester City 0 (1-1 on agg; Groclin win away goals); Levski Sofia 0 Slavia Prague 0 (2-2 on agg; Levski win on away goals)

December 11

Maccabi Haifa 0 Valencia 4 (Valencia win 4-0 on agg)

THIRD ROUND

First legs, February 26

Benfica 1 Rosenborg 0; Valencia 3 Besiktas 2; Sochaux 2 Inter Milan 2; Liverpool 2 Levski Sofia 0; Celtic 3 FK Teplice 0; Brondby 0 Barcelona 1; FC Bruges 1 Debrecen 0; Auxerre 0 Panathinaikos 0; Parma 0 Genclerbirligi 1; Perugia 0 PSV Eindhoven 2; Galatasaray 2 Villarreal 2; Marseilles 1 Dnipro 0; Gaziantepspor 1 AS Roma 0; Groclin Dyskobolia 0 Bordeaux 1; Spartak Moscow 0 Mallorca 3; Valerenga 1 Newcastle United 1

Second legs, March 3

Villarreal 3 Galatasaray 0 (Villarreal win 5-2 on agg); Barcelona 2 Brondby 1 (Barcelona win 3-1 on agg); Real Mallorca 0 Spartak Moscow 1 (Mallorca win 3-1 on agg); Newcastle United 3 Valerenga 1 (Newcastle win 4-2 on agg); Rosenborg 2 Benfica 1 (2-2 on agg; Benfica win on away goals); Inter Milan 0 Sochaux 0 (2-2 on agg; Inter win on away goals); PSV Eindhoven 3 Perugia 1 (PSV win 3-1 on agg); Panathinaikos 0 Auxerre 1 (Auxerre win 1-0 on agg); Levski Sofia 2 Liverpool 4 (Liverpool win 6-2 on agg); Besiktas 0 Valencia 2 (Valencia win 5-2 on agg); Debrecen 0 FC Bruges 0 (Bruges win 1-0 on agg); Bordeaux 4 Groclin Dyskobolia 1 (Bordeaux win 5-1 on agg); FK Teplice 1 Celtic 0 (Celtic win 3-1 on agg); AS Roma 2 Gaziantepspor 0 (Roma win 2-1 on agg); Dnipro 0 Marseilles 0 (Marseilles win 1-0 on agg); Genclerbirligi 3 Parma 0 (Genclerbirligi win 3-0 on agg)

MATCH OF THE SEASON

Newcastle United 2 PSV Eindhoven 1 *(Newcastle won 3-2 on agg)*
St James' Park, Wednesday April 14 2004
George Caulkin

NEWCASTLE UNITED did not slip seamlessly into their second European semi-final, but after negotiating the peaks and troughs that this sapping season has offered them, it is a wonder they retained the energy to stagger past PSV Eindhoven last night. Resilience is their watchword, however, and at the end of nine months that can most charitably be described as character-building, it has become a fiery strength.

In spite of grasping an early lead in this Uefa Cup quarter-final, second leg through Alan Shearer, Sir Bobby Robson's side were clinging to their last hope of a trophy with rabid-eyed desperation by the time the final whistle shrilled. While Gary Speed had negated PSV'S equaliser — a penalty from Mateja Kezman — they carried the knowledge that another concession would put them out of the competition via the away-goal ruling.

They were to be grateful to Shay Given, who punched away a 30-yard free kick from Wilfred Bouma in the 88th minute, but they clung on manfully. Newcastle will face Marseilles in the last four; memories of their Fairs Cup triumph in 1969 have been resurrected. But not for the manager. "We can't run ahead of ourselves," Robson said. "Marseilles is a difficult hurdle. We've got to get over that one. This was a big, big victory in a big game." Robson's steadfast attitude is now matched by his players. "We've become a durable team," he said. The 1-1 draw they took back from the first leg in the Netherlands was remarkable for its stern defending.

In both fixtures against the Dutch champions, a single error at the back cost Newcastle a goal, an unfortunate ratio that surely cannot continue. While Robson conceded that the tie was "never over, never safe", there was also rich praise for Given, Jonathan Woodgate et al. "At this level, one mistake per match means you have a fantastic team. You won't lose many," Robson added.

That the architects of this win were Shearer and Speed (supplemented by Laurent Robert, whose delivery was once again dead-eye), was also fitting because few players have sweated more profusely for the Tyneside cause. "Well done to our two old-timers," Robson said. "Three, if I include me. Except that I'm an old, old, old-timer." For once, the 71-year-old probably felt his age, even if his trepidation was slow in coming. Within nine minutes, Newcastle were ahead through Shearer's 27th goal since August. At the near post, the captain clambered above Bouma and Ronald Wattereus, the flapping goalkeeper, to glance Robert's fine inswinging corner into the net. Yet they failed to capitalise on their advantage.

PSV had seen possession, yet by the advent of half-time had not manufactured anything approaching a meaningful attack.

Shearer rises — and Newcastle are heading for the Uefa Cup semi-finals

Newcastle had pressed them relentlessly, restricting their options in midfield and harrying their defenders without mercy. But their job was half-done. It was undone through an act of carelessness. When Young-Pyo Lee slung the ball into the 18-yard-box after 51 minutes, Olivier Bernard had scope to clear, but the left back instead chose to chest it down. His control was less than perfect and as Ji-Sung Park strained to reach it, Bernard caught him in the midriff. The Spanish referee had little hesitation in pointing to the spot. Kezman struck his penalty with venom and suddenly PSV appeared forceful.

The single consistency was Robert. In too many matches the winger has failed to beat the first man with his crosses, but this was a return to form. Sixty-six minutes had elapsed when he stroked in another elegant corner and Speed delayed his run to perfection before thrusting his head at the ball. It was, Robson said, "one of the most important goals of his career".

Given went on to make his crucial save. "If we hadn't turned the screw again, we could have gone out," Robson said. Instead, they welcome Marseilles next Thursday and where the manager refuses to tread, his chairman has no such qualms. "We can now scent silverware in Europe," Freddy Shepherd said.

NEWCASTLE UNITED (4-4-2): S Given — A Hughes, J Woodgate, T Bramble (sub: A O'Brien, 77min), O Bernard — D Ambrose (sub: F Ameobi, 81), J Jenas, G Speed, L Robert (sub: H Viana, 90) — A Shearer, C Bellamy. **Substitutes not used:** R Elliott, K Dyer, S Harper, M Bridges.
PSV EINDHOVEN (4-1-4-1): R Wattereus — K Bogelund, J Colin, W Bouma, Y-P Lee — J Vogel (sub: J Vonlanthen, 76) — D Rommedahl (sub: J Vennegoor of Hesselink, 46), M van Bommel, J de Jong, J-S Park — M Kezman. **Substitutes not used:** R van Dijk, E Addo, J Wuytens, R van der Schaaf, Leandro.

FOURTH ROUND

First legs, March 11

Villarreal 2 AS Roma 0
Benfica 0 Inter Milan 0
Celtic 1 Barcelona 0
Liverpool 1 Marseilles 1
Newcastle 4 Real Mallorca 1
Auxerre 1 PSV Eindhoven 1
Genclerbirligi 1 Valencia 0
Bordeaux 3 FC Bruges 1

Second legs, March 25

Valencia 2 Genclerbirligi 0
(aet; Valencia win 2-1 on agg, silver goal)

Barcelona 0 Celtic 0
(Celtic win 1-0 on agg)

Inter Milan 4 Benfica 3
(Inter Milan win 4-3 on agg)

Real Mallorca 0 Newcastle United 3
(Newcastle United win 7-1 on agg)

Marseilles 2 Liverpool 1
(Marseilles win 3-2 on agg)

AS Roma 2 Villarreal 0
(Villarreal win 3-2 on agg)

PSV Eindhoven 3 Auxerre 0
(PSV Eindhoven win 4-1 on agg)

FC Bruges 0 Bordeaux 1
(Bordeaux win 4-1 on agg)

QUARTER-FINALS

First legs, April 8

Celtic 1 Villarreal 1
Marseilles 1 Inter Milan 0
PSV Eindhoven 1 Newcastle United 1
Bordeaux 1 Valencia 2

Second legs, April 14

Valencia 2 Bordeaux 1
(Valencia win 4-2 on agg)
Inter Milan 0 Marseilles 1
(Marseilles win 2-0 on agg)
Newcastle United 2 PSV Eindhoven 1
(Newcastle United win 3-2 on agg)
Villarreal 2 Celtic 0
(Villarreal win 3-1 on agg)

SEMI-FINALS

First legs, April 22

Villarreal 0 Valencia 0
Newcastle United 0 Marseilles 0

Second legs, May 6

Valencia 1 Villarreal 0
(Valencia win 1-0 on agg)
Marseilles 2 Newcastle United 0
(Marseilles win 2-0 on agg)

Final details page 352

PLAYER OF THE SEASON
Didier Drogba Marseilles

It was little wonder that Chelsea and Manchester United should start sniffing around after witnessing the damage that Didier Drogba is capable of inflicting on Premiership defences. Liverpool and Newcastle United would reluctantly testify to the fearsome talent of the Marseilles forward, who also scored five goals in six Champions League matches last season. Drogba alone could not save Marseilles from a first-round exit from the Champions League, but that competition's loss proved to be the Uefa Cup's gain. Blessed with pace, power and poise, the striker, born in Ivory Coast, claimed a goal in each leg to vanquish Liverpool in the quarter-finals and scored twice in a virtuoso performance in the semi-final, second leg against Newcastle, though Valencia had the final word.

Oliver Kay

The fate of the Uefa Cup final is sealed as Barthez brings down Mista

FINAL
Wednesday May 19 (Gothenburg)

VALENCIA (1) **2**   **MARSEILLES** (0) **0**
Vicente 45 (pen), Mista 57   40,000

Valencia added the Uefa Cup to their Spanish league title with a victory over a Marseilles side that was forced to play the second half with ten men after Fabien Barthez, the former Manchester United goalkeeper, was sent off. Barthez received a red card for bringing down Mista, the Valencia striker, at the end of the first half and Vicente, the Spain midfield player, scored from the penalty spot past Gavanon, Barthez's replacement. Mista finished the match as a contest with a superb strike just before the hour mark. It was Valencia's first European trophy since they won the Cup Winners' Cup in 1980, although they reached the European Cup final in 2000 and 2001, losing on both occasions.

VALENCIA (4-4-2): S Canizares — Curro Torres, R Ayala, C Marchena (sub: M Pellegrino, 86min), A Carboni — F Rufete (sub: P Aimar, 64), D Albelda, R Baraja, Vicente — M A Angulo (sub: M Sissoko, 83), Mista. **Substitutes not used:** D Rangel, J Sanchez, J Garrido, Xisco. **Booked:** Vicente, Carboni.
MARSEILLES (5-4-1): F Barthez — A Meite, B Hemdani, H Beye, M Dos Santos, D Ferreira — S N'Diaye (sub: F Celestini, 84), M Flamini (sub: L Batlles, 71), C Meriem (sub: J Gavanon, 45), S Marlet — D Drogba. **Substitutes not used:** P Christanval, S Vachousek, J Ecker, N Cicut. **Booked:** Marlet, Drogba. **Sent off:** Barthez (45).
Referee: P Collina (Italy).

LEADING SCORERS

Didier Drogba	Marseilles	6
Mateja Kezman	PSV Eindhoven	6
Alan Shearer	Newcastle United	6
Sonny Anderson	Villarreal	6
Craig Bellamy	Newcastle United	5
Mista	Valencia	5
Albert Riera	Bordeaux	5

EUROPEAN LEAGUES

SPAIN
Valencia

ITALY
AC Milan

GERMANY
Werder Bremen

FRANCE
Lyons

THE NETHERLANDS
Ajax

PORTUGAL
FC Porto

BELGIUM
Anderlecht

Brazilian blend: Cafu and his compatriot Kaka enjoyed fine seasons as AC Milan returned to the summit of Italian football

FINAL TABLES

SPAIN

	P	W	D	L	F	A	Pts
Valencia	38	23	8	7	71	27	77
Barcelona	38	21	9	8	63	39	72
Deportivo La Coruna	38	21	8	9	60	34	71
Real Madrid	38	21	7	10	72	54	70
Athletic Bilbao	38	15	11	12	53	49	56
Seville	38	15	10	13	56	45	55
Atletico Madrid	38	15	10	13	51	53	55
Villarreal	38	15	9	14	47	49	54
Real Betis	38	13	13	12	46	43	52
Malaga	38	15	6	17	50	55	51
Real Mallorca	38	15	6	17	54	66	51
Osasuna	38	11	15	12	38	37	48
Real Zaragoza	38	13	9	16	46	55	48
Albacete	38	13	8	17	40	48	47
Real Sociedad	38	11	13	14	49	53	46
Espanyol	38	13	4	21	48	64	43
Racing Santander	38	11	10	17	48	63	42
Valladolid	38	10	11	17	46	56	41
Celta Vigo	38	9	12	17	48	68	39
Murcia	38	5	11	22	29	57	26

ITALY

	P	W	D	L	F	A	Pts
AC Milan	34	25	7	2	65	24	82
AS Roma	34	21	8	5	68	19	71
Juventus	34	21	6	7	67	42	69
Inter Milan	34	17	8	9	59	37	59
Parma	34	16	10	8	57	46	58
Lazio	34	16	8	10	52	38	56
Udinese	34	13	11	10	44	40	50
Sampdoria	34	11	13	10	40	42	46
Chievo	34	11	11	12	36	37	44
Lecce	34	11	8	15	43	56	41
Brescia	34	9	13	12	52	57	40
Bologna	34	10	9	15	45	53	39
Siena	34	8	10	16	41	54	34
Reggina	34	6	16	12	29	45	33
Perugia	34	6	14	14	44	56	32
Modena	34	6	12	16	27	46	30
Empoli	34	7	9	18	26	54	29
Ancona	34	2	7	25	21	70	13

A BIG-BANG THEORY HAS emerged in the football universe. Fill your attack and midfield with *galacticos* but neglect the defence and reserve team — and eventually the whole thing will blow up in your face. At least that is Real Madrid's experience after a season in which they united David Beckham with Zinedine Zidane, Luis Figo, Ronaldo and Raul, yet gained no reward.

A frail defence was exposed while a lack of decent alternatives in the squad meant that the big names eventually faded through fatigue. Real shipped 31 goals in their final 13 games, during which they lost the Spanish Cup final, were eliminated from the European Cup by AS Monaco and relinquished an eight-point lead over Valencia in the league. They finished fourth and had to play a qualifying match to try to reach the Champions League. Real admitted that they bought Beckham rather than Ronaldinho because his handsome features offered more commercial opportunities, so it was satisfying that the Brazil forward's brilliance enabled Barcelona to finish two positions above Real in the table.

Those appreciative of traditional team-building methods delighted in Valencia's triumph in both La Liga and the Uefa Cup. "We are a team, with capital letters," Rafael Benitez, their coach, said, emphasising the difference between his side and Real. Liverpool were impressed enough to appoint him as Gerard Houllier's successor.

Pablo Aimar, Argentina's creative genius, was the closest thing to a *galactico* at Valencia, but injuries meant that he missed a third of the league campaign. Vicente proved a driving influence on the left wing, as he would for Spain during their ill-fated Euro 2004 challenge, while Roberto Ayala, the Argentina hard-man, again showed himself to be one of the world's best defenders.

Deportivo La Coruna also booked a return to the Champions League, a competition in which they pulled off an extraordinary 4-0 win against AC Milan in last season's competition, overturning a 4-1 deficit from the first leg. It was a rare stumble for the Italian side, who secured their first Serie A title of the 21st century after dominating the 1990s. Inspired by Kaka', the Brazil playmaker, Milan stood out, only suffering their second and final league defeat after clinching the title with a 1-0 home win over AS Roma, their closest rivals. So relentless was their march that they recorded a better points-per-game ratio than Arsenal managed in their unbeaten Premiership campaign.

As so often in Italy, though, the football was only part of the story. Crowd trouble caused the decisive Milan-Roma match to be held up and the Lazio-Roma fixture to be abandoned, while summer saw

Werder Bremen celebrate their unlikely title triumph in Germany

GERMANY

	P	W	D	L	F	A	Pts
Werder Bremen	34	22	8	4	79	38	74
Bayern Munich	34	20	8	6	70	39	68
B Leverkusen	34	19	8	7	73	39	65
VfB Stuttgart	34	18	10	6	52	24	64
VfL Bochum	34	15	11	8	57	39	56
B Dortmund	34	16	7	11	59	48	55
Schalke 04	34	13	11	10	49	42	50
SV Hamburg	34	14	7	13	47	60	49
Hansa Rostock	34	12	8	14	55	54	44
VfL Wolfsburg	34	13	3	18	56	61	42
B Moncheng'dbach	34	10	9	15	40	49	39
Hertha Berlin	34	9	12	13	42	59	39
SC Freiburg	34	10	8	16	42	67	38
Hannover 96	34	9	10	15	49	63	37
Kaiserslautern	34	11	6	17	39	62	36
Frankfurt	34	9	5	20	36	53	32
1860 Munich	34	8	8	18	32	55	32
FC Cologne	34	6	5	23	32	57	23

FRANCE

	P	W	D	L	F	A	Pts
Lyons	38	24	7	7	64	26	79
PSG	38	22	10	6	50	28	76
AS Monaco	38	21	12	5	59	30	75
Auxerre	38	19	8	11	60	34	65
FC Sochaux	38	18	9	11	54	42	63
FC Nantes	38	17	9	12	47	35	60
Marseilles	38	17	6	15	51	45	57
Lens	38	15	8	15	34	48	53
Rennes	38	14	10	14	56	44	52
Lille	38	14	9	15	41	41	51
Nice	38	11	17	10	42	39	50
Bordeaux	38	13	11	14	40	43	50
Strasbourg	38	10	13	15	43	50	43
Metz	38	11	9	18	34	42	42
Ajaccio	38	10	10	18	33	55	40
Toulouse	38	9	12	17	31	44	39
Bastia	38	9	12	17	33	49	39
Guingamp	38	10	8	20	36	58	38
Le Mans	38	9	11	18	35	57	38
Montpellier	38	8	7	23	41	74	31

THE NETHERLANDS

	P	W	D	L	F	A	Pts
Ajax	34	25	5	4	79	31	80
PSV Eindhoven	34	23	5	6	92	30	74
Feyenoord	34	20	8	6	71	38	68
SC Heerenveen	34	17	7	10	45	35	58
AZ Alkmaar	34	17	6	11	65	42	57
Roda JC	34	14	11	9	60	41	53
Willem II	34	13	10	11	47	54	49
FC Twente	34	15	3	16	56	53	48
NAC Breda	34	12	10	12	58	55	46
FC Utrecht	34	13	7	14	42	52	46
RKC Waalwijk	34	10	10	14	47	55	40
RBC Roosendaal	34	10	10	14	34	47	40
FC Groningen	34	9	10	15	38	53	37
NEC	34	10	4	20	44	62	34
ADO Den Haag	34	9	7	18	36	61	34
Vitesse Arnhem	34	4	16	14	39	56	28
FC Volendam	34	7	6	21	31	79	27
FC Zwolle	34	5	11	18	27	67	26

PORTUGAL

	P	W	D	L	F	A	Pts
FC Porto	34	25	7	2	63	19	82
Benfica	34	22	8	4	62	28	74
Sporting Lisbon	34	23	4	7	60	33	73
CD Nacional	34	17	5	12	56	35	56
SC Braga	34	15	9	10	36	38	54
Rio Ave	34	12	12	10	42	37	48
CS Maritimo	34	12	12	10	35	33	48
Boavista	34	12	11	11	32	31	47
Moreirense	34	12	10	12	33	33	46
Uniao Leiria	34	11	12	11	43	45	45
SC Beira-Mar	34	11	8	15	36	45	41
Gil Vicente	34	10	10	14	43	40	40
Academica	34	11	5	18	40	42	38
Vitoria Guimaraes	34	9	10	15	31	40	37
Alverca	34	10	5	19	33	49	35
Belenenses	34	8	11	15	35	54	35
Pacos de Ferreira	34	8	4	22	27	53	28
Amadora	34	4	5	25	22	74	17

BELGIUM

	P	W	D	L	F	A	Pts
Anderlecht	34	25	6	3	77	27	81
FC Bruges	34	22	6	6	77	31	72
Standard Liege	34	18	11	5	68	31	65
Genk	34	17	8	9	58	40	59
Mouscron	34	15	14	5	64	42	59
Westerlo	34	14	10	10	51	45	52
Germinal Beerschot	34	11	11	12	34	40	44
La Louviere	34	14	10	14	45	46	44
AA Gent	34	8	16	10	33	34	40
Lokeren	34	10	9	15	45	54	39
Lierse	34	8	15	11	33	40	39
Beveren	34	11	5	18	45	58	38
Sint-Truiden	34	9	11	14	36	50	38
Cercle Bruges	34	7	14	13	28	52	35
Charleroi	34	8	9	17	35	47	33
Mons	34	7	12	15	29	52	33
Heusden	34	7	7	20	36	68	28
Royal Antwerp	34	7	6	21	30	67	27

Double delight for Valencia, who won the Uefa Cup and Spanish league

investigations into allegations of match-fixing in the top three divisions. To add to the sense of upheaval, Milan, guided by Carlo Ancelotti, were the only top-six club to have retained their coach as the new season approached.

Bayern Munich also changed their coach after surrendering their Bundesliga crown to Werder Bremen, the most surprising champions among Europe's leading leagues. Felix Magath was recruited from VfB Stuttgart to replace Ottmar Hitzfeld after Bayern finished runners-up to a club that had finished sixth a year earlier. Led by Thomas Schaaf, who lifted the championship shield as a player with Bremen in 1988 and 1993, they thrived with a settled side that included unlikely title-winning defenders such as Valerien Ismael, once of Crystal Palace, and Paul Stalteri, the Canada midfield player. Johan Micoud, rescued from Parma after a miserable spell, has been reborn in midfield, while Ailton's 28 goals constituted the best total in the Bundesliga.

Bremen's achievement on a low budget was underlined when Ailton and Mladen Krstajic, the Serbia and Montenegro defender, joined Schalke 04 in the summer, forgoing the Champions League to play for a better-paying club that would be competing in the InterToto Cup.

Big spending has helped Lyons to the top of the tree in France and they are proving difficult to dislodge. Having managed their first league triumph in 2001-02, they collected a third successive championship. Paris Saint-Germain pushed them hard.

No team, though, could sustain a challenge to FC Porto, who were only denied a second consecutive treble by defeat to Benfica in the Portuguese Cup final. Domestic competition became too small a challenge for Jose Mourinho, who, after overseeing 33 home league wins in a row as coach, left to join Chelsea. His team-building skills would have been welcome in Madrid.

PLAYER OF THE SEASON
Kaka' AC Milan

AC Milan have fielded seven Brazilians during the past two seasons, but none has made as great an impact as Ricardo Izecson Santos Leite, otherwise known as Kaka'. Arriving in the summer of 2003, the attacking midfield player was expected to be an understudy to Rui Costa and Rivaldo, yet his outstanding form relegated the Portugal player to the bench and prompted Rivaldo to return to Brazil. With ten league goals and a hand in countless others, Kaka', 21, inspired Milan's stroll to the Serie A title and helped them to gain them a reputation for thrilling football.   **Bill Edgar**

LEADING LEAGUE GOALSCORERS

ITALY

Andrei Shevchenko (AC Milan)	24
Alberto Gilardino (Parma)	23
Francesco Totti (AS Roma)	20
Javier Chevanton (Lecce)	19
Adriano (Parma and Inter Milan)	17
David Trezeguet (Juventus)	16
Antonio Cassano (AS Roma)	14
Christian Vieri (Inter Milan)	13

SPAIN

Ronaldo (Real Madrid)	24
Julio Baptista (Seville)	20
Mista (Valencia)	19
Salva (Malaga)	19
Raul Tamudo (Espanyol)	19
Fernando Torres (Atletico Madrid)	19
Samuel Eto'o (Real Mallorca)	17
David Villa (Real Zaragoza)	17
Nihat Kahveci (Real Sociedad)	14
Savo Milosevic (Celta Vigo)	14

GERMANY

Ailton (Werder Bremen)	28
Roy Makaay (Bayern Munich)	23
Martin Max (Hansa Rostock)	20
Dimitar Berbatov (B Leverkusen)	16
Vahid Hashemian (VfL Bochum)	16
Jan Koller (Borussia Dortmund)	16
Ewerthon (Borussia Dortmund)	16
Diego Klimowicz (VfL Wolfsburg)	15
Franca (Bayer Leverkusen)	14

FRANCE

Djibril Cisse (Auxerre)	26
Alexander Frei (Rennes)	19
Didier Drogba (Marseilles)	18
Pauleta (Paris Saint-Germain)	18
Pierre-Alain Frau (Sochaux)	17

THE NETHERLANDS

Mateja Kezman (PSV Eindhoven)	31
Dirk Kuijt (Feyenoord)	20
Gerald Sibon (SC Heerenveen)	15
T Buffel (Feyenoord)	15
Ali Elkhattabi (AZ Alkmaar)	14
B N'Kufo (FC Twente)	14

PORTUGAL

Benni McCarthy (FC Porto)	20
Adriano (Nacional)	19
Evandro (Rio Ave)	15
Liedson (Sporting Lisbon)	15
Ricardo Sousa (Boavista)	14
Derlei (FC Porto)	13

SWITZERLAND

	P	W	D	L	F	A	Pts
FC Basle	36	26	7	3	86	32	85
Young Boys	36	22	6	8	75	48	72
Servette	36	15	7	14	61	62	52
FC Zurich	36	14	8	14	58	52	50
St Gallen	36	14	8	14	54	57	50
FC Thun	36	13	10	13	51	57	49
Grasshopper	36	12	5	19	62	74	41
Aarau	36	9	11	16	57	69	38
Neuchatel Xamax	36	10	6	20	46	63	36
FC Wil	36	7	8	21	37	73	29

WALES

	P	W	D	L	F	A	Pts
Rhyl	32	23	8	1	76	26	77
TNS	32	24	4	4	77	28	76
Haverfordwest	32	17	11	4	40	23	62
Aberystwyth	32	18	5	9	59	39	59
Caersws	32	15	10	7	63	41	55
Bangor	32	16	6	10	72	47	54
Cwmbran	32	15	3	14	51	44	48
Connah's Quay	32	11	9	12	58	55	42
Caernarfon	32	11	9	12	65	65	42
Newtown	32	12	5	15	43	50	41
Port Talbot	32	11	6	15	41	51	39
Porthmadog	32	11	3	18	41	55	36
Flexys	32	11	2	19	44	59	35
Afan Lido	32	8	8	16	31	54	32
Welshpool	32	6	7	19	35	71	25
Carmarthen	32	3	11	18	28	69	20
Barry	32	3	7	22	30	77	16

NORTHERN IRELAND

	P	W	D	L	F	A	Pts
Linfield	30	22	7	1	67	16	73
Portadown	30	22	4	4	71	22	70
Lisburn Distillery	30	16	7	7	45	30	55
Coleraine	30	14	9	7	48	36	51
Glentoran	30	15	5	10	48	27	50
Ballymena United	30	13	8	9	41	35	47
Limavady United	30	12	5	13	41	44	41
Ards	30	9	11	10	36	46	38
Crusaders	30	10	6	14	33	38	36
Dungannon Swifts	30	10	6	14	36	48	36
Institute	30	9	7	14	38	53	34
Newry Town	30	8	9	13	35	53	33
Omagh Town	30	9	4	17	37	58	31
Larne	30	7	8	15	42	51	29
Cliftonville	30	6	8	16	27	45	26
Glenavon	30	4	4	22	24	67	16

VORSPRUNG DURCH BUNDESLIGA

Bill Edgar

CLOSE YOUR EYES AND imagine this: Manchester City clinch the title at the home of their nearest rivals. Everton also qualify for the Champions League — pipping their last-day opponents to the prize — a year after narrowly avoiding relegation. Meanwhile, Manchester United, the country's best-supported club, fail to make even the Uefa Cup. Open your eyes and welcome to another routine season in the wonderful Bundesliga.

Fantasy in England is fact in Germany. Werder Bremen, like City in the Premiership, were ranked eighth in the pre-season title betting for 2003-04 yet somehow they secured the crown, sealing the feat away to Bayern Munich, the champions and favourites. Bayer Leverkusen shrugged off a battle against the drop 12 months earlier to book a Champions League place ahead of VfB Stuttgart, against whom they gained the required victory on the season's closing day. Borussia Dortmund, who drew a phenomenal average attendance of more than 75,000, were left to contemplate the InterToto Cup.

Of the strongest five European leagues, England's was founded in 1888, Spain's in 1929, Italy's in 1930 and France's in 1932. Lagging well behind came the Germans, who finally created a national and professional championship in 1963. The Bundesliga lacks a deep history, but there is compensation in its glorious present. Germany's national team may struggle to raise the pulse, but the same charge cannot be levelled at its clubs. Given its dramatic climaxes, unpredictability, huge diversity of nationalities on the pitch, spectacular stadiums and playing strength in depth, it possesses an irresistible cocktail unmatched by any other European league. The locals are certainly impressed: the country boasts the highest average top-flight attendances in world football.

The Bundesliga has not been plagued by the huge ability gap between the best and the rest that exists in many other leagues. Remarkable as they were, the rises of Bremen and Leverkusen last season — from sixth place to first and from fifteenth to third respectively —

are firmly overshadowed by Kaiserslautern's achievement in 1997-98, when they won the title in their first season after promotion. Naturally, this uncertainty also applies in opposite circumstances. Dortmund were almost relegated in 2000 having finished fourth the year before and having won the European Cup in 1997.

In the past five seasons, 11 different clubs have finished in the top five: Bremen, Bayern, Leverkusen, Stuttgart, Dortmund, VfL Bochum, SV Hamburg, Hertha Berlin, Schalke 04, TSV 1860 Munich and Kaiserslautern. Over the same period in Spain, nine different teams have penetrated the top five, while only seven have done so in England and Italy.

As for close finishes, they are almost a Bundesliga trademark. The title was decided on the final day in five successive seasons from 1991 to 1995 and again on three consecutive occasions from 2000 to 2002. Eintracht

Ailton, the Bremen striker, topped the Bundesliga goal chart

Crowds at the Westfalenstadion averaged more than 75,000 even though Borussia Dortmund were well off the title pace

Frankfurt, Stuttgart and Dortmund began the last round of matches in 1991-92 level on points, with Frankfurt ahead on goal difference. Dortmund soon moved into pole position and spent most of the afternoon there, only for Stuttgart to collect the championship with a winning goal four minutes from time away to Leverkusen by Guido Buchwald, the Germany defender.

The climax was even more extraordinary in 2001, when Schalke knew that they would beat Bayern to the championship if they could defeat Unterhaching at home while the Munich side lost away to Hamburg. Schalke recovered from 3-2 down after 70 minutes to win 5-3 and then Bayern fell 1-0 behind in stoppage time. For three minutes, Schalke's first title in 43 years seemed a certainty — until Patrik Andersson equalised for Bayern from an indirect free kick inside the penalty area.

True, Bremen won last season's title with two matches to spare, but there was great excitement in the late tussle for the last Champions League place and the fact that three teams fought to avoid the final relegation position on the closing day. The campaign also finished with spectacular results. In consecutive weeks in May, Bremen thrashed Hamburg 6-0, Dortmund lost 6-2 away to Hertha, who were battling to avoid relegation, and Bremen were beaten 6-2 at home by Leverkusen. Such scorelines are not unfamiliar. As so often, the German league finished well clear of its main European rivals last season in goals per game.

The Bundesliga seems to be a magnet for quirkiness. While the lithe frame of Thierry Henry topped the Premiership's goalscoring charts, the equivalent in Germany was Ailton, whose green Bremen shirt almost burst at the seams. In April Hans-Jorg Butt, the Leverkusen goalkeeper, was out of his goal celebrating his penalty against Schalke when Mike Hanke scored from the centre circle at the restart.

Players from all corners of the globe have thrived in Germany. South America has provided three successive leading or joint leading goalscorers in the league in Marcio Amoroso, Giovane Elber and Ailton, all Brazilians. North America has been represented by several United States players and Paul Stalteri, the Canada defender, missed only one match in Bremen's championship campaign last season. Africa supplied the Bundesliga's joint leading goalscorer for consecutive seasons in the 1990s in Anthony Yeboah, of Frankfurt, and Sammy Kuffour, his Ghanaian compatriot, has won the league five times with Bayern.

So compelling is the mix that the average attendance record for the Bundesliga has just been broken for the third season in a row, the latest a rise of more than three thousand to 37,481. With terracing still permitted, fans watch from a greater variety of stadiums, in contrast to the increasingly uniform arenas of the Premiership.

Popular ideas such as marking a goal with music over the Tannoy appeared in Germany long before England while, for supporters at home, innovative television coverage has added to the Bundesliga's appeal. Germany had cameras trained on individual players or coaches before England did and TV directors take a light-hearted approach. A snowball hitting a player's head as he takes a throw-in or a manager tripping over his chair on the touchline will be repeated in slow motion from different angles. German football: functional, dull and humourless? Absolutely not. Forget the stereotype and enjoy the show.

EUROPEAN QUALIFIERS

CHAMPIONS LEAGUE

Albania KF Tirana
Armenia FC Pyunik
Austria AK Graz
Azerbaijan FK Neftchi
Belarus FC Gomel
Belgium Anderlecht, FC Bruges
Bosnia NK Siroki Brijeg
Bulgaria Lokomotiv Plovdiv
Croatia Hajduk Split
Cyprus Apoel Nicosia
Czech Republic Banik Ostrava, Sparta Prague
Denmark FC Copenhagen
England Arsenal, Chelsea, Manchester United, Liverpool
Estonia FC Flora Tallinn
Faeroe Isles HB Torshavn
Finland HJK Helsinki
France Lyons, Paris Saint-Germain, AS Monaco
Georgia FC WIT Georgia
Germany Werder Bremen, Bayern Munich, Bayer Leverkusen
Greece Panathinaikos, Olympiakos, PAOK Salonika
Hungary Ferencvaros
Iceland KR Reykjavik
Ireland Shelbourne
Israel AC Milan, AS Roma, Juventus, Inter Milan
Latvia Skonto Riga
Lithuania FBK Kaunas
Luxembourg Jeunesse Esch
Macedonia FK Pobeda
Malta Sliema Wanderers
Moldova FC Sheriff
Netherlands Ajax, PSV Eindhoven
Northern Ireland Linfield
Norway Rosenborg
Poland Wisla Krakow
Portugal FC Porto, Benfica
Romania Dinamo Bucharest
Russia CSKA Moscow
Scotland Celtic, Rangers
Serbia and Montenegro Red Star Belgrade
Slovakia MSK Zilina
Slovenia NK Gorica

Spain Valencia, Barcelona, Real Madrid, Deportivo La Coruna
Sweden Djurgardens
Switzerland FC Basle, Young Boys
Turkey Fenerbahce, Trabzonspor
Ukraine Dinamo Kiev, Shakhtar Donetsk
Wales Rhyl

UEFA CUP

Albania FK Partizani, Dinamo Tirana
Andora Santa Coloma
Armenia FC MIKA, FC Shirak, FC Banants
Austria Austria Vienna, Rapid Vienna
Azerbaijan FK Shamkir, FK Karabakh
Belarus FC Shakhtyor Soligorsk, FC BATE Borisov
Belgium KSK Beveren, Standard Liege
Bosnia FK Modrica, NK Zeljeznicar
Bulgaria Levski Sofia, CSKA Sofia, Litex Lovech
Croatia Dinamo Zagreb, HHNK Rijeka
Cyprus AC Omonia, AEK Larnaca
Czech Republic Sigma Olomouc, Slavia Prague
Denmark Brondby, Aalborg BK
England Newcastle United, Middlesborough, Milwall
Estonia Levadia Tallinn, TVMK Tallinn
Faeroe Isles B36, B68
Finland FC Haka, AC Allianssi
France Auxerre, FC Sochaux, LB Chateauroux
Georgia Dinamo Tiblisi, FC Tiblisi
Germany VfB Stuttgart, VfL Bochum, TSV Alemannia Aachen
Greece AEK Athens, Egaleo, Panionios NFC
Hungary FC Honved Budapest, Ujpesti TE
Iceland IA Akranes, FH Hafnarfjordur

Ireland Longford Town, Bohemians
Israel Hapoel Bnei Sakhnin, Maccabi Petach-Tikva
Italy Lazio, Parma, Udinese
Latvia FK Ventspils, FHK Liepajas Metalurgs
Lithuania FK Zalgiris Vilinus, FK Ekranas
Liechtenstein FC Vaduz
Luxembourg F91 Dudelange, Etzella Ettelbruck
Macedonia FK Sloga Jugomagnat, FK Sileks
Malta Birkirkara, Marsaxiokk
Moldova FC Nistru Otaci, FC Tiraspol
Netherlands Utrecht, Feyenoord, SC Heerenveen, AZ Alkmaar
Northern Ireland Glentoran, Portadown
Norway Bodo Glimt, Stabaek IF, Odd Grenland
Poland Amica Wronki, Legia Warsaw
Portugal Sporting Lisbon, CD Nacional, SC Braga, CS Maritimo
Romania FC Otelui Galati, Steaua Bucharest
Russia Terek Grozny, Zenit St Petersburg, Rubin Kazan
San Marino SS Pennarossa
Scotland Dunfermline Athletic, Heart of Midlothian
Serbia and Montenegro FK Partisan, FK Zeleznik, Buducnost Banatski Dvor
Slovakia FK Dukla Banska Bystrica, Artmedia Bratislava
Slovenia NK Maribor, NK Primorje
Spain Real Zaragoza, Athletic Bilbao, Seville
Sweden Osters IF, IF Elfsborg, Hammarby
Switzerland FC Wil, Servette
Turkey Genclerbirligi, Besiktas
Ukraine FC Illychivets Mariupil, Metalurgh Donetsk
Wales Total Network Solutions, Haverfordwest County

INTERNATIONAL FOOTBALL

Dragon-slayers: John Hartson despairs after Wales lose to Russia in their European Championship play-off

ENGLAND
Pages 362-369

NORTHERN IRELAND
Pages 370-373

SCOTLAND
Pages 374-377

WALES
Pages 378-381

IRELAND
Pages 382-385

INTERNATIONAL DATES
Page 386

THE GAMES

Wednesday August 20 2003
Friendly
CROATIA (h)
Portman Road
Won 3-1   HT **1-0**   Att **27,000**
ENGLAND D James (West Ham United; sub: **P Robinson**, Leeds United, ht) — **P Neville** (Manchester United; sub: **D Mills**, Middlesbrough, 81min), **R Ferdinand** (Manchester United; sub: **M Upson**, Birmingham City, 60), **J Terry** (Chelsea), **A Cole** (Arsenal; sub: **W Bridge**, Chelsea, 60) — **D Beckham** (Real Madrid; sub: **T Sinclair**, Manchester City, 60), **S Gerrard** (Liverpool; sub: **D Murphy**, Liverpool, 81), **P Scholes** (Manchester United; sub: **J Cole**, Chelsea, 60), **N Butt** (Manchester United; sub: **F Lampard**, Chelsea, 27) — **E Heskey** (Liverpool; sub: **J Beattie**, Southampton, 76), **M Owen** (Liverpool; sub: **K Dyer**, Newcastle United, 60)
Substitute not used **C Kirkland** (Liverpool)
Scorers **Beckham 10** (pen), **Owen 51, Lampard 80**
Booked **Gerrard**

CROATIA S Pletikosa (sub: T Butina, 70) — D Simic (sub: M Babic, ht), J Simunic (sub: A Seric, 72), S Tomas — R Kovac, B Zivkovic (sub: J Agic, 72), M Rapaic (sub: I Mornar, ht), J Leko (sub: D Rosso, 60), M Maric (sub: D Srna, ht) — N Kovac, I Olic
Scorer **Mornar 78**
Referee **C Bo Larsen** (Denmark)

Saturday September 6
European Championship qualifier
MACEDONIA (a)
Skopje
Won 2-1   HT **0-1**   Att **20,500**
MACEDONIA P Milosevski — I Mitrevski, M Stojanovski, G Stavreski — V Grozdanovski (sub: A de Jesus Braga, 56min), V Sumulikovski, V Trajanov, A Sakiri — G Pandev (sub: I Gjuzelov, 47), I Naumoski — G Hristov (sub: D Dimitrovski, 88). *Substitutes not used* J Nikoloski, D Kapinkovski, S Georgievski, P Kjumbev
Scorer **Hristov 28**
Booked **Sakiri, Naumoski, Hristov, Braga**

ENGLAND D James (West Ham United) — **G Neville** (Manchester United), **J Terry** (Chelsea), **S Campbell** (Arsenal), **A Cole** (Arsenal) — **D Beckham** (Real Madrid), **N Butt** (Manchester United), **F Lampard** (Chelsea; sub: **E Heskey**, Liverpool, ht), **O Hargreaves** (Bayern Munich) — **M Owen** (Liverpool; sub: **K Dyer**, Newcastle United, 85), **W Rooney** (Everton; sub: **P Neville**, Manchester United, 74). *Substitutes not used* **P Robinson** (Leeds United), **M Upson** (Birmingham City), **W Bridge** (Chelsea), **J Cole** (Chelsea)
Scorers **Rooney 53, Beckham 63** (pen)
Booked **Campbell, Beckham**
Referee **F de Bleeckere** (Belgium)

CHAOS WAS CLAMPED TO THE England team like a shadow. A contentious suspension, a purported players' strike, botched call-ups, scuffles in a tunnel, upheaval at the Football Association, the uncertain future of Sven-Goran Eriksson and a slow withering on the vine for friendly matches combined to ensure a season of controversy for the national side. Their reaction utterly lacked hysteria. When it mattered, the shadow lifted.

Of nine matches, only four brought victory, yet two were in qualifying fixtures for the European Championship and there was greater glory in the disciplined 0-0 draw away to Turkey that ensured England's participation in Portugal. Questions were still asked of the head coach and his side, but not on that most fundamental of matters. The results came and their spirits soared.

Even in the best of circumstances, it would have been regarded as a sound achievement. After a 3-1 win over Croatia at Portman Road notable for the full debut of John Terry, who would become a mainstay at centre half, England negotiated slippery competitive ties against Macedonia and Liechtenstein (Wayne Rooney scored in both). A point in Istanbul would be good enough to reach Euro 2004 without recourse to a play-off. Yet the circumstances were far from normal. When Eriksson's squad assembled at Sopwell House, it was with an air of militancy.

Unhappy at the FA's handling of Rio Ferdinand's failure to attend a routine drugs test, talks were convened and shelved, unresolved. A boycott of the game was mooted, the barricades were manned and the tabloids screamed betrayal. It was a troubling introduction for Mark Palios, Adam Crozier's replacement as the FA's chief executive, but calamity was averted and, in spite of a missed penalty by David Beckham, England ground out a fine goalless draw in bitter conditions. Opposing players jostled as they sought the dressing-rooms at half-time, missiles rained down and no one henceforth would question the desire and motivation of Eriksson's team.

A sense of unease would linger, however. In attempting to create a moral platform for team selection (Ferdinand's ban was the backdrop to everything, but there had been a spate of unsavoury off-field incidents), the FA caused further disgruntlement when Alan Smith was called up and sent back to Leeds United before the friendly against Denmark at Old Trafford. England were on the way to winning the rugby World Cup and comparisons were awkward.

It was another week of bluster and controversy, leading to a game lacking in tension, featuring eight England substitutions and amounting to little. Away to Portugal (nine substitutes), Ledley King scored a goal, performed soundly in the centre of defence and

Beckham and Lampard get that uplifting feeling in Istanbul

Wednesday September 10
European Championship qualifier
LIECHTENSTEIN (h)
Old Trafford
Won 2-0   HT 0-0   Att 64,931
ENGLAND D James (West Ham United) — **G Neville**
(Manchester United), **J Terry** (Chelsea), **M Upson**
(Birmingham City), **W Bridge** (Chelsea) — **D Beckham**
(Real Madrid; sub: **O Hargreaves**, Bayern Munich, 58min),
S Gerrard (Liverpool; sub: **P Neville**, Manchester United,
58), **F Lampard** (Chelsea) — **W Rooney** (Everton; sub:
J Cole, Chelsea, 69) — **M Owen** (Liverpool), **J Beattie**
(Southampton) *Substitutes not used* **P Robinson** (Leeds
United), **S Campbell** (Arsenal), **K Dyer** (Newcastle United),
E Heskey (Liverpool)
Scorers **Owen 46, Rooney 52**
Booked **Bridge**

LIECHTENSTEIN P Jehle — M Telser, D Hasler, C Ritter,
Martin Stocklasa (sub: S Maierhofer, ht) — Michael
Stocklasa, A Gerster — R Beck (sub: T Beck, 57), M Frick,
F Burgmeier — F D'Elia (sub: R Buchel, 73). *Substitutes
not used* M Heeb, J Ospelt, M Beck, F-J Vogt
Booked **Martin Stocklasa, Jehle, Gerster**
Referee **K Fisker** (Denmark)

Saturday October 11
European Championship qualifier
TURKEY (a)
Istanbul
Drew 0-0   HT 0-0   Att 42,000
TURKEY Rustu Recber — Fatih Akyel, Alpay Ozalan, Bulent
Korkmaz, Ibrahim Uzulmez— Okan Buruk (sub: Ilhan
Mansiz, 68min), Tugay Kerimoglu, Emre Belozoglu — Nihat
Kahveci, Sergen Yalcin (sub: Tuncay Sanil, 61), Hakan
Sukur *Substitutes not used* Omer Catkic, Ergun Penbe,
Yildiray Basturk, Emre Asik, Umit Davala
Booked **Rustu, Tugay**

ENGLAND D James (West Ham United) — **G Neville**
(Manchester United), **J Terry** (Chelsea), **S Campbell**
(Arsenal), **A Cole** (Arsenal) — **D Beckham** (Real Madrid),
S Gerrard (Liverpool), **P Scholes** (Manchester United;
sub: **F Lampard**, Chelsea, 88), **N Butt** (Manchester
United) — **E Heskey** (Liverpool; sub: **D Vassell**, Aston
Villa, 67), **W Rooney** (Everton; sub: **K Dyer**, Newcastle
United, 71) *Substitutes not used* **P Robinson** (Leeds
United), **P Neville** (Manchester United), **M Upson**
(Birmingham City), **W Bridge** (Chelsea)
Booked **Butt**
Referee **P Collina** (Italy)

GROUP SEVEN
FINAL TABLE

	P	W	D	L	F	A	Pts
England	8	6	2	0	14	5	20
Turkey	8	6	1	1	17	5	19
Slovakia	8	3	1	4	11	9	10
Macedonia	8	1	3	4	11	14	6
Liechtenstein	8	0	1	7	2	22	1

Sunday November 16
Friendly
Old Trafford
DENMARK (h)
Lost 2-3   HT 2-2   Att 64,159
ENGLAND D James (West Ham United; sub: **P
Robinson**, Leeds United, ht) — **G Neville** (Manchester
United; sub: **G Johnson**, Chelsea, 16min), **J Terry**
(Chelsea), **M Upson** (Birmingham City), **A Cole** (Arsenal;
sub: **W Bridge**, Chelsea, ht) — **D Beckham** (Real Madrid;
sub: **J Jenas**, Newcastle United, 66), **N Butt** (Manchester
United; sub: **P Neville**, Manchester United, ht), **F
Lampard** (Chelsea) — **J Cole** (Chelsea; sub: **D Murphy**,
Liverpool, 76) — **W Rooney** (Everton; sub: **S Parker**,
Charlton Athletic, 66), **E Heskey** (Liverpool; sub: **J
Beattie**, Southampton, ht) *Substitutes not used* **D Mills**
(Leeds United), **I Walker** (Leicester City)
Scorers **Rooney 4, J Cole 9**
Booked **James, Johnson**

DENMARK T Sorensen — T Helveg (sub: B Priske, ht),
R Henriksen, P Nielsen (sub: T Gaardsoe, 71), N Jensen
— J Gronkjaer (sub: P Lovenkrands, 62), T Gravesen,
M Wieghorst (sub: D Jensen, 29), D Rommedahl (sub:
K Perez, 20) — E Sand (sub: J D Tomasson, ht), M
Jorgensen (sub: P Madsen, 84) *Substitutes not used* T
Roll, P Skov-Jensen
Scorers **Jorgensen 8, 30 (pen), Tomasson 82**
Booked **D Jensen**
Referee **V Hrinak** (Slovakia)

Wednesday February 18 2004
Friendly
Faro
PORTUGAL (a)
Drew 1-1   HT 0-0   Att 27,000
PORTUGAL Ricardo — P Ferreira, F Couto (sub: Beto,
83min), J Andrade (sub: R Carvalho, 75), R Jorge (sub:
N Valente, ht) — Costinha (sub: Deco, ht), Petit (sub:
H Viana, 83) — L Figo (sub: L Boa Morte, 66), R Costa
(sub: Tiago, 61), Simao (sub: C Ronaldo, ht) — Pauleta
(sub: H Almeida, 78) *Substitutes not used* Quim, Miguel
Scorer **Pauleta 70**
Booked **Petit**

ENGLAND D James (Manchester City) — **P Neville**
(Manchester United; sub: **D Mills**, Middlesbrough, ht),
G Southgate (Middlesbrough), **L King** (Tottenham
Hotspur), **A Cole** (Arsenal; sub: **W Bridge**, Chelsea, 18;
sub: **J Carragher**, Liverpool, 88) — **D Beckham** (Real
Madrid; sub: **O Hargreaves**, Bayern Munich, 86), **N Butt**
(Manchester United; sub: **J Jenas**, Newcastle United, 86),
P Scholes (Manchester United; sub: **K Dyer**, Newcastle
United, ht), **F Lampard** (Chelsea; sub: **J Cole**, Chelsea,
ht) — **W Rooney** (Everton; sub: **E Heskey**, Liverpool, 71),
M Owen (Liverpool; sub: **A Smith**, Leeds United, 71)
Substitute not used **P Robinson** (Leeds United)
Scorer **King 47**
Referee **V Kassai** (Hungary)

Artim Sakiri, Macedonia's captain, makes a point to Beckham in Skopje

never appeared destined to seize a regular place. In Sweden (eight),
Alan Thompson made a belated debut on the left of midfield and
disappointed. The phoney wars were depressing. With Ferdinand
unavailable and Jonathan Woodgate and Gareth Southgate injured,
Eriksson's back four picked itself. Michael Owen and Rooney were
virtually guaranteed to start in attack and the outstanding question
in midfield was whether Frank Lampard, who enjoyed a dynamic
season with Chelsea, would be chosen ahead of Nicky Butt.

If the build-up was dreary, it was again left to Eriksson — contrary
to his placid demeanour but in keeping with his love life — to
provide much of the drama. Having been spotted taking tea with
Roman Abramovich, Chelsea's billionaire owner, it had long been
assumed that he would be decamping to Stamford Bridge, especially
as some of the club's new signings bore a suspicious twinge of
Swedish influence. Yet if Palios had been stung by the Ferdinand
episode, his response to feverish speculation about his most
high-profile employee was astute. By openly initiating negotiations

Sol Campbell gets the better of Helgi Sigurdsson, of Iceland, in the air

with Eriksson, Chelsea's interest was flushed out. Eriksson appeared daunted by questions about loyalty and a contract extension was finally agreed. Although the terms of his lucrative new deal stretched until 2006, he would now remain in his position until the next World Cup. Definitely. Probably. But, whatever else, England would not be travelling to Portugal with Eriksson's position under scrutiny, with a replacement frantically sought and with the squad unsettled before World Cup qualifying matches against Wales, Northern Ireland, Austria, Poland and Azerbaijan.

A sequence of five matches without a win caused murmurs of unhappiness, yet there could be no outright dissent. Not yet. As Gary Neville put it: "We haven't been great in friendlies for the last two or three years, but when the real games come along, we haven't often failed to deliver."

Between the contentiousness and with the caveats, the feeling was of quiet progress being made. As they embarked for Portugal and the European Championship, proof would be provided either way.

Wednesday March 31
Friendly
Gothenburg
SWEDEN (a)
Lost 0-1   **HT 0-0**   Att **40,464**
SWEDEN A Isaksson (sub: M Kihlstedt, ht) — T Lucic, O Mellberg, J Mjallby (sub: T Linderoth, ht), E Edman — M Nilsson, A Svensson (sub: M Jonson, ht), A Andersson (sub: K Kallstrom, ht), C Wilhelmsson — Z Ibrahimovic (sub: A Ostlund, 90), J Elmander (sub: P Hansson, ht) *Substitutes not used* M Hedman, C Andersson, P Farnerud, M Dorsin
Scorer **Ibrahimovic 54**
Booked **Edman**

ENGLAND D James (Manchester City) — **P Neville** (Manchester United), **J Terry** (Chelsea; sub: **A Gardner**, Tottenham Hotspur, ht), **J Woodgate** (Newcastle United; sub: **G Southgate**, Middlesbrough, ht), **J Carragher** (Liverpool) — **O Hargreaves** (Bayern Munich; sub: **J Jenas**, Newcastle United, 60), **N Butt** (Manchester United; sub: **S Parker**, 78), **S Gerrard** (Liverpool; sub: **J Cole**, Chelsea, 60), **A Thompson** (Celtic; sub: **E Heskey**, Liverpool, 60) — **D Vassell** (Aston Villa; sub: **J Defoe**, Tottenham Hotspur, 12), **W Rooney** (Everton; sub: **A Smith**, Leeds United, 60) *Substitutes not used* **R Green** (Norwich City), **D Mills** (Middlesbrough), **P Robinson** (Leeds United), **J Samuel** (Aston Villa), **I Walker** (Leicester City), **S Wright-Phillips** (Manchester City)
Booked **Neville**
Referee **T Ovrebo** (Norway)

Tuesday June 1
FA Summer Tournament
City of Manchester Stadium
JAPAN (h)
Drew 1-1   **HT 1-0**   Att **38,581**
ENGLAND D James (Manchester City) — sub: **P Neville**, Manchester United, 86min); **J Terry** (Chelsea; sub: **L King**, Tottenham Hotspur, 88), **S Campbell** (Arsenal), **A Cole** (Arsenal) — **D Beckham** (Real Madrid; sub: **J Cole**, Chelsea, 82), **F Lampard** (Chelsea; sub: **N Butt**, Manchester United, 82), **S Gerrard** (Liverpool; sub: **O Hargreaves**, Bayern Munich, 82) — **P Scholes** (Manchester United; sub: **K Dyer**, Newcastle United, 77) — **W Rooney** (Everton; sub: **E Heskey**, Birmingham City, 77), **M Owen** (Liverpool; sub: **D Vassell**, Aston Villa, 77) *Substitutes not used* **W Bridge** (Chelsea), **J Carragher** (Liverpool), **J Defoe** (Tottenham Hotspur), **P Robinson** (Tottenham Hotspur), **I Walker** (Leicester City)
Scorer **Owen 22**

JAPAN S Narazaki — K Tsuboi, T Miyamoto, Y Nakazawa — A Kaji, J Inamoto (sub: T Fukunishi, 90), S Ono, A Santos — S Nakamura — K Tamada (sub: T Suzuki, 60), T Kubo (sub: A Yanagisawa, 60) *Substitutes not used* A Miura, M Tanaka, T Chano, T Fujita, M Ogasawara, Y Endo, M Motoyama, Y Doi, Y Kawaguchi
Scorer **Ono 53**
Referee **R Rosetti** (Italy)

Saturday June 5
FA Summer Tournament
City of Manchester Stadium
ICELAND (h)
Won 6-1   HT 3-1   Att 43,500

ENGLAND P Robinson (Tottenham Hotspur; sub: **I Walker**, Leicester City, 62min) — **G Neville** (Manchester United; sub: **P Neville**, Manchester United, ht), **J Carragher** (Liverpool; sub: **J Defoe**, Tottenham Hotspur, 85), **S Campbell** (Arsenal; sub: **L King**, Tottenham Hotspur, ht), **A Cole** (Arsenal; sub: **W Bridge**, Chelsea, ht) — **D Beckham** (Real Madrid; sub: **K Dyer**, Newcastle United, ht), **F Lampard** (Chelsea; sub: **N Butt**, Manchester United, ht), **S Gerrard** (Liverpool; sub: **O Hargreaves**, Bayern Munich, ht), **P Scholes** (Manchester United; sub: **J Cole**, Chelsea, ht) — **W Rooney** (Everton; sub: **E Heskey**, Birmingham City, ht), **M Owen** (Liverpool; sub: **D Vassell**, Aston Villa, ht) *Substitute not used* **D James** (Manchester City)
Scorers **Lampard 25, Rooney 27, 38, Vassell 57, 77, Bridge 68**

ICELAND A Arason — I Ingimarsson, P Marteinsson (sub: K Sigurdsson, ht), H Hreidarsson — T Gudjonsson (sub: H Jonsson, 78), J Gudjonsson, A Gretarsson, I Sigurdsson (sub: J Gudmundsson, 78) — E Gudjohnsen — H Helguson (sub: T Gudmundsson, 85), H Sigurdsson (sub: B Gudjonsson, 69) *Substitutes not used* K Finnbogason, A Helgason, M Baldvinsson
Scorer **Helguson 42**
Referee **J Wegereef** (Netherlands)

■ *Full details of the 2004 European Championship are on pages 41-54*

MATCH OF THE SEASON

Turkey 0 England 0
Sukru Saracoglu Stadium, Saturday October 11 2003
From Matt Dickinson

THEY HAD PREACHED TOGETHERNESS all week, so, when Alpay Ozalan and David Beckham were at each other's throats in the tunnel, England's big men rushed to the defence of their captain like rugby forwards rushing to the aid of a vulnerable wing three-quarter. John Terry, Sol Campbell and even mild-mannered Emile Heskey went wading in to what one player described as a "fair old ding-dong". Whether striking, fighting or defiantly keeping out the Turks, England stayed united ever since 20 of them ticked their ballot papers on Tuesday night.

Only 20 out of 24? A split? Fearful that they might be accused of coercing the rest of the players into taking a stand for Rio Ferdinand, the Manchester United players offered to abstain. Some of their team-mates may have wished that they had all kept their heads down when they picked up the papers the next day and the headlines screamed that they were a disgrace to their country.

Training on Thursday morning was flat as all the nervous excitement of their unprecedented stand against the FA gave way to fatigue and, with Sven-Goran Eriksson unable to hide his troubled mind and even contemplating resignation if England lost, there were concerns within the party as they boarded the flight to Istanbul. A warning light signalled that the adrenalin tanks had run dry.

Whatever the rights and wrongs of their argument with the FA, for the players to have found it within themselves to produce such a gritty display spoke loudly for their fortitude under pressure. Under Eriksson, their head coach and amateur psychologist, they are developing a steeliness of mind that will ensure that they can cope with just about every setback. If the World Cup quarter-final was played against Brazil tomorrow, England might still be shown up for some technical deficiencies — although they more than matched the Turks in that department — but they would not surrender at half-time. Their moral victory in Istanbul can be put on the mantelpiece with the triumphs over Germany, Argentina and the mauling of the Turks in Sunderland in April. England are starting to frighten teams, top ones, too. How else to explain Turkish inhibitions that paralysed the players and, by the end of the match, silenced Europe's rowdiest fans?

Some of them even meekly applauded England off the field after the players had danced deliriously around the centre circle because there were no supporters to run to. "It was lonely out there," Steven Gerrard said. There was not a trace of Englishness in the stadium: not a banner or flag and, apart from the spontaneous but quickly stifled roar from the press box at the final whistle, not a single cry of support. Terry and Wayne Rooney were not fazed and England's

David Beckham was taunted by Alpay after his penalty miss, but it was a jubilant England who had the last laugh in Istanbul

Beckham skies his penalty over the bar, but the miss proved irrelevant as England got the draw they needed to qualify

youth can no longer be regarded as an obstacle to winning a leading tournament.

Team spirit, according to Steve Archibald, the former Tottenham Hotspur striker, is an illusion in the aftermath of victory. This was a draw for England, but there was nothing illusory about the unity of the team. Eriksson has surrounded himself with players he can trust. Steve McManaman and Robbie Fowler have been packed off like naughty schoolboys. Alan Smith has yet to return from exile after suffering the only sending-off of Eriksson's reign. Even Gareth Southgate's mild challenge to the Swede's authority has been met with the axe.

"The players come from different clubs, but when they come together they help each other," Eriksson said and their expectation of victory was evident from the first few passes; England's were slick and accurate, Turkey's hurried and often bound for touch. Eriksson's most important tactical instruction had been for Paul Scholes to harass Tugay, Turkey's playmaker. "We did what we planned to do," he said. "Scholes didn't score, but he did a marvellous job."

England did everything right in the first half apart from end the contest with a couple of goals. Michael Owen must have longed to have been running into all the space behind the Turkey defence, although Beckham's missed penalty after Gerrard was tripped was the most glaring failure as he lost his footing and skied the ball high into the stands. "We've been telling him that he's been spending too much time with Jonny Wilkinson," Gerrard said. "You can't call that a miss, surely?" Beckham pleaded.

Alpay rushed to taunt Beckham and the Aston Villa

defender continued his baiting as they ran off at half-time and he stuck a finger into the England captain's nose. In the ensuing brawl, Ashley Cole is said to have been struck in the face with spittle. Pierluigi Collina halted the 30-man free-for-all with one blow on his whistle and ordered Beckham and Alpay into his room for a dressing down. The Italian had once again proved that he is the world's leading referee because there was barely a squeak from anyone in the second half.

Perhaps fearful that Turkey had been roused by the brawl, England retreated too deep after the break, but Terry and Campbell were heroic in defence, albeit assisted by Senol Gunes. The Turkey coach lost the plot, overloading his team with strikers at a rate not seen since Holland went to Dublin and Louis van Gaal finished with Ruud van Nistelrooy, Pierre van Hooijdonk, Patrick Kluivert and Jimmy Floyd Hasselbaink tripping over each other in the box.

"We don't have the mentality to play 0-0," Eriksson had said, but it was reassuring to discover that they had the capacity to do so.

TURKEY (4-3-3): **Rustu Recber** (Barcelona) — **Fatih Akyel** (Fenerbahce), **Alpay Ozalan** (Aston Villa), **Bulent Korkmaz** (Galatasaray), **Ibrahim Uzulmez** (Besiktas) — **Okan Buruk** (Inter Milan; sub: **Ilhan Mansiz**, Besiktas, 68min), **Tugay Kerimoglu** (Blackburn Rovers), **Emre Belozoglu** (Inter Milan) — **Nihat Kahveci** (Real Sociedad), **Sergen Yalcin** (Besiktas; sub: **Tuncay Sanli**, Fenerbahce, 61), **Hakan Sukur** (Galatasaray). **Substitutes not used:** Omer Catkic (Gaziantepspor), **Ergun Penbe** (Galatasaray), **Yildiray Basturk** (Bayer Leverkusen), **Emre Asik** (Besiktas), **Umit Davala** (Werder Bremen). **Booked:** Rustu, Tugay.

ENGLAND (4-4-2): **D James** (West Ham United) — **G Neville** (Manchester United), **J Terry** (Chelsea), **S Campbell** (Arsenal), **A Cole** (Arsenal) — **S Gerrard** (Liverpool), **D Beckham** (Real Madrid), **P Scholes** (Manchester United; sub: **F Lampard**, Chelsea, 88), **N Butt** (Manchester United) — **E Heskey** (Liverpool; sub: **D Vassell**, Aston Villa, 67), **W Rooney** (Everton; sub: **K Dyer**, Newcastle United, 71). **Substitutes not used:** **P Robinson** (Leeds United), **P Neville** (Manchester United), **M Upson** (Birmingham City), **W Bridge** (Chelsea). **Booked:** Butt.

PLAYER OF THE SEASON
Wayne Rooney

He was not fit when England's season began with victory against Croatia at Portman Road, but by the time that Sven-Goran Eriksson's squad set off for the European Championship finals, Wayne Rooney was already established as the hero-in-waiting. He was not to disappoint. A goal against Macedonia in September earned the teenager a place in the record books as well as the supporters' hearts as, at 17 years and 317 days, he replaced Michael Owen as the youngest scorer in his country's history. Another goal against Liechtenstein enabled England to reach a postwar landmark of eight successive victories, and while Rooney may not have scored in Istanbul, by keeping a cool head he silenced the doubters who claimed that his suspect temperament could cost England dear. A goal and an assist meant that Rooney was immune from criticism after defeat to Denmark and it was his double against Iceland — the second a stunning effort that encapsulated his speed of thought and power of shot — that helped to send England to Euro 2004 in high spirits. The rest, as they say, is hysteria ...
George Caulkin

THE GAMES

Saturday September 6 2003
European Championship qualifier
UKRAINE (a)
Donetsk
Drew 0-0   HT 0-0   Att 24,000
UKRAINE O Shovkovskyi — O Luzhny, S Fedorov, A
Tymoschuk, A Nesmachnyi — O Horshkov, S Rebrov (sub:
O Melaschenko, 73min), A Husin (sub: O Husev, 17),
H Zubov — A Voronin, A Vorobei *Substitutes not used*
V Reva, V Shevchuk, Y Dmytrulin, S Serebrennikov,
O Guy

NORTHERN IRELAND M Taylor (Birmingham City) — **C
Baird** (Southampton), **A Hughes** (Newcastle United), **G
McCartney** (Sunderland), **P Kennedy** (Wigan Athletic) —
K Gillespie (Leicester City), **D Johnson** (Birmingham
City), **G Doherty** (Tottenham Hotspur; sub: **P Mulryne**,
Norwich City, 67), **D Griffin** (Stockport County), **M
Hughes** (Crystal Palace; sub: **S Jones**, Crewe Alexandra,
81) — **D Healy** (Preston North End; sub: **A Smith**,
Glentoran, 62) *Substitutes not used* **E Morris**
(Glentoran), **G McCann** (Cheltenham Town), **P McVeigh**
(Norwich City), **G Hamilton** (Portadown)
Booked Doherty, Griffin, Hughes
Referee **W Stark** (Germany)

Wednesday September 10
European Championship qualifier
ARMENIA (h)
Windsor Park
Lost 0-1   HT 0-0   Att 8,616
NORTHERN IRELAND M Taylor (Birmingham City) — **C
Baird** (Southampton), **A Hughes** (Newcastle United), **G
McCartney** (Sunderland), **G McCann** (Cheltenham Town)
— **K Gillespie** (Leicester City; sub: **S Jones**, Crewe
Alexandra, 29min), **D Griffin** (Dundee United), **T Doherty**
(Bristol City; sub: **P Mulryne**, Norwich City, 29), **D
Johnson** (Birmingham City) — **D Healy** (Preston North
End; sub: **P McVeigh**, Norwich City, 78), **A Smith**
(Glentoran) *Substitutes not used* **R Carroll** (Manchester
United), **C Murdock** (Hibernian), **A Kirk** (Heart of
Midlothian), **G Hamilton** (Portadown)
Booked Johnson

ARMENIA R Berezovski — S Hovsepyan, T-M Zechu,
J A Bilibio — A Sarkisian, A Petrosyan (sub: A Karamyan,
13), A Voskanyan, R Khachatryan, Y Melikyan —
A Karamyan (sub: E Partiskyan, 87) — A Mousesyan
(sub: A Hakobyan, 75) *Substitutes not used*
A Ambertsumyan, A Morozov, A Mkrtchyan, R Jenebyan
Scorer **Karamyan 27**
Booked Melikyan
Referee **A Stredak** (Slovakia)

THE ENGLISH LANGUAGE HAS flourished in our national game over the years, inspiring several worthy additions to the dictionary of catchphrases. "One-nil to the Arsenal" and "Sack the board" are among the cliches now in general use. As the qualifying matches in the European Championship drew to a close, another one entered the vocabulary: "Northern Ireland nil".

Despite a splendid effort in Ukraine to eke out a draw and a narrow defeat away to Greece, who went on to win the European Championship, Northern Ireland were unable to muster a single goal during their doomed campaign to reach Portugal. Worse still, in between those two matches, Windsor Park witnessed a miserable performance at home to Armenia, the only team capable of replacing Northern Ireland at the bottom of the group. Instead of an uplifting victory, a 1-0 defeat merely emphasised how low they had slipped, not only in the global scheme of things but also in morale.

Seldom have Northern Ireland been accused of lacking the spirit and vigour to tackle even the most daunting of opponents, but on that grey, dank Wednesday night in September, the green shirts appeared pallid. It was a squad that had forgotten how to celebrate even a consolation goal, never mind a victory. They had given up the ghost. And when you tire of treading water, the only way is down.

It was then that Sammy McIlroy, the manager, decided that he would not be responsible for the situation any longer. McIlroy had been a dignified presence in the most trying of circumstances during his tenure of almost four years. Working with willing but raw materials, he had frequently suffered the indignity of almost farcical travel arrangements that saw essential team baggage either lost or misdirected in transit. Players withdrawing at the eleventh hour had become part of the job and, although he waited until the European Championship qualifying saga had run its course, his resignation, two days after the final game in Athens in September, came as no surprise.

McIlroy left to manage Stockport County, but it would be several months before the Irish FA appointed his successor. In keeping with its *modus operandi*, the subsequent announcement in January was anything but predictable. Lawrie Sanchez seems an unlikely name for a Northern Ireland manager, but his three caps for the Province, by virtue of his mother's birthright, lent some authenticity to his claim to be taken as a serious candidate for the vacancy.

Jimmy Nicholl, the Dunfermline Athletic assistant manager who was capped 73 times for Northern Ireland and turned down the post while manager of Raith Rovers, had attracted 49 per cent of the

Andy Smith takes on Magne Hoset, of Norway, during February's defeat

vote during a local television poll and was the overwhelming favourite to get the job. But Sanchez prevailed. True to form, really, since his finest moment in football was the headed goal for Wimbledon that defeated Liverpool in the 1988 FA Cup Final, a memorable triumph for the underdogs. In 2001, he also guided Wycombe Wanderers, then in the Nationwide League second division, to the FA Cup semi-finals.

"In my career as a player and a manager, I have caused one or two upsets," Sanchez said. "I hope, in a situation like this, I can cause one or two upsets as well." If that was fighting talk, then at least Sanchez knew that things could not get much worse. As it transpired, his first few games were encouraging.

A 4-1 defeat by Norway at Windsor Park in February scarcely did justice to the visiting side's dominance of the game, but at least one unwanted millstone was lifted from the home side's shoulders when David Healy scored. It was Northern Ireland's first goal in 1,298 minutes of play — a world record dating back to a friendly match against Poland in Cyprus in February 2002. Healy's effort was his ninth goal for his country and a tenth followed in March to nudge him closer to Colin Clark's record of 13.

Of equal significance was the 1-0 victory over Estonia in Tallinn that it brought. Healy's finish was impeccable, a dazzling right-foot shot that fizzed into the top corner of the net. The reward for Sanchez, in his second match at the helm, was Northern Ireland's first victory in 16 games since a World Cup qualifying match success away to Malta in October 2001.

Back in Belfast, a draw with Serbia and Montenegro confirmed that resilience had been restored and another forward with previously latent predatory talents was unearthed. When James Quinn equalised, it was his first goal for his country in four years.

MATCH OF THE SEASON

Wednesday March 31
Friendly
ESTONIA (a)
Tallinn
Won 1-0   HT 1-0   Att 2,000
ESTONIA M Kaalma — E Jaager, A Stepanov, R Piiroja
(sub: T Rahn, 82min), R Klavan — M Smirnov (sub: O
Reinumae, 85), M Reim, M Kristal, T Kink (sub: S
Terehov, 71) — I Zelinski (sub: I Teever, 64), M Rooba
(sub: J Lindpere, 73) *Substitutes not used* R Kaas,
A Purje, E Saviauk, A Dmitrijev
Booked **Reim, Piiroja, Rahn**

NORTHERN IRELAND M Taylor (Birmingham City) — **C
Baird** (Southampton), **M Williams** (Wimbledon), **S
Craigan** (Motherwell), **A Capaldi** (Plymouth Argyle) — **S
Jones** (Crewe Alexandra; sub: **G McCann**, Cheltenham
Town, 68), **D Sonner** (Nottingham Forest; sub: **M Duff**,
Cheltenham Town, 78), **J Whitley** (Sunderland), **P
Mulryne** (Norwich City) — **D Healy** (Preston North End), **A
Smith** (Glentoran) *Substitutes not used* A Fettis (Hull
City), **C Toner** (L Orient), **A Kirk** (Heart of Midlothian)
Scorer **Healy 43**
Booked **Sonner, Healy, Williams**
Referee **P Kari** (Finland)

Wednesday April 28
Friendly
SERBIA AND MONTENEGRO (h)
Windsor Park
Drew 1-1   HT 1-1   Att 9,690
NORTHERN IRELAND M Taylor (Birmingham City; sub: **R
Carrroll**, Manchester United, ht) — **C Baird**
(Southampton), **M Williams** (Wimbledon), **S Craigan**
(Motherwell), **T Capaldi** (Plymouth Argyle) — **K Gillespie**
(Leicester City; sub: **S Jones**, Crewe Alexandra, ht), **T
Doherty** (Bristol City; sub: **M Hughes**, Crystal Palace,
78), **J Whitley** (Sunderland; sub: **D Sonner**, Nottingham
Forest, 78), **P Mulryne** (Norwich City; sub: **P McVeigh**,
Norwich City, ht) — **D Healy** (Preston North End; sub: **G
Hamilton**, Portadown, ht), **J Quinn** (Willem II; sub: **A
Smith**, Glentoran, 78) *Substitutes not used* P Kennedy
(Wigan Athletic), **C Murdock** (Hibernian)
Scorer **Quinn 18**
Booked **Whitley, Doherty, Quinn**

SERBIA AND MONTENEGRO Z Banovic — M Cirkovic
(sub: J Markoski, 82), D Petkovic, M Krstajic, I
Dragutinovic (sub: M Vitakic, ht) — G Trobok (sub: N Ivic,
ht), G Gavrancic, A Nadj, Z Vukic, V Paunovic (sub: M
Kolakovic, 69) — M Kezman *Substitutes not used* O
Kovacevic, M Dudic, N Djordevic
Scorer **Paunovic 7**
Booked **Nadj, Paunovic, Krstajic**
Referee **C Richards** (Wales)

Sunday May 30
Friendly
BARBADOS (a)
Bridgetown
Drew 1-1   HT 0-1   Att 8,000
BARBADOS A Chase — R Braithwaite, J Parris, D James, W
Burrowes — K Hall, N Forde, S Lovell, R Grosvenor — K
Skinner (sub: L Riley, 65min), R Lucas *Substitutes not used*
Howell, Boyce, Burgess, Hawkesworth, Goodridge, Neblett
Scorer **Skinner 40**
Booked **Lovell, Lucas, James**

NORTHERN IRELAND M Taylor (Birmingham City) — **C
Baird** (Southampton; sub: **S Jones**, Crewe Alexandra,
67), **M Williams** (Wimbledon; sub: **S Craigan** (Motherwell), **T
Capaldi** (Plymouth Argyle; sub: **S Elliott**, Hull City, 67); **K
Gillespie** (Leicester City; sub: **C Murdock**, Hibernian, ht),
D Johnson (Birmingham City), **D Sonner** (Nottingham
Forest; sub: **P McVeigh**, Norwich City, 67), **P Mulryne**
(Norwich City; sub: **A Smith**, Glentoran, ht); **J Quinn**
(Willem II), **D Healy** (Preston North End; sub: **G Hamilton**,
Portadown, 80) *Substitutes not used* M Ingham
(Sunderland), **J Whitley** (Sunderland), **G Doherty**
(Tottenham Hotspur)
Scorer **Healy 71**
Sent off **Williams**
Referee **N Brizan** (Trinidad and Tobago)

Estonia 0 Northern Ireland 1
A Le Coq Arena, Tallinn, Wednesday March 31 2004
Ian Winrow

DAVID HEALY is rapidly emerging as Lawrie Sanchez's talisman
after the Preston North End forward hit the first-half winner that
secured a deserved victory for Northern Ireland — their first in 16
matches. Healy had marked Sanchez's first game in charge, against
Norway last month, with the goal that ended his team's agonising
and humiliating 1,298-minute goal drought. Now Sanchez has
overseen the removal of yet another unwanted mark — Northern
Ireland previously tasted victory when Healy struck the only goal
against Malta in October 2001.

The win over a team ranked No 66 in Fifa's world rankings, 58
places higher than Northern Ireland, was just reward for their
impressive efforts, which belied recent history. "It's nice to win a
football match again because it has been a long time for us," Sanchez
said. "And it was nice to score again. It was a great goal to win a
game with and I think we deserved it. It's my first win in charge and,
hopefully, it is the first of many."

Sanchez's plans had been torn apart in the build-up when his
already experimental squad was further depleted by a spate of
withdrawals. But his patched-up team unexpectedly took the game
to their hosts from the opening whistle. With Andy Smith, the
Glentoran forward, matching Healy's pace and vigour up front and
Steve Jones and Jeff Whitley advancing from midfield at every
opportunity, Estonia struggled to emerge from their own half in the
first 45 minutes. Then, with the interval looming, Healy produced
the moment of genuine quality that decided the match.

Jones collected the ball on the right flank and made yet another
surge forward before picking out Healy on the left-hand side of the
penalty area with an accurate crossfield pass. Healy shifted inside on
to his right foot and sent a fierce curling effort into the top left-hand
corner of Martin Kaalma's goal.

The second half was never likely to be as one-sided, but although
the visiting team's attacks were less frequent, Whitley spurned two
good opportunities to add to the lead, particularly in the 63rd
minute when he drove a volley straight at Kaalma from 12 yards.

ESTONIA (4-4-2): **M** Kaalma (Flora Tallinn) — **E** Jaager (Flora Tallinn), **A** Stepanov (Torpedo Moscow),
R Piiroja (Flora Tallin; sub: **T** Rahn, Volyn Lutsk, 82min), **R** Klavan (Flora Tallinn) — **M** Smirnov (TVMK
Tallinn; sub: **O** Reinumae, Flora Tallinn, 85), **M** Reim (Flora Tallinn), **M** Kristal (Flora Tallinn), **T** Kink
(Spartak Moscow; sub: **S** Terehov, Haka, 71) — **I** Zelinski (Frem; sub: **I** Teever, TVMK Tallinn, 64),
M Rooba (Flora Tallinn; sub: **J** Lindpere, Flora Tallinn, 73). **Substitutes not used:** R Kaas (Flora
Tallinn), A Purje (Levadia Tallinn), E Saviauk (Flora Tallinn), A Dmitrijev (Levadia Tallinn). **Booked:**
Reim, Piiroja, Rahn.
NORTHERN IRELAND (4-4-2): **M** Taylor (Birmingham City) — **C** Baird (Southampton), **M** Williams
(Wimbledon), **S** Craigan (Motherwell), **A** Capaldi (Plymouth Argyle) — **S** Jones (Crewe Alexandra; sub:
G McCann, Cheltenham Town, 68), **D** Sonner (Nottingham Forest; sub: **M** Duff, Cheltenham Town,
78), **J** Whitley (Sunderland), **P** Mulryne (Norwich City) — **D** Healy (Preston North End), **A** Smith
(Glentoran). **Substitutes not used:** A Fettis (Hull City), C Toner (Leyton Orient), A Kirk (Heart of
Midlothian). **Booked:** Sonner, Healy, Williams.
Referee: P Kari (Finland).

PLAYER OF THE SEASON
David Healy

It would be impossible not to mention the contribution of Maik Taylor, the Birmingham City goalkeeper, to the cause and his appointment as captain for the victory in Estonia was merited. However, David Healy takes the honour because of his unrelenting quest to end not only his personal goal drought but also the team's. Forwards must show courage by not hiding in times of crisis and the Preston North End striker demonstrated an abundance of that particular virtue. He may have fluffed several easy chances at vital times, but his just rewards at last arrived, hopefully to spur him on to greater deeds.
David McVay

Wednesday June 2
Friendly
ST KITTS & NEVIS (a)
Basseterre
Won 2-0   HT 0-0   Att 2,000
NORTHERN IRELAND M Taylor (Birmingham City) — **C Baird** (Southampton), **A Capaldi** (Plymouth Argyle), **S Craigan** (Motherwell), **C Murdock** (Hibernian) — **D Sonner** (Nottingham Forest; sub: **S Jones**, Crewe Alexandra, 52min), **J Whitley** (Sunderland; sub: **K Gillespie**, Leicester City, 65), **S Elliott** (Hull City; sub: **P Mulryne**, Norwich City, 65), **G Hamilton** (Portadown; sub: **D Healy**, Preston North End, 65) — **P McVeigh** (Norwich City), **A Smith** (Glentoran)
Scorers **Healy 81, Jones 86**

Sunday June 6
Friendly
TRINIDAD & TOBAGO (a)
Bacolet
Won 3-0   HT 2-0   Att 7,500
NORTHERN IRELAND M Taylor (Birmingham City; sub: **A Mannus**, Linfield, 83min) — **C Baird** (Southampton), **A Capaldi** (Plymouth Argyle), **S Craigan** (Motherwell), **M Williams** (Wimbledon) — **S Elliott** (Hull City; sub: **S Jones**, Crewe Alexandra, ht), **D Johnson** (Birmingham City; sub: **K Gillespie**, Leicester City, 72), **P Mulryne** (Norwich City; sub: **D Sonner**, Nottingham Forest, 72), **J Whitley** (Sunderland) — **D Healy** (Preston North End), **J Quinn** (Willem II; sub: **A Smith**, Glentoran, ht)
Scorers **Healy 4, 65, Elliott 41**

THE GAMES

Wednesday August 20 2003
Friendly
NORWAY (a)
Oslo
Drew 0-0   HT 0-0   Att 12,858
NORWAY E Johnsen — C Basma (sub: A Aas, 70min), H Berg (sub: R Johnsen, ht), C Lundekvam, A Bergdolmo (sub: S Iversen, 68) — M Andresen, F Johnsen (sub: J Solli, ht), B Hangeland (sub: T Andersen, ht), J A Riise — O G Solskjaer — J Carew *Substitutes not used* F Olsen, R Strand, H Flo
SCOTLAND R Douglas (Celtic) — **M Ross** (Rangers; sub: **D Fletcher**, Manchester United, 60), **A Webster** (Heart of Midlothian), **S Pressley** (Heart of Midlothian), **C Dailly** (West Ham United) — **C Cameron** (Wolverhampton Wanderers; sub: **G Rae**, Dundee, 84), **P Lambert** (Celtic), **B Ferguson** (Blackburn Rovers), **G Naysmith** (Everton) — **S Crawford** (Dunfermline Athletic; sub: **P Devlin**, Birmingham City, 79), **D Hutchison** (West Ham United) *Substitutes not used* N Alexander (Cardiff City), L Wilkie (Dundee), G Alexander (Preston North End), S Maloney (Celtic), B Kerr (Newcastle United), S Caldwell (Newcastle United), P Gallacher Dundee United)
Referee **M Vuorela** (Finland)

Saturday September 6
European Championship qualifier
FAEROE ISLES (h)
Hampden Park
Won 3-1   HT 2-1   Att 40,109
SCOTLAND R Douglas (Celtic) — **J McNamara** (Celtic), **L Wilkie** (Dundee), **A Webster** (Heart of Midlothian), **G Naysmith** (Everton) — **P Devlin** (Birmingham City; sub: **J McFadden**, Everton, 58min), **C Cameron** (Wolverhampton Wanderers), **B Ferguson** (Blackburn Rovers), **N McCann** (Southampton) — **P Dickov** (Leicester City; sub: **G Rae**, Dundee, 67), **S Crawford** (Dunfermline Athletic; sub: **S Thompson**, Rangers, 74) *Substitutes not used* P Gallacher (Dundee United), G Alexander (Preston North End), M Ross (Rangers), S Caldwell (Newcastle United)
Scorers **McCann** 8, **Dickov** 45, **McFadden** 74
Booked **Crawford**
FAEROE ISLES J Mikkelsen — J I Petersen, O Johanessen, J R Jacobsen, P Thorsteinsson — J Johnsson (sub: A Danielsen, 84), F Benjaminsen, J Petersen, R Jacobsen — J Borg (sub: C Holst, 84), H Petersen (sub: T Askelsen, 65) *Substitutes not used* J Knudsen, S Olsen, A Flotum, H Hansen
Scorer **Johnsson** 36
Booked **Benjaminsen, R Jacobsen**
Referee **D Seferin** (Slovenia)

Wednesday September 10
European Championship qualifier
GERMANY (a)
Dortmund
Lost 1-2   HT 1-0   Att 67,000
GERMANY O Kahn — A Freidrich, C Worns, F Baumann, T Rau — B Schneider (sub: S Kehl, 80min), C Ramelow, M Ballack, M Rehmer — F Bobic (sub: M Klose, 75), K Kuranyi *Substitutes not used* J Lehmann, B Lauth, M Hartmann, A Hinkel, C Rahn
Scorers **Bobic** 25, **Ballack** 50 (pen)
Booked **Rau**
SCOTLAND R Douglas (Celtic) — **J McNamara** (Celtic), **S Pressley** (Heart of Midlothian), **C Dailly** (West Ham United), **G Naysmith** (Everton) — **J McFadden** (Everton; sub: **G Rae**, Dundee, 53), **P Lambert** (Celtic; sub: **M Ross**, Rangers, ht), **B Ferguson** (Blackburn Rovers), **C Cameron** (Wolverhampton Wanderers) — **S Thompson** (Rangers), **N McCann** (Southampton) *Substitutes not used* P Gallacher (Dundee United), **A Webster** (Heart of Midlothian), **L Wilkie** (Dundee), **P Devlin** (Birmingham City), **P Dickov** (Leicester City)
Scorer **McCann** 59
Booked **Dailly, Ross, Pressley, Ferguson**
Sent off **Ross**
Referee **A Frisk** (Sweden)

BERTI VOGTS KNOWS HE IS AN ERSATZ Scot, but that has not stopped him trying to remind the rest of his adopted country about its roots. He has ordered his players to parade the Saltire before games and hired a rock band to play *Flower Of Scotland* to stir up the crowd. The little German, though, had to wait until November before he discovered what it really means to be Scottish. Just four days separated two games that summed up the rollercoaster of emotions that is handed down as a birthright to the Tartan Army.

From the peak of wild optimism, after defeating Holland 1-0 in the first leg of their Euro 2004 play-off, Scotland plunged down a ravine of unfathomable despair. A 6-0 thrashing from one of the world's top sides in Amsterdam left Vogts's team so disfigured that a proper post mortem was not possible for several months.

It was a classic example of Scotland's capricious football tradition. It echoed 1962, when Denis Law and Co humbled Czechoslovakia 3-0 in a World Cup qualifying group match only to be thrashed 6-2 by the same opponents in a play-off; the Czechs went on to reach the final against Brazil. Or what about the summer of 1978? Ally MacLeod — who, sadly, died last winter — took his team to the World Cup finals and saw them held 1-1 by Iran before inflicting a memorable, Archie Gemmill-inspired defeat upon Holland. The Dutch went on to the final; Scotland caught the first flight home.

In truth, everyone knew that Vogts had taken his 2003 team as far as he could. Scotland reached the play-offs by finishing second in their group behind Germany. Outright qualification was put beyond their reach when Rudi Voller's team won 2-1 in Dortmund in September, when injury robbed Scotland of Paul Lambert, their captain.

That left them needing a win over Lithuania in the last match of the group, in October, to claim second place and a play-off berth. Darren Fletcher settled a nervy affair with his first international goal in only his second game, though the Manchester United teenager must have wondered if it was all worth it after he and his bemused colleagues stumbled from the pitch in Amsterdam a month later as Ruud van Nistelrooy claimed a hat-trick.

So, for the third time in a row, Scotland were onlookers in a finals. Whether that sequence is extended to four, only time and the World Cup campaign — Italy, the group favourites, seem certain to leave the Scots scavenging for scraps yet again — will tell.

"Judge me on competitive games, not friendlies," Vogts implored. He somehow managed to squeeze in 16 during his first 27 months in charge. but they brought an alarming run of defeats. When Wales carried on in February where Holland had left off, winning 4-0 in

Patrick Kluivert is shut out as Scotland beat Holland at Hampden Park

Cardiff, it was the ninth defeat in a dozen friendlies and reopened the debate about Vogts's future. Wales romped to their biggest win in the 128-year history of the fixture and this time the man who helped himself to a hat-trick was not someone such as Van Nistelrooy but Robert Earnshaw, of Cardiff City.

A month later, the pressure on Vogts began to grow even more. Friendly No 13 was unlucky for John Kennedy. The young Celtic central defender's debut lasted just 15 minutes, Kennedy being taken off on a stretcher after a cynical stamp by Ioan Ganea, the Wolverhampton Wanderers striker. The 2-1 defeat was overshadowed by the news that Kennedy — who had helped to snuff out Barcelona in the Nou Camp a week earlier for his club in a Uefa Cup tie — would miss the next 18 months with a dreadful cruciate injury.

Vogts was condemned for showing precious little concern for Kennedy at the time. The tetchiness with the media surfaced in the next friendly, away to Denmark in Copenhagen, which the Scots lost narrowly 1-0, when Vogts banned his players from being interviewed by the press. Next, television suffered, with Sky being refused interviews because of criticism from Charlie Nicholas, the former Scotland player.

Scotland wrapped up their long campaign with more friendlies, winning 1-0 away to Estonia, where James McFadden scored for the third time in six games, then 4-1 against Trinidad and Tobago at Easter Road.

"There was only one really bad defeat, against Wales," Vogts insisted. "All the others came against the top teams in the world — Holland, Germany, Romania — but I am optimistic about my team and the World Cup. We have great young players in McFadden and Fletcher. The future looks good, but we need time."

Saturday October 11
European Championship qualifier
LITHUANIA (h)
Hampden Park
Won 1-0   HT 0-0   Att 50,343
SCOTLAND R Douglas (Celtic) — **J McNamara** (Celtic), **S Pressley** (Heart of Midlothian), **C Dailly** (West Ham United), **G Naysmith** (Everton) — **G Rae** (Dundee), **C Cameron** (Wolverhampton Wanderers; sub: **D Fletcher**, Manchester United, 65min), **B Ferguson** (Blackburn Rovers), **J McFadden** (Everton; sub: **G Alexander**, Preston North End, 89) — **S Crawford** (Dunfermline Athletic), **K Miller** (Wolverhampton Wanderers; sub: **D Hutchison**, West Ham United, 65) *Substitutes not used* **N Alexander** (Cardiff City), **A Webster** (Heart of Midlothian), **L Wilkie** (Dundee), **K Harper** (Portsmouth)
Scorer **Fletcher 69**
Booked **McNamara, Naysmith**

LITHUANIA G Stauce — R Dziaukstas, T Zvirgzdauskas, I Dedura, D Regelskis (sub: R Beniusis, 85) — N Barasa, D Vencevicius (sub: D Maciulevicius, 79), T Razanauskas, G Baravicius (sub: D Cesnauskis, ht) — E Jankauskas, R Poskus *Substitutes not used:* V Zutautasm, V Alunderis, O Buitkus, A Skerla
Booked **Vencevicius, Poskus**
Referee C Colombo (France)

**GROUP FIVE
FINAL TABLE**

	P	W	D	L	F	A	Pts
Germany	8	5	3	0	13	4	18
Scotland	8	4	2	2	12	8	14
Iceland	8	4	1	3	11	9	13
Lithuania	8	3	1	4	7	11	10
Faeroe Isles	8	0	1	7	7	18	1

Saturday November 15
European Championship qualifying play-off, first leg
HOLLAND (h)
Hampden Park
Won 1-0   HT 1-0   Att 50,670
SCOTLAND R Douglas (Celtic) — **J McNamara** (Celtic), **S Pressley** (Heart of Midlothian), **L Wilkie** (Dundee), **G Naysmith** (Everton) — **C Dailly** (West Ham United) — **D Fletcher** (Manchester United), **B Ferguson** (Blackburn Rovers), **N McCann** (Southampton; sub: **S Pearson**, Motherwell, 70min) — **P Dickov** (Leicester City; sub: **K Miller**, Wolverhampton Wanderers, 65), **J McFadden** (Everton; sub: **D Hutchison**, West Ham United, 90) *Substitutes not used* **J Gould** (Preston North End), **G Alexander** (Preston North End), **S Caldwell** (Newcastle United), **S Crawford** (Dunfermline Athletic)
Scorer **McFadden 22**
Booked **McFadden, Dailly**

HOLLAND E van der Sar — A Ooijer, J Stam, F de Boer, G van Bronckhorst (sub: C Seedorf, ht) — A van der Meyde, P Cocu, E Davids (sub: R van der Vaart, 60), M Overmars — P Kluivert (sub: R Makaay, 76) — R van Nistelrooy *Substitutes not used* R Waterreus, B Zenden, M Reiziger, P van Hooijdonk
Booked **Stam, Ooijer**
Referee T Hauge (Norway)

Wednesday November 29
European Championship qualifying play-off, second leg
HOLLAND (a)
Amsterdam
Lost 0-6   HT **0-3**   Att **51,000**
Holland won 6-1 on aggregate
HOLLAND E van der Sar — M Reiziger, A Ooijer (sub: F de Boer, ht), W Bouma (sub: C Seedorf, 66) — P Cocu, W Sneijder, R van der Vaart, E Davids — A van der Meyde, R van Nistelrooy (sub: P Kluivert, 77), M Overmars *Substitutes not used* R Waterreus, A Robben, P van Hooijdonk, R Makaay
Scorers **Sneijder 15, Ooijer 33, Van Nistelrooy 36, 50, 66, De Boer 64**
Booked **Davids, Van Nistelrooy**

SCOTLAND R Douglas (Celtic) — **J McNamara** (Celtic), **S Pressley** (Heart of Midlothian), **L Wilkie** (Dundee), **G Naysmith** (Everton; sub: **M Ross**, Rangers, ht) — **D Fletcher** (Manchester United), **G Rae** (Dundee), **B Ferguson** (Blackburn Rovers), **N McCann** (Southampton; sub: **K Miller**, Wolverhampton Wanderers, 62) — **P Dickov** (Leicester City; sub: **S Crawford**, Dunfermline Athletic, ht), **J McFadden** (Everton) *Substitutes not used* **J Gould** (Preston North End), **G Alexander** (Preston North End), **S Caldwell** (Newcastle United), **D Hutchison** (West Ham United)
Booked **Naysmith, Pressley, Dickov**
Referee **L Michel** (Slovakia)

Wednesday February 18 2004
Friendly
WALES (a)
Cardiff
Lost 0-4   HT **0-2**   Att **47,124**
SCOTLAND R Douglas (Celtic) — **J McNamara** (Celtic), **S Caldwell** (Newcastle United), **P Ritchie** (Walsall), **G Naysmith** (Everton; sub: **G Murty**, Reading, ht) — **C Dailly** (West Ham United) — **D Fletcher** (Manchester United; sub: **A Webster**, Heart of Midlothian, 86), **C Cameron** (Wolverhampton Wanderers; sub: **P Gallagher**, Blackburn Rovers, 68), **S Pearson** (Celtic; sub: **J McFadden**, Everton, ht) — **K Miller** (Wolverhampton Wanderers), **P Dickov** (Leicester City) *Substitutes not used* **G Caldwell** (Hibernian), **G Teale** (Wigan Athletic), **P Gallacher** (Dundee United)
Wales details on page 380

Wednesday March 31
Friendly
ROMANIA (h)
Hampden Park
Lost 1-2   HT **0-1**   Att **20,433**
SCOTLAND P Gallacher (Dundee United) — **C Dailly** (West Ham United), **S Pressley** (Heart of Midlothian), **J Kennedy** (Celtic; sub: **S Crainey**, Southampton, 18min) — **G Alexander** (Preston North End), **G Caldwell** (Hibernian), **G Rae** (Rangers), **C Cameron** (Wolverhampton Wanderers), **N McCann** (Southampton) — **K Miller** (Wolverhampton Wanderers; sub: **J McFadden**, Everton, 51), **S Thompson** (Rangers; sub: **S Crawford**, Dunfermline Athletic, 63) *Substitutes not used* **C Gordon** (Heart of Midlothian), **S Caldwell** (Newcastle United), **P Ritchie** (Walsall), **R Hughes** (Portsmouth), **G Murty** (Reading), **S Shearer** (Coventry City)
Scorer **McFadden 56**

ROMANIA B Stelea (sub: B Lobont, ht) — F Stoican, A Iensci, C Chivu, R Rat — F Petre (sub: N Mitea, ht), O Petre, D Pancu (sub: I Danciulescu, 89), F Cernat (sub: F Soava, 63) — I Ganea (sub: A Cristea, 81), A Mutu *Substitutes not used* I Stancu, M Constantin
Scorers **Chivu 36, Pancu 50**
Booked **Mutu, Cernat**
Referee **J Hyytia** (Finland)

MATCH OF THE SEASON

Scotland 1 Holland 0
Hampden Park, Saturday November 15 2003
Phil Gordon

IT SAYS MUCH ABOUT THE SCOTLAND team's recent inglorious past that the best nights out at Hampden Park have involved Robbie Williams and Rod Stewart. Finally, a real footballer has given the celebrated stadium its soul back.

Apart from the one-off gig by Zinedine Zidane and the Real Madrid *galacticos* at the European Cup final of 2002, Hampden has struggled to regain the raucous passion it once housed. It was no longer the world's largest ground when it reopened in 1999 after a £60 million facelift had stripped out its vertiginous terraces to make way for 50,000 seats, but you would not have known the difference at 5pm on Saturday.

No sooner had Terje Hauge's whistle signalled the end than the Hampden sound system pumped up the volume with Status Quo's *Rockin' All Over The World.* Corny? Yes. Effective? Certainly. James McFadden was not tempted to play air guitar, but make no mistake, if he did, 50,000 would stand and watch him. Perhaps the young Everton forward is saving that for Amsterdam on Wednesday, if Scotland can complete this Euro 2004 play-off encounter by protecting the precious lead that has offered a glimpse of the finals.

McFadden is the cult hero of the Scotland fans and symbolises the remarkable transformation that Berti Vogts's team has made over the past 14 months. Both began calamitously. For Vogts, it was the 2-2 draw in the Faeroe Isles at the start of the European Championship qualifying campaign; for McFadden, it was a rebuke from his new coach after his debut in the Far East, when he missed the flight home after a night on the tiles in Hong Kong. Vogts, though, kept faith in McFadden, just as the Scottish public did with its new German manager, even though morale plunged lower than the Fifa ranking of No 63 after a series of desperate defeats in friendlies. Now everyone is in tune and the only voices cracking are Dutch ones.

Holland may believe that their stellar squad will recover the situation in the Amsterdam ArenA, but they cannot be certain, as heated debate between Dutch journalists and Dick Advocaat on Saturday indicated. Advocaat has stated that he will resign on Thursday if Holland fail to make the finals. The former Rangers manager must be a touch uneasy about the way Vogts second-guessed his game-plan at Hampden and must fear that the Scotland national coach is capable of repeating it.

Christian Dailly sat in front of the back four and stayed inside Patrick Kluivert's shirt all day. Even if the West Ham United defender is suspended from the second leg — Hauge told Dailly that he would consider recommending to Uefa that his harsh caution be

PLAYER OF THE SEASON
Darren Fletcher

The breath of fresh air on the Scotland national scene is represented by Darren Fletcher and James McFadden, who have shown great skill and a youthful lack of respect for more vaunted opponents. Fletcher, 20, became Scotland's youngest captain in over a century when he led out the team against Estonia and Berti Vogts is convinced that the composed youngster will eventually replace Roy Keane in the Manchester United engine room.

Phil Gordon

rescinded — Vogts believes that he has others capable of fulfilling the "team function" that he prophesied would overcome the Dutch fame academy. "The pressure is on the Dutch now," Vogts said.

While Holland dominated the second half, they created only two genuine chances. Andy van der Meyde thrashed one against the bar and Lee Wilkie's vigilance snuffed out Ruud van Nistelrooy in the other. Even so, Scotland, as Advocaat acknowledged, remained "dangerous on the break". That will gnaw away at Advocaat, who knows that the damage to his "golden generation" by two unheralded Scots might just be irreparable.

McFadden did not quite dance around as many Dutch tackles as Archie Gemmill did with his celebrated goal in 1978, but from the same angle of the box he left Giovanni van Bronckhorst for dead, exchanged passes with Darren Fletcher via a sublime backheel from the Manchester United teenager, and scored with a composed left-foot shot of which Gemmill would have been proud. Perhaps, 25 years late, Scotland will finally make the Dutch pay.

SCOTLAND (4-1-3-2): R Douglas (Celtic) — J McNamara (Celtic), S Pressley (Heart of Midlothian), L Wilkie (Dundee), G Naysmith (Everton) — C Dailly (West Ham United) — D Fletcher (Manchester United), B Ferguson (Blackburn Rovers), N McCann (Southampton; sub: S Pearson, Motherwell, 70min) — P Dickov (Leicester City; sub: K Miller, Wolverhampton Wanderers, 65), J McFadden (Everton; sub: D Hutchison, West Ham United, 90). **Substitutes not used:** J Gould (Preston North End), G Alexander (Preston North End), S Caldwell (Newcastle United), S Crawford (Dunfermline Athletic). **Booked:** McFadden, Dailly.

HOLLAND (4-4-1-1): E van der Sar (Fulham) — A Ooijer (PSV Eindhoven), J Stam (Lazio), F de Boer (Galatasaray), G van Bronckhorst (Barcelona; sub: C Seedorf, AC Milan, ht) — A van der Meyde (Inter Milan), P Cocu (Barcelona), E Davids (Juventus; sub: R van der Vaart, Ajax, 60), M Overmars (Barcelona) — P Kluivert (Barcelona; sub: R Makaay, Bayern Munich, 76) — R van Nistelrooy (Manchester United). **Substitutes not used:** R Waterreus (PSV Eindhoven), B Zenden (Middlesbrough), M Reiziger (Barcelona), P van Hooijdonk (Fenerbahce). **Booked:** Stam, Ooijer.

Wednesday April 28
Friendly
DENMARK (a)
Copenhagen
Lost 0-1   HT 0-0   Att 22,885
DENMARK T Sorenson — T Helveg, R Henriksen (sub: P Kroldrup, 66min), M Laursen, N Jensen (sub: K Perez, ht) — D Jensen, C Jensen (sub: A Sennels, ht), M Wieghorst (sub: M Retov, 80) — J Gronkjaer (sub: T Rasmussen, 88), J D Tomasson (sub: E Sand, ht), M Jorgensen (sub: D Rommedahl, 66) *Substitutes not used* P Neilsen, B Priske, P Skov-Jensen, S Andersen, P Madsen
Scorer Sand 60

SCOTLAND P Gallacher (Dundee United) — G Caldwell (Hibernian), S Pressley (Heart of Midlothian), M Mackay (Norwich City), S Crainey (Southampton; sub: N McCann, Southampton, ht), D Fletcher (Manchester United), C Dailly (West Ham United), G Holt (Norwich City), P Canero (Leicester City, 16) — K Kyle (Sunderland), J McFadden (Everton) *Substitutes not used* C Gordon (Heart of Midlothian), S Caldwell (Newcastle United), K Miller (Wolverhampton Wanderers), G Alexander (Preston North End), S Thompson (Rangers), A Webster (Heart of Midlothian), D McNamee (Livingston), D Marshall (Celtic)
Booked G Caldwell, McFadden
Referee M Ingvarsson (Sweden)

Thursday May 27
Friendly
ESTONIA (a)
Tallinn
Won 1-0   HT 0-0   Att 4,000
ESTONIA M Kaalma — T Allas, A Stepanov, E Jaager, R Klavan — T Rahn, S Terehhov (sub: O Reinumae, 85min), M Reim, K Viikmae — A Oper, J Lindpere (sub: T Kink, 75)
SCOTLAND P Gallacher (Dundee United) — D McNamee (Livingston), G Caldwell (Hibernian), M Mackay (Norwich City), S Pressley (Heart of Midlothian; sub: A Webster, Heart of Midlothian, ht), R Hughes (Portsmouth), D Fletcher (Manchester United), G Holt (Norwich City), K Miller (Wolverhampton Wanderers; sub: S Crawford, Dunfermline Athletic, 79), J McFadden (Everton; sub: B Kerr, Newcastle United, 89), N Quashie (Portsmouth) *Substitutes not used* C Gordon (Heart of Midlothian), S Caldwell (Newcastle United), J McAllister (Livingston), L McCulloch (Wigan Athletic), S Shearer (Coventry City)
Scorer McFadden 76
Referee T Poulsen (Denmark)

Sunday May 30
Friendly
TRINIDAD AND TOBAGO (h)
Easter Road
Won 4-1   HT 4-0   Att 16,187
SCOTLAND C Gordon (Heart of Midlothian) — J McNamara (Celtic), S Pressley (Heart of Midlothian), M Mackay (Norwich City; sub: D McNamee, Livingston, 85), J McAllister (Livingston) — N Quashie (Portsmouth; sub: R Hughes, Portsmouth, 72), G Caldwell (Hibernian; sub: S Caldwell, Newcastle United, 80), D Fletcher (Manchester United), G Holt (Norwich City; sub: B Kerr, Newcastle United, 54) — S Crawford (Dunfermline Athletic; sub: K Miller, Wolverhampton Wanderers, 69), J McFadden (Everton; sub: A Webster, Heart of Midlothian, 85) *Substitutes not used* P Gallacher (Dundee United), L McCulloch (Wigan Athletic), S Shearer (Coventry City)
Scorers Fletcher 6, Holt 14, G Caldwell 23, Quashie 34
TRINIDAD AND TOBAGO Ince — Sancho, Cox, Andrews — Edwards (sub: Theobald, 90), Eve (sub: Jemmot, 82), Jones, Dwarika (sub: Nixon, 75), Mason — John, Glen (sub: Boucaud, 28) *Substitutes not used* Rojas, King, Baptiste, Williams
Scorer John 55
Referee P Vink (the Netherlands)

THE GAMES

Wednesday August 20 2003
European Championship qualifier
SERBIA AND MONTENEGRO (a)
Belgrade
Lost 0-1   HT 0-0   Att 30,000
SERBIA AND MONTENEGRO D Jevric — G Gavrancic, M Krstajic, D Stefanovic — M Cirkovic, D Mladenovic, D Stankovic (sub: P Djordjevic, 81min), I Dragutinovic — Z Vukic (sub: S Ilic, 68) — D Kovacevic, M Kezman (sub: S Milosevic, 71) *Substitutes not used* N Djordjevic, G Bunjevcevic, B Boskovic, D Zilic
Scorer **Mladenovic 73**
Booked **Vukic, Stankovic, Jevric, Milosevic**
WALES P Jones (Southampton) — M Delaney (Aston Villa), R Page (Sheffield United), D Gabbidon (Cardiff City), G Speed (Newcastle United) — S Davies (Tottenham Hotspur), M Pembridge (Everton), R Savage (Birmingham City) — C Bellamy (Newcastle United), R Giggs (Manchester United) — N Blake (Wolverhampton Wanderers; sub: R Earnshaw, Cardiff City, 78) *Substitutes not used* R Weston (Cardiff City), A Williams (Reading), A Johnson (West Bromwich Albion), J Koumas (West Bromwich Albion), N Roberts (Wigan Athletic), M Crossley (Fulham)
Booked **Delaney**
Referee **A Frisk** (Sweden)

Saturday September 6
European Championship qualifier
ITALY (a)
Milan
Lost 0-4   HT 0-0   Att 70,000
ITALY G Buffon — C Panucci (sub: M Oddo, 58min), A Nesta, F Cannavaro, G Zambrotta — M Camoranesi, S Perrotta (sub: S Fiore, 86), C Zanetti, A Del Piero — C Vieri, F Inzaghi (sub: G Gattuso, 74) *Substitutes not used* N Legrottaglie, B Corradi, M Delvecchio, F Toldo
Scorers **Inzaghi 59, 62, 70, Del Piero 76 (pen)**
Booked **Buffon**
WALES P Jones (Southampton) — S Davies (Tottenham Hotspur), M Delaney (Aston Villa), R Page (Sheffield United), G Speed (Newcastle United) — J Koumas (West Bromwich Albion; sub: R Earnshaw, Cardiff City, 71), M Pembridge (Fulham; sub: A Johnson, West Bromwich Albion, 79), R Savage (Birmingham City) — C Bellamy (Newcastle United), R Giggs (Manchester United) — J Hartson (Celtic; sub: N Blake, Wolverhampton Wanderers, 82) *Substitutes not used* A Williams (Reading), D Barnard (Grimsby Town), J Oster (Sunderland), M Crossley (Fulham)
Booked **Savage, Bellamy, Delaney**
Referee **M Merk** (Germany)

Wednesday September 10
European Championship qualifier
FINLAND (h)
Millennium Stadium
Drew 1-1   HT 1-0   Att 73,441
WALES P Jones (Southampton) — R Weston (Cardiff City; sub: A Johnson, West Bromwich Albion, 73min), A Melville (Fulham), R Page (Sheffield United), G Speed (Newcastle United) — S Davies (Tottenham Hotspur), M Pembridge (Fulham), J Koumas (West Bromwich Albion) — R Earnshaw (Cardiff City), R Giggs (Manchester United) — J Hartson (Celtic; sub: N Blake, Wolverhampton Wanderers, 82) *Substitutes not used* A Williams (Reading), D Barnard (Grimsby Town), C Robinson (Portsmouth), J Oster (Sunderland), M Crossley (Fulham)
Scorer **Davies 3**
Booked **Koumas, Melville** Sent off **Koumas (64)**
FINLAND A Niemi — P Pasanen (sub: P Kopteff, 82), H Tihinen, S Hyypia, J Saarinen (sub: J Reini, ht) — A Riihilahti, T Tainio — M Nurmela, J Kolkka, M Vayrynen (sub: S Kuqi, 57) — M Forssell *Substitutes not used* T Kuivasto, S Valakari, J Johansson, J Jaaskelainen
Scorer **Forssell 80**
Booked **Pasanen**
Referee **A Dauden Ibanez** (Spain)

IN THE LINE OF NATIONAL DUTY, Mark Hughes spent two weeks this summer at the European Championship finals, but, by the time the competition arrived, there was nowhere on earth he would have less liked to be. Having dreamt of travelling to Portugal as the manager of a team playing in their first leading tournament for 46 years, he ended up taking the trip alone, observing matches in a scouting capacity and unable to shrug off the bitter feeling that he should have been an active participant rather than an envious onlooker.

It was not until May 12, six months after an acrimonious play-off defeat by Russia, that Hughes wearily waved the white flag. It was then that the Court of Arbitration for Sport in Switzerland rejected an appeal by the Football Association of Wales to have the Russians expelled from the competition on the basis that one of their players, Egor Titov, had tested positive for a banned substance, bromantan, after the play-off first leg. "Cheats have been allowed to prosper," Hughes said through gritted teeth after hearing the court's verdict.

The pain of failure is nothing new for Wales, but, for Hughes, this was the bitterest pill. It was death by a thousand cuts, relatively few of them self-inflicted. Even when they led their qualifying group after winning their first four matches, Wales could feel the fates conspiring against them. Hughes could accept the injuries and suspensions that deprived him of key players at vital times, but harder to swallow were the succession of non-football issues that came to subvert their campaign.

Hughes was repeatedly told that it was "typical Welsh bad luck", but this was no ordinary qualifying campaign, a sob story of myopic referees and tragicomic penalty misses. This time, alternative scapegoats were found, most notably Titov but also Fifa, the sport's world governing body, which was unsympathetic on a variety of issues arising from the postponement of a qualifying match against Serbia and Montenegro at five days' notice.

The match in Belgrade was to be the turning point in Wales' hitherto perfect qualifying campaign. Initially scheduled for March 2003, when their confidence was at an all-time high, it was postponed for security reasons and rearranged for August 20, four days into the new domestic season. Without two of their most influential players, Andy Melville and John Hartson, Wales toiled admirably, but Dragan Mladenovic's late goal inflicted the first setback of their campaign, one from which they never recovered.

Seventeen days later, Hughes and his players headed to Italy for their most critical game of the campaign without either of their first-choice central defenders, Melville and Danny Gabbidon, and

Delaney, right, and Sennikov tangle as Russia triumph in Cardiff

with doubts creeping into their heads for the first time. Predictably, in the hostile atmosphere of the San Siro, they were overrun by an Italy team thirsty for revenge.

From that moment on, Wales were concerned only with claiming the point they needed to secure second place, having weeks earlier been in a commanding position to win the group. In the event, with Italy drawing in Belgrade, victories in their last two games, both at home, would have seen Wales finish top, but they did not get close. A tense 1-1 draw with Finland ensured a place in the play-offs before a largely academic 3-2 home defeat by Serbia and Montenegro.

The play-off draw sent Wales on a daunting mission to Moscow in mid-November, but, belatedly rediscovering the qualities that had served them so well in their first four qualifying matches, they returned with what seemed a highly creditable 0-0 draw. As so often, though, their nerve deserted them on their day of reckoning. Unsure whether to stick or twist in the second leg, they ended up doing neither, their fate sealed by an early goal from Vadim Evseev. At the final whistle, the strains of U2's *I Still Haven't Found What I'm Looking For* filled the stadium.

Although news of Titov's positive test gave them renewed hope of reaching Portugal, it was with an eye on the World Cup that Hughes arranged a series of friendlies in the spring, including a 4-0 victory over Scotland, with Robert Earnshaw scoring a hat-trick. Paul Parry, his Cardiff City team-mate, headed the winning goal against Canada in Wrexham. That should have sent Hughes to Portugal in better spirits, but the memories of Russia — of Titov, Evseev and bromantan — were still too fresh. They still haven't found what they're looking for, but, with Hughes having vowed to fight on, they will not give up.

Saturday October 11
European Championship qualifier
SERBIA AND MONTENEGRO (h)
Millennium Stadium
Lost 2-3 HT **1-1** Att **72,414**
WALES P Jones (Southampton) — **R Weston** (Cardiff City; sub: **R Edwards**, Aston Villa, 73min), **M Delaney** (Aston Villa), **D Gabbidon** (Cardiff City), **D Barnard** (Grimsby Town) — **C Robinson** (Portsmouth; sub: **J Oster**, Sunderland, 88), **G Speed** (Newcastle United) — **R Earnshaw** (Cardiff City), **R Giggs** (Manchester United), **C Bellamy** (Newcastle United) — **J Hartson** (Celtic; sub: **N Blake**, Wolverhampton Wanderers, 86) *Substitutes not used* **A Melville** (Fulham), **A Williams** (Reading), **M Pembridge** (Fulham), **M Crossley** (Fulham)
Scorers **Hartson 25, Earnshaw 90**
Booked **Bellamy**

SERBIA AND MONTENEGRO D Jevric — G Gavrancic, G Bunjevcevic, N Djordjevic — M Cirkovic (sub: M Brnovic, 75), D Mladenovic, B Boskovic, D Sarac — Z Vukic — D Kovacevic (sub: D Ljuboja, 79), M Kezman (sub: S Milosevic, 60) F Stuchlik *Substitutes not used* M Dudic, B Vaskovic, S Markovic, D Zilic
Scorers **Vukic 10, Milosevic 81, Ljuboja 86**
Booked **Bunjevcevic, Gavrancic, Kezman, Djordjevic, Kovacevic**

Referee **F Stuchlik** (Austria)

GROUP NINE
FINAL TABLE

	P	W	D	L	F	A	Pts
Italy	8	5	2	1	17	4	17
Wales	8	4	1	3	13	10	13
Serbia & M	8	3	3	2	11	11	12
Finland	8	3	1	4	9	10	10
Azerbaijan	8	1	1	6	5	20	4

Saturday November 15
European Championship qualifying play-off, first leg
RUSSIA (a)
Moscow
Drew 0-0 HT **0-0** Att **29,000**
RUSSIA S Ovchinnikov — V Evseev, S Ignashevitch, V Onopko, D Sennikov — A Smertin (sub: R Gusev, 59min), A Mostovoi, D Alenichev — D Loskov — D Sytchev (sub: M Izmailov, ht), D Bulykin *Substitutes not used* A Solomatin, E Aldonin, E Titov, A Kerzhakov, V Malafeev
Booked **Ovchinnikov, Mostovoi**

WALES P Jones (Southampton) — **M Delaney** (Aston Villa), **A Melville** (Fulham), **D Gabbidon** (Cardiff City), **D Barnard** (Grimsby Town) — **G Speed** (Newcastle United) — **J Koumas** (West Bromwich Albion), **A Johnson** (West Bromwich Albion), **R Savage** (Birmingham City), **R Giggs** (Manchester United) — **J Hartson** (sub: **N Blake**, Wolverhampton Wanderers, 80) *Substitutes not used* **K Symons** (Crystal Palace), **R Edwards** (Aston Villa), **C Robinson** (Portsmouth), **J Oster** (Sunderland), **R Earnshaw** (Cardiff City), **M Crossley** (Fulham)
Booked **Delaney, Koumas, Speed**
Referee **L Cortez Batista** (Portugal)

Wednesday November 19
European Championship qualifying play-off, second leg
RUSSIA (h)
Millennium Stadium
Lost 0-1   HT 0-1   Att 73,062
Russia won 1-0 on aggregate
WALES P Jones (Southampton) — **M Delaney** (Aston Villa), **A Melville** (Fulham), **D Gabbidon** (Cardiff City), **D Barnard** (Grimsby Town) — **G Speed** (Newcastle United) — **J Koumas** (West Bromwich Albion; sub: **N Blake**, Wolverhampton Wanderers, 74min), **A Johnson** (West Bromwich Albion; sub: **R Earnshaw**, Cardiff City, 58), **R Savage** (Birmingham City), **R Giggs** (Manchester United) — **J Hartson** (Celtic) *Substitutes not used* **K Symons** (Crystal Palace), **R Edwards** (Aston Villa), **C Robinson** (Portsmouth), **J Oster** (Sunderland), **M Crossley** (Fulham)
Booked **Savage, Barnard**

RUSSIA V Malafeev — V Evseev, S Ignashevitch, V Onopko, D Sennikov — A Smertin — R Gusev, E Titov (sub: V Radimov, 59), D Alenichev, M Izmailov — D Bulykin *Substitutes not used* A Solomatin, E Aldonin, D Loskov, D Sytchev, A Kerzhakov, I Akinfeev
Scorer **Evseev 22**
Booked **Alenichev, Bulykin, Radimov**
Referee **M E Mejuto Gonzalez** (Spain)

Wednesday February 18 2004
Friendly
SCOTLAND (h)
Millennium Stadium
Won 4-0   HT 2-0   Att 47,124
WALES M Crossley (Fulham; sub: **D Ward**, Nottingham Forest, ht) — **R Edwards** (Aston Villa), **A Melville** (West Ham United; sub: **K Symons**, Crystal Palace, 87min), **R Page** (Sheffield United), **D Gabbidon** (Cardiff City) — **J Oster** (Sunderland), **R Savage** (Birmingham City; sub: **C Fletcher**, Bournemouth, 72), **G Speed** (Newcastle United; sub: **C Robinson**, Portsmouth, 72), **S Davies** (Tottenham Hotspur; sub: **P Parry**, Cardiff City, 33) — **R Earnshaw** (Cardiff City), **R Giggs** (Manchester United; sub: **G Taylor**, Nottingham Forest, ht) *Substitutes not used* **R Weston** (Cardiff City), **N Roberts** (Wigan Athletic)
Scorer **Earnshaw 1, 35, 58, Taylor 78**
Referee **M Ross** (Northern Ireland)
Scotland details on page 376

Wednesday March 31
Friendly
HUNGARY (a)
Budapest
Won 2-1   HT 1-1   Att 15,00
HUNGARY G Babos — Z Peto, P Stark, A Komlosi (sub: Z Dveri, 89min) — L Bodnar, B Molnar, K Lisztes (sub: B Toth, 52), Z Geram, Z Low (sub: B Bodor, 89) — K Kenesei (sub: I Szabics, ht), S Torghelle (sub: J Sebok, 69) *Substitutes not used* L Szucs, A Bojte
Scorer **Kenesei 9**
Booked **Lisztes, Torghelle**

WALES P Jones (Wolverhampton Wanderers; sub: **D Coyne**, Leicester City, ht) — **D Gabbidon** (Cardiff City), **R Page** (Sheffield United), **A Melville** (West Ham United), **B Thatcher** (Leicester City; sub: **R Edwards**, Aston Villa, 54) — **J Koumas** (West Bromwich Albion), **R Savage** (Birmingham City), **C Robinson** (Portsmouth; sub: **C Fletcher**, Bournemouth, 89), **D Vaughan** (Crewe Alexandra; sub: **G Roberts**, Tranmere Rovers, 64) — **R Earnshaw** (Cardiff City), **G Taylor** (Nottingham Forest) *Substitutes not used* **D Barnard** (Grimsby Town), **K Symons** (Crystal Palace), **J Collins** (Cardiff City), **N Roberts** (Wigan Athletic), **M Margetson** (Cardiff City)
Scorers **Koumas 20, Earnshaw 81**
Booked **Thatcher, Vaughan**
Referee **F Meyer** (Germany)

MATCH OF THE SEASON

Wales 4 Scotland 0
Millennium Stadium, Wednesday February 18 2004
Oliver Kay

THE SCOTLAND SQUAD HAVE SPENT the past few days canvassing against Berti Vogts's plan to introduce "foreign" players into the national team, but their case was undermined by their wretched performance in Cardiff last night and by three goals from Robert Earnshaw, Wales' Zambia-born forward. If Earnshaw's hat-trick, increasing his international strike rate to six goals in only ten appearances, gave Wales the perfect tonic after their failure in the European Championship play-offs, it also exposed the paucity of talent at Vogts's disposal.

Vogts looked aghast as he reflected on a result that gave his team another unwanted record — their heaviest defeat in 103 meetings with Wales since 1876. Scotland could certainly do with unearthing a player such as Earnshaw, who far outshone their own prodigies, Darren Fletcher and James McFadden, before Gareth Taylor scored Wales' fourth goal.

Earnshaw was acclaimed by Vogts and Mark Hughes, the Wales manager, as the difference between the teams, but he was by no means the only one. Wales, who had not won in their previous seven matches, rediscovered the purpose and swagger that took them so agonisingly close to qualification for their first leading tournament since 1958, whereas Scotland gave ammunition to those who feel they have failed to progress in two years under Vogts.

Vogts faced a hostile inquisition during the post-match press conference and, much as he spoke of his efforts to rejuvenate his squad, few of his other responses gave the impression of a man who is hopeful of taking Scotland forward. "What can I do?" he asked repeatedly before declaring that it was "not possible" for tactics to counteract the pace of Earnshaw and Ryan Giggs, who did such damage in the absence of John Hartson. For Hughes, this summer's finals in Portugal remain a remote possibility — with an appeal to Uefa on March 19 against the qualification of Russia, whose victorious team in the play-offs included Egor Titov, who tested positive for a banned substance — but, more realistically, they will be hopeful of causing England some difficulties during the forthcoming World Cup qualifying campaign.

It took only 43 seconds for Earnshaw to get off the mark, beating a leaden-footed defence to a pass by Gary Speed before slipping the ball past Rab Douglas, who was to have a wretched evening in the Scotland goal. Earnshaw claimed his second goal in the 35th minute, a diving header from Giggs's cross, possibly with the benefit of a deflection off Gary Naysmith. With Paul Ritchie and Stephen Caldwell, the Scotland central defenders, playing like strangers, there was always space for Earnshaw to run into. He secured his

PLAYER OF THE SEASON
Robert Earnshaw

As a sense of woe and weariness began to descend on the Wales squad, spirits were raised by the emergence of Robert Earnshaw. He had played and scored for his country before, but it was only last season, with five goals in four starts for Wales, that the Cardiff City forward came of age. The highlight was a hat-trick against Scotland in February, which was stunning in its execution but no surprise to those who have charted his progress. No longer is he Wales' secret weapon, but Earnshaw, with his explosive pace and clinical finishing, is now ready to be a frontline player for his country.

Oliver Kay

hat-trick in the 58th minute, racing on to Robbie Savage's pass before cutting inside Ritchie and shooting past Douglas. If there was a question mark over Earnshaw's claim to his second goal, he had the backing of his manager. "He left the field with the ball under his arm and he was entitled to," Hughes said. "He is a great talent and, if he continues to listen, he can be anything he wants to be."

Earnshaw's appetite had been sated, but there was further embarrassment to follow for Scotland as Taylor, the Nottingham Forest forward, came off the bench to score his first international goal. If its conception was impressive, with the ball passed at speed through the heart of the Scotland defence, its execution again reflected badly on Douglas, who was beaten at his near post. It was that kind of an evening for Scotland, whose 5,000-strong Tartan Army headed north armed only with the meagre consolation that things, surely, can only get better.

WALES (4-4-2): M Crossley (Fulham; sub: **D Ward**, Nottingham Forest, ht) — **R Edwards** (Aston Villa), **A Melville** (West Ham United; sub: **K Symons**, Crystal Palace, 87min), **R Page** (Sheffield United), **D Gabbidon** (Cardiff City) — **J Oster** (Sunderland), **R Savage** (Birmingham City; sub: **C Fletcher**, Bournemouth, 72), **G Speed** (Newcastle United; sub: **C Robinson**, Portsmouth, 72), **S Davies** (Tottenham Hotspur; sub: **P Parry**, Cardiff City, 33) — **R Earnshaw** (Cardiff City), **R Giggs** (Manchester United; sub: **G Taylor**, Nottingham Forest, ht). *Substitutes not used:* **R Weston** (Cardiff City), **N Roberts** (Wigan Athletic).

SCOTLAND (4-1-3-2): **R Douglas** (Celtic) — **J McNamara** (Celtic), **S Caldwell** (Newcastle United), **P Ritchie** (Walsall), **G Naysmith** (Everton; sub: **G Murty**, Reading, ht) — **C Dailly** (West Ham United) — **D Fletcher** (Manchester United; sub: **A Webster**, Heart of Midlothian, 86), **C Cameron** (Wolverhampton Wanderers; sub: **P Gallagher**, Blackburn Rovers, 68), **S Pearson** (Celtic; sub: **J McFadden**, Everton, ht) — **K Miller** (Wolverhampton Wanderers), **P Dickov** (Leicester City). *Substitutes not used:* **G Caldwell** (Hibernian), **G Teale** (Wigan Athletic), **P Gallacher** (Dundee United).

Thursday May 27
Friendly
NORWAY (a)
Oslo
Drew 0-0   HT 0-0   Att 14,137
NORWAY T Myhre — C Basma, H Berg (sub: C Lundekvam, 17min), R Johnsen (sub: M Andersen, 88), J A Riise — T Helstad (sub: T A Flo, 61), M Andresen, M Hoset, M Pedersen (sub: A Bergdolmo, ht), O G Solskjaer (sub: J G Solli, 61), B Saeternes (sub: R Lange, ht) *Substitutes not used* J Larsen, J Hoiland
Booked Solskjaer

WALES D Coyne (Leicester City) — **M Delaney** (Aston Villa), **J Collins** (Cardiff City), **D Gabbidon** (Cardiff City), **B Thatcher** (Leicester City) — **J Oster** (Sunderland; sub: **D Barnard**, Grimsby Town, 90), **C Fletcher** (Bournemouth), **C Robinson** (Portsmouth; sub: **R Edwards**, Aston Villa, 75), **P Parry** (Cardiff City; sub: **G Roberts**, Tranmere Rovers, 71) — **R Earnshaw** (Cardiff City; sub: **N Roberts**, Wigan Athletic, 71), **C Bellamy** (Newcastle United; sub: **C Llewellyn**, Wrexham, 80) *Substitutes not used* **M Margetson** (Cardiff City), **A Williams** (Reading), **D Vaughan** (Crewe Alexandra), **J Koumas** (West Bromwich Albion)
Referee **M Hansson** (Sweden)

Sunday May 30
Friendly
CANADA (h)
Racecourse Ground
Won 1-0   HT 1-0   Att 10,805
WALES D Coyne (Leicester City; sub: **M Margetson**, Cardiff City, ht) — **M Delaney** (Aston Villa), **J Collins** (Cardiff City), **D Gabbidon** (Cardiff City), **B Thatcher** (Leicester City) — **J Oster** (Sunderland), **C Fletcher** (Bournemouth), **C Robinson** (Portsmouth; sub: **R Edwards**, Aston Villa, 79), **P Parry** (Cardiff City; sub: **R Earnshaw**, Cardiff City, 67) — **C Bellamy** (Newcastle United; sub: **C Llewellyn**, Wrexham, 89) *Substitutes not used* **A Williams** (Reading), **D Barnard** (Grimsby Town), **G Roberts** (Tranmere Rovers), **D Vaughan** (Crewe Alexandra), **N Roberts** (Wigan Athletic)
Scorer **Parry 21**

CANADA P Onstad — D Imhof, M Watson, J De Vos, A Jazic — I Hulme (sub: O Occean, 79), J De Guzman, A Hutchinson (sub: P Peschisolido, ht), J Brennan (sub: M Bircham, ht) — T Radzinski (sub: K McKenna, 72), D De Rosario (sub: M Klukowski, 83) *Substitute not used* L Hirschfeld
Referee **P McKeon** (Ireland)

Tuesday August 19 2003
Friendly
AUSTRALIA (h)
Lansdowne Road
Won 2-1   HT 0-0   Att 40,000
IRELAND N Colgan (Stockport County) — **S Carr** (Tottenham Hotspur; sub: **I Harte**, Leeds United, 57min), **G Breen** (Sunderland; sub: **A O'Brien**, Newcastle United, ht), **K Cunningham** (Birmingham City; sub: **R Dunne**, Manchester City, 84), **J O'Shea** (Manchester United) — **S Finnan** (Liverpool; sub: **K Kilbane**, Sunderland, 66), **M Kinsella** (Aston Villa), **M Holland** (Charlton Athletic; sub: **C Healy**, Sunderland, 19), **D Duff** (Chelsea; sub: **A Quinn**, Sheffield Wednesday, 80) — **G Doherty** (Tottenham Hotspur; sub: **C Morrison**, Birmingham City, 57), **R Keane** (Tottenham Hotspur; sub: **D Connolly**, West Ham United, ht) *Substitutes not used* **J Murphy** (West Bromwich Albion), **S Given** (Newcastle United)
Scorers **O'Shea 74, Morrison 80**
AUSTRALIA M Schwarzer — L Neill, H Foxe, T Popovic — S Lazaridis, B Emerton, P Okon (sub: V Grella, 66), M Bresciano, D Tiatto (sub: A Vidmar, 69) — M Viduka (sub: J Aloisi, 78), S Chipperfield *Substitutes not used* K Muscat, J Skoko, Z Kalac, L Wilkshire
Scorer **Viduka 49**
Booked **Okon**
Referee **K Vidlak** (Czech Republic)

Saturday September 6
European Championship qualifier
RUSSIA (h)
Lansdowne Road
Drew 1-1   HT 1-1   Att 36,000
IRELAND S Given (Newcastle United) — **S Carr** (Tottenham Hotspur), **G Breen** (Sunderland), **K Cunningham** (Birmingham City), **J O'Shea** (Manchester United; sub: **I Harte**, Leeds United, 25min) — **L Carsley** (Everton; sub: **S Reid**, Blackburn Rovers, ht), **M Holland** (Charlton Athletic), **C Healy** (Sunderland), **K Kilbane** (Everton) — **D Duff** (Chelsea) — **C Morrison** (Birmingham City; sub: **G Doherty**, Tottenham Hotspur, 73) *Substitutes not used* **S Finnan** (Liverpool), **M Kinsella** (Aston Villa), **N Colgan** (Stockport County), **D Connolly** (West Ham United)
Scorer **Duff 35**
Booked **Cunningham, Kilbane**
RUSSIA S Ovchinnikov — V Evseev, S Ignashevitch, V Onopko, D Sennikov — R Gusev, V Esipov (sub: A Kerzhakov, 34), A Smertin, A Mostovoi, D Alenichev (sub: E Aldonin, 39) — D Bulykin *Substitutes not used* V Malafeev, G Nizhegorodov, V Radimov, D Loskov, D Sychev
Scorer **Ignashevitch 42**
Booked **Gusev, Ignashevitch, Evseev, Mostovoi**
Referee **L Michel** (Slovakia)

Tuesday September 9
Friendly
TURKEY (h)
Lansdowne Road
Drew 2-2   HT 1-0   Att 27,200
IRELAND N Colgan (Stockport County; sub: **J Murphy**, West Bromwich Albion, 72min) — **S Finnan** (Liverpool), **G Breen** (Sunderland; sub: **C Morrison**, Birmingham City, 86), **A O'Brien** (Newcastle United; sub: **R Dunne**, Manchester City, 72), **I Harte** (Leeds United; sub: **S Carr**, Tottenham Hotspur, 90) — **M Kinsella** (Aston Villa), **C Healy** (Sunderland; sub: **S McPhail**, Nottingham Forest, 86), **K Kilbane** (Everton) — **D Duff** (Chelsea; sub: **S Reid**, Blackburn Rovers, ht) — **D Connolly** (West Ham United), **G Doherty** (Tottenham Hotspur) *Substitutes not used:* **M Holland** (Charlton Athletic), **A Quinn** (Sheffield Wednesday), **G Crowe** (Bohemians)
Scorers **Connolly 35, Dunne 90**
TURKEY Rustu (sub: Omer, 61; sub: Zafer, 86) — Fatih, Bulent (sub: Umit, 86), Alpay (sub: Okan Buruk, ht), Ergun — Tayfun (sub: Deniz, ht), Tugay (sub: Ahmet, 72), Emre (sub: Gokdeniz, 61), Hasan Sas (sub: Ibrahim, ht) — Tuncay (sub: Okan Yilmaz, 72), Hakan Sukur (sub: Tumer, 86)
Scorers **Hakan Suker 51, Okan Yilmaz 86**
Booked **Alpay, Emre**
Referee **J Wegereef** (Netherlands)

IT WAS NOT LONG BEFORE the chants of "Kean-o" rang loud around Lansdowne Road. As Roy Maurice Keane warmed up for the friendly against Romania on May 27, the fans poured forth their relief and appreciation. Two years after he had walked away from international football, the son of Cork was back and ready for action again. He nodded to acknowledge the welcome. It felt good.

In the intervening period, after Keane had strode off into self-imposed exile on the eve of the 2002 World Cup finals, forests of Irish newsprint had been devoted to championing the cause of his return. Many trees had perished, too, to satisfy the lust of the anti-Keane brigade, still miffed by his behaviour on the remote Pacific island of Saipan. "Stay away, Roy. We don't need you" was the tone of their protests. But Ireland did. "I'm glad that one of the greatest players ever to play for Ireland has chosen this path," Brian Kerr, the manager, said. "It cannot have been an easy decision for him, but his desire to represent his country is immense. He will bring quality and experience to a potentially excellent squad of players whose sole focus is the 2006 World Cup qualifying matches."

Keane won his 60th cap against Romania, the startling 5-1 conquerors of Germany in Bucharest the previous month, and played with typical aplomb, pushing and prodding his young team-mates to a notable 1-0 victory. His reintegration was almost complete, the circus could now leave town. The spat with Mick McCarthy, Kerr's predecessor, in Saipan could also be consigned to history. "I felt I was fighting a losing battle," Keane said, "and it was right for me not to be there because it was a waste of time. I was frustrated with what was going on around me and felt that people didn't have the same targets as me.

"I was never looking for perfection with the Irish team, but I was always looking for progress. Things had to change and that has happened in the last year or two. That is very important. Everybody is entitled to their opinions, but it wasn't ever about popularity. I was just trying to do what I felt was right. I now feel it's right to come back and I'm looking forward to the challenge in the World Cup qualifiers."

Keane's body may be ailing, with hip and hamstring injuries the worst of his worries, but his mind is still sharp. He no longer rampages like a bull — and Kenny Cunningham has kept the captaincy — but he should provide a guiding hand, a calming or inspiring influence, in times of need.

Keane's absence was felt particularly badly in the closing games of the 2004 European Championship qualifying campaign, against Russia and Switzerland. Kerr had revived hopes of reaching the

Roy Keane leads from the front at he returns to the international fold

finals, Ireland rising impressively from the ashes left behind by McCarthy, but a tame 1-1 draw against Russia in Dublin left doubts.

They were confirmed in Basle in October in a dreadful 2-0 defeat against Switzerland, Kerr's first loss in ten matches in charge. Subsequently, the indomitable Irish spirit resurfaced. In eight friendly matches, including seven against countries rated in the top 50 in the world, Kerr's evolving side lost only once. That it was against Nigeria in London, two days after their exertions against Romania and with a youthful and much-depleted line-up, applies perspective. More significant was the eye-catching 0-0 draw against Brazil, the world champions, complete with Ronaldo, Ronaldinho et al, in February and the 2-1 victory against the Czech Republic, who boasted an undefeated record of 20 matches, the next month.

Ireland ended their 2003-04 campaign with four matches in ten days, taking in fixtures against Romania, then Nigeria and Jamaica in the Unity Cup at The Valley, then a trip to play Holland. A 1-0 win against the Dutch courtesy of Robbie Keane's superb solo effort — his 20th international goal, one short of Niall Quinn's Ireland record — highlighted their progress.

Kerr was without, among others, Roy Keane, Damien Duff, Stephen Carr and Kevin Kilbane in the Amsterdam ArenA, yet the likes of Alan Maybury, Graham Barrett and Alan Quinn proved more than capable deputies against a full-strength Holland side bound for Portugal. With Clive Clarke, Martin Rowlands, Michael Doyle and Aiden McGeady now blooded and hovering on the fringes, Ireland's future appears bright. It is what Kerr has worked towards since his appointment in January 2003. And it is what has refired the patriotism within Roy Keane, the desire to deal with "unfinished business". The dark days of Saipan are no more.

Saturday October 11
European Championship qualifier
SWITZERLAND (a)
Berne
Lost 0-2   HT 0-1   Att 30,006
SWITZERLAND J Stiel — B Haas, Murat Yakin, P Muller, C Spycher — B Huggel, J Vogel, R Wicky — Hakan Yakin (sub: F Celestini, 56min) — A Frei (sub: S Henchoz, 90), S Chapuisat (sub: M Streller, 69) *Substitutes not used* P Zuberbuhler, M Zwyssig, B Berner, M Rama
Scorers **Hakan Yakin 6, Frei 60**
Booked **Haas, Wicky**
IRELAND S Given (Newcastle United) — **S Carr** (Tottenham Hotspur), **G Breen** (Sunderland), **J O'Shea** (Manchester United), **I Harte** (Leeds United) — **D Duff** (Chelsea), **M Holland** (sub: M Kinsella, 74), **C Healy** (Sunderland), **K Kilbane** (Everton; sub: S Finnan, Liverpool, 74) — **R Keane** (Tottenham Hotspur), **D Connolly** (West Ham United; sub: C Morrison, Birmingham City, 58) *Substitutes not used* A O'Brien (Newcastle United), L Carsley (Everton), N Colgan (Stockport County), G Doherty (Tottenham Hotspur)
Booked **Carr, Kinsella, Harte**
Referee **A Frisk** (Sweden)

GROUP TEN
FINAL TABLE

	P	W	D	L	F	A	Pts
Switzerland	8	4	3	1	15	11	15
Russia	8	4	2	2	19	12	14
Ireland	8	3	2	3	10	11	11
Albania	8	3	2	4	11	15	8
Georgia	8	2	1	5	8	14	7

Tuesday November 18
Friendly
CANADA (h)
Lansdowne Road
Won 3-0   HT 1-0   Att 30,000
IRELAND S Given (Newcastle United; sub: N Colgan, Stockport County, 82min) — **S Carr** (Tottenham Hotspur; sub: I Harte, Leeds United, ht), K Cunningham (Birmingham City), **R Dunne** (Manchester City), **J O'Shea** (Manchester United; sub: J Thompson, Nottingham Forest, 87) — **S Reid** (Blackburn Rovers; sub: R Delap, Southampton, 61), **G Kavanagh** (Cardiff City; sub: M Holland, Charlton Athletic, 11), **A Reid** (Nottingham Forest; sub: S McPhail, Nottingham Forest, 73), **D Duff** (Chelsea; sub: K Kilbane, Everton, 87) — **G Doherty** (Tottenham Hotspur; sub: C Morrison, Birmingham City, ht), **R Keane** (Tottenham Hotspur) *Substitute not used* J Murphy (West Bromwich Albion)
Scorers **Duff 23, Keane 60, 84**
CANADA L Hirschfeld — P Stalteri, J De Vos (sub: M Rogers, 82), K McKenna, A Jazic — J Bent, M Bircham (sub: M Nash, 79), D Imhof, R Hastings (sub: P Fenwick, 87) — P Peschisolido (sub: P Bernier, 75), T Radzinski *Substitutes not used:* N Dasovic, K Stamatopoulos
Booked **Bircham**
Referee **M Whitby** (Wales)

Wednesday February 18 2004
Friendly
BRAZIL (h)
Lansdowne Road
Drew 0-0   HT 0-0   Att 44,000
IRELAND S Given (Newcastle United) — **S Carr** (Tottenham Hotspur), **A O'Brien** (Newcastle United), **K Cunningham** (Birmingham City), **J O'Shea** (Manchester United) — **M Holland** (Charlton Athletic), **G Kavanagh** (Cardiff City), **K Kilbane** (Everton), **A Reid** (Nottingham Forest; sub: J McAteer, Sunderland, 64min) — **C Morrison** (Birmingham City), **R Keane** (Tottenham Hotspur) *Substitutes not used* S Finnan (Liverpool), G Doherty (Tottenham Hotspur), I Harte (Leeds United), P Kenny (Sheffield United), L Carsley (Everton), R Delap (Southampton), D Connolly (West Ham United), A Lee (Cardiff City), G Stack (Arsenal)
Booked **Kavanagh**
BRAZIL Dida — Cafu, Lucio, Roque Junior, Roberto Carlos — Kleberson (sub: Julio Baptista, ht), Gilberto Silva (sub: Edmilson, 14) — Ronaldinho, Kaka', Ze Roberto — Ronaldo *Substitutes not used* Marcos, Belletti, Juan, Junior, Fabio Rochemback, Juninho, Luis Fabiano, Adriano
Booked **Cafu, Roque Junior**
Referee **A Frisk** (Sweden)

Friendly
CZECH REPUBLIC (h)
Lansdowne Road
Won 2-1   HT 0-0   Att 42,000
IRELAND S Given (Newcastle United; sub: **P Kenny**, Sheffield United, 82min) — **A Maybury** (Heart of Midlothian), **G Doherty** (Tottenham Hotspur; sub: **L Miller**, Celtic, 70), **K Cunningham** (Birmingham City), **I Harte** (Leeds United) — **A Reid** (Nottingham Forest; sub: **R Delap**, Southampton, 66), **M Holland** (Charlton Athletic), **K Kilbane** (Everton), **D Duff** (Chelsea; sub: **M Kinsella**, West Bromwich Albion, 76) — **R Keane** (Tottenham Hotspur), **C Morrison** (Birmingham City; sub: **A Lee**, Cardiff City, 76) *Substitutes not used* **J Thompson** (Nottingham Forest), **S Kelly** (Tottenham Hotspur), **L Carsley** (Everton), **J Murphy** (West Bromwich Albion)
Scorers **Harte** 52, **Keane** 90
Booked **Kilbane**
CZECH REPUBLIC P Cech (sub: M Vaniak, ht) — M Jiranek (sub: J Plasil, 69), R Bolf (sub: D Rozehnal, 58), T Ujfalusi, M Jankulovski — L Sionko (sub: J Stajner, ht), T Galasek, R Tyce — P Nedved (sub: M Heinz, ht) — M Baros (sub: P Vorisek, 84), J Koller (sub: V Lokvenc, ht) *Substitutes not used* A Kinsky, Z Grygera
Scorer **Baros** 81
Booked **Sionko**
Referee E K Fisker (Denmark)

Wednesday April 28
Friendly
POLAND (a)
Bydgoszcz
Drew 0-0   HT 0-0   Att 18,000
POLAND J Dudek (sub: A Boruc, 58min) — M Zewlakow (sub: P Kaczorowski, 83), T Klos (sub: B Bosacki, 80), A Glowacki (sub: T Hajto, ht), T Rzasa — M Lewandowski — M Zurawski, M Szymkowiak (sub: A Radomski, 85), S Mila (sub: E Smolarek, 65), J Krzynowek (sub: K Kosowski, ht) — E Olisadebe (sub: A Niedzielan, ht) *Substitutes not used* D Gorawski, G Rasiak
IRELAND S Given (Newcastle United; sub: **N Colgan**, Hibernian, 70) — **J O'Shea** (Manchester United), **G Doherty** (Tottenham Hotspur; sub: **A O'Brien**, Newcastle United, 80), **K Cunningham** (Birmingham City), **I Harte** (Leeds United; sub: **A Maybury**, Heart of Midlothian, 63) — **S Reid** (Blackburn Rovers), **L Miller** (Celtic), **M Kinsella** (West Bromwich Albion), **A Reid** (Nottingham Forest; sub: **J Douglas**, Blackburn Rovers, 80) — **A Lee** (Cardiff City; sub: **G Barrett**, Coventry City, 63), **C Morrison** (Birmingham City; sub: **J Byrne**, Shelbourne, 89) *Substitutes not used:* **M Doyle** (Coventry City), **A Quinn** (Sheffield Wednesday)
Booked **Maybury, Barrett**
Referee S Shebek (Ukraine)

Thursday May 27
Friendly
ROMANIA (h)
Lansdowne Road
Won 1-0   HT 0-0   Att 42,356
IRELAND S Given (Newcastle United; sub: **S Finnan** (Liverpool), **A O'Brien** (Newcastle United), **K Cunningham** (Birmingham City), **A Maybury** (Heart of Midlothian) — **L Miller** (Celtic), **Roy Keane** (Manchester United), **M Holland** (Charlton Athletic), **A Reid** (Nottingham Forest; sub: **M Rowlands**, Queens Park Rangers, 78min) — **C Morrison** (Birmingham City), **Robbie Keane** (Tottenham Hotspur) *Substitutes not used* **G Doherty** (Tottenham Hotspur), **C Clarke** (Stoke City), **M Kinsella** (West Bromwich Albion), **J Douglas** (Blackburn Rovers), **N Colgan** (Hibernian), **S McPhail** (Leeds United), **G Barrett** (Coventry City), **A Lee** (Cardiff City), **M Doyle** (Coventry City), **P Kenny** (Sheffield United), **A Quinn** (Sheffield Wednesday), **A McGeady** (Celtic)
Scorer **Holland** 85
ROMANIA B Labont (sub: B Stelea, ht) — M Radoi (sub: M Constianin, 84), A Icensi (sub: C Barcauan, 90), S Ghianes, C Dancia (sub: M Petre, 78) — C Soava (sub: O Petre, 90), D Florentin, P Plesan (sub: M Aliuta, 61) — N Dica (sub: D Alexa, 78), D Danciulescu (sub: A Neaga, 71), I Ganea (sub: D Niculae, 88)
Referee J Jara (Czech Republic)

MATCH OF THE SEASON

Ireland 0 Brazil 0
Lansdowne Road, Wednesday February 18 2004
Russell Kempson

THAT IRELAND WILL NOT BE TAKING part in the European Championship finals in Portugal still sticks in the craw here. Not having to plan for the Algarve hurts. A goalless draw in the friendly against Brazil at Lansdowne Road last night might offer scant consolation, but it is time that the Irish stopped beating themselves up.

This was a highly creditable display against the world champions. Brazil wanted to win and took the match seriously. Cafu and Roque Junior were booked, illustrating how committed they were to the cause, and Roberto Carlos became an increasingly frustrated figure. How often — for club or country — is the Real Madrid left back seen throwing the ball to the ground in a temper tantrum?

Carlos Alberto Parreira, the coach, has a World Cup qualifying programme to think of and when Brazil resume their campaign against Paraguay, the South America group leaders, at the end of next month, he wants them finely honed. It is why he fielded eight of the stars who started in the World Cup final against Germany in 2002; it is why he avoided a mass of substitutions.

Brian Kerr, the Ireland manager, took a similar stance, using only one replacement, and it made for as competitive a friendly as there can have been. Ireland disrupted the smooth-flowing style of the Brazilians from the kick-off and if the tackle by Graham Kavanagh on Gilberto Silva in the fifth minute bordered on the dangerous, it was more through overenthusiasm than any malicious intent.

The Arsenal midfield player left the pitch in the fourteenth minute and is now likely to miss Saturday's match against Chelsea at Stamford Bridge in the Barclaycard Premiership because of the injury to his right ankle. However, he might be fit for the trip to Celta Vigo in the last 16 of the European Cup on Tuesday. "I think it felt worse than it actually was," Gilberto said. "It felt a little better once I'd got off the pitch and I think it's OK."

Parreira apportioned no blame to Kavanagh. "I don't think it was intentional," he said. "It was not a dirty game, Ireland were just strong and tough, as we knew they would be. For a 0-0 game, it was very exciting. We did not get much space and after Gilberto left it took us a long time to settle."

Kerr has a series of friendlies, continuing with the visit of the Czech Republic to Dublin next month, to hone his side for the World Cup qualifiers against Cyprus and Switzerland in September. They then face France, the second-ranked side in the world, in October, so to have held the first-ranked side to a 0-0 draw has to be a boost for morale.

"Parreira said that Brazil don't do friendlies and we simply agreed

PLAYER OF THE SEASON
John O'Shea

A calm, self-assured defender, John O'Shea has risen through the youth ranks for club and country to become one of the first names that Sir Alex Ferguson and Brian Kerr write down on their teamsheets. Though used at left back by both Manchester United and Ireland, O'Shea would prefer to play in central defence, a position that he should grow into. A member of the Ireland under-16 side that won the European Championship in 1998, he was given his senior debut by Mick McCarthy against Croatia in August 2001 and has played, when available, in every game since Kerr took over in January 2003. Was an influential figure in the return of Roy Keane from international retirement.

Russell Kempson

with them," Kerr said. "We had to get in among them and scrap for everything and that's what we did. Brazil are a class act, make no mistake about that, but we gave a good disciplined performance and I'm proud of them."

All the *galacticos* were there — Ronaldo, Ronaldinho, Roberto Carlos — but they played second fiddle to the tigerish Irish for much of the first half. Clinton Morrison gave his best display in a green shirt, giving the much heralded Lucio a torrid time, while Andy O'Brien made the most of a rare start.

Robbie Keane was guilty of a glaring miss in the 54th minute. How he headed over from Morrison's cross will haunt him for some time to come. Still, O'Brien can tell the lads back at Newcastle United how he snuffed out Ronaldo and the memories of missing out on the Euro 2004 finals will fade a little bit more. Nil-nil against the world champions is not to be sneezed at.

IRELAND (4-4-2): **S Given** (Newcastle United) — **S Carr** (Tottenham Hotspur), **A O'Brien** (Newcastle United), **K Cunningham** (Birmingham City), **J O'Shea** (Manchester United) — **M Holland** (Charlton Athletic), **G Kavanagh** (Cardiff City), **K Kilbane** (Everton), **A Reid** (Nottingham Forest; sub: **J McAteer**, Sunderland, 64min) — **C Morrison** (Birmingham City), **R Keane** (Tottenham Hotspur). Substitutes not used: **S Finnan** (Liverpool), **G Doherty** (Tottenham Hotspur), **I Harte** (Leeds United), **P Kenny** (Sheffield United), **L Carsley** (Everton), **R Delap** (Southampton), **D Connolly** (West Ham United), **A Lee** (Cardiff City), **G Stack** (Arsenal). Booked: Kavanagh.
BRAZIL (4-2-3-1): **Dida** (AC Milan) — **Cafu** (AC Milan), **Lucio** (Bayer Leverkusen), **Roque Junior** (Siena), **Roberto Carlos** (Real Madrid) — **Kleberson** (Manchester United; sub: **Julio Baptista**, Seville, ht), **Gilberto Silva** (Arsenal; sub: **Edmilson**, Lyons, 14) — **Ronaldinho** (Barcelona), **Kaka'** (AC Milan), **Ze Roberto** (Bayern Munich) — **Ronaldo** (Real Madrid). Substitutes not used: **Marcos** (Palmeiras), **Belletti** (Villarreal), **Juan** (Bayer Leverkusen), **Junior** (Siena), **Fabio Rochemback** (Sporting Lisbon), **Juninho** (Middlesbrough), **Luis Fabiano** (Sao Paulo), **Adriano** (Inter Milan). Booked: Cafu, Roque Junior.

Saturday May 29
Unity Cup
NIGERIA
The Valley
Lost 0-3   HT 0-1   Att **7,438**
IRELAND N Colgan (Hibernian) — **S Finnan** (Liverpool), **G Doherty** (Tottenham Hotspur), **K Cunningham** (Birmingham City), **A Maybury** (Heart of Midlothian; sub: **C Clarke**, Stoke City, ht) — **L Miller** (Celtic, sub: **M Rowlands**, Queens Park Rangers, ht), **M Kinsella** (West Bromwich Albion), **M Holland** (Charlton Athletic; sub: **J Douglas**, Coventry City, 66), **S McPhail** (Leeds United) — **R Keane** (Tottenham Hotspur; sub: **G Barrett**, Coventry City, 83), **A Lee** (Cardiff City) *Substitutes not used* **A Quinn** (Sheffield Wednesday), **A O'Brien** (Newcastle United), **P Kenny** (Sheffield United), **J Thompson** (Nottingham Forest), **A Reid** (Nottingham Forest), **S Given** (Newcastle United), **C Morrison** (Birmingham City), **M Doyle** (Coventry City), **A McGeady** (Celtic)
NIGERIA S Rotimi — G Abbey (sub: Y Adamu, 90), S Olajengbesi, J Enakhire, G Lawal — J Utaka, S Olofinjana (sub: P Obiefule, 86), C Obodo, I Ekwueme — O Martins (sub: I Showunmi, 84), B Ogbeche (sub: R Baita, 72)
Scorers Ogbeche 36, 70, Martins 51
Referee A D'Urso (England)

Wednesday June 2
Unity Cup
JAMAICA
The Valley
Won 1-0   HT 1-0   Att **6,155**
IRELAND P Kenny (Sheffield United) — **A Maybury** (Heart of Midlothian), **G Doherty** (Tottenham Hotspur), **A O'Brien** (Newcastle United), **J O'Shea** (Manchester United; sub: **C Clarke**, Stoke City, ht) — **G Barrett** (Coventry City), **M Kinsella** (West Bromwich Albion; sub: **M Holland**, 83), **A Reid** (Nottingham Forest; sub: **M Rowlands**, Queens Park Rangers, 77) — **C Morrison** (Birmingham City), **A Lee** (Cardiff City; sub: **A McGeady**, Celtic, 83) *Substitutes not used* **N Colgan** (Hibernian), **S Finnan** (Liverpool), **J Thompson** (Nottingham Forest), **S McPhail** (Leeds United), **M Doyle** (Coventry City), **R Keane** (Tottenham Hotspur)
Scorer Barrett 26
JAMAICA D Ricketts — G Neil, D Stewart, I Goodison, G Reid — F Davis, C Chin-Sue (sub: R Langley, 66), M Hyde — D Burton (sub: N Bernard, 83), K Lisbie (sub: J Johnson, 83), M King (sub: C Dobson, 85)
Referee R Styles (England)

Saturday June 5
Friendly
HOLLAND (a)
Won 1-0   HT 1-0   Att **45,500**
HOLLAND E van der Sar — M Reiziger (sub: J Heitinga, ht), J Stam, W Bouma (sub: P van Hooijdonk, 83), G van Bronckhorst — W Sneijder (sub: C Seedorf, ht; sub: P Bosvelt, 63), P Cocu, R van der Vaart, E Davids (sub: A Robben, 63), R van Nistelrooy (sub: R Makaay, 66), P Kluivert (sub: A van der Meyde, ht)

IRELAND S Given (Newcastle United) — **S Finnan** (Liverpool), **A O'Brien** (Newcastle United), **K Cunningham** (Birmingham City), **A Maybury** (Heart of Midlothian; sub: **M Doyle**, Coventry City, 88) — **G Barrett** (Coventry City), **M Holland** (Charlton Athletic), **A Quinn** (Sheffield Wednesday), **A Reid** (Nottingham Forest; sub: **A Lee**, Cardiff City, 82), **R Keane** (Tottenham Hotspur) — **C Morrison** (Birmingham City; sub: **A Lee**, Cardiff City, 82) *Substitutes not used* **J Thompson** (Nottingham Forest), **G Doherty** (Tottenham Hotspur), **M Rowlands** (Queens Park Rangers), **N Colgan** (Hibernian), **C Clarke** (Stoke City), **S McPhail** (Leeds United), **A McGeady** (Celtic)
Scorer Keane 45
Referee M Dean (England)

INTERNATIONAL DATES

AUGUST
2004

Wednesday 18
Friendlies
England v Ukraine
Latvia v Wales
Scotland v Hungary
Ireland v Bulgaria

SEPTEMBER

Friday 3
Under-21 Championship qualifiers
Austria v England
Azerbaijan v Wales
Ireland v Cyprus

Saturday 4
World Cup qualifiers
Group 4
France v Israel
Ireland v Cyprus
Switzerland v Faeroe Isles
Group 5
Italy v Norway
Slovenia v Moldova
Group 6
Austria v England
Azerbaijan v Wales
Northern Ireland v Poland

Tuesday 7
Under-21 qualifiers
Poland v England
Scotland v Slovenia
Switzerland v Ireland
Wales v Germany

Wednesday 8
World Cup qualifiers
Group 4
Faeroe Isles v France
Israel v Cyprus
Switzerland v Ireland
Group 5
Moldova v Italy
Norway v Belarus
Scotland v Slovenia
Group 6
Austria v Azerbaijan
Poland v England
Wales v Northern Ireland

OCTOBER

Friday 8
Under-21 qualifiers
England v Wales
France v Ireland
Scotland v Norway

Saturday 9
World Cup qualifiers
Group 4
Cyprus v Faeroe Isles
France v Ireland
Israel v Switzerland

Group 5
Belarus v Moldova
Scotland v Norway
Slovenia v Italy
Group 6
Austria v Poland
Azerbaijan v Northern Ireland
England v Wales

Tuesday 12
Under-21 qualifiers
Azerbaijan v England
Moldova v Scotland
Wales v Poland

Wednesday 13
World Cup qualifiers
Group 4
Cyprus v France
Ireland v Faeroe Isles
Group 5
Italy v Belarus
Moldova v Scotland
Norway v Slovenia
Group 6
Azerbaijan v England
Northern Ireland v Austria
Wales v Poland

NOVEMBER

Wednesday 17
World Cup qualifier
Group 4
Cyprus v Israel
Friendly
Scotland v Sweden

FEBRUARY 2005

February 9
Friendly
Wales v Hungary

MARCH

Friday 25
Under-21 qualifiers
England v Germany
Israel v Ireland
Italy v Scotland
Wales v Austria

Saturday 26
World Cup qualifiers
Group 4
France v Switzerland
Israel v Ireland
Group 5
Italy v Scotland
Group 6
England v Northern Ireland
Poland v Azerbaijan
Wales v Austria

Tuesday 29
Under-21 qualifiers
Austria v Wales
England v Azerbaijan

Wednesday 30
World Cup qualifiers
Group 4
Israel v France
Switzerland v Cyprus
Group 5
Moldova v Norway
Slovenia v Belarus
Group 6
Austria v Wales
England v Azerbaijan
Poland v Northern Ireland

JUNE

Friday 3
Under-21 qualifiers
Ireland v Israel
Scotland v Moldova

Saturday 4
World Cup qualifiers
Group 4
Faeroe Isles v Switzerland
Ireland v Israel
Group 5
Belarus v Slovenia
Norway v Italy
Scotland v Moldova
Group 6
Azerbaijan v Poland

Tuesday 7
Under-21 qualifier
Belarus v Scotland

Wednesday 8
World Cup qualifiers
Group 4
Faeroe Isles v Ireland
Group 5
Belarus v Scotland

AUGUST

Wednesday 17
World Cup qualifier
Group 4
Faeroe Isles v Cyprus

SEPTEMBER

Friday 2
Under-21 qualifiers
Scotland v Italy
Wales v England

Saturday 3
World Cup qualifiers
Group 4
France v Faeroe Isles
Switzerland v Israel
Group 5
Moldova v Belarus
Slovenia v Norway
Scotland v Italy
Group 6
Northern Ireland v Azerbaijan
Poland v Austria

Wales v England

Tuesday 6
Under-21 qualifiers
Germany v England
Ireland v France
Norway v Scotland
Poland v Wales

Wednesday 7
World Cup qualifiers
Group 4
Cyprus v Switzerland
Faeroe Isles v Israel
Ireland v France
Group 5
Belarus v Italy
Moldova v Slovenia
Norway v Scotland
Group 6
Azerbaijan v Austria
Northern Ireland v England
Poland v Wales

OCTOBER

Friday 7
Under-21 qualifiers
England v Austria
Cyprus v Ireland
Germany v Wales
Scotland v Belarus

Saturday 8
World Cup qualifiers
Group 4
Cyprus v Ireland
Israel v Faeroe Isles
Switzerland v France
Group 5
Italy v Slovenia
Norway v Moldova
Scotland v Belarus
Group 6
England v Austria
Northern Ireland v Wales

Tuesday 11
Under-21 qualifiers
England v Poland
Ireland v Switzerland
Slovenia v Scotland
Wales v Azerbaijan

Wednesday 12
World Cup qualifiers
Group 4
France v Cyprus
Ireland v Switzerland
Group 5
Belarus v Norway
Italy v Moldova
Slovenia v Scotland
Group 6
Austria v Northern Ireland
England v Poland
Wales v Azerbaijan

Compiled by Daniel Crewe

George Hardwick, distinguished former captain of Middlesbrough and England, died in April, aged 84. His obituary is on page 390

TED BATES
Page 389

RONNIE SIMPSON
Page 391

BOB STOKOE
Page 392

JOHN CHARLES
Page 393

LIVES IN BRIEF

UMBERTO AGNELLI
Born November 1, 1934
Died May 27, 2004

A member of the dynasty that owns the Fiat motor company, Umberto Agnelli became chairman of Juventus at the age of 22. His purchase of stars such as Omar Sivori and John Charles helped to bring the team championship wins in 1958, 1960 and 1961.

DEREK BIRNAGE
Born June 13, 1913
Died January 18, 2004

Derek Birnage was the first editor of the *Tiger* comic, which starred Roy of the Rovers, and he wrote about the star for six years, taking ideas from interviewing Bobby Charlton.

LEONIDAS DA SILVA
Born 1913
Died January 24, 2004

Nicknamed "the rubber man", the powerful centre forward Leonidas da Silva was one of the first players to try the overhead kick and he was also the first player to score four goals in a match in the World Cup finals, when Brazil beat Poland 6-5 in 1938. He mysteriously did not play in the semi-final against Italy, but netted twice in the match for third place and became the tournament's leading scorer. After retiring he served as manager of Sao Paulo before becoming a radio commentator and the proprietor of a furniture shop.

JOHN ASTON
Born September 3, 1921 **Died** July 31, 2003
Career Manchester United/England

Of the 30 goals that John Aston scored for United in almost 300 games, half came in 1950-51 when he was moved to centre forward. He had made his league debut as an inside forward in 1946, but eventually moved to full back. Aston, who won 17 caps, won the League with United in 1951-52 and was later chief scout. His son, John Jr, was a member of the 1968 European Cup-winning team.

JOE BAKER
Born July 17, 1940 **Died** October 6, 2003
Career Hibernian/Torino/Arsenal/Nottingham Forest/
Sunderland/Hibernian/England

"The greatest difficulty I had was in making myself understood," Joe Baker, the feisty centre forward, said of winning eight caps for England despite having grown up in Scotland. During four initial seasons at Hibernian he scored 159 goals and after a brief stint at Torino he signed for Arsenal, scoring 93 goals in 156 games.

BERT BARLOW
Born July 22, 1916 **Died** March 21, 2004
Career Barnsley/Wolverhampton Wanderers/Portsmouth/
Leicester City/Colchester United

When Portsmouth caused a sensation by defeating Wolves in the 1939 FA Cup Final, their opening goal was scored by Bert Barlow, who had left the West Midlands club the previous summer. Ten years later, when Pompey were crowned League champions, he was the only member of the Cup-winning team still at Fratton Park.

TED BATES

Born May 3, 1918 **Died** November 28, 2003
Career Southampton

After joining Southampton on his 19th birthday in 1937, Ted Bates prospered in the postwar years as an inside right, scoring 64 goals in 202 League games. He became manager in 1955 and guided the club into the top flight for the first time in 1966. In 1973 he became chief executive and five years later joined the board as director, becoming club president in 1998. He was the subject of a biography entitled, appropriately, *Dell Diamond*.

Bates, second left, laps the pitch with his team-mates in January 1951

JACK BURKITT

Born January 19, 1926 **Died** September 12, 2003
Career Nottingham Forest

"The best slow player I have ever seen," was Joe Mercer's description of the Nottingham Forest wing half, but his touch and tenacity more than compensated for this handicap. During the 1950s, Jack Burkitt helped the club to rise to the first division and was captain in 1959 when, with ten men, Forest won the FA Cup. He was the first player to make more than 500 league appearances for the club.

HENRY COCKBURN

Born September 14, 1923 **Died** February 2, 2004
Career Manchester United/Bury/England

Henry Cockburn was only 5ft 6in and played left half though right-footed, but his pace and enthusiasm made him the backbone of the Manchester United side during the late 1940s and early 1950s. The team finished runners-up three times in four seasons in the first division before eventually securing the title in 1952. He won 13 caps.

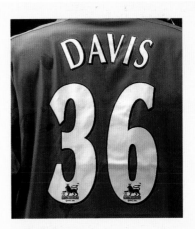

JIMMY DAVIS

Born February 6, 1982
Died August 9, 2003

A fast, hard-running midfield player, Jimmy Davis had yet to make a first-team breakthrough at Manchester United, but he had made a big impact on loan at Swindon Town and was due to begin a loan spell at Watford when he was killed in a car crash while driving to their opening game of the season. In tribute, United players donned shirts bearing his squad number for their FA Cup Final lap of honour.

LOTHAR EMMERICH

Born November 29, 1941
Died August 14, 2003

At Villa Park during the 1966 World Cup finals, Lothar "Emma" Emmerich, the West Germany outside left, struck a fierce, rising drive against Spain from the byline which Franz Beckenbauer described as the best World Cup goal ever scored. The final, in which he set up the controversial late equaliser, was the last of his five internationals.

JESUS GIL

Born March 12, 1933
Died May 14, 2004

A populist Mayor of Marbella, Jesus Gil was also, from 1987, the president of Atletico Madrid, overseeing the arrival of many managers — and their frequently swift departures. When Atletico won the league and Cup double in 1996 he rode through the streets of Madrid on his horse.

JIM KENNEDY
Born January 31 1934
Died December 2, 2003

A dedicated Celtic fan, he could hardly believe his good fortune that he ended up playing at left back for his beloved team. Jim Kennedy played for Celtic for almost ten years and won six caps for Scotland.

TONY PEET
Born May 5, 1922
Died August 27, 2003

A colonial civil servant, Tony Peet was a founder member of the Pegasus football club, made up of Oxford and Cambridge Blues. He also played cricket for Kenya's European team.

ROQUE MASPOLI
Born October 12, 1917
Died February 22, 2004

Roque Maspoli was the goalkeeper who helped Uruguay to an unthinkable victory over Brazil in the deciding match of the 1950 World Cup and also went on to manage his national side. At Penarol he won the championship five times as a player and three times as a manager.

HELMUT RAHN
Born August 16, 1929
Died August 14, 2003

In the World Cup final of 1954, Rahn first side-footed West Germany's equaliser against Hungary and then, with the score at 2-2 and six minutes remaining, hit the winner. The victory gave his nation a huge psychological boost and Rahn was feted for weeks. But while he scored 21 goals in 40 internationals, he was seen by many fans as an exhibitionist, served two prison terms for drink-driving and was the first player to be sent off in the new Bundesliga, for head-butting. He later ran a car business and worked for a building waste disposal company.

GEORGE HARDWICK
Born February 2, 1920 **Died** April 19, 2004
Career Middlesbrough/Oldham Athletic/England

George Hardwick may have had the looks of a Hollywood idol, but he was one of England's most formidable and toughest captains, leading his country in 13 games between 1946 and 1948. His one defeat came away to Switzerland and the heavy press criticism that followed helped to inspire the team to the legendary 10-0 win over Portugal in Lisbon in their next match. "The Errol Flynn of football" joined Middlesbrough at the age of 13 and remained there until he was 30. His proudest moment, he insisted, was leading the Great Britain XI that defeated Europe 6-1 at Hampden Park in 1947. His statue stands outside the Riverside Stadium.

RAY HARFORD
Born June 1, 1945 **Died** August 9, 2003
Career Charlton Athletic/Exeter City/Lincoln City/Mansfield Town/ Port Vale/Colchester United

After an undistinguished playing career, Ray Harford became one of Britain's most respected coaches. In 1988 his Luton Town side won the League Cup, defeating Arsenal in a dramatic Wembley final. After taking Wimbledon to seventh in the first division in 1991, he was invited to become No 2 to Kenny Dalglish at Blackburn Rovers — backed by Jack Walker's millions — and with Harford proving an innovative as well as an effective coach, Blackburn won the Premiership title in 1995. He was less successful when taking over from Dalglish and later had spells in charge of West Bromwich Albion, Queens Park Rangers, Derby County and Millwall.

EDDIE HOPKINSON
Born October 29, 1935 **Died** April 25, 2004
Career Oldham Athletic/Bolton Wanderers/England

Known for his tenacity and cat-like reflexes, Eddie Hopkinson played a record 508 league games for Bolton Wanderers and also appeared in the 1958 FA Cup Final victory over a post-Munich Manchester United side. "Hoppy", who won 14 caps, made his full debut for Bolton in 1956 and remained there until he retired in 1969. He became a coach at the club, also serving Stockport County.

FRANK LARGE
Born January 26, 1940 **Died** August 2003
Career Halifax Town/Queens Park Rangers/Northampton Town/ Carlisle United/Oldham Athletic/Northampton Town/Leicester City/ Fulham/Northampton Town/Chesterfield

The journalistic cliche "much-travelled" might have been invented for Frank Large, who nevertheless scored more than 200 senior goals in a career spanning 16 years. He tasted promotion success at Northampton in 1962-63 and Carlisle in 1964-65.

ALLY MacLEOD

Born February 26, 1931 **Died** February 1, 2004
Career Third Lanark/St Mirren/Blackburn Rovers/Hibernian/Third Lanark/Ayr United

"I'm going to prove the best manager in the world," Ally MacLeod said when he was appointed Scotland manager in 1977 and many believed him when his team qualified for the 1978 World Cup finals. But after leaving for Argentina on a tidal wave of euphoria, Scotland returned in ignominy after failing to reach the second stage. His spell at Blackburn included an appearance in the 1960 FA Cup Final.

JOHN ROBSON

Born July 15, 1950 **Died** May 2004
Career Derby County/Aston Villa

Tough and reliable, John Robson was one of the mainstays of Brian Clough's Derby County side that won promotion to the first division in 1969 and then the League championship in 1972. At Aston Villa he won a further promotion and two League Cup winner's medals. He retired in 1978 after being diagnosed with multiple sclerosis.

JIM SANDERS

Born July 5, 1920
Died August 14, 2003
Career West Bromwich Albion/Coventry City

After a wartime career in the RAF, during which he turned out for Charlton Athletic, Jim Sanders joined West Bromwich Albion and was the club's regular goalkeeper for the next decade, making

Jim Sanders, second left, inspects the pitch the day before the 1954 Cup Final

more than 350 appearances. The highlight of his career came in 1953-54 when the club won the FA Cup and finished runners-up in the first division.

RONNIE SIMPSON

Born October 11, 1930 **Died** April 19, 2004
Career Queen's Park/Newcastle United/Hibernian/Celtic/Scotland

Ronnie Simpson had reached the veteran's age of 36 when he became immortalised not only as one of the Celtic team that won the European Cup, but also as part of a Scotland side that defeated England at Wembley. For good measure, 1967 also saw him voted Footballer of the Year in Scotland. Not that these were the first successes of his career — he won FA Cup winner's medals with Newcastle United in 1952 and 1955 and was a member of the Great Britain squad at the 1948 Olympic Games.

GIL REECE

Born July 2, 1942
Died December 20, 2003

Between 1965 and 1972 Gil Reece, a fast, tricky winger, scored 58 goals for Sheffield United in 197 games. He also played for Cardiff City and Swansea City and won 29 caps for Wales before returning to plumbing and running a hotel in Cardiff.

DERRICK ROBINS

Born June 27, 1914
Died December 20, 2003

As chairman of Coventry City in the 1960s, working in partnership with Jimmy Hill, the manager, Derrick Robins successfully piloted the club's rise through the divisions. Moreover, the two men achieved this with an emphasis on marketing and public relations that had not been seen before in a staid and moribund sport. A self-made businessman in the building industry, Robins was also well known in the world of cricket for the touring teams that bore his name and he spent the last 30 years of his life in South Africa.

REG SMITH

Born January 20, 1912
Died January 6, 2004

A strong winger capped twice by England, Reg Smith was part of the Millwall side, then in the third division, that reached the FA Cup semi-final in 1937. He went on to manage the club and also converted The Den from gas to electricity.

PROFESSOR SIR ROLAND SMITH
Born October 1, 1928
Died November 20, 2003

Roland Smith became chairman of Manchester United in 1991 and presided over the club's expansion into a world-famous brand which, when he retired in 2002, was valued at £1 billion.

GUY THYS
Born December 6, 1922
Died August 1, 2003

After taking charge of the Belgium national team in 1976, Guy Thys steered his side to the European Championship final in 1980, the World Cup semi-finals in 1986 and quarter-finals in 1990. Latterly he was public relations manager for the Belgian FA.

PERCY YOUNG
Born May 17, 1912
Died May 9, 2004

As well as being a composer and the author of a seminal book on Elgar, Percy Young was a football historian and most notably wrote *A History of British Football*. His other books included a history of his favourite club, Wolverhampton Wanderers.

TREVOR SMITH
Born April 13, 1936 **Died** August 9, 2003
Career Birmingham City/England

The rock-solid Trevor Smith played 430 games at the heart of Birmingham City's defence and was a master of the sliding tackle. For 11 years from 1953 he had a permanent place in the first team and during this time he also won two England caps. He helped Birmingham to win the second division championship in 1955 and reach the FA Cup Final in 1956.

BOB STOKOE
Born September 21, 1930
Died February 1, 2004
Career Newcastle United/Bury

"Once you've had that funny feeling that football gives up here, nowhere else seems to matter," Bob Stokoe once said, summing up his relationship with the North East. Famed for the raincoat and trilby he wore when managing Sunderland to their stunning FA Cup Final victory over Leeds United in 1973, he had already tasted glory in the competition as a defender in the Newcastle United team that lifted the trophy in 1955.

WILLIE WATSON
Born March 7, 1920 **Died** April 24, 2004
Career Huddersfield Town/Sunderland/Halifax Town/England

Although he was good enough to play cricket for Yorkshire, football was considered his stronger suit and he joined Sunderland after the Second World War, winning the first of his four England caps in 1949. After his century against Australia at Lord's in 1953, he was chosen to tour the West Indies and his football career ended.

DENNIS WILSHAW
Born March 11, 1926 **Died** May 10, 2004
Career Wolverhampton Wanderers/Walsall/Stoke City/England

An inside forward, Dennis Wilshaw scored 172 goals in 378 games for Wolves, including 25 when the club won the championship in 1953-54. He had trained to be a teacher, but signed for Wolves in 1944 and on his debut in 1949 scored a hat-trick. He scored ten goals in 12 games for England, including four against Scotland in 1955.

JOHN CHARLES

Born December 27, 1931
Died February 21, 2004
Career Leeds United/
Juventus/Leeds United/AS
Roma/Cardiff City/Wales

Known as "the Gentle Giant" —
for although he was 6ft 2in and
frequently heavily marked, he
was never cautioned, let alone
sent off — John Charles was the
complete footballer, equally at
home leading the forward line or
at centre half. He was the
youngest player to be capped by
Wales, at 18, and scored 15 goals
in 38 internationals. Charles
made his League debut for Leeds
as a centre half at the age of 17
and after finishing as the leading
goalscorer in the first division in
1957 he moved to Juventus for a
record £65,000. After his first
game, an Italian newspaper
wrote that he was "half a team"
and the club went on to win the
title, with Charles voted the
league's player of the season. He
scored 105 goals in 168 games for
Juventus in Italian competitions
and years later would still top
polls of the club's greatest
foreign players — no mean feat
at such an illustrious club. When
Charles returned to Leeds he
missed Italy and went back to
Roma. His autobiography, *King
John,* and a biography, *Gentle
Giant,* were published recently,
although his final years were
blighted by Alzheimer's disease,
an illness all too common in
players of his generation.

**John Charles, in his pomp, goes
through his paces for the benefit of
a photographer at Elland Road on
a dank and dismal 1950s day**

KEY DATES

AUGUST 2004

Saturday 7
Coca-Cola Football League starts
Sunday 8
FA Community Shield: Arsenal
v Manchester United
Tuesday 10
InterToto Cup finals (first legs)
Tuesday 10 and Wednesday 11
Champions League third qualifying
round (first legs)
Thursday 12
Uefa Cup second qualifying round
(first legs)
Saturday 14
Barclays Premiership starts
Nationwide Conference starts
Sunday 15
FA Women's Premier League starts
Tuesday 24
InterToto Cup finals (second legs)
Tuesday 24 and Wednesday 25
Champions League third qualifying
round (second legs)
Carling Cup first round
Thursday 26
Uefa Cup second qualifying round
(second legs)
Friday 27
Uefa Super Cup: FC Porto v Valencia
Saturday 28
FA Cup extra preliminary round
Sunday 29
FA Nationwide Women's Premier League
Cup preliminary round

SEPTEMBER

Saturday 4
FA Cup preliminary round
Sunday 5
FA Women's Cup first qualifying round
Saturday 11
FA Vase first qualifying round
Sunday 12
FA Women's Premier League Cup
first round
Tuesday 14 and Wednesday 15
Champions League group matches
Thursday 16
Uefa Cup first round (first legs)
Saturday 18
FA Cup first qualifying round
Tuesday 21 and Wednesday 22
Carling Cup second round
Saturday 25
FA Vase second qualifying round
Sunday 26
FA Women's Cup second qualifying round

Monday 27
Football League Trophy first round starts
Tuesday 28 and Wednesday 29
Champions League group matches
Thursday 30
Uefa Cup first round (second legs)

OCTOBER

Saturday 2
FA Cup second qualifying round
Saturday 9
FA Trophy preliminary round
Sunday 10
FA Sunday Cup first round
FA Women's Premier League Cup
second round
Saturday 16
FA Cup third qualifying round
Tuesday 19 and Wednesday 20
Champions League group matches
Thursday 21
Uefa Cup group matches
Saturday 23
FA Vase first round
Sunday 24
FA Women's Cup first round
Tuesday 26 and Wednesday 27
Carling Cup third round
Saturday 30
FA Cup fourth qualifying round

NOVEMBER

Monday 1
Football League Trophy second
round starts
Tuesday 2 and Wednesday 3
Champions League group matches
Thursday 4
Uefa Cup group matches
Saturday 6
FA Trophy first round
Sunday 7
FA Women's Premier League Cup
third round
Tuesday 9 and Wednesday 10
Carling Cup fourth round
Saturday 13
FA Cup first round
Sunday 14
FA Women's Cup second round
Saturday 20
FA Vase second round
Sunday 21
FA Sunday Cup second round
Tuesday 23 and Wednesday 24
Champions League group matches
FA Cup first-round replays

Thursday 25
Uefa Cup group matches
Saturday 27
FA Trophy second round
Monday 29
Football League Trophy area quarter-finals
Tuesday 30
Carling Cup fifth round

DECEMBER

Wednesday 1
Carling Cup fifth round
Wednesday 1 and Thursday 2
Uefa Cup group matches
Saturday 4
FA Cup second round
Sunday 5
FA Women's Cup third round
Tuesday 7 and Wednesday 8
Champions League group matches
Saturday 11
FA Vase third round
Sunday 12
Intercontinental Cup
FA Sunday Cup third round
FA Women's Premier League Cup
semi-finals
Wednesday 15
FA Cup second-round replays
Wednesday 15 and Thursday 16
Uefa Cup group matches

JANUARY 2005

Saturday 8
FA Cup third round
Sunday 9
FA Women's Cup fourth round
Wednesday 12
Carling Cup semi-finals (first legs)
Saturday 15
FA Trophy third round
Wednesday 19
FA Cup third-round replays
Saturday 22
FA Vase fourth round
Sunday 23
FA Sunday Cup fourth round
Monday 24
Football League Trophy area semi-finals
Wednesday 26
Carling Cup semi-finals (second legs)
Saturday 29
FA Cup fourth round
Sunday 30
FA Women's Cup fifth round

FEBRUARY

Saturday 5
FA Trophy fourth round

Wednesday 9
FA Cup fourth-round replays
Saturday 12
FA Vase fifth round
Sunday 13
FA Sunday Cup fifth round
FA Women's Cup sixth round
Wednesday 16
Football League Trophy area finals
   (first legs)
Wednesday 16 and Thursday 17
Uefa Cup first knockout round (first legs)
Saturday 19
FA Cup fifth round
Tuesday 22 and Wednesday 23
Champions League first knockout round
   (first legs)
Thursday 24
Uefa Cup first knockout round
   (second legs)
Saturday 26
FA Trophy fifth round
Sunday 27
Carling Cup final

MARCH
Wednesday 2
FA Cup fifth-round replays
Saturday 5
FA Vase sixth round
Tuesday 8 and Wednesday 9
Champions League first knockout round
   (second legs)
Wednesday 9
Football League Trophy area finals
   (second legs)
Thursday 10
Uefa Cup second knockout round
   (first legs)
Saturday 12
FA Cup sixth round
FA Trophy sixth round
Sunday 13
FA Women's Cup semi-finals
Wednesday 16 and Thursday 17
Uefa Cup second knockout round
   (second legs)
Saturday 19
FA Vase semi-finals (first legs)
Sunday 20
FA Sunday Cup semi-finals
Tuesday 22
FA Cup sixth-round replays
Saturday 26
FA Vase semi-finals (second legs)
Sunday 27
FA Nationwide Women's Premier League
   Cup final (provisional)

APRIL
Saturday 2
FA Trophy semi-finals (first legs)
Tuesday 5 and Wednesday 6
Champions League quarter-finals (first legs)
Thursday 7
Uefa Cup quarter-finals (first legs)

Will Patrick Vieira be splashing out on champagne again at the end of 2004-05?

Saturday 9
FA Trophy semi-finals (second legs)
Sunday 10
Football League Trophy final
Tuesday 12 and Wednesday 13
Champions League quarter-finals
   (second legs)
Thursday 14
Uefa Cup quarter-finals (second legs)
Saturday 16
FA Cup semi-finals
Sunday 24
FA Sunday Cup final (provisional)
Tuesday 26 and Wednesday 27
Champions League semi-finals
   (first legs)
Thursday 28
Uefa Cup semi-finals (first legs)

MAY
Monday 2
FA Women's Cup final
Tuesday 3 and Wednesday 4
Champions League semi-finals
   (second legs)
Thursday 5
Uefa Cup semi-finals (second legs)

Saturday 7
Coca-Cola Football League ends
Saturday 14
Barclays Premiership ends
FA Vase final
Coca-Cola Football League play-offs
   semi-finals (first legs)
Wednesday 18
Uefa Cup final
Coca-Cola Football League play-offs
   semi-finals (second legs)
Saturday 21
FA Cup Final
Sunday 22
FA Trophy final
Wednesday 25
Champions League final
Saturday 28
Coca-Cola League Two play-offs final
Sunday 29
Coca-Cola League One play-offs final
Monday 30
Coca-Cola Championship play-offs final

Dates to be announced
FA Youth Cup final
FA County Youth Cup final

FROM THE FIRST KICK . . .

THEGAME
Two halves and a whole lot more 11 AUGUST 2003 www.timesonline.co.uk/thegame — THE TIMES MONDAYS

KICK OFF NEW SEASON - NEW ERA PAGES 2-3

O'NEILL AT DOUBLE	FINAL ANALYSIS	FINISHED ARTICLE	03 TONY CASCARINO
The manager shaped by his playing days in Europe 4-5	Matt Dickinson and Simon Barnes, plus the Cup stories of 2003 9-15	Simon Kuper on the genius – and anguish – of Pavel Nedved 20-25	14 SAM HAMMAM
			16 MARK POUGATCH
			18 FRANK SKINNER

EVERY KICK, EVERY PASS, EVERY TACKLE, EVERY SAVE, EVERY GOAL, EVERY BLADE OF GRASS, EVERY MONDAY.

THEGAME
To the point 15 DECEMBER 2003 www.timesonline.co.uk/thegame — THE TIMES MONDAYS

NEEDLED TONY CASCARINO COMES CLEAN PAGES 2-3

WILKINSON BORED	JUST WONDERFUL	FEVER PITCHES	03 GABRIELE MARCOTTI
Gabby Logan on the hypocrites who hijacked a World Cup win 4	Why I knew Bolton could beat Chelsea, by Sam Allardyce 6	Arsenal snatch back top spot as Leeds win five-goal thriller 12-13	09 THE MONEY GAME
			16 AKI RIIHILAHTI
			11 EXTRA TIME

EVERY KICK, EVERY PASS, EVERY TACKLE, EVERY SAVE, EVERY GOAL, EVERY BLADE OF GRASS, EVERY MONDAY.

THEGAME
Appealing 22 DECEMBER 2003 www.timesonline.co.uk/thegame — THE TIMES MONDAYS

RIO PASSES THE TEST MATT DICKINSON PAGES 12-13

UNITED YOU FALL	STAUNCH SUPPORT	COUNTING THE COST	04 GABRIELE MARCOTTI
Simon Barnes on the arrogance driving football to despair 3	Ferdinand is lucky compared with me, says Paolo Di Canio 8	Why sponsors could pull the plug on defenders top desir 13	05 ALAN DAVIES
			09 THE MONEY GAME
			11 MARK POUGATCH

EVERY KICK, EVERY PASS, EVERY TACKLE, EVERY SAVE, EVERY GOAL, EVERY BLADE OF GRASS, EVERY MONDAY.

THEGAME
White hot 29 DECEMBER 2003 www.timesonline.co.uk/thegame — THE TIMES MONDAYS

IN THE ZONE SPURS PRAYING FOR A NEW YEAR'S REVOLUTION PAGE 7

THE BOO BOYS	STRANGE TIMES	BABY TALK	03 DAVID ELLERAY
Being a referee is a thankless task, says Matt Dickinson 2-3	Gabby Logan reflects on an extraordinary year in football 4	West Ham spring a surprise in the their youth policy 8	06 SAM ALLARDYCE
			10 THE MONEY GAME
			20 AKI RIIHILAHTI

EVERY KICK, EVERY PASS, EVERY TACKLE, EVERY SAVE, EVERY GOAL, EVERY BLADE OF GRASS, EVERY MONDAY.

THEGAME
Striking 12 JANUARY 2004 www.timesonline.co.uk/thegame — THE TIMES MONDAYS

MANE ATTRACTION BATIGOL'S LIGHT BURNS ON PAGES 2-3

NORTHERN SOUL	ALL FOUR NONE	GO ON, SON	05 SAM ALLARDYCE
Brian Clarke finds a club in crisis as he returns home after 40 years 4-8	Chelsea stick together to thrash Leicester City 6	Ferguson facing new inquiry as FA investigate Howard transfer 12-13	10 TONY CASCARINO
			12 GABBY LOGAN

EVERY KICK, EVERY PASS, EVERY TACKLE, EVERY SAVE, EVERY GOAL, EVERY BLADE OF GRASS, EVERY MONDAY.

THEGAME
Understood 19 JANUARY 2004 www.timesonline.co.uk/thegame — THE TIMES MONDAYS

Oi, Nicolas, what's the matter now?

Le Gaffer ne me comprend pas

LOST IN TRANSLATION TONY CASCARINO PAGES 4-5

TOFFEE CRUNCH	SAFE KEEPING	DOUBLE TOPS	09 BRYAN GUNN
Everton and Rooney David Moyes explains the balancing act 2-3	Alan Davies and Mark Pougatch on Seamark legacy 6-7	Arsenal strike twice at Villa Park to push in front of United 12-13	05 MATT DICKINSON
			20 THE WIVES
			11 EXTRA TIME

EVERY KICK, EVERY PASS, EVERY TACKLE, EVERY SAVE, EVERY GOAL, EVERY BLADE OF GRASS, EVERY MONDAY.

THEGAME
Clear headed 26 JANUARY 2004 www.timesonline.co.uk/thegame — THE TIMES MONDAYS

TREASURE CHEST WHY MONEY CAN'T BUY VIEIRA PAGES 2-3

COLD TRAFFORD	ALL FOR ONE	UP FOR THE CUP	02 TONY CASCARINO
Trouble is brewing at Manchester United 4-5	Unity could be the best asset Leeds United have, says Gabby Logan 8	West Charlton are leading the way with their fourth round 8-10	06 AKI RIIHILAHTI
			12 SAM ALLARDYCE
			20 GABRIELE MARCOTTI

EVERY KICK, EVERY PASS, EVERY TACKLE, EVERY SAVE, EVERY GOAL, EVERY BLADE OF GRASS, EVERY MONDAY.

THEGAME
Heavyweight FEBRUARY 2004 www.timesonline.co.uk/thegame — THE TIMES MONDAYS

PUNCH BALL COLE ESCAPES RED CARD AS ARSENAL GO TOP PAGES 12-13

NERVE CENTRE	PASSING LEGEND	FERGUSON FEARS	04 GABRIELE MARCOTTI
Ashling O'Connor spies the top secret future of fitness in football 2-3	Simon Barnes on the fingering torment of Ally MacLeod 7	Manchester United manager's son may quit career 8-9	05 TONY CASCARINO
			06 ALAN DAVIES
			11 MARK POUGATCH

EVERY KICK, EVERY PASS, EVERY TACKLE, EVERY SAVE, EVERY GOAL, EVERY BLADE OF GRASS, EVERY MONDAY.

THEGAME
No sweat 9 FEBRUARY 2004 www.timesonline.co.uk/thegame — THE TIMES MONDAYS

OFF THE HOOK GIGGS LETS WEAKENED CHELSEA GET AWAY 12-13

THE PASSING OF TIME	MOUTH OF GOD	THE MIDDLE MEN	04 MARK HODKINSON
What happens when it's quicker than you, says Tony Cascarino 2-3	Gabriele Marcotti on Diego Maradona's latest incarnation 6	Why I much prefer Keith to Collina, says Aki Riihilahti 8	05 GABBY LOGAN
			06 SAM ALLARDYCE
			09 THE MONEY GAME

EVERY KICK, EVERY PASS, EVERY TACKLE, EVERY SAVE, EVERY GOAL, EVERY BLADE OF GRASS, EVERY MONDAY.